KT-473-993

ECONOMICS

the **Sloman Economics** news site

Visit the Sloman website at **www.pearsoned.co.uk/sloman** to find valuable **student** learning material including:

- a new, searchable **economic news blog**, with news items, analysis and accompanying **podcasts** added several times per month and referenced to the relevant chapter in this book;
- a new **student revision centre** with an online revision guide to help you prepare for your economics exam, self-assessment questions to test your knowledge, an online glossary, revision flashcards and hints and tips for doing well in exams;
- hotlinks to over 200 sites;
- links to the book's **MyEconLab** site.

With your purchase of a new copy of this textbook, you received a Student Access Kit to **MyEconLab** for *Economics*, Seventh Edition. Follow the instructions on the card to register successfully and start making the most of the online resources.

MyEconLab provides a variety of tools to enable students to assess and progress their own learning, including questions and tests for each chapter of the book. A personalised Study Plan identifies areas to concentrate on to improve grades. Specific tools are provided to each student to direct their studies in the most efficient way. MyEconLab also includes:

- a highly interactive online workbook;
- guided solutions that break problems into component steps and guide you through them with hints;
- extra case studies with questions: several per chapter;
- maths cases with exercises, related to the Looking at the Maths boxes in the book;
- answers to all in-chapter questions;
- a comprehensive glossary with flashcards to check students' knowledge;
- animations of key models with audio explanations.

See **Getting Started with MyEconLab** on page xxii for more details.

To activate your registration go to **www.pearsoned.co.uk/sloman**, click on the *Economics*, Seventh Edition cover, select MyEconLab registration, log-in and follow the instructions on-screen to register as a new user.

We work with leading authors to develop the
strongest educational materials in economics,
bringing cutting-edge thinking and best learning
practice to a global market.

Under a range of well-known imprints, including
Financial Times Prentice Hall, we craft high-quality
print and electronic publications which help readers
to understand and apply their content, whether
studying or at work.

To find out more about the complete range of our
publishing, please visit us on the World Wide Web at
www.pearsoned.co.uk.

ECONOMICS

Seventh Edition

John Sloman
The Economics Network, University of Bristol

Alison Wride
University of Exeter

FT Prentice Hall
FINANCIAL TIMES

An imprint of **Pearson Education**

Harlow, England • London • New York • Boston • San Francisco • Toronto • Sydney • Singapore • Hong Kong
Tokyo • Seoul • Taipei • New Delhi • Cape Town • Madrid • Mexico City • Amsterdam • Munich • Paris • Milan

Pearson Education Limited
Edinburgh Gate
Harlow
Essex CM20 2JE
England

and Associated Companies throughout the world

Visit us on the World Wide Web at:
www.pearsoned.co.uk

First edition published 1991
Second edition published 1994
Updated second edition published 1995
Third edition published 1997
Updated third edition published 1998
Fourth edition published 2000
Fifth edition published 2003
Sixth edition published 2006
Seventh edition published 2009

© John Sloman 1991
© John Sloman, Alison Bird and Mark Sutcliffe 1994, 1997
© John Sloman, Alison Sloman and Mark Sutcliffe 2000, 2003
© John Sloman 2006
© John Sloman, Alison Wride 2009

The rights of John Sloman and Alison Wride to be identified as
authors of this work have been asserted by them in accordance with
the Copyright, Designs and Patents Act 1988.

All rights reserved. No part of this publication may be reproduced,
stored in a retrieval system, or transmitted in any form or by any
means, electronic, mechanical, photocopying, recording or
otherwise, without either the prior written permission of the
publisher or a licence permitting restricted copying in the
United Kingdom issued by the Copyright Licensing Agency Ltd,
Saffron House, 6–10 Kirby Street, London EC1N 8TS.

All trademarks used herein are the property of their respective
owners. The use of any trademark in this text does not vest in the
author or publisher any trademark ownership rights in such
trademarks, nor does the use of such trademarks imply any
affiliation with or endorsement of this book by such owners.

ISBN 978-0-273-71562-7

British Library Cataloguing-in-Publication Data
A catalogue record for this book is available from the British Library

Library of Congress Cataloguing-in-Publication Data
Sloman, John, 1947–
    Economics / John Sloman, Alison Wride. – 7th ed.
      p. cm.
    ISBN 978-0-273-71562-7 (pbk.)
    1. Economics. I. Wride, Alison. II. Title.
  HB171.5.S635 2009
  330—dc22
                                      2009003561

10 9 8 7 6 5 4 3 2 1
13 12 11 10 09

Typeset in 8/12pt Stone Serif by 35

Printed and bound by Rotolito Lombarda, Italy
*The publisher's policy is to use paper manufactured from sustainable
forests.*

About the Authors

John Sloman is Director of the Economics Network (www.economicsnetwork.ac.uk) of the UK Higher Education Academy. The Economics Network is based at the University of Bristol and provides a range of services designed to promote and share good practice in learning and teaching economics. The Network is one of 24 subject centres covering the range of disciplines taught in UK Higher Education. The HE Academy is backed by grants from the four UK higher education funding councils.

John is also visiting professor at the University of the West of England, Bristol where, from 1992 to 1999, he was Head of School of Economics. He taught at UWE until 2007. John has taught a range of courses, including economic principles on social science and business studies degrees, development economics, comparative economic systems, intermediate macroeconomics and managerial economics. He has also taught economics on various professional courses.

He is also the author of *Essentials of Economics* (Pearson Education, 4th edition 2007) and *Economics and the Business Environment* (2nd edition 2008). He is also co-author, with Kevin Hinde from the University of Durham, of *Economics for Business* (Pearson Education, 4th edition 2007) and with Peter Smith from the University of Southampton of the *Economics Workbook* designed to accompany *Economics* 7th edition. Translations or editions of the various books are available for a number of different countries with the help of co-authors around the world.

John is very interested in promoting new methods of teaching economics, including group exercises, experiments, role playing, computer-aided learning and the use of audience response systems and podcasting in teaching. He has organised and spoken at conferences for both lecturers and students of economics throughout the UK and in many other countries.

As part of his work with the Economics Network he has contributed to its two sites for students and prospective students of economics: Study Economics (www.studyeconomics.org) and Why Study Economics? (www.whystudyeconomics.ac.uk)

From March to June 1997, John was a visiting lecturer at the University of Western Australia. In July and August 2000, he was again a visiting lecturer at the University of Western Australia and also at Murdoch University in Perth.

In 2007, John received a Lifetime Achievement Award as 'outstanding teacher and ambassador of economics' prsented jointly by the Higher Education Academy, the Government Economic Service and the Scottish Economic Society.

Alison Wride is Deputy Director of the University of Exeter Business School and an Associate Professor in Economics. Prior to her appointment as Deputy Head, she was Head of Undergraduate Studies within the School.

Her areas of interest include the student experience and the relationship between skills, employability and education. She is acknowledged as having expertise in understanding the factors that influence student satisfaction, particularly relevant given the School's position as number one business school in the UK for 2006, 2007 and 2008.

In 2006 Alison received the Student Nominated Award for Teaching Excellence from the Economics Network of the UK Higher Education Academy. This was followed by the University of Exeter Vice Chancellor's Award for Excellence in 2007, in recognition of both her role in leading on the transformation of the student experience in the Business School and her own teaching. Her work in this area has lead to requests for talks at a number of conferences and other events.

Alison has taught economics at a variety of levels: A level, undergraduate and MBA. Her teaching ethos is based on enthusing students and bringing economics to life and setting the theory in context. She still believes that 'the best decision I ever made – in terms of my career – was choosing to take A level economics. I fell in love with the subject within an hour and that was entirely due to the excellence and enthusiasm of my teacher.'

Alison's external interests include work with the Treasury and Government Economic Service on economics training for non-economists working in Government; she is currently involved in a similar initiative with the Scottish Government. This work focuses on furnishing those at the cutting edge of developing policy with the tools and economic understanding to ensure that both the formulation of aims and the choice of methods result in coherent strategies that enhance efficiency and equity.

Brief Contents

Custom Publishing   **xv**
Guided Tour   **xvi**
Getting Started with MyEconLab   **xxii**
Preface   **xxv**
Student Resources Flowchart   **xxx**
Lecturer Resources Flowchart   **xxxi**
Acknowledgements   **xxxii**
Publisher's Acknowledgements   **xxxiii**

Part A   INTRODUCTION

1   **Introducing Economics**   **3**

Part B   FOUNDATIONS OF MICROECONOMICS

2   **Supply and Demand**   **31**
3   **Markets in Action**   **56**

Part C   MICROECONOMIC THEORY

4   **Background to Demand**   **95**
5   **Background to Supply**   **123**
6   **Profit Maximising under Perfect Competition and Monopoly**   **163**
7   **Profit Maximising under Imperfect Competition**   **185**
8   **Alternative Theories of the Firm**   **213**
9   **The Theory of Distribution of Income**   **236**

Part D   MICROECONOMIC POLICY

10   **Inequality, Poverty and Policies to Redistribute Income**   **275**
11   **Markets, Efficiency and the Public Interest**   **304**
12   **Environmental Policy**   **341**
13   **Government Policy towards Business**   **367**

Part E   FOUNDATIONS OF MACROECONOMICS

| 14 | The National Economy | 385 |
| 15 | Macroeconomic Issues and Analysis: An Overview | 415 |

Part F   MACROECONOMICS

16	The Roots of Modern Macroeconomics	453
17	Short-run Macroeconomic Equilibrium	474
18	Money and Interest Rates	502
19	The Relationship between the Money and Goods Markets	535
20	Fiscal and Monetary Policy	561
21	Aggregate Supply, Unemployment and Inflation	611
22	Long-term Economic Growth	638
23	Supply-side Policies	650

Part G   THE WORLD ECONOMY

24	International Trade	669
25	The Balance of Payments and Exchange Rates	705
26	Global and Regional Interdependence	742
27	Economic Problems of Developing Countries	761

	Postscript: The Castaways or Vote for Caliban	792
	Appendix 1: Some Techniques of Economic Analysis	A:1
	Appendix 2: Websites	A:14
	Threshold Concepts and Key Ideas	T:1
	Glossary	G:1
	Index	I:1

Contents

Custom Publishing — xv
Guided Tour — xvi
Getting Started with MyEconLab — xxii
Preface — xxv
Student Resources Flowchart — xxx
Lecturer Resources Flowchart — xxxi
Acknowledgements — xxxii
Publisher's Acknowledgements — xxxiii

Part A INTRODUCTION

1 Introducing Economics — 3

1.1 What do economists study? — 4
1.2 Different economic systems — 16
1.3 The nature of economic reasoning — 25

Boxes

1.1 *What's the latest economics news?* — 5
1.2 *Looking at macroeconomic data* — 7
1.3 *The opportunity costs of studying* — 11
1.4 *Scarcity and abundance* — 13
1.5 *The rise and fall of planning in the former Soviet Union* — 18
1.6 *Adam Smith and the 'invisible hand' of the market* — 22
1.7 *Ceteris paribus* — 26

Part B FOUNDATIONS OF MICROECONOMICS

2 Supply and Demand — 31

2.1 Demand — 32
2.2 Supply — 39
2.3 Price and output determination — 42
2.4 The control of prices — 51

Boxes

2.1 The demand for lamb — 36
2.2 *UK house prices* — 46
2.3 *Stock market prices* — 48
2.4 *Underground markets* — 53

3 Markets in Action — 56

3.1 Elasticity — 57
3.2 The time dimension — 71
3.3 Indirect taxes — 77
3.4 Government rejection of market allocation — 80
3.5 Agriculture and agricultural policy — 82

Boxes

3.1 *Advertising and its effect on demand curves* — 62
3.2 *Pricing on the buses* — 63
3.3 Using calculus to calculate the price elasticity of demand — 65
3.4 *Short selling* — 74
3.5 *Dealing in futures markets* — 76
3.6 *A moral dilemma of tobacco taxes* — 79
3.7 *The fallacy of composition* — 84

Part C MICROECONOMIC THEORY

4 Background to Demand — 95

4.1 Marginal utility theory — 96
4.2 Demand under conditions of risk and uncertainty — 105
*4.3 Indifference analysis — 109

Boxes

*4.1 *Using calculus to derive a marginal utility function* — 98
4.2 *The marginal utility revolution* — 102
4.3 *Is economics the study of selfish behaviour?* — 103
4.4 *Taking account of time* — 104
4.5 *Problems with insurance markets* — 108
*4.6 *Love and caring* — 116
*4.7 *Consumer theory: characteristics theory* — 120

5 Background to Supply — 123

5.1 The short-run theory of production — 124
5.2 Costs in the short run — 130
5.3 The long-run theory of production — 136
5.4 Costs in the long run — 146
5.5 Revenue — 150
5.6 Profit maximisation — 155

Boxes

5.1 *Malthus and the dismal science of economics* — 126
5.2 *Diminishing returns in the bread shop* — 128
5.3 *The relationship between averages and marginals* — 129
*5.4 *The relationship between TPP, MPP and APP* — 130
5.5 *The fallacy of using historic costs* — 131
5.6 *Cost curves in practice* — 135

*5.7	The Cobb–Douglas production function	141
5.8	Minimum efficient scale	150
*5.9	Using calculus to find the maximum profit output	158
5.10	The logic of logistics	160

6 Profit Maximising under Perfect Competition and Monopoly — **163**

6.1	Alternative market structures	164
6.2	Perfect competition	165
6.3	Monopoly	173
6.4	The theory of contestable markets	179

Boxes

6.1	Concentration ratios	166
6.2	Is perfect best?	167
6.3	E-commerce and perfect competition	170
6.4	Breaking Sky's monopoly on live football coverage	177
6.5	X inefficiency	178
6.6	Airline deregulation in the USA and Europe	180

7 Profit Maximising under Imperfect Competition — **185**

7.1	Monopolistic competition	186
7.2	Oligopoly	189
7.3	Game theory	201
7.4	Price discrimination	206

Boxes

7.1	Selling ice cream as a student	187
7.2	Is beer becoming more concentrated?	191
7.3	OPEC	194
7.4	The prisoners' dilemma	203
7.5	What's the train fare to London?	207
7.6	Peak-load pricing	207
7.7	Price discrimination in the cinema	209

8 Alternative Theories of the Firm — **213**

8.1	Problems with traditional theory	214
8.2	Alternative maximising theories	218
8.3	Multiple aims	228
8.4	Pricing in practice	231

Boxes

8.1	The organisational structure of firms	214
8.2	What do you maximise?	217
8.3	When is a theory not a theory?	219
8.4	Enron	224
8.5	Merger activity	226
8.6	Stakeholder power?	229
8.7	How do companies set prices?	232

9 The Theory of Distribution of Income — **236**

9.1	Wage determination under perfect competition	237
9.2	Wage determination in imperfect markets	246
9.3	Capital and profit	258
9.4	Land and rent	268

Boxes

9.1	Labour as a factor of production	238
*9.2	Using indifference curve analysis to derive the individual's supply curve of labour	240
9.3	Immigration and the UK labour market	241
9.4	Monopsony in Victorian times	247
9.5	The rise and decline of the labour movement in the UK	249
9.6	How useful is marginal productivity theory?	251
9.7	Equal pay for equal work?	252
9.8	Flexible labour markets and the flexible firm	254
9.9	Stocks and flows	260
9.10	The economics of non-renewable resources	269

Part D   MICROECONOMIC POLICY

10 Inequality, Poverty and Policies to Redistribute Income — **275**

10.1	Inequality and poverty	276
10.2	Taxes, benefits and the redistribution of income	288

Boxes

10.1	Poverty in the past	284
10.2	How to reverse the UK's increased inequality	285
10.3	Minimum wage legislation	287
10.4	The Laffer curve	296
*10.5	Tax cuts and incentives	298
10.6	UK tax credits	301

11 Markets, Efficiency and the Public Interest — **304**

11.1	Efficiency under perfect competition	305
11.2	The case for government intervention	313
11.3	Forms of government intervention	323
*11.4	Cost–benefit analysis	329
11.5	Government failure and the case for the market	336

Boxes

11.1	The police as a public service	316
11.2	A commons solution	318
11.3	Should health-care provision be left to the market?	322
11.4	Deadweight loss from taxes on goods and services	325
*11.5	What price a human life?	332
*11.6	Meeting the Kyoto Protocol	334
11.7	Mises, Hayek and the Mont Pelerin Society	338

12 Environmental Policy — **341**

12.1	Economics of the environment	342
12.2	Policies to tackle pollution and its effects	347
12.3	The economics of traffic congestion	356
12.4	Urban transport policies	361

Boxes

12.1	A Stern warning	344
12.2	Green taxes	350
12.3	Are we all green now?	352
12.4	Selling the environment	352
12.5	Trading our way out of climate change	355
12.6	Restricting car access to Athens	362
12.7	Road pricing in Singapore	364

13 Government Policy towards Business — 367

| 13.1 | Competition policy | 368 |
| 13.2 | Privatisation and regulation | 375 |

Boxes

13.1	A lift to profits?	371
13.2	School fees in the UK	372
13.3	What price for peace of mind?	374
13.4	Selling power to the people	380

Part E   FOUNDATIONS OF MACROECONOMICS

14 The National Economy — 387

14.1	The scope of macroeconomics	388
14.2	The circular flow of income	390
14.3	Measuring national income and output	393
14.4	Short-term economic growth and the business cycle	398
14.5	Long-term economic growth	403
	Appendix: Calculating GDP	409

Boxes

14.1	Which country is better off?	396
14.2	How big is the underground economy?	397
14.3	Output gaps	398
14.4	Is stability always desirable?	402
14.5	Theories of growth	405
14.6	The costs of economic growth	406
14.7	When higher GDP can lead to lower welfare	410

15 Macroeconomic Issues and Analysis: An Overview — 415

15.1	Unemployment	416
15.2	Aggregate demand and supply and the level of prices	425
15.3	Inflation	428
15.4	The balance of payments and exchange rates	439
15.5	Postscript to Part E: The relationship between the four macroeconomic objectives	447

Boxes

15.1	The costs of unemployment	420
15.2	Hyperinflation	430
15.3	Cost-push illusion	433
15.4	Is inflation dead?	434
15.5	The Phillips curve	436
15.6	Dealing in foreign exchange	445
15.7	The political business cycle (Part I)	448

Part F   MACROECONOMICS

16 The Roots of Modern Macroeconomics — 453

16.1	Setting the scene: three key issues	454
16.2	Classical macroeconomics	456
16.3	The Keynesian revolution	462
16.4	The monetarist–Keynesian debate	466
16.5	The current position: an emerging consensus?	469

Boxes

16.1	Balance the budget at all costs	460
16.2	The crowding-out effect	461
16.3	Will wage cuts cure unemployment?	463

17 Short-run Macroeconomic Equilibrium — 474

17.1	Background to the theory	475
17.2	The determination of national income	486
17.3	The simple Keynesian analysis of unemployment and inflation	492
17.4	The Keynesian analysis of the business cycle	495

Boxes

*17.1	Using calculus to derive the MPC	479
17.2	Consumption and saving in practice	480
17.3	Business expectations and their effect on investment	484
17.4	Deriving the multiplier formula	490
17.5	The paradox of thrift	492
17.6	Has there been an accelerator effect over the past thirty years?	498

18 Money and Interest Rates — 502

18.1	The meaning and functions of money	503
18.2	The financial system	504
18.3	The supply of money	519
18.4	The demand for money	526
18.5	Equilibrium	531

Boxes

18.1	Money supply, national income and national wealth	503
18.2	Residential mortgages and securitisation	512
18.3	Tackling the credit crunch	516
18.4	UK and eurozone monetary aggregates	520
*18.5	Calculating the money multiplier	523
18.6	Are the days of cash numbered?	527

19 The Relationship between the Money and Goods Markets — 535

19.1	The effects of monetary changes on national income	536
19.2	The monetary effects of changes in the goods market	544
*19.3	ISLM analysis: the integration of the goods and money market models	548
19.4	Taking inflation into account	556

Boxes

19.1	Choosing the exchange rate or the money supply	541
19.2	The stability of the velocity of circulation	542
19.3	Crowding out in an open economy	546
*19.4	Environmentally sustainable macroeconomic equilibrium	554

20 Fiscal and Monetary Policy 561

20.1	Fiscal policy	562
20.2	Monetary policy	574
*20.3	*ISLM* analysis of fiscal and monetary policy	589
20.4	Fiscal and monetary policy in the UK	591
20.5	Rules versus discretion	601

Boxes

20.1	Managing the US economy	566
20.2	Riding a switchback	570
20.3	Following the golden rule	572
20.4	The operation of monetary policy in The UK	578
20.5	Central banking and monetary policy in the USA	580
20.6	Monetary policy in the eurozone	582
20.7	Goodhart's law	586
20.8	Using interest rates to control both aggregate demand and the exchange rate	587
20.9	Quantitative easing	588
20.10	Inflation targeting	602
20.11	Interest rate responses and the financial crisis of 2007/8	604
*20.12	How do inflation targets work in practice?	606

21 Aggregate Supply, Unemployment and Inflation 611

21.1	Aggregate supply	612
21.2	The expectations-augmented Phillips curve	619
21.3	Inflation and unemployment: the new classical position	626
21.4	Inflation and unemployment: the modern Keynesian position	632
21.5	Postscript: Common ground among economists?	636

Boxes

21.1	Cost-push inflation and supply shocks	617
*21.2	Analysing demand-pull and cost-push inflation using the ADI/ASI model	618
*21.3	Basing expectations on the past	622
21.4	The political business cycle (Part II)	625
21.5	The rational expectations revolution	628
21.6	Forecasting the weather	629
21.7	The boy who cried 'Wolf'	631

22 Long-term Economic Growth 638

22.1	Long-run economic growth in industrialised countries	639
22.2	Economic growth without technological progress	642
22.3	Economic growth with technological progress	645

Box

| 22.1 | Productivity and economic growth | 646 |

23 Supply-side Policies 650

23.1	Supply-side policies and the macroeconomy	651
23.2	Approaches to supply-side policy	652
23.3	Market-orientated supply-side policies	654
23.4	Interventionist supply-side policy	661

Boxes

23.1	The supply-side revolution in the USA	655
23.2	Assessing PFI	658
23.3	Alternative approaches to training and education	662
23.4	Unemployment and supply-side policies	665
23.5	A new approach to industrial policy	666

Part G   THE WORLD ECONOMY

24 International Trade 671

24.1	The advantages of trade	672
24.2	Arguments for restricting trade	683
24.3	Preferential trading	692
24.4	The European Union	697

Boxes

24.1	Sharing out the jobs	674
24.2	Trade as exploitation?	676
24.3	Free trade and the environment	683
24.4	Strategic trade theory	685
*24.5	The optimum tariff or export tax	687
24.6	Giving trade a bad name	688
24.7	The Doha development agenda	690
24.8	Mutual recognition	699
24.9	Features of the single market	701
24.10	The Internal Market Scoreboard	702

25 The Balance of Payments and Exchange Rates 705

25.1	Alternative exchange rate regimes	706
25.2	Fixed exchange rates	716
25.3	Free-floating exchange rates	720
25.4	Exchange rate systems in practice	729
	Appendix: The open economy and *ISLM* analysis	737

Boxes

25.1	Balance of trade and the public finances	708
25.2	The UK's balance of payments deficit	711
25.3	The effectiveness of fiscal and monetary policies under fixed exchange rates	718
25.4	The price of a Big Mac	722
25.5	The euro/dollar seesaw	724
25.6	The effectiveness of monetary and fiscal policies under floating exchange rates	728
25.7	How significant are inflation differentials?	733

26 Global and Regional Interdependence   742

26.1   Globalisation and the problem of instability   743
26.2   European economic and monetary union (EMU)   748
26.3   Achieving greater currency stability   755

Boxes

26.1   *Globalisation and the US trade imbalance*   *744*
26.2   *Attempts at harmonisation: the G8*   *748*
26.3   *Optimal currency areas*   *754*
26.4   *The Tobin tax*   *756*

27 Economic Problems of Developing Countries   761

27.1   The problem of underdevelopment   762
27.2   International trade and development   766
27.3   Structural problems within developing
        countries   776
27.4   The problem of debt   783

Boxes

27.1   *The Human Development Index*   *765*
27.2   *When driving and alcohol do mix*   *770*
27.3   *The Chinese economic miracle*   *774*
27.4   Unemployment in developing countries   *780*
27.5   *The building BRICs of development*   *782*
27.6   *Argentina in crisis*   *784*
27.7   *Debt and the environment*   *786*
27.8   *Swapping debt*   *789*

Postscript: The Castaways or Vote for Caliban   792
Appendix 1: Some Techniques of Economic Analysis   A:1
Appendix 2: Websites   A:14
Threshold Concepts and Key Ideas   T:1
Glossary   G:1
Index   I:1

Supporting Resources

Visit **www.pearsoned.co.uk/sloman** click on the *Economics*, Seventh Edition cover at the top of the page, select MyEconLab registration and log-in to access MyEconLab.

MyEconlab for students

MyEconLab for *Economics*, Seventh Edition enables you to assess your learning and provides you with a personalised Study Plan, which identifies areas you need to concentrate on to improve your grades. Specific tools are provided to direct your study in the most efficient way. Access to MyEconLab is provided with every new purchase of the main text.

MyEconLab contains the following resources:

- a personalised Study Plan, with extensive self-testing material and homework that can be set by your tutor;
- a complete online workbook for use alongside the textbook as you learn;
- multiple choice questions to test your learning;
- extra case studies with questions per chapter;
- maths cases with exercises, related to the Looking at the Maths boxes in the book;
- answers to all in-chapter questions;
- an economics news blog updated several times per month. Each news item has an introduction, links to a range of news articles, questions and references to the relevant chapter of the book;
- animations of all key models with audio explanations. These can be downloaded to your iPod or MP4 player;
- extensive annotated Hotlinks to relevant sites on the Internet, regularly updated;
- an online glossary to explain key terms with flashcards to test your knowledge.

MyEconLab for lecturers

- MyEconLab's gradebook automatically records each student's time spent and performance on the tests and Study Plan and generates reports you can use to monitor your students' progress.
- You can use MyEconLab to build your own tests, quizzes and homework assignments from the question base provided to set for your students' assessment.
- Questions are generated algorithmically so that they use different values each time they are used.
- If you want to devote the time, you can create your own exercises by using the econ exercise builder.

For lecturers wanting more information about the MyEconLab product, please contact your local Pearson Education sales representative at **www.pearsoned.co.uk/replocator** or visit **www.myeconlab.com**.

Additional lecturer resources:

- tutor guide to using chapters and discussion of learning/teaching issues;
- customisable testbank of question material;
- customisable lecture plans in PowerPoint with questions for use in lectures with or without an audience response system;
- key models animated as full-colour PowerPoint slide shows;
- downloadable PowerPoint slides of all figures and tables from the book;
- a range of teaching and learning case studies;
- workshops with answers;
- answers to end-of-chapter questions;
- answers to the case studies found in MyEconLab.

These lecturer resources can be downloaded from the lecturer website at **www.pearsoned.co.uk/sloman**. Click on the *Economics*, Seventh Edition cover and select lecturer resources. Most are open access, but answers are password protected.

The lecturer resources are also available on a memory stick from your Pearson Education sales representative.

Custom Publishing

Custom publishing allows academics to pick and choose content from one or more textbooks for their course and combine it into a definitive course text.

Here are some common examples of custom solutions which have helped over 1000 courses across Europe:

- different chapters from across our publishing imprints combined into one book;
- lecturer's own material combined together with textbook chapters or published in a separate booklet;
- third-party cases and articles that you are keen for your students to read as part of the course;
- any combination of the above.

The Pearson Education custom text published for your course is professionally produced and bound – just as you would expect from any Pearson Education text. Since many of our titles have online resources accompanying them we can even build a Custom website that matches your course text.

If you are teaching a first year Economics course you may have a large teaching team with different lecturers teaching the micro and macroeconomics sections. Do you find that it can be difficult to agree on one textbook? If you do, you might find combining the macro and micro halves from different Pearson textbooks, either in one volume or two separate volumes, a useful solution. If you like to spend slightly longer on any one topic, you might like to provide some additional chapters as further reading online for your students.

Custom publishing has enabled adopters of this text to employ these different solutions.

If, once you have had time to review this title, you feel Custom publishing might benefit you and your course, please do get in contact. However minor, or major the change – we can help you out.

For more details on how to make your chapter selection for your course please go to www.pearsoned.co.uk/sloman and select the custom publishing link.

You can contact us at: **www.pearsoncustom.co.uk** or via your local representative at: **www.pearsoned.co.uk/replocator**.

Guided Tour

The book is divided into seven **parts**, each with a full page introduction and part map to help you navigate around the book.

Full page **chapter openers** provide an overview of the topics to be covered in each chapter, and a map of all chapter sections and sub-sections. These overviews, as well as full learning objectives per chapter, can be found in MyEconLab.

PRACTISING AND TESTING YOUR LEARNING

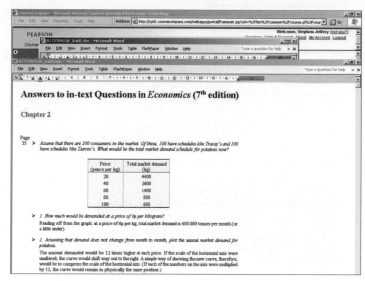

Questions throughout the text enable you to test your understanding of what you have just read. Answers appear in MyEconLab.

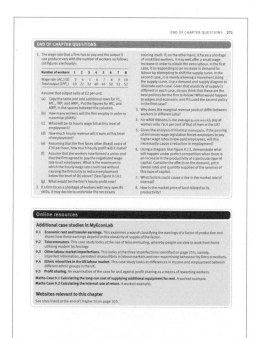

End-of-chapter questions can be used for self-testing or in class.

Take the **Chapter Tests in MyEconLab** to generate a personalised Study Plan. You will then be directed to specific resources in MyEconLab to help you focus your studies and improve your grades. For details on how to access MyEconLab, see the access card that is packaged with every new copy of this book.

Graphical problems help you explore economic concepts visually.

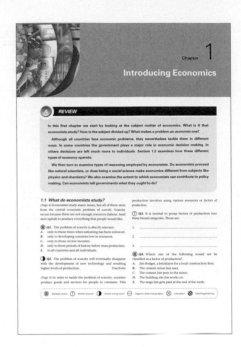

A printed **Workbook** is available for purchase
(from www.pearson-books.com,
ISBN 978-0-273-72916-7), which contains
over 1500 questions of various types, carefully
matched to the content of the main text.

AIDING YOUR UNDERSTANDING

Threshold Concept boxes cover the fundamental concepts
that you need to grasp in order to think like an economist.
An icon appears in the margin when these concepts are
referred to later in the text, and highlights the links between
different parts of the subject.

Section Summaries allow you to recap on your learning at
frequent intervals and provide an important revision tool.

The **Key Ideas** in an economist's toolkit are highlighted and explained where they first appear. Again, an icon appears in the margin whenever they recur later in the book.

All **economic terms** are printed in bold where they first appear in the text, and **definitions** of them are given at the bottom of the page. All terms also appear in the comprehensive glossary that appears at the back of the book and in MyEconLab.

You can use your **personalised MyEconLab Study Plan** to assess how well you are doing, and areas you need to concentrate on to improve.

Extra resources such as animated graphs with audio explanations are provided to further explain the topics you need to focus on improving your grades. For details on how to access MyEconLab, see the access card that is packaged with every new copy of this book.

APPLYING ECONOMICS TO THE REAL WORD

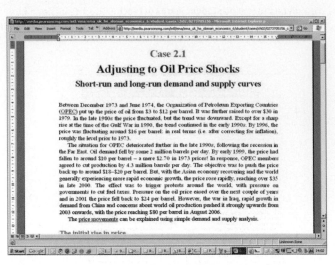

Additional Case Studies relevant to each chapter can be found in MyEconLab. These cases are listed at the end of each chapter.

Case Studies and Applications boxes include examples, data and scenarios from the real world to show you why this subject really matters in everyday life.

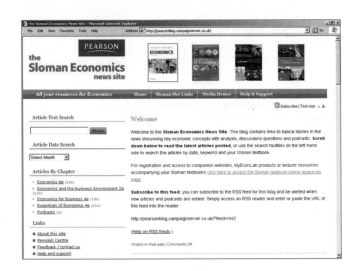

A news blog site. New items are added several times per month. These link to articles in the press and there are questions on each news item and references to the book. There is also a powerful search feature that lets you search for articles by chapter of the book, by topic or by month.

Websites relevant to each chapter are listed at the end of the chapter and are linked to the chapter resources area of MyEconLab.

FLEXIBLE LEARNING

We understand that no student learns or teacher teaches in the same way. Hence, with this seventh edition, we have endeavoured to make the book and its accompanying resources as flexible as possible to use. The in-text features and accompanying online resources allow you to study at your own pace and focus on topics where you need the most help.

Starred sections contain optional, more advanced material. These can be omitted without interrupting the flow of the argument.

Optional **Looking at the Maths** boxes are designed for students on more rigorous courses, which make use of maths. They express mathematically what is also covered in words or graphically. Most link to Maths Cases with worked mathematical examples and numerical questions that can be found in MyEconLab.

See **Suggestions for Shorter or Less Advanced Courses** in the Preface for different ideas of how best to use the book for different courses.

Getting Started with MyEconLab

The seventh edition of *Economics* comes with a new, improved and updated version of MyEconLab. MyEconLab is personalised and innovative online study and testing resource that provides a variety of tools to enable you to assess and progress your own learning. In addition to the exercises interspersed in the text, which you are encouraged to tackle as you go along, you should log-on to this new online tool and practise further.

To get started, take out your **access kit** included inside this book to register online.

Registration and log-in

Go to **www.pearsoned.co.uk/sloman** and click on the *Economics*, Seventh Edition cover, select MyEconLab registration and log-in and follow the instructions on-screen using the code inside your access kit, which will look like this:

Example
SIMPLE-FRILL-TONLE-WEIRS-CHOIR-FLEES

The log-in screen will look like this:

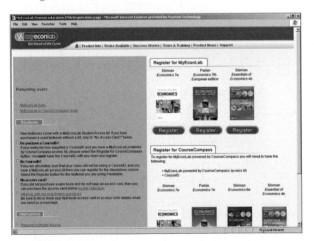

Now you should be registered with your own password ready to log-in directly to your own course.

When you log-in to your course for the first time, the course home page will look like this:

Now follow the steps below for the chapter you are studying.

Step 1: Take a sample test

Sample tests (two for each chapter) enable you to test yourself to see how much you already know about a particular topic and identify the areas in which you need more practice. Click on the Study Plan button in the menu and take **sample test a** for the chapter you are studying. Once you have completed a chapter, go back and take **sample test b** to see how much you have learned.

Step 2: Review your study plan

To help you make the most efficient use of your self-study time, the results of the sample tests you have taken will be incorporated into your Study Plan showing you what sections you have mastered and what sections you need to study further.

Step 3: Have a go at an exercise

From the Study Plan, click on the section of the book you are studying and have a go at the series of interactive **Exercises**. (Exercises with page references are based on end-of-chapter questions in the book.)

When required, use the **Grapher** on the right-hand side to select the graphing tools you need to complete the question. For help using the grapher click on the question icon.

Additional study tools such as **Guided Solutions** and **Examples** break the question down step-by-step to help you to complete the exercises successfully. You can try the same exercises over and over again, and each time the values will change, giving you unlimited practice.

Step 4: Use the e-book and additional multimedia tools found in Textbook Resources to help you further

Use the online workbook for an interactive way to review what you have learned in the text and to practise further with additional support before you attempt the questions in MyEconlab.

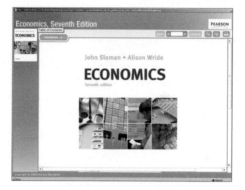

If you are struggling with a question, you can click on the textbook icon to read the relevant part of your textbook again.

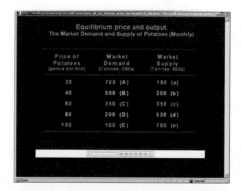

You can also click on the animation icon to help you visualise and improve your understanding of key concepts.

Good luck getting started with *MyEconLab*.

For an online tour go to **www.myeconlab.com**.

For any help and advice contact the 24-hour online support at **www.myeconlab.com** and click on student support.

Preface

Economics affects all our lives. As consumers we try to make the best of our limited incomes. As workers – or future workers! – we take our place in the job market. As citizens of a country our lives are affected by the decisions of our government: decisions over taxes, decisions over spending on health and education, decisions on interest rates, decisions that affect unemployment, inflation and growth. As dwellers on the planet Earth we are affected by the economic decisions of each other: the air we breathe, the water we drink and the environment we leave to our children are all affected by the economic decisions taken by the human race.

Economics thus deals with some of the most challenging issues we face. It is this that still excites the authors about economics after many years of teaching the subject. We hope that some of this excitement rubs off on you.

The first six editions of *Economics* have been widely used in Britain and throughout the world. Like them, this new edition is suitable for all students of economics at first-year degree level, A level or on various professional courses where a broad grounding in both principles and applications is required. It is structured to be easily understood by those of you who are new to the subject, with various sections and boxes that can be left out on first reading or on shorter courses; yet it also has sufficient depth to challenge those of you who have studied the subject before, with starred sections (*) and case studies that will provide much that is new. There are also optional short mathematical sections for those of you studying a more rigorous course.

The book gives a self-contained introduction to the world of economics and is thus ideal for those who will not study the subject beyond introductory level. But by carefully laying a comprehensive foundation and by the inclusion of certain materials in starred sections that bridge the gap between introductory and second-level economics, it provides the necessary coverage for those of you going on to specialise in economics.

The book is designed with one overriding aim: to make this exciting and highly relevant subject as clear to understand as possible. To this end the book has a number of important features (see also the Guided Tour):

- A full and consistent colour design is used to guide you through the text and make the structure easy to follow.
- The text is written in a direct and straightforward style, with short paragraphs to aid rapid comprehension.
- Key ideas are highlighted and explained where they first appear. These ideas are key elements in the economist's 'toolkit' and whenever they recur later in the book, an icon appears in the margin and you are referred back to the page where they are defined and explained.
- Fifteen 'threshold concepts' are presented and explained in separate panels. Grasping these fundamental concepts that recur throughout the subject will help you to 'think like an economist'. Like the key ideas, an icon is used to refer to them whenever they occur.
- Full-page chapter introductions raise the key issues of the chapter and also give a map to help you 'navigate' through the contents of the various sections.
- Numerous examples from around the world are given: some serious, some lighthearted.
- Summaries appear at the end of each section (rather than each chapter).
- Definitions of all economic terms can be found at the bottom of the page where they first appear.
- A comprehensive index is provided, including reference to all defined terms.
- Through the text, questions (typically one or two per page) are posed to test comprehension and stimulate thought while you are learning. Answers to all these questions are in MyEconLab.
- Questions at the end of each chapter can be used for either individual or class use.
- Boxes provide case studies, institutional material, news items, contemporary and historical debates and issues, anecdotes and advanced topics.
- Advanced material in starred sections/boxes is included, which can be omitted without affecting the flow of argument.
- Additional case studies, which are listed at the end of each chapter, can be accessed in MyEconLab.
- Many issues are examined in their historical as well as contemporary context.

- 'Looking at the maths' sections are designed for students on more rigorous courses that make use of mathematics. These sections express things mathematically that have just been covered in words and/or graphically. Most of them link to Maths Cases on the book's website. These cases give worked mathematical examples and also include one or more numerical questions for you to work through, either at home or in class.
- Extensive website references are given at the end of each chapter. These refer you to the websites listed at the end of the book in Appendix 2. These can all be accessed directly from MyEconLab at www.coursecompass.com.

All these features are designed to make your studies more interesting and to help you learn in a deeper and more active way.

The book looks at the world of the early 21st century. Despite huge advances in technology and despite the comfortable lives led by many people in the industrialised world, we still suffer from unemployment, poverty and inequality, and in many countries (the UK included) the gap between rich and poor has grown much wider; our environment is polluted; our economy still goes through periodic recessions; conflict and disagreement often dominate over peace and harmony.

What is more, the world order has been changing. With a growing interdependence of the economies of the world; with an inexorable process of 'globalisation', which links us all through a web of telecommunications and international trade into a world of Coca-Cola, Nike trainers, Microsoft, football and American chat shows; with repeated bouts of turmoil on international financial markets culminating in the banking crisis of 2008/9; with evidence that economic problems have spread like a contagion around the world, resulting in what might prove to be a paralysing recession; with Chinese economic growth increasingly becoming the powerhouse of the global economy; with the move away from the ideological simplicity of a 'free-market' solution to all economic problems; with a powerful but economically sluggish 'eurozone' and a rapidly evolving European Union with new members; with an uncertain future for the USA with its ever-growing level of debt; and with an ever deepening crisis for many developing countries; so there are many new economic challenges that face us. Economists are called on to offer solutions.

But despite our changing environment, there are certain economic fundamentals that do not change. Despite disagreements among economists – and there are plenty – there is a wide measure of agreement on how to analyse these fundamentals.

We hope that this book will give you an enjoyable introduction to the economist's world and that it will equip you with the tools to understand and criticise the economic policies that others pursue.

Good luck and have fun.

TO LECTURERS AND TUTORS

This new edition retains many of the popular features of the previous edition (see also the Guided Tour):

- A style that is direct and to the point, with the aim all the time to provide maximum clarity. There are numerous examples to aid comprehension.
- All economic terms highlighted in the text where they first appear and defined at the foot of that page. Each term is also highlighted in the index, so that the student can simply look up a given definition as required. By defining them on the page where they appear, the student can also see the terms used in context in the text.
- Key ideas highlighted and explained when they first appear. There are 38 of these ideas, which are fundamental to the study of economics. Students can see them recurring throughout the book, and an icon appears in the margin to refer back to the page where the idea first appears.
- Fifteen 'threshold concepts'. Understanding and being able to relate and apply these core economic concepts helps students to 'think like an economist' and to relate the different parts of the subject to each other.

- A wealth of applied material in boxes (176 in all), making learning more interesting for students and, by relating economics to the real world, bringing the subject alive. The boxes allow the book to be comprehensive without the text becoming daunting and allow more advanced material to be introduced where appropriate. Many of the boxes can be used as class exercises and virtually all have questions at the end.
- Full-page chapter introductions. These set the scene for the chapter by introducing the students to the topics covered and relating them to the everyday world. The introductions also include a 'chapter map'. This provides a detailed contents listing, helping students to see how the chapter is structured and how the various topics relate to each other.
- A consistent use of colour in graphs and diagrams, with explanations in panels where appropriate. These features make them easier to comprehend and more appealing.
- Starred sections and boxes for more advanced material. These can be omitted without interrupting the flow of the argument. This allows the book to be used by students with different abilities and experience, and on courses of different levels of difficulty.

- 'Looking at the maths' sections. These short sections express a topic mathematically. Some use calculus; some do not. They are designed to be used on more rigorous courses and go further than other textbooks at introductory level in meeting the needs of students on such courses. Most refer students to worked examples in Maths Cases in MyEconLab. Some of these use simultaneous equations; some use simple unconstrained optimisation techniques; others use constrained optimisation, using both substitution and Lagrange multipliers. The 'Looking at the maths' sections are short and can be omitted by students on non-mathematical courses without any loss of continuity.
- An open learning approach, with questions incorporated into the text so as to test and reinforce students' understanding as they progress. This makes learning a much more active process.
- End-of-chapter questions. These can be set as work for students to do in class or at home. Alternatively, students can simply use them to check their comprehension at the end of a topic.
- Summaries given at the end of each section, thus providing a point for reflection and checking on comprehension at reasonably frequent intervals.
- An even micro/macro split.
- The book is divided into seven parts. This makes the structure transparent and makes it easier for the student to navigate.

Despite retaining these popular features, there have been many changes to this seventh edition.

Extensive revision

Economics (seventh edition) uses a lot of applied material, both to illustrate theory and policy, and to bring the sub-

ject alive for students by relating it to contemporary issues. This has meant that, as with the previous edition, much of the book has had to be rewritten to reflect contemporary issues. Specifically this means that:

- Many of the boxes are new or extensively revised.
- There are many new examples given in the text.
- All policy sections reflect the changes that have taken place in the last three years. For example, changes in environmental policy and competition policy are fully discussed in the new Chapters 12 and 13; previously these were brought together in a single chapter. The impact of the extensive turmoil experienced in the financial markets and the banking sector in 2008/9 has been covered, as has the subsequent recession, allowing us to consider fully the implications for monetary and fiscal policy, particularly in an updated and expanded Chapter 20.
- All tables and charts have been updated, as have factual references in the text.
- Theoretical coverage has been strengthened at various points of the books. For example, there is an expanded section on game theory in Chapter 7, which now includes discussion of the multiple move games. The chapter on money and interest rates and further sections on the links between money and goods markets have been expanded and strengthened in the light of the collapse of the banking system in 2008/9. Particular attention has been paid to the role of securitisation and the issues of capital adequacy liquidity and risk.

Most importantly, every single section and every single sentence of the book has been carefully considered, and if necessary redrafted, to ensure both maximum clarity and contemporary relevance. The result, we hope, is a text that your students will find exciting and relevant to today's world.

SUGGESTIONS FOR SHORTER OR LESS ADVANCED COURSES

The book is designed to be used on a number of different types of course. Because of its comprehensive nature, the inclusion of a lot of optional material and the self-contained nature of many of the chapters and sections, it can be used very flexibly.

It is suitable for one-year principles courses at first-year degree level, two-year economics courses on non-economics degrees, A level, HND and professional courses. It is also highly suitable for single-semester courses, either with a micro or a macro focus, or giving a broad outline of the subject.

The following suggests chapters which are appropriate to different types of course and gives some guidance on chapters that can be omitted while retaining continuity:

Alternative 1: Less advanced but comprehensive courses

Omit all starred sections, starred sub-sections and starred boxes.

Example of a comprehensive course, omitting some of these chapters: Chapters 1–7, 9, 11–13, 14, 15, 17–22, 24–25.

Alternative 2: Economics for Business courses

Chapters 1–3, 5–9, 12–15, 18, 20, 23–6.

Example of an Economics for Business course, omitting some of these chapters: Chapters 1–3, 5–9, 13, 14, 15, 18, 20, 24–25.

Alternative 3: Introduction to microeconomics

Chapters 1–13, 24. The level of difficulty can be varied by including or omitting starred sections and boxes from these chapters.

Example of an Introduction to Microeconomics course, omitting some of these chapters: Chapters 1–7, 9, 11–13, 24.

Alternative 4: Introduction to macroeconomics

Chapters 1, 2, 14–26. The level of difficulty can be varied by including or omitting starred sections and boxes from these chapters.

Example of an Introduction to Macroeconomics course, omitting some of these chapters: Chapters 1, 2, (If micro-economics has not previously been covered) 14, 15, 17–23, 25.

Alternative 5: Outline courses

Chapters 1, 2, 5, 6, 14, 15, 17, 18, 24, 25 (section 25.1). Omit boxes at will.

Alternative 6: Courses with a theory bias

Chapters 1, 2, 4–9, 11, 14–19, 21, 22, 24, 25. The level of difficulty can be varied by including or omitting starred sections and boxes from these chapters.

Alternative 7: Courses with a policy bias (and only basic theory)

Chapters 1–3, 5, 6, 10–15, (17), 20, 23–6.

COMPANION BOOKS AND MATERIALS

Student Workbook, Seventh Edition (by John Sloman and Peter Smith)

A new edition of the Student Workbook has been designed to accompany this text. Each chapter of the workbook matches a chapter of *Economics* and consists of four sections.

A. Review questions. This section is a mixture of narrative and questions and goes through all the key material in the text-book chapter. Questions are a mixture of multiple choice, true/false, either/or, filling in blank words or phrases, matching a series of answers to a series of questions, short written answers and brief calculations. Each type of question is clearly marked with an appropriate symbol.
B. Problems, exercises and projects. This section includes multiple-part calculations and exercises, and student projects (including data search exercises, games, role playing and questionnaires).
C. Discussion topics and essays. This includes various thought-provoking questions that can be used for class discussion and more traditional essay questions.
D. Answers and comments. This includes answers to *and* comments on all questions in section A of each chapter (answers to section B questions are given on the memory stick and in the lecturer's resources at **www.pearsoned.co.uk/sloman**).

MyEconLab (for students)

MyEconLab is a comprehensive set of online resources developed for the seventh edition of *Economics*. Access is provided with every new purchase of this text. MyEconLab provides a variety of tools to enable students to assess their own learning, including exercises, quizzes and tests.

A personalised Study Plan identifies areas to concentrate on to improve grades, and specific tools are provided to each student to direct their studies in the most efficient way.

In addition, a large range of other resources are available in MyEconLab, including:

- A highly interactive online workbook;
- Animations of key models with audio explanations;
- A news blog with news items added several times each month;
- A comprehensive glossary with flashcards to check students' knowledge;
- 154 case studies with questions for self study, ordered chapter by chapter and referred to in the text;
- Maths cases with exercises, related to the 'Looking at the Maths' sections in the book;
- 20 self-test questions per chapter;
- Updated list of over 260 hotlinks to sites of use for economics;
- Answers to all in-chapter questions;
- Profiles of famous historical economists;
- Learning objectives for each chapter written in 'student-friendly' language.

Note that the news blog and hotlinks can also be accessed directly from **www.pearsoned.co.uk/sloman**.

See Guided Tour (pages xvi–xxi) for more details.

For lecturers

MyEconLab

MyEconLab can be set up by you as a complete virtual learning environment for your course or embedded into Blackboard, WebCT or Moodle. You can customise its look and feel and its availability to students. You can use it to provide support to your students in the following ways:

- MyEconLab's gradebook automatically records each student's time spent and performance on the tests and Study Plan. It also generates reports you can use to monitor your students' progress.
- You can use MyEconLab to build your own tests, quizzes and homework assignments from the question base provided to set for your students' assessment.
- Questions are generated algorithmically so that they use different values each time they are used.
- You can create your own exercises by using the econ exercise builder.

Memory stick

The CD produced for tutors using the 6th edition of *Economics* proved very popular. The materials on the CD have been updated, revised and extended for the 7th edition and are now available on a memory stick, free of charge from Pearson Education to tutors using the book as a course text. The memory stick contains the following:

- PowerPoint® slide shows in full colour for use with a data projector in lectures and classes. These can also be made available to students by loading them on to a local network. The memory stick contains several types of these slide shows:
  - All figures from the book and most of the tables. Each figure is built up in a logical sequence, thereby allowing tutors to show them in lectures in an animated form. They are also available in a simple version suitable for printing onto acetate for OHPs.
  - A range of models. There are 39 files, each containing one of the key models from the book, developed in an animated sequence of between 20 and 80 screens.
  - Customisable lecture plans. These are a series of bullet-point lecture plans. There is one for each chapter of the book. Each one can be easily edited, with points added, deleted or moved, so as to suit particular lectures. A consistent use of colour is made to show how the points tie together. They come in various versions:
    - Lecture plans with integrated diagrams. These lecture plans include animated diagrams and charts at the appropriate points.
    - Lecture plans with integrated diagrams and questions. These allow lectures to become more interactive and can be used with or without an audience response system (ARS). ARS versions are available for InterWrite PRS® and for TurningPoint®.
    - Lecture plans are also without the diagrams so that you can construct your own on the blackboard or whiteboard or use an OHP.

- Tutor's Guide in Word®. This contains the following features:
  - Answers to all questions in *Economics* (7th edition): i.e. questions embedded in the text, box questions and end-of-chapter questions. These can be edited as desired and distributed to students.
  - Answers to the case studies and maths cases found in MyEconLab.
  - Suggestions on how to use the text.
  - Learning objectives that can be used for syllabus design and course planning.
- Multiple-choice questions. This test bank have been revised and contains many new questions. It is flexible and easy to use.
- Case studies. These, also available in MyEconLab, can be reproduced and used for classroom exercises or for student assignments. Answers are also provided.
- Workshops. There are 20 of these (10 micro and 10 macro/international). They are in Word® and can be reproduced for use with large groups of students (up to 200). Suggestions for use are given on the memory stick. Answers to all workshop questions are given in separate Word® files.
- Teaching/learning case studies. These examine various ways to improve student learning of introductory economics.

Lecturer website

All the materials on the memory stick are available to download from the lecturer section of the website (**www.pearsoned.co.uk/sloman**). Click on the book image to take you to the link to the lecturer site. Most of the materials are open access, but all answers are in a secure password protected area of the site.

The site is regularly updated.

WinEcon (Sloman version)

The widely acclaimed *WinEcon* software, produced and authored by the Economics Consortium of the Teaching and Learning Technology Programme (TLTP) and designed to support courses in introductory economics, is now available to download in a version specially designed for *Economics* (7th edition).

There is a separate chapter in the Sloman version of *WinEcon* to correspond with the relevant chapter in the book. The software is highly interactive and is attractive to use and is regularly updated. It has been redesigned in a new attractive format.

For details of WinEcon and how to download a copy, go to **www.winecon.com/sloman-economics**.

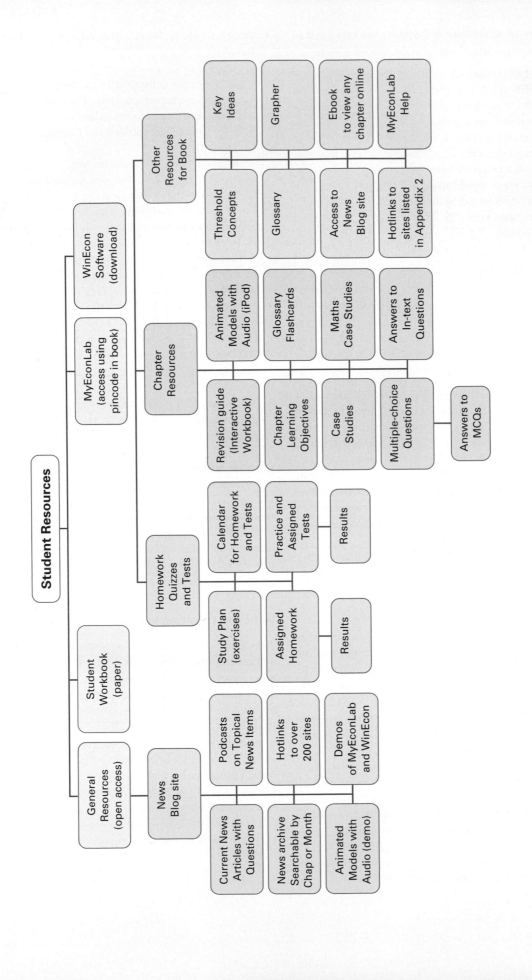

Student Resources

- General Resources (open access)
  - News Blog site
    - Current News Articles with Questions
    - Podcasts on Topical News Items
    - News archive Searchable by Chap or Month
    - Hotlinks to over 200 sites
    - Animated Models with Audio (demo)
    - Demos of MyEconLab and WinEcon

- Student Workbook (paper)

- MyEconLab (access using pincode in book)
  - Homework Quizzes and Tests
    - Study Plan (exercises)
    - Calendar for Homework and Tests
    - Assigned Homework
      - Results
    - Practice and Assigned Tests
      - Results
  - Chapter Resources
    - Revision guide (Interactive Workbook)
    - Animated Models with Audio (iPod)
    - Chapter Learning Objectives
    - Glossary Flashcards
    - Case Studies
    - Maths Case Studies
    - Multiple-choice Questions
      - Answers to MCQs
    - Answers to In-text Questions

- WinEcon Software (download)

- Other Resources for Book
  - Threshold Concepts
  - Key Ideas
  - Glossary
  - Grapher
  - Access to News Blog site
  - Ebook to view any chapter online
  - Hotlinks to sites listed in Appendix 2
  - MyEconLab Help

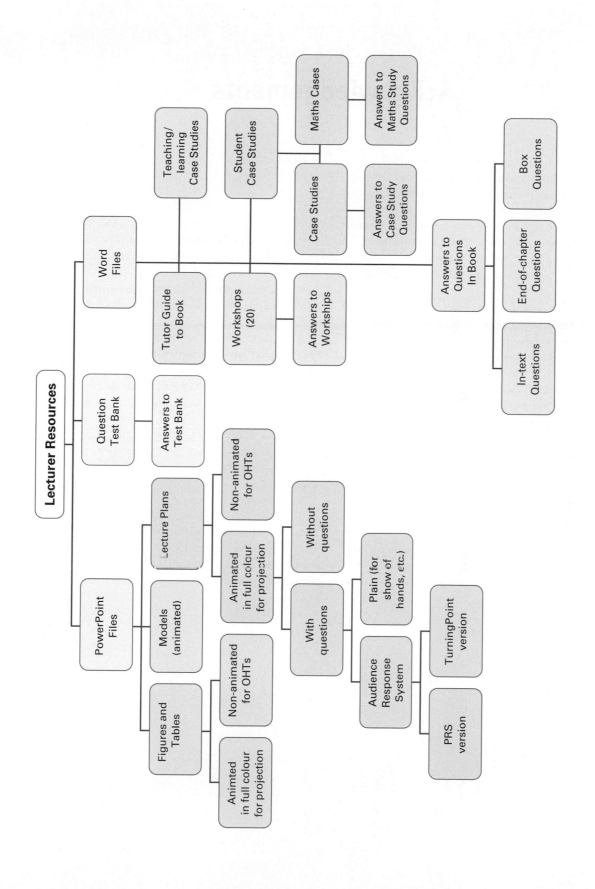

Acknowledgements

As with previous editions, we owe a debt to various people. The whole team from Pearson has, as always, been very helpful and supportive. Thanks in particular to Ellen Morgan, who has been of tremendous help at every stage of revising the book and to Joe Vella who has steered the book smoothly through production. Thanks also to Margaret Christie, who meticulously copy-edited the manuscript, Joan Dale Lace, proofreader and Isobel McLean who prepared the Index.

Thanks too to colleagues and students from many universities who have been helpful and encouraging and, as in previous editions, have made useful suggestions for improvement. We have attempted to incorporate their ideas wherever possible. Please do write or email if you have any suggestions. Especially we should like to thank the following reviewers of the previous editions. Their analysis and comments have helped to shape this new edition.

Dr Christopher J. Gerry, University College London SSESS, UK

David Ho

Ian Jackson, Staffordshire University, UK

Lars Bach, The International Business Academy, Kolding, Denmark

Leslie Christensen, Copenhagen Business School (CBS), Denmark

Professor Mark J. Holmes, University of Waikato, New Zealand

Pamela Siler, University of Abertay Dundee, UK

Richard O'Doherty, University of the West of England, UK

Roy Bailey, University of Essex, UK

Stuart Sayer, University of Edinburgh, UK

Professor Sue Bowden, University of York, UK

Tony McGough, Course Director, Cass Business School, City University London, UK

Walter Vanthielen, Hasselt University, Belgium

Wilfried Pauwels, University of Antwerp, Belgium

A special thanks to Peter Smith from the University of Southampton who has revised the Workbook to accompany this edition of the book and has contributed to the Tutor Guide and the MyEconLab online course. It's great to have his input and ideas for improvements to the books and supplements.

A special thanks too to Mark Sutcliffe from the Cardiff School of Management. Mark provided considerable help and support on earlier editions and it's still much appreciated.

John: My biggest thanks go to my family, and especially to Alison, my wife and soulmate, and our daughter Ellie. As always they have been patient and supportive, despite my long hours at the computer.

Alison: I'd like to offer thanks to my husband, Chris, without his support and love none of this would have been possible.

Publishers Acknowledgements

We are grateful to the following for permission to reproduce copyright material:

Figures

Figure on page 254 adapted from *Flexibility, Uncertainty and Manpower Management*, IMS Report No. 89, Institute of Manpower Studies (Atkinson, J., 1984), Institute for Employment Studies (IES); Figure 10.1 adapted from 'T he effects of taxes and benefits on household income' 2006/07, *Economic & Labour Market Review*, July, National Statistics, 2008, © Crown copyright 2008. Published with the permission of the Office for Public Sector Information (OPSI); Figures 10.5, 10.7, 10.8, 12.4 after *Family Spending*, National Statistics, 2008, © Crown Copyright 2008. Published with the permission of the Office for Public Sector Information (OPSI); Figures 10.14a, 10.14b after Eurostat, Statistics in Focus http://epp.eurostat.ec.europa.eu, Commission of the European Communities, 2008; Figure on page 344 from *Stern Review on the Economics of Climate Change*, Office of Climate Change (OCC) Stern Review, 2006, Executive Summary, Figure 1, based on data drawn from World Resources Institute Climate Analysis Indicators Tool (CAIT) online database version 3.0., © Crown copyright 2006; Figure on page 380 after 'Electricity supply: reorganisation and privatisation', *The Economic Review*, March, Vol. 7, No. 4 (Green, R., 1991), Reprinted by permission of Philip Allan Updates; Figures A14.1, A14.2 after *United Kingdom National Accounts: The Blue Book 2008 Edition*, National Statistics, 2008, www.statistics.gov.uk Crown copyright material is reproduced with the permission of the Controller Office of Public Sector Information (OPSI); Figure on page 411 after *Quality of Life Briefing*, New Economics Foundation/Friends of the Earth (Mayo, E., MacGillivray, A. and McLaren, D., 1998), copyright © The New Economics Foundation; Figure on page 430 from Yugoslavian banknote, 1994, copyright © National Bank of Serbia, Treasury Department; Figure on page 485 after *Business and Consumer Surveys* Commission of the European Communities, 2008; Figure on page 573 after *Pre-Budget Report 2008* H. M. Treasury, 2005; Figure on page 606 after *Inflation Report*, November, Bank of England, 2008, copyright © The Bank of England; Figure 21.16 after *Budget Report 2008* H.M. Treasury, 2008, Chart 2.1; Figure on page 646 after *Productivity in the UK: 7, Securing long-term prosperity*, November, HM Treasury and Department for Business Enterprise and Regulatory Reform, 2007; Figure 24.7 adapted from *The Competitive Advantage of Nations*, The Free Press (Porter M. E., 1998) p. 127, Reprinted with the permission of The Free Press, a Division of Simon & Schuster, Inc., copyright © 1990, 1998 by Michael E. Porter. All rights reserved; and figure on page 782 after Forecast by Morgan Stanley, *The Economist*, 5 June 2008, copyright © The Economist 2008.

Tables

Tables on page 7, 396, 484 and tables 15.5, 20.1, 22.1, 22.2, 23.1, 24.1 adapted from *Statistical Annex of the European Economy*, Commission of the European Communities, 2007; Table on page 166 after *United Kingdom Input-Output Analyses, 2006 Edition*, National Statistics, 2006, Table 8.31, © Crown copyright 2008. Published with the permission of the Office for Public Sector Information (OPSI); Tables on page 252 after *Annual Survey of Hours and Earnings*, National Statistics © Crown copyright 2008. Published with the permission of the Office for Public Sector Information (OPSI); Table 10.1 after *Family Spending*, National Statistics, 2008, © Crown copyright 2008. Published with the permission of the Office for Public Sector Information (OPSI); Table 10.2 adapted from Based on HMRC personal wealth statistics www.hmrc.gov.uk/stats/personal_wealth/menu.htm, Table 13.5 HM Revenue & Customs, © Crown copyright 2008; Tables on page 334, 335 after *The costs and benefits of lowering the sulphur content of petrol and diesel to less than 10 ppm*, Commission of the European Communities, DG Environment, 2001 Tables 4, 5 and 9; Table 12.1 after *OECD Environmental Outlook*, Organisation for Economic Co-operation and Development, 2002; Table 12.3 after *Transport Statistics of Great Britain, 2007*, Department for Transport, 2007, Crown Copyright material is reproduced with permission under the terms of the Click-Use License; Table on page 410 from *An Index of Sustainable Economic Welfare for the UK 1950–96*, Centre for Environmental Strategy, University of Surrey (Jackson, T., Marks, N., Ralls, J. and Stymne, S.); Table A14.1 after *United Kingdom National Accounts: The Blue Book 2008 Edition*, National Statistics, 2008, www.statistics.gov.uk. Crown copyright material is reproduced with the permission of the Controller Office of Public Sector Information (OPSI); Table A14.2 after *UK National Income and Expenditure*, National Statistics, 2008, www.statistics.gov.uk. Crown copyright material is reproduced with the permission of the Controller Office of Public Sector Information (OPSI); Table on page 431 after Based on data in IMF International Financial Statistics (IFS) database www.imfstatistics.org International Monetary Fund; Tables 15.2, 15.3 after *Economic and Labour Market Review* National Statistics, © Crown copyright 2008. Published with the permission of the Office for Public Sector Information (OPSI); Table 15.4 after Eurostat, Statistics in Focus http://epp.eurostat.ec.europa.eu Commission of the European Communities, 2008; Tables 15.7, 15.8 after Based on data in the Statistical Interactive Database www.bankofengland.co.uk/mfsd/iadb/NewIntermed.asp Bank of England, copyright © The Bank of England; Table on page 484 after *Business and Consumer Surveys* Commission of the European Communities, DG for Financial and Economic Affairs, 2007; Tables on page 520, 18.2 and 18.7 adapted from *Bankstats,* Bank of England, 2008 Table in A and B: money and lending, and Table B1.1.1, copyright © The Bank of England; Table 20.6 after From the National Statistics website www.statistics.gov.uk National Statistics, © Crown copyright. Reproduced with the permission of the Controller Office of Public Sector Information (OPSI); Table 24.5 adapted from The competition effects of the single market in Europe, *Economic Policy* (Allen, C., Gasiorek, M. and Smith, A., 1998), copyright © Wiley-Blackwell; Table 25.2 after Based on data in the IMF International Financial Statistics (IFS) database www.imfstatistics.org International Monetary Fund; Table 26.1 after *OECD Economic Outlook,*

Organisation for Economic Co-operation and Development, 2007; Table 27.1 after *World Development Statistics,* World Bank, 2005; Table on page 765 adapted from *UNDP Human Development Report 2007/2008,* United Nations Development Program, published 2007, reproduced with permission of Palgrave Macmillan; Tables 27.4, 27.5 after *Global Development Finance* World Bank, 2008; Tables 2.1, 2.2 after *Times Series Data,* National Statistics, 2008, © Crown copyright. Reproduced with the permission of the Controller Office of Public Sector Information (OPSI); Table 2.3 after *The effects of taxes and benefits on household income, 2006/07* National Statistics, 2008, © Crown copyright 2008. Published with the permission of the Office for Public Sector Information (OPSI); Table 2.5 after *Economic Trends* National Statistics, © Crown copyright 2006. Published with the permission of the Controller of Her Majesty's Stationery Office (HMSO).

Text
Box 19.4 after *A proposal for greening of textbook macro: 'IS-LM-EE'*, Royal Holloway College, University of London, Working Paper (Heyes, A., 1998); Extract on page 665 from Intricate workings, *The Economist*, 17 June 2006, copyright © The Economist 2006.

In some instances we have been unable to trace the owners of copyright material, and we would appreciate any information that would enable us to do so.

Introduction

1 Introducing Economics

In this opening part of the book you will get a glimpse of what the subject of economics is all about. One thing should be stressed right from the outset: economics is not just a set of facts or theories to be memorised. Studying economics gives you a way of thinking about the world. It helps you to make sense of the decisions people are making all the time: decisions we make about what to buy or what job to do; decisions our government makes about how much to tax us or what to spend those taxes on. This makes economics a fascinating and relevant subject for everyone, not just those who are going on to further study. You will be able to apply this 'way of thinking' to your daily life and to work; this helps explain why the subject enhances employability.

Economics contains some core ideas. These ideas are simple, but can be applied to a wide range of economic problems. We start examining these ideas in Chapter 1.

Chapter 1

Introducing Economics

CHAPTER MAP

1.1 What do economists study?   **4**
The problem of scarcity   4
Demand and supply   5
Dividing up the subject   5
Macroeconomics   6
Microeconomics   7
Illustrating economic issues: the production
    possibility curve   11
Illustrating economic issues: the circular flow
    of goods and incomes   14

1.2 Different economic systems   **16**
The classification of economic systems   16
The command economy   18
Assessment of the command economy   19
The free-market economy   20
Assessment of the free-market economy   23
The mixed economy   24

1.3 The nature of economic reasoning   **25**
Economics as a science   25
Economics as a social science   26
Economics and policy   26

You may never have studied economics before, and yet when you open a newspaper what do you read? – a report from 'our economics correspondent'. Turn on the television news and what do you see? – an item on the state of the economy. Talk to friends and often the topic will turn to the price of this or that product, or whether you have got enough money to afford to do this or that.

The fact is that economics affects our daily lives. We are continually being made aware of local, national and international economic issues, whether price increases, interest rate changes, fluctuations in exchange rates, unemployment, economic recessions or the effects of globalisation.

We are also continually faced with economic problems and decisions of our own. What should I buy in the supermarket? Should I save up for a summer holiday, or spend more on day-to-day living? Should I go to university, or should I try to find a job now? If I go to university, should I work part time?

So just what is economics about? In this chapter we will attempt to answer this question and give you some insights into the subject that you will be studying. We will see how the subject is divided up, and in particular we will distinguish between the two major branches of economics: microeconomics and macroeconomics.

We will also look at the ways in which different types of economy operate, from the centrally planned economies of the former communist countries to the largely free-market economies of most of the world today. We will ask just how 'markets' work.

1.1 WHAT DO ECONOMISTS STUDY?

Many people think that economics is about *money*. Well, to some extent this is true. Economics has a lot to do with money: with how much money people are paid; how much they spend; what it costs to buy various items; how much money firms earn; how much money there is in total in the economy. But as we will see later in the book, money is only important because of what it allows us to do; money is a tool and economics is more than just the study of money.

It is concerned with the following:

- The *production* of goods and services: how much the economy produces, both in total and of individual items; how much each firm or person produces; what techniques of production are used; how many people are employed.
- The *consumption* of goods and services: how much the population as a whole spends (and how much it saves); what the pattern of consumption is in the economy; how much people buy of particular items; what particular individuals choose to buy; how people's consumption is affected by prices, advertising, fashion and other factors.

 Could production and consumption take place without money? If you think they could, give some examples.

But we still have not quite got to the bottom of what economics is about. What is the crucial ingredient that makes a problem an economic one? The answer is that there is one central problem faced by all individuals and all societies. From this one problem stem all the other economic problems we shall be looking at throughout this book.

This central economic problem is the problem of scarcity. This applies not only in countries like Ethiopia and the Sudan, but also in the UK, the USA, Japan, France and all other countries of the world. For an economist, scarcity has a very specific definition.

 Before reading on, how would you define 'scarcity'? Must goods be at least temporarily unattainable to be scarce?

The problem of scarcity

Ask people if they would like more money, and the vast majority would answer 'Yes'. They want more money so that they can buy more goods and services; and this applies not only to poor people but also to most wealthy people too. The point is that human wants are virtually unlimited.

Yet the means of fulfilling human wants are limited. At any one time the world can only produce a limited amount of goods and services. This is because the world only has a limited amount of *resources*. These resources, or *factors of production* as they are often called, are of three broad types:

- Human resources: *labour*. The labour force is limited in number, but also in skills. This limits the productivity of labour.
- Natural resources: *land and raw materials*. The world's land area is limited, as are its raw materials.
- Manufactured resources: *capital*. Capital consists of all those inputs that have each had to be produced in the first place. The world has a limited stock of capital: a limited supply of factories, machines, transportation and other equipment. The productivity of capital is limited by the state of technology.

 Could each of these types of resources be increased in quantity or quality? Is there a time dimension to your answer?

So here is the reason for scarcity: human wants are virtually unlimited, whereas the resources available to satisfy these wants are limited. We can thus define scarcity as follows:

Definitions

Production The transformation of inputs into outputs by firms in order to earn profit (or to meet some other objective).

Consumption The act of using goods and services to satisfy wants. This will normally involve purchasing the goods and services.

Factors of production (or resources) The inputs into the production of goods and services: labour, land and raw materials, and capital.

Labour All forms of human input, both physical and mental, into current production.

Land and raw materials Inputs into production that are provided by nature: e.g. unimproved land and mineral deposits in the ground.

Capital All inputs into production that have themselves been produced: e.g. factories, machines and tools.

BOX 1.1 **WHAT'S THE LATEST ECONOMICS NEWS?** CASE STUDIES AND APPLICATIONS

- Budget news: Chancellor cuts 2p off the basic rate of income tax while abolishing the lowest 10p band. The resulting reaction from MPs and the public requires a rethink on tax allowances.
- Mortgage companies require housebuyers to pay larger deposits: impact on the housing market is expected to result in lower house prices.
- Despite predictions of a recession, cinemas and takeaway pizza chains report record turnover.
- Smoking banned in public places: pubs and cafes concerned about the impact on trade.
- Food prices soar across the world: an increase in mortality in developing countries is predicted.
- Prices rise: unions demand higher wages to compensate.

- Unemployment increases: consumer spending falls.
- Increased expenditure on primary and secondary education is announced while tuition fees for university degrees are increased. The government claims that this will help reduce poverty and increase productivity. Opponents claim that students from low-income households will be priced out of higher education.
- Oil prices hit a record high level: Shell's share price rises, while those of Ford Motor Company fall.
- Banking crisis: lack of credit triggers recession.

 What is it that makes each one of the above news items an economics item?

 KEY IDEA 1 *Scarcity* is the excess of human wants over what can actually be produced. Because of scarcity, various choices have to be made between alternatives.

 If we would all like more money, why does the government not print a lot more? Could it not thereby solve the problem of scarcity 'at a stroke'?

Of course, we do not all face the problem of scarcity to the same degree. A poor person unable to afford enough to eat or a decent place to live will hardly see it as a 'problem' that a rich person cannot afford a second BMW. But economists do not claim that we all face an equal problem of scarcity. In fact this is one of the major issues economists study: how resources are distributed, whether between different individuals, different regions of a country or different countries of the world.

But given that people, both rich and poor, want more than they can have, this makes them behave in certain ways. Economics studies that behaviour. It studies people at work, producing the goods that people want. It studies people as consumers, buying the goods that they themselves want. It studies governments influencing the level and pattern of production and consumption. In short, it studies anything to do with the process of satisfying human wants.

Demand and supply

We said that economics is concerned with consumption and production. Another way of looking at this is in terms of *demand* and *supply*. In fact, demand and supply and the relationship between them lie at the very centre of economics. But what do we mean by the terms, and what is their relationship with the problem of scarcity?

Demand is related to wants. If goods and services were free, people would simply demand whatever they wanted. Such wants are virtually boundless, perhaps only limited by people's imagination. *Supply*, on the other hand, is limited. It is related to resources. The amount that firms can supply depends on the resources and technology available.

Given the problem of scarcity, given that human wants exceed what can actually be produced, *potential* demands will exceed *potential* supplies. Society therefore has to find some way of dealing with this problem, to try to match demand with supply. This applies at the level of the economy overall: *aggregate* demand will need to be balanced against *aggregate* supply. In other words, total spending in the economy should balance total production. It also applies at the level of individual goods and services. The demand and supply of cabbages should balance, and so should the demand and supply of digital cameras, cars, houses and package holidays.

But if potential demand exceeds potential supply, how are *actual* demand and supply to be made equal? Either demand has to be curtailed, or supply has to be increased, or a combination of the two. Economics studies this process. It studies how demand adjusts to available supplies, and how supply adjusts to consumer demands.

KI 1 p5

Dividing up the subject

Economics is traditionally divided into two main branches – *macroeconomics* and *microeconomics*, where 'macro' means big and 'micro' means small.

Definition

Scarcity The excess of human wants over what can actually be produced to fulfil these wants.

Macroeconomics is concerned with the economy as a whole. It is thus concerned with *aggregate demand* and *aggregate supply*. By 'aggregate demand' we mean the total amount of spending in the economy, whether by consumers, by customers outside the country for our exports, by the government, or by firms when they buy capital equipment or stock up on raw materials. By 'aggregate supply' we mean the total national output of goods and services.

Microeconomics is concerned with the individual parts of the economy. It is concerned with the demand and supply of particular goods, services and resources such as cars, butter, clothes, haircuts, electricians, secretaries, blast furnaces, computers and oil.

 Which of the following are macroeconomic issues, which are microeconomic ones and which could be either depending on the context?
(a) Inflation.
(b) Low wages in certain service industries.
(c) The rate of exchange between the pound and the euro.
(d) Why the price of cabbages fluctuates more than that of cars.
(e) The rate of economic growth this year compared with last year.
(f) The decline of traditional manufacturing industries.
(g) The influx of workers from eastern Europe.

Macroeconomics

Because things are scarce, societies are concerned that their resources should be used *as fully as possible* and that over time their national output should grow.

Why should resources be used as fully as possible? If resources are 'saved' in one time period surely they can be used in the next time period? The answer is that not all resources can be saved. If workers don't go to work one week then that resource is lost: labour can't be saved up for the future.

Why do societies want growth? To understand this, think back to the discussion of endless wants: if our output grows, then more of our wants can be satisfied over time.

The achievement of growth and the full use of resources is not easy, however, as demonstrated by the periods of high unemployment and stagnation that have occurred from time to time throughout the world (for example, in the 1930s, the early 1980s, the early 1990s and the period from early 2008). Furthermore, attempts by government to stimulate growth and employment have often resulted in inflation and a large rise in imports. Even when societies do achieve growth, it can be short-lived. Economies have often experienced cycles where periods of growth alternate with periods of stagnation, such periods varying from a few months to a few years. This is known as the 'business cycle'.

Macroeconomic problems are closely related to the balance between aggregate demand and aggregate supply.

If aggregate demand is too *high* relative to aggregate supply, inflation and trade deficits are likely to result.

- **Inflation** refers to a general rise in the level of prices throughout the economy. If aggregate demand rises substantially, firms are likely to respond by raising their prices. After all, if demand is high, they can probably still sell as much as before (if not more) even at the higher prices, and thus make more profits. If firms in general put up their prices, inflation results.
- **Balance of trade** deficits are the excess of imports over exports. If aggregate demand rises, people are likely to buy more imports. In other words, part of the extra expenditure will go on Japanese LCD TVs, German cars, French wine, etc. Also, if inflation is high, home-produced goods will become uncompetitive with foreign goods. We are likely to buy more foreign imports and people abroad are likely to buy fewer of our exports.

If aggregate demand is too low relative to aggregate supply, unemployment and recession may well result.

- **Recession** is where output in the economy declines: in other words, growth becomes negative. A recession is associated with a low level of consumer spending. If people spend less, shops are likely to find themselves with unsold stock. As a result they will buy less from the manufacturers, which in turn will cut down on production.

Definitions

Macroeconomics The branch of economics that studies economic aggregates (grand totals): e.g. the overall level of prices, output and employment in the economy.

Aggregate demand The total level of spending in the economy.

Aggregate supply The total amount of output in the economy.

Microeconomics The branch of economics that studies individual units: e.g. households, firms and industries. It studies the interrelationships between these units in

determining the pattern of production and distribution of goods and services.

Rate of inflation The percentage increase in the level of prices over a 12-month period.

Balance of trade Exports of goods and services minus imports of goods and services. If exports exceed imports, there is a 'balance of trade surplus' (a positive figure). If imports exceed exports, there is a 'balance of trade deficit' (a negative figure).

Recession A period where national output falls for six months or more.

KI 1
p5

| **BOX 1.2** | **LOOKING AT MACROECONOMIC DATA** | CASE STUDIES AND APPLICATIONS |

Assessing different countries' macroeconomic performance

Rapid economic growth, low unemployment, low inflation and the avoidance of current account deficits[1] are major macroeconomic policy objectives of most governments round the world. To help them achieve these objectives they employ economic advisers. But when we look at the performance of various economies, the success of government macroeconomic policies seems decidedly 'mixed'.

The table shows data for the USA, Japan, Germany[2] and the UK from 1961 to 2008.

Macroeconomic performance of four industrialised economies (average annual figures)

	Unemployment (% of workforce)				Inflation (%)				Economic growth (%)				Balance on current account (% of national income)			
	USA	Japan	Germany	UK	USA	Japan	Germany	UK	USA	Japan	Germany	UK	USA	Japan	Germany	UK
1961–70	4.8	1.3	0.6	1.7	2.4	5.6	2.7	3.9	4.2	10.1	4.4	3.0	0.5	0.6	0.7	0.2
1971–80	6.4	1.8	2.2	3.8	7.0	8.8	5.1	13.2	3.2	4.4	2.8	2.0	0.9	0.5	1.1	−0.7
1981–90	2.5	2.5	6.0	9.6	4.5	2.2	2.5	6.2	3.2	3.9	2.3	2.6	−1.7	2.3	2.6	−1.4
1991–2000	3.3	3.3	7.9	7.9	2.2	0.4	2.3	3.3	3.3	1.5	1.9	2.4	−1.6	2.5	−0.7	−1.5
2001–10	6.3	4.7	8.7	5.7	2.1	−0.7	1.9	1.8	1.7	0.8	1.0	1.6	−4.8	3.7	4.6	−3.0

Note: Years 2009 and 2010 forecasts.

Source: Statistical Annex of the European Economy (Commission of the European Communities, 2007), various tables.

1. *Has the UK generally fared better or worse than the other three countries?*
2. *Was there a common pattern in the macroeconomic performance of each of the four countries over these 50 years?*

If the government does not have much success in managing the economy, it could be for the following reasons:

- Economists have incorrectly analysed the problems and hence have given the wrong advice.
- Economists disagree and hence have given conflicting advice.

- Economists have based their advice on inaccurate forecasts.
- Governments have not heeded the advice of economists.
- There is little else that governments could have done: the problems were insoluble or could not have been predicted.

[1] The current account balance is the trade balance plus any incomes earned from abroad minus any incomes paid abroad. These incomes could be wages, investment incomes or government revenues (see section 15.4 for details).
[2] West Germany from 1961 to 1991.

- *Unemployment* is likely to result from cutbacks in production. If firms are producing less, they will need to employ fewer people.

Macroeconomic policy, therefore, tends to focus on the balance of aggregate demand and aggregate supply. It can be *demand-side policy*, which seeks to influence the level of spending in the economy. This in turn will affect the level of production, prices and employment. Or it can be *supply-side policy*. This is designed to influence the level of production directly: for example, by trying to create more incentives for firms to innovate.

Microeconomics

Microeconomics and choice

Because resources are scarce, choices have to be made. There are three main categories of choice that must be made in any society:

KI 1
p5

Definitions

Unemployment The number of people who are actively looking for work but are currently without a job. (Note that there is much debate as to who should officially be counted as unemployed.)

Demand-side policy Government policy designed to alter the level of aggregate demand, and thereby the level of output, employment and prices.

Supply-side policy Government policy that attempts to alter the level of aggregate supply directly.

- *What* goods and services are going to be produced and in what quantities, since there are not enough resources to produce all the things people desire? How many cars, how much wheat, how much insurance, how many video games etc. will be produced?

- *How* are things going to be produced? What resources are going to be used and in what quantities? What techniques of production are going to be adopted? Will cars be produced by robots or by assembly line workers? Will electricity be produced from coal, oil, gas, nuclear fission, renewable resources or a mixture of these?

- *For whom* are things going to be produced? In other words, how will the nation's income be distributed? After all, the higher your income, the more you can consume of the nation's output. What will be the wages of farm workers, printers, footballers and accountants? How much will pensioners receive? How much of the nation's income will go to shareholders or landowners?

All societies have to make these choices, whether they are made by individuals, groups or the government. These choices can be seen as microeconomic choices, since they are concerned not with the total amount of national output, but with the individual goods and services that make it up: what they are, how they are made, and who gets the incomes to buy them.

Choice and opportunity cost

Choice involves sacrifice. The more food you choose to buy, the less money you will have to spend on other goods. The more food a nation produces the fewer resources will there be for producing other goods. In other words, the production or consumption of one thing involves the sacrifice of alternatives. This sacrifice of alternatives in the production (or consumption) of a good is known as its *opportunity cost*.

KEY IDEA 2 | The *opportunity cost* of any activity is the sacrifice made to do it. It is the best thing that could have been done as an alternative.

KI 1
p5

| THRESHOLD CONCEPT 1 | CHOICE AND OPPORTUNITY COST | THINKING LIKE AN ECONOMIST |

Scarcity, as we have seen, is at the heart of economics.

We face scarcity as individuals. Each of us has a limited income and hence we cannot buy everything we want. Also, there are only 24 hours in a day and we all have a limited lifespan. So even if we had the money, we would not be able to enjoy every possible good we would like to consume or take part in every possible activity.

The same applies to nations. A country has limited resources and hence cannot produce everything people would like. So too with the world. Our planet has finite resources, and the technology and human abilities to exploit these resources are also limited.

We thus have to make choices. In fact, virtually every time we do something, we are making a choice between alternatives. If you choose to spend your time staying in and watching television, you are choosing not to go out. If you buy a DVD for £10, you are choosing not to spend that £10 on something else. Likewise, if a nation devotes more of its resources to producing manufactured goods, there will be less to devote to the provision of services or the production of agricultural goods. If we devote more resources to producing a cleaner environment, we may have to produce less of the material goods that people want to consume.

What we give up in order to do something is known as its *opportunity cost*. Opportunity cost is the cost of doing something measured in terms of the best alternative forgone. It's what you would have chosen to do with your time or money if you had not made the choice you did. This is one of the most fundamental concepts in economics. It is a threshold concept: once you have seen its importance, it affects the way you look at economic problems. When you use the concept of opportunity cost, you are thinking like an economist. And this may be different from thinking like an accountant or from the way you thought before. We will come across this concept many times throughout this book.

By looking at opportunity cost we are recognising that we face trade-offs. To do more of one thing involves doing less of something else. For example, we trade off work and leisure. The more we work, the less leisure time we will have. In other words, the opportunity cost of working is the leisure we have sacrificed. Nations trade off producing one good against others. The more a country spends on defence, whether on weapons or employing military personnel, the less it will have to spend on consumer goods and services. This has become known as the 'guns versus butter' trade-off. In other words, if a country decides to use more of its resources for defence, the opportunity cost is the consumer goods sacrificed. We examine such trade-offs at a national level on pages 12–3, when we look at the 'production possibility curve'.

We thus have to make decisions between alternatives. To make sensible decisions we must weigh up the benefits of doing something against its opportunity cost. This is known in economics as 'rational decision making'. It is another of our threshold concepts (no. 8): see page 100.

1. *Think of three things you did last week. What was the opportunity cost of each one?*
2. *Assume that a supermarket has some fish that has reached its sell-by date. It was originally priced at £10, but yesterday was marked down to £5 'for quick sale'. It is now the end of the day and it still has not been sold. The supermarket is about to close and there is no one in the store who wants fish. What is the opportunity cost for the store of throwing the fish away?*

If the workers on a farm can produce either 1000 tonnes of wheat or 2000 tonnes of barley, then the opportunity cost of producing 1 tonne of wheat is the 2 tonnes of barley forgone. The opportunity cost of buying a textbook is the new pair of jeans you also wanted that you have had to go without. The opportunity cost of working overtime is the leisure you have sacrificed.

Opportunity cost as the basis for choice is the first of our 'Threshold Concepts' (see page 8). There are fifteen of these threshold concepts, which we shall be exploring throughout the book. Once you have grasped these concepts and seen their significance, they will affect the way that you understand and analyse economic problems. They will help you to 'think like an economist'.

Rational choices

Economists often refer to **rational choices**. This simply means the weighing up of the *costs* and *benefits* of any activity, whether it be firms choosing what and how much to produce, workers choosing whether to take a particular job or to work extra hours, or consumers choosing what to buy.

Imagine you are doing your shopping in a supermarket and you want to buy a chicken. Do you spend a lot of money and buy a free-range organic chicken, or do you buy a cheap battery hen instead? To make a rational (i.e. sensible) decision, you will need to weigh up the costs and benefits of each alternative. The free-range chicken may taste better and it may meet your concerns about animal welfare, but it has a high opportunity cost: because it is expensive, you will need to sacrifice quite a lot of consumption of other goods if you decide to buy it. If you buy the cheap battery-farmed chicken, however, although you will not enjoy it so much, you will have more money left over to buy other things: it has a lower opportunity cost.

Thus rational decision making, as far as consumers are concerned, involves choosing those items that give you the best value for money – i.e. the *greatest benefit relative to cost*.

The same principles apply to firms when deciding what to produce. For example, should a car firm open up another production line? A rational decision will again involve weighing up the benefits and costs. The benefits are the revenues the firm will earn from selling the extra cars. The costs will include the extra labour costs, raw material costs, costs of component parts, etc. It will be profitable to open up the new production line only if the revenues earned exceed the costs entailed: in other words, if it adds to profit.

In the more complex situation of deciding which model of car to produce, or how many of each model, the firm must weigh up the relative benefits and costs of each – i.e. it will want to produce the most profitable product mix.

 Assume that you are looking for a job and are offered two. One is more pleasant to do, but pays less. How would you make a rational choice between the two jobs?

Marginal costs and benefits

In economics we argue that rational choices involve weighing up **marginal costs** and **marginal benefits**. These are the costs and benefits of doing a little bit more or a little bit less of a specific activity. They can be contrasted with the total costs and benefits of the activity.

Take a familiar example. What time will you set the alarm clock to go off tomorrow morning? Let us say that you have to leave home at 8.30. Perhaps you will set the alarm for 7.00. That will give you plenty of time to get up and get ready, but it will mean a relatively short night's sleep. Perhaps you will decide to set it for 7.30 or even 8.00. That will give you a longer night's sleep, but much more of a rush in the morning to get ready.

So how do you make a rational decision about when the alarm should go off? What you have to do is to weigh up the costs and benefits of *additional* sleep. Each extra minute in bed gives you more sleep (the marginal benefit), but gives you more of a rush when you get up (the marginal cost). The decision is therefore based on the costs and benefits of *extra* sleep, not on the total costs and benefits of a whole night's sleep.

This same principle applies to rational decisions made by consumers, workers and firms. For example, the car firm we were considering just now will weigh up the marginal costs and benefits of producing cars: in other words, it will compare the costs and revenue of producing *additional* cars. If additional cars add more to the firm's revenue than to its costs, it will be profitable to produce them.

Rational decision making, then, involves weighing up the marginal benefit and marginal cost of any activity.

Definitions

Opportunity cost The cost of any activity measured in terms of the best alternative forgone.

Rational choices Choices that involve weighing up the benefit of any activity against its opportunity cost.

Marginal costs The additional cost of doing a little bit more (or 1 unit more if a unit can be measured) of an activity.

Marginal benefits The additional benefits of doing a little bit more (or 1 unit more if a unit can be measured) of an activity.

Rational decision making Doing more of an activity if its marginal benefit exceeds its marginal cost and doing less if its marginal cost exceeds its marginal benefit.

If the marginal benefit exceeds the marginal cost, it is rational to do the activity (or to do more of it). If the marginal cost exceeds the marginal benefit, it is rational not to do it (or to do less of it).

Rational decision making is Threshold Concept 8 and this is examined in Chapter 4, page 100.

 How would the principle of weighing up marginal costs and benefits apply to a worker deciding how much overtime to work in a given week?

Microeconomic objectives

Microeconomics is concerned with the allocation of scarce resources: with the answering of the *what, how* and *for whom* questions. But how satisfactorily will these questions be answered? Clearly this depends on society's objectives. There are two major objectives that we can identify: *efficiency* and *equity*.

Efficiency.   If altering what was produced or how it was produced could make us all better off (or at least make some of us better off without anyone losing), then it would be efficient to do so. For a society to achieve full *economic efficiency*, three conditions must be met:

- Efficiency in production (**productive efficiency**). This is where production of each item is at minimum cost. Producing any other way would cost more.
- Efficiency in consumption. This is where consumers allocate their expenditures so as to get maximum satisfaction from their income. Any other pattern of consumption would make people feel worse off.
- Efficiency in specialisation and exchange. This is where firms specialise in producing goods for sale to consumers, and where individuals specialise in doing jobs in order to buy goods, so that everyone maximises the benefits they achieve relative to the costs of achieving them.

These last two are collectively known as **allocative efficiency**. In any economic activity, allocative efficiency will be increased as long as doing more of that activity (and hence less of an alternative) involves a greater marginal benefit than marginal cost. Full efficiency will be achieved when all such improvements have been made.

 KEY IDEA 3 *Economic efficiency* is achieved when each good is produced at the minimum cost and where individual people and firms get the maximum benefit from their resources.

Equity.   Even though the current levels of production and consumption might be efficient, they might be regarded as unfair, if some people are rich while others are poor. Another microeconomic goal, therefore, is that of **equity**. Income distribution is regarded as equitable if it is considered to be fair or just. The problem with this objective, however, is that people have different notions of fairness. A rich person may well favour a much higher degree of inequality than will a poor person. Likewise socialist governments will generally be in favour of a larger redistribution of income from the rich to the poor than will conservative governments.

 KEY IDEA 4 *Equity* is where income is distributed in a way that is considered to be fair or just. Note that an equitable distribution is not the same as an equal distribution and that different people have different views on what is equitable.

 Would it ever be desirable to have total equality in an economy?

The social implications of choice

In practice, the consequences of the choices that people make may be neither efficient nor equitable. Firms may use inefficient techniques or be poorly managed; people often make wrong decisions about what to buy or what job to take; governments may be wasteful or inefficient in their use of tax revenues; there may be considerable inequality and injustice.

What is more, the effects of people's choices often spill over to other people. Take the case of pollution. It might be profitable for a firm to tip toxic waste into a river. But what is profitable for the firm will not necessarily be 'profitable' for society. Such an action may have serious environmental consequences.

Definitions

Economic efficiency A situation where each good is produced at the minimum cost and where individual people and firms get the maximum benefit from their resources.

Productive efficiency A situation where firms are producing the maximum output for a given amount of inputs, or producing a given output at the least cost.

Allocative efficiency A situation where the current combination of goods produced and sold gives the maximum satisfaction for each consumer at their current levels of income. Note that a redistribution of income would lead to a different combination of goods that was allocatively efficient.

Equity A distribution of income that is considered to be fair or just. Note that an equitable distribution is not the same as an equal distribution and that different people have different views on what is equitable.

KI 2
p8

BOX 1.3	THE OPPORTUNITY COSTS OF STUDYING	CASE STUDIES AND APPLICATIONS

What are you sacrificing?

You may not have realised it, but you probably consider opportunity costs many times a day. The reason is that we are constantly making choices: what to buy, what to eat, what to wear, whether to go out, how much to study, and so on. Each time we make a choice to do something, we are in effect rejecting doing some alternative. This alternative forgone is the opportunity cost of the action we choose.

Sometimes the opportunity costs of our actions are the direct monetary costs we incur. Sometimes it is more complicated.

Take the opportunity costs of your choices as a student of economics.

Buying a textbook costing £49.99

This does involve a direct money payment. What you have to consider is the alternatives you could have bought with the £49.99. You then have to weigh up the benefit from the best alternative against the benefit of the textbook.

What might prevent you from making the best decision?

Coming to classes

You may or may not be paying your own course fees, but even if you are, there is no extra (marginal) monetary cost in coming to classes once the fees have been paid. You will not get a refund by skipping classes!

So are the opportunity costs zero? No: by coming to classes you are not working in the library; you are not sitting drinking coffee with friends; you are not able to undertake paid work during that time. If you are making a rational decision to come to classes, then you will consider such possible alternatives.

Choosing to study at university or college

What are the opportunity costs of being a student in higher education?

1. *If there are several other things you could have done, is the opportunity cost the sum of all of them?*
2. *What is the opportunity cost of spending an evening revising for an economics exam? What would you need to know in order to make a sensible decision about what to do that evening?*

At first it might seem that the costs of higher education would include the following:

- Tuition fees.
- Books, stationery, etc.
- Accommodation, food, entertainment, travel and other living expenses.

But adding these up does not give the opportunity cost. The opportunity cost is the *sacrifice* entailed by going to university or college *rather than* doing something else. Let us assume that the alternative is to take a job that has been offered. The correct list of opportunity costs of higher education would include:

- Books, stationery, etc.
- Additional accommodation and travel expenses over what would have been incurred by taking the job.
- Wages that would have been earned in the job less any income received as a student.
- The proportion of tuition fees paid by the student.

1. *Why is the cost of food not included?*
2. *Make a list of the benefits of higher education.*
3. *Is the opportunity cost to the individual of attending higher education different from the opportunity costs to society as a whole? Do the benefits of higher education for society differ from those for the individual*

Throughout the book we will be considering how well the economy meets various economic and social objectives, whether micro or macro. We will examine why problems occur and what can be done about them.

Illustrating economic issues: the production possibility curve

Economics books and articles frequently contain diagrams. The reason is that diagrams are very useful for illustrating economic relationships. Ideas and arguments that might take a long time to explain in words can often be expressed clearly and simply in a diagram.

Two of the most common types of diagram used in economics are graphs and flow diagrams. In this and the next section we will look at one example of each. These examples are chosen to illustrate the distinction between microeconomic and macroeconomic issues.

We start by having a look at a *production possibility curve*. This diagram is a graph. Like many diagrams in economics it shows a simplified picture of reality – a picture stripped of all details that are unnecessary to illustrate the

Definition

Production possibility curve A curve showing all the possible combinations of two goods that a country can produce within a specified time period with all its resources fully and efficiently employed.

Figure 1.1 A production possibility curve

Table 1.1	Maximum possible combinations of food and clothing that can be produced in a given time period

Units of food (millions)	Units of clothing (millions)
8.0	0.0
7.0	2.2
6.0	4.0
5.0	5.0
4.0	5.6
3.0	6.0
2.0	6.4
1.0	6.7
0.0	7.0

points being made. Of course, there are dangers in this. In the attempt to make a diagram simple enough to understand, we run the risk of oversimplifying. If this is the case, the diagram may be misleading.

A production possibility curve is shown in Figure 1.1. The graph is based on the data shown in Table 1.1.

Assume that some imaginary nation devotes all its resources – land, labour and capital – to producing just two goods, food and clothing. Various possible combinations that could be produced over a given period of time (e.g. a year) are shown in the table. Thus the country, by devoting all its resources to producing food, could produce 8 million units of food but no clothing. Alternatively by producing, say, 7 million units of food it could release enough resources – land, labour and capital – to produce 2.2 million units of clothing. At the other extreme, it could produce 7 million units of clothing with no resources at all being used to produce food.

The information in the table can be transferred to a graph (Figure 1.1). We measure units of food on one axis (in this case the vertical axis) and units of clothing on the other. The curve shows all the combinations of the two

goods that can be produced with all the nation's resources fully and efficiently employed. For example, production could take place at point *x*, with 6 million units of food and 4 million units of clothing being produced. Production cannot take place beyond the curve. For example, production is not possible at point *w*: the nation does not have enough resources to do this.

Note that there are two simplifying assumptions in this diagram. First, it is assumed that there are just two types of good that can be produced. We have to assume this because we only have two axes on our graph. The other assumption is that there is only one type of food and one type of clothing. This is implied by measuring their output in particular units (e.g. tonnes). If food differed in type, it would be possible to produce a greater tonnage of food for a given amount of clothing simply by switching production from one foodstuff to another.

These two assumptions are obviously enormous simplifications when we consider the modern complex economies of the real world. But despite this, the diagram still allows important principles to be illustrated simply. In fact, this is one of the key advantages of using diagrams.

Microeconomics and the production possibility curve

A production possibility curve illustrates the microeconomic issues of choice and opportunity cost.

If the country chose to produce more clothing, it would have to sacrifice the production of some food. This sacrifice of food is the opportunity cost of the extra clothing.

The fact that to produce more of one good involves producing less of the other is illustrated by the downward-sloping nature of the curve. For example, the country could move from point *x* to point *y* in Figure 1.2. In doing so it would be producing an extra 1 million units of clothing, but 1 million units less of food. Thus the opportunity cost of the 1 million extra units of clothing would be the 1 million units of food forgone.

| Figure 1.2 | Increasing opportunity costs |

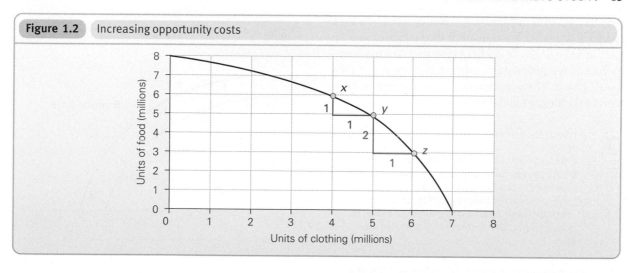

KI 1
p5

| BOX 1.4 | SCARCITY AND ABUNDANCE | CASE STUDIES AND APPLICATIONS |

Is lunch ever free?

The central economic problem is scarcity. But are *all* goods and services scarce? Is anything we desire truly abundant?

First, what do we mean by *abundance*? In the economic sense we mean something where supply exceeds demand at a *zero* price. In other words, even if it is free, there is no shortage. What is more, there must be no opportunity cost in supplying it. For example, if the government supplies health care free to the sick, it is still scarce in the economic sense because there is a cost to the government (and hence the taxpayer).

Two things that might seem to be abundant are air and water.

Air

In one sense air *is* abundant. There is no shortage of air to breathe for most people for most of the time.

But if we define air as clean, unpolluted air, then in some parts of the world it is scarce. In these cases, resources have to be used to make clean air available. If there is pollution in cities or near industrial plants, it will cost money to clean it up. The citizen may not pay directly – the cleaned-up air may be free to the 'consumer' – but the taxpayer or industry (and hence its customers) will have to pay.

Another example is when extractor fans have to be installed to freshen up air in buildings.

Even if you live in a non-polluted part of the country, you may well have spent money moving there to escape the pollution. Again there is an opportunity cost to obtain the clean air.

Water

Whether water is abundant depends again on where you live. It also depends on what the water is used for.

Water for growing crops in a country with plentiful rain *is* abundant. In drier countries, resources have to be spent on irrigation.

Water for drinking is not abundant. Reservoirs have to be built. The water has to be piped, purified and pumped.

1. *There is a saying in economics, 'There is no such thing as a free lunch' (hence the sub-title for this box). What does this mean?*
2. *Are any other (desirable) goods or services truly abundant?*

It also illustrates the phenomenon of ***increasing opportunity costs***. By this we mean that as a country produces more of one good it has to sacrifice ever-increasing amounts of the other. The reason for this is that different factors of production have different properties. People have different skills; land differs in different parts of the country; raw materials differ one from another; and so on. Thus as the nation concentrates more and more on the production of one good, it has to start using resources that are less and less suitable – resources that would have been better suited to producing other goods. In our example, then, the production of more and more clothing will involve a growing *marginal cost*: ever-increasing amounts of food have to be sacrificed for each additional unit of clothing produced.

It is because opportunity costs increase that the production possibility curve is bowed outward rather than being a

Definition

Increasing opportunity costs of production When additional production of one good involves ever-increasing sacrifices of another.

straight line. Thus in Figure 1.2 as production moves from point x to y to z, so the amount of food sacrificed rises for each additional unit of clothing produced. The opportunity cost of the fifth million units of clothing is 1 million units of food. The opportunity cost of the sixth million units of clothing is 2 million units of food.

1. What is the opportunity cost of the seventh million units of clothing?
2. If the country moves upward along the curve and produces more food, does this also involve increasing opportunity costs?
3. Under what circumstances would the production possibility curve be (a) a straight line; (b) bowed in towards the origin? Are these circumstances ever likely?

Macroeconomics and the production possibility curve

There is no guarantee that resources will be fully employed, or that they will be used in the most efficient way possible. The nation may thus be producing at a point inside the curve: for example, point v in Figure 1.3.

What we are saying here is that the economy is producing less of both goods than it is possible for it to produce, either because some resources are not being used (for example, workers may be unemployed), or because it is not using the most efficient methods of production possible, or a combination of the two. By using its resources to the full, however, the nation could move out on to the curve: to point x or y, for example. It could thus produce more clothing and more food.

Here we are concerned not with the combination of goods produced (a microeconomic issue), but with whether the total amount produced is as much as it could be (a macroeconomic issue).

Over time, the production possibilities of a nation are likely to increase. **Investment** in new plant and machinery will increase the stock of capital; new raw materials may be

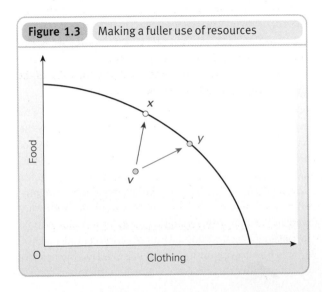

Figure 1.3   Making a fuller use of resources

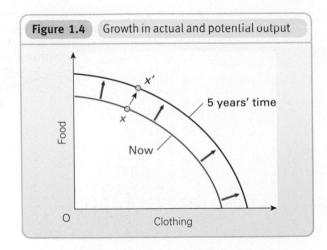

Figure 1.4   Growth in actual and potential output

discovered; technological advances are likely to take place; through education and training, labour is likely to become more productive. This growth in potential output is illustrated by an outward shift in the production possibility curve. This will then allow actual output to increase: for example, from point x to point x' in Figure 1.4.

Will economic growth necessarily involve a parallel outward shift of the production possibility curve?

Illustrating economic issues: the circular flow of goods and incomes

The process of satisfying human wants involves producers and consumers. The relationship between them is two-sided and can be represented in a flow diagram (see Figure 1.5).

The consumers of goods and services are labelled 'households'. Some members of households, of course, are also workers, and in some cases are the owners of other factors of production too, such as land. The producers of goods and services are labelled 'firms'.[1]

Firms and households are in a twin 'demand and supply' relationship with each other.

---

[1] In practice, much of society's production takes place *within* the household for its members' own consumption. Examples include cooking, washing, cleaning, growing vegetables, do-it-yourself activities and childcare. Also, firms buy from and sell to each other – whether it be raw materials, capital goods or semi-finished goods. Nevertheless, it is still useful to depict the flows of goods and services and money *between* households and firms when explaining the operation of markets.

Definition

Investment The production of items that are not for immediate consumption.

Figure 1.5	Circular flow of goods and incomes

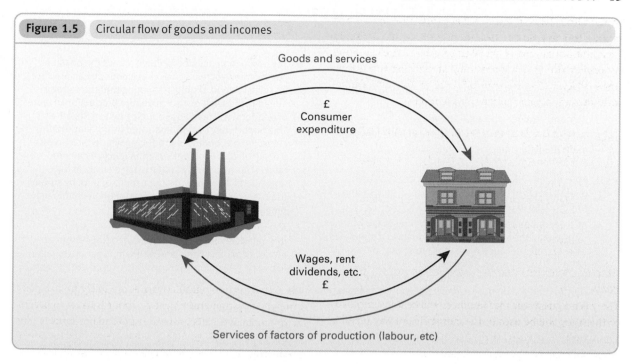

First, in the top part of the diagram, households demand goods and services, and firms supply goods and services. In the process, exchange takes place. In a money economy (as opposed to a *barter economy*), firms exchange goods and services for money. In other words, money flows from households to firms in the form of consumer expenditure, while goods and services flow the other way – from firms to households.

This coming together of buyers and sellers is known as a *market* – it could be a street market, a shop, a website offering online shopping or whatever. Thus we talk about the market for apples, for oil, for cars, for houses, for televisions, and so on.

Second, firms and households come together in the market for factors of production. This is illustrated in the bottom half of Figure 1.5. This time the demand and supply roles are reversed. Firms demand the use of factors of production owned by households – labour, land and capital. Households supply them. Thus the services of labour and other factors flow from households to firms, and in exchange firms pay households money – namely, wages,

rent, dividends and interest. Just as we referred to particular goods markets, so we can also refer to particular factor markets – the market for bricklayers, for secretaries, for footballers, for land, and so on.

There is thus a circular flow of incomes. Households earn incomes from firms and firms earn incomes from households. The money circulates. There is also a circular flow of goods and services, but in the opposite direction. Households supply factor services to firms which then use them to supply goods and services to households.

This flow diagram, like the production possibility curve, can help us to distinguish between microeconomics and macroeconomics.

Microeconomics is concerned with the composition of the circular flow: what combinations of goods make up the goods flow; how the various factors of production are combined to produce these goods; for whom the wages, dividends, rent and interest are paid out.

Macroeconomics is concerned with the total size of the flow and what causes it to expand and contract.

Definitions

Barter economy An economy where people exchange goods and services directly with one another without any payment of money. Workers would be paid with bundles of goods.

Market The interaction between buyers and sellers.

Section summary

1. The central economic problem is that of scarcity. Given that there is a limited supply of factors of production (labour, land and capital), it is impossible to provide everybody with everything they want. Potential demands exceed potential supplies.

2. The subject of economics is usually divided into two main branches, macroeconomics and microeconomics.

3. Macroeconomics deals with aggregates such as the overall levels of unemployment, output, growth and prices in the economy.

4. Microeconomics deals with the activities of individual units within the economy: firms, industries, consumers, workers, etc. Because resources are scarce, people have to make choices. Society has to choose by some means or other *what* goods and services to produce, *how* to produce them and *for whom* to produce them. Microeconomics studies these choices.

5. Rational choices involve weighing up the marginal benefits of each activity against its marginal opportunity costs. If the marginal benefits exceed the marginal costs, it is rational to choose to do more of that activity.

6. The production possibility curve shows the possible combinations of two goods that a country can produce in a given period of time. Assuming that the country is already producing on the curve, the production of more of one good will involve producing less of the other. This opportunity cost is illustrated by the slope of the curve. If the economy is producing within the curve as a result of idle resources or inefficiency, it can produce more of both goods by taking up this slack. In the longer term it can only produce more of both by shifting the curve outwards through investment, technological progress, etc.

7. The circular flow of goods and incomes shows the interrelationships between firms and households in a money economy. Firms and households come together in markets. In goods markets, firms supply goods and households demand goods. In the process, money flows from households to firms in return for the goods and services that the firms supply. In factor markets, firms demand factors of production and households supply them. In the process, money flows from firms to households in return for the services of the factors that households supply.

1.2 DIFFERENT ECONOMIC SYSTEMS

The classification of economic systems

All societies are faced with the problem of scarcity. They differ considerably, however, in the way they tackle the problem. One important difference between societies is in the degree of government control of the economy: the extent to which government decides 'what', 'how' and 'for whom' to produce.

At the one extreme lies the completely *planned or command economy*, where all the economic decisions are taken by the government.

At the other extreme lies the completely *free-market economy*. In this type of economy there is no government intervention at all. All decisions are taken by individuals and firms. Households decide how much labour and other factors to supply, and what goods to consume. Firms decide what goods to produce and what factors to employ. The pattern of production and consumption that results depends on the interactions of all these individual demand and supply decisions in free markets.

In practice, all economies are a mixture of the two. It is therefore the degree of government intervention that distinguishes different economic systems. Thus in the former communist countries of eastern Europe, the government played a large role, whereas in the USA, the government plays a much smaller role.

It is nevertheless useful to analyse the extremes, in order to put the different *mixed economies* of the real world into perspective. The mixture of government and the market can be shown by the use of a spectrum diagram such as Figure 1.6. It shows where particular economies of the real world lie along the spectrum between the two extremes.

Definitions

Centrally planned or command economy An economy where all economic decisions are taken by the central authorities.

Free-market economy An economy where all economic decisions are taken by individual households and firms and with no government intervention.

Mixed economy An economy where economic decisions are made partly by the government and partly through the market.

| **Figure 1.6** | Classifying economic systems |

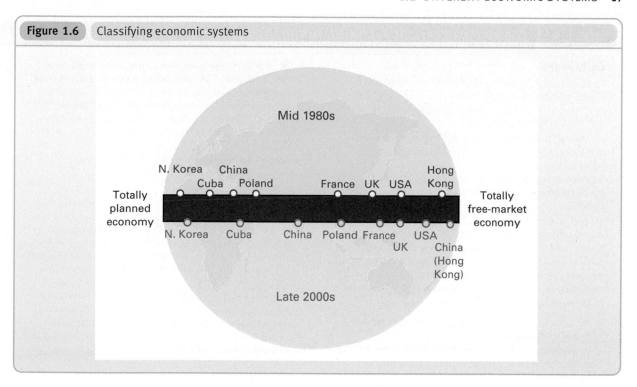

The diagram is useful in that it provides a simple picture of the mixture of government and the market that exists in various economies. It can also be used to show changes in the mixture over time.

The problem with this type of classification is that it is 'unidimensional', and thus rather simplistic. Countries differ in the *type* of government intervention as well as the level. For example, governments intervene through planning, public ownership, regulation, taxes and subsidies, partnership schemes with private industry, and so on. Thus two countries could be in a similar position along the spectrum but have quite different types of government intervention.

Notice that there has been a general movement to the right along the spectrum since the early 1980s. In former communist countries this has been a result of the abandonment of central planning and the adoption of a large measure of private enterprise, especially since the late 1980s. In western economies it has been a result of deregulation of private industry and privatisation (the selling of nationalised industries to the private sector).

 Do you agree with the positions that the eight countries have been given in the spectrum diagram? Explain why or why not.

The informal sector: a third dimension

In all societies, many economic decisions are made, whether individually or in groups, which involve neither the government nor the market. For example, many of the activities taking place in the home, such as cooking, cleaning, decorating, making clothes, gardening and care for children or the elderly, can be seen as 'economic' activities. There is an output (such as a meal or a service provided) and there is an opportunity cost to the provider (in terms of alternative activities forgone). And yet no money changes hands. Similarly, many of the activities done in groups, such as clubs, societies and charities, involve the provision of goods and/or services, but again, no money changes hands.

These activities are taking place in the **informal sector**. The relative size of the informal sector varies from one country to another and over time. In rich countries, as more and more mothers go out to work and as working hours have increased, many people employ others to do the jobs, such as cleaning and childcare, that they once did themselves. What was once part of the informal sector is now part of the market sector.

In many developing countries, much of the economic activity in poorer areas involves **subsistence production**. This is where people grow their own food, build their own

Definitions

Informal sector The parts of the economy that involve production and/or exchange, but where there are no money payments.

Subsistence production Where people produce things for their own consumption.

BOX 1.5   THE RISE AND FALL OF PLANNING IN THE FORMER SOVIET UNION

Early years

The Bolsheviks under the leadership of Lenin came to power in Russia with the October revolution of 1917. The Bolsheviks, however, were opposed by the White Russians and civil war ensued.

During this period of war communism, the market economy was abolished. Industry and shops were nationalised; workers were told what jobs to do; there were forced requisitions of food from peasants to feed the towns; workers were allocated goods from distribution depots.

With the ending of the civil war in 1921, the economy was in bad shape. Lenin embarked on the New Economic Policy. This involved a return to the use of markets. Smaller businesses were returned to private hands, and peasants were able to sell their food rather than having it requisitioned. The economy began to recover. Lenin died in 1924 and Stalin came to power.

The Stalinist system

The Soviet economy underwent a radical transformation from 1928 onwards. The key features of the Stalinist approach were collectivisation, industrialisation and central planning.

Collectivisation of agriculture

Peasant farms were abolished and replaced by large-scale collective farms where land was collectively owned and worked. This initially caused massive disruption and famine, with peasants slaughtering their animals rather than giving them up to the collective. People died in their thousands. Despite an initial fall in output, more food was provided for the towns, and many workers left the land to work in the new industries.

In addition to the collective farms, state farms were established. These were owned by the state and were run by managers appointed by the state. Both collective and state farms were given quotas of output that they were supposed to deliver, for which the state would pay a fixed price.

Industry and central planning

A massive drive to industrialisation took place. To achieve this a vast planning apparatus was developed. At the top was *Gosplan*, the central planning agency. This prepared five-year plans and annual plans. The five-year plans specified the general direction in which the economy was to move. The annual plans gave the details of just what was to be produced and with what resources for some 200 or so key products. The effect was that all factories were given targets that had to be achieved. It was the task of the planning authorities to ensure that the targets were realistic: that there were sufficient resources to meet the targets. The system operated without the aid of the price mechanism and the profit motive. The main incentive was the *bonus*: bonuses were paid to managers and workers if targets were achieved.

Stalin died in 1953. The planning system, however, remained largely unchanged until the late 1980s. In the early years, very high growth rates were achieved, but this was at a cost of low efficiency. The poor flow of information from firms to the planners led to many inconsistencies in the plans. The targets were often totally unrealistic, and as a result there were frequent shortages and sometimes surpluses. With incentives purely geared to meeting targets, there was little product innovation and goods were frequently of poor quality.

A large 'underground economy' flourished in which goods were sold on the black market and in which people

---

shelter, make their own clothes, etc. Whilst some of the inputs (e.g. material) may have to be purchased through the market, much of this production is in the informal sector and involves no exchange of money. The importance of the informal sector, particularly to developing countries, should not be underestimated. This is an area of increasing interest to many economists, particularly as some of the downsides of economic growth become apparent.

The command economy

The command economy is usually associated with a socialist or communist economic system, where land and capital are collectively owned. The state plans the allocation of resources at three important levels:

- It plans the allocation of resources between current consumption and investment for the future. By sacrificing some present consumption and diverting resources into investment, it could increase the economy's growth rate.

The amount of resources it chooses to devote to investment will depend on its broad macroeconomic strategy: the importance it attaches to growth as opposed to current consumption.

- At a microeconomic level, it plans the output of each industry and firm, the techniques that will be used, and the labour and other resources required by each industry and firm.

In order to ensure that the required inputs are available, the state would probably conduct some form of **input–output analysis**. All industries are seen as users of

Definition

Input–output analysis This involves dividing the economy into sectors where each sector is a user of inputs from and a supplier of outputs to other sectors. The technique examines how these inputs and outputs can be matched to the total resources available in the economy.

did second 'unofficial' jobs (e.g. as plumbers, electricians or garment makers).

Gorbachev's reforms

During the 1970s growth had slowed down and by the time Gorbachev came to power in 1985 many people were pressing for fundamental economic reforms. Gorbachev responded with his policy of *perestroika* (economic reconstruction), which among other things included the following:

- Making managers more involved in preparing their own plans rather than merely being given instructions.
- Insisting that firms become more efficient and cover their costs of production. If they could not, the state might refuse to bale them out and they could be declared bankrupt.
- Improving the incentive system by making bonuses more related to genuine productivity. Workers had come to expect bonuses no matter how much or how little was produced.
- Organising workers into small teams or 'brigades' (typically of around 10–15 workers). Bonuses were then awarded to the whole brigade according to its productivity. The idea was to encourage people to work more effectively together.
- Stringent checks on quality by state officials and the rejection of substandard goods.
- Allowing one-person businesses and co-operatives (owned by the workers) to be set up.
- A greater willingness by the state to raise prices if there were substantial shortages.

These reforms, however, did not halt the economic decline. What is more, there was now an unhappy mix of planning and the market, with people unclear as to what to expect from the state. Many managers resented the extra responsibilities they were now expected to shoulder. Queues lengthened in the shops and people increasingly became disillusioned with *perestroika*.

Following the failed coup of 1991, in which hard-line communists had attempted to reimpose greater state control, both the Soviet Union and the system of central planning came to an end.

Russia, under its new leader Boris Yeltsin, embarked upon a radical programme of market reforms in which competition and enterprise were intended to replace state central planning (see Case Studies 13.6, *Privatisation in transition economies*, and 13.7, *Forms of transition in transition countries*, in MyEconLab. See also Case Study 1.5 in MyEconLab, *Free-market medicine in Russia*.)

The Russian economy today

Twenty years after the end of the Soviet Union the Russian economy is booming. Moscow's streets are filled with BMWs and Mercedes and shoppers throng to GUM, the huge shopping mall that runs along the east side of Red Square. Annual growth has averaged 7% over the past decade and Russia has the second-largest oil reserves in the world and the fourth-largest reserves of gold.

Yet the story in not one of unalloyed success; outside Moscow in many areas incomes and wealth remain low, with the majority of households unable to afford luxuries. Road and rail services remain poor and much of the housing stock is in a state of disrepair. The challenge that faces the Russian leadership is to increase people's income and consumption while at the same time investing in an infrastructure that remains damaged by decades of neglect.

---

inputs from other industries and as producers of output for consumers or other industries. For example, the steel industry uses inputs from the coal and iron-ore industries and produces output for the vehicle and construction industries. Input–output analysis shows, for each industry, the sources of all its inputs and the destination of all its output. By using such analysis the state attempts to match up the inputs and outputs of each industry so that the planned demand for each industry's product is equal to its planned supply.

- It plans the distribution of output between consumers. This will depend on the government's aims. It may distribute goods according to its judgement of people's needs; or it may give more to those who produce more, thereby providing an incentive for people to work harder.

It may distribute goods and services directly (for example, by a system of rationing); or it may decide the distribution of money incomes and allow individuals to decide how to spend them. If it does the latter, it may still seek to influence the pattern of expenditure by setting appropriate prices: low prices to encourage consumption, and high prices to discourage consumption.

Assessment of the command economy

With central planning, the government could take an overall view of the economy. It could direct the nation's resources in accordance with specific national goals.

High growth rates could be achieved if the government directed large amounts of resources into investment. Unemployment could be largely avoided if the government carefully planned the allocation of labour in accordance with production requirements and labour skills. National income could be distributed more equally or in accordance with needs. The social repercussions of production and consumption (e.g. the effects on the environment) could be taken into account, provided the government was able to predict these effects and chose to take them into account.

KI 4
p10

In practice, a command economy could achieve these goals only at considerable social and economic cost. The reasons are as follows:

- The larger and more complex the economy, the greater the task of collecting and analysing the information essential to planning, and the more complex the plan. Complicated plans are likely to be costly to administer and involve cumbersome bureaucracy.

- If there is no system of prices, or if prices are set arbitrarily by the state, planning is likely to involve the inefficient use of resources. It is difficult to assess the relative efficiency of two alternative techniques that use different inputs, if there is no way in which the value of those inputs can be ascertained. For example, how can a rational decision be made between an oil-fired and a coal-fired furnace if the prices of oil and coal do not reflect their relative scarcity?

- It is difficult to devise appropriate incentives to encourage workers and managers to be more productive without a reduction in quality. For example, if bonuses are given according to the quantity of output produced, a factory might produce shoddy goods, since it can probably produce a larger quantity of goods by cutting quality. To avoid this problem, a large number of officials may have to be employed to check quality.

- Complete state control over resource allocation would involve a considerable loss of individual liberty. Workers would have no choice where to work; consumers would have no choice what to buy.

- The government might enforce its plans even if they were unpopular.

- If production is planned, but consumers are free to spend money incomes as they wish, there will be a problem if the wishes of consumers change. Shortages will occur if consumers decide to buy more; surpluses will occur if they decide to buy less.

Most of these problems were experienced in the former Soviet Union and the other Eastern bloc countries, and were part of the reason for the overthrow of their communist regimes (see Box 1.5).

The free-market economy

Free decision making by individuals

In a free market, individuals are free to make their own economic decisions. Consumers are free to decide what to buy with their incomes: free to make demand decisions. Firms are free to choose what to sell and what production methods to use: free to make supply decisions. The demand and supply decisions of consumers and firms are transmitted to each other through their effect on prices: through the *price mechanism*. The prices that result are the prices that firms and consumers have to accept.

The price mechanism

The price mechanism works as follows. Prices respond to shortages and surpluses. Shortages result in prices rising. Surpluses result in prices falling. Let us take each in turn.

If consumers decide they want more of a good (or if producers decide to cut back supply), demand will exceed supply. The resulting shortage will cause the price of the good to rise. This will act as an incentive to producers to supply more, since production will now be more profitable. At the same time it will discourage consumers from buying so much. *Price will continue rising until the shortage has thereby been eliminated.*

If, on the other hand, consumers decide they want less of a good (or if producers decide to produce more), supply will exceed demand. The resulting surplus will cause the price of the good to fall. This will act as a disincentive to producers, who will supply less, since production will now be less profitable. It will encourage consumers to buy more. *Price will continue falling until the surplus has thereby been eliminated.*

This price, where demand equals supply, is called the *equilibrium price*. By *equilibrium* we mean a point of balance or a point of rest: in other words, a point towards which there is a tendency to move.

The same analysis can be applied to labour (and other factor) markets, except that here the demand and supply roles are reversed. Firms are the demanders of labour. Individuals are the suppliers. If the demand for a particular type of labour exceeded its supply, the resulting shortage would drive up the wage rate (i.e. the price of labour), thus reducing firms' demand for that type of labour and encouraging more workers to take up that type of job. Wages would continue rising until demand equalled supply: until the shortage was eliminated.

Likewise if there were a surplus of a particular type of labour, the wage would fall until demand equalled supply. As with price, the wage rate where the demand for labour equals the supply is known as the equilibrium wage rate.

Definitions

Price mechanism The system in a market economy whereby changes in price in response to changes in demand and supply have the effect of making demand equal to supply.

Equilibrium price The price where the quantity demanded equals the quantity supplied: the price where there is no shortage or surplus.

Equilibrium A position of balance. A position from which there is no inherent tendency to move away.

Can you think of any examples where prices and wages do not adjust very rapidly to a shortage or surplus? For what reasons might they not do so?

The response of demand and supply to changes in price illustrates a very important feature of how economies work: *people respond to incentives*. It is important, therefore, that incentives are appropriate and have the desired effect. This is the fifth of our fifteen threshold concepts (see Chapter 2, page 52).

The effect of changes in demand and supply

How will the price mechanism respond to changes in consumer demand or producer supply? After all, the pattern of consumer demand changes: for example, people may decide they want more mountain bikes and fewer racers. Likewise the pattern of supply changes: for example, changes in technology may allow the mass production of microchips at lower cost, while the production of hand-built furniture becomes relatively expensive.

In all cases of changes in demand and supply, the resulting changes in price act as both signals and incentives.

A change in demand.   A rise in demand is signalled by a rise in price. This then acts as an incentive for supply to rise. What in effect is happening is that the high price of these goods relative to their costs of production is signalling that consumers are willing to see resources diverted from other uses. This is just what firms do. They divert resources from goods with lower prices relative to costs (and hence lower profits) to those goods that are more profitable.

A fall in demand is signalled by a fall in price. This then acts as an incentive for supply to fall. The goods are now less profitable to produce.

A change in supply.   A rise in supply is signalled by a fall in price. This then acts as an incentive for demand to rise. A fall in supply is signalled by a rise in price. This then acts as an incentive for demand to fall.

 KEY IDEA 5 *Changes in demand or supply cause markets to adjust.* Whenever such changes occur, the resulting 'disequilibrium' will bring an automatic change in prices, thereby restoring equilibrium (i.e. a balance of demand and supply).

The fact that markets adjust so as to equate demand and supply is our fourth 'Threshold Concept', which is discussed in Chapter 2, page 44.

 1. *Why do the prices of fresh vegetables fall when they are in season? Could an individual farmer prevent the price falling?*
2. *If you were the manager of a supermarket, how would you set about deciding what prices to charge for food approaching its sell-by date?*
3. *The number of owners of MP3 players has grown rapidly and hence the demand for downloaded music files has also grown rapidly. Yet the prices of downloads have fallen. Why?*

The interdependence of markets

The interdependence of goods and factor markets.   A rise in demand for a good will raise its price and profitability. Firms will respond by supplying more. But to do this they will need more inputs. Thus the demand for the inputs will rise, which in turn will raise the price of the inputs. The suppliers of inputs will respond to this incentive by supplying more. This can be summarised as follows:

KI 5 p21

1. Goods market
   • Demand for the good rises.
   • This creates a shortage.
   • This causes the price of the good to rise.
   • This eliminates the shortage by choking off some of the demand and encouraging firms to produce more.
2. Factor market
   • The increased supply of the good causes an increase in the demand for factors of production (i.e. inputs) used in making it.
   • This causes a shortage of those inputs.
   • This causes their prices to rise.
   • This eliminates their shortage by choking off some of the demand and encouraging the suppliers of inputs to supply more.

It can thus be seen that changes in goods markets will cause changes in factor markets. Figure 1.7 summarises this sequence of events. (It is common in economics to summarise an argument like this by using symbols.)

Interdependence exists in the other direction too: factor markets affect goods markets. For example, the discovery of raw materials will lower their price. This will lower the costs of production of firms using these raw materials and will increase the supply of the finished goods. The resulting surplus will lower the price of the good, which will encourage consumers to buy more.

 Summarise this last paragraph using symbols like those in Figure 1.7.

The interdependence of different goods markets.   A rise in the price of one good will encourage consumers to buy alternatives. This will drive up the price of alternatives. This in turn will encourage producers to supply more of the alternatives.

 Are different factor markets similarly interdependent? What would happen if the price of capital equipment rose?

Conclusion

Even though all individuals are merely looking to their own self-interest in the free-market economy, they are in fact being encouraged to respond to the wishes of others through the incentive of the price mechanism. (See Case Study 1.4, *The interdependence of markets*, in MyEconLab; see also Box 1.6.)

Figure 1.7	The price mechanism: the effect of a rise in demand

Goods market

$$D_g \uparrow \longrightarrow \text{shortage} \longrightarrow \boxed{P_g \uparrow} \diagdown \begin{array}{l} S_g \uparrow \\ \\ D_g \downarrow \end{array} \quad \text{until } D_g = S_g$$
$$(D_g > S_g)$$

Factor market

$$S_g \uparrow \longrightarrow D_f \uparrow \longrightarrow \text{shortage} \longrightarrow \boxed{P_f \uparrow} \diagdown \begin{array}{l} S_f \uparrow \\ \\ D_f \downarrow \end{array} \quad \text{until } D_f = S_f$$
$$(D_f > S_f)$$

BOX 1.6 **ADAM SMITH (1723–90)** EXPLORING ECONOMICS

And the 'invisible hand' of the market

Many economists would argue that modern economics dates from 1776. That was the year in which Adam Smith's *An Inquiry into the Nature and Causes of the Wealth of Nations* was published – one of the most important books on economics ever written.

Adam Smith was born in 1723 in Kirkcaldy, a small coastal town north of Edinburgh. After graduating from Glasgow University at the age of 17, he first became a fellow of Balliol College, Oxford, but then returned to Scotland and at the age of 29 became professor of moral philosophy at the University of Glasgow. At the age of 40 he resigned and spent three years touring the continent, where he met many influential economists and philosophers. He then returned to Scotland, to his home town of Kirkcaldy, and set to work on *The Wealth of Nations*.

The work, in five books, is very wide ranging, but the central argument is that market economies generally serve the public interest well. Markets guide production and consumption like an *invisible hand*. Even though everyone is looking after their own private self-interest, their interaction in the market will lead to the social good.

In book I, chapter 2, he writes:

Man has almost constant occasion for the help of his brethren and it is in vain for him to expect it from their benevolence only . . . It is not from the benevolence of the butcher, the brewer, or the baker that we expect our dinner, but from their regard to their own interest. We address ourselves, not to their humanity but to their self-love, and never talk to them of our own necessities, but of their advantages.

Later, in book IV, chapter 2, he continues:

Every individual is continually exerting himself to find out the most advantageous employment of whatever capital he can command. It is his own advantage, indeed, and not that of the society, which he has in view. But the study of his own advantage naturally, or rather necessarily, leads him to prefer that employment which is most advantageous to the society . . . he intends only his own gain, and he is in this, as in many other cases, led by an invisible hand to promote an end which was no part of his intention. Nor is it always the worse for the society that it was no part of it. By pursuing his own interest he frequently promotes that of society more effectually than when he really intends to promote it.

He argued, therefore, with one or two exceptions, that the state should not interfere with the functioning of the economy. It should adopt a laissez-faire or 'hands-off' policy. It should allow free enterprise for firms and free trade between countries.

This praise of the free market has led many on the political right to regard him as the father of the 'libertarian movement' – the movement that advocates the absolute minimum amount of state intervention in the economy (see Box 11.7 on page 338). In fact one of the most famous of the libertarian societies is called the Adam Smith Institute.

But Smith was not blind to the drawbacks of unregulated markets. In book I, chapter 7, he looks at the problem of monopoly:

A monopoly granted either to an individual or to a trading company has the same effect as a secret in trade or manufactures. The monopolists, by keeping the market constantly under-stocked, by never fully supplying the effectual demand, sell their commodities much above the natural price, and raise their emoluments, whether they consist in wages or profit, greatly above their natural rate.

Later on he looks at the dangers of firms getting together to pursue their mutual interest:

People of the same trade seldom meet together, even for merriment or diversion, but the conversation ends in a conspiracy against the public or in some contrivance to raise prices.

KI 5
p21

Assessment of the free-market economy

The fact that a free-market economy functions automatically is one of its major advantages. There is no need for costly and complex bureaucracies to co-ordinate economic decisions. The economy can respond quickly to changing demand and supply conditions.

When markets are highly competitive, no one has great power. Competition between firms keeps prices down and acts as an incentive to firms to become more efficient. The more firms there are competing, the more responsive they will be to consumer wishes.

The more efficiently firms can combine their factors of production, the more profit they will make. The more efficiently workers work, the more secure will be their jobs and the higher their wages. The more carefully consumers decide what to buy, the greater the value for money they will receive.

Thus people pursuing their own self-interest through buying and selling in competitive markets helps to minimise the central economic problem of scarcity, by encouraging the efficient use of the nation's resources in line with consumer wishes. From this type of argument, the following conclusion is often drawn by defenders of the free market: 'The pursuit of private gain results in the social good.'

This claim is the subject of much debate and has profound moral implications (see Threshold Concept 2 below).

In practice, however, markets do not achieve maximum efficiency in the allocation of scarce resources, and governments feel it necessary to intervene to rectify this and other problems of the free market. The problems of a free market are as follows:

- Competition between firms is often limited. A few giant firms may dominate an industry. In these cases they may charge high prices and make large profits. Rather than merely responding to consumer wishes, they may attempt to persuade consumers by advertising. Consumers are particularly susceptible to advertisements for products that are unfamiliar to them.
- Lack of competition and high profits may remove the incentive for firms to be efficient.
- Power and property may be unequally distributed. Those who have power and/or property (e.g. big business, unions and landlords) will gain at the expense of those without power and property.
- The practices of some firms may be socially undesirable. For example, a chemical works may pollute the environment.

KI 5
p21

KI 1
p5

KI 4
p10

| THRESHOLD CONCEPT 2 | PEOPLE GAIN FROM VOLUNTARY ECONOMIC INTERACTION | THINKING LIKE AN ECONOMIST |

Economic interaction between people can take a number of different forms. Sometimes it takes place in markets. For example, when goods are exchanged, there is interaction between the consumer and the shop. When someone is employed, there is interaction between the employer and the employee. When a firm buys raw materials, there is interaction between the purchasing firm and the selling firm.

In each case there is a mutual gain. If there wasn't, the interaction would not take place. If you choose to go on a package holiday costing £400, then assuming the holiday turns out as you expected, you will have gained. You would rather have the holiday than spend the £400 on something else. The marginal benefit to you exceeds the marginal cost. The travel agent and tour operator also gain. They make a profit on selling you the holiday. It is a 'win–win situation'. This is sometimes called a *positive sum game*: an interaction where there is a positive net gain.

Another example is international trade (the subject of Chapter 24). If two countries trade with each other, there will be a net gain to both of them. If there wasn't, they would not trade. Both countries will end up consuming a greater value of products than they could without trade. The reason is that each country can specialise in the products it is relatively good at producing (compared to the other country) and export them, and import from the other country the goods it is relatively poor at producing.

And it's not just in markets that human interaction results in a net gain. If you go out with friends, normally you will all benefit – unless you end up falling out or something else goes wrong! If you are a member of a football team, a political party or a choir, you hope that it's not just you that gains, but the other members too.

That there is a net gain from voluntary interaction is a *threshold concept* because realising this tends to change the way we look at economic activity. Often it is important to identify what these overall gains are so that we can compare them with alternative forms of interaction. For example, even though both workers and their employer respectively gain from the wages currently paid and the output currently produced, it might still be possible to reorganise the workforce in a way that increases production. This could allow the employer to pay higher wages and still gain an increase in profits. Both sides could thus gain from constructive negotiation about wages and new work practices.

Sometimes it may appear that voluntary interaction results in one side gaining and the other losing. For example, a firm may raise its price. It gains and the consumer loses. But is this strictly true? Consumers are certainly worse off than before, but as long as they are still prepared to buy the product, they must consider that they are still gaining more by buying it than by not. There is still a gain to both sides: it's just that the firm is gaining more and the consumer is gaining less.

1. *Would you ever swap things with friends if both of you did not gain? Explain your answer.*
2. *Give one or two examples of involuntary (i.e. compulsory) economic interaction, where one side gains but the other loses.*

Although market forces can automatically equate demand and supply, and although the outcomes of the process may often be desirable, they are by no means always so. Unbridled market forces can result in severe problems for individuals, society and the environment.

Markets tend to reflect the collective actions of individual consumers and firms. But when consumers and firms make their decisions, they may fail to take account of the broader effects of their actions. They may act selfishly. If people want to buy guns and knives, market forces will make it profitable for firms to supply them. If people want to drive fuel-hungry cars and fit bullbars to them, then this will create the market for firms to supply them. Market forces are not kind and caring. They mechanically reflect human behaviour.

And it's not just selfish behaviour that markets reflect; it's ignorance too. You may be blissfully unaware that a toy that you buy for a child is dangerous, but by doing so, you are encouraging unscrupulous firms to supply them. A firm may be unaware that a piece of machinery it uses is dangerous until an accident happens. In the meantime, it continues using it because it is profitable to do so.

If wages are determined purely by demand and supply, then some people, such as pop stars, footballers and accountants, may be very well paid. Others, such as cleaners, bar staff and security guards, may be very poorly paid. If the resulting inequality is seen as unfair, then market forces alone will not be enough to achieve a fair society.

Recognising the limitations and failings of markets is a *threshold concept*. It helps us to understand how laws or taxes or subsidies could be framed to counteract such failings. It helps us to relate the mechanical operation of demand and supply to a whole range of social objectives and ask whether the market system is the best way of meeting such objectives.

But to recognise market failures is only part of the way to finding a solution. Can the government and various public agencies, such as the police and the health services, put things right, and if so, how? Or do the limitations of government mean that the solution is sometimes worse than the problem? We examine these issues in many parts of the book. We set the scene in Threshold Concept 6 on page 52.

1. *If global warming affects all of us adversely, why in a purely market economy would individuals and firms continue with activities that contribute towards global warming?*
2. *In what ways do your own consumption patterns adversely affect other people?*

- Some socially desirable goods would simply not be produced by private enterprise. What firm would build and operate a lighthouse unless the government was involved in the funding?
- A free-market economy may lead to macroeconomic instability. There may be periods of recession with high unemployment and falling output, and other periods of rising prices.
- Finally, there is the ethical objection, that a free-market economy, by rewarding self-interested behaviour, may encourage selfishness, greed, materialism and the acquisition of power.
- The fact that free markets may fail to meet various social objectives is Threshold Concept 3.

The mixed economy

Because of the problems of both free-market and command economies, all real-world economies are a mixture of the two systems.

In *mixed market economies*, the government may control the following:

- *Relative prices* of goods and inputs, by taxing or subsidising them or by direct price controls.
- Relative incomes, by the use of income taxes, welfare payments or direct controls over wages, profits, rents, etc.
- The pattern of production and consumption, by the use of legislation (e.g. making it illegal to produce unsafe goods), by direct provision of goods and services (e.g. education and defence), by taxes and subsidies or by nationalisation.
- The macroeconomic problems of unemployment, inflation, lack of growth, balance of trade deficits and exchange rate fluctuations, by the use of taxes and government expenditure, the control of bank lending and interest rates, the direct control of prices and the control of the foreign exchange rate.

The fact that government intervention can be used to rectify various failings of the market is Threshold Concept 6 (see Chapter 2, page 52). It is important to realise, however, that that governments are not perfect and their actions may bring adverse as well as beneficial consequences. For more on government intervention in the mixed economy see Chapters 10 to 13.

Just how the government intervenes, and what the effects of the various forms of intervention are, will be examined in detail in later chapters.

Definitions

Mixed market economy A market economy where there is some government intervention.

Relative price The price of one good compared with another (e.g. good X is twice the price of good Y).

Section summary

1. The economic systems of different countries vary according to the extent to which they rely on the market or the government to allocate resources.

2. At the one extreme, in a command economy, the state makes all the economic decisions. It plans amounts of resources to allocate for present consumption and amounts for investment for future output. It plans the output of each industry, the methods of production it will use and the amount of resources it will be allocated. It plans the distribution of output between consumers.

3. A command economy has the advantage of being able to address directly various national economic goals, such as rapid growth and the avoidance of unemployment and inequality. A command economy, however, is likely to be inefficient: a large bureaucracy will be needed to collect and process information; prices and the choice of production methods are likely to be arbitrary; incentives may be inappropriate; shortages and surpluses may result.

4. At the other extreme is the free-market economy. In this economy, decisions are made by the interaction of demand and supply. Price changes act as the mechanism whereby demand and supply are balanced. If there is a shortage, price will rise until the shortage is eliminated. If there is a surplus, price will fall until that is eliminated.

5. A free-market economy functions automatically and if there is plenty of competition between producers this can help to protect consumers' interests. In practice, however, competition may be limited; there may be great inequality; there may be adverse social and environmental consequences; there may be macroeconomic instability.

6. In practice, all economies are some mixture of the market and government intervention. It is the degree and form of government intervention that distinguishes one type of economy from another.

1.3 THE NATURE OF ECONOMIC REASONING

Economics is one of the social sciences. So in what sense is it a *science*? Is it like the natural sciences such as physics and astronomy? What is the significance of the word 'social' in social science? What can economists do, and what is their role in helping governments devise economic policy?

Economics as a science

The methodology employed by economists has a lot in common with that employed by natural scientists. Both attempt to construct theories or **models** which are then used to *explain* and *predict*. An astronomer, for example, constructs models of planetary movements to *explain* why planets are in the position they are and to *predict* their position in the future.

Models in economics

In order to explain and predict, the economist constructs models of the economy or parts of the economy. These models show simplified relationships between various economic phenomena. For example, a model of a market shows the relationships between demand, supply and price. Although most models can be described verbally, they can normally be represented more precisely in graphical or mathematical form.

Building models

Models are constructed by making general hypotheses about the causes of economic phenomena: for example, that consumer demand will rise when consumer incomes

rise. These hypotheses will often be based on observations. This process of making general statements from particular observations is known as **induction**.

Using models

Explanation.   Models explain by showing how things are caused: what the causes of inflation are, why workers in some industries earn more than others, and so on.

Prediction.   Models are sometimes used to make simple forecasts: for example, inflation will be below 5 per cent next year. Usually, however, predictions are of the 'If . . . then . . .' variety: for example, if demand for good *x* rises, its price will rise. This process of drawing conclusions from models is known as **deduction**.

When making such deductions it has to be assumed that nothing else that can influence the outcome has changed in the meantime. For example, if demand for good *x* rises, its price will rise *assuming* the cost of producing good *x* has

Definitions

Economic model A formal presentation of an economic theory.

Induction Constructing general theories on the basis of specific observations.

Deduction Using a theory to draw conclusions about specific circumstances.

BOX 1.7   *CETERIS PARIBUS*

Because of the complexities of the real world, economic models have to make various simplifying assumptions. Sometimes, however, economists are criticised for making unrealistic assumptions, assumptions that make their models irrelevant. The following joke illustrates the point.

There were three people cast away on a desert island: a chemist, an engineer and an economist. There was no food on the island and their plight seemed desperate.

Then they discovered a crate of canned food that had been washed up on the island. When they realised that

they had no means of opening the cans, they decided that each of them should use their expertise to find a solution.

The chemist searched around for various minerals that could be heated up to produce a compound that would burn through the lids of the cans.

The engineer hunted around for rocks and then worked out what height of tree they would have to be dropped from in order to smash open the cans.

Meanwhile the economist sat down and thought 'Assuming we had a can opener . . .'.

---

not fallen. This is known as the *ceteris paribus* assumption. *Ceteris paribus* is Latin for 'other things being equal'.

Assessing models

Models can be judged according to how successful they are in explaining and predicting.

If the predictions are wrong, the first thing to do is to check whether the deductions were correctly made. If they were, the model must be either adapted or abandoned in favour of an alternative model with better predictive ability.

Sometimes an economist will want to retain a model with poor predictive powers if it nevertheless helps to give some insight into the workings of the economy. For example, a model of some ideal world in which the goals of efficiency, growth and equality were all met might be extremely useful as a yardstick against which to compare the real world and to understand its shortcomings.

Economics as a social science

Economics concerns human behaviour. One problem here is that individuals often behave in very different ways. People have different tastes and different attitudes. This problem, however, is not as serious as it may seem at first sight. The reason is that people *on average* are likely to behave more predictably. For example, if the price of a product goes up by 5 per cent, we might be able to predict, *ceteris paribus*, that the quantity demanded will fall by approximately 10 per cent. This does not mean that every single individual's demand will fall by 10 per cent, only

that *total* demand will. Some people may demand a lot less; others may demand the same as before.

Even so, there are still things about human behaviour that are very difficult to predict, even when we are talking about whole groups of people. How, for example, will firms react to a rise in interest rates when making their investment decisions? This will depend on things such as the state of business confidence, something that is notoriously difficult to predict. How will a business respond to price changes by its rivals? This will often depend on how it thinks its rivals themselves will react to its own response.

For these reasons there is plenty of scope for competing models in economics, each making different assumptions and leading to different policy conclusions. As a result, economics can often be highly controversial. As we shall see later on in the book, different political parties may adhere to different schools of economic thought. Thus the political left may adhere to a model which implies that governments must intervene if unemployment is to be cured, whereas the political right may adhere to a model which implies that unemployment will be reduced if the government intervenes less and relies more on the free market.

One branch of economics that has seen considerable growth in recent years is 'behavioural economics'. This sets up experiments and simulations to see how people respond to different sets of circumstances.

The fact that there are different economic theories does not mean that economists always disagree. Despite the popular belief that 'if you laid all the economists of the world end to end they would still not reach a conclusion', there is in fact a large measure of agreement between economists about how to analyse the world and what conclusions to draw.

Definition

Ceteris paribus Latin for 'other things being equal'. This assumption has to be made when making deductions from theories.

Economics and policy

Economists play a major role in helping governments to devise economic policy. In order to understand this role, it is necessary to distinguish between positive and normative statements.

A **_positive statement_** is a statement of fact. It may be right or wrong, but its accuracy can be tested by appealing to the facts. 'Unemployment is rising', 'Inflation will be over 6 per cent by next year', and 'If the government cuts taxes, imports will rise' are all examples of positive statements.

A **_normative statement_** is a statement of value: a statement about what ought or ought not to be, about whether something is good or bad, desirable or undesirable. 'It is right to tax the rich more than the poor', 'The government ought to reduce inflation', and 'Old-age pensions ought to be increased' are all examples of normative statements. They cannot be proved or disproved by a simple appeal to the facts.

Economists can only contribute to questions of policy in a positive way. That is, they can analyse the consequences of following certain policies. They can say which of two policies is more likely to achieve a given aim, but they should not, as economists, say whether the aims of the policy are desirable. For example, economists may argue that a policy of increasing government expenditure will reduce unemployment and raise inflation, but they cannot, as economists, decide whether such a policy is desirable.

 KEY IDEA 6

The importance of the positive/normative distinction. Economics can only contribute to policy issues in a positive way. Economists, as scientists, should not make normative judgements. They can make them only as individual people, with no more moral right than any other individual.

> **?**
>
> *Which of the following are positive statements and which are normative?*
> *(a) Cutting the higher rates of income tax will redistribute incomes from the poor to the rich.*
> *(b) It is wrong that inflation should be reduced if this means that there will be higher unemployment.*
> *(c) It is incorrect to state that putting up interest rates will reduce inflation.*
> *(d) The government should introduce road pricing to address the issue of congestion.*
> *(e) Current government policies should be aimed at reducing unemployment.*

Definitions

Positive statement A value-free statement which can be tested by an appeal to the facts.

Normative statement A value judgement.

Section summary

1. The methodology used by economists is similar to that used by natural scientists. Economists construct models which they use to explain and predict economic phenomena. These models can be tested by appealing to facts and seeing how successfully they have been predicted or explained by the model. Unsuccessful models can be either abandoned or amended.

2. Being a social science, economics is concerned with human actions. Making accurate predictions in economics is very difficult given that economics has to deal with a constantly changing environment.

3. Economists can help governments to devise policy by examining the consequences of alternative courses of action. In doing this, it is important to separate positive questions about what the effects of the policies are, from normative ones as to what the goals of policy should be. Economists in their role as economists have no superior right to make normative judgements. They do, however, play a major role in assessing whether a policy meets the political objectives of government (or opposition).

END OF CHAPTER QUESTIONS

1. Imagine that a country can produce just two things: goods and services. Assume that over a given period it could produce any of the following combinations:

			Units of goods							
0	10	20	30	40	50	60	70	80	90	100
			Units of services							
80	79	77	74	70	65	58	48	35	19	0

   (a) Draw the country's production possibility curve.

   (b) Assuming that the country is currently producing 40 units of goods and 70 units of services, what is the opportunity cost of producing another 10 units of goods?

   (c) Explain how the figures illustrate the principle of increasing opportunity cost.

   (d) Now assume that technical progress leads to a 10 per cent increase in the output of goods for any given amount of resources. Draw the new production possibility curve. How has the opportunity cost of producing extra units of services altered?

2. Imagine that you won millions of pounds on the National Lottery. Would your 'economic problem' be solved?

3. Assume that in a household one parent currently works full time and the other stays at home to look after the family. How would you set about identifying and calculating the opportunity costs of the second parent now taking a full-time job? How would such calculations be relevant in deciding whether it is worth taking that job?

4. When you made the decision to study economics, was it a 'rational' decision (albeit based on the limited information you had available at the time)? What additional information would you like to have had in order to ensure that your decision was the right one?

5. In what way does specialisation reduce the problem of scarcity?

6. Would redistributing incomes from the rich to the poor reduce the overall problem of scarcity?

7. Assume that oil begins to run out and that extraction becomes more expensive. Trace through the effects of this on the market for oil and the market for other fuels.

8. Give two examples of positive statements about the economy, and two examples of normative ones. Now give two examples that are seemingly positive, but which have normative implications or undertones.

Online resources

Additional case studies in MyEconLab

1.1 **Buddhist economics.** A different perspective on economic problems and economic activity.

1.2 **Green economics.** This examines some of the environmental costs that society faces today. It also looks at the role of economics in analysing these costs and how the problems can be tackled.

1.3 **Global economics.** This examines how macroeconomics and microeconomics apply at the global level and identifies some key issues.

1.4 **The interdependence of markets.** A case study in the operation of markets, examining the effects on a local economy of the discovery of a large coal deposit.

1.5 **Free-market medicine in Russia.** This examines the operating of the fledgling market economy in Russia and the successes and difficulties in moving from a planned to a market economy.

Websites relevant to this chapter

Numbers and sections refer to websites listed in the Web Appendix and hotlinked from this book's website at **www.pearsoned.co.uk/sloman**.

- For news articles relevant to this chapter, see the *Economics News Articles* link from the book's website.

- For a tutorial on finding the best economics websites, see site C8 (*The Internet Economist*).

- For general economics news sources, see websites in section A of the Web Appendix at the end of the book, and particularly A1–9, 24, 38, 39. See also A38, 39, 43 and 44 for links to newspapers worldwide; and A41 and 42 for links to economics news articles from newspapers worldwide.

- For sources of economic data, see sites in section B and particularly B1–4, 33, 34.

- For general sites for students of economics, see sites in section C and particularly C1–7.

- For sites giving links to relevant economics websites, organised by topic, see sites I4, 7, 8, 11, 12, 17, 18.

- For news on the Russian economy (Box 1.5 and Case Study 1.5 in MyEconLab), see sites A14, 15. See also the *Economic Systems and Theories* and *Transition Economies* sections of sites I7 and 11.

- For an excellent site giving details of the lives, works and theories of famous economists from the history of economic thought (including Adam Smith from Box 1.6), see C18

Foundations of Microeconomics

2 Supply and Demand 31

3 Markets in Action 56

In the first half of the book, we focus on microeconomics. Despite being 'small economics' – in other words, the economics of the individual parts of the economy, rather than the economy as a whole – it is still concerned with many of the big issues of today. To understand how the economy works at this micro level, we must understand how markets work. This involves an understanding of demand and supply.

In Chapter 2, we look at how demand and supply interact to determine prices in a free-market economy. Markets, however, are not always free: governments frequently intervene in markets and Chapter 2 considers the impact of some forms of government intervention. In Chapter 3, we take the analysis of markets further to look at markets in action. We will see just how responsive they are to changing circumstances.

2 Chapter

Supply and Demand

CHAPTER MAP

2.1 Demand   **32**
The relationship between demand and price   32
The demand curve   33
Other determinants of demand   34
Movements along and shifts in the demand curve   35

2.2 Supply   **39**
Supply and price   39
The supply curve   39
Other determinants of supply   40
Movements along and shifts in the supply curve   41

2.3 Price and output determination   **42**
Equilibrium price and output   42
Movement to a new equilibrium   44
Incentives in markets   50
*Identifying the position of demand and
   supply curves   50

2.4 The control of prices   **51**
Setting a minimum (high) price   52
Setting a maximum (low) price   54

As we saw in Chapter 1, in a free-market economy prices play a key role in transmitting information from buyers to sellers and from sellers to buyers. This chapter examines this 'price mechanism' in more detail.

We examine what determines demand, what determines supply and what the relationship is between demand, supply and price. We see how the price mechanism transmits information both from consumers to producers, and from producers to consumers; and how prices act as incentives – for example, if consumers want more mobile phones, how this increased demand leads to an increase in their price and hence to an incentive for firms to increase their production.

What we will see is just how the free market responds to changes in demand or supply – and responds in a way that balances demand and supply at a position of 'equilibrium'.

In practice, not all prices are determined in the free market. After all, we live in a mixed economy. Sometimes the government or some other agency attempts to control prices. In the final section of this chapter, we see what would happen if the government sets about *controlling* prices. Why will shortages occur if it sets a low price, or surpluses if it sets a high one? When might governments feel that it is a good idea to fix prices?

The markets we will be examining are highly competitive ones, with many firms competing against each other. In economics we call this *perfect competition*. This is where consumers and producers are too numerous to have any control over prices: they are *price takers*.

In the case of consumers, this means that they have to accept the prices as given for the things that they buy. On most occasions this is true; when you get to the supermarket checkout you cannot start haggling with the checkout operator over the price of a can of beans or a tub of margarine.

In the case of firms, perfect competition means that producers are too small and face too much competition from other firms to be able to raise prices. Take the case of farmers selling wheat. They have to sell it at the current market price. If individually they try to sell at a higher price, no one will buy, since purchasers of wheat (e.g. flour millers) can get all the wheat they want at the market price.

Of course, many firms *do* have the power to choose their prices. This does not mean that they can simply charge whatever they like. They will still have to take account of overall consumer demand and their competitors' prices. Ford, when setting the price of its Focus cars, will have to ensure that they remain competitive with

Astras, Golfs, Civics, etc. Nevertheless, most firms have some flexibility in setting their prices: they have a degree of 'market power'.

If this is the case, then why do we study *perfect* markets, where firms are price takers? One reason is that they provide a useful approximation to the real world and give us many insights into how a market economy works. Many markets do function very similarly to the markets we shall be describing.

Another is that perfect markets provide an ideal against which to compare the real world. It is often argued that perfect markets benefit the consumer, whereas markets dominated by big business may operate against the consumer's interests. Although these are normative issues, the economist can nevertheless compare the behaviour of prices, output, profit, etc. in different types of market. For example, will the consumer end up paying higher prices in a market dominated by just a few firms than in one operating under perfect competition? Will BT respond to an increase in demand for telephone services in the same way as a farmer does to an increase in the demand for cauliflowers?

Markets with powerful firms are examined in Chapters 6 and 7. For now we concentrate on price takers.

2.1 DEMAND

The relationship between demand and price

The headlines announce 'Major crop failures in Brazil and East Africa: coffee prices soar'. Shortly afterwards you find that coffee prices have doubled in the shops. What do you do? Presumably you will cut back on the amount of coffee you drink. Perhaps you will reduce it from, say, six cups per day to two. Perhaps you will give up drinking coffee altogether.

This is simply an illustration of the general relationship between price and consumption: *when the price of a good*

rises, the quantity demanded will fall. This relationship is known as the *law of demand*. There are two reasons for this law:

- People will feel poorer. They will not be able to afford to buy so much of the good with their money. The purchasing power of their income (their *real income*) has fallen. This is called the *income effect* of a price rise.
- The good will now cost more than alternative or 'substitute' goods, and people will switch to these. This is called the *substitution effect* of a price rise.

Definitions

Perfect competition (preliminary definition) A situation where the consumers and producers of a product are price takers. (There are other features of a perfectly competitive market; these are examined in Chapter 6.)

Price taker A person or firm with no power to be able to influence the market price.

Law of demand The quantity of a good demanded per period of time will fall as price rises and will rise as price falls, other things being equal (*ceteris paribus*).

Income effect The effect of a change in price on quantity demanded arising from the consumer becoming better or worse off as a result of the price change.

Substitution effect The effect of a change in price on quantity demanded arising from the consumer switching to or from alternative (substitute) products.

Similarly, when the price of a good falls, the quantity demanded will rise. People can afford to buy more (the income effect), and they will switch away from consuming alternative goods (the substitution effect).

Therefore, returning to our example of the increase in the price of coffee, we will not be able to afford to buy as much as before, and we will probably drink more tea, cocoa, fruit juices or even water instead.

 KEY IDEA 7 — **The income and substitution effects** are useful concepts as they help to explain why people react to a price rise by buying less. The size of these effects depends on a range of factors. These factors determine the shape of the demand curve.

A word of warning: be careful about the meaning of the words **quantity demanded**. They refer to the amount that consumers are willing and able to purchase at a given price over a given period (e.g. a week, or a month, or a year). They do not refer to what people would simply *like* to consume. You might like to own a luxury yacht, but your demand for luxury yachts will almost certainly be zero at the current price.

The demand curve

Consider the hypothetical data in Table 2.1, which shows how many kilograms of potatoes per month would be purchased at various prices.

Columns (2) and (3) show the **demand schedules** for two individuals, Kate and Simon. Column (4) shows the total **market demand schedule**. This is the total demand by all consumers. To obtain the market demand schedule for potatoes, we simply add up the quantities demanded at each price by *all* consumers: i.e. Kate, Simon and everyone else who demands potatoes. Notice that we are talking about demand *over a period of time* (not at *a point* in time). Thus we could talk about daily demand or weekly demand or annual demand.

 Assume that there are 200 consumers in the market. Of these, 100 have schedules like Kate's and 100 have schedules like Simon's. What would be the total market demand schedule for potatoes now?

The demand schedule can be represented graphically as a **demand curve**. Figure 2.1 shows the market demand curve for potatoes corresponding to the schedule in Table 2.1. The price of potatoes is plotted on the vertical axis. The quantity demanded is plotted on the horizontal axis.

Point *E* shows that at a price of 100p per kilo, 100 000 tonnes of potatoes are demanded each month. When the price falls to 80p we move down the curve to point *D*. This shows that the quantity demanded has now risen to 200 000 tonnes per month. Similarly, if the price falls to 60p we move down the curve again to point *C*: 350 000 tonnes are now demanded. The five points on the graph (*A–E*) correspond to the figures in columns (1) and (4) of Table 2.1. The graph also enables us to read off the likely quantities demanded at prices other than those in the table.

 1. How much would be demanded at a price of 30p per kilogram?
2. Assuming that demand does not change from month to month, plot the annual market demand for potatoes.

A demand curve could also be drawn for an individual consumer. Like market demand curves, individuals' demand curves generally slope downwards from left to right: they have negative slope. The lower the price of the product, the more a person is likely to buy.

 1. Draw Kate's and Simon's demand curves for potatoes on one diagram. Note that you will use the same vertical scale as in Figure 2.1, but you will need a quite different horizontal scale.
2. At what price is their demand the same?
3. What explanations could there be for the quite different shapes of their two demand curves? (This question is explored in section 3.1 below.)

Two points should be noted at this stage:

- In textbooks, demand curves (and other curves too) are only occasionally used to plot specific data. More frequently they are used to illustrate general theoretical arguments. In such cases the axes will simply be price and quantity, with the units unspecified.

Definitions

Quantity demanded The amount of a good that a consumer is willing and able to buy at a given price over a given period of time.

Demand schedule for an individual A table showing the different quantities of a good that a person is willing and able to buy at various prices over a given period of time.

Market demand schedule A table showing the different total quantities of a good that consumers are

willing and able to buy at various prices over a given period of time.

Demand curve A graph showing the relationship between the price of a good and the quantity of the good demanded over a given time period. Price is measured on the vertical axis; quantity demanded is measured on the horizontal axis. A demand curve can be for an individual consumer or group of consumers, or more usually for the whole market.

	Price (pence per kg) (1)	Kate's demand (kg) (2)	Simon's demand (kg) (3)	Total market demand (tonnes: 000s) (4)
A	20	28	16	700
B	40	15	11	500
C	60	5	9	350
D	80	1	7	200
E	100	0	6	100

Table 2.1 The demand for potatoes (monthly)

Figure 2.1 Market demand curve for potatoes (monthly)

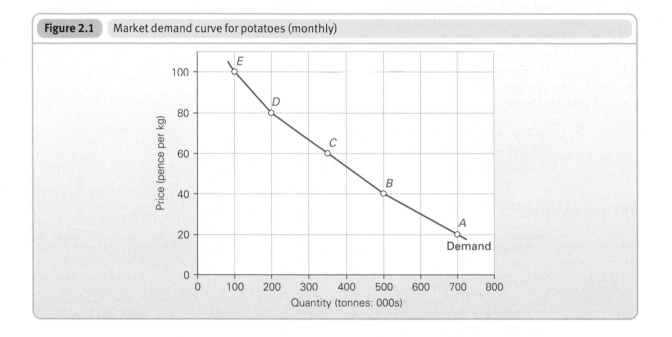

- The term 'curve' is used even when the graph is a straight line! In fact when using demand curves to illustrate arguments we frequently draw them as straight lines – it's easier.

Other determinants of demand

Price is not the only factor that determines how much of a good people will buy. Demand is also affected by the following.

Tastes. The more desirable people find the good, the more they will demand. Tastes are affected by advertising, by fashion, by observing other consumers, by considerations of health and by the experiences from consuming the good on previous occasions.

The number and price of substitute goods (i.e. competitive goods). The higher the price of **substitute goods**, the higher will be the demand for this good as people switch from the substitutes. For example, the demand for coffee will depend on the price of tea. If tea goes up in price, the demand for coffee will rise.

The number and price of complementary goods. **Complementary goods** are those that are consumed together: cars

Definitions

Substitute goods A pair of goods which are considered by consumers to be alternatives to each other. As the price of one goes up, the demand for the other rises.

Complementary goods A pair of goods consumed together. As the price of one goes up, the demand for both goods will fall.

and petrol, shoes and polish, fish and chips. The higher the price of complementary goods, the fewer of them will be bought and hence the less will be the demand for the good under consideration. For example, the demand for batteries will depend on the price of handheld games. If the price of handheld games comes down, so that more are bought, the demand for batteries will rise.

Income. As people's incomes rise, their demand for most goods will rise. Such goods are called **normal goods**. There are exceptions to this general rule, however. As people get richer, they spend less on **inferior goods**, such as supermarket 'value' ranges, and switch to better quality goods.

Distribution of income. If national income were redistributed from the poor to the rich, the demand for luxury goods would rise. At the same time, as the poor got poorer they might have to buy more inferior goods, whose demand would thus rise too.

Expectations of future price changes. If people think that prices are going to rise in the future, they are likely to buy more now before the price does go up.

Movements along and shifts in the demand curve

A demand curve is constructed on the assumption that 'other things remain equal' (*ceteris paribus*). In other words, it is assumed that none of the determinants of demand, other than price, changes. The effect of a change in price is then simply illustrated by a movement along the demand curve: for example, from point B to point D in Figure 2.1 when the price of potatoes rises from 40p to 80p per kilo.

What happens, then, when one of these other determinants does change? The answer is that we have to construct a whole new demand curve: the curve shifts. If a change in one of the other determinants causes demand to rise – say, income rises – the whole curve will shift to the right. This shows that at each price more will be demanded than before. Thus, in Figure 2.2, at a price of P, a quantity of Q_0

Figure 2.2 An increase in demand

was originally demanded. But now, after the increase in demand, Q_1 is demanded. (Note that D_1 is not necessarily parallel to D_0.)

If a change in a determinant other than price causes demand to fall, the whole curve will shift to the left.

To distinguish between shifts in and movements along demand curves, it is usual to distinguish between a change in *demand* and a change in the *quantity demanded*. A shift in the demand curve is referred to as a **change in demand**, whereas a movement along the demand curve as a result of a change in price is referred to as a **change in the quantity demanded**.

1. *Assume that in Table 2.1 the total market demand for potatoes increases by 20 per cent at each price – due, say, to substantial increases in the prices of bread and rice. Plot the old and the new demand curves for potatoes. Is the new curve parallel to the old one?*
2. *The price of blueberries rises and yet it is observed that the sales of blueberries increase. Does this mean that the demand curve for blueberries is upward sloping? Explain.*

Definitions

Normal good A good whose demand rises as people's incomes rise.

Inferior good A good whose demand falls as people's incomes rise.

Change in demand The term used for a shift in the demand curve. It occurs when a determinant of demand other than price changes.

Change in the quantity demanded The term used for a movement along the demand curve to a new point. It occurs when there is a change in price.

*BOX 2.1 | THE DEMAND FOR LAMB

A real-world demand function[1]

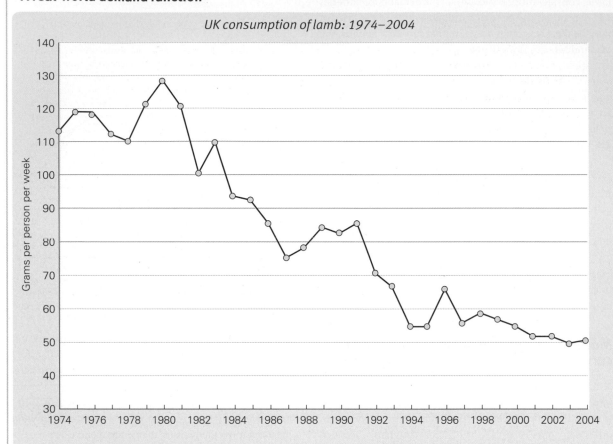

UK consumption of lamb: 1974–2004

Grams per person per week

The diagram shows what happened to the consumption of lamb in the UK over the period 1974–2004. How can we explain this dramatic fall in consumption? One way of exploring this issue is to make use of a regression model, which should help us to see which variables are relevant and how they are likely to affect demand.

The following is an initial model fitted (using the *Microfit* statistical software package) to annual data for the years 1974–2004.

$$Q_L = 170.2 - 0.197P_L - 0.069P_B + 0.280P_P - 0.0094Y \quad (1)$$

where Q_L is the quantity of lamb sold in grams per person per week;

P_L is the 'real' price of lamb (in pence per kg, 1985 prices);

P_B is the 'real' price of beef (in pence per kg, 1985 prices);

P_P is the 'real' price of pork (in pence per kg, 1985 prices);

Y is households' real disposable income per head (£ per year, 2002 prices).

This model makes it possible to predict what would happen to the demand for lamb if any one of the four explanatory variables changed, assuming that the other variables remained constant.

 Using equation (1), calculate what would happen – ceteris paribus – to the demand for lamb if:
(a) the real price of lamb went up by 10p per kg;
(b) the real price of beef went up by 10p per kg;
(c) the real price of pork fell by 10p per kg;
(d) real disposable income per head rose by £100 per annum.
Are the results as you would expect?

There is a serious problem with estimated demand functions like these: they assume that *other* determinants of demand (i.e. those not included in the model) have not changed. In the case of this demand-for-lamb function, one of the other determinants *did* change. This was tastes – during the 1980s and 1990s there was a shift in demand away from lamb and other meats, partly for health reasons, and partly because of an expansion in the availability of and demand for vegetarian and low-meat alternatives.

On the assumption that this shift in taste took place steadily over time, a new demand equation was estimated for the same years:

$$Q_L = 148.7 - 0.278P_L - 0.030P_B + 0.116P_P + 0.0062Y \\ - 3.787TIME \qquad (2)$$

where $TIME = 1$ in 1974, 2 in 1975, 3 in 1976, etc.

1. How does the introduction of the variable TIME affect the relationship between the demand for lamb and (a) its real price; (b) real disposable income per head?
2. Does lamb now appear to be a normal good or an inferior good?
3. What does the negative coefficient of P_B indicate?

Model (2) is a better model than model (1) in two major respects. The first point is that it has a better 'goodness of fit'. This can be shown by the 'R-squared'. $R^2 = 1$ represents a perfect fit, whereas $R^2 = 0$ shows that the model has no explanatory power whatsoever. In model (2), $R^2 = 0.925$ compared with 0.908 for model (1). This means that model (2) can explain 92.5 per cent of the variation in the consumption of lamb during the period 1974 to 2004, whereas model (1) can explain only 90.8 per cent.

Secondly, the coefficient of Y is now positive, suggesting that lamb is a normal good, which seems sensible. By omitting a measure of consumers' tastes from model (1), we mis-specified that model and introduced a bias into the estimated coefficient of Y. In effect, the income variable was picking up the effects of changing tastes and its coefficient ended up being negative rather than positive. By including $TIME$, we eliminated that bias.

Whilst model (2) is clearly an improvement on model (1), it is by no means perfect. One problem is that its R^2 is still somewhat below 1. Another problem is that P_B should have a positive coefficient, since beef is surely a substitute for lamb. More importantly, the model takes no account of the fact that consumers' purchases of lamb this year are likely to be strongly influenced by what they were consuming last year. Finally, whilst the model includes the real prices of two substitutes for lamb, it does not include the real prices of any complements.

To take the above points into account, the following third model was estimated, using data for 1975 to 2004.

$$Q_L = 2.657 - 0.237P_L + 0.071P_B + 0.145P_P + 0.0113Y \\ - 3.298TIME + 0.572LQ_L - 0.084P_C \qquad (3)$$

where LQ_L is the lagged consumption of lamb (i.e. consumption in the previous year) and P_C is the real price of a complement (potatoes). $R^2 = 0.954$.

1. To what extent is model (3) an improvement on model (2)?
2. Use the three equations and also the data given in the table below to estimate the demand for lamb in 1996 and 2004. (First you will need to fill in the missing figures in the TIME column.) Which model works the best in each case? Why? Explain why the models are all subject to error in their predictions. Note: 1996 was unusual in the sense that there was the BSE scare, which caused an abrupt shift in demand from beef to lamb. Can you discern this BSE effect in the graph?

	Q_L	LQ_L	P_L	P_B	P_P	Y	TIME	P_C
1975	119	113	274.0	348.2	310.1	5 873	2	27.3
1996	65	54	295.0	325.3	280.5	10 203		25.9
2004	50	51	318.3	324.6	274.3	12 491		37.1

Nominal food prices were calculated by dividing expenditure by consumption. These nominal prices in pence per kg were then adjusted to 'real' prices by dividing by the RPI (retail price index) for total food (1985 – 100) and multiplying by 100.

Sources: http://statistics.defra.gov.uk/esg/publications/efs/datasets/efsexpd.xls (expenditure);

http://statistics.defra.gov.uk/esg/publications/efs/datasets/efscons.xls (consumption);

http://www.statistics.gov.uk/downloads/theme_economy/ETSupp2005.pdf (income & RPI food);

Economic Trends Annual Supplement 2005, Tables 1.5 & 2.1.

3. Use model (3) and the data given in the table to explain why the demand for lamb fell so dramatically between 1975 and 2004.
4. The formula for the elasticity of demand (price elasticity, income elasticity or cross elasticity) can be written as $dQ/dX \div Q/X$, where dQ/dX represents the coefficient for a given variable, X. For example, in equation (3), 0.071 gives the value of the term dQ_L/dP_B when working out the cross-price elasticity of demand for lamb with respect to changes in the price of beef. Using equation (3) and the table above, work out the following for 2004:
   (a) the price elasticity of demand for lamb;
   (b) the income elasticity of demand for lamb;
   (c) the cross-price elasticity of demand for lamb with respect to (i) beef, (ii) pork, (iii) potatoes.

[1] Thanks to Tony Flegg, John's 'office mate' at UWE, for writing this box.

*LOOKING AT THE MATHS

We can represent the relationship between the market demand for a good and the determinants of demand in the form of an equation. This is called a *demand function*. It can be expressed either in general terms or with specific values attached to the determinants.

Simple demand functions

Demand equations are often used to relate quantity demanded to just one determinant. Thus an equation relating quantity demanded to price could be in the form

$$Q_d = a - bP \tag{1}$$

For example, the actual equation might be:

$$Q_d = 10\ 000 - 200P \tag{2}$$

From this can be calculated a complete demand schedule or demand curve, as shown in the table and diagram. As price (P) changes, the equation tells us how much the quantity demanded (Q_d) changes.

Demand schedule for equation (2)

P	Q_d
5	9000
10	8000
15	7000
20	6000
25	5000

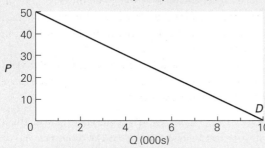

Demand curve for equation (2)

1. Complete the demand schedule in the table up to a price of 50.
2. What is it about equation (2) that makes the demand curve (a) downward sloping; (b) a straight line?

This equation is based on a *ceteris paribus* assumption: it is assumed that all the other determinants of demand remain constant. If one of these other determinants changed, the equation itself would change. There would be a shift in the curve: a change in demand. If the *a* term alone changed, there would be a parallel shift in the curve. If the *b* term changed, the slope of the curve would change.

Simple equations can be used to relate demand to other determinants too. For example, an equation relating quantity demanded to income would be in the form

$$Q_d = a + bY \tag{3}$$

1. Referring to equation (3), if the term 'a' has a value of −50 000 and the term 'b' a value of 0.001, construct a demand schedule with respect to total income (Y). Do this for incomes between £100 million and £300 million at £50 million intervals.
2. Now use this schedule to plot a demand curve with respect to income. Comment on its shape.

More complex demand functions

In a similar way, we can relate the quantity demanded to two or more determinants. For example, a demand function could be of the form:

$$Q_d = a - bP + cY + dP_s - eP_c \tag{4}$$

This equation says that the quantity demanded (Q_d) will fall as the price of the good (P) rises, will rise as the level of consumer incomes (Y) rises, will rise as the price of a particular substitute (P_s) rises and will fall as the price of a particular complement (P_c) rises, by amounts b, c, d and e respectively.

Estimated demand equations

Surveys can be conducted to show how demand depends on each one of a number of determinants, while the rest are held constant. Using statistical techniques called *regression analysis*, a demand equation can be estimated.

For example, assume that it was observed that the demand for butter (measured in 250g units) depended on its price (P_b), the price of margarine (P_m) and total annual consumer incomes (Y). The estimated weekly demand equation may then be something like

$$Q_d = 2\ 000\ 000 - 50\ 000P_b + 20\ 000P_m + 0.01Y \tag{5}$$

Thus if the price of butter were 50p, the price of margarine were 35p and consumer incomes were £200 million, and if P_b and P_m were measured in pence and Y was measured in pounds, then the demand for butter would be 2 200 000 units. This is calculated as follows:

$$\begin{aligned} Q_d &= 2\ 000\ 000 - (50\ 000 \times 50) + (20\ 000 \times 35) \\ &\quad + (0.01 \times 200\ 000\ 000) \\ &= 2\ 000\ 000 - 2\ 500\ 000 + 700\ 000 + 2\ 000\ 000 \\ &= 2\ 200\ 000 \end{aligned}$$

The branch of economics that applies statistical techniques to economic data is known as *econometrics*. Econometrics is beyond the scope of this book. It is worth noting, however, that econometrics, like other branches of statistics, cannot produce equations and graphs that allow totally reliable predictions to be made. The data on which the equations are based are often incomplete or unreliable, and the underlying relationships on which they are based (often ones of human behaviour) may well change over time.

Definitions

Demand function An equation which shows the mathematical relationship between the quantity demanded of a good and the values of the various determinants of demand.

Regression analysis A statistical technique which allows a functional relationship between two or more variables to be estimated.

Econometrics The science of applying statistical techniques to economic data in order to identify and test economic relationships.

Section summary

1. When the price of a good rises, the quantity demanded per period of time will fall. This is known as the 'law of demand'. It applies both to individuals' demand and to the whole market demand.

2. The law of demand is explained by the income and substitution effects of a price change.

3. The relationship between price and quantity demanded per period of time can be shown in a table (or 'schedule') or as a graph. On the graph, price is plotted on the vertical axis and quantity demanded per period of time on the horizontal axis. The resulting demand curve is downward sloping (negatively sloped).

4. Other determinants of demand include tastes, the number and price of substitute goods, the number

and price of complementary goods, income, distribution of income and expectations of future price changes.

5. If price changes, the effect is shown by a movement along the demand curve. We call this effect 'a change in the quantity demanded'.

6. If any other determinant of demand changes, the whole curve will shift. We call this effect 'a change in demand'. A rightward shift represents an increase in demand; a leftward shift represents a decrease in demand.

7. *The relationship between the quantity demanded and the various determinants of demand (including price) can be expressed as an equation.

2.2 SUPPLY

Supply and price

Imagine you are a farmer deciding what to do with your land. Part of your land is in a fertile valley, while part is on a hillside where the soil is poor. Perhaps, then, you will consider growing vegetables in the valley and keeping sheep on the hillside.

Your decision will depend to a large extent on the price that various vegetables will fetch in the market and likewise the price you can expect to get from sheep and wool. As far as the valley is concerned, you will plant the vegetables that give the best return. If, for example, the price of potatoes is high, you might use a lot of the valley for growing potatoes. If the price gets higher, you may well use the whole of the valley, being prepared maybe to run the risk of potato disease. If the price is very high indeed, you may even consider growing potatoes on the hillside, even though the yield per acre is much lower there.

In other words, the higher the price of a particular farm output, the more land will be devoted to it. This illustrates the general relationship between supply and price: *when the price of a good rises, the quantity supplied will also rise.* There are three reasons for this:

- As firms supply more, they are likely to find that beyond a certain level of output, costs rise more and more rapidly. In the case of the farm just considered, if more and more potatoes are grown, then land progressively less suitable to potato cultivation has to be used. This raises the cost of producing extra potatoes. It is the same for manufacturers. Beyond a certain level of output, costs are likely to rise rapidly as workers have to be paid overtime and as machines approach capacity working. If higher output involves higher costs of producing each

unit, producers will need to get a higher price if they are to be persuaded to produce extra output.

- The higher the price of the good, the more profitable it becomes to produce. Firms will thus be encouraged to produce more of it by switching from producing less profitable goods.

- Given time, if the price of a good remains high new producers will be encouraged to set up in production. Total market supply thus rises.

The first two determinants affect supply in the short run. The third affects supply in the long run. We distinguish between short-run and long-run supply in section 3.2 on page 71.

The supply curve

The amount that producers would like to supply at various prices can be shown in a *supply schedule*. Table 2.2 shows a monthly supply schedule for potatoes, both for an individual farmer (farmer X) and for all farmers together (the whole market).

Definition

Supply schedule A table showing the different quantities of a good that producers are willing and able to supply at various prices over a given time period. A supply schedule can be for an individual producer or group of producers, or for all producers (the market supply schedule).

Table 2.2	The supply of potatoes (monthly)		
	Price of potatoes (pence per kg)	Farmer X's supply (tonnes)	Total market supply (tonnes: 000s)
a	20	50	100
b	40	70	200
c	60	100	350
d	80	120	530
e	100	130	700

The supply schedule can be represented graphically as a *supply curve*. A supply curve may be an individual firm's supply curve or a market curve (i.e. that of the whole industry).

Figure 2.3 shows the *market* supply curve of potatoes. As with demand curves, price is plotted on the vertical axis and quantity on the horizontal axis. Each of the points *a–e* corresponds to a figure in Table 2.2. Thus, for example, a price rise from 60p per kilogram to 80p per kilogram will cause a movement along the supply curve from point *c* to point *d*: total market supply will rise from 350 000 tonnes per month to 530 000 tonnes per month.

1. *How much would be supplied at a price of 70p per kilo?*
2. *Draw a supply curve for farmer X. Are the axes drawn to the same scale as in Figure 2.3?*

Not all supply curves will be upward sloping (positively sloped). Sometimes they will be vertical, or horizontal or even downward sloping. This will depend largely on the time period over which firms' response to price changes is considered. This question is examined in the section on the elasticity of supply (see section 3.1 below) and in more detail in Chapters 5 and 6.

Other determinants of supply

Like demand, supply is not simply determined by price. The other determinants of supply are as follows.

The costs of production. The higher the costs of production, the less profit will be made at any price. As costs rise, firms will cut back on production, probably switching to alternative products whose costs have not risen so much.

The main reasons for a change in costs are as follows:

- Change in input prices: costs of production will rise if wages, raw material prices, rents, interest rates or any other input prices rise.
- Change in technology: technological advances can fundamentally alter the costs of production. Consider, for example, how the microchip revolution has changed production methods and information handling in virtually every industry in the world.
- Organisational changes: various cost savings can be made in many firms by reorganising production.
- Government policy: costs will be lowered by government subsidies and raised by various taxes.

The profitability of alternative products (substitutes in supply). If a product which is a **substitute in supply** becomes more

---

Definitions

Supply curve A graph showing the relationship between the price of a good and the quantity of the good supplied over a given period of time.

Substitutes in supply These are two goods where an increased production of one means diverting resources away from producing the other.

Figure 2.3	Market supply curve of potatoes (monthly)

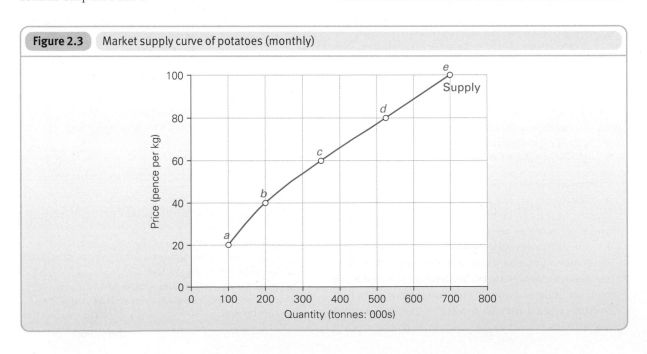

profitable to supply than before, producers are likely to switch from the first good to this alternative. Supply of the first good falls. Other goods are likely to become more profitable if their prices rise and/or their costs of production fall. For example, if the price of carrots goes up, or the cost of producing carrots comes down, farmers may decide to cut down potato production in order to produce more carrots.

The profitability of goods in joint supply. Sometimes when one good is produced, another good is also produced at the same time. These are said to be **goods in joint supply**. An example is the refining of crude oil to produce petrol. Other grade fuels will be produced as well, such as diesel and paraffin. If more petrol is produced, due to a rise in demand and hence its price, then the supply of these other fuels will rise too.

Nature, 'random shocks' and other unpredictable events. In this category we would include the weather and diseases affecting farm output, wars affecting the supply of imported raw materials, the breakdown of machinery, industrial disputes, earthquakes, floods and fire, etc.

The aims of producers. A profit-maximising firm will supply a different quantity from a firm that has a different aim, such as maximising sales. For most of the time we shall assume that firms are profit maximisers. In Chapter 8, however, we consider alternative aims.

Expectations of future price changes. If price is expected to rise, producers may temporarily reduce the amount they sell. They are likely to build up their stocks and only release them on to the market when the price does rise. At the same time they may install new machines or take on more labour, so that they can be ready to supply more when the price has risen.

The number of suppliers. If new firms enter the market, supply is likely to increase.

 By referring to each of the above determinants of supply, identify what would cause (a) the supply of potatoes to fall and (b) the supply of leather to rise.

Movements along and shifts in the supply curve

The principle here is the same as with demand curves. The effect of a change in price is illustrated by a movement along the supply curve: for example, from point *d* to point *e* in Figure 2.3 when price rises from 80p to 100p. Quantity supplied rises from 530 000 to 700 000 tonnes per month.

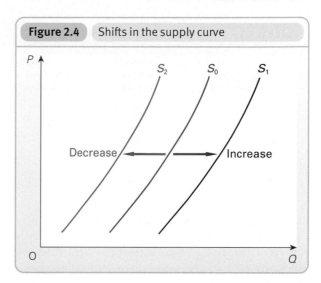

Figure 2.4 Shifts in the supply curve

If any other determinant of supply changes, the whole supply curve will shift. A rightward shift illustrates an increase in supply. A leftward shift illustrates a decrease in supply. Thus in Figure 2.4, if the original curve is S_0, the curve S_1 represents an increase in supply (more is supplied at each price), whereas the curve S_2 represents a decrease in supply (less is supplied at each price).

A movement along a supply curve is often referred to as a **change in the quantity supplied**, whereas a shift in the supply curve is simply referred to as a **change in supply**.

 This question is concerned with the supply of oil for central heating. In each case consider whether there is a movement along the supply curve (and in which direction) or a shift in it (and whether left or right).
(a) New oil fields start up in production.
(b) The demand for central heating rises.
(c) The price of gas falls.
(d) Oil companies anticipate an upsurge in demand for central-heating oil.
(e) The demand for petrol rises.
(f) New technology decreases the costs of oil refining.
(g) All oil products become more expensive.

Definitions

Joint supply goods These are two goods where the production of more of one leads to the production of more of the other.

Change in the quantity supplied The term used for a movement along the supply curve to a new point. It occurs when there is a change in price.

Change in supply The term used for a shift in the supply curve. It occurs when a determinant other than price changes.

*LOOKING AT THE MATHS

Using survey data and regression analysis, equations can be estimated relating supply to some of its determinants. Note that not all determinants can be easily quantified (e.g. nature and the aims of firms), and they may thus be left out of the equation.

The simplest form of supply equation relates supply to just one determinant. Thus a function relating supply to price would be of the form

$$Q_s = c + dP \tag{1}$$

Using regression analysis, values can be estimated for c and d. Thus an actual supply equation might be something like

$$Q_s = 500 + 1000P \tag{2}$$

1. *If P was originally measured in pounds, what would happen to the value of the d term in equation (2) if P were now measured in pence?*

2. *Draw the schedule (table) and graph for equation (2) for prices from £1 to £10. What is it in the equation that determines the slope of the supply 'curve'?*

If any determinant other than price changed, a new equation would result. For example, if costs of production fell, the equation might then be

$$Q_s = 1000 + 1500P \tag{3}$$

More complex supply equations would relate supply to more than one determinant. For example:

$$Q_s = 200 + 80P - 20a_1 - 15a_2 + 30j \tag{4}$$

where P is the price of the good, a_1 and a_2 are the profitabilities of two alternative goods that could be supplied instead, and j is the profitability of a good in joint supply.

Explain why the P and j terms have a positive sign, whereas the a_1 and a_2 terms have a negative sign.

Section summary

1. When the price of a good rises, the quantity supplied per period of time will usually also rise. This applies both to individual producers' supply and to the whole market supply.

2. There are two reasons in the short run why a higher price encourages producers to supply more: (a) they are now willing to incur the higher costs per unit associated with producing more; (b) they will switch to producing this product and away from now less profitable ones. In the long run, there is a third reason: new producers will be attracted into the market.

3. The relationship between price and quantity supplied per period of time can be shown in a table (or schedule) or as a graph. As with a demand curve, price is plotted on the vertical axis and quantity per period of time on the horizontal axis. The resulting supply curve is upward sloping (positively sloped).

4. Other determinants of supply include the costs of production, the profitability of alternative products, the profitability of goods in joint supply, random shocks and expectations of future price changes.

5. If price changes, the effect is shown by a movement along the supply curve. We call this effect 'a change in the quantity supplied'.

6. If any determinant *other* than price changes, the effect is shown by a shift in the whole supply curve. We call this effect 'a change in supply'. A rightward shift represents an increase in supply; a leftward shift represents a decrease in supply.

7. *The relationship between the quantity supplied and the various determinants of supply can be expressed in the form of an equation.

2.3   PRICE AND OUTPUT DETERMINATION

Equilibrium price and output

We can now combine our analysis of demand and supply. This will show how the actual price of a product and the actual quantity bought and sold are determined in a free and competitive market.

Let us return to the example of the market demand and market supply of potatoes, and use the data from Tables 2.1 and 2.2. These figures are given again in Table 2.3.

What will be the price and output that actually prevail? If the price started at 20p per kilogram, demand would exceed supply by 600 000 tonnes ($A - a$). Consumers would

Table 2.3	The market demand and supply of potatoes (monthly)	
Price of potatoes (pence per kg)	**Total market demand (tonnes: 000s)**	**Total market supply (tonnes: 000s)**
20	700 (A)	100 (a)
40	500 (B)	200 (b)
60	350 (C)	350 (c)
80	200 (D)	530 (d)
100	100 (E)	700 (e)

be unable to obtain all they wanted and would thus be willing to pay a higher price. Producers, unable or unwilling to supply enough to meet the demand, will be only too happy to accept a higher price. The effect of the shortage, then, will be to drive up the price. The same would happen at a price of 40p per kilogram. There would still be a shortage; price would still rise. But as the price rises, the quantity demanded falls and the quantity supplied rises. The shortage is progressively eliminated.

 Explain the process by which the price of houses would rise if there were a shortage.

What would happen if the price of potatoes started at a much higher level: say, at 100p per kilogram? In this case supply would exceed demand by 600 000 tonnes (*e* – *E*). The effect of this surplus would be to drive the price down as farmers competed against each other to sell their excess supplies. The same would happen at a price of 80p per kilogram. There would still be a surplus; price would still fall.

In fact, only one price is sustainable – the price where demand equals supply: namely, 60p per kilogram, where both demand and supply are 350 000 tonnes. When supply matches demand the market is said to **clear**. There is no shortage and no surplus.

As we have already seen in section 1.2, the price where demand equals supply is called the *equilibrium price* and we return to this in more detail in Threshold Concept 4 on page 44. In Table 2.3, if the price starts at anything other than 60p per kilogram, it will tend to move towards 60p. The equilibrium price is the only price at which producers' and consumers' wishes are mutually reconciled: where the producers' plans to supply exactly match the consumers' plans to buy.

 KEY IDEA 8 *Equilibrium is the point where conflicting interests are balanced.* Only at this point is the amount that demanders are willing to purchase the same as the amount that suppliers are willing to supply. It is a point that will be automatically reached in a free market through the operation of the price mechanism.

Demand and supply curves

The determination of equilibrium price and output can be shown using demand and supply curves. Equilibrium is where the two curves intersect.

Figure 2.5 shows the demand and supply curves of potatoes corresponding to the data in Table 2.3. Equilibrium price is P_e (60p) and equilibrium quantity is Q_e (350 000 tonnes).

At any price above 60p, there would be a surplus. Thus at 80p there is a surplus of 330 000 tonnes (*d* – *D*). More is supplied than consumers are willing and able to purchase at that price. Thus a price of 80p fails to clear the market. Price will fall to the equilibrium price of 60p. As it does so, there will be a movement along the demand curve from point *D* to point *C*, and a movement along the supply curve from point *d* to point *c*.

At any price below 60p, there would be a shortage. Thus at 40p there is a shortage of 300 000 tonnes (*B* – *b*). Price will rise to 60p. This will cause a movement along the supply curve from point *b* to point *c* and along the demand curve from point *B* to point *C*.

Definition

Market clearing A market clears when supply matches demand, leaving no shortage or surplus.

Figure 2.5 The determination of market equilibrium (potatoes: monthly)

| THRESHOLD CONCEPT 4 | MARKETS EQUATE DEMAND AND SUPPLY | THINKING LIKE AN ECONOMIST |

'Leave things up to the market.' 'The market will sort it out.' 'It's what the market wants.' 'You can't buck the market.'

These are typical sayings about the market and emphasise the power of market forces. The point is that our lives are affected massively by markets. Market forces affect the prices of the things we buy and the incomes we earn. Even governments find it difficult to control many key markets. Governments might not like it when stock market prices plummet or when oil prices soar, but there is precious little they can do about it.

In many ways a market is like a democracy. People, by choosing to buy goods, are voting for them to be produced. Firms finding 'a market' for their products are happy to oblige and produce them. The way it works is simple. If people want more of a product, they buy more and thereby 'cast their votes' (i.e. their money) in favour of more being produced. The resulting shortage drives up the price, which gives firms the incentive to produce more of the product. In other words, firms are doing what consumers want – not because of any 'love' for consumers, or because they are being told to produce more by the government – but because it is in their own self-interest. They supply more because the higher price has made it profitable to do so.

This is a *threshold concept* because to understand market forces – the forces of demand and supply – is to go straight to the heart of a market economy and understand what makes it tick. And in this process, prices are the key. It is changes in price that balance demand and supply. If demand exceeds supply, price will rise. This will choke off some of the demand and encourage more supply until demand equals supply – until an equilibrium has been reached. If supply exceeds demand, price will fall. This will discourage firms from supplying so much and encourage consumers to buy more, until, once more, an equilibrium has been reached.

In this process, markets act like an 'invisible hand' – a term coined by the famous economist Adam Smith (see

Box 1.6 on page 22). Market prices guide both producers to respond to consumer demand and consumers to respond to changes in producer supply.

In many circumstances, markets bring outcomes that people want. As we have seen, if consumers want more, then market forces will lead to more being produced. Sometimes, however, market forces can bring adverse effects. We explore these at various parts of the book. It is important, at this stage, however, to recognise that markets are rarely perfect. Market failures, from pollution to the domination of our lives by big business, are very real. Understanding this brings us to Threshold Concept 6 (see page 52).

Partial equilibrium

The type of equilibrium we will be examining for the next few chapters is known as 'partial equilibrium'. It is partial because what we are doing is examining just one tiny bit of the economy at a time: just one market (e.g. that for eggs). It is even partial within the market for eggs because we are assuming that price is the *only* thing that changes to balance demand and supply: that nothing else changes. In other words, when we refer to equilibrium price and quantity, we are assuming that all the other determinants of both demand and supply are held constant.

If another determinant of demand or supply *does* change, there would then be a new partial equilibrium as price adjusts and both demanders and suppliers respond. For example, if a health scare connected with egg consumption causes the demand for eggs to fall, the resulting surplus will lead to a fall in the equilibrium price and quantity.

1. *If there is a shortage of certain skilled workers in the economy, how will market forces lead to an elimination of the skills shortage?*
2. *If consumers want more of a product, is it always desirable that market forces result in more being produced?*

Point *Cc* is the equilibrium: where demand equals supply.

Movement to a new equilibrium

The equilibrium price will remain unchanged only so long as the demand and supply curves remain unchanged. If either of the curves shifts, a new equilibrium will be formed.

A change in demand

If one of the determinants of demand changes (other than price), the whole demand curve will shift. This will lead to a movement *along* the *supply* curve to the new intersection point.

For example, in Figure 2.6, if a rise in consumer incomes led to the demand curve shifting to D_2, there would be a shortage of *h–g* at the original price P_{e_1}. This would cause price to rise to the new equilibrium P_{e_2}. As it did so, there would be a movement along the supply curve from point *g* to point *i*, and along the new demand curve (D_2) from point *h* to point *i*. Equilibrium quantity would rise from Q_{e_1} to Q_{e_2}.

The effect of the shift in demand, therefore, has been a movement *along* the supply curve from the old equilibrium to the new: from point *g* to point *i*.

What would happen to price and quantity if the demand curve shifted to the left? Draw a diagram to illustrate your answer.

Figure 2.6   Effect of a shift in the demand curve

 What will happen to the equilibrium price and quantity of butter in each of the following cases? You should state whether demand or supply (or both) have shifted and in which direction. (In each case assume ceteris paribus.)
(a) A rise in the price of margarine.
(b) A rise in the demand for yoghurt.
(c) A rise in the price of bread.
(d) A rise in the demand for bread.
(e) An expected rise in the price of butter in the near future.
(f) A tax on butter production.
(g) The invention of a new, but expensive, process for removing all cholesterol from butter, plus the passing of a law which states that all butter producers must use this process.

A change in supply

Likewise, if one of the determinants of supply changes (other than price), the whole supply curve will shift. This will lead to a movement *along* the *demand* curve to the new intersection point.

For example, in Figure 2.7, if costs of production rose, the supply curve would shift to the left: to S_2. There would be a shortage of *g–j* at the old price of P_{e_1}. Price would rise from P_{e_1} to P_{e_3}. Quantity would fall from Q_{e_1} to Q_{e_3}. In other words, there would be a movement along the demand curve from point *g* to point *k*, and along the new supply curve (S_2) from point *j* to point *k*.

To summarise: a shift in one curve leads to a movement along the other curve to the new intersection point.

Sometimes a number of determinants might change. This might lead to a shift in *both* curves. When this happens, equilibrium simply moves from the point where the old curves intersected to the point where the new ones intersect.

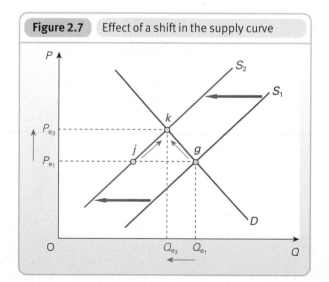

Figure 2.7   Effect of a shift in the supply curve

*LOOKING AT THE MATHS

We saw on pages 36 and 42 how demand and supply curves can be represented by equations. Assume that the equations for the supply and demand curves in a particular market are as follows:

$$Q_D = a - bP \qquad (1)$$

$$Q_S = c + dP \qquad (2)$$

We can find the market equilibrium price by setting the two equations equal to each other, since, in equilibrium, the quantity supplied (Q_S) equals the quantity demanded (Q_D). Thus:

$$c + dP = a - bP$$

Subtracting *c* from and adding *bP* to both sides gives:

$$dP + bP = a - c$$
$$\therefore (d + b)P = a - c$$
$$\therefore P = \frac{a - c}{d + b} \qquad (3)$$

We can then solve for equilibrium quantity (Q_e) by substituting equation (3) in either equation (1) or (2) (since $Q_D = Q_S$).

Thus, from equation (1):

$$Q_e = a - b\left(\frac{a - c}{d + b}\right)$$

$$= \frac{a(d + b) - b(a - c)}{d + b}$$

$$= \frac{ad + ab - ba + bc}{d + b} = \frac{ad + bc}{d + b} \qquad (4)$$

or, from equation (2):

$$Q_e = c + d\left(\frac{a - c}{d + b}\right)$$

$$= \frac{cd + cb + da - dc}{d + b} = \frac{cb + da}{d + b} \qquad (5)$$

Thus:

$$Q_e = \frac{ad + bc}{d + b}\text{(equation (4))} = \frac{cb + da}{d + b}\text{(equation (5))}$$

A worked example is given in Maths Case 2.1 in MyEconLab.

BOX 2.2   UK HOUSE PRICES

The ups and downs of the housing market

If you are thinking of buying a house sometime in the future, then you may well follow the fortunes of the housing market with some trepidation. In the late 1980s there was a housing price explosion in the UK: in fact, between 1984 and 1989 house prices *doubled*. After several years of falling or gently rising house prices in the early and mid 1990s, there was another boom from 1996 to 2007, with house prices rising by 26 per cent per year at the peak (in the 12 months to January 2003). Although incomes grew in the same period, they did not 'keep up' with house price growth and thus affordability fell. Many households, particularly first-time buyers, found that they were priced out of the market. Then in 2008, things changed dramatically; house prices plummeted. By the end of the year they were falling at an annual rate of 19 per cent (see chart).

House prices since the early 1980s

The diagram shows what happened to house prices in the period 1983 to 2008. The vertical axis measures the annual percentage increase in average house prices. The figures are adjusted quarterly.

You can see that house price inflation was very high in the late 1980s, reaching a peak of 34 per cent per annum in the fourth quarter of 1988. In their rush to buy a house before prices rose any further, many people in this period borrowed as much as they were able. Building societies and banks at that time had plenty of money to lend and were only too willing to do so. Many people, therefore,

took out very large mortgages. In 1983 the average new mortgage was 2.08 times average annual earnings. By 1989 this figure had risen to 3.44.

After 1989 there followed a period of *falling* prices. From 1990 to 1995, house prices fell by 12.2 per cent. Many people now found themselves in a position of *negative equity*, where the size of their mortgage was greater than the value of their house. In other words, if they sold their house, they would end up still owing money. The people most likely to be in this position were first-time buyers who had borrowed a large amount relative to the price of their house.

From 1996, however, house prices began to recover and by 2003 house price inflation had returned to rates similar to those in the 1980s. This boom in house prices continued until late 2007. Was this good news or bad news? For those who had been trapped in negative equity in the early 1990s, it was good news. It was also good news for old people who wished to move into a retirement home and who had a house to sell. It was bad news, however, for first-time buyers, for whom house purchase was becoming increasingly unaffordable. As we shall see in many parts of this book, what is good news for one person is often bad news for another.

In the mid 2000s, many first-time buyers had taken out mortgages of 100 per cent (or even more) of the value of the house. Mortgages had been plentiful and there were many introductory offers of low interest rates to tempt

UK house price inflation (annual percentage rates, adjusted quarterly)

Source: Based on *Halifax House Price Index* (HBOS).

purchasers. In 1997, house prices for first-time buyers averaged 1.75 times their annual income. By 2007, this had risen to 3.5 times.

Then in 2008, the house market turned. After 12 years of rising house prices, prices were now falling – and rapidly too. With the 'credit crunch', which began in 2007, where lending between banks dwindled, mortgages became less available and at higher interest rates and requiring a large deposit. By November 2008, the number of new mortgage approvals was only 33 per cent of that in November of the previous year.

The determinants of house prices

House prices are determined by demand and supply. If demand rises (i.e. shifts to the right) or if supply falls (i.e. shifts to the left), the equilibrium price of houses will rise. Similarly, if demand falls or supply rises, the equilibrium price will fall.

So why did house prices rise so rapidly in the 1980s and again in the late 1990s and 2000s, but fall in the early 1990s and from 2008? The answer lies primarily in changes in the *demand* for housing. Let us examine the various factors that affected the demand for houses.

Incomes (actual and anticipated).   The second half of the 1980s and from 1997 to 2007 were periods of rapidly rising incomes. The economy was experiencing an economic 'boom'. Many people wanted to spend their extra incomes on housing: either buying a house for the first time, or moving to a better one. What is more, many people thought that their incomes would continue to grow, and were thus prepared to stretch themselves financially in the short term by buying an expensive house, confident that their mortgage payments would become more and more affordable over time.

The early 1990s and 2008/9, by contrast, were periods of recession, with rising unemployment and either falling or much more slowly growing incomes. People had much less confidence about their ability to afford large mortgages.

The desire for home ownership.   Mrs Thatcher (prime minister from 1979 to 1991) put great emphasis on the virtues of home ownership: a home-owning democracy. Certainly, from the 1980s onward it became generally accepted that it was very desirable to own one's own home.

The cost of mortgages.   During the second half of the 1980s, mortgage interest rates were generally falling. This meant that people could afford larger mortgages, and thus afford to buy more expensive houses. In 1989, however, this trend was reversed. Mortgage interest rates were now rising. Many people found it difficult to maintain existing payments, let alone to take on a larger mortgage. From 1996 to 2003 mortgage rates were generally reduced again, once more fuelling the demand for houses. Even when interest rates rose gradually over the period from 2004 to 2007 they didn't come close to the rates reached in the early 1990s. By 2008, however, higher mortgage interest rates were becoming increasingly unaffordable for many people and this was one factor contributing to the initial downturn in house prices.

The availability of mortgages.   In the two housing boom periods of the late 1980s and from 1997 to 2007, mortgages were readily available. With house prices rising, banks and building societies were prepared to accept smaller deposits on houses, and to lend a larger multiple of people's income. After all, if borrowers were to default, lenders would still have a very good chance of getting all their money back.

In the early 1990s, however, and again from 2008, banks and building societies were more cautious about granting mortgages. They were aware that, with falling house prices, rising unemployment and the growing problem of negative equity, there was an increased danger that borrowers would default on payments. In 2008/9 the problem was compounded by the credit crunch, meaning that banks had less money to lend.

Speculation.   In the two housing boom periods, people generally believed that house prices would continue rising. This encouraged people to buy as soon as possible, and to take out the biggest mortgage possible, before prices went up any further. There was also an effect on supply. Those with houses to sell held back until the last possible moment in the hope of getting a higher price. The net effect was a rightward shift in the demand curve for houses and a leftward shift in the supply curve. The effect of this speculation, therefore, was to help bring about the very effect that people were predicting (for more on speculation see section 3.2).

In the early 1990s, and again from 2008, the opposite occurred. People thinking of buying houses held back, hoping to buy at a lower price. People with houses to sell tried to sell as quickly as possible before prices fell any further. Again the effect of this speculation was to aggravate the change in prices – this time a fall in prices.

Speculation in recent years has been compounded by the growth in the 'buy-to-let' industry, with mortgage lenders entering this market in large numbers and a huge amount of media attention focused on the possibilities for individuals to make very high returns.

What of the future?

At the time of writing, the credit crunch has resulted in a huge decline of mortgage advances and a rapid decline in house prices. Will this continue? As central banks, governments and the finance industry around the world take measures to improve the flow of credit, so mortgages should become more available again and interest rates should remain low. At the same time, the long-term growth in demand for houses is likely to outstrip the growth in supply. This is a recipe for rising house prices once more.

1. *Draw supply and demand diagrams to illustrate what was happening to house prices (a) in the second half of the 1980s and the period from 1997 to 2007; (b) in the early 1990s and the period from 2008.*
2. *Are there any factors on the supply side that influence house prices?*
3. *Find out what forecasters are predicting for house prices over the next year and attempt to explain their views.*

BOX 2.3 STOCK MARKET PRICES

Demand and supply in action

Firms that are quoted on the stock market can raise money by issuing shares. These are sold on the 'primary stock market'. People who own the shares receive a 'dividend' on them, normally paid six-monthly. The amount varies with the profitability of the company.

People or institutions that buy these shares, however, may not wish to hold on to them forever. This is where the 'secondary stock market' comes in. It is where existing shares are bought and sold. There are stock markets, primary and secondary, in all the major countries of the world.

There are more than 3200 shares and other securities listed on the London Stock Exchange and trading in them takes place each Monday to Friday (excluding Bank Holidays). The prices of shares depend on demand and supply. For example, if the demand for Tesco shares at any one time exceeds the supply on offer, the price will rise until demand and supply are equal. Share prices fluctuate throughout the trading day and sometimes price changes can be substantial.

To give an overall impression of share price movements, stock exchanges publish share price indices. The best known one in the UK is the FTSE ('footsie') 100, which stands for the 'Financial Times Stock Exchange'

index of the 100 largest companies' shares. The index represents an average price of these 100 shares. The chart shows movements in the FTSE 100 from 1995 to 2008. The index was first calculated on 3 January 1984 with a base level of 1000 points. It reached a peak of 6930 points on 30 December 1999 and fell to 3287 on 12 March 2003.

But what causes share prices to change? Why were they so high in 1999, but only just over half that value just three years later? The answer lies in the determinants of the demand and supply of shares.

Demand

There are five main factors that affect the demand for shares.

The dividend yield. This is the dividend on a share as a percentage of its price. The higher the dividend yields on shares the more attractive they are as a form of saving. One of the main explanations of rising stock market prices from 2003 to 2007 was high profits and resulting high dividends. Similarly, the slowdown in the world economy after 2007 led to falling profits and falling dividends.

Financial Times Stock Exchange Index (FTSE) (3/1/1984 = 1000)

The price of and/or return on substitutes.　The main substitutes for shares in specific companies are other shares. Thus if, in comparison with other shares, Tesco shares are expected to pay high dividends relative to the share price, people will buy Tesco shares. As far as shares in general are concerned, the main substitutes are other forms of saving. Thus if the interest rate on savings accounts in banks and building societies fell, people with such accounts would be tempted to take their money out and buy shares instead.

Another major substitute is property. If house prices rise rapidly, as they did in 2002 and 2003, this will reduce the demand for shares as many people switch to buying property in anticipation of even higher prices. If house prices level off, as they did in 2005/6, this makes shares relatively more attractive as an investment and can boost the demand for them. Of course, other factors may affect *both* house prices *and* shares in the same way. Thus the 'credit crunch' that started in 2007, when finance became both harder to obtain and more expensive, resulted in both falling house prices *and* falling share prices as the economy slowed down and profits fell.

Incomes.　If the economy is growing rapidly and people's incomes are thus rising rapidly, they are likely to buy more shares. Thus in the mid to late 1990s, when UK incomes were rising at an average annual rate of over 3 per cent, share prices rose rapidly (see chart). As the economy slowed in the early 2000s and again in 2008, so share prices fell.

Wealth.　'Wealth' is people's accumulated savings and property. Wealth rose in the 1990s and many people used their increased wealth to buy shares. It was a similar picture in the mid 2000s. Much of the wealth worldwide was in relatively 'liquid' form – i.e. in a form that can easily be turned into cash (and hence used to buy shares).

Expectations.　In the mid to late 1990s, people expected share prices to go on rising. They were optimistic about continued growth in the economy and that certain sectors, such as leisure and high-tech industries, would grow particularly strongly. But as people bought shares, this pushed their prices up even more, thereby fuelling further speculation that they would go on rising and encouraging further share buying.

In the early 2000s, by contrast, confidence was shaken. Most countries experienced a slowing down in economic growth, or even a recession (a fall in national output). This, combined with other negative factors, such as the 11 September 2001 attack on the World Trade Center and various corporate scandals such as the accounting fraud concerning the giant US company Enron, caused share prices to plummet. As people anticipated further price falls, so they held back from buying, thereby pushing prices even lower. Conversely, as share prices began rising again

from 2003 onwards, so this boosted the demand for shares, thereby fuelling the surge in share prices.

Then with the credit crunch and falling profits from 2007, share prices fell, with the falls resulting in further selling and further falls as confidence waned. Things reached crisis point in October 2008, as people feared banking collapses and the onset of recession. On 10 October, the FTSE fell as low as 3874, 31 per cent down on early September and 42 per cent down from October of the previous year. However, with a bank rescue plan announced by governments around the world (see Box 18.3), expectations became more positive and the FTSE rose by 17 per cent in just two days.

But as recession deepened and as more news about banks' bad debts emerged, so share prices remained volatile. Banks shares, particularly, were very vulnerable to speculation, with growing worries in early 2009 that further bank bailouts by governments would be necessary. We examine speculation in detail in section 3.2.

Supply

The factors affecting supply are largely the same as those affecting demand, but in the opposite direction.

If the return on alternative forms of saving falls, people with shares are likely to hold on to them, as they represent a better form of saving. The supply of shares to the market will fall. If incomes or wealth rise, people again are likely to want to hold on to their shares.

As far as expectations are concerned, if people believe that share prices will rise, they will hold on to the shares they have. Supply to the market will fall, thereby pushing up prices. If, however, they believe that prices will fall, they will sell their shares now before prices do fall. Supply will increase, driving down the price.

Share prices and business

Companies are crucially affected by their share price. If a company's share price falls, this is taken as a sign that 'the market' is losing confidence in the company. This will make it more difficult to raise finance, not only by issuing additional shares in the primary market, but also from banks. It will also make the company more vulnerable to a takeover bid. This is where one company seeks to buy out another by offering to buy all its shares. A takeover will succeed if the owners of more than half of the company's shares vote to accept the offered price. Shareholders are more likely to agree to the takeover if the company's shares have not being doing very well recently.

1.　*If the rate of economic growth in the economy is 3 per cent in a particular year, why are share prices likely to rise by more than 3 per cent that year?*
2.　*Find out what has happened to the FTSE 100 index over the past 12 months and explain why (see site B27 on the hotlinks part of the website).*

Incentives in markets

Throughout this chapter we have seen that people and firms respond to incentives. In all cases of changes in demand and supply, the resulting changes in price act as both signals and incentives. This is Threshold Concept 5.

*Identifying the position of demand and supply curves

Both demand and supply depend on price, and yet their interaction determines price. For this reason it is difficult to identify just what is going on when price and quantity change, and to identify just what the demand and supply curves look like.

Let us say that we want to identify the demand curve for good X. We observe that when the price was 20p, 1000 units were purchased. At a later date the price has risen to 30p and 800 units are now purchased. What can we conclude from this about the demand curve? The answer is that without further information we can conclude very little. Consider Figures 2.8 and 2.9. Both are consistent with the facts.

In Figure 2.8 the demand curve has not shifted. The rise in price and the fall in sales are due entirely to a shift in the supply curve. The movement from point *a* to point *b* is thus a movement along the demand curve. If we can be certain that the demand curve has not shifted, then the evidence allows us to identify its position (or, at least, two points on it).

In Figure 2.9, however, not only has the supply curve shifted, but so also has the demand curve. Let us assume that people's tastes for the product have increased. In this case a movement from *a* to *b* does *not* trace out the demand curve. We cannot derive the demand curve(s) from the evidence of price and quantity alone.

| THRESHOLD CONCEPT 5 | PEOPLE RESPOND TO INCENTIVES | THINKING LIKE AN ECONOMIST |

It is important, therefore, that these have the desired effect

When there is a shortage of a good, its market price will rise. There will thus be an incentive for us to consume less. After all, the opportunity cost has risen. It might be better to switch to a cheaper alternative or simply to consume less and use the money saved to buy something entirely different.

Similarly, when the price of a good rises, there is an incentive for firms to produce more. After all, the good is now more profitable to produce and thus firms might consider producing more of this and cutting down the production of less profitable products.

These two incentives of a rise in price could be seen as desirable, as they result in the shortage being eliminated and consumers being able to buy more of a good where demand initially exceeds supply.

Incentives, however, could be 'perverse'. In other words, they could have undesirable effects. For example, if a particular course or module on your degree is assessed by two pieces of coursework, this may act as an incentive for you to concentrate solely on these two pieces and do little work on the remainder of the course!

There are plenty of other examples where incentives can be perverse. For example, making insurance compulsory may encourage people to take risks. Making cars safer may encourage people to drive faster. Increasing top rates of income tax may encourage high earners to work less or to evade paying taxes by not declaring income – tax revenues may end up falling.

If an economic system is to work well, it is important, therefore, that the incentives are appropriate and do not bring about undesirable side-effects. This is a *threshold concept* because virtually every action taken by households or firms is influenced by incentives. We need to understand just what the incentives are, what their effects are likely to be, and how the incentives could be improved.

This was something increasingly recognised in the former Soviet Union in the days of central planning – but too late! The targets given to factory managers (see Box 1.5 on pages 18–19) were often inappropriate. For example, if targets were specified in tonnes, the incentive was to produce heavy products. Soviet furniture and cooking utensils tended to be very heavy! If targets were set in area (e.g. sheet glass), then the incentive was to produce thin products. If targets were set simply in terms of number of units, then the incentive was to produce shoddy products.

The lessons of Soviet planning, however, have been lost on many in the West. Today across the public sector, and large parts of the private sector too, people are set targets. Thus if hospitals are given the target to reduce waiting lists, the incentive is to cut down on the quality of treatment so that as many patients as possible can be seen. If the target for universities is to reduce failure rates, then the incentive is to make it easier for students to pass.

One crucial incentive we shall be examining is that of profit. In a competitive environment, firms striving for increased profit may result in better products and a lower price for consumers as firms seek to undercut each other. In other cases, however, firms may be able to make bigger profits by controlling the market and keeping competitors out or by colluding with them. Here the profit incentive has a perverse effect: it leads to higher prices for consumers and less choice.

1. *Give two other examples of perverse incentives. How could the incentives be improved?*
2. *Find out just what the learning objectives are of the economics course or module that you are studying. What positive incentives are there for you to meet these learning objectives? Identify any perverse incentives and how you would change them.*

Figure 2.8	Problems in identifying the position and shape of the demand curve: shift in supply curve alone

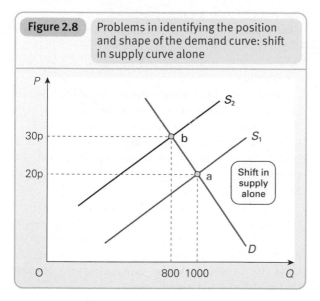

Figure 2.9	Problems in identifying the position and shape of the demand curve: shift in supply *and* demand curves

The problem is that when the supply curve shifts, we often cannot know whether or not the demand curve has shifted, and if so by how much. How would we know, for example, just how much people's tastes have changed?

The problem works the other way round too. It is difficult to identify a supply curve when the demand curve shifts. Is the change in price and quantity entirely due to the shift in the demand curve, or has the supply curve shifted too?

This is known as the **identification problem**. It is difficult to identify just what is causing the change in price and quantity.

Section summary

1. If the demand for a good exceeds the supply, there will be a shortage. This will lead to a rise in the price of the good.

2. If the supply of a good exceeds the demand, there will be a surplus. This will lead to a fall in the price.

3. Price will settle at the equilibrium. The equilibrium price is the one that clears the market: the price where demand equals supply.

4. If the demand or supply curve shifts, this will lead either to a shortage or to a surplus. Price will therefore either rise or fall until a new equilibrium is reached at the position where the supply and demand curves now intersect.

5. *It is difficult to identify the position of a real-world supply (or demand) curve simply by looking at the relationship between price and quantity at different points in time. The problem is that the other curve may have shifted (by an unknown amount).

2.4 THE CONTROL OF PRICES

TC 3
p24

At the equilibrium price, there will be no shortage or surplus. The equilibrium price, however, may not be the most desirable price. The government, therefore, may prefer to keep prices above or below the equilibrium price.

If the government sets a **minimum price** above the equilibrium (a price floor), there will be a surplus: $Q_s - Q_d$ in Figure 2.10. Price will not be allowed to fall to eliminate this surplus.

TC 6
p52

Definitions

Identification problem The problem of identifying the relationship between two variables (e.g. price and quantity demanded) from the evidence when it is not known whether or how the variables have been affected by other determinants. For example, it is difficult to identify the shape of a demand curve simply by observing price and quantity when it is not known whether changes in other determinants have shifted the demand curve.

Minimum price A price floor set by the government or some other agency. The price is not allowed to fall below this level (although it is allowed to rise above it).

Figure 2.10 Minimum price: price floor

Figure 2.11 Maximum price: price ceiling

If the government sets a **maximum price** below the equilibrium (a price ceiling), there will be a shortage: $Q_d - Q_s$ in Figure 2.11. Price will not be allowed to rise to eliminate this shortage.

Setting a minimum (high) price

The government sets minimum prices to prevent them from falling below a certain level. It may do this for various reasons:

- To protect producers' incomes. If the industry is subject to supply fluctuations (e.g. fluctuations in weather affecting crops), prices are likely to fluctuate severely. Minimum prices will prevent the fall in producers'

incomes that would accompany periods of low prices. (This is examined further in section 3.5.)

- To create a surplus (e.g. of grains) – particularly in periods of glut – which can be stored in preparation for possible future shortages.
- In the case of wages (the price of labour), minimum wage legislation can be used to prevent workers' wage rates from falling below a certain level (see Box 10.3).

Definition

Maximum price A price ceiling set by the government or some other agency. The price is not allowed to rise above this level (although it is allowed to fall below it).

THRESHOLD CONCEPT 6 **GOVERNMENTS CAN SOMETIMES IMPROVE MARKET OUTCOMES** THINKING LIKE AN ECONOMIST

Threshold Concept 3 was that markets may fail to meet social objectives. This is where government economic policy comes in. Governments have a number of policy instruments that they can use, either to influence markets or to replace them altogether. These policy instruments include taxation, benefits and subsidies, laws and regulations, licences and permits, and direct provision by government departments or agencies (such as the ministry of defence or the national health service).

The threshold concept here is not merely that governments intervene, but that they can correct, or at least lessen, market failures. Once we have understood the nature of a market failure, we can then set about designing a policy to correct it. For example, if we could identify that the cost to society of producing a product in a way which created pollution was £20 per unit more than the benefit that society gained from the product, then the government could tax the producer £20 per unit. This could be an argument for imposing taxes on airline tickets to reflect the adverse effects of air travel on the atmosphere.

In Chapters 10 to 13 we consider a number of these policy instruments and seek to identify the *optimum* level of government intervention to meet social objectives. In this chapter and the next we have a preliminary look at some of these instruments.

Governments themselves, however, are not perfect – as opposition parties frequently remind us! For an economic adviser to recommend a particular policy as the best means of correcting a market failure does not mean that the government will carry it out efficiently or, indeed, carry it out at all.

1. *How may welfare benefits be seen as a means of correcting market failures? Does the payment of such benefits create any problems for society?*
2. *Assume that the government sees litter as a market failure that requires government action. Give some examples of policies it could adopt to reduce litter.*

Draw a supply and demand diagram with the price of labour (the wage rate) on the vertical axis and the quantity of labour (the number of workers) on the horizontal axis. What will happen to employment if the government raises wages from the equilibrium to some minimum wage above the equilibrium?

The government can use various methods to deal with the surpluses associated with minimum prices.

- The government could buy the surplus and store it, destroy it or sell it abroad in other markets.
- Supply could be artificially lowered by restricting producers to particular quotas. In Figure 2.10, supply could therefore be reduced to Q_d.
- Demand could be raised by advertising, by finding alternative uses for the good, or by reducing consumption of substitute goods (e.g. by imposing taxes or quotas on substitutes, such as imports).

BOX 2.4   UNDERGROUND MARKETS

CASE STUDIES AND APPLICATIONS

A consequence of low fixed prices

When the government sets maximum prices, an underground market[1] is likely to result. An underground market is one where sellers ignore the government's price restrictions. But why is it in their interest to do so, given that they probably run the risk of fines or even imprisonment?

Effect of price control on underground-market prices

No underground market

Price ceiling

← shortage →

If dealers buy all the supplies at P_g, the underground market equilibrium price will be P_b

Price ceiling

Take the case of price controls used in the Second World War. The government set maximum prices for many essential items that were in short supply. This is illustrated in the diagram.

The unacceptably high equilibrium price is P_e. The price fixed by the government is P_g. But at P_g there is a shortage of $Q_d - Q_s$. To deal with the shortage, either the government will have to accept queues, or shops selling only to 'regular' customers; or alternatively a system of rationing will have to be introduced.

But whichever system is adopted, one thing is clear: many consumers would be prepared to pay a price considerably above P_g in order to get hold of the good. The demand curve shows this: the less the supply, the higher up the demand curve will the equilibrium price be.

This is where people dealing in the underground market come in. Provided they can get supplies (maybe by some shady dealing), provided they can have access to consumers, provided consumers are willing to break the law, and provided they can escape detection, dealers can charge a price considerably above P_g. But what price can they charge?

Take the extreme case. Assume that the dealers buy up all the supply (Q_s) from the producers at the official price and then sell it at a price that clears the market. The underground-market price will be P_b: at that price, demand is equal to Q_s. The dealers gain the extra revenue shown by the shaded area.

In practice, of course, many people will get their supplies from official sources, and pay only P_g. On the other hand, if dealers are few in number and have only limited supplies, they could sell them at very high prices, above P_b.

During the Second World War, 'spivs' (as these dealers were called) could often charge extortionately high prices for such items as nylon stockings and coffee.

1. *What would be the effect on underground-market prices of a rise in the official price?*
2. *Will a system of low official prices plus an underground market be more equitable or less equitable than a system of free markets?*

[1] In the past they were known as 'black markets'.

One of the problems with minimum prices is that firms with surpluses on their hands may try to evade the price control and cut their prices.

Another problem is that high prices may cushion inefficiency. Firms may feel less need to find more efficient methods of production and to cut their costs if their profits are being protected by the high price. Also, the high price may discourage firms from producing alternative goods which they could produce more efficiently or which are in higher demand, but which nevertheless have a lower (free-market) price.

Setting a maximum (low) price

The government may set maximum prices to prevent them from rising above a certain level. This will normally be done for reasons of fairness. In wartime, or times of famine, the government may set maximum prices for basic goods so that poor people can afford to buy them.

The resulting shortages, however, create further problems. If the government merely sets prices and does not intervene further, the shortages will lead to the following:

- Allocation on a 'first come, first served' basis. This is likely to lead to queues developing, or firms adopting waiting lists. Queues were a common feature of life in the former communist east European countries where governments kept prices below the level necessary to equate demand and supply. In the 1990s, as part of their economic reforms, they lifted price controls; this had the obvious benefit of reducing or eliminating queues. However, the consequential sharp increase in food prices made life very hard for those on low incomes.
- Firms deciding which customers should be allowed to buy: for example, giving preference to regular customers.

Neither of the above may be considered fair since some people in need may be forced to go without. Therefore, the government may adopt a system of **rationing**. People could be issued with a set number of coupons for each item rationed.

A major problem with maximum prices is likely to be the emergence of **underground markets**, where customers, unable to buy enough in legal markets, may well be prepared to pay very high prices: prices above P_e in Figure 2.11 (see Box 2.4).

Another problem is that the maximum prices reduce the quantity produced of an already scarce commodity. For example, artificially low prices in a famine are likely to reduce food supplies: if not immediately, then at the next harvest, because of less being sown. In many developing countries, governments control the price of basic foodstuffs in order to help the urban poor. The effect, however, is to reduce incomes for farmers, who are then encouraged to leave the land and flock into the ever-growing towns and cities.

To minimise these types of problem the government may attempt to reduce the shortage by encouraging supply: by drawing on stores, by direct government production, or by giving subsidies or tax relief to firms. Alternatively, it may attempt to reduce demand: by the production of more alternative goods (e.g. homegrown vegetables in times of war) or by controlling people's incomes.

Another example of maximum prices is where the government imposes rent controls in an attempt to make rented accommodation more affordable. Here the 'price' is the rent people are charged. The danger of this policy is that it will create a shortage of rental property. The policy is examined in Case Study 2.4 in MyEconLab.

 Think of some examples where the price of a good or service is kept below the equilibrium (e.g. rent controls). In each case, consider the advantages and disadvantages of the policy.

Definitions

Rationing Where the government restricts the amount of a good that people are allowed to buy.

Underground markets Where people ignore the government's price and/or quantity controls and sell illegally at whatever price equates illegal demand and supply.

Section summary

1. There are several ways in which the government intervenes in the operation of markets. It can fix prices, tax or subsidise products, regulate production, or produce goods directly itself.

2. The government may fix minimum or maximum prices. If a minimum price is set above the equilibrium, a surplus will result. If a maximum price is set below the equilibrium price, a shortage will result.

3. Minimum prices are set as a means of protecting the incomes of suppliers or creating a surplus for storage in case of future reductions in supply. If the government is not deliberately trying to create a surplus, it must decide what to do with it.

4. Maximum prices are set as a means of keeping prices down for the consumer. The resulting shortage will cause queues, waiting lists or the restriction of sales by firms to favoured customers. Alternatively, the government could introduce a system of rationing. With maximum prices, underground markets are likely to arise. This is where goods are sold illegally above the maximum price.

END OF CHAPTER QUESTIONS

1. The weekly demand and supply schedules for T-shirts (in millions) in a free market are as follows:

Price (£)	8	7	6	5	4	3	2	1
Quantity demanded	6	8	10	12	14	16	18	20
Quantity supplied	18	16	14	12	10	8	6	4

   (a) What are the equilibrium price and quantity?
   (b) Assume that changes in fashion cause the demand for T-shirts to rise by 4 million at each price. What will be the new equilibrium price and quantity? Has equilibrium quantity risen as much as the rise in demand? Explain why or why not.
   (c) Now plot the data in the table and mark the equilibrium. Also plot the new data corresponding to (b).

2. On separate demand and supply diagrams for bread, sketch the effects of the following: (a) a rise in the price of wheat; (b) a rise in the price of butter and margarine; (c) a rise in the price of rice, pasta and potatoes. In each case, state your assumptions.

3. For what reasons might the price of foreign holidays rise? In each case, identify whether these are reasons affecting demand, supply, or both.

4. If both demand and supply change, and if we know which direction they have shifted but not how much, why is it that we will be able to predict the direction in which *either* price *or* quantity will change, but not both? (Clue: consider the four possible combinations and sketch them if necessary: (a) *D* left, *S* left; (b) *D* right, *S* right; (c) *D* left, *S* right; (d) *D* right, *S* left.)

5. If you were the owner of a clothes shop, how would you set about deciding what prices to charge for each garment at the end-of-season sale?

6. Is there any truth in the saying that the price of a good is a reflection of its quality?

7. Assume that the (weekly) market demand and supply of tomatoes are given by the following figures:

Price (£ per kilo)	4.00	3.50	3.00	2.50	2.00	1.50	1.00
Q_d (000 kilos)	30	35	40	45	50	55	60
Q_s (000 kilos)	80	68	62	55	50	45	38

   (a) What are the equilibrium price and quantity?
   (b) What will be the effect of the government fixing a *minimum* price of (i) £3 per kilo; (ii) £1.50 per kilo?
   (c) Suppose that the government paid tomato producers a subsidy of £1 per kilo.
      (i) Give the new supply schedule.
      (ii) What will be the new equilibrium price?
      (iii) How much will this cost the government?
   (d) Alternatively, suppose that the government guaranteed tomato producers a price of £2.50 per kilo.
      (i) How many tomatoes would it have to buy in order to ensure that all the tomatoes produced were sold?
      (ii) How much would this cost the government?
   (e) Alternatively, suppose it bought *all* the tomatoes produced at £2.50.
      (i) At what single price would it have to sell them in order to dispose of the lot?
      (ii) What would be the net cost of this action?

8. Assume that oil begins to run out and that extraction becomes more expensive. Trace through the effects of this on the market for oil and the market for other fuels.

Online resources

Additional case studies in MyEconLab

2.1 **Adjusting to oil price shocks**. A case study showing how demand and supply analysis can be used to examine the price changes in the oil market since 1973.

2.2 **Coffee prices**. An examination of the coffee market and the implications of fluctuations in the coffee harvest for growers and coffee drinkers.

2.3 **Rationing**. A case study in the use of rationing as an alternative to the price mechanism. In particular, it looks at the use of rationing in the UK during the Second World War.

2.4 **Rent control**. The effect of government control of rents on the market for rental property.

Maths Case 2.1 Finding equilibrium price and quantity using algebra. This gives an example of solving equilibrium price and quantity from a demand and a supply equation using the method of simultaneous equations.

Websites relevant to this chapter

Numbers and sections refer to websites listed in the Web Appendix and hotlinked from this book's website at **www.pearsoned.co.uk/sloman**.

- For news articles relevant to this chapter, see the *Economics News Articles* link from the book's website.
- For general news on markets, see websites in section A, and particularly A2, 3, 4, 5, 8, 9, 18, 24, 25, 26, 36. See also links to newspapers worldwide in A38, 39, 43 and 44, and the news search feature in Google at A41.
- For links to sites on markets, see the relevant sections of I4, 7, 11, 17.
- For data on the housing market (Box 2.2), see sites B7, 8, 11.
- For sites favouring the free market, see C17 and E34.
- For student resources relevant to this chapter, see sites C1–7, 9, 10, 19.
- For a range of classroom games and simulations of markets, see sites C24 (computer-based) and C20 (non-computer-based).

Markets in Action

CHAPTER MAP

3.1 Elasticity	**57**
Price elasticity of demand	57
Measuring the price elasticity of demand	57
Interpreting the figure for elasticity	58
Determinants of price elasticity of demand	58
Price elasticity of demand and consumer expenditure	59
The measurement of elasticity: arc elasticity	61
*The measurement of elasticity: point elasticity	63
Price elasticity of supply	65
Income elasticity of demand	67
Cross-price elasticity of demand	69
3.2 The time dimension	**71**
Short-run and long-run adjustment	71
Price expectations and speculation	71
Dealing with uncertainty and risk	75
3.3 Indirect taxes	**77**
The effect of imposing taxes on goods	77
Elasticity and the incidence of taxation	78
3.4 Government rejection of market allocation	**80**
Providing goods and services free at the point of delivery: the case of hospital treatment	80
Prohibiting the sale of certain goods and services: the case of illegal drugs	81
3.5 Agriculture and agricultural policy	**82**
Why intervene?	82
Government intervention	85
The Common Agricultural Policy of the EU	88
Criticisms of the CAP	88
Reforming the CAP	89

In Chapters 1 and 2 we demonstrated that changes in price affect the quantity demanded and supplied. But how much? How much will the demand for DVDs go up if the price of DVDs comes down? How much will the supply of new houses go up if the price of houses rises? In Chapter 3 we develop the concept of *elasticity* of demand and supply to examine this responsiveness.

We then look at how quickly markets adjust and also examine how people's expectations of price changes affect what actually happens to prices. In particular, we look at speculation – people attempting to gain from anticipated price changes.

In Chapter 1 we identified that the real world is one of mixed economies. The government intervenes in many markets, even highly competitive ones. This intervention can take a number of forms:

- Fixing prices, either above or below the free-market equilibrium. We looked at this in Chapter 2.

- Taxing the production or sale of various goods, such as petrol.

- Subsidising the production or sale of various goods, such as public transport.

- Producing goods or services directly (e.g. defence and health care).

- Regulation. Various laws could be passed to regulate the behaviour of firms. For example, some activities, such as the dumping of toxic waste, could be made illegal; or licences or official permission might have to be obtained to produce certain goods; or a regulatory body could supervise the activities of various firms and prevent any that it felt to be against the public interest (e.g. the production of unsafe toys).

Supply and demand analysis is a useful tool for examining the effects of government intervention. First we examine what could happen if a government seeks to do away with a market system of allocation, either by providing things free to consumers, or by banning certain harmful activities. We then examine government intervention in agriculture – a sector that has received massive government support in many countries of the world. We look at the economic arguments for such intervention and then examine some specific measures that governments have taken.

The role of government in the economy is examined further in Chapters 10 to 13.

3.1 **ELASTICITY**

Price elasticity of demand

When the price of a good rises, the quantity demanded will fall. That much is fairly obvious. But in most cases we will want to know more than this. We will want to know by just *how much* the quantity demanded will fall. In other words, we will want to know how *responsive* demand is to a rise in price.

Take the case of two products: oil and cabbages. In the case of oil, a rise in price is likely to result in a relatively small fall in the quantity demanded. If people want to continue driving, they have to pay the higher prices for fuel. A few may turn to riding bicycles, and some people may try to make fewer journeys, but for most people, a rise in the price of petrol and diesel will make little difference in the short term to how much they use their cars.

In the case of cabbages, however, a rise in price may lead to a substantial fall in the quantity demanded. The reason is that there are alternative vegetables that people can buy. Many people, when buying vegetables, are very conscious of their prices and will buy whatever is reasonably priced.

We call the responsiveness of demand to a change in price the *price elasticity of demand*, and as we shall see on many occasions throughout this book, it is one of the most important concepts in economics. For example, if we know the price elasticity of demand for a product, we can predict the effect on price and quantity of a shift in the *supply* curve for that product.

Figure 3.1 shows the effect of a shift in supply with two quite different demand curves (*D* and *D′*). Curve *D′* is more elastic than curve *D* over any given price range. In other words, for any given change in price, there will be a larger change in quantity demanded along curve *D′* than along curve *D*.

Assume that initially the supply curve is S_1, and that it intersects with both demand curves at point *a*, at a price of P_1 and a quantity of Q_1. Now supply shifts to S_2. What will happen to price and quantity? In the case of the less elastic demand curve *D*, there is a relatively large rise in price (to P_2) and a relatively small fall in quantity (to Q_2): equilibrium is at point *b*. In the case of the more elastic demand curve *D′*, however, there is only a relatively small rise in price (to P_3), but a relatively large fall in quantity (to Q_3): equilibrium is at point *c*.

Measuring the price elasticity of demand

What we want to compare is the size of the change in quantity demanded with the size of the change in price. But since price and quantity are measured in different units, the only sensible way we can do this is to use percentage or proportionate changes. This gives us the following *formula for the price elasticity of demand ($P\epsilon_D$)* for a product: percentage (or proportionate) change in quantity demanded divided by the percentage (or proportionate) change in price. Putting this in symbols gives:

$$P\epsilon_D = \frac{\%\Delta Q_D}{\%\Delta P}$$

where ϵ (the Greek epsilon) is the symbol we use for elasticity, and Δ (the capital Greek delta) is the symbol we use for a 'change in'.

Thus if a 40 per cent rise in the price of oil caused the quantity demanded to fall by a mere 10 per cent, the price elasticity of oil over this range will be

$-10\%/40\% = -0.25$

whereas, if a 5 per cent fall in the price of cabbages caused a 15 per cent rise in the quantity demanded, the price elasticity of demand for cabbages over this range would be

$15\%/-5\% = -3$

| **Figure 3.1** | Market supply and demand |

The effect on price of a shift in supply depends on the responsiveness of demand to a change in price

---

Definitions

Price elasticity of demand The responsiveness of quantity demanded to a change in price.

Formula for price elasticity of demand ($P\epsilon_D$) The percentage (or proportionate) change in quantity demanded divided by the percentage (or proportionate) change in price: $\%\Delta Q_D \div \%\Delta P$.

Cabbages have a more elastic demand than oil, and this is shown by the figures. But just what do these two figures show? What is the significance of minus 0.25 and minus 3?

Interpreting the figure for elasticity

The use of proportionate or percentage measures

Elasticity is measured in proportionate or percentage terms for the following reasons:

- It allows comparison of changes in two qualitatively different things, which are thus measured in two different types of unit: i.e. it allows comparison of *quantity* changes with *monetary* changes.

- It is the only sensible way of deciding *how big* a change in price or quantity is. Take a simple example. An item goes up in price by £1. Is this a big increase or a small increase? We can answer this only if we know what the original price was. If a can of beans goes up in price by £1 that is a huge price increase. If, however, the price of a house goes up by £1 that is a tiny price increase. In other words, it is the percentage or proportionate increase in price that determines how big a price rise is.

The sign (positive or negative)

Demand curves are generally downward sloping. This means that price and quantity change in opposite directions. A *rise* in price (a positive figure) will cause a *fall* in the quantity demanded (a negative figure). Similarly a *fall* in price will cause a *rise* in the quantity demanded. Thus when working out price elasticity of demand, we either divide a negative figure by a positive figure, or a positive figure by a negative. Either way, we end up with a negative figure.

The value (greater or less than 1)

If we now ignore the negative sign and just concentrate on the value of the figure, this tells us whether demand is **elastic** or **inelastic**.

Elastic ($\epsilon > 1$). This is where a change in price causes a proportionately larger change in the quantity demanded. In this case the value of elasticity will be greater than 1, since we are dividing a larger figure by a smaller figure.

Inelastic ($\epsilon < 1$). This is where a change in a price causes a proportionately smaller change in the quantity demanded. In this case elasticity will be less than 1, since we are dividing a smaller figure by a larger figure.

Unit elastic ($\epsilon = 1$). **Unit elasticity of demand** occurs where price and quantity demanded change by the same proportion. This will give an elasticity equal to 1, since we are dividing a figure by itself.

Determinants of price elasticity of demand

The price elasticity of demand varies enormously from one product to another. For example, the demand for a holiday in any given resort typically has a price elasticity greater than 5, whereas the demand for electricity has a price elasticity less than 0.5 (ignoring the negative signs). But why do some products have a highly elastic demand, whereas others have a highly *in*elastic demand? What determines price elasticity of demand?

The number and closeness of substitute goods. This is the most important determinant. The more substitutes there are for a good and the closer they are, the more people will switch to these alternatives when the price of the good rises: the greater, therefore, will be the price elasticity of demand.

Returning to our examples of oil and cabbages, there is no close substitute for oil and thus demand is relatively inelastic. There are plenty of alternatives to cabbages, however, and thus demand is relatively elastic.

 Why will the price elasticity of demand for holidays in Crete be greater than that for holidays in general? Is this difference the result of a difference in the size of the income effect or the substitution effect? Is there anything the suppliers of holidays in Crete can do to reduce this higher price elasticity?

The proportion of income spent on the good. The higher the proportion of our income we spend on a good, the more we will be forced to cut consumption when its price rises: the bigger will be the income effect and the more elastic will be the demand.

Thus salt has a very low price elasticity of demand. Part of the reason is that there is no close substitute. But part is that we spend such a tiny fraction of our income on salt that we would find little difficulty in paying a relatively large percentage increase in its price: the income effect of a price rise would be very small. By contrast, there will be a much bigger income effect when a major item of expenditure rises in price. For example, if mortgage interest rates rise (the 'price' of loans for house purchase), people may have to cut down substantially on their demand for

---

Definitions

Elastic demand Where quantity demanded changes by a larger percentage than price. Ignoring the negative sign, it will have a value greater than 1.

Unit elasticity of demand Where quantity demanded changes by the same percentage as price. Ignoring the negative sign, it will have a value equal to 1.

housing – being forced to buy somewhere much smaller and cheaper, or to live in rented accommodation.

 Will a general item of expenditure such as food or clothing have a price-elastic or inelastic demand? (Consider both the determinants we have considered so far.)

The time period. When price rises, people may take a time to adjust their consumption patterns and find alternatives. The longer the time period after a price change the more elastic the demand is likely to be.

To illustrate this, let us return to our example of oil. Between December 1973 and June 1974 the price of crude oil quadrupled, which led to large increases in the prices of petrol and central-heating oil. Over the next few months, there was only a very small reduction in the consumption of oil products. Demand was highly inelastic. The reason was that people still wanted to drive their cars and heat their houses.

Over time, however, as the higher oil prices persisted, new fuel-efficient cars were developed and many people switched to smaller cars or moved closer to their work. Similarly, people switched to gas or solid fuel central heating, and spent more money insulating their houses to save on fuel bills. Demand was thus much more elastic in the long run.

In 2007 and 2008 oil prices again were increasing very sharply (see Box 7.3 on page 194). If the high oil price had persisted, we might have expected to see patterns of demand changing over the next few years as consumers adjusted to these higher prices. In fact, within months there were signs of these effects beginning to occur as demand for large fuel-hungry cars in the USA (such as Hummers and other SUVs) fell and demand for smaller European and Japanese models rose. But as recession swept the world, so the oil price rapidly fell. We would have to wait for recovery to see soaring oil prices again.

 Demand for oil might be relatively elastic over the longer term, and yet it could still be observed that over time people consume more oil (or only very slightly less) despite rising oil prices. How can this apparent contradiction be explained?

Price elasticity of demand and consumer expenditure

One of the most important applications of price elasticity of demand concerns its relationship with the total amount of money consumers spend on a product. ***Total consumer expenditure*** (TE) is simply price multiplied by quantity purchased.

$$TE = P \times Q$$

For example, if consumers buy 3 million units (Q) at a price of £2 per unit (P), they will spend a total of £6 million (TE).

Total consumer expenditure will be the same as the ***total revenue*** (TR) received by firms from the sale of the product (before any taxes or other deductions).

What will happen to consumer expenditure (and hence firms' revenue) if there is a change in price? The answer depends on the price elasticity of demand.

Elastic demand

As price rises, so quantity demanded falls and vice versa. When demand is elastic, quantity demanded changes proportionately more than price. Thus the change in quantity has a bigger effect on total consumer expenditure than does the change in price. For example, when the price rises, there will be such a large fall in consumer demand that *less* will be spent than before. This can be summarised as follows:

- P rises; Q falls proportionately more; thus TE falls.
- P falls; Q rises proportionately more; thus TE rises.

In other words, total expenditure changes in the same direction as *quantity*.

This is illustrated in Figure 3.2. The areas of the rectangles in the diagram represent total expenditure. Why? The area of a rectangle is its height multiplied by its length. In this case, this is price multiplied by quantity bought, which is total expenditure. Demand is elastic between points *a* and *b*. A rise in price from £4 to £5 causes a proportionately larger fall in quantity demanded: from 20 million to 10 million. Total expenditure *falls* from £80 million (the striped area) to £50 million (the pink area).

When demand is elastic, then, a rise in price will cause a fall in total consumer expenditure and thus a fall in the total revenue that firms selling the product receive. A reduction in price, however, will result in consumers spending more, and hence firms earning more.

Inelastic demand

When demand is inelastic, it is the other way around. Price changes proportionately more than quantity. Thus the change in price has a bigger effect on total consumer

Definitions

Total consumer expenditure on a product (*TE*) (per period of time) The price of the product multiplied by the quantity purchased: $TE = P \times Q$.

Total revenue (*TR*) (per period of time) The total amount received by firms from the sale of a product, before the deduction of taxes or any other costs. The price multiplied by the quantity sold. $TR = P \times Q$.

Inelastic demand Where quantity demanded changes by a smaller percentage than price. Ignoring the negative sign, it will have a value less than 1.

Figure 3.2 Price elasticity of demand and total expenditure: elastic demand between two points

Figure 3.3 Price elasticity of demand and total expenditure: inelastic demand between two points

expenditure than does the change in quantity. To summarise the effects:

- *P* rises; *Q* falls proportionately less; *TE* rises.
- *P* falls; *Q* rises proportionately less; *TE* falls.

In other words, total consumer expenditure changes in the same direction as *price*.

This is illustrated in Figure 3.3. Demand is inelastic between points *a* and *c*. A rise in price from £4 to £8 causes a proportionately smaller fall in quantity demanded: from 20 million to 15 million. Total expenditure *rises* from £80 million (the striped area) to £120 million (the pink area).

In this case, firms' revenue will increase if there is a rise in price and fall if there is a fall in price.

 Assume that demand for a product is inelastic. Will consumer expenditure go on increasing as price rises? Would there be any limit?

Special cases

Figure 3.4 shows three special cases: (a) a totally inelastic demand ($P\epsilon_D = 0$), (b) an infinitely elastic demand ($P\epsilon_D = \infty$) and (c) a unit elastic demand ($P\epsilon_D = -1$).

Totally inelastic demand. This is shown by a vertical straight line. No matter what happens to price, quantity demanded remains the same. It is obvious that the more the price rises, the bigger will be the level of consumer expenditure. Thus in Figure 3.4(a), consumer expenditure will be higher at P_2 than at P_1.

 Can you think of any examples of goods which have a totally inelastic demand (a) at all prices; (b) over a particular price range?

Infinitely elastic demand. This is shown by a horizontal straight line. At any price above P_1 in Figure 3.4(b), demand is zero. But at P_1 (or any price below) demand is 'infinitely' large.

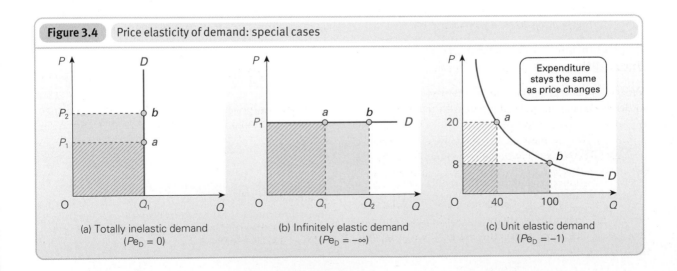

Figure 3.4 Price elasticity of demand: special cases

(a) Totally inelastic demand ($Pe_D = 0$)

(b) Infinitely elastic demand ($Pe_D = -\infty$)

(c) Unit elastic demand ($Pe_D = -1$)

This seemingly unlikely demand curve is in fact relatively common for an *individual producer*. In a perfect market, as we have seen, firms are small relative to the whole market (like the small-scale grain farmer). They have to accept the price as given by supply and demand in the *whole market*, but at that price they can sell as much as they produce. (Demand is not *literally* infinite, but as far as the firm is concerned it is.) In this case, the more the individual firm produces, the more revenue will be earned. In Figure 3.4(b), more revenue is earned at Q_2 than at Q_1.

Unit elastic demand. This is where price and quantity change in exactly the same proportion. Any rise in price will be exactly offset by a fall in quantity, leaving total consumer expenditure unchanged. In Figure 3.4(c), the striped area is exactly equal to the pink area: in both cases, total expenditure is £800.

You might have thought that a demand curve with unit elasticity would be a straight line at 45° to the axes. Instead it is a curve called a *rectangular hyperbola*. The reason for its shape is that the proportionate *rise* in quantity must equal the proportionate *fall* in price (and vice versa). As we move down the demand curve, in order for the *proportionate* change in both price and quantity to remain constant there must be a bigger and bigger *absolute* rise in quantity and a smaller and smaller absolute fall in price. For example, a rise in quantity from 200 to 400 is the same proportionate change as a rise from 100 to 200, but its absolute size is double. A fall in price from £5 to £2.50 is the same percentage as a fall from £10 to £5, but its absolute size is only half.

To illustrate these figures, draw the demand curve corresponding to the following table.

P	Q	TE
£2.50	400	£1000
£5	200	£1000
£10	100	£1000
£20	50	£1000
£40	25	£1000

If the curve had an elasticity of −1 throughout its length, what would be the quantity demanded (a) at a price of £1; (b) at a price of 10p; (c) if the good were free?

The measurement of elasticity: arc elasticity

We have defined price elasticity as the percentage or proportionate change in quantity demanded divided by the percentage or proportionate change in price. But how, in practice, do we measure these changes for a specific demand curve? We shall examine two methods. The first is called the *arc method*. The second (in an optional section) is called the *point method*.

A common mistake that students make is to think that you can talk about the elasticity of a *whole curve*. The mistake here is that in most cases the elasticity will vary along the length of the curve.

Figure 3.5 Different elasticities along different portions of a demand curve

Take the case of the demand curve illustrated in Figure 3.5. Between points *a* and *b*, total expenditure rises ($P_2Q_2 > P_1Q_1$): demand is thus elastic between these two points. Between points *b* and *c*, however, total expenditure falls ($P_3Q_3 < P_2Q_2$). Demand here is inelastic.

Normally, then, we can only refer to the elasticity of a *portion* of the demand curve, not of the *whole* curve. There are, however, two exceptions to this rule.

The first is when the elasticity just so happens to be the same all the way along a curve, as in the three special cases illustrated in Figure 3.4. The second is where two curves are drawn on the same diagram, as in Figure 3.1. Here we can say that demand curve D is less elastic than demand curve D′ at any given price. Note, however, that each of these two curves will still have different elasticities along its length.

Although we cannot normally talk about the elasticity of a whole curve, we can nevertheless talk about the elasticity between any two points on it. This is known as *arc elasticity*. In fact the formula for price elasticity of demand that we have used so far is the formula for arc elasticity. Let us examine it more closely. Remember the formula we used was:

$$\frac{\text{Proportionate } \Delta Q}{\text{Proportionate } \Delta P} \text{ (where } \Delta \text{ means 'change in')}$$

The way we measure a proportionate change in quantity is to divide that change by the level of Q: $\Delta Q/Q$. Similarly,

Definition

Arc elasticity The measurement of elasticity between two points on a curve.

BOX 3.1 | **ADVERTISING AND ITS EFFECT ON DEMAND CURVES** |

How to increase sales and price

When we are told that brand X will make us more beautiful, enrich our lives, wash our clothes whiter, help us attract more friends, give us a new taste sensation or allow us to save the planet, just what are the advertisers up to? 'Trying to sell the product', you may reply.

In fact there is a bit more to it than this. Advertisers are trying to do two things:

- Shift the product's demand curve to the right.
- Make it less price elastic.

This is illustrated in the diagram.

Effect of advertising on the demand curve

D_1 shows the original demand curve with price at P_1 and sales at Q_1. D_2 shows the curve after an advertising campaign. The rightward shift allows an increased quantity (Q_2) to be sold at the original price. If the demand is also made highly inelastic, the firm can also raise its price and still have a substantial increase in sales. Thus in the diagram, price can be raised to P_2 and sales will be Q_3 – still substantially above Q_1. The total gain in revenue is shown by the shaded area.

How can advertising bring about this new demand curve?

Shifting the demand curve to the right

This can occur in two ways. First, if the advertising brings the product to more people's attention, then the market for the good grows and the demand curve shifts to the right. Second, if the advertising increases people's desire for the product, they will be prepared to pay a higher price for each unit purchased.

Making the demand curve less elastic

This will occur if the advertising creates greater brand loyalty. People must be led to believe (rightly or wrongly) that competitors' brands are inferior. This can be done directly by comparing the brand being advertised with a competitor's product. Alternatively, the advertisements may concentrate on making the product seem so distinctive that it implies that no other product can compete. These approaches will allow the firm to raise its price above that of its rivals with no significant fall in sales. The substitution effect will have been lessened because consumers have been led to believe that there are no close substitutes.

1. *Think of some advertisements which deliberately seek to make demand less elastic.*
2. *Imagine that 'Sunshine' sunflower margarine, a well-known brand, is advertised with the slogan 'It helps you live longer'. What do you think would happen to the demand curve for a supermarket's own brand of sunflower margarine? Consider both the direction of shift and the effect on elasticity. Will the elasticity differ markedly at different prices? How will this affect the pricing policy and sales of the supermarket's own brand? What do you think might be the response of government to the slogan*

---

we measure a proportionate change in price by dividing that change by the level of P: $\Delta P/P$. Price elasticity of demand can thus now be rewritten as

$$\frac{\Delta Q}{Q} \div \frac{\Delta P}{P}$$

But just what value do we give to P and Q? Consider the demand curve in Figure 3.6. What is the elasticity of demand between points m and n? Price has fallen by £2 (from £8 to £6), but what is the proportionate change? Is it $-2/8$ or $-2/6$? The convention is to express the change as a proportion of the average of the two prices, £8 and £6: in other words, to take the midpoint price, £7. Thus the proportionate change is $-2/7$.

Figure 3.6 Measuring elasticity

BOX 3.2   ANY MORE FARES?

Pricing on the buses

Imagine that a local bus company is faced with increased costs and fears that it will make a loss. What should it do?

The most likely response of the company will be to raise its fares. But this may be the wrong policy, especially if existing services are underutilised. To help it decide what to do, it commissions a survey to estimate passenger demand at three different fares: the current fare of 50p per mile, a higher fare of 60p and a lower fare of 40p. The results of the survey are shown in the first two columns of the table.

Demand turns out to be elastic. This is because of the existence of alternative means of transport. As a result of the elastic demand, total revenue can be increased by reducing the fare from the current 50p to 40p. Revenue would rise from £2m to £2.4m per annum.

But what will happen to the company's profits? Its profit is the difference between the total revenue from

passengers and its total costs of operating the service. If buses are currently underutilised, it is likely that the extra passengers can be carried without the need for extra buses, and hence at no extra cost.

At a fare of 50p, the old profit was £0.2m (£2.0m – £1.8m). After the increase in costs, a 50p fare now gives a loss of £0.2m (£2.0m – £2.2m).

By raising the fare to 60p, the loss is increased to £0.4m. But by lowering the fare to 40p, a profit of £0.2m can again be made.

1. *Estimate the price elasticity of demand between 40p and 50p and between 50p and 60p.*
2. *Was the 50p fare the best fare originally?*
3. *The company considers lowering the fare to 30p, and estimates that demand will be 8.5 million passenger miles. It will have to put on extra buses, however. How should it decide?*

Fare (£ per mile) (1)	Estimated demand (passenger miles per year: millions) (2)	Total revenue (£ millions per year) (3)	Old total cost (£ millions per year) (4)	New total cost (£ millions per year) (5)
0.40	6	2.4	1.8	2.2
0.50	4	2.0	1.8	2.2
0.60	3	1.8	1.8	2.2

Similarly, the proportionate change in quantity between points *m* and *n* is $^{10}/_{15}$, since 15 is midway between 10 and 20.

Thus using the **average (or 'midpoint') formula**, elasticity between *m* and *n* is given by:

$$\frac{\Delta Q}{\text{average } Q} \div \frac{\Delta P}{\text{average } P} = \frac{10}{15} \div \frac{-2}{7} = 2.33$$

Since 2.33 is greater than 1, demand is elastic between *m* and *n*.

Referring to Figure 3.6, use the midpoint formula to calculate the price elasticity of demand between (a) P = 6 and P = 4; (b) P = 4 and P = 2. What do you conclude about the elasticity of a straight-line demand curve as you move down it?

*The measurement of elasticity: point elasticity

Rather than measuring elasticity between two points on a demand curve, we may want to measure it at a single point: for example, point *r* in Figure 3.7. In order to measure **point elasticity** we must first rearrange the terms in the formula $\Delta Q/Q \div \Delta P/P$. By doing so we can rewrite the formula for price elasticity of demand as:

$$\frac{\Delta Q}{\Delta P} \times \frac{P}{Q}$$

Since we want to measure price elasticity at a *point* on the demand curve, rather than between two points, it is necessary to know how quantity demanded would react to an *infinitesimally small* change in price. In the case of

Definitions

Average (or 'midpoint') formula for price elasticity of demand $\Delta Q_D/\text{average} Q_D \div \Delta P/\text{average} P$.

Point elasticity The measurement of elasticity at a point on a curve. The formula for price elasticity

of demand using the point elasticity method is $dQ/dP \times P/Q$, where dQ/dP is the inverse of the slope of the tangent to the demand curve at the point in question.

point r in Figure 3.7, we want to know how the quantity demanded would react to an infinitesimally small change from a price of 30.

An infinitesimally small change is signified by the letter d. The formula for price elasticity of demand thus becomes

$$\frac{dQ}{dP} \times \frac{P}{Q}$$

where dQ/dP is the differential calculus term for the rate of change of quantity with respect to a change in price (see Appendix 1). And conversely, dP/dQ is the rate of change of price with respect to a change in quantity demanded. At any given point on the demand curve, dP/dQ is given by the *slope* of the curve (its rate of change). The slope is found

by drawing a tangent to the curve at that point and finding the slope of the tangent.

The tangent to the demand curve at point r is shown in Figure 3.7. Its slope is –50/100. Thus, dP/dQ is –50/100 and dQ/dP is the inverse of this, –100/50 = –2.

Returning to the formula $dQ/dP \times P/Q$, elasticity at point r equals

$$-2 \times 30/40 = -1.5$$

Rather than having to draw the graph and measure the slope of the tangent, the technique of differentiation can be used to work out point elasticity as long as the equation for the demand curve is known. An example of the use of this technique is given in Box 3.3 (on page 65).

---

*LOOKING AT THE MATHS

Elasticity of a straight-line demand curve

A straight-line demand curve has a different elasticity at each point on it. The only exceptions are a vertical demand curve ($P\epsilon_D = 0$) and a horizontal demand curve ($P\epsilon_D = \infty$). The reason for this differing elasticity can be demonstrated using the equation for a straight-line demand curve:

$$Q = a - bP$$

The term '$-b$' would give the slope of the demand curve if we were to plot Q on the vertical axis and P on the horizontal. Since we plot them the other way around,[1] the term 'b' gives the inverse of the slope as plotted. The slope of the curve as plotted is given by dP/dQ; the inverse of the slope is given by $dQ/dP = -b$).

The formula for price elasticity of demand (using the point elasticity method) is

$$P\epsilon_D = \frac{dQ}{dP} \cdot \frac{P}{Q}$$

This can thus be rewritten as

$$P\epsilon_D = -b\frac{P}{Q}$$

This is illustrated in the diagram, which plots the following demand curve:

$$Q = 50 - 5P$$

The slope of the demand curve (dP/dQ) is constant (i.e. –10/50 or –0.2). The inverse of the slope (dQ/dP) is thus –5, where 5 is the 'b' term in the equation. In this example, therefore, price elasticity of demand is given by

$$P\epsilon_D = -5\frac{P}{Q}$$

The value of P/Q, however, differs along the length of the demand curve. At point n, $P/Q = 8/10$. Thus

$$P\epsilon_D = -5(8/10) = -4$$

At point m, however, $P/Q = 6/20$. Thus

$$P\epsilon_D = -5(6/20) = -1.5$$

Different elasticities along a straight-line demand curve

These questions refer to the diagram.
1. *What is the price elasticity of demand at points l and k?*
2. *What is the price elasticity of demand at the point (a) where the demand curve crosses the vertical axis; (b) where it crosses the horizontal axis?*
3. *As you move down a straight-line demand curve, what happens to elasticity? Why?*
4. *Calculate price elasticity of demand between points n and l using the arc method. Does this give the same answer as the point method? Would it if the demand curve were actually curved?*

[1] It is contrary to normal convention to plot the independent variable (P) on the vertical axis and the dependent variable (Q) on the horizontal axis. The reason why we do this is because there are many other diagrams in economics where Q is the *independent* variable. Such diagrams include cost curves and revenue curves, which we will consider in Chapter 5. As you will see, it is much easier if we *always* plot Q on the horizontal axis even when, as in the case of demand curves, Q is the dependent variable.

Figure 3.7 Measuring elasticity at a point

$$P\epsilon_d = (1 / \text{slope}) \times P/Q$$

Price elasticity of supply ($P\epsilon_s$)

When price changes, there will be not only a change in the quantity demanded, but also a change in the quantity supplied. Frequently we will want to know just how responsive quantity supplied is to a change in price. The measure we use is the **price elasticity of supply**.

> ### Definition
>
> **Price elasticity of supply** The responsiveness of quantity supplied to a change in price.

---

*BOX 3.3   **USING CALCULUS TO CALCULATE THE PRICE ELASTICITY OF DEMAND**   EXPLORING ECONOMICS

(A knowledge of the rules of differentiation is necessary to understand this box. See Appendix 1.)

The following is an example of an equation for a demand curve:

$$Q_d = 60 - 15P + P^2$$

(where Q_d is measured in thousands of units). From this the following table and the graph can be constructed.

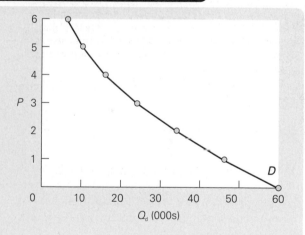

P	60	−15P	+P²	=	Q_d(000s)
0	60	− 0	+ 0	=	60
1	60	−15	+ 1	=	46
2	60	−30	+ 4	=	34
3	60	−45	+ 9	=	24
4	60	−60	+16	=	16
5	60	−75	+25	=	10
6	60	−90	+36	=	6

Point elasticity can be easily calculated from such a demand equation using calculus. To do this you will need to know the rules of differentiation (see pages A:9–12). Remember the formula for point elasticity:

$$P\epsilon_D = dQ/dP \times P/Q$$

The term dQ/dP can be calculated by differentiating the demand equation:

Given $Q_d = 60 - 15P + P^2$
then $dQ/dP = -15 + 2P$

Thus at a price of 3, for example,

$$dQ/dP = -15 + (2 \times 3)$$
$$= -9$$

Thus price elasticity of demand at a price of 3

$$= -9 \times P/Q$$
$$= -9 \times 3/24$$
$$= -9/8 \text{ (which is elastic)}$$

 Calculate the price elasticity of demand on this demand curve at a price of (a) 5; (b) 2; (c) 0.

Figure 3.8 Supply curves with different price elasticity of supply

Figure 3.8 shows two supply curves. Curve S_2 is more elastic between any two prices than curve S_1. Thus, when price rises from P_1 to P_2 there is a larger increase in quantity supplied with S_2 (namely, Q_1 to Q_3) than there is with S_1 (namely, Q_1 to Q_2). For any shift in the demand curve there will be a larger change in quantity supplied and a smaller change in price with curve S_2 than with curve S_1. Thus the effect on price and quantity of a shift in the demand curve will depend on the price elasticity of supply.

The *formula for the price elasticity of supply ($P\epsilon_s$)* is: the percentage (or proportionate) change in quantity supplied divided by the percentage (or proportionate) change in price. Putting this in symbols gives

$$P\epsilon_s = \frac{\%\Delta Q_s}{\%\Delta P}$$

In other words, the formula is identical to that for the price elasticity of demand, except that quantity in this case is quantity *supplied*. Thus if a 10 per cent rise in price caused a 25 per cent rise in the quantity supplied, the price elasticity of supply would be

$25\%/10\% = 2.5$

and if a 10 per cent rise in price caused only a 5 per cent rise in the quantity, the price elasticity of supply would be

$5\%/10\% = 0.5$

Definition

Formula for price elasticity of supply (PεS) The percentage (or proportionate) change in quantity supplied divided by the percentage (or proportionate) change in price: $\%\Delta Q_s \div \%\Delta P$.

In the first case, supply is elastic ($P\epsilon_s > 1$); in the second it is inelastic ($P\epsilon_s < 1$). Notice that, unlike the price elasticity of demand, the figure is positive. This is because price and quantity supplied change in the *same* direction.

Determinants of price elasticity of supply

The amount that costs rise as output rises. The less the additional costs of producing additional output, the more firms will be encouraged to produce for a given price rise: the more elastic will supply be.

Supply is thus likely to be elastic if firms have plenty of spare capacity, if they can readily get extra supplies of raw materials, if they can easily switch away from producing alternative products and if they can avoid having to introduce overtime working, at higher rates of pay. The less these conditions apply, the less elastic will supply be.

Time period

- Immediate time period. Firms are unlikely to be able to increase supply by much immediately. Supply is virtually fixed, or can only vary according to available stocks. Supply is highly inelastic.
- Short run. If a slightly longer period of time is allowed to elapse, some inputs can be increased (e.g. raw materials) while others will remain fixed (e.g. heavy machinery). Supply can increase somewhat.
- Long run. In the long run, there will be sufficient time for all inputs to be increased and for new firms to enter the industry. Supply, therefore, is likely to be highly elastic in many cases. In some circumstances the long-run supply curve may even slope downwards. (See the section on economies of scale in Chapter 5, pages 136–8.)

The measurement of price elasticity of supply

A vertical supply has zero elasticity. It is totally unresponsive to a change in price. A horizontal supply curve has infinite elasticity. There is no limit to the amount supplied at the price where the curve crosses the vertical axis.

When two supply curves cross, the steeper one will have the lower price elasticity of supply (e.g. curve S_1 in Figure 3.8). Any straight-line supply curve starting at the origin, however, will have an elasticity equal to 1 throughout its length, *irrespective of its slope*. This perhaps rather surprising result is illustrated in Figure 3.9. This shows three supply curves, each with a different slope, but each starting from the origin. On each curve two points are marked. In each case there is the *same* proportionate rise in Q as in P. For example, with curve S_1 a doubling in price from £3 to £6 leads to a doubling of output from 1 unit to 2 units.

This demonstrates nicely that it is not the *slope* of a curve that determines its elasticity, but its proportionate change.

Other supply curves' elasticities will vary along their length. In such cases we have to refer to the elasticity either

Figure 3.9 Unit elastic supply curves

Given the following supply schedule:

P:	2	4	6	8	10
Q:	0	10	20	30	40

(a) Draw the supply curve.
(b) Using the arc method, calculate price elasticity of supply (i) between $P = 2$ and $P = 4$; (ii) between $P = 8$ and $P = 10$.
(c) *Using the point method, calculate price elasticity of supply at $P = 6$.
(d) Does the elasticity of the supply curve increase or decrease as P and Q increase? Why?
(e) What would be the answer to (d) if the supply curve were a straight line but intersecting the horizontal axis to the right of the origin?

between two points on the curve, or at a specific point. Calculating elasticity between two points will involve the **arc method**. Calculating elasticity at a point will involve the point method. These two methods are just the same for supply curves as for demand curves: the formulae are the same, only the term Q now refers to quantity supplied rather than quantity demanded.

*LOOKING AT THE MATHS

We can use a supply equation to demonstrate why a straight-line supply curve through the origin has an elasticity equal to 1. Assume that the supply equation is

$$Q_s = a + bP \qquad (1)$$

If the supply curve passes through the origin, the value of $a = 0$. Thus:

$$Q_s = bP \qquad (2)$$

The point elasticity formula for price elasticity of supply is similar to that for price elasticity of demand (see pages 63–4) and is given by

$$P\epsilon_s = \frac{dQ_s}{dP} \cdot \frac{P}{Q_s} \qquad (3)$$

But

$$b = \frac{dQ_s}{dP} \qquad (4)$$

since this is the slope of the equation (the inverse of the slope of the curve). Substituting equation (4) in equation (3) gives

$$P\epsilon_s = b \cdot \frac{P}{Q_s} \qquad (5)$$

Substituting equation (2) in equation (5) gives:

$$P\epsilon_s = b \cdot \frac{P}{bP}$$

$$= \frac{bP}{bP}$$

$$= 1$$

Income elasticity of demand (Y∈D)

So far we have looked at the responsiveness of demand and supply to a change in price. But price is just one of the determinants of demand and supply. In theory, we could look at the responsiveness of demand or supply to a change in *any* one of their determinants. We could have a whole range of different types of elasticity of demand and supply.

KEY IDEA 9

Elasticity. The responsiveness of one variable (e.g. demand) to a change in another (e.g. price). This concept is fundamental to understanding how markets work. The more elastic variables are, the more responsive is the market to changing circumstances.

In practice there are just two other elasticities that are particularly useful to us, and both are demand elasticities.

The first is the ***income elasticity of demand (Y∈D)***. This measures the responsiveness of demand to a change in consumer incomes (Y). It enables us to predict how much the demand curve will shift for a given change in income. The **formula for the income elasticity of demand** is: the percentage (or proportionate) change in demand divided by the percentage (or proportionate) change in income. Putting this in symbols gives

$$Y\epsilon_D = \frac{\%\Delta Q_D}{\%\Delta Y}$$

Definitions

Formula for price elasticity of supply (arc method) ΔQ_s/average $Q_s \div \Delta P$/average P.

Income elasticity of demand The responsiveness of demand to a change in consumer incomes.

Formula for income elasticity of demand (Y∈D) The percentage (or proportionate) change in demand divided by the percentage (or proportionate) change in income: $\%\Delta Q_D \div \%\Delta Y$.

In other words, the formula is identical to that for the price elasticity of demand, except that we are dividing the change in demand by the change in income that caused it rather than by a change in price. Thus if a 2 per cent rise in income caused an 8 per cent rise in a product's demand, then its income elasticity of demand would be:

$$8\%/2\% = 4$$

THRESHOLD CONCEPT 7 — ELASTICITY: OF A VARIABLE TO A CHANGE IN A DETERMINANT

THINKING LIKE AN ECONOMIST

As we have seen in the case of price elasticity of demand, elasticity measures the responsiveness of one variable (e.g. quantity demanded) to change in another (e.g. price). This concept is fundamental to understanding how markets work. The more elastic variables are, the more responsive is the market to changing circumstances.

Elasticity is more than just a technical term. It's not difficult to learn the formula

$$P\epsilon_D = \frac{\%\Delta Q_D}{\%\Delta P}$$

in the case of price elasticity of demand, and then to interpret this as

$$P\epsilon_D = \frac{\Delta Q_D}{\text{average } Q_D} \div \frac{\Delta P}{\text{average } P}$$

using the arc elasticity method, or as

$$P\epsilon_D = \frac{dQ_D}{dP} \times \frac{P}{Q}$$

using the point elasticity method.

We can also very simply state the general formula for any elasticity as

$$\epsilon_{XY} = \frac{\%\Delta X}{\%\Delta Y}$$

where the formula refers to the responsiveness of variable X to a change in variable Y (where X could be quantity supplied or demanded, and Y could be price, income, the price of substitutes, or any other determinant of demand or supply). Again, we could use the arc or point elasticity methods. Although students often find it hard at first to use the formulae, it's largely a question of practice in mastering them. No doubt, if you are attending classes, you will be given practice in working out elasticities!

What makes elasticity a *threshold concept* is that it lies at the heart of how economic systems operate. In a market economy, prices act as signals that demand or supply has changed. They also act as an incentive for people to respond to the new circumstances. The greater the elasticity of demand, the bigger will be the response to a change in supply; the greater the elasticity of supply, the bigger will be the response to a change in demand.

Understanding elasticity and what determines its magnitude helps us understand how an economy is likely to respond to the ever-changing circumstances of the real world.

In a perfect market economy, firms face an infinitely elastic (horizontal) demand curve: they are price takers (see page 32 and Figure 3.4(b)). What this means is that they have no power to affect prices: they are highly dependent on market forces.

By contrast, big businesses (and some small ones too) are in a very different position. If there are only one or two firms in a market, each is likely to face a relatively inelastic demand. This gives them the power to raise prices and make more profit. As we have seen, if demand is price inelastic, then raising price will increase the firm's revenue (see Figure 3.4(b)). Even if demand is elastic (but still downward sloping) the firm could still increase profit by raising prices, provided that the fall in revenue was less than the reduction in costs from producing less. The general point here is that the less elastic is the firm's demand curve, the greater will be its power to raise prices and make a bigger profit.

It's not just price elasticity of demand that helps us understand how market economies operate. In a perfect market, market supply is likely to be highly elastic, especially in the long run after firms have had time to enter the industry. Thus if a new lower-cost technique is discovered, which increases profits in an industry, new firms will enter the market, attracted by the higher profits. This increased supply will then have the effect of driving prices down and hence profit rates will fall back. What this means is that in highly competitive industries firms are very responsive to changing economic circumstances. If they are not, they are likely to be forced out of business; it's a question of survival of the fittest. We explore this process in more detail in section 6.2.

If there is less competition, firms are likely to have a much easier life. But what is good for them may be bad for us as consumers. We may end up paying higher prices and having poorer quality goods – although not necessarily. We explore this in sections 6.3 and 6.4 and in Chapter 7.

So, getting to grips with elasticity is not just about doing calculations. It's about understanding the very essence of how economies operate.

1. *What would you understand by the 'wage elasticity of demand for labour'? How would the magnitude of this elasticity affect the working of the market for (a) plumbers and (b) footballers?*
2. *How is the concept of income elasticity of demand relevant in understanding how the structure of economies changes over the years?*

The major determinant of income elasticity of demand is the degree of 'necessity' of the good. In a developed country, the demand for luxury goods expands rapidly as people's incomes rise, whereas the demand for basic goods rises only a little. Thus items such as cars and foreign holidays have a high income elasticity of demand, whereas items such as vegetables and bus journeys have a low income elasticity of demand.

The demand for some goods actually *decreases* as people's incomes rise beyond a certain level. These are inferior goods such as cheap margarine. As people earn more, so they switch to butter or better quality margarine. Unlike **normal goods**, which have a positive income elasticity of demand, **inferior goods** have a negative income elasticity of demand.

 Look ahead to Table 3.1 (page 83). It shows the income elasticity of demand for various foodstuffs. Explain the difference in the figures for milk, bread and fresh fish.

Income elasticity of demand is an important concept to firms considering the future size of the market for their product. If the product has a high income elasticity of demand, sales are likely to expand rapidly as national income rises, but may also fall significantly if the economy moves into recession. (See Case Study 3.2, *Income elasticity of demand and the balance of payments*, in MyEconLab: This shows how the concept of income elasticity of demand can help us understand why so many developing countries have chronic balance of payments problems.)

Cross-price elasticity of demand ($C\epsilon_{D_{AB}}$)

This is often known by its less cumbersome title of **cross elasticity of demand**. It is a measure of the responsiveness of demand for one product to a change in the price of another (either a substitute or a complement). It enables us to predict how much the demand curve for the first product will shift when the price of the second product changes.

The **formula for the cross-price elasticity of demand** ($C\epsilon_{D_{AB}}$) is: the percentage (or proportionate) change in demand for good A divided by the percentage (or proportionate) change in price of good B. Putting this in symbols gives

$$C\epsilon_{D_{AB}} = \frac{\%\Delta Q_{D_A}}{\%\Delta P_B}$$

If good B is a *substitute* for good A, A's demand will *rise* as B's price rises. In this case, cross elasticity will be a positive figure. For example, if the demand for butter rose by 2 per cent when the price of margarine (a substitute) rose by 8 per cent, then the cross elasticity of demand for butter with respect to margarine would be

$$2\%/8\% = 0.25$$

If good B is *complementary* to good A, however, A's demand will *fall* as B's price rises and thus as the quantity of B demanded falls. In this case, cross elasticity of demand will be a negative figure. For example, if a 4 per cent rise in the price of bread led to a 3 per cent fall in demand for butter, the cross elasticity of demand for butter with respect to bread would be

$$-3\%/4\% = -0.75$$

The major determinant of cross elasticity of demand is the closeness of the substitute or complement. The closer it is, the bigger will be the effect on the first good of a change in the price of the substitute or complement, and hence the greater the cross elasticity – either positive or negative.

Firms need to know the cross elasticity of demand for their product when considering the effect on the demand for their product of a change in the price of a rival's product or of a complementary product. These are vital pieces of information for firms when making their production plans.

Another application of the concept of cross elasticity of demand is in the field of international trade and the balance of payments. How does a change in the price of domestic goods affect the demand for imports? If there is a high cross elasticity of demand for imports (because they are close substitutes for home-produced goods), and if prices at home rise due to inflation, the demand for imports will rise substantially, thus worsening the balance of trade.

 Which are likely to have the highest cross elasticity of demand: two brands of coffee, or coffee and tea?

Definitions

Normal goods Goods whose demand increases as consumer incomes increase. They have a positive income elasticity of demand. Luxury goods will have a higher income elasticity of demand than more basic goods.

Inferior goods Goods whose demand decreases as consumer incomes increase. Such goods have a negative income elasticity of demand.

Cross-price elasticity of demand The responsiveness of demand for one good to a change in the price of another.

Formula for cross-price elasticity of demand ($C\epsilon_{D_{AB}}$) The percentage (or proportionate) change in demand for good a divided by the percentage (or proportionate) change in price of good b: $\%\Delta Q_{D_A} \div \%\Delta P_B$.

*LOOKING AT THE MATHS

Calculating income and cross-price elasticities from a demand equation

The following demand equation relates quantity demanded (Q_A) for good A to its own price (P_A), consumer income (Y) and the price of a substitute good B (P_B).

$$Q_A = a - bP_A + cY + eP_B$$

Note that this is a 'linear' equation because it has no power terms, such as P^2 or Y^2. The formula[1] for income elasticity of demand for good A will be

$$Y\epsilon_\Delta = \frac{\partial Q_A}{\partial Y} \cdot \frac{Y}{Q_A}$$

But since the term $\partial Q_A/\partial Y$ represents the amount that Q_A will change for a given change in Y (i.e. the value of c), then

$$Y\epsilon_D = c \frac{Y}{Q_A}$$

Similarly, the formula for cross-price elasticity of demand for good A with respect to good B will be

$$C\epsilon_{D_{AB}} = \frac{\partial Q_A}{\partial P_B} \cdot \frac{P_B}{Q_A} = e \frac{P_B}{Q_A}$$

A worked example of these two formulae is given in Maths Case 3.1 in MyEconLab. We can also use calculus to work out the two elasticities for both linear and non-linear demand equations. A worked example of this is given in Maths Case 3.2 in MyEconLab.

---

[1] Note that in this case we use the symbol '∂' rather than 'd' to represent an infinitely small change. This is the convention when the equation contains more than one independent variable (in this case P_A, Y and P_B). The term $\partial Q_A/\partial Y$ is the 'partial derivative' (see page A13) and refers to the rate of change of Q_A to just *one* of the three variables (in this case Y).

Section summary

1. Elasticity is a measure of the responsiveness of demand (or supply) to a change in one of the determinants.

2. It is defined as the proportionate change in quantity demanded (or supplied) divided by the proportionate change in the determinant.

3. If quantity changes proportionately more than the determinant, the figure for elasticity will be greater than 1 (ignoring the sign): it is elastic. If the quantity changes proportionately less than the determinant, the figure for elasticity will be less than 1: it is inelastic. If they change by the same proportion, the elasticity has a value of 1: it is unit elastic.

4. Price elasticity of demand measures the responsiveness of demand to a change in price. Given that demand curves are downward sloping, price elasticity of demand will have a negative value. Demand will be more elastic the greater the number and closeness of substitute goods, the higher the proportion of income spent on the good and the longer the time period that elapses after the change in price.

5. When demand is price elastic, a rise in price will lead to a reduction in total expenditure on the good and hence a reduction in the total revenue of producers.

6. Demand curves normally have different elasticities along their length. We can thus normally refer only to the specific value for elasticity between two points on the curve or at a single point.

7. Elasticity measured between two points is known as arc elasticity. When applied to price elasticity of demand the formula is

$$\frac{\Delta Q_d}{\text{average } Q_d} \div \frac{\Delta P}{\text{average } P}$$

8. *Elasticity measured at a point is known as *point elasticity*. When applied to price elasticity of demand the formula is

$$\frac{dQ}{dP} \times \frac{P}{Q}$$

   where dQ/dP is the inverse of the slope of the tangent to the demand curve at the point in question.

9. Price elasticity of supply measures the responsiveness of supply to a change in price. It has a positive value. Supply will be more elastic the less costs per unit rise as output rises and the longer the time period.

10. Income elasticity of demand measures the responsiveness of demand to a change in income. For normal goods it has a positive value. Demand will be more income elastic the more luxurious the good and the less rapidly demand is satisfied as consumption increases. For inferior goods, income elasticity has a negative value.

11. Cross-price elasticity of demand measures the responsiveness of demand for one good to a change in the price of another. For substitute goods the value will be positive; for complements it will be negative. The cross-price elasticity will be higher the closer the two goods are as substitutes or complements.

3.2 THE TIME DIMENSION

KI 5
p21

The full adjustment of price, demand and supply to a situation of disequilibrium will not be instantaneous. It is necessary, therefore, to analyse the time path which supply takes in responding to changes in demand, and which demand takes in responding to changes in supply.

Short-run and long-run adjustment

As we saw in the previous section, elasticity varies with the time period under consideration. The reason is that producers and consumers take time to respond to a change in price. The longer the time period, the bigger the response, and thus the greater the elasticity of supply and demand.

TC 7
p68

This is illustrated in Figures 3.10 and 3.11. In both cases, as equilibrium moves from points a to b to c, there is a large short-run price change (P_1 to P_2) and a small short-run quantity change (Q_1 to Q_2), but a small long-run price change (P_1 to P_3) and a large long-run quantity change (Q_1 to Q_3).

Price expectations and speculation

In a world of shifting demand and supply curves, prices do not stay the same. Sometimes they go up; sometimes they come down.

If prices are likely to change in the foreseeable future, this will affect the behaviour of buyers and sellers *now*. If, for example, it is now December and you are thinking of buying a new television, you might decide to wait until the January sales, and in the meantime make do with your set. If, on the other hand, in December you see a summer

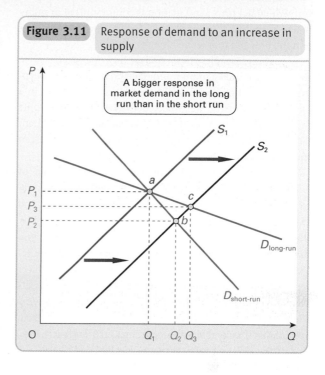

Figure 3.11 Response of demand to an increase in supply

A bigger response in market demand in the long run than in the short run

holiday advertised that you like, you might well book it then and not wait until nearer the summer for fear that the price will have gone up by then. Thus a belief that prices will go up will cause people to buy now; a belief that prices will come down will cause them to wait.

The reverse applies to sellers. If you are thinking of selling your house and prices are falling, you will want to sell it as quickly as possible. If, on the other hand, prices are rising sharply, you will wait as long as possible so as to get the highest price. Thus a belief that prices will come down will cause people to sell now; a belief that prices will go up will cause them to wait.

> **KEY IDEA 10**
>
> *People's actions are influenced by their expectations.* People respond not just to what is happening now (such as a change in price), but to what they anticipate will happen in the future.

This behaviour of looking into the future and making buying and selling decisions based on your predictions is called *speculation*. Speculation is often based on current trends in prices. If prices are currently rising, people may try to decide whether they are about to peak and go back

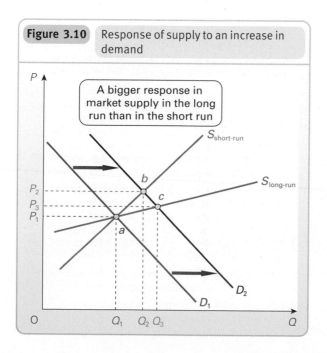

Figure 3.10 Response of supply to an increase in demand

A bigger response in market supply in the long run than in the short run

Definition

Speculation Where people make buying or selling decisions based on their anticipations of future prices.

down again, or whether they are likely to go on rising. Having made their prediction, they will then act on it. Their actions will then affect demand and supply, which in turn will affect price. Speculation is commonplace in many markets: the stock exchange, the foreign exchange market and the housing market are three examples.

Sometimes people will take advantage of expected price rises purely to make money and have no intention of keeping the item they have bought. For example, if shares in a particular company are expected to rise in price, people may buy them now while they are cheap and sell them later when the price has risen, thereby making a profit from the difference in price.

Similarly, people will sometimes take advantage of expected price reductions by selling something now only to buy it back later. For example, if you own shares and expect their price to fall, you may sell them now and buy them back later when their price has fallen. Again, you make a profit from the difference in price.

Sometimes the term *speculation* is used in this narrower sense of buying (or selling) commodities or financial assets simply to make money from later selling them (or buying them back) again at a higher (or lower) price. The term *speculators* usually refers to people engaged in such activities.

In the extreme case, speculators need not part with any money. If they buy an item and sell it back fairly soon at a higher price, they may be able to use the money from the sale to pay the original seller: the speculator merely pockets the difference! Alternatively, speculators may sell an item they do not even possess, as long as they can buy it back in time (at a lower price) to hand it over to the original purchaser. Again, they simply pocket the difference in price.

It may sound as if speculators are on to a good thing, and often they are, but speculation does carry risks: the predictions of individual speculators may turn out to be wrong, and then they could make losses rather than profits.

Nevertheless, speculators on average tend to gain rather than lose. The reason is that speculation tends to be *self-fulfilling*. In other words, the actions of speculators tend to bring about the very effect on prices that they had anticipated. For example, if speculators believe that the price of British Airways shares is about to rise, they will buy BA shares. But by doing this they will contribute to an increase in demand and ensure that the price *will* rise; the prophecy has become self-fulfilling.

Speculation can either help to reduce price fluctuations or aggravate them: it can be stabilising or destabilising.

Figure 3.12 Stabilising speculation: initial price fall

Speculators believe that the fall in price to P_2 is only temporary

Stabilising speculation

Speculation will tend to have a *stabilising* effect on price fluctuations when suppliers and/or demanders believe that a change in price is only *temporary*.

An initial fall in price. In Figure 3.12 demand has shifted from D_1 to D_2; equilibrium has moved from point *a* to point *b*, and price has fallen to P_2. How do people react to this fall in price?

Given that they believe this fall in price to be only temporary, suppliers *hold back*, expecting prices to rise again: supply shifts from S_1 to S_2. After all, why supply now when, by waiting, they could get a higher price?

Buyers *increase* their purchases, to take advantage of the temporary fall in price. Demand shifts from D_2 to D_3.

The equilibrium moves to point *c*, with price rising back towards P_1.

An initial rise in price. In Figure 3.13 demand has shifted from D_1 to D_2. Price has risen from P_1 to P_2.

Suppliers bring their goods to market now, before price falls again. Supply shifts from S_1 to S_2. Demanders, however, hold back until price falls. Demand shifts from D_2 to D_3. The equilibrium moves to point *c*, with price falling back towards P_1.

An example. A good example of stabilising speculation is that which occurs in agricultural commodity markets. Take the case of wheat. When it is harvested in the autumn,

Definitions

Speculators People who buy (or sell) commodities or financial assets with the intention of profiting by selling them (or buying them back) at a later date at a higher (lower) price.

Self-fulfilling speculation The actions of speculators tend to cause the very effect that they had anticipated.

Stabilising speculation Where the actions of speculators tend to reduce price fluctuations.

Figure 3.13 Stabilising speculation: initial price rise

Destabilising speculation

Speculation will tend to have a *destabilising* effect on price fluctuations when suppliers and/or buyers believe that a change in price heralds similar changes to come.

An initial fall in price. In Figure 3.14 demand has shifted from D_1 to D_2 and price has fallen from P_1 to P_2. This time, believing that the fall in price heralds further falls in price to come, suppliers sell now before the price does fall. Supply shifts from S_1 to S_2. And demanders wait: they wait until price does fall further. Demand shifts from D_2 to D_3.

Their actions ensure that price does fall further: to P_3.

An initial rise in price. In Figure 3.15 a price rise from P_1 to P_2 is caused by a rise in demand from D_1 to D_2. Suppliers wait until price rises further. Supply shifts from S_1 to S_2. Demanders buy now before any further rise in price. Demand shifts from D_2 to D_3. As a result, price continues to rise: to P_3.

there will be a plentiful supply. If all this wheat were to be put on the market, the price would fall to a very low level. Later in the year, when most of the wheat would have been sold, the price would then rise to a very high level. This is all easily predictable.

So what do farmers do? The answer is that they speculate. When the wheat is harvested, they know price will tend to fall, and so instead of bringing it all to market they put a lot of it into store. The more price falls, the more they will put into store *anticipating that the price will later rise*. But this holding back of supplies prevents prices from falling. In other words, it stabilises prices.

Later in the year, when the price begins to rise, they will gradually release grain onto the market from the stores. The more the price rises, the more they will release on to the market *anticipating that the price will fall again by the time of the next harvest*. But this releasing of supplies will again stabilise prices by preventing them from rising so much.

Rather than the farmers doing the speculation, it could be done by grain merchants. When there is a glut of wheat in the autumn, and prices are relatively low, they buy wheat on the grain market and put it into store. When there is a shortage in the spring and summer they sell wheat from their stores. In this way they stabilise prices just as the farmers did when they were the ones who operated the stores.

 In Figures 3.12 and 3.13, the initial change in price was caused by a shift in the demand curve. Redraw these two diagrams to illustrate the situation where the initial change in price was caused by a shift in the supply curve (as would be the case in the wheat market that we have just considered).

Figure 3.14 Destabilising speculation: initial price fall

Figure 3.15 Destabilising speculation: initial price rise

Definition

Destabilising speculation Where the actions of speculators tend to make price movements larger.

BOX 3.4 SHORT SELLING

Gambling on a fall in share prices

A form of speculation that can be very damaging to stock markets is the practice of **short selling**. This is where people take advantage of anticipated falls in share prices by selling shares they do not possess! How does this work?

Assume that a share price is currently £10 per share and traders on the stock market believe that the price is about to fall. They want to take advantage of this but don't possess any. What they do is borrow shares from dealers who do own some and agree to return them on a specified date. They pay a fee for doing this. In the meantime they sell the shares on the market at the current price of £10 and wait for it to fall. They are now 'short' of the shares (i.e. they don't possess them but still owe them).

Assume that just before the agreed time comes for returning the shares the price has fallen to £8. The trader then buys the shares, returns them to the dealer who had lent them and pockets the difference of £2 (minus the fee).

Although anyone can short sell shares, it is largely traders from various financial institutions who engage in this practice. Huge bonuses can be earned from their employers if the short selling is profitable. This encourages an atmosphere of risk-taking and looking to short-term gains rather than providing long-term capital to firms.

Short selling in the banking crisis of 2008

The practice of short selling had become rife in recent years and added to the instability of markets, driving share prices down that were anticipated to fall. This was a particular problem in 2008, when worries about bad debts and losses in the banking sector led many traders to short sell the shares of banks and other financial institutions felt to be most at risk.

The short selling of Halifax Bank of Scotland (HBOS) shares in September 2008 was a major contributing factor to the collapse in its share price. HBOS, the UK's largest mortgage lender, had been suffering losses as a result of

falling house prices and difficulties of many house owners in keeping up with their monthly mortgage payments. The share price plummeted by over 70 per cent in the space of a few days. The fall was driven on by speculation, much of it short selling. On 17 September it was announced that HBOS would be taken over by Lloyds TSB.

Concerns about the practice of short selling driving instability in financial markets led the Financial Services Authority, the industry's regulator, to announce, 18 September, on a four-month ban on the practice. At the same time, the US financial regulator, the Securities and Exchange Commission, announced a similar move.

Is short selling always profitable?

Short selling, as with other forms of speculation, is a form of gambling. If you gamble on a price fall and the price does fall, your gamble pays off and you make a profit. If you get it wrong, however, and the price rises, you will make a loss. In the case of short selling, you would have to buy the shares (to give back to the lender) at a higher price than you sold them.

This is just what happened in September 2008. With central banks around the world supporting markets, with the US government announcing that it would take over the bad debts of banks and with future short selling temporarily banned, share prices rapidly increased. The FTSE rose by a record 8.8 per cent on 19 September. Those with 'short positions' – i.e. those who had sold shares they had borrowed – then had to buy them back at a much higher price. Losses of hundreds of millions of pounds were made by short sellers. But they gained little sympathy from the general public, who blamed their 'greed' for much of the falls in share prices of the previous weeks.

 Why would owners of shares, such as pension funds, lend them to short sellers rather than selling the shares themselves and then buying them back later?

In Chapter 2 we examined the housing market (see Box 2.2). In this market, speculation is frequently destabilising. Assume that people see house prices beginning to move upwards. This might be the result of increased demand brought about by a cut in mortgage interest rates or by growth in the economy. People may well believe that the rise in house prices signals a boom in the housing market: that prices will go on rising. Potential buyers will thus try

to buy as soon as possible before prices rise any further. This will increase demand (as in Figure 3.15) and will thus lead to even bigger price rises. This is precisely what happened in the UK housing market in 1999–2007. Then in early 2008 prices started to fall; potential buyers believed that they would fall further and thus held off entering the market, leading to even bigger price falls.

Definition

Short selling (or **shorting**) Where investors borrow an asset, such as shares, oil contracts or foreign currency; sell the asset, hoping the price will soon fall; then buy it back later and return it to the lender. Assuming the price has fallen, the short seller will make a profit of the difference (minus any fees). There is always the danger, however, that the price may have risen, in which case the short seller will make a loss.

Conclusion

In some circumstances, then, the action of speculators can help to keep price fluctuations to a minimum (stabilising speculation). This is most likely when markets are relatively stable in the first place, with only moderate underlying shifts in demand and supply.

In other circumstances, however, speculation can make price fluctuations much worse. This is most likely in times of uncertainty, when there are significant changes in the determinants of demand and supply. Given this uncertainty, people may see price changes as signifying some trend. They then 'jump on the bandwagon' and do what the rest are doing, further fuelling the rise or fall in price.

 Redraw Figures 3.14 and 3.15 assuming, as in the previous question, that the initial change in price was caused by a shift in the supply curve.

Dealing with uncertainty and risk

When price changes are likely to occur, buyers and sellers will try to anticipate them. Unfortunately, on many occasions no one can be certain just what these price changes will be. Take the case of stocks and shares. If you anticipate that the price of, say, Marks & Spencer shares is likely to go up substantially in the near future, you may well decide to buy some now and then sell them later after the price has risen. But you cannot be certain that they will go up in price: they may fall instead. If you buy the shares, therefore, you will be taking a gamble.

Now gambles can be of two types. The first is where you know the odds. Let us take the simplest case of a gamble on the toss of a coin. Heads you win; tails you lose. You know that the odds of winning are precisely 50 per cent. If you bet on the toss of a coin, you are said to be operating under conditions of **risk**. *Risk is when the probability of an outcome is known.* Risk itself is a measure of the *variability* of an outcome. For example, if you bet £1 on the toss of a coin, such that heads you win £1 and tails you lose £1, then the variability is –£1 to +£1.

The second form of gamble is the more usual. This is where the odds are not known or are known only roughly. Gambling on the stock exchange is like this. You may have a good idea that a share will go up in price, but is it a 90 per cent chance, an 80 per cent chance or what? You are not certain. Gambling under this sort of condition is known as operating under **uncertainty**. *This is when the probability of an outcome is not known.*

You may well disapprove of gambling and want to dismiss people who engage in it as foolish or morally wrong. But 'gambling' is not just confined to horses, cards, roulette and the like. Risk and uncertainty pervade the whole of economic life, and decisions are constantly having to be made whose outcome cannot be known for certain. Even the most morally upright person will still have to decide which career to go into, whether and when to buy a house, or even something as trivial as whether or not to take an umbrella when going out. Each of these decisions and thousands of others are made under conditions of uncertainty (or occasionally risk).

 KEY IDEA 11 *People's actions are influenced by their attitudes towards risk.* Many decisions are taken under conditions of risk or uncertainty. Generally, the lower the probability of (or the more uncertain) the desired outcome of an action, the less likely people will be to undertake the action.

 Give some examples of decisions you have taken recently that were made under conditions of uncertainty. With hindsight do you think you made the right decisions?

We shall be examining how risk and uncertainty affect economic decisions on several occasions throughout the book. For example, in Chapter 4 we will see how it affects people's attitudes and actions as consumers and how taking out insurance can help to reduce their uncertainty. At this point, however, let us focus on firms' attitudes when supplying goods.

Stock holding as a way of reducing the problem of uncertainty

A simple way that suppliers can reduce the problem of uncertainty is by holding stocks. Take the case of the wheat farmers we saw in the previous section. At the time when they are planting the wheat in the spring, they are uncertain as to what the price of wheat will be when they bring it to market. If they keep no stores of wheat, they will just have to accept whatever the market price happens to be at harvest time. If, however, they have storage facilities, they can put the wheat into store if the price is low and then wait until the price goes up. Alternatively, if the price of wheat is high at harvest time, they can sell the wheat straight away. In other words, they can choose the time to sell.

Definitions

Risk When a (desirable) outcome of an action may or may not occur, but the probability of its occurring is known. The lower the probability, the greater the risk involved in taking the action.

Uncertainty When an outcome may or may not occur and its probability of occurring is not known.

BOX 3.5 | **DEALING IN FUTURES MARKETS** |

A way of reducing uncertainty

One way of reducing or even eliminating uncertainty is by dealing in **futures** or **forward markets**. Let us examine first the activities of sellers and then those of buyers.

Sellers

Suppose you are a farmer and want to store grain to sell at some time in the future, expecting to get a better price then than now. The trouble is that there is a chance that the price will go down. Given this uncertainty, you may be unwilling to take a gamble.

An answer to your problem is provided by the *commodity futures market*. This is a market where prices are agreed between sellers and buyers today for delivery at some specified date in the future.

For example, if it is 20 October today, you could be quoted a price today for delivery in six months' time (i.e. on 20 April). This is known as the six-month **future price**. Assume that the six-month future price is £160 per tonne. If you agree to this price and make a six-month forward contract, you are agreeing to sell a specified amount of wheat at £160 on 20 April. No matter what happens to the **spot price** (i.e. the current market price) in the meantime, your selling price has been agreed. The spot price could have fallen to £140 (or risen to £180) by April, but your selling price when 20 April arrives is fixed at £160. There is thus *no risk to you whatsoever of the price going down*. You will, of course, have lost out if the spot price is *more* than £160 in April.

Buyers

Now suppose that you are a flour miller. In order to plan your expenditures, you would like to know the price you will have to pay for wheat, not just today, but also at various future dates. In other words, if you want to take delivery of wheat at some time in the future, you would like a price quoted *now*. You would like the risks removed of prices going *up*.

Let us assume that today (20 October) you want to *buy* the same amount of wheat on 20 April that a farmer wishes to sell on that same date. If you agree to the £160 future price, a future contract can be made with the farmer. You are then guaranteed that purchase price, no matter what happens to the spot price in the meantime. There is thus *no risk to you whatsoever of the price going up*. You will, of course, have lost out if the spot price is *less* than £160 in April.

The determination of the future price

Prices in the futures market are determined in the same way as in other markets: by demand and supply.

For example, the six-month wheat price or the three-month coffee price will be that which equates the demand for those futures with the supply. If the five-month sugar price is currently £220 per tonne and people expect by then, because of an anticipated good beet harvest, that the spot price for sugar will be £170 per tonne, there will be few who want to buy the futures at £220 (and many who want to sell). This excess of supply of futures over demand will push the price down.

Speculators

Many people operate in the futures market who never actually handle the commodities themselves. They are neither producers nor users of the commodities. They merely speculate. Such speculators may be individuals, but they are more likely to be financial institutions.

Let us take a simple example. Suppose that the six-month (April) coffee price is £1300 per tonne and that you, as a speculator, believe that the spot price of coffee is likely to rise above that level between now (October) and six months' time. You thus decide to buy 20 tonnes of April coffee futures now.

But you have no intention of taking delivery. After four months, let us say, true to your prediction, the spot price (February) has risen and as a result the April price (and other future prices) have risen too. You thus decide to *sell* 20 tonnes of April (two-month) coffee futures, whose price, let us say, is £1500. You are now 'covered'.

When April comes, what happens? You have agreed to buy 20 tonnes of coffee at £1300 per tonne and to sell 20 tonnes of coffee at £1500 per tonne. All you do is to hand the futures contract to buy to the person to whom you agreed to sell. They sort out delivery between them and you make £200 per tonne profit.

If, however, your prediction had been wrong and the price had *fallen*, you would have made a loss. You would have been forced to sell coffee contracts at a lower price than you bought them.

Speculators in the futures market thus incur risks, unlike the sellers and buyers of the commodities, for whom the futures market eliminates risk. Financial institutions offering futures contracts will charge for the service: for taking on the risks.

 If speculators believed that the price of cocoa in six months was going to be below *the six-month future price quoted today, how would they act?*

Definitions

Futures or forward market A market in which contracts are made to buy or sell at some future date at a price agreed today.

Future price A price agreed today at which an item (e.g. commodities) will be exchanged at some set date in the future.

Spot price The current market price.

Section summary

1. A complete understanding of markets must take into account the time dimension.

2. Given that producers and consumers take a time to respond fully to price changes, we can identify different equilibria after the lapse of different lengths of time. Generally, short-run supply and demand tend to be less price elastic than long-run supply and demand. As a result, any shifts in *D* or *S* curves tend to have a relatively bigger effect on price in the short run and a relatively bigger effect on quantity in the long run.

3. People often anticipate price changes and this will affect the amount they demand or supply. This

speculation will tend to stabilise price fluctuations if people believe that the price changes are only temporary. However, speculation will tend to destabilise these fluctuations (i.e. make them more severe) if people believe that prices are likely to continue to move in the same direction as at present (at least for some time).

4. Many economic decisions are taken under conditions of risk or uncertainty. Uncertainty over future prices can be tackled by holding stocks. When prices are low, the stocks can be built up. When they are high, stocks can be sold.

3.3 INDIRECT TAXES

The effect of imposing taxes on goods

TC 6
p52

In section 2.4 we started looking at government intervention in markets and considered the impact of setting maximum and minimum prices. We now turn to another example of government intervention – the imposition of taxes on goods. These **indirect taxes**, as they are called, include taxes such as value added tax (VAT) and excise duties on cigarettes, petrol and alcoholic drinks.

These taxes can be a fixed amount per unit sold – a **specific tax**. An example is the tax per litre of petrol. Alternatively, they can be a percentage of the price or value added at each stage of production – an **ad valorem tax**. An example is VAT.

When a tax is levied on a good, this has the effect of shifting the supply curve upwards by the amount of the tax (see Figure 3.16). In the case of a specific tax, it will be a parallel shift, since the amount of the tax is the same at all prices. In the case of an *ad valorem* tax, the curve will *swing* upwards. At a zero price there would be no tax and hence no shift in the supply curve. As price rises, so the gap between the original and new supply curves will widen,

since a given *percentage* tax will be a larger *absolute* amount the higher the price.

But why does the supply curve shift upwards by the amount of the tax? This is illustrated in Figure 3.17. To be persuaded to produce the same quantity as before the imposition of the tax (i.e. Q_1), firms must now receive a price which allows them fully to recoup the tax they have to pay (i.e. $P_1 + \text{tax}$).

Definitions

Indirect tax A tax on the expenditure on goods. Indirect taxes include value added tax (VAT) and duties on tobacco, alcoholic drinks and petrol. These taxes are not paid directly by the consumer, but indirectly via the sellers of the good. Indirect taxes contrast with direct taxes (such as income tax) which are paid directly out of people's incomes.

Specific tax An indirect tax of a fixed sum per unit sold.

Ad valorem tax An indirect tax of a certain percentage of the price of the good.

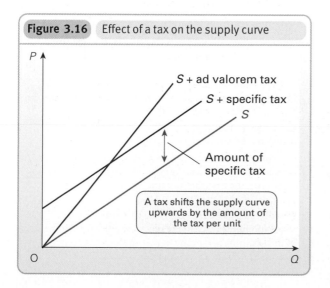

Figure 3.16 Effect of a tax on the supply curve

S + ad valorem tax
S + specific tax
S

Amount of specific tax

A tax shifts the supply curve upwards by the amount of the tax per unit

Figure 3.17 Effect of a tax on price and quantity

Figure 3.18   The incidence of an indirect tax

Case (1)	Case (2)	Case (3)	Case (4)
Inelastic demand	Elastic demand	Inelastic supply	Elastic supply

*LOOKING AT THE MATHS

Assume that a specific tax per unit of t is imposed on producers of a good. This is then added to the pre-tax price of P_1. The price paid by consumers is thus $P_1 + t$.

Assuming linear demand and supply equations (see page 45), these can be written as:

$$Q_D = a - b(P_1 + t) \qquad (1)$$

$$Q_S = c + dP_1 \qquad (2)$$

In equilibrium, $Q_D = Q_S$. Thus:

$$a - b(P_1 + t) = c + dP_1$$

We can rearrange this equation to give:

$$bP_1 + dP_1 = a - c - bt$$

Thus:

$$P_1 = \frac{a - c - bt}{b + d} \qquad (3)$$

Take the following example. If the demand and supply equations were

$$Q_D = 120 - 10(P_1 + t) \qquad (4)$$

and

$$Q_S = 10 + 5P_1 \qquad (5)$$

and $t = 2$, then from equation (3):

$$P_1 = \frac{120 - 10 - (10 \times 2)}{10 + 5} = 6$$

and from equations (4) and (5):

$$Q_D = 120 - 80 = Q_S = 10 + 30 = 40$$

The market price will be

$$P_1 + t = 6 + 2 = 8$$

 Assuming that the pre-tax equations were

$$Q_D = 120 - 10P$$

and

$$Q_S = 10 - 5P$$

what is (a) the consumer share of the tax and (b) the producer share?

The effect of the tax is to raise price and reduce quantity. Price will not rise by the full amount of the tax, however, because the demand curve is downward sloping. In Figure 3.17, price rises only to P_2. Thus the burden or *incidence* of such taxes is distributed between consumers and producers. Consumers pay to the extent that price rises. Producers pay to the extent that this rise in price is not sufficient to cover the tax.

Elasticity and the incidence of taxation

The incidence of indirect taxes depends on the elasticity of demand and supply of the commodity in question. Consider cases (1)–(4) in Figure 3.18. In each of the diagrams (which are all drawn to the same scale), the size of the tax is the same: the supply curve shifts upwards by the same amount. Price rises to P_2 in each case and quantity falls to Q_2, but, as you can see, the size of this increase in price and decrease in quantity differs in each case, depending on the price elasticity of demand and supply.

The total tax revenue is given by the amount of tax per unit (the vertical difference between the two supply curves) multiplied by the new amount sold (Q_2). This is shown as the total shaded area in each case in Figure 3.18.

The rise in price from P_1 to P_2 multiplied by the number of goods sold (Q_2) (the pink area) is the amount of the tax passed on to consumers and thus represents the *consumers' share* of the tax. The remainder (the green area) is the *producers' share*. This is the amount by which the producers'

Definitions

Incidence of tax The distribution of the burden of tax between sellers and buyers.

Consumers' share of a tax on a good The proportion of the revenue from a tax on a good that arises from an increase in the price of the good.

Producers' share of a tax on a good The proportion of the revenue from a tax on a good that arises from a reduction in the price to the producer (after the payment of the tax).

| BOX 3.6 | ASHES TO ASHES? | CASE STUDIES AND APPLICATIONS |

A moral dilemma of tobacco taxes

Consider the following dilemma. Cigarettes have a fairly price-inelastic demand (approximately –0.6), and thus placing a tax on them is an effective means of generating revenue. In the UK in 2007/8, tobacco duties raised just under £8.1 billion or 1.8 per cent of total tax revenue. This compares with 5.5 per cent for fuel duties and 1.8 per cent for alcohol duties.

Clearly, then, tobacco duties are a major source of revenue for the government. The less people can be put off smoking by the tax, the more revenue will be raised. In fact, if the government were to encourage people to smoke, it could thereby raise more revenue! The dilemma is that there is strong pressure on governments around the world to discourage people from smoking and the more governments succeed in this, the less will be their tax revenue.

This is not a new problem. Cabinet papers released in May 2008 revealed that in 1956 the Chancellor, Harold Macmillan, argued against issuing a government health warning about cigarettes, despite being presented with statistical evidence that it was harmful. He was concerned that an official warning would lead to reduced tax revenue from tobacco.

But would a reduction in smoking represent a cost to the government? Clearly it would represent a cut in tax revenue, but it would also reduce spending on smoking-related diseases. The amount spent by the National Health Service on smoking-related illness is around £1.8 billion per year. This, however, is considerably less than the revenue raised from tobacco taxes. Clearly smokers more than pay for their own treatment. Indeed, the state and the NHS may acquire further financial benefit from smokers. The benefits stem from the fact that smokers die younger. The NHS gains from avoiding many of the high-cost treatments required by elderly patients and the state gains from having to pay out less in pensions and other benefits.

The costs of smoking, however, are not limited to health-care costs and other costs to the exchequer. There are also costs in terms of lost output as a result of smoking-related illnesses. Then there are savings in human costs from reduced suffering and deaths. Smoking kills over 100 000 people per year in the UK, with an additional 3000 or more killed by the effects of passive smoking. More than 17 000 children each year are admitted to hospital because of the effects of passive smoking.

So perhaps raising tobacco taxes would be doubly beneficial. Not only would it raise revenue, but also it would help to back up other anti-smoking measures. There are, however, three problems with this.

The first concerns smuggling and tobacco-related crime. Smuggled cigarettes account for around 20 per cent of the UK market. Not only is the high price differential between tobacco prices in the UK and abroad encouraging criminality, but smuggled tobacco products are losing the government over £2 billion each year in tax revenue.

Another issue concerns the poorest households. The poorer people are, the larger the proportion of their income is spent on tobacco (and hence tobacco taxes). The poorest 10 per cent of the population spend approximately 15 per cent of their disposable income on tobacco. This compares with a figure of just 2 per cent for the population as a whole. As such, the higher the tax on tobacco, the more it redistributes incomes from the poor to the rich.

The third problem is that raising tobacco taxes does *not* have a very marked effect on the consumption of cigarettes; taxes are an ineffective way of discouraging smoking. Why is this? Think back to the discussion on elasticity in section 3.1; demand for cigarettes is inelastic because there are few substitutes and cigarette smokers are often addicted to their habit.

Thus when taxes on tobacco are raised there are three consequences: smuggling is more profitable; low-income households are affected more than high-income households; and, finally, tax revenues go up substantially while smoking is reduced only a little.

This dilemma helps explain the move away from using taxes as a method of reducing smoking and towards policies that more directly impact on smokers' behaviour. In 2006 and 2007 legislation came into force in the UK banning smoking in workplaces and public places such as shops, bars and restaurants. This followed similar moves in other countries and was supported by an earlier report by the Chief Medical Officer,[1] which suggested that such a ban would save up to £2.7 billion from a healthier workforce.

If the ban is successful and smokers give up in substantial numbers – and early indications suggest that this is likely – then the government will find itself having to look elsewhere for a source of replacement tax revenue.

1. *You are a government minister. What arguments might you put forward in favour of maximising the revenue from cigarette taxation?*
2. *What is the likely impact on businesses and individuals of the ban on smoking in public places?*
3. *Many people think that if tobacco were to be discovered today it would be an illegal substance, as is the case with cannabis. What problems would face a government trying to ban smoking completely (see section 3.4)?*

[1] Annual Report of the Chief Medical Officer 2003 (http://www.publications.doh.gov.uk/cmo/annualreport2003/smokefree.htm).

net price ($P_2 - t$) is below the original price (P_1) multiplied by Q_2.

The following conclusions can be drawn:

- Quantity will fall less, and hence tax revenue for the government will be greater, the less elastic are demand and supply (cases (1) and (3)).
- Price will rise more, and hence the consumers' share of the tax will be larger, the less elastic is demand and the more elastic is supply (cases (1) and (4)).
- Price will rise less, and hence the producers' share will be larger, the more elastic is demand and the less elastic is supply (cases (2) and (3)).

Cigarettes, petrol and alcohol have been major targets for indirect taxes. Demand for each of them is high and fairly inelastic. Thus the tax will not curb demand greatly. They are good sources, therefore, of tax revenue to the government (see Box 3.6).

Supply tends to be more elastic in the long run than in the short run. Assume that a tax is imposed on a good that was previously untaxed. How will the incidence of this tax change as time passes? How will the incidence be affected if demand too becomes more elastic over time?

Section summary

1. If the government imposes a tax on a good, this will cause its price to rise to the consumers, but it will also cause the revenue to producers (after the tax has been paid) to fall.

2. The 'incidence of tax' will depend on the price elasticity of demand and supply of the good.

3. The consumers' burden will be higher and the producers' burden correspondingly lower, the less elastic the demand and the more elastic the supply of the good. The total tax revenue for the government will be higher the less elastic are both demand and supply.

3.4 GOVERNMENT REJECTION OF MARKET ALLOCATION

TC 6
p52

Sometimes the government may consider that certain products or services are best not allocated through the market at all. This section examines two extreme cases. The first is goods or services that are provided free at the point of delivery, such as treatment in National Health Service hospitals and education in state schools. The second is goods and services whose sale is banned, such as certain drugs, weapons and pornography.

Providing goods and services free at the point of delivery: the case of hospital treatment

KI 4
p10

When the government provides goods and services free to consumers, this often reflects the public's view that they have a *right* to such things. Most people believe that it would be wrong to charge parents for their children's schooling or for having treatment in a hospital, certainly emergency treatment. However, there are also economic reasons that lie behind the provision: for example, educating children brings a benefit to *all* society.

But what are the consequences of not charging for a service such as health? The analysis is similar to that of a maximum price, only here the maximum price is zero. Figure 3.19 illustrates the situation. It shows a demand and a supply curve for a specific type of treatment in a given hospital.

The demand curve is assumed to be downward sloping. If people had to pay, the amount of treatment demanded would fall as the price went up – partly because some people would feel that they could not afford it (the income effect), and partly because people would turn to alternative treatments, such as prescription drugs. The fewer the alternatives, and the less close they are to hospital treatment, the less elastic would be the demand curve.

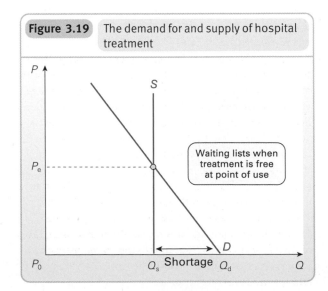

Figure 3.19 The demand for and supply of hospital treatment

The supply curve is assumed to be totally inelastic, at least in the short run, given current space and equipment. In the longer run, the supply curve may be upward sloping, but only if any charges made could be used to employ extra staff and buy more equipment, and even build extra wards and theatres, rather than the money simply going to the government.

At a price of zero, there is a shortage of $Q_d - Q_s$. Only at the equilibrium price of P_e will demand equal supply.

The shortage will have to be dealt with and some form of rationing will be required. One way to ration health care is to have a waiting list system. Most hospitals in the UK have waiting lists for non-emergency treatments. The trouble with this 'solution', however, is that waiting lists will continue to lengthen unless the shortage is reduced. There is also the problem that some people on the waiting list may require urgent treatment; these cases will get faster treatment than non-urgent cases. A consequence is that people waiting for non-urgent treatments, such as hip replacements or the treatment of varicose veins, may have to wait a very long time. Public health-care systems that do not make any charges for treatment are sometimes criticised for being unresponsive to the needs of patients.

Changes in demand and supply

One of the problems for the provision of health care is that the demand has grown more rapidly than people's incomes. Unless an increasing proportion of a nation's income is devoted to health care, shortages are likely to get worse. The demand curve in Figure 3.19 will shift to the right faster than the supply curve.

But why has demand grown so rapidly? There are two main reasons. The first has to do with demography. People in developed countries are living longer and the average age of the population is rising. But elderly people require a larger amount of medical treatment than younger people. The second has to do with advances in medical science and technology. More and more medical conditions are now treatable, so there is now a demand for such treatment where none existed before.

What is the solution? The answer for most people would be to increase supply, while keeping treatment free. Partly this can be done by increases in efficiency, and, indeed, various initiatives have been taken by government and health managers to try to reduce costs and increase the amount of treatment offered. Often, however, such measures are highly controversial; examples include reducing the length of time people are allowed to stay in hospital after an operation, or moving patients to hospitals, often at a distance, where operations can be done more cheaply. The only other way of increasing supply is to allocate more funds to health care, and this means either increasing taxes or diverting resources from other forms of public expenditure, such as education or social security. But then, as we know, scarcity involves choices!

TC 1
p8

Schooling is free in state schools in most countries. If parents are given a choice of schools for their children, there will be a shortage of places at popular schools (the analysis will be the same as in Figure 3.19, with the number of places in a given school measured on the horizontal axis). What methods could be used for dealing with this shortage? What are their relative merits?

Prohibiting the sale of certain goods and services: the case of illegal drugs

It is illegal to sell certain goods and services, and yet many of these goods have flourishing markets. Billions of pounds change hands worldwide in the illegal drugs, arms and pornography trades. What, then, is the impact of making certain products illegal? How would the effect compare with other policies, such as taxing these products?

Note that as economists we can examine the effects of such policies and hence help to inform public debate: we cannot, however, *as economists* make judgements as to whether such policies are *morally* right or wrong (see pages 26–7 on the distinction between positive and normative statements).

KI 6
p27

The market for illegal products

Figure 3.20 illustrates the market for a product such as a drug. If it were not illegal, the demand and supply curves would look something like D_{legal} and S_{legal}. The equilibrium price and quantity would be P_{legal} and Q_{legal}.

Now assume that the drug is made illegal. The effect will be to reduce supply and demand (i.e. shift both curves to the left), as both suppliers and users of the drug fear being caught and paying the penalty (fines or imprisonment). Also some people will stop supplying or using the drug simply because it is illegal and irrespective of any penalty. The harsher the penalties for supplier or user, and the more likely they are to get caught, and also the more law-abiding people are, the bigger will be the leftward shift in the respective supply or demand curve.

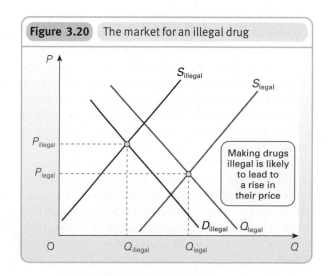

Figure 3.20   The market for an illegal drug

Making drugs illegal is likely to lead to a rise in their price

In Figure 3.20, the supply curve shifts to $S_{illegal}$ and the demand curve shifts to $D_{illegal}$. The quantity sold will fall to $Q_{illegal}$ and the price will rise to $P_{illegal}$. It is assumed that there will be a bigger shift in the supply curve (and hence a rise in price) as the penalties for supplying drugs are usually higher than those for merely possessing them.

 Under what circumstances would making a product illegal (a) cause a fall in its price; (b) cause the quantity sold to fall to zero?

A comparison of prohibition with taxing the product

Cocaine is illegal. Other drugs, such as tobacco and alcohol, are taxed. But the effect in both cases is to reduce consumption. So are there any differences in the results of using taxation and prohibition?

A *tax* on a product, like making a product illegal, will have the effect of shifting the supply curve upwards to the left (as we saw in Figure 3.17). Unlike making the product illegal, however, a tax will not shift the demand curve. A bigger shift in the supply curve would therefore be needed

than in Figure 3.20 for a tax to have the same effect as prohibition on the level of consumption. It would also result in a higher price for any given level of consumption.

So why not simply use taxes rather than making goods illegal? Those in favour of legalising various drugs argue that this would avoid the associated criminal activity that goes with illegal products (such as drugs gangs, violence and money laundering) and the resulting costs of law enforcement. It would also bring in tax revenue for the government.

The reason given by governments for keeping drugs illegal is that it sends out important messages to society and reflects what the majority wants. Taxing something, by contrast, implies that the product is acceptable. Also, if taxes were to be set high enough to reduce legal consumption to a politically acceptable level, there would then develop a large illegal market in the drugs as people sought to evade the tax.

 What are the arguments for and against making the sale of alcoholic drinks illegal? To what extent can an economist help to resolve the issue?

Section summary

1. Sometimes the government will want to avoid allocation by the market for a particular good or service. Examples include things provided free at the point of use and products that are prohibited by the government.

2. If products are provided free to consumers, demand is likely to exceed supply. This is a particular problem in the case of health care, where demand is growing rapidly.

3. If products such as drugs are prohibited, an illegal market is likely to develop. Demand and supply would be less than in a free market. The price could be either higher or lower, depending on who faces the harshest penalties and the greatest likelihood of being caught – suppliers or users.

4. A similar reduction in consumption could be achieved by using taxation. Other effects, however, such as on the price, on allied crime and on public perceptions of the acceptability of the product, will be different.

3.5 AGRICULTURE AND AGRICULTURAL POLICY

TC 4
p44
If markets for agricultural products were free from government intervention, they would be about as close as one could get to perfect competition in the real world. There are thousands of farmers, each insignificantly small relative to the total market. As a result, farmers are price takers.

Yet despite this high degree of competition, there is more government intervention in agriculture throughout the world than in virtually any other industry. For example, nearly half of the EU budget is spent on agricultural support. Agricultural markets therefore pose something of a paradox. If they are so perfect, why is there so much government intervention?

Why intervene?

TC 6
p52

The following are the most commonly cited problems of a free market in agricultural products.

Agricultural prices are subject to considerable fluctuations. This has a number of effects:

- Fluctuating prices cause fluctuating farm incomes. In some years, farm incomes may be very low.
- In other years, the consumer will suffer by having to pay very high prices.
- Fluctuating prices make the prediction of future prices very difficult. This in turn makes rational economic

decision making very difficult. How is a farmer to choose which of two or more crops to plant if their prices cannot be predicted?

- This uncertainty may discourage farmers from making long-term investment plans. A farmer may be reluctant to invest in, say, a new milking parlour, if in a couple of years it might be more profitable to switch to arable farming. A lack of investment by farmers will reduce the growth of efficiency in agriculture.

Low incomes for those in farming. Over the years, farm incomes have tended to decline relative to those in other sectors of the economy. What is more, farmers have very little market power. A particular complaint of farmers is that they have to buy their inputs (tractors, fertilisers, etc.) from non-competitive suppliers who charge high prices. Then they often have to sell their produce at very low prices to food processors, packers, distributors and supermarkets. Farmers thus feel squeezed from both directions.

Traditional rural ways of life may be destroyed. The pressure on farm incomes may cause unemployment and bankruptcies; smaller farms may be taken over by larger ones; village life may be threatened – with the break-up of communities and the closure of schools, shops and other amenities.

Competition from abroad. Farming may well be threatened by cheap food imports from abroad. This may drive farmers out of business.

Against all these arguments must be set the argument that intervention involves economic costs. These may be costs to the taxpayer in providing financial support to farmers, or costs to the consumer in higher prices of foodstuffs, or costs to the economy as a whole by keeping resources locked into agriculture that could have been more efficiently used elsewhere.

Then there is the question of recent trends in food prices. With the rise in demand for food from rapidly growing countries, such as China and India, and with the increased use of land for growing biofuels rather than food crops, world food prices have risen. Farming in many parts of the world is becoming more profitable.

Causes of short-term price fluctuations

Supply problems. A field is not like a machine. It cannot produce a precisely predictable amount of output according to the inputs fed in. The harvest is affected by a number of unpredictable factors such as the weather, pests and diseases. Fluctuating harvests mean that farmers' incomes will fluctuate.

Demand problems. Food, being a basic necessity of life, has no substitute. If the price of food in general goes up, people cannot switch to an alternative: they have either to pay the higher price or to consume less food. They might consume a bit less, but not much! The price elasticity for food in general, therefore, is very low, as Table 3.1 shows.

It is not quite so low for individual foodstuffs because if the price of one goes up, people can always switch to an alternative. If beef goes up in price, people can buy pork or lamb instead. Note, that lamb is the one foodstuff in Table 3.1 with an elastic demand. Nevertheless, certain foodstuffs still have a low price elasticity, especially if they are considered to be basic foods rather than luxuries, there are no close substitutes, or they account for a relatively small portion of consumers' income.

With an inelastic demand curve, any fluctuations in supply will cause large fluctuations in price. This is illustrated in Figure 3.21.

 Why is the supply curve drawn as a vertical straight line in Figure 3.21?

Causes of declining farm incomes

Demand problems. There is a limit to the amount people wish to eat. As people get richer, they might buy better cuts

Table 3.1	Price and income elasticities of demand in the UK for various foodstuffs	
Foodstuff	**Price elasticity of demand (average 1988–2000)**	**Income elasticity of demand (1998–2000)**
Bread	−0.40	0.12
Milk	−0.17	−0.17
Cheese	−0.35	0.23
Lamb	−1.29	0.15
Pork	−0.82	0.13
Fresh fish	−0.80	0.31
Eggs	−0.28	−0.01
Fresh potatoes	−0.12	0.09
Fresh green vegetables	−0.66	0.27
Frozen peas	−0.68	0.06
Bananas	−0.32	0.12
Cakes and biscuits	−0.56	0.13
All foods	n.a.	0.20

Source: National Food Survey 2000 (National Statistics, 2001), extracted from Tables 6.1, 6.3, 6.4 and 6.5.

Figure 3.21 Inelastic demand for food

Large price fluctuations from supply shifts

of meat, or more convenience foods, but they will spend very little extra on basic foodstuffs. Their income elasticity of demand for basic foods is very low (see Table 3.1).

 Why don't farmers benefit from a high income elasticity of demand for convenience foods?

This very low income elasticity of demand has a crucial effect on farm incomes. It means that a rise in national income of 1 per cent leads to a rise in food consumption of considerably less than 1 per cent. As a result, total farm incomes will grow much more slowly than the incomes of other sectors, farmers' incomes will grow less rapidly than those of the owners of other businesses, and farm workers' wages will grow less rapidly than those of other workers.

BOX 3.7 THE FALLACY OF COMPOSITION EXPLORING ECONOMICS

Or when good is bad

Ask farmers whether they would like a good crop of potatoes this year, or whether they would rather their fields be ravaged by pests and disease, and the answer is obvious. After all, who would wish disaster upon themselves!

And yet, what applies to an individual farmer does not apply to farmers as a whole. Disaster for all may turn out not to be disaster at all.

Why should this be? The answer has to do with price elasticity. The demand for food is highly price inelastic. A fall in supply, due to a poor harvest, will therefore cause a proportionately larger rise in price. Farmers' incomes will therefore rise, not fall.

Look at diagram (a). Farmer Giles is a price taker. If he alone has a bad harvest, price will not change. He simply sells less (Q_2) and thus earns less. His revenue falls by the amount of the shaded area. But if all farmers have a bad harvest the picture is quite different, as shown in diagram (b).

(b) *All farmers*

Bad harvest for all farmers: price rises; revenue rises

(a) *Farmer Giles*

Bad harvest for farmer Giles alone: revenue falls

Supply falls from Q_1 to Q_2, and consequently price rises from P_1 to P_2. Revenue thus rises from areas (1 + 2) to areas (1 + 3).

And so what applies to a single farmer in isolation (a fall in revenue) does not apply to farmers in general. This is known as the 'fallacy of composition'.

KEY IDEA 12 *The fallacy of composition.* What applies in one case will not necessarily apply when repeated in all cases.

1. *Can you think of any other (non-farming) examples of the fallacy of composition?*
2. *Would the above arguments apply in the case of foodstuffs that can be imported as well as being produced at home?*

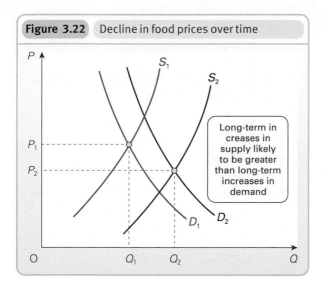

Figure 3.22 Decline in food prices over time

Long-term increases in supply likely to be greater than long-term increases in demand

Figure 3.23 Buffer stocks to stabilise prices

Supply problems. Farming productivity has grown dramatically over the years as farmers have invested in new technology and improved farming methods. (Increases in crop yields in various EU countries are shown in Table 3.2 on page 88.) But, given the price-inelastic demand for food, increased supply will have the effect of driving down agricultural prices, thus largely offsetting any reduction in costs. And given the income-inelastic demand for food, the long-term rise in demand will be less than the long-term rise in supply.

Figure 3.22 shows a basic foodstuff like potatoes or other vegetables. Rising productivity leads to an increase in supply from S_1 to S_2. But given that demand is price inelastic and shifts only slightly to the right over time, from D_1 to D_2, price falls from P_1 to P_2.

As we saw above, this national effect of low price and income elasticities of demand and rising supply has been offset in recent years by growing *world* demand for food and problems with world supply, such as poor harvests, rising input costs (such as diesel and fertilisers) and the diversion of land to growing biofuels – by 2010, some 30 per cent of the US maize (corn) crop is on course for being used for ethanol production. The effect of all this is a substantial increase in the prices of many foodstuffs, and in particular wheat, rice, maize and soya.

Government intervention

There are five main types of government intervention that can be used to ease the problems for farmers.

Buffer stocks

Buffer stocks involve the government buying food and placing it in store when harvests are good, and then releasing the food back on to the market when harvests are bad. They can thus only be used with food that can be stored: i.e. non-perishable foods, such as grain; or food that can be put into frozen storage, such as butter. The idea of buffer stocks is a very ancient one, as Case Study 3.5 in MyEconLab, *Seven years of plenty and seven years of famine*, demonstrates.

What the government does is to fix a price. Assume that this is P_g in Figure 3.23. At this price demand is Q_{d_1}. If there is a good harvest (S_{a_1}), the government buys up the surplus, $Q_{s_1} - Q_d$, and puts it into store. If there is a bad harvest (S_{a_2}), it releases $Q_d - Q_{s_2}$ from the store on to the market.

This system clearly stabilises price, at P_g. At this price, though, farm incomes will still fluctuate with the size of the harvest. It is possible, however, to have a buffer stock system that stabilises *incomes*. Such a system is examined in Case Study 3.6 in MyEconLab, *Buffer stocks to stabilise farm incomes*.

To prevent stores mounting over time, the government price will have to be the one that balances demand and supply over the years. Surpluses in good years will have to match shortages in bad years. Buffer stocks, therefore, can only *stabilise* prices or incomes; they do not *increase* farm incomes over the long term.

Subsidies

The government can pay subsidies or grant tax relief to farmers to compensate for low market prices. Subsidies can be used to increase farm incomes as well as to stabilise them. The simplest form of subsidy is one known as **direct income support** or **direct aid**. Here farmers are

---

Definitions

Buffer stocks Stocks of a product used to stabilise its price. In years of abundance, the stocks are built up. In years of low supply, stocks are released on to the market.

Direct income support or **direct aid** A fixed grant to farmers that does not vary with current output. It may be based on acreage, number of livestock or past output.

paid a fixed sum of money irrespective of output. Given that such subsidies are unrelated to output, they do not provide an incentive to produce more.

An alternative system is to pay a subsidy *per unit of output*. This, of course, will encourage farmers to produce more, which in turn will depress the market price.

Figure 3.24 illustrates the case of an agricultural product in which the country is self-sufficient. Without a subsidy the market price would be P_e, where supply equals demand.

Assume now that the government wishes farmers to receive a price of P_g. If farmers do receive this price, they will plan to increase production to Q_1, which will push the market price down to P_m. The size of the subsidy that the government must pay, therefore, will be $P_g - P_m$. The total amount of taxpayers' money spent will be the shaded area. The effect of the subsidy is to shift the effective supply curve downwards by the amount of the subsidy, to S + subsidy.

When some of the product is imported, the effect is slightly different. Let us assume, for simplicity, that a country is a price taker in world markets. It will face a horizontal world supply curve of the product at the world price. In other words, consumers can buy all they want at the world price. In Figure 3.25 the world price is P_w. Without a subsidy, domestic supply is Q_{s_1}. Domestic demand is Q_d. Imports are therefore the difference: $Q_d - Q_{s_1}$.

Assume now that the government wants farmers to receive a price of P_g. At that price, domestic supply increases to Q_{s_2}, but the price paid by the consumer does not fall. It remains at P_w. The subsidy paid per unit is $P_g - P_w$. The cost to the taxpayer is again shown by the shaded area.

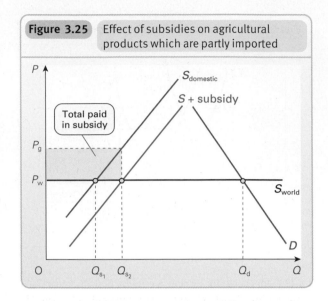

Figure 3.25 Effect of subsidies on agricultural products which are partly imported

A problem with subsidies of a fixed amount per unit is that the price the farmer receives will fluctuate along with the market price. An alternative, therefore, would be to let the size of the subsidy vary with the market price. The lower the price, the bigger the subsidy.

An advantage of subsidies is that they result in lower prices for the consumer. On the other hand, they have to be paid from tax revenues and therefore result in higher taxes.

High minimum prices

If the government considers agricultural prices to be too low, it can set a minimum price for each product above the free-market level. This was the traditional approach adopted in the EU. In recent years, however, forms of intervention in the EU have become more diverse.

The effect of high minimum prices will vary between products, depending on whether the country is a net importer or self-sufficient. Let us consider each case in turn.

Agricultural products where the country is a net importer. Assuming that the minimum price is above the world price, the government will need to impose customs duties (known alternatively as *tariffs* or *import levies*) on imported products to bring them up to the required price. Given that the world price will fluctuate, these import levies would need to be variable.

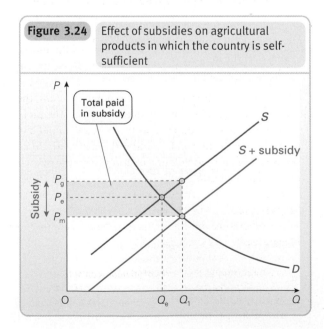

Figure 3.24 Effect of subsidies on agricultural products in which the country is self-sufficient

Definition

Tariffs or **import levies** Taxes on imported products: i.e. customs duties.

Figure 3.26 Minimum price where some of the product is imported

The effects of this system are illustrated in Figure 3.26. If trade took place freely at the world price P_w, Q_{d_1} would be demanded and Q_{s_1} supplied domestically. The difference $(Q_{d_1} - Q_{s_1})$ would be imported.

If a minimum price P_{min} is now set and a levy imposed on imports to raise their price to P_{min}, domestic prices will also rise to this level. Demand will fall to Q_{d_2}. Domestic supply will rise to Q_{s_2}. Imports will fall to $Q_{d_2} - Q_{s_2}$. The amount paid in import levies is shown by the shaded area.

Agricultural products where the country is self-sufficient. The effects of a minimum price in this situation are illustrated in Figure 3.27. Assume that the world price is P_w. This will be the equilibrium price, since any domestic surplus at P_w (i.e. $b - a$) will be exported at that price.

Now assume that the government sets a minimum price of P_{min}. Given that this is above the equilibrium (world) price, there will be an unsold surplus of $d - e$ (i.e. $Q_{s_2} - Q_{d_2}$).

But what will happen to this surplus? If farmers are to be helped, and not merely find that they cannot sell all they

produce, the government will have to buy up this surplus. This is what happens in the EU. 'Intervention Boards' buy up the surpluses and in most cases (e.g. grains, milk powder and beef) put them into storage. In Figure 3.27, the cost to the government of buying the surplus is shown by the total shaded area ($edQ_{s_2}Q_{d_2}$). Unless the food is thrown away or otherwise disposed of, there will obviously then be the additional costs of storing this food: costs that could be very high over time, especially if the food has to be frozen.

An alternative to storing the food is for the government to sell the surpluses on the world market. In this case, the net cost would only be area *edcf*.

What would be the amount paid in Figure 3.27 if instead of the government buying the surpluses, export subsidies were given to farmers so as to guarantee them a price (plus subsidy) of P_{min}?

Reductions in supply

An alternative approach would be to find some way of reducing supply. This would lead to a higher market price and could avoid the cost to the taxpayer of buying surpluses or paying subsidies.

In open markets, however, a reduction in domestic supply could simply lead to an increase in imports, with the result that the price would not rise to the desired level. In such a case, a combination of a reduction in domestic supply and import levies (or other import restrictions) would be required. This can be illustrated using Figure 3.27. First, by the use of various restrictions on output, the domestic supply curve could be shifted to the left, so that it intersected the demand curve at point *e*. Second, an import levy of $P_{min} - P_w$ would need to be imposed to bring the price up to the desired level.

But how could supply be reduced to Q_{d_2}? The simplest way would be to give farmers a quota of how much each was allowed to produce. The effect would be to make the domestic supply curve vertical above point *x*. Milk quotas, which have been in force in the EU since 1984, are an example of this system.

Alternatively, farmers could be required to limit the amount of *land* they use for a particular product. The problem with this is that supply, and hence price, would still vary according to the yield. Another alternative would be to require farmers to withdraw a certain percentage of their land from agricultural use. This would shift supply curves for food to the left generally, but they would still be upward sloping because farmers could still switch from one product to another on their remaining land, according to which products gave the best price.

Compare the relative merits of (a) quotas on output, (b) limits to the amount of land used for a particular product and (c) farmers being required to take land out of food production.

Figure 3.27 Minimum price for an agricultural product where the country is self-sufficient

Structural policies

The government could provide retraining or financial help for people to leave agriculture. It could provide grants or other incentives for farmers to diversify into forestry, tourism, rural industry or different types of food, such as organically grown crops, or other foods with a high income elasticity of demand.

The Common Agricultural Policy of the EU

Imagine public reaction if the government decided that the car industry needed protection from foreign competition and as a result decided to fix car prices some 20 per cent above current levels, and also agreed to buy up any unsold cars and put them into giant car parks, selling some of them off later on world markets at a knock-down price. There would be public uproar. And yet this is very similar to the type of support that has, until relatively recently, been the main one given to farmers under the EU's Common Agricultural Policy (CAP).

It involves setting an intervention price for each product above the free-market equilibrium, with any surpluses being bought by Intervention Boards and then either stored or sold on world markets. If products are exported, then export subsidies are paid to make up the difference between export prices and the intervention price. In addition to high minimum prices, the CAP has involved various subsidies, primarily in the beef and sheep sectors but also in the arable sector.

The objectives of the CAP were set out in 1957 in Article 39 of the Treaty of Rome. They included the following:

- Assured supplies of food.
- A fair standard of living for those working in agriculture.
- A growth in agricultural productivity.
- Stable prices.
- Reasonable prices for consumers.

How successful has the CAP been in meeting these objectives? It has certainly helped to increase the self-sufficiency of the EU in many agricultural products, which could be valuable if world food prices were to rise. Also, by fixing prices that do not fluctuate with demand and supply, stable prices are guaranteed – at least for a year. It has also directly increased farm incomes. Indeed, some larger farmers have benefited greatly from the CAP. Nevertheless, average incomes in farming have continued to lag behind those of other sectors of the economy, and many farmers face periodic losses.

Agricultural productivity has grown rapidly, as illustrated by Table 3.2. This has been in large part the result of technological improvements and a greater use of chemicals. It is difficult, however, to judge the extent to which this has resulted directly from higher food prices rather than the simple availability of new techniques, or competition from other farmers.

Table 3.2	Yields of selected crops (average annual, 100 kg/hectare)			
	Year	Wheat	Barley	Potatoes
Belgium	1970	39.0	31.0	293
	2003–6	85.2	73.9	431
France	1970	34.5	27.8	223
	2003–6	70.8	62.6	421
Germany	1970	37.9	32.2	272
	2003–6	73.4	58.9	393
Netherlands	1970	45.0	31.9	354
	2003–6	86.9	61.7	425
UK	1970	42.0	33.6	276
	2003–6	79.0	58.9	415

Source: Data from *Agriculture in the European Union* (Commission of the European Communities, DG for Agriculture and Rural Development, 2008), selected tables.

What of the final objective: 'reasonable prices for consumers'? In the short run, a policy of high prices is inconsistent with reasonable prices for consumers (if 'reasonable' is defined as 'low' or at any rate 'not high'). In the long run, however, it can be argued that, if prices above the market equilibrium encourage investment and productivity increases, then after a number of years they will end up lower than they would have been without the policy.

Criticisms of the CAP

If the arguments in favour of the CAP's system of price support are questionable, the arguments against are substantial.

Agricultural surpluses (not sold on world markets)

The costs of the surpluses are borne by consumers and taxpayers. They can be illustrated by referring back to Figure 3.27. Assume that the intervention is P_{min}.

- The cost to the taxpayer is shown by the shaded area.
- The cost to the consumer arises from having to pay the higher price P_{min}.
- There will be a gain to farmers, however, from the extra profits resulting from the rise in price.

The costs and benefits of this system of high minimum prices are compared with those of a system of per-unit subsidies in Case Study 3.7 in MyEconLab.

Over the longer term, surpluses were increasing. The reason is that higher prices encouraged more investment in farming and therefore greater increases in long-run supply. The attendant costs to taxpayers therefore tended to rise over time.

By the early 1990s, European butter, grain and beef 'mountains' and wine 'lakes' had become symbols of a failed policy.

Inequity

The system of high support prices as it operated in the EU is inequitable at three levels.

KI 4
p10

Increase in inequalities in agriculture. The degree of price support has varied enormously from one product to another and has tended to favour farmers in the richer northern countries of the EU – those producing arable crops and those with the largest farms.

Increase in inequalities generally. Poor people spend a larger proportion of their income on food than the rich, but pay a lower proportion of their income in taxes than the rich. A system of high prices for food therefore directly penalises the poor and reduces the burden on richer taxpayers.

A system of subsidies, on the other hand, leads to lower prices for the consumer, the cost being borne entirely by the taxpayer. It therefore leads to greater equality.

Inequity between member countries of the EU. Countries that import the most food from outside the EU – countries like the UK – have paid the most in import levies into the EAGGF (European Agricultural Guidance and Guarantee Fund). The countries with the greatest food surpluses have drawn most from the EAGGF.

Harmful effects on the environment

By encouraging increased output, the CAP has encouraged the destruction of hedgerows, and the increased use of chemical fertilisers and pesticides. Many of these chemicals have caused pollution. This issue is examined in Case Study 3.8 in MyEconLab.

Effects on the rest of the world

The CAP has had a very damaging effect on agriculture in non-EU countries in two ways.

Import levies. Levies on imported food substantially reduce the amount of food that other countries have been able to export to the EU. For example, Australia, a low-cost producer of butter, and once a major exporter to the UK, has found it impossible to export any butter at all to the EU.

'Dumping' surpluses on world markets. Export subsidies have allowed EU surpluses to be sold at very low prices on world markets. This has a doubly damaging effect on agriculture in developing countries: (a) exporters of foodstuffs find it very difficult to compete with subsidised EU exports; (b) farmers in developing countries who are producing for their domestic market find that they cannot compete with cheap imports of food.

Agriculture in the developing world thus declines. Farmers' incomes are too low to invest in the land. Many migrate to the overcrowded cities and become slum dwellers in shanty towns, with little or no paid employment (see Chapter 27). The neglect of agriculture can then lead to famines if there is poor rainfall in any year.

One of the major sticking points in the protracted international trade talks under the so-called 'Doha round'[1] has been the insistence of developing countries that Europe and North America abandon their policies of protecting their farmers.

Reforming the CAP

Proposals for reforming the CAP have been debated within the EU for a number of years. Most have focused on the growing problem of food surpluses and on the resulting demands made on the EU budget. Reforms can be grouped into two broad categories: those that seek to lower prices and those that seek to reduce supply.

Early reforms

Early reforms focused on reductions in supply. There were two main reforms.

Production quotas. These were introduced in the mid 1980s for sugar and milk. They involve imposing limits (or 'quotas') on the amount that farmers are permitted to produce. It is not practical, however, to have a quota system for grains and vegetables where yields fluctuate with the harvest. But if quotas are applied only to a limited range of products, this merely encourages farmers to switch to other products which may already be in surplus.

Acreage controls (set-aside). Another way of reducing cereal production has been to reduce the area cultivated. Subsidies are paid to farmers to leave their land fallow. Under this **set-aside** scheme, which was introduced in 1988, farmers are required to withdraw part of their arable land from production, and in return are paid compensation. From 2000/1 farmers were required to set aside 10 per cent of their land. This land, however, could be used for products not intended for human or animal consumption (e.g. biofuels).

A problem with set-aside was that farmers tended to set aside their least productive land, thereby making little difference to total output. Another problem was that farmers tended to put in extra effort on the remaining land, again hoping to maintain total output. If they were successful, supply would not be reduced and the problem of surpluses

---

[1] The Doha round of trade talks began in Doha, Qatar, in 2001 and continued without agreement for the next seven years. Developing countries wanted substantial reductions in agricultural support by the USA and the EU in order to allow greater access to these markets. They also wanted to retain the right to levy substantial tariffs on food imports from the rich world.

> ### Definition
>
> **Set-aside** A system in the EU of paying farmers not to use a certain proportion of their land.

would remain. To increase yields they would probably use more chemicals with the attendant problems of pollution.

With rising world food prices, the EU announced in 2008 that it would abolish set-aside (see below).

The MacSharry reforms

In 1992 a major reform package was introduced. These 'MacSharry reforms' (named after the EU agriculture commissioner) included a substantial cut in intervention prices (including a 29 per cent cut in cereal prices) phased in over three years. There was also a corresponding cut in export subsidies. (Intervention prices were still somewhat above world prices.)

Farmers were then paid compensation for their resulting loss of income. Since this income support (or 'direct aid', as it is known) is based on average historical yields in each farming region, it is independent of any changes in production by individual farmers. It thus provides no direct incentive to increase production. In order to receive direct aid, all except small farmers had to abide by the set-aside system and incentives were paid for farmers to switch to less intensive farming methods, with less use of chemical pesticides and fertilisers, and fewer livestock per hectare.

The effect of these measures was to reduce farm surpluses and in the first three years after these reforms, annual cereal output fell from 180 million tonnes to 160 million tonnes, and intervention stocks all but disappeared. Set-aside land had increased by 30 per cent, and, contrary to the predictions of some analysts, yields had not increased (this was partly the result of poor weather).

Further reforms

In July 1997, as part of its proposed plans for expansion of the EU, the European Commission published a document entitled *Agenda 2000*. In response to this document, it was agreed to cut intervention prices for cereals by 15 per cent, for beef by 20 per cent and, in 2005/6, for butter and skimmed milk powder by 15 per cent. It was also agreed to provide more support for rural development and the environment.

Critics claimed that the agreement was not sufficiently radical. Since the system of intervention prices was to continue, albeit at lower levels, surpluses were likely to remain. Also, there was no overall cut in the cost of the CAP, which was set to continue absorbing nearly half of the EU budget.

In June 2003, EU farm ministers adopted more fundamental reforms. It had been proposed to abolish all production-related subsidies and replace them with direct aid, but in the end a compromise deal was reached. This allowed countries to retain up to 25 per cent of support linked to production for cereals, 50 per cent for sheep and 100 per cent for beef.

Most countries, however, have moved to a system of direct aid. This involves making annual 'single farm pay-ments'. The UK adopted this system in January 2005. It has the following features:

- Annual payments to each farm based on the average of the EU funds it received over the three years from 2000 to 2002.
- Payments conditional on farmers making environmental improvements to their land.
- Payments to large farms gradually reduced, with 80 per cent of the money saved in each country being diverted to rural development.

The 10 per cent set-aside requirement was retained, but with greater flexibility to trade set-aside entitlements (along with their corresponding payments).

Despite the obvious advantages to many developing countries from the cuts in intervention prices, not all have gained. Take the case of sugar. Some sugar producers in Africa and the Caribbean had been given preferential access to European markets and were able to sell at the high guaranteed prices. They would clearly lose from the fall in prices. The EU offered some support to such countries, but not enough to prevent a fall in their income.

The gradual shift from price support to direct aid did reduce food prices and hence help EU consumers, benefiting low-income families relatively more than high-income ones. Taxpayers still have to finance the direct aid to farmers, but, with less incentive to expand production, this is less of a burden than that of paying high intervention prices for large food surpluses.

2008 reforms

In May 2008 proposals were made for further reforms to the CAP. These included further decoupling of financial support from output, phasing out of milk quotas and the ending of set-aside.

The budgetary impact of these reforms was estimated to be neutral; they were not designed to reduce the cost of the CAP; rather they reinforce a shift in emphasis towards viewing agriculture as part of the whole rural environment. This has involved increasing the grants available for setting up alternative rural industries and 'environmentally friendly' farm activities.

In practice, the sharp increases in food prices seen in 2007 and early 2008 raised the whole question of the need for agricultural support in times of high free-market prices for food.

With the onset of recession from mid 2008, however, food prices fell rapidly. There were calls from many parts of agriculture for additional support from the EU. The EU responded in various ways. For example, in the dairy sector, export subsidies for butter, cheese and whole and skimmed milk powder were reintroduced in January 2009; and in March 2009, the EU resumed intervention buying of butter and skimmed milk powder.

Section summary

1. Despite the fact that a free market in agricultural produce would be highly competitive, there is large-scale government intervention in agriculture throughout the world. The aims of intervention include preventing or reducing price fluctuations, encouraging greater national self-sufficiency, increasing farm incomes, encouraging farm investment, and protecting traditional rural ways of life and the rural environment generally.

2. Price fluctuations are the result of fluctuating supply combined with a price-inelastic demand. The supply fluctuations are due to fluctuations in the harvest.

3. The demand for food is generally income inelastic and thus grows only slowly over time. Supply, on the other hand, has generally grown rapidly as a result of new technology and new farm methods. This puts downward pressure on prices – a problem made worse for farmers by the price inelasticity of demand for food.

4. Government intervention can be in the form of buffer stocks, subsidies, price support, quotas and other ways of reducing supply, and structural policies.

5. Buffer stocks can be used to stabilise prices. They cannot be used to increase farm incomes over time.

6. Subsidies will increase farm incomes but will lower consumer prices to the world price level (or to the point where the market clears).

7. In the EU prices have been kept high to both farmer and consumer. In the case of partly imported foodstuffs, this is achieved by imposing variable import levies. In cases where the EU is self-sufficient, surpluses are purchased at an intervention price.

8. The CAP system of high intervention prices has been justified as providing assured supplies of food, a fair standard of living for farmers, incentives to increase productivity, stable prices, and, in the long term, possibly lower prices for consumers.

9. The CAP has been criticised, however, on a number of counts: it leads to food surpluses, the static costs of which are greater than those of subsidies; price support has been unequal as between foodstuffs, with a resulting misallocation of resources; it has aggravated inequalities within agriculture; it has been inequitable between member countries; it has encouraged environmental damage; import levies and the surpluses 'dumped' on world markets have had a damaging effect on the agricultural sector of non-EU countries.

10. Reforms have included the following: reductions in intervention prices and, in return, paying farmers compensation unrelated to output; acreage controls; increasing expenditure on rural diversification and restructuring; encouraging the use of less intensive farming methods.

END OF CHAPTER QUESTIONS

1. Why are both the price elasticity of demand and the price elasticity of supply likely to be greater in the long run?

2. Which of the following will have positive signs and which will have negative ones: (a) price elasticity of demand; (b) income elasticity of demand (normal good); (c) income elasticity of demand (inferior good); (d) cross elasticity of demand (with respect to changes in price of a substitute good); (e) cross elasticity of demand (with respect to changes in price of a complementary good); (f) price elasticity of supply?

3. What are the advantages and disadvantages of speculation from the point of view of (a) the consumer; (b) firms?

4. Think of two things that are provided free of charge. In each case, identify whether and in what form a shortage might occur. In what ways are/could these shortages be dealt with? Are they the best solution to the shortages?

5. If the government increases the tax on a litre of petrol by 5p, what will determine the amount by which the price of petrol will go up as a result of this tax increase?

6. Illustrate on four separate diagrams (as in Figure 3.18) the effect of different elasticities of demand and supply on the incidence of a subsidy.

7. Why are agricultural prices subject to greater fluctuations than those of manufactured products?

8. Compare the relative benefits of subsidies and high minimum prices (as under the CAP) to (a) the consumer; (b) the farmer.

9. The EU is more than self-sufficient in a number of commodities. Does this mean that the objectives of the CAP have been achieved? What has been the cost of achieving this success? What do you think would have happened in the absence of the CAP?

10. Do rising world food prices make the CAP unnecessary?

Online resources

Additional case studies in MyEconLab

3.1 Shall we put up our price? This uses the concept of price elasticity of demand to explain why prices are higher where firms face little or no competition.

3.2 Income elasticity of demand and the balance of payments. This examines how a low income elasticity of demand for the exports of many developing countries can help to explain their chronic balance of payments problems.

3.3 The role of the speculator. This assesses whether the activities of speculators are beneficial or harmful to the rest of society.

3.4 The cobweb model. Illustrating the effect of time lags in production.

3.5 Seven years of plenty and seven years of famine. This looks at how buffer stocks were used by Joseph in biblical Egypt.

3.6 Buffer stocks to stabilise farm incomes. This theoretical case shows how the careful use of buffer stocks combined with changes in set prices can be used to stabilise farm incomes.

3.7 Agricultural subsidies. This considers who gains and who loses from the use of subsidies on the production of agricultural products.

3.8 The CAP and the environment. This case shows how the system of high intervention prices had damaging environmental effects. It also examines the more recent measures the EU has adopted to reverse the effects.

Maths Case 3.1 Calculating income and cross-price elasticities from a demand equation: a worked example (Part 1: not using calculus). This gives an example of working out cross and income elasticities from a particular demand function.

Maths Case 3.2 Calculating income and cross-price elasticities from a demand equation: a worked example (Part 2: using calculus), This shows how simple differentiation can be used to work out elasticity values. It gives an example of working out cross and income elasticities from a particular demand function.

Websites relevant to this chapter

Numbers and sections refer to websites listed in the Web Appendix and hotlinked from this book's website at **www.pearsoned.co.uk/sloman**.

- For news articles relevant to this chapter, see the *Economics News Articles* link from the book's website.
- For general news on markets and market intervention, see websites in section A, and particularly A1–5, 7–9, 18, 24, 25, 26, 33, 36. See also A38 and 39 for links to newspapers worldwide; and A42 for links to economics news articles from newspapers worldwide.
- For information on taxes in the UK, see sites 30 and 36.
- For information on agriculture and the Common Agricultural Policy, see sites E14 and G9.
- For sites favouring the free market, see C17 and E34.
- For student resources relevant to this chapter, see sites C1–7, 9, 10, 19.
- For a simulation of running a farm, see site D3.
- For a range of classroom games and simulations of markets and market intervention, see sites C24 (computer-based) and C20 (non-computer-based).
- Site D3 contains simulations on elasticity, house prices and the relationships between markets.

Microeconomic Theory

4   **Background to Demand**   95

5   **Background to Supply**   123

6   **Profit Maximising under Perfect Competition and Monopoly**   163

7   **Profit Maximising under Imperfect Competition**   185

8   **Alternative Theories of the Firm**   213

9   **The Theory of Distribution of Income**   236

We now examine in more detail how economies function at a micro level. In doing so, we look at some of the big questions of our time. How do consumers choose between different goods? Why do some firms make such large profits? Why is there such a gap between the rich and the poor?

Chapters 4 and 5 examine demand and supply in more detail. Then in Chapters 6 to 8 we look at how the degree of competition a firm faces affects its prices and profits. Finally, in Chapter 9 we look at the distribution of income: why some are rich while others are poor.

Background to Demand

CHAPTER MAP

4.1 Marginal utility theory   **96**
Total and marginal utility   96
The optimum level of consumption: the simplest
  case – one commodity   98
Marginal utility and the demand for a good   100
The optimum combination of goods consumed   101
The multi-commodity version of marginal utility
  and the demand curve   102

**4.2 Demand under conditions of risk and
    uncertainty**   **105**
The problem of imperfect information   105
Attitudes towards risk and uncertainty   106
Diminishing marginal utility of income and
  attitudes towards risk taking   106
Insurance: a way of removing risks   107

*4.3 Indifference analysis   **109**
The limitations of the marginal utility approach
  to demand   109
Indifference curves   110
The budget line   112
The optimum consumption point   113
The effect of changes in income   114
The effect of changes in price   115
Deriving the individual's demand curve   115
The income and substitution effects of a price
  change   116
The usefulness of indifference analysis   119

In this chapter we take a more detailed look at consumer demand. If we had unlimited income and time we could consume as much as we wanted. We would not have to be careful with our money. In the real world, however, given limited incomes and the problem of scarcity, we have to make choices about what to buy. You may have to choose between that new economics textbook you feel you ought to buy and going to a festival, between a new pair of jeans and a meal out, between saving up for a car and having more money to spend on everyday items.

We will be assuming in this chapter that consumers behave 'rationally'. Remember from Chapter 1 how we defined rational choices. They are choices that involve the weighing up of the costs and benefits of our actions. As far as consumption is concerned, rational action involves considering the relative costs and benefits to us of the alternatives we could spend our money on. We do this in order to gain the maximum satisfaction possible from our limited incomes.

Of course this does not mean that you get a calculator out every time you go shopping. When you go round the supermarket, you are hardly likely to look at every item on the shelf and weigh up the satisfaction you think you would get from it against the price on the label. Nevertheless, you have probably learned over time the sort of things you like and what they cost. You can probably make out a 'rational' shopping list quite quickly.

There are two main approaches to analysing consumer behaviour: the marginal utility approach and the indifference approach. We examine both of them in this chapter. We also look at the problem of making rational choices when we have only limited information.

As we are going to be examining the **rational consumer**, it is important to understand what we mean by the term. It means a person who attempts to get the best value for money from his or her purchases. Given that we have limited income, we do not want to waste our money. Thus most of the time we try to ensure that the benefits of what we are buying are worth the expense to us.

Sometimes we may act 'irrationally'. We may purchase goods impetuously or out of habit, with little thought to their price or quality. In general, however, it is reasonable to assume that people behave rationally.

> 1. *Do you ever purchase things irrationally? If so, what are they and why is your behaviour irrational?*
> 2. *If you buy something in the shop on the corner when you know that the same item could have been bought more cheaply two miles up the road in the supermarket, is your behaviour irrational? Explain.*

Two words of warning before we go on. First, don't confuse irrationality and ignorance. We are going to assume that consumers behave rationally, but that does not mean that they have perfect information. How often have you been disappointed after buying something when you find that it is not as good as you had been led to believe by advertisements or by its packaging, or when you find later that you could have bought an alternative more cheaply? Take the case of a foreign holiday. It may not turn out to be nearly as good as the brochure led you to believe. This is a problem of ignorance. You probably nevertheless behaved rationally in the first place, believing (albeit wrongly) that you were getting value for money.

Second, the term 'rational' does not imply any moral approval. It is simply referring to behaviour that is consistent with your own particular goals, behaviour directed to getting the most out of your limited income. People may well disapprove of the things that others buy – their clothes, their cars, their cigarettes – but that is making a judgement about their goals, tastes or morality. As economists we cannot make judgements about what people's goals should be. We can, however, look at the implications of people behaving rationally in pursuit of those goals. This is what we are doing when we examine rational consumer behaviour: we are looking at its implications for consumer demand.

4.1 MARGINAL UTILITY THEORY

Total and marginal utility

People buy goods and services because they get satisfaction from them. Economists call this satisfaction 'utility'.

An important distinction must be made between *total utility* and *marginal utility*.

Total utility (*TU*) is the total satisfaction a person gains from all those units of a commodity consumed within a given time period. Thus if Lucy drank ten cups of tea a day, her daily total utility from tea would be the satisfaction derived from those ten cups.

Marginal utility (*MU*) is the additional satisfaction gained from consuming one *extra* unit within a given period of time. Thus we might refer to the marginal utility that Lucy gains from her third cup of tea of the day or her eleventh cup.

A difficulty arises immediately with the utility approach to explaining demand: how do you measure utility? Utility is subjective. There is no way of knowing what another person's experiences are really like. Just how satisfying does Nick find his first cup of tea in the morning? How does his utility compare with Lucy's? We do not have utility meters that can answer these questions!

For the moment, we will ignore this problem and assume that a person's utility can be measured in utils, where a **util** is one unit of satisfaction.

Diminishing marginal utility

Up to a point, the more of a commodity you consume, the greater will be your total utility. However, as you become more satisfied, each *extra* unit that you consume will probably give you less additional utility than previous units. In other words, your marginal utility falls, the more you consume. This is known as the **principle of diminishing marginal utility**.

> ### Definitions
>
> **Rational consumer** A person who weighs up the costs and benefits to him or her of each additional unit of a good purchased.
>
> **Total utility** The total satisfaction a consumer gets from the consumption of all the units of a good consumed within a given time period.
>
> **Marginal utility** The extra satisfaction gained from consuming one extra unit of a good within a given time period.
>
> **Util** An imaginary unit of satisfaction from the consumption of a good.
>
> **Principle of diminishing marginal utility** As more units of a good are consumed, additional units will provide less additional satisfaction than previous units.

TC 1
p8

KI 6
p27

KEY IDEA 13 *The principle of diminishing marginal utility.* The more of a product a person consumes, the less will be the additional utility gained from one more unit.

Table 4.1 Ollie's utility from consuming crisps (daily)

Packets of crisps consumed	*TU* in utils	*MU* in utils
0	0	–
1	7	7
2	11	4
3	13	2
4	14	1
5	14	0
6	13	−1

For example, the second cup of tea in the morning gives you less additional satisfaction than the first cup. The third cup gives less satisfaction still.

At some level of consumption, your total utility will be at a maximum. No extra satisfaction can be gained by the consumption of further units within that period of time. Thus marginal utility will be zero. Your desire for tea may be fully satisfied at seven cups per day. An eighth cup will yield no extra utility. It may even give you displeasure (i.e. negative marginal utility).

 Are there any goods or services where consumers do not experience diminishing marginal utility?

Total and marginal utility curves

If we could measure utility, we could construct a table showing how much total and marginal utility a person would gain at different levels of consumption of a particular commodity. This information could then be transferred to a graph. Table 4.1 and Figure 4.1 do just this. They show the imaginary utility that Ollie gets from consuming packets of crisps.

Referring first to the table, if Ollie consumes no crisps, he obviously gets no satisfaction from crisps: his total utility is zero. If he now consumes one packet a day, he gets 7 utils of satisfaction. (Sorry if this sounds silly, but we will tackle this question of measurement later.) His total utility

is 7, and his marginal utility is also 7. They must be equal if only one unit is consumed.

If he now consumes a second packet, he gains an extra 4 utils (*MU*), giving him a total utility of 11 utils (i.e. 7 + 4). His marginal utility has fallen because, having already eaten one packet, he has less craving for a second. A third packet gives him less extra utility still: marginal utility has fallen to 2 utils, giving a total utility of 13 utils (i.e. 11 + 2).

By the time he has eaten five packets, he would rather not eat any more. A sixth actually reduces his utility (from 14 utils to 13): its marginal utility is negative.

The information in Table 4.1 is plotted in Figure 4.1. Notice the following points about the two curves:

- The *MU* curve slopes downwards. This is simply illustrating the principle of diminishing marginal utility.
- The *TU* curve starts at the origin. Zero consumption yields zero utility.
- It reaches a peak when marginal utility is zero. When marginal utility is zero (at five packets of crisps), there is no addition to total utility. Total utility must be at the maximum – the peak of the curve.

Figure 4.1 Ollie's utility from consuming crisps (daily)

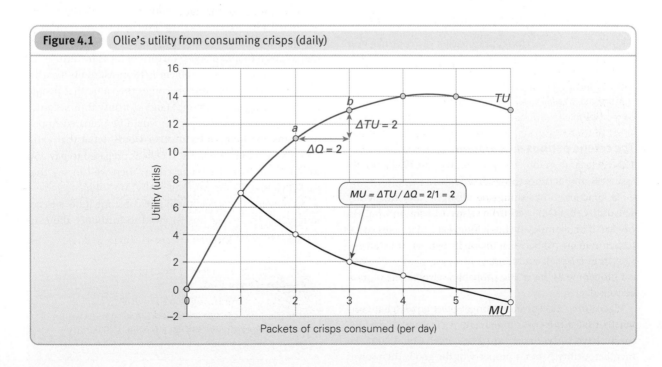

*BOX 4.1 USING CALCULUS TO DERIVE A MARGINAL UTILITY FUNCTION

The relationship between total utility and marginal utility can be shown using calculus. If you are not familiar with the rules of calculus, ignore this box (or see Appendix 1, pages A9–13).

A consumer's typical utility function for a good might be of the form

$$TU = 60Q - 4Q_2$$

where Q is the quantity of the good consumed.

This would give the figures shown in the following table.

Q	60Q	$-4Q^2$	=	TU
1	60	−4	=	56
2	120	−16	=	104
3	180	−36	=	144
4	240	−64	=	176
.	.	.		.

 Complete this table to the level of consumption at which TU is at a maximum.

Marginal utility is the first derivative of total utility. In other words, it is the rate of change of total utility. Differentiating the *TU* function gives

$$MU = \frac{dTU}{dQ} = 60 - 8Q$$

This gives the figures shown in the following table.

Q	60	−8Q	=	MU
1	60	−8	=	52
2	60	−16	=	44
3	60	−24	=	36
4	60	−32	=	28
.	.	.		.

Note that the marginal utility diminishes.

The *MU* function we have derived is a straight-line function. If, however, the *TU* function contained a cubed term (Q^3), the *MU* function would be a curve.

 Derive the MU function from the following TU function:

$$TU = 200Q - 25Q^2 + Q^3$$

From this MU function, draw up a table (like the one above) up to the level of Q where MU becomes negative. Graph these figures.

- Marginal utility can be derived from the *TU* curve. It is the slope of the line joining two adjacent quantities on the curve. For example, the marginal utility of the third packet of crisps is the slope of the line joining points *a* and *b*. The slope of such a line is given by the formula

$$\frac{\Delta TU}{\Delta Q}(= MU)$$

In our example $\Delta TU = 2$ (total utility has risen from 11 to 13 utils), and $\Delta Q = 1$ (one more packet of crisps has been consumed). Thus $MU = 2$.

 If Ollie were to consume more and more crisps, would his total utility ever (a) fall to zero; (b) become negative? Explain.

The ceteris paribus assumption

The table and graph we have drawn are based on the assumption that other things do not change.

In practice, other things *do* change – and frequently. The utility that Ollie gets from crisps depends on what else he eats. If on Saturday he has a lot to eat and nibbles snacks (other than crisps) between meals, he will get little satisfaction from crisps. If on Monday, however, he is too busy to eat proper meals, he would probably welcome one or more packets of crisps.

Each time the consumption of *other* goods changed – whether substitutes or complements – a new utility schedule would have to be drawn up. The curves would shift. Remember, utility is not a property of the goods themselves.

Utility is in the mind of the consumer, and consumers change their minds. Their tastes change; their circumstances change; their consumption patterns change.

The optimum level of consumption: the simplest case – one commodity

Just how much of a good should people consume if they are to make the best use of their limited income? To answer this question we must tackle the problem of how to measure utility, given that in practice we cannot measure 'utils'.

One solution to the problem is to measure utility with money. In this case, utility becomes the value that people place on their consumption. Marginal utility thus becomes the amount of money a person would be prepared to pay to obtain one more unit: in other words, what that extra unit is worth to that person. If Ollie is prepared to pay 45p to obtain an extra packet of crisps, then we can say that packet yields him 45p worth of utility: $MU = 45\text{p}$.

So how many packets should he consume if he is to act rationally? To answer this we need to introduce the concept of *consumer surplus*.

Definition

Consumer surplus The excess of what a person would have been prepared to pay for a good (i.e. the utility) over what that person actually pays.

Marginal consumer surplus

Marginal consumer surplus (*MCS*) is the difference between what you are willing to pay for one more unit of a good and what you are actually charged. If Ollie were willing to pay 45p for another packet of crisps which in fact only cost him 40p, he would be getting a marginal consumer surplus of 5p.

$$MCS = MU - P$$

Total consumer surplus

Total consumer surplus (*TCS*) is the sum of all the marginal consumer surpluses that you have obtained from all the units of a good you have consumed. It is the difference between the total utility from all the units and your expenditure on them. If Ollie consumes four packets of crisps, and if he would have been prepared to spend £1.60 on them and only had to spend £1.20, then his total consumer surplus is 40p.

$$TCS = TU - TE$$

where *TE* is the total expenditure on a good: i.e. $P \times Q$.

Let us define **rational consumer behaviour** as the attempt to maximise consumer surplus. How do people set about doing this?

People will go on purchasing additional units as long as they gain additional consumer surplus: in other words, as long as the price they are prepared to pay exceeds the price they are charged ($MU > P$). But as more units are purchased, so they will experience diminishing marginal utility. They will be prepared to pay less and less for each additional unit. Their marginal utility will go on falling until $MU = P$: i.e. until no further consumer surplus can be gained. At that point, they will stop purchasing additional units. Their optimum level of consumption has been reached: consumer surplus has been maximised. If they continue to purchase beyond this point, *MU* would be less than *P*, and thus they would be paying more for the last units than they were worth to them.

The process of maximising consumer surplus can be shown graphically. Let us take the case of Tanya's annual purchases of petrol. Tanya has her own car, but as an alternative she can use public transport or walk. To keep the analysis simple, let us assume that Tanya's parents bought her the car and pay the licence duty, and that Tanya does

Figure 4.2 Tanya's consumer surplus from petrol

not have the option of selling the car. She does, however, have to buy the petrol. The current price is £1.20 per litre. Figure 4.2 shows her consumer surplus.

If she were to use just a few litres per year, she would use them for very important journeys for which no convenient alternative exists. For such trips she may be prepared to pay up to £1.50 per litre. For the first few litres, then, she is getting a marginal utility of around £1.50 per litre, and hence a marginal consumer surplus of around 30p (i.e. £1.50 – £1.20).

By the time her annual purchase is around 200 litres, she would be prepared to pay only around £1.40 for additional litres. The additional journeys, although still important, would be less vital. Perhaps these are journeys where she could have taken public transport, albeit at some inconvenience. Her marginal consumer surplus at 200 litres is 20p (i.e. £1.40 – £1.20).

Gradually, additional litres give less and less additional utility as less and less important journeys are undertaken. The 500th litre yields £1.30 worth of extra utility. Marginal consumer surplus is now 10p (i.e. £1.30 – £1.20).

By the time she gets to the 900th litre, Tanya's marginal utility has fallen to £1.20. There is no additional consumer surplus to be gained. Her total consumer surplus is at a maximum. She thus buys 900 litres, where $P = MU$.

Her total consumer surplus is the sum of all the marginal consumer surpluses: the sum of all the 900 vertical lines between the price and the *MU* curve. This is shown by the total *area* between *P* and *MU* up to 900 litres (i.e. the pink shaded area in Figure 4.2).

This analysis can be expressed in general terms. In Figure 4.3, if the price of a commodity is P_1, the consumer will consume Q_1. The person's total expenditure (*TE*) is $P_1 Q_1$, shown by area 1. Total utility (*TU*) is the area under the marginal utility curve: i.e. areas 1 + 2. Total consumer surplus ($TU - TE$) is shown by area 2.

KI 13
p97

KI 13 **p97**

Definitions

Marginal consumer surplus The excess of utility from the consumption of one more unit of a good (*MU*) over the price paid: $MCS = MU - P$.

Total consumer surplus The excess of a person's total utility from the consumption of a good (*TU*) over the total amount that person spends on it (*TE*): $TCS = TU - TE$.

Rational consumer behaviour The attempt to maximise total consumer surplus.

If a good were free, why would total consumer surplus equal total utility? What would be the level of marginal utility at the equilibrium level of consumption?

THRESHOLD CONCEPT 8   RATIONAL DECISION MAKING INVOLVES CHOICES AT THE MARGIN

Rational decision making involves weighing up the marginal benefit and marginal cost of any activity. If the marginal benefit exceeds the marginal cost, it is rational to do the activity (or to do more of it). If the marginal cost exceeds the marginal benefit, it is rational not to do it (or to do less of it).

Let's take the case of when you go to the supermarket to do shopping for the week. Assume that you have £30 to spend. Clearly, you will want to spend it wisely. With each item you consider buying, you should ask yourself what its marginal benefit is to you: in other words, how much you would be prepared to spend on it. This will depend on the prices and benefits of alternatives. Thus if you were considering spending £2 from the £30 on wholemeal bread, you should ask yourself whether the £2 would be better spent on some alternative, such as white bread, rolls or crackers. The *best* alternative (which might be a combination of products) is the marginal opportunity cost. If the answer is that you feel you are getting better value for money by spending it on the wholemeal bread, then you are saying that the marginal benefit exceeds the marginal opportunity cost. It is an efficient use of your money to buy the wholemeal bread and forgo the alternatives.

Most decisions are more complex than this, as they involve buying a whole range of products. In fact, that is what you are doing in the supermarket. But the principle is still the same. In each case, a rational decision involves weighing up marginal benefits and marginal costs. Is buying an extra jar of this, or packet of that, worth the sacrifice of the alternative you could have purchased with the money?

This is another example of a *threshold concept* because it is a way of thinking about economic problems. It is a general principle that can be applied in a whole host of contexts: whether it is individuals deciding what to buy, how much to work, what job to apply for, or whether to study for a degree or take a job; or firms deciding how much to produce, whether to invest in new capacity or new products, or what type of people to employ and how many; or governments deciding how much to spend on various projects, such as roads, hospitals and schools, or what rates of tax to impose on companies that pollute the environment.

In each case, better decisions will be made by weighing up marginal costs and marginal benefits.

1. *Assume that a firm is selling 1000 units of a product at £20 each and that each unit on average costs £15 to produce. Assume also that to produce additional units will cost the firm £19 each and that the price will remain at £20. To produce additional products will therefore reduce the average profit per unit. Should the firm expand production? Explain.*

2. *Assume that a ferry has capacity for 500 passengers. Its operator predicts that it will typically have only 200 passengers on each of its midweek sailings over the winter. Assume also that each sailing costs the company £10 000. This means that midweek winter sailings cost the company an average of £10 000/200 = £50 per passenger. Currently tickets cost £60. Should the company consider selling stand-by tickets during the winter for (a) less than £60; (b) less than £50? (Clue: think about the marginal cost of taking additional passengers.)*

Figure 4.3   Consumer surplus

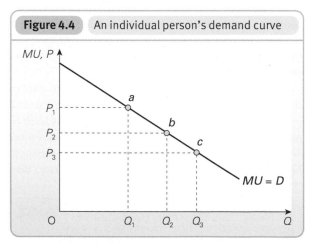

Figure 4.4   An individual person's demand curve

Marginal utility and the demand curve for a good

An individual's demand curve

Individual people's demand curve for any good will be the same as their marginal utility curve for that good, where utility is measured in money.

This is demonstrated in Figure 4.4, which shows the marginal utility curve for a particular person and a particular good. If the price of the good were P_1, the person would consume Q_1, where $MU = P_1$. Thus point a would be one point on that person's demand curve. If the price fell to P_2, consumption would rise to Q_2, since this is where $MU = P_2$.

Thus point *b* is a second point on the demand curve. Likewise if price fell to P_3, Q_3 would be consumed. Point *c* is a third point on the demand curve.

Thus as long as individuals seek to maximise consumer surplus and hence consume where $P = MU$, their demand curve will be along the same line as their marginal utility curve.

The market demand curve

The market demand curve will simply be the (horizontal) sum of all individuals' demand curves and hence *MU* curves.

The shape of the demand curve. The price elasticity of demand will reflect the rate at which *MU* diminishes. If there are close substitutes for a good, it is likely to have an elastic demand, and its *MU* will diminish slowly as consumption increases. The reason is that increased consumption of this product will be accompanied by *decreased* consumption of the alternative product(s). Since total consumption of this product *plus* the alternatives has increased only slightly (if at all), the marginal utility will fall only slowly.

For example, the demand for a certain brand of petrol is likely to have a fairly high price elasticity, since other brands are substitutes. If there is a cut in the price of Texaco petrol (assuming the prices of other brands stay constant), consumption of Texaco petrol will increase a lot. The *MU* of Texaco petrol will fall slowly, since people consume less of other brands. Petrol consumption *in total* may be only slightly greater, and hence the *MU* of petrol only slightly lower.

> Why do we get less total consumer surplus from goods where our demand is relatively elastic?

Shifts in the demand curve. How do *shifts* in demand relate to marginal utility? For example, how would the marginal utility of (and hence demand for) margarine be affected by a rise in the price of butter? The higher price of butter would cause less butter to be consumed. This would increase the marginal utility of margarine, since if people are using less butter, their desire for margarine is higher. The *MU* curve (and hence the demand curve) for margarine thus shifts to the right.

> How would marginal utility and market demand be affected by a rise in the price of a complementary good?

Weaknesses of the one-commodity version of marginal utility theory

A change in the consumption of one good will affect the marginal utility of substitute and complementary goods. It will also affect the amount of income left over to be spent on other goods. Thus a more satisfactory explanation of demand would involve an analysis of choices between goods, rather than looking at one good in isolation.

What is more, deriving a demand curve from a marginal utility curve measured in money assumes that money itself has a constant marginal utility. The trouble is that it does not. If people have a rise in income, they will consume more. Other things being equal, the marginal utility of the goods that they consume will diminish. Thus an extra £1 of consumption will bring less satisfaction than previously. In other words, it is likely that the *marginal utility of money diminishes as income rises.*

Unless a good occupies only a tiny fraction of people's expenditure, a fall in its price will mean that their real income has increased: i.e. they can afford to purchase more goods in general. As they do so, the marginal utility of their money will fall. We cannot, therefore, legitimately use money to measure utility in an absolute sense. We can, however, still talk about the relative utility that we get from various goods for a given increase in expenditure.

The following sections thus look at the choice between goods, and how it relates to marginal utility.

The optimum combination of goods consumed

We can use marginal utility analysis to show how a rational person decides what combination of goods to buy. Given that we have limited incomes, we have to make choices. It is not just a question of choosing between two obvious substitutes (like carrots and peas or a holiday in Greece and one in Spain), but about allocating our incomes between all the goods and services we might like to consume. If you have, say, an income of £15 000 per year, what is the optimum 'bundle' of goods and services for you to spend it on?

The rule for rational consumer behaviour is known as the *equi-marginal principle*. This states that a consumer will get the highest utility from a given level of income when the ratio of the marginal utilities is equal to the ratio of the prices. Algebraically, this is when, for any pair of goods, A and B, that are consumed:

$$\frac{MU_A}{MU_B} = \frac{P_A}{P_B} \tag{1}$$

To see the sense of this, say that the last unit of good A you consumed gave three times as much utility as the last

---

Definition

Equi-marginal principle (in consumption)
Consumers will maximise total utility from their incomes by consuming that combination of goods where
$$\frac{MU_A}{MU_B} = \frac{P_A}{P_B}$$

> ### BOX 4.2 THE MARGINAL UTILITY REVOLUTION: JEVONS, MENGER, WALRAS
> EXPLORING ECONOMICS
>
> #### Solving the diamonds–water paradox
>
> What determines the market value of a good? We already know the answer: demand and supply. So if we find out what determines the position of the demand and supply curves, we will at the same time be finding out what determines a good's market value.
>
> This might seem obvious. Yet for years economists puzzled over just what determines a good's value.
>
> Some economists like Karl Marx and David Ricardo concentrated on the supply side. For them, value depended on the amount of resources used in producing a good. This could be further reduced to the amount of labour time embodied in the good. Thus, according to the labour theory of value, the more labour that was directly involved in producing the good, or indirectly in producing the capital equipment used to make the good, the more valuable would the good be.
>
> Other economists looked at the demand side. But here they came across a paradox.
>
> Adam Smith in the 1760s gave the example of water and diamonds. 'How is it', he asked, 'that water which is so essential to human life, and thus has such a high "value-in-use", has such a low market value (or "value-in-exchange")? And how is it that diamonds which are relatively so trivial have such a high market value?' The answer to this paradox had to wait over a hundred years until the marginal utility revolution of the 1870s. William Stanley Jevons (1835–82) in England, Carl Menger (1840–1921) in Austria, and Léon Walras (1834–1910) in Switzerland all independently claimed that the source of the market value of a good was its marginal utility, not its total utility.
>
> This was the solution to the diamonds–water paradox. Water, being so essential, has a high total utility: a high 'value in use'. But for most of us, given that we consume so much already, it has a very low marginal utility. Do you leave the cold tap running when you clean your teeth? If you do, it shows just how trivial water is to you at the
>
> margin. Diamonds, on the other hand, although they have a much lower total utility, have a much higher marginal utility. There are so few diamonds in the world, and thus people have so few of them, that they are very valuable at the margin. If, however, a new technique were to be discovered of producing diamonds cheaply from coal, their market value would fall rapidly. As people had more of them, so their marginal utility would rapidly diminish.
>
> Marginal utility still only gives the demand side of the story. The reason why the marginal utility of water is so low is that supply is so plentiful. Water is very expensive in Saudi Arabia! In other words, the full explanation of value must take into account both demand and supply.
>
>
>
> *The diagram illustrates a person's* MU *curves of water and diamonds. Assume that diamonds are more expensive than water. Show how the* MU *of diamonds will be greater than the* MU *of water. Show also how the* TU *of diamonds will be less than the* TU *of water. (Remember:* TU *is the area under the* MU *curve.)*

---

unit of B. Yet good A only cost twice as much as good B. You would obviously gain by increasing your consumption of A and cutting your purchases of B. But as you switched from B to A, the marginal utility of A would fall due to diminishing marginal utility, and conversely the marginal utility of B would rise. To maximise utility you would continue this substitution of A for B until the ratios of the marginal utilities (MU_A/MU_B) equalled the ratio of the prices of the two goods (P_A/P_B). At this point, no further gain can be made by switching from one good to another. This is the optimum combination of goods to consume.

 KI 13 p97

Equation (1) is a specific example of the general equi-marginal principle in economics, which applies to all rational choices between two alternatives, whether in production, consumption, employment or whatever:

> KEY IDEA 14
>
> *The equi-marginal principle.* The optimum amount of two alternatives consumed (or produced) will be where the marginal benefit ratios of the two alternatives are equal to their marginal cost ratios:
>
> $$\frac{MB_A}{MB_B} = \frac{MC_A}{MC_B}$$

The multi-commodity version of marginal utility and the demand curve

How can we derive a demand curve from the above analysis?

Let us simply reinterpret equation (1) so that it relates the *MU* and *P* of good A to the *MU* and *P* of *any* other good.

BOX 4.3   **IS ECONOMICS THE STUDY OF SELFISH BEHAVIOUR?**   CASE STUDIES AND APPLICATIONS

Is what's best for the individual best for others?

Many of the choices we make are not made as individuals purely for ourselves. If you are a member of a family or living with friends, many of your 'consumption' decisions will affect the other members of the household and many of their decisions will affect you.

Some things will be decided jointly: what to have for dinner, what colour to paint the hall, whether to have a party. Put this another way: when you gain utility, the other members of the household will often gain too (e.g. from things 'jointly' consumed, such as central heating).

Sometimes, however, it is the other way round. When things are jointly purchased, such as food, then one person's consumption will often be at the expense of other members of the household. 'Who's finished all the milk?' 'I want to watch a different television programme.'

What we are saying is that when individuals are in a group, such as a family, a club or an outing with a group of friends, their behaviour will affect and be affected by the other members of the group. For this reason, we have to amend our simple analysis of 'rational' choice. Let us consider two situations. The first is where people are trying to maximise their own self-interest within the group. The second is where people are genuinely motivated by the interests of the other members – whether from feelings of love, friendship, moral duty or whatever. We will consider these two situations within a family.

Self-interested behaviour

If you do not consider the other members of the family, this could rebound on you. For example, if you do not clean out the bath after yourself, or do not do your share of the washing up, then you may have to 'pay the price'. Other family members may get cross with you, or behave equally selfishly themselves.

When considering doing things for their own benefit, therefore, the 'rational' person would at the very least consider the reactions of the other members of the family. We could still use the concept of marginal utility, however, to examine such behaviour. If marginal utility were greater than the price ($MU > P$), it would be 'rational' to do more of any given activity. Here, though, marginal utility would include utility not only from directly consuming goods or services within the household, but also from the favourable reactions to you from other family members. Likewise, marginal utility would be reduced if there were any unfavourable reaction from other family members. The 'price' (i.e. the marginal cost to you) would include not only the monetary costs to you of consuming something, but also any other sacrifice you make in order to consume it. In other words, the price would be the full opportunity cost.

Take first the case of goods or services jointly consumed, such as a family meal. Do you offer to cook dinner? If you were motivated purely by self-interest, you would do so if the marginal benefit (i.e. marginal utility) to you exceeded the marginal cost to you. The marginal benefit would include the benefit to you of consuming the meal, plus any pleasure you got from the approval of other family members, plus any entitlement to being let off other chores. The marginal cost to you would include any monetary costs to you (e.g. of purchasing the ingredients)

and the sacrifice of any alternative pleasurable activities that you had to forgo (such as watching television). Whether the actual preparation of the meal was regarded as a marginal benefit or a marginal cost would depend on whether the individual saw it as a pleasure or a chore.

Clearly, these benefits and costs are highly subjective: they are as you perceive them. But the principle is simple: if you were behaving purely out of self-interest, you would cook the meal if you felt that you would gain more from doing so than it cost you.

Now take the case of consuming something individually where it deprives another household member of consuming it (such as taking the last yoghurt from the fridge). Again, if you were behaving purely out of self-interest, you would have to weigh up the pleasure from that yoghurt against the cost to you of incurring the irritation of other family members.

Behaviour in the interests of the family as a whole

However, most people are not totally selfish, especially when it comes to relating to other members of their family. In fact, family members are often willing to make personal sacrifices or put in considerable effort (e.g. with household chores or child rearing) for the sake of other family members, without being motivated by what they individually can get out of it.

In such cases, consumption decisions can be examined at two levels: that of the individual and that of the whole family.

As far as individuals are concerned, analysis in terms of their own marginal benefit and marginal cost would be too simplistic. Often it is a more accurate picture to see household members, rather than behaving selfishly, instead behaving in the self-interest of the whole household. So a decision about what food to buy for the family at the supermarket, if taken by an individual member, is likely to take into account the likes and dislikes of other family members, and the costs to the whole household budget. In other words, it is the whole family's marginal benefits and marginal costs that the individual family member is considering.

Other forms of altruism

It is not only within the circle of family and friends that we see altruistic behaviour take place. Individuals choose to give money to charity, to return other people's property when they find it and to give blood that will help save strangers. This behaviour has been a focus for economic research and the apparent contradiction between utility maximisation and the actions of individuals provides an opportunity to think further about motivation and utility.

1. *Imagine that you are going out for the evening with a group of friends. How would you decide where to go? Would this decision-making process be described as 'rational' behaviour?*

2. *Think of some examples of altruistic behaviour towards strangers. In each case list some of the reasons why individuals might behave 'unselfishly'.*

In other words, the equation would be the same for goods B, C, D, E and any other good. For any given income, and given prices for good A and all other goods, the quantity a person will demand of good A will be that which satisfies equation (1). One point on the individual's demand curve for good A has been determined.

If the price of good A now falls, such that

$$\frac{MU_A}{MU_B} > \frac{P_A}{P_B} \quad \text{(and similarly for goods C, D, E, etc.)}$$

the person would buy more of good A and less of all other goods (B, C, D, E, etc.), until equation (1) is once more satisfied. A second point on the individual's demand curve for good A has been determined.

Further changes in the price of good A would bring further changes in the quantity demanded, in order to satisfy equation (1). Further points on the individual's demand curve would thereby be derived.

If the price of *another* good changed, or if the marginal utility of any good changed (including good A), then again the quantity demanded of good A (and other goods) would change, until again equation (1) were satisfied. These changes in demand will be represented by a *shift* in the demand curve for good A.

BOX 4.4 **TAKING ACCOUNT OF TIME** CASE STUDIES AND APPLICATIONS

Do you take a taxi or go by bus? How long do you spend soaking in the bath? Do you go to the bother of cooking a meal or will you get a take-away?

We have argued that such decisions, if they are to be rational, should involve weighing up the relative marginal utilities of these activities against their relative marginal costs.

One crucial dimension we have ignored up to now is the time dimension. One of the opportunity costs of doing any activity is the sacrifice of time.

A take-away meal may be more expensive than a home-cooked one, but it saves you time. Part of the cost of the home-cooked meal, therefore, is the sacrifice of time involved. The full cost is therefore not just the cost of the ingredients and the fuel used, but also the opportunity cost of the alternative activities you have sacrificed while you were cooking.

Given the high-pressured lives many people lead in affluent countries, a high value is often put on time saved. Increased sales of ready meals and the success of firms specialising in domestic flights are consequences of this lifestyle.

Even pleasurable activities involve a time cost. The longer you spend doing pleasurable activity 'a', the less time you will have for doing pleasurable activity 'b'. The longer you laze in the bath, the less TV will you be able to watch (unless you have a TV in the bathroom!).

Section summary

1. The satisfaction people get from consuming a good is called 'utility'. Total utility is the satisfaction gained from the total consumption of a particular good over a given period of time. Marginal utility is the extra satisfaction gained from consuming one more unit of the good.

2. The marginal utility tends to fall the more that people consume. This is known as the 'principle of diminishing marginal utility'.

3. The utility that people get from consuming a good will depend on the amount of other goods they consume. A change in the amount of other goods consumed, whether substitutes or complements, will shift the total and marginal utility curves.

4. 'Rational' consumers will attempt to maximise their consumer surplus. Consumer surplus is the excess of people's utility (measured in money terms) over their expenditure on the good. This will be maximised by purchasing at the point where the *MU* of a good is equal to its price.

5. In the simple case where the price and consumption of other goods is held constant, a person's *MU* curve will lie along the same line as that person's demand curve.

6. The market demand curve is merely the horizontal sum of the demand curves of all the individual consumers. The elasticity of the market demand curve will depend on the rate at which marginal utility diminishes as more is consumed. This in turn depends on the number and closeness of substitute goods. If there are close substitutes, people will readily switch to this good if its price falls, and thus marginal utility will fall only slowly. The demand will be elastic.

7. Measuring the marginal utility of a good in money avoids the problem of using some imaginary unit such as utils, but it assumes that money has a constant utility. In reality, the marginal utility of money is likely to decrease as income rises.

8. A more satisfactory way of analysing the demand for goods is to look at people's choices between goods. A consumer will maximise utility from a given income by consuming according to the 'equi-marginal principle'. This states that goods should be consumed in that combination which equates the *MU/P* ratio for each good.

4.2 DEMAND UNDER CONDITIONS OF RISK AND UNCERTAINTY

The problem of imperfect information

So far we have assumed that when people buy goods and services, they know exactly what price they will pay and how much utility they will gain. In many cases this is a reasonable assumption. When you buy a bar of chocolate, you clearly do know how much you are paying for it and have a very good idea how much you will like it. But what about a mobile phone, or a car, or a laptop computer, or any other *consumer durable*? In each of these cases you are buying something that will last you a long time, and the further into the future you look, the less certain you will be of its costs and benefits to you.

Take the case of a washing machine costing you £300. If you pay cash, your immediate outlay involves no uncertainty: it is £300. But washing machines can break down. In two years' time you could find yourself with a repair bill of £100. This cannot be predicted and yet it is a price you will have to pay, just like the original £300. In other words, when you buy the washing machine, you are uncertain as to the full 'price' it will entail over its lifetime.

If the costs of the washing machine are uncertain, so too are the benefits. You might have been attracted to buy it in the first place by the manufacturer's glossy brochure, or by the look of it, or by adverts on TV, in magazines, etc. When you have used it for a while, however, you might discover things you had not anticipated. Perhaps the cycle takes longer than you had hoped; perhaps the machine is noisy, or it leaks, or the door sticks; and so on.

Buying consumer durables thus involves uncertainty. So too does the purchase of assets, whether a physical asset such as a house or financial assets such as shares. In the case of assets, the uncertainty is over their future *price*. If you buy shares in a company, what will happen to their price? Will it shoot up, thus enabling you to sell them at a large profit, or will it fall? You cannot know for certain.

Definition

Consumer durable A consumer good that lasts a period of time, during which the consumer can continue gaining utility from it.

THRESHOLD CONCEPT 9 | **PEOPLE'S ACTIONS DEPEND ON THEIR EXPECTATIONS** | THINKING LIKE AN ECONOMIST

Many, if not most, economic actions are taken before the benefits are enjoyed. Thus, you work first and get paid later – at the end of the week or month, or whatever. Similarly, you buy something in a shop today, and consume it later. In the case of a product like a food item from the supermarket, you will probably consume it fairly soon and pretty well all at once. In the case of many 'consumer durables', such as cars or electrical goods, you enjoy them over a much longer period.

It is the same with firms. What they produce today will be sold at some point in the future. In other words, firms typically incur costs first and receive revenues later. In the case of investing in new buildings or equipment, it may be a very long time before the firm starts seeing profits from the investment.

In each of these cases, then, the decision is made to do something now in anticipation of what will happen in the future. The threshold concept here is that decision making is only as good as the information on which it is based. If your expectations turn out to be wrong, a seemingly good decision may turn out disastrously – as many failed businesses bear witness! Part of what we do as economists is to examine how people get information and on what basis they form their expectations; part of what we do is to forecast the future.

Whenever information about the future is imperfect, as it nearly always will be, then there are risks involved in basing decisions on such information. Businesses constantly have to live with risk: risk that market prices will decline, that costs will rise, that supplies will not arrive, that machinery will break down, that competitors will launch new and better products, and so on. But in our everyday lives, we too face risks because of poor information about the future. Do you spend money on a holiday in this country and risk having a wet week? Do you go to the cinema to see a film, only to find out that you don't enjoy it?

Sometimes you lack information simply because you have not taken the time or paid the money to acquire it. This could apply to the specifications of a product. A little research could give you the information you require. Sometimes, however, the information is simply not available – at least not in the form that will give you certainty. A firm may do market research to find out what consumers want, but until a product is launched, it will not be certain how much will be sold. A market analyst may give you a forecast of what will happen to stock market prices or to the dollar/euro exchange rate, but analysts frequently get it wrong.

1. *What risks are involved in buying a house?*
2. *Give some examples of ways in which it is possible to buy better information. Your answer should suggest that there is profitable business to be made in supplying information.*
3. *Is there a role for government intervention in the provision of information? (We return to this in Chapter 11).*

> **KEY IDEA 15** Good decision making requires good information. Where information is poor, decisions and their outcomes may be poor.

The problems surrounding making decisions today based on expectations of the future are explored in Threshold Concept 9.

Attitudes towards risk and uncertainty

So how will uncertainty affect people's behaviour? The answer is that it depends on their attitudes towards taking a gamble. To examine these attitudes let us assume that a person does at least know the *odds* of the gamble. In other words, the person is operating under conditions of *risk* rather than *uncertainty*.

 KI 11 p75

 Define 'risk' and 'uncertainty' (see Chapter 3, pages 75–6).

To illustrate different attitudes towards risk, consider the case of gambling that a particular number will come up on the throw of a dice. There is a one in six chance of this happening. Would you gamble? It depends on what odds you were offered and on your attitude to risk.

Odds can be of three types. They can be *favourable* odds. This is where on average you will gain. If, for example, you were offered odds of 10 to 1 on the throw of a dice, then for a £1 bet you would get nothing if you lost, but you would get £10 (plus your £1 stake) if your number came up. Since your number should come up on average one time in every six, on average you will gain. The longer you go on playing, the more money you are likely to win. If the odds were 5 to 1 (i.e. you win £5 plus get your £1 stake back), they would be *fair* odds. On average you would break even. If, however, they were less than 5 to 1, they would be described as *unfavourable*. On average you would lose.

 Give some examples of gambling (or risk taking in general) where the odds are (a) unfavourable; (b) fair; (c) favourable.

There are three possible categories of attitude towards risk.

Risk neutral. This is where a person will take a gamble if the odds are favourable; not take a gamble if the odds are unfavourable; and be indifferent about taking a gamble if the odds are fair.

Risk loving. Such a person is prepared to take a gamble even if the odds are unfavourable. The more risk loving a person is, the worse the odds he or she will be prepared to accept.

Risk averse. Such a person may not be prepared to take a gamble even if the odds are favourable. The more risk averse people are, the better the odds would have to be to entice them to take a gamble. Few people are *totally risk averse* and thus totally unwilling to take a gamble. If I offered people a bet on the toss of a coin such that tails they pay me 10p and heads I pay them £100, few would refuse (unless on moral grounds).

Diminishing marginal utility of income and attitudes towards risk taking

 KI 13 p97

Avid gamblers may be risk lovers. People who spend hours in the betting shop or at the race track may enjoy the risks, knowing that there is always the chance that they might win. On average, however, such people will lose. After all, the bookies have to take their cut and thus the odds are generally unfavourable.

Most people, however, for most of the time are risk averse. We prefer to avoid insecurity. But why? Is there a simple reason for this? Economists use marginal utility analysis to explain why.

They argue that the gain in utility to people from an extra £100 is less than the loss of utility from forgoing £100. Imagine your own position. You have probably adjusted your standard of living to your income, or are trying to do so. If you unexpectedly gained £100, that would be very nice: you could buy some new clothes or have a weekend away. But if you lost £100, it could be very hard indeed and you might have serious difficulties in making ends meet. Thus if you were offered the gamble of a 50:50 chance of winning or losing £100, you would probably decline the gamble.

 Which gamble would you be more likely to accept, a 60:40 chance of gaining or losing £10 000, or a 40:60 chance of gaining or losing £1? Explain why.

This risk-averting behaviour accords with the principle of *diminishing marginal utility*. Up to now in this chapter we have been focusing on the utility from the consumption of individual goods: Lucy and her cups of tea; Ollie and his packets of crisps. In the case of each individual good, the more we consume, the less satisfaction we gain from each additional unit: the marginal utility falls. But the same principle applies if we look at our *total* consumption. The higher our level of total consumption, the less additional satisfaction will be gained from each additional £1 spent. What we are saying here is that there is a **diminishing marginal utility of income**. The more you earn, the lower

> ## Definition
>
> **Diminishing marginal utility of income** Where each additional pound earned yields less additional utility.

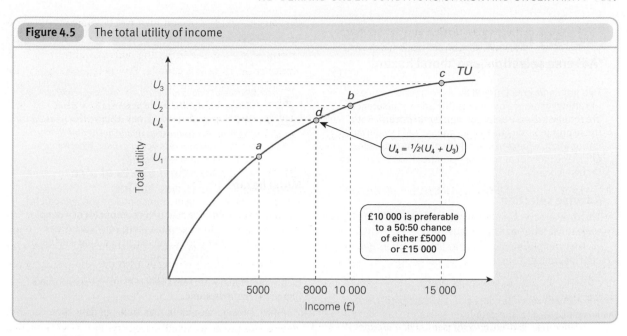

Figure 4.5   The total utility of income

will be the utility gained from each *extra* £1. If people on low incomes earn an extra £100, they will feel a lot better off: their marginal utility from that income will be very high. If rich people earn an extra £100, however, their gain in utility will be less.

 Do you think that this provides a moral argument for redistributing income from the rich to the poor? Does it prove that income should be so redistributed?

Why, then, does a diminishing marginal utility of income make us risk averse? The answer is illustrated in Figure 4.5, which shows the *total* utility you get from your income.

The slope of this curve gives the *marginal* utility of your income. As the marginal utility of income diminishes, so the curve gets flatter. A rise in income from £5000 to £10 000 will cause a movement along the curve from point *a* to point *b*. Total utility rises from U_1 to U_2. A similar rise in income from £10 000 to £15 000, however, will lead to a move from point *b* to point *c*, and hence a *smaller* rise in total utility from U_2 to U_3.

Now assume that your income is £10 000 and you are offered a chance of gambling £5000 of it. You are offered the fair odds of a 50:50 chance of gaining an extra £5000 (i.e. doubling it) or losing it. Effectively, then, you have an equal chance of your income rising to £15 000 or falling to £5000.

At an income of £10 000, your total utility is U_2. If your gamble pays off and raises your income to £15 000, your total utility will rise to U_3. If it does not pay off, you will be left with only £5000 and a utility of U_1. Given that you have a 50:50 chance of winning, your *average* expected utility will be midway between U_1 and U_3 (i.e. U_4). But this is the utility that would be gained from an income of £8000. Given that you would prefer U_2 to U_4 you will choose not to take the gamble.

Thus risk aversion is part of rational utility-maximising behaviour.

 If people are generally risk averse, why do so many around the world take part in national lotteries?

On most occasions we do not know the odds of taking a gamble. In other words, we will be operating under conditions of *uncertainty*. This could make us very cautious indeed. The more pessimistic we are, the more cautious we are.

Insurance: a way of removing risks

Insurance is the opposite of gambling. It takes the risk away. If, for example, you risk losing your job if you are injured, you can remove the risk of loss of income by taking out an appropriate insurance policy.

Since people are generally risk averse, they will be prepared to pay the premiums even though they give them 'unfair odds'. The total premiums paid to an insurance company will be *more* than the amount it pays out: that is how such companies make a profit.

But does this mean that an insurance company is less risk averse than its customers? Why is it prepared to shoulder the risks that its customers were not? The answer is that the insurance company is able to **pool its risks**.

KI 11
p75

Definition

Pooling risks (for an insurance company) The more policies an insurance company issues and the more independent the risks of claims from these policies are, the more predictable will be the number of claims.

BOX 4.5 PROBLEMS WITH INSURANCE MARKETS

EXPLORING ECONOMICS

'Adverse selection' and 'moral hazard'

Two problems encountered by insurance companies in setting insurance premiums (the price of insurance) are termed **adverse selection** and **moral hazard**. Both these problems arise as a consequence of asymmetric information, when the insurance company knows less about the individual seeking insurance than the person themself does.

Adverse selection

This is where the people who take out insurance are likely to be those who have the highest risk.

For example, suppose that a company offers health-care insurance. It surveys the population and works out that the average person requires £200 of treatment per year. The company thus sets the premium at £250 (the extra £50 to cover its costs and provide a profit). But it is probable that the people most likely to take out the insurance are those most likely to fall sick: those who have been ill before, those whose families have a history of illness, those in jobs that are hazardous to health, etc. These people on average may require £500 of treatment per year. The insurance company would soon make a loss.

But cannot the company then simply raise premiums to £550 or £600? It can, but the problem is that the higher premiums will only be attractive to the high-risk individuals. If the company raises the premium it will thereby be depriving the person of average health of reasonably priced insurance and reducing the potential to sell insurance to people who value it.

The answer is for the company to obtain information that will allow it to discriminate more carefully between people. This process is known as 'screening'. There are several methods that the company can adopt. It can ask for personal information about those seeking insurance. For example, if you are applying for health-care insurance, you may have to fill out a questionnaire giving details of your lifestyle and family history. The company may even ask for a medical so that they can have an expert opinion on your level of risk and set an appropriate premium.

The second form of screening occurs when an insurance company makes use of market data to assess risk. For example, companies offering life insurance can make use of life expectancy tables produced annually by the National Office of Statistics.

1. *What details does an insurance company require to know before it will insure a person to drive a car?*
2. *The European Commission has proposed on occasion that insurance companies should not be able to vary premiums according to age or gender. What would be the impact of such legislation?*

Moral hazard

This occurs when having insurance makes you less careful and thus increases your risk to the company. For example, if your bicycle is insured against theft, you may be less concerned to go through the hassle of chaining it up each time you leave it. This is an example of an information failure, because the insurance company cannot determine for any individual whether taking out insurance will make him or her more careless.

Again, if insurance companies work out risks by looking at the total number of bicycle thefts, these figures will understate the risks to the company because they will include thefts from uninsured people who are likely to be more careful. One answer is for insurance companies to write contracts that allow them to reduce the incidence of moral hazard.

How will the following reduce moral hazard?
(a) A no-claims bonus.
(b) An excess, which means that the claimant has to pay the first so many pounds of any claim.
(c) Offering lower premiums to those less likely to claim (e.g. lower house contents premiums for those with burglar alarms).

The problem of moral hazard occurs in many other walks of life. A good example is that of debt. If someone else is willing to pay your debts (e.g. your parents) it is likely to make you less careful in your spending! This has been used by some rich countries as an argument for not cancelling the debts of poor countries (see section 27.4).

Insurance market failure

If the problems of adverse selection and moral hazard cannot be overcome by screening and carefully written contracts then this is not a problem for them alone. Most people in society are risk averse and are willing to pay others to reduce the risk that they face. Insurance markets have grown up in response to this. If insurance markets fail, then society suffers as a consequence.

Definitions

Adverse selection The tendency of those who are at greatest risk to take out insurance.

Moral hazard The temptation to take more risk when you know that other people (e.g. insurers) will cover the risks.

The pooling of risks

Suppose that each year there is a one in a hundred chance of your house burning down. Although this is only a small chance, it would be so disastrous that you are simply not prepared to take the risk. You thus take out house insurance and are prepared to pay a premium of *more than* 1 per cent (one in a hundred).

The insurance company, however, is not just insuring you. It is insuring thousands of others at the same time. If your house burns down, there will be approximately 99 others that do not. The premiums the insurance company has collected will be more than enough to cover its payments. The more houses it insures, the smaller will be the variation in the proportion that actually burn down each year.

This is an application of the *law of large numbers*. What is unpredictable for an individual becomes highly predictable in the mass. The more people the insurance company insures, the more predictable is the total outcome.

What is more, the insurance company is in a position to estimate just what the risks are. It can thus work out what premiums it must charge in order to make a profit. Insurance companies even share data amongst themselves to make the estimation of such risk more accurate. With individuals, however, the precise risk is rarely known. Do you know your chances of living to 80? Almost certainly you do not. But a life assurance company has the statistical data to work out precisely the chances of a person of your age, sex and occupation living to 80! It can convert your *uncertainty* into the company's *risk*.

The pooling of risks does not just require a large number of policies. It also requires the risks to be **independent**. If an insurance company insured 1000 houses *all in the same neighbourhood*, and then there were a major fire in the area, the claims would be enormous. The risks of fire were not independent. The company would, in fact, have been taking a gamble on a single event. If, however, it provides fire insurance for houses scattered all over the country, the risks *are* independent.

1. *Why are insurance companies unwilling to provide insurance against losses arising from war or 'civil insurrection'?*
2. *Name some other events where it would be impossible to obtain insurance.*

Another way in which insurance companies can spread their risks is by **diversification**. The more types of insurance a company offers (car, house, life, health, etc.), the greater is likely to be the independence of the risks.

Definitions

Law of large numbers The larger the number of events of a particular type, the more predictable will be their average outcome.

Independent risks Where two risky events are unconnected. The occurrence of one will not affect the likelihood of the occurrence of the other.

Diversification Where a firm expands into new types of business

---

Section summary

1. When people buy consumer durables, they may be uncertain of their benefits and any additional repair and maintenance costs. When they buy financial assets, they may be uncertain of what will happen to their price in the future. Buying under these conditions of imperfect knowledge is therefore a form of gambling. When we take such gambles, if we know the odds we are said to be operating under conditions of risk. If we do not know the odds, we are said to be operating under conditions of uncertainty.

2. People can be divided into risk lovers, those who are risk averse and those who are risk neutral. Because of the diminishing marginal utility of income, it is rational for people to be risk averse (unless gambling is itself pleasurable).

3. Insurance is a way of eliminating risks for policy holders. Being risk averse, people are prepared to pay premiums in order to obtain insurance. Insurance companies, on the other hand, are prepared to take on these risks because they can spread them over a large number of policies. According to the law of large numbers, what is unpredictable for a single policy holder becomes highly predictable for a large number of them provided that their risks are independent of each other.

---

*4.3 INDIFFERENCE ANALYSIS

The limitations of the marginal utility approach to demand

Even though the multi-commodity version of marginal utility theory is useful in demonstrating the underlying logic of consumer choice, it still has a major weakness.

Utility cannot be measured in any absolute sense. We cannot really say, therefore, by *how much* the marginal utility of one good exceeds another.

An alternative approach is to use *indifference analysis*. This does not involve measuring the *amount* of utility a person gains, but merely *ranking* various combinations of goods in order of preference. In other words, it assumes that consumers can decide whether they prefer one combination of goods to another. For example, if you were asked to choose between two baskets of fruit, one containing 4 oranges and 3 pears and the other containing 2 oranges and 5 pears, you could say which you prefer or whether you are indifferent between them. It does not assume that you can decide just *how much* you prefer one basket to another or just how much you like either.

The aim of indifference analysis, then, is to analyse, *without having to measure utility*, how a rational consumer chooses between two goods. As we shall see, it can be used to show the effect on this choice of (a) a change in the consumer's income and (b) a change in the price of one or both goods. It can also be used to analyse the income and substitution effects of a change in price.

Indifference analysis involves the use of *indifference curves* and *budget lines*.

Indifference curves

An **indifference curve** shows all the various combinations of two goods that give an equal amount of satisfaction or utility to a consumer.

To show how one can be constructed, consider the following example. Imagine that a supermarket is conducting a survey about the preferences of its customers for different types of fruit. One of the respondents is Ali, a student who likes a healthy diet and regularly buys fresh fruit. He is asked his views about various combinations of oranges and pears. Starting with the combination of 10 pears and 13 oranges, he is asked what other combinations he would

Table 4.2	Combinations of pears and oranges that Ali likes the same amount as 10 pears and 13 oranges	
Pears	**Oranges**	**Point in Figure 4.6**
30	6	a
24	7	b
20	8	c
14	10	d
10	13	e
8	15	f
6	20	g

like the same amount as this one. From his answers a table is constructed (Table 4.2). What we are saying here is that Ali would be equally happy to have any one of the combinations shown in the table.

This table is known as an **indifference set**. It shows alternative combinations of two goods that yield the same level of satisfaction. From this we can plot an indifference curve. We measure units of one good on one axis and units of the other good on the other axis. Thus in Figure 4.6, which is based on Table 4.2, pears and oranges are measured on the two axes. The curve shows that Ali is indifferent as to whether he consumes 30 pears and 6 oranges (point *a*) or 24 pears and 7 oranges (point *b*) or any other combination of pears and oranges along the curve.

Notice that we are not saying *how much* Ali likes pears and oranges; merely that he likes all the combinations along the indifference curve the same amount. All the combinations thus yield the same (unspecified) utility.

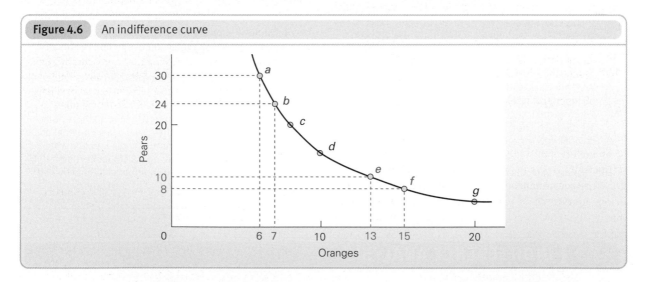

Figure 4.6 An indifference curve

Definitions

Indifference curve A line showing all those combinations of two goods between which a consumer is indifferent: i.e. those combinations that give the same level of utility.

Indifference set A table showing the same information as an indifference curve.

The shape of the indifference curve

As you can see, the indifference curve we have drawn is not a straight line. It is bowed in towards the origin. In other words, its slope gets shallower as we move down the curve. Indifference curves are normally drawn this shape. But why?

Let us see what the slope of the curve shows us. It shows the rate at which the consumer is willing to exchange one good for the other, holding his or her level of satisfaction the same. For example, consider the move from point *a* to point *b* in Figure 4.6. Ali gives up 6 units of pears and requires 1 orange to compensate for the loss. The slope of the indifference curve is thus −6/1 = −6. Ignoring the negative sign, the slope of the indifference curve (that is, the rate at which the consumer is willing to substitute one good for the other) is known as the *marginal rate of substitution* (*MRS*). In this case, therefore, the *MRS* = 6.

Note that as we move down the curve, the marginal rate of substitution diminishes as the slope of the curve gets less. For example, look at the move from point *e* to point *f*. Here the consumer gives up 2 pears and requires 2 oranges to compensate. Thus along this section of the curve, the slope is −2/2 = −1 (and hence the *MRS* = 1).

The reason for a *diminishing marginal rate of substitution* is related to the *principle of diminishing marginal utility* that we looked at in section 4.1. This stated that individuals will gain less and less additional satisfaction the more of a good that they consume. This principle, however, is based on the assumption that the consumption of other goods is held *constant*. In the case of an indifference curve, this is not true. As we move down the curve, more of one good is consumed but *less* of the other. Nevertheless the effect on consumer satisfaction is similar. As Ali consumes more pears and fewer oranges, his marginal utility from pears will diminish, while that from oranges will increase. He will thus be prepared to give up fewer and fewer pears for each additional orange. *MRS* diminishes.

The relationship between the marginal rate of substitution and marginal utility

In Figure 4.6, consumption at point *a* yields equal satisfaction with consumption at point *b*. Thus the utility sacrificed by giving up 6 pears must be equal to the utility gained by consuming one more orange. In other words, the marginal utility of an orange must be six times as great as that of a pear. Therefore, $MU_{oranges}/MU_{pears} = 6$. But this is the same as the marginal rate of substitution. With X measured on the horizontal axis and Y on the vertical axis, then

$$MRS = \frac{MU_X}{MU_Y} = \frac{\text{slope of indifference curve}}{\text{(ignoring negative sign)}}$$

 Although indifference curves will normally be bowed in towards the origin, on odd occasions they might not be. Which of the following diagrams correspond to which of the following? Explain the shape of each curve.

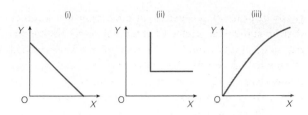

(a) *X and Y are left shoes and right shoes.*
(b) *X and Y are two brands of the same product, and the consumer cannot tell them apart.*
(c) *X is a good but Y is a 'bad' – like household refuse.*

An indifference map

More than one indifference curve can be drawn. For example, referring back to Table 4.2, Ali could give another set of combinations of pears and oranges that all give him a higher (but equal) level of utility than the set shown in the table. This could then be plotted in Figure 4.6 as another indifference curve.

Although the actual amount of utility corresponding to each curve is not specified, indifference curves further out to the right would show combinations of the two goods that yield a higher utility, and curves further in to the left would show combinations yielding a lower utility.

In fact, a whole *indifference map* can be drawn, with each successive indifference curve showing a higher level of utility. Combinations of goods along I_2 in Figure 4.7 give a higher utility to the consumer than those along I_1. Those along I_3 give a higher utility than those along I_2, and so on. The term 'map' is appropriate here, because the indifference curves are rather like contours on a real map. Just as a contour joins all those points of a particular height, so an indifference curve shows all those combinations yielding a particular level of utility.

 Draw another two indifference curves on Figure 4.6, one outward from and one inward from the original curve. Read off various combinations of pears and oranges along these two new curves and enter them on a table like Table 4.2.

Definitions

Marginal rate of substitution (between two goods in consumption) The amount of one good (Y) that a consumer is prepared to give up in order to obtain one extra unit of another good (X): i.e. $\Delta Y/\Delta X$.

Diminishing marginal rate of substitution The more a person consumes of good X and the less of good Y, the less additional Y will that person be prepared to give up in order to obtain an extra unit of X: i.e. $\Delta Y/\Delta X$ diminishes.

Indifference map A graph showing a whole set of indifference curves. The further away a particular curve is from the origin, the higher the level of satisfaction it represents.

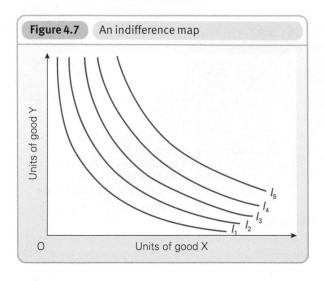

Figure 4.7 An indifference map

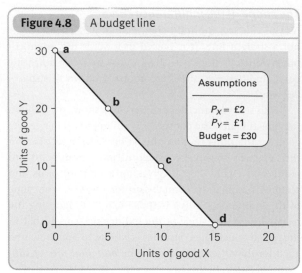

Figure 4.8 A budget line

Assumptions

$P_X = £2$
$P_Y = £1$
Budget = £30

The budget line

We turn now to the **budget line**. This is the other important element in the analysis of consumer behaviour.
Whereas indifference maps illustrate people's preferences,
the *actual* choices they make will depend on their *incomes*.
The budget line shows what combinations of two goods
you are *able* to buy, given (a) your income available to
spend on them and (b) their prices.

Just as we did with an indifference curve, we can construct a budget line from a table. The first two columns of
Table 4.3 show various combinations of two goods X and Y
that can be purchased assuming that (a) the price of X is
£2 and the price of Y is £1 and (b) the consumer has a
budget of £30 to be divided between the two goods.

In Figure 4.8, then, if you are limited to a budget of
£30, you can consume any combination of X and Y along
the line (or inside it). You cannot, however, afford to buy
combinations that lie outside it: i.e. in the darker shaded
area. This area is known as the *infeasible region* for the given
budget.

We have said that the amount people can afford to buy
will depend on (a) their budget and (b) the prices of the two
goods. We can show how a change in either of these two
determinants will affect the budget line.

A change in income

If the consumer's income (and hence budget) increases,
the budget line will shift outwards, parallel to the old one.
This is illustrated in the last two columns of Table 4.3 and
in Figure 4.9, which show the effect of a rise in the consumer's budget from £30 to £40. (Note that there is no
change in the prices of X and Y, which remain at £2 and
£1 respectively.)

Table 4.3 Consumption possibilities for budgets of £30 and £40

	Budget of £30		Budget of £40	
Units of good X	Units of good Y	Point on budget line in Figure 4.8	Units of good X	Units of good Y
0	30	a	0	40
5	20	b	5	30
10	10	c	10	20
15	0	d	15	10
			20	0

Note: It is assumed that $P_X = £2$, $P_Y = £1$.

Definitions

Budget line A graph showing all the possible
combinations of two goods that can be purchased
at given prices and for a given budget.

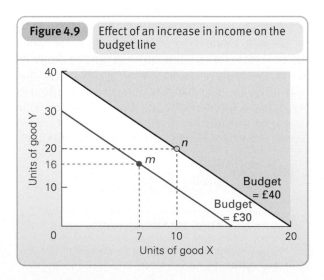

Figure 4.9 Effect of an increase in income on the budget line

Figure 4.10 Effect on the budget line of a fall in the price of good X

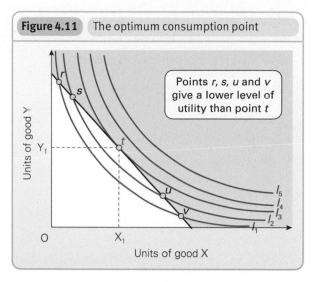

Figure 4.11 The optimum consumption point

Points *r*, *s*, *u* and *v* give a lower level of utility than point *t*

More can now be purchased. For example, if the consumer was originally purchasing 7 units of X and 16 units of Y (point *m*), this could be increased with the new budget of £40, to 10 units of X and 20 units of Y (point *n*) or any other combination of X and Y along the new higher budget line.

A change in price

The relative prices of the two goods are given by the *slope* of the budget line. The slope of the budget line in Figure 4.8 is 30/15 = 2. (We are ignoring the negative sign: strictly speaking, the slope should be –2.) Similarly, the slope of the new higher budget line in Figure 4.9 is 40/20 = 2. But in each case this is simply the ratio of the *price* of X (£2) to the *price* of Y (£1).

Thus the slope of the budget line equals

$$\frac{P_X}{P_Y}$$

If the price of either good changes, the slope of the budget line will change. This is illustrated in Figure 4.10 which, like Figure 4.8, assumes a budget of £30 and an initial price of X of £2 and a price of Y of £1. The initial budget line is B_1.

Now let us assume that the price of X falls to £1 but that the price of Y remains the same (£1). The new budget line will join 30 on the Y axis with 30 on the X axis. In other words, the line pivots outwards on point *a*. If, instead, the price of Y changed, the line would pivot on point *b*.

1. Assume that the budget remains at £30 and the price of X stays at £2, but that Y rises in price to £3. Draw the new budget line.
2. What will happen to the budget line if the consumer's income doubles and the prices of both X and Y double?

The optimum consumption point

We are now in a position to put the two elements of the analysis together: the indifference map and a budget line.

This will enable us to show how much of each of the two goods the 'rational' consumer will buy from a given budget. Let us examine Figure 4.11.

The consumer would like to consume along the highest possible indifference curve. This is curve I_3 at point *t*. Higher indifference curves, such as I_4 and I_5, although representing higher utility than curve I_3, are in the infeasible region: they represent combinations of X and Y that cannot be afforded with the current budget. The consumer *could* consume along curves I_1 and I_2, between points *r* and *v*, and *s* and *u* respectively, but they give a lower level of utility than consuming at point *t*.

The optimum consumption point for the consumer, then, is where the budget line touches (is 'tangential to') the highest possible indifference curve. At any other point along the budget line, the consumer would get a lower level of utility.

If the budget line is tangential to an indifference curve, they will have the same slope. (The slope of a curve is the slope of the tangent to it at the point in question.) But as we have seen, the slope of the budget line is

$$\frac{P_X}{P_Y}$$

and the slope of the indifference curve is

$$MRS = \frac{MU_X}{MU_Y}$$

Therefore, at the optimum consumption point

$$\frac{P_X}{P_Y} = \frac{MU_X}{MU_Y}$$

But this is the *equi-marginal principle* that we established in the first part of this chapter: only this time, using the indifference curve approach, there has been no need to measure utility. All we have needed to do is to observe, for any two combinations of goods, whether the consumer preferred one to the other or was indifferent between them.

TC 8 p100

KI 14 p102

*LOOKING AT THE MATHS

We can express the optimum consumption point algebraically. With a limited budget of B, the objective is to maximise utility subject to this budget constraint. This can be expressed as

$$\text{Max } TU(X, Y) \qquad (1)$$

subject to the budget constraint that

$$P_X X + P_Y Y = B \qquad (2)$$

Equation (1) is known as the 'objective function' and says that the objective is to maximise utility, which depends on the consumption of two goods, X and Y. For example, assume that the utility function is

$$TU = X^{3/4} Y^{1/4}$$

This is known as a 'Cobb–Douglas utility function' and will give smooth convex indifference curves. Assume also that the price of X is 4, the price of Y is 2 and the budget is 64. Thus:

$$4X + 2Y = 64$$

Rearranging this constraint to express X in terms of Y gives

$$X = 16 - \frac{Y}{2}$$

By first substituting this value of X into the utility function (so that it is expressed purely in terms of Y) and then differentiating the resulting equation and setting it equal to zero, we can solve for the value of Y and then X that yields the maximum utility for the given budget. The answer is:

$$X = 12 \text{ and } Y = 8$$

The workings of this are given in Maths Case 4.1 in MyEconLab.

An alternative method, which is slightly longer but is likely to involve simpler calculations, involves the use of 'Lagrangian multipliers'. This method is explained, along with a worked example, in Maths Case 4.2.

Figure 4.12   Effect on consumption of a change in income

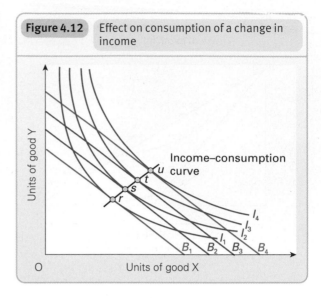

In Figure 4.12 a series of budget lines are drawn representing different levels of consumer income. The corresponding optimum consumption points (r, s, t, u) are shown. Each point is where the new higher budget line just touches the highest possible indifference curve.[1] The line joining these points is known as the *income–consumption curve*.

If your money income goes up and the price of goods does not change, we say that your *real income* has risen. In other words, you can buy more than you did before. But your real income can also rise even if you do not earn any more money. This will happen if prices fall. For the same amount of money, you can buy more goods than previously. We analyse the effect of a rise in real income caused by a fall in prices in just the same way as we did when money income rose and prices stayed the same. Provided the *relative* prices of the two goods stay the same (i.e. provided they fall by the same percentage), the budget line will shift outwards parallel to the old one.

The effect of changes in income

As we have seen, an increase in income is represented by a parallel shift outwards of the budget line (assuming no change in the price of X and Y). This will then lead to a new optimum consumption point on a higher indifference curve. A different consumption point will be found for each different level of income.

[1] We can always draw in an indifference curve that will be tangential to a given budget line. Just because we only draw a few indifference curves on a diagram, it does not mean that there are only a few possible ones. We could draw as many as we liked. Again it is rather like the contours on a real map. They may be drawn at, say, 10 metre intervals. We could, however, if we liked, draw them at 1 metre or even 1 cm intervals, or at whatever height was suitable to our purpose. For example, if the maximum height of a lake were 32.45 metres above sea level, it might be useful to draw a contour at that height to show what land might be liable to flooding.

Definitions

Income–consumption curve A line showing how a person's optimum level of consumption of two goods changes as income changes (assuming the prices of the goods remain constant).

Real income Income measured in terms of how much it can buy. If your *money* income rises by 10 per cent, but prices rise by 8 per cent, you can buy only 2 per cent more goods than before. Your *real* income has risen by 2 per cent.

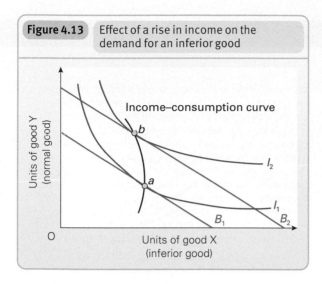

Figure 4.13 Effect of a rise in income on the demand for an inferior good

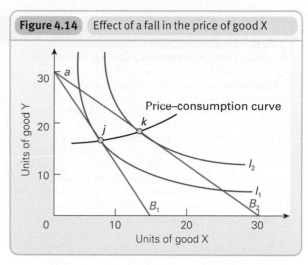

Figure 4.14 Effect of a fall in the price of good X

Income elasticity of demand and the income–consumption curve

The income–consumption curve in Figure 4.12 shows that the demand for both goods rises as income rises. Thus both goods have a positive income elasticity of demand: they are both normal goods.

 Now let us focus just on good X. If the income–consumption curve became flatter at higher levels of income, it would show an increasing proportion of income being spent on X. The flatter it became, the higher would be the income elasticity of demand for X.

If, by contrast, X were an inferior good, such as cheap margarine, its demand would fall as income rose; its income elasticity of demand would be negative. This is illustrated in Figure 4.13. Point *b* is to the left of point *a*, showing that at the higher income B_2, less X is purchased.

1. *The income–consumption curve in Figure 4.13 is drawn as positively sloped at low levels of income. Why?*
2. *Show the effect of a rise in income on the demand for X and Y, where this time Y is the inferior good and X is the normal good. Is the income–consumption curve positively or negatively sloped?*

The effect of changes in price

If either X or Y changes in price, the budget line will 'pivot'. Take the case of a reduction in the price of X (but no change in the price of Y). If this happens, the budget line will swing outwards. We saw this effect in Figure 4.10 (on page 113). These same budget lines are reproduced in Figure 4.14, but this time we have added indifference curves.

The old optimum consumption point was at *j*. After the reduction in the price of good X, a new optimum consumption point is found at *k*.

Illustrate on an indifference diagram the effects of the following:
(a) *A rise in the price of good X (assuming no change in the price of Y).*
(b) *A fall in the price of good Y (assuming no change in the price of X).*

A series of budget lines could be drawn, all pivoting round point *a* in Figure 4.14. Each one represents a different price of good X, but with money income and the price of Y held constant. The flatter the curve, the lower the price of X. At each price, there will be an optimum consumption point. The line that connects these points is known as the *price–consumption curve*.

Deriving the individual's demand curve

We can use the analysis of price changes to show how in theory a person's demand curve for a product can be derived. To do this we need to modify the diagram slightly.

Let us assume that we want to derive a person's demand curve for good X. What we need to show is the effect on the consumption of X of a change in the price of X assuming the prices of all other goods are held constant. To do this we need to redefine good Y. Instead of being a *single* good, Y becomes the total of *all other* goods. But what units are we to put on the vertical axis? Each of these other goods

Definition

Price–consumption curve A line showing how a person's optimum level of consumption of two goods changes as the price of one of the two goods changes (assuming that income and the price of the other good remain constant).

*BOX 4.6   LOVE AND CARING

An economic approach to family behaviour

We have been using indifference analysis to analyse a single individual's choices between two goods. The principles of rational choice, however, can be extended to many other fields of human behaviour. These include situations where people are members of groups and where one person's behaviour affects another. Examples include how friends treat each other, how sexual partners interrelate, how parents treat children, how chores are shared out in a family, how teams are organised, how people behave to each other at work, and so on.

In all these cases, decisions are constantly having to be made. Generally people try to make the 'best' decisions, decisions which will maximise the interests of the individual or the members of the group, decisions that are 'rational'. This will involve weighing up (consciously or subconsciously) the costs and benefits of alternative courses of action to find out which is in the individual's or group's best interests.

One of the pioneers of this approach has been Gary Becker (1930–). Becker has been a professor at Chicago University since 1970 and is regarded as a member of the 'Chicago school', a group of economists from the university who advocate the market as the best means of solving economic problems. He is also a member of the free-market pressure group called the Mont Pelerin Society (see Box 11.7).

Gary Becker has attempted to apply simple economic principles of rational choice to a whole range of human activities, including racial and sexual discrimination, competition in politics, and criminal behaviour. Much of his work, however, has focused on the family, a field previously thought to be the domain of sociologists, anthropologists and psychologists. Even when family members are behaving lovingly and unselfishly, they nevertheless, according to Becker, tend to behave

'rationally' in the economists' sense of trying to maximise their interests, only in this case their 'interests' include the welfare of the other members of their family.

A simple illustration of this approach is given in the diagram below. It assumes, for simplicity, that there are just two members of the family, Judy and Warren. Warren's consumption is measured on the horizontal axis; Judy's on the vertical. Their total joint income is given by Y_T. The line $Y_T Y_T$ represents their consumption possibilities. If Warren were to spend their entire joint income on himself, he would consume at point g. If Judy were to spend their entire joint income on herself, she would consume at point f.

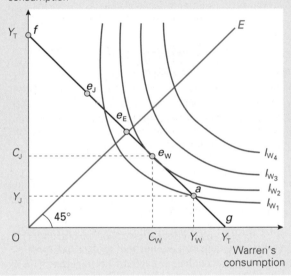

will be in different units: litres of petrol, loaves of bread, kilograms of cheese, numbers of haircuts, etc. We cannot add them all up unless we first convert them to a common unit. The answer is to measure them as the total amount of money spent on them: i.e. what is *not* spent on good X.

With expenditure on all other goods plotted on the vertical axis and with income, tastes and the price of all other goods held constant, we can now derive the demand curve for X. This is demonstrated in Figure 4.15.

We illustrate the changes in the price of X by pivoting the budget line on the point where it intersects the vertical axis. It is then possible, by drawing a price–consumption line, to show the amount of X demanded at each price. It is then a simple matter of transferring these price–quantity relationships on to a demand curve. In Figure 4.15, each of the points *a*, *b*, *c* and *d* on the demand curve in the lower part of the diagram corresponds to one of the four points on the price–consumption curve. (Note that P_2 is half of P_1, P_3 is one-third of P_1 and P_4 is one-quarter of P_1.)

 As quantity demanded increases from Q_1 to Q_2 in Figure 4.15, the expenditure on all other goods decreases. (Point b is lower than point a.) This means, therefore, that the person's total expenditure on X has correspondingly increased. What, then, can we say about the person's price elasticity of demand for X between points a and b? What can we say about the price elasticity of demand between points b and c, and between points c and d?

The income and substitution effects of a price change

In Chapter 2 we argued that when the price of a good rises, consumers will purchase less of it for two reasons:

- They cannot afford to buy so much. This is the *income effect*.
- The good is now more expensive relative to other goods. Therefore consumers substitute alternatives for it. This is the *substitution effect*.

Let us assume that Warren works full time and Judy works part time. As a result Warren earns more than Judy. He earns Y_W; she earns Y_J. If each spent their own incomes on themselves alone, they would consume at point a.

But now let us assume that Warren loves Judy, and that he would prefer to consume less than Y_W to allow her to consume more than Y_J. His preferences are shown by the indifference curves. Each curve shows all the various combinations of consumption between Warren and Judy that give Warren equal satisfaction. (Note that because he loves Judy, he gets satisfaction from her consumption: her happiness gives him pleasure.)

Warren's optimum distribution of consumption between himself and Judy is at point e_W. This is the highest of his indifference curves that can be reached with a joint income of Y_T. At this point he consumes C_W; she consumes C_J.

If he loved Judy 'as himself' and wanted to share their income out equally, then the indifference curves would be shallower. The tangency point to the highest indifference curve would be on the 45° line OE. Consumption would be at point e_E.

Similar indifference curves could be drawn for Judy. Her optimum consumption point might be at point e_J. But if she loved Warren 'as herself', her optimum point would then be at point e_E.

Some interesting conclusions can be drawn from this analysis:

- Income redistribution (i.e. consumption redistribution) within the family can be to the benefit of all the members. In the case we have been considering, both Warren and Judy gain from a redistribution of income from point a to point e_W. The only area of

contention is between points e_W and e_J. Here negotiation would have to take place. This might be in return for some favour. 'If you'll let me have the money I need for that new coat, I'll do the washing up for a whole month.'

- In the case of each one loving the other as him- or herself, there is no area of contention. They are both happiest with consumption at point e_E.
- In the case of 'extreme love', where each partner would prefer the other to have more than him- or herself, point e_W would be above point e_E, and point e_J would be below point e_E. In this case, each would be trying to persuade the other to have more than he or she wanted. Here a different type of negotiation would be needed. 'I'll only let you buy me that coat if you let me do the washing up for a whole month.'
- Some forms of consumption benefit both partners. Household furniture or a new car would be cases in point. Any such purchases would have the effect of shifting the consumption point out beyond line $Y_T Y_T$, and could lead to both partners consuming on a higher indifference curve. This shows the 'economic' advantages of the collective consumption that can be experienced in households or other groups (such as clubs).

1. *If Judy earned more than Warren, show how much income she would redistribute to him if (a) she cared somewhat for him; (b) she loved him 'as herself'. Draw her indifference curves in each of these two cases.*
2. *In the case where they both love each other 'as themselves', will their two sets of indifference curves be identical?*

We can extend our arguments from Chapter 2 by demonstrating the income and substitution effects with the use of indifference analysis. Let us start with the case of a normal good and show what happens when its price changes.

A normal good

In Figure 4.16 the price of **normal good** X has *risen* and the budget line has pivoted *inwards* from B_1 to B_2. The con-

sumption point has moved from point f to point h. Part of this shift in consumption is due to the substitution effect and part is due to the income effect.

The substitution effect. To separate these two effects a new budget line is drawn, parallel to B_2 but tangential to the original indifference curve I_1. This is the line B_{1a}. Being parallel to B_2, it represents the new price ratio (i.e. the higher price of X). Being tangential to I_1, however, it enables the consumer to obtain the *same utility* as before: in other words, there is no loss in *real* income to the consumer. By focusing, then, on B_{1a}, which represents no change in real income, we have excluded the income effect. The movement from point f to point g is due *purely* to a change in the relative prices of X and Y. The movement from Q_{X_1} to Q_{X_2} is the *substitution* effect.

The income effect. In reality, the budget line has shifted to B_2 and the consumer is forced to consume on a lower

Definitions

Income effect of a price change That portion of the change in quantity demanded that results from the change in real income.

Substitution effect of a price change That portion of the change in quantity demanded that results from the change in the relative price of the good.

Normal good A good whose demand increases as income increases.

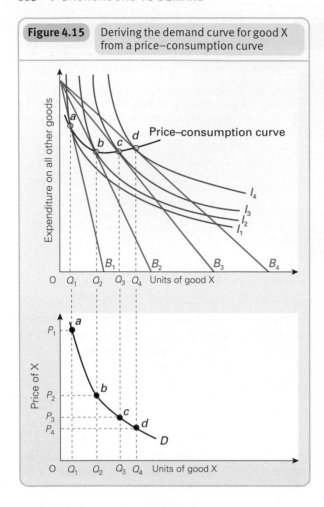

Figure 4.15   Deriving the demand curve for good X from a price–consumption curve

Figure 4.16   The income and substitution effects of a rise in the price of good X if X is a normal good

← Substitution effect
← Income effect
Units of good X

An inferior good

As we saw above, when people's incomes rise, they will buy less of **inferior goods** such as poor-quality margarine and cheap powdered instant coffee, since they will now be able to afford better-quality goods instead. Conversely, when their income falls, they will have to reduce their living standards: their consumption of inferior goods will thus rise.

The substitution effect.   If the *price* of an inferior good (good X) rises, the substitution effect will be in the same direction as for a normal good: i.e. it will be negative. People will consume less X relative to Y, since X is now more expensive relative to Y. For example, if the price of inferior-quality margarine (good X) went up, people would tend to use better-quality margarine or butter (good Y) instead. This is illustrated in Figure 4.17 by a movement along the original indifference curve (I_1) from point *f* to point *g*. The quantity of X demanded falls from Q_{X_1} to Q_{X_2}.

The income effect.   The income effect of the price rise, however, will be the opposite of that for a normal good: it will be *positive*. The reduction in real income from the rise in price of X will tend to *increase* the consumption of X, since with a fall in real income *more* inferior goods will now be purchased – including more X. Thus point *h* is to the *right* of point *g*: the income effect increases quantity back from Q_{X_2} to Q_{X_3}.

indifference curve I_2: real income has fallen. Thus the movement from Q_{X_2} to Q_{X_3} is the *income* effect.

In the case of a normal good, therefore, the income and substitution effects of a price change reinforce each other. They are both negative: they *both* involve a *reduction* in the quantity demanded as price *rises* (and vice versa).[1]

The bigger the income and substitution effects, the higher will be the price elasticity of demand for good X.

Illustrate on two separate indifference diagrams the income and substitution effects of the following:
(a) A decrease in the price of good X (and no change in the price of good Y).
(b) An increase in the price of good Y (and no change in the price of good X).

---

[1] It is important not to confuse the income effect of a price change from the simple effect on demand of an increase in income. In the latter case, a rise in income will cause a rise in demand for a normal good – a positive effect (and hence there will be a positive income elasticity of demand). In the case of a price reduction, although for a normal good the resulting rise in real income will still cause a rise in demand, it is in *the opposite* direction from the change in price – a negative effect *with respect to price* (and hence there will be a negative price elasticity of demand).

Definition

Inferior good A good whose demand decreases as income increases.

Figure 4.17 The income and substitution effects of a rise in the price of good X if X is an inferior (non-Giffen) good

A Giffen good: a particular type of inferior good

If the inferior good were to account for a very large proportion of a consumer's expenditure, a change in its price would have a significant effect on the consumer's real income, resulting in a large income effect. It is conceivable, therefore, that this large abnormal income effect could outweigh the normal substitution effect. In such a case, a rise in the price of X would lead to *more* X being consumed!

This is illustrated in Figure 4.18, where point *h* is to the *right* of point *f*. In other words, the fall in consumption (Q_{X_1} to Q_{X_2}) as a result of the substitution effect is more than offset by the rise in consumption (Q_{X_2} to Q_{X_3}) as a result of the large positive income effect.

Figure 4.18 The income and substitution effects of a rise in the price of good X if X is a Giffen good

Such a good is known as a ***Giffen good***, after Sir Robert Giffen (1837–1910), who is alleged to have claimed that the consumption of bread by the poor rose when its price rose. Bread formed such a large proportion of poor people's consumption that, if its price went up, the poor could not afford to buy so much meat, vegetables, etc. and had to buy more bread instead. It is possible that in countries in Africa today with very low incomes, staple foods such as manioc and maize are Giffen goods. Naturally, such cases must be very rare indeed and some economists remain unconvinced of their existence, except as a theoretical possibility.

 Could you conceive of any circumstances in which one or more items of your expenditure would become Giffen goods?

The usefulness of indifference analysis

Indifference analysis has made it possible to demonstrate the logic of 'rational' consumer choice, the derivation of the individual's demand curve, and the income and substitution effects of a price change. All this has been done without having to measure utility.

Nevertheless there are limitations to the usefulness of indifference analysis:

- In practice it is virtually impossible to derive indifference curves, since it would involve a consumer having to imagine a whole series of different combinations of goods and deciding in each case whether a given combination gave more, equal or less satisfaction than other combinations.
- Consumers may not behave 'rationally', and hence may not give careful consideration to the satisfaction they believe they will gain from consuming goods. They may behave impetuously.
- Indifference curves are based on the satisfaction that consumers *believe* they will gain from a good. This belief may well be influenced by advertising. Consumers may be disappointed or pleasantly surprised, however, when they actually consume the good. In other words, consumers are not perfectly knowledgeable. Thus the 'optimum consumption' point may not in practice give consumers maximum satisfaction for their money.
- Certain goods are purchased only now and again, and then only one at a time. Examples would include consumer durables such as cars, televisions and washing machines. Indifference curves are based on the assumption that marginal increases in one good can be traded off against marginal decreases in another. This will not be the case with consumer durables.

TC 9
p105

Definition

Giffen good An inferior good whose demand increases as its price increases as a result of a positive income effect larger than the normal negative substitution effect.

*BOX 4.7 **CONSUMER THEORY: A FURTHER APPROACH** EXPLORING ECONOMICS

Characteristics theory

Characteristics theory was developed in the mid 1960s by Kelvin Lancaster. He argued that people demand goods not for their own sake, but for the characteristics they possess.

Take cars, for example. When choosing between the different makes, consumers do not just consider their relative prices, they also consider their attributes: comfort, style, performance, durability, reliability, fuel consumption, etc. It is these characteristics that give rise to utility.

Characteristics theory, then, is based on four crucial assumptions:

- All goods possess various characteristics.
- Different brands possess them in different proportions.
- The characteristics are measurable: they are 'objective'.
- The characteristics (along with price and income) determine consumer choice.

Let us assume that you are choosing between three different goods or brands of a good (e.g. a foodstuff). Each one has a different combination of two characteristics (e.g. protein and calories). Your choices can be shown graphically.

The choice between brands of a product: each brand has different characteristics

The levels of two characteristics are shown on the two axes. An indifference map can be constructed, showing the different combinations of the two characteristics that yield given levels of utility. Thus any combination of the two characteristics along indifference curve I_4 in the diagram gives a higher level of utility than those along I_3, and so on. The shape of the indifference curves (bowed in)

illustrates a diminishing marginal rate of substitution between the two characteristics.

The amounts of the two characteristics given by the three brands are shown by the three rays. The more that is consumed of each brand, the further up the respective ray will the consumer be. Thus at x_1, the consumer is gaining Q_{a_1} of characteristic A and Q_{b_1} of characteristic B.

Assume that, for the same money, the consumer could consume at x_1 with brand (1), x_2 with brand (2) and x_3 with brand (3). The consumer will consume brand (1): x_1 is on a higher indifference curve than x_2 or x_3.

Now assume that the price of brand (2) falls. For a given expenditure, the consumer can now move up the brand (2) ray. But not until the price has fallen enough to allow consumption at point x_4 will the consumer consider switching from brand (1). If price falls enough for consumption to be at point x_5, clearly the consumer will switch.

The characteristics approach has a number of advantages over conventional indifference curve analysis in explaining consumer behaviour.

- It helps to explain brand loyalty. When price changes, people will not necessarily gradually move from one brand to another. Rather they will stick with a brand until a critical price is reached. Then they will switch brands all at once.
- It allows the choice between several goods to be shown on the same diagram. Each good or brand has its own ray.
- It helps to explain the nature of substitute goods. The closer substitutes are, the more similar will be their characteristics and hence the closer will be their rays. The closer the rays, the more likely it is that there will be a shift in consumption to one good when the price of the other good changes.
- A change in the quality of a good can be shown by rotating its ray.

There are weaknesses with the approach, however:

- Some characteristics cannot be measured. Such characteristics as beauty, taste and entertainment value are subjective: they are in the mind of the consumer.
- Only two characteristics can be plotted. Most goods have several characteristics.

1. *Make a list of the characteristics of shoes. Which are 'objective' and which are 'subjective'?*
2. *If two houses had identical characteristics, except that one was near a noisy airport and the other was in a quiet location, and if the market price of the first house were £180 000 and that of the second £200 000, how would that help us to put a value on the characteristic of peace and quiet?*

Characteristics theory is examined in more detail in Case Study 4.6 in MyEconLab.

Section summary

1. The indifference approach to analysing consumer demand avoids having to measure utility.

2. An indifference curve shows all those combinations of two goods that give an equal amount of satisfaction to a consumer. An indifference map can be drawn with indifference curves further to the north-east representing higher (but still unspecified) levels of satisfaction.

3. Indifference curves are usually drawn convex to the origin. This is because of a diminishing marginal rate of substitution between the two goods. As more of one good is purchased, the consumer is willing to give up less and less of the other for each additional unit of the first. The marginal rate of substitution is given by the slope of the indifference curve, which equals MU_X/MU_Y.

4. A budget line can be drawn on an indifference diagram. A budget line shows all those combinations of the two goods that can be purchased for a given amount of money, assuming a constant price of the two goods. The slope of the budget line depends on the relative price of the two goods. The slope is equal to P_X/P_Y.

5. The consumer will achieve the maximum level of satisfaction for a given income (budget) by consuming at the point where the budget line just touches the highest possible indifference curve. At this point of tangency, the budget line and the indifference curve have the same slope. Thus $MU_X/MU_Y = P_X/P_Y$, which is the 'equi-marginal principle' for maximising utility from a given income that was established in section 4.1.

6. If the consumer's real income (and hence budget) rises, there will be a parallel outward shift of the budget line. The 'rational' consumer will move to the point of tangency of this new budget line with the highest indifference curve. The line that traces out these optimum positions for different levels of income is known as the 'income–consumption curve'.

7. If the price of one of the two goods changes, the budget line will pivot on the axis of the other good. An outward pivot represents a fall in price; an inward pivot represents an increase in price. The line that traces the tangency points of these budget lines with the appropriate indifference curves is called a 'price–consumption curve'.

8. By measuring the expenditure on all other goods on the vertical axis and by holding their price constant and money income constant, a demand curve can be derived for the good measured on the horizontal axis. Changes in its price can be represented by pivoting the budget line. The effect on the quantity demanded can be found from the resulting price–consumption curve.

9. The effect of a change in price on quantity demanded can be divided into an income and a substitution effect. The substitution effect is the result of a change in relative prices alone. The income effect is the result of the change in real income alone.

10. For a normal good, the income and substitution effects of a price rise will both be negative and will reinforce each other. With an inferior good, the substitution effect will still be negative but the income effect will be positive and thus will to some extent offset the substitution effect. If the good is 'very' inferior and the (positive) income effect is bigger than the (negative) substitution effect, it is called a Giffen good. A rise in the price of a Giffen good will thus cause a rise in the quantity demanded.

11. Indifference analysis, although avoiding having to measure utility, nevertheless has limitations. Indifference curves are difficult to derive in practice; consumers may not behave rationally; the 'optimum' consumption point may not be optimum if the consumer lacks knowledge of the good; indifference curves will not be smooth for items where single units each account for a large proportion of income.

END OF CHAPTER QUESTIONS

1. Imagine that you had £10 per month to allocate between two goods, A and B. Imagine that good A cost £2 per unit and good B cost £1 per unit. Imagine also that the utilities of the two goods are those set out in the table below. (Note that the two goods are not substitutes for each other, so that the consumption of one does not affect the utility gained from the other.)

   (a) What would be the marginal utility ratio (MU_A/MU_B) for the following combinations of the two goods: (i) 1A, 8B; (ii) 2A, 6B; (iii) 3A, 4B; (iv) 4A, 2B? (Each combination would cost £10.)

   (b) Show that where the marginal utility ratio (MU_A/MU_B) equals the price ratio (P_A/P_B), total utility is maximised.

   (c) If the two goods were substitutes for each other, why would it not be possible to construct a table like the one given here?

The utility gained by a person from various quantities of two goods: A and B

Good A			Good B		
Units per month	MU (utils)	TU (utils)	Units per month	MU (utils)	TU (utils)
0	–	0.0	0	–	0.0
1	11.0	11.0	1	8.0	8.0
2	8.0	19.0	2	7.0	15.0
3	6.0	25.0	3	6.5	21.5
4	4.5	29.5	4	5.0	26.5
5	3.0	32.5	5	4.5	31.0
			6	4.0	35.0
			7	3.5	38.5
			8	3.0	41.5
			9	2.6	44.1
			10	2.3	46.4

2. Is it reasonable to assume that people seek to equate the marginal utility/price ratios of the goods that they purchase, if (a) they have never heard of 'utility', let alone 'marginal utility'; (b) marginal utility cannot be measured in any absolute way?

3. Consider situations where you might consider swapping items with someone. Why are such situations relatively rare? Can you think of circumstances in which this might be more common?

4. Explain why the price of a good is no reflection of the total value that consumers put on it.

5. A country's central bank (e.g. the Bank of England or the US Federal Reserve Bank) has a key role in ensuring the stability of the banking system. In many countries the central bank is prepared to bail banks out which find themselves in financial difficulties. Although this has the benefit of reducing the chance of banks going bankrupt and depositors losing their money, it can create a moral hazard. Explain why.

*6. Sketch a person's indifference map for two goods X and Y. Mark the optimum consumption point. Now illustrate the following (you might need to draw a separate diagram for each):

(a) A rise in the price of good X, but no change in the price of good Y.

(b) A shift in the person's tastes from good Y to good X.

(c) A fall in the person's income and a fall in the price of good Y, with the result that the consumption of Y remains constant (but that of X falls).

*7. Distinguish between a normal good, an inferior good and a Giffen good. Use indifference curves to illustrate your answer.

*8. Assume that commuters regard bus journeys as an inferior good and car journeys as a normal good. Using indifference curves, show how (a) a rise in incomes and (b) a fall in bus fares will affect the use of these two modes of transport. How could people's tastes be altered so that bus journeys were no longer regarded as an inferior good? If tastes were altered in this way, what effect would it have on the indifference curves?

Online resources

Additional case studies in MyEconLab

4.1 **Bentham and the philosophy of utilitarianism**. This looks at the historical and philosophical underpinning of the ideas of utility maximisation.

4.2 **Utility under attack**. This looks at the birth of indifference analysis, which was seen as a means of overcoming the shortcomings of marginal utility analysis.

4.3 **Applying indifference curve analysis to taxes on goods**. Assume that the government wants to raise extra revenue from an expenditure tax. Should it put a relatively small extra tax on all goods, or a relatively large one on just certain selected goods?

4.4 **Income and substitution effects: the Slutsky approach**. This looks at an alternative way of using indifference analysis to analyse income and substitution effects.

4.5 **Deriving an Engel curve**. Income elasticity of demand and the income–consumption curve.

4.6 **The characteristics approach to analysing consumer demand**. This is an extension of the analysis of Box 4.7.

Maths Case 4.1 Finding the optimum consumption point: Part 1. This case looks at how the utility maximisation point can be discovered with a Cobb–Douglas utility function with given prices and a given budget constraint.

Maths Case 4.2 Finding the optimum consumption point: Part 2. This case uses the Lagrange method to solve the same problem as in Maths Case 4.1

Websites relevant to this chapter

Numbers and sections refer to websites listed in the Web Appendix and hotlinked from this book's website a **www.pearsoned.co.uk/sloman**.

- For news articles relevant to this chapter, see the Economics News Articles link from the book's website.

- For general news on demand and consumers, see websites in section A, and particularly A2, 3, 4, 8, 9, 11, 12, 23, 25, 36. See also site A41 for links to economics news articles on particular search topics (e.g. consumer demand and advertising).

- For data, information and sites on products and marketing, see sites B2, 10; I7, 11, 13, 17.

- For student resources relevant to Part C, see sites C1–7, 19.

Background to Supply

CHAPTER MAP

5.1 The short-run theory of production   **124**
Short- and long-run changes in production   124
The law of diminishing returns   125
The short-run production function: total product   125
The short-run production function: average and
   marginal product   127

5.2 Costs in the short run   **130**
Measuring costs of production   130
Costs and inputs   132
Total cost   132
Average and marginal costs   133

5.3 The long-run theory of production   **136**
The scale of production   136
Location   138
The size of the whole industry   139
The optimum combination of factors:
   the marginal product approach   139
*The optimum combination of factors: the
   isoquant/isocost approach   140
Postscript: decision making in different time
   periods   145

5.4 Costs in the long run   **146**
Long-run average costs   146
Long-run marginal costs   147
Long-run and short-run average cost curves   148
Long-run cost curves in practice   148
*Derivation of long-run costs from an
   isoquant map   148

5.5 Revenue   **150**
Total, average and marginal revenue   150
Revenue curves when price is not affected by
   the firm's output   152
Revenue curves when price varies with output   153
Shifts in revenue curves   155

5.6 Profit maximisation   **155**
Short-run profit maximisation: using total curves   155
Short-run profit maximisation: using average
   and marginal curves   156
Some qualifications   157

So far we have assumed that supply curves are upward sloping: that a higher price will encourage firms to supply more. But just how much will firms choose to supply at each price? It depends largely on the amount of profit they will make. If a firm can increase its profits by producing more, it will normally do so.

Profit is made by firms earning more from the sale of goods than they cost to produce. A firm's total profit ($T\Pi$) is thus the difference between its total sales revenue (TR) and its total costs of production (TC):

$$T\Pi = TR - TC$$

In order then to discover how a firm can maximise its profit or even get a sufficient level of profit, we must first consider what determines costs and revenue.

The first four sections build up a theory of short-run and long-run costs. They show how output depends on the inputs used, and how costs depend on the amount of output produced. Section 5.5 then looks at revenue. Finally, in section 5.6, we bring cost and revenue together to see how profit is determined. In particular, we shall see how profit varies with output and how the point of maximum profit is found.

Chapter 4 went behind the demand curve. It saw how the 'rational' consumer weighs up the *benefits* (utility) of consuming various amounts of goods or combinations of goods against their *costs* (their price).

We now need to go behind the supply curve and find out just how the **rational producer** (or 'firm' as we call all producers) will behave.

In this case, we shall be looking at the benefits and costs to the firm of producing various quantities of goods and using various alternative methods of production. We shall be asking:

- How much will be produced?
- What combination of inputs will be used?
- How much profit will be made?

Profit and the aims of a firm

The traditional theory of supply, or **theory of the firm**, assumes that firms aim to *maximise profit*; this is a realistic assumption in many cases. The traditional profit-maximising theory of the firm is examined in this and the following two chapters. First we examine the general principles that govern how much a firm supplies. Then, in Chapters 6 and 7, we look at how supply is affected by the amount of competition a firm faces.

In some circumstances, however, firms may not seek to maximise profits. Instead they may seek to maximise sales, or the rate of growth of sales. Alternatively, they may have no *single* aim, but rather a series of potentially conflicting aims held by different managers in different departments of the firm. Sometimes there may be a conflict between the owners of the firm and those running it. Not surprisingly, a firm's behaviour will depend on just what its aims are. Chapter 8 looks at various **alternative theories** to profit maximisation, each theory depending on the particular aims of the firm.

5.1   THE SHORT-RUN THEORY OF PRODUCTION

The cost of producing any level of output will depend on the amount of inputs (or 'factors of production') used and the price the firm must pay for them. Let us first focus on the quantity of factors used.

KEY IDEA 16

Output depends on the amount of resources and how they are used. Different amounts and combinations of inputs will lead to different amounts of output. If output is to be produced efficiently, then inputs should be combined in the optimum proportions.

Short- and long-run changes in production

If a firm wants to increase production, it will take time to acquire a greater quantity of certain inputs. For example, a manufacturer can use more electricity by turning on switches, but it might take a long time to obtain and install more machines, and longer still to build a second or third factory.

If, then, the firm wants to increase output in a hurry, it will only be able to increase the quantity of certain inputs. It can use more raw materials, more fuel, more tools and possibly more labour (by hiring extra workers or offering overtime to its existing workforce). But it will have to make do with its existing buildings and most of its machinery.

The distinction we are making here is between **fixed factors** and **variable factors**. A *fixed* factor is an input that cannot be increased within a given time period (e.g. buildings). A *variable* factor is one that can.

The distinction between fixed and variable factors allows us to distinguish between the **short run** and the **long run**.

Definitions

Rational producer behaviour When a firm weighs up the costs and benefits of alternative courses of action and then seeks to maximise its net benefit.

Traditional theory of the firm The analysis of pricing and output decisions of the firm under various market conditions, assuming that the firm wishes to maximise profit.

Alternative theories of the firm Theories of the firm based on the assumption that firms have aims other than profit maximisation.

Fixed factor An input that cannot be increased in supply within a given time period.

Variable factor An input that can be increased in supply within a given time period.

Short run The period of time over which at least one factor is fixed.

Long run The period of time long enough for *all* factors to be varied.

The short run is a time period during which at least one factor of production is fixed. In the short run, then, output can be increased only by using more variable factors. For example, if an airline wanted to carry more passengers in response to a rise in demand, it could possibly accommodate more passengers on existing flights if there was space. It could possibly increase the number of flights with its existing fleet, by hiring more crew and using more fuel. But in the short run it could not buy more planes: there would not be time for them to be built.

The long run is a time period long enough for all inputs to be varied. Given long enough, a firm can build additional factories and install new machines.

The actual length of the short run will differ from firm to firm. It is not a fixed period of time. Thus if it takes a farmer a year to obtain new land, buildings and equipment, the short run is any time period up to a year and the long run is any time period longer than a year. If it takes an airline two years to obtain an extra plane, the short run is any period up to two years and the long run is any period longer than two years.

1. *How will the length of the short run for the airline depend on the state of the aerospace industry?*
2. *Up to roughly how long is the short run in the following cases?*
   (a) A firm supplying DJs for clubs and parties
   (b) Nuclear power generation
   (c) A small grocery retailing business
   (d) 'Superstore Hypermarkets Ltd'
   In each case specify your assumptions.

For the remainder of this section we will concentrate on short-run production.

The law of diminishing returns

Production in the short run is subject to *diminishing returns*. You may well have heard of 'the law of diminishing returns': it is one of the most famous of all 'laws' of economics. To illustrate how this law underlies short-run production let us take the simplest possible case where there are just two factors: one fixed and one variable.

Take the case of a farm. Assume the fixed factor is land and the variable factor is labour. Since the land is fixed in supply, output per period of time can be increased only by increasing the amount of workers employed. But imagine what would happen as more and more workers crowd on to a fixed area of land. The land cannot go on yielding more and more output indefinitely. After a point the additions to output from each extra worker will begin to diminish.

We can now state the *law of diminishing (marginal) returns*.

The law of diminishing marginal returns states that when increasing amounts of a variable factor are used with a given amount of a fixed factor, there will come a point when each extra unit of the variable factor will produce less extra output than the previous unit.

A good example of the law of diminishing returns is given in Case Study 5.1 in MyEconLab. It looks at diminishing returns to the application of nitrogen fertiliser on farmland.

The short-run production function: total product

Let us now see how the law of diminishing returns affects total output, or *total physical product* (TPP) as it is sometimes called.

The relationship between inputs and output is shown in a *production function*. In the simple case of the farm with only two factors – namely, a fixed supply of land ($\bar{L}n$) and a variable supply of farm workers (Lb) – the production function would be

$$TPP = f(\bar{L}n, Lb)$$

This states that total physical product (i.e. the output of the farm) over a given period of time is a function of (i.e. depends on) the quantity of land and labour employed. We could express the precise relationship using an equation (an example is given in Box 5.4).

Definitions

Law of diminishing (marginal) returns When one or more factors are held fixed, there will come a point beyond which the extra output from additional units of the variable factor will diminish.

Total physical product The total output of a product per period of time that is obtained from a given amount of inputs.

Production function The mathematical relationship between the output of a good and the inputs used to produce it. It shows how output will be affected by changes in the quantity of one or more of the inputs.

BOX 5.1 MALTHUS AND THE DISMAL SCIENCE OF ECONOMICS

Population growth + diminishing returns = starvation

The law of diminishing returns has potentially cataclysmic implications for the future populations of the world.

If the population of the world grows rapidly, then food output may not keep pace with it. There could be diminishing returns to labour as more and more people crowd on to the limited amount of land available.

This is already a problem in some of the poorest countries of the world, especially in sub-Saharan Africa. The land is barely able to support current population levels. Only one or two bad harvests are needed to cause mass starvation – witness the appalling famines in recent years in Ethiopia and Sudan.

The relationship between population and food output was analysed as long ago as 1798 by the Reverend Thomas Robert Malthus (1766–1834) in his *Essay on the Principle of Population*. This book was a bestseller and made Robert Malthus perhaps the best known of all social scientists of his day.

Malthus argued as follows:

> I say that the power of population is indefinitely greater than the power in the earth to produce subsistence for man.
>
> Population when unchecked, increases in a geometrical ratio. Subsistence increases only in an arithmetical ratio. A slight acquaintance with numbers will show the immensity of the first power in comparison with the second.[1]

What Malthus was saying is that world population tends to double about every 25 years or so if unchecked. It grows geometrically, like the series 1, 2, 4, 8, 16, 32, 64, etc. But food output, because of diminishing returns, cannot keep pace with this. It is likely to grow at only an arithmetical rate, like the series 1, 2, 3, 4, 5, 6, 7, etc. It is clear that population, if unchecked, will soon outstrip food supply.

So what is the check on population growth? According to Malthus, it is starvation. As population grows, so food output per head will fall until, with more and more people starving, the death rate will rise. Only then will population growth stabilise at the rate of growth of food output.

Have Malthus' predictions been borne out by events? Two factors have mitigated the forces that Malthus described:

- The rate of population growth tends to slow down as countries become more developed. Although improved health prolongs life, this tends to be more than offset by a decline in the birth rate as people choose to have smaller families. This is illustrated in the table below. Population growth peaked in the 1960s, has fallen substantially since then and is projected to fall further in future decades.
- Technological improvements in farming have greatly increased food output per hectare. (See Case Study 5.1 in MyEconLab for an example.)

The growth in food output has thus exceeded the rate of population growth in developed countries. Also certain developing countries have seen significant advances in agriculture. These include the 'green revolution' of the 1960s, whereby new high-yielding crop varieties were developed (especially in the cases of wheat and rice), and the development of genetically modified crops in recent

	Number of workers (Lb)	**TPP**	**APP** (= TPP/Lb)	**MPP** (= ΔTPP/ΔLb)
a	0	0	–	
				3
	1	3	3	
				7
b	2	10	5	
				14
	3	24	8	
				12
c	4	36	9	
				4
	5	40	8	
				2
	6	42	7	
d				0
	7	42	6	
				−2
	8	40	5	

Table 5.1 Wheat production per year from a particular farm

Alternatively, the production function could be expressed in the form of a table or a graph. Table 5.1 and Figure 5.1 show a hypothetical production function for a farm producing wheat. The first two columns of Table 5.1 and the top diagram in Figure 5.1 show how total wheat output per year varies as extra workers are employed on a fixed amount of land.

With nobody working on the land, output will be zero (point *a*). As the first farm workers are taken on, wheat output initially rises more and more rapidly. The assumption behind this is that with only one or two workers efficiency is low, since the workers are spread too thinly. With more workers, however, they can work together – each, perhaps, doing some specialist job – and thus they can use the land more efficiently. In Table 5.1, output rises more and more rapidly up to the employment of the third worker (point *b*). In Figure 5.1 the *TPP* curve gets steeper up to point *b*.

After point *b*, however, diminishing marginal returns set in: output rises less and less rapidly, and the *TPP* curve correspondingly becomes less steeply sloped.

When point *d* is reached, wheat output is at a maximum: the land is yielding as much as it can. Any more

EXPLORING
ECONOMICS

years. In some countries food output growth has outstripped population growth. India, for example, now exports grain.

Nevertheless, the Malthusian spectre is very real for some of the poorest developing countries, which are simply unable to feed their populations satisfactorily. It is these poorest countries of the world which have some of the highest rates of population growth – around 3 per cent per annum in many African countries.

A further cause for concern arises from the move in Asia towards a westernised diet, with meat and dairy products playing a larger part. This further increases pressure on the land, since cattle require considerably more grain to produce meat than would be needed to feed humans a vegetarian diet.

A third factor is cited by some commentators, who remain unconvinced of the strength of Malthus' gloomy prognostication for the world. They believe that he seriously underestimated humankind's capacity to innovate; perhaps human ingenuity is one resource that doesn't suffer from diminishing returns.

1. Why might it be possible for there to be a zero marginal productivity of labour on many family farms in poor countries and yet just enough food for all the members of the family to survive? (Illustrate using MPP and APP curves.)
2. The figures in the following table are based on the assumption that birth rates will fall faster than death rates. Under what circumstances might these forecasts underestimate the rate of growth of world population?

World population levels and growth: actual and projected

Year	World population (billions)	Average annual rate of increase (%)		
		World	More developed regions	Less developed regions
1950	2.5			
		1.8	1.2	2.1
1960	3.0			
		2.0	1.0	2.4
1970	3.7			
		1.9	0.7	2.2
1980	4.5			
		1.7	0.6	2.1
1990	5.3			
		1.4	0.3	1.7
2000	6.1			
		1.2	0.3	1.4
2010	6.9			
		1.0	0.2	1.2
2020	7.7			
		0.8	0.1	1.0
2030	8.3			
		0.6	0.0	0.7
2040	8.8			
		0.4	−0.1	0.5
2050	9.2			

Sources: Various.

[1] T. R. Malthus, *First Essay on Population* (Macmillan, 1926), pp. 13–14.

---

workers employed after that are likely to get in each other's way. Thus beyond point *d*, output is likely to fall again: eight workers produce less than seven workers.

The short-run production function: average and marginal product

In addition to total physical product, two other important concepts are illustrated by a production function: namely, *average physical product* (*APP*) and *marginal physical product* (*MPP*).

Average physical product

This is output (*TPP*) per unit of the variable factor (Q_v). In the case of the farm, it is the output of wheat per worker.

$$APP = TPP/Q_v$$

Thus in Table 5.1 the average physical product of labour when four workers are employed is $36/4 = 9$ tonnes per year.

Marginal physical product

This is the *extra* output (Δ*TPP*) produced by employing *one more* unit of the variable factor.

Definitions

Average physical product Total output (*TPP*) per unit of the variable factor in question: $APP = TPP/Q_v$.

Marginal physical product The extra output gained by the employment of one more unit of the variable factor: $MPP = \Delta TPP/\Delta Q_v$.

Figure 5.1   Wheat production per year (tonnes)

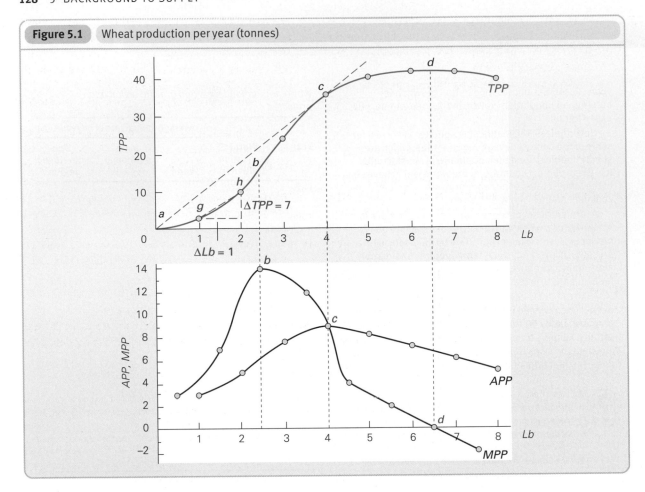

CASE STUDIES AND APPLICATIONS

BOX 5.2   DIMINISHING RETURNS IN THE BREAD SHOP

Is the baker using his loaf?

Just up the road from where John lives is a bread shop. Like many others, he buys his bread there on a Saturday morning. Not surprisingly, Saturday morning is the busiest time of the week for the shop and as a result it takes on extra assistants.

During the week only one assistant serves the customers, but on a Saturday morning there used to be five serving. But could they serve five times as many customers? No, they could not. There were diminishing returns to labour.

The trouble is that certain factors of production in the shop are fixed:

- The shop is a fixed size. It gets very crowded on Saturday morning. Assistants sometimes had to wait while customers squeezed past each other to get to the counter, and with five serving, the assistants themselves used to get in each other's way.

- There is only one cash till. Assistants frequently had to wait while other assistants used it.

- There is only one pile of tissue paper for wrapping the bread. Again the assistants often had to wait.

The fifth and maybe even the fourth assistant ended up serving very few extra customers.

John is still going to the same bread shop and they still have only one till and one pile of tissue paper. But now only three assistants are employed on a Saturday! The shop, however, is just as busy.

 How would you advise the baker as to whether he should (a) employ four assistants on a Saturday; (b) extend his shop, thereby allowing more customers to be served on a Saturday morning?

Thus in Table 5.1 the marginal physical product of the fourth worker is 12 tonnes. The reason is that by employing the fourth worker, wheat output has risen from 24 tonnes to 36 tonnes: a rise of 12 tonnes.

In symbols, marginal physical product is given by

$$MPP = \Delta TPP / \Delta Q_v$$

Thus in our example:

$$MPP = 12/1 = 12$$

The reason why we divide the increase in output (ΔTPP) by the increase in the quantity of the variable factor (ΔQ_v) is that some variable factors can be increased only in multiple units. For example, if we wanted to know the MPP of fertiliser and we found out how much extra wheat was produced by using an extra 20 kg bag, we would have to divide this output by 20 (ΔQ_v) to find the MPP of *one* more kilogram.

Note that in Table 5.1 the figures for MPP are entered in the spaces between the other figures. The reason is that MPP can be seen as the *difference* in output *between* one level of input and another. Thus in the table the difference in output between five and six workers is 2 tonnes.

The figures for APP and MPP are plotted in the lower diagram of Figure 5.1. We can draw a number of conclusions from these diagrams:

- The MPP between two points is equal to the slope of the TPP curve between those two points. For example, when the number of workers increases from 1 to 2 ($\Delta Lb = 1$),

TPP rises from 3 to 10 tonnes ($\Delta TPP = 7$). MPP is thus 7: the slope of the line between points g and h.
- MPP rises at first: the slope of the TPP curve gets steeper.
- MPP reaches a maximum at point b. At that point the slope of the TPP curve is at its steepest.
- After point b, diminishing returns set in. MPP falls. TPP becomes less steep.
- APP rises at first. It continues rising as long as the addition to output from the last worker (MPP) is greater than the average output (APP): the MPP pulls the APP up (see Box 5.3). This continues beyond point b. Even though MPP is now falling, the APP *goes on* rising as long as the MPP is still above the APP. Thus APP goes on rising to point c.
- Beyond point c, MPP is below APP. New workers add less to output than the average. This pulls the average down: APP falls.
- As long as MPP is greater than zero, TPP will go on rising: new workers add to total output.
- At point d, TPP is at a maximum (its slope is zero). An additional worker will add nothing to output: MPP is zero.
- Beyond point d, TPP falls. MPP is negative.

KI 17
p125

1. What is the significance of the slope of the line *ac* in the top part of Figure 5.1?
2. Given that there is a fixed supply of land in the world, what implications can you draw from Figure 5.1 about the effects of an increase in world population for food output per head? (See Box 5.1.)

BOX 5.3 | **THE RELATIONSHIP BETWEEN AVERAGES AND MARGINALS** | **EXPLORING ECONOMICS**

In this chapter we have just examined the concepts of *average* and *marginal* physical product. We shall be coming across several other average and marginal concepts later on. It is useful at this stage to examine the general relationship between averages and marginals. In all cases there are three simple rules that relate them.

To illustrate these rules, consider the following example.

Imagine a room with ten people in it. Assume that the *average* age of those present is 20.

Now if a 20-year-old enters the room (the *marginal* age), this will not affect the average age. It will remain at 20. If a 56-year-old now comes in, the average age will rise: not to 56, of course, but to 23. This is found by dividing the sum of everyone's ages (276) by the number of people (12). If then a child of 10 were to enter the room, this would pull the average age down.

From this example we can derive the three universal rules about averages and marginals:

- If the marginal equals the average, the average will not change.
- If the marginal is above the average, the average will rise.
- If the marginal is below the average, the average will fall.

A cricketer scores the following number of runs in five successive innings:

Innings:	1	2	3	4	5
Runs:	20	20	50	10	0

These can be seen as the marginal number of runs from each innings. Calculate the total and average number of runs after each innings. Show how the average and marginal scores illustrate the three rules above.

*BOX 5.4 THE RELATIONSHIP BETWEEN *TPP*, *MPP* AND *APP*

Using calculus again

The total physical product of a variable factor (e.g. fertiliser) can be expressed as an equation. For example:

$$TPP = 100 + 32Q_f + 10Q_f^2 - Q_f^3 \qquad (1)$$

where *TPP* is the output of grain in tonnes per hectare, and Q_f is the quantity of fertiliser applied in kilograms per hectare.

From this we can derive the *APP* function. *APP* is simply TPP/Q_f: i.e. output per kilogram of fertiliser. Thus:

$$APP = \frac{100}{Q_f} + 32 + 10Q_f - Q_f^2 \qquad (2)$$

We can also derive the *MPP* function. *MPP* is the rate of increase in *TPP* as additional fertiliser is applied. It is thus the first derivative of *TPP*: $dTPP/dQ_f$. Thus:

$$MPP = 32 + 20Q_f - 3Q_f^2 \qquad (3)$$

From these three equations we can derive the table shown.

 Check out some figures by substituting values of Q_f into each of the three equations.

Maximum output (484 tonnes) is achieved with 8 kg of fertiliser per hectare. At that level, *MPP* is zero: no additional output can be gained.

Q_f	*TPP*	*APP*	*MPP*
1	141	141	49
2	196	98	60
3	259	86	65
4	324	81	64
5	385	77	57
6	436	72	44
7	471	67	25
8	484	60	0
9	469	52	−31

This maximum level of *TPP* can be discovered from the equations by using a simple technique. If *MPP* is zero at this level, then simply find the value of Q_f where

$$MPP = 32 + 20Q_f - 3Q_f^2 = 0 \qquad (4)$$

Solving this equation[1] gives $Q_f = 8$.

[1] By applying the second derivative test (see Appendix 1) you can verify that $Q_f = 8$ gives the *maximum TPP* rather than the *minimum*. (Both the maximum *and* the minimum point of a curve have a slope equal to zero.)

Section summary

1. A production function shows the relationship between the amount of inputs used and the amount of output produced from them (per period of time).

2. In the short run it is assumed that one or more factors (inputs) are fixed in supply. The actual length of the short run will vary from industry to industry.

3. Production in the short run is subject to diminishing returns. As greater quantities of the variable factor(s) are used, so each additional unit of the variable factor will add less to output than previous units: marginal physical product will diminish and total physical product will rise less and less rapidly.

4. As long as marginal physical product is above average physical product, average physical product will rise. Once *MPP* has fallen below *APP*, however, *APP* will fall.

5.2 COSTS IN THE SHORT RUN

We have seen how output changes as inputs are varied in the short run. We now use this information to show how costs vary with the amount a firm produces. Obviously, before deciding how much to produce, it has to know the precise level of costs for each level of output.

But first we must be clear on just what we mean by the word 'costs'. The term is used differently by economists and accountants.

Measuring costs of production

When measuring costs, economists always use the concept of *opportunity cost*. Remember from Chapter 1 how we

defined opportunity cost. It is the cost of any activity measured in terms of the *sacrifice* made in doing it: in other words, the cost measured in terms of the opportunities forgone.

How do we apply this principle of opportunity cost to a firm? First we must discover what factors of production it is

Definition

Opportunity cost Cost measured in terms of the next best alternative forgone.

using. Then we must measure the sacrifice involved. To do this it is necessary to put factors into two categories.

Factors not owned by the firm: explicit costs

The opportunity cost of using factors not already owned by the firm is simply the price that the firm has to pay for them. Thus if the firm uses £100 worth of electricity, the opportunity cost is £100. The firm has sacrificed £100 which could have been spent on something else. These costs are called *explicit costs* because they involve direct payment of money by firms.

Factors already owned by the firm: implicit costs

When the firm already owns factors (e.g. machinery), it does not as a rule have to pay out money to use them. Their opportunity costs are thus *implicit costs*. They are equal to what the factors could earn for the firm in some alternative use, either within the firm or hired out to some other firm.

Here are some examples of implicit costs:

* A firm owns some buildings. The opportunity cost of using them is the rent it could have received by letting them out to another firm.
* A firm draws £100 000 from the bank out of its savings in order to invest in new plant and equipment. The opportunity cost of this investment is not just the

£100 000 (an explicit cost), but also the interest it thereby forgoes (an implicit cost).

* The owner of the firm could have earned £20 000 per annum by working for someone else. This £20 000 is then the opportunity cost of the owner's time.

If there is no alternative use for a factor of production, as in the case of a machine designed to produce a specific product, and if it has no scrap value, the opportunity cost of using it is *zero*. In such a case, if the output from the machine is worth more than the cost of all the *other* inputs involved, the firm might as well use the machine rather than let it stand idle.

What the firm paid for the machine – its *historic cost* – is irrelevant. Not using the machine will not bring that money back. It has been spent. These are sometimes referred to as 'sunk costs'.

 The *'bygones' principle* states that sunk (fixed) costs should be ignored when deciding whether to produce or sell more or less of a product. Only variable costs should be taken into account.

Likewise the *replacement cost* is irrelevant. That should be taken into account only when the firm is considering replacing the machine.

BOX 5.5   **THE FALLACY OF USING HISTORIC COSTS**   **EXPLORING ECONOMICS**

Or there's no point crying over spilt milk

If you fall over and break your leg, there is little point in saying 'If only I hadn't done that I could have gone on that skiing holiday; I could have taken part in that race; I could have done so many other things (sigh).' Wishing things were different won't change history. You have to manage as well as you can with your broken leg.

It is the same for a firm. Once it has purchased some inputs, it is no good then wishing it hadn't. It has to accept that it has now got them, and make the best decisions about what to do with them.

Take a simple example. The local greengrocer decides in early December to buy 100 Christmas trees for £10 each. At the time of purchase, this represents an opportunity cost of £10 each, since the £10 could have been spent on something else. The greengrocer estimates that there is enough local demand to sell all

100 trees at £20 each, thereby making a reasonable profit.

But the estimate turns out to be wrong. On 23 December there are still 50 trees unsold. What should be done? At this stage the £10 that was paid for the trees is irrelevant. It is a historic cost. It cannot be recouped: the trees cannot be sold back to the wholesaler!

In fact, the opportunity cost is now zero. It might even be negative if the greengrocer has to pay to dispose of any unsold trees. It might, therefore, be worth selling the trees at £10, £5 or even £1. Last thing on Christmas Eve it might even be worth giving away any unsold trees.

 Why is the correct price to charge (for the unsold trees) the one at which the price elasticity of demand equals −1? (Assume no disposal costs.)

Definitions

Explicit costs The payments to outside suppliers of inputs.

Implicit costs Costs that do not involve a direct payment of money to a third party, but which nevertheless involve a sacrifice of some alternative.

Historic costs The original amount the firm paid for factors it now owns.

Replacement costs What the firm would have to pay to replace factors it currently owns.

Costs and inputs

A firm's costs of production will depend on the factors of production it uses. The more factors it uses, the greater will its costs be. More precisely, this relationship depends on two elements:

- The productivity of the factors. The greater their physical productivity, the smaller will be the quantity of them required to produce a given level of output, and hence the lower will be the cost of that output. In other words, there is a direct link between *TPP*, *APP* and *MPP* and the costs of production.
- The price of the factors. The higher their price, the higher will be the costs of production.

In the short run, some factors are fixed in supply. Their total costs, therefore, are fixed, in the sense that they do not vary with output. Rent on land is a ***fixed cost***. It is the same whether the firm produces a lot or a little.

The total cost of using variable factors, however, does vary with output. The cost of raw materials is a ***variable cost***. The more that is produced, the more raw materials are used and therefore the higher is their total cost.

The following are some costs incurred by a shoe manufacturer. Decide whether each one is a fixed cost or a variable cost or has some element of both.
(a) The cost of leather
(b) The fee paid to an advertising agency
(c) Wear and tear on machinery
(d) Business rates on the factory
(e) Electricity for heating and lighting
(f) Electricity for running the machines
(g) Basic minimum wages agreed with the union
(h) Overtime pay
(i) Depreciation of machines as a result purely of their age (irrespective of their condition)

Table 5.2	Total costs for firm X		
Output (Q)	TFC (£)	TVC (£)	TC (£)
0	12	0	12
1	12	10	22
2	12	16	28
3	12	21	33
4	12	28	40
5	12	40	52
6	12	60	72
7	12	91	103
.	.	.	.

Total cost

The ***total cost*** (*TC*) of production is the sum of the *total variable costs* (*TVC*) and the *total fixed costs* (*TFC*) of production:

$$TC = TVC + TFC$$

Consider Table 5.2 and Figure 5.2. They show the total costs for firm X of producing different levels of output (*Q*). Let us examine each of the three cost curves in turn.

Definitions

Fixed costs Total costs that do not vary with the amount of output produced.

Variable costs Total costs that do vary with the amount of output produced.

Total cost The sum of total fixed costs and total variable costs: $TC = TFC + TVC$.

| Figure 5.2 | Total costs for firm X |

Total fixed cost (TFC)

In our example, total fixed cost is assumed to be £12. Since this does not vary with output, it is shown by a horizontal straight line.

Total variable cost (TVC)

With a zero output, no variable factors will be used. Thus $TVC = 0$. The TVC curve, therefore, starts from the origin.

The shape of the TVC curve follows from the law of diminishing returns. Initially, *before* diminishing returns set in, TVC rises less and less rapidly as more variable factors are added. Take the case of a factory with a fixed supply of machinery: initially as more workers are taken on the workers can do increasingly specialist tasks and make a fuller use of the capital equipment. This corresponds to the portion of the TPP curve that rises more rapidly (up to point b in Figure 5.1 on p. 128).

As output is increased beyond point m in Figure 5.2, diminishing returns set in. Since extra workers (the extra variable factors) are producing less and less extra output, the extra units of output they do produce will cost more and more in terms of wage costs. Thus TVC rises more and more rapidly. The TVC curve gets steeper. This corresponds to the portion of the TPP curve that rises less rapidly (between points b and d in Figure 5.1).

Total cost (TC)

Since $TC = TVC + TFC$, the TC curve is simply the TVC curve shifted vertically upwards by £12.

Average and marginal costs

Average cost (AC) is cost per unit of production:

$$AC = TC/Q$$

Thus if it cost a firm £2000 to produce 100 units of a product, the average cost would be £20 for each unit (£2000/100).

Like total cost, average cost can be divided into the two components, fixed and variable. In other words, average cost equals *average fixed cost* ($AFC = TFC/Q$) plus *average variable cost* ($AVC = TVC/Q$):

$$AC = AFC + AVC$$

Marginal cost (MC) is the *extra* cost of producing *one more unit*: that is, the rise in total cost per one unit rise in output:

$$MC = \frac{\Delta TC}{\Delta Q}$$

For example, assume that a firm is currently producing 1 000 000 boxes of matches a month. It now increases output by 1000 boxes (another batch): $\Delta Q = 1000$. As a result, its total costs rise by £30: $\Delta TC = £30$. What is the cost of producing one more box of matches? It is

$$\frac{\Delta TC}{\Delta Q} = \frac{£30}{1000} = 3p$$

(Note that all marginal costs are variable, since, by definition, there can be no extra fixed costs as output rises.)

Given the TFC, TVC and TC for each output, it is possible to derive the AFC, AVC, AC and MC for each output using the above definitions.

For example, using the data of Table 5.2, Table 5.3 can be constructed.

 Fill in the missing figures in Table 5.3. (Note that the figures for MC come in the spaces between each level of output.)

What will be the shapes of the MC, AFC, AVC and AC curves? These follow from the nature of the MPP and APP curves that we looked at in section 5.1 above. You may recall that the typical shapes of the APP and MPP curves are like those illustrated in Figure 5.3.

Marginal cost (MC)

The shape of the MC curve follows directly from the law of diminishing returns. Initially, in Figure 5.4, as more of the variable factor is used, extra units of output cost less than previous units. MC falls. This corresponds to the rising portion of the MPP curve in Figure 5.3 and the portion of the TVC curve in Figure 5.2 to the left of point m.

Definitions

Average (total) cost Total cost (fixed plus variable) per unit of output: $AC = TC/Q = AFC + AVC$.

Average fixed cost Total fixed cost per unit of output: $AFC = TFC/Q$.

Average variable cost Total variable cost per unit of output: $AVC = TVC/Q$.

Marginal cost The extra cost of producing one more unit of output: $MC = \Delta TC/\Delta Q$.

Table 5.3 Total, average and marginal costs for firm X

Output (Q) (units)	TFC (£)	AFC (TFC/Q) (£)	TVC (£)	AVC (TVC/Q) (£)	TC (TFC+TVC) (£)	AC (TC/Q) (£)	MC (ΔTC/ΔQ) (£)
0	12	–	0	–	12	–	
							10
1	12	12	10	10	22	22	
							...
2	12	6	16	...	28	14	
							5
3	...	...	21	7	...	...	
							7
4	...	3	28	...	40	...	
							12
5	...	2.4	...	8	52	10.4	
							...
6	...	...	...	10	...	12	
							31
7	...	1.7	91	13	103	14.7	

Figure 5.3 Average and marginal physical product

Beyond a certain level of output, diminishing returns set in. This is shown as point *x* in Figure 5.4 and corresponds to point *b* in Figure 5.3 (and point *m* in Figure 5.2). Thereafter *MC* rises as *MPP* falls. Additional units of output cost more and more to produce, since they require ever-increasing amounts of the variable factor.

Average fixed cost (AFC)

This falls continuously as output rises, since *total* fixed costs are being spread over a greater and greater output.

Average variable cost (AVC)

The shape of the *AVC* curve depends on the shape of the *APP* curve. As the average product of workers rises (up to point *c* in Figure 5.3), the average labour cost per unit of output (the *AVC*) falls: as far as point *y* in Figure 5.4. Thereafter, as *APP* falls, *AVC* must rise.

Figure 5.4 Average and marginal costs

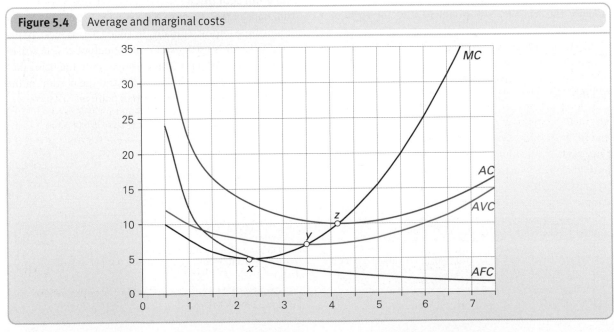

BOX 5.6 **COST CURVES IN PRACTICE**

When fixed factors are divisible

Are cost curves always the shape depicted in this chapter? The answer is no. Sometimes, rather than being U-shaped, the *AVC* and *MC* curves are flat-bottomed, like the curves in the diagram below. Indeed, they may be constant (and equal to each other) over a substantial range of output.

The reason for this is that fixed factors may sometimes not have to be in full use all the time. Take the case of a firm with 100 identical machines, each one requiring one person to operate it. Although the firm cannot use more than the 100 machines, it could use fewer: in other words, some of the machines could be left idle. Assume, for example, that instead of using 100 machines, the firm

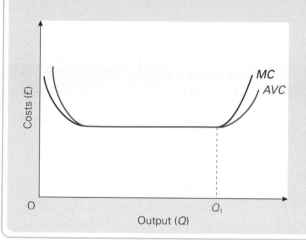

uses only 90. It would need only 90 operatives and 90 per cent of the raw materials.

Similarly, if it used only 20 machines, its total variable costs (labour and raw materials) would be only 20 per cent. What we are saying here is that average variable cost remains constant – and over a very large range of output, using anything from 1 machine to 100 machines.

The reason for the constant *AVC* (and *MC*) is that by varying the amount of fixed capital used, the proportions used of capital, labour and raw materials can be kept the same and hence the average and marginal productivity of labour and raw materials will remain constant.

Only when all machines are in use (at Q_1) will *AVC* start to rise if output is further expanded. Machines may then have to work beyond their optimal speed, using more raw materials per unit of output (diminishing returns to raw materials), or workers may have to work longer shifts with higher (overtime) pay.

1. *Assume that a firm has five identical machines, each operating independently. Assume that with all five machines operating normally, 100 units of output are produced each day. Below what level of output will* AVC *and* MC *rise?*
2. *Manufacturing firms like the one we have been describing will have other fixed costs (such as rent and managerial overheads). Does the existence of these affect the argument that the* AVC *curve will be flat-bottomed?*

Average (total) cost (AC)

This is simply the vertical sum of the *AFC* and *AVC* curves. Note that as *AFC* gets less, the gap between *AVC* and *AC* narrows.

The relationship between average cost and marginal cost

This is simply another illustration of the relationship that applies between *all* averages and marginals (see Box 5.3).

As long as new units of output cost less than the average, their production must pull the average cost down. That is, if *MC* is less than *AC*, *AC* must be falling. Likewise, if new units cost more than the average, their production must drive the average up. That is, if *MC* is greater than *AC*, *AC* must be rising. Therefore, the *MC* crosses the *AC* at its minimum point (point *z* in Figure 5.4).

Since all marginal costs are variable, the same relationship holds between *MC* and *AVC*.

Why is the minimum point of the AVC curve at a lower level of output than the minimum point of the AC curve?

*LOOKING AT THE MATHS

The total, average and marginal cost functions can be expressed algebraically as follows:

$$TFC = a \tag{1}$$

$$TVC = bQ - cQ^2 + dQ^3 \tag{2}$$

$$TC = a + bQ - cQ^2 + dQ^3 \tag{3}$$

where *a* is the constant term representing fixed costs, and the signs of the terms in the *TVC* equation have been chosen to give *TVC* and *TC* curves shaped like those in Figure 5.2. Dividing each of the above by *Q* gives:

$$AFC = \frac{a}{Q} \tag{4}$$

$$AVC = b - cQ + dQ^2 \tag{5}$$

$$AC = \frac{a}{Q} + b - cQ + dQ^2 \tag{6}$$

Differentiating equation (3) or (2) gives:

$$MC = b - 2cQ + 3dQ^2 \tag{7}$$

A worked example of each of these is given in Maths Case 5.1 in MyEconLab.

Section summary

1. When measuring costs of production, we should be careful to use the concept of opportunity cost. In the case of factors not owned by the firm, the opportunity cost is simply the explicit cost of purchasing or hiring them. It is the price paid for them. In the case of factors already owned by the firm, it is the implicit cost of what the factor could have earned for the firm in its next best alternative use.

2. In the short run, some factors are fixed in supply. Their total costs are thus fixed with respect to output. In the case of variable factors, their total cost will increase as more output is produced and hence as more of the variable factor is used.

3. Total cost can be divided into total fixed and total variable costs. Total variable cost will tend to increase less rapidly at first as more is produced, but then, when diminishing returns set in, it will increase more and more rapidly.

4. Marginal cost is the cost of producing one more unit of output. It will probably fall at first (corresponding to the part of the *TVC* curve where the slope is getting shallower), but will start to rise as soon as diminishing returns set in.

5. Average cost, like total cost, can be divided into fixed and variable costs. Average fixed cost will decline as more output is produced. The reason is that the total fixed cost is being spread over a greater and greater number of units of output. Average variable cost will tend to decline at first, but once the marginal cost has risen above it, it must then rise.

5.3 THE LONG-RUN THEORY OF PRODUCTION

In the long run, *all* factors of production are variable. There is time for the firm to build a new factory (maybe in a different part of the country), to install new machines, to use different techniques of production, and in general to combine its inputs in whatever proportion and in whatever quantities it chooses.

In the long run, then, there are several decisions that a firm has to make: decisions about the scale and location of its operations and what techniques of production it should use. These decisions affect the costs of production. It is important, therefore, to get them right.

The scale of production

If a firm were to double all of its inputs – something it could do in the long run – would it double its output? Or will output more than double or less than double? We can distinguish three possible situations:

Constant returns to scale.   This is where a given percentage increase in inputs will lead to the *same* percentage increase in output.

Increasing returns to scale.   This is where a given percentage increase in inputs will lead to a *larger* percentage increase in output.

Decreasing returns to scale.   This is where a given percentage increase in inputs will lead to a *smaller* percentage increase in output.

Notice the terminology here. The words 'to scale' mean that *all* inputs increase by the same proportion. Decreasing returns *to scale* are therefore quite different from diminishing *marginal* returns (where only the *variable* factor increases). The differences between marginal returns to a variable factor and returns to scale are illustrated in Table 5.4.

Table 5.4	Short-run and long-run increases in output				
Short run			**Long run**		
Input 1	**Input 2**	**Output**	**Input 1**	**Input 2**	**Output**
3	1	25	1	1	15
3	2	45	2	2	35
3	3	60	3	3	60
3	4	70	4	4	90
3	5	75	5	5	125

In the short run, input 1 is assumed to be fixed in supply (at 3 units). Output can be increased only by using more of the variable factor (input 2). In the long run, however, both input 1 and input 2 are variable.

Referring still to Table 5.4, are there diminishing or increasing marginal returns, and are there decreasing or increasing returns to scale?

Economies of scale

The concept of increasing returns to scale is closely linked to that of *economies of scale*. A firm experiences economies

Definition

Economies of scale When increasing the scale of production leads to a lower cost per unit of output.

of scale if costs per unit of output fall as the scale of production increases. Clearly, if a firm is getting increasing returns to scale from its factors of production, then as it produces more it will be using smaller and smaller amounts of factors per unit of output. Other things being equal, this means that it will be producing at a lower unit cost.

There are several reasons why firms are likely to experience economies of scale. Some are due to increasing returns to scale; some are not.

Specialisation and division of labour. In large-scale plants workers can do more simple, repetitive jobs. With this **specialisation and division of labour** less training is needed; workers can become highly efficient in their particular job, especially with long production runs; there is less time lost in workers switching from one operation to another; and supervision is easier. Workers and managers can be employed who have specific skills in specific areas.

Indivisibilities. Some inputs are of a minimum size: they are indivisible. The most obvious example is machinery. Take the case of a combine harvester. A small-scale farmer could not make full use of one. They only become economical to use, therefore, on farms above a certain size. The problem of **indivisibilities** is made worse when different machines, each of which is part of the production process, are of a different size. For example, if there are two types of machine, one producing 6 units a day, and the other packaging 4 units a day, a minimum of 12 units would have to be produced, involving two production machines and three packaging machines, if all machines are to be fully utilised.

The 'container principle'. Any capital equipment that contains things (blast furnaces, oil tankers, pipes, vats, etc.) tends to cost less per unit of output the larger its size. The reason has to do with the relationship between a container's volume and its *surface area*. A container's cost depends largely on the materials used to build it and hence roughly on its surface area. Its output depends largely on its *volume*. Large containers have a bigger volume relative to surface area than do small containers. For example, a container with a bottom, top and four sides, with each side measuring 1 metre, has a volume of 1 cubic metre and a surface area of 6 square metres (six surfaces of 1 square metre

each). If each side were now to be doubled in length to 2 metres, the volume would be 8 cubic metres and the surface area 24 square metres (six surfaces of 4 square metres each). Thus an eightfold increase in capacity has been gained at only a fourfold increase in the container's surface area, and hence an approximate fourfold increase in cost.

Greater efficiency of large machines. Large machines may be more efficient in the sense that more output can be gained for a given amount of inputs. For example, only one worker may be required to operate a machine whether it be large or small. Also, a large machine may make more efficient use of raw materials.

By-products. With production on a large scale, there may be sufficient waste products to enable some by-product or by-products to be made.

Multi-stage production. A large factory may be able to take a product through several stages in its manufacture. This saves time and cost in moving the semi-finished product from one firm or factory to another. For example, a large cardboard-manufacturing firm may be able to convert trees or waste paper into cardboard and then into cardboard boxes in a continuous sequence.

All the above are examples of **plant economies of scale**. They are due to an individual factory or workplace or machine being large. There are other economies of scale, however, that are associated with the *firm* being large – perhaps with many factories.

Organisational economies. With a large firm, individual plants can specialise in particular functions. There can also be centralised administration of the firm; for example, one human resources department could administer all the wages. Often, after a merger between two firms, savings can be made by **rationalising** their activities in this way.

Spreading overheads. Some expenditures are economic only when the *firm* is large: for example, research and development – only a large firm can afford to set up a research laboratory. This is another example of indivisibilities, only this time at the level of the firm rather than the

---

Definitions

Specialisation and division of labour Where production is broken down into a number of simpler, more specialised tasks, thus allowing workers to acquire a high degree of efficiency.

Indivisibility The impossibility of dividing a factor into smaller units.

Plant economies of scale Economies of scale that arise because of the large size of a factory.

Rationalisation The reorganising of production (often after a merger) so as to cut out waste and duplication and generally to reduce costs.

plant. The greater the firm's output, the more these **overhead** costs are spread.

Financial economies. Large firms are often able to obtain finance at lower interest rates than small firms. They may be able to obtain certain inputs cheaper by buying in bulk.

Economies of scope. Often a firm is large because it produces a range of products. This can result in each individual product being produced more cheaply than if it was produced in a single-product firm. The reason for these **economies of scope** is that various overhead costs and financial and organisational economies can be shared among the products. For example, a firm that produces a whole range of CD players, amplifiers and tuners can benefit from shared marketing and distribution costs and the bulk purchase of electronic components.

1. *Which of the economies of scale we have considered are due to increasing returns to scale and which are due to other factors?*
2. *What economies of scale is a large department store likely to experience?*

Diseconomies of scale

When firms get beyond a certain size, costs per unit of output may start to increase. There are several reasons for such **diseconomies of scale**:

- Management problems of co-ordination may increase as the firm becomes larger and more complex, and as lines of communication get longer. There may be a lack of personal involvement by management.
- Workers may feel 'alienated' if their jobs are boring and repetitive, and if they feel that they are an insignificantly small part of a large organisation. Small- to medium-sized companies often report that workers feel they 'make a difference'; this may be lost in a large firm and as a consequence lower motivation may lead to shoddy work.
- Industrial relations may deteriorate as a result of these factors and also as a result of the more complex interrelationships between different categories of worker. More levels of 'people management' may therefore be required.
- Production-line processes and the complex interdependencies of mass production can lead to great disruption if there are hold-ups in any one part of the firm.

Whether firms experience economies or diseconomies of scale will depend on the conditions applying in each individual firm.

Why are firms likely to experience economies of scale up to a certain size and then diseconomies of scale after some point beyond that?

Location

In the long run, a firm can move to a different location. The location will affect the cost of production since locations differ in terms of the availability and cost of raw materials, suitable land and power supply, the qualifications, skills and experience of the labour force, wage rates, transport and communications networks, the cost of local services, and banking and financial facilities. In short, locations differ in terms of the availability, suitability and cost of the factors of production.

Transport costs will be an important influence on a firm's location. Ideally, a firm will wish to be as near as possible to both its raw materials and the market for its finished product. When market and raw materials are in different locations, the firm will minimise its transport costs by locating somewhere between the two. In general, if the raw materials are more expensive to transport than the finished product, the firm should be located as near as possible to the raw materials. This will normally apply to firms whose raw materials are heavier or more bulky than the finished product. Thus heavy industry, which uses large quantities of coal and various ores, tends to be concentrated near the coal fields or near the ports. If, on the other hand, the finished product is more expensive to transport (e.g. bread and beer), the firm will probably be located as near as possible to its market.

When raw materials or markets are in many different locations, transport costs will be minimised at the 'centre of gravity'. This location will be nearer to those raw materials and markets whose transport costs are greater per mile.

How is the opening up of trade and investment between eastern and western Europe likely to affect the location of industries within Europe that have (a) substantial economies of scale; (b) little or no economies of scale?

Definitions

Overheads Costs arising from the general running of an organisation, and only indirectly related to the level of output.

Economies of scope When increasing the range of products produced by a firm reduces the cost of producing each one.

Diseconomies of scale Where costs per unit of output increase as the scale of production increases.

The size of the whole industry

As an *industry* grows in size, this can lead to **external economies of scale** for its member firms. This is where a firm, whatever its own individual size, benefits from the *whole industry* being large. For example, the firm may benefit from having access to specialist raw material or component suppliers, labour with specific skills, firms that specialise in marketing the finished product, and banks and other financial institutions with experience of the industry's requirements. What we are referring to here is the **industry's infrastructure**: the facilities, support services, skills and experience that can be shared by its members.

1. *Name some industries where external economies of scale are gained. What are the specific external economies in each case?*
2. *Would you expect external economies to be associated with the concentration of an industry in a particular region?*

The member firms of a particular industry might experience **external diseconomies of scale**. For example, as an industry grows larger, this may create a growing shortage of specific raw materials or skilled labour. This will push up their prices, and hence the firms' costs.

The optimum combination of factors: the marginal product approach

In the long run, all factors can be varied. The firm can thus choose what techniques of production to use: what design of factory to build, what types of machine to buy, how to organise the factory, whether to use highly automated processes or more labour-intensive techniques. It must be very careful in making these decisions. Once it has built its factory and installed the machinery, these then become fixed factors of production, maybe for many years: the subsequent 'short-run' time period may in practice last a very long time!

For any given scale, how should the firm decide what technique to use? How should it decide the optimum 'mix' of factors of production?

The profit-maximising firm will obviously want to use the least costly combination of factors to produce any given output. It will therefore substitute factors, if by so doing it can reduce the cost of a given output. What then is the optimum combination of factors?

The simple two-factor case

Take first the simplest case where a firm uses just two factors: labour (L) and capital (K). The least-cost combination of the two will be where

$$\frac{MPP_L}{P_L} = \frac{MPP_K}{P_K}$$

– in other words, where the extra product (MPP) from the last pound spent on each factor is equal. But why should this be so? The easiest way to answer this is to consider what would happen if they were not equal.

If they were not equal, it would be possible to reduce cost per unit of output, by using a different combination of labour and capital. For example, if

$$\frac{MPP_L}{P_L} > \frac{MPP_K}{P_K}$$

more labour should be used relative to capital, since the firm is getting a greater physical return for its money from extra workers than from extra capital. As more labour is used per unit of capital, however, diminishing returns to labour set in. Thus MPP_L will fall. Likewise, as less capital is used per unit of labour, MPP_K will rise. This will continue until

$$\frac{MPP_L}{P_L} = \frac{MPP_K}{P_K}$$

At this point, the firm will stop substituting labour for capital.

Since no further gain can be made by substituting one factor for another, this combination of factors or 'choice of technique' can be said to be the most efficient. It is the least-cost way of combining factors for any given output. Efficiency in this sense of using the optimum factor proportions is known as **productive efficiency**.

The multi-factor case

Where a firm uses many different factors, the least-cost combination of factors will be where

$$\frac{MPP_a}{P_a} = \frac{MPP_b}{P_b} = \frac{MPP_c}{P_c} \cdots = \frac{MPP_n}{P_n}$$

where a . . . n are different factors. This is a variant of the equi-marginal principle that we examined on page 102.

Definitions

External economies of scale Where a firm's costs per unit of output decrease as the size of the whole industry grows.

Industry's infrastructure The network of supply agents, communications, skills, training facilities, distribution channels, specialised financial services, etc. that supports a particular industry.

External diseconomies of scale Where a firm's costs per unit of output increase as the size of the whole industry increases.

Productive efficiency The least-cost combination of factors for a given output.

The reasons are the same as in the two-factor case. If any inequality exists between the *MPP/P* ratios, a firm will be able to reduce its costs by using more of those factors with a high *MPP/P* ratio and less of those with a low *MPP/P* ratio until they all become equal.

A major problem for a firm in choosing the least-cost technique is in predicting future factor price changes.

If the price of a factor were to change, the *MPP/P* ratios would cease to be equal. The firm, to minimise costs, would then like to alter its factor combinations until the *MPP/P* ratios once more became equal. The trouble is that, once it has committed itself to a particular technique, it may be several years before it can switch to an alternative one. Thus if a firm invests in labour-intensive methods of production and is then faced with an unexpected wage rise, it may regret not having chosen a more capital-intensive technique.

 If factor X costs twice as much as factor Y ($P_X/P_Y = 2$), what can be said about the relationship between the MPPs of the two factors if the optimum combination of factors is used?

*LOOKING AT THE MATHS

We can express the long-run production function algebraically. In the simple two-factor model, where capital (K) and labour (L) are the two factors, the production function is

$$TPP = f(K, L)$$

A simple and widely used production function is the **Cobb–Douglas production function**. This takes the form

$$TPP = AK^{\alpha}L^{\beta}$$

Box 5.7 demonstrates that where $\alpha + \beta = 1$, there are constant returns to scale; where $\alpha + \beta > 1$, there are increasing returns to scale; and where $\alpha + \beta < 1$, there are decreasing returns to scale.

A multiple-factor Cobb–Douglas production function would take the form

$$TPP = AF_1^{\alpha}F_2^{\beta}F_3^{\gamma} \ldots F_n^{\omega}$$

where $F_1, F_2, F_3 \ldots F_n$ are all the factors. For example, if there were six factors, n would be factor 6. Again, it can be shown that where $\alpha + \beta + \gamma + \ldots + \omega = 1$, there are constant returns to scale; where $\alpha + \beta + \gamma + \ldots + \omega > 1$, there are increasing returns to scale; and where $\alpha + \beta + \gamma + \ldots + \omega < 1$, there are decreasing returns to scale.

*The optimum combination of factors: the isoquant/isocost approach

This section is optional. You can skip straight to page 145 without loss of continuity.

A firm's choice of optimum technique can be shown graphically. This graphical analysis takes the simplest case

of just two variable factors – for example, labour and capital. The amount of labour used is measured on one axis and the amount of capital used is measured on the other.

The graph involves the construction of *isoquants* and *isocosts*.

Isoquants

Imagine that a firm wants to produce a certain level of output: say, 5000 units per year. Let us assume that it estimates all the possible combinations of labour and capital that could produce that level of output. Some of these estimates are shown in Table 5.5.

Table 5.5	Various capital and labour combinations to produce 5000 units of output per year				
	a	**b**	**c**	**d**	**e**
Units of capital (K)	40	20	10	6	4
Number of workers (L)	5	12	20	30	50

Technique *a* is a capital-intensive technique, using 40 units of capital and only 5 workers. As we move towards technique *e*, labour is substituted for capital. The techniques become more labour intensive.

These alternative techniques for producing a given level of output can be plotted on a graph. The points are joined to form an **isoquant**. Figure 5.5 shows the 5000 unit isoquant corresponding to Table 5.5.

The isoquant shows the whole *range* of alternative ways of producing a given output. Thus Figure 5.5 shows not only points *a* to *e* from the table, but all the intermediate points too.

Like an indifference curve, an isoquant is rather like a contour on a map. As with contours and indifference curves, a whole series of isoquants can be drawn, each one representing a different level of output (*TPP*). The higher the output, the further out to the right will the isoquant be.

Definitions

Cobb–Douglas production function Like other production functions, this shows how output (*TPP*) varies with inputs of various factors (F_1, F_2, F_3, etc.). In the simple two-factor case it takes the following form:

$$TPP = f(F_1, F_2) = AF_1^{\alpha}F_2^{\beta}$$

If $\alpha + \beta = 1$, there are constant returns to scale; if $\alpha + \beta > 1$, there are increasing returns to scale; if $\alpha + \beta < 1$, there are decreasing returns to scale.

Isoquant A line showing all the alternative combinations of two factors that can produce a given level of output.

Figure 5.5 An isoquant

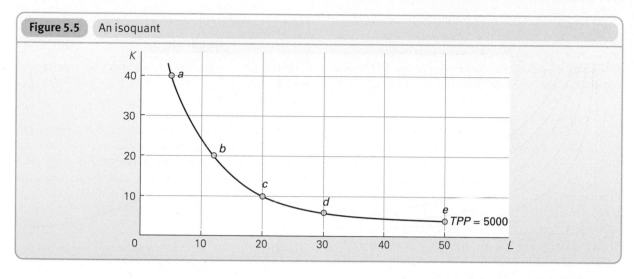

---

*BOX 5.7 **THE COBB–DOUGLAS PRODUCTION FUNCTION** EXPLORING ECONOMICS

Exploring its properties

Let us take the simple Cobb–Douglas production function (see opposite):

$$TPP = AK^{\alpha}L^{\beta} \qquad (1)$$

Returns to scale and the Cobb–Douglas production function

What would happen if you were to double the amount of K and L used (in other words, the scale of production doubles)? If output doubles, there are constant returns to scale. If output more than doubles, there are increasing returns to scale; if it less than doubles, there are decreasing returns to scale. Let us see what happens when we double the amount of K and L in equation (1).

$$TPP = A(2K^{\alpha})(2L^{\beta})$$
$$= A2^{\alpha}K^{\alpha}2^{\beta}L^{\beta}$$
$$= A2^{\alpha+\beta}K^{\alpha}L^{\beta}$$

If $\alpha + \beta = 1$, then $2^{\alpha+\beta} = 2$. Thus

$$TPP = 2AK^{\alpha}L^{\beta}$$

In other words, doubling the amount of K and L used has doubled output: there are constant returns to scale.

If $\alpha + \beta > 1$, then $2^{\alpha+\beta} > 2$. In this case, doubling inputs will more than double output: there are increasing returns to scale. Similarly, if $\alpha + \beta < 1$, then $2^{\alpha+\beta} < 2$ and there are decreasing returns to scale.

Finding the marginal physical products of labour and capital

The marginal physical product (MPP) of a factor is the additional output obtained by employing one more unit of that factor, while holding other factors constant. The MPP of either factor in the above Cobb–Douglas production function can be found by differentiating the function with respect to that factor (see page A13 for the rules of partial differentiation). Thus

$$MPP_K = \frac{\partial (TPP)}{\partial K} = \alpha AK^{\alpha-1}L^{\beta} \qquad (2)$$

and

$$MPP_L = \frac{\partial (TPP)}{\partial L} = \beta AK^{\alpha}L^{\beta-1} \qquad (3)$$

For example, if the production function were

$$TPP = 4K^{3/4}L^{1/2} \qquad (4)$$

and if $K = 81$ and $L = 36$, then, from equations (2) and (4),

$$MPP_K = \alpha AK^{\alpha-1}L^{\beta}$$
$$= \frac{3}{4} \times 4(81^{-1/4})(36^{1/2})$$
$$= 3 \times \frac{1}{3} \times 6 = 6$$

$$MPP_L = \beta AK^{\alpha}L^{\beta-1}$$
$$\text{and} = \frac{1}{2} \times 4(81^{3/4})(36^{-1/2})$$
$$= 2 \times 27 \times \frac{1}{6} = 9$$

In other words, an additional unit of capital will produce an extra 6 units of output and an additional unit of labour will produce an extra 9 units of output.

  Assume that the production function is given by

$$TPP = 36K^{1/3}L^{1/2}R^{1/4}$$

where R is the quantity of a particular raw material used.
(a) Are there constant, increasing or decreasing returns to scale?
(b) What is the marginal productivity of the raw material if $K = 8$, $L = 16$ and $R = 81$?

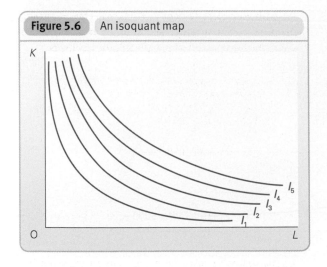

Figure 5.6   An isoquant map

Thus in Figure 5.6, isoquant I_5 represents a higher level of output than I_4, and I_4 a higher output than I_3, and so on.

1. *Could isoquants ever cross?*
2. *Could they ever slope upwards to the right?*
    Explain your answers.

The shape of the isoquant.   Why is the isoquant 'bowed in' towards the origin? This illustrates a diminishing ***marginal rate of factor substitution*** (*MRS*). This, as we shall see very soon, is due to the law of diminishing returns.

The MRS[1] is the amount of one factor (e.g. K) that can be replaced by a 1 unit increase in the other factor (e.g. L), if output is to be held constant. So if 2 units of capital ($\Delta K = 2$) could be replaced by 1 unit of labour ($\Delta L = 1$) the MRS would be 2. Thus:

$$MRS = \frac{\Delta K}{\Delta L} = \frac{2}{1} = 2$$

The MRS between two points on the isoquant will equal the slope of the line joining those two points. Thus in Figure 5.7, the MRS between points g and h is 2 ($\Delta K/\Delta L = 2/1$). But this is merely the slope of the line joining points g and h (ignoring the negative sign).

---

[1] Note that we use the same letters *MRS* to refer to the marginal rate of *factor* substitution as we did in the previous chapter to refer to the marginal rate of substitution *in consumption*. Sometimes we use the same words too – just 'marginal rate of substitution' rather than the longer title. In this case we must rely on the context in order to tell which is being referred to.

Definition

Marginal rate of factor substitution The rate at which one factor can be substituted by another while holding the level of output constant:

$$MRS = \Delta F_1/\Delta F_2 = MPPF_2/MPPF_1$$

Figure 5.7   Diminishing marginal rate of factor substitution

When the isoquant is bowed in towards the origin, the slope of the isoquant will diminish as one moves down the curve, and so too, therefore, will the MRS diminish. Referring again to Figure 5.7, between points g and h the $MRS = 2$. Lower down the curve between points j and k, it has fallen to 1.

Calculate the MRS moving up the curve in Figure 5.5 between each pair of points: e–d, d–c, c–b and b–a. Does the MRS diminish moving in this direction?

The relationship between MRS and MPP.   As one moves down the isoquant, total output, by definition, will remain the same. Thus the loss in output due to less capital being used (i.e. $MPP_K \times \Delta K$) must be exactly offset by the gain in output due to more labour being used (i.e. $MPP_L \times \Delta L$). Thus:

$$MPP_L \times \Delta L = MPP_K \times \Delta K$$

This equation can be rearranged as follows:

$$\frac{MPP_L}{MPP_K} = \frac{\Delta K}{\Delta L} \quad (= MRS)$$

Thus the MRS is equal to the inverse of the marginal productivity ratios of the two factors.

Diminishing MRS and the law of diminishing returns.   The principle of diminishing MRS is related to the law of diminishing returns. As one moves down the isoquant, increasing amounts of labour are being used relative to capital. This, given diminishing returns, would lead the MPP of labour to fall relative to the MPP of capital. But since $MRS = MPP_L/MPP_K$, if MPP_L/MPP_K diminishes, then, by definition, so must MRS.

The less substitutable factors are for each other, the faster MRS will diminish, and therefore the more bowed in will be the isoquant.

Isocosts

We have seen how factors combine to produce different levels of output, but how do we choose the level of output? This will involve taking costs into account.

Assume that factor prices are fixed. A table can be constructed showing the various combinations of factors that a firm can use for a particular sum of money.

For example, assuming that P_K is £20 000 per unit per year and P_L is £10 000 per worker per year, Table 5.6 shows various combinations of capital and labour that would cost the firm £300 000 per year.

Table 5.6	Combinations of capital and labour costing the firm £300 000 per year			
Units of capital (at £20 000 per unit)	0	5	10	15
No. of workers (at a wage of £10 000)	30	20	10	0

These figures are plotted in Figure 5.8. The line joining the points is called an **isocost**. It shows all the combinations of labour and capital that cost £300 000.

Definition

Isocost A line showing all the combinations of two factors that cost the same to employ.

As with isoquants, a series of isocosts can be drawn. Each one represents a particular cost to the firm. The higher the cost, the further out to the right will the isocost be.

1. *What will happen to an isocost if the prices of both factors rise by the same percentage?*
2. *What will happen to the isocost in Figure 5.8 if the wage rate rises to £15 000?*

The slope of the isocost equals

$$\frac{P_L}{P_K}$$

This can be shown in the above example. The slope of the isocost in Figure 5.8 is $15/30 = {}^1/_2$. But this is P_L/P_K (i.e. £10 000/£20 000).

Isoquants and isocosts can now be put on the same diagram. The diagram can be used to answer either of two questions: (a) What is the least-cost way of producing a particular level of output? (b) What is the highest output that can be achieved for a given cost of production?

These two questions are examined in turn.

The least-cost combination of factors to produce a given level of output

First the isoquant is drawn for the level of output in question: for example, the 5000 unit isoquant in Figure 5.5. This is reproduced in Figure 5.9.

Then a series of isocosts are drawn representing different levels of total cost. The higher the level of total cost, the further out will be the isocosts.

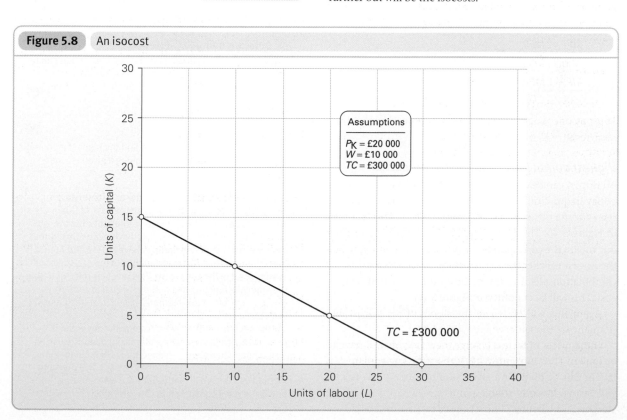

Figure 5.8 An isocost

Assumptions

P_K = £20 000
W = £10 000
TC = £300 000

TC = £300 000

Units of capital (K)

Units of labour (L)

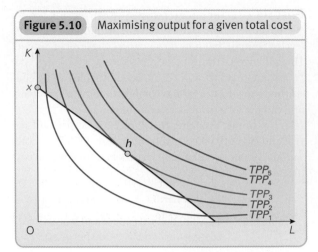

Figure 5.9 The least-cost method of production

Figure 5.10 Maximising output for a given total cost

The least-cost combination of labour and capital is shown at point r, where $TC = £400\ 000$. This is where the isoquant just touches the lowest possible isocost. Any other point on the isoquant (e.g. s or t) would be on a higher isocost.

Comparison with the marginal productivity approach. We showed earlier that the least-cost combination of labour and capital was where

$$\frac{MPP_L}{P_L} = \frac{MPP_K}{P_K}$$

In this section it has just been shown that the least-cost combination is where the isoquant is tangential to an isocost (i.e. point r in Figure 5.9). Thus their slope is the same. The slope of the isoquant equals MRS, which equals MPP_L/MPP_K; and the slope of the isocost equals P_L/P_K.

$$\therefore \quad \frac{MPP_L}{P_K} = \frac{MPP_L}{P_K}$$

$$\therefore \quad \frac{MPP_L}{P_L} = \frac{MPP_K}{P_K}$$

Thus, as one would expect, the two approaches yield the same result.

Highest output for a given cost of production

An isocost can be drawn for the particular level of total cost outlay in question. Then a series of isoquants can be drawn, representing different levels of output (*TPP*). This is shown in Figure 5.10. The higher the level of output, the further out will lie the corresponding isoquant. The point at which the isocost touches the highest isoquant will give the factor combination yielding the highest output for that level of cost. This will be at point h in Figure 5.10.

Again this will be where the slopes of the isocost and isoquant are the same: where $P_L/P_K = MRS$.

If the prices of factors change, new isocosts will have to be drawn. Thus in Figure 5.10, if the wage rate goes up, less labour can be used for a given sum of money. The isocost will swing inwards round point x. The isocost will get steeper. Less labour will now be used relative to capital.

*LOOKING AT THE MATHS

We can express the optimum production point algebraically. This can be done in either of two ways, corresponding to Figures 5.9 or 5.10. The method is similar to that used for finding the optimum consumption point that we examined on page 114.

(a) Corresponding to Figure 5.9

The first way involves finding the least-cost method of producing a given output (Q). This can be expressed as

$$\text{Min } P_K K + P_L L \qquad (1)$$

subject to the output constraint that

$$Q = Q(K,L) \qquad (2)$$

In other words, the objective is to find the lowest isocost (equation 1) to produce on a given isoquant (equation 2).

(b) Corresponding to Figure 5.10

The second involves finding the highest output that can be produced for a given cost. This can be expressed as

$$\text{Max } Q(K,L) \qquad (3)$$

subject to the cost constraint that

$$P_K K + P_L L = C \qquad (4)$$

In other words, the objective is to find the highest isoquant (equation 3) that can be reached along a given isocost (equation 4).

There are two methods of solving (a) and (b) for any given value of P_K, P_L and either Q (in the case of (a)) or C (in the case of (b)). The first involves substituting the constraint equation into the objective function (to express K in terms of L) and then finding the value of L and then K that minimises the objective function in the case of (a) or maximises it in the case of (b). This involves differentiating the objective function and setting it equal to zero. A worked example of this method is given in Maths Case 5.2 in MyEconLab.

The second method, which is slightly longer but is likely to involve simpler calculations, involves the use of 'Lagrangian multipliers'. This method is explained, along with a worked example, in Maths Case 5.3. It is the same method as we used in Maths Case 4.2 when finding the optimal level of consumption of two products.

Postscript: decision making in different time periods

We have distinguished between the short run and the long run. Let us introduce two more time periods to complete the picture. The complete list then reads as follows.

Very short run (immediate run). All factors are fixed. Output is fixed. The supply curve is vertical. On a day-to-day basis, a firm may not be able to vary output at all. For example, a flower seller, once the day's flowers have been purchased from the wholesaler, cannot alter the amount of flowers available for sale on that day. In the very short run, all that may remain for a producer to do is to sell an already produced good.

 Why are Christmas trees and fresh foods often sold cheaply on Christmas Eve? (See Box 5.5.)

Short run. At least one factor is fixed in supply. More can be produced, but the firm will come up against the law of diminishing returns as it tries to do so.

Long run. All factors are variable. The firm may experience constant, increasing or decreasing returns to scale. But although all factors can be increased or decreased, they are of a fixed *quality*.

Very long run. All factors are variable, *and* their quality and hence productivity can change. Labour productivity can increase as a result of education, training, experience and social factors. The productivity of capital can increase as a result of new inventions (new discoveries) and innovation (putting inventions into practice).

Improvements in factor quality will increase the output they produce: *TPP*, *APP* and *MPP* will rise. These curves will shift vertically upwards.

Just how long the 'very long run' is will vary from firm to firm. It will depend on how long it takes to develop new techniques, new skills or new work practices.

It is important to realise that decisions *for* all four time periods can be made *at* the same time. Firms do not make short-run decisions *in* the short run and long-run

decisions *in* the long run. They can make both short-run and long-run decisions today. For example, assume that a firm experiences an increase in consumer demand and anticipates that it will continue into the foreseeable future. It thus wants to increase output. Consequently, it makes the following four decisions *today*:

- (*Very short run*) It accepts that for a few days it will not be able to increase output. It informs its customers that they will have to wait. In some markets the firm may temporarily raise prices to choke off some of the demand.
- (*Short run*) It negotiates with labour to introduce overtime working as soon as possible, to tide it over the next few weeks. It orders extra raw materials from its suppliers. It launches a recruitment drive for new labour so as to avoid paying overtime longer than is necessary.
- (*Long run*) It starts proceedings to build a new factory. What would this involve? In some cases the firm may talk to the bank directly about finance and start investigating sites. A different approach might be to discuss requirements with a firm of consultants.
- (*Very long run*) It institutes a programme of research and development and/or training in an attempt to increase productivity.

 1. Could the long run and the very long run ever be the same length of time?
2. What will the long-run and very-long-run market supply curves for a product look like? How will the shape of the long-run curve depend on returns to scale?
*3. In the very long run, new isoquants will have to be drawn as factor productivity changes. An increase in productivity will shift the isoquants inwards towards the origin: less capital and labour will be required to produce any given level of output. Will this be a parallel inward shift of the isoquants? Explain.

Although we distinguish these four time periods, it is the middle two we are primarily concerned with. The reason for this is that there is very little the firm can do in the *very* short run. And concerning the *very* long run, although the firm will obviously want to increase the productivity of its inputs, it will not be in a position to make precise calculations of how to do it. It will not know precisely what inventions will be made, or just what will be the results of its own research and development.

Section summary

1. In the long run, a firm is able to vary the quantity it uses of all factors of production. There are no fixed factors.

2. If it increases all factors by the same proportion, it may experience constant, increasing or decreasing returns to scale.

3. Economies of scale occur when costs per unit of output fall as the scale of production increases. This can be due to a number of factors, some of which result directly from increasing (physical) returns to scale. These include the benefits of specialisation and

▶

division of labour, the use of larger and more efficient machines, and the ability to have a more integrated system of production. Other economies of scale arise from the financial and administrative benefits of large-scale organisations.

4. Long-run costs are also influenced by a firm's location. The firm will have to balance the needs to be as near as possible both to the supply of its raw materials and to its market. The optimum balance will depend on the relative costs of transporting the inputs and the finished product.

5. To minimise costs per unit of output, a firm should choose that combination of factors which gives an equal marginal product for each factor relative to its price: i.e. $MPP_a/P_a = MPP_b/P_b = MPP_c/P_c$, etc. (where a, b and c are different factors). If the MPP/P ratio for one factor is greater than for another, more of the first should be used relative to the second.

6. An isoquant shows the various combinations of two factors to produce a given output. A whole map of such isoquants can be drawn with each isoquant representing a different level of output. The slope of the isoquant ($\Delta K/\Delta L$) gives the marginal rate of factor substitution (MPP_L/MPP_K). The bowed-in shape of

isoquants illustrates a diminishing marginal rate of factor substitution, which in turn arises because of diminishing marginal returns.

7. An isocost shows the various combinations of two factors that cost a given amount to employ. It will be a straight line. Its slope is equal to the price ratio of the two factors (P_L/P_K).

8. The tangency point of an isocost with an isoquant represents the optimum factor combination. It is the point where MPP_L/MPP_K (the slope of the isoquant) = P_L/P_K (the slope of the isocost). By drawing a single isoquant touching the lowest possible isocost, we can show the least-cost combination of factors for producing a given output. By drawing a single isocost touching the highest possible isoquant, we can show the highest output obtainable for a given cost of production.

9. Four distinct time periods can be distinguished. In addition to the short- and long-run periods, we can also distinguish the very-short- and very-long-run periods. The very short run is when all factors are fixed. The very long run is where not only the quantity of factors but also their quality is variable (as a result of changing technology, etc.).

5.4 COSTS IN THE LONG RUN

We turn now to *long-run* cost curves. Since there are no fixed factors in the long run, there are no long-run fixed costs. For example, the firm may rent more land in order to expand its operations. Its rent bill therefore goes up as it expands its output. All costs, then, in the long run are variable costs.

 KEY IDEA 19 *Fixed costs and the time period.* Fixed costs occur only in the short run, since in the long run all inputs can be varied.

Long-run average costs

Long-run average cost (LRAC) curves can take various shapes, but a typical one is shown in Figure 5.11.

Definition

Long-run average cost curve A curve that shows how average cost varies with output on the assumption that *all* factors are variable. (It is assumed that the least-cost method of production will be chosen for each output.)

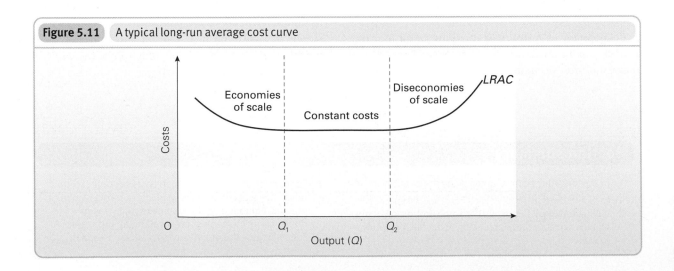

Figure 5.11 A typical long-run average cost curve

It is often assumed that as a firm expands, it will initially experience economies of scale and thus face a downward-sloping *LRAC* curve. After a point, however, all such economies will have been achieved and thus the curve will flatten out. Then (possibly after a period of constant *LRAC*) the firm will get so large that it will start experiencing diseconomies of scale and thus a rising *LRAC*. At this stage, production and financial economies will begin to be offset by the managerial problems of running a giant organisation.

 Given the LRAC curve in Figure 5.11, what would the firm's long-run total cost curve look like?

Assumptions behind the long-run average cost curve

We make three key assumptions when constructing long-run average cost curves.

Factor prices are given. At each level of output, it is assumed that a firm will be faced with a given set of factor prices. If factor prices *change*, therefore, both short- and long-run cost curves will shift. Thus an increase in nationally negotiated wage rates would shift the curves upwards.

However, factor prices might be different at *different* levels of output. For example, one of the economies of scale that many firms enjoy is the ability to obtain bulk discount on raw materials and other supplies. In such cases, the curve does *not* shift. The different factor prices are merely experienced at different points along the curve, and are reflected in the shape of the curve. Factor prices are still given for any particular level of output.

The state of technology and factor quality are given. These are assumed to change only in the *very* long run. If a firm gains economies of scale, it is because it is being able to exploit *existing* technologies and make better use of the existing availability of factors of production.

Firms choose the least-cost combination of factors for each output. The assumption here is that firms operate efficiently: that they choose the cheapest possible way of producing any level of output. In other words, at every point along the *LRAC* curve, the firm will adhere to the cost-minimising formula (see page 139):

$$\frac{MPP_a}{P_a} = \frac{MPP_b}{P_b} = \frac{MPP_c}{P_c} \cdots \frac{MPP_n}{P_n}$$

where a . . . n are the various factors the firm uses.

If the firm did not choose the optimum factor combination, it would be producing at a point above the *LRAC* curve.

Long-run marginal costs

The relationship between long-run average and **long-run marginal cost** curves is just like that between any other averages and marginals (see Box 5.3). This is illustrated in Figure 5.12.

If there are economies of scale (diagram (a)), additional units of output will add less to costs than the average. The *LRMC* curve must be below the *LRAC* curve and thus pulling the average down as output increases. If there are diseconomies of scale (diagram (b)), additional units of output will cost more than the average. The *LRMC* curve must

---

Definition

Long-run marginal cost The extra cost of producing one more unit of output assuming that all factors are variable. (It is assumed that the least-cost method of production will be chosen for this extra output.)

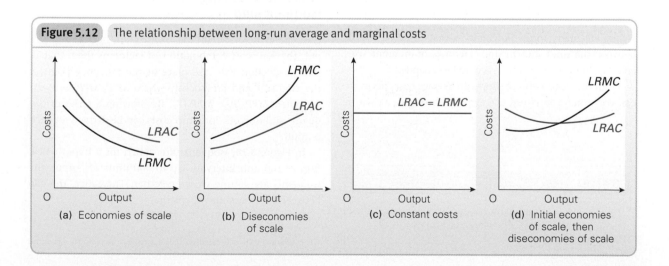

Figure 5.12 The relationship between long-run average and marginal costs

(a) Economies of scale
(b) Diseconomies of scale
(c) Constant costs
(d) Initial economies of scale, then diseconomies of scale

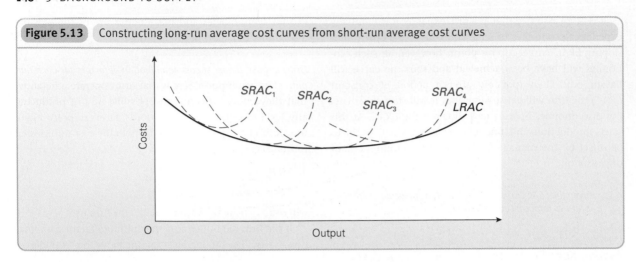

Figure 5.13 Constructing long-run average cost curves from short-run average cost curves

be above the *LRAC* curve, pulling it up. If there are no economies or diseconomies of scale, so that the *LRAC* curve is horizontal, any additional units of output will cost the same as the average and thus leave the average unaffected (diagram (c)).

1. *Explain the shape of the LRMC curve in diagram (d) in Figure 5.12.*
2. *What would the LRMC curve look like if the LRAC curve were 'flat-bottomed', as in Figure 5.11?*

The relationship between long-run and short-run average cost curves

Take the case of a firm which has just one factory and faces a short-run average cost curve illustrated by $SRAC_1$ in Figure 5.13.

In the long run, it can build more factories. If it thereby experiences economies of scale (due, say, to savings on administration), each successive factory will allow it to produce with a new lower *SRAC* curve. Thus with two factories it will face $SRAC_2$, with three factories $SRAC_3$, and so on. Each *SRAC* curve corresponds to a particular amount of the factor that is fixed in the short run: in this case, the factory. (There are many more *SRAC* curves that could be drawn between the ones shown, since factories of different sizes could be built or existing ones could be expanded.)

From this succession of short-run average cost curves we can construct a long-run average cost curve, as shown in

Figure 5.13. This is known as the ***envelope curve***, since it envelopes the short-run curves.

Will the envelope curve be tangential to the bottom of each of the short-run average cost curves? Explain why it should or should not be.

Long-run cost curves in practice

Firms do experience economies of scale. Some experience continuously falling *LRAC* curves, as in Figure 5.12(a). Others experience economies of scale up to a certain output and thereafter constant returns to scale.

Evidence is inconclusive on the question of diseconomies of scale. There is little evidence to suggest the existence of *technical* diseconomies, but the possibility of diseconomies due to managerial and industrial relations problems cannot be ruled out.

Some evidence on economies of scale in the UK is considered in Box 5.8 (on pages 150–1).

*Derivation of long-run costs from an isoquant map[1]

Cost curves are drawn on the assumption that, for any output, the least-cost combination of factors is used: that is, that production will take place at the tangency point of the isoquant and an isocost, where $MPP_L/MPP_K = P_L/P_K$: i.e. where $MPP_L/P_L = MPP_K/P_K$. By drawing a series of isoquants and isocosts, long-run costs can be derived for each output.

In Figure 5.14, isoquants are drawn for a hypothetical firm at 100 unit intervals. Up to 400 units of output, the isoquants are getting closer together. Thereafter, the gap between the isoquants widens again.

Definition

Envelope curve A long-run average cost curve drawn as the tangency points of a series of short-run average cost curves.

[1] This optional section is based on the material in the optional section on pages 140–4.

Figure 5.14   Deriving an *LRAC* curve from an isoquant map

The line from *a* to *g* is known as the ***expansion path***. It traces the tangency points of the isoquants and isocosts, and thus shows the minimum-cost combinations of labour and capital to produce each output: the (long-run) total cost being given by the isocost.

Definition

Expansion path   The line on an isoquant map that traces the minimum-cost combinations of two factors as output increases. It is drawn on the assumption that both factors can be varied. It is thus a long-run path.

Up to point *d*, less and less *extra* capital (*K*) and labour (*L*) are required to produce each extra 100 units of output. Thus long-run marginal cost is falling. Above point *d*, more and more extra *K* and *L* are required and thus *LRMC* rises.

Thus the isoquant map of Figure 5.14 gives an *LRMC* curve that is ⌣-shaped. The *LRAC* curve will therefore also be ⌣-shaped (only shallower) with the *LRMC* coming up through the bottom of the *LRAC*.

 What would the isoquant map look like if there were (a) continuously increasing returns to scale; (b) continuously decreasing returns to scale?

Section summary

1. In the long run, all factors are variable. There are thus no long-run fixed costs.

2. When constructing long-run cost curves, it is assumed that factor prices are given, that the state of technology is given and that firms will choose the least-cost combination of factors for each given output.

3. The *LRAC* curve can be downward sloping, upward sloping or horizontal, depending in turn on whether there are economies of scale, diseconomies of scale or neither. Typically, *LRAC* curves are drawn saucer-shaped or ⌣-shaped. As output expands, initially there are economies of scale. When these are exhausted, the curve will become flat. When the firm becomes very large, it may begin to experience

diseconomies of scale. If this happens, the *LRAC* curve will begin to slope upwards again.

4. The long-run marginal cost curve will be below the *LRAC* curve when *LRAC* is falling, above it when *LRAC* is rising and equal to it when *LRAC* is neither rising nor falling.

5. An envelope curve can be drawn which shows the relationship between short-run and long-run average cost curves. The *LRAC* curve envelops the short-run *LRAC* curves: it is tangential to them.

6. Costs can be derived from an isoquant map. Long-run total costs are found from the expansion path, which shows the least-cost combination of factors to produce any given output. It traces out the tangency points of the isocosts and isoquants.

BOX 5.8 | MINIMUM EFFICIENT SCALE

The extent of economies of scale in practice

Two of the most important studies of economies of scale are those made by C. F. Pratten[1] in the late 1980s and by a group advising the European Commission[2] in 1997. Both studies found strong evidence that many firms, especially in manufacturing, experienced substantial economies of scale.

In a few cases, long-run average costs fell continuously as output increased. For most firms, however, they fell up to a certain level of output and then remained constant.

The extent of economies of scale can be measured by looking at a firm's *minimum efficient scale* (*MES*). The *MES* is the size beyond which no significant additional economies of scale can be achieved: in other words, the point where the *LRAC* curve flattens off. In Pratten's studies, he defined this level as the minimum scale above which any possible doubling in scale would reduce average costs by less than 5 per cent (i.e. virtually the bottom of the *LRAC* curve). In the diagram, *MES* is shown at point *a*.

The *MES* can be expressed in terms either of an individual factory or of the whole firm. Where it refers to the minimum efficient scale of an individual factory, the *MES* is known as the *minimum efficient plant size* (*MEPS*).

The *MES* can then be expressed as a percentage of the total size of the market or of total domestic production. Table (a), based on the Pratten study, shows *MES* for plants and firms in various industries. The first column shows *MES* as a percentage of total UK production. The second column shows *MES* as a percentage of total EU production. Table (b), based on the 1997 study, shows *MES* for various plants.

Expressing *MES* as a percentage of total output gives an indication of how competitive the industry could be.

Table (a)

Product	MES as % of production		% additional cost at $^1/_2$ MES
	UK	EU	
Individual plants			
Cellulose fibres	125	16	3
Rolled aluminium semi-manufactures	114	15	15
Refrigerators	85	11	4
Steel	72	10	6
Electric motors	60	6	15
TV sets	40	9	9
Cigarettes	24	6	1.4
Ball-bearings	20	2	6
Beer	12	3	7
Nylon	4	1	12
Bricks	1	0.2	25
Carpets	0.3	0.04	10
Footwear	0.3	0.03	1
Firms			
Cars	200	20	9
Lorries	104	21	7.5
Mainframe computers	>100	n.a.	5
Aircraft	100	n.a.	5
Tractors	98	19	6

Source: See footnote 1 below.

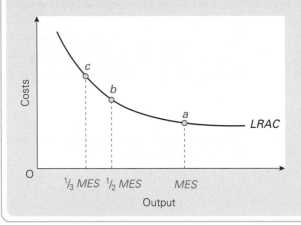

5.5 | REVENUE

Remember that we defined a firm's total profit as its total revenue minus its total costs of production. So far in this chapter we have examined costs. We now turn to revenue.

As with costs, we distinguish between three revenue concepts: total revenue (*TR*), average revenue (*AR*) and marginal revenue (*MR*).

Total, average and marginal revenue

Total revenue (TR)

Total revenue is the firm's total earnings per period of time from the sale of a particular amount of output (*Q*). For

example, if a firm sells 1000 units (*Q*) per month at a price of £5 each (*P*), then its monthly total revenue will be £5000: in other words, £5 × 1000 (*P × Q*). Thus

$$TR = P \times Q$$

Definition

Total revenue A firm's total earnings from a specified level of sales within a specified period: $TR = P \times Q$.

CASE STUDIES AND
APPLICATIONS

Table (b)

Plants	MES as % of total EU production
Aerospace	12.19
Agricultural machinery	6.57
Electric lighting	3.76
Steel tubes	2.42
Shipbuilding	1.63
Rubber	1.06
Radio and TV	0.69
Footwear	0.08
Carpets	0.03

Source: See footnote 2 below.

In some industries (such as footwear and carpets), economies of scale were exhausted (i.e. *MES* was reached) with plants or firms that were still small relative to total UK production and even smaller relative to total EU production. In such industries, there would be room for many firms and thus scope for considerable competition.

In other industries, however, even if a single plant or firm were large enough to produce the whole output of the industry in the UK, it would still not be large enough to experience the full potential economies of scale: the *MES* is greater than 100 per cent. Examples from Table (a) include factories producing cellulose fibres, and car manufacturers. In these industries, there is no possibility of competition from within the country. In fact, as long as the *MES* exceeds 50 per cent, there will not be room for more than one firm large enough to gain full economies of scale (unless they export). In this case, the industry is said to be a natural monopoly.

As we shall see in the next few chapters, when competition is lacking, consumers may suffer by firms charging prices considerably above costs.

A second way of measuring the extent of economies of scale is to see how much costs would increase if

production were reduced to a certain fraction of *MES*. The normal fractions used are $^1/_2$ or $^1/_3$ *MES*. This is illustrated in the diagram. Point *b* corresponds to $^1/_2$ *MES*; point to C $^1/_3$ *MES*. The greater the percentage by which *LRAC* at point *b* or *c* is higher than at point *a*, the greater will be the economies of scale to be gained by producing at *MES* rather than at $^1/_2$ *MES* or $^1/_3$ *MES*. For example, in Table (a) there are greater economies of scale to be gained from moving from $^1/_2$ *MES* to *MES* in the production of electric motors than in cigarettes.

The main purpose of the studies was to determine whether the single EU market is big enough to allow both economies of scale and competition. The tables suggest that in all cases, other things being equal, the EU market is indeed large enough for this to occur. The second study also found that 47 of the 53 manufacturing sectors analysed had scope for further exploitation of economies of scale.

In 2007 and 2008 the European Commission agreed to fund a number of research projects to conduct further investigations of *MES* across different industries and to consider the impact of the expansion of the EU.

1. *Why might a firm operating with one plant achieve MEPS and yet not be large enough to achieve MES? (Clue: are all economies of scale achieved at plant level?)*
2. *Why might a firm producing bricks have an MES which is only 0.2 per cent of total EU production and yet face little effective competition from other EU countries?*

[1] C. F. Pratten, 'A survey of the economies of scale', in *Research into the 'Costs of Non-Europe'*, Volume 2 (Commission of the European Communities, Luxembourg, 1988).
[2] European Commission/Economists Advisory Group Ltd, 'Economies of Scale', *The Single Market Review*, Subseries V, Volume 4 (Commission of the European Communities, Luxembourg, 1997).

Average revenue (AR)

Average revenue is the amount the firm earns per unit sold. Thus

$$AR = TR/Q$$

So if the firm earns £5000 (*TR*) from selling 1000 units (*Q*), it will earn £5 per unit. But this is simply the price! Thus

$$AR = P$$

(The only exception to this is when the firm is selling its products at different prices to different consumers. In this case, *AR* is simply the (weighted) average price.)

Marginal revenue (MR)

Marginal revenue is the extra total revenue gained by selling one more unit (per time period). So if a firm sells an extra 20 units this month compared with what it expected

Definitions

Average revenue Total revenue per unit of output. When all output is sold at the same price, average revenue will be the same as price: $AR = TR/Q = P$.

Marginal revenue The extra revenue gained by selling one more unit per period of time: $MR = \Delta TR/\Delta Q$.

to sell, and in the process earns an extra £100, then it is getting an extra £5 for each extra unit sold: $MR = £5$. Thus

$MR = \Delta TR / \Delta Q$

We now need to see how each of these three revenue concepts (*TR*, *AR* and *MR*) varies with output. We can show this graphically in the same way as we did with costs.

The relationships will depend on the market conditions under which a firm operates. A firm that is too small to be able to affect market price will have different-shaped revenue curves from a firm that is able to choose the price it charges. Let us examine each of these two situations in turn.

Revenue curves when price is not affected by the firm's output

Average revenue

If a firm is very small relative to the whole market, it is likely to be a **price taker**. That is, it has to accept the price given by the intersection of demand and supply in the whole market. But, being so small, it can sell as much as it is capable of producing at that price. This is illustrated in Figure 5.15.

The left-hand part of the diagram shows market demand and supply. Equilibrium price is £5. The right-hand part of the diagram looks at the demand for an individual firm that is tiny relative to the whole market. (Look at the differences in the scale of the horizontal axes in the two parts of the diagram.)

Being so small, any change in its output will be too insignificant to affect the market price. It thus faces a

horizontal demand 'curve' at the price. It can sell 200 units, 600 units, 1200 units or whatever without affecting this £5 price.

Average revenue is thus constant at £5. The firm's average revenue curve must therefore lie along exactly the same line as its demand curve.

Marginal revenue

In the case of a horizontal demand curve, the marginal revenue curve will be the same as the average revenue curve, since selling one more unit at a constant price (*AR*) merely adds that amount to total revenue. If an extra unit is sold at a constant price of £5, an extra £5 is earned.

Total revenue

Table 5.7 shows the effect on total revenue of different levels of sales with a constant price of £5 per unit. As price is constant, total revenue will rise at a constant rate as more is sold. The *TR* 'curve' will therefore be a straight line through the origin, as in Figure 5.16.

 What would happen to the TR curve if the market price rose to £10? Try drawing it.

Table 5.7	Deriving total revenue for a price-taking firm	
Quantity (units)	**Price ≡ AR = MR (£)**	**TR (£)**
0	5	0
200	5	1000
400	5	2000
600	5	3000
800	5	4000
1000	5	5000
1200	5	6000
.	.	.

Definition

Price taker A firm that is too small to be able to influence the market price.

Figure 5.15   Deriving a firm's *AR* and *MR*: price-taking firm

(a) The market

(b) The firm

Figure 5.16 Total revenue for a price-taking firm

Revenue curves when price varies with output

The three curves (*TR*, *AR* and *MR*) look quite different when price does vary with the firm's output. If a firm has a relatively large share of the market, it will face a downward-sloping demand curve. This means that if it is to sell more, it must lower the price. It could also choose to raise its price. If it does so, however, it will have to accept a fall in sales.

Average revenue

Remember that average revenue equals price. If, therefore, price has to be lowered to sell more output, average revenue will fall as output increases.

Table 5.8 gives an example of a firm facing a downward-sloping demand curve. The demand curve (which shows how much is sold at each price) is given by the first two columns.

Note that, as in the case of a price-taking firm, the demand curve and the *AR* curve lie along exactly the same line. The reason for this is simple: *AR* = *P*, and thus the curve relating price to quantity (the demand curve) must be the same as that relating average revenue to quantity (the *AR* curve).

Table 5.8 Revenues for a firm facing a downward-sloping demand curve

Q (units)	P = AR (£)	TR (£)	MR (£)
1	8	8	
2	7	14	6
3	6	18	4
4	5	20	2
5	4	20	0
6	3	18	−2
7	2	14	−4
.	.	.	.

Marginal revenue

When a firm faces a downward-sloping demand curve, marginal revenue will be less than average revenue, and may even be negative. But why?

If a firm is to sell more per time period, it must lower its price (assuming it does not advertise). This will mean lowering the price not just for the extra units it hopes to sell, but also for those units it would have sold had it not lowered the price.

Thus the marginal revenue is the price at which it sells the last unit, *minus* the loss in revenue it has incurred by reducing the price on those units it could otherwise have sold at the higher price. This can be illustrated with Table 5.8.

Assume that the price is currently £7. Two units are thus sold. The firm now wishes to sell an extra unit. It lowers the price to £6. It thus gains £6 from the sale of the third unit, but loses £2 by having to reduce the price by £1 on the two units it could otherwise have sold at £7. Its net gain is therefore £6 − £2 = £4. This is the marginal revenue: it is the extra revenue gained by the firm from selling one more unit. (Notice that in Table 5.8 the figures for *MR* are entered in the spaces between the figures for the other three columns.)

There is a simple relationship between marginal revenue and *price elasticity of demand*. Remember from Chapter 3 (pages 58–9) that if demand is price elastic, a *decrease* in price will lead to a proportionately larger increase in the quantity demanded and hence an *increase* in revenue. Marginal revenue will thus be positive. If, however, demand is inelastic, a decrease in price will lead to a proportionately smaller increase in sales. In this case, the price reduction will more than offset the increase in sales and as a result revenue will fall. Marginal revenue will be negative.

If, then, at a particular quantity sold marginal revenue is a positive figure (i.e. if sales per time period are 4 units or less in Figure 5.17), the demand curve will be elastic at that quantity, since a rise in quantity sold (as a result of a reduction in price) would lead to a rise in total revenue. If, on the other hand, marginal revenue is negative (i.e. at a level of sales of 5 or more units in Figure 5.17), the demand curve

Figure 5.17 AR and MR curves for a firm facing a downward-sloping demand curve

Figure 5.18 Total revenue for a firm facing a downward-sloping demand curve

will be inelastic at that quantity, since a rise in quantity sold would lead to a *fall* in total revenue.

Thus the demand (*AR*) curve in Figure 5.17 is elastic to the left of point *r* and inelastic to the right.

Total revenue

Total revenue equals price times quantity. This is illustrated in Table 5.8. The *TR* column from Table 5.8 is plotted in Figure 5.18.

Unlike the case of a price-taking firm, the *TR* curve is not a straight line. It is a curve that rises at first and then falls. But why? As long as marginal revenue is positive (and hence demand is price elastic), a rise in output will raise total revenue. However, once marginal revenue becomes negative (and hence demand is inelastic), total revenue will fall. The peak of the *TR* curve will be where *MR* = 0. At this point, the price elasticity of demand will be equal to 1.

*LOOKING AT THE MATHS

As with cost curves (see page 135), we can express revenue curves algebraically.

Price-taking firms

Let us take *TR*, *AR* and *MR* in turn. They will take the following forms:

$$TR = bQ \tag{1}$$

This equation will give an upward-sloping straight-line *TR* 'curve', with a slope of *b*. Note that the absence of a constant (*a*) term means that the line passes through the origin. This is obviously the case, given that if sales (*Q*) are zero, total revenue will be zero.

$$AP = \frac{TR}{Q} = b \tag{2}$$

This will give a horizontal *AR* curve at an *AR* (i.e. price) of *b*.

$$MR = \frac{d(TR)}{dQ} = b \tag{3}$$

Differentiating the *TR* function gives a value of *b*. As we have seen, *AR* = *MR* when the firm is a price taker and faces a horizontal demand curve (at the market price).

Price-making firms: a straight-line demand 'curve'

'Price makers' face a downward-sloping demand curve. If this is a straight-line demand curve, the revenue equations will be as follows:

$$TR = bQ - cQ^2 \tag{4}$$

The negative cQ^2 term will give a revenue curve whose slope gets less until a peak is reached (see Figure 5.18). Thereafter, as the cQ^2 term becomes bigger than the bQ term, *TR* will fall.

$$AP = \frac{TR}{Q} = b - cQ \tag{5}$$

This gives a straight-line downward-sloping *AR* curve (demand curve) with a slope of −*c*, which crosses the horizontal axis when *cQ* becomes bigger than *b*.

$$MR = \frac{d(TR)}{dQ} = b - 2cQ \tag{6}$$

This again gives a straight downward-sloping line, this time with a slope of −2*c*. Note that this means that the slope of the *MR* curve is twice that of the *AR* curve.

But what if the demand curve is actually curved? What will the three revenue equations be then? We explore this in Maths Case 5.4 in MyEconLab and relate the equations to the relevant diagrams.

The relationship between marginal revenue and price elasticity of demand

You can see from Figure 5.17 how price elasticity of demand and marginal revenue are related. We can express this relationship algebraically as follows:

$$MR = P(1 + (1/P\epsilon_D)) \tag{7}$$

or

$$P = \frac{MR}{1 + (1/P\epsilon_D)}$$

Proof of this relationship is given in Maths Case 6.2 in MyEconLab, but for now we can see how equation (7) relates to Figure 5.17. The *P* term must be positive. If demand is elastic, then $P\epsilon_D$ must have a value less than −1 (i.e. the figure for elasticity, ignoring the negative sign, must be greater than 1). Thus the term $1/P\epsilon_D$ must have a negative value between 0 and −1. This means, therefore, that the term $(1 + (1/P\epsilon_D))$ must be positive, and hence *MR* must be positive.

If, however, demand is inelastic, then $P\epsilon_D$ must have a value between −1 and zero. Thus the term $1/P\epsilon_D$ must have a negative value less than −1 (i.e. an absolute value, ignoring the negative sign, that is greater than 1). This means, therefore, that the term $(1 + (1/P\epsilon_D))$ must be negative, and hence *MR* must be negative.

Finally, if demand is unit elastic, then the term $1/P\epsilon_D$ must have a value of −1 and hence the term $(1 + (1/P\epsilon_D))$ must have a value of zero. *MR* must be zero.

Shifts in revenue curves

We saw in Chapter 2 that a change in *price* will cause a movement along a demand curve. It is similar with revenue curves, except that here the causal connection is in the other direction. Here we ask what happens to revenue when there is a change in the firm's *output*. Again the effect is shown by a movement along the curves.

A change in any *other* determinant of demand, such as tastes, income or the price of other goods, will shift the demand curve. By affecting the price at which each level of output can be sold, there will be a shift in all three revenue curves. An increase in revenue is shown by a shift upwards; a decrease by a shift downwards.

 Copy Figures 5.17 and 5.18 (which are based on Table 5.8). Now assume that incomes have risen and that, as a result, two more units per time period can be sold at each price. Draw a new table and plot the resulting new AR, MR and TR curves on your diagrams. Are the new curves parallel to the old ones? Explain.

Section summary

1. Total revenue (*TR*) is the total amount a firm earns from its sales in a given time period. It is simply price times quantity: $TR = P \times Q$.

2. Average revenue (*AR*) is total revenue per unit: $AR = TR/Q$. In other words, $AR = P$.

3. Marginal revenue is the extra revenue earned from the sale of one more unit per time period.

4. The *AR* curve will be the same as the demand curve for the firm's product. In the case of a price taker, the demand curve and hence the *AR* curve will be a horizontal straight line and will also be the same as the *MR* curve. The *TR* curve will be an upward-sloping straight line from the origin.

5. A firm that faces a downward-sloping demand curve must obviously also face the same downward-sloping *AR* curve. The *MR* curve will also slope downwards, but will be below the *AR* curve and steeper than it. The *TR* curve will be an arch shape starting from the origin.

6. When demand is price elastic, marginal revenue will be positive and the *TR* curve will be upward sloping. When demand is price inelastic, marginal revenue will be negative and the *TR* curve will be downward sloping.

7. A change in output is represented by a movement along the revenue curves. A change in any other determinant of revenue will shift the curves up or down.

5.6 PROFIT MAXIMISATION

We are now in a position to put costs and revenue together to find the output at which profit is maximised, and also to find out how much that profit will be.

There are two ways of doing this. The first and simpler method is to use total cost and total revenue curves. The second method is to use marginal and average cost and marginal and average revenue curves. Although this method is a little more complicated (but only a little!), it is more useful when we come to compare profit maximising under different market conditions.

We will look at each method in turn. In both cases, we will concentrate on the short run: namely, that period in which one or more factors are fixed in supply. In both cases, we take the instance of a firm facing a downward-sloping demand curve.

Short-run profit maximisation: using total curves

Table 5.9 shows the total revenue figures from Table 5.8. It also shows figures for total cost. These figures have been chosen so as to produce a *TC* curve of a typical shape.

Total profit (*TΠ*) is found by subtracting *TC* from *TR*. Check this out by examining the table. Where *TΠ* is negative, the firm is making a loss. Total profit is maximised at an output of 3 units, where there is the greatest gap between total revenue and total costs. At this output, total profit is £4 (£18 – £14).

The *TR*, *TC* and *TΠ* curves are plotted in Figure 5.19. The size of the maximum profit is shown by the arrows.

 What can we say about the slope of the TR and TC curves at the maximum profit point? What does this tell us about marginal revenue and marginal cost?

Table 5.9	Total revenue, total cost and total profit		
Q (units)	TR (£)	TC (£)	TΠ (£)
0	0	6	−6
1	8	10	−2
2	14	12	2
3	18	14	4
4	20	18	2
5	20	25	−5
6	18	36	−18
7	14	56	−42
.	.	.	.

Figure 5.19   Finding maximum profit using totals curves

Figure 5.20   Finding the profit-maximising output using marginal curves

Short-run profit maximisation: using average and marginal curves

Table 5.10 is based on the figures in Table 5.9.

1. *Fill in the missing figures (without referring to Table 5.8 or 5.9).*
2. *Why are the figures for MR and MC entered in the spaces between the lines in Table 5.10?*

Finding the maximum profit that a firm can make is a two-stage process. The first stage is to find the profit-maximising output. To do this we use the *MC* and *MR* curves. The second stage is to find out just how much profit is at this output. To do this we use the *AR* and *AC* curves.

Stage 1: Using marginal curves to arrive at the profit-maximising output

There is a very simple ***profit-maximising rule***: if profits are to be maximised, *MR must equal MC*. From Table 5.10 it can be seen that *MR* = *MC* at an output of 3. This is shown as point *e* in Figure 5.20.

But why are profits maximised when *MR* = *MC*? The simplest way of answering this is to see what the position would be if *MR* did not equal *MC*.

Referring to Figure 5.20, at a level of output below 3, *MR* exceeds *MC*. This means that by producing more units there will be a bigger addition to revenue (*MR*) than to cost (*MC*). Total profit will *increase*. As long as MR exceeds MC, *profit can be increased by increasing production.*

At a level of output above 3, *MC* exceeds *MR*. All levels of output above 3 thus add more to cost than to revenue and

Definition

Profit-maximising rule Profit is maximised where marginal revenue equals marginal cost.

Table 5.10   Revenue, cost and profit

Q (units)	P=AR (£)	TR (£)	MR (£)	TC (£)	AC (£)	MC (£)	TΠ (£)	AΠ (£)
0	9	0		6	–		−6	–
			8			4		
1	8	8		10	10		...	−2
			...			2		
2	7	14		12	...		2	1
			4			2		
3	6	18		14	$4^2/_3$		4	$1^1/_3$
			2			4		
4	5	20		18	$4^1/_2$		2	$^1/_2$
			0			7		
5	4	20		25	5		−5	−1
			−2			...		
6	3	18		36	...		...	...
			...			20		
7	2	14		56	8		−42	−6
.	.	.		.	.	.	.	.

TC 8
p100

hence *reduce* profit. *As long as MC exceeds MR, profit can be increased by cutting back on production.*

Profits are thus maximised where *MC = MR*: at an output of 3. This can be confirmed by reference to the *TΠ* column in Table 5.10.

Students worry sometimes about the argument that profits are maximised when *MR = MC*. Surely, they say, if the last unit is making no profit, how can profit be at a *maximum*? The answer is very simple. If you cannot *add* anything more to a total, the total must be at the maximum. Take the simple analogy of going up a hill. When you cannot go any higher, you must be at the top.

Figure 5.21 Measuring the maximum profit using average curves

*LOOKING AT THE MATHS

As we have seen, the rule for profit maximisation is that firms should produce where *MC = MR*. This can be derived algebraically as follows. Profit is defined as

$$TΠ = TR - TC \qquad (1)$$

Profit is maximised at the point where an additional unit of output will add no more to profit – that is, where

$$\frac{ΔTΠ}{ΔQ} = MΠ = 0 \qquad (2)$$

or, from (1), where

$$\frac{ΔTR}{ΔQ} - \frac{ΔTC}{ΔQ} = 0 \qquad (3)$$

or

$$\frac{ΔTR}{ΔQ} = \frac{ΔTC}{ΔQ} \qquad (4)$$

i.e. where *MR = MC*.

Equation (2) can be related to Figure 5.19. Profits are maximised at the highest point of the *TΠ* curve. At the top of any curve (or bottom for that matter), its slope is zero. Thus *ΔTΠ/Q = MΠ = 0*. Put another way, the tangent to the top of the *TΠ* curve is horizontal.

Stage 2: Using average curves to measure the size of the profit

Once the profit-maximising output has been discovered, we use the average curves to measure the *amount* of profit at the maximum. Both marginal and average curves corresponding to the data in Table 5.10 are plotted in Figure 5.21.

First, average profit (*AΠ*) is found. This is simply *AR − AC*. At the profit-maximising output of 3, this gives a figure for *AΠ* of £6 − £4²/3 = £1¹/3. Then total profit is obtained by multiplying average profit by output:

$$TΠ = AΠ × Q$$

This is shown as the shaded area. It equals £1¹/3 × 3 = £4. This can again be confirmed by reference to the *TΠ* column in Table 5.10.

 From the information for a firm given in the table below, construct a table like 5.10.

Q	0	1	2	3	4	5	6	7
P	12	11	10	9	8	7	6	5
TC	2	6	9	12	16	21	28	38

Use your table to draw diagrams like Figures 5.19 and 5.21. Use these two diagrams to show the profit-maximising output and the level of maximum profit. Confirm your findings by reference to the table you have constructed.

Some qualifications

Long-run profit maximisation

Assuming that the *AR* and *MR* curves are the same in the long run as in the short run, long-run profits will be maximised at the output where *MR* equals the *long-run MC*. The reasoning is the same as with the short-run case.

The meaning of 'profit'

One element of cost is the opportunity cost to the owners of the firm of being in business. This is the minimum return the owners must make on their capital in order to prevent them from eventually deciding to close down and perhaps move into some alternative business. It is a *cost* because, just as with wages, rent, etc., it has to be covered if the firm is to continue producing. This opportunity cost to the owners is sometimes known as **normal profit**, and is *included in the cost curves.*

Definition

Normal profit The opportunity cost of being in business: the profit that could have been earned in the next best alternative business. It is counted as a cost of production.

What determines this normal rate of profit? It has two components. First, someone setting up in business invests capital in it. There is thus an opportunity cost. This is the interest that could have been earned by lending it in some riskless form (e.g. by putting it in a savings account in a bank). Nobody would set up a business unless they expected to earn at least this rate of profit. Running a business is far from riskless, however, and hence a second element is a return to compensate for risk. Thus:

normal profit (%) – rate of interest on a riskless loan
+ a risk premium

The risk premium varies according to the line of business. In those with fairly predictable patterns, such as food retailing, it is relatively low. Where outcomes are very uncertain, such as mineral exploration or the manufacture of fashion garments, it is relatively high.

| *BOX 5.9 | USING CALCULUS TO FIND THE MAXIMUM PROFIT OUTPUT | EXPLORING ECONOMICS |

Imagine that a firm's total revenue and total cost functions were

$$TR = 48Q - Q^2$$

$$TC = 12 + 16Q + 3Q^2$$

From these two equations the following table can be derived.

Q	TR	TC	$T\Pi\ (= TR - TC)$
0	0	12	−12
1	47	31	16
2	92	56	36
3	135	87	48
4	176	124	52
5	215	167	48
6	252	216	36
7	287	271	16
.	.	.	.

1. How much is total fixed cost?
2. Continue the table for Q = 8 and Q = 9.
3. Plot TR, TC and TΠ on a diagram like Figure 5.19.

It can clearly be seen from the table that profit is maximised at an output of 4, where $T\Pi = 52$.

This profit-maximising output and the level of profit can be calculated without drawing up a table. The calculation involves calculus. There are two methods that can be used.

Finding where $MR = MC$

Marginal revenue can be found by differentiating the total revenue function.

$$MR = dTR/dQ$$

The reason is that marginal revenue is the rate of change of total revenue. Differentiating a function gives its rate of change.

Similarly, marginal cost can be found by differentiating the total cost function:

$$MC = dTC/dQ$$

Differentiating TR and TC gives

$$dTR/dQ = 48 - 2Q = MR$$

and

$$dTC/dQ = 16 + 6Q = MC$$

Profit is maximised where $MR = MC$: in other words, where

$$48 - 2Q = 16 + 6Q$$

Solving this for Q gives

$$32 = 8Q$$

$$\therefore Q = 4$$

The equation for total profit ($T\Pi$) is

$$T\Pi = TR - TC$$
$$= 48Q - Q^2 - (12 + 16Q + 3Q^2)$$
$$= -12 + 32Q - 4Q^2$$

Substituting $Q = 4$ into this equation gives

$$T\Pi = -12 + (32 \times 4) - (4 \times 4^2)$$

$$\therefore T\Pi = 52$$

These figures can be confirmed from the table.

Maximising the total profit equation

To maximise an equation we want to find the point where the slope of the curve derived from it is zero. In other words, we want to find the top of the $T\Pi$ curve.

The slope of a curve gives its rate of change and is found by differentiating the curve's equation. Thus to find maximum $T\Pi$ we differentiate it (to find the slope) and set it equal to zero (to find the top).

$$T\Pi = -12 + 32Q - 4Q^2 \text{ (see above)}$$

$$\therefore dT\Pi/dQ = 32 - 8Q$$

Setting this equal to zero gives

$$32 - 8Q = 0$$

$$\therefore 8Q = 32$$

$$\therefore Q = 4$$

This is the same result as was found by the first method. Again $Q = 4$ can be substituted into the $T\Pi$ equation to give

$$T\Pi = 52$$

Given the following equations:

$$TR = 72Q - 2Q^2; TC = 10 + 12Q + 4Q^2$$

calculate the maximum profit output and the amount of profit at that output using both methods.

Thus if owners of a business earn normal profit, they will (just) be content to remain in that industry. If they earn more than normal profit, they will also (obviously) prefer to stay in this business. If they earn less than normal profit, then after a time they will consider leaving and using their capital for some other purpose. We will see in Chapter 6 that the level of profits that a firm can make plays a pivotal role in the way markets are structured.

 How will the size of 'normal profit' vary with the general state of the economy?

Given that normal profits are included in costs, any profit that is shown diagrammatically (e.g. the shaded area in Figure 5.21) must therefore be over and above normal profit. It is known by several alternative names: ***supernormal profit***, ***pure profit***, ***economic profit*** or sometimes simply ***profit***. They all mean the same thing: the excess of total profit over normal profit.

Loss minimising

It may be that there is no output at which the firm can make a profit. Such a situation is illustrated in Figure 5.22: the AC curve is above the AR curve at all levels of output.

In this case, the output where $MR = MC$ will be the loss-minimising output. The amount of loss at the point where $MR = MC$ is shown by the shaded area in Figure 5.22. Even though the firm is making losses, there is no 'better' level of output at this point.

Whether or not to produce at all

The short run. Fixed costs have to be paid even if the firm is producing nothing at all. Rent and business rates have to be paid, etc. Providing, therefore, that the firm is able to cover its *variable* costs, it is no worse off and therefore will continue to produce. Of course, if the firm's revenues are more than its variable costs, then it is able to go some way to covering the fixed costs and again it will continue to produce.

What happens if the firm's revenue is not enough to cover its variable costs: that is, if the AVC curve is above, or the AR curve below, the position illustrated in Figure 5.23? In that case the firm is worse off than if it only has fixed costs and it will shut down production. This situation is known as the ***short-run shut-down point***.

The long run. All costs are variable in the long run. If, therefore, the firm cannot cover its long-run average costs (which include normal profit), it will close down. The ***long-run shut-down point*** will be where the AR curve is tangential to the $LRAC$ curve.

KI 18
p131

Figure 5.22 Loss-minimising output

Figure 5.23 The short-run shut-down point

Definitions

Supernormal profit (also known as **pure profit, economic profit** or simply **profit**) The excess of total profit above normal profit.

Short-run shut-down point Where the AR curve is tangential to the AVC curve. The firm can only just cover its variable costs. Any fall in revenue below this level will cause a profit-maximising firm to shut down immediately.

Long-run shut-down point Where the AR curve is tangential to the $LRAC$ curve. The firm can just make normal profits. Any fall in revenue below this level will cause a profit-maximising firm to shut down once all costs have become variable.

BOX 5.10   THE LOGIC OF LOGISTICS

Driving up profits

One key to a company's success is the logistics of its operations. 'Logistics' refers to the management of the inflow of resources to a company and the outflow of finished goods from it; in other words, it refers to 'supply-chain management'. This includes the purchasing of raw materials, transporting them, production sequencing, stock control, delivery to wholesalers or retailers, and so on.

Logistics depends on the provision of high quality and timely information. As IT systems have become increasingly sophisticated, they have enabled modern developments in logistics to transform the operation of many industries.

Driving down costs

With the widespread use of containerisation and development of giant distribution companies, such as UPS and DHL, transporting materials and goods around the world has become much faster and much cheaper. Instead of having to make parts in-house, companies can now use the logistics industry to obtain them at lower cost elsewhere, often from the other side of the world.

With improved systems for ordering materials, and deliveries becoming more and more reliable, firms no longer need keep large stocks of parts; they simply buy them as they need them. The same opportunity to save costs lies with the finished product: a company can keep lower levels of stocks when its own delivery mechanisms are more efficient.

The globalisation of logistics, with increasing use of the Internet, has resulted in a hugely complex logistics industry. Firms that were once solely concerned with delivery are now employed to manage companies' supply chains and achieve substantial cost savings for them.

Driving up revenues

Efficient logistics has not just resulted in lower costs. The flexibility it has given firms has allowed many to increase their sales.

Carrying lower levels of stocks and switching from supplier to supplier, with the process often being managed by a logistics company, can allow companies to change the products they offer more rapidly. They can be more responsive to consumer demand and thereby increase their sales.

A well-known example of a company benefiting from this approach is Primark. This low-cost fashion retailer focuses much more on buying, logistics and supply-chain management than on branding or advertising.

1. *What dangers are there in keeping stocks to a minimum and relying on complex supply chains?*
2. *Which industries do you think would benefit most from reduced transport times for their finished products? Think of an industry, other than low-cost fashion, which would benefit from the ability to switch rapidly the products offered.*

*LOOKING AT THE MATHS

We can state the short- and long-run shut-down points algebraically. Remember that total profit ($T\Pi$) is defined as

$$T\Pi = TR - TC = TR - (TFC + TVC) \qquad (1)$$

A negative value for $T\Pi$ means that the firm makes a loss. This will occur when

$$TR - (TFC + TVC) < 0$$

or

$$TR < (TFC + TVC)$$

But when should the firm shut down?

Short-run shut-down point

If the firm shuts down, TR and TVC will be zero, but in the short run it will still incur total fixed costs (TFC) and thus

$$T\Pi = -TFC \qquad (2)$$

In other words, it will make a loss equal to total fixed costs. From this it can be seen that the firm should close in the short run only if

$$T\Pi < -TFC$$

i.e.

$$(TR - TFC - TVC) < -TFC \qquad (3)$$

In other words, the loss should not exceed fixed costs. Put another way (i.e. by rearranging (3)), it should continue in production as long as

$$TR \geq TVC \qquad (4)$$

or, dividing both sides of (4) by quantity, where

$$AR \geq AVC \qquad (5)$$

The firm, therefore, should shut down if

$$AR < AVC$$

This is shown in Figure 5.23.

Long-run shut-down point

In the long run, there are no fixed costs. Thus

$$T\Pi = TR - TVC = TR - TC \qquad (6)$$

If the firm shuts down, it will earn no revenue, but incur no costs. Thus

$$T\Pi = TR - TC = 0 - 0 = 0$$

The firm should therefore continue in production as long as

$$(TR - TC) \geq 0$$

i.e.

$$TR \geq TC$$

or, dividing both sides by quantity, as long as

$$AR \geq AC$$

(where AC in this case is long-run average cost)

The firm, therefore, should shut down if

$$AR < AC$$

Section summary

1. Total profit equals total revenue minus total cost. By definition, then, a firm's profits will be maximised at the point where there is the greatest gap between total revenue and total cost.

2. Another way of finding the maximum profit point is to find the output where marginal revenue equals marginal cost. Having found this output, the level of maximum profit can be found by finding the average profit ($AR - AC$) and then multiplying it by the level of output.

3. Normal profit is the minimum profit that must be made to persuade a firm to stay in business in the long run. It is counted as part of the firm's costs. Supernormal profit is any profit over and above normal profit.

4. For a firm that cannot make a profit at any level of output, the point where $MR = MC$ represents the loss-minimising output.

5. In the short run, a firm will close down if it cannot cover its variable costs. In the long run, it will close down if it cannot make normal profits.

END OF CHAPTER QUESTIONS

1. The following table shows the average cost and average revenue (price) for a firm at each level of output.

Output	1	2	3	4	5	6	7	8	9	10
AC (£)	7.00	5.00	4.00	3.30	3.00	3.10	3.50	4.20	5.00	6.00
AR (£)	10.00	9.50	9.00	8.50	8.00	7.50	7.00	6.50	6.00	5.50

(a) Construct a table to show TC, MC, TR and MR at each level of output (put the figures for MC and MR midway between the output figures).

(b) Using MC and MR figures, find the profit-maximising output.

(c) Using TC and TR figures, check your answer to (b).

(d) Plot the AC, MC, AR and MR figures on a graph.

(e) Mark the profit-maximising output and the AR and AC at this output.

(f) Shade in an area to represent the level of profits at this output.

*2. Draw the isoquant corresponding to the following table, which shows the alternative combinations of labour and capital required to produce 100 units of output per day of good X.

K	16	20	$26^2/_3$	40	60	80	100
L	200	160	120	80	$53^1/_3$	40	32

(a) Assuming that capital costs are £20 per day and the wage rate is £10 per day, what is the least-cost method of producing 100 units? What will the daily total cost be? (Draw in a series of isocosts.)

(b) Now assume that the wage rate rises to £20 per day. Draw a new set of isocosts. What will be the least-cost method of producing 100 units now? How much labour and capital will be used?

3. Choose two industries that you believe are very different. Identify factors used in those industries that in the short run are (a) fixed; (b) variable.

4. Taking the same industries, identify as many economies of scale as you can.

5. 'Both short-run and long-run average cost curves may be ⌣-shaped, but the explanations for their respective shapes are quite different.' Explain this statement.

6. Why do marginal cost curves intersect both the average variable cost curve and the average cost curve at their lowest point?

7. Draw a diagram like that in Figure 5.21. Now illustrate the effect of a rise in demand for the product. Mark the new profit-maximising price and output. Will the profit-maximising output, price, average cost and profit necessarily be higher than before?

8. Why might it make sense for a firm which cannot sell its output at a profit to continue in production for the time being? For how long should the firm continue to produce at a loss?

Online resources

Additional case studies in MyEconLab

5.1 **Diminishing returns to nitrogen fertiliser**. This case study provides a good illustration of diminishing returns in practice by showing the effects on grass yields of the application of increasing amounts of nitrogen fertiliser.

5.2 **Deriving cost curves from total physical product information**. This shows how total, average and marginal costs can be derived from total product information and the price of inputs.

5.3 **Division of labour in a pin factory**. This is the famous example of division of labour given by Adam Smith in his *Wealth of Nations* (1776).

5.4 **Followers of fashion**. This case study examines the effects of costs on prices of fashion-sensitive goods.

5.5 **Putting on a duplicate**. This examines the effects on marginal costs of additional passengers on a coach journey.

5.6 **Comparing the behaviour of long-run and short-run costs**. This is an application of isoquant analysis.

Maths Case 5.1 Total, average and marginal cost. Looking at the mathematical functions for these curves and deriving specific types of cost from a total cost equation.

Maths Case 5.2 Finding the optimum production point: Part 1. Examples using the method of substituting the constraint equation into the objective function.

Maths Case 5.3 Finding the optimum production point: Part 2. The same examples as in Maths Case 5.2, but this time using the Lagrangian methods.

Maths Case 5.4 Total, average and marginal revenue. Looking at the mathematical functions for these curves for both price-taking and price-making firms and relating them to revenue curves.

Websites relevant to this chapter

Numbers and sections refer to websites listed in the Web Appendix and hotlinked from this book's website at **www.pearsoned.co.uk/sloman**.

- For news articles relevant to this chapter, see the *Economics News Articles* link from the book's website.
- For student resources relevant to this chapter, see sites C1–7, 9, 10, 14, 19, 20.
- For a case study examining costs, see site D2.
- For sites that look at companies, their scale of operation and market share, see B2 (third link); E4, 10; G7, 8.
- For links to sites on various aspects of production and costs, see the sections *Microeconomics: Production* in sites I7 and 11.

Profit Maximising under Perfect Competition and Monopoly

CHAPTER MAP

6.1 Alternative market structures   164

6.2 Perfect competition   165
Assumptions of perfect competition   165
The short run and the long run   165
The short-run equilibrium of the firm   167
The short-run supply curve   168
The long-run equilibrium of the firm   169
The long-run industry supply curve   169
The incompatibility of perfect competition and
    substantial economies of scale   171
Perfect competition and the public interest   172

6.3 Monopoly   173
What is a monopoly?   173
Barriers to entry   173
Equilibrium price and output   175
Monopoly and the public interest   176

6.4 The theory of contestable markets   179
Potential competition or monopoly?   179
The importance of costless exit   182
Assessment of the theory   182
Contestable markets and the public interest   182

As we saw in Chapter 5, a firm's profits are maximised where its marginal cost equals its marginal revenue: $MC = MR$. But we will want to know more than this.

- What determines the amount of profit that a firm will make? Will profits be large, or just enough for the firm to survive, or so low that it will be forced out of business?

- Will the firm produce a high level of output or a low level?

- Will it be producing efficiently, making best use of resources?

- Will the price charged to the consumer be high or low?

- More generally, will the consumer benefit from the decisions a firm makes? This is, of course, a normative question (see section 1.3). Nevertheless, economists can still identify and analyse the effects these decisions have on consumers.

The answers to these questions largely depend on the amount of competition that a firm faces. A firm in a highly competitive environment will behave quite differently from a firm facing little or no competition. In particular, a firm facing competition from many other firms will be forced to keep its prices down and be as efficient as possible, simply to survive. If, however, the firm faces little or no competition (like a local water company or a major pharmaceutical company), it may have considerable power over prices, and we may end up paying considerably more as a result.

In this chapter and the next, we consider different types of market structure. Here we focus on the extremes: perfect competition (very many firms competing) and monopoly (only one firm in the industry).

6.1 ALTERNATIVE MARKET STRUCTURES

It is traditional to divide industries into categories according to the degree of competition that exists between the firms within the industry. There are four such categories.

At one extreme is **perfect competition**, where there are very many firms competing. Each firm is so small relative to the whole industry that it has no power to influence price. It is a price taker. At the other extreme is **monopoly**, where there is just one firm in the industry, and hence no competition from within the industry. In the middle come **monopolistic competition**, which involves quite a lot of firms competing and where there is freedom for new firms to enter the industry, and **oligopoly**, which involves only a few firms and where entry of new firms is restricted.

To distinguish more precisely between these four categories, the following must be considered:

- How freely firms can enter the industry. Is entry free or restricted? If it is restricted, just how great are the barriers to the entry of new firms?
- The nature of the product. Do all firms produce an identical product, or do firms produce their own particular brand or model or variety?
- The firm's degree of control over price. Is the firm a price taker or can it choose its price, and if so, how will changing its price affect its profits? What we are talking about here is the nature of the demand curve it faces. How elastic is it? If the firm puts up its price, will it lose (a) all its sales (a horizontal demand curve), or (b) a large

proportion of its sales (a relatively elastic demand curve), or (c) just a small proportion of its sales (a relatively inelastic demand curve)?

> **KEY IDEA 20**
>
> **Market power.** When firms have market power over prices, they can use this to raise prices and profits above the perfectly competitive level. Other things being equal, the firm will gain at the expense of the consumer. Similarly, if consumers or workers have market power, they can use this to their own benefit.

Table 6.1 shows the differences between the four categories.

> 1. Give one more example in each category.
> 2. Would you expect builders and restaurateurs to have the same degree of control over price?

The market structure under which a firm operates will determine its behaviour. Firms under perfect competition will behave quite differently from firms which are monopolists, which will behave differently again from firms under oligopoly or monopolistic competition.

TC 5 p50

This behaviour (or 'conduct') will in turn affect the firm's performance: its prices, profits, efficiency, etc. In many cases, it will also affect other firms' performance: *their* prices, profits, efficiency, etc. The collective conduct of all the firms in the industry will affect the whole industry's performance.

Economists thus see a causal chain running from market structure to the performance of that industry.

Structure → Conduct → Performance

First we shall look at the two extreme market structures: perfect competition and monopoly. Then in Chapter 7 we shall look at the two intermediate cases of monopolistic competition and oligopoly.

The two intermediate cases are sometimes referred to collectively as **imperfect competition**. The vast majority of firms in the real world operate under imperfect competition. It is still worth studying the two extreme cases, however, because they provide a framework within which to understand the real world. Some industries tend more to the competitive extreme, and thus their performance corresponds to some extent to perfect competition. Other industries tend more to the other extreme: for example, when there is one dominant firm and a few much smaller firms. In such cases, their performance corresponds more to monopoly.

Chapters 6 and 7 assume that firms, under whatever market structure, are attempting to maximise profits. Chapter 8 questions this assumption. It looks at alternative theories of the firm: theories based on assumptions *other* than profit maximising.

KI 9 p67

Definitions

Perfect competition A market structure where there are many firms, none of which is large; where there is freedom of entry into the industry; where all firms produce an identical product; and where all firms are price takers.

Monopoly A market structure where there is only one firm in the industry. (Note that this is the economic definition of a pure monopoly. In UK competition law, the part that applies to the abuse of monopoly power covers firms that are in a position of 'market dominance'. Such firms will have a large share, but not necessarily a 100 per cent share of the market. See Chapter 13 for more on this.)

Monopolistic competition A market structure where, as with perfect competition, there are many firms and freedom of entry into the industry, but where each firm produces a differentiated product and thus has some control over its price.

Oligopoly A market structure where there are few enough firms to enable barriers to be erected against the entry of new firms.

Imperfect competition The collective name for monopolistic competition and oligopoly.

Table 6.1	Features of the four market structures				
Type of market	**Number of firms**	**Freedom of entry**	**Nature of product**	**Examples**	**Implication for demand curve for firm**
Perfect competition	Very many	Unrestricted	Homogeneous (undifferentiated)	Cabbages, carrots (these approximate to perfect competition)	Horizontal. The firm is a price taker
Monopolistic competition	Many/several	Unrestricted	Differentiated	Builders, restaurants	Downward sloping, but relatively elastic. The firm has some control over price
Oligopoly	Few	Restricted	1. Undifferentiated 2. Differentiated	1. Petrol 2. Cars, electrical appliances	Downward sloping, relatively inelastic but depends on reactions of rivals to a price change
Monopoly	One	Restricted or completely blocked	Unique	Many prescription drugs, local water companies	Downward sloping, more inelastic than oligopoly. The firm has considerable control over price

6.2 PERFECT COMPETITION

Assumptions of perfect competition

The model of perfect competition is built on four assumptions:

- Firms are *price takers*. There are so many firms in the industry that each one produces an insignificantly small portion of total industry supply, and therefore has no power whatsoever to affect the price of the product. It faces a horizontal demand 'curve' at the market price: the price determined by the interaction of demand and supply in the whole market.
- There is complete *freedom of entry* into the industry for new firms. Existing firms are unable to stop new firms setting up in business. Setting up a business takes time, however. Freedom of entry, therefore, applies in the long run.
- All firms produce an *identical product*. (The product is 'homogeneous'.) There is therefore no branding or advertising.
- Producers and consumers have *perfect knowledge* of the market. That is, producers are fully aware of prices, costs and market opportunities. Consumers are fully aware of the price, quality and availability of the product.

These assumptions are very strict. Few, if any, industries in the real world meet these conditions. Certain agricultural markets are perhaps closest to perfect competition. The market for fresh vegetables is an example.

Nevertheless, despite the lack of real-world cases, the model of perfect competition plays a very important role in economic analysis and policy. Its major relevance is as an 'ideal type' and many people, particularly those on the political right, argue that achieving perfect competition would bring a number of important advantages. The model can thus be used as a standard against which to judge the shortcomings of real-world industries. It can help governments to formulate policies towards industry.

1. It is sometimes claimed that the market for various stocks and shares is perfectly competitive, or nearly so. Take the case of the market for shares in a large company like Ford. Go through each of the four assumptions above and see if they apply in this case. (Don't be misled by the first assumption. The 'firm' in this case is not Ford itself.)
2. Is the market for gold perfectly competitive?

The short run and the long run

Before we can examine what price, output and profits will be, we must first distinguish between the short run and the long run as they apply to perfect competition.

In the **short run**, the number of firms is fixed. Depending on its costs and revenue, a firm might be making large profits, small profits, no profits or a loss; and in the short run, it may continue to do so.

> ### Definition
>
> **Short run under perfect competition** The period during which there is insufficient time for new firms to enter the industry.

BOX 6.1	CONCENTRATION RATIOS	EXPLORING ECONOMICS

Measuring the degree of competition

We can get some indication of how competitive a market is by observing the number of firms: the more the firms, the more competitive the market would seem to be. However, this does not tell us anything about how *concentrated* the market might be. There may be *many* firms (suggesting a situation of perfect competition or monopolistic competition), but the largest two firms might produce 95 per cent of total output. This would make these two firms more like oligopolists.

Thus, even though a large number of producers may make the market *seem* highly competitive, this could be deceiving. Another approach, therefore, to measuring

5-firm concentration ratios for various industries (by output)

Industry	5-firm ratio	15-firm ratio
Sugar	99	99
Tobacco products	99	99
Oils and fats	88	95
Confectionery	81	91
Gas distribution	82	87
Soft drinks, mineral water	75	93
Postal/courier services	65	75
Telecommunications	61	75
Inorganic chemicals	57	80
Pharmaceuticals	57	74
Alcoholic beverages	50	78
Soap and toiletries	40	64
Accountancy services	36	47
Motor vehicles	34	54
Glass and glass products	26	49
Fishing	16	19
Advertising	10	20
Wholesale distribution	6	11
Furniture	5	13
Construction	5	9

Source: Based on data in of *United Kingdom Input-Output Analyses, 2006 Edition* (National Statistics, 2006), Table 8.31.

the degree of competition is to focus on the level of concentration of firms.

The simplest measure of industrial concentration involves adding together the market share of the largest so many firms: e.g. the largest 3, 5 or 15. This would give what is known as the '3-firm', '5-firm' or '15-firm' 'concentration ratio'. There are different ways of estimating market share: by revenue, by output, by profit, etc.

The table shows the 5-firm and 15-firm concentration ratios of selected industries in the UK by output. As you can see, there is an enormous variation in the degree of concentration from one industry to another.

One of the main reasons for this is differences in the percentage of total industry output at which economies of scale are exhausted. If this occurs at a low level of output, there will be room for several firms in the industry which are all benefiting from the maximum economies of scale.

The degree of concentration will also depend on the barriers to entry of other firms into the industry (see pages 173–5) and on various factors such as transport costs and historical accident. It will also depend on how varied the products are within any one industrial category. For example, in categories as large as furniture and construction there is room for many firms, each producing a specialised range of products.

So is the degree of concentration a good guide to the degree of competitiveness of the industry? The answer is that it is *some* guide, but on its own it can be misleading. In particular, it ignores the degree of competition from abroad.

1. *What are the advantages and disadvantages of using a 5-firm concentration ratio rather than a 15-firm, a 3-firm or even a 1-firm ratio?*
2. *Why are some industries, such as bread baking and brewing, relatively concentrated, in that a few firms produce a large proportion of total output (see Box 7.2 and Case Study 7.4 in MyEconLab), and yet there are also many small producers?*

In the **long run**, however, the level of profits affects entry and exit from the industry. If supernormal profits are made (see page 159), new firms will be attracted into the industry, whereas if losses are being made, firms will leave.

Note that although we shall be talking about the *level* of profit (since that makes our analysis of pricing and output

decisions simpler to understand), in practice it is usually the *rate* of profit that determines whether a firm stays in the industry or leaves. The **rate of profit** (*r*) is the level of profit ($T\Pi$) as *a proportion of the level of capital (K) employed*: $r = T\Pi/K$. As you would expect, larger firms will require to make a larger *total* profit to persuade them to stay in an industry. Total normal profit is thus larger for them than

Definitions

Long run under perfect competition The period of time that is long enough for new firms to enter the industry.

Rate of profit Total profit ($T\Pi$) as a proportion of the capital employed (K): $r = T\Pi/K$.

BOX 6.2   **IS PERFECT BEST?**

EXPLORING ECONOMICS

Be careful of the word 'perfect'.

'Perfect competition' refers to competition that is complete. Perhaps 'complete competition' would be a better term. There is a complete absence of power, a complete absence of entry barriers, a complete absence of product differentiation between producers, and complete information for producers and consumers on the market. It is thus useful for understanding the effects of power, barriers, product differentiation and lack of information.

Perfect does not mean 'best', however.

Just because it is at the extreme end of the competition spectrum, it does not follow that perfect competition is desirable. You could have a perfect bomb – i.e. one that kills everyone in the world. You could have a perfect killer virus – i.e. one that is totally immune to drugs, and against which humans have no natural protection at all. Such things, though perfect, are hardly desirable!

To say that perfect competition is desirable and that it is a goal towards which government policy should be directed are normative statements. Economists, in their role as economists, cannot make such statements.

This does not mean, of course, that economists cannot identify the effects of perfect competition, but whether these effects are *desirable* or not is an ethical question.

The danger is that by using perfect competition as a yardstick, and by using the word 'perfect' rather than 'complete', economists may be surreptitiously persuading their audience that perfect competition is a goal we *ought* to be striving to achieve.

for a small firm. The *rate* of normal profit, however, will probably be similar.

1. *Why do economists treat normal profit as a cost of production?*
2. *What determines (a) the level and (b) the rate of normal profit for a particular firm?*

Thus whether the industry expands or contracts in the long run will depend on the rate of profit. Naturally, since the time a firm takes to set up in business varies from industry to industry, the length of time before the long run is reached also varies from industry to industry.

The short-run equilibrium of the firm

The determination of price, output and profit in the short run under perfect competition can best be shown in a diagram.

Figure 6.1 shows a short-run equilibrium for both an industry and a firm under perfect competition. Both parts of the diagram have the same scale for the vertical axis. The horizontal axes have totally different scales, however. For example, if the horizontal axis for the firm were measured in, say, thousands of units, the horizontal axis for the whole industry might be measured in millions or tens of millions of units, depending on the number of firms in the industry.

Let us examine the determination of price, output and profit in turn.

Price

The price is determined in the industry by the intersection of demand and supply. The firm faces a horizontal demand (or average revenue) 'curve' at this price. It can sell all it can produce at the market price (P_e), but nothing at a price above P_e.

| **Figure 6.1** | Short-run equilibrium of an industry and a firm under perfect competition |

(a) Industry

(b) Firm

Figure 6.2   Loss minimising under perfect competition

Output

The firm will maximise profit where marginal cost equals marginal revenue ($MR = MC$), at an output of Q_e. Note that, since the price is not affected by the firm's output, marginal revenue will equal price (see page 152 and Figure 5.15).

Profit

If the average cost (AC) curve (which includes normal profit) dips below the average revenue (AR) 'curve', the firm will earn supernormal profit. Supernormal profit *per unit* at Q_e is the vertical difference between AR and AC at Q_e. *Total* supernormal profit is the shaded rectangle in Figure 6.1.

What happens if the firm cannot make a profit at *any* level of output? This situation would occur if the AC curve were above the AR curve at all points. This is illustrated in Figure 6.2, where the market price is P_1. In this case, the point where $MC = MR$ represents the *loss-minimising* point (where loss is defined as anything less than normal profit). The amount of the loss is represented by the shaded rectangle.

As we saw in section 5.6, whether the firm is prepared to continue making a loss in the short run or whether it will close down immediately depends on whether it can cover its *variable* costs.

Provided price is above average variable cost (AVC), the firm will still continue producing in the short run: it can pay its variable costs and go some way to paying its fixed costs. It will shut down in the short run only if the market price falls below P_2 in Figure 6.2.

The short-run supply curve

The *firm's* short-run supply curve will be its (short-run) marginal cost curve.

A supply curve shows how much will be supplied at each price: it relates quantity to price. The marginal cost curve relates quantity to marginal cost. But under perfect competition, given that $P = MR$, and $MR = MC$, P must equal MC. Thus the supply curve and the MC curve will follow the same line.

For example, in Figure 6.3(b), if price were P_1, profits would be maximised at Q_1 where $P_1 = MC$. Thus point *a* is one point on the supply curve. At a price of P_2, Q_2 would be produced. Thus point *b* is another point on the supply curve, and so on.

So, under perfect competition, the firm's supply curve is entirely dependent on costs of production. This demonstrates why the firm's supply curve is upward sloping.

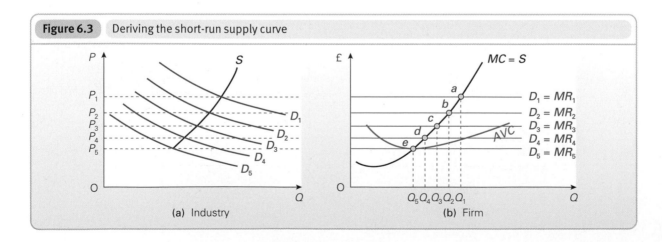

Figure 6.3   Deriving the short-run supply curve

Given that marginal costs rise as output rises (due to diminishing marginal returns), a higher price will be necessary to induce the firm to increase its output.

Note that the firm will not produce at a price below *AVC*. Thus the supply curve is only that portion of the *MC* curve above point *e*.

What will be the short-run supply curve of the whole *industry*? This is simply the sum of the short-run supply curves (and hence *MC* curves) of all the firms in the industry. Graphically this will be a *horizontal* sum, since it is *quantities* that are being added.

Will the industry supply be zero below a price of P_s in Figure 6.3?

The long-run equilibrium of the firm

TC 5
p50

In the long run, if typical firms are making supernormal profits, new firms will be attracted into the industry. Likewise, if established firms can make supernormal profits by increasing the scale of their operations, they will do so, since all factors of production are variable in the long run.

KI 5
p21

The effect of the entry of new firms and/or the expansion of existing firms is to increase industry supply. This is illustrated in Figure 6.4. At a price of P_1 supernormal profits are earned. This causes industry supply to expand (the industry supply curve shifts to the right). This in turn leads to a fall in price. Supply will go on increasing and price falling until firms are making only normal profits. This will be when price has fallen to the point where the demand 'curve' for the firm just touches the bottom of its long-run average cost curve. Q_L is thus the long-run equilibrium output of the firm, with P_L the long-run equilibrium price.

Illustrate on a diagram similar to Figure 6.4 what would happen in the long run if price were initially below P_L.

*LOOKING AT THE MATHS

As we have seen, the long-run equilibrium output is where long-run average cost is minimised. If we know the equation for *LRAC*, we can simply use the techniques of minimisation (see pages A11–12) to find the equilibrium output. Assume that the long-run average cost function is

$$LRAC = a - bQ + cQ^2$$

The technique is to differentiate this function and set it equal to zero, i.e.

$$\frac{d(LRAC)}{dQ} = -b + 2cQ = 0 \qquad (1)$$

Solving equation (1) for *Q* gives the long-run equilibrium output. Once we have found the value of *Q*, we can substitute it back into equation (1) to find the value of *LRAC* and hence the equilibrium price (since *P = LRAC*).

We can then use the second derivative test (see page A12) to check that this indeed does represent a minimum, not a maximum, *LRAC*. An example of this is given in Maths Case 6.1 in MyEconLab.

Since the *LRAC* curve is tangential to all possible short-run *AC* curves (see section 5.4), the full long-run equilibrium will be as shown in Figure 6.5 where

$$LRAC = AC = MC = MR = AR$$

The long-run industry supply curve

If industry demand increased, what would happen to industry price and output in the long run? The long-run supply curve gives the answer.

Each of the diagrams in Figure 6.6 shows an increase in demand. The demand curve shifts from D_1 to D_2. Equilibrium in the short run moves from point *a* to point *b*, where D_2 and S_1 intersect. After the initial rise in price, the resulting supernormal profit attracts new firms into

---

Figure 6.4 Long-run equilibrium under perfect competition

(a) Industry

(b) Firm

Figure 6.5 Long-run equilibrium of the firm under perfect competition

long-run supply curve will pass through points *a* and *c*. This is illustrated in each of the three diagrams.

If price falls back to its original level (i.e. points *a* and *c* are at the *same* price) the *long-run* supply curve will be horizontal (see diagram (a) in Figure 6.6). This would occur if there were no change in firms' average cost curves. Price would simply return to the bottom of firms' *LRAC* curve.

If, however, the entry of new firms creates a shortage of factors of production, this will bid up factor prices. Firms' *LRAC* curve will shift vertically upwards, and so the long-run equilibrium price will be higher. The long-run supply curve of the industry, therefore, will slope upwards, as in diagram (b) in Figure 6.6. This is the case of *increasing industry costs* or *external diseconomies of scale*: i.e. diseconomies external to the firm (see section 5.3).

If the expansion of the industry lowers firms' *LRAC* curve, due, say, to the building up of an industrial infrastructure (distribution channels, specialist suppliers, banks, communications, etc.), the long-run supply curve will slope downwards, as in diagram (c) in Figure 6.6. This is the case of *decreasing industry costs* or *external economies of scale*.

the industry. The short-run supply curve shifts to S_2 and equilibrium moves to point *c*. Thus the long-run effect of the increase in demand has been to move the equilibrium from point *a* to point *c*. This means, therefore, that the

---

BOX 6.3   E-COMMERCE AND PERFECT COMPETITION

A return of power to the people?

The relentless drive towards big business in recent decades has seen many markets become more concentrated and increasingly dominated by large producers. And yet forces are at work that are undermining this dominance and bringing more competition to markets. One of these forces is *e-commerce*.

In this case study, we will consider just how far e-commerce is returning 'power to the people'.

Moving markets back towards perfect competition?

To see the extent to which e-commerce is making markets more competitive, let's look at the assumptions of perfect competition.

Large number of firms. The growth of e-commerce has led to many new firms starting up in business. It's not just large firms like Amazon.com that are providing increased competition for established firms, but the thousands of small online companies that are being established every day. Many of these firms are selling directly to us as consumers. This is known as 'B2C' (business-to-consumers) e-commerce. But many more are selling to other firms ('B2B'). More and more companies, from the biggest to the smallest, are transferring their purchasing to the Web and are keen to get value for money.

The reach of the Web is global. This means that firms, whether conventional or web-based, have to keep an eye on the prices and products of competitors in the rest of the world, not just in the local neighbourhood. Firms' demand curves are thus becoming very price elastic. This is especially so for goods that are cheap to transport, or

for services such as insurance and banking where no transport is required.

Perfect knowledge. There are various ways in which e-commerce is adding to the consumer's knowledge. There is greater price transparency, with consumers able to compare prices online. Online shopping agents, such as Kelkoo and DealTime, can quickly locate a list of alternative suppliers. There is greater information on product availability and quality and this information is available at very little cost to the consumer. Virtual shopping malls, full of e-retailers, place the high street retailer under intense competitive pressure.

The pressure is even greater in the market for intermediate products. Many firms are constantly searching for cheaper sources of supply, and the Internet provides a cheap and easy means of conducting such searches.

Freedom of entry. Internet companies often have lower start-up costs than their conventional rivals. Their premises are generally much smaller, with no 'shop-front' costs and lower levels of stockholding; in fact many of these businesses are initially operated from their owners' homes. Marketing costs can also be relatively low, especially given the ease with which companies can be located with search engines. Internet companies are often smaller and more specialist, relying on Internet 'outsourcing' (buying parts, equipment and other supplies through the Internet), rather than making everything themselves. They are also more likely to use delivery firms rather than having their own transport fleet. All this makes it relatively cheap for new firms to set up and begin trading over the Internet.

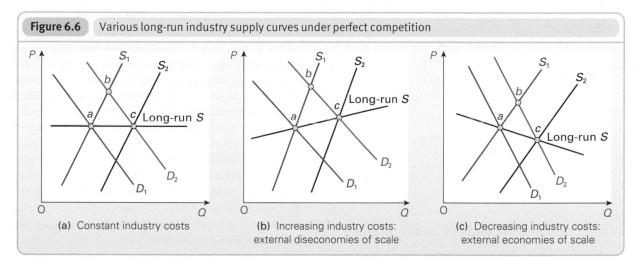

Figure 6.6   Various long-run industry supply curves under perfect competition

(a) Constant industry costs

(b) Increasing industry costs: external diseconomies of scale

(c) Decreasing industry costs: external economies of scale

The incompatibility of perfect competition and substantial economies of scale

Why is perfect competition so rare in the real world – if it even exists at all? One important reason for this has to do with economies of scale.

In many industries, firms may have to be quite large if they are to experience the full potential economies of scale. But perfect competition requires there to be *many* firms and that each one is a price taker. Firms must therefore be small under perfect competition: too small in most cases for economies of scale.

CASE STUDIES AND APPLICATIONS

One consequence of the rise of e-commerce is that the distinction between firms and consumers is becoming increasingly blurred. With the rise of eBay, more and more people are finding going into business incredibly easy. Some people are finding a market for all the junk they've collected over the years, while others are selling products they produce at home and yet others specialise in selling on products using the marketing power of eBay. As a consequence there are some 84 million active eBay users worldwide, and hundreds of thousands of people make a full-time living from buying and selling on eBay. Annual sales on eBay are worth over £30 billion.

Not only do these factors make markets more price competitive, they also bring other benefits. Costs are driven down, as firms economise on stockholding, rely more on outsourcing and develop more efficient relationships with suppliers. 'Procurement hubs', online exchanges and trading communities are now well established in many industries. The competition also encourages innovation, which improves quality and the range of products.

What are the limits to e-commerce?

In twenty years, will we be doing all our shopping on the Internet? Will the only shopping malls be virtual ones? Although e-commerce is revolutionising some markets, it is unlikely that things will go anything like that far.

The benefits of 'shop shopping' are that you get to see the good, touch it and use it. You can take instant possession of it: you don't have to wait. Many people like wandering round the shops, meeting friends, seeing what

takes their fancy, trying on clothes, browsing through DVDs and so on. 'Retail therapy' for many is a leisure activity.

Online shopping is limited by current technology; Internet access may be slow and frustrating; 'surfing' may instead become 'wading'; you have to wait for goods to be delivered; and what if deliveries are late or fail completely? Online shopping requires access to a credit or debit card, which might not be available to everyone, particularly younger consumers and those on low incomes.

Also, costs might not be as low as expected. How efficient is it to have many small deliveries of goods? How significant are the lost cost savings from economies of scale that larger producers or retailers are likely to generate?

Nevertheless, e-commerce has made many markets, both retail and B2B, more competitive. This is especially so for services and for goods whose quality is easy to identify online. Many firms are being forced to face up to having their prices determined by the market.

1. *Why may the Internet work better for replacement buys than for new purchases?*
2. *Give three examples of products that are particularly suitable for selling over the Internet and three that are not. Explain your answer.*
3. *In 2008 eBay sellers called for a boycott of the site, following changes in the fees being charged and the removal of their ability to leave feedback on buyers. Explain how eBay can both increase competition across the economy and simultaneously acquire very substantial monopoly power.*

Once a firm expands sufficiently to achieve economies of scale, it will usually gain market power. It will be able to undercut the prices of smaller firms, which will thus be driven out of business. Perfect competition is destroyed.

Perfect competition could only exist in any industry, therefore, if there were no (or virtually no) economies of scale.

1. *What other reasons can you think of why perfect competition is so rare?*
2. *Why does the market for fresh vegetables approximate to perfect competition, whereas that for aircraft does not?*

Perfect competition and the public interest

There are a number of features of perfect competition which, it could be argued, benefit society:

- Price equals marginal cost. As we shall see in Chapter 11, this has important implications for the allocation of resources between alternative products. Given that price equals marginal utility (see Chapter 4), marginal utility will equal marginal cost. This is argued to be an *optimal* position.

  To demonstrate why, consider what would happen if they were not equal. If price were greater than marginal cost, this would mean that consumers were putting a higher value ($P = MU$) on the production of extra units than they cost to produce (MC). Therefore more ought to be produced. If price were less than marginal cost, consumers would be putting a lower value on extra units than they cost to produce. Therefore less ought to be produced. When they are equal, therefore, production levels are just right. But, as we shall see later, it is only under perfect competition that $MC = P$.

- Long-run equilibrium is at the bottom of the firm's long-run AC curve. That is, for any *given* technology, the firm, in the long run, will produce at the least-cost output.

- Perfect competition is a case of 'survival of the fittest'. Inefficient firms will be driven out of business, since they will not be able to make even normal profits. This encourages firms to be as efficient as possible and, where possible, to invest in new improved technology.

- The combination of (long-run) production being at minimum average cost and the firm making only normal profit keeps prices at a minimum.

- If consumer tastes change, the resulting price change will lead firms to respond (purely out of self-interest). An increased consumer demand will call forth extra supply with only a short-run increase in profit.

Because of these last two points, perfect competition is said to lead to ***consumer sovereignty***. Consumers, through the market, determine what and how much is to be produced. Firms have no power to manipulate the market. They cannot control price. The only thing they can do to increase profit is to become more efficient, and that benefits the consumer too.

Even under perfect competition, however, the free market has various limitations. For example, there is no guarantee that the goods produced will be distributed to the members of society in the *fairest* proportions. There may be considerable inequality of income. (We examine this issue in Chapter 10.) What is more, a redistribution of income would lead to a different pattern of consumption and hence production. Thus there is no guarantee that perfect competition will lead to the optimum combination of goods being produced when society's views on equity are taken into account.

Another limitation is that the production of certain goods may lead to various undesirable side-effects, such as pollution. Perfect competition cannot safeguard against this either.

What is more, perfect competition may be less desirable than other market structures such as monopoly.

- Even though firms under perfect competition may seem to have an incentive to develop new technology (in order to gain supernormal profits, albeit temporarily), the long-run normal profits they make may not be sufficient to fund the necessary research and development. Also, they will be aware that, with complete information available, if they did develop new more efficient methods of production, their rivals would merely copy them, in which case the investment would have been a waste of money.

- Perfectly competitive industries produce undifferentiated products. This lack of variety might be seen as a disadvantage to the consumer. Under monopolistic competition and oligopoly there is often intense competition over the quality and design of the product. This can lead to pressure on firms to innovate and to improve their products. This pressure will not exist under perfect competition.

The issue of the efficiency or otherwise of perfect markets and the various failings of real-world markets is examined in more detail in Chapters 11–13.

At this stage, however, it is important to emphasise that the whole question of advantages and disadvantages is a normative one, and as such it is a question to which the economist cannot give a definitive answer. After all, people have very different views as to what constitutes 'good' or 'bad'.

Definition

Consumer sovereignty A situation where firms respond to changes in consumer demand without being in a position in the long run to charge a price above average cost.

Section summary

1. The assumptions of perfect competition are: a very large number of firms, complete freedom of entry, a homogeneous product and perfect knowledge of the good and its market on the part of both producers and consumers.

2. In the short run, there is not time for new firms to enter the market, and thus supernormal profits can persist. In the long run, however, any supernormal profits will be competed away by the entry of new firms.

3. The short-run equilibrium for the firm will be where the price, as determined by demand and supply in the market, is equal to marginal cost. At this output, the firm will be maximising profit. The firm's short-run supply curve is the same as its marginal cost curve (that portion of it above the *AVC* curve).

4. The long-run equilibrium will be where the market price is just equal to firms' long-run average cost. The long-run industry supply curve will thus depend on what happens to firms' *LRAC* curves as industry output expands. If their *LRAC* curves shift upwards (due to external diseconomies of scale), the long-run industry

supply curve will slope upwards. If their *LRAC* curves shift downwards (due to external economies of scale), the long-run industry supply curve will slope downwards.

5. There are no substantial (internal) economies of scale to be gained by perfectly competitive firms. If there were, the industry would cease to be perfectly competitive as the large, low-cost firms drove the small, high-cost ones out of business.

6. Under perfect competition, production will be at the point where $P = MC$. This can be argued to be optimal. Perfect competition can act as a spur to efficiency and bring benefits to the consumer in terms of low costs and low prices.

7. On the other hand, perfectly competitive firms may be unwilling to invest in research and development or may have insufficient funds to do so. They may also produce a lack of variety of goods. Finally, perfect competition does not necessarily lead to a fair distribution of income or guarantee an absence of harmful side-effects of production.

6.3 MONOPOLY

What is a monopoly?

This may seem a strange question because the answer seems obvious. A monopoly exists when there is only one firm in the industry.

But whether an industry can be classed as a monopoly is not always clear. It depends how narrowly the industry is defined. For example, a textile company may have a monopoly on certain types of fabric, but it does not have a monopoly on fabrics in general. The consumer can buy fabrics other than those supplied by the company. A pharmaceutical company may have a monopoly of a certain drug, but there may be alternative drugs for treating a particular illness.

To some extent, the boundaries of an industry are arbitrary. What is more important for a firm is the amount of monopoly *power* it has, and that depends on the closeness of substitutes produced by rival industries. The Post Office in the UK before 2006 had a monopoly over the delivery of letters under a certain weight, but it faced competition in communications from phones, faxes and email.

 As an illustration of the difficulty in identifying monopolies, try to decide which of the following are monopolies: British Telecom; your local evening newspaper; the village post office; a rail company; Interflora; the London Underground; ice creams in the cinema; Guinness; food sold in a university outlet; the board game 'Monopoly'. (As you will quickly realise in each case, it depends how you define the industry.)

Barriers to entry

For a firm to maintain its monopoly position, there must be **barriers to entry** of new firms. Barriers also exist under oligopoly, but in the case of monopoly they must be high enough to block the entry of new firms. Barriers can be of various forms.

Economies of scale. If a monopoly experiences substantial economies of scale, the industry may not be able to support more than one producer. In Figure 6.7, D_1 represents the industry demand curve, and hence the demand curve for the firm under monopoly. The monopolist can gain supernormal profit at any output between points *a* and *b*. If there were two firms, however, each charging the same price and supplying half the industry output, they would both face the demand curve D_2. There is no price that would allow them to cover costs.

This case is known as **natural monopoly**. It is particularly likely if the market is small. For example, two bus

Definitions

Barrier to entry Anything that prevents or impedes the entry of firms into an industry and thereby limits the amount of competition faced by existing firms.

Natural monopoly A situation where long-run average costs would be lower if an industry were under monopoly than if it were shared between two or more competitors.

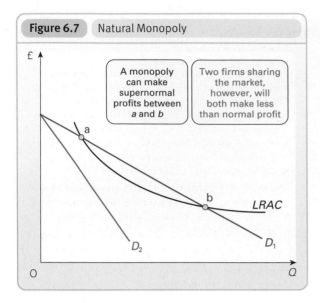

Figure 6.7 Natural Monopoly

A monopoly can make supernormal profits between *a* and *b*

Two firms sharing the market, however, will both make less than normal profit

companies might find it unprofitable to serve the same routes, each running with perhaps only half-full buses, whereas one company with a monopoly of the routes could make a profit. Electricity transmission via a national grid is another example of a natural monopoly.

Even if a market could support more than one firm, a new entrant is unlikely to be able to start up on a very large scale. Thus a monopolist already experiencing economies of scale can charge a price below the cost of the new entrant and drive it out of business. If, however, the new entrant is a firm already established in another industry, it may be able to survive this competition.

Network economies. When a product or service is used by everyone in the market, there are benefits to all users from having access to other users. Thus eBay, by providing such large **network economies**, makes it very difficult for other online auction houses to compete. Similar network economies apply to Microsoft's Windows (see Case Study 6.4 in MyEconLab), Adobe's Acrobat (for PDF files) and airlines operating interconnecting routes (see Box 6.6).

Economies of scope. A firm that produces a range of products is also likely to experience a lower average cost of production. For example, a large pharmaceutical company producing a range of drugs and toiletries can use shared research, marketing, storage and transport facilities across its range of products. These lower costs make it difficult for a new single-product entrant to the market, since the large

Definition

Network economies The benefits to consumers of having a network of other people using the same product or service.

firm will almost certainly be able to undercut its price and drive it out of the market.

Product differentiation and brand loyalty. If a firm produces a clearly differentiated product, where the consumer associates the product with the brand, it will be very difficult for a new firm to break into that market. Rank Xerox invented, and patented, the plain paper photocopier. After their legal monopoly (see below) ran out, people still associated photocopiers with Rank Xerox. It is still not unusual to hear someone say that they are going to 'Xerox the article' or, for that matter, 'Hoover their carpet'. Other examples of strong brand image include Guinness, Kellogg's Cornflakes, Coca-Cola, Nescafé and Sellotape. In most cases, such loyalty would not be enough to *block* entry, but it might well reinforce other barriers.

Lower costs for an established firm. An established monopoly is likely to have developed specialised production and marketing skills. It is more likely to be aware of the most efficient techniques and the most reliable and/or cheapest suppliers. It is likely to have access to cheaper finance. It is thus operating on a lower cost curve. New firms would therefore find it hard to compete and would be likely to lose any price war.

Ownership of, or control over, key inputs. If a firm governs the supply of vital inputs (say, by owning the sole supplier of some component part), it can deny access to these inputs to potential rivals. On a world scale, the de Beers company has a monopoly in fine diamonds because all diamond producers market their diamonds through de Beers.

Ownership of, or control over, wholesale or retail outlets. Similarly, if a firm controls the outlets through which the product must be sold, it can prevent potential rivals from gaining access to consumers. For example, Coca-Cola supplies chilled display units free of charge to shops on the condition that they stock only Coca-Cola's range of drinks in them.

Legal protection. The firm's monopoly position may be protected by patents on essential processes, by copyright, by various forms of licensing (allowing, say, only one firm to operate in a particular area) and by tariffs (i.e. customs duties) and other trade restrictions to keep out foreign competitors. Examples of monopolies protected by patents include most new medicines developed by pharmaceutical companies (e.g. anti-AIDS drugs), Microsoft's Windows operating systems, and agro-chemical companies, such as Monsanto, with various genetically modified plant varieties and pesticides.

Mergers and takeovers. The monopolist can put in a takeover bid for any new entrant. The mere threat of takeovers may discourage new entrants.

Aggressive tactics. An established monopolist can probably sustain losses for longer than a new entrant. Thus it can start a price war, mount massive advertising campaigns, offer an attractive after-sales service, introduce new brands to compete with new entrants, and so on.

Intimidation. The monopolist may resort to various forms of harassment, legal or illegal, to drive a new entrant out of business.

Equilibrium price and output

Since there is, by definition, only one firm in the industry, the firm's demand curve is also the industry demand curve.

Compared with other market structures, demand under monopoly will be relatively inelastic at each price. The monopolist can raise its price and consumers have no alternative firm in the industry to turn to. They either pay the higher price or go without the good altogether.

Unlike the firm under perfect competition, the monopoly firm is a 'price maker'. It can choose what price to charge. Nevertheless, it is still constrained by its demand curve. A rise in price will lower the quantity demanded. Be careful not to fall into the trap of thinking that a monopoly can control both price *and* output simultaneously.

As with firms in other market structures, a monopolist will maximise profit where $MR = MC$. In Figure 6.8, profit is maximised at Q_m. The supernormal profit obtained is shown by the shaded area.

These profits will tend to be larger the less elastic is the demand curve (and hence the steeper is the MR curve), and thus the bigger is the gap between MR and price (AR). The actual elasticity will depend on whether reasonably close substitutes are available in *other* industries. The demand for a rail service will be much less elastic (and the potential for profit greater) if there is no bus service to the same destination.

Since there are barriers to the entry of new firms, these supernormal profits will not be competed away in the long run. The only difference, therefore, between short-run and long-run equilibrium is that in the long run the firm will produce where $MR = long$-$run MC$.

 Try this brain teaser. A monopoly would be expected to face an inelastic demand. After all, there are no direct substitutes. And yet, if it produces where $MR = MC$, MR must be positive and demand must therefore be elastic. Therefore the monopolist must face an elastic demand! Can you solve this conundrum?

Limit pricing

If the barriers to the entry of new firms are not total, and if the monopolist is making very large supernormal profits, there may be a danger in the long run of potential rivals breaking into the industry. In such cases, the monopolist may keep its price down and thereby deliberately restrict the size of its profits so as not to attract new entrants. This practice is known as **limit pricing**.

*LOOKING AT THE MATHS

From Figure 6.8, it can be seen that the less elastic the demand at the output where $MC = MR$, the greater will be the gap between AR and MR, and hence the further above MR will the price be. The relationship between price, MR (or MC) and price elasticity of demand ($P\epsilon_D$) is given by the following formula:

$$P = \frac{MR}{1 + (1/P\epsilon_D)}$$

Thus if $MR = MC = £12$ and $P\epsilon_D = -4$, the profit-maximising price would be

$$\frac{£12}{1 + (1/-4)} = \frac{£12}{1 - 1/4} = \frac{£12}{0.75} = £16$$

Proof of this rule is given in Maths Case 6.2 in MyEconLab. You can see simply by examining the formula, however, that the lower the elasticity, the greater will be the price relative to MR or MC.[1]

 What is the profit-maximising price if $MR = MC = £12$ and $P\epsilon_D = -2$?

[1] Note that this formula works only if demand is elastic, as it must be if MR is positive (which it will be, since MC must be positive).

In Figure 6.9, two AC curves are drawn: one for the monopolist and one for a potential entrant. The monopolist, being established, has a lower AC curve. The new entrant, if it is to compete successfully with the monopolist, must charge the same price or a lower one. Thus,

Definition

Limit pricing Where a monopolist (or oligopolist) charges a price below the short-run profit maximising level in order to deter new entrants.

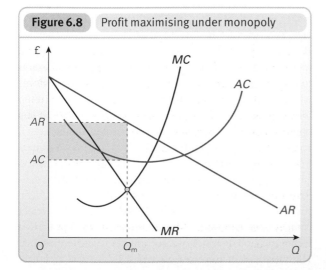

Figure 6.8 Profit maximising under monopoly

Figure 6.9   Limit pricing

Provided price is kept below the limit price (P_L), new firms cannot make a profit

Figure 6.10   Equilibrium of the industry under perfect competition and monopoly: with the same *MC* curve

provided the monopolist does not raise price above P_L, the other firm, unable to make supernormal profit, will not be attracted into the industry.

P_L may well be below the monopolist's short-run profit-maximising price, but the monopolist may prefer to limit its price to P_L to protect its long-run profits from damage by competition.

Fear of government intervention to curb the monopolist's practices (e.g. the Office of Fair Trading referring the firm to the Competition Commission: see section 13.1) may have a similar restraining effect on the price that the monopolist charges.

1. *On a diagram like Figure 6.9, by drawing in MR and MC curves, demonstrate that P_L could be below the short-run profit-maximising price.*
2. *What does this analysis assume about the price elasticity of demand for the new entrant (a) above P_L; (b) below P_L?*

Monopoly and the public interest

Disadvantages of monopoly

There are several reasons why monopolies may be against the public interest. As we shall see in Chapter 13, these

TC 3
p24

have given rise to legislation to regulate monopoly power and/or behaviour.

KI 20
p164

Higher price and lower output than under perfect competition (short run). Figure 6.10 compares the profit-maximising position for an industry under monopoly with that under perfect competition. The monopolist will produce Q_1 at a price of P_1. This is where $MC = MR$.

If the same industry operated under perfect competition, however, it would produce at Q_2 and P_2 – a higher output and a lower price. This is where industry supply under perfect competition equals industry demand. (Remember, we showed in section 6.2 that the firm's supply curve under perfect competition is its *MC* curve and thus the industry's supply curve is simply the *industry MC* curve: the *MC* curve shown in Figure 6.10.)

This analysis is based on the assumption that the industry has the *same AC* and *MC* curves whether under perfect competition or run as a monopoly. For example, suppose some potato farmers initially operate under perfect competition. The market price is P_2 in Figure 6.10. Then they set up a marketing agency through which they all sell their potatoes. The agency therefore acts as a monopoly supplier to the market and charges a price of P_1. Since it is the same farmers before and after, production costs are unlikely to have changed much. But as we shall see below, even if an industry has *lower AC* and *MC* curves under monopoly than under perfect competition, it is still likely to charge a higher price and produce a lower output.

When we were looking at the advantages of perfect competition, we said that the level where $P = MC$ could be argued to be the *optimum* level of production. Clearly, if a monopolist is producing below this level (e.g. at Q_1 in Figure 6.10 – where $P > MC$), the monopolist can be argued to be producing at *less* than optimal output. Consumers would be prepared to pay more for additional units than they cost to produce.

Higher price and lower output than under perfect competition (long run). Under perfect competition, freedom of entry eliminates supernormal profit and forces firms to produce at the bottom of their *LRAC* curve. The effect, therefore, is to keep long-run prices down. Under monopoly, however, barriers to entry allow profits to remain supernormal in the long run. The monopolist is not forced to operate at the bottom of the *AC* curve. Thus, other things being equal, long-run prices will tend to be higher, and hence output lower, under monopoly.

Possibility of higher cost curves due to lack of competition. The sheer survival of a firm in the long run under perfect competition requires that it uses the most efficient known technique, and develops new techniques wherever possible. The monopolist, however, sheltered by barriers to entry, can still make large profits even if it is not using the most efficient technique. It has less incentive, therefore, to be efficient (see Box 6.4).

On the other hand, if it can lower its costs by using and developing more efficient techniques, it can gain extra supernormal profits which will not be competed away.

KI 4
p10

Unequal distribution of income. The high profits of monopolists may be considered as unfair, especially by competitive firms, or anyone on low incomes for that matter.

The scale of this problem obviously depends on the size of the monopoly and the degree of its power. The monopoly profits of the village store may seem of little consequence when compared to the profits of a giant national or international company.

If the shares in a monopoly (such as a water company) were very widely distributed among the population, would the shareholders necessarily want the firm to use its monopoly power to make larger profits?

BOX 6.4 | **BREAKING SKY'S MONOPOLY ON LIVE FOOTBALL COVERAGE** | CASE STUDIES AND APPLICATIONS

The impact of opening up the market

The early days of Sky

The structure of English football was changed with the formation of the FA Premier League for the 1992/3 football season. One justification for this was the promise of higher payments by TV companies. Live league football had been shown on free-to-air television throughout the 1980s and the clubs were very aware that this was potentially a very lucrative source of revenue.

The first contract to acquire the live and exclusive FA Premier League football broadcasting rights for the United Kingdom and the Republic of Ireland was worth £191m over five seasons. A consequence of Sky being awarded the contract was that live top-flight English league football was no longer available on terrestrial and free-to-air television. Those who wanted to watch live football matches on television had to sign up with Sky, buying both a basic package and the additional Sky sports channels; Sky thus had a monopoly.

Attempts to reduce monopoly power

Both the Premier League and Sky's coverage proved to be hugely successful with viewers and advertisers and this was reflected in the price paid for subsequent packages. The one starting in 1997 cost Sky £670m for four seasons, while in 2003 BSkyB, as the company was now formally known, paid over £1 billion for exclusive rights for three seasons.

However, over this period the European Commission was expressing increasing concern about the extent of Sky's monopoly. The Commission started legal proceedings in 2002, filing a statement of objections, but was thwarted when the League agreed a new contract with Sky before ironing out an EC-approved deal.

At this time Sky did agree to sub-license up to eight 'top quality Premier League matches' each season to another broadcaster in order to win European approval. The Commission trumpeted this pledge as meaning 'that for the first time in the history of the Premier League free-to-air television will have a realistic opportunity to show live Premier League matches'. These hopes were dashed, however, when no rival broadcaster met the asking price set by Sky.

In 2005 the European Commission announced that Sky's monopoly would be broken. From 2007, the next set of rights, for a three-season period, would be sold in

six 'balanced' packages of 23 games per season, with no broadcaster allowed more than five packages. The Commission claimed that the deal would give fans 'greater choice and better value'.

However, concern was expressed about the impact on the incomes of the Premiership clubs. While some commentators expected a more competitive process to result in roughly the same total income as was paid by Sky in 2003, just over £1 billion, others suggested that Sky paid a premium for the guarantee that it would be the sole broadcaster. Thus one effect of the new process might be reduced revenues for the clubs.

The outcome of the EC ruling

In May 2006 the bidding process for the rights for 2007–10 was completed. The outcome was that Sky won four of the six available packages and would show 92 live Premiership matches per season, while Setanta, an Irish-based satellite broadcaster, won the remaining two packages and would have 46 games.

Much to the surprise of many, the total amount paid by the two companies far exceeded the previous contract, with the Premier League receiving more than £1.7 billion over the three years. However, the outcome for fans was seen as rather less positive; although there would now be more live games than in previous seasons, fans wishing to watch all of them would have to buy two packages.

Overall the packaging of media rights for English top-flight football has been hugely influential in the development of the game. Revenues for the Premier League exceeded £1.9 billion for 2007/8 and it remains the biggest-earning league in world football. English football contributes over £700 million in taxes, and overseas sales have a positive impact on the UK's balance of payments. Fans now have access to more than 120 live games each season and attendances at matches remain buoyant. The monopoly power that accrued initially to Sky, and that is currently shared with Sentanta, may well have proved the making of the Premier League.

1. *What other examples of monopoly power exist in football? Could this power be reduced?*
2. *Assess the impact of the pay broadcasters' emergence over the last fifteen years on (a) football fans, (b) other viewers.*

TC 5
p50

In addition to these problems, monopolies may lack the incentive to introduce new product varieties, and large monopolies may be able to exert political pressure and thereby get favourable treatment from governments.

Advantages of monopoly

Despite these arguments, monopolies can have some advantages.

Economies of scale. The monopoly may be able to achieve substantial economies of scale due to larger plant, centralised administration and the avoidance of unnecessary duplication (e.g. a monopoly water company would eliminate the need for several sets of rival water mains under each street). If this results in an *MC* curve substantially below that of the same industry under perfect competition, the monopoly will produce a *higher* output at a *lower* price. In Figure 6.11, the monopoly produces Q_1 at a price of P_1, whereas the perfectly competitive industry produces Q_2 at the higher price P_2.

Note that this result follows only if the monopoly *MC* curve is below point *x* in Figure 6.11. Note also that an industry cannot exist under perfect competition if substantial economies of scale can be gained. It is thus somewhat hypothetical to compare a monopoly with an alternative situation that could not exist. What is more, were the monopolist to follow the $P = MC$ rule observed by perfectly competitive firms, it would charge an even lower price (P_3) and produce an even higher output (Q_3).

Figure 6.11 Equilibrium of the industry under perfect competition and monopoly: with different *MC* curves

Possibility of lower cost curves due to more research and development and more investment. Although the monopolist's sheer survival does not depend on its finding ever more efficient methods of production, it can use part of its supernormal profits for research and development and investment. It thus has a greater ability to become efficient than has the small firm with limited funds.

KI 3
p10

Competition for corporate control. Although a monopoly faces no competition in the goods market, it may face an

---

KI 3
p10

BOX 6.5   X INEFFICIENCY

EXPLORING ECONOMICS

The cost of a quiet life

The major criticism of monopoly has traditionally been that of the monopoly's power in selling the good. The firm charges a price above *MC* (see Figure 6.10). This is seen as *allocatively inefficient* because at the margin consumers are willing to pay more than it is costing to produce ($P > MC$); and yet the monopolist is deliberately holding back, so as to keep its profits up. Allocative inefficiency is examined in detail in section 11.1.

Monopolies may also be inefficient for another reason: they may have higher costs. But why?

Higher costs may be the result of *X inefficiency*[1] (sometimes known as *technical inefficiency*). Without competitive pressure on profit margins, cost controls may become lax. The result may be overstaffing and spending on prestige buildings and equipment, as well as less effort to keep technologically up to date, scrap old plant, research new products, or develop new domestic and export markets.

Thus the more comfortable the situation, the less may be the effort which is expended to improve it. The effect of this X inefficiency is to make the *AC* and *MC* curves higher than they would otherwise be.

During the early 1980s, there were significant reductions in X inefficiency in many countries. With a worldwide recession, and a fall in both sales and profits, many firms embarked on cost-cutting programmes. Much out-of-date plant was closed down, and employment was reduced. Those firms that survived the recession (and many did not) tended to emerge both more competitive and more efficient.

Another factor causing a reduction in X inefficiency has been the growth in international competition. As markets have increasingly become global in scale, as e-commerce has increased and as customs duties and other barriers to trade have been reduced (see section 24.2), so many companies are facing fiercer competition from abroad.

1. *How might you measure X inefficiency?*
2. *Another type of inefficiency is productive inefficiency. What do you think this is? (Clue: it has to do with the proportions in which factors are used.)*

[1] This term was coined by Harvey Leibenstein, 'Allocative efficiency or X efficiency', *American Economic Review*, June 1966.

alternative form of competition in financial markets. A monopoly, with potentially low costs, which is currently run inefficiently, is likely to be subject to a takeover bid from another company. This **competition for corporate control** may thus force the monopoly to be efficient in order to avoid being taken over.

Innovation and new products. The promise of supernormal profits, protected perhaps by patents, may encourage the development of new (monopoly) industries producing new products.

Monopoly and price discrimination

One further characteristic of monopoly is that it allows firms to price discriminate: to charge different prices either to all customers or to different groups of customers. Firms undertake this as a way of further increasing profits. The ability to price discriminate rests on the firm having some monopoly power, although this need not be a complete monopoly. Price discrimination is discussed in more detail in section 7.4, pages 206–11.

Section summary

1. A monopoly is where there is only one firm in an industry. In practice, it is difficult to determine that a monopoly exists because it depends on how narrowly an industry is defined.

2. Barriers to the entry of new firms are usually necessary to protect a monopoly from competition. Such barriers include economies of scale (making the firm a natural monopoly or at least giving it a cost advantage over new (small) competitors), control over supplies of inputs or over outlets, patents or copyright, and tactics to eliminate competition (such as takeovers or aggressive advertising).

3. Profits for the monopolist (as for other firms) will be maximised where $MC = MR$. In the case of monopoly, this will probably be at a higher price relative to

marginal cost than for other firms, due to the less elastic nature of its demand at any given price.

4. Monopolies may be against the public interest to the extent that they charge a higher price relative to cost than do competitive firms; if they cause a less desirable distribution of income; if a lack of competition removes the incentive to be efficient and innovative; and if they exert undesirable political pressures on governments.

5. On the other hand, any economies of scale will in part be passed on to consumers in lower prices, and the monopolist's high profits may be used for research and development and investment, which in turn may lead to better products at possibly lower prices.

6.4 THE THEORY OF CONTESTABLE MARKETS

Potential competition or monopoly?

In recent years, economists have developed the theory of contestable markets. This theory argues that what is crucial in determining price and output is not whether an industry is *actually* a monopoly or competitive, but whether there is the real *threat* of competition.

If a monopoly is protected by high barriers to entry – if, for example, it owns all the relevant raw materials – then it will be able to make supernormal profits with no fear of competition.

If, however, another firm *could* take over from it with little difficulty, it will behave much more like a competitive firm. The threat of competition has a similar effect to actual competition.

As an example, consider a catering company engaged by a factory to run its canteen. The catering company has a monopoly over the supply of food to the workers in that factory. If, however, it starts charging high prices or providing a poor service, the factory could offer the running of the canteen to an alternative catering company. This threat

may force the original catering company to charge 'reasonable' prices and offer a good service.

Perfectly contestable markets

A market is **perfectly contestable** when the costs of entry and exit by potential rivals are zero, and when such entry can be made very rapidly. In such cases, the moment it becomes possible to earn supernormal profits, new firms will enter, thus driving profits down to a normal level. The sheer threat of this happening, so the theory goes, will ensure that the firm already in the market will (a) keep its

---

Definitions

Competition for corporate control The competition for the control of companies through takeovers.

Perfectly contestable market A market where there is free and costless entry and exit.

BOX 6.6	AIRLINE DEREGULATION IN THE USA AND EUROPE

A case study of contestable markets

If a market is highly contestable, the mere threat of competition may be successful in keeping prices and profits down. Of course, established firms would not like this! They would be keen to erect barriers to entry and to make exit more costly for any firm that did enter.

Governments around the world are generally in favour of increased competition and frown on the erection of entry barriers (see section 13.1). This means that they generally prefer not to intervene if markets are competitive or highly contestable, but may attempt to regulate the prices, profits or behaviour of firms where competition or contestability is limited. Conversely, if markets have been regulated and yet are potentially competitive, many governments have then deregulated them (i.e. removed regulations).

A good case study of deregulation and contestability (or lack of it) is the airline industry.

The USA

The airline industry in the United States has been deregulated since 1978. Prior to this, air routes were allocated by the government, with the result that many airlines operated as monopolies or shared the route with just one other airline. Now there exists a policy of 'open skies'.

Initially the consequences were dramatic, with lower fares and, over many routes, a greater choice of airlines. The Brookings Institute calculated that, in the first ten years of deregulation, the lower fares saved consumers some $100 billion. One consequence of the increased competition was that many US airlines went out of business.

Even where routes continued to be operated by just one or two airlines, fares still fell if the route was *contestable*: if the entry and exit costs remained low. In 1992, despite the bankruptcies, 23 new carriers were established in North America, and many routes were taken over by existing carriers.

But deregulation did not make all routes more contestable. In some cases the reverse happened. In a situation of rising costs and falling revenues, there were mergers and takeovers of the vulnerable airlines. By 2000 just seven airlines accounted for over 90 per cent of American domestic air travel, compared with fifteen in

1984. With this move towards greater monopolisation, some airlines managed to make their routes *less* contestable. The result was that air fares over the 1990s rose faster than prices in general.

A key ingredient in making routes less contestable was the development of a system of air routes radiating out from about 30 key or 'hub' airports. With waves of flights scheduled to arrive and depart within a short space of time, passengers can make easy connections at these hub airports.

The problem is that several of these hub airports became dominated by single airlines which, through economies of scale and the ownership or control of various airport facilities, such as boarding gates or check-in areas, could effectively keep out potential entrants. By 2002, at fifteen of the hub airports, including some of the busiest, the dominant airline had a market share in excess of 70 per cent.

The airlines have also used measures to increase 'customer loyalty' and thereby make entry barriers higher. These measures include frequent flier rewards, deals with travel agents, and code sharing with 'partner' airlines.

In the 2000s, however, the domestic US airlines market became more competitive again, thanks to the growth of low-cost carriers (LCCs). These accounted for just 7 per cent of US domestic passengers in 1990; by 2008 this had risen to over 30 per cent. The response of the major airlines was to create their own low-cost carriers, such as Delta's 'Song' in 2004 and United's 'Ted' in 2004.

A danger here is that big airlines may use their LCCs to undercut the prices of small new entrants so as to drive them out of the market. Such 'predatory pricing' (see page 210), however, is illegal, and the Department of Justice has begun investigating several cases.

With the rise in fuel prices in 2006–8, some of these new LCCs went out of business. Delta shut its Song division in 2006 and United shut Ted in 2008. Southwest, which started as a low-cost airline, continued in its position of market dominance.

Europe

Until the early 1990s, the European air transport industry was highly regulated, with governments controlling

prices down, so that it just makes normal profits, and (b) produce as efficiently as possible, taking advantage of any economies of scale and any new technology. If it did not do this, rivals would enter, and potential competition would become actual competition.

This is illustrated in Figure 6.12. Assume that there is only one firm in the industry, which faces a long-run average cost curve given by *LRAC*. Assume that profits are maximised at a price of P_1, with supernormal profits being shown by the shaded area. If entry and exit costs are high,

the price will remain at this level. If entry and exit costs are low, however, rival firms may be tempted to enter and take over the monopoly. To avert this, the existing firm will have to lower its price. In the case of zero entry and exit costs, the monopolist will have to lower its price to P_2, where price equals *LRAC*, and where, therefore, profits are normal and would not attract rival firms to enter. At the same time, the monopolist will have to ensure that its *LRAC* curve is as low as possible (i.e. that it avoids any X inefficiency (see Box 6.5)).

routes. National routes were often licensed to the national airline and international routes to the two respective national airlines. Since 1993, the industry has been progressively deregulated and competition has increased, with a growing availability of discount fares. Now, within the EU, airlines are free to charge whatever they like, and any EU airline can fly on any route it wants, providing it can get the slots at the airports at either end.

As in the USA, however, whilst increased competition has benefited passengers, many of the airlines have tried to make their routes less contestable by erecting entry barriers. Predatory pricing occurred, as the established airlines tried to drive out new competitors. The proliferation of fare categories made it hard for consumers to compare prices, and established carriers' highly publicised fares often had many restrictions, with most people having to pay considerably higher fares. As in the USA, code sharing and airline alliances have reduced competition. Finally, at busy airports, such as Heathrow, the shortage of check-in and boarding gates, runways and airspace provided a major barrier to new entrants.

Nevertheless, new low-cost airlines, such as easyJet, Ryanair and Flybe, provided effective competition for the established national and short-haul international carriers, which were forced to cut fares on routes where they directly competed. British Airways went as far as re-badging their loss-making subsidiary regional airline as BA Connect in 2006, adopting a low-cost model and pledging to 'cut one third from standard domestic fares'. However, the company accrued further losses that year and was sold to Flybe in early 2007.

Low-cost airlines have been able to enter the market by using other airports, such as Stansted and Luton in the case of London, and various regional airports throughout Europe. Many passengers showed themselves willing to travel further at the beginning and end of their journey if the overall cost remained much lower.

Lower costs

How could the LCCs compete? The airline industry does not on the face of it seem to be a highly contestable one. Apart from anything else, aircraft would appear to be a high-cost input.

The answer lies in a variety of cost-saving opportunities. The LCCs are able to lease planes rather than buy them; even when they own their own planes, the aircraft are generally older and more basic, offering a standard accommodation rather than different classes. The result is reduced exit costs, increasing contestability. In addition, by charging extra for each item of luggage, they reduce the amount they carry, thus saving fuel.

The large hub-and-spoke carriers have also found that the very nature of their operations constricts their ability to compete with the LCCs on city-to-city routes. Not only are the hubs themselves expensive, but the movement of passengers in and out of the terminals takes longer than with smaller airports. Thus the LCCs, with operating costs some 25 to 50 per cent lower than the traditional carriers, have become a highly effective competitive force on these routes between various city pairs and have forced down prices.

Despite these successes, some commentators suggest that the current LCCs are unlikely to survive a period of increasing fuel prices and falling consumer demand. In July 2008 Ryanair reported a fall in profits of 85 per cent and other carriers look vulnerable, with routes being cut. Nevertheless, it seems likely that the airline market will remain highly contestable.

1. *Make a list of those factors that determine the contestability of a particular air route.*
2. *In the UK, train operators compete for franchises to run services on a particular route. The franchises are normally for 7, 10, 12 or 15 years. The franchise specifies prices and minimum levels of services (frequency, timing and quality). Would this be a good system to adopt in the airline market over particular routes? How is the airline market similar to/different from the rail market in this regard?*
3. *In a period of rising fuel prices, and thus higher air fares, do you think that the low-cost carriers are more or less vulnerable than the traditional carriers in the short term? Would your answer differ when we look at the longer-term decisions of passengers?*

Contestable markets and natural monopolies

So why in such cases are the markets not *actually* perfectly competitive? Why do they remain monopolies?

The most likely reason has to do with economies of scale and the size of the market. To operate on a minimum efficient scale, the firm may have to be so large relative to the market that there is only room for one such firm in the industry. If a new firm does come into the market, then one or other of the two firms will not survive the competition. The market is simply not big enough for both of them.

This is the case in Figure 6.12. The industry is a natural monopoly, given that the *LRAC* curve is downward sloping even at output *c*.

If, however, there are no entry or exit costs, new firms will be perfectly willing to enter even though there is only room for one firm, provided they believe that they are more efficient than the established firm. The established firm, knowing this, will be forced to produce as efficiently as possible and with only normal profit.

Figure 6.12 A contestable monopoly

Costless exit, therefore, encourages firms to enter an industry, knowing that, if unsuccessful, they can always transfer their capital elsewhere.

The lower the exit costs, the more contestable the market. This implies that firms already established in other similar markets may provide more effective competition against monopolists, since they can simply transfer capital from one market to another. For example, studies of airlines in the USA show that entry to a particular route may be much easier for an established airline, which can simply transfer planes from one route to another (see Box 6.6).

In which of the following industries are exit costs likely to be low: (a) steel production; (b) market gardening; (c) nuclear power generation; (d) specialist financial advisory services; (e) production of a new drug; (f) mobile hairdressers; (g) car ferry operators? Do these exit costs depend on how narrowly the industry is defined?

The importance of costless exit

Setting up in a new business usually involves large expenditures on plant and machinery. Once this money has been spent, it becomes fixed costs. If these fixed costs are no higher than those of the existing firm, then the new firm could win the battle. But, of course, there is always the risk that it might lose.

But does losing the battle really matter? Can the firm not simply move to another market?

It does matter if there are substantial costs of exit. This will be the case if the capital equipment cannot be transferred to other uses, as would be the case, for example, with a power station. In this case, these fixed costs are known as *sunk costs*. The losing firm is left with capital equipment that it cannot use. The firm may therefore be put off entering in the first place. The market is not perfectly contestable, and the established firm can make supernormal profit.

If, however, the capital equipment can be transferred, the exit costs will be zero (or at least very low), and new firms will be more willing to take the risks of entry. For example, a rival coach company may open up a service on a route previously operated by only one company, and where there is still only room for one operator. If the new firm loses the resulting battle, it can still use the coaches it has purchased. It simply uses them for a different route. The cost of the coaches is not a sunk cost.

Assessment of the theory

The theory of contestable markets is an improvement on simple monopoly theory, which merely focuses on the existing structure of the industry and makes no allowance for potential competition: no allowance for the size of the barriers to entry and the costs of exit.

Perfectly contestable markets may exist only rarely. But like perfect competition they provide an *ideal type* against which to judge the real world. It can be argued that they provide a more useful ideal type than perfect competition, since the extent of divergence from this ideal provides a better means of predicting firms' price and output behaviour than does the simple portion of the market currently supplied by the existing firm.

One criticism of the theory, however, is that it does not take sufficient account of the possible reactions of the established firm. There may be no cost barriers to entry or exit (i.e. a perfectly contestable market), but the established firm may let it be known that any firm that dares to enter will face all-out war! This may act as a deterrent to entry. In the meantime, the established firm may charge high prices and make supernormal profits.

Contestable markets and the public interest

If a monopoly operates in a perfectly contestable market, it might bring the 'best of both worlds'. Not only will it be able to achieve low costs through economies of scale, but also the potential competition will keep profits and hence prices down.

For this reason, the theory has been seized on by politicians on the political right to justify a policy of *laissez-faire* (non-intervention) and deregulation (e.g. coach and air routes). They argue that the theory vindicates the free market. There are two points in reply to this:

Definition

Sunk costs Costs that cannot be recouped (e.g. by transferring assets to other uses). Examples include specialised machinery or the costs of an advertising campaign.

- Few markets are *perfectly* contestable. If entry and exit are not costless, a monopoly can still make supernormal profits in the long run.
- There are other possible failings of the market beside monopoly power (e.g. inequality, pollution). These failings are examined in Chapters 10 and 11.

Nevertheless the theory of contestable markets has highlighted the importance of entry barriers in determining monopoly behaviour. The size of the barriers has therefore become the focus of attention of many politicians and academics when considering anti-monopoly policy.

Section summary

1. Potential competition may be as important as actual competition in determining a firm's price and output strategy.

2. The threat of this competition increases as entry and exit costs to and from the industry diminish. If the entry and exit costs are zero, the market is said to be *perfectly* contestable. Under such circumstances, an existing monopolist will be forced to keep its profits down to the normal level if it is to resist entry by new firms. Exit costs will be lower, the lower are the sunk costs of the firm.

3. The theory of contestable markets provides a more realistic analysis of firms' behaviour than theories based simply on the *existing* number of firms in the industry.

END OF CHAPTER QUESTIONS

1. A perfectly competitive firm faces a price of £14 per unit. It has the following short-run cost schedule:

Output	0	1	2	3	4	5	6	7	8
TC (£)	10	18	24	30	38	50	66	91	120

   (a) Copy the table and put in additional rows for average cost and marginal cost at each level of output. (Enter the figures for marginal cost in the space between each column.)

   (b) Plot *AC*, *MC* and *MR* on a diagram.

   (c) Mark the profit-maximising output.

   (d) How much (supernormal) profit is made at this output?

   (e) What would happen to the price in the long run if this firm were typical of others in the industry? Why would we need to know information about long-run average cost in order to give a precise answer to this question?

2. If the industry under perfect competition faces a downward-sloping demand curve, why does an individual firm face a horizontal demand curve?

3. If supernormal profits are competed away under perfect competition, why will firms have an incentive to become more efficient?

4. Is it a valid criticism of perfect competition to argue that it is incompatible with economies of scale?

5. On a diagram similar to Figure 6.4, show the long-run equilibrium for both firm and industry under perfect competition. Now assume that the demand for the product falls. Show the short-run and long-run effects.

6. Why is the profit-maximising price under monopoly greater than marginal cost? In what way can this be seen as inefficient?

7. On three diagrams like Figure 6.8, illustrate the effect on price, quantity and profit of each of the following: (a) a rise in demand; (b) a rise in fixed costs; (c) a rise in variable costs. In each case, show only the *AR*, *MR*, *AC* and *MC* curves.

8. Think of three examples of monopolies (local or national) and consider how contestable their markets are.

Online resources

Additional case studies in MyEconLab

6.1 **B2B electronic marketplaces.** This case study examines the growth of firms trading with each other (business to business or 'B2B') over the Internet and considers the effects on competition.

6.2 **Measuring monopoly power.** This case study examines how the degree of monopoly power possessed by a firm can be measured.

6.3 **Competition in the pipeline?** This examines monopoly in the supply of gas.

6.4 **Windows cleaning.** This discusses the examination of Microsoft's market dominance by the US Justice Department and the European Commission.

Maths Case 6.1 Long-run equilibrium under perfect competition. Using calculus to find equilibrium output and price.

Maths Case 6.2 Price elasticity of demand and the profit-maximising price. A proof of the profit-maximising rule relating price elasticity of demand, price and marginal revenue.

Websites relevant to this chapter

See sites listed at the end of Chapter 7 on page 212.

Profit Maximising under Imperfect Competition

CHAPTER MAP

7.1 Monopolistic competition — 186
Assumptions of monopolistic competition — 186
Equilibrium of the firm — 186
Limitations of the model — 187
Non-price competition — 188
Monopolistic competition and the public interest — 188

7.2 Oligopoly — 189
The two key features of oligopoly — 189
Competition and collusion — 190
Industry equilibrium under collusive oligopoly — 190
Tacit collusion: price leadership — 192
Tacit collusion: rules of thumb — 193
Factors favouring collusion — 196
Non-collusive oligopoly: the breakdown of
collusion — 196
Non-collusive oligopoly: assumptions
about rivals' behaviour — 196
Oligopoly and the public interest — 200

7.3 Game theory — 201
Single-move games — 201
Multiple-move games — 204
The importance of threats and promises — 204
The importance of timing — 204
Assessing the theory of games — 205

7.4 Price discrimination — 206
Conditions necessary for price discrimination
to operate — 206
Advantages to the firm — 208
Profit-maximising prices and output — 208
Price discrimination and the public interest — 210

Very few markets in practice can be classified as perfectly competitive or as a pure monopoly. The vast majority of firms do compete with other firms, often quite aggressively, and yet they are not price takers: they do have some degree of market power. Most markets, therefore, lie between the two extremes of monopoly and perfect competition, in the realm of 'imperfect competition'.

There are two types of imperfect competition: namely, monopolistic competition and oligopoly.

Under monopolistic competition, there will normally be quite a large number of relatively small firms. Think of the large number of car repair garages, builders, hairdressers, restaurants and other small traders that you get in any large town or city. They are in fierce competition with each other, and yet competition is not perfect. They are all trying to produce a product that is different from their rivals.

Under oligopoly, there will be only a few firms competing. Most of the best-known companies, such as Ford, Coca-Cola, Nike, BP and Nintendo, are oligopolists. Sometimes oligopolists will attempt to collude with each other to keep prices up. On other occasions, competition will be intense, with rival firms trying to undercut each other's prices, or developing new or better products in order to gain a larger share of the market. We will examine both collusion and competition between oligopolists and show when each is more likely to occur.

7.1 MONOPOLISTIC COMPETITION

We will start by looking at monopolistic competition. This was a theory developed in the 1930s by the American economist Edward Chamberlin. Monopolistic competition is nearer to the competitive end of the spectrum. It can best be understood as a situation where there are a lot of firms competing, but where each firm does nevertheless have some degree of market power (hence the term 'monopolistic' competition): each firm has some choice over what price to charge for its products.

Assumptions of monopolistic competition

- There are *quite a large number of firms*. As a result, each firm has an insignificantly small share of the market, and therefore its actions are unlikely to affect its rivals to any great extent. This means that when each firm makes its decisions it does not have to worry how its rivals will react. It assumes that what its rivals choose to do will *not* be influenced by what it does.

  This is known as the assumption of **independence**. (As we shall see later, this is not the case under oligopoly. There we assume that firms believe that their decisions *do* affect their rivals, and that their rivals' decisions will affect them. Under oligopoly, we assume that firms are *inter*dependent.)

- There is *freedom of entry* of new firms into the industry. If any firm wants to set up in business in this market, it is free to do so.

In these two respects, therefore, monopolistic competition is like perfect competition.

- The situation differs from perfect competition, however, in that each firm produces a product or provides a service in some way different from those of its rivals. As a result, it can raise its price without losing all its customers. Thus its demand curve is downward sloping, albeit relatively elastic given the large number of competitors to whom customers can turn. This is known as the assumption of **product differentiation**.

Definitions

Independence (of firms in a market) Where the decisions of one firm in a market will not have any significant effect on the demand curves of its rivals.

Product differentiation Where one firm's product is sufficiently different from its rivals' to allow it to raise the price of the product without customers all switching to the rivals' products. A situation where a firm faces a downward-sloping demand curve.

Restaurants, hairdressers and builders are all examples of monopolistic competition.

 Give some other examples of monopolistic competition. (Try looking at www.yell.com if you are stuck.)

A typical feature of monopolistic competition is that, although there are many firms in the industry, there is only one firm in a particular location. This applies particularly in retailing. There may be many hairdressers in a town, but only one in a particular street. In a sense, therefore, it has a local monopoly. People may be prepared to pay higher prices for their haircuts there to avoid having to go elsewhere.

Equilibrium of the firm

Short run

As with other market structures, profits are maximised at the output where $MC = MR$. The diagram will be the same as for the monopolist, except that the AR and MR curves will be more elastic. This is illustrated in Figure 7.1(a). As with perfect competition, it is possible for the monopolistically competitive firm to make supernormal profit in the short run. This is shown as the shaded area.

Just how much profit the firm will make in the short run depends on the strength of demand: the position and elasticity of the demand curve. The further to the right the demand curve is relative to the average cost curve, and the less elastic the demand curve is, the greater will be the firm's short-run profit. Thus a firm facing little competition and whose product is considerably differentiated from that of its rivals may be able to earn considerable short-run profits.

1. *Why may a food shop charge higher prices than supermarkets for 'essential items' and yet very similar prices for delicatessen items?*
2. *Which of these two items is a petrol station more likely to sell at a discount: (a) oil; (b) sweets? Why?*

Long run

If typical firms are earning supernormal profit, new firms will enter the industry in the long run. As they do, they will take some of the customers away from established firms. The demand for the established firms will therefore fall. Their demand (AR) curve will shift to the left, and will continue doing so as long as supernormal profits remain and thus new firms continue entering.

Long-run equilibrium is reached when only normal profits remain: when there is no further incentive for new firms to enter. This is illustrated in Figure 7.1(b). The firm's demand curve settles at D_L, where it is tangential to the firm's $LRAC$ curve. Output will be Q_L: where $AR_L = LRAC$. (At any other output, $LRAC$ is greater than AR and thus less than normal profit would be made.)

Figure 7.1   Equilibrium of the firm under monopolistic competition

(a) Short run

(b) Long run

1. Why does the LRMC curve cross the MRL curve directly below the tangency point of the LRAC and ARL curves?
2. Assuming that supernormal profits can be made in the short run, will there be any difference in the long-run and short-run elasticity of demand? Explain.

Limitations of the model

There are various problems in applying the model of monopolistic competition to the real world:

- Information may be imperfect. Firms will not enter an industry if they are unaware of what supernormal profits are being made, or if they underestimate the demand for the particular product they are considering selling.

- Given that the firms in the industry produce different products, it is difficult if not impossible to derive a demand curve for the industry as a whole. Thus the analysis has to be confined to the level of the firm.

- Firms are likely to differ from each other not only in the product they produce or the service they offer, but also in their size and cost structure. What is more, entry may not be *completely* unrestricted. Two petrol stations could not set up in exactly the same place – on a busy cross-roads, say. Thus although the typical or 'representative' firm may earn only normal profit in the long run, other firms may be able to earn long-run supernormal profit. They may have some cost advantage or produce something that is impossible to duplicate perfectly.

- One of the biggest problems with the simple model shown in Figure 7.1 is that it concentrates on price and output decisions. In practice, the profit-maximising firm

---

BOX 7.1   **SELLING ICE CREAM AS A STUDENT**   CASE STUDIES AND APPLICATIONS

John's experience of monopolistic competition

When I was a student, my parents lived in Exeter in Devon, and at that time, the city's bypass became completely jammed on a summer Saturday as holidaymakers made their way to the coast. Traffic queues were several miles long.

For a summer job, I drove a small ice-cream van. Early on, I had the idea of selling ice cream from a tray to the people queuing in their cars. I made more money on a Saturday than the rest of the week put together. I thought I was on to a good thing.

But news of this lucrative market soon spread, and each week new ice-cream sellers appeared – each one reducing my earnings! By the middle of August there were over thirty ice-cream sellers from five different ice-cream companies. Most tried to get to the beginning of the queue, to get ahead of their rivals.

Imagine the scene. A family driving to the coast rounds a bend and is suddenly met by a traffic jam and several ice-cream sellers all jostling to sell them an ice cream. It was quite surreal. Not surprisingly, many of the potential customers refused to buy, feeling somewhat intimidated by the spectacle. It was not long before most of us realised that it was best to disperse and find a section of the road where there were no other sellers.

But with so many ice-cream sellers, no one made much money. My supernormal earnings had been reduced to a normal level. I made about the same on Saturday to people stuck in queues as I would have done if I had driven my van around the streets.

1. Was there totally free entry to this market?
2. What forms of product differentiation were there?

under monopolistic competition also has to decide the exact variety of product to produce and how much to spend on advertising it. This will lead the firm to take part in non-price competition.

Non-price competition

Non-price competition involves two major elements: product development and advertising.

The major aims of *product development* are to produce a product that will sell well (i.e. one in high or potentially high demand) and that is different from rivals' products (i.e. has a relatively inelastic demand due to lack of close substitutes). For shops or other firms providing a service, 'product development' takes the form of attempting to provide a service which is better than, or at least different from, that of rivals: personal service, late opening, certain lines stocked and so on.

The major aim of *advertising* is to sell the product. This can be achieved not only by informing the consumer of the product's existence and availability, but also by deliberately trying to persuade consumers to purchase the good. Like product development, successful advertising will not only increase demand, but also make the firm's demand curve less elastic since it stresses the specific qualities of this firm's product over its rivals' (see Box 3.1 on page 62).

Product development and advertising not only increase a firm's demand and hence revenue, they also involve increased costs. So how much should a firm advertise to maximise profits?

For any given price and product, the optimal amount of advertising is where the revenue from *additional* advertising (MR_A) is equal to its cost (MC_A). As long as $MR_A > MC_A$, additional advertising will add to profit. But extra amounts spent on advertising are likely to lead to smaller and smaller increases in sales. Thus MR_A falls, until $MR_A = MC_A$. At that point, no further profit can be made. It is at a maximum.

> *Why will additional advertising lead to smaller and smaller increases in sales?*

Two problems arise with this analysis:

- The effect of product development and advertising on demand will be difficult for a firm to forecast.
- Product development and advertising are likely to have different effects at different prices. Profit maximisation,

therefore, will involve the more complex choice of the optimum combination of price, type of product, and level and variety of advertising.

Monopolistic competition and the public interest

Comparison with perfect competition

It is often argued that monopolistic competition leads to a less efficient allocation of resources than perfect competition.

Figure 7.2 compares the long-run equilibrium positions for two firms. One firm is under perfect competition and thus faces a horizontal demand curve. It will produce an output of Q_1 at a price of P_1. The other is under monopolistic competition and thus faces a downward-sloping demand curve. It will produce the lower output of Q_2 at the higher price of P_2. A crucial assumption here is that a firm would have the *same* long-run average cost (*LRAC*) curve in both cases. Given this assumption, monopolistic competition has the following disadvantages:

- Less will be sold and at a higher price.
- Firms will not be producing at the least-cost point.

By producing more, firms would move to a lower point on their *LRAC* curve. Thus firms under monopolistic competition are said to have **excess capacity**. In Figure 7.2 this excess capacity is shown as $Q_1 - Q_2$. In other words, monopolistic competition is typified by quite a large number of firms (e.g. petrol stations), all operating at an output less than that necessary to achieve minimum cost, and thus being forced to charge a price above that which they could charge if they had a bigger turnover. How often have you been to a petrol station and had to queue for the pumps?

> *Does this imply that if, say, half of the petrol stations were closed down, the consumer would benefit? (Clue: what would happen to the demand curves of the remaining stations?)*

Definitions

Non-price competition Competition in terms of product promotion (advertising, packaging, etc.) or product development.

Excess capacity (under monopolistic competition) In the long run, firms under monopolistic competition will produce at an output below their minimum-cost point.

Figure 7.2 Long-run equilibrium of the firm under perfect and monopolistic competition

On the other hand, it is often argued that these wastes of monopolistic competition may be insignificant. In the first place, although the firm's demand curve is downward sloping, it is still likely to be highly elastic due to the large number of substitutes. In the second place, although the firm under monopolistic competition will not be operating quite at the bottom of its *LRAC* curve, the nature of the industry may allow some economies of scale to be gained. The *LRAC* curve would thus be lower than in the case of the larger number of smaller firms that would be necessary to keep the industry perfectly competitive. The size of the economies of scale, if any, will obviously vary from industry to industry.

Furthermore, consumers are likely to benefit from monopolistic competition by having a greater variety of products to choose from. Each firm may satisfy some particular requirement of particular consumers.

 Which would you rather have: five restaurants to choose from, each with very different menus and each having spare tables so that you could always guarantee getting one; or just two restaurants to choose from, charging less but with less choice and making it necessary to book well in advance?

Comparison with monopoly

The arguments here are very similar to those comparing perfect competition and monopoly.

On the one hand, freedom of entry for new firms and hence the lack of long-run supernormal profits under monopolistic competition are likely to help keep prices down for the consumer and encourage cost saving. On the other hand, monopolies are likely to achieve greater economies of scale and have more funds for investment and research and development.

Section summary

1. Monopolistic competition occurs where there is free entry to the industry and quite a large number of firms operating independently of each other, but where each firm has some market power as a result of producing differentiated products or services.

2. In the short run, firms can make supernormal profits. In the long run, however, freedom of entry will drive profits down to the normal level. The long-run equilibrium of the firm is where the (downward-sloping) demand curve is tangential to the long-run average cost curve.

3. The long-run equilibrium is one of excess capacity. Given that the demand curve is downward sloping, its tangency point with the *LRAC* curve will not be at the bottom of the *LRAC* curve. Increased production would thus be possible at *lower* average cost.

4. In practice, supernormal profits may persist into the long run: firms have imperfect information; entry may not be completely unrestricted; firms may use non-price competition to maintain an advantage over their rivals.

5. Non-price competition may take the form of product development or product promotion (advertising, etc.).

6. Monopolistically competitive firms, because of excess capacity, may have higher costs than perfectly competitive firms, but consumers may gain from a greater diversity of products.

7. Monopolistically competitive firms may have fewer economies of scale than monopolies and conduct less research and development, but the competition may keep prices lower than under monopoly.

7.2 # OLIGOPOLY

Oligopoly occurs when just a few firms between them share a large proportion of the industry.

There are, however, significant differences in the structure of industries under oligopoly and similarly significant differences in the behaviour of firms. The firms may produce a virtually identical product (e.g. metals, chemicals, sugar, petrol). Most oligopolists, however, produce differentiated products (e.g. cars, soap powder, soft drinks, electrical appliances). Much of the competition between such oligopolists is in terms of the marketing of their particular brand. Marketing practices may differ considerably from one industry to another.

The two key features of oligopoly

Despite the differences between oligopolies, two crucial features distinguish oligopoly from other market structures.

Barriers to entry

In contrast to the situation under monopolistic competition, there are various barriers to the entry of new firms. These are similar to those under monopoly (see pages 173–5). The size of the barriers, however, varies from industry to industry. In some cases entry is relatively easy, whereas in others it is virtually impossible.

Interdependence of the firms

Because there are only a few firms under oligopoly, each has to take account of the others. This means that they are mutually dependent: they are *interdependent*. Each firm is affected by its rivals' actions. If a firm changes the price or specification of its product, for example, or the amount of its advertising, the sales of its rivals will be affected. The rivals may then respond by changing their price, specification or advertising. No firm can afford to ignore the actions and reactions of other firms in the industry.

KEY IDEA 21

People often think and behave strategically. How you think others will respond to your actions is likely to influence your own behaviour. Firms, for example, when considering a price or product change will often take into account the likely reactions of their rivals.

It is impossible, therefore, to predict the effect on a firm's sales of, say, a change in its price without first making some assumption about the reactions of other firms. Different assumptions yield different predictions. For this reason there is no one single theory of oligopoly. Firms may react differently and unpredictably.

KI 10
p71

Competition and collusion

Oligopolists are pulled in two different directions:

- The interdependence of firms may make them wish to *collude* with each other. If they could club together and act as if they were a monopoly, they could jointly maximise industry profits.
- On the other hand, they will be tempted to *compete* with their rivals to gain a bigger share of industry profits for themselves.

These two policies are incompatible. The more fiercely firms compete to gain a bigger share of industry profits, the smaller these industry profits will become! For example, price competition will drive down the average industry price, while competition through advertising will raise industry costs. Either way, industry profits will fall.

Sometimes firms collude, sometimes not. The following sections examine first **collusive oligopoly** (both open and tacit), and then **non-collusive oligopoly**.

Industry equilibrium under collusive oligopoly

When firms under oligopoly engage in collusion, they may agree on output, prices, market share, advertising expenditure, etc. Such collusion reduces the uncertainty they face. It reduces the fear of engaging in competitive price cutting or retaliatory advertising, both of which could reduce total industry profits.

A formal collusive agreement is called a **cartel**. The cartel will maximise profits if it acts like a monopoly: if the members behave as if they were a single firm. This is illustrated in Figure 7.3.

KI 20
p164

The total market demand curve is shown with the corresponding market *MR* curve. The cartel's *MC* curve is the *horizontal* sum of the *MC* curves of its members (since we are adding the *output* of each of the cartel members at each level of marginal cost). Profits are maximised at Q_1 where $MC = MR$. The cartel must therefore set a price of P_1 (at which Q_1 will be demanded).

TC 8
p100

Having agreed on the cartel price, the members may then compete against each other using *non-price competition*, to gain as big a share of resulting sales (Q_1) as they can.

How will advertising affect the cartel's MC and AR curves? How will this affect the profit-maximising output? Is there any problem here for the cartel in fixing the price?

Figure 7.3 Profit-maximising cartel

Definitions

Interdependence (under oligopoly) One of the two key features of oligopoly. Each firm will be affected by its rivals' decisions. Likewise its decisions will affect its rivals. Firms recognise this interdependence. This recognition will affect their decisions.

Collusive oligopoly Where oligopolists agree (formally or informally) to limit competition between themselves. They may set output quotas, fix prices, limit product promotion or development, or agree not to 'poach' each other's markets.

Non-collusive oligopoly Where oligopolists have no agreement between themselves, formal, informal or tacit.

Cartel A formal collusive agreement.

BOX 7.2   IS BEER BECOMING MORE CONCENTRATED?

Oligopoly in the brewing industry

At first glance, the UK brewing industry might appear to be highly competitive, with many pubs in close proximity to one another and with many brands of beer and lager offered for sale. However, in reality most pubs are owned by the major brewers. These 'tied houses' sell only a limited range of the beers and lagers that are available. Consumer choice is clearly constrained.

The oligopolistic nature of the brewing industry can be seen when we consider the market shares of the leading brewers (see the table below). In 1985 the three largest brewers held 47 per cent of the market. By 2001 this had grown to 73 per cent. What is also significant is that small independent brewers, which generally operate within a local or regional market, saw a dramatic fall in their market share. With this huge growth in the market power of the major brewers have come large rises in the price of beer sold in pubs (even after taking inflation and tax increases into account). Prices in the UK have risen faster than anywhere else in Europe.

In 1987, the Monopolies and Mergers Commission, the forerunner to the Competition Commission (see section 13.1), investigated the brewing industry and in 1989 issued the 'Beer Orders', requiring the large brewers to sell many of their pubs. The objective was to increase competition as smaller brewers and other companies and individuals bought these pubs and then stocked a range of beers.

However, the hopes were ill-founded. The pubs that were sold were the least profitable, and many have since closed. There is thus now less competition between pubs and about 40 per cent of UK pubs are now owned by large pub chains.

The Beer Orders also required that over 10 000 pubs owned by the big breweries should stock 'guest beers' from rival breweries. But the big breweries responded by selling most of these pubs. In pubs not owned by the big breweries, and where there is the threat of genuine competition, the big breweries often supply their beers at lower prices, thus making it impossible for the smaller breweries to compete.

The brewers, finding a reduction in their scope for achieving economies of scale from *vertical* integration

(owning both breweries and pubs), have sought to gain economies of scale from *horizontal* integration (having a larger share of total brewing). Mergers and takeovers in the brewing industry have been common. For example, in May 2000 Interbrew (the Belgian brewer and owners of the Stella Artois brand) acquired Whitbread, the UK's third largest brewer, and a month later acquired Bass, the second largest. This gave Interbrew nearly one-third of the market. The acquisitions were referred to the Competition Commission, which recommended a break-up of the new giant: a recommendation accepted by the government. In response, at the end of 2001 Interbrew (then called InBev) sold most of the Whitbread division, including brands such as Carling, Caffrey's and Worthington, to the US brewer Coors.

In the light of this splitting of Interbrew, and feeling that this proved that competition policy was effective, the government in 2002 decided to scrap the Beer Orders. This was greeted with dismay by small independent brewers, which were already reluctant to expand, faced with the power of such massive competitors in both production and retail, with heavily advertised brands gaining larger and larger shares of the market.

In the spring of 2008, Scottish & Newcastle was taken over in a joint deal by Dutch brewers Heineken and Danish company, Carlsberg. As a consequence, Heineken became Britain's largest brewer and reported a healthy increase in its annual profits following the takeover.

However, the large breweries have found their profits under pressure as they face higher costs and lower volumes of sales. Their focus has moved to the eastern European markets, where there exist many opportunities for integration and growth. Meanwhile, in the UK there is some evidence that the number of independent and local brewers is growing each year, bucking the trend of the previous twenty years.

1. What are the barriers to entry in (a) brewing; (b) opening new pubs?
2. Do small independent brewers have any market advantages?

Market shares of the largest brewers

	1985 (%)		2008 (%)
Bass	22	Heineken-S&N (Foster's, Kronenbourg)	28
Allied Lyons (Carlsberg)	13	Coors/SABMiller (Carling, Grolsch, Caffrey's)	22
Grand Met (Watneys)	12	Anheuser-Busch Inbev (Bass, Beck's, Stella)	20
Whitbread	11	Carlsberg UK (Carlsberg, Tetley's)	13
Scottish and Newcastle	10	Diageo (Guinness)	6
Courage	9		
Others	23	Others	11
	100	Total	100
3-firm concentration ratio	47	3-firm concentration ratio	70
5-firm concentration ratio	68	5-firm concentration ratio	89

Source: Various newspaper articles.

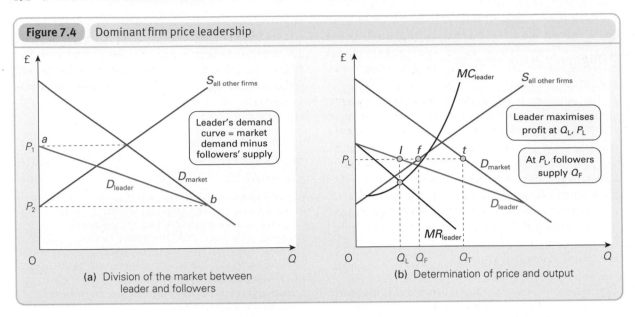

Figure 7.4   Dominant firm price leadership

(a) Division of the market between leader and followers

(b) Determination of price and output

Alternatively, the cartel members may somehow agree to divide the market between them. Each member would be given a *quota*. The sum of all the quotas must add up to Q_1. If the quotas exceeded Q_1, either there would be output unsold if price remained fixed at P_1, or the price would fall.

But if quotas are to be set by the cartel, how will it decide the level of each individual member's quota? The most likely method is for the cartel to divide the market between the members according to their current market share. This is the solution most likely to be accepted as 'fair'.

 If this 'fair' solution were adopted, what effect would it have on the industry MC curve in Figure 7.3?

In many countries, cartels are illegal – being seen by the government as a means of driving up prices and profits, and thereby as being against the public interest (see section 13.1). Where open collusion is illegal, however, firms may simply break the law, or get round it. Alternatively, firms may stay within the law, but still *tacitly* collude by watching each other's prices and keeping theirs similar. Firms may tacitly 'agree' to avoid price wars or aggressive advertising campaigns.

Tacit collusion: price leadership

One form of *tacit collusion* is where firms keep to the price set by an established leader. The leader may be the largest firm: the one dominating the industry. This is known as *dominant firm price leadership*. Alternatively, the price leader may simply be the one that has proved to be the most reliable one to follow: the one that is the best barometer of market conditions. This is known as *barometric firm price leadership*. Let us examine each of these two types of price leadership in turn.

Dominant firm price leadership

How in theory does the leader set the price? The leader will maximise profits where its marginal revenue is equal to its marginal cost. Figure 7.4(a) shows the total market demand curve and the supply curve of all followers. These firms, like perfectly competitive firms, accept the price as given, only in this case it is the price set by the leader, and thus their joint supply curve is simply the sum of their *MC* curves – the same as under perfect competition.

The leader's demand curve can be seen as that portion of market demand unfilled by the other firms. In other words, it is market demand minus other firms' supply. At P_1 the

---

Definitions

Quota (set by a cartel) The output that a given member of a cartel is allowed to produce (production quota) or sell (sales quota).

Tacit collusion Where oligopolists take care not to engage in price cutting, excessive advertising or other forms of competition. There may be unwritten 'rules' of collusive behaviour such as price leadership.

Dominant firm price leadership Where firms (the followers) choose the same price as that set by a dominant firm in the industry (the leader).

Barometric firm price leadership Where the price leader is the one whose prices are believed to reflect market conditions in the most satisfactory way.

whole of market demand is satisfied by the other firms, and so the demand for the leader is zero (point *a*). At P_2 the other firms' supply is zero, and so the leader faces the full market demand (point *b*). The leader's demand curve thus connects points *a* and *b*.

The leader's profit will be maximised where its marginal cost equals its marginal revenue. This is shown in Figure 7.4(b). The diagram is the same as Figure 7.4(a) but with the addition of *MC* and *MR* curves for the leader. The leader's marginal cost equals its marginal revenue at an output of Q_L (giving a point *l* on its demand curve). The leader thus sets a price of P_L, which the other firms then duly follow. They supply Q_F (i.e. at point *f* on their supply curve). Total market demand at P_L is Q_T (i.e. point *t* on the market demand curve), which must add up to the output of both leader and followers (i.e. $Q_L + Q_F$).

> *Draw a pair of diagrams like those in Figure 7.4. Illustrate what would happen if market demand rose but the costs of neither leader nor followers rose. Would there be an equal percentage increase in the output of both leader and followers?*

In practice, however, it is very difficult for the leader to apply this theory. The leader's demand and *MR* curves depend on the followers' supply curve – something the leader will find virtually impossible to estimate with any degree of accuracy. The leader will thus have to make a rough estimate of what its profit-maximising price and output will be, and simply choose that. That is the best it can do!

A simpler model is where the leader assumes that it will maintain a constant *market share* (say, 50 per cent). It makes this assumption because it also assumes that all other firms will follow its price up and down. This is illustrated in Figure 7.5. It knows its current position on its demand curve (say, point *a*). It then estimates how responsive its demand will be to industry-wide price changes and

thus constructs its demand and *MR* curves accordingly. It then chooses to produce Q_L at a price of P_L: at point *l* on its demand curve (where *MC* = *MR*). Other firms then follow that price. Total market demand will be Q_T, with followers supplying that portion of the market not supplied by the leader, namely $Q_T - Q_L$.

*LOOKING AT THE MATHS

In Figure 7.4, the various curves can be represented by equations and this would allow us to solve for P_L, Q_L, Q_F and Q_T. An example of this is given in Maths Case 7.1 in MyEconLab.

Note that we derived all the curves in Figure 7.4 from just three: the market demand curve, the followers' supply curve and the leader's *MC* curve. It follows that, if we know the functions for these three curves, we can derive the functions for the remainder.

There is one problem with this model: the assumption that the followers will want to maintain a constant market share. If the leader raises its price, the followers may want to supply more, given that the new price (= *MR* for a price-taking follower) may well be above their marginal cost. On the other hand, the followers may decide merely to maintain their market share for fear of retaliation from the leader, in the form of price cuts or an aggressive advertising campaign.

Barometric firm price leadership

A similar exercise can be conducted by a barometric firm. Although such a firm does not dominate the industry, its price will be followed by the others. It merely tries to estimate its demand and *MR* curves – assuming, again, a constant market share – and then produces where *MR* = *MC* and sets price accordingly.

In practice, which firm is taken as the barometer may frequently change. Whether we are talking about oil companies, car producers or banks, any firm may take the initiative in raising prices. Then, if the other firms are merely waiting for someone to take the lead – say, because costs have risen – they will all quickly follow suit. For example, if one of the banks raises its mortgage rates by 1 per cent, then this is likely to stimulate the others to follow suit.

Tacit collusion: rules of thumb

An alternative to following an established leader is to follow an established set of simple 'rules of thumb'. These rules do not involve setting *MC* equal to *MR*, and thus may involve an immediate loss of profit. They do, however, help to prevent an outbreak of competition, and thus help to maintain profits into the longer term.

Figure 7.5 Price leader aiming to maximise profits for a given market share

Leader maximises profit at Q_L and thus sets price of P_L

BOX 7.3 OPEC

The history of the world's most famous cartel

OPEC is probably the best known of all cartels. It was set up in 1960 by the five major oil-exporting countries: Saudi Arabia, Iran, Iraq, Kuwait and Venezuela. Today it has twelve members, including Nigeria, Angola, Libya and Ecuador. Its stated objectives were as follows:

- The co-ordination and unification of the petroleum policies of member countries.
- The organisation of means to ensure the stabilisation of prices, eliminating harmful and unnecessary fluctuations.

The years leading up to 1960 had seen the oil-producing countries increasingly in conflict with the international oil companies, which extracted oil under 'concessionary agreement'. Under this scheme, oil companies were given the right to extract oil in return for royalties. This meant that the oil-producing countries had little say over output and price levels.

The early years

Despite the formation of OPEC in 1960, it was not until 1973 that control of oil production was effectively transferred from the oil companies to the oil countries, with OPEC making the decisions on how much oil to produce and thereby determining its oil revenue. By this time OPEC consisted of thirteen members.

OPEC's pricing policy over the 1970s consisted of setting a market price for Saudi Arabian crude (the market leader), and leaving other OPEC members to set their prices in line with this. This was a form of dominant 'firm' price leadership.

As long as demand remained buoyant, and was price inelastic, this policy allowed large price increases with consequent large revenue increases. In 1973/4, after the Arab–Israeli war, OPEC raised the price of oil from around $3 per barrel to over $12. The price was kept at roughly this level until 1979. And yet the sales of oil did not fall significantly.

 Illustrate what was happening here on a demand and supply diagram. Remember that demand was highly inelastic and was increasing over time.

After 1979, however, following a further increase in the price of oil from around $15 to $40 per barrel, demand did fall. This was largely due to the recession of the early 1980s (although, as we shall see later on when we look at macroeconomics, this recession was in turn largely caused by governments' responses to the oil price increases).

The use of quotas

Faced by declining demand, OPEC after 1982 agreed to limit output and allocate production quotas in an attempt

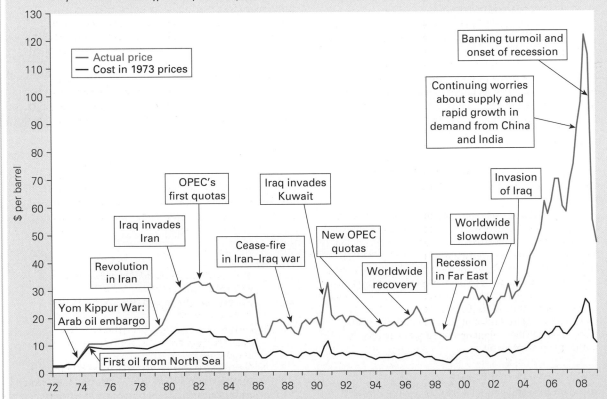

Oil prices and the effects of OPEC quotas, wars and the ups and downs of the world economy

Source: Energy Informational Administration database (http:tonto.eia.doe.gov/dnav/pet/hist/rbrteM.htm).

to keep the price up. A production ceiling of 16 million barrels per day was agreed in 1984.

The cartel was beginning to break down, however, due to the following:

- The world recession and the resulting fall in the demand for oil.
- Growing output from non-OPEC members.
- 'Cheating' by some OPEC members who exceeded their quota limits.

With a glut of oil, OPEC could no longer maintain the price. The 'spot' price of oil (the day-to-day price at which oil was trading on the open market) was falling, as the graph shows.

The trend of lower oil prices was reversed in the late 1980s. With the world economy booming, the demand for oil rose and along with it the price. Then in 1990 Iraq invaded Kuwait and the Gulf War ensued. With the cutting-off of supplies from Kuwait and Iraq, the supply of oil fell and there was a sharp rise in its price.

But with the ending of the war and the recession of the early 1990s, the price rapidly fell again and only recovered slowly as the world economy started expanding once more.

On the demand side, the development of energy-saving technology plus increases in fuel taxes led to a relatively slow growth in consumption. On the supply side, the growing proportion of output supplied by non-OPEC members, plus the adoption in 1994 of a relatively high OPEC production ceiling of 24.5 million barrels per day, meant that supply more than kept pace with demand.

The situation for OPEC deteriorated further in the late 1990s, following the recession in the Far East. Oil demand fell by some 2 million barrels per day. By early 1999, the price had fallen to around $10 per barrel – a mere $2.70 in 1973 prices! In response, OPEC members agreed to cut production by 4.3 million barrels per day. The objective was to push the price back up to around $18–20 per barrel. But, with the Asian economy recovering and the world generally experiencing more rapid economic growth, the price rose rapidly and soon overshot the $20 mark. By early 2000 it had reached $30: a tripling in price in just 12 months. With the world economy then slowing down, however, the price rapidly fell back, reaching $18 in November 2001.

However, in late 2001 the relationship between OPEC and non-OPEC oil producers changed. The ten members of the OPEC cartel decided to cut production by 1.5 million barrels a day. This followed an agreement with five of the major oil producers outside of the cartel to reduce their output too, the aim being to push oil prices upwards and then stabilise them at around $25 per barrel. The alliance between OPEC and non-OPEC oil producers is the first such instance of its kind in the oil industry. As a result, it seemed that OPEC might now once again be able to control the market for oil.

The price surge of 2003–8

But how successfully could this alliance cope with crisis? With worries over an impending war with Iraq and a strike in Venezuela, the oil price rose again in late 2002, passing the $30 mark in early 2003. OPEC claimed that it could maintain supply and keep prices from surging even with an Iraq war, but with prices rising rapidly above $30, many doubted that it could. In 2004 the situation worsened with supply concerns related to the situation in Iraq, Saudi Arabia, Russia and Nigeria, and the oil price rose to over $50 in October 2004. OPEC tried to relax the quotas, but found it difficult to adjust supply sufficiently quickly to make any real difference to the price.

From 2006, oil prices increased more sharply than they ever had before and, for the first time in years, the real price of oil exceeded that seen in the 1970s. The major cause of the increases was very substantial increases in demand, particularly from India and China, coupled with continuing concerns about supply. The implications of the sharp price increases were substantial: inflationary pressures built up across the world, while the income of OPEC nations doubled in the first half of 2008.

By July 2008 the price reached $147. Some analysts were predicting a price of over $200 per barrel by the end of the year.

. . . and then the fall

But then, with the growing banking turmoil and fears of a recession, the price began to fall – and rapidly so. When the price dropped below $100 in September 2008 the majority of the world breathed a sigh of relief. But as the economic outlook became gloomier and the demand for oil fell, so the price plummeted, reaching $34 by the end of the year – less than a quarter of the price just five months previously. Whilst this was good news for the consumer, it was potentially damaging for investment in oil exploration and development and also for investment in alternative energy supplies.

OPEC responded to the falling price by announcing cuts in production, totalling some 14 per cent between August 2008 and January 2009. But with OPEC producing less than a third of global oil output, this represented less than 5 per cent of global production.

The recent history of OPEC illustrates the difficulty of using supply quotas to achieve a particular price. With demand being price inelastic but income elastic (responsive to changes in world income, such as rising demand from China), and with considerable speculative movements in demand, the equilibrium price for a given supply quota can fluctuate wildly.

1. *What conditions facilitate the formation of a cartel? Which of these conditions were to be found in the oil market in (a) the early 1970s; (b) the mid 1980s; (c) the mid 2002?*
2. *Could OPEC have done anything to prevent the long-term decline in real oil prices seen from 1981 to 2002?*
3. *Does the increased demand seen from China and India imply that the era of cheap energy is over? What impact could technology have in the long run on (a) demand; (b) supply?*

One example of a rule of thumb is *average cost pricing*. Here, producers simply add a certain percentage for profit on top of average costs. Thus, if average costs rise by 10 per cent, prices will automatically be raised by 10 per cent. This is a particularly useful rule of thumb in times of inflation, when all firms will be experiencing similar cost increases.

If a firm has a typically shaped average cost curve and sets prices 10 per cent above average cost, what will its supply curve look like?

Another rule of thumb is to have certain **price benchmarks**. Thus clothes may sell for £9.95, £14.95 or £19.95 (but not £12.31 or £16.42). If costs rise, then firms simply raise their price to the next benchmark, knowing that other firms will do the same.

Rules of thumb can also be applied to advertising (e.g. you do not criticise other firms' products, only praise your own); or to the design of the product (e.g. lighting manufacturers tacitly agreeing not to bring out an everlasting light bulb).

Factors favouring collusion

Collusion between firms, whether formal or tacit, is more likely when firms can clearly identify with each other or some leader and when they trust each other not to break agreements. It will be easier for firms to collude if the following conditions apply:

- There are only very few firms all well known to each other.
- They are not secretive with each other about costs and production methods.
- They have similar production methods and average costs, and are thus likely to want to change prices at the same time and by the same percentage.
- They produce similar products and can thus more easily reach agreements on price.
- There is a dominant firm.
- There are significant barriers to entry and therefore little fear of disruption by new firms.
- The market is stable. If industry demand or production costs fluctuate wildly, it will be difficult to make agreements, partly due to difficulties in predicting and partly because agreements may frequently have to be amended. There is a particular problem in a declining market where firms may be tempted to undercut each other's prices in order to maintain their sales.
- There are no government measures to curb collusion.

In which of the following industries is collusion likely to occur: bricks, beer, margarine, cement, crisps, washing powder, blank DVDs, carpets?

Non-collusive oligopoly: the breakdown of collusion

In some oligopolies, there may only be a few (if any) factors favouring collusion. In such cases, the likelihood of price competition is greater.

Even if there is collusion, there will always be the temptation for individual oligopolists to 'cheat', by cutting prices or by selling more than their allotted quota.

Let us take the case of a cartel consisting of five equal-sized firms. The whole cartel is illustrated in Figure 7.6(a). Assume that the cartel sets the industry profit-maximising price of £10. This will give an industry output of 1000 units, which the cartel divides equally between its five members: i.e. each member is assigned a quota of 200 units.

Now consider Figure 7.6(b). This shows the position for one of the members of the cartel, firm A. Provided the cartel's price remains fixed at £10, then £10 would also be the marginal revenue for the individual firm. This will create an incentive for cartel members to cheat: to sell more than their allotted quota. Firm A would maximise its own profits by selling 600 units, where $MC = P \ (= MR)$, provided it could do this by taking market share off the other members, and thus leaving total industry output (and hence price) unaffected.

Alternatively, individual members might be tempted to undercut the cartel's price. Again, provided the rest of the cartel maintained its price at £10, firm A would face a relatively elastic demand curve (shown by AR in Figure 7.6(b)). A modest cut in its price would attract considerable custom away from the other members of the cartel. Firm A would maximise its profit by cutting its price to £8 and thereby increasing its sales to 400 units.

The danger, of course, with either selling above quota or cutting price is that this would invite retaliation from the other members of the cartel, with a resulting price war. Price would then fall and the cartel could well break up in disarray.

Non-collusive oligopoly: assumptions about rivals' behaviour

Even though oligopolists might not collude, they will still need to take account of rivals' likely behaviour when

---

Definitions

Average cost pricing Where a firm sets its price by adding a certain percentage for (average) profit on top of average cost.

Price benchmark A price that is typically used. Firms, when raising a price, will usually raise it from one benchmark to another.

Figure 7.6 The incentive for a firm to produce more than its quota, or undercut the cartel's price

(a) The industry

(b) Firm A

TC 9
p105

deciding their own strategy. In doing so, they will probably look at rivals' past behaviour and make assumptions based on it. There are three well-known models, each based on a different set of assumptions.

Assumption that rivals produce a given quantity: the Cournot model

One assumption is that rivals will produce a particular *quantity*. This is most likely when the market is stable and the rivals have been producing a relatively constant quantity for some time. The task, then, for the individual oligopolist is to decide its own price and quantity given the presumed output of its competitors.

The earliest model based on this assumption was developed by the French economist Augustin Cournot[1] in 1838. The ***Cournot model*** takes the simple case of just two firms (a ***duopoly***) producing an identical product: for example, two electricity generating companies supplying the whole country.

This is illustrated in Figure 7.7(a), which shows the profit-maximising price and output for firm A. The total

market demand curve is shown as D_M. Assume that firm A believes that its rival, firm B, will produce Q_{B_1} units. Thus firm A perceives its own demand curve (D_{A_1}) to be Q_{B_1} units less than total market demand. In other words, the horizontal gap between D_M and D_{A_1} is Q_{B_1} units. Given its perceived demand curve of D_{A_1}, its marginal revenue curve will be MR_{A_1} and the profit-maximising output will be Q_{A_1}, where $MR_{A_1} = MC_A$. The profit-maximising price will be P_{A_1}.

If firm A believed that firm B would produce *more* than Q_{B_1}, its perceived demand and *MR* curves would be further to the left and the profit-maximising quantity and price would both be lower.

Figure 7.7(b) illustrates the ***reaction functions*** of firm A and firm B. Each curve shows the amount of output the respective firm will produce in the light of how much it perceives the other firm will produce. Take the reaction curve for firm A. If it assumes that firm B will produce Q_{B_1} (as in Figure 7.7(a)) it will choose to produce Q_{A_1}: i.e. at point *x* on its reaction curve.

We can now conduct a similar analysis for firm B, again using a diagram like Figure 7.7(a). If it assumes that firm A will produce a particular level of output, it will then decide its profit-maximising price and output in the light of this. Firm B's reaction curve in Figure 7.7(b) shows all the profit-maximising outputs for firm B for each output of firm A.

TC 8
p100

---

[1] See http://cepa.newschool.edu/het/profiles/cournot.htm for a profile of Cournot and his work.

Definitions

Cournot model A model of duopoly where each firm makes its price and output decisions on the assumption that its rival will produce a particular quantity.

Duopoly An oligopoly where there are just two firms in the market.

Reaction function (or curve) This shows how a firm's optimal output varies according to the output chosen by its rival (or rivals).

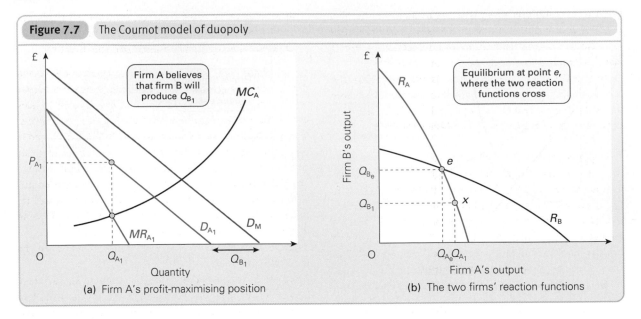

Figure 7.7   The Cournot model of duopoly

(a) Firm A's profit-maximising position

(b) The two firms' reaction functions

What will the market equilibrium be? This will be at point *e* in Figure 7.7(b). It is known as the ***Cournot equilibrium***. Only at this point will neither firm choose to adjust its output. How will the equilibrium be reached if production is currently *not* at equilibrium?

Assume that production is at point *x*. Although firm A is on its reaction curve, firm B is not. Given production of Q_{A_1} by firm A, firm B will produce at a point on its reaction curve vertically above this (i.e. an output *greater* than Q_{B_1}). This will cause firm A to move up its reaction curve. The process will continue until point *e* is reached.

Profits in the Cournot model. Industry profits will be *less* than under a monopoly or a cartel. The reason is that price will be lower than the monopoly price. This can be seen from Figure 7.7(a). If this were a monopoly, then to find the profit-maximising output, we would need to construct an *MR* curve corresponding to the market demand curve (D_M). This would intersect with the *MC* curve at a higher output than Q_{A_1} and a *higher* price (given by D_M).

Nevertheless, profits in the Cournot model will be higher than under perfect competition, since price is still above marginal cost.

Maths Case 7.2 in MyEconLab shows how the Cournot equilibrium can be derived algebraically from the market demand function and the cost functions of the two firms.

Assumption that rivals set a particular price: the Bertrand model

An alternative assumption is that rival firms set a particular price and stick to it. This scenario is more realistic when firms do not want to upset customers by frequent price changes or when they want to produce catalogues which specify prices. The task, then, for a given oligopolist is to choose its own price and quantity in the light of the prices set by rivals.

The most famous model based on this assumption was developed by another French economist, Joseph Bertrand, in 1883. Bertrand again took the simple case of a duopoly, but its conclusions apply equally to oligopolies with three or more firms.

The outcome is one of price cutting until all supernormal profits are competed away. The reason is simple. If firm A assumes that its rival, firm B, will hold price constant, then firm A should undercut this price by a small amount and as a result gain a large share of the market. At this point, firm B will be forced to respond by cutting its price. What we end up with is a price war until price is forced down to the level of average cost, with only normal profits remaining. This is discussed in more detail in section 7.3 below.

Nash equilibrium. The equilibrium outcome in either the Cournot or Bertrand models is not in the *joint* interests of the firms. In each case, total profits are less than under a monopoly or cartel. But, in the absence of collusion, the outcome is the result of each firm doing the best it can,

Definition

Cournot equilibrium Where the outputs chosen by each firm are consistent with each other: where the two firms' reaction curves cross.

given its assumptions about what its rivals are doing. The resulting equilibrium is known as a *Nash equilibrium*, after John Nash, a US mathematician (and subject of the film *A Beautiful Mind*) who introduced the concept in 1951.

In practice, when competition is intense, as in the Bertrand model, the firms may seek to collude long before profits have been reduced to a normal level. Alternatively, firms may put in a *takeover bid* for their rival(s).

The kinked demand curve assumption

In 1939 a theory of non-collusive oligopoly was developed simultaneously on both sides of the Atlantic: in the USA by Paul Sweezy and in Britain by R. L. Hall and C. J. Hitch. This *kinked demand theory* has since become perhaps the most famous of all theories of oligopoly. The model seeks to explain how it is that, even when there is no collusion at all between oligopolists, prices can nevertheless remain stable.

The theory is based on two asymmetrical assumptions:

- If an oligopolist cuts its price, its rivals will feel forced to follow suit and cut theirs, to prevent losing customers to the first firm.

- If an oligopolist raises its price, however, its rivals will *not* follow suit since, by keeping their prices the same, they will thereby gain customers from the first firm.

On these assumptions, each oligopolist will face a demand curve that is *kinked* at the current price and output (see Figure 7.8). A rise in price will lead to a large fall in sales as customers switch to the now relatively lower-priced rivals. The firm will thus be reluctant to raise its price. Demand is relatively elastic above the kink. On the other hand, a fall in price will bring only a modest increase in sales, since rivals lower their prices too and therefore customers do not switch. The firm will thus also be reluctant to lower its price. Demand is relatively inelastic below the kink. Thus oligopolists will be reluctant to change prices at all.

This price stability can be shown formally by drawing in the firm's marginal revenue curve, as in Figure 7.9.

To see how this is done, imagine dividing the diagram into two parts, one on either side of Q_1. At quantities less than Q_1 (the left-hand part of the diagram), the *MR* curve will correspond to the shallow part of the *AR* curve. At quantities greater than Q_1 (the right-hand part), the *MR*

KI 9
p67

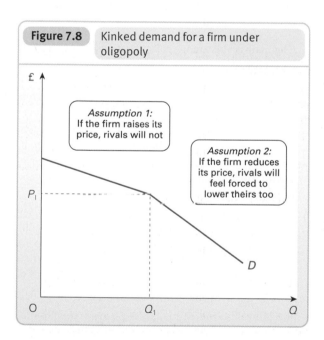

Figure 7.8 Kinked demand for a firm under oligopoly

Assumption 1:
If the firm raises its price, rivals will not

Assumption 2:
If the firm reduces its price, rivals will feel forced to lower theirs too

P_1

D

O Q_1 Q

£

Figure 7.9 Stable price under conditions of a kinked demand curve

If *MC* is anywhere between MC_1 and MC_2, profit is maximised at Q_1

MC_2

MC_1

P_1

a

b

$D = AR$

O Q_1 Q

MR

£

Definitions

Nash equilibrium The position resulting from everyone making their optimal decision based on their assumptions about their rivals' decisions. Without collusion, there is no incentive for any firm to move from this position.

Takeover bid Where one firm attempts to purchase another by offering to buy the shares of that company from its shareholders.

Kinked demand theory The theory that oligopolists face a demand curve that is kinked at the current price, demand being significantly more elastic above the current price than below. The effect of this is to create a situation of price stability.

curve will correspond to the steep part of the *AR* curve. To see how this part of the *MR* curve is constructed, imagine extending the steep part of the *AR* curve back to the vertical axis. This and the corresponding *MR* curve are shown by the dotted lines in Figure 7.9.

As you can see, there will be a gap between points *a* and *b*. In other words, there is a vertical section of the *MR* curve between these two points.

Profits are maximised where $MC = MR$. Thus, if the *MC* curve lies anywhere between MC_1 and MC_2 (i.e. between points *a* and *b*), the profit-maximising price and output will be P_1 and Q_1. Thus prices will remain stable *even with a considerable change in costs*.

Despite its simple demonstration of the real-world phenomenon of price stability, the model does have two major limitations:

- Price stability may be due to *other* factors. Firms may not want to change prices too frequently as this involves modifying price lists, working out new revenue predictions and revaluing stocks of finished goods, and it may upset customers. Price stability, therefore, is not proof of the accuracy of the model.
- Although the model can help to explain price stability, it does not explain how prices are set in the first place. To do this, some other model would be required. This is a serious limitation in times of inflation, when oligopolists, like other firms, raise prices in response to higher costs and higher demand. What the model does predict, however, is that the price will be raised only after marginal cost has risen above MC_2 in Figure 7.9, and that once it has been raised, a new kink will form at that price. Price will then remain fixed at that level until higher costs once more force a further price rise.

Oligopoly and the public interest

If oligopolists act collusively and jointly maximise industry profits, they will in effect be acting together as a monopoly. In such cases, the disadvantages to society experienced under monopoly will also be experienced under oligopoly (see section 6.3).

Furthermore, in two respects, oligopoly may be more disadvantageous than monopoly:

- Depending on the size of the individual oligopolists, there may be less scope for economies of scale to mitigate the effects of market power.
- Oligopolists are likely to engage in much more extensive advertising than a monopolist (see Case Study 7.8 in MyEconLab).

These problems will be less, however, if oligopolists do not collude, if there is some degree of price competition and if barriers to entry are weak.

Also, the power of oligopolists in certain markets may to some extent be offset if they sell their product to other powerful firms. Thus oligopolistic producers of baked beans sell a large proportion of their output to giant supermarket chains, which can use their market power to keep down the price at which they purchase the beans. This phenomenon is known as ***countervailing power***.

 Which of the following are examples of effective countervailing power?
(a) Tour operators purchasing seats on charter flights.
(b) A large office hiring a photocopier from Rank Xerox.
(c) Marks & Spencer buying clothes from a garment manufacturer.
(d) A small village store (but the only one for miles around) buying food from a wholesaler.

The power of oligopolists will also be reduced if the market in which they operate is contestable (see section 6.4). The lower the entry and exit costs for new firms, the more difficult it will be for oligopolists to collude and make supernormal profits.

 Which of the following markets do you think are contestable: (a) credit cards; (b) brewing; (c) petrol retailing; (d) insurance services; (e) compact discs?

In some respects, oligopoly may have *advantages* to society over other market structures:

- Oligopolists, like monopolists, can use part of their supernormal profit for research and development. Unlike monopolists, however, oligopolists will have a considerable *incentive* to do so. If the product design is improved, this may allow the firm to capture a larger share of the market, and it may be some time before rivals can respond with a similarly improved product. If, in addition, costs are lowered by technological improvement, the resulting higher profits will improve the firm's capacity to withstand any price war.
- Non-price competition through product differentiation may result in greater choice for the consumer. Take the case of stereo equipment. Non-price competition has led to a huge range of different products of many different specifications, each meeting the specific requirements of different consumers.

It is difficult, however, to draw any general conclusions, since oligopolies differ so much in their performance.

Definition

Countervailing power Where the power of a monopolistic/oligopolistic seller is offset by powerful buyers who can prevent the price from being pushed up.

Section summary

1. An oligopoly is where there are just a few firms in the industry with barriers to the entry of new firms. Firms recognise their mutual dependence.

2. Oligopolists will want to maximise their joint profits. This will tend to make them collude to keep prices high. On the other hand, they will want the biggest share of industry profits for themselves. This will tend to make them compete.

3. They are more likely to collude if there are few of them; if they are open with each other; if they have similar products and cost structures; if there is a dominant firm; if there are significant entry barriers; if the market is stable; and if there is no government legislation to prevent collusion.

4. Collusion can be open or tacit.

5. A formal collusive agreement is called a 'cartel'. A cartel aims to act as a monopoly. It can set price and leave the members to compete for market share, or it can assign quotas. There is always a temptation for cartel members to 'cheat' by undercutting the cartel price if they think they can get away with it and not trigger a price war.

6. Tacit collusion can take the form of price leadership. This is where firms follow the price set by either a dominant firm in the industry or a firm seen as a reliable 'barometer' of market conditions. Alternatively, tacit collusion can simply involve following various rules of thumb such as average cost pricing and benchmark pricing.

7. Even when firms do not collude, they will still have to take into account their rivals' behaviour. In the Cournot model, firms assume that their rivals' output is given and then choose the profit-maximising price and output in the light of this assumption. The resulting price and profit are lower than under monopoly, but still higher than under perfect competition.

8. In the Bertrand model, firms assume that their rivals' price is given. This will result in prices being competed down until only normal profits remain.

9. In the kinked demand curve model, firms are likely to keep their prices stable unless there is a large shift in costs or demand.

10. Whether oligopoly behaviour is in the public interest depends on the particular oligopoly and how competitive it is; whether there is any countervailing power; whether the firms engage in extensive advertising and of what type; whether product differentiation results in a wide range of choice for the consumer; how much of the profits are ploughed back into research and development; and how contestable the market is. Since these conditions vary substantially from oligopoly to oligopoly, it is impossible to state just how well or how badly oligopoly in general serves the public interest.

7.3 GAME THEORY

TC 9 p105

As we have seen, the behaviour of a firm under non-collusive oligopoly will depend on how it thinks its rivals will react to its policies. When considering whether to cut prices in order to gain a larger market share, a firm will ask itself two key questions: first, how much it can get away with, without inciting retaliation; second, if its rivals do retaliate and a price war ensues, whether it will be able to 'see off' some or all of its rivals, while surviving itself.

KI 21 p190

It is not unreasonable to compare rival firms in an oligopoly to the players in a game or generals in a battle. They will need to choose the appropriate strategy with respect to price, advertising and product development. The firm's choice of strategy will depend both on how it thinks its rivals will react and on how willing it is to take risks.

Economists have developed *game theory* to look at this strategic approach in more depth. It examines the best strategy that each firm can adopt for each assumption about its rivals' behaviour.

Single-move games

The simplest type of 'game' is a single-move or single-period game, sometimes known as a normal-form game. This involves just one 'move' by each firm involved. For example, if two or more firms are bidding for a contract which will be awarded to the lowest bidder, when the bids are all made the contract will be awarded to the lowest bidder: the 'game' is over.

Definition

Game theory A mathematical method of decision making in which alternative strategies are analysed to determine the optimal course of action for the interested party, depending on assumptions about rivals' behaviour. Widely used in economics, game theory is also used as a tool in biology, psychology and politics.

Simple dominant-strategy games

Many single-period games have predictable outcomes, no matter what assumptions each firm makes about its rivals' behaviour. Such games are known dominant-strategy games. The simplest case is where there are just two firms with identical costs, products and demand. They are both considering which of two alternative prices to charge. Table 7.1 shows typical profits they could each make.

Let us assume that at present both firms (X and Y) are charging a price of £2 and that they are each making a profit of £10 million, giving a total industry profit of £20 million. This is shown in cell A in Table 7.1.

Now assume they are both (independently) considering reducing their price to £1.80. First they must take into account what their rival might do, and how this will affect them. Let us consider X's position. In our simple example, we assume that there are just two things that its rival, firm Y, might do. Either Y could cut its price to £1.80, or it could leave its price at £2. What should X do?

One alternative is to go for the *cautious* approach and think of the worst thing that its rival could do. If X kept its price at £2, the worst thing for X would be if its rival Y cut its price. This is shown by cell C: X's profit falls to £5 million. If, however, X cut its price to £1.80, the worst outcome would again be for Y to cut its price, but this time X's profit only falls to £8 million. In this case, then, if X is cautious, it will *cut its price to £1.80*. Note that Y will argue along similar lines, and if it is cautious it too will cut its price to £1.80. This policy of adopting the safer strategy is known as **maximin**. Following a maximin approach, the firm will opt for the alternative that will *maxi*mise its *mini*mum possible profit.

An alternative is to go for the *optimistic* approach and assume that your rivals react in the way most favourable to you. Here the firm goes for the strategy that yields the highest possible profit. In X's case, this again means cutting its price, only this time on the optimistic assumption that firm Y will leave its price unchanged. If firm X is correct in its assumption, it will move to box B and achieve the maximum possible profit of £12 million. This approach of going for the maximum possible profit is known as **maximax**. Note that again the same argument applies to Y. Its maximax strategy is to cut price and hopefully end up in cell C.

Given that in this 'game' *both* approaches, maximin and maximax, lead to the *same* strategy (namely cutting price), this is known as a **dominant-strategy game**.

As we saw above, the equilibrium outcome of a game where there is no collusion between the players is known as a *Nash equilibrium*. The Nash equilibrium in this game is cell D.

But, given that both X and Y will be tempted to lower prices, they will both end up earning a lower profit (£8 million profit each in cell D) than if they had charged the higher price (£10 million profit each in cell A). Thus collusion, rather than a price war, would have benefited both, and yet both would be tempted to cheat and cut prices. This is known as the **prisoners' dilemma** (see Box 7.4).

More complex games with no dominant strategy

More complex 'games' can be devised with more than two firms, many alternative prices, differentiated products and various forms of non-price competition (e.g. advertising). Table 7.2 illustrates a more complex game.

Definitions

Maximin The strategy of choosing the policy whose worst possible outcome is the least bad.

Maximax The strategy of choosing the policy that has the best possible outcome.

Dominant-strategy game Where different assumptions about rivals' behaviour lead to the adoption of the same strategy.

Prisoners' dilemma Where two or more firms (or people), by attempting independently to choose the best strategy for whatever the other(s) are likely to do, end up in a worse position than if they had co-operated in the first place.

Table 7.1	Profits for firms X and Y at different prices

		X's price	
		£2	**£1.80**
Y's price	**£2**	A £10m each	B £ 5m for Y £12m for X
	£1.80	C £12m for Y £5m for X	D £8m each

Table 7.2	Profit possibilities for firm X (£m)

		Other firms' responses						
		a	**b**	**c**	**d**	**e**	**f**	
Strategies for firm X	1	100	60	−20	10	30	80	(maximax – a)
	2	40	50	20	30	25	60	(maximin – c)
	3	90	15	30	25	20	50	(best compromise)

KI 21
p190

| **BOX 7.4** | **THE PRISONERS' DILEMMA** | CASE STUDIES AND APPLICATIONS |

Game theory is not just relevant to economics. A famous non-economic example is the prisoners' dilemma.

Nigel and Amanda have been arrested for a joint crime of serious fraud. Each is interviewed separately and given the following alternatives:

- First, if they say nothing, the court has enough evidence to sentence both to a year's imprisonment.
- Second, if either Nigel or Amanda *alone* confesses, he or she is likely to get only a three-month sentence but the partner could get up to ten years.
- Third, if both confess, they are likely to get three years each.

What should Nigel and Amanda do?

		Amanda's alternatives	
		Not confess	Confess
Nigel's alternatives	**Not confess**	**A** Each gets 1 year	**C** Nigel gets 10 years Amanda gets 3 months
	Confess	**B** Nigel gets 3 months Amanda gets 10 years	**D** Each gets 3 years

Let us consider Nigel's dilemma. Should he confess in order to get the short sentence (the maximax strategy)? This is better than the year he would get for not confessing. There is, however, an even better reason for confessing. Suppose Nigel doesn't confess but, unknown to him, Amanda does confess. Then Nigel ends up with the long sentence. Better than this is to confess and to get no more than three years: this is the safest (maximin) strategy.

Amanda is in the same dilemma. The result is simple. When both prisoners act selfishly by confessing, they both end up in position D with relatively long prison terms. Only when they collude will they end up in position A with relatively short prison terms, the best combined solution.

Of course, the police know this and will do their best to prevent any collusion. They will keep Nigel and Amanda in separate cells and try to persuade each of them that the other is bound to confess.

Thus the choice of strategy depends on:

- Nigel's and Amanda's risk attitudes: i.e. are they 'risk-lovers' or 'risk averse'?
- Nigel's and Amanda's estimates of how likely the other is to own up.

1. *Why is this a dominant-strategy 'game'?*
2. *How would Nigel's choice of strategy be affected if he had instead been involved in a joint crime with Rikki, Kate, Amrita and Dave, and they had all been caught?*

The prisoners' dilemma is a good illustration of *the fallacy of composition* that we examined in Box 3.7 (see page 84). What applies at the level of the individual does not apply to the group as a whole. It might be in the individual's interests to confess. It is clearly not in the interests of both, however, for both to confess.

Let us now look at two real-world examples of the prisoners' dilemma.

Standing at concerts

When people go to some public event, such as a concert or a match, they often stand in order to get a better view. But once people start standing, everyone is likely to do so: after all, if they stayed sitting, they would not see at all. In this Nash equilibrium, most people are worse off, since, except for tall people, their view is likely to be worse and they lose the comfort of sitting down.

Too much advertising

Why do firms spend so much on advertising? If they are aggressive, they do so to get ahead of their rivals (the maximax approach). If they are cautious, they do so in case their rivals increase their advertising (the maximin approach). Although in both cases it may be in the individual firm's best interests to increase advertising, the resulting Nash equilibrium is likely to be one of excessive advertising: the total spent on advertising (by all firms) is not recouped in additional sales.

Give some other non-economic examples of the prisoners' dilemma.

It shows the profits that will result from three alternative strategies that firm X can pursue (e.g. price cut, advertising campaign, new model) and six possible responses from rivals (e.g. all rivals cutting price, some cutting price, all increasing advertising). It is assumed that firm X can calculate the effects on its profits of these various reactions.

Which strategy will X choose? It may go for the safe strategy – *maximin*. Here it will choose strategy 2. The worst outcome from strategy 2 (response c) will still give a profit of £20 million, whereas the worst outcome from strategy 3 (response b) is a profit of only £15 million, and the worst outcome from strategy 1 (response c) is a loss of £20 million.

Alternatively, firm X may go for a high-risk strategy: the one with highest maximum profit – *maximax*. Here it would choose strategy 1. This has a potential maximum profit of £100 million (response a), whereas the best outcome from strategy 3 is only £90 million (response a), and for strategy 2 only £60 million (response f).

Alternatively, it may go for a **compromise strategy** and choose strategy 3. The best outcome from strategy 3 (response a) is only slightly lower than strategy 1 (response a) – £90 million compared with £100 million. The worst outcome (response b) is only slightly lower than strategy 2 (response c) – £15 million compared with £20 million.

It is also likely to weigh up the *likelihood* of each outcome occurring. For example, in Table 7.2, firm X is much more likely to adopt the maximax solution if the chances of response *a* occurring are very high and the chances of outcome *c* occurring are very low.

Multiple-move games

In many situations firms will *react* to what their rivals do; their rivals, in turn, will react to what they do. In other words, the game moves back and forth from one 'player' to the other like a game of chess or cards. Firms will still have to think strategically (as you do in chess), considering the likely responses of their rivals to their own actions. These multiple-move games are known as **repeated games** or **extensive-form games**.

One of the simplest repeated games is the **tit-for-tat**. This is where a firm will *only* cut prices, or make some other aggressive move, if the rival does so first. To illustrate this in a multiple-move situation let us look again at the example we considered in Table 7.1, but this time we will extend it beyond one time period.

Assume that firm X is adopting the tit-for-tat strategy. If firm Y cuts its price from £2.00 to £1.80, then firm X will respond in round 2 by also cutting its price. The two firms will end up in cell D – worse off than if neither had cut their price. If, however, firm Y had left its price at £2.00 then firm X would respond by leaving its price unchanged too. Both firms would remain in cell A with a higher profit than in cell D.

As long as firm Y knows that firm X will respond in this way, it has an incentive not to cut its price. Thus it is in X's interests to make sure that Y clearly 'understands' how X will react to any price cut. In other words, X will make a threat.

The importance of threats and promises

TC 5
p50

In many situations, an oligopolist will make a threat or promise that it will act in a certain way. As long as the threat or promise is *credible* (i.e. its competitors believe it), the firm can gain and it will influence its rivals' behaviour.

Take the simple situation where a large oil company, such as Esso, states that it will match the price charged by any competitor within a given radius. Assume that competitors believe this 'price promise' but also that Esso will not try to *undercut* their price. In the simple situation where there is only one other filling station in the area, what price should it charge? Clearly it should charge the price that would maximise its profits, assuming that Esso will charge the *same* price. In the absence of other filling stations in the area, this is likely to be a relatively high price.

Now assume that there are several filling stations in the area. What should the company do now? Its best bet is probably to charge the same price as Esso and hope that no other company charges a lower price and forces Esso to cut its price. Assuming that Esso's threat is credible, other companies are likely to reason in a similar way.

Assume that there are two major oil companies operating filling stations in an area. The first promises to match the other's prices. The other promises always to sell at 1p per litre cheaper than the first. Describe the likely sequence of events in this 'game' and the likely eventual outcome. Could the promise of the second company be seen as credible?

The importance of timing

Most decisions by oligopolists are made by one firm at a time rather than simultaneously by all firms. Sometimes a firm will take the initiative. At other times it will respond to decisions taken by other firms.

Take the case of a new generation of large passenger aircraft that can fly further without refuelling. Assume that there is a market for a 500-seater version of this type of aircraft and a 400-seater version, but that the market for each size of aircraft is not big enough for the two manufacturers, Boeing and Airbus, to share it profitably. Let us also assume that the 400-seater market would give an annual profit of £50 million to a single manufacturer and the 500-seater would give an annual profit of £30 million, but that if both manufacturers produced the same version, they would each make an annual loss of £10 million.

Assume that Boeing announces that it is building the 400-seater plane. What should Airbus do? The choice is illustrated in Figure 7.10. This diagram is called a **decision tree** and shows the sequence of events. The small square at the left of the diagram is Boeing's decision point (point A). If it decided to build the 500-seater plane, we would move up

---

Definitions

Compromise strategy A strategy whose worst outcome is better than under the maximax strategy and whose best outcome is better than under the maximin strategy.

Credible threat (or promise) One that is believable to rivals because it is in the threatener's interests to carry it out.

Decision tree (or game tree) A diagram showing the sequence of possible decisions by competitor firms and the outcome of each combination of decisions.

Figure 7.10 A decision tree

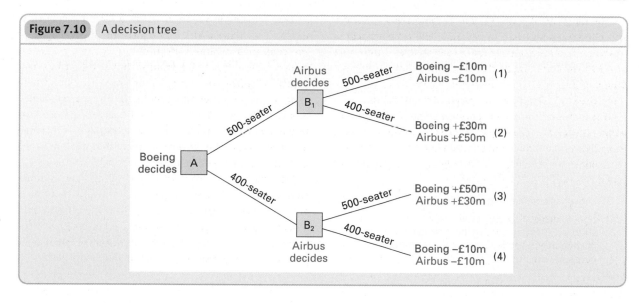

the top branch. Airbus would now have to make a decision (point B_1). If it too built the 500-seater plane, we would move to outcome 1: a loss of £10 million for both manufacturers. Clearly, with Boeing building a 500-seater plane, Airbus would choose the 400-seater plane: we would move to outcome 2, with Boeing making a profit of £30 million and Airbus a profit of £50 million. Airbus would be very pleased!

Boeing's best strategy at point A, however, would be to build the 400-seater plane. We would then move to Airbus's decision point B_2. In this case, it is in Airbus's interests to build the 500-seater plane. Its profit would be only £30 million (outcome 3), but this is better than a £10 million loss if it too built the 400-seater plane (outcome 4). With Boeing deciding first, the Nash equilibrium will thus be outcome 3.

There is clearly a ***first-mover advantage*** here. Once Boeing has decided to build the more profitable version of the plane, Airbus is forced to build the less profitable one. Naturally, Airbus would like to build the more profitable one and be the first mover. Which company succeeds in going first depends on how advanced they are in their research and development and in their production capacity.

More complex decision trees

The aircraft example is the simplest version of a decision tree, with just two companies and each one making only one key decision. In many business situations, much more complex trees could be constructed. The 'game' would be more like one of chess, with many moves and several options on each move. If there were more than two companies, the decision tree would be more complex still.

Definition

First-mover advantage When a firm gains from being the first one to take action.

 Give an example of decisions, other than those about pricing, which two firms could make in sequence, each one affecting the other's next decision.

Assessing the theory of games

The advantage of the game theory approach is that the firm does not need to know which response its rivals will make. However, it must be able to measure the effect of each possible response. This will be virtually impossible to do with many firms competing and many different possible responses. The approach is useful, therefore, only in relatively simple cases, and even here the estimates of profit from each outcome may amount to no more than a rough guess.

It is thus difficult for an economist to predict with any accuracy what price, output and level of advertising the firm will choose. This problem is compounded by the difficulty in predicting the type of strategy – safe, high-risk, compromise – that the firm will adopt.

In some cases, firms may compete hard for a time (in price or non-price terms) and then realise that maybe no one is winning. Firms may then start to collude and jointly raise prices and reduce advertising. Later, after a period of tacit collusion, competition may break out again. This may be sparked off by the entry of a new firm, by the development of a new product design, by a change in market demand, or simply by one or more firms no longer being able to resist the temptation to 'cheat'. In short, the behaviour of particular oligopolists may change quite radically over time.

Finally, we have been assuming that people behave selfishly. In reality, people's actions are likely to be influenced by their moral values. Businesspeople will often be unwilling to behave ruthlessly or dishonestly, or to undertake profitable activities that they regard as unfair. In Chapter 8 we examine some of the consequences of pursuing goals other than ruthless profit maximisation.

Section summary

1. Game theory is a way of modelling behaviour in strategic situations where the outcome for an individual or firm depends on the choices made by others. Thus game theory examines various strategies that firms can adopt when the outcome of each is not certain.

2. The simplest type of 'game' is a single-move or single-period game, sometimes known as a normal-form game. Many single-period games have predictable outcomes, no matter what assumptions each firm makes about its rivals' behaviour. Such games are known as dominant-strategy games.

3. Non-collusive oligopolists will have to work out a price strategy. They can adopt a low-risk 'maximin' strategy of choosing the policy that has the least-bad worst outcome, or a high-risk 'maximax' strategy of choosing

the policy with the best possible outcome, or some compromise. Either way, a 'Nash' equilibrium is likely to be reached which is not in the best interests of the firms collectively. It will entail a lower level of profit than if they had colluded.

4. In multiple-move games play is passed from one 'player' to the other sequentially. Firms will respond not only to what firms do, but what they say they will do. To this end, a firm's threats or promises must be credible if they are to influence rivals' decisions.

5. A firm may gain a strategic advantage over its rivals by being the first one to take action (e.g. launch a new product). A decision tree can be constructed to show the possible sequence of moves in a multiple-move game.

7.4 PRICE DISCRIMINATION

Up to now we have assumed that a firm will sell its output at a single price. Sometimes, however, firms may practise **price discrimination**. This is where a firm sells the same product to different consumers at different prices *even though production costs are the same*. There are three major varieties of price discrimination:

- **First-degree price discrimination** is where the firm charges each consumer the maximum price he or she is prepared to pay for each unit. For example, stallholders in a street market will attempt to do this when bartering with their customers.

- **Second-degree price discrimination** is where the firm charges customers different prices according to how much they purchase. It may charge a high price for the first so many units, a lower price for the next so many units, a lower price again for the next, and so on. For example, electricity companies in some countries charge a high price for the first so many kilowatts. This is the amount of electricity that would typically be used for lighting and running appliances: in other words, the

uses for which there is no substitute fuel. Additional kilowatts are charged at a much lower rate. This is electricity that is typically used for heating and cooking, where there are alternative fuels.

- **Third-degree price discrimination** is where consumers are grouped into two or more independent markets and a separate price is charged in each market. Examples include different bus fares for adults and children, and different prices charged by a firm for the same product in different countries. Third-degree price discrimination is much more common than first- or second-degree discrimination.

Conditions necessary for price discrimination to operate

As we shall see, a firm will be able to increase its profits if it can engage in price discrimination. But under what circumstances will it be able to charge discriminatory prices? There are three conditions that must be met:

Definitions

Price discrimination Where a firm sells the same product at different prices.

First-degree price discrimination Where a firm charges each consumer for each unit the maximum price which that consumer is willing to pay for that unit.

Second-degree price discrimination Where a firm charges a consumer so much for the first so many units purchased, a different price for the next so many units purchased, and so on.

Third-degree price discrimination Where a firm divides consumers into different groups and charges a different price to consumers in different groups, but the same price to all the consumers within a group.

Peak-load pricing Price discrimination (second or third degree) where a higher price is charged in peak periods and a lower price in off-peak periods.

BOX 7.7 | **JUST THE TICKET?**

Price discrimination in the cinema

One of the commonest forms of price discrimination is where children are charged a lower price than adults, whether on public transport or for public entertainment. Take the case of cinema tickets. In most cinemas, children pay less than adults during the day. In the evening, however, many cinemas charge both adults and children the same price.

But why do cinemas charge children less during the day? After all, the child is seeing the same film as the adult and occupying a whole seat. In other words, there is no difference in the 'product' that they are 'consuming'. And why are children charged the higher price in the evenings, given that the seat and the film are the same as during the day?

The answer has to do with revenue maximisation and the price elasticity of demand. Once a cinema has decided to show a film, the marginal costs of an additional customer are zero. There are no additional staffing, film-hire, electricity or other costs. With marginal costs equal to zero, profits will be maximised where marginal revenue is also equal to zero: in other words, where total revenue is maximised.

Take the case of a cinema with 500 seats. This is illustrated in the diagrams, which show the demand and marginal revenue curves for both adults and children. It is assumed that the elasticity of demand for children's tickets is greater than that for adults' tickets. Diagram (a) shows demand during the late afternoon (i.e. after school). Here the demand by children is relatively high compared with adults, but the overall demand is low. Diagram (b) shows demand during the evening. Here there is a higher overall level of demand, especially by adults, many of whom work during the day.

(a) Number of tickets (afternoon)

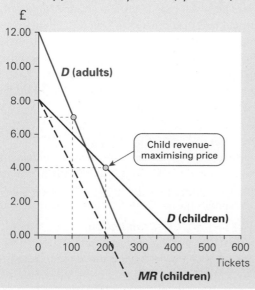

(b) Number of tickets (evening and total)

For the afternoon screening (diagram (a)), revenue is maximised from children by charging them a price of £4.00, i.e. at the point on the demand curve where $MR = 0$. At this price, 200 child tickets will be sold.

Assuming that the same adult price is charged in both the afternoon and the evening, we need to look at the *total* demand for full-priced tickets (i.e. for both afternoon and evening screenings) in order to ascertain the revenue-maximising price. This will be a price of £7.00, where total adult $MR = 0$ (see diagram (b)). This will lead to 100 adult tickets being sold in the afternoon and 500 in the evening.

But why are reduced-price tickets not available for children in the evening? In diagram (b), the sale of low-priced tickets for children would lead to demand exceeding the 500-seat capacity of the cinema. Each time an adult was turned away because the seat had already been sold to a child, the cinema would lose.

1. Which type of price discrimination is the cinema pursuing: first, second or third degree? Could it pursue either of the other two types?
2. If all cinema seats could be sold to adults in the evenings at the end of the week, but only a few on Mondays and Tuesdays, what price discrimination policy would you recommend to the cinema in order for it to maximise its weekly revenue?
3. Would the cinema make more profit if it could charge adults a different price in the afternoon and the evenings?
4. Would you advise that the cinema extend its practice of price discrimination to include other groups? If so, which groups should be targeted?

Figure 7.14 Profit-maximising output under third-degree price discrimination

(a) Market X

(b) Market Y

(c) Total (markets X + Y)

---

example, with output of 1000 units in market X and 2000 in market Y, making 3000 in total, revenue would increase by £5 if one extra unit were sold, whether in market X or Y.

Total profit is maximised where $MC = MR$: i.e. at an output of 3000 units in total. This output must then be divided between the two markets so that MC is equal to MR in each market: i.e. $MC = MR = £5$ in each market. MR must be the same in both markets, otherwise revenue could be increased by switching output to the market with the higher MR.

The profit-maximising price in each market is given by the relevant demand curve. Thus, in market X, 1000 units will be sold at £9 each, and in market Y, 2000 units will be sold at £7 each. Note that the higher price is charged in the market with the less elastic demand curve.

 How would profit-maximising output and price be determined under third-degree price discrimination if there were three separate markets? Draw a diagram to illustrate your answer.

---

*LOOKING AT THE MATHS

We can use calculus to work out the profit-maximising prices and outputs in each of the two markets X and Y in Figure 7.14. If we know the demand functions in each of the two markets, X and Y, we can derive the total revenue functions in each market (TR_X and TR_Y) and hence in the two markets together ($TR = TR_X + TR_Y$). Total profit is given by

$$T\Pi = TR_X + TR_Y - TC$$

To find the maximum-profit output in each market, we (partially) differentiate the total profit equation with respect to output in each of X and Y and set each equal to zero and solve for Q_X and Q_Y (pages A9–12 for how calculus is used to find a maximum value). We can then substitute these values of Q_X and Q_Y in the respective demand functions to work out P_X and P_Y.

Maths Case 7.3 in MyEconLab shows how this is done by using a worked example.

Price discrimination and the public interest

It is tempting to think that anything that increases firms' profits must be at the expense of consumers' welfare. However, this is not necessarily the case and no clear-cut decision can be made over the social desirability of price discrimination. Some people benefit from it; others lose. This can be illustrated by considering the effects of price discrimination on the following aspects of the market.

Distribution

Those paying the higher price will certainly have a lower consumer surplus and may well feel that price discrimination is unfair to them. On the other hand, those charged the lower price will have a greater consumer surplus than they would have had otherwise. They will consume more of the good and in some cases they may be able to obtain a good or service they could not otherwise afford, as with, for example, concessionary rail fares for pensioners. Price discrimination is likely to increase output and make the good or service available to more people.

Competition

As explained above, a firm may use price discrimination to drive competitors out of business. This is known as **predatory pricing**. For example, in many towns, large bus companies have used profits they make in *other* towns where they have

---

Definition

Predatory pricing Where a firm sets its prices below average cost in order to drive competitors out of business.

a monopoly to subsidise their bus fares and thereby drive competitors out of business, only then to raise prices above those that the competitors had been charging. On the other hand, a firm might use the profits from its high-priced market to break into another market and withstand a possible price war. Competition is thereby increased.

Profits

Price discrimination raises a firm's profits. This could be seen as an undesirable redistribution of income in society, especially if the average price of the product is raised. On the other hand, the higher profits may be reinvested and lead to innovation or lower costs in the future.

Section summary

1. Price discrimination is where a firm sells the same product at different prices even though costs are the same. It can be first-degree, second-degree or third-degree price discrimination.

2. Price discrimination allows the firm to earn a higher revenue from a given level of sales.

3. Under first-degree price discrimination, the profit-maximising output is where $MC = P$. Under third-degree price discrimination, profit-maximising output is where the firm's MC is equal to the overall MR (found by adding horizontally the MR curves in each of the separate markets). This is then divided between the markets by selling that amount in each market where $MC = MR$, at a price given by the demand curve in each market.

4. Some people will gain from price discrimination; others will lose.

END OF CHAPTER QUESTIONS

1. Assume that firm X is considering four possible strategies: 1, 2, 3 and 4. Assume that firm X estimates that there are five possible responses (a, b, c, d and e) that its rivals might make to its actions. It estimates the effects on its profits in the case of each of these five responses to each of its four strategies. Its estimates are given in the following table.

Profit possibilities for firm X (£m)

		Rivals' responses				
		a	b	c	d	e
	1	30	20	80	−10	100
Alternative strategies	2	−5	105	40	100	30
for firm X	3	90	0	50	45	60
	4	30	15	10	20	25

(a) Which of the strategies (1, 2, 3 or 4) should it adopt if it is hoping to make the maximum possible profit (maximax)?

(b) Which of the strategies should it adopt if it is very cautious and decides to assume that the worst will happen (maximin)?

(c) Which of the strategies might be the best compromise between these two extreme positions? Explain.

2. Assume that a monopolistically competitive industry is in long-run equilibrium. On a diagram like Figure 7.1(b), show the effect of a fall in demand on a firm's price and profit in (a) the short run and (b) the long run.

3. In what ways is a monopolistically competitive firm likely to be less efficient than one under perfect competition?

4. Are there any shops in your area that stay open later than others? If so, does this affect the prices they charge? Why do you think this is?

5. Give three examples of oligopolistic industries. In what ways do the firms in each of these industries compete? Why do they choose to compete in the way that they do?

6. Why, under oligopoly, might a particular industry be collusive at one time and yet highly price competitive at another?

7. What is meant by the *prisoners' dilemma game* when applied to the behaviour of oligopolists? What will determine the outcome of the game?

8. Think of two examples of price discrimination. In what ways do the consumers gain or lose? What information would you need to be certain in your answer?

Online resources

Additional case studies in MyEconLab

7.1 **The motor vehicle repair and servicing industry.** A case study of monopolistic competition.

7.2 **The corner shop and the hypermarket.** A case study in non-price competition: how the corner shop can survive competition from the big supermarkets.

7.3 **Curry wars.** Monopolistic competition in the take-away food market.

7.4 **Bakeries: oligopoly or monopolistic competition.** A case study on the bread industry, showing that small-scale local bakeries can exist alongside giant national bakeries.

7.5 **'Rip-off Britain'.** This examines the evidence for oligopolistic collusion in the car, supermarket and banking industries.

7.6 **Fair wars in the skies?** The effect of the entry of low-cost airlines on air fares.

7.7 **A product's life cycle.** How market conditions vary at different stages in a product's life.

7.8 **Advertising and the public interest.** Does the consumer benefit from advertising?

Maths Case 7.1 Calculating the profit-maximising price of a price leader. Using equations for demand, revenue and cost curves.

Maths Case 7.2 Deriving the Cournot equilibrium. An algebraic example.

Maths Case 7.3 Calculating the profit-maximising prices under third-degree price discrimination. Using calculus to find the profit-maximising output and price in each market and to compare the profit with and without price discrimination.

Websites relevant to Chapters 6 and 7

Numbers and sections refer to websites listed in the Web Appendix and hotlinked from this book's website at **www.pearsoned.co.uk/sloman**.

- For news articles relevant to this and the previous chapter, see the *Economics News Articles* link from the book's website.

- For general news on companies and markets, see websites in section A, and particularly A2, 3, 4, 5, 8, 9, 18, 24, 25, 26, 36. See also A38, 39, 40, 43 and 44 for links to newspapers worldwide; and A41 and 42 for links to economics news articles from newspapers worldwide.

- For sites that look at competition and market power, see B2 (third link); E4, 10, 18; G7, 8. See also links in I7, 11, 14 and 17.

- For information on OPEC (Box 7.3), see site H6.

- For a site on game theory, see A40 including its home page. See also D4; C20; I17 and 4 (in the EconDirectory section).

- For a site that contains a number of open-access computer-based games on oligopoly and game theory that can be played between students, see site C24.

- For a simulation of running a farm (under perfect competition), see site D12.

- For a simulation on third-degree price discrimination, see site D3.

Alternative Theories
of the Firm

CHAPTER MAP

8.1 Problems with traditional theory   **214**
Difficulties in maximising profit   214
Alternative aims   216
The principal–agent problem   216
Survival and attitudes towards risk   217

8.2 Alternative maximising theories   **218**
Long-run profit maximisation   218
Managerial utility maximisation   219
Sales revenue maximisation (short-run)   219
Growth maximisation   221
Growth by internal expansion   221
Growth by merger   222
Growth through strategic alliances   223
Growth through going global   225
Equilibrium for a growth-maximising firm   225
Alternative maximising theories and the
   public interest   225

8.3 Multiple aims   **228**
Satisficing and the setting of targets   228
Organisational slack   229
Multiple goals: predictions of behaviour   230
Satisficing and the public interest   230

8.4 Pricing in practice   **231**
Cost-based pricing   231

The traditional theories of the firm that we have been looking at in the previous three chapters assume that firms aim to maximise profits. Although this is an accurate assumption for many firms, for many it is not.

Some firms would *like* to maximise profits, but have insufficient information to enable them to do so. Others do not even want to maximise profits, if that means sacrificing achieving some other aim, such as rapid growth or increased market share.

In this chapter, we first examine some of the weaknesses of traditional theory. We then turn to look at various aims that firms might pursue as an alternative to maximum profits: aims such as maximum sales revenue or maximum growth. We also examine the implications of pursuing alternative aims for the profitability of the firm and for the prices paid by the consumer.

Many firms, especially larger ones, are complex organisations, with different individuals and departments pursuing their own agenda. What happens when these various goals come into conflict? How does conflict get resolved? What are the implications for consumers and other 'stakeholders'? We examine these issues in section 8.3.

Finally we ask how prices get determined in practice. If firms do not use marginal revenue and marginal cost concepts in setting their prices, or if they are not aiming to achieve maximum profits, how do they choose the price to charge? As we shall see, firms often base their prices on average cost.

8.1 PROBLEMS WITH TRADITIONAL THEORY

The traditional profit-maximising theories of the firm have been criticised for being unrealistic. The criticisms are mainly of two sorts: (a) that firms wish to maximise profits but for some reason are unable to do so; or (b) that firms have aims other than profit maximisation. Let us examine each in turn.

Difficulties in maximising profit

One criticism of traditional theory sometimes put forward is that firms do not use *MR* and *MC* concepts. This may be true, but firms could still arrive at maximum profit by trial and error adjustments of price, or by finding the output where *TR* and *TC* are furthest apart. Provided they end up maximising profits, they will be equating *MC* and *MR*, even if they did not adopt that as a strategy. In this case, traditional models will still be useful in predicting price and output.

Lack of information

The main difficulty in trying to maximise profits is a *lack of information*.

TC 9
p105

Firms may well use accountants' cost concepts not based on opportunity cost. If it were thereby impossible

to measure true profit, a firm would not be able to maximise profit except by chance.

 What cost concepts are there other than those based on opportunity cost? Would the use of these concepts be likely to lead to an output greater or less than the profit-maximising one?

More importantly, firms are unlikely to know precisely (or even approximately) their demand curves and hence their *MR* curves. Even though (presumably) they will know how much they are selling at the moment, this only gives them one point on their demand curve and no point at all on their *MR* curve. In order to make even an informed guess of marginal revenue, they must have some idea of how responsive demand will be to a change in price. But how are they to estimate this price elasticity? Market research may help. But even this is frequently very unreliable.

KI 15
p106

KI 9
p67

The biggest problem in estimating the firm's demand curve is in estimating the actions and reactions of *other* firms and their effects. Collusion between oligopolists or price leadership would help, but there will still be a considerable area of uncertainty, especially if the firm faces competition from abroad or from other industries.

BOX 8.1 INSIDE THE FIRM

The organisational structure of firms

KI 22
p216

The internal operating structure of firms is frequently governed by their size. Small firms tend to be centrally managed, with decision making operating through a clear managerial hierarchy. In large firms, however, the organisational structure tends to be more complex, although technological change is forcing many organisations to reassess the most suitable organisational structure for their business.

U-form

Medium-sized firms are often broken up into separate departments, such as marketing, finance and production. The managers of each department are normally directly responsible to a chief executive, whose function is to co-ordinate their activities, relaying the firm's overall strategy to them and being responsible for inter-departmental communication. We call this type of structure *U (unitary) form* (see figure (a)).

When firms expand beyond a certain size, however, a U-form structure is likely to become inefficient. This inefficiency arises from difficulties in communication, co-ordination and control. It becomes too difficult to manage the whole organisation from the centre.

M-form

To overcome these organisational problems, the firm can adopt an *M (multi-divisional) form* of managerial structure (see figure (b)).

(b) *M-form business organisation*

This suits larger firms. The firm is divided into a number of 'divisions'. Each division could be responsible for a particular product or group of products, or a particular market (e.g. a specific country). The day-to-day running and even certain long-term decisions of each division would be the responsibility of the divisional manager(s).

(a) *U-form business organisation*

Game theory may help a firm decide its price and output strategy: it may choose to sacrifice the chance of getting the absolute maximum profit (the high-risk, maximax option), and instead go for the safe strategy of getting probably at least reasonable profits (maximin). But even this assumes that it knows the consequences for its profits of each of the possible reactions of its rivals. In reality, it will not even have this information to any degree of certainty, because it will not be able to predict how consumers will respond to each of its rivals' alternative reactions.

Time period

Finally there is the problem of deciding the *time period* over which the firm should be seeking to maximise profits. Firms operate in a changing environment. Demand curves shift; supply curves shift. Some of these shifts occur as a result of factors outside the firm's control, such as changes in competitors' prices and products. Some, however, change as a direct result of a firm's policies, such as an advertising campaign or the installation of new equipment. The firm is not, therefore, faced with static cost and revenue curves from which it can read off its profit-maximising price and output. Instead it is faced with a changing (and often highly unpredictable) set of curves. If it chooses a price and output that maximises profits *this* year, it may as a result jeopardise profits in the future.

Take a simple example. The firm may be considering whether to invest in new expensive equipment. If it does, its costs will rise in the short run and thus short-run profits will fall. On the other hand, if the quality of the product thereby increases, demand is likely to increase over the longer run. Also, variable costs are likely to decrease if the

---

Definitions

U-form (unitary form) of corporate organisation Where the managers of the various departments of a firm are directly responsible to a head office, and normally to a chief executive.

M-form (multi-divisional form) of corporate organisation Where the firm is split into a number of separate divisions (e.g. different products or countries), with each division then split into a number of departments.

Flat organisation Where the senior management communicate directly with those lower in the organisational structure, bypassing middle management.

H-form organisation (holding company) Where the parent company holds interests in a number of subsidiary companies.

CASE STUDIES AND APPLICATIONS

There are a number of benefits:

- Reduced length of information flows.
- The chief executive being able to concentrate on overall strategic planning.
- An enhanced level of control by managers, with each division being run as a mini 'firm', each competing with other divisions for the limited amount of company resources available.

One of the major problems with M-form organisations is that they can become very bureaucratic with many layers of management. Managers might pursue goals that conflict with those of shareholders or head office (see the section on the principal–agent problem below). As a result, some companies in recent years have moved back towards simpler structures. These *flat organisations*, as they are called, dispense with various layers of middle management. Recent technological innovations, especially in respect to computer systems such as email and management information systems, have enabled senior managers to communicate easily and directly with those lower in the organisational structure.

In many respects, the flat organisation represents a return to the U-form structure. It is yet to be seen whether we also have a return to the problems associated with this type of organisation.

H-form

As many businesses have expanded their operations, often on a global scale, so further more complex forms of business organisation have evolved. One such is the *H form* or *holding company*. A holding company (or parent company) is one that owns a controlling interest in other subsidiary companies. These subsidiaries, in turn, may also have controlling interests in other companies. There may thus be a complex web of interlocking holdings.

While the parent company has ultimate control over its various subsidiaries, it is likely that both tactical and strategic decision making is left to the individual companies within the organisation. Many multinationals are organised along the lines of an international holding company, where overseas subsidiaries pursue their own independent strategy.

As the organisational structures of companies and their forms of governance become more complex, so it becomes increasingly difficult to identify simple company aims. Different managers or departments may have different objectives. What predictions, then, can we make about firms' behaviour? We will examine this question throughout this chapter.

 What advantages might the consumer gain from a large M- or H-form company?

new equipment is more efficient. In other words, long-run profit is likely to increase, but probably by a highly uncertain amount.

Given these extreme problems in deciding profit-maximising price and output, firms may fall back on simple rules of thumb for pricing (see page 193).

Alternative aims

An even more fundamental attack on the traditional theory of the firm is that firms do not even *aim* to maximise profits (even if they could).

The traditional theory of the firm assumes that it is the *owners* of the firm who make price and output decisions. It is reasonable to assume that owners *will* want to maximise profits: this much most of the critics of the traditional theory accept. The question is, however, whether the owners do in fact make the decisions.

In **public limited companies** the shareholders are the owners and presumably will want the firm to maximise profits so as to increase their dividends and the value of their shares. Shareholders elect directors. Directors in turn employ professional managers who are often given considerable discretion in making decisions. There is therefore a *separation between the ownership and control* of a firm. (See Case Study 8.1 in MyEconLab for an examination of the legal structure of firms.)

But what are the objectives of managers? Will *they* want to maximise profits, or will they have some other aim?

Managers may be assumed to want to *maximise their own utility*. This may well involve pursuits that conflict with profit maximisation. They may, for example, pursue higher salaries, greater power or prestige, better working conditions, greater sales, etc. Different managers in the same firm may well pursue different aims.

Managers will still have to ensure that *sufficient* profits are made to keep shareholders happy, but that may be very different from *maximising* profits.

Alternative theories of the firm to those of profit maximisation, therefore, tend to assume that large firms are **profit satisficers**. That is, managers strive hard for a minimum target level of profit, but are less interested in profits above this level.

Such theories fall into two categories: first, those theories that assume that firms attempt to maximise some other aim, provided that sufficient profits are achieved (these are

examined in section 8.2); and second, those theories that assume that firms pursue a number of potentially conflicting aims, of which sufficient profit is merely one (these are examined in section 8.3).

 The nature of institutions and organisations is likely to influence behaviour. There are various forces influencing people's decisions in complex organisations. Assumptions that an organisation will follow one simple objective (e.g. short-run profit maximisation) are thus too simplistic in many cases.

 Make a list of six possible aims that a manager of a high street department store might have. Identify some conflicts that might arise between these aims.

The principal–agent problem

Can the owners of a firm ever be sure that their managers will pursue the business strategy most appropriate to achieving the owners' goals (i.e. maximisation of profit)? This is an example of what is known in economics as the **principal–agent problem**. One of the features of a complex modern economy is that people (principals) have to employ others (agents) to carry out their wishes. If you want to go on holiday, it is easier to go to a travel agent to sort out the arrangements than to do it all yourself. Likewise, if you want to buy a house, it is more convenient to go to an estate agent. The point is that these agents have specialist knowledge and can save you, the principal, a great deal of time and effort. It is merely an example of the benefits of the specialisation and division of labour.

It is the same with firms. They employ people with specialist knowledge and skills to carry out specific tasks. Companies frequently employ consultants to give them advice or engage the services of specialist firms such as an advertising agency. It is the same with the employees of the company. They can be seen as 'agents' of their employer. In the case of workers, they can be seen as the agents of management. Junior managers are the agents of senior management. Senior managers are the agents of the directors, who are themselves agents of the shareholders. Thus in large firms there is often a complex chain of principal–agent relationships.

Definitions

Public limited comoany A company owned by its shareholders. Shareholders' liability is limited to the value of their shares. Shares may be bought and sold publicly – on the stock market.

Profit satisficing Where decision makers in a firm aim for a target level of profit rather than the absolute maximum level.

Principal–agent problem Where people (principals), as a result of lack of knowledge, cannot ensure that their best interests are served by their agents.

BOX 8.2   **WHAT DO YOU MAXIMISE?**   CASE STUDIES AND APPLICATIONS

Managers are only human too

You are a student studying economics. So what do you maximise?

Do you attempt to maximise the examination marks you will get? If so, you will probably have to spend most of each week studying. Obviously you will have to have breaks for food and sleep, and you will need some recreation, but you will probably still spend a lot more time studying than you do now!

What is more likely is that you will, in some rather vaguely defined way, try to maximise your happiness. Getting a good mark in your exams is just one element contributing to your happiness, and you will have to weigh it against the opportunity cost of studying – namely, time not spent out with friends, watching television, playing sport, working for money, etc.

To argue that managers seek to maximise profits to the exclusion of everything else is rather like arguing that you seek to maximise your exam marks. Managers' happiness (or utility) will depend on their salaries, the pleasantness of their job, their power, their respect, the friendship of their colleagues, etc.

Achieving profits may be an important aim (after all, it does contribute to a manager's utility), but the effort required to make extra profits involves an opportunity cost to the manager. For example, the manager may have to work longer hours or fire a close colleague and friend.

1. *When are increased profits in the manager's personal interest?*
2. *Does the way you allocate your time between study and leisure vary at different times of the year? If so, why?*

TC 9 p105

But these relationships have an inherent danger for the principal: there is **asymmetric information** between the two sides.

The agent knows more about the situation than the principal – in fact this is part of the reason why the principal employs the agent in the first place. The danger is that the agent may well not act in the principal's best interests, and may be able to get away with it because of the principal's imperfect knowledge. The estate agent may try to convince the vendor that it is necessary to accept a lower price, while the real reason is to save the agent time, effort and expense.

In firms too, agents frequently do not act in the best interests of their principals. For example, workers may be able to get away with not working very hard, preferring instead a quiet life. Similarly, given the divorce between the ownership and control of a company, managers (agents) may pursue goals different from those of shareholders (principals). Thus *X inefficiency* is likely to occur (see Box 6.5).

> **KEY IDEA 23**
>
> *The principal–agent problem*. Where people (principals), as a result of a lack of knowledge, cannot ensure that their best interests are served by their agents. Agents may take advantage of this situation to the disadvantage of the principals.

Definition

Asymmetric information Where one party in an economic relationship (e.g. an agent) has more information than another (e.g. the principal).

So how can principals tackle the problem? There are two elements in the solution:

- The principals must have some way of *monitoring* the performance of their agents. For example, a company might employ efficiency experts to examine the operation of its management. KI 15 p106

- There must be *incentives* for agents to behave in the principals' interests. For example, managers' salaries could be closely linked to the firm's profitability. TC 5 p50

Alternative theories of the firm therefore place considerable emphasis on incentive mechanisms in explaining the behaviour of managers and the resulting performance of their companies.

In a competitive market, managers' and shareholders' interests are more likely to coincide. Managers have to ensure that the company remains efficient or it may not survive the competition and they might lose their jobs. In monopolies and oligopolies, however, where supernormal profits can often be relatively easily earned, the interests of shareholders and managers are likely to diverge. Here it will be in shareholders' interests to institute incentive mechanisms that ensure that their agents, the managers, are motivated to strive for profitability.

Survival and attitudes towards risk

Aiming for profits, sales, salaries, power, etc. will be useless if the firm does not survive! Trying to *maximise* any of the various objectives may be risky. For example, if a firm tries to maximise its market share by aggressive advertising or price cutting, it might invoke a strong response from its rivals. The resulting war may drive it out of business. Concern with survival, therefore, may make firms cautious.

KI 11
p75

Not all firms, however, make survival the top priority. Some are adventurous and are prepared to take risks. Adventurous firms are most likely to be those dominated by a powerful and ambitious individual – an individual prepared to take gambles.

The more dispersed the decision-making power is in the firm, however, and the more worried managers are about their own survival, the more cautious are their policies likely to be: preferring collusion to competition, preferring to stick with products that have proved to be popular, and preferring to expand slowly and steadily. If a firm is too cautious, however, it may not in fact survive. It may find that it loses markets to more aggressive competitors.

KI 22
p216

Section summary

1. There are two major types of criticism of the traditional profit-maximising theory: (a) firms may not have the information to maximise profits; (b) they may not even want to maximise profits.

2. Lack of information on demand and costs and on the actions and reactions of rivals, and a lack of use of opportunity cost concepts, may mean that firms adopt simple 'rules of thumb' for pricing.

3. In large companies, there is likely to be a separation between ownership and control. The shareholders (the owners) may want maximum profits, but it is the managers who make the decisions, and managers are likely to aim to maximise their own utility rather than that of the shareholders. This leads to profit 'satisficing'.

4. The problem of managers not pursuing the same goals as the owners is an example of the *principal–agent problem*. Agents (in this case, the managers) may not always carry out the wishes of their principals (in this case, the owners). Because of asymmetric information, managers are able to pursue their own aims, just so long as they produce results that will satisfy the owners. The solution for owners is to monitor the performance of managers, and create incentives for managers to behave in the owners' interests.

5. Some alternative theories assume that there is a single alternative aim that firms seek to maximise. Others assume that managers have a series of (possibly conflicting) aims.

8.2 ALTERNATIVE MAXIMISING THEORIES

Long-run profit maximisation

The traditional theory of the firm is based on the assumption of *short-run* profit maximisation. Many actions of firms may be seen to conflict with this aim and yet could be consistent with the aim of **long-run profit maximisation**. For example, policies to increase the size of the firm or the firm's share of the market may involve heavy advertising or low prices to the detriment of short-run profits. But if this results in the firm becoming larger, with a bigger share of the market, the resulting economic power may enable the firm to make larger profits in the long run.

At first sight, a theory of long-run profit maximisation would seem to be a realistic alternative to the traditional short-run profit-maximisation theory. In practice, however, the theory is not a very useful predictor of firms' behaviour and is very difficult to test.

Definition

Long-run profit maximisation An alternative theory which assumes that managers aim to shift cost and revenue curves so as to maximise profits over some longer time period.

A claim by managers that they were attempting to maximise long-run profits could be an excuse for virtually any policy. When challenged as to why the firms had, say, undertaken expensive research or high-cost investment, or had engaged in a damaging price war, the managers could reply 'Ah, yes, but in the long run it will pay off.' This is very difficult to refute (until it is too late!).

Even if long-run profit maximisation *is* the prime aim, the means of achieving it are extremely complex. The firm will need a plan of action for prices, output, investment, etc., stretching from now into the future. But today's pricing and marketing decisions affect tomorrow's demand. Therefore, future demand curves cannot be taken as given. Today's investment decisions will affect tomorrow's costs. Therefore, future cost curves cannot be taken as given either. These shifts in demand and cost curves will be very difficult to estimate with any precision. Quite apart from this, the actions of competitors, suppliers, unions and so on are difficult to predict. Thus the picture of firms making precise calculations of long-run profit-maximising prices and outputs is an unrealistic one.

TC 9
p105

It may be useful, however, simply to observe that firms, when making current price, output and investment decisions, try to judge the approximate effect on new entrants, consumer demand, future costs, etc., and try to avoid

BOX 8.3   **WHEN IS A THEORY NOT A THEORY?**   EXPLORING ECONOMICS

Have you heard the joke about the man sitting in a railway carriage who was throwing pieces of paper out of the window? A fellow traveller was curious and asked him why he kept doing this.

'It keeps the elephants down,' was the reply.

'But,' said the other man, 'there are no elephants around here.'

'I know,' said the first man. 'Effective, isn't it?'

Let's reformulate this joke.

Once upon a time there was this boss of a company who kept doing strange things. First he would spend a massive amount of money on advertising, and then stop. Then he would pay a huge wage increase 'to keep his workforce happy'. Then he would close the factory for two

months to give everyone a break. Then he would move the business, lock, stock and barrel, to a new location.

One day he was talking to an accountant friend, who asked, 'Why do you keep doing these strange things?'

'I have to do them to make the business profitable,' was the reply.

'But your business is profitable,' said the accountant.

'I know. It just goes to show how effective my policies are.'

1. *Why might it be difficult to refute a theory of long-run profit maximisation?*
2. *If a theory cannot in principle be refuted, is it a useful theory?*

---

decisions that would appear to conflict with long-run profits. Often this will simply involve avoiding making decisions (e.g. cutting price) that may stimulate an unfavourable result from rivals (e.g. rivals cutting their price).

Managerial utility maximisation

One of the most influential of the alternative theories of the firm has been that developed by O. E. Williamson[1] in the 1960s. Williamson argued that, provided satisfactory levels of profit are achieved, managers often have the discretion to choose what policies to pursue. In other words, they are free to pursue their *own* interests. And what are the managers' interests? To maximise their own utility, argued Williamson.

Williamson identified a number of factors that affect a manager's utility. The four main ones were salary, job security, dominance (including status, power and prestige) and professional excellence.

Of these only salary is *directly* measurable. The rest have to be measured indirectly. One way of doing this is to examine managers' expenditure on various items, and in particular on *staff*, on *perks* (such as a company car and a plush office) and on *discretionary investment*. The greater is the level of expenditure by managers on these items, the greater is likely to be their status, power, prestige, professional excellence and job security, and hence utility.

Having identified the factors that influence a manager's utility, Williamson developed several models in which managers seek to maximise their utility. He used these models to predict managerial behaviour under various conditions and argued that they performed better than traditional profit-maximising theory.

One important conclusion was that average costs are likely to be higher when managers have the discretion to pursue their own utility. For example, perks and unneces-

sarily high staffing levels add to costs. On the other hand, the resulting 'slack' allows managers to rein in these costs in times of low demand (see page 229). This enables them to maintain their profit levels. To support these claims he conducted a number of case studies. These did indeed show that staff and perks were cut during recessions and expanded during booms, and that new managers were frequently able to cut staff without influencing the productivity of firms.

Sales revenue maximisation (short-run)

Perhaps the most famous of all alternative theories of the firm is that developed by William Baumol in the late 1950s. This is the theory of *sales revenue maximisation*. Unlike the theories of long-run profit maximisation and managerial utility maximisation, it is easy to identify the price and output that meet this aim – at least in the short run.

So why should managers want to maximise their firm's sales revenue? The answer is that the success of managers, and in particular sales managers, may be judged according to the level of the firm's sales. Sales figures are an obvious barometer of the firm's health. Managers' salaries, power and prestige may depend directly on sales revenue. The firm's sales representatives may be paid commission on their sales. Thus sales revenue maximisation may be a more dominant aim in the firm than profit maximisation, particularly if it has a dominant sales department.

Sales revenue will be maximised at the top of the *TR* curve at output Q_1 in Figure 8.1. Profits, by contrast, would be maximised at Q_2. Thus, for given total revenue and total

---

Definition

Sales revenue maximisation An alternative theory which assumes that managers aim to maximise the firm's short-run total revenue.

Figure 8.1   Sales revenue maximising output

cost curves, sales revenue maximisation will tend to lead to a higher output and a lower price than profit maximisation.

 Draw a diagram with MC and MR curves. Mark the output (a) at which profits are maximised; (b) at which sales revenue is maximised.

The firm will still have to make sufficient profits, however, to keep the shareholders happy. Thus firms can be seen to be operating with a profit constraint. They are *profit satisficers*.

The effect of this profit constraint is illustrated in Figure 8.2. The diagram shows a total profit ($T\Pi$) curve. (This is found by simply taking the difference between TR and TC at each output.) Assume that the minimum acceptable profit is Π (whatever the output). Any output greater than Q_3 will give a profit less than Π. Thus the sales revenue maximiser who is also a profit satisficer will produce Q_3, not Q_1. Note, however, that this output is still greater than the profit-maximising output Q_2.

Figure 8.2   Sales revenue maximising with a profit constraint

Total profit

If the firm could maximise sales revenue and still make more than the minimum acceptable profit, it would probably spend this surplus profit on advertising to increase revenue further. This would have the effect of shifting upwards the TR curve and also the TC curve (since advertising costs money).

*LOOKING AT THE MATHS

We can express sales revenue maximisation algebraically. We start with the situation with no profit constraint.

Unconstrained sales revenue maximisation

Assume that the total revenue function is given by

$$TR = bQ - cQ^2 \tag{1}$$

This will give a straight-line MR function given by

$$MR = \frac{dTR}{dQ} = b - 2cQ$$

Total revenue is maximised where $MR = 0$, since, when total revenue is maximised, any increase in output will give a zero rise in total revenue. In other words, at the top of the total revenue curve in Figures 8.1 and 8.2, the slope of the curve is zero (the tangent to the curve is horizontal). Thus:

$$MR = b - 2cQ = 0$$

i.e.

$$2cQ = b$$

i.e.

$$Q = \frac{b}{2c} \tag{2}$$

Thus, if the total revenue function were

$$TR = 120Q - 3Q^2$$

then, from equation (2), total revenue would be maximised at an output (Q), where

$$Q = \frac{b}{2c} = \frac{120}{2 \times 3} = 20$$

Constrained sales revenue maximisation

If there is a profit constraint, we can write the objective function as Max TR, subject to $TR - TC \geq T\Pi^*$ where $T\Pi^*$ is the minimum profit that must be achieved. Assume that the TR and TC functions are given by

$$TR = bQ - cQ^2$$

and

$$TC = a + dQ - eQ^2 + gQ^3$$

Note that these two equations match the shapes of the TR and TC curves in Figures 8.1 and 8.2. The constraint can now be written:

$$TR - TC = -a + (b - d)Q + (e - c)Q^2 - gQ^3 \geq T\Pi^*$$

We can use this to solve for Q. An example of this is given in Maths Case 8.1 in MyEconLab.

Sales revenue maximisation will tend to involve more advertising than profit maximisation. Ideally the profit-maximising firm will advertise up to the point where the marginal revenue of advertising equals the marginal cost of advertising (assuming diminishing returns to advertising). The firm aiming to maximise sales revenue will go beyond this, since further advertising, although costing more than it earns the firm, will still add to total revenue. The firm will continue advertising until surplus profits above the minimum have been used up.

 Since advertising increases a firm's costs, will prices necessarily be lower with sales revenue maximisation than with profit maximisation?

Growth maximisation

Rather than aiming to maximise *short-run* revenue, managers may take a longer-term perspective and aim for **growth maximisation** in the size of the firm. They may directly gain utility from being part of a rapidly growing 'dynamic' organisation; promotion prospects are greater in an expanding organisation since new posts tend to be created; larger firms may pay higher salaries; managers may obtain greater power in a larger firm.

Growth is probably best measured in terms of a growth in sales revenue, since sales revenue (or 'turnover') is the simplest way of measuring the size of a business. An alternative would be to measure the capital value of a firm, but this will depend on the ups and downs of the stock market and is thus a rather unreliable method.

If a firm is to maximise growth, it needs to be clear about the time period over which it is setting itself this objective. For example, maximum growth over the next two or three years might be obtained by running factories to absolute maximum capacity, cramming in as many machines and workers as possible, and backing this up with massive advertising campaigns and price cuts. Such policies, however, may not be sustainable in the longer run. The firm may simply not be able to finance them. A longer-term perspective (say, five to ten years) may require the firm to 'pace' itself, and perhaps to direct resources away from current production and sales into the development of new products that have a potentially high and growing long-term demand.

Growth may be achieved either by internal expansion or by merger.

Growth by internal expansion

Internal growth requires an increase in sales, which in turn requires an increase in the firm's productive capacity. In order to increase its *sales*, the firm is likely to engage in extensive product promotion and to try to launch new products. In order to increase *productive capacity*, the firm will require new investment. Both product promotion and investment will require finance.

In the short run, the firm can finance growth by borrowing, by retaining profits or by a new issue of shares. What limits the amount of finance that a firm can acquire, and hence the rate at which it can grow? If the firm *borrows* too much, the interest payments it incurs will make it difficult to maintain the level of dividends to shareholders. Similarly, if the firm *retains* too much *profit*, there will be less available to pay out in dividends. Also, if it attempts to raise capital by a *new issue of shares*, the distributed profits will have to be divided between a larger number of shares. Whichever way it finances investment, therefore, the more it invests, the more the dividends on shares in the short run will probably fall.

This could lead shareholders to sell their shares, unless they are confident that *long-run* profits and hence dividends will rise again, thus causing the share price to remain high in the long run. If shareholders do sell their shares, this will cause share prices to fall. If they fall too far, the firm runs the risk of being taken over and of certain managers losing their jobs. The **takeover constraint** therefore requires that the growth-maximising firm distribute sufficient profits to avoid being taken over.

In the long run, a rapidly growing firm may find its profits increasing, especially if it can achieve economies of scale and a bigger share of the market. These profits can then be used to finance further growth.

Growth through vertical integration

If market conditions make growth through increased sales difficult, then a firm may choose to grow through vertical integration. This has a number of advantages.

Economies of scale. These can occur by the business performing *complementary* stages of production within a single business unit. The classic example of this is the steel manufacturer combining the furnacing and milling stages of production, saving the costs that would have been required to reheat the iron had such operations been undertaken by independent businesses. Clearly, for most firms, the performing of more than one stage on a single site is likely to reduce transport costs, as semi-finished products no longer have to be moved from one plant to another.

Reduced uncertainty. A business that is not vertically integrated may find itself subject to various uncertainties in the marketplace. Examples include uncertainty over future

> ### Definitions
>
> **Growth maximisation** An alternative theory which assumes that managers seek to maximise the growth in sales revenue (or the capital value of the firm) over time.
>
> **Takeover constraint** The effect that the fear of being taken over has on a firm's willingness to undertake projects that reduce distributed profits.

price movements, over supply reliability or over access to markets.

Barriers to entry. Vertical integration may give the firm greater power in the market by enabling it to erect entry barriers to potential competitors. For example, a firm that undertakes backward vertical integration and acquires a key input resource can effectively close the market to potential new entrants, either by simply refusing to supply a competitor, or by charging a very high price for the input, such that new firms face an absolute cost disadvantage.

 See if you can identify two companies that are vertically integrated and what advantages they gain from such integration.

The major problem with vertical integration is that it may reduce the firm's ability to respond to changing market demands. A business that integrates may find itself tied to its own supply source. If, by contrast, it were free to choose between suppliers, inputs might be obtained at a lower price than the firm could achieve by supplying itself.

Many firms are finding that it is better *not* to be vertically integrated but to focus on their core business and to outsource their supplies, their marketing and many other functions. That way they put alternative suppliers and distributors in competition with each other.

Growth through diversification

An alternative internal growth strategy to vertical integration is that of diversification. A good example of a highly diversified company is Virgin. Its interests include planes, trains, cars, finance, music, mobile phones, holidays, wedding venues, wine, cinemas, radio, television, online gambling, cosmetics, publishing, balloon flights and even space travel.

If the current market is saturated, stagnant or in decline, diversification might be the only avenue open to the business if it wishes to maintain a high growth performance. In other words, it is not only the level of profits that may be limited in the current market, but also the growth of sales.

Diversification also has the advantage of spreading risks. So long as a business produces a single product in a single market, it is vulnerable to changes in that market's conditions. If a farmer produces nothing but potatoes and the potato harvest fails, the farmer is ruined. If, however, the farmer produces a whole range of vegetable products, or even diversifies into livestock, then he or she is less subject to the forces of nature and the unpredictability of the market.

Growth by merger

A merger may be the result of the mutual agreement of two firms to come together. Alternatively, one firm may put in a takeover bid for another. This involves the first firm offering to buy the shares of the second for cash, to swap them for shares in the acquiring company, or to issue fixed-interest securities (debentures). The shareholders of the second firm then vote on whether to accept the offer. (Technically this is an 'acquisition' or 'takeover' rather than a merger, but the term 'merger' is generally used to include both mutual agreements and acquisitions.)

There are three types of merger:

- A **horizontal merger** is where firms in the same industry and at the same stage of production merge: e.g. two car manufacturers.
- A **vertical merger** is where firms in the same industry but at different stages in the production of a good merge: e.g. a car manufacturer with a car component parts producer.
- A **conglomerate merger** is where firms in different industries merge: e.g. when British Aerospace acquired Austin Rover.

Motives for merger

But why do firms want to take over others? Economists have identified a number of possible motives.

Merger for growth. Mergers provide a much quicker means to growth than does internal expansion. Not only does the firm acquire new capacity, it also acquires additional consumer demand. There is a danger for growth-maximising firms, however, from being taken over themselves. If they are growing rapidly and yet have a relatively low profit and a low stock market value, they will be attractive to predators.

Merger for economies of scale. Once the merger has taken place, the constituent parts can be reorganised through a process of 'rationalisation'. The result can be a reduction in costs. For example, only one head office will now be needed. Reduced costs are a way of increasing profits and thereby increasing the rate of growth.

In fact the evidence suggests that most mergers result in few if any cost savings: either potential economies of scale are not exploited due to a lack of rationalisation, or diseconomies result from the disruptions of reorganisation. New managers installed by the parent company are often seen as unsympathetic, and morale may go down.

Definitions

Horizontal merger Where two firms in the same industry at the same stage in the production process merge.

Vertical merger Where two firms in the same industry at different stages in the production process merge.

Conglomerate merger Where two firms in different industries merge.

Merger for monopoly power. Here the motive is to reduce competition and thereby gain greater market power and larger profits. With less competition, the firm will face a less elastic demand and will be able to charge a higher percentage above marginal cost. This obviously fits well with the traditional theory of the firm.

 Which of the three types of merger (horizontal, vertical and conglomerate) are most likely to lead to (a) reductions in average costs; (b) increased market power?

Merger for increased market valuation. A merger can benefit shareholders of *both* firms by leading to a potential increase in the stock market valuation of the merged firm. If both sets of shareholders believe that they will make a capital gain, then they are more likely to give the go-ahead to the merger.

In practice, however, there is little evidence to suggest that mergers lead to a capital gain. One possible reason for this is the increases in costs referred to above. In the early stages of a merger boom, as in 2005–6, when some good deals may be had, the share price of acquiring firms may rise. But as the merger boom develops, more marginal firms are acquired. Take the merger boom of the late 1990s. In some 80 per cent of cases, there was a significant fall in the share value of the acquiring firm.

 Merger to reduce uncertainty. There are two major sources of uncertainty for firms. The first is the behaviour of rivals. Mergers, by reducing the number of rivals, can correspondingly reduce uncertainty. At the same time they can reduce the costs of competition (e.g. by reducing advertising). The second source of uncertainty is the economic environment. In a period of rapid change, such as often accompanies a boom, firms may seek to protect themselves by merging with others.

Merger due to opportunity. Sometimes mergers occur simply as a consequence of opportunities that suddenly and unexpectedly arise. Such mergers are largely unplanned and thus virtually impossible to predict. Dynamic business organisations are constantly on the lookout for such opportunities.

Other motives. Other motives for mergers include:

- Getting bigger so as to become less likely to be taken over oneself.
- Merging with another firm to prevent it being taken over by an unwanted predator (the 'White Knight' strategy).
- Asset stripping. This is where a firm buys another and then breaks it up, selling off the profitable bits and probably closing down the remainder.
- Empire building. This is where owners or managers like the power or prestige of owning or controlling several (preferably well-known) companies.
- Broadening the geographical base of the company by merging with a firm in a different part of the country or the world.

These theories, alongside the general area of mergers and acquisitions, are the subject of ongoing research, but most are in need of greater empirical investigation and support.

 1. *Which of the above theories overlap and in what way?*
2. *Why do you think it is difficult to find adequate empirical support for any of them?*

Mergers and the relationship between growth and profit

In order for a firm to be successful in a takeover bid, it must be sufficiently profitable to finance the takeover. Thus the faster it tries to grow and the more takeovers it attempts, the higher must be its profitability.

In addition to being an obvious means to the growth of the firm, mergers may be a means of increasing profits, since mergers can lead to both lower average costs through economies of scale and higher average revenue through increased market power over prices. These profits in turn may be seen as a means of financing further growth.

It can therefore be seen that, whichever way it is financed, growth is closely linked to profits. High profits can help a firm grow. Rapid growth can lead to a rapid growth in profits.

These are not inevitable links, however. For example, long-run profits may not increase if a firm, as part of its growth policy, invests in risky projects or projects with a low rate of return. Expansion alone is no guarantee of profits. Also, high profits will not necessarily lead to growth if a large proportion is distributed to shareholders and only a small proportion is reinvested. High profits may help growth, but they do not guarantee it.

Growth through strategic alliances

One means of achieving growth is through the formation of *strategic alliances* with other firms. They are a means whereby business operations can be expanded relatively quickly and at relatively low cost, and are a common way in which firms can deepen their involvement in global markets.

There are many types of strategic alliance between businesses, covering a wide range of alternative collaborative arrangements.

Joint ventures. A *joint venture* is where two or more firms decide to create, and jointly own, a new independent organisation. The creation of O_2, originally called Cellnet, by BT and Securicor is an example of such a strategy.

> ### Definitions
>
> **Strategic alliance** Where two firms work together, formally or informally, to achieve a mutually desirable goal.
> **Joint venture** Where two or more firms set up and jointly own a new independent firm.

Consortia. In recent years, many consortia have been created. Camelot, the company that runs the UK National Lottery, and Trans Manche Link, the company that built the Channel Tunnel, are two examples. A *consortium* is usually created for very specific projects, such as a large civil engineering work. As such they have a very focused objective, and once the project is completed, the consortium is usually dissolved.

Franchising. A less formal strategic alliance is where a business agrees to *franchise* its operations to third parties. McDonald's and Coca-Cola are good examples of businesses that use a franchise network. In such a relationship, the franchisee is responsible for manufacturing and/or selling, and the franchiser retains responsibility for branding and marketing.

Subcontracting. Like franchising, **subcontracting** is a less formal source of strategic alliance, where companies maintain their independence. When a business subcontracts, it employs an independent business to manufacture or

---

Definitions

Consortium Where two or more firms work together on a specific project and create a separate company to run the project.

Franchise A formal agreement whereby a company uses another company to produce or sell some or all of its product.

Subcontracting Where a firm employs another firm to produce part of its output or some of its input(s).

BOX 8.4 ENRON

A cautionary tale of business growth

Not many companies come bigger than Enron did, and none bigger has ever filed for bankruptcy, as Enron did on 1 December 2001.

Enron seemed to have everything going for it, being the largest energy trader in the USA with 25 per cent of the market. In 2000, Enron earned $100 billion in revenue and turned a profit of $1 billion. But by the time it filed for bankruptcy, the seventh largest company in the USA had seen its market value collapse from $80 billion to less than $400 million. Its shares fell from a high of $89.50 in the previous year to a meagre 26 cents. How did it all go so wrong so quickly?

Enron was created in 1986, following the merger of two gas pipeline companies, Houston Natural Gas and InterNorth. As US energy and utility markets were deregulated, Enron diversified rapidly into alternative sources of energy supply such as electricity, and established interests in areas such as water. This diversification in Enron's interests was not restricted to the US market. Enron embarked upon a global growth strategy, which involved it acquiring interests in utilities throughout the world.

As Enron grew, it also shifted its business focus. It gradually reduced its role in gas and oil production, its traditional core business activities, and moved into the new world of online energy trading. This appeared to have been a wise move, as by November 1999 it had traded more than $1 trillion of electricity and gas online. Enron was, at this time, the largest business on the Internet. So what went wrong?

The weaknesses in Enron's growth strategy lay both in the speed of its expansion and, most crucially, in how its growth was financed. On declaring bankruptcy in December 2001, the scale of Enron's debts was revealed to be both massive and global. Creditors were estimated to be owed some $18.7 billion.

Clearly, Enron had financed an overwhelming part of its growth through borrowing. As a source of finance for business growth, this only becomes a problem if revenue

begins to fall and you are unable to meet the payments on the money owed. Given the public picture presented by Enron, and its apparent success, revenue and profits seemed to be guaranteed. The business was a clear winner. Such a picture would certainly have helped Enron to attract significant amounts of capital to fund its expansion plans.

However, everything was not as it seemed. Enron's financial position was precarious. In October 2001, Enron announced unexpected losses, which led it to reduce capital by $1.2 billion. A series of bad investments overseas were held to be the main reason for this decision. The announcement of losses was swiftly followed by the revelation that Enron was to be investigated by the US Securities and Exchange Commission for financial irregularities. It was subsequently revealed that through some accounting loophole Enron had been overstating its earnings since 1997 to the value of some $600 million. Predictably many of Enron's trading partners had by this stage begun to lose confidence in the business and started to pull out of deals.

At this point Dynegy, one of Enron's smaller rivals, agreed to buy the company for $9 billion in stock. However, as more losses were disclosed, and the need to get regulatory approval for the acquisition was established, Dynegy pulled out of the deal. Shareholder confidence had by this point totally collapsed and Enron's credit rating plummeted.

Enron's rise and fall reveals a tale of unsustainable growth and expansion that was bought on debt. It reveals not only the folly of such a strategy, but the need to have a strong system of financial regulation to ensure that a business's true financial position is reflected in its balance sheet.

1. *Why might a business favour borrowing, as a means of financing growth, over other sources of finance?*
2. *What are the strengths and weaknesses of diversification as a business growth strategy?*

supply some service rather than conduct the activity itself. Car manufacturers are major subcontractors. Given the multitude and complexity of components that are required to manufacture a car, the use of subcontractors to supply specialist items, such as brakes and lights, seems a logical way to organise the business.

Networks.   **Networks** are less formal than any of the above alliances. A network is where two or more businesses work collaboratively but without any formal relationship binding one to the other. Such a form of collaboration is highly prevalent in Japan. Rather than a formal contract regulating the behaviour of the partners to the agreement, their relationship is based upon an understanding of trust and loyalty.

Why form strategic alliances?

As a business expands, possibly internationally, it may well be advantageous to join with an existing player in the market. Such a business would have local knowledge and an established network of suppliers and distributors.

In addition, strategic alliances allow firms to share risk. The Channel Tunnel and the consortium of firms that built it is one such example. The construction of the Channel Tunnel was a massive undertaking and far too risky for any single firm to embark upon. With the creation of a consortium, risk was spread and the various consortium members were able to specialise in their areas of expertise.

They also allow firms to pool capital. Projects that might have prohibitively high start-up costs, or running costs, may become feasible if firms co-operate and pool their capital. In addition, an alliance of firms, with their combined assets and credibility, may find it easier to generate finance, whether from investors in the stock market or from the banking sector.

The past 25 years have seen a flourishing of strategic alliances. They have become a key growth strategy for business both domestically and internationally. They are seen as a way of expanding business operations quickly without the difficulties associated with the more aggressive approach of acquisition or the more lengthy process of merger.

Growth through going global

In many respects, a firm's global strategy is simply an extension of its strategy within its own domestic market. However, opening up to global markets can provide an obvious means for a business to expand its markets and spread its risks. It is also a means of reducing costs, whether

through economies of scale or from accessing cheap sources of supply or low-wage production facilities.

A firm's global growth strategy may involve simply exporting or opening up factories abroad, or it may involve merging with businesses abroad or forming strategic alliances. As barriers to trade and the international flow of capital have come down, so more and more businesses have sought to become multinational. The result is that the global business environment has tended to become more and more competitive.

Equilibrium for a growth-maximising firm

What will a growth-maximising firm's price and output be? Unfortunately there is no simple formula for predicting this.

In the short run, the firm may choose the profit-maximising price and output – so as to provide the greatest funds for investment. On the other hand, it may be prepared to sacrifice some short-term profits in order to mount an advertising campaign. It all depends on the strategy it considers most suitable to achieve growth.

In the long run, prediction is more difficult still. The policies that a firm adopts will depend crucially on the assessments of market opportunities made by managers. But this involves judgement, not fine calculation. Different managers will judge a situation differently.

One prediction can be made. Growth-maximising firms are likely to diversify into different products, especially as they approach the limits to expansion in existing markets.

Alternative maximising theories and the public interest

It is difficult to draw firm conclusions about the public interest.

In the case of sales revenue maximisation, a higher output will be produced than under profit maximisation, but the consumers will not necessarily benefit from lower prices, since more will be spent on advertising – costs that will be reflected in a higher price.

In the case of growth and long-run profit maximisation, there are many possible policies that a firm could pursue. To the extent that a concern for the long run encourages firms to look to improved products, new products and new techniques, the consumer may benefit from such a concern. To the extent, however, that growth encourages a greater level of industrial concentration through merger, the consumer may lose from the resulting greater level of monopoly power.

As with the traditional theory of the firm, the degree of competition a firm faces is a crucial factor in determining just how responsive it will be to the wishes of the consumer.

 How will competition between growth-maximising firms benefit the consumer?

Definition

Network An informal arrangement between businesses to work together towards some common goal.

| BOX 8.5 | MERGER ACTIVITY |

A worldwide perspective

What have been the trends, patterns and driving factors in mergers and acquisitions[1] (M&A) around the world over the past ten years? An overview is given in chart (a). The 1990s saw a rapid growth in M&A as the world economy boomed. Then with a slowing down in economic growth after 2000, M&A activity declined, both in value and in the number of deals, only to pick up again after 2003 as the world economy surged ahead again. By 2006, the value of M&A had reached a record $4 trillion, surpassing the previous record in 2000.

The 1990s

The early 1990s saw relatively low M&A activity as the world was in recession, but as world economic growth picked up, so worldwide M&A activity increased. Economic growth was particularly rapid in the USA, which became the major target for acquisitions.

There was also an acceleration in the process of 'globalisation'. With the dismantling of trade barriers around the world and increasing financial deregulation, international competition increased. Companies felt the need to become bigger in order to compete more effectively.

In Europe, M&A activity was boosted by the development of the Single Market, which came into being in January 1993. Companies took advantage of the abolition of trade barriers in the EU, which made it easier for them to operate on an EU-wide basis. As 1999 approached, and with it the arrival of the euro, so European merger activity reached fever pitch, stimulated also by the strong economic growth experienced throughout the EU.

By the end of the 1990s, annual worldwide M&A activity was three times the level of the beginning of the decade. At this time there were some very large mergers indeed. These included a €29.4 billion marriage of pharmaceutical companies Zeneca of the UK and Astra of Sweden in 1998, a €205 billion takeover of telecoms giant Mannesmann of Germany by Vodafone of the UK in 1999 and a €50.8 billion takeover of Orange of the UK by France Telecom in 2000.

Other sectors in which merger activity was rife included financial services and the privatised utilities sector. In the UK, in particular, most of the privatised water and electricity companies were taken over, with buyers attracted by the sector's monopoly profits. French and US buyers were prominent.

The 2000s

Then, with a worldwide economic slowdown after 2000, there was a fall in both the number and value of mergers throughout most of the world. What is more, the worldwide pattern of M&A activity was changing. Increasingly, both European and US companies were looking to other parts of the world to expand their activities. This is illustrated in chart (b).

The two major target regions have been (a) the rest of Europe, especially the ten countries joining the EU in 2004 plus Russia, and (b) Asian countries, especially India and China. These new markets have the twin attractions of rapidly growing demand and low costs, including cheap skilled labour and low tax rates.

M&A activity has become more widespread across industrial sectors. In the 1997–2000 boom, the

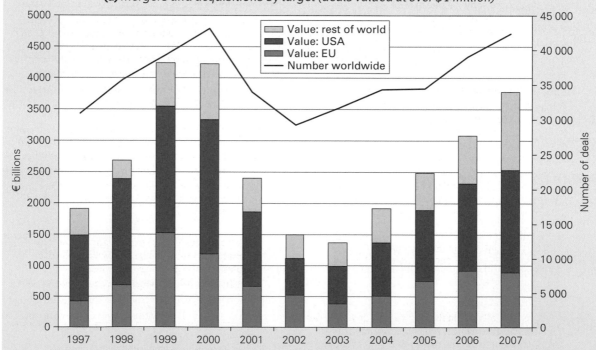

(a) *Mergers and acquisitions by target (deals valued at over $1 million)*

Value: rest of world
Value: USA
Value: EU
Number worldwide

Source: Mergers & Acquisitions Note, April (Commission of the European Communities, DG for Economics and Financial Affairs, 2007); various newspaper articles.

(b) *Mergers and acquisitions by target region (percentage of total number)*

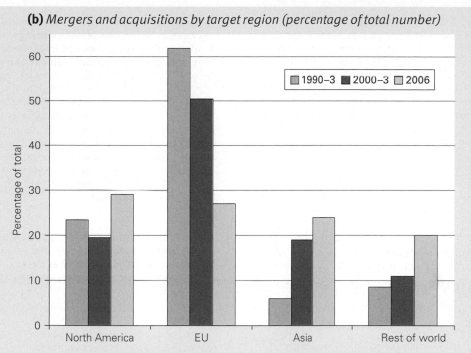

Source: Mergers & Acquisitions Note, June (Commission of the European Communities, DG for Economics and Financial Affairs, 2007).

companies targeted were predominantly in the telecoms and media sectors. The boom of the mid 2000s, by contrast, saw companies involved in M&A from across the range of industries. According to a 2006 survey of Chief Executive Officers around the world,[2] 47 per cent were actively engaged to some degree in M&A activity. The figure rises to 61 per cent for CEOs of large companies (those with revenue of more than $10 billion).

> Overwhelmingly, gaining access to new markets and customers is the main purpose given for cross-border M&A, cited by nearly two-thirds of CEOs. However, CEOs do not underestimate the difficulties faced in cross-border acquisition and integration. Cultural issues and conflicts, differences in regulations and unexpected costs are the main obstacles to cross-border M&A activity cited by CEOs. . . . The global winners of tomorrow are those that can change their outlook from local to global in the true sense, and learn to operate in a world now subject to far more influences from a wider array of sources than ever before.[3]

In 2008, as the world economy slid into recession, so M&A activity slowed. In the first nine months of 2008, global M&A activity was 25 per cent down on the same period in 2007.

Types of M&A activity

Some 12 per cent of M&A deals are 'hostile' (up from 2 per cent in 2000). In other words, the company being taken over does not want to be. The deals are often concluded after prolonged boardroom battles, with bosses of the acquiring company seeking opportunities to build

empires, and bosses of the target company attempting all sorts of manoeuvres to avoid being taken over. This may involve them seeking deals with alternative, more 'friendly' companies. Generally companies are increasingly using the services of investment banks to help them in the process of making or warding off deals.

Despite the growing number of horizontal mergers, there has also been a tendency for companies to become more focused, by selling off parts of their business that are not seen as 'core activities'. For example, not long after its takeover of Wellcome, Glaxo decided to concentrate on the production of prescription drugs, and as a consequence to sell its share of Warner Wellcome, which produced non-prescription drugs.

This trend of horizontal mergers and conglomerate and vertical de-mergers has allowed companies to increase their market power in those specific sectors where they have expertise. Consumers may gain from lower costs, but the motives of the companies are largely to gain increased market power – something of dubious benefit to consumers.

 Are the motives for merger likely to be different in a recession from those in a period of rapid economic growth? What would you predict about the pattern of mergers over the next few years, given the current state of the economy?

[1] By 'acquisitions' we mean takeovers or the acquiring of at least 5 per cent of a company's shares.
[2] *Global CEO Survey 2006*, PricewaterhouseCoopers.
[3] 'Global CEOs' Business Confidence Reaches Record Levels', PricewaterhouseCoopers Press Release, 24 January 2007.

Section summary

1. Rather than seeking to maximise short-run profits, a firm may take a longer-term perspective. It is very difficult, however, to predict the behaviour of a long-run profit-maximising firm, since (a) different managers are likely to make different judgements about how to achieve maximum profits and (b) demand and cost curves may shift unpredictably both in response to the firm's own policies and as a result of external factors.

2. Managers may seek to maximise their own utility, which, in turn, will depend on factors such as salary, job security, power within the organisation and the achieving of professional excellence. Given, however, that managerial utility depends on a range of variables, it is difficult to use the theory to make general predictions of firms' behaviour.

3. Managers may gain utility from maximising sales revenue. They will still have to ensure that a satisfactory level of profit is achieved, however. The output of a firm which seeks to maximise sales revenue will be higher than that for a profit-maximising firm. Its level of advertising will also tend to be higher. Whether price will be higher or lower depends on the relative effects on demand and cost of the additional advertising.

4. Many managers aim for maximum growth of their organisation, believing that this will help their salaries, power, prestige, etc.

5. Growth may be by internal expansion. This can be financed by ploughing back profits, by share issue, or by borrowing. Whichever method a firm uses, it will require sufficient profits to avoid becoming vulnerable to a takeover.

6. Vertical integration can reduce a firm's costs through various economies of scale. It can also help to reduce uncertainty, as the vertically integrated business can hopefully secure supply routes and/or retail outlets.

7. Growth may be by merger. Mergers can be horizontal, vertical or conglomerate. Merger activity tends to occur in waves. Various motives have been suggested for mergers, including growth, economies of scale, market power, increased share values, reduction in uncertainty, and simply taking advantage of opportunities as they occur.

8. One means of achieving growth is through the formation of strategic alliances with other firms. They have the advantage of allowing easier access to new markets, risk sharing and capital pooling.

9. Many firms' growth strategy includes expansion abroad.

10. As with long-run profit-maximising theories, it is difficult to predict the price and output strategies of a growth-maximising firm. Much depends on the judgements of particular managers about growth opportunities.

11. Alternative aims will benefit the consumer to the extent that they encourage firms to develop new products and to find more efficient methods of production. They may be against the consumer's interest to the extent that they lead firms to engage in extensive advertising or to merge with a resulting increased concentration of market power.

8.3 MULTIPLE AIMS

Satisfising and the setting of targets

KI 22
p216

Large firms are often complex institutions with several departments (sales, production, design, purchasing, personnel, finance, etc.). Each department is likely to have its own specific set of aims and objectives, which may come into conflict with those of other departments. These aims in turn will be constrained by the interests of shareholders, workers, customers and creditors (collectively known as *stakeholders*), who will need to be kept sufficiently happy.

Definition

Stakeholders (in a company) People who are affected by a company's activities and/or performance (customers, employees, owners, creditors, people living in the neighbourhood, etc.). They may or may not be in a position to take decisions, or influence decision taking, in the firm.

In many firms, targets are set for production, sales, profit, stockholding, etc. If, in practice, target levels are not achieved, a 'search' procedure will be started to find what went wrong and how to rectify it. If the problem cannot be rectified, managers will probably adjust the target downwards. If, on the other hand, targets are easily achieved, managers may adjust them upwards. Thus the targets to which managers aspire depend to a large extent on the success in achieving *previous* targets. Targets are also influenced by expectations of demand and costs, by the achievements of competitors and by expectations of competitors' future behaviour. For example, if it is expected that the economy is likely to move into recession, sales and profit targets may be adjusted downwards.

TC 9
p105

If targets conflict, the conflict will be settled by a bargaining process between managers. The outcome of the bargaining, however, will depend on the power and ability of the individual managers concerned. Thus a similar set of conflicting targets may be resolved differently in different firms.

BOX 8.6   STAKEHOLDER POWER?

Who governs the firm?

KI 22
p216

The concept of the 'stakeholder economy' became fashionable in the late 1990s. Rather than the economy being governed by big business, and rather than businesses being governed in the interests of shareholders (many of whom are big institutions, such as insurance companies and pension funds), the economy should serve the interests of everyone. But what does this mean for the governance of firms?

The stakeholders of a firm include customers, employees (from senior managers to the lowest-paid workers), shareholders, suppliers, lenders and the local and national communities.

The supporters of a stakeholding economy argue that *all* these interest groups ought to have a say in the decisions of the firm. Trade unions or workers' councils ought to be included in decisions affecting the workforce, or indeed all company decisions. They could be represented on decision-making bodies and perhaps have seats on the board of directors. Alternatively, the workforce might be given the power to elect managers.

Banks or other institutions lending to firms ought to be included in investment decisions. In Germany, where banks finance a large proportion of investment, banks are represented on the boards of most large companies.

Local communities ought to have a say in any projects (such as new buildings or the discharge of effluent) that affect the local environment. Customers ought to have more say in the quality of products being produced: for example, by being given legal protection against the production of shoddy or unsafe goods.

Where interest groups cannot be directly represented in decision making, companies ought to be regulated by the government in order to protect the interests of the various groups. For example, if farmers and other suppliers to supermarkets are paid very low prices, then the purchasing behaviour of the supermarkets could be regulated by some government agency.

But is this vision of a stakeholder economy likely to become reality? Trends in the international economy suggest that the opposite might be occurring. The growth of multinational corporations, with their ability to move finance and production to wherever it is most profitable, has weakened the power of employees, local interest groups and even national governments.

Employees in one part of the multinational may have little in the way of common interests with employees in another. In fact, they may vie with each other: for example, over which plant should be expanded or closed down. What is more, many firms are employing a larger and larger proportion of casual, part-time, temporary or agency workers. With these new 'flexible labour markets', such employees have far less say in the company than permanent members of staff: they are 'outsiders' to decision making within the firm (see Box 9.8).

Also, the widespread introduction of share incentive schemes for managers (whereby managers are rewarded with shares) has increasingly made profits their driving goal. Finally, the policies of opening up markets and deregulation – policies that have been adopted by many governments round the world in recent years – have again weakened the power of many stakeholders.

Nevertheless, many firms in recent years have put greater emphasis on 'corporate social responsibility' (CSR), seeing it as important to have an ethical dimension to their business practices. Whether this is a genuine commitment to the interests of society, or simply an attempt to win a larger market by gaining a good public image, clearly varies from firm to firm. CSR and business ethics are explored in Case Study 8.3 in MyEconLab.

 Are customers' interests best served by profit-maximising firms, answerable primarily to shareholders, or by firms where various stakeholder groups are represented in decision making?

Organisational slack

Since changing targets often involves search procedures and bargaining processes and is therefore time-consuming, and since many managers prefer to avoid conflict, targets tend to be changed fairly infrequently. Business conditions, however, often change rapidly. To avoid the need to change targets, therefore, managers will tend to be fairly conservative in their aspirations. This leads to the phenomenon known as *organisational slack*.

When the firm does better than planned, it will allow slack to develop. This slack can then be taken up if the firm does worse than planned. For example, if the firm produces more than it planned, it will build stocks of finished goods and draw on them if subsequently production falls. It would not, in the meantime, increase its sales target or reduce its production target. If it did, and production then fell below target, the production department might not be able to supply the sales department with its full requirement.

Thus keeping targets fairly low and allowing slack to develop allows all targets to be met with minimum conflict.

Organisational slack, however, adds to a firm's costs. If firms are operating in a competitive environment, they may be forced to cut slack in order to survive. In the 1970s, many Japanese firms succeeded in cutting slack by using *just-in-time* methods of production. These involve keeping stocks to a minimum and ensuring that inputs are delivered

Definitions

Organisational slack Where managers allow spare capacity to exist, thereby enabling them to respond more easily to changed circumstances.

Just-in-time methods Where a firm purchases supplies and produces both components and finished products as they are required. This minimises stockholding and its associated costs.

as required. Clearly, this requires that production is tightly controlled and that suppliers are reliable. Many firms today have successfully cut their warehouse costs by using such methods. These methods are examined in Box 9.8.

Multiple goals: predictions of behaviour

Conservatism

Some firms may be wary of unnecessary change. Change is risky. They may prefer to stick with tried and tested practices. 'If it works, stick with it.' This could apply to pricing policies, marketing techniques, product design and range, internal organisation of the firm, etc.

If something does not work, managers will probably change it, but again they may be conservative and only try a cautious change: perhaps imitating successful competitors.

This safe, satisficing approach makes prediction of any given firm's behaviour relatively easy. You simply examine its past behaviour. Making generalisations about all such cautious firms, however, is more difficult. Different firms are likely to have established different rules of behaviour depending on their own particular experiences of their market.

Comparison with other firms

Managers may judge their success by comparing their firm's performance with that of rival firms. For example, growing market share may be seen as a more important indicator of 'success' than simple growth in sales. Similarly, they may compare their profits, their product design, their technology or their industrial relations with those of rivals. To many managers it is *relative* performance that matters, rather than absolute performance.

What predictions can be made if this is how managers behave? The answer is that it depends on the nature of competition in the industry. The more profitable, innovative and efficient are the competitors, the more profitable, innovative and efficient will managers try to make their particular firm.

The further ahead of their rivals that firms try to stay, the more likely it is that there will be a 'snowballing' effect, with each firm trying to outdo the other.

 Will this type of behaviour tend to lead to profit maximisation?

Satisficing and the public interest

Firms with multiple goals will be satisficers. The greater the number of goals of the different managers, the greater is the chance of conflict, and the more likely it is that organisational slack will develop. Satisficing firms are therefore likely to be less responsive to changes in consumer demand and changes in costs than profit-maximising firms. They may thus be less efficient.

On the other hand, such firms may be less eager to exploit their economic power by charging high prices, or to use aggressive advertising, or to pay low wages.

The extent to which satisficing firms do act in the public interest will, as in the case of other types of firm, depend to a large extent on the amount and type of competition they face, and their attitudes towards this competition. Firms that compare their performance with that of their rivals are more likely to be responsive to consumer wishes than firms that prefer to stick to well-established practices. On the other hand, they may be more concerned to 'manipulate' consumer tastes than the more traditional firm.

 Are satisficing firms more likely to suffer from X inefficiency (see Box 6.5) than firms which seek to maximise profit or sales revenue?

Section summary

1. In large firms, decisions are taken by or influenced by a number of different people, including various managers, shareholders, workers, customers, suppliers and creditors. If these different people have different aims, a conflict between them is likely to arise. A firm cannot maximise more than one of these conflicting aims. The alternative is to seek to achieve a satisfactory target level of a number of aims.

2. If targets were easily achieved last year, they are likely to be made more ambitious next year. If they were not achieved, a search procedure will be conducted to identify how to rectify the problem. This may mean adjusting targets downwards, in which case there will be some form of bargaining process between managers.

3. Life is made easier for managers if conflict can be avoided. This will be possible if slack is allowed to develop in various parts of the firm. If targets are not being met, the slack can then be taken up without requiring adjustments in other targets.

4. Satisficing firms may be less innovative, less aggressive and less willing to initiate change. If they do change, it is more likely to be in response to changes made by their competitors. Managers may judge their performance by comparing it with that of rivals.

5. Satisficing firms may be less aggressive in exploiting a position of market power. On the other hand, they may suffer from greater X inefficiency.

What is the typical procedure by which firms set prices? Do they construct marginal cost and marginal revenue curves (or equations) and find the output where they are equal? Do they then use an average revenue curve (or equation) to work out the price at that output?

As we saw in section 8.1, firms often do not have the information to do so, even if they wanted to. In practice, firms look for rules of pricing that are relatively simple to apply.

Cost-based pricing

One approach is *average cost or mark-up pricing*. Here producers work out the price by simply adding a certain percentage (mark-up) for profit on top of average costs (average fixed costs plus average variable costs).

$$P = AFC + AVC + \text{profit mark-up}$$

Choosing the mark-up

The level of profit mark-up on top of average cost will depend on the firm's aims: whether it is aiming for high or even maximum profits, or merely a target based on previous profit. It will also depend on the likely actions of rivals and their responses to changes in this firm's price and how these responses will affect demand.

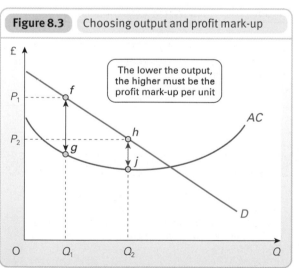

Figure 8.3 Choosing output and profit mark-up

The lower the output, the higher must be the profit mark-up per unit

If a firm could estimate its demand curve, it could then set its output and profit mark-up at levels that will avoid a shortage or surplus. Thus in Figure 8.3 it could choose a lower output (Q_1) with a higher mark-up (fg) or a higher output (Q_2) with a lower mark-up (hj), depending on its aims. If the firm could not estimate its demand curve, it could adjust its mark-up and output over time by a process

of trial and error, according to its success in meeting profit and sales aims.

The equilibrium price and output

Is it possible to identify an equilibrium price and output for the firm that sets its prices by adding a mark-up to average cost? To answer this we can identify a supply curve for the firm.

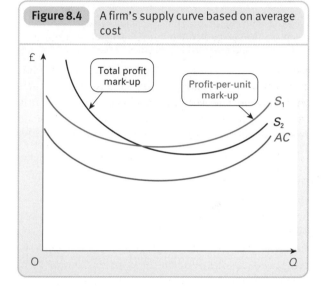

Figure 8.4 A firm's supply curve based on average cost

If a firm is aiming for a particular profit *per unit* of output and does not adjust this target, the firm's supply curve is derived by adding the mark-up to the *AC* curve. This is shown by curve S_1 in Figure 8.4. If, however, a firm is aiming for a particular level of *total* profit, and does not adjust this target, its supply curve will be like curve S_2. The greater the output, the less the profit per unit needs to be (and hence the less the mark-up) to give a particular level of total profit.

In either case, price and quantity can be derived from the intersection of demand and supply. Price and output will change if the demand or cost (and hence supply) curve shifts.

The main problem here is in predicting the demand curve, since it depends not only on consumer tastes but on the prices and behaviour of competitors. In practice, firms will usually base their assumptions about future sales on

Definition

Average cost or **mark-up pricing** Where firms set the price by adding a profit mark-up to average cost.

BOX 8.7   HOW DO COMPANIES SET PRICES?

KI 22
p216

In 1996 the Bank of England published a survey of price-setting behaviour in 654 UK companies.[1] Among other things, the survey sought to establish what factors influenced companies' pricing decisions. The results are shown in table (a).

Companies were asked to rank alternative methods of pricing of their main product . . . The most popular response was that prices were set with respect to market conditions. The top preference[2] for almost 40 per cent of respondents was that prices were set at the highest level that the market could bear. An additional 25 per cent of respondents stated that they set prices in relation to their competitors – this was the second choice most popular among companies . . .

The survey also confirmed the importance of company-specific factors. The first preference of about 20 per cent of respondents was that price was made up of a direct cost per unit plus a variable percentage mark-up . . . A further 17 per cent of companies, particularly retailing companies, stated that they priced on the basis of costs plus a fixed percentage mark-up.

Cost plus mark-ups tended to be more important for small companies . . . which cannot afford expensive market research.

The survey also sought to establish those factors which could cause prices to change – either up or down (see table (b)).

The Bank survey asked companies to rank those factors most likely to push prices up or down. It found

that there were substantial differences between the factors that influenced price increases and those that influenced price decreases. First, many more companies said that cost rises were likely to push prices up than said that cost reductions were likely to push prices down. Second, a rise in demand seemed less likely to lead to a price increase than a fall in demand was to lead to a price cut . . .

The importance of strategic interaction with competitors suggests that when contemplating a price cut, companies need to consider the chance of sparking off a price war . . . The finding that companies were much more likely to match rival price falls than they are to follow rival price rises appears to support the importance of strategic behaviour.

KI 21
p190

Recent surveys

Europe-wide survey. A European study of 2006 reported similar results to the 1996 UK survey. This European study brought together surveys conducted by nine Eurosystem national central banks on the price-setting behaviour of over 11 000 European firms[3].

The research found that price-setting behaviour is consistent across Europe, with mark-up pricing the dominant strategy in the eurozone and price discrimination widely practised. The asymmetries noted above with respect to price increases and decreases were also seen.

Further Bank of England survey. In 2008, the Bank of England conducted another survey of price-setting behaviour. This time 693 firms responded, with a spread

(a) How are prices determined?

	1st	%	2nd	%	3rd	%
Market level	257	39	140	21	78	12
Competitors' prices	161	25	229	35	100	15
Direct cost plus variable mark-up	131	20	115	18	88	14
Direct cost plus fixed mark-up	108	17	49	8	42	6
Set by customer	33	5	52	8	47	7
Regulatory agency	11	2	3	1	5	1

Source: How do UK companies set prices? *Bank of England Quarterly Bulletin*, May (Hall, S., Walsh, M. and Yates, T., 1996), Table D, p. 188.

(b) Factors leading to a rise or fall in price

Rise	Number[a]	%	Fall	Number[a]	%
Increase in material costs	421	64	Decrease in material costs	186	28
Rival price rise	105	16	Rival price fall	235	36
Rise in demand	101	15	Fall in demand	146	22
Prices never rise	26	4	Prices never fall	75	12
Increase in interest rates	18	3	Decrease in interest rates	8	1
Higher market share	14	2	Lower market share	69	11
Fall in productivity	5	1	Rise in productivity	22	3

[a] Numbers citing a scenario as most important.

Note: Top preferences only.

Source: How do UK companies set prices? *Bank of England Quarterly Bulletin*, May (Hall, S., Walsh, M. and Yates, T., 1996), Table E, p. 189.

(c) Most important factors leading to a rise or fall in price

Price rise	Rank	Price reduction	Rank
Increase in cost of labour	1	Actual decline in demand	1
Increase in the prices of fuel, raw materials or other inputs	2	Actual price reduction by domestic competitor(s)	2
Actual rise in demand	3	Expected decline in demand	3
Increasing costs arising out of regulation	4	Significant reduction in market share	4
Actual price increase by domestic competitor(s)	5	Expected price reduction by domestic competitor(s)	5
Expected rise in demand	6	Decrease in the prices of fuel, raw materials or other inputs	6

Source: Bank of England Quarterly Bulletin, Q4 (Bank of England, 2008).

across industry consistent with shares in UK GDP. The findings broadly supported those of the 1996 survey.

The survey revealed that different factors influence price rises and price falls. Higher costs – in particular, labour costs and raw materials – are the most important driver behind price rises, whereas lower demand and competitors' prices are the main factor resulting in price falls.[4]

Companies were asked to rank the importance of eleven factors in determining both price rises and price reductions. Table (c) shows the most important six in determining price changes (based on share of companies responding 'important' or 'very important').

Unlike the 1996 survey, companies were asked about *expected* changes in key variables, including demand, costs and rivals' prices. These were important determinants for many companies.

The survey confirmed that a majority of firms use mark-up pricing, with 58 per cent describing it as 'very important'. More than half of these firms *adjust* their mark-up according to market conditions. Competitors' prices and market demand are the two most important factors leading to a fall in price. The increase in the cost of labour and prices of fuel and raw materials are the two most important factors leading to a price rise.

Price flexibility

Evidence from the USA[5] and the eurozone study suggests that the frequency and magnitude of price changes varies enormously from product to product.

Generally speaking, the greater the share of raw materials in a product, the more often its price moves: petrol prices change, on average, in five months out of six in both America and Europe; the prices of fresh food are altered far more frequently than those of processed food. The prices of services are stickier than those of goods. This may be because services tend to be more labour-intensive than goods, and because wages are stickier (downwards, anyway) than other prices.[6]

For most products, prices change relatively infrequently in Europe, with retail prices changing on average just over once per year. In the USA, sales are much more common, especially with clothes, furniture

and processed food. The prices of services also change more frequently in the USA. In Europe services are more regulated and wages (a large proportion of the cost of most services) are less flexible.

How often individual prices move is an important question. Shifts in prices are like the traffic lights of an economy, signalling to people to buy more of this and less of that, to spend or to save, or to find new jobs. If the lights change readily, resources can be redirected smoothly; if they get stuck, so does the economy. In particular, if neither prices nor wages fall easily, the cost in output and jobs of reducing inflation can be high. Sticky prices also mean that an inflationary shock – an increase in oil prices, say – can take a long time to work its way through the system.[7]

As far as the magnitude of price changes is concerned, in both the USA and Europe, price changes are typically much bigger than the rate of inflation. In Europe, average price increases are 8 per cent and average price reductions 10 per cent.

1. Which of the following is more likely to be consistent with the aim of maximising profits: pricing on the basis of (a) cost per unit plus a variable percentage mark-up; (b) cost per unit plus a fixed percentage mark-up?
2. Explain the differences between the importance attached to the different factors leading to price increases and those leading to price reductions.
3. Why do you think percentage price changes are bigger than the rate of inflation?

[1] Simon Hall, Mark Walsh and Tony Yates, 'How do UK companies set prices?', *Bank of England Quarterly Bulletin*, May 1996.
[2] Companies were able to show more than one response as their top preference. This means the total percentage of companies expressing first preferences for all of the explanations of price determination exceeds 100%.
[3] Silvia Fabiani et al., 'What firms' surveys tell us about price-setting behavior in the euro area', *International Journal of Central Banking*, September 2006.
[4] Jennifer Greenslade and Miles Parker, 'Price-setting behaviour in the United Kingdom', *Bank of England Quarterly Bulletin*, 2008 Q4.
[5] Emi Nakamura and Jón Steinsson, 'Five facts about prices: a reevaluation of menu cost models', Harvard University, May 2007.
[6] 'Sticky situations', *The Economist*, 9 Nov 2006.
[7] *Ibid.*

current figures, add a certain percentage to allow for growth in demand and then finally adjust this up or down if they decide to change the mark-up.

Variations in the mark-up

In most firms, the mark-up is not rigid. In expanding markets, or markets where firms have monopoly/oligopoly power, the size of the mark-up is likely to be greater. In contracting markets, or under conditions of rising costs and constant demand, a firm may well be forced to accept lower profits and thus reduce the mark-up.

Multi-product firms often have different mark-ups for their different products depending on their various market conditions. Such firms will often distribute their overhead costs unequally between their products. The potentially most profitable products, often those with the least elastic demands, will probably be required to make the greatest contribution to overheads.

The firm is likely to take account of the actions and possible reactions of its competitors. It may well be unwilling to change prices when costs or demand change, for fear of the reactions of competitors (see the discussion of kinked demand curve theory on pages 199–200). If prices are kept constant but costs change, either due to a movement along the *AC* curve in response to a change in demand, or due to a shift in the *AC* curve, the firm must necessarily change the size of the mark-up.

All this suggests that, whereas the mark-up may well be based on a target profit, firms are often prepared to change their target and hence their mark-up, according to market conditions.

1. *If the firm adjusts the size of its mark-up according to changes in demand and the actions of competitors, could its actions approximate to setting price and output where MC = MR?*
2. *Some firms set their prices by adding a mark-up to average variable cost (the mark-up would be larger to include an element to cover fixed cost). Why might this make pricing easier for the firm? (See Box 5.6.)*

---

*LOOKING AT THE MATHS

Using a mark-up approach to find the profit-maximising price

Could the firm use a mark-up approach to set the *profit-maximising* price? It could, provided it bases its mark-up on marginal cost (*MC*), rather than average cost, and provided it knows the price elasticity of demand ($P\epsilon_D$) for its product. The rule is:

$$P = \frac{MC}{1 + (1/P\epsilon_D)}$$

This is simply the formula for profit-maximising price that we derived in section 6.3 (see page 175), except that we have used *MC* rather than *MR* (where profits are maximised,

MC = *MR*). Proof of this formula is given in Maths Case 6.2 in MyEconLab.

Thus if *MC* = £10 and $P\epsilon_D = -5$, the firm should charge a price of

$$\frac{£10}{1 + (1/-5)} = \frac{£10}{1 - 1/5} = \frac{£10}{0.8} = £12.50$$

The weakness of this pricing rule is that it applies only at the profit-maximising output. If the firm is currently a long way from that output, *MC* and $P\epsilon_D$ may diverge considerably from the values that the firm should use in its calculation. If, however, the firm is producing relatively near to its profit-maximising output, the rule can give a price that is a close approximation to the profit-maximising price.

Section summary

1. Many firms set prices by adding a profit mark-up to average cost. This cost-plus pricing is most likely when firms are profit satisficers or when they do not have the information to find the price that will equate marginal cost and marginal revenue.
2. The mark-up could be based on achieving a target level of either *total* profit or profit per unit. In either

case, a supply curve can be derived by adding the corresponding mark-up to the average cost curve.
3. For firms keen to increase profit, the size of the mark-up can be varied as market conditions permit the target profit to be increased.

END OF CHAPTER QUESTIONS

1. Assume that a firm faces a downward-sloping demand curve. Draw a diagram showing the firm's *AR, MR, AC* and *MC* curves. (Draw them in such a way that the firm can make supernormal profits.) Mark the following on the diagram:

   (a) The firm's profit-maximising output and price.

   (b) Its sales-revenue-maximising output and price.

   (c) Its sales-maximising output and price (subject to earning at least normal profit).

   Could the answer to (a) and (b) ever be the same?

   Could the answer to (b) and (c) ever be the same?

2. Would it be possible for firms to calculate their maximum-profit output if they did not use marginal cost and marginal revenue concepts?

3. What is meant by the principal–agent problem? Give two examples of this problem that you have come across in your own experience.

4. 'A firm will always prefer to make more profit rather than less.' Do you agree with this statement? Is it compatible with alternatives to the profit-maximising theory of the firm?

5. A firm under monopoly or oligopoly that aims to maximise sales revenue will tend to produce more than a firm that aims to maximise profits. Does this conclusion also apply under (a) perfect competition and (b) monopolistic competition, given that there is freedom of entry?

6. What are the potential costs and benefits of mergers to (a) shareholders; (b) managers; (c) customers?

7. Why is it difficult to test the assumption that firms seek to maximise *long-run* profits?

8. Do behavioural theories of the firm allow us to make any predictions about firms' prices and output?

9. Is mark-up pricing likely to benefit consumers?

Online resources

Additional case studies in MyEconLab

8.1 **The legal structure of firms**. A study of the different types of legal identity that a firm can take – from the sole proprietor to the partnership to the limited company.

8.2 **The Body Shop**. A case study of 'alternative business values'.

8.3 **Corporate social responsibility**. An examination of social responsibility as a goal of firms and its effect on business performance.

8.4 **The global information economy and strategic alliances**. The way forward for companies such as America Online?

8.5 **Downsizing and business organisation**. The case of IBM.

Maths Case 8.1 Sales revenue maximising with a profit constraint. Part 1: Using simple algebra to find the sales-revenue-maximising output.

Maths Case 8.2 Sales revenue maximising with a profit constraint. Part 2: Using the Lagrangian approach.

Websites relevant to this chapter

Numbers and sections refer to websites listed in the Web Appendix and hotlinked from this book's website at **www.pearsoned.co.uk/sloman**.

- For news articles relevant to this chapter, see the *Economics News Articles* link from the book's website.

- For general news relevant to alternative strategies, see websites in section A, and particularly A2, 3, 8, 9, 23, 24, 25, 26, 35, 36. See also A38, 39, 43 and 44 for links to newspapers worldwide, and A42 and 43 for links to economics news articles on particular search topics from newspapers worldwide.

- For student resources relevant to this chapter, see sites C1–7, 9, 10, 19.

- For information on mergers, see sites E4, 10, 18, 20.

- For data on small and medium-sized enterprises, see the database in B3 or E10.

- For information on pricing, see site E10 and the sites of the regulators of the privatised industries: E16, 19, 21, 22, 25.

- Sites I7 and 11 in the Business section contain links to *Business > Management > Organisational Management*.

- Site D3 has a simulation on sales revenue versus profit maximisation.

The Theory of Distribution of Income

CHAPTER MAP

9.1 Wage determination under perfect competition **237**
Perfect labour markets 237
The supply of labour 238
The demand for labour: the marginal
  productivity theory 242
Wages and profits under perfect competition 244
Equality and inequality under perfect competition 244
Who are the poor? Who are the rich? 245

9.2 Wage determination in imperfect markets **246**
Firms with market power in employing labour 246
Labour with market power 247
Firms and labour with market power 248
Collective bargaining 248
The efficiency wage hypothesis 251
Other labour market imperfections 255
Discrimination 256
Who are the poor? Who are the rich? 257

9.3 Capital and profit **258**
The non-human factors of production 258
The demand for capital services 259
The supply of capital services 259
Determination of the price of capital services 261
*Demand for and supply of capital for purchase 261
*Determination of the rate of interest 264
Capital and profit 264
Financing investment 264
The role of the stock market 265

9.4 Land and rent **268**
Rent: the reward to landowners 268
The price of land 268
Who are the poor? Who are the rich? 270

Why do film stars, footballers and stockbrokers earn such large incomes? Why, on the other hand, do cleaners, hospital porters and workers in clothing factories earn very low incomes? These are the types of question that the theory of distribution seeks to answer. It attempts to explain why some people are rich and others poor.

The explanation for differences in wages lies in the working of labour markets. In sections 9.1 and 9.2, we will consider how labour markets operate. In particular, we will focus on the determination of wage rates in different types of market: ones where employers are wage takers, ones where they can choose the wage rate, and ones where wage rates are determined by a process of collective bargaining. In the final two sections, we turn to capital and land and ask what determines the rewards that their owners receive.

This chapter examines the theory of income distribution by showing how the rewards to factors of production (labour, capital and land) depend on market conditions. Chapter 10, on the other hand, looks at income distribution in practice. It looks at inequality and poverty and at government policies to tackle the problem.

9.1 WAGE DETERMINATION UNDER PERFECT COMPETITION

Perfect labour markets

When looking at the market for labour, it is useful to make a similar distinction to that made in the theory of the firm: the distinction between perfect and imperfect markets. Although in practice few labour markets are totally perfect, many are at least approximately so.

The assumptions of perfect labour markets are similar to those of perfect goods markets. The main one is that everyone is a *wage taker*. In other words, neither employers nor employees have any economic power to affect wage rates. This situation is not uncommon. Small employers are likely to have to pay the 'going wage rate' to their employees, especially when the employee is of a clearly defined type, such as an electrician, a bar worker, a secretary or a porter. As far as employees are concerned, being a wage taker means not being a member of a union and therefore not being able to use collective bargaining to push up the wage rate.

The other assumptions of a perfect labour market are as follows:

Freedom of entry. There are no restrictions on the movement of labour. For example, workers are free to move to different jobs or to areas of the country where wage rates are higher. There are no barriers erected by, say, unions, professional associations or the government. Of course, it takes time for workers to change jobs and maybe to retrain. This assumption therefore applies only in the long run.

Definition

Wage taker An employer or employee who has no power to influence the market wage rate.

Perfect knowledge. Workers are fully aware of what jobs are available at what wages and with what conditions of employment. Likewise, employers know what labour is available and how productive that labour is.

Homogeneous labour. It is usually assumed that, in perfect markets, workers of a given category are identical in terms of productivity. For example, it would be assumed that all bricklayers are equally skilled and motivated.

 Which of the above assumptions do you think would be correct in each of the following cases?
(a) *Supermarket checkout operators.*
(b) *Agricultural workers.*
(c) *Crane operators.*
(d) *Economics teachers.*
(e) *Call-centre workers.*
(f) *Professional footballers.*

Wage rates and employment under perfect competition are determined by the interaction of the market demand and supply of labour. This is illustrated in Figure 9.1(a).

Generally it would be expected that the supply and demand curves slope the same way as in goods markets. The higher the wage paid for a certain type of job, the more workers will want to do that job. This gives an upward-sloping supply curve of labour. On the other hand, the higher the wage that employers have to pay, the less labour they will want to employ. Either they will simply produce less, or they will substitute other factors of production, like machinery, for labour. Thus the demand curve for labour slopes downwards.

Figure 9.1(b) shows how an individual employer has to accept this wage. The supply of labour to that employer is infinitely elastic. In other words, at the market wage W_m, there is no limit to the number of workers available to that

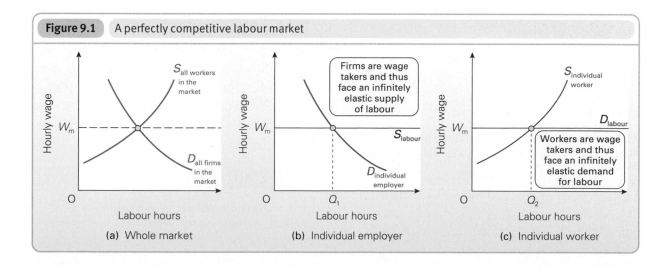

| Figure 9.1 | A perfectly competitive labour market |

(a) Whole market
(b) Individual employer
(c) Individual worker

BOX 9.1   **LABOUR AS A FACTOR OF PRODUCTION**   EXPLORING ECONOMICS

Is this any way to treat a worker?

The theory that wages depend on demand and supply is often referred to as the 'neoclassical' theory of wages. Treated as pure theory it is value free and does not involve moral judgements. It does not say, for example, whether the resulting distribution of income is fair or just.

In practice, however, the neoclassical theory is often used in such a way as to imply moral judgements. It is a theory that tends to be associated with the political right and centre: those who are generally in favour of markets and the capitalist system. Many on the political left are critical of its implied morality. They make the following points:

- By treating labour as a 'factor of production', it demeans labour. Labour is not the same as a piece of land or a machine.
- It somehow legitimises the capitalist system, where some people own land and capital whereas others have only their own labour. It seems to imply that people have a right to the incomes from their property even if that property is very unequally distributed among the population.
- It implies that labour has no rights to the goods that it produces. These goods are entirely the property of the employer, even though it is the workers who made them.

Karl Marx (1818–83) was highly critical of these values and the way that the capitalist system led to extremes of wealth and poverty. He argued that labour was the only true source of value. After all, it is labour that makes machines, labour that tills the land and makes it yield, labour that mines coal and other natural resources. Property, he argued, is therefore a form of theft. When capitalists extract profits from their enterprises, he continued, they are stealing part of the value produced by labour.

Neoclassical economists defend their position against the Marxist 'labour theory of value' by arguing the following:

- They are merely describing the world. If people want to draw pro-capitalist conclusions from their theory, then that is up to them.
- If the labour theory of value is used in any practical way to evaluate costs and output, it will lead to a misallocation of resources. Labour is not the only scarce resource. Land, for example, is also scarce and needs to be included in calculations of costs, otherwise it will be used wastefully.

 Assume that it is agreed by everyone that it is morally wrong to treat labour as a mere 'factor of production', with no rights over the goods produced. Does this make the neoclassical theory wrong?

employer (but no workers at all will be available below it: they will all be working elsewhere). At the market wage W_m, the employer will employ Q_1 hours of labour.

Figure 9.1(c) shows how an individual worker also has to accept this wage. In this case it is the demand curve for that worker that is infinitely elastic. In other words, there is as much work as the worker cares to do at this wage (but none at all above it).

We now turn to look at the supply and demand for labour in more detail.

The supply of labour

We can look at the supply of labour at three levels: the supply of hours by an individual worker, the supply of workers to an individual employer, and the total market supply of a given category of labour. Let us examine each in turn.

The supply of hours by an individual worker

Work involves two major costs (or 'disutilities') to the worker:

- When people work they sacrifice leisure.
- The work itself may be unpleasant.

Each extra hour worked will involve additional disutility. This *marginal disutility of work* (*MDU*) will tend to *increase* as people work more hours. There are two reasons for this.

First, the less leisure they have left, the greater is the disutility they experience in sacrificing a further hour of leisure. Second, any unpleasantness they experience in doing the job tends to increase due to boredom or tiredness.

This increasing marginal disutility (see Figure 9.2(a)) will tend to give an upward-sloping supply curve of hours by an individual worker (see Figure 9.2(b)). The reason is that, in order to persuade people to work more hours, a higher hourly wage must be paid to compensate for the higher marginal disutility incurred. This helps to explain why overtime rates are higher than standard rates.

Under certain circumstances, however, the supply of hours curve might bend backwards (see Figure 9.3). The reason is that when wage rates go up, two opposing forces operate on the individual's labour supply.

On the one hand, with higher wage rates people tend to work more hours, since time taken in leisure now involves a greater sacrifice of income and hence consumption. They

TC 1 p8

Definition

Marginal disutility of work The extra sacrifice/ hardship to a worker of working an extra unit of time in any given time period (e.g. an extra hour per day).

Figure 9.2 Marginal disutility of work and an individual's supply of labour

(a) The marginal disutility of
hours worked

(b) The supply of hours worked

Figure 9.3 Backward-bending supply curve of labour

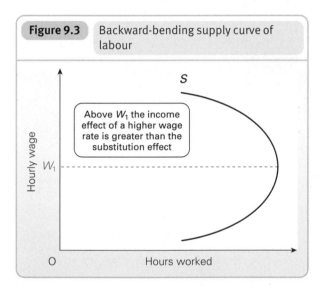

Above W_1 the income
effect of a higher wage
rate is greater than the
substitution effect

substitute income (i.e. work) for leisure. This is called the *substitution effect* of the increase in wage rates.

On the other hand, people may feel that with higher wage rates they can afford to work less and have more leisure. This is called the *income effect*.

The relative magnitude of these two effects determines the slope of the individual's supply curve. It is normally assumed that the substitution effect outweighs the income effect, especially at lower wage rates. A rise in the wage rate acts as an incentive: it encourages a person to work more hours. It is possible, however, that the income effect might

outweigh the substitution effect. Particularly at very high wage rates people say 'There's not so much point now in doing overtime. I can afford to spend more time at home.'

If the wage rate becomes high enough for the income effect to dominate, the supply curve will begin to slope backwards. This occurs above a wage rate of W_1 in Figure 9.3.

These considerations are particularly important for a government considering tax cuts. The Conservative governments of the 1980s argued that cuts in income taxes are like giving people a pay rise, and thus provide an incentive for people to work harder. This analysis is only correct, however, if the substitution effect dominates. If the income effect dominates, people will work *less* after the tax cut. These questions are examined in Chapter 10.

The supply of labour to an individual employer

Under perfect competition, the supply of labour to a particular firm will be perfectly elastic, as in Figure 9.1(b). The firm is a 'wage taker' and thus has no power to influence wages. Take the case of a small firm that wishes to employ a temporary typist via a secretarial agency. It has to pay the 'going rate', and presumably will be able to employ as many typists as it likes (within reason) at that wage rate.

The market supply of a given type of labour

This will typically be upward sloping, as in Figure 9.1(a). The higher the wage rate offered in a particular type of job, the more people will want to do that job.

KI 7
p33

Definitions

Substitution effect of a rise in wage rates Workers will tend to substitute income for leisure as leisure now has a higher opportunity cost. This effect leads to *more* hours being worked as wage rates rise.

Income effect of a rise in wage rates Workers get a higher income for a given number of hours worked and may thus feel they need to work *fewer* hours as wage rates rise.

*BOX 9.2 USING INDIFFERENCE CURVE ANALYSIS TO DERIVE THE INDIVIDUAL'S SUPPLY CURVE OF LABOUR

Indifference curve analysis (see section 4.3) can be used to derive the individual's supply curve of labour. The analysis can show why the supply curve may be backward bending.

Assume that an individual can choose the number of hours to work and has twelve hours a day to divide between work and leisure (the remaining twelve being for sleep, shopping, travelling, etc.). In the diagram, with an hourly wage rate of £5, budget line B_1 shows all the possible combinations of daily income and leisure hours. For example, at point x the individual has an income of £40 by working eight hours and having four hours of leisure.

The choice of hours worked at different wage rates

At an hourly wage of £10, the budget line becomes B_2, and at an hourly wage of £12.50 it becomes B_3.

The diagram also shows three indifference curves. Each indifference curve shows all those combinations of income and leisure that give the individual a particular level of utility. The curves are bowed in towards the origin, showing that increasingly higher incomes are necessary to compensate for each hour of leisure sacrificed. Curve I_3 shows a higher level of utility than I_2, and I_2 a higher level than I_1.

At a wage rate of £5 per hour, the individual can move along budget line B_1. Point x shows the highest level of utility that can be achieved. The individual thus supplies eight hours of labour (and has four hours of leisure).

At the higher wage rate of £10 per hour, the individual is now on budget line B_2 and maximises utility at point y by working nine hours. Thus the higher wage has encouraged the individual to work one more hour. So far, then, the individual's supply curve would be upward sloping: a higher wage rate leads to more labour hours supplied.

At the still higher wage rate of £12.50 per hour, the individual is on budget line B_3, and now maximises utility at point z. But this means that only eight hours are now worked. The supply curve has begun to bend backwards. In other words, the individual is now in a position to be able to afford to take more time off in leisure. The income effect has begun to offset the substitution effect.

1. *Using the analysis developed in Chapter 4, try to show the size of the income and substitution effects when moving from point x to point y and from point y to point z.*
2. *Illustrate on an indifference diagram the effect on the hours a person works of (a) a cut in the rate of income tax; (b) an increase in child benefit (assuming the person has children).*

The *position* of the market supply curve of labour depends on the number of people willing and able to do the job at each given wage rate. This depends on three things:

- The number of qualified people. Of course if the job is unskilled then a large number of people will be 'qualified'.
- The non-wage benefits or costs of the job, such as the pleasantness or otherwise of the working environment, job satisfaction or dissatisfaction, status, power, the degree of job security, holidays, perks and other fringe benefits.
- The wages and non-wage benefits in alternative jobs.

A change in the wage rate will cause a movement along the supply curve. A change in any of these other three determinants will shift the whole curve.

 Which way will the supply curve shift if the wage rates in alternative jobs rise?

The elasticity of the market supply of labour

How responsive will the supply of labour be to a change in the wage rate? If the market wage rate goes up, will a lot more labour become available or only a little? This responsiveness (elasticity) depends on (a) the difficulties and costs of changing jobs and (b) the time period under consideration.

Another way of looking at the elasticity of supply of labour is in terms of the **mobility of labour**: the willingness and ability of labour to move to another job, whether in a

Definition

Mobility of labour The willingness and ability of labour to move to another job.

BOX 9.3   **IMMIGRATION AND THE UK LABOUR MARKET**

Free movement of people and the single European market

Eight former communist states (the 'A8' or 'Accession 8' countries) joined the European Union in May 2004. Many of the existing members, however, decided not to open up their labour markets fully to workers from these countries for fear of being overwhelmed by an inflow of economic migrants.

But the UK, alongside some others including Sweden and Ireland, chose to adopt an open borders policy, allowing workers from countries including Poland, Slovakia and the Czech Republic to take up jobs. There would be no requirement to seek work permits, although a Workers Registration Scheme (WRS) was set up to allow the UK to monitor the numbers coming into the country.

The expansion of the EU did raise questions about the impact on the UK labour market, and concerns were raised by those who predicted that an inflow of workers would result in increased unemployment and lower wages. Other issues raised included the view that immigrants would be a drain on the economy, requiring increased spending on education, health care and benefits.

Those in favour of allowing eastern European workers free access pointed to the buoyant state of the UK economy at the time. Since the late 1990s the country had experienced a period of sustained growth, with low levels of unemployment and a growing number of unfilled job vacancies. The UK, like other western European countries, was facing an ageing population, with the ratio of workers to pensioners predicted to fall sharply over the next two decades. Immigration was seen as one solution to this problem.

In the three years following the accession of the A8 countries, the UK saw very substantial inflows of workers; by 2007 over 750 000 had registered on the WRS. These figures were much higher than the original projections of

around 13 000 per year. The UK responded restrictions on workers from the next two count the EU (in January 2007), Bulgaria and Romania. Wo from these countries were granted work permits only in sectors where there was a skills shortage.

Those coming in were employed across a range of sectors including hospitality and catering, agriculture, health and manufacturing. Around two-thirds were from Poland and the majority were young and brought no dependants with them, easing fears that they would be a burden on the welfare state. However, by 2007 higher inflation, increasing wages in Poland and the weakening value of the pound combined to make the UK less attractive, and the numbers arriving started to fall.

There have been a number of studies attempting to quantify the impact of immigration on the economy. At the microeconomic level we would expect an increase both in labour supply and in the elasticity of supply as the pool of available workers expands to include those across Europe. A 2007 Ernst & Young study,[1] suggested that there had been a positive effect on growth. Peter Spencer, chief economic adviser to the ITEM Club, explained, 'Without a million and a half foreign workers since 1997 the UK economy would have suffered slower GDP growth, higher inflation and interest rates.'

Draw a diagram illustrating the UK's decision to open up labour markets to workers from the A8 countries. Show the situation both before and after. Consider both the position and slope of the labour supply curve and the impact on the number employed and on wages. Would you expect there to be any movement in the demand for labour?

[1] 'Migration and the UK Economy', Ernst and Young ITEM Club, December 2007.

---

different location (geographical mobility) or in a different industry (occupational mobility). The mobility of labour (and hence the elasticity of supply of labour) will be higher when there are alternative jobs in the same location, when alternative jobs require similar skills, and when people have good information about these jobs. It is also much higher in the long run, when people have the time to acquire new skills and when the education system has time to adapt to the changing demands of industry.

If the demand for a particular category of worker increases, the wage rate will rise. The more inelastic the supply of labour, the higher the rise will be. Workers already employed in that industry will get the benefit of that rise, even though they are doing the same job as before. They are now earning a premium above the wage that was necessary to attract them into the industry in the first place. This premium is called *economic rent*. Case Study 9.1 in MyEconLab explores this concept and its relationship with the elasticity of supply of labour.

1. *Assume that there is a growing demand for computer programmers. As a result more people train to become programmers. Does this represent a rightward shift in the supply curve of programmers, or merely the supply curve becoming more elastic in the long run, or both? Explain.*
2. *Which is likely to be more elastic, the supply of coal miners or the supply of shop assistants? Explain.*

Definition

Economic rent The excess that a factor of production is paid over the amount necessary to keep it in its current employment.

mand for labour: the marginal
ductivity theory

traditional 'neoclassical' theory of the firm assumes that firms aim to maximise profits. The same assumption is made in the neoclassical theory of labour demand. This theory is generally known as the **marginal productivity theory**.

The profit-maximising approach

How many workers will a profit-maximising firm want to employ? The firm will answer this question by weighing up the costs of employing extra labour against the benefits. It will use exactly the same principles as in deciding how much output to produce.

In the goods market, the firm will maximise profits where the marginal cost of an extra unit of *goods* produced equals the marginal revenue from selling it: $MC = MR$.

In the labour market, the firm will maximise profits where the marginal cost of employing an extra *worker* equals the marginal revenue that the worker's output earns for the firm: MC of labour = MR of labour. The reasoning is simple. If an extra worker adds more to a firm's revenue than to its costs, the firm's profits will increase. It will be worth employing that worker. But as more workers are employed, diminishing returns to labour will set in (see page 125). Each extra worker will produce less than the previous one, and thus earn less revenue for the firm. Eventually the marginal revenue from extra workers will fall to the level of their marginal cost. At that point, the firm will stop employing extra workers. There are no additional profits to be gained. Profits are at a maximum.

Measuring the marginal cost and revenue of labour

Marginal cost of labour (MC$_L$). This is the extra cost of employing one more worker. Under perfect competition, the firm is too small to affect the market wage. It faces a horizontal supply curve (see Figure 9.1(b) on page 237). Thus the additional cost of employing one more person will simply be the wage: $MC_L = W$.

Marginal revenue of labour (MRP$_L$). The marginal revenue that the firm gains from employing one more worker is called the **marginal revenue product** of labour. The MRP_L is found by multiplying two elements – the *marginal physical*

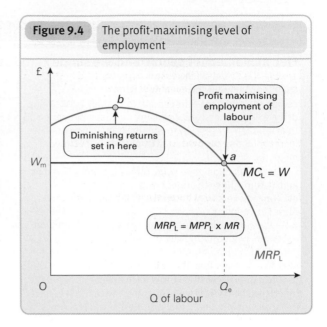

Figure 9.4 The profit-maximising level of employment

product of labour (MPP_L) and the marginal revenue gained by selling one more unit of output (MR):

$$MRP_L = MPP_L \times MR$$

The MPP_L is the extra output produced by the last worker. Thus if the last worker produces 100 tonnes of output per week (MPP_L), and if the firm earns an extra £2 for each additional tonne sold (MR), then the worker's MRP is £200. This extra worker is adding £200 to the firm's revenue.

The profit-maximising level of employment for a firm

The MPP curve was illustrated in Figure 5.3 (see page 134). As more workers are employed, there will come a point when diminishing returns set in (point *b*). The MPP_L curve thus slopes down after this point. The MRP_L curve will be a similar shape to the MPP_L curve, since it is merely being multiplied by a constant figure, MR. (Under perfect competition MR equals P and does not vary with output.) The MRP_L curve is illustrated in Figure 9.4, along with the MC_L 'curve'.

 Why is the MC$_L$ curve horizontal?

Definitions

Marginal productivity theory The theory that the demand for a factor depends on its marginal revenue product.

Marginal revenue product (of a factor) The extra revenue that a firm earns from employing one more unit of a variable factor: $MRP_{factor} = MPP_{factor} \times MR_{good}$.

*LOOKING AT THE MATHS

The marginal product of labour can be expressed using calculus. It is the rate of increase in output of good X with respect to changes in the quantity of labour:

$$MPP_L = \frac{\partial X}{\partial L}$$

The marginal revenue product of labour is thus given by

$$MPP_L = MR\frac{\partial X}{\partial L}$$

Profits are maximised at the level of employment (L) where $W = MRP_L$: i.e. where

$$W = MR\frac{\partial X}{\partial L} \tag{1}$$

We can easily move from this to the level of profit-maximising *output* of good X (where $MC = MR$). Rearranging equation (1), we get

$$\frac{W}{\partial X/\partial L} = MR \tag{2}$$

But, assuming that labour is the only variable factor, marginal cost (of output) is the extra cost of employing labour (the only extra cost) *per unit of output*. In other words:

$$MC = \frac{W}{\partial X/\partial L} \tag{3}$$

i.e.

$$MC = MR$$

Thus, not surprisingly, the profit-maximising employment of labour (where $W = MRP_L$) will yield the profit-maximising output (where $MC = MR$).

Figure 9.5 Deriving the fi
labour

 TC 8
p100

Profits will be maximised at an employment level of Q_e, where MC_L (i.e. W) = MRP_L. Why? At levels of employment below Q_e, MRP_L exceeds MC_L. The firm will increase profits by employing more labour. At levels of employment above Q_e, MC_L exceeds MRP_L. In this case, the firm will increase profits by reducing employment.

Derivation of the firm's demand curve for labour

No matter what the wage rate, the quantity of labour demanded will be found from the intersection of W and MRP_L (see Figure 9.5). At a wage rate of W_1, Q_1 labour is demanded; at W_2, Q_2 is demanded; at W_3, Q_3 is demanded.

Thus the MRP_L curve will show the quantity of labour employed at each wage rate. But this is just what the demand curve for labour shows. Thus the MRP_L curve is the demand curve for labour.

There are three determinants of the demand for labour:

- The wage rate. This determines the position *on* the demand curve. (Strictly speaking, we should refer here to the wage rate determining the 'quantity demanded' rather than the 'demand'.)
- The productivity of labour (MPP_L). This determines the position *of* the demand curve.

- The demand for the good. The higher the market demand for the good, the higher will be its market price, and hence the higher will be the MR, and thus the MRP_L. This too determines the position of the demand curve. It shows how the demand for labour (and other factors) is a **derived demand**: i.e. one derived from the demand for the good. For example, the higher the demand for houses, and hence the higher their price, the higher will be the demand for bricklayers.

A change in the wage rate is represented by a movement *along* the demand curve for labour. A change in the productivity of labour or the demand for the good *shifts* the curve.

Derivation of the industry demand curve for labour

This is not simply the sum of the demand curves of the individual firms. The firm's demand curve is based on a constant P and MR, no matter how many workers the firm employs (this is one of the assumptions of perfect competition). In Figure 9.6, when the wage rate falls from W_1 to W_2 the firm will employ more labour by moving from a to b along its demand curve MRP_1.

The trouble with this analysis is that when the wage rate falls, it will affect *all* employers. They will all want to employ more labour. But when they do, the total industry output will increase, and hence P (and MR) will be pushed down. This will shift the firm's MRP curve to the left and lead to a lower level of employment at point c. Therefore, when we allow for the effect of lower wages on the market price of the good, the firm's demand curve for labour will be the *green* line passing through points a and c.

Definition

Derived demand Demand for a factor of production that depends on the demand for the good that uses it.

Using the firm's demand curves for labour to derive the industry demand curves for labour

The industry demand curve for labour is derived from the line connecting points *a* and *c*

Thus the *industry* demand curve for labour is the (horizontal) sum of the *green* lines for each firm, and is therefore less elastic than the firm's MRP curve.

What will determine the elasticity of this curve?

The elasticity of demand for labour

The elasticity of demand for labour (with respect to changes in the wage rate) will be greater:

KI 9
p67

- The greater the price elasticity of demand for the good. A fall in W leads to higher employment and more output. This will drive P down. If the market demand for the good is elastic, this fall in P will lead to a lot more being sold and hence to a lot more people being employed.

KI 7
p33

- The easier it is to substitute labour for other factors and vice versa. If labour can be readily substituted for other factors, then a reduction in W will lead to a large increase in labour used to replace these other factors.
- The greater the elasticity of supply of complementary factors. If the wage rate falls, a lot more labour will be demanded if plenty of complementary factors can be obtained at little increase in their price.
- The greater the elasticity of supply of substitute factors. If the wage rate falls and more labour is used, less substitute factors will be demanded and their price will fall. If their supply is elastic, a lot less will be supplied and therefore a lot more labour will be used instead.
- The greater the wage cost as a proportion of total costs. If wages are a large proportion of total costs and the wage rate falls, total costs will fall significantly; therefore production will increase significantly, and so too will the demand for labour.
- The longer the time period. Given sufficient time, firms can respond to a fall in wage rates by reorganising their

production processes to make use of the now relatively cheap labour.

For each of the following jobs, check through the above list of determinants (excluding the last), and try to decide whether demand would be relatively elastic or inelastic: firefighters; telesales operators; carpenters; bus drivers; accountants; farm workers; car workers.

Wages and profits under perfect competition

The wage rate (W) is determined by the interaction of demand and supply in the labour market. It will be equal to the value of the output that the last person produces (MRP_L).

Profits to the individual firm arise from the fact that the MRP_L curve slopes downwards (diminishing returns). Thus the last worker adds less to the revenue of firms than was added previously by workers already employed.

If *all* workers in the firm receive a wage equal to the MRP of the *last* worker, everyone but the last worker will receive a wage less than their MRP. This excess of MRP_L over W of previous workers provides a surplus to the firm over its wages bill (see Figure 9.7). Part of this will be required for paying non-wage costs; part will be profits for the firm.

Perfect competition between firms ensures that profits are kept down to *normal* profits. If the surplus over wages is such that *supernormal* profits are made, new firms will enter the industry. The price of the good (and hence MRP_L) will fall, and the wage rate will be bid up, until only normal profits remain.

Equality and inequality under perfect competition

The mythical world of perfect wage equality

Under certain very strict assumptions, a perfectly competitive market will lead to perfect equality of wage rates. All workers will earn exactly the same. These strict assumptions are as follows:

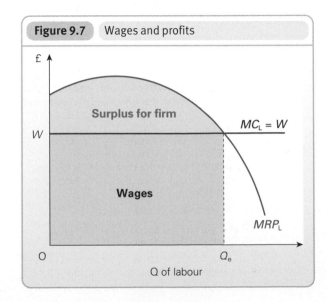

Figure 9.7 Wages and profits

- All workers have identical abilities.
- There is perfect mobility of labour.
- All jobs are equally attractive to all workers.
- All workers and employers have perfect knowledge.
- Wages are determined entirely by demand and supply.

Given these assumptions, if consumer demand rose in any industry, the demand for labour would rise. As a result, wage rates would begin to rise. Immediately workers would flood into this industry, attracted by the higher wages. Very quickly, then, wage rates would be competed back down to the level in the rest of the economy. Likewise if wage rates began to fall in any industry, workers would leave, thereby eliminating any labour surplus and preventing the fall in wage rates.

Under these conditions, therefore, not only would the labour supply curve to a *firm* be infinitely elastic, but so too would the labour supply curve to each *industry* at the universal wage rate.

Of course, in the real world these conditions do not hold. Huge inequalities of wages exist. A financial dealer in the City can earn 50 times as much as a shop assistant. But even if markets *were* perfect, inequality would be expected to persist.

Causes of inequality under perfect competition

In the short run, inequality will exist under perfect competition because of the time it takes for changes in demand and supply conditions to bring new long-run equilibria. Thus expanding industries will tend to pay higher wage rates than contracting industries.

But even after enough time has elapsed for all adjustments to be made to changes in demand and supply, long-run wage differentials will still exist for the following reasons:

- Workers do not have identical abilities.
- Workers are not perfectly mobile, even in the long run. People have different preferences about where they want to live and the jobs they like to do.

- Jobs differ enormously in terms of the skills they require and in terms of their pleasantness or unpleasantness.

What is more, since demand and supply conditions are constantly changing, long-run general equilibrium throughout the economy will never be reached.

Who are the poor? Who are the rich?

The low paid will be those whose labour is in low demand or high supply. Low demand will be due to low demand for the good or low labour productivity. High supply will be due to low mobility out of industries in decline or to a surplus of people with the same skills or qualifications. Thus, for example, workers who possess few skills, are unfit, are working in contracting industries, do not want to move from the area and will not or cannot retrain, will be low paid.

The highly paid will be those whose labour is in high demand or low supply. Thus workers who possess skills or talents that are in short supply, especially if those skills take a long time for others to acquire, and those who are working in expanding industries, will tend to earn high wages.

Although the movement of labour from low-paid to high-paid jobs will tend to reduce wage differentials, considerable inequality will persist even under perfect competition. It is a fallacy, therefore, to believe that it is possible to eliminate poverty and inequality simply by 'freeing up' markets and encouraging workers to 'stand on their own feet' or 'get on their bikes'.

What is more, in the real world there exist many market imperfections. These tend to make inequality greater. These imperfections are examined in the next section.

Finally, income inequality under capitalism will also be due to unequal distribution of the ownership of land and capital. Even under perfect competition, considerable inequality will therefore exist if wealth is concentrated in the hands of the few.

Section summary

1. Wages in a perfect market are determined by supply and demand.

2. The supply curve of hours by an individual worker reflects the increasing marginal disutility of work. Its shape depends on the relative sizes of the substitution and income effects of a wage change. The substitution effect is positive. A higher wage encourages people to work more by substituting wages for leisure. The income effect, however, is negative. A higher wage makes people feel that they can afford to work less. If the income effect is bigger than the substitution effect, the supply curve for labour hours will bend backwards.

3. The supply of labour to a particular employer under perfect competition is infinitely elastic.

4. The market supply is typically upward sloping. Its elasticity depends on labour mobility.

5. The demand for labour depends on a worker's marginal revenue product. This is the extra revenue that a firm will gain from the output of an extra worker. The profit-maximising firm will continue taking on extra workers until MRP_L is equal to MC_L (= W under perfect competition).

6. The elasticity of demand for labour depends on the elasticity of demand for the good being produced, the ease of substituting labour for other factors and vice versa, the elasticity of supply of substitute and complementary factors, wages as a proportion of total costs, and the time period involved.

7. Although market forces will tend to lead to the elimination of differentials as workers move from low-paid to high-paid jobs, nevertheless inequality can persist even under perfect competition. People have different abilities and skills; people are not perfectly mobile; and jobs differ in their labour requirements.

8. Inequality is also caused by market imperfections and by unequal ownership of land and capital.

TC 3
p24

9.2 WAGE DETERMINATION IN IMPERFECT MARKETS

In the real world, firms and/or workers are likely to have the power to influence wage rates: they are not wage takers. This is one of the major types of labour market imperfection.

When a firm is the only employer of a certain type of labour, this situation is called a **monopsony**. The Post Office is a monopsony employer of postal workers. A monopsony is more likely to occur in a local market. Thus a factory may be the only employer of certain types of labour in that district. When there are just a few employers, this is called **oligopsony**.

Workers may have market power as members of unions. When a single union bargains on behalf of a certain type of labour, it is acting as a monopolist. When there is more than one union, they are oligopolists.

When a monopsonist employer faces a monopolist union, the situation is called **bilateral monopoly**.

Firms with market power in employing labour (monopsony, etc.)

KI 20
p164

Monopsonists (and oligopsonists too) are 'wage setters', not 'wage takers'. A large employer in a small town, for example, may have considerable power to resist wage increases or even to force wage rates down.

Such firms face an upward-sloping supply curve of labour. This is illustrated in Figure 9.8. If the firm wants to take on more labour, it will have to pay a higher wage rate to attract workers away from other industries. But conversely, by employing less labour it can get away with paying a lower wage rate.

The supply curve shows the wage rate that must be paid to attract a given quantity of labour. The wage it pays is the *average cost* to the firm of employing labour (AC_L). The supply curve is also therefore the AC_L curve.

The *marginal cost* of employing one more worker (MC_L) will be above the wage (AC_L). The reason is that the wage rate has to be raised to attract extra workers. The MC_L will thus be the new higher wage paid to the new employee *plus* the small rise in the total wages bill for existing employees: after all, they will be paid the higher wage too.

The profit-maximising employment of labour would be at Q_1, where $MC_L = MRP_L$. The wage paid would thus be W_1.

If this had been a perfectly competitive labour market,

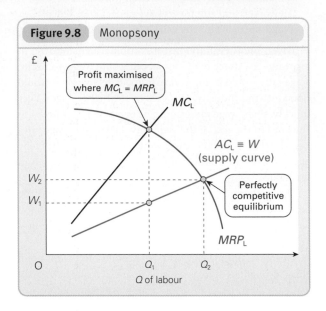

Figure 9.8 Monopsony

employment would have been at the higher level Q_2, with the wage rate at the higher level W_2, where $W = MRP_L$. What in effect the monopsonist is doing, therefore, is forcing the wage rate down by restricting the number of workers employed.

1. *The following table shows data for a monopsonist employer. Fill in the missing figures. How many workers should the firm employ if it wishes to maximise profits?*

Number of workers	Wage rate (£)	Total cost of labour (£)	Marginal cost of labour (£)	Marginal revenue product (£)
1	100	100		
			110	230
2	105	210		
			120	240
3	110	330		
4	115	. . .	. . .	240
5	120	. . .	. . .	230
6	125	. . .	. . .	210
7	130	. . .	. . .	190
8	135	. . .	. . .	170
9	140	. . .	. . .	150

2. *Will a monopsony typically also be a monopoly? Give examples of monopsonists that are not monopolists, and monopolists that are not monopsonists.*

Definitions

Monopsony A market with a single buyer or employer.

Oligopsony A market with just a few buyers or employers.

Bilateral monopoly Where a monopsony buyer faces a monopoly seller.

Labour with market power (union monopoly or oligopoly)

The extent to which unions will succeed in pushing up wage rates depends on their power and militancy. It also depends on the power of firms to resist and on their ability to pay higher wages. In particular, the scope for unions to gain a better deal for their members depends on the sort of market in which the employers are producing.

If the employers are producing under perfect or monopolistic competition, unions can raise wage rates only at the expense of employment. Firms are earning only normal profit. Thus if unions force up wage rates, the marginal firms will make losses and eventually leave the industry. Fewer workers will be employed. The fall in output will lead to higher prices. This will enable the remaining firms to pay a higher wage rate.

Figure 9.9 illustrates these effects. If unions force the wage rate up from W_1 to W_2, employment will fall from Q_1 to Q_2. There will be a surplus of people $(Q_3 - Q_2)$ wishing to work in this industry for whom no jobs are available.

The union is in a doubly weak position. Not only will jobs be lost as a result of forcing up the wage rate, but there is also a danger that the people who are unemployed as a result of the job losses might undercut the union wage, unless the union can prevent firms employing non-unionised labour.

Wage rates can be increased without a reduction in the level of employment only if, as part of the bargain, the productivity of labour is increased. This is called a ***productivity deal***. The *MRP* curve, and hence the demand curve in Figure 9.9, shifts to the right.

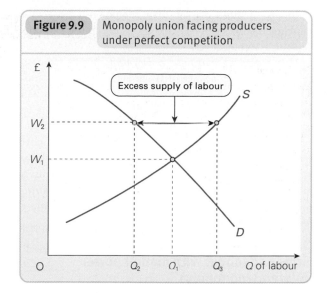

Figure 9.9 Monopoly union facing producers under perfect competition

Which of the following unions find themselves in a weak bargaining position for the above reasons?
(a) The seafarers' union (Nautilus)
(b) The shopworkers' union (USDAW)
(c) The National Union of Mineworkers
(d) The farm workers' union (part of the Transport and General Workers' Union)

Definition

Productivity deal Where, in return for a wage increase, a union agrees to changes in working practices that will increase output per worker.

BOX 9.4 **LIFE AT THE MILL** CASE STUDIES AND APPLICATIONS

Monopsony in Victorian times

A dramatic illustration of the effects of extreme monopsony power is that of the textile mill in nineteenth-century England. When a mill was the only employer in a small town, or when factory owners colluded as oligopsonists, and when there was no union to counterbalance the power of the employer, things could be very bad for the worker. Very low pay would be combined with often appalling working conditions.

Friedrich Engels described the life of the textile factory worker as follows:

> The factory worker is condemned to allow his physical and mental powers to become atrophied. From the age of eight he enters an occupation which bores him all day long. And there is no respite from this boredom. The machine works ceaselessly. Its wheels, belts and spindles hum and rattle ceaselessly in his ears, and if he thinks of taking even a moment's rest, the

overlooker is always there to punish him with a fine. It is nothing less than torture of the severest kind to which the workers are subjected by being condemned to a life-sentence in the factory, in the service of a machine which never stops. It is not only the body of the worker which is stunted, but also his mind. It would indeed be difficult to find a better way of making a man slow-witted than to turn him into a factory worker.[1]

1. *Why did competition between employers not force up wages and improve working conditions?*
2. *Were the workers making a 'rational economic decision' when they chose to work in such factories?*

[1] F. Engels, *The Condition of the Working Class in England*, translated by W. O. Henderson and W. H. Chaloner (Basil Blackwell, 1971), pp. 199–200.

In a competitive market, then, the union is faced with the choice between wages and jobs. Its actions will thus depend on its objectives.

If it wants to *maximise employment*, it will have to content itself with a wage of W_1 in Figure 9.9, unless productivity deals can be negotiated. At W_1, Q_1 workers will be employed. Above W_1 fewer than Q_1 workers will be *demanded*. Below W_1 fewer than Q_1 workers will be *supplied*.

If the union is more concerned with securing a higher wage rate, it may be prepared to push for a wage rate above W_1 and accept some reduction in employment. This is more likely if the reduction can be achieved through **natural wastage**. This is where people retire, or take voluntary redundancy, or simply leave for another job.

Firms and labour with market power (bilateral monopoly)

What happens when a union monopoly faces a monopsony employer? What will the wage rate be? What will the level of employment be? Unfortunately, economic theory cannot give a precise answer to these questions. There is no 'equilibrium' level as such. Ultimately, the wage rate and the level of employment will depend on the relative bargaining strengths and skills of unions and management.

Strange as it may seem, unions may well be in a stronger position to make substantial gains for their members when they are facing a powerful employer. There is often considerable scope for them to increase wage rates *without* this leading to a reduction in employment, or even for them to increase both the wage rate *and* employment. Figure 9.10 shows how this can be so.

Assume first that there is no union. The monopsonist will maximise profits by employing Q_1 workers at a wage rate of W_1. (Q_1 is where $MRP_L = MC_L$.)

What happens when a union is introduced into this situation? Wage rates will now be set by negotiation between unions and management. Once the wage rate has been agreed, the employer can no longer drive the wage rate down by employing fewer workers. If it tried to pay less than the agreed wage, it could well be faced by a strike, and thus have a zero supply of labour!

Similarly, if the employer decided to take on *more* workers, it would not have to *increase* the wage rate, as long as the negotiated wage were above the free-market wage: as long as the wage rate were above that given by the supply curve S_1.

The effect of this is to give a new supply curve that is horizontal up to the point where it meets the original

Definition

Natural wastage Where a firm wishing to reduce its workforce does so by not replacing those who leave or retire.

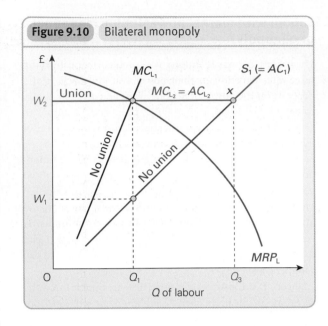

Figure 9.10 Bilateral monopoly

supply curve. For example, let us assume that the union succeeds in negotiating a wage rate of W_2 in Figure 9.10. The supply curve will be horizontal at this level to the left of point x. To the right of this point it will follow the original supply curve S_1, since to acquire more than Q_3 workers the employer would have to raise the wage rate above W_2.

If the supply curve is horizontal to the left of point x at a level of W_2, so too will be the MC_L curve. The reason is simply that the extra cost to the employer of taking on an extra worker (up to Q_3) is merely the wage rate: no rise has to be given to existing employees. If MC_L is equal to the wage, the profit-maximising level of employment ($MC_L = MRP_L$) will now be where $W = MRP_L$. At a negotiated wage rate of W_2, the firm will therefore choose to employ Q_1 workers.

What this means is that the union can push the wage rate right up from W_1 to W_2 and the firm will still *want* to employ Q_1. In other words, a wage rise can be obtained *without* a reduction in employment.

 If the negotiated wage rate were somewhere between W_1 and W_2, what would happen to employment?

The union could go further still. By threatening industrial action, it may be able to push the wage rate above W_2 and still insist that Q_1 workers are employed (i.e. no redundancies). The firm may be prepared to see profits drop right down to normal level rather than face a strike and risk losses. The absolute upper limit to wages will be that at which the firm is forced to close down.

Collective bargaining

Sometimes when unions and management negotiate, *both* sides can gain from the resulting agreement. For example, the introduction of new technology may allow higher

| BOX 9.5 | THE RISE AND DECLINE OF THE LABOUR MOVEMENT IN THE UK | CASE STUDIES AND APPLICATIONS |

Modern trade unionism had its birth with the industrial revolution of the eighteenth and nineteenth centuries. Unions were seen as a means of improving the lot of industrial workers, most of whom suffered low pay, long hours and poor working conditions. But with great hostility from employers and from the legal system, membership grew slowly. By the end of the nineteenth century, only just over 10 per cent of manual workers were in an effective union.

The big change came after the First World War. Many working men, on returning from France, began to demand that their sacrifice for their country should be rewarded. The trade union movement was seen as one way to improve wages and working conditions. Membership soared. By 1920, 45 per cent of the total labour force (8.3 million workers) were in trade unions.

But it was after the Second World War that the trade union movement in the UK really became established as a substantial economic and political force. This can be explained by three crucial trends:

- The growth in the public sector meant that government was itself becoming increasingly responsible for determining wages and conditions of service for many workers.
- In their attempt to control inflation in the 1960s and 1970s, governments sought to impose an 'incomes policy' constraining wage increases. To be successful, this required acceptance by the trade union movement.
- The philosophy of many post-war governments was to govern by consent. Social contracts and pacts, and tripartite discussions between government, employers and unions, gave the union movement considerable influence over economic decision making.

Union power grew steadily during the 1950s and 1960s, so much so that attempts were made by successive governments to curb its influence. However, such moves attracted fierce and widespread opposition, and as a result legislation was in many cases abandoned or modified. The trade union movement had by the late 1970s become very powerful with over 13 million members.

The election of the Conservative government in 1979 ushered in a new wave of trade union reform, eroding and removing many rights and privileges acquired by unions over the years. Trade union membership began to fall. Since 1979 it has fallen by over 5 million. This can be explained in part by the shift from a manufacturing to a service-based economy, since the services sector is far less unionised than manufacturing. The main explanation, however, lies in the attitudes of new firms to union recognition: in many cases a more aggressive management style and a highly competitive environment have made it virtually impossible for unions to gain bargaining rights.

With continued privatisation and the introduction of private-sector management practices, local pay bargaining and contracted-out services into many of the remaining parts of the public sector, trade unionism is still further under threat.

The future of the union movement is unclear. The creation of mega-unions is one possibility, as groups of unions merge in an attempt to retain some form of power and influence. For example, in 1993 a new union, UNISON, was created by an amalgamation of various public-sector unions. It has some 1.3 million members. Many unions have adopted a 'new realism', accepting single-union agreements and supporting flexible working practices and individualised pay packets based on performance (see Box 9.8). Some commentators have suggested that unions may become little more than advisers to individual employees on questions of law and rights, their influence over pay bargaining simply withering away. Unions are being forced to reconsider their role, however uncertain it may appear to be.

 What factors, other than the ones identified above, could account for the decline in union membership in recent years?

UK trade union membership as percentage of total employed plus unemployed

Sources: The Trade Union Movement in the UK 1992, Malthouse Press (Marsh, A. and Cox, B., 1992) and Trade Union Membership (BERR).

wages, improved working conditions and higher profits. Usually, however, one side's gain is the other's loss. Higher wages mean lower profits. Either way, both sides will want to gain the maximum for themselves.

In collective bargaining, there are various threats or promises that either side can make. Union *threats* might include strike action, **picketing**, **working to rule** or refusing to co-operate with management: for example, in the introduction of new technology. Alternatively, in return for higher wages or better working conditions, unions might *offer* no-strike agreements (or an informal promise not to take industrial action), increased productivity, reductions in the workforce, or long-term deals over pay.

In turn, employers might *threaten* employees with plant closure, **lock-outs**, redundancies or the employment of non-union labour. Alternatively, they might *offer*, in return for lower wage increases, various 'perks', such as productivity bonuses, profit-sharing schemes, better working conditions, more overtime, more holiday entitlement or more security of employment.

The outcome of negotiations. The success of a union in achieving its demands depends on its financial strength, the determination of its members and the level of support from other unions and the public in general. It also depends on the willingness of the firm to concede and on its profitability. Firms earning substantial supernormal profits are in a much better position to pay wage increases than firms operating in a highly competitive environment.

The wage settlement may be higher if the union represents only **core workers**. It may be able to secure a higher wage rate at the expense of non-members, who might lose their jobs or be replaced by part-time or temporary workers. The core workers can be seen as **insiders**. Their union(s) can prevent the unemployed – the **outsiders** – from competing wages down.

Industrial action imposes costs on both unions and firms. Unions lose pay. Firms lose revenue. It is usually in both sides' interests, therefore, to settle by negotiation. Nevertheless, to gain the maximum advantage, each side must persuade the other that it will carry out its threats if pushed.

The approach described so far has essentially been one of confrontation. The alternative is for both sides to concentrate on increasing the total net income of the firm by co-operating on ways to increase efficiency or the quality of the product. This approach is more likely when unions and management have built up an atmosphere of trust over time.

 Recall the various strategies that rival oligopolists can adopt. What parallels are there in union and management strategies?

The role of government in collective bargaining

The government can influence the outcome of collective bargaining in a number of ways. One is to try to set an example. It may take a tough line in resisting wage demands by public-sector workers, hoping thereby to persuade employers in the private sector to do likewise.

Alternatively, it could set up arbitration or conciliation machinery. For example, in the UK, the Advisory, Conciliation and Arbitration Service (ACAS) conciliates in over 1000 disputes each year.

Another approach is to use legislation. The government could pass laws that restrict the behaviour of employers or unions. It could pass laws that set a minimum wage rate (see Box 10.3), or prevent discrimination against workers on various grounds. Similarly, it could pass laws that curtail the power of unions. The UK Conservative governments between 1979 and 1997 put considerable emphasis on reducing the power of trade unions and making labour markets more 'flexible'. Several Acts of Parliament were passed. These included the following measures:

- Employees were given the right to join any union. This effectively ended **closed-shop** agreements.
- Secret postal ballots of the union membership were made mandatory for the operation of a political fund, the election of senior union officials, and strikes and other official industrial action.
- Political strikes, sympathy action and action against other non-unionised companies were made illegal.

Definitions

Picketing Where people on strike gather at the entrance to the firm and attempt to dissuade workers or delivery vehicles from entering.

Working to rule Workers do the bare minimum they have to, as set out in their job descriptions.

Lock-outs Union members are temporarily laid off until they are prepared to agree to the firm's conditions.

Core workers Workers, normally with specific skills, who are employed on a permanent or long-term basis.

Insiders Those in employment who can use their privileged position (either as members of unions or because of specific skills) to secure pay rises despite an excess supply of labour (unemployment).

Outsiders Those out of work or employed on a casual, part-time or short-term basis, who have little or no power to influence wages or employment.

Closed shop Where a firm agrees to employ only union members.

- Lawful action would be confined to that against workers' own direct employers, even to their own particular place of work. All *secondary action* was made unlawful.
- It was made unlawful for employers to penalise workers for choosing to join or refusing to join a trade union. It was also made unlawful for employers to deny employment on the grounds that an applicant does not belong to a union.

The effect of these measures was considerably to weaken the power of trade unions in the UK.

The efficiency wage hypothesis

We have seen that a union may be able to force an employer to pay a wage above the market-clearing rate. But wage rates above the equilibrium are not just the result of union power. It may well be in firms' interests to pay higher wage rates, even in non-unionised sectors.

One explanation for this phenomenon is the *efficiency wage hypothesis*. This states that the productivity of workers rises as the wage rate rises. As a result, employers are

---

Definitions

Secondary action Industrial action taken against a company not directly involved in a dispute (e.g. a supplier of raw materials to a firm whose employees are on strike).

Efficiency wage hypothesis The hypothesis that the productivity of workers is affected by the wage rate that they receive.

BOX 9.6   HOW USEFUL IS MARGINAL PRODUCTIVITY THEORY?

EXPLORING ECONOMICS

Reality or the fantasy world of economists?

The marginal productivity theory of income distribution has come in for a lot of criticisms. Are they justified?

To start with, you cannot criticise something unless you know precisely what it is you are criticising. Marginal productivity theory has been criticised for assuming perfect competition. It doesn't!

Marginal productivity theory merely states that to maximise profits an employer will employ workers up to the point where the worker's marginal cost equals the extra revenue added by that worker: $MC_L = MRP_L$. This applies equally under perfect competition, monopsony and oligopoly.

What it does say is that, if there is perfect competition, then the worker's wage will equal MRP_L. It certainly does not say that there will always be perfect competition, or that $W = MRP_L$ in other market structures.

A second criticism is that employers simply do not behave in this 'marginal way', weighing up each additional worker's costs and revenues for the firm. There are three possible reasons for this.

Ignorance of the theory of profit maximisation. The employer may use some rule of thumb, but nevertheless is attempting to maximise profits.

This is a criticism of the theory only if the theory is supposed to describe how employers actually behave. It does not. It merely states that, if firms are attempting to maximise profits, they will in fact be equating MC_L and MRP_L, whether they realise it or not!

A worker's marginal productivity cannot be calculated. When workers are part of a team, it is not usually possible to separate out the contribution to output of each individual. What is the marginal productivity of a cleaner, a porter, a secretary, a security guard, or even a member of a production line? Similarly, it may not be possible to separate the contribution of workers from that of their tools. A lathe operator is useless without a lathe, as is a lathe without a lathe operator.

This is a more fundamental criticism. Nevertheless it is possible to amend the theory to take this into account. First, an employer can look at the composition of the team, or the partnership of worker and tools, and decide whether any reorganisations or alternative production methods will increase the firm's profitability (i.e. increase revenue more than costs). Second, the employer can decide whether to expand or contract the overall size of the team, or the number of workers plus machines. Here the whole team or the worker plus machine is the 'factor of production' whose marginal productivity must be weighed against its costs.

Firms are not always profit maximisers. This is a criticism only if the theory states that firms are. As long as the theory is merely used to describe what would happen if firms maximised profits, there is no problem.

This criticism, then, is really one of how the theory is used. And even if it is used to predict what will actually happen in the real world, it is still relatively accurate in the large number of cases where firms' behaviour diverges only slightly from profit maximising. It is clearly wrong in other cases.

Moral issues. A final criticism is the moral one. If economists focus their attention exclusively on how to maximise profits, it might be concluded that they are putting their seal of approval on this sort of behaviour. Of course, economists will respond by saying that they are doing no such thing: they are confining themselves to positive economics. Nevertheless the criticism has some force. What an economist chooses to study is in part a normative decision.

 Do any of the following contradict marginal productivity theory: (a) wage scales related to length of service (incremental scales); (b) nationally negotiated wage rates; (c) discrimination; (d) firms taking the lead from other firms in determining this year's pay increase?

frequently prepared to offer wage rates above the market-clearing level, attempting to balance increased wage costs against gains in productivity. But why may higher wage rates lead to higher productivity? There are three main explanations.

Less 'shirking'

In many jobs it is difficult to monitor the effort individuals put into their work. Workers may thus get away with shirking or careless behaviour. This is an example of the principal–agent problem (see page 217). The worker, as an agent of the employer (the principal), is not necessarily going to act in the principal's interest.

The business could attempt to reduce shirking by imposing a series of sanctions, the most serious of which would be dismissal. The greater the wage rate currently received, the greater will be the cost to the individual of dismissal, and the less likely it is, therefore, that workers will shirk. The business will benefit not only from the additional output but also from a reduction in the costs of having

---

| BOX 9.7 | **EQUAL PAY FOR EQUAL WORK?** |

(a) Average hourly pay, excluding overtime, for full-time UK employees, aged 18 and over, 1970–2007 (£ per hour)

	1970	1974	1978	1982	1986	1990	1994	1998	2002	2004	2006	2007
Men	0.67	1.05	2.00	3.55	4.82	6.89	8.65	10.65	12.92	13.73	14.29	14.95
Women	0.42	0.71	1.48	2.62	3.58	5.28	6.88	8.39	10.32	11.21	11.24	12.42
Women's pay as percentage of men's	62.7	67.6	74.0	73.8	74.3	76.6	79.5	78.8	79.9	81.6	78.7	83.1

Source: Annual Survey of Hours and Earnings (National Statistics, 2008).

(b) Average hourly pay, excluding overtime, for selected occupations, full-time UK employees on adult rates, 2007 (£ per hour)

Occupation	Men	Women	Women's pay as percentage of men's
Social workers	14.98	15.56	103.9
Bar staff	6.33	6.21	98.1
Nurses	14.46	14.13	97.7
Chefs, cooks	8.16	7.54	92.4
Secondary school teachers	22.13	19.98	90.3
Sales and retail assistants	7.78	6.94	89.2
Telephonists	10.01	8.80	87.9
Librarians	15.39	13.24	86.0
Police officers (sergeant and below)	16.90	14.48	85.7
Laboratory technicians	12.35	10.42	84.4
Directors/chief executives of major organisations	66.74	55.41	83.0
Solicitors, lawyers and judges	30.47	24.97	81.9
Medical practitioners	35.24	28.39	80.6
Personnel managers	27.29	21.91	80.3
Assemblers and routine operatives	9.61	7.61	79.2
Management consultants and economists	25.32	19.10	75.4
Hairdressers/barbers	8.44	6.32	74.9
All occupations	14.95	12.42	83.1
Average *gross weekly* pay (incl. overtime)	606.10	462.80	76.4
Average weekly hours worked (incl. overtime)	40.7	37.4	
Average weekly overtime	1.9	0.7	

Source: Annual Survey of Hours and Earnings (National Statistics, 2008).

Women earn less than men. How much less depends on how earnings are measured, but on the most widely used definition (see table (a)), women in the UK earn about 20 per cent less than men. The gender wage gap narrowed over the years until the mid 2000s. In the past few years, however, the gap has persisted at around 20 per cent or slightly above.

A similar picture can be seen throughout the EU. In 2005, women's average hourly pay was 85 per cent of men's. The figure varies from one country to another. In Germany it was 78 per cent, whereas in Belgium it was 93 per cent.

The inequality between male and female earnings can in part be explained by the fact that men and women are occupationally segregated. Seeing that women predominate in poorly paid occupations, the difference in earnings is somewhat to be expected. But if you consider table (b), you can see that quite substantial to monitor workers' performance. As a consequence the *efficiency wage rate* for the business will lie above the market-determined wage rate.

Definition

Efficiency wage rate The profit-maximising wage rate for the firm after taking into account the effects of wage rates on worker motivation, turnover and recruitment.

Reduced labour turnover

If workers receive on-the-job training or retraining, then to lose a worker once the training has been completed is a significant cost to the business. Labour turnover, and hence its associated costs, can be reduced by paying a wage above the market-clearing rate. By paying such a wage rate the business is seeking a degree of loyalty from its employees.

Morale

A simple reason for offering wage rates above the market-clearing level is to motivate the workforce – to create the

TC 5
p50

CASE STUDIES AND APPLICATIONS

earnings differentials persist within particular occupations.

1. *If we were to look at weekly rather than hourly pay and included the effects of overtime, what do you think would happen to the pay differentials in table (a)?*
2. *In table (b), which of the occupations have a largely female workforce?*

So why has this inequality persisted? There are a number of possible reasons:

- The marginal productivity of labour in typically female occupations may be lower than in typically male occupations. This may in part be due to simple questions of physical strength. Very often, however, it is due to the fact that women tend to work in more labour-intensive occupations. If there is less capital equipment per female worker than there is per male worker, then it would be expected that the marginal product of a woman would be less than that of a man. Evidence from the EU as a whole suggests that occupational segregation is a significant factor in explaining pay differences.

- Many women take career breaks to have children. For this reason, employers are sometimes more willing to invest money in training men (thereby increasing their marginal productivity), and more willing to promote men.

- Women tend to be less geographically mobile than men. If social norms are such that the man's job is seen as somehow more 'important' than the woman's, then a couple will often move if necessary for the man to get promotion. The woman, however, will have to settle for whatever job she can get in the same locality as her partner.

- A smaller proportion of women workers are members of unions than men. Even when they are members of unions, these are often in jobs where unions are weak (e.g. clothing industry workers and shop assistants).

- Part-time workers (mainly women) have less bargaining power, less influence and less chance of obtaining promotion.

- Custom and practice. Despite equal pay legislation, many jobs done wholly or mainly by women continue to be low-paid, irrespective of productivity.

- Prejudice. In many jobs women are discriminated against when it comes to promotion, especially to senior positions. Women are seriously underrepresented in boardrooms. This phenomenon is known as the 'glass ceiling'. It is very difficult to legislate against when the employer can simply claim that the 'better' person was promoted.

Which of the above reasons could be counted as economically 'irrational' (i.e. paying different wage rates to women and men for other than purely economic reasons)? Certainly the last two would classify. Paying different wage rates on these grounds would not be in the profit interests of the employer.

Some of the others, however, are more difficult to classify. The causes of the inequality in wage rates may be traced back beyond the workplace: perhaps to the educational system, or to a culture that discourages women from being so aggressive in seeking promotion or 'self-advertisement'.

It is interesting to consider the role that maternity pay and leave may play in the continuation of unequal incomes between women and men. In July 2008 Nicola Brewer, chief executive of the Equality and Human Rights Commission, gave a speech in which she called for a rethinking of family policy. In particular she suggested that overgenerous treatment of mothers, compared with fathers, was a contributory factor in continuing inequality. By 2010 mothers in the UK will have become entitled to 52 weeks' paid maternity leave while fathers receive two weeks' paternity pay. Ms Brewer argued that this policy perpetuated the view that childcare was a women's issue rather than a parental one. The right to request flexible working until the point where a child reaches the age of 16 (a right that is much more likely to be invoked by women than men) is likely to strengthen the view of many employers that women are less valuable employees.

1. *If employers were forced to give genuinely equal pay for equal work, how would this affect the employment of women and men? What would determine the magnitude of these effects?*
2. *How could family policy ensure that parents are able to work, while reducing pay differentials?*
3. *What measures could a government introduce to increase the number of women getting higher-paid jobs?*

KI 22
p216

BOX 9.8   FLEXIBLE LABOUR MARKETS AND THE FLEXIBLE FIRM

New work practices for old?

The past 25 years have seen sweeping changes in the ways that firms organise their workforce. Two world recessions combined with rapid changes in technology have led many firms to question the wisdom of appointing workers on a permanent basis to specific jobs. Instead, they want to have the greatest flexibility possible to respond to new situations. If demand falls, they want to be able to 'shed' labour without facing large redundancy costs. If demand rises, they want rapid access to additional labour supplies. If technology changes (say, with the introduction of new computerised processes), they want to have the flexibility to move workers around, or to take on new workers in some areas and lose workers in others.

What many firms seek, therefore, is flexibility in employing and allocating labour. What countries are experiencing is an increasingly flexible labour market, as workers and employment agencies respond to the new 'flexible firm'.

There are three main types of flexibility in the use of labour:

- **Functional flexibility.** This is where an employer is able to transfer labour between different tasks within the production process. It contrasts with traditional forms of organisation where people were employed to do a specific job, and then stuck to it. A functionally flexible labour force will tend to be multi-skilled and relatively highly trained.
- **Numerical flexibility.** This is where the firm is able to adjust the size and composition of its workforce according to changing market conditions. To achieve this, the firm is likely to employ a large proportion of its labour on a part-time or casual basis, or even subcontract specialist requirements.
- **Financial flexibility.** This is where the firm has flexibility in its wage costs. In large part it is a result of functional and numerical flexibility. Financial flexibility can be achieved by rewarding individual effort and

productivity rather than paying a given rate for a particular job. Such rates of pay are increasingly negotiated at the local level rather than being nationally set. The result is not only a widening of pay differentials between skilled and unskilled workers, but also growing differentials in pay between workers within the same industry but in different parts of the country.

The diagram shows how these three forms of flexibility are reflected in the organisation of a *flexible firm*, an organisation quite different from that of the traditional firm. The most significant difference is that the labour force is segmented. The core group, drawn from the *primary labour market*, will be composed of functionally

The flexible firm

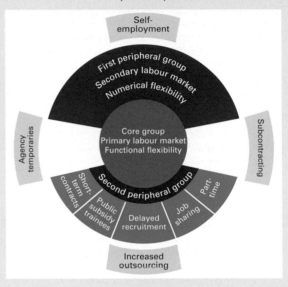

Source: Flexibility, Uncertainty and Manpower Management, Institute of Manpower Studies (Atkinson, J., 1984), IMS Report No. 89.

feeling that the firm is a 'good' employer that cares about its employees. As a consequence, workers might be more industrious and more willing to accept the introduction of new technology (with the reorganisation and retraining that it involves).

The paying of efficiency wages above the market-clearing wage will depend upon the type of work involved. Workers who occupy skilled positions, especially where the business has invested time in their training (thus making them costly to replace) are likely to receive efficiency wages

Definitions

Functional flexibility Where employers can switch workers from job to job as requirements change.

Numerical flexibility Where employers can change the size of their workforce as their labour requirements change.

Financial flexibility Where employers can vary their wage costs by changing the composition of their workforce or the terms on which workers are employed.

Flexible firm A firm that has the flexibility to respond to changing market conditions by changing the composition of its workforce.

Primary labour market The market for permanent full-time core workers.

flexible workers, who have relatively secure employment and are generally on full-time permanent contracts. Such workers will be relatively well paid and receive wages reflecting their scarce skills.

The periphery, drawn from the **secondary labour market**, is more fragmented than the core, and can be subdivided into a first and a second peripheral group. The first peripheral group is composed of workers with a lower level of skill than those in the core, skills that tend to be general rather than firm-specific. Thus workers in the first peripheral group can usually be drawn from the external labour market, often through agencies. Such workers may be employed on full-time contracts, but they will generally face less secure employment than those workers in the core.

The business gains a greater level of numerical flexibility by drawing labour from the second peripheral group. Here workers are employed on a variety of short-term, part-time contracts, often again through agencies. Some of these workers may be working from home, or online from another country, such as India, where wage rates are much lower. Workers in the second peripheral group have little job security.

As well as supplementing labour in the first peripheral group, the second periphery can also provide high-level specialist skills. In this instance the business can subcontract or hire self-employed labour, minimising its commitment to such workers. The business thereby gains both functional and numerical flexibility simultaneously.

The Japanese model

The application of new flexible working patterns is becoming more prevalent in businesses in the UK and elsewhere in Europe and North America. In Japan, flexibility has been part of the business way of life for many years and was crucial in shaping the country's economic success in the 1970s and 1980s. In fact we now talk of a Japanese model of business organisation, which many of its competitors seek to emulate.

The model is based around four principles:

- *Total quality management (TQM)*. This involves all employees working towards continuously improving all aspects of quality, both of the finished product and of methods of production.

- *Elimination of waste*. According to the 'just-in-time' (JIT) principle, businesses should take delivery of just sufficient quantities of raw materials and parts, at the right time and place. Stocks are kept to a minimum and hence the whole system of production runs with little, if any, slack. For example, supermarkets today have smaller storerooms relative to the total shopping area than they did in the past, and take more frequent deliveries.

- *A belief in the superiority of team work*. Collective effort is a vital element in Japanese working practices. Team work is seen not only to enhance individual performance, but also to involve the individual in the running of the business and thus to create a sense of commitment.

- *Functional and numerical flexibility*. Both are seen as vital components in maintaining high levels of productivity.

The principles of this model are now widely accepted as being important in creating and maintaining a competitive business in a competitive marketplace.

Within the EU, the UK has been one of the most successful countries in cutting unemployment and creating jobs. Much of this has been attributed to increased labour market flexibility. As a result, other EU member states, such as Italy and Germany, are seeking to emulate many of the measures the UK has adopted.

1. Is a flexible firm more likely or less likely to employ workers up to the point where their $MRP = MC_L$?
2. How is the advent of flexible firms likely to alter the gender balance of employment and unemployment?

---

considerably above the market wage. By contrast, workers in unskilled positions, where shirking can be easily monitored, where little training takes place and where workers can be easily replaced, are unlikely to command an 'efficiency wage premium'. In such situations, rather than keeping wage rates high, the business will probably try to pay as little as possible.

Definition

Secondary labour market The market for peripheral workers, usually employed on a temporary or part-time basis, or a less secure 'permanent' basis.

Other labour market imperfections

The possession of power by unions and/or firms is not the only way in which real-world labour markets diverge from the perfectly competitive model.

- Workers or employers may have imperfect information.
- Wages may respond very slowly to changes in demand and supply, causing disequilibrium in labour markets to persist.
- Firms may not be profit maximisers. Likewise workers may not seek to maximise their 'worker surplus' – the excess of benefits from working (i.e. wages) over the disutility of working (displeasure in doing the job and lost leisure).

Some of the forms and effects of these three imperfections are examined in Case Study 9.3. in MyEconLab.

Discrimination

Discrimination can be another major factor in determining wages. It can take many forms: it can be by race, sex, age, class, dress, etc.; it can occur in many different aspects of society. This section is concerned with *economic discrimination.* This is defined as a situation where workers of identical ability receive different pay for doing the same job, or are given different chances of employment or promotion.

Take the case of racial discrimination by employers. Figure 9.11 illustrates the wages and employment of both black and white workers by a firm with monopsony power which practises racial discrimination against black workers. Let us assume that there is no difference in the productivity of black and white workers. Let us also assume for simplicity that there is an equal number of black workers and white workers available at any given wage rate. Finally, let us assume that there are no laws to prevent the firm discriminating in terms of either wages or employment.

Figure 9.11(a) shows the MC and MRP curves for black workers. If there were no discrimination, employment of black workers would be at Q_{B_1}, where $MRP_B = MC_B$. The wage rate paid to black workers would be W_{B_1}.

Figure 9.11(b) shows the position for white workers. Again, if there were no discrimination, Q_{W_1} white workers would be employed at a wage of W_{W_1}: the same wage as that of black workers. (Note that in each case the MRP curve is drawn on the assumption that the number of workers employed from the other ethnic group is constant.)

If the firm now discriminates against black workers, it will employ workers along a lower curve, $MRP_B - x$ (where x can be seen as the discriminatory factor). Employment of black workers will thus be at the lower level of Q_{B_2} and the wage they receive will be at the lower level of W_{B_2}.

How will discrimination against black workers affect wages and employment of white workers? Let us consider two cases.

In the first case, assume that the employer practises economic discrimination purely in the negative sense: i.e. it discriminates against black workers but employs white workers on profit-maximising principles. Thus white workers would be employed up to that point where their MC equals their MRP. But the fact that fewer black workers are now being employed will mean that for any given quantity of white workers there will be fewer workers employed in total, and therefore the MRP of white workers will have increased. In Figure 9.11(b) the white workers' MRP curve has shifted to MRP_{W_2}. This has the effect of raising employment of white workers to Q_{W_2} and the wage rate to W_{W_2}.

Firms may, however, also practise economic discrimination *in favour* of certain groups. Figure 9.11(b) also illustrates this second case, where the employer practises economic discrimination in favour of white workers. Here the firm will employ workers along a higher curve, $MRP_{W_2} + y$, where y is the discriminatory factor. The effect is further to increase the wage rate and level of employment of white workers, to W_{W_3} and Q_{W_3} respectively.

KI 4
p10

Definition

Economic discrimination Where workers of identical *ability* are paid different wages or are otherwise discriminated against because of race, age, sex, etc.

 What effect will the discrimination by the firm have on the wages and employment of black workers in other firms in the area if (a) these other firms discriminate against black workers; (b) they do not discriminate?

Figure 9.11 The effect of racial discrimination by a monopsonist employer

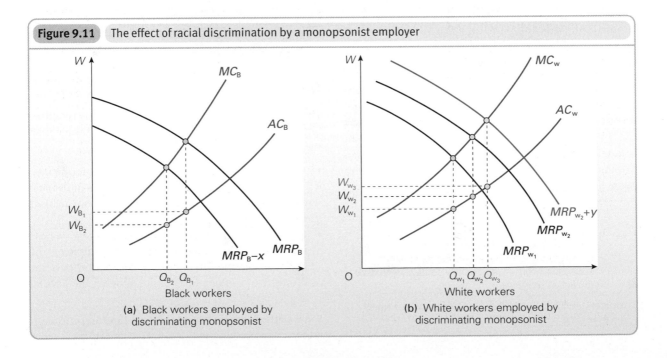

(a) Black workers employed by discriminating monopsonist

(b) White workers employed by discriminating monopsonist

If the government now insists on equal pay for equal work, then employers that discriminate will respond by further cutting back on black workers. The answer to *this* problem would seem to be for the government to pass laws that insist not only that black workers be paid the same as white workers for doing the same job, but also that they be treated equally when applying for jobs. The problem here is that an employer which wants to continue discrimination can always claim that the black applicants were less well qualified than the white applicant who got the job. Such laws are therefore difficult to enforce.

The type of discrimination considered so far can be seen as 'irrational' if the firm wants to maximise profits. After all, to produce a given amount of output, it would be paying out more in wages to employ white workers than black workers. In a competitive market environment, such firms may be forced to end discrimination simply to survive the competition from non-discriminating rivals. If, however, the firm has market power, it will probably be making sufficient profits to allow it to continue discriminating. The main pressure to end discrimination is then likely to come from unions, customers, shareholders or race relations organisations.

Other examples of non-economic discrimination stem from unequal educational opportunities. If the educational system discriminates against black children, they are likely to end up with poorer qualifications. They have less *human capital* invested in them. Under these circumstances, employers, preferring to employ the best-qualified applicants, are likely to choose white people. This is particularly so in the more highly paid jobs that require a higher level of educational attainment. Tackling this problem at source means tackling weaknesses in the education system

and breaking what has come to be known as the cycle of deprivation.

Who are the poor? Who are the rich?

To the list we made at the end of section 9.1 we can now add the following factors that will tend to make people poor:

- Lack of economic power, not belonging to a union or belonging to a union with only weak bargaining power.
- Ignorance of better job opportunities.
- Lack of will or ability to search for a better job.
- Discrimination against them by employers or fellow workers.

Thus before the advent of the minimum wage many people of Asian origin, especially women, working in the garment industry in back-street 'sweatshops' earned pitifully low wages.

Conversely, belonging to a powerful union, working for a profitable employer which nevertheless is not a ruthless profit maximiser, being aware of new job opportunities and having the 'get up and go' to apply for better jobs, and being white, male and middle-class are all factors that help to contribute to people earning high wages.

Definition

Human capital The qualifications, skills and expertise that contribute to a worker's productivity.

Section summary

1. If a firm is a monopsony employer, it will employ workers to the point where $MRP_L = MC_L$. Since the wage is below MC_L, the monopsonist, other things being equal, will employ fewer workers at a lower wage than would be employed in a perfectly competitive labour market.

2. If a union has monopoly power, its power to raise wage rates will be limited if the employer operates under perfect or monopolistic competition in the goods market. A rise in wage rates will force the employer to cut back on employment.

3. In a situation of bilateral monopoly (where a monopoly union faces a monopsony employer), the union may have considerable scope to raise the wage rate above the monopsony level, without the employer wishing to reduce the level of employment. There is no unique equilibrium wage. The wage will depend on the outcome of a process of collective bargaining between union and management.

4. Each side can make various threats or promises. The outcome of the bargaining will depend on the relative power, attitudes and bargaining skills of both sides, the firm's profitability and the information each side has about the other. The outcome also depends on the legal framework within which the negotiations take place.

5. Power is not the only factor that makes actual wage determination different from the perfectly competitive model. Firms and workers may have imperfect knowledge of the labour market; disequilibrium in labour markets may persist; firms may not be profit maximisers (see Case Study 9.3 in MyEconLab).

6. Firms may exercise discrimination (by race, sex, age, etc.) in their employment policy. By discriminating against a particular group, an employer with market power can drive down the wages of the members of that group. Unless firms are forced not to discriminate, equal pay legislation may well lead to a reduction in the employment of members of groups that are discriminated against.

9.3   CAPITAL AND PROFIT

The non-human factors of production

In the final two sections of the chapter, we consider the market for *other* factors of production. These can be divided into two broad groups.

Land. This includes all those productive resources supplied by nature: in other words, not only land itself, but also all natural resources. (We examine land in section 9.4.)

Capital. This includes all manufactured products that are used to produce goods and services. Thus capital includes such diverse items as a blast furnace, a bus, a cinema projector, a computer, a factory building and a screwdriver.

The capital goods described above are physical assets and are known as *physical* capital. The word 'capital' is also used to refer to various *paper* assets, such as shares and bonds. These are the means by which firms raise finance to purchase physical capital, and are known as *financial* capital. Being merely paper assets, however, they do not count as factors of production. Nevertheless, financial markets have an important role in determining the level of investment in physical capital, and we shall be examining these markets in the final part of section 9.3.

Factor prices versus the price of factor services

A feature of most non-human factors is that they last a period of time. A machine may last ten years; a coal mine may last fifty years before it is exhausted; farmland will last for ever if properly looked after. We must therefore distinguish between the income the owner will get from *selling* the factor and that which the owner will get from *using* it or *hiring* it out.

- The income from selling the factor is the factor's *price*. Thus a machine might sell for £10 000, or a hectare of land for £20 000.
- The income gained from using a factor is its *return*, and the income gained from hiring a factor out is its *rental*. This income represents the value or price of the factor's *services*, expressed per period of time. Thus a machine might earn a firm £1000 per year. A hectare of land might earn a landowner £2000 rent per year.

Obviously the price of a factor will be linked to the value of its services. The price that a hectare of land will fetch if sold will depend on the return or rent that can be earned on that land. If it is highly productive farmland, it will sell for a higher price than a piece of scrubby moorland.

 When we were looking at wage rates, were we talking about the price of labour or the price of labour services? Is this distinction between the price of a factor and the price of factor services a useful one in the case of labour? Was it in Roman times?

The profit-maximising employment of land and capital

On the demand side, the same rules apply for land and capital as for labour, if a firm wishes to maximise profits. Namely, it should demand factors up to the point where the marginal cost of the factor equals its marginal revenue product: $MC_f = MRP_f$. This same rule applies whether the firm is buying the factor outright, or merely renting it.

Figure 9.12 illustrates the two cases of perfect competition and monopsony. In both cases the *MRP* curve slopes downwards. This is another illustration of the law of diminishing returns, but this time applied to land or

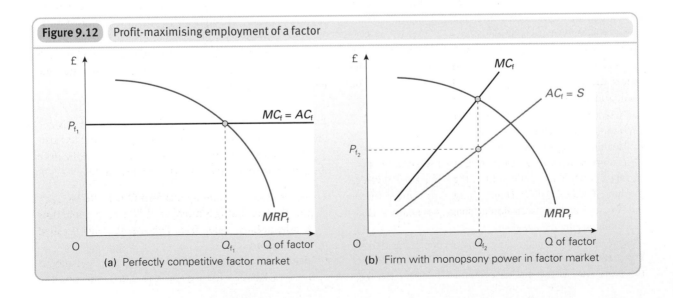

Figure 9.12   Profit-maximising employment of a factor

(a) Perfectly competitive factor market

(b) Firm with monopsony power in factor market

capital. For example, if a farmer increases the amount of land farmed while *holding other factors constant*, diminishing returns to land will occur. If the same number of farm workers and the same amount of agricultural machinery and fertilisers are used but on a larger area, then returns per hectare will fall.

In Figure 9.12(a) the firm is a price taker. The factor price is given at P_{f_1}. Profits are maximised at Q_{f_1} where $MRP_f = P_f$ (since $P_f = MC_f$).

In Figure 9.12(b) the firm has monopsony power. The factor price will vary, therefore, with the amount that the firm uses. The firm will again use factors to the point where $MRP_f = MC_f$. In this case, it will mean using Q_{f_2} at a price of P_{f_2}.

What is the difference between buying a factor and renting it? Although the $MRP_f = MC_f$ rule remains the same, there are differences. As far as buying the factors is concerned, the MC_f is the extra outlay for the firm in *purchasing* one more unit of the factor; and the MRP_f is all the revenue produced by that factor over its *whole life* (but measured in terms of what this is worth when purchased: see pages 261–3). In the case of renting, MC_f is the extra outlay for the firm in rent *per period*, while MRP_f is the extra revenue earned from it *per period*.

The demand for capital services

What we are talking about in this section is the hiring of capital equipment for a period of time (as opposed to buying it outright). The analysis is virtually identical to that of the demand for labour. As with labour, we can distinguish between an individual firm's demand and the whole market demand.

Individual firm's demand
Take the case of a small painting and decorating firm thinking of hiring some scaffolding in order to complete a job. It could use ladders, which it already owns, but the job would take longer to complete. If it hires the scaffolding for one day, it can perhaps shorten the job by, say, two or three days. If it hires it for a second day, it can perhaps save another one or two days. Hiring it for additional days may save extra still. But diminishing returns are occurring: the longer the scaffolding is up, the less intensively it will be used, and the less additional time it will save. Perhaps for some of the time it will be used when ladders could have been used equally easily.

The time saved allows the firm to take on extra work. Thus each extra day the scaffolding is hired gives the firm extra revenue. This is the scaffolding's marginal revenue product of capital (MRP_K). Diminishing returns mean that it has the normal downward-sloping shape (see Figure 9.12).

Market demand
The market demand for capital services is derived in exactly the same way as the market demand for labour (see Fig-

ure 9.6 on page 244). It is the horizontal sum of the MRP_K curves of the individual firms, corrected for the fact that increased use of capital will increase output, drive down the price of the good and hence reduce MRP. This means that the market demand curve for capital is steeper than the horizontal sum of the demand curves (MRP_K) of all the firms in the market.

Under what circumstances would the market demand for renting a type of capital equipment be (a) elastic; (b) inelastic? (Clue: turn back to page 244 and see what determines the elasticity of demand for labour.)

The supply of capital services

It is necessary to distinguish (a) the supply *to* a single firm, (b) the supply *by* a single firm and (c) the market supply.

Supply to a single firm
This is illustrated in Figure 9.13(a) (page 260). The small firm renting capital equipment is probably a price taker. If so, it faces a horizontal supply curve at the going rental rate (R_e). If, however, it has monopsony power, it will face an upward-sloping supply curve as in Figure 9.12(b).

Supply by a single firm
This is illustrated in Figure 9.13(b). On the demand side, the firm is likely to be a price taker. It has to accept the going rental rate (R_e) established in the market. If it tries to charge more, then customers are likely to turn to rival suppliers.

But what will the individual supplier's *supply* curve look like? The theory here has a lot in common with perfect competition in the goods market (see page 168): the supply curve is the firm's MC curve, only here the MC is the extra cost of supplying one more unit of capital equipment for rent over a given time period.

The problem with working out the marginal cost of renting out capital equipment is that the equipment probably cost a lot to buy in the first place, but lasts a long time. How then are these large costs to be apportioned to each new rental? The answer is that it depends on the time period under consideration.

The short run. In the short run, the hire company is not buying any new equipment: it is simply hiring out its existing stock of equipment. In the case of the scaffolding hire firm, the marginal costs of doing this will be as follows:

• Depreciation. Scaffolding has second-hand value. Each time the scaffolding is hired out it deteriorates, and thus its second-hand value falls. This loss in value is called 'depreciation'.

• Maintenance and handling. Hiring out equipment involves labour time (e.g. in the office) and possibly

Figure 9.13   Long-run equilibrium rental rate for the services of a particular type of capital

(a) Individual user of capital services

(b) Individual supplier of capital services

(c) Market for capital services

transport costs; the equipment may need servicing after being hired out.

These marginal costs are likely to rise relatively slowly. For each extra day a piece of equipment is hired out, the company will incur the same or only slightly higher additional costs. This gives a relatively flat supply curve of capital services in Figure 9.13(b) up to the hire company's maximum capacity. Once the scaffolding firm is hiring out all its scaffolding, the supply curve becomes vertical.

 Assume now that the firm has monopoly power in hiring out equipment, and thus faces a downward-sloping demand curve. Draw in two such demand curves on a diagram like Figure 9.13(b), one crossing the MC curve in the horizontal section, and one in the vertical section. How much will the firm supply in each case and at what price? (You will need to draw in MR curves too.) Is the MC curve still the supply curve?

The long run. In the long run, the hire company will consider purchasing additional equipment. It can therefore

---

BOX 9.9   **STOCKS AND FLOWS**

EXPLORING ECONOMICS

The discussion of the rewards to capital and land leads to a very important distinction: that between stocks and flows.

A stock is a quantity of something held. A landowner may own 200 hectares. A farmer may have a barn with 500 tonnes of grain. You may have £1000 in a savings account. These are all stocks: they are all quantities held at a given point in time.

A flow is an increase or decrease in quantity over a specified period. The landowner may buy another 10 hectares during the year. The farmer may use 10 tonnes of grain from the barn each week as animal feed. You may save £10 per month.

Wages, rent and interest are all rewards to flows. Wages are the amount paid for the services of a person's labour for a week or month. Rent is the amount paid per period of time to use the services of land. Likewise interest is the reward paid to people per year for the use of their money.

If an asset is sold, its value is the value of the stock. It is a simple payment at a single point in time for the transfer of a whole asset. Thus the price of land and the price of capital are stock concepts.

An important example of stocks and flows arises with capital and investment. If a firm has 100 machines, that is a stock of capital. It may choose to build up its stock by investing. Investment is a flow concept. The firm may choose to invest in 10 new machines each year. This may not add 10 to the stock of machines, however, as some may be wearing out (a negative flow).

 KEY IDEA 24 **Stocks and flows.** A stock is a quantity of something at a given point in time. A flow is an increase or decrease in something over a specified period of time. This is an important distinction and a common cause of confusion.

 Which of the following are stocks and which are flows?
(a) Unemployment
(b) Redundancies
(c) Profits
(d) A firm's stock market valuation
(e) The value of property after a period of inflation

supply as much as it likes in the long run. The supply curve will be relatively elastic, or if it is a price taker itself (i.e. if the scaffolding firm simply buys scaffolding at the market price), the supply curve will be horizontal. This long-run supply curve will be vertically higher than the short-run curve, since the long-run *MC* includes the cost of purchasing each additional piece of equipment.

Maths Case 9.1 in MyEconLab shows how this marginal cost can be calculated.

Market supply

This is illustrated in Figure 9.13(c). The market supply curve of a particular type of capital service is the sum of the quantities supplied by all the individual firms.

In the short run, the market supply will be relatively inelastic, given that it takes time to manufacture new equipment and that stocks of equipment currently held by manufacturers are likely to be relatively small. Also, capital is *heterogeneous*: i.e. one piece of capital equipment is not the same as another. If there is a shortage of scaffolding, you cannot use a cement mixer instead: people would fall off! Finally, hire companies may be unwilling to purchase (expensive) new equipment immediately there is a rise in demand: after all, the upsurge in demand may turn out to be short-lived.

 If supply is totally inelastic, what determines the rental value of capital equipment in the short run?

In the *long run*, the supply curve of capital services will be more elastic because extra capital equipment can be produced. It will not be horizontal, however, but upward sloping. Its elasticity will depend on the elasticity of supply of capital equipment to the hire companies.

Determination of the price of capital services

As Figure 9.13(c) shows, in a perfect market the market rental rate for capital services will be determined by the interaction of market demand and supply. Note that the analysis here parallels that of the determination of the equilibrium wage in a given labour market (see Figure 9.1 on page 237).

 What will happen to the demand for capital services and the equilibrium rental if the price of some other factor, say labour, changes? Assume that wage rates fall. Trace through the effects on a three-section diagram like Figure 9.13. (Clue: a fall in wages will reduce costs and hence the price of the product, so that more will be sold; and it will make labour cheaper relative to capital.)

If there is monopsony power on the part of the users of hired capital, this will have the effect of depressing the rental rate below the *MRP*$_K$ (see Figure 9.12(b)). If, on the other hand, there is monopoly power on the part of hire companies, the analysis is similar to that of monopoly in the goods market (see Figure 6.8 on page 175). The firm, by reducing the supply of capital for hire, can drive up the rental rate. It will maximise profit where the marginal revenue from hiring out the equipment is equal to the marginal cost of so doing: at a rental rate (price) *above* the marginal cost.

*Demand for and supply of capital for purchase

The alternative to hiring capital is to buy it outright. This section examines the demand and supply of capital for purchase.

The demand for capital: investment

How many computers will an engineering firm want to buy? Should a steelworks install another blast furnace? Should a removal firm buy another furniture lorry? These are all *investment* decisions. Investment involves purchasing of additional capital.

The demand for capital, or 'investment demand', by a profit-maximising firm is based on exactly the same principles as the demand for labour or the demand for capital services. The firm must weigh up the marginal revenue product of that investment (i.e. the money it will earn for the firm) against its marginal cost.

The problem is that capital is durable. It goes on producing goods, and hence yielding revenue for the firm, for a considerable period of time. Calculating these benefits therefore involves taking account of their timing.

There are two ways of approaching the problem: the *present value* approach and the *rate of return* approach. In both cases, the firm is comparing the marginal benefits with the marginal costs of the investment.

Present value approach. To work out the benefit of an investment (its *MRP*), the firm must estimate all the future earnings it will bring and then convert them to a **present value**. It can then compare this with the cost of the investment. Let us take a simple example.

Assume that a firm is considering buying a machine. It will produce £1000 per year (net of operating costs) for four years and then wear out and sell for £1000 as scrap. What is the benefit of this machine to the firm? At first sight the answer would seem to be £5000. This, after all, is the total

Definitions

Investment The purchase by the firm of equipment or materials that will add to its stock of capital.

Present value approach to appraising investment This involves estimating the value *now* of a flow of future benefits (or costs).

income earned from the machine. Unfortunately, it is not as simple as this. The reason is that money earned in the future is less beneficial to the firm than having the same amount of money today: if the firm has the money today, it can earn interest on it by putting it in the bank or reinvesting it in some other project.

To illustrate this, assume that you have £100 today and can earn 10 per cent interest by putting it in a bank. In one year's time that £100 will have grown to £110, in two years' time to £121, in three years' time to £133.10 and so on. This process is known as *compounding*.

It follows that if someone offered to give you £121 in two years' time, that would be no better than giving you £100 today, since, with interest, £100 would grow to £121 in two years. What we say, then, is that, with a 10 per cent interest rate, £121 in two years' time has a *present value* of £100.

The procedure of reducing future value back to a present value is known as *discounting*.

> **KEY IDEA 25**
>
> **The principle of discounting.** People generally prefer to have benefits today rather than in the future. Thus future benefits have to be reduced (discounted) to give them a present value.

When we do discounting, the rate we use is called the *rate of discount*: in this case, 10 per cent. The formula for discounting is as follows:

$$PV = \sum \frac{R_t}{(1+r)^t}$$

where PV is the present value, R_t is the revenue from the investment in year t, r is the rate of discount (expressed as a decimal: e.g. 10% = 0.1) and $\sum$ is the sum of each of the years' discounted earnings.

So what is the present value of the investment in the machine that produced £1000 for four years and then is sold as scrap for £1000 at the end of the four years? According to the formula it is:

Year 1　Year 2　Year 3　Year 4

$$= \frac{£1000}{1.1} + \frac{£1000}{(1.1)^2} + \frac{£1000}{(1.1)^3} + \frac{£2000}{(1.1)^4}$$

$$= £909 + £826 + £751 + £1366$$

$$= £3852$$

Thus the present value of the investment (i.e. its *MRP*) is £3852, *not* £5000 as it might seem at first sight. In other words, if the firm had £3852 today and deposited it in a bank at a 10 per cent interest rate, the firm would earn exactly the same as it would by investing in the machine.

So is the investment worthwhile? It is now simply a question of comparing the £3852 benefit with the cost of buying the machine. If the machine costs less than £3852, it will be worth buying. If it costs more, the firm would be better off keeping its money in the bank.

The difference between the present value of the benefits (PV_b) of the investment and its cost (C) is known as the *net present value* (*NPV*).

$$NPV = PV_b - C$$

If the *NPV* is positive, the investment is worthwhile.

 What is the present value of a machine that lasts three years, earns £100 in year 1, £200 in year 2 and £200 in year 3, and then has a scrap value of £100? Assume that the rate of discount is 5 per cent. If the machine costs £500, is the investment worthwhile? Would it be worthwhile if the rate of discount were 10 per cent?

Rate of return approach. The alternative approach when estimating whether an investment is worthwhile is to calculate the investment's *rate of return*. This rate of return is known as the firm's *marginal efficiency of capital* (*MEC*) or *internal rate of return* (*IRR*).

> **KI 25**
> **p262**

We use the same formula as for calculating present value:

$$PV = \sum \frac{R_1}{(1+r)^t}$$

and then calculate what value of r would make the PV equal to the cost of investment: in other words, the rate of discount that would make the investment just break even. Say this worked out at 20 per cent. What we would be saying is that the investment would just cover its costs if the current rate of interest (rate of discount) were 20 per cent. In other words, this investment is equivalent to receiving 20 per cent interest: it has a 20 per cent rate of return (*MEC*).

Details of how to calculate the internal rate of return, along with a worked example, are given in Maths Case 9.2 in MyEconLab.

Definitions

Compounding The process of adding interest each year to an initial capital sum.

Discounting The process of reducing the value of future flows to give them a present valuation.

Rate of discount The rate that is used to reduce future values to present values.

Net present value of an investment The discounted benefits of an investment minus the cost of the investment.

Marginal efficiency of capital or internal rate of return The rate of return of an investment: the discount rate that makes the net present value of an investment equal to zero.

Figure 9.14   The profit-maximising stock of capital

% rate per year (vertical axis)

i

MEC

O   *Q₁*

Quantity of capital

So should the investment go ahead? Yes, if the actual rate of interest (*i*) is less than 20 per cent. The firm is better off investing its money in this project than keeping it in the bank: i.e. if *MEC* > *i* the investment should proceed.

TC 8
p100

This is just one more application of the general rule that if $MRP_f > MC_f$ then more of the factor should be used: only in this case, *MRP* is expressed as a rate of return (*MEC*), and *MC* is expressed as a rate of interest (*i*).

The profit-maximising position is illustrated in Figure 9.14. As the firm invests more, and thus builds up its stock of capital, so *MEC* will fall due to diminishing returns. As long as *MEC* is greater than *i*, the firm should invest more. It should stop when the stock of capital has reached Q_1. Thereafter it should cut investment to a level just sufficient to replace worn-out machines, and thus keep the capital stock at Q_1.

KI 17
p125

KI 11
p75

The risks of investment.   One of the problems with investment is that the future is uncertain. The return on an investment will depend on the value of the goods it produces, which will depend on the goods market. But future markets cannot be predicted with accuracy: they depend on consumer tastes, the actions of rivals and the whole state of the economy. Investment is thus risky.

Risk may also be incurred in terms of the output from an investment. Take the case of prospecting for oil. An oil company may be lucky and have a major strike, but it may simply drill dry well after dry well. If it does get a major strike, and hence earn a large return on its investment, these profits will not be competed away by competitors prospecting in other fields, because they too still run the risk of drilling dry holes.

How is this risk accounted for when calculating the benefits of an investment? The answer is to use a higher rate of discount. The higher the risk, the bigger the premium that must be added to the rate.

The supply of capital

It is necessary to distinguish the supply of *physical* capital from the supply of *finance* to be used by firms for the purchase of capital.

Supply of physical capital.   The principles here are just the same as those in the goods market. It does not matter whether a firm is supplying lorries (capital) or cars (a consumer good): it will still produce up to the point where *MC* = *MR* if it wishes to maximise profits.

Supply of finance.   An economy will have a stock of financial capital (or 'loanable funds') held in banks and other financial institutions. These funds can be borrowed by firms for investment in new physical capital.

When people save, this will build up the stock of loanable funds. This flow of saving represents the resources released when people refrain from consumption. Among other things, saving depends on the rate of interest. This is illustrated in Figure 9.15. A rise in the interest rate will encourage people to save more, thereby increasing the supply (i.e. the stock) of loanable funds (a movement up along the supply curve).

KI 24
p260

This supply curve will be relatively inelastic in the short run, since the flow of saving over a short time period (say, a month) will have only a relatively small effect on the total stock of funds. Over a year, however, the effect would be twelve times bigger. The longer the time period, therefore, the more elastic the supply curve.

Saving also depends on the level of people's incomes, their expectations of future price changes, and their willingness to forgo present consumption in order to be able to have more in the future. A change in any of these other determinants will shift the supply curve.

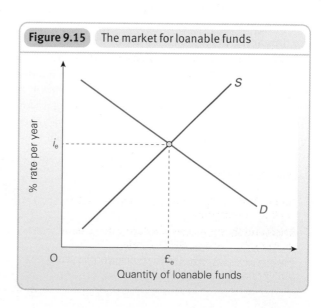

Figure 9.15   The market for loanable funds

% rate per year (vertical axis)

S

iₑ

D

O   *fₑ*

Quantity of loanable funds

*Determination of the rate of interest

The rate of interest is determined by the interaction of supply and demand in the market for loanable funds. This is illustrated in Figure 9.15. As we have seen, supply represents accumulated savings.

The demand curve includes the demand by households for credit and the demand by firms for funds to finance their investment. The curve slopes downwards for two reasons. First, households will borrow more at lower rates of interest. It effectively makes goods cheaper for them to buy. Second, it reflects the falling rate of return on investment as investment increases. This is simply due to diminishing returns to investment. As rates of interest fall, it will become profitable for firms to invest in projects that have a lower rate of return: the quantity of loanable funds demanded thus rises.

Equilibrium will be achieved where demand equals supply at an interest rate of i_e and a quantity of loanable funds $£_e$.

How will this market adjust to a change in demand or supply? Assume that there is a rise in demand for capital equipment, due, say, to an improvement in technology that increases the productivity of capital. There is thus an increase in demand for loanable funds. The demand curve shifts to the right in Figure 9.15. The equilibrium rate of interest will rise and this will encourage more savings. The end result is that more money will be spent on capital equipment.

Capital and profit

What does the analysis so far tell us about the amount of profit that firms will earn? After all, profit is the reward that the owners of firms get from having and using capital.

Remember from Chapter 6 the distinction between normal and supernormal profit. In a perfectly competitive world, all supernormal profits will be competed away in the long run.

Another way of putting this is that a perfectly competitive firm in the long run will earn only a **normal rate of return** on capital. This means that the return on capital (after taking risk into account) will be just the same as if the owners of capital had simply deposited their money in a bank instead. If a firm's capital yields a higher rate of return than this normal level (i.e. supernormal returns), other firms will be attracted to invest in similar capital. The resulting increased level of capital will increase the supply of goods. This in turn will lower the price of the goods and hence lower the rate of return on capital until it has fallen back to the normal level.

 Can a perfectly competitive firm earn a supernormal rate of return on capital if it continuously innovates?

If, however, capital owners have monopoly/oligopoly power and can thus restrict the entry of new firms or the copying of innovations – for example, by having a patent on a particular process – they can continue to get a supernormal return on their capital.

Financing investment

Sources of business finance

A firm can finance capital investment in one of three major ways:

- Internal funds (i.e. retained profits).
- Borrowing from the banking sector.
- Issuing new shares (equities) or debentures (fixed-interest loan stock).

The largest source of finance for investment in the UK is firms' own internal funds (i.e. ploughed-back profits). Given, however, that business profitability depends in large part on the general state of the economy, internal funds as a source of business finance are likely to show considerable cyclical variation. When profits are squeezed in a recession, this source of investment will decline.

Other sources of finance, which include borrowing and the issue of shares and debentures, are known as 'external funds'. These are then categorised as short-term, medium-term or long-term sources of finance.

- Short-term finance is usually in the form of a short-term bank loan or overdraft facility, and is used by business as a form of working capital to aid it in its day-to-day business operations.
- Medium-term finance, again provided largely by banks, is usually in the form of a loan with set repayment targets. It is common for such loans to be made at a fixed rate of interest, with repayments being designed to fit in with the business's expected cash flow. Bank lending has been the most volatile source of business finance, and has been particularly sensitive to the state of the economy. While part of the reason is the lower demand for loans during a recession, part of the reason is the caution of banks in granting loans if prospects for the economy are poor. In 2008 there was a reduction in the willingness of banks to grant loans to businesses following the credit crunch. This is examined in more detail in Boxes 18.2 and 18.3 on pages 512 and 516.
- Long-term finance, especially in the UK, tends to be acquired through the stock market. It will usually be in

---

Definition

Normal rate of return The rate of return (after taking risks into account) that could be earned elsewhere.

the form of **shares** (or **equities**). This is where members of the public or institutions (such as pension funds) buy a part ownership in the company and, as a result, receive dividends on those shares. The dividends depend on the amount of profit the company makes and distributes to shareholders. The proportion of business financing from this source clearly depends on the state of the stock market. In the late 1990s, with a buoyant stock market, the proportion of funds obtained through share issue increased. Then with a decline in stock market prices from 2000 to 2003, this proportion fell. In 2008 there were very substantial falls in the values of shares, further reducing the ability of firms to raise finance.

Alternatively, firms can issue **debentures** (or **company bonds**). These securities are fixed-interest loans to firms. Debenture holders have a prior claim on company shares. Their interest must be paid in full before shareholders can receive any dividends.

Despite the traditional reliance on the stock market for external long-term sources of finance, there has been a growing involvement of banks in recent years. Banks have become more willing to provide finance for business start-ups and for diversification. Nevertheless, there is a concern that banks are still relatively cautious. This results in a problem of 'short-termism', with bankers often demanding a quick return on their money or charging high interest rates, and being less concerned to finance long-term investment.

Comparison of the UK with other European countries. In other European countries, notably Germany and France, the attitude towards business funding is quite different from that in the UK. In these countries banks provide a significant amount of long-term, fixed-rate finance. This provides a much more stable source of finance and creates an environment where banks are much more committed to the long-run health of companies.

The role of the stock market

The London Stock Exchange operates as both a primary and secondary market in capital.

As a **primary market**, it is where public limited companies (see Case Study 8.1 in MyEconLab) can raise finance by issuing new shares, whether to new shareholders or to existing ones. To raise finance on the Stock Exchange a business must be 'listed'. The Listing Agreement involves directors agreeing to abide by a strict set of rules governing behaviour and levels of reporting to shareholders. Companies must have at least three years' trading experience and make at least 25 per cent of their shares available to the public. In August 2008, there were 1213 UK and 333 international companies on the Official List. During 2007 £469.8 billion's worth of new capital was raised by selling equity (ordinary shares) and fixed-interest securities on the London Stock Exchange.

As well as those on the Official List, there are over 1600 companies on what is known as the Alternative Investment Market (AIM). Companies listed here tend to be young but with growth potential, and do not have to meet the strict criteria or pay such high costs as companies on the Official List.

As a **secondary market**, the Stock Exchange enables investors to sell *existing* shares and debentures to one another. In the financial year ending March 2008, on an average day's trading, £9 billion's worth of trading in UK equities took place.

The advantages and disadvantages of using the stock market to raise capital

As a market for raising capital, the stock market has a number of advantages:

- It brings together those that wish to invest and companies that seek investment, and does so in a relatively low-cost way. It thus represents a way that savings can be mobilised to generate output.
- Firms that are listed on the Stock Exchange are subject to strict regulations. This is likely to stimulate investor confidence, making it easier for business to raise finance.
- The process of merger and acquisition is facilitated by having a share system, which in turn increases competition for corporate control (see pages 178–9).

The main weaknesses of the stock market for raising capital are:

- The cost to a business of getting listed can be immense, not only in a financial sense, but also in being open to public scrutiny. Directors' and senior managers' decisions will often be driven by how the market is likely to react, rather than by what they perceive to be in the business's best interests. They always have to think about the reactions of those large shareholders in the City that control a large proportion of their shares.

Definitions

Shares (equities) A part ownership of a company. Companies' distributed profits are paid to shareholders in the form of dividends according to the number of shares held.

Debentures (company bonds) Fixed-interest loans to firms. These assets can be traded on the stock market and their market price is determined by demand and supply.

Primary market in capital Where shares are sold by the issuer of the shares (i.e. the firm) and where, therefore, finance is channelled directly from the purchasers (i.e. the shareholders) to the firm.

Secondary market in capital Where shareholders sell shares to others. This is thus a market in 'second-hand' shares.

- In the UK, it is often claimed that the market suffers from *short-termism*. Investors on the Stock Exchange are mainly concerned with a company's short-term performance and its share value. In responding to this, the business might neglect its long-term performance and potential.

Is the stock market efficient?

One of the arguments made in favour of the stock market is that it acts as an arena within which share values can be accurately or efficiently priced. If new information comes onto the market concerning a business and its performance, this will be quickly and rationally transferred into the business's share value. This is known as the *efficient market hypothesis*. So, for example, if an investment analyst found that, in terms of its actual and expected dividends, a particular share was underpriced and thus represented a 'bargain', the analyst would advise investors to buy. As people then bought the shares, their price would rise, pushing their value up to their full worth. So by attempting to gain from inefficiently priced securities, investors will encourage the market to become more efficient.

So how efficient is the stock market in pricing securities? Is information rationally and quickly conveyed into the share's price? Or are investors able to prosper from the stock market's inefficiencies?

We can identify three levels of efficiency.

The weak form of efficiency. Share prices often move in cycles that do not reflect the underlying performance of the firm. If information is imperfect, those with a better understanding of such cycles gain from buying shares at the trough and selling them at the peak of the cycles. They are taking advantage of the market's inefficiency.

The technical analysis used by investment analysts to track share cycles is a complex science, but more and more analysts are using the techniques. As they do so and knowledge becomes more perfect, so the market will become more efficient and the cycles will tend to disappear. But why?

As more people buy a company's shares as the price falls towards its trough, so this extra demand will prevent the price falling so far. Similarly, as people sell as the price rises towards its peak, so this extra supply will prevent the price rising so far. This is an example of stabilising speculation

(see pages 72–3). As more and more people react in this way, so the cycle all but disappears. When this happens, *weak efficiency* has been achieved.

The semi-strong form of efficiency. **Semi-strong efficiency** is when share prices adjust fully to publicly available information. In practice, not all investors will interpret such information correctly: their knowledge is imperfect. But as investors become more and more sophisticated, and as more and more advice is available to shareholders (through stockbrokers, newspapers, published accounts, etc.), and as many shares are purchased by professional fund managers, so the interpretation of public information becomes more and more perfect and the market becomes more and more efficient in the semi-strong sense.

If the market were efficient in the semi-strong sense, then no gain could be made from studying a company's performance and prospects, as any such information would *already* be included in the current share price. In selecting shares, you would do just as well by pinning the financial pages of a newspaper on the wall, throwing darts at them, and buying the shares the darts hit!

The strong form of efficiency. If the stock market showed the **strong form of efficiency**, then share prices would fully reflect *all* available information – whether public or not. For this to be so, all 'inside' information would have to be reflected in the share price the moment the information became available.

If the market is *not* efficient at this level, then people who have access to privileged information will be able to make large returns from their investments by acting on such information. For example, directors of a company would know if the company was soon to announce better-than-expected profits. In the meantime, they could gain by buying shares in the company, knowing that the share price would rise when the information about the profits became public. Gains made from such 'insider dealing' are illegal. However, proving whether individuals are engaging in it is very difficult. In 2007 the Financial Services Authority brought just three criminal cases, prompting criticism that it was toothless. Nevertheless, there are people in prison for insider dealing: so it does happen!

Definitions

Short-termism Where firms and investors take decisions based on the likely short-term performance of a company, rather than on its long-term prospects. Firms may thus sacrifice long-term profits and growth for the sake of a quick return.

Efficient (capital) market hypothesis The hypothesis that new information about a company's current or future performance will be quickly and accurately reflected in its share price.

Weak efficiency (of share markets) Where share dealing prevents cyclical movements in shares.

Semi-strong efficiency (of share markets) Where share prices adjust quickly, fully and accurately to publicly available information.

Strong efficiency (of share markets) Where share prices adjust quickly, fully and accurately to all available information, both public and that only available to insiders.

Given the penalties for insider dealing and the amount of private information that firms possess, it is unlikely that all such information will be reflected in share prices. Thus the strong form of stock market efficiency is unlikely to hold.

 Would the stock market be more efficient if insider dealing were made legal?

If stock markets were fully efficient, the expected returns from every share would be the same. The return is referred to as the *yield*: this is measured as the dividends paid on the share as a percentage of the share's market price. For example, if you hold shares whose market price is £1 per share and you receive an annual dividend of 3p per share, then the yield on the shares is 3 per cent. But why should the expected returns on shares be the same? If any share was expected to yield a higher-than-average return, people would buy it; its price would rise and its yield would correspondingly fall.

It would only be unanticipated information, therefore, that would cause share prices to deviate from that which reflected expected average yields. Such information must, by its nature, be random, and as such would cause share prices to deviate randomly from their expected price, or follow what we call a *random walk*. Evidence suggests that share prices do tend to follow random patterns.

Definitions

Yield on a share The dividend received per share expressed as a percentage of the current market price of the share.

Random walk Where fluctuations in the value of a share away from its 'correct' value are random, i.e. have no systematic pattern. When charted over time, these share price movements would appear like a 'random walk': like the path of someone staggering along drunk!

Section summary

1. It is necessary to distinguish between buying the services of land (by renting) or capital (by hiring) and buying them outright.

2. The profit-maximising employment of land and capital services will be where the factor's *MRP* is equal to its price (under perfect competition) or its *MC* (where firms have monopsony power).

3. The demand for capital services will be equal to MRP_K. Due to diminishing returns, this will decline as more capital is used.

4. The supply of capital services to a firm will be horizontal or upward sloping depending on whether the firm is perfectly competitive or has monopsony power. The supply of capital services by a firm in the short run is likely to be relatively elastic up to its maximum use, and then totally inelastic. In the long run, the supplying firm can purchase additional capital equipment for hiring out. The long-run supply curve will therefore be very elastic, but at a higher rental rate than in the short run, given that the cost of purchasing the equipment must be taken into account in the rental rate.

5. The market supply of capital services is likely to be highly inelastic in the short run, given that capital equipment tends to have very specific uses and cannot normally be transferred from one use to another. In the long run, it will be more elastic.

6. The price of capital services is determined by the interaction of demand and supply.

7. The demand for capital for purchase will depend on the return it earns for the firm. To calculate this return, all future earnings from the investment have to be reduced to a present value by discounting at a market rate of interest (discount). If the present value exceeds the cost of the investment, the investment is worthwhile. Alternatively, a rate of return from the investment can be calculated and then this can be compared with the return that the firm could have earned by investing elsewhere.

8. The supply of finance for investment depends on the supply of loanable funds, which in turn depends on the rate of interest, on the general level of thriftiness and on expectations about future price levels and incomes.

9. The rate of interest will be determined by the demand and supply of loanable funds. When deciding whether to make an investment, a firm will use this rate for discounting purposes. If, however, an investment involves risks, the firm will require a higher rate of return on the investment than current market interest rates.

10. Business finance can come from internal sources (ploughed-back profits) or from external ones. External sources of finance include borrowing and the issue of shares.

11. The stock market operates as both a primary and a secondary market in capital. As a primary market it channels finance to companies as people purchase new shares and debentures. It is also a market for existing shares and debentures.

12. The stock market helps to stimulate growth and investment by bringing together companies and people who want to invest in them. By regulating firms and by keeping transaction costs of investment low, it helps to ensure that investment is efficient.

13. The stock market does impose costs on firms, however. It is expensive for firms to be listed and the public exposure may make them too keen to 'please' the market. It can also foster short-termism.

14. The stock market is relatively efficient. It achieves weak efficiency by reducing cyclical movements in share prices. It achieves semi-strong efficiency by allowing share prices to respond quickly and fully to publicly available information. Whether it achieves strong efficiency by adjusting quickly and fully to all information (both public or insider), however, is more doubtful.

9.4 LAND AND RENT

Rent: the reward to landowners

We turn now to land. The income it earns for landowners is the *rent* charged to the users of the land. This rent, like the rewards to other factors, is determined by demand and supply.

What makes land different from other factors of production is that it has an inelastic supply. In one sense, this is obvious. The total supply of land in any area is fixed. It is in the very nature of land that it cannot be moved from one place to another!

In another sense, supply is not *totally* inelastic. Land can be improved. It can be cleared, levelled, drained, fertilised, etc. Thus the supply of a certain type of land can be increased by expending human effort on improving it. The question is whether *land* has thereby increased, or whether the improvements constitute *capital* invested in land, and if so whether the higher rents that such land can earn really amount to a return on the capital invested in it.

To keep the analysis simple, let us assume that land *is* fixed. Let us take the case of an area of 10 000 hectares surrounding the village of Oakleigh. This is shown as a vertical supply 'curve' in Figure 9.16. The demand curve for that land will be like the demand curve for other factors of production. It is the *MRP* curve and slopes down due to diminishing returns from land. The equilibrium rent is r_e, where demand and supply intersect.

Notice that the level of this rent depends entirely on *demand*. If a new housing development takes place in Oakleigh, due perhaps to a growth in employment in a nearby town, the demand curve will shift to D_1 and the equilibrium rent will rise to r_{e1}. But the supply of land remains fixed at 10 000 hectares. Landowners will earn more rent, but they themselves have done nothing: the higher rent is a pure windfall gain.

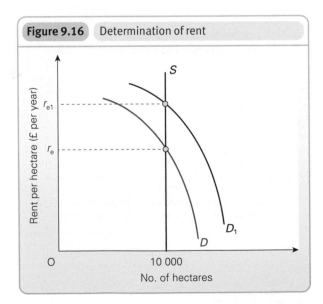

Figure 9.16 Determination of rent

Rent per hectare (£ per year)

r_{e1}

r_e

S

D_1

D

O   10 000

No. of hectares

So why are rents in the centre of London many times higher per hectare than they are in the north of Scotland? The answer is that demand is very much higher in London.

Demand for land depends on its marginal revenue product. Thus it is differences in the *MRP* of land that explain the differences in rent from one area to another. There are two reasons for differences in *MRP*. Remember that *MRP* = *MPP* (marginal physical product of the factor) × *MR* (marginal revenue of the good produced by that factor).

Differences in MPP. Land differs in productivity. Fertile land will produce a higher output than deserts or moorland. Similarly, land near centres of population will be of much more use to industry than land in the middle of nowhere.

 What other factors will determine the MPP of land for industry?

Differences in MR. The higher the demand for a particular good, the higher its price and marginal revenue, and hence the higher the demand and rent for the land on which that good is produced. Thus if the demand for housing rises relative to the demand for food, the rent on land suitable for house building will rise relative to the rent on agricultural land.

To summarise: rents will be high on land that is physically productive (high *MPP*) and produces goods in high demand (high *MR*).

1. *We defined the factor of production 'land' to include raw materials. Does the analysis of rent that we have just been looking at apply to raw materials?*
2. *The supply of land in a particular area may be totally inelastic, but the supply of land in that area for a specific purpose (e.g. growing wheat) will be upward sloping: the higher the price of wheat and thus the higher the rent that wheat producers are prepared to pay, the more will be made available for wheat production. What will determine the elasticity of supply of land for any particular purpose?*

The price of land

Not all land is rented: much of it is bought and sold outright. Its price will depend on what the purchaser is prepared to pay, and this will depend on the land's rental value.

Let us say that a piece of land can earn £1000 per year. What would a person be prepared to pay for it? There is a simple formula for working this out:

$$P = \frac{R}{i} \qquad (1)$$

where P is the price of the land, R is the rent per year and i is the market rate of interest.

BOX 9.10 **THE ECONOMICS OF NON-RENEWABLE RESOURCES** **EXPLORING ECONOMICS**

What happens as stocks diminish?

As world population inexorably rises, so the demands on our planet's resources continue to grow. Some of these resources are renewable. Water resources are replenished by rain. The soil, if properly managed, can continue to grow crops. Felled forests can be replanted. Of course, if we use these resources more rapidly than they are replenished, stocks will run down. We are all aware of the problems of seas that are overfished, or rainforests that are cleared, or reservoirs that are inadequate to meet our growing demand for water.

But whereas these resources can be replenished, others cannot. These are known as non-renewable resources. What determines the price of such resources and their rate of depletion? Will we eventually run out of resources such as oil, coal, gas and various minerals? To answer these questions, we need to distinguish between the available stock of such resources, and their use (a flow). The greater their use, the faster the stocks will run down.

Price increases over time

As stocks run down, so the price of the resources will tend to increase. Thus we can all expect to pay more for fossil fuels as remaining reserves are depleted. Owners of the reserves (e.g. mine owners and owners of oil wells) will thus find the value of their assets increasing. But how quickly will prices rise? In a perfect market, they will rise at the market rate of return on other assets (of equivalent risk). This is known as the Hotelling rule, named after Harold Hotelling who developed the argument in the early 1930s.

To understand why this is so, consider what would happen if the price of oil rose more slowly than the rate of return on other assets. People who owned oil wells would find that the value of their oil reserves was increasing less rapidly than the value of other assets. They might as well sell more oil now and invest the money in other assets, thereby getting a higher return. The extra oil coming to the market would depress the current oil price, but also reduce reserves, thereby creating a bigger shortage for the future and hence a higher future price. This would cause oil prices to rise more quickly over time (from the new lower base). Once the rate of price increase has risen to equal the rate of return on other assets, equilibrium has occurred. There will no longer be an incentive for the oil to be extracted faster.

The current price

But what determines the current price level (as opposed to its rate of increase)? This will be determined by supply and demand for the extracted resource (its flow).

In the case of a resource used by households, demand will depend on consumer tastes, the price of other goods, income, etc. Thus the greater the desire for using private cars, the greater the demand for petrol. In the case of

minerals used by firms, demand will depend on the marginal revenue product of the resources. In either case, a rise in demand will cause a rise in the resource's price.

Supply will depend on three things:

- The rate of interest on other assets. As we have seen, the higher the rate of interest, the faster will the resource be extracted, in order that the mine owners (or well owners) can reinvest their profits at these higher rates of interest.
- The stock of known reserves. As new reserves are discovered, this will push down the price.
- The costs of extraction. The lower the costs, the greater will be the amount extracted, and hence the lower will be the market price of the resource.

Are we extracting non-renewable resources at the optimum rate?

If there are limited reserves of fossil fuels and other minerals, are we in danger that they will soon run out? Should we be more concerned with conservation?

In fact, the market provides an incentive to conserve such resources. As reserves run down, so the price of non-renewable resources will rise. This will create an incentive to discover alternatives. For example, as fossil fuels become more expensive, so renewable sources of energy, such as solar power, wind power and wave power, will become more economical. There will also be a greater incentive to discover new techniques of power generation and to conserve energy.

Markets, however, are imperfect. As we shall see in Chapter 11, when we consume natural resources, we do not take into account the full costs. For example, the burning of fossil fuels creates harmful environmental effects in the form of acid rain and the greenhouse effect, but these 'external' costs are not included in the price we pay.

Then there is the question of the distribution of income between present and future generations. If non-renewable resources are going to be expensive in the future, should we not be conserving these resources today in order to help our descendants? The problem is that consumers may well act totally selfishly, saying, 'Why should we conserve resources? By the time they run out, we will be dead.' We almost certainly do care about the welfare of our children and grandchildren, but what about our great-great-grandchildren, whom we will never meet?

? 1. Will the market provide incentives for firms to research into energy-conserving techniques, if energy prices at present are not high enough to make the use of such techniques profitable?
2. How will the existence of monopoly power in the supply of resources influence their rate of depletion?

KI 24 p260

TC 5 p50

TC 3 p24

KI 4 p10

Let us assume that the market rate of interest is 10 per cent (i.e. 0.1). Then according to the formula, a purchaser would be prepared to pay

$$\frac{£1000}{0.1} = £10\ 000$$

Why should this be so? If a person deposits £10 000 in the bank, with an interest rate of 10 per cent this will earn that person £1000 per year. Assuming our piece of land is guaranteed to earn a rent of £1000 per year, then provided it costs less than £10 000 to buy, it is a better investment than putting money in the bank. The competition between people to buy this land will drive its price up until it reaches £10 000.

This is just another example of equilibrium being where marginal cost equals marginal benefit. This can be demonstrated by rearranging equation (1) to give

$$Pi = R$$

Remember that the equilibrium price of the land (P) is £10 000 and that the rate of interest (i) is 0.1. If you borrow the £10 000 to buy the land, it will cost you £1000 per year in interest payments (i.e. Pi). This is your annual marginal cost. The annual marginal benefit will be the rent (R) you will earn from the land.

1. *What price would the same piece of land sell for if it still earned £1000 rent per year, but if the rate of interest were now (a) 5 per cent; (b) 20 per cent?*
2. *What does this tell us about the relationship between the price of an asset (like land) and the rate of interest?*

Who are the poor? Who are the rich?

We have been building up an answer to these questions as this chapter has progressed. The final part of the answer concerns the ownership of land and capital. Many people own no land or capital at all. These people will therefore earn no profit, rent or interest.

For those who are fortunate enough to own productive assets, their income from them will depend on (a) the quantity they own and (b) their rental value.

The quantity of assets owned

This will depend on the following:

- Inheritance. Some people have rich parents who leave them substantial amounts of land and capital.
- Past income and savings. If people have high incomes and save a large proportion of them, this helps them to build up a stock of assets.
- Skill in investment (entrepreneurial skill). The more skilful people are in investing and in organising production, the more rapidly will their stock of assets grow.
- Luck. When people open up a business, there are usually substantial risks. The business might flourish or fail.

The rental value

This is the income earned per unit of land and capital. It will depend on the following:

- The level of demand for the factor. This depends on the factor's *MRP*, which in turn depends on its physical productivity (*MPP*) and the demand for the good it produces and hence the good's *MR*.
- The elasticity of demand for the good. The greater the monopoly power that capital owners have in the goods market, the less elastic will be the demand for the product and the greater will be the supernormal returns they can earn on their capital.
- The elasticity of supply of the factor. The less elastic its supply, the more factor owners can gain from a high demand. The high demand will simply push up the level of economic rent that the factor will earn.
- The total factor supply by other factor owners. The further to the left the total factor supply curve, the higher the level of economic rent that each unit of the factor can earn for any given level of demand.

Thus if you are lucky enough to have rich parents who leave you a lot of money when you are relatively young; if you are a skilful investor and save and reinvest a large proportion of your earnings; if you own assets that few other people own, and which produce goods in high demand: then you may end up very rich.

If you have no assets, you will have no property income at all. If at the same time you are on a low wage or are unemployed, then you may be very poor indeed.

Section summary

1. Rent on land, like the price of other factor services, is determined by the interaction of demand and supply. Its supply is totally inelastic (or nearly so). Its demand curve is downward sloping and will equal the *MRP* of land.

2. The price of land depends on its potential rental value (its marginal benefit) and the repayment costs of borrowing to pay for the land (its marginal cost). Equilibrium is where the two are equal.

3. People's income depends not only on their wages but on whether they own any land or capital, and, if they do, the rental value of these assets. This is the final element in determining the distribution of income in the economy.

END OF CHAPTER QUESTIONS

1. The wage rate that a firm has to pay and the output it can produce vary with the number of workers as follows (all figures are hourly):

Number of workers	1	2	3	4	5	6	7	8
Wage rate (AC_L) (£)	3	4	5	6	7	8	9	10
Total output (TPP_L)	10	22	32	40	46	50	52	52

Assume that output sells at £2 per unit.

(a) Copy the table and add additional rows for TC_L, MC_L, TRP_L and MRP_L. Put the figures for MC_L and MRP_L in the spaces between the columns.

(b) How many workers will the firm employ in order to maximise profits?

(c) What will be its hourly wage bill at this level of employment?

(d) How much hourly revenue will it earn at this level of employment?

(e) Assuming that the firm faces other (fixed) costs of £30 per hour, how much hourly profit will it make?

(f) Assume that the workers now formed a union and that the firm agreed to pay the negotiated wage rate to all employees. What is the maximum to which the hourly wage rate could rise without causing the firm to try to reduce employment below the level of (b) above? (See Figure 9.10.)

(g) What would be the firm's hourly profit now?

2. If a firm faces a shortage of workers with very specific skills, it may decide to undertake the necessary training itself. If, on the other hand, it faces a shortage of unskilled workers, it may well offer a small wage increase in order to obtain the extra labour. In the first case, it is responding to an increase in demand for labour by attempting to shift the supply curve. In the second case, it is merely allowing a movement along the supply curve. Use a demand and supply diagram to illustrate each case. Given that elasticity of supply is different in each case, do you think that these are the best policies for the firm to follow? What would happen to wages and economic rent if it used the second policy in the first case?

3. Why does the marginal revenue product differ between workers in different jobs?

4. For what reasons is the average gross weekly pay of women only 76.4 per cent of that of men in the UK?

5. Given the analysis of bilateral monopoly, if the passing of minimum wage legislation forces employers to pay higher wage rates to low-paid employees, will this necessarily cause a reduction in employment?

6. Using a diagram like Figure 9.13, demonstrate what will happen under perfect competition when there is an increase in the productivity of a particular type of capital. Consider the effects on the demand, price (rental rate) and quantity supplied of the services of this type of capital.

7. What factors could cause a rise in the market rate of interest?

8. How is the market price of land related to its productivity?

Online resources

Additional case studies in MyEconLab

9.1 Economic rent and transfer earnings. This examines a way of classifying the earnings of a factor of production and shows how these earnings depend on the elasticity of supply of the factor.

9.2 Telecommuters. This case study looks at the rise of telecommuting, whereby people are able to work from home utilising modern technology.

9.3 Other labour market imperfections. This looks at the three imperfections identified on page 255: namely, imperfect information, persistent disequilibria in labour markets and non-maximising behaviour by firms or workers.

9.4 Ethnic minorities in the UK labour market. This case study looks at differences in income and employment between different ethnic groups in the UK.

9.5 Profit sharing. An examination of the case for and against profit sharing as a means of rewarding workers.

Maths Case 9.1 Calculating the long-run cost of supplying additional equipment for rent. A worked example.

Maths Case 9.2 Calculating the internal rate of return. A worked example.

Websites relevant to this chapter

See sites listed at the end of Chapter 10 on page 303.

Microeconomic Policy

10 Inequality, Poverty and Policies to Redistribute Income   275

11 Markets, Efficiency and the Public Interest   304

12 Environmental Policy   341

13 Government Policy towards Business   367

We now turn to the application of microeconomics and its role in government policy. In Part C we looked at *how* market economies function at a micro level. In Part D we examine the various policies that can be adopted to deal with shortcomings of the market system.

There are various questions that governments will ask. How much monopoly power is too much? How equal do we want the distribution of income to be? How can we make markets more efficient? How can we protect the environment and prevent the depletion of resources? How can we prevent climate change?

In Chapter 10 we look at policies that address the distribution of income. In Chapter 11 we examine the issue of market failure and consider the potential for government intervention. Finally in Chapters 12 and 13 we turn to government policies with respect to the environment and business.

10 Chapter

Inequality, Poverty and Policies to Redistribute Income

CHAPTER MAP

10.1 Inequality and poverty   **276**
Types of inequality   276
The size distribution of income in the UK   277
Measuring the size distribution of income   277
The functional distribution of income in the UK   280
Other determinants of income inequality   282
The distribution of wealth   283
Causes of inequality   284
Government attitudes towards inequality   286

10.2 Taxes, benefits and the redistribution of income   **288**
The use of taxation and government expenditure
   to redistribute income   288
The requirements of a good tax system   288
Types of tax   289
Taxes as a means of redistributing income   292
Problems with using taxes to redistribute
   incomes   293
Taxation and incentives   294
Benefits   298
Benefits and the redistribution of income   298
The tax/benefit system and the problem of
   disincentives: the poverty trap   299
Conclusions   299

In Chapter 9 we saw that there are considerable differences in wage rates, and that these depend on market conditions. Similarly, we saw that differences in rewards to owners of capital and land also depend on their respective markets.

But differences in factor rewards are only part of the explanation of inequality. In this chapter, we open out the analysis. We take a more general look at why some people are rich while others are poor, and consider the overall degree of inequality in our society: a society that includes the super-rich, with their luxury yachts and their villas abroad, and people living in slum conditions, with not enough to feed and clothe themselves or their children properly: a society where people begging in the streets are an all too familiar sight. We will see how the gap between rich and poor has tended to widen over time.

We will show how inequality can be measured. We will also look at how incomes are distributed between particular groups, whether by occupation, age, sex, household composition or geographical area.

The second part of the chapter considers what can be done to reduce inequality. Is the solution to tax the rich very heavily, so that the money can be redistributed to the poor? Or might this discourage people from working so hard? Would it be better, then, to focus on benefits and increase the support for the poor? Or might this discourage people from taking on work for fear of losing their benefits? We look at the attitudes of governments and at some of the debates taking place today over how to reduce inequality without discouraging effort or initiative.

10.1 INEQUALITY AND POVERTY

Inequality is one of the most contentious issues in the world of economics and politics. Some people have incomes far in excess of what they need to enjoy a luxurious lifestyle, while others struggle to purchase even the basic necessities.

The need for some redistribution from rich to poor is broadly accepted across the political spectrum. Thus the government taxes the rich more than the poor and then transfers some of the proceeds to the poor, either as cash benefits or in kind. Nevertheless there is considerable disagreement as to the appropriate *amount* of redistribution.

Whether the current distribution of income is desirable or not is a normative question. Economists therefore cannot settle the debate between politicians over how much the government should redistribute incomes from rich to poor. Nevertheless economists do have a major role to play in the analysis of inequality. They can do the following:

- Identify the extent of inequality and analyse how it has changed over time.
- Explain why a particular level of income distribution occurs and what causes inequality to grow or to lessen.
- Examine the relationship between equality and other economic objectives such as efficiency.
- Identify various government policies to deal with problems of inequality and poverty.
- Examine the effects of these policies, both on inequality itself and on other questions such as efficiency, inflation and unemployment.

Types of inequality

There are a number of different ways of looking at the distribution of income and wealth. Each way highlights a different aspect of inequality.

The distribution of income

There are three broad ways of examining the distribution of income. First we can look at how evenly incomes are distributed among the population. This is known as the **size distribution of income**. It can be expressed between *households*, or between *individual earners*, or between *all individuals*. It can be expressed either *before* or *after* the deduction of taxes and the receipt of benefits. For example, we might want to know the proportion of pre-tax national income going to the richest 10 per cent of households.

Then there is the question of distribution between different *factors of production*. This is known as the **functional distribution of income**. At the *broader* level, we could look at the distribution between the general factor categories: labour, land and capital. For example, there is the question of the relative shares of wages and profits in national income. At a *narrower* level, we could look at distribution within the factor categories. Why are some jobs well paid while others are badly paid? Why are rents higher in some areas than in others? This is the type of distribution we looked at in Chapter 9.

Finally there is the question of the **distribution of income by class of recipient**. This can be by *class of person*: women, men, single people, married people, people within a particular age group or ethnic group, and so on. Alternatively, it can be by *geographical area*. Typically, this is expressed in terms of differences in incomes between officially defined regions within a country.

The distribution of wealth

Income is a *flow*. It measures the receipt of money per period of time (e.g. £10 000 per year). Wealth, by contrast, is a stock (see Box 9.9). It measures the value of a person's assets at a particular point in time. The distribution of wealth can be measured as a size distribution (how evenly it is distributed among the population); as a functional distribution (the proportion of wealth held in various forms, such as dwellings, land, company shares, bank deposits, etc.); or according to the holders of wealth, classified by age, sex, geographical area, etc.

Analysis of incomes below a certain level: the analysis of poverty

A major problem here is in defining just what is meant by poverty. The dividing line between who is poor and who is not is necessarily arbitrary. Someone who is classed as poor in the UK may seem comparatively rich to an Ethiopian.

The extent and nature of poverty can be analysed in a number of ways:

- The number or proportion of people or households falling into the category.
- The occupational distribution of poverty.
- The geographical distribution of poverty.

Definitions

Size distribution of income Measurement of the distribution of income according to the levels of income received by individuals (irrespective of source).

Functional distribution of income Measurement of the distribution of income according to the source of income (e.g. from employment, from profit, from rent, etc.).

Distribution of income by class of recipient Measurement of the distribution of income between the classes of person who receive it (e.g. homeowners and non-homeowners or those in the north and those in the south).

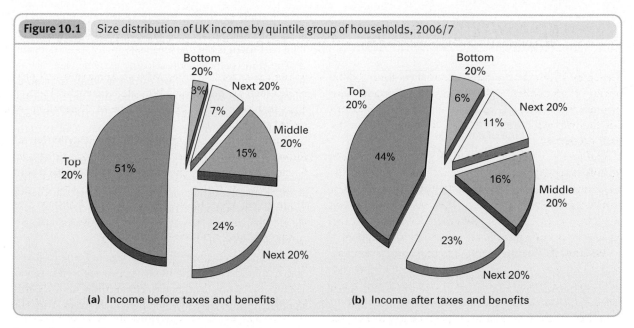

Figure 10.1 Size distribution of UK income by quintile group of households, 2006/7

(a) Income before taxes and benefits

(b) Income after taxes and benefits

Source: From The effect of taxes and benefits on household income, 2006/07, *Economic & Labour Market Review*, July (National Statistics, 2008).

- The distribution of poverty according to age, sex, ethnic origin, marital status, educational attainment, etc.

It is not possible in this chapter to look at all aspects of inequality in the UK. Nevertheless some of the more important facts are considered, along with questions of their measurement and interpretation.

The size distribution of income in the UK

Figure 10.1 shows the size distribution of income in the UK. It covers income from all sources. In each chart, households are grouped into five equal-sized groups or *quintiles*, from the poorest 20 per cent of households up to the richest 20 per cent. (The general term for division into equal-sized groups is *quantiles*.) The following points can be drawn from these statistics:

- In 2006/7 the richest 20 per cent of households earned 51 per cent of national income, and even after the deduction of taxes this was still 44 per cent.
- The poorest 20 per cent, by contrast, earned a mere 3 per cent of national income, and even after the receipt of benefits this had risen only to 6 per cent.

Inequality grew dramatically in the 1980s and did not begin to reduce again until 2000, and then only very slightly. Between 1977 and 2006/7 the post-tax-and-benefits share of national income of the bottom 40 per cent of households fell from 23 per cent to 17 per cent, while the share of the top 20 per cent grew from 37 per cent to 44 per cent.

As we shall see in section 10.2, by taxing the rich proportionately more than the poor, taxes can be used as a means of reducing inequality. In the UK, however, indirect

taxes (e.g. on tobacco and alcohol) are paid proportionately more by the poor and so have the opposite effect. In 2006/7, the lowest-earning 20 per cent of households paid 38.6 per cent of their gross income in taxes, while the highest-earning 20 per cent paid only 34.8 per cent of their income. When we look at indirect taxes we see that the poorest quintile paid 27.8 per cent of their income while the richest quintile paid only 10.1 per cent. This more than offsets the redistributive effect from income tax being paid proportionately more by the rich.

Redistribution of income in the UK, therefore, is achieved mainly through the benefits system.

Measuring the size distribution of income

Apart from tables and charts, two of the most widely used methods for measuring inequality are the *Lorenz curve* and the *Gini coefficient*.

Lorenz curve

Figure 10.2 shows the **Lorenz curve** for the UK based on pre-tax (but post-benefit) incomes.

Definitions

Quintiles Divisions of the population into five equal-sized groups (an example of a quantile).

Quantiles Divisions of the population into equal-sized groups.

Lorenz curve A curve showing the proportion of national income earned by any given percentage of the population (measured from the poorest upwards).

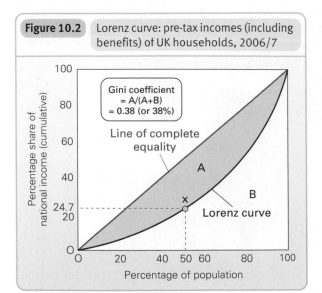

Figure 10.2 Lorenz curve: pre-tax incomes (including benefits) of UK households, 2006/7

The horizontal axis measures percentages of the population from the poorest to the richest. Thus the 40 per cent point represents the poorest 40 per cent of the population. The vertical axis measures the percentage of national income they receive.

The curve starts at the origin: zero people earn zero incomes. If income were distributed totally equally, the Lorenz curve would be a straight 45° line. The 'poorest' 20 per cent of the population would earn 20 per cent of national income; the 'poorest' 60 per cent would earn 60 per cent, and so on. The curve ends up at the top right-hand corner, with 100 per cent of the population earning 100 per cent of national income.

In practice, the Lorenz curve will 'hang below' the 45° line. Point *x*, for example, shows that the poorest 50 per cent of UK households, even after the receipt of benefits, received only 24.7 per cent of national income. The further the curve drops below the 45° line, the greater will be the level of inequality.

The Lorenz curve is quite useful for showing the change in income distribution over time. From 1949 to 1979 the curve moved inwards towards the 45° line, suggesting a lessening of inequality. Then from 1979 to 1990 it moved downwards away from the 45° line, suggesting a deepening of inequality. Since 1990 it has remained approximately the same.

The problem with simply comparing Lorenz curves by eye is that it is imprecise. This problem is overcome by using Gini coefficients.

Gini coefficient

The **Gini coefficient** is a precise way of measuring the position of the Lorenz curve. It is the ratio of the area between the Lorenz curve and the 45° line to the whole area below the 45° line. In Figure 10.2 this is the ratio of the shaded area *A* to the whole area (*A* + *B*), sometimes expressed as a percentage.

If income is totally equally distributed so that the Lorenz curve follows the 45° line, area *A* disappears and the Gini coefficient is zero. As inequality increases, so does area *A*. The Gini coefficient rises. In the extreme case of total inequality, where one person earns the whole of national income, area *B* would disappear and the Gini coefficient would be 1. Thus the Gini coefficient will be between 0 and 1. The higher it is, the greater is the inequality. In 1979 the pre-tax Gini coefficient in the UK was 0.30. With the growth in inequality during the 1980s, the coefficient steadily increased and stood at 0.38 in 1990. Since then it has remained at approximately that level (fluctuating between 0.36 and 0.39). The post-tax coefficient rose even more dramatically – from 0.29 in 1979 to 0.40 in 1990. It was 0.39 in 2006/7.

Gini coefficients have the advantage of being relatively simple to understand and use. They provide a clear way of comparing income distribution either in the same country at different times, or between different countries. They suffer two main drawbacks, however.

First, a single measure cannot take into account all the features of inequality. Take the case of the two countries illustrated in Figure 10.3. If area *X* is equal to area *Y*, they will have the same Gini coefficient, and yet the pattern of their income distribution is quite different.

In which country in Figure 10.3 would you expect to find the highest number of poor people? Describe how income is distributed in the two cases.

Second, there is the problem of what statistics are used in the calculation. Are they pre-tax or post-tax; do they

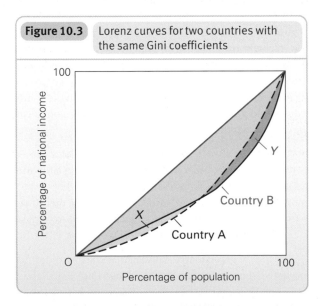

Figure 10.3 Lorenz curves for two countries with the same Gini coefficients

Definition

Gini coefficient The area between the Lorenz curve and the 45° line divided by the total area under the 45° line.

Figure 10.4 Ratio of income shares of bottom 40% to top 20% of households (after taxes and benefits)

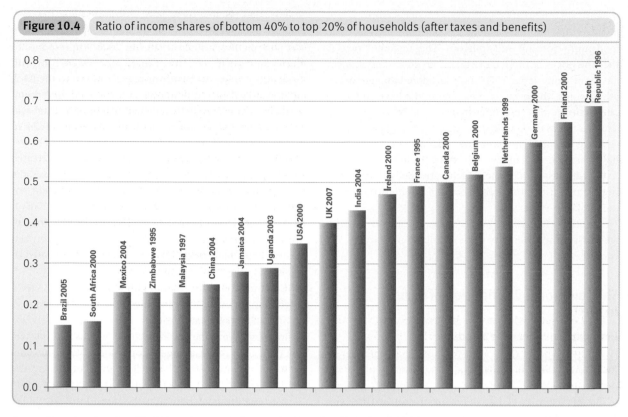

Source: Based on data from World Development Indicators database (World Bank, 2008).

include benefits; do they include non-monetary incomes (such as food grown for own consumption: a major item in many developing countries); are they based on individuals, households or tax units? Unfortunately, different countries use different types of statistics. International comparisons of inequality are thus fraught with difficulties.

Ratios of the shares in national income of two quantile groups

This is a very simple method of measuring income distribution. A ratio quite commonly used is that of the share of national income of the *bottom 40 per cent* of the population to that of the *top 20 per cent*. Thus if the bottom 40 per cent earned 15 per cent of national income and the top 20 per cent earned 50 per cent of national income, the ratio would be 15/50 = 0.3. The lower the ratio, therefore, the greater the inequality. Figure 10.4 gives some examples of this ratio from different countries.

1. Why do you think that the ratios for developing countries are lower than those for developed countries?
2. Make a list of reasons why the ratios in Figure 10.4 may not give an accurate account of relative levels of inequality between countries.
3. What would the ratio be if national income were absolutely equally distributed?

Do earnings statistics give a true representation of inequality?

Although the size distribution of income gives a good first indication of inequality, there are various factors that need to be taken into account when interpreting the statistics.

The first is the diminishing marginal utility of income. If a rich person spends twice as much as a poor person, does that mean that they get twice as much utility? The answer is probably no. The more you earn and spend, the less additional utility you will get for each extra amount spent (see pages 106–7). Part of the reason is the obvious one that you increasingly tire of more of the same products. Part of the reason is that you buy more luxurious versions of products. The argument here is that a car costing £20 000 will not give you four times as much utility as one costing £5000.

The second factor concerns the interpretation of changes in inequality over time. The past thirty years have seen income increases skewed towards the rich, with the top 10 per cent of income earners getting a lot richer, while the incomes of the poor have risen very little. As we have seen, from 1979 to 2006/7 the Gini coefficient of post-tax income in the UK rose from 0.29 to 0.39.

Yet inequality may not have grown as rapidly as the figures suggest. As people earn more, so the pattern of their spending changes. They spend proportionately more on services, such as childcare, financial advice and personal trainers, and on luxury goods such as designer clothing and fast cars, and proportionately less on items such as basic foodstuffs, clothing and toiletries. The argument here is that the prices of these more luxurious goods and services has been rising faster than those of more basic goods. In other words, the poor have experienced a lower inflation rate than the rich, meaning that inequality has not been rising as fast as the simple statistics would suggest.

More recently, however, the inflation rate of the poor has overtaken that of the rich. Prices of food and energy have risen faster than those of luxury goods. This would suggest that the statistics have been *understating* the growth in inequality.

The third factor that needs to be taken into account when assessing inequality is the distribution of *wealth*. We consider this below (pages 283–4).

The functional distribution of income in the UK

Distribution of income by source

Figure 10.5 shows the sources of household incomes in 1975 and 2006/7. Wages and salaries constitute by far the largest element. However, their share fell from 77 per cent to 67 per cent of national income between 1975 and 2006/7. Conversely, the share coming from social security benefits and pensions rose from 12 per cent to 19 per cent, reflecting the growing proportion of the population past retirement age.

In contrast to wages and salaries, investment income (dividends, interest and rent) accounts for a relatively small percentage of household income – a mere 3 per cent in

2006/7. Nevertheless, some groups, typically elderly people, rely on savings interest as a key source of income. With the plummeting of interest rates in 2008/9 in response to the credit crunch, so many of these people were badly hit. Conversely, those with large mortgages linked to the Bank of England's Bank Rate ('tracker mortgages'), found themselves with much smaller payments each month. There was thus a major redistributive effect away from net savers to net borrowers.

With the growth of small businesses and the increased numbers of people being 'employed' on a freelance basis, the proportion of incomes coming from self-employment has grown. It rose from 6 per cent in 1975 to 9 per cent in 2006/7.

The overall shares illustrated in Figure 10.5 hide the fact that the sources of income differ quite markedly between different income groups. These differences are shown in Table 10.1.

Column (1) shows that higher-income groups get a larger proportion of their income from wages and salaries than do lower-income groups. This can be largely explained by examining column (5). As would be expected, the poor tend to get a larger proportion of their incomes in social security benefits than do people further up the income scale.

It is interesting to note that the second poorest 20 per cent of households have a larger proportion of their income from pensions and annuities than any other group. Pensioners are clustered in this group because they tend to be fairly poor (pensions being less than wages), but not as poor as unemployed people or as families on low incomes.

One perhaps surprising feature to note is that the proportion of income coming from profits, rent and interest

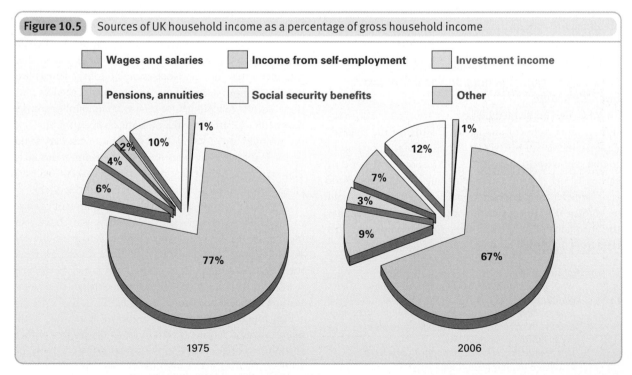

Figure 10.5   Sources of UK household income as a percentage of gross household income

Source: Based on data in *Family Spending* (National Statistics, 2008).

Table 10.1 Sources of UK household income as a percentage of total household income by quintile groups: 2006

Gross household weekly incomes (quintiles)	Wages and salaries (1)	Income from self-employment (2)	Income from investments (3)	Pensions and annuities (4)	Social security benefits (5)	Other (6)	Total (7)
Lowest 20%	6	3	3	9	77	2	100
Next 20%	32	4	4	16	43	2	100
Middle 20%	61	7	3	11	17	2	100
Next 20%	75	8	3	7	7	1	100
Highest 20%	79	11	4	4	2	1	100
All households	67	9	3	7	12	1	100

Source: *Family Spending* (National Statistics, 2008).

(column (3)) varies little between the income groups. In fact only for those people in the top 1 or 2 per cent is it significantly higher. The conclusion from this, plus the fact that investment incomes account for only 3 per cent of household incomes in total, is that incomes from capital and land are of only relatively minor significance in explaining income inequality.

The major cause of differences in incomes between individuals in employment is the differences in wages and salaries between different occupations.

Distribution of wages and salaries by occupation

Differences in full-time wages and salaries are illustrated in Figure 10.6. This shows the average gross weekly pay of full-

time adult workers in selected occupations in 2007. As you can see, there are considerable differences in pay between different occupations. The causes of differences in wage rates from one occupation to another were examined in Chapter 9.

 If fringe benefits (such as long holidays, company cars, free clothing/uniforms, travel allowances and health insurance) were included, do you think the level of inequality would increase or decrease? Explain why.

Since the late 1970s, wage differentials have widened. Part of the explanation lies in a shift in the demand

Figure 10.6 Average gross weekly earnings of UK full-time adult employees (£): 2007

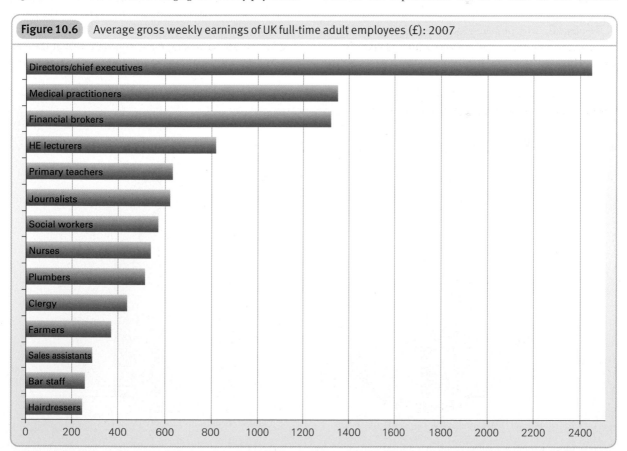

Source: *Annual Survey of Hours and Earnings* (National Statistics, 2008).

for labour. Many firms have adopted new techniques which require a more highly educated workforce. Wage rates in some of these skilled occupations have increased substantially.

At the same time, there has been a decline in the number of unskilled jobs in industry and, along with it, a decline in the power of unions to represent such people. Where low-skilled jobs remain, there will be intense pressure on employers to reduce wage costs if they are competing with companies based in developing countries, where wage rates are much lower.

As prospects for unskilled people decline in industry, so people with few qualifications increasingly compete for low-paid, service-sector jobs (e.g. in supermarkets and fast-food outlets). The growth in people seeking part-time work has also kept wage rates down in this sector.

Other determinants of income inequality

Differences in household composition

Other things being equal, the more dependants there are in a household, the lower the income will be *per member* of that household. Figure 10.7 gives an extreme example of this. It shows the average household income in the UK in 2006 of four different categories of household.

Households with two adults and four or more children had approximately the same income as households with only one man and one woman. This means that they had a very much lower income *per member* of the household.

There is a twin problem for many large households. Not only may there be relatively more children and elderly dependants, but also the total household income will be reduced if one of the adults stays at home to look after the family, or works only part time.

Differences by sex

Box 9.7 on pages 252–3 looked at some of the aspects of income inequality between the sexes. In 2007, the average gross weekly pay for full-time female employees was £462.80. For male employees it was £606.10. There are three important factors to note:

- Women are paid less than men in the same occupations. You will see this if you compare some of the occupations in Table (b) in Box 9.7.
- Women tend to be employed in lower-paid occupations than men.
- Women do much less overtime than men (on average, 0.7 hours per week, compared with 1.9 for men).

 List the reasons for each of the three factors above. (Re-read section 9.2 and Box 9.7 if you need help.)

Differences in the geographical distribution of income

Figure 10.8 shows the gross weekly household incomes in different regions of the UK in 2006. Differences in incomes between the regions reflect regional differences in industrial structure, unemployment and the cost of living. As can be seen from the figure, average incomes are significantly lower in the north-east than in the south-east of England.

On a more local level, there are considerable differences in incomes between affluent areas and deprived areas. It is

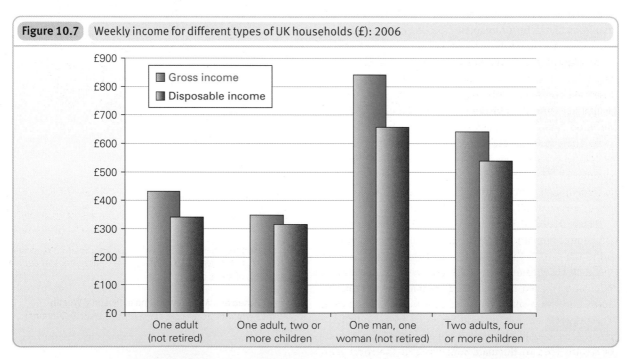

Figure 10.7 Weekly income for different types of UK households (£): 2006

Source: Based on data in *Family Spending* (National Statistics, 2008).

Figure 10.8 Gross weekly household income, selected UK regions (£), 2006

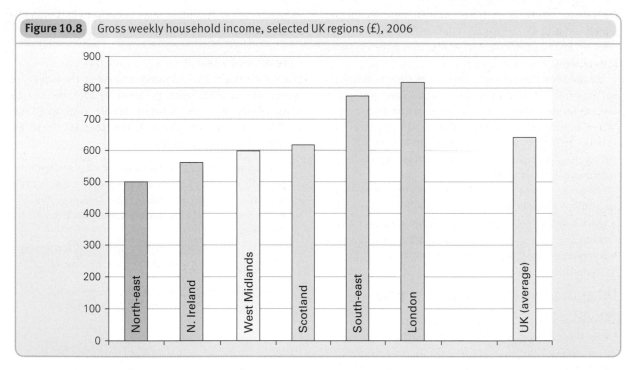

Source: *Family Spending* (National Statistics, 2008).

at this level that some of the most extreme examples of inequality can be observed, with 'leafy' affluent suburbs only a mile or two away from run-down estates. Regional inequality and local inequality are explored in Case Study 23.10 in MyEconLab.

The distribution of wealth

Wealth is difficult to measure. Being a *stock* of assets (such as a house, land, furniture, personal possessions and investments), it has an easily measurable value only when it is sold. What is more, individuals are not required to keep any record of their assets. Only when people die and their assets are assessed for inheritance tax does a record become available. Official statistics are thus based on Inland Revenue data of the assets of those who have died that year. These statistics are suspect for two reasons. First, the people who have died are unlikely to be a representative sample of the population. Second, many items are excluded, such as household and personal items, and items passed automatically to the surviving spouse.

Figure 10.9 and Table 10.2 give official statistics on the UK composition and distribution of wealth. As can be seen from Table 10.2, inequality of wealth is far greater than inequality of income. The wealthiest 1 per cent of the adult population owned 21 per cent of the marketable wealth in 2003, and the wealthiest 10 per cent owned 53 per cent. These figures do not include pension rights, which are much more equally distributed. The level and distribution of wealth tend to fluctuate somewhat in the short term with movements in share prices and house prices.

Figure 10.9 Composition of UK gross personal wealth, 2003

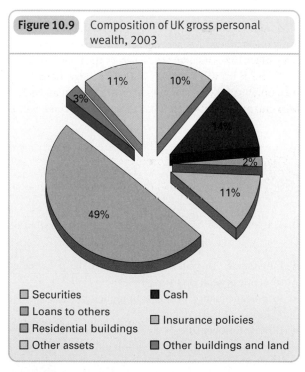

- □ Securities
- □ Loans to others
- □ Residential buildings
- □ Other assets
- ■ Cash
- □ Insurance policies
- ■ Other buildings and land

Note: The figures are for gross wealth. To get net wealth we would have to deduct mortgage and other debts. These debts amount to nearly 10% of gross debt.

Source: Based on HMRC Distribution of Personal Wealth Statistics (www.hmrc.gov.uk/stats) (HM Revenue & Customs), Table 13.1.

| BOX10.1 | POVERTY IN THE PAST | CASE STUDIES AND APPLICATIONS |

Consider from the following passage whether it is reasonable or even possible to compare poverty today with poverty in the 1800s.

> Every great city has one or more slums, where the working class is crowded together. True, poverty often dwells in hidden alleys close to the palaces of the rich; but, in general, a separate territory has been assigned to it, where, removed from the sight of the happier classes, it may struggle along as it can.
>
> The houses are occupied from cellar to garret, filthy within and without, and their appearance is such that no human being could possibly wish to live in them . . . the filth and tottering ruin surpass all description. Scarcely a whole window-pane can be found, the walls are crumbling, doorposts and window-frames loose and broken, doors of old boards nailed together, or altogether wanting in this thieves' quarter, where no doors are needed, there being nothing to steal. Heaps of garbage and ashes lie in all directions, and the foul

liquids emptied before the doors gather in stinking pools. Here live the poorest of the poor, the worst-paid workers with thieves and the victims of prostitution indiscriminately huddled together . . . and those who have not yet sunk in the whirlpool of moral ruin which surrounds them, sinking daily deeper, losing daily more and more of their power to resist the demoralising influence of want, filth, and evil surroundings.[1]

1. If we were to measure poverty today and in the nineteenth century in absolute terms, in which would there be the greater number of poor?
2. If we measure poverty in relative terms, must a society inevitably have a problem of poverty, however rich it is?

[1] F. Engels, *The Condition of the Working Class in England* (Progress Publishers, 1973), pp. 166–7.

| Table 10.2 | Size distribution of UK wealth |

	Proportion of marketable wealth (%)			
	1971	**1981**	**1991**	**2003**
Wealthiest 1%	31	18	17	21
Wealthiest 5%	52	36	35	40
Wealthiest 10%	65	50	47	53
Wealthiest 25%	86	73	71	72
Wealthiest 50%	97	92	92	93
Gini coefficient	0.80	0.67	0.64	0.70

Source: Based on HMRC Distribution of Personal Wealth Statistics (www.hmrc.gov.uk/stats) (HM Revenue & Customs), Table 13.5.

The four major causes of inequality in the distribution of wealth are as follows:

- Inheritance. This allows inequality to be perpetuated from one generation to another.
- Income inequality. People with higher incomes can save more.
- Different propensities to save. People who save a larger proportion of their income will build up a bigger stock of wealth.
- Entrepreneurial and investment talent/luck. Some people are successful in investing their wealth and making it grow rapidly.

Even though wealth is still highly concentrated, there was a significant reduction in inequality of wealth up to the early 1990s. From 1971 to 1991 the Gini coefficient of wealth fell a full 16 percentage points from 0.80 to 0.64. A major reason for this was the increased taxation of

inherited wealth. Since 1991, however, this reduction in inequality has been reversed somewhat. This can be explained by lower levels of inheritance tax and substantial rises in property prices and share values.

Causes of inequality

We turn now to identify the major causes of inequality. The problem has many dimensions and there are many factors that determine the pattern and depth of inequality. It is thus wrong to try to look for a single cause, or even the major one. The following are possible determinants of inequality:

- Inequality of wealth. People with wealth are able to obtain an income other than from their own labour. The greater the inequality of wealth, the greater is the inequality of income likely to be.
- Differences in ability. People differ in intelligence, strength, dexterity, etc. Some of these differences are innate and some are acquired through the process of 'socialisation' – education, home environment, peer group, etc.
- Differences in attitude. Some people are adventurous, willing to take risks, willing to move for better jobs, keen to push themselves forward. Others are much more cautious.
- Differences in qualifications. These are reflections of a number of things: ability, attitudes towards study, access to educational establishments, the quality of tuition, attitudes and income of parents, etc.
- Differences in hours worked. Some people do a full-time job plus overtime, or a second job; others work only part time.

| BOX 10.2 | HOW TO REVERSE THE UK'S INCREASED INEQUALITY | CASE STUDIES AND APPLICATIONS |

Has policy succeeded?

In February 1995 the Rowntree Foundation published the results of a comprehensive inquiry into the UK's growing inequality since 1979.[1] The findings made grim reading. Inequalities in income had widened further and faster than in any other period in history. The rich had got substantially richer, while the poor had become not only relatively poorer, but absolutely poorer.

This growing divide, the report argued, was threatening the whole fabric of society. There was a growing underclass of people with little hope of clawing their way out of their desperate poverty, frequently seeing crime as their only escape route. The poor include the long-term unemployed, pensioners, families dependent on state benefits and young people without the educational attainment to compete in the increasingly competitive labour market. And it is not just the poor who are affected by poverty. Do we want a society, asks the report, where the rich have to build fortresses to protect themselves?

The report recommended various remedies. The thrust of them was to encourage employment and improve the lot of low-paid workers. Suggested measures included increased government expenditure on training schemes, top-up benefits for those on low wages and tax cuts targeted at the poor. These were seen as much better alternatives than simply increasing unemployment benefits, which could well make people more reluctant to get a job.

Have such recommendations been heeded and is inequality in the UK now in decline?

Policies and their effects since 1997

After coming to office in 1997, the Labour government put the reduction of poverty, especially child and pensioner poverty, high on its agenda. In 1999 the Prime Minister, Tony Blair, pledged to cut child poverty by a quarter by 2004/5, halve child poverty by 2010/11 and eliminate it within a generation. The focus was on eliminating the 'cycle of deprivation', where children in poor households are more likely to leave school early, less likely to get good jobs and more likely to be unemployed themselves as adults, and thus to bring up their children in poverty.

A number of measures were taken, including making work more financially worthwhile for poor families by the use of tax credits (see Box 10.6) and increasing benefits for poor families with children. The government also extended means-tested benefits for pensioners, although there remains a problem of lack of take-up of some of these benefits.

In 2005 the Joseph Rowntree Foundation was optimistic that the policy was proving effective:

Simulation modelling shows that tax and benefit reforms have reduced child poverty quickly enough to give the government a good chance of hitting its 2004/5 targets. Pensioner poverty should be falling by 2004/5, and tax and benefit policies have at least stopped overall income inequality growing (as it would otherwise have done).[2]

However, the rate of progress slowed and it soon became clear that the government was in danger of missing its targets. In 2006 an independent report for the Department of Work and Pensions was published.[3] This highlighted the need to increase benefit/tax credits further if the UK's child poverty levels were to approach the best in Europe. It identified a substantial number of children who remained in workless households, for whom there was no end to poverty in sight.

Since then the government has continued to increase benefits and to offer further support to parents wishing to work by the extension of family policies, including parental leave and the right to request flexible working. However, the changing macroeconomic climate in the late 2000s did cause some campaigners to express concern about the government's ability to sustain the momentum on child poverty reduction.

One criticism of current policy is that there has been no specific aim of reducing income inequality. The result is that it has remained roughly the same as in 1997. Although substantial numbers of families have seen incomes increase, the general growth in *all* incomes since 2000 has meant that inequality persists.

1. *Suggest a range of 'direct' policies that the government might pursue in order to reduce inequality and poverty within the UK.*
2. *If the government concentrates on eliminating child and pensioner poverty, what is likely to happen to other vulnerable groups? Which groups might this include?*

[1] *Income and Wealth* (Joseph Rowntree Foundation, 1995).
[2] Policies towards poverty, inequality and exclusion since 1997, http://www.jrf.org.uk/knowledge/findings/socialpolicy/0015.asp. This report from the Joseph Rowntree Foundation summarises the findings of a book, *A More Equal Society? New Labour, Poverty, Inequality and Exclusion*, edited by John Hills and Kitty Stewart (The Policy Press, 2005).
[3] Lisa Harker for the Department of Work and Pensions, *Delivering on Child Poverty: What Would It Take?* (November 2006).

- Differences in job utility/disutility. Other things being equal, unpleasant, arduous or dangerous jobs will need to pay higher wages.
- Differences in power. Monopoly power in the supply of factors or goods, and monopsony power in the demand for factors, is unequally distributed in the economy.
- Differences in the demand for goods. Factors employed in expanding industries will tend to have a higher

marginal revenue product because their output has a higher market value.
- Differences in household composition. The greater the number of dependants relative to income earners, the poorer the average household member will be (other things being equal).
- Discrimination by race, sex, age, social background, etc.

- Degree of government support. The greater the support for the poor, the less will be the level of inequality in the economy.
- Unemployment. When unemployment levels are high, this is one of the major causes of poverty.

 Which of the above causes are reflected in differences in the marginal revenue product of factors?

Government attitudes towards inequality

The political right sees little problem with inequality as such. In fact, inequality has an important economic function. Factor price differences are an essential part of a dynamic market economy. They are the price signals that encourage resources to move to sectors of the economy where demand is growing, and away from sectors where demand is declining. If the government interferes with this process by taxing high incomes and subsidising low incomes, working people will not have the same incentive to gain better qualifications, to seek promotion, to do over-time, or to move for better jobs. Similarly, owners of capital will not have the same incentive to invest.

If inequality is to be reduced, claims the political right, it is better done by encouraging greater factor mobility. If factor supply curves are more elastic (greater mobility), then any shifts in demand will cause smaller changes in factor prices and thus less inequality. But how is greater mobility to be encouraged? The answer, they say, is to create a culture of self-help: where people are not too reliant on state support; where they will 'get on their bikes' and look for higher incomes. At the same time, they argue that the monopoly power of unions to interfere in labour markets should be curtailed. The net effect of these two policies, they claim, would be to create a more competitive labour market which would help to reduce inequality as well as promoting economic growth and efficiency.

State support, say those on the right, should be confined to the relief of 'genuine' poverty. Benefits should be simply a minimum safety net for those who cannot work (e.g. the sick or disabled), or on a temporary basis for those who, through no fault of their own, have lost their jobs. Even at this basic level, however, the right argues that state support can discourage people from making more effort.

Although many on the political left accept that there is some possibility of a trade-off between equality and efficiency, they see it as a far less serious problem. Questions of efficiency and growth, claims the left, are best dealt with by encouraging investment. This, they argue, is best achieved by creating an environment of industrial democracy where workers participate in investment decisions. This common purpose is in turn best achieved in a more equal and less individualistically competitive society. The left also sees a major role for government in providing support for investment: for example, through government-sponsored research, by investment grants, by encouraging firms to get together and plan a co-ordinated strategy, or by maintaining low interest rates that make borrowing cheaper for investment.

These policies to achieve growth and efficiency, claims the left, will leave the government freer to pursue a much more active policy on redistribution.

Section summary

1. Inequality can be examined by looking at the size distribution of income, the functional distribution of income (whether by broad factor categories, narrow factor categories, occupation or other individual factor reward), the distribution of income by recipient (whether by class of person or geographical area), the distribution of wealth, or the extent and nature of poverty.

2. An analysis of the size distribution of income in the UK shows that inequality has grown.

3. The size distribution of income can be illustrated by means of a Lorenz curve. The greater the inequality, the more bowed the curve will be towards the bottom right-hand corner.

4. Size distribution can also be measured by a Gini coefficient. This will give a figure between 0 (total equality) and 1 (total inequality). Income distribution can also be measured as the ratio of the share of national income of a given lower income quantile to that of a higher income quantile.

5. Wages and salaries constitute by far the largest source of income, and thus inequality can be explained mainly in terms of differences in wages and salaries. Nevertheless state benefits are an important moderating influence on inequality and constitute the largest source of income for the poorest 20 per cent of households. Investment earnings are only a minor determinant of income except for the richest 1 or 2 per cent.

6. Other determinants of income inequality include differences in household composition, sex and where people live.

7. The distribution of wealth is less equal than the distribution of income.

8. Attitudes towards government redistribution of income vary among political parties. The political right stresses the danger that redistributive policies may destroy incentives. The best approach to inequality, according to the right, is to 'free up' markets so as to encourage greater mobility. The left, by contrast, sees fewer dangers in reducing incentives and stresses the moral and social importance of redistribution from rich to poor.

| BOX 10.3 | MINIMUM WAGE LEGISLATION | CASE STUDIES AND APPLICATIONS |

A way of helping the poor?

The Labour government introduced a statutory UK minimum wage in April 1999. The rate was £3.60 per hour for those aged 22 and over, and £3.00 for those between 18 and 21. In 2004 an additional rate was introduced for 16- and 17-year-olds. The rates have been increased every year and in 2008/9 were £5.73, £4.77, and £3.53. These compare with the following adult rates in Europe (at exchange rates as of 2008 Q3): Belgium, £5.90; France, £6.80; Ireland, £6.75; Netherlands, £5.94; Poland, £1.48.

The call for a minimum wage in the UK had grown stronger during the 1990s as the number of low-paid workers increased. There were many people working as cleaners, kitchen hands, garment workers, security guards and shop assistants who were receiving pittance rates of pay, sometimes less than £2 per hour. There were several factors explaining the growth in the size of the low-pay sector.

- *Unemployment.* Very high rates of unemployment since the early 1980s had shifted the balance of power from workers to employers. Employers were able to force many wage rates downwards, especially those of unskilled and semi-skilled workers.
- *Growth in part-time employment.* Changes in the structure of the UK economy, particularly the growth in the service sector and the growing proportion of women seeking work, had led to an increase in part-time employment, with many part-time workers not receiving the same rights, privileges and hourly pay as their full-time equivalents.
- *Changes in labour laws.* The abolition of 'wages councils' in 1993, which had set legally enforceable minimum hourly rates in various low-paid industries, and the introduction of various new laws to reduce the power of labour (see pages 250–1) had left low-paid workers with little protection.

Assessing the arguments

The principal argument against imposing a national minimum wage concerns its impact on employment. If you raise wage rates above the equilibrium level, there will be surplus labour: i.e. unemployment (see Figure 9.9 on page 247). However, the impact of a national minimum wage on employment is not so simple.

In the case of a firm operating in competitive labour and goods markets, the demand for low-skilled workers is relatively wage sensitive. Any rise in wage rates, and hence prices, by this firm alone would lead to a large fall in sales and hence to employment. But given that all firms face the minimum wage, individual employers are more able to pass on higher wages in higher prices, knowing that their competitors are doing the same.

When employers have a degree of monopsony power, however, it is not even certain that they would want to reduce employment. Remember what we argued in Figure 9.10 (on page 248) when we were examining the effects of unions driving up wages. The argument is the same with a minimum wage. The minimum wage can be as high as W_2 and the firm will still want to employ as many workers as at W_1. The point is that the firm can no longer drive down the wage rate by employing fewer workers, so the incentive to cut its workforce has been removed. Indeed, if the minimum wage rate were above W_1 but below W_2, the firm would now want to employ more workers (where the minimum wage rate ($= MC_L$) is equal to the MRP_L). What is effectively happening is that the minimum wage is redistributing the firm's income from profits to wages.

In the long run, the effect on unemployment will depend on the extent to which the higher wages are compensated by higher labour productivity.

Evidence from the USA and other countries suggests that modest increases in the minimum wage have had a neutral effect upon employment. Similarly in the UK, there is little evidence to suggest that employers have responded by employing fewer workers. In fact, unemployment rates have fallen. This, however, can be explained by the fact that the minimum wage was introduced during a period when there was a buoyant economy and increasing labour market flexibility (see Box 9.8).

Whether there would continue to be little effect if the minimum wage were to rise substantially is another matter. The issue, then, seems to be how high can the minimum wage be set before unemployment begins to rise.

Impact of the minimum wage in the UK

Some 1.3 million workers benefit from the minimum wage. The main beneficiaries have been women, the majority of whom work part time and many of whom are lone parents, and people from ethnic minorities. Even the Conservative Party, previously a staunch opponent of a minimum wage, has dropped its opposition.

The biggest weakness of a minimum wage as a means of relieving poverty is that it only affects the employed. One of the main causes of poverty is unemployment. Clearly the unemployed would not benefit from a minimum wage.

Another cause of poverty is a large number of dependants in a family. If there is only one income earner, he or she may be paid above the minimum wage rate and yet the family could be very poor. By contrast, many of those who would be helped by a minimum wage are second income earners in a family.

These are not arguments against minimum wage legislation. They merely suggest that a minimum wage rate cannot be the sole answer to poverty and must be considered in conjunction with benefits.

In the UK, the TUC estimated that there are around 150 000 workers who receive less than the minimum wage and whose employers are breaking the law. It is likely that these workers do not report this as they feel intimidated and fear that they will lose their jobs.

As the economy moved towards recession in 2008, employers called for only moderate increases in the minimum wage in order to reduce the likelihood of increased unemployment.

1. *If an increase in wage rates for low-paid workers leads to their being more motivated, how would this affect the marginal revenue product and the demand for such workers? What implications does your answer have for the effect on employment in such cases? (See pages 251–5 on the efficiency wage hypothesis.)*
2. *If a rise in the minimum wage encourages employers to substitute machines for workers, will this necessarily lead to higher long-term unemployment in (a) that industry and (b) the economy in general?*

10.2   TAXES, BENEFITS AND THE REDISTRIBUTION OF INCOME

In this section, we will look at policies to redistribute incomes more equally, and in particular we will focus on the use of government expenditure and taxation. Redistribution is just one of three major roles for government expenditure and taxation. The second is to compensate for the failure of the market to allocate resources efficiently. We examine this role in the following three chapters. The third is to influence the overall level of activity in the economy. Adjusting government expenditure and/or taxation for this purpose is known as *fiscal policy* and is examined in Chapter 20.

The use of taxation and government expenditure to redistribute income

Taxation.   If the rich are taxed proportionately more than the poor, the post-tax distribution of income will be more equal than the pre-tax distribution.

Subsidies.   Subsidies are of two broad types. First, *cash benefits* can be seen as subsidies to people's incomes. They include such things as child benefit and old-age pensions. Second, *benefits in kind* provide subsidised goods and services, which may be provided free (e.g. education or bus travel) or at a reduced price (e.g. NHS dental treatment). Subsidies will lessen inequality if they account for a larger proportion of a poor person's income than a rich person's.

Although we shall focus mainly on the use of taxes and benefits, there are two other types of redistributive policy.

Legislation.   Examples include minimum wage legislation (see Box 10.3) and anti-discrimination legislation.

Structural policies.   These are policies where the government tries to alter those institutions and attitudes of society that increase or at least perpetuate inequalities. Examples of such policies include attacking privileges, encouraging widening participation in higher education, promoting worker share ownership, encouraging industries to move to areas of high unemployment and encouraging the provision of crèche facilities at work.

Before we turn to look at the use of taxation and government expenditure to redistribute incomes, we must first look at what taxes are available to a government and what are the requirements of a good tax system.

The requirements of a good tax system

Whatever the purpose of taxation, when it comes to devising and administering particular taxes there are various principles that many people argue should be observed.

Horizontal equity.   According to the principle of ***horizontal equity***, people in the *same circumstances* should be taxed equally. In other words, taxes should be levied impartially. For example, people earning the same level of income and with the same personal circumstances (e.g. number and type of dependants, size of mortgage, etc.) should pay the same level of income tax.

    Is it horizontally equitable for smokers and drinkers to pay more tax than non-smokers and non-drinkers?

Vertical equity.   According to the principle of ***vertical equity***, taxes should be 'fairly' apportioned between rich and poor. What constitutes fairness here is highly controversial. No one likes paying taxes and thus a rich person's concept of a fair tax is unlikely to be the same as a poor person's. This whole question of using taxes as a means of redistributing incomes will be examined in detail below.

Equity between recipients of benefits.   Under the ***benefit principle***, it is argued that those who receive the most benefits from government expenditure ought to pay the most in taxes. For example, it can be argued that roads should be paid for from fuel tax. That way those who use the roads the most will pay the most towards their construction and maintenance.

1. *Does the benefit principle conflict with either vertical or horizontal equity?*
2. *Would this be a good principle to apply in the case of health care?*

In most cases, the benefits principle would be difficult to put into practice. There are two reasons why. First, a specific tax would have to be devised for each particular good and service provided by the state. Second, in the case of many goods and services provided by the state, it would be difficult to identify the amount of benefit received by each individual. Just how much benefit (in money terms) do you derive from street lighting, from the police, from the navy, from clean air, etc.?

Cheapness of collection.   Taxes cost money to collect. These costs should be kept to a minimum relative to the revenue they yield.

Definitions

Horizontal equity The equal treatment of people in the same situation.

Vertical equity The redistribution from the better off to the worse off. In the case of taxes, this means the rich paying proportionately more taxes than the poor.

Benefit principle of taxation The principle that people ought to pay taxes in proportion to the amount that they use government services.

Difficulty of evasion. If it is desirable to have a given tax, people should not be able to escape paying. A distinction is made between ***tax evasion*** and ***tax avoidance***:

- Tax evasion is illegal. This is where, for example, people do not declare income to the tax authorities.
- Tax avoidance is legal, albeit from the government's point of view undesirable. This is where people try to find ways of managing their affairs so as to reduce their tax liability. It has been estimated that this cost the UK government in excess of £13 billion in 2007/8. Tax avoidance is more likely to be practised by the rich than the poor – in part because they stand to gain more; in part because they can afford to pay for the specialist advice required.

Non-distortion. Taxes alter market signals: taxes on goods and services alter market prices; taxes on income alter wages. They should not do this in an undesirable direction.

If prices are not distorted in the first place, it is best to use taxes that have the same percentage effect on prices of all goods and services. That way *relative* prices remain the same. For example, VAT in the UK is levied on most goods and services at a single rate of 17.5 per cent (15 per cent in 2009). If goods were taxed at different rates, this would create distortions, switching consumption and production from goods with high taxes to goods with low taxes.

If, however, the government feels that market prices *are* distorted in the first place, taxes can be used to alter price signals in the desired direction.

How can the market distortions argument be used to justify putting excise duties on specific goods such as petrol, alcohol and tobacco? Is this the only reason why excise duties are put on these particular products?

Convenience to the taxpayer. Taxes should be *certain* and *clearly understood* by taxpayers so that they can calculate their tax liabilities. The method of payment should be *straightforward*.

Convenience to the government. Governments use tax changes as an instrument for managing the economy. Tax rates should thus be *simple to adjust*. Also, the government will need to be able to *calculate* as accurately as possible the effects of tax changes, both on the total tax yield and on the distribution of the burden between taxpayers.

Minimal disincentive effects. Taxes may discourage people from working longer or harder, from saving, from investing or from taking initiative. For example, a high rate of income tax may discourage people from seeking promotion or from doing overtime. 'What is the point,' they may say, 'if a large proportion of my extra income is taken away in taxes?' It is desirable that these disincentives should be kept to a minimum.

Of course, not all these requirements can be met at the same time. There is no perfect tax. The government thus has to seek a compromise when there is a conflict between any of the requirements. One of the most serious conflicts is between vertical equity and the need to keep disincentives to a minimum. The more steeply the rich are taxed, it is argued, the more serious are the disincentive effects on them likely to be. This particular conflict is examined below.

Types of tax

Taxes can be divided into two broad categories. ***Direct taxes*** are paid directly by the taxpayer to the tax authorities. Such taxes include personal income tax, tax on companies' income and tax on capital and wealth. ***Indirect taxes***, on the other hand, are paid via a middle person. For example, value added tax (VAT) is designed to be a tax on consumption. But you the consumer do not pay it to the authorities: it is paid by firms, which then pass it on to consumers in higher prices (see section 3.3). You are thus taxed indirectly when you buy goods and services.

Direct taxes

Personal income tax. All types of income are included – wages, salaries, interest, dividends and rent. In most countries, people can earn a certain amount of income free of tax: this is known as their personal ***tax allowance***. In many countries, employees' income tax is paid directly on their behalf by their employers. In the UK this is known as the pay-as-you-earn scheme (PAYE).

The marginal rate of income tax is the rate that people pay on additional income. In most countries, the marginal rate increases in bands as people earn more. In many countries, there is a main marginal rate of tax that most people pay. This is known as the standard or ***basic rate of tax***.

The *average* rate is a person's total income tax as a fraction of total income. This will always be less than the

---

Definitions

Tax evasion The illegal non-payment of taxes (e.g. by not declaring income earned).

Tax avoidance The rearrangement of one's affairs so as to reduce one's tax liability.

Direct taxes Taxes on income and wealth. Paid directly to the tax authorities on that income or wealth.

Indirect taxes Taxes on expenditure. Paid to the tax authorities not by the consumer, but indirectly by the suppliers of the goods or services.

Tax allowance An amount of income that can be earned tax free. Tax allowances vary according to a person's circumstances.

Basic rate of tax The main marginal rate of tax, applying to most people's incomes.

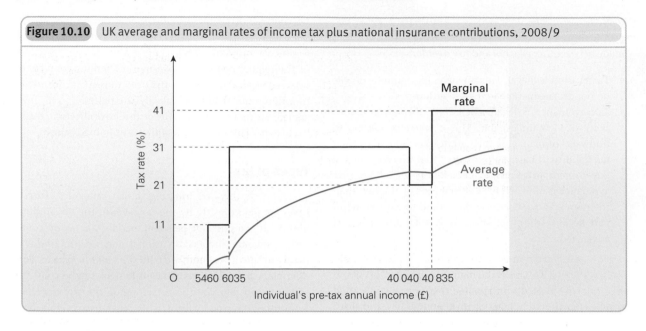

Figure 10.10 UK average and marginal rates of income tax plus national insurance contributions, 2008/9

Table 10.3 UK marginal income tax and national insurance contribution rates: 2008/9

Income per annum (£)	Marginal income tax rate (%)	Marginal NIC rate (%)	Marginal income tax plus NIC rate (%)
0–5460	0	0	0
5461–6035	0	11	11
6036–40 040	20	11	31
40 041–40 835	20	1	21
Above 40 835	40	1	41

marginal rate, since part of a person's income will be tax-free; and for higher tax rate payers, part will be taxed at lower rates.

Individuals' social security contributions. In the UK these are known as national insurance contributions (NICs). These are like income taxes in that they are generally charged as a percentage of a person's income, the marginal rate varying with income. Unlike other taxes, which are paid into a common fund to finance government expenditure, they are used to finance *specific* expenditure: namely, pensions and social security. Although they do not officially count as 'taxes', to all intents and purposes they are so.

Table 10.3 and Figure 10.10 show the marginal and average rates of income tax and social security contributions in the UK (in 2008/9). Notice the effect of the marginal national insurance rate falling to a mere 1 per cent on incomes above £40 040.

Employers' social security contributions. Employers also have to pay social security contributions on behalf of their employees. These are paid per employee. In some countries, small firms pay reduced rates.

Tax on corporate income. In the UK this is known as corporation tax. It is a tax on the profits of limited companies. In most countries, there are lower rates for small companies. Profits can usually be offset against capital expenditure and interest payments when working out the tax liability. This effectively means that profits that are reinvested are not taxed.

Tax on capital gains. This is a tax payable when a person sells assets, such as property or shares. It is payable on the gain in value of these assets since a set date in the past, or since they were purchased if this was after the set date.

Taxes on wealth. These are taxes on assets held or acquired by individuals. One form of wealth tax in most countries is that on inherited assets or assets transferred before a person's death. Another is taxes based on the value of a person's property. This is a particularly common form of local taxation (the others being local income tax, local business tax and local sales tax).

Poll taxes. These are fixed-sum charges per head of the population, irrespective of the person's income. Very few countries use such taxes as they are regarded as grossly unfair. A poll tax (or 'community charge') was introduced in Scotland in 1989 and in England and Wales in 1990 as the new form of local tax, replacing the property tax called 'rates' (which was based on property values). But it was massively unpopular with the electorate and was replaced by 'council tax' (again based on property values) in 1993.

Indirect taxes

There are three main types of indirect tax, all of which are taxes on *expenditure*.

Table 10.4 Calculating VAT: an example where the rate of VAT is 10%

	Value added	VAT	Value added plus VAT	Price sold to next stage
	(1)	(2)	(3)	(4)
Firm A sells raw materials to firm B for £11 000	£10 000	£1000	£11 000	£11 000
Firm B processes them and sells them to a manufacturer, firm C, for £19 800	£8 000	£800	£8 800	£19 800
Firm C sells the manufactured goods to a wholesaler, firm D, for £27 500	£7 000	£700	£7 700	£27 500
Firm D sells them to a retailer, firm E, for £33 000	£5 000	£500	£5 500	£33 000
Firm E sells them to consumers for £44 000	£10 000	£1000	£11 000	£44 000
	£40 000 +	**£4000** =	**£44 000**	

General expenditure taxes. An example of this is *value added tax (VAT)*. This is the main indirect tax throughout the EU. VAT is paid on the value that firms add to goods and services at each stage of their production and distribution. For example, if a firm purchases supplies costing £10 000 and with them produces goods that it sells for £15 000 (before VAT), it is liable to pay VAT on the £15 000 minus £10 000: in other words, on the £5000 value it has added. Suppliers must provide invoices to show that the VAT has already been paid on all the inputs.

The example in Table 10.4 can be used to show how the tax eventually gets passed on to the consumer. For simplicity's sake, assume that the rate of VAT is 10 per cent and that each firm uses only one supplier.

The value added at each stage plus VAT adds up to the total amount paid by the consumer: £44 000 in this case. The total VAT paid, therefore, amounts to a tax on the consumer. In the example, the £4000 VAT is 10 per cent of the (pre-tax) consumer price of £40 000.

The rates of VAT in the various EU countries are shown in the table in Box 24.9 on page 701. Each country has a standard rate and up to two lower rates for basic goods and services.

Many other countries levy general expenditure taxes at a *single* stage (either wholesale or retail). These taxes are called *purchase taxes* and will normally be a percentage of the price of the good at that stage.

Excise duties. These are taxes on particular goods and services: for example, petrol and diesel, alcoholic drinks, tobacco products and gambling. They are a single-stage tax levied on the manufacturer. They are paid in addition to VAT.

VAT is an *ad valorem tax*. This means that the tax is levied at a *percentage* of the value of the good. The higher the value of the good, the higher the tax paid. Excise duties, by contrast, are a *specific tax*. This means that they are levied at a *fixed amount*, irrespective of the value of the good. Thus the duty on a litre of unleaded petrol is the same for a cut-price filling station as for a full-price one.

Customs duties. Economists normally refer to these as *tariffs*. They are duties on goods imported from outside the country.

 To what extent do (a) income tax, (b) VAT and (c) a poll tax meet the various requirements for a good tax system on pages 288–9 above? (Some of the answers to this question are given below.)

Details of tax rates in the UK are given in Case Study 10.3 in MyEconLab. This case study also examines how progressive or regressive the various types of tax are.

The balance of taxation

Table 10.5 shows the balance of the different types of tax in selected countries. Some striking differences can be seen between the countries. In France, income taxes account for only 18.3 per cent of tax revenue, whereas in the USA they account for over 35 per cent. In the UK, social security contributions (national insurance) are a much lower percentage of total taxes than in other countries, whereas indirect taxes are a much higher percentage. In most countries, taxes on property and wealth are a very small proportion of total taxation. In the USA and France, however, they are somewhat larger.

The table also shows total taxes as a percentage of gross domestic product or GDP. (GDP is a measure of the nation's income: we will be examining how it is measured

Definitions

Value added tax (VAT) A tax on goods and services, charged at each stage of production as a percentage of the value added at that stage.

***Ad valorem* tax** A tax on a good levied as a percentage of its value. It can be a single-stage tax or a multi-stage tax (as with VAT).

Specific tax A tax on a good levied at a fixed amount per unit of the good, irrespective of the price of that unit.

Tariff A tax on imported goods.

Table 10.5   Balance of taxation in selected countries (2006)

Types of tax as percentage of total tax[1]	France	Germany	Sweden	UK	USA
Personal income	18.3	23.2	27.8	28.1	35.2
Social security	42.2	43.8	34.8	21.2	27.6
Corporate taxes	7.0	5.6	9.6	10.5	9.7
Property and wealth	8.9	1.9	3.7	5.9	9.2
Expenditure	23.6	25.5	24.1	34.3	18.3
Total taxes[1] as percentage of GDP	44.5	35.7	50.1	37.4	28.2

[1] 'Taxes' in this table include social security contributions.
Source: Extracted from various tables in *Government Finance Statistics* (International Monetary Fund [IMF]).

in the appendix to Chapter 14.) In Sweden just over half of the nation's income is paid in tax, whereas in the USA the figure is not much over a quarter.

Taxes as a means of redistributing income

If taxes are to be used as a means of achieving greater equality, the rich must be taxed proportionately more than the poor. The degree of redistribution will depend on the degree of 'progressiveness' of the tax. In this context, taxes may be classified as follows:

- ***Progressive tax***. As people's income (Y) rises, the percentage of their income paid in the tax (T) rises. In other words, the *average* rate of tax (T/Y) rises.
- ***Regressive tax***. As people's income rises, the percentage of their income paid in the tax falls: T/Y falls.
- ***Proportional tax***. As people's income rises, the percentage of their income paid in the tax stays the same: T/Y is constant.

In other words, progressiveness is defined in terms of what happens to the average rate of tax as incomes rise. (Note that it is not defined in terms of the *marginal* rate of tax.)

1. *If a person earning £5000 per year pays £500 in a given tax and a person earning £10 000 per year pays £800, is the tax progressive or regressive?*
2. *A proportional tax will leave the distribution of income unaffected. Why should this be so, given that a rich person will pay a larger absolute amount than a poor person?*

An extreme form of regressive tax is a lump-sum tax (e.g. a poll tax). This is levied at a fixed *amount* (not rate) irrespective of income.

Figure 10.11 illustrates these different categories of tax. Diagram (a) shows the total amount of tax that a person pays. With a progressive tax, the curve gets progressively steeper, showing that the average rate of tax (T/Y) rises. The

Definitions

Progressive tax   A tax whose average rate with respect to income rises as income rises.

Regressive tax   A tax whose average rate with respect to income falls as income rises.

Proportional tax   A tax whose average rate with respect to income stays the same as income rises.

Figure 10.11   Different categories of tax

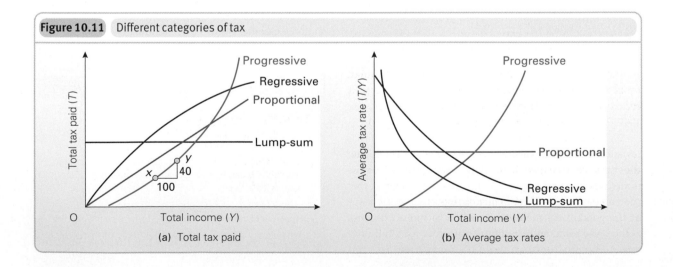

(a) Total tax paid

(b) Average tax rates

marginal rate of tax ($\Delta T/\Delta Y$) is given by the slope. Thus between points x and y the marginal tax rate is 40 per cent.

Diagram (b) shows the average rates. With a proportional tax, a person pays the same amount of tax on each pound earned. With a progressive tax, a larger proportion is paid by a rich person than by a poor person, and vice versa with a regressive tax.

The more steeply upward sloping the average tax curve, the more progressive is the tax, and the more equal will be the post-tax incomes of the population.

Problems with using taxes to redistribute incomes

How successfully can taxes redistribute income, and at what economic cost?

Problems in achieving redistribution

How to help the very poor. Taxation takes away income. It can thus reduce the incomes of the rich. But no taxes, however progressive, can *increase* the incomes of the poor. This will require subsidies (i.e. benefits).

But what about tax cuts? Can bigger tax cuts not be given to the poor? This is possible only if the poor are already paying taxes in the first place. Take the two cases of income tax and taxes on goods and services.

- Income tax. If the government cuts income tax, then anyone currently paying it will benefit. A cut in tax *rates* will give proportionately more to the rich, since they have a larger proportion of taxable income relative to total income. An increase in personal *allowances*, on the other hand, will give the same *absolute* amounts to everyone above the new tax threshold. This will therefore represent a smaller proportionate gain to the rich. In either case, however, there will be no gain at all to those people below the tax threshold. They paid no income tax in the first place. These poorest people of all therefore gain nothing at all from income tax cuts.
- Taxes on goods and services. Since these taxes are generally regressive, any cut in their rate will benefit the poor proportionately more than the rich. A more dramatic effect would be obtained by cutting the rate most on those goods consumed relatively more by the poor.

The government may not wish to cut the overall level of taxation, given its expenditure commitments. In this case, it can switch the burden from regressive to progressive taxes. That way at least some benefit is gained by the very poor.

Tax evasion and tax avoidance. The higher the rates of tax, the more likely are people to try to escape paying some of their taxes.

People who are subject to higher rates of income tax will be more tempted not to declare all their income. This tax *evasion* will be much easier for people not paying all their taxes through a pay-as-you-earn (PAYE) scheme. This will

include the self-employed and people doing casual work on top of their normal job ('moonlighting'). Furthermore, richer people can often reduce their tax liability – engage in *tax avoidance* – by a careful use of various legal devices such as trusts and tax loopholes such as being allowed to offset 'business expenses' against income.

Part of the government's justification for abolishing income tax rates above 40 per cent in 1988 was that many people escaped paying these higher taxes.

Why may a steeply progressive income tax which is designed to achieve greater vertical equity lead to a reduction in horizontal equity?

Undesired incidence of tax. High rates of income tax on high wage earners may simply encourage employers to pay them higher wages. At the other end of the scale, tax cuts for low-paid workers may simply allow employers to cut wages. In other words, part of the incidence of income taxes will be borne by the employer and only part by the employee. Thus attempting to make taxes more 'progressive' will fail if employers simply adjust wages to compensate.

The incidence of income tax is determined by the elasticity of supply and demand for labour. In Figure 10.12, the initial supply and demand curves for labour (before the imposition of the tax) intersect at point (1), giving Q_1 labour employed at a wage of W_1. Now an income tax is imposed. This shifts the labour supply curve vertically upwards by the amount of the tax, giving the new labour supply curve, S + tax. The new equilibrium is reached at point (2) with Q_2 labour employed at a (gross) wage of W_2.

The incidence of the tax is as follows:

- The total tax revenue for the government is shown by the total shaded area.
- Workers' take-home pay is cut from W_1 to W_2 – tax. Their share of the tax is thus area A.
- Employers have to pay workers a rise of $W_2 - W_1$. They pay area B.

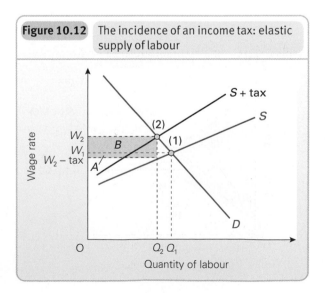

Figure 10.12 The incidence of an income tax: elastic supply of labour

If the supply curve of labour of well-paid workers is relatively elastic, as shown in Figure 10.12, there will only be a relatively slight fall in take-home pay (the workers' share of the tax is relatively small). The tax will, therefore, have only a relatively slight redistributive effect away from this group of workers.

1. *Do poor people gain more from a cut in income tax with an elastic or an inelastic supply of labour? Is the supply of unskilled workers likely to be elastic or inelastic?*
2. *Draw two diagrams like Figure 10.12, one with a steep demand curve and one with a shallow demand curve. How does the elasticity of demand affect the incidence of the income tax?*

Of course, income taxes are not imposed on workers in one industry alone. People, therefore, cannot move to another industry to avoid paying taxes. This fact will cause a relatively inelastic supply response to any rise in income tax, since the only alternative to paying the income tax is to work less. The less elastic this response, the more will the burden of the tax fall on the taxpayer and the more effectively can income taxes be used to redistribute incomes.

The economic costs of redistribution

KI 3
p10

If redistribution is to be achieved through *indirect* taxes, this can lead to market distortions.

Take first the case of an indirect tax applied to one good only. Assume for simplicity that there is universal perfect competition. Raising the price of this good relative to other goods will introduce a market distortion. Consumption will shift away from this good towards other goods that people preferred less at the original prices. What is more, the loss to consumers and producers (other things being equal) will be greater than the gain to the community from the tax revenue. This is illustrated in Figure 10.13.

With no tax, price will be at P_1 and output at Q_1, where demand equals supply. By imposing a tax on the good, the supply curve shifts upwards to S + tax. Price rises to P_2 and

output falls to Q_2. Producers are left with P_2 – tax. What are the various losses and gains?

Consumers, by having to pay a higher price, lose consumer surplus (see section 4.1). Originally their consumer surplus was areas $A + B + C$. With the price now at P_2, the consumer surplus falls to area C alone. The loss to consumers is areas $A + B$.

Producers, by receiving a lower price after tax and selling fewer units, lose profits. In the simple case where there are no fixed costs of production, total profits are simply the sum of all the marginal profits ($P (= MR) – MC$) on each of the units sold. Thus before the tax is imposed, firms receive total profits of areas $D + E + F$. After the tax is imposed, they receive a profit of area F alone. The loss in profits to producers is therefore areas $D + E$.

The total loss to consumers and producers is areas $A + B + D + E$. The gain to the government in tax revenue is areas $B + E$: the tax rate times the number of units sold (Q_2). There is thus a net loss to the community of areas $A + D$. This is known as the *deadweight loss of the tax*.

However, if the money raised from the tax is redistributed to the poor, their gain in welfare is likely to exceed the loss in welfare from the higher tax. The reason is that a pound sacrificed by the average consumer is probably of less value to him or her than a pound gained by a poor person.

What is more, if the tax is applied at a uniform rate to *all* goods, there is no distortion resulting from reallocation between goods. This is one of the major justifications for having a single rate of VAT.

Of course, in the real world, markets are highly imperfect and there is no reason why taxes will necessarily make these imperfections worse. In fact, it might be desirable on efficiency grounds to tax certain goods and services, such as cigarettes, alcohol, petrol and gambling, at higher rates than other goods and services. We will examine these arguments in the next chapter.

Although there are costs of redistribution, there are also benefits extending beyond those to whom income is redistributed. If redistribution to the poor reduces crime, vandalism and urban squalor, then it is not just the poor who gain: it is everyone, both financially in terms of reduced policing and social work costs, and more generally in terms of living in a happier and less divided society.

Taxation and incentives

TC 5 **p50**

Another possible economic cost of high tax rates is that they may act as a disincentive to work, thereby reducing

---

Figure 10.13 Indirect tax applied to good X

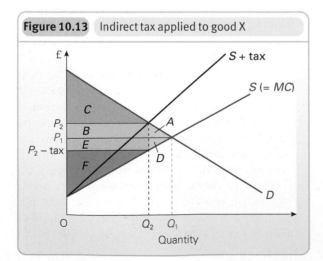

> **Definition**
>
> **Deadweight loss of an indirect tax** The net loss of consumer plus producer surplus (after adding in the tax revenue) from the imposition of an indirect tax.

BOX 10.4 **THE LAFFER CURVE**

Having your cake and eating it

Professor Art Laffer was one of President Reagan's advisers during his first administration (1981–4). He was a strong advocate of income tax cuts, arguing that substantial increases in output would result.

He went further than this. He argued that tax cuts would actually increase the amount of tax revenue that the government earned.

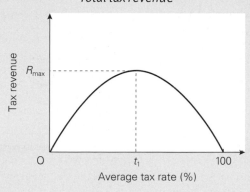

If tax cuts cause income to rise (due to incentives) proportionately more than the tax rate has fallen, then

tax revenues will increase. These effects are illustrated by the now famous 'Laffer' curve.

If the average tax rate were zero, no revenue would be raised. As the tax rate is raised above zero, tax revenues will increase. The curve will be upward sloping. Eventually, however, the curve will peak (at tax rate t_1). Thereafter tax rates become so high that the resulting fall in output more than offsets the rise in tax rate. When the tax rate reaches 100 per cent, the revenue will once more fall to zero, since no one will bother to work.

The curve may not be symmetrical. It may peak at a 40 per cent, 50 per cent, 60 per cent or even 90 per cent rate. Nevertheless, Laffer and others on the political right argued that tax rates were above t_1. In fact most evidence suggests that tax rates in most countries were well below t_1 in the 1980s and certainly are now, given the cuts in income tax rates that have been made around the world over the past twenty years.

1. What is the elasticity of supply of output with respect to changes in tax rates at a tax rate of t_1? What is it below t_1? What is it above t_1?
2. If the substitution effect of a tax cut outweighs the income effect, does this necessarily mean that the economy is to the right of point t_1?

---

national output and consumption. This whole question of incentives is highly charged politically. According to the political right, there is a trade-off between output and equity. High and progressive income taxes can lead to a more equal distribution of income, but a smaller national output. Alternatively, if taxes are cut there will be a bigger national output, but less equally divided. If many on the left are correct, however, we can have both a more equal society and a bigger national output: there is no trade-off.

The key to analysing these arguments is to distinguish between the *income effect* and the *substitution effect* of a tax rise. Raising taxes does two things:

KI 7 p33

- It reduces incomes. People may therefore work *more* in an attempt to maintain their consumption of goods and services. This is the *income effect*.
- It reduces the opportunity cost of leisure. An extra hour taken in leisure now involves a smaller sacrifice in consumption, since each hour less worked involves less

sacrifice in after-tax income. Thus people may substitute leisure for consumption, and work *less*. This is the *substitution effect*.

The relative size of the income and substitution effects is likely to differ for different types of people and different types of tax change.

Different types of people

The *income* effect is likely to dominate for people with long-term commitments: for example, those with families, or those with mortgages and other debts. They may feel forced to work *more* to maintain their disposable income. Clearly for such people, higher taxes are *not* a disincentive to work. The income effect is also likely to be relatively large for people on higher incomes, for whom an increase in tax rates represents a substantial cut in income.

The *substitution* effect is likely to dominate for those with few commitments: those whose families have left home, the single, and second income earners in families where that second income is not relied on for 'essential' consumption. A rise in tax rates for these people is likely to encourage them to work less.

Although high income earners may work more when there is a tax *rise*, they may still be discouraged by a steeply progressive tax *structure*. If they have to pay very high marginal rates of tax, it may simply not be worth their while seeking promotion or working harder (see Boxes 10.4 and 10.5).

Definitions

Income effect of a tax rise Tax increases reduce people's incomes and thus encourage people to work more.

Substitution effect of a tax rise Tax increases reduce the opportunity cost of leisure and thus encourage people to work less.

*BOX 10.5   TAX CUTS AND INCENTIVES

An application of indifference curve analysis[1]

Will tax cuts provide an incentive for people to work more? This question can be analysed using indifference curves (see section 4.3). The analysis is similar to that developed in Box 9.2. It is assumed that individuals can choose how many hours a day to work.

The position with no income tax
Diagram (a) shows the situation without income tax.

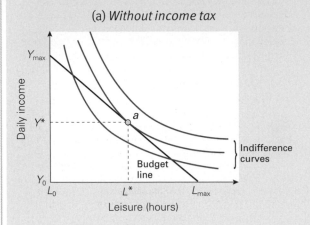

(a) *Without income tax*

The budget line shows the various combinations of leisure and income open to an individual at a given wage rate.

 Why is the budget line straight? What would it look like if overtime were paid at higher rates per hour?

The indifference curves show all the combinations of income and leisure that give the person equal satisfaction. The optimum combination of income and leisure is at Y^* and L^* where the individual is on the highest possible indifference curve: point a.

The position with income tax
Now let us introduce a system of income taxes. This is illustrated in diagram (b).

(b) *With income tax*

Assume that the tax has the following features:

- Up to an income of Y_1 no tax is paid: Y_1 is the individual's personal allowance.
- From Y_1 to Y_2 the basic rate of tax is paid. The budget line is flatter, since less extra income is earned for each extra hour of leisure sacrificed.
- Above Y_2 the higher rate of tax is paid. The budget line becomes flatter still.

The individual illustrated in the diagram will now choose to earn a take-home pay of Y^{**} and have L^{**} hours of leisure: point b. Note that this is more leisure than in the no-tax situation (point a). In this diagram, then, the tax has acted as a disincentive. The substitution effect has outweighed the income effect.

 Redraw diagram (b), but in such a way that the income effect outweighs the substitution effect.

1. *Who is likely to work harder as a result of a cut in income tax rates, a rich person or a poor person? Why? Would your answer be different if personal allowances were zero?*
2. *How will tax cuts affect the willingness of women to return to employment after having brought up a family?*

Different types of tax change
If the government wishes to raise income taxes in order to redistribute incomes, there are three main ways it can do it: raising the higher rates of tax; raising the basic rate; and reducing tax allowances.

Raising the higher rates of tax.   This may seem the most effective way of redistributing incomes: after all, it is only the rich who will suffer. There are, however, serious problems:

- The income effect will be relatively small, since it is only that part of incomes subject to the higher rates that will be affected. The substitution effect, however, could be relatively high. Rich people are likely to put a higher premium on leisure, and may well feel that it is not worth working so hard if a larger proportion of any increase in income is taken in taxes.
- It may discourage risk-taking by businesspeople.

KI 11
p75

A cut in the basic tax rate

We can now analyse the effects of tax cuts. A cut in the basic rate is shown in diagram (c).

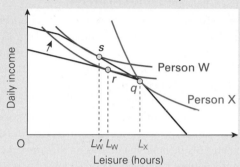

(c) *Cut in the basic rate of tax*

The tax cut makes the budget line steeper above point *q* (the tax threshold).

For people on the tax threshold – like person X – the cut in the basic rate makes no difference. Person X was originally taking L_X hours of leisure (point *q*) and will continue to do so.

For people above the tax threshold – like person W – the tax cut will enable them to move to a higher indifference curve. Person W will move from point *r* to point *s*. The way this diagram is drawn, point *s* is to the left of point *r*. This means that person W will work more: the substitution effect is greater than the income effect.

 Try drawing two or three diagrams like diagram (c), with the tangency point at different points along the budget line to the left of q*. You will find that the further to the left you move, the less likely is the substitution effect to outweigh the income effect: i.e. the more likely are people to work less when given a tax cut.*

A rise in the tax threshold

Diagram (d) shows a rise in personal allowances while the tax rates stay the same.

(d) *Increase in the tax threshold*

The point at which people start paying taxes rises from point *t* to point *u*. The slope of the budget line remains the same, however, since the tax rates have not changed.

For people paying taxes, the increase in allowances represents a lump-sum increase in income: there will thus be an income effect. But since tax rates have not changed, there is no substitution effect. People therefore work less. The person in the diagram moves from point *m* to point *n*, taking L_2 rather than L_1 hours in leisure.

 Will people actually on the old tax threshold (i.e. those whose indifference curve/budget line tangency point is at t*) work more or less? Try drawing it.*

A cut in the higher rate of tax

It is likely that the income effect of this will be quite small except for those on very high incomes. The substitution effect is therefore likely to outweigh the income effect, causing people to work more.

 All the above analysis assumes that taxes will not affect people's gross wage rates. If part of the incidence of taxes is borne by the employer, so that gross wages fall, after-tax wages will fall less. There will therefore be a smaller shift in the budget line. How will this affect the argument for tax cuts?

[1] This box is based on D. Ulph, 'Tax cuts: will they work?', *Economic Review*, March 1987.

- The rich may be more mobile internationally, so there may be a 'brain drain'.

Raising the basic rate of tax. As we have seen, the income effect is likely to be relatively large for those with higher incomes, especially if they have substantial commitments like a large mortgage. For such people, a rise in tax rates is likely to act as an incentive.

For those just above the tax threshold, there will be very little extra to pay on *existing* income, since most of it is tax-free. However, each *extra* pound earned will be taxed at the new higher rate. The substitution effect, therefore, is likely to outweigh the income effect. For these people, a rise in tax rates will act as a disincentive.

For those below the tax threshold, the marginal rate remains at zero. A rise in the basic rate might nevertheless deter them from undertaking training in order to get a better wage.

For those people who are not employed, a rise in tax rates may make them feel that it is no longer worth looking for a job.

Reducing tax allowances. For all those above the old tax threshold, there is no *substitution* effect at all. The rate of tax has not changed. However, there is an *income* effect. The effect is like a lump-sum tax. Everyone's take-home pay is cut by a fixed sum, and people will need to work harder to make up some of the shortfall. This type of tax change, however, is highly regressive. If everyone pays the same *amount* of extra tax, this represents a bigger percentage for poorer people than richer people. In other words, there may be no negative incentive effects, but it is not suitable as part of a policy to redistribute incomes more equally!

The conclusion from the theoretical arguments is that tax changes will have very different effects depending on (a) whom they affect and (b) the nature of the change.

1. *Go through each of the above types of tax change and consider the effects of a tax cut.*
2. *What tax changes (whether up or down) will have a positive incentive effect and also redistribute incomes more equally?*

One final point should be stressed. For many people, there is no choice in the amount they work. The job they do dictates the number of hours worked, irrespective of changes in taxation.

Evidence

All the available evidence suggests that the effects of tax changes on output are relatively small. Labour supply curves seem highly inelastic to tax changes.

Benefits

Benefits can be either cash benefits or benefits in kind.

Cash benefits

Means-tested benefits. **Means-tested benefits** are available only to those whose income (and savings in some instances) fall below a certain level. To obtain such benefits, therefore, people must apply for them and declare their personal circumstances to the authorities.

The benefits could be given as grants or merely as loans. They could be provided as general income support or for the meeting of specific needs, such as rents, fuel bills and household items.

Universal benefits. **Universal benefits** are those that everyone is entitled to, irrespective of their income, if they fall into a certain category or fulfil certain conditions. Examples include state pensions, and certain unemployment, sickness and invalidity benefits.

Benefits in kind

Individuals receive other forms of benefit from the state, not as direct monetary payments, but in the form of the provision of free or subsidised goods or services. These are known as **benefits in kind**. The two largest items in most

countries are health care and education. They are distributed very unevenly, however, largely due to the age factor. Old people use a large proportion of health services, but virtually no education services.

Benefits in kind tend to be consumed roughly equally by the different income groups. Nevertheless they still have some equalising effect, since they represent a much larger proportion of poor people's income than rich people's. They still have a far smaller redistributive effect, however, than cash benefits.

Figure 10.14 on page 300 shows the expenditure on social protection benefits in selected European countries. These include unemployment, sickness, invalidity, maternity, family, survivors' and housing benefits and state pensions. They are mainly cash benefits, but do include some benefits in kind. They exclude health and education. As you can see, the benefits vary significantly from one country to another. Part of the reason for this is that countries differ in their rates of unemployment and in the age structure of their population. Thus Ireland has the lowest percentage of people over 65 in the EU and the smallest share of benefits devoted to pensions. Despite this, however, the generosity and coverage of benefits varies considerably from country to country, reflecting, in part, the level of income per head.

The system of benefits in the UK and their redistributive effects are examined in Case Study 10.5 in MyEconLab.

Benefits and the redistribution of income

It might seem that means-tested benefits are a much more efficient system for redistributing income from the rich to the poor: the money is directed to those most in need. With universal benefits, by contrast, many people may receive them who have little need for them. Do families with very high incomes need child benefit? Would it not be better for the government to redirect the money to those who are genuinely in need?

There are, however, serious problems in attempting to redistribute incomes by the use of means-tested benefits:

Definitions

Means-tested benefits Benefits whose amount depends on the recipient's income or assets.

Universal benefits Benefits paid to everyone in a certain category irrespective of their income or assets.

Benefits in kind Goods or services that the state provides directly to the recipient at no charge or at a subsidised price. Alternatively, the state can subsidise the private sector to provide them.

- Not everyone entitled to means-tested benefits applies for them, whether from ignorance of what is available, from the complexities of claiming or from reluctance to reveal personal circumstances or from a feeling that it is demeaning to claim. Thus some of the poorest families receive no support.
- The level of income above which people become ineligible for benefits may be set too low. Even if it were raised, there will always be some people just above the level who will still find difficulties.
- Means tests based purely on *income* (or even universal benefits based on broad categories) ignore the very special needs of many poor people. A person earning £120 a week and living in a small, well-appointed flat with a low rent will have less need of assistance than another person who also earns £120 per week but lives in a cold, draughty and damp house with large bills to meet. If means tests are to be fair, *all* of a person's circumstances need to be taken into account.

The tax/benefit system and the problem of disincentives: the poverty trap

When means-tested benefits are combined with a progressive income tax system, there can be a serious problem of disincentives. As poor people earn more money, not only will they start paying income taxes and national insurance, but also they will begin losing means-tested benefits. Theoretically, it is possible to have a marginal tax-plus-lost-benefit rate in excess of 100 per cent. In other words, for every extra £1 earned, taxes and lost benefits add up to more than £1. High marginal tax-plus-lost-benefit rates obviously act as a serious disincentive. What is the point of getting a job or trying to earn more money, if you end up earning little more or even losing money?

This situation is known as the *poverty trap*. People are trapped on low incomes with no realistic means of bettering their position.

The problem of the poverty trap would be overcome by switching to a system of universal benefits unrelated to income. For example, *everyone* could receive a flat payment from the state fixed at a sufficiently high level to cover their basic needs. There would still be *some* disincentive, but this would be confined to an income effect: people would not have the same need to work if the state provided a basic income. But there would no longer be the disincentive to work caused by a resulting *loss* of benefits (a substitution

effect). In addition a system of universal benefits is relatively cheap to administer, avoiding the need for costly means-testing.

The big drawback with universal benefits, however, is their cost. If they were given to everyone and were large enough to help the poor, their cost would be enormous. Thus although the benefits themselves would not create much disincentive effect, the necessary taxation to fund them probably would.

There is no ideal solution to this conundrum. On the one hand, the more narrowly benefits are targeted on the poor, the greater is the problem of the poverty trap. On the other hand, the more widely they are spread, the greater is the cost of providing any given level of support to individuals. A compromise proposal is that of a *negative income tax*. This is examined in Case Study 10.6 in MyEconLab. Box 10.6 examines the use of tax credits – which have similarities with a negative income tax – in the UK.

Conclusions

Redistribution is not costless. Whether it takes place through taxes or benefits or both, it can pose a problem of disincentives. Nevertheless the size of the disincentive problem varies enormously from one tax to another and from one benefit to another, and in some cases there may even be an incentive effect: for example, when the income effect of a tax outweighs the substitution effect. It is therefore important to estimate the particular effects of each type of proposal not only on income distribution itself, but also on economic efficiency.

Ultimately, the questions of how much income should be redistributed and whether the costs are worth bearing are normative questions, and ones therefore that an economist cannot answer. They are moral and political questions. It would be nice if the 'utility' gained by the poor and lost by the rich could be quantified so that any net gain from redistribution could be weighed up against lost output. But such 'interpersonal comparisons of utility' are not possible. For example, the benefit that a person receives from a cooker or an electric fire cannot be measured in 'utils' or any other 'psychic unit'. What people are prepared to pay for the items is no guide either, since a poor person obviously cannot afford to pay nearly as much as a rich person, and yet will probably get the same if not more personal benefit from them.

Yet decisions have to be made!

Definitions

Poverty trap Where poor people are discouraged from working or getting a better job because any extra income they earn will be largely or entirely taken away in taxes and lost benefits.

Negative income tax A combined system of tax and benefits. As people earn more, they gradually lose their benefits until beyond a certain level they begin paying taxes.

Figure 10.14   Social protection benefits in various European countries

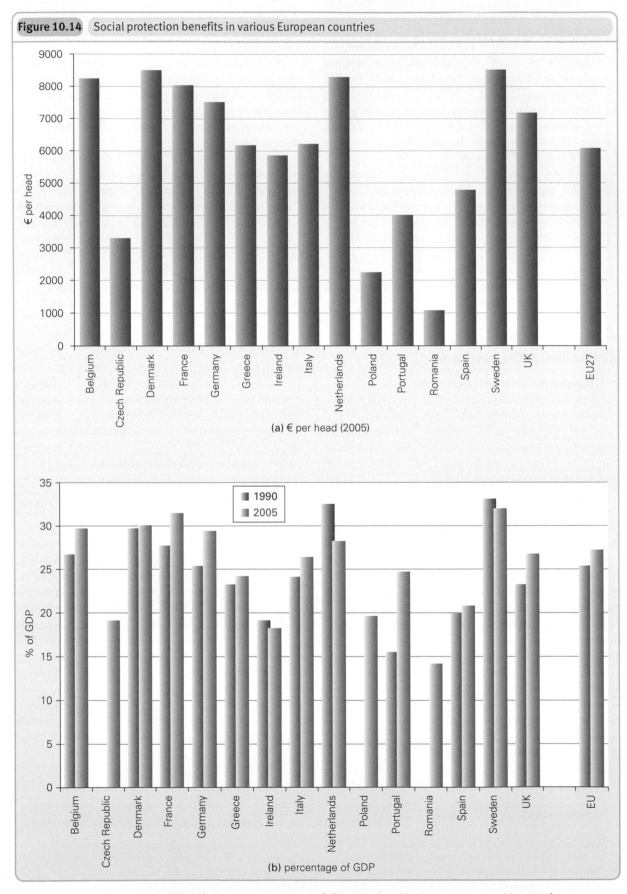

(a) € per head (2005)

(b) percentage of GDP

Source: Eurostat, Statistics in Focus (http://epp.eurostat.ec.europa.eu), (Commission of the European Communities, 2008).

| BOX 10.6 | UK TAX CREDITS | CASE STUDIES AND APPLICATIONS |

An escape from the poverty trap?

Tax credits (which share characteristics with negative income taxes) were introduced in the UK in 1999 in the form of Working Families Tax Credit, which was replaced in 2003 by Working Tax Credit (WTC) and Child Tax Credit (CTC). These credits are paid as a cash benefit.

Working Tax Credit is designed for working people on low incomes. To be eligible for the basic amount (see the table), people without children must be aged 25 or over and work at least 30 hours per week. People with children, the over 50s returning to work and the disabled must work at least 16 hours per week. Couples and lone parents receive an additional amount. There is a further addition for anyone with children who works at least 30 hours per week, or for couples who jointly work at least 30 hours per week. This is designed as an incentive for people to move from part-time to full-time work. Recipients of WTC also get paid 80 per cent of eligible childcare costs up to £175 per week for one child and £300 for two or more children. For each pound earned above a threshold amount, relief is reduced by 39p.

Child Tax Credit provides support to families with children, whether or not anyone in the family works. It is paid in addition to WTC and child benefit. There is a basic rate and an additional amount per child. Relief tapers off for incomes over a threshold amount although the full adult element is awarded to households with an income of up to £50 000 (2008/9). (See table for rates of WTC and CTC.)

WTC and CTC rates (£ annual): 2008/9

Working tax credit (WTC)	
Basic element	1 800
Addition for couples and lone parents	1 770
Addition for those working 30 hours or more	735
Income threshold (above which WTC is reduced)	6 420
Child tax credit (CTC)	
Family element	545
Baby addition	545
Additional amount per child	2 085
Income threshold (above which CTC is reduced)	15 575

Source: Inland Revenue.

Apart from targeting support at poorer families, these tax credits are intended to improve incentives to work, by reducing the poverty trap (see page 299). In other words, the aim is to reduce the financial penalties for parents working by tapering off more slowly the rate at which benefits are lost. With a lost-benefit rate of 39 per cent, the combined marginal tax-plus-lost-benefit rate (the 'marginal deduction rate') is typically around 70 per cent, depending on a person's marginal rate of tax and other means-tested benefits received.

Although the introduction of these tax credits has reduced the typical marginal deduction rate for poor families, the rate is still very high. For many poor parents, therefore, the incentive to work is still relatively low.

There is another effect from reducing the rate at which benefit tapers off. Some benefit will now be available to slightly less poor families. Although this is good in terms of providing support for them, there is now more of a disincentive for parents in such families to work extra hours, or to take a better job, since the marginal deduction rate is now higher. In other words, although they are better off, they will take home less for each extra hour worked.

WTC and CTC illustrate the general problem of providing support to poor people which is affordable for taxpayers without creating disincentives to work. The more gently the support tapers off (and hence the less the disincentive to earn extra money), the more costly it is to finance, and hence higher tax rates are needed elsewhere. The problems with using negative income taxes are explored in Case Study 10.6 in MyEconLab.

WTC and CTC are major elements of the UK Labour government's policy on poverty, which is focused on families. The policy concentrates on eliminating worklessness in households where children are living, lifting them out of poverty and breaking the 'cycle of deprivation'. (More details of the policy are contained in Box 10.2. on page 285.)

A major criticism of tax credits lies in the complexity of the system. This has two consequences: first, it is estimated that of the 7 million households eligible for the benefits, around 2 million fail to claim them; second, the system is administratively costly and prone to errors. Despite this, tax credits have contributed to reductions in the number of children living in poverty in the UK since 2000.

Economists sometimes refer to an 'unemployment trap'. People are discouraged from taking work in the first place. Explain how such a 'trap' arises. Do working tax credits and child tax credits create an unemployment trap? What are the best ways of eliminating, or at least reducing, the unemployment trap?

Section summary

1. Government intervention in the economy through taxation and government expenditure has a number of purposes including redistribution, the correction of market distortions and macroeconomic stabilisation.

2. There are various requirements of a good tax system, including horizontal and vertical equity; payment according to the amount of benefit received; being cheap to collect, difficult to evade, non-distortionary and convenient to the taxpayer and the government; and having the minimum disincentive effects.

3. Taxes can be divided into those paid directly to the authorities (direct taxes: e.g. income tax) and those paid via a middle person (indirect taxes: e.g. VAT).

4. Taxes can be categorised as progressive, regressive or proportional. Progressive taxes have the effect of reducing inequality. The more steeply progressive they are, the bigger is the reduction in inequality.

5. There are various limitations to using taxes to redistribute incomes. First, they cannot on their own increase the incomes of the poor. (Cutting taxes, however, can help the poor if the cuts are carefully targeted.) Second, high taxes on the rich may encourage evasion or avoidance. Third, higher income taxes on the rich will probably lead to their employers paying higher (gross) wages.

6. Using indirect taxes to redistribute incomes involves costs of resource reallocation.

7. Raising taxes has two effects on the amount that people wish to work. On the one hand, people will be encouraged to work more in order to maintain their incomes. This is the income effect. On the other hand, they will be encouraged to substitute leisure for income (i.e. to work less), since an hour's leisure now costs less in forgone income. This is the substitution effect. The relative size of the income and substitution effects will depend on the nature of the tax change. The substitution effect of a tax rise is more likely to outweigh the income effect for those with few commitments, for people just above the tax threshold and in cases where the highest rates of tax are increased.

8. Benefits can be cash benefits or benefits in kind. Means-tested cash benefits include support for poor families and for low-paid people. Universal benefits include state pensions and child benefit. Benefits in kind include health care, education and free school meals.

9. Means-tested benefits can be specifically targeted to those in need and are thus more 'cost-effective'. However, there can be serious problems with such benefits, including limited take-up, some relatively needy people falling just outside the qualifying limit, and inadequate account being taken of all relevant circumstances affecting a person's needs.

10. The poverty trap occurs when the combination of increased taxes and reduced benefits removes the incentive for poor people to earn more. The more steeply progressive this combined system is at low incomes, the bigger is the disincentive effect.

END OF CHAPTER QUESTIONS

1. Using the data shown on the pie charts in Figure 10.1, construct two Lorenz curves (on the same diagram), corresponding to the before- and after-tax income figures. Interpret and comment on the diagram you have drawn.

2. Can taxes be used to relieve poverty?

3. In what ways might the views of different politicians on what constitutes a 'good' tax system conflict?

4. Distinguish between proportional, progressive and regressive taxation. Could a progressive tax have a constant marginal rate?

5. Consider the cases for and against a poll tax.

6. Under what circumstances would a rise in income tax act as (a) a disincentive and (b) an incentive to effort?

7. What is meant by the poverty trap? What design of benefit system would offer the best solution to the problem of the poverty trap?

8. How would you go about deciding whether person A or person B gets more personal benefit from each of the following: (a) an electric fire; (b) a clothing allowance of £x; (c) free higher education; (d) child benefit? Do your answers help you in deciding how best to allocate benefits?

Online resources

Additional case studies in MyEconLab

10.1   **How can we define poverty?** This examines different definitions of poverty and, in particular, distinguishes between absolute and relative measures of poverty.

10.2   **Adam Smith's maxims of taxation.** This looks at the principles of a good tax system as identified by Adam Smith.

10.3   **Taxation in the UK.** This case study looks at the various types of tax in the UK. It gives the current tax rates and considers how progressive the system is.

10.4   **The poll tax.** This case charts the introduction of the infamous poll tax (or 'community charge') in the UK and its subsequent demise.

10.5   **The system of benefits in the UK.** A description of the various benefits used in the UK and their redistributive effects.

10.6   **Negative income tax and redistribution.** How effectively can a negative income tax redistribute income without causing adverse incentive effects?

Websites relevant to Chapters 9 and 10

Numbers and section refer to websites listed in the Web Appendix and hotlinked from this book's website at **www.pearsoned.co.uk/sloman**.

- For news articles relevant to this and the previous chapter, see the *Economics News Articles* link from the book's website.

- For general news on labour markets, see websites in section A, and particularly A1, 2, 4, 5 and 7. See also A41 and 42 for links to economics news articles from newspapers worldwide.

- For data on labour markets, see links B1 or 2, especially to *Labour Market Trends* on the National Statistics site. Also see B9 and links in B19. Also see the labour topic in B33 and the *resources > statistics* links in H3. For international data on labour markets, see the ILO datasets in the ESDS International site (B35) (you will need to log in, available free to all students in UK higher education).

- For information on international labour standards and employment right, see site H3.

- Sites I7 and 11 contain links to *Labour Economics*, *Labour Force and Markets* and *Labour Unions* in the Microeconomics section and to *Distribution of Income and Wealth* in the Macroeconomics section. Site I4 has links in the *Directory* section to *Labour* and *Labour Economics*. Site I17 in the *Labour Economics* section has links to various topics, such as *Labour Unions, Minimum Wage, Poverty and Work*.

- Links to the TUC and Confederation of British Industry sites can be found at E32 and 33.

- For information and poverty and the redistribution of income, see E9, 30, 36; G5, 13. See also *The Virtual Economy* at D1.

- For student resources relevant to these two chapters, see sites C1–7, 9, 10, 19.

- For simulations on *Labour market reforms and Tackling child poverty,* see site D3.

Markets, Efficiency and the Public Interest

CHAPTER MAP

11.1 Efficiency under perfect competition   **305**
Social efficiency: 'Pareto optimality'   305
The simple analysis of social efficiency: marginal
   benefit and marginal cost   305
Achieving social efficiency through the market   306
The simple analysis of general equilibrium   308
*The intermediate analysis of social efficiency:
   marginal benefit and marginal cost ratios   310
*Efficiency in the goods market   311
*Efficiency in the factor market   312
*The intermediate analysis of general equilibrium   312

11.2 The case for government intervention   **313**
Externalities   313
Public goods   315
Common resources   316
Market power   317
Other market failures   320
Conclusions   321

11.3 Forms of government intervention   **323**
Taxes and subsidies   323
Changes in property rights   326
Laws prohibiting undesirable behaviour   327
Regulatory bodies   327
Price controls   327
Provision of information   328
The direct provision of goods and services   328
Public ownership   328

*11.4 Cost–benefit analysis   **329**
The procedure   329
Identifying the costs and benefits   331
Measuring the costs and benefits   331
Risk and uncertainty   332
Discounting future costs and benefits   333
The distribution of costs and benefits   333

**11.5 Government failure and the case for
   the market**   **336**
Drawbacks of government intervention   337
Advantages of the free market   337
Should there be more or less intervention?   338

In Chapter 10 we examined the problem of inequality. In this chapter we turn to examine another major area of concern. This is the question of the efficiency (or inefficiency) of markets in allocating resources.

First we show how a perfect market economy could under certain conditions lead to 'social efficiency'. In section 11.2 we examine the real world and show how markets in practice fail to meet social goals. These failures provide the major arguments in favour of government intervention in a market economy. We then turn to discuss the alternative ways in which a government can intervene to correct these various market failings.

If the government is to replace the market and provide goods and services directly, it will need some way of establishing their costs and benefits. Section 11.4 looks at 'cost–benefit analysis'. This is a means of establishing the desirability of a public project such as a new motorway or a new hospital. Finally, in section 11.5, we look at the case for restricting government intervention. We examine the advantages of real-world markets and the drawbacks of government intervention.

11.1 EFFICIENCY UNDER PERFECT COMPETITION

Perfect competition has been used by many economists and policy makers as an ideal against which to compare the benefits and shortcomings of real-world markets.

As was shown in Chapter 6, perfect competition has various advantages for society. Under perfect competition, firms' supernormal profits are competed away in the long run by the entry of new competitors. As a result, firms are forced to produce at the bottom of their average cost curves. What is more, the fear of being driven out of business by the entry of new firms forces existing firms to try to find lower-cost methods of production, thus shifting their *AC* curves downwards.

Perhaps the most wide-reaching claim for perfect competition is that under certain conditions it will lead to a *socially efficient* use of a nation's resources.

KI 3
p10

Social efficiency: 'Pareto optimality'

If it were possible to make changes in the economy – changes in the combination of goods produced or consumed, or changes in the combination of inputs used – and if such changes benefited some people without anyone else being made worse off, economists would describe this as an *improvement in social efficiency*, or a **Pareto improvement**, after Vilfredo Pareto, the Italian social scientist (see Person Profile in MyEconLab).

Do you agree that, if some people gain and if no one loses, then this constitutes an 'improvement' in the well-being of society? Would it be possible to improve the well-being of society without a Pareto improvement?

When all Pareto improvements have been made – in other words, when any additional changes in the economy would benefit some people only by making others worse off – the economy is said to be **socially efficient**, or Pareto optimal. What we shall show is that under certain conditions a perfect market will lead to **Pareto optimality**.

But a word of caution. Just because social efficiency is achieved in a particular market environment, it does not necessarily make that environment *ideal*. It may be a *necessary* condition for an ideal allocation of resources that all Pareto improvements are made. It is not *sufficient*, however. If, for example, the government redistributed income from the rich to the poor, there would be no Pareto improvement, since the rich would lose. Thus both an equal and a highly unequal distribution of income could be Pareto optimal, and yet it could be argued that a more equal distribution is socially more desirable. For the moment, however, we will ignore questions of fairness and just focus on social efficiency.

KI 4
p10

So why may a perfect market lead to social efficiency? The following sections explain.

The simple analysis of social efficiency: marginal benefit and marginal cost

Remember how we defined 'rational' choices. A rational person will choose to do an activity if the gain from so doing exceeds any sacrifice involved. In other words, whether as a producer, a consumer or a worker, a person will gain by expanding any activity whose marginal benefit (*MB*) exceeds its marginal cost (*MC*) and by contracting any activity whose marginal cost exceeds its marginal benefit. Remember that when economists use the term 'cost', they are referring to 'opportunity cost': in other words, the *sacrifice* of alternatives. Thus when we say that the marginal benefit of an activity is greater than its marginal cost, we mean that the additional benefit gained exceeds any sacrifice in terms of alternatives forgone.

KI 2
p8

Thus the economist's rule for **rational economic behaviour** is that a person should expand or contract the level of any activity until its marginal benefit is equal to its marginal cost. At that point, the person will be acting efficiently in his or her own private interest. Only when *MB* = *MC* can no further gain be made. This is known as a situation of **private efficiency**.

TC 8
p100

By analogy, *social* efficiency will be achieved where, for any activity, the marginal benefit to *society* (*MSB*) is equal to the marginal (opportunity) cost to *society* (*MSC*).

$$MSB = MSC$$

Definitions

Pareto improvement Where changes in production or consumption can make at least one person better off without making anyone worse off.

Social efficiency A situation of Pareto optimality.

Pareto optimality Where all possible Pareto improvements have been made: where, therefore, it is impossible to make anyone better off without making someone else worse off.

Rational economic behaviour Doing more of those activities whose marginal benefit exceeds their marginal cost and doing less of those activities whose marginal cost exceeds their marginal benefit.

Private efficiency Where a person's marginal benefit from a given activity equals the marginal cost.

KEY IDEA 26 Allocative efficiency (simple formulation) in any activity is achieved where marginal benefit equals marginal cost. Private efficiency is achieved where marginal private benefit equals marginal private cost ($MB = MC$). Social efficiency is achieved where marginal social benefit equals marginal social cost ($MSB = MSC$).

But why is social efficiency (i.e. Pareto optimality) achieved at this point? If MSB were greater than MSC, there would be a Pareto improvement if there were an increase in the activity. For example, if the benefits to consumers from additional production of a good exceed the cost to producers, the consumers could fully meet the cost of production in the price they pay, and so no producer loses, and yet there would still be a net gain to consumers. Thus society has gained. Likewise if MSC were greater than MSB, society would gain from a decrease in production.

Economists argue that under certain circumstances the achievement of *private* efficiency will result in *social* efficiency also. Two major conditions have to be fulfilled, however:

- There must be *perfect competition* throughout the economy. This is examined in the following sections.
- There must be *no externalities*. Externalities are additional costs or benefits to society, *over and above* those experienced by the individual producer or consumer. Pollution is an example. It is a cost that society experiences from production, but it is not a cost that the individual producer has to pay. In the *absence* of externalities, the only costs or benefits to society are the ones that the individual producer or consumer experiences: i.e. marginal social benefit (MSB) is the same as marginal private benefit (MB), and marginal social cost (MSC) is the same as marginal private cost (MC).

To understand just how social efficiency is achieved, we must look at how people maximise their interests through the market.

Achieving social efficiency through the market

Consumption: $MU = P$

The marginal benefit to a consumer from the consumption of any good is its marginal utility. The marginal cost is the price the consumer has to pay.

> ### Definition
> **Externalities** Costs or benefits of production or consumption experienced by society but not by the producers or consumers themselves. Sometimes referred to as 'spillover' or 'third-party' costs or benefits.

Figure 11.1 Maximum total surplus under perfect competition

As demonstrated in section 4.1, the 'rational' consumer will maximise consumer surplus where $MU = P$: in other words, where the marginal benefit from consumption is equal to the marginal cost of consumption. Do you remember the case of Tanya and her purchases of petrol? (See page 99.) She goes on making additional journeys and hence buying extra petrol as long as she feels that the journeys are worth the money she has to spend: in other words, as long as the marginal benefit she gets from buying extra petrol (its marginal utility to her) exceeds its marginal cost (its price). She will stop buying extra petrol when its marginal utility has fallen (the law of diminishing marginal utility) to equal its price. At that point, her consumer surplus is maximised: she has an 'efficient' level of consumption.

 Assume that the price of the good falls. How will an 'efficient' level of consumption be restored?

As we have seen, an individual's consumer surplus is maximised at the output where $MU = P$. With all consumers doing this, and all facing the same market price, their collective consumer surplus will be maximised. This is illustrated in Figure 11.1. Consumers' total utility is given by the area under the demand (MU) curve (areas $A + B + C$). Consumers' total expenditure is $P \times Q$ (areas $B + C$). Consumer surplus is the difference between total utility and total expenditure: in other words, the area between the price and the demand curve (area A).

Production: $P = MC$

The marginal benefit to a producer from the production of any good is its marginal revenue (which under perfect competition will be the same as the price of the good). As demonstrated in Chapter 6, the 'rational' firm will maximise its profit where its marginal revenue (i.e. the price under conditions of perfect competition) is equal to its marginal cost of production. This is the same thing as

When all markets are in balance

In previous chapters we have been looking at individual markets: goods markets and factor markets. But any change in one market is likely to have repercussions in other markets. And changes in these other markets will probably affect other markets, and so on.

The point about a market economy is that it is like an interconnected web. Understanding these connections helps us understand the concept of an 'economy'.

If we started with an economy where all markets were in equilibrium, we would have a state of **general equilibrium**. Then let's assume that a change occurs in just one market – say a rise in oil prices resulting from increased demand from China, India and other rapidly growing newly industrialised countries. This will have knock-on effects throughout the economy. Costs, and hence prices, will rise in oil-consuming industries. Consumption will fall for the products of these industries and rise for substitute products which do not use oil, or use less of it. Some motorists will be encouraged to use public transport or cycle. This could have knock-on effects on the demand for houses, with people choosing to live nearer to their work. This could then have effects on the various parts of the construction industry. You can work out some of these effects for yourself.

You will quickly see that a single change in one industry can set off a chain reaction throughout the economy. If there is just the one initial change, things will settle to a new general equilibrium where all markets are back in balance with demand equal to supply. In practice, of course, economic 'shocks' are occurring all the time and thus the economy is in a constant state of flux with no stable general equilibrium.

The concept of general equilibrium is a *threshold concept* because it gives us an insight into how market forces apply to a *whole* economy, and not just to its individual parts. It is about seeing how the whole jigsaw fits together and how changes ripple throughout the economy.

Many other subjects use the concept of general equilibrium. Take meteorology. We could study a single weather system, such as a low pressure area or a cold front. But, to make sense of the development and movement of such systems, we would need to see them as part of a bigger picture: as part of the whole world's weather system, which at any time is moving towards a general equilibrium in response to various changes.

For instance, in the short term, we can see how weather systems respond to the changing seasons: for example, how pressure systems move northwards in the northern hemisphere summer. In the longer term we could model how world weather systems will respond to climate change. Will the resulting general equilibrium be one where sea levels rise; where the Gulf Stream is turned off, with much of north-western Europe becoming colder; where the deserts of north Africa spread to southern Europe; and so on?

The human body is another example of general equilibrium. Another is the operation of various ecosystems, such as a jungle or the tundra. Various natural events or human intervention can profoundly affect such ecosystems and result in a new general equilibrium. For example, cutting down rainforests can affect a vast range of plant and animal life, as well as the climate.

But in economics, understanding general equilibrium is not just about understanding and predicting the output of the various industries that make up the economy. It can help us make value judgements and formulate policy. As we shall see in Threshold Concept 11 (see page 310), under certain conditions, general equilibrium can be seen as *socially efficient*. These conditions are (a) perfect competition and (b) an absence of externalities.

If social efficiency is seen as desirable, then one policy implication might be to try to make markets as perfect as possible and to 'internalise' externalities. In this chapter we examine whether such policies should be adopted and, if so, what form should they take?

1. *If general equilibrium is achieved when all markets have responded to a change and its knock-on effects, and if such changes are constantly occurring, will general equilibrium actually be achieved? Does your answer have any implications for policy?*
2. *If social efficiency is seen as desirable (a normative issue), should policy necessarily be geared to achieving this?*

---

saying that it will produce where the marginal benefit from production is equal to the marginal cost from production.

Profit is the excess of total revenue over total costs. A related concept is that of **total producer surplus** (*TPS*). This is the excess of total revenue over total *variable* costs: $TPS = TR - TVC$. In other words, total producer surplus is total

Definition

Total producer surplus Total revenue minus total variable costs $(TR - TVC)$: in other words, total profit plus total fixed costs $(T\Pi + TFC)$.

profit plus fixed costs: $TPS = T\Pi + TFC$. But since there are no marginal fixed costs (by definition), both producer surplus and profit will be maximised at the same output.

Total producer surplus for all firms in the market is shown in Figure 11.1. Total revenue (i.e. total expenditure) is $P \times Q$ (areas $B + C$). Total variable cost is the area under the *MC* curve (area C): i.e. it is the sum of all the marginal costs of each unit produced. Producer surplus is thus the area between the price and the *MC* curve (area B).

Private efficiency in the market: MU = MC

In Figure 11.1, both consumer surplus and producer surplus are maximised at output Q_e. This is the equilibrium

KI 26
p306

TC 2
p23

output under perfect competition. Thus, under perfect competition, the market will ensure that **total surplus** (areas *A* + *B*), sometimes called **total private surplus**, is maximised. At this output, $MU = P = MC$.

At any output other than Q_e total surplus will be less. If output were below Q_e, then MU would be above MC: total surplus would be increased by producing more. If output were above Q_e, then MU would be below MC: total surplus would be increased by producing less.

Social efficiency in the market: MSB = MSC

Provided the two conditions of (a) perfect competition and (b) the absence of externalities are fulfilled, Pareto optimality (i.e. social efficiency) will be achieved. Let us take each condition in turn.

KI 26
p306

Perfect competition. Perfect competition will ensure that private efficiency is achieved:

$$MU = MC \text{ (for all producers and all consumers)}$$

No externalities. In the absence of externalities, $MSB = MU$ (i.e. the benefits of consumption within society are confined to the direct consumers) and $MSC = MC$ (i.e. the costs of production to society are simply the costs paid by the producers). Thus

$$MSB = MU = P = MC = MSC$$

i.e.

$$MSB = MSC$$

With no externalities, the total surplus shown in Figure 11.1 will represent **total social surplus**.

TC 3
p24

Inefficiency would arise if (a) competition were not perfect and hence if marginal revenue were *not* equal to price and as a result marginal cost were not equal to price; or (b) there were externalities and hence either marginal social benefit were different from marginal utility (i.e. marginal *private* benefit) or marginal social cost were different from marginal (private) cost. We examine such 'market failures' in section 11.2.

1. If monopoly power existed in an industry, would production be above or below the socially efficient level (assuming no externalities)? Which would be greater, MSB or P?

Definitions

Total (private) surplus Total consumer surplus *(TU – TE)* plus total producer surplus *(TR – TVC)*.

Total social surplus Total benefits to society from consuming a good minus total costs to society from producing it. In the absence of externalities, total social surplus is the same as total (private) surplus.

---

2. Assuming perfect competition and no externalities, social efficiency will also be achieved in factor markets. Demonstrate that this will be where

$$MSB_f = MRP_f = P_f = MDU_f = MSC_f$$

(where MRP is the marginal revenue product of a factor, MDU is the marginal disutility of supplying it, and f is any factor – see section 9.1).

3. Why will marginal social benefit not equal marginal social costs in the labour market if there exists (a) union monopoly power and/or (b) firms with monopsony power?

Interdependence, efficiency and the 'invisible hand': the simple analysis of general equilibrium

TC 10
p307

If there is perfect competition and an absence of externalities throughout the economy, then the whole economy, when in equilibrium, will be socially efficient. A state of general Pareto optimality will exist.

No economy, however, is static. Conditions of demand and supply are constantly changing. Fashions change, technology changes and so on. Thus old patterns of consumption and production will cease to be Pareto optimal. Nevertheless, provided there is perfect competition and no externalities, forces will come into play to restore Pareto optimality.

In this perfect market economy, Pareto optimality is restored not by government action, but rather by the individual actions of producers, consumers and factor owners all seeking their own self-interest. It is as if an 'invisible hand' were working to guide the economy towards social efficiency (see Box 1.6).

KI 5
p21

The economic system will respond to any change in demand or supply by a whole series of subsequent changes in various interdependent markets. Social efficiency will thereby be restored. The whole process can be illustrated with a diagram showing the circular flow of income (see Figure 11.2).

Assume, for example, that tastes change such that the marginal utility of a particular good rises. This is illustrated on the right-hand side of the diagram by a shift in the MU curve (i.e. the demand curve) from MU_1 to MU_2 (i.e. D_1 to D_2). This will lead to the following sequence of events, which you can follow round the diagram in an anticlockwise direction.

Consumer demand

The rise in marginal utility (i.e. the rise in marginal social benefit of the good, MSB_g) leads to increased consumption. The resulting shortage will drive up the market price.

Producer supply

The rise in the market price will mean that price is now above the marginal (social) cost of production. It will thus be profitable for firms to increase their production. This in turn will lead to an increase in marginal cost (a movement

Figure 11.2 The interdependence of goods and factor markets

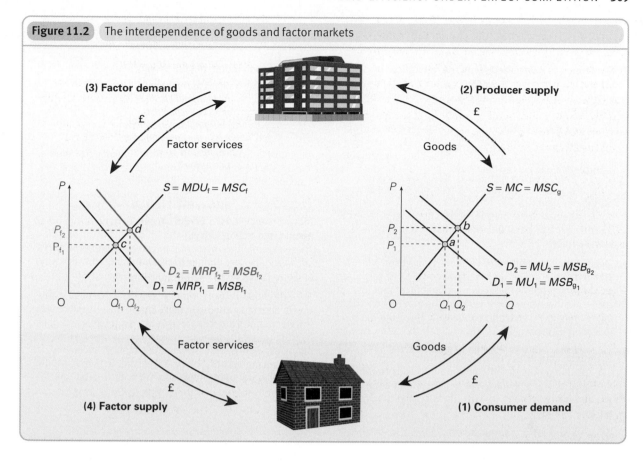

up along the marginal cost curve) due to diminishing returns. There is a movement up along the supply curve from point *a*. Price will continue to rise until equilibrium is reached at P_2Q_2 (point *b*), where $MSB_{g_2} = MSC_g$.

Factor demand

The rise in the price of the good will lead to an increase in the marginal revenue product of factors that are employed in producing the good. The reason for this is that the marginal *revenue* product of a factor is its marginal *physical* product multiplied by the *price* of the good (see section 9.1). But since the price of the good has now gone up, the output of factors will be worth correspondingly more. The following takes just one factor (*f*) as an example.

A rise in the value of the factor's output (due to the higher price of the good) will make its marginal revenue product higher than its marginal cost to the firm. This will increase the demand for the factor. Factor demand shifts to D_2 (= $MRP_{f_2} = MSB_{f_2}$). This in turn will drive up the price of the factor.

Factor supply

The rise in the price of the factor will raise the marginal benefit of supplying it (and hence the marginal social benefit). This will mean that the marginal benefit now exceeds the marginal cost (the marginal disutility, MDU_f) of supplying the factor. There is thus a movement up along the factor supply curve from point *c* as more units of the

factor are supplied. The price of the factor will continue to rise until equilibrium is reached at $P_{f_2}Q_{f_2}$ (point *d*), where $MSB_{f_2} = MSC_f$.

The process of adjustment does not end here. If supernormal profits are made, new firms will enter. Similarly, if factor rewards are supernormal, new factors will be attracted from other industries. This in turn will affect prices and hence quantities in *other* industries in both goods and factor markets.

In other words, a single change in tastes will create a ripple effect throughout the economy, through a whole series of interdependent markets. Eventually, long-run equilibrium will be restored with $MSB = MSC$ in all markets. The economy has returned to a position of Pareto optimality. And all this has taken place with no government intervention. It is the 'invisible hand' of the market that has achieved this state of social efficiency.

These arguments form a central part of the neoclassical case for *laissez-faire*: the philosophy of non-intervention by the government. Under ideal conditions, it is argued, the free pursuit of individual self-interest will lead to the social good.

1. *Trace through the effects in both factor and goods markets of the following: (a) an increase in the productivity of a particular type of labour; (b) an increase in the supply of a particular factor.*
2. *Show in each case how social efficiency will initially be destroyed and then how market adjustments will restore social efficiency.*

Economics is concerned with the allocation of scarce resources. Whenever choices are made, whether by consumers, firms, the government or any other agency, a choice is being made about the allocation of resources.

When you buy a CD costing £10, you are choosing to allocate £10 of your money to the purchase – £10 that could have been spent on something else. But have you allocated your money in the best way?

Similarly, when a firm chooses to produce one product rather than another, or to use technique A rather than some alternative technique, it is choosing to allocate its resources in particular ways. But are these the best ways?

The question is whether the resources have been allocated *efficiently*. We define an efficient allocation of resources as one which brings the maximum benefit for that level of costs. In other words, no gain would be made by reallocating resources in some alternative way. Thus your decision to spend £10 on a CD is an efficient allocation of your resources, if it brings you more benefit (i.e. utility) for the £10 than could any other purchase. The firm's decision to use technique A is an efficient one if it leads to a higher rate of profit: if the marginal benefit (i.e. marginal revenue) relative to the marginal cost is greater than for any other technique.

> KI 14
> p102

What we are talking about here is 'allocative efficiency'. It is a *threshold concept* because to understand it is to understand how to make the most of scarce resources: and scarcity is the core problem of economics for all of us.

It is obvious that poor people on very limited incomes will want to spend their money as efficiently as possible. But even exceedingly rich people, who can buy anything they want, are still likely to have limited time or opportunities. They too will probably want to use their time efficiently so that they can make best use of their wealth!

Allocative efficiency is a threshold concept for another reason. We need to see how it relates to *social* objectives. If people all individually achieve their own *private efficiency*, does this mean that society will have an efficient allocation of resources? The answer is no. The reason is that our decisions often have consequences for *other* people: our actions have external costs and/or benefits. These externalities mean that private efficiency and *social efficiency* diverge. We need to understand how and why, and how social efficiency can be achieved.

> KI 4
> p10

Then there is the question of equity. Just because everyone is allocating their resources in the best possible way for them, and even if there were no externalities, it does not follow that the allocation of resources is *fair*. However efficiently rich people spend their money, most people would still argue that it is socially desirable to redistribute part of rich people's income to the poor through the tax and benefit system.

1. *Why might consumers not always make efficient consumption decisions?*
2. *Explain the meaning of social efficiency using the concept of Pareto improvements.*

The following pages examine social efficiency in more detail. You may omit these and skip straight to section 11.2 (page 313) if you want to.

*The intermediate analysis of social efficiency: marginal benefit and marginal cost ratios

In practice, consumers do not consider just one good in isolation. They make choices between goods. Likewise firms make choices as to which goods to produce and which factors to employ. A more satisfactory analysis of social efficiency, therefore, considers the choices that firms and households make.

> TC 11
> p310

Whether as a producer, consumer or worker, a person will gain by expanding activity X relative to activity Y if

$$\frac{MB_X}{MB_Y} > \frac{MC_X}{MC_Y}$$

The reason is straightforward. Activity X is giving a greater benefit relative to its cost than is activity Y. Only when

> KI 14
> p102

$$\frac{MB_X}{MB_Y} = \frac{MC_X}{MC_Y}$$

can no further gain be made by switching from the one activity to the other. At this point, people will be acting efficiently in their own private interest.

By analogy, social efficiency is achieved where the social marginal benefit ratio of two goods is equal to the social marginal cost ratio.

> **KEY IDEA 27**
>
> Social efficiency (equi-marginal formulation) is achieved where the marginal social benefit ratios are equal to the marginal social cost ratios for any two alternatives. In the case of two alternatives X and Y, this will be where
>
> $$\frac{MSB_X}{MSB_Y} = \frac{MSC_X}{MSC_Y}$$

As with the simple analysis of social efficiency, it can be shown that, provided there is perfect competition and no externalities, the achievement of private efficiency will result in social efficiency also. This will be demonstrated in the following sections.

*Efficiency in the goods market (intermediate analysis)

TC 11 p310

Private efficiency under perfect competition

Consumption. The optimum combination of two goods X and Y consumed for any consumer is where

KI 14 p102

$$\frac{MU_X}{MU_Y} \text{ (i.e. } MRS) = \frac{P_X}{P_Y}$$

The *marginal rate of substitution in consumption (MRS)* (see page 111) is the amount of good Y that a consumer would be willing to sacrifice for an increase in consumption of good X (i.e. $\Delta Y/\Delta X$). $MRS = MU_X/MU_Y$ since, if X gave twice the marginal utility of Y, the consumer would be prepared to give up two of Y to obtain one of X (i.e. $MRS = 2/1$).

If MU_X/MU_Y were greater than P_X/P_Y, how would consumers behave? What would bring consumption back to equilibrium where $MU_X/MU_Y = P_X/P_Y$?

Production. The optimum combination of two goods X and Y produced for any producer is where

KI 14 p102

$$\frac{MC_X}{MC_Y} \text{ (i.e. } MRT) = \frac{P_X}{P_Y}$$

The *marginal rate of transformation in production (MRT)* is the amount of good Y that the producer will have to give up producing for an increase in production of good X (i.e. $\Delta Y/\Delta X$) if total costs of production are to remain unchanged. $MRT = MC_X/MC_Y$ since, if the marginal cost of good X were twice that of Y, the firm's costs would remain constant if it gave up producing two of Y in order to produce an extra X (i.e. $MRT = 2/1$).

If MC_X/MC_Y were greater than P_X/P_Y, how would firms behave? What would bring production back into equilibrium where $MC_X/MC_Y = P_X/P_Y$?

Social efficiency under perfect competition

In each of the following three cases, it will be assumed that there are no externalities.

Social efficiency between consumers. If MU_X/MU_Y for person a is greater than MU_X/MU_Y for person b, *both* people would gain if person a gave person b some of good Y in exchange for some of good X. There would be a Pareto improvement. The Pareto optimal distribution of consumption will therefore be where

KI 27 p310

$$\frac{MU_X}{MU_Y} \text{ person a} = \frac{MU_X}{MU_Y} \text{ person b} = \frac{MU_X}{MU_Y} \text{ person c} \dots \text{etc.}$$

i.e. *MRS* is the same for all consumers.

But this will be achieved *automatically* under perfect competition, since each consumer will consume that combination of goods where $MU_X/MU_Y = P_X/P_Y$ and all consumers face the *same* (market) prices and hence the *same* P_X/P_Y.

Social efficiency between producers. If MC_X/MC_Y for producer g is greater than MC_X/MC_Y for producer h, then if producer g produced relatively more Y and producer h produced relatively more X, the same output could be produced at a lower total cost (i.e. with less resources). There would be a Pareto improvement. The Pareto optimal distribution of production between firms is therefore where

KI 27 p310

$$\frac{MC_X}{MC_Y} \text{ producer g} = \frac{MC_X}{MC_Y} \text{ producer h} = \frac{MC_X}{MC_Y} \text{ producer i} \dots \text{etc.}$$

i.e. *MRT* is the same for all producers.

This too will be achieved *automatically* under perfect competition, since each producer will maximise profits where $MC_X/MC_Y = P_X/P_Y$ and all producers face the *same* (market) prices and hence the *same* P_X/P_Y.

Social efficiency in exchange. If MU_X/MU_Y (i.e. *MRS*) for all consumers is greater than MC_X/MC_Y (i.e. *MRT*) for all producers, then there would be a Pareto improvement if resources were reallocated to produce relatively more X and less Y.

Assume the *MRS* (i.e. $\Delta Y/\Delta X$) = 3/1 and the *MRT* (i.e. $\Delta Y/\Delta X$) = 2/1. Consumers will be prepared to give up three units of Y to obtain one unit of X, and yet producers only have to sacrifice producing two units of Y to produce one unit of X. Thus consumers can pay producers in full for extra units of X they produce and there will still be a net gain to consumers. There has been a Pareto improvement.

The Pareto optimal allocation of resources is where

Social MRS (SMRS) = Social MRT (SMRT)

KI 27 p310

Assuming no externalities, this will be achieved automatically under perfect competition, since (a) with no externalities, social and private marginal rates of substitution will be the same, and similarly social and private marginal rates of transformation will be the same, and (b) P_X/P_Y is the same for all producers and consumers. In other words:

$$SMRS = MRS_{\text{all consumers}} = \frac{MU_X}{MU_Y} \text{ all consumers} = \frac{P_X}{P_Y}$$

and

$$SMRT = MRT_{\text{all producers}} = \frac{MC_X}{MC_Y} \text{ all producers} = \frac{P_X}{P_Y}$$

i.e.

SMRS = SMRT

KI 27 p310

Thus the pursuit of private gain, it is argued, has led to the achieving of social efficiency. This is a momentous conclusion. It is clearly very attractive to people to think that, simply by looking after their own interests, social efficiency will thereby be achieved!

This is illustrated graphically in Figure 11.3. A production possibility curve (the red line) shows the various

Figure 11.3 Social efficiency under perfect competition

Socially efficient output:
$MRS = P_X/P_Y = MRT$

Good Y

S

Slope = MRS

Slope = P_X/P_Y
Slope = MRT

I_3
I_2
I_1

O   Good X

combinations of two goods X and Y that can be produced (see pages 11–12). Its slope is given by $\Delta Y/\Delta X$ and shows how much Y must be given up to produce 1 more of X. Its slope, therefore, is the marginal rate of transformation (*MRT*).

Social indifference curves can be drawn showing the various combinations of X and Y that give particular levels of satisfaction to consumers as a whole. Their slope is given by $\Delta Y/\Delta X$ and shows how much Y consumers are prepared to give up to obtain one more unit of X. Their slope, therefore, is the marginal rate of substitution in consumption (*MRS*).

The Pareto optimal combination of goods is at point S, where the production possibility curve is tangential to the highest possible indifference curve. At any other point on the production possibility curve, a lower level of consumer satisfaction is achieved. The slope of the tangent at S is equal to both *MRT* and *MRS*, and hence also to P_X/P_Y.

 If production were at a point on the production possibility curve below point S, describe the process whereby market forces would return the economy to point S.

*Efficiency in the factor market (intermediate analysis)

TC 11
p310

A similar analysis can be applied to factor markets, showing that perfect competition and the absence of externalities will lead to efficiency in the use of factors between firms. Assume that there are two factors: labour (L) and capital (K).

If MPP_L/MPP_K for firm g is greater than MPP_L/MPP_K for firm h, then if firm g were to use relatively more labour and firm h relatively more capital, more could be produced for the same total input. There would be a Pareto improvement.

The Pareto optimum distribution of factors between firms will therefore be where

$$\frac{MPP_L}{MPP_K} \text{ firm g} = \frac{MPP_L}{MPP_K} \text{ firm h} = \frac{MPP_L}{MPP_K} \text{ firm i} \ldots \text{etc.}$$

But this will be achieved automatically under perfect competition since, as we saw in section 5.3, each producer will be producing where $MPP_L/MPP_K = P_L/P_K$ and each producer will face the same factor prices and hence P_L/P_K.

Provided there are no externalities, the marginal private benefit of labour to a firm (MPP_L) will equal the marginal social benefit of labour (MSB_L). The same applies to capital. Thus $MPP_L/MPP_K = MSB_L/MSB_K = P_L/P_K$. Similarly on the cost side, if there are no externalities, then $MC_L/MC_K = MSC_L/MSC_K = P_L/P_K$. Therefore:

$$\frac{MSB_L}{MSB_K} = \frac{MSC_L}{MSC_K}$$

 KI 27 p310

*The intermediate analysis of general equilibrium

 TC 10 p307

General equilibrium is where equilibrium exists in all markets. Under perfect competition and in the absence of externalities, general equilibrium will give Pareto optimality.

If any change in the conditions of demand or supply occurs, this disequilibrium will automatically create a whole series of interdependent reactions in various markets.

KI 5 p21

Assume, for example, that tastes change such that MU_X rises and MU_Y falls. This will lead to the following sequence of events in the goods market.

MU_X/MU_Y will now be greater than P_X/P_Y. Thus consumers buy more X relative to Y. This causes MU_X/MU_Y to fall (due to diminishing marginal utility) and P_X/P_Y to rise (due to a relative shortage of X and a surplus of Y), helping to restore equilibrium where $MU_X/MU_Y = P_X/P_Y$. The rise in P_X/P_Y causes P_X/P_Y to be greater than MC_X/MC_Y. Thus firms produce more X relative to Y. This causes MC_X/MC_Y to rise (due to diminishing returns), helping to restore equilibrium where $P_X/P_Y = MC_X/MC_Y$. This process of price and quantity adjustment thus continues until once more

$$\frac{MU_X}{MU_Y} = \frac{P_X}{P_Y} = \frac{MC_X}{MC_Y}$$

 KI 14 p102

Similar adjustments will take place in the factor market. The price of those factors used in producing good X will be bid up and those used in producing Y will be bid down. This will encourage factors to move from industry Y and into industry X. The whole process of adjustment continues until equilibrium and Pareto optimality are restored in all goods and factor markets.

Definition

General equilibrium Where all the millions of markets throughout the economy are in a simultaneous state of equilibrium.

Section summary

1. Social efficiency (Pareto optimality) will be achieved when it is not possible to make anyone better off without making someone else worse off. This will be achieved if people behave 'rationally' under perfect competition providing there are no externalities.

2. Rational behaviour involves doing more of any activity whose marginal benefit *(MB)* exceeds its marginal cost *(MC)* and less of any activity whose marginal cost exceeds its marginal benefit. The optimum level of consumption or production for the individual consumer or firm will be where $MB = MC$. This is called a situation of 'private efficiency'.

3. In a perfectly competitive goods market, the consumer will achieve private efficiency where $MU = P$, and the producer where $P = MC$. Thus $MU = MC$. In the absence of externalities, private benefits and costs will equal social benefits and costs. Thus $MU = MSB$ and $MC = MSC$. Thus $MSB = MSC$: a situation of social efficiency (Pareto optimality).

4. Given perfect competition and an absence of externalities, if the equality of marginal benefit and marginal cost is destroyed in any market (by shifts in demand or supply), price adjustments will take place until general equilibrium is restored where $MSB = MSC$ in all markets: a situation of general Pareto optimality.

*5. The rational producer or consumer will choose the combination of any two pairs of goods where their marginal benefit ratio is equal to their marginal cost ratio. Consumers will achieve private efficiency where

$$\frac{MU_X}{MU_Y} \text{ (i.e. } MRS) = \frac{P_X}{P_Y}$$

Producers will achieve private efficiency where

$$\frac{P_X}{P_Y} = \frac{MC_X}{MC_Y} \text{ (i.e. } MRT)$$

Thus:

$$\frac{MU_X}{MU_Y} = \frac{MC_X}{MC_Y}$$

In the absence of externalities, this will give a situation of social efficiency where

$$\frac{MSB_X}{MSB_Y} = \frac{MSC_X}{MSC_Y}$$

*6. Similarly, in factor markets, social efficiency will be achieved if there is perfect competition and an absence of externalities. This will be where the *MSB* ratio for any two factors is equal to their *MSC* ratio.

*7. Again assuming perfect competition and an absence of externalities, general equilibrium will be achieved where there is a socially efficient level of production, consumption and exchange in all markets: where the *MSB* ratio for any pair of goods or factors is equal to the *MSC* ratio.

11.2 THE CASE FOR GOVERNMENT INTERVENTION

TC 3
p24

In the real world, markets fail to achieve social efficiency. Part of the problem is the existence of externalities, part is a lack of perfect competition and part is the fact that markets may take a long time to adjust to any disequilibrium given the often considerable short-run immobility of factors. What is more, social efficiency (i.e. Pareto optimality) is not the only economic goal of society. Markets may also fail to the extent that they fail to achieve other objectives such as greater equality and faster growth. In this section we explore the various categories of market failure.

> **KEY IDEA 28**
> Markets generally fail to achieve social efficiency. There are various types of market failure. Market failures provide one of the major justifications for government intervention in the economy.

Externalities

The market will not lead to social efficiency if the actions of producers or consumers affect people other than themselves: in other words, when there are *externalities* (side-effects).

> **KEY IDEA 29**
> **Externalities are spillover costs or benefits.** Where these exist, even an otherwise perfect market will fail to achieve social efficiency.

Whenever other people are affected beneficially, there are said to be ***external benefits***. Whenever other people are affected adversely, there are said to be ***external costs***.

Thus the full cost to society (the ***social cost***) of the production of any good is the private cost faced by firms plus any externalities of production. Likewise the full benefit to

Definitions

External benefits Benefits from production (or consumption) experienced by people *other* than the producer (or consumer).

External costs Costs of production (or consumption) borne by people *other* than the producer (or consumer).

Social cost Private cost plus externalities in production.

Figure 11.4 External costs and benefits in production

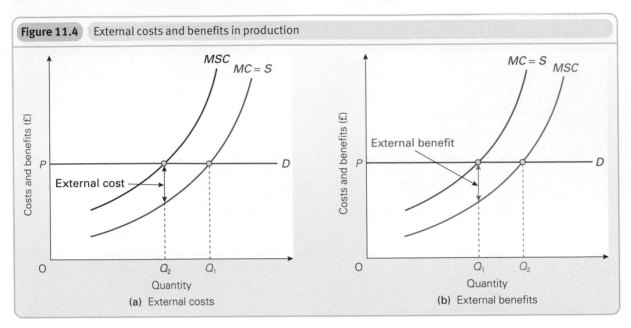

(a) External costs

(b) External benefits

society (the *social benefit*) from the consumption of any good is the private benefit enjoyed by consumers plus any externalities of consumption.

There are four major types of externality. (In each case, we will assume that the market is in other respects perfect.)

External costs of production (MSC > MC)

When a chemical firm dumps waste in a river or pollutes the air, the community bears costs additional to those borne by the firm. The marginal *social* cost (*MSC*) of chemical production exceeds the marginal private cost (*MC*). Diagrammatically, the *MSC* curve is above the *MC* curve. This is shown in Figure 11.4(a), which assumes that the firm in other respects is operating in a perfect market, and is therefore a price taker (i.e. faces a horizontal demand curve).

The *socially* optimal output would be Q_2, where $P = MSC$. The firm, however, produces Q_1, which is more than the optimum. Thus external costs lead to overproduction from society's point of view.

The problem of external costs arises in a free-market economy because no one has legal ownership of the air or rivers and no one can prevent or charge for their use as a dump for waste. Such a 'market' is missing. Control must, therefore, be left to the government or local authorities.

Other examples are extensive farming that destroys hedgerows and wildlife, and climate change caused by CO_2 emissions from power stations.

Definition

Social benefit Private benefit plus externalities in consumption.

External benefits of production (MSC < MC)

If a forestry company plants new woodlands, there is a benefit not only to the company itself, but also to the world through a reduction of CO_2 in the atmosphere (forests are a carbon sink). The marginal *social* cost of providing timber, therefore, is less than the marginal *private* cost.

In Figure 11.4(b), the *MSC* curve is *below* the *MC* curve. The level of output provided by the forestry company is Q_1, where $P = MC$, a *lower* level than the social optimum, Q_2, where $P = MSC$.

Another example of external benefits in production is that of research and development. If other firms have access to the results of the research, then clearly the benefits extend beyond the firm that finances it. Since the firm receives only the private benefits, it will conduct a less than optimal amount of research.

External costs of consumption (MSB < MB)

When people use their cars, other people suffer from their exhaust, the added congestion, the noise, etc. These 'negative externalities' make the marginal social benefit of using cars less than the marginal private benefit (i.e. marginal utility).

Figure 11.5(a) shows the marginal utility and price to a consumer of using a car. The distance travelled by this motorist will be Q_1 miles: i.e. where $MU = P$ (where price is the cost of petrol, oil, wear and tear, etc. per mile). The *social* optimum, however, would be less than this, namely Q_2, where $MSB = P$.

Other examples are noisy radios in public places, the smoke from cigarettes, and litter.

 Is it likely that the MSB curve will be parallel to the MU curve? Explain your reasoning.

Figure 11.5   External costs and benefits in consumption

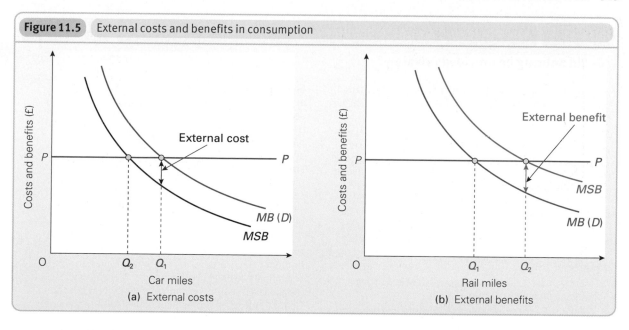

(a) External costs

(b) External benefits

External benefits of consumption (MSB > MB)

When people travel by train rather than by car, other people benefit by there being less congestion and exhaust and fewer accidents on the roads. Thus the marginal social benefit of rail travel is *greater* than the marginal private benefit (i.e. marginal utility). There are external benefits from rail travel. In Figure 11.5(b), the *MSB* curve is *above* the private *MB* curve. The actual level of consumption (Q_1) is thus below the socially optimal level of consumption (Q_2).

Other examples include the beneficial effects for other people of deodorants, vaccinations and attractive clothing.

To summarise: whenever there are external benefits, there will be too little produced or consumed. Whenever there are external costs, there will be too much produced or consumed. The market will not equate *MSB* and *MSC*.

1. Give other examples of each of the four types of externality.
2. Redraw Figures 11.4(a) and 11.5(a), only this time assume that the producer (in the first diagram) or the consumer (in the second) has economic power and is thus not a price taker. How does the existence of power affect the relationship between the private and the social optimum positions?

Public goods

There is a category of goods where the positive externalities are so great that the free market, whether perfect or imperfect, may not produce at all. They are called *public goods*. Examples include lighthouses, pavements, flood-control dams, public drainage, public services such as the police and even government itself.

Public goods have two important characteristics: *non-rivalry* and *non-excludability*.

- If I consume a bar of chocolate, it cannot then be consumed by someone else. If, however, I walk along a pavement or enjoy the benefits of street lighting, it does not prevent you or anyone else doing the same. There is thus what we call *non-rivalry* in the consumption of such goods. These goods have large external benefits relative to private benefits. This makes them socially desirable, but privately unprofitable. No one person alone would pay to have a pavement built along his or her street. The private benefit would be too small relative to the cost. And yet the social benefit to all the other people using the pavement may far outweigh the cost.

Which of the following have the property of non-rivalry: (a) a can of drink; (b) public transport; (c) a commercial radio broadcast; (d) the sight of flowers in a public park?

- If I spend money erecting a flood-control dam to protect my house, my neighbours will also be protected by the dam. I cannot prevent them enjoying the benefits of my expenditure. This feature of *non-excludability* means

Definitions

Public good A good or service that has the features of non-rivalry and non-excludability and as a result would not be provided by the free market.

Non-rivalry Where the consumption of a good or service by one person will not prevent others from enjoying it.

Non-excludability Where it is not possible to provide a good or service to one person without it thereby being available for others to enjoy.

Could policing be provided privately?

A good example of a public good or service is that of the police. Take the case of police officers on the beat. They are providing a general service to the community by deterring and detecting crime.

If individuals had to employ their own police officers privately, this would create considerable external benefits relative to private benefits. One police officer can provide protection to *many* individuals. But for most people it would be out of the question to employ their own police officer: the private cost would hugely exceed the private benefit. Also, once such privately employed police were on duty catching and deterring criminals, people who did not employ their own police officers could not be excluded from these benefits. There would be a 'free-rider' problem.

It obviously makes sense, therefore, that policing should be provided as a public service.

But do all aspects of policing come into this category? The answer is no. When there is a *specific* task of guarding specific property, policing could be provided by the market. This is in fact done by security firms. Security guards are employed by banks, shops, factories, etc. to prevent theft or criminal damage to their property. In these cases, the private benefits are perceived to exceed the private costs.

Should such security services be provided privately or are they better provided by the police? Since the *private*

benefits in such cases are large, there is a strong argument for charging the recipient. But why should the service be provided by private security firms? Could the police not charge firms for specific guard duties? The problem here is that, if private security firms were not allowed to operate, the police would have a monopoly and could charge very high prices unless the prices were regulated by the government. Also, the quality of the service might be poorer than that provided by private security companies which were competing against each other for business.

On the other hand, the police are likely to bring greater expertise to the job. There are also economies of scale to be gained: for example, the police may have knowledge of criminal activities in other parts of the area which may pose a threat to the particular property in question. Finally, there is the problem that private security guards may not show the same level of courtesy as the police in dealing with the public (or criminals for that matter).

1. *The police charge football clubs for policing inside football grounds. Do you think this is a good idea?*
2. *Some roads could be regarded as a public good, but some could be provided by the market. Which types of road could be provided by the market? Why? Would it be a good idea?*

---

that they would get the benefits free, and would therefore have no incentive to pay themselves. This is known as the *free-rider problem*.

KEY IDEA 30

The free-rider problem. People are often unwilling to pay for things if they can make use of things other people have bought. This problem can lead to people not purchasing things that it would be to the benefit of them and other members of society to have.

When goods have these two features the free market will simply not provide them. Thus these public goods can be provided only by the government or by the government subsidising private firms. (Note that not all goods produced by the public sector are public goods.)

1. *Give some other examples of public goods. Does the provider of these goods (the government or local authority) charge for their use? If so, is the method of charging based on the amount of the good that people use? Is it a good method of charging? Could you suggest a better method?*
2. *Name some goods or services provided by the government or local authorities that are not public goods.*

Common resources

Common resources are not owned but are available free of charge to anyone. Examples include the air we breathe and the oceans for fishing. Like public goods, they are non-excludable. For example, fishing boats can take as many fish as they are able from the open seas. There is no 'owner' of the fish to stop them. As long as there are plentiful stocks of fish, there is no problem.

But as more people fish the seas, so fish stocks are likely to run down. This is where common resources differ from public goods. There *is* rivalry. One person's use of a common resource diminishes the amount available for others. This result is an overuse of common resources. This is why fish stocks in many parts of the world are severely depleted, why virgin forests are disappearing (cut down for timber or firewood), why many roads are so congested and why the atmosphere is becoming so polluted (being used as a common 'dump' for emissions). In each case, a resource that is

---

Definition

Free-rider problem When it is not possible to exclude other people from consuming a good that someone has bought.

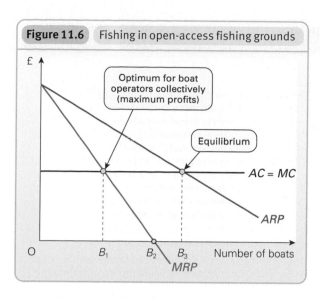

Figure 11.6 Fishing in open-access fishing grounds

the revenue actually earned by the additional boat. The extra boat gets an average catch (which has been reduced somewhat because of the additional boat) and hence gains the average revenue product of all the boats.

What will be the equilibrium? Note first that the optimal number of boats for the boat operators collectively is B_1, where the marginal cost of an extra boat equals its marginal revenue product. In other words, this maximises the collective profit. At point B_1, however, there will be an incentive for extra boats to enter the fishery because the average revenue product (that is, the return that an additional boat gets) is greater than the cost of operating the boat.

More boats will enter as long as the value earned by each boat (ARP) is greater than the cost of operating it: as long as the ARP curve is above the $AC = MC$ line. Equilibrium is reached with B_3 boats: considerably above the collective profit-maximising number. Note also that the way the diagram is drawn, marginal revenue product is negative. The last boat has *decreased* the total value of the catch.

In many parts of the world, fish stocks have become so severely depleted that governments, individually or collectively, have had to act. Measures have included quotas on catches or the number of boats, minimum net mesh sizes (to allow young fish to escape), or banning fishing altogether in certain areas.

 To what extent can the following be regarded as common resources? (a) rainforests; (b) children's playgrounds in public parks; (c) silence in a library; (d) the Internet.

freely available is overused. This has become known as the **tragedy of the commons**.

 How can we analyse the overuse of common resources? The simplest way is in terms of externalities. When I use a common resource, I am reducing the amount available for others. I am imposing a cost on other people: an external cost. If I am motivated purely by self-interest, I will not take these external costs into account. In terms of Figure 11.4(a), I will produce Q_1, which is above the socially optimal amount, Q_2. Overuse of the resource thus occurs.

 Another way of analysing it is to examine the effect of one person's use of a resource on other people's output. Take the case of fishing grounds. In Figure 11.6 the horizontal axis measures the use of this common resource, say in terms of the number of fishing boats per day. The average cost of operating a boat (e.g. the wages of the crew and the fuel) is taken to be constant and is thus equal to the marginal cost. For the sake of simplicity, the price of fish is also assumed to be constant.

As the number of boats increases and fish stocks decline, so each extra boat entering will add less and less to the total catch. The revenue added by each extra boat – the marginal revenue product (MRP) – thus declines. Eventually, at point B_2, no more fish can be caught: $MRP = 0$. The catch is at the maximum. The average revenue product (ARP) is the revenue earned per boat: i.e. the total value of the catch divided by the number of boats.

The average and marginal revenue product curves have to be interpreted with care. Say one additional boat enters the fishing ground. The MRP curve shows the extra revenue accruing to the boat operators collectively. It does *not* show

Market power

Lack of Pareto optimality

Whenever markets are imperfect, whether as pure monopoly or monopsony or as some form of imperfect competition, the market will fail to equate MSB and MSC. Pareto optimality will not be achieved.

 This is illustrated in Figure 11.7, which shows revenue and cost curves for a monopolist. It assumes no externalities. The socially efficient (Pareto optimal) output is Q_2, where $MSB = MSC$. The monopolist, however, produces the lower output Q_1, where $MR = MC$.

 Referring back to Figure 9.8 on page 246, and assuming that the MRP_L curve represents the marginal social benefit from the employment of a factor, and that the price of the factor represents its marginal social cost (i.e. assuming no externalities), show that a monopsony will employ less than the Pareto optimal amount of factors.

Deadweight loss under monopoly

Another way of analysing the welfare loss that occurs under monopoly is to use the concepts of *consumer* and *producer surplus*. The two concepts are illustrated in Figure 11.8, which is similar to Figure 11.7. The diagram shows an industry that is initially under perfect competition and then becomes a monopoly (but faces the same revenue and cost curves).

Definition

Tragedy of the commons When resources are commonly available at no charge, people are likely to overexploit them.

KI 4
p10

BOX 11.2 A COMMONS SOLUTION

Making the best use of common resources

To avoid the tragedy of the commons, one solution is to change the status of such resources. There are two obvious ways of doing this.

The first is for the government or an inter-governmental agency either to take over the resources or to regulate their use. Thus a national or local government could pass laws preventing people from tipping waste onto common land or into rivers. Alternatively, groups of governments could act collectively to regulate activities. An example here is the EU's common fisheries policy or international agreements to ban whaling.

The second is to privatise such resources. Common land could be sold or given to private landowners. Such land would then have the property of excludability. This solution clearly raises questions of fairness. How should the land be divided up? If it is sold, how should the previous users of the resource be compensated – if at all? In the 'enclosure movement' in Britain in the eighteenth and nineteenth centuries, common lands were often acquired by wealthy aristocracy and hedges put around them. Poor peasants, who had previously used the land, either had to rent it from the landlords or left the land and were forced to take low-paid work in the cities.

But is there any way for resources to stay as common resources without them being overexploited? After all, economic theory would seem to suggest that the overexploitation of such resources is inevitable: that common ownership will end in tragedy.

Social attitudes towards common resources

In practice, many common resources are used sustainably without government regulation.

When economists began to look at how systems of commonly managed resources actually worked, they found to their surprise that they often worked quite well. Swiss Alpine pastures; Japanese forests; irrigation systems in Spain and the Philippines. All these were examples of commons that lasted for decades. Some irrigation networks held in common were more efficiently run than the public and private systems that worked alongside them. Though there were failures, too, it seemed as if good management could stave off the tragedy.[1]

The crucial factor here is whether a sense of individual responsibility can be engendered and whether some mechanism can be found for the users to act collectively to manage the resources – a form of quasi-government. Also there has to be some agreement about what is a fair use of such resources and, in many cases, rules will have to be developed.

In *Governing the Commons*, which was published in 1990, Elinor Ostrom of Indiana University described the rules needed to keep a commons going. She showed that there are almost always elaborate conventions over who can use resources and when. What you take out of a commons has to be proportional to what you put in. Usage has to be compatible with the commons' underlying health (i.e., you cannot just keep grazing your animals regardless). Everyone has to have some say in the rules. And people usually pay more attention to monitoring abuses and to conflict resolution than to sanctions and punishment.[2]

Sometimes the rules of behaviour can be deeply embedded in culture. Thus indigenous peoples operating on marginal lands, such as the Aborigines in Australia or the San in the Kalahari, have a culture that respects common resources and puts sustainability at the heart of its philosophy.

Land is fundamental to the wellbeing of Aboriginal people. The land is not just soil or rocks or minerals, but a whole environment that sustains and is sustained by people and culture. For Indigenous Australians, the land is the core of all spirituality and this relationship and the spirit of 'country' is central to the issues that are important to Indigenous people today.[3]

But if rules are not embedded in culture, how can they be made to stick? One way is through the development of pressure groups, such as Friends of the Earth or local community action groups.

Mrs Ostrom suggests the so-called 'miracle of the Rhine' – the clean-up of Europe's busiest waterway – should be seen as an example of successful commons management because it was not until local pressure groups, city and regional governments and non-governmental organisations got involved that polluters were willing to recognise the costs they were imposing on others, and cut emissions. An inter-governmental body (the International Commission for the Protection of the Rhine) did not have the same effect.[4]

 Is there any way in which people's behaviour towards the global commons can be changed so as to reduce the problem of climate change?

[1] 'Commons Sense', *The Economist*, 31 July 2008.
[2] *Ibid.*
[3] Australian Indigenous cultural heritage (http://www.cultureandrecreation.gov.au/articles/indigenous/)
[4] 'Commons Sense', *The Economist*, 31 July 2008.

KI 4
p10

Under *perfect competition* the industry will produce an output of Q_{pc} at a price of P_{pc}, where $MC (= S) = P (= AR)$: i.e. at point *a*. Consumer surplus is shown by areas 1 + 2 + 3, and producer surplus by areas 4 + 5. Total surplus (i.e. consumer plus producer surplus) is maximised at this output (see Figure 11.1 on page 306).

What happens when the industry is under *monopoly*? The firm will produce where $MC = MR$, at an output of Q_m and a price of P_m (at point *b* on the demand curve). Total revenue is $P_m \times Q_m$ (areas 2 + 4 + 6). Total cost is the area under the MC curve (area 6). Thus the producer surplus is areas 2 + 4. This is clearly a *larger* surplus than under perfect

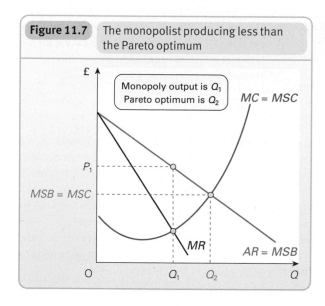

Figure 11.7 The monopolist producing less than the Pareto optimum

Monopoly output is Q_1
Pareto optimum is Q_2

$MC = MSC$

P_1

$MSB = MSC$

MR

$AR = MSB$

O Q_1 Q_2 Q

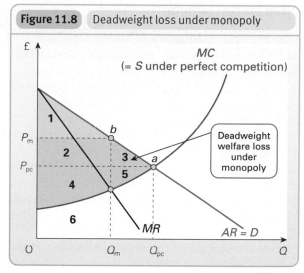

Figure 11.8 Deadweight loss under monopoly

MC
$(= S$ under perfect competition)

P_m

P_{pc}

Deadweight welfare loss under monopoly

MR $AR = D$

O Q_m Q_{pc} Q

competition (since area 2 is larger than area 5). The consumer surplus, however, will fall dramatically. With consumption at Q_m, total utility is given by areas $1 + 2 + 4 + 6$, whereas consumer expenditure is given by areas $2 + 4 + 6$. Consumer surplus, then, is simply area 1. (Note that area 2 has been transformed from consumer surplus to producer surplus.)

Total surplus under monopoly is therefore areas $1 + 2 + 4$: a smaller surplus than under perfect competition. 'Monopolisation' of the industry has resulted in a loss of total surplus of areas $3 + 5$. The producers' gain has been more than offset by the consumers' loss. This loss of surplus is known as the **deadweight welfare loss** of monopoly.

KI 28
p313

*LOOKING AT THE MATHS

Total consumer surplus (*TCS*) equals total utility minus total expenditure (i.e. total revenue). Total producer surplus (*TPS*) equals total revenue minus total variable cost. Thus total surplus (*TS*) is given by:

$$TS = TCS + TPS = (TU - TR) + (TR - TVC) = TU - TVC$$

Assuming that the demand curve traces out the marginal utility curve (see pages 100–1), this allows us to derive the total utility function. To do this, you would need to use the technique of integration. Assuming that the total utility function is

$$TU = bQ - cQ^2$$

and that the total variable cost function is

$$TVC = jQ - kQ^2 + lQ^3$$

this will give a total surplus function of

$$TS = (bQ - cQ^2) - (jQ - kQ^2 + lQ^3) \qquad (1)$$

To find the level of deadweight welfare loss, we would then subtract total surplus under perfect competition from that under monopoly. To do this, we would solve equation (1) first for Q_{pc} and then for Q_m and then subtract the second from the first. A worked example of this is given in Maths Case 11.1 in MyEconLab.

Conclusions

The firm with market power uses fewer factors and produces less output than the Pareto optimum. It also causes deadweight welfare loss. To the extent, however, that the firm seeks aims *other* than profit maximisation and thus may produce more than the profit-maximising output, so these criticisms must be relaxed.

As was shown in Chapter 6, there are possible social *advantages* from powerful firms: advantages such as economies of scale and more research and development. These advantages may outweigh the lack of Pareto optimality. It can be argued that an ideal situation would be where firms are large enough to gain economies of scale and yet are somehow persuaded or compelled to produce where $P = MC$ (assuming no externalities).

With oligopoly and monopolistic competition, further wastes may occur because of possibly substantial resources involved in non-price competition. Advertising is the major example. It is difficult to predict just how much oligopolists will diverge from the Pareto optimum, since their pricing and output depends on their interpretation of the activities of their rivals.

? *Why will Pareto optimality not be achieved in markets where there are substantial economies of scale in production?*

Definition

Deadweight welfare loss The loss of consumer plus producer surplus in imperfect markets (when compared with perfect competition).

Other market failures

Ignorance and uncertainty

Perfect competition assumes that consumers, firms and factor suppliers have perfect knowledge of costs and benefits. In the real world, there is often a great deal of ignorance and uncertainty. Thus people are unable to equate marginal benefit with marginal cost.

Consumers purchase many goods infrequently. Cars, washing machines and other consumer durables fall into this category, as do houses. Consumers may not be aware of the quality of such goods until they have purchased them, by which time it is too late. Advertising may contribute to people's ignorance by misleading them as to the benefits of a good.

Firms are often ignorant of market opportunities, prices, costs, the productivity of factors (especially white-collar workers), the activity of rivals, etc.

Many economic decisions are based on expected future conditions. Since the future can never be known for certain, many decisions may turn out to be wrong.

In some cases, it may be possible to obtain the information through the market. There may be an agency that will sell you the information or a newspaper or magazine that contains the information. In this case, you will have to decide whether the cost to you of buying the information is worth the benefit it will provide you. A problem here is that you may not have sufficient information to judge how reliable the information is that you are buying!

1. Assume that you wanted the following information. In which cases might you (i) buy perfect information, (ii) buy imperfect information, (iii) be able to obtain information without paying for it, (iv) not be able to obtain information?
    (a) Which washing machine is the most reliable?
    (b) Which of two vacant jobs is more satisfying?
    (c) Which builder will repair my roof most cheaply?
    (d) Which builder is the best value for money?
    (e) How big a mortgage would it be wise for me to take out?
    (f) What course of higher education should I follow?
    (g) What brand of washing powder washes whiter?
    (h) Will a house need any work done on it over the next few years?
2. Make a list of pieces of information that a firm might want to know, and consider whether it could buy the information and how reliable that information might be.

Immobility of factors and time lags in response

Even under conditions of perfect competition, factors may be very slow to respond to changes in demand or supply. Labour, for example, may be highly immobile both occupationally and geographically. This can lead to large price changes and hence to large supernormal profits and high wages for those in the sectors of rising demand or falling costs. The long run may be a very long time coming!

KEY IDEA 31

The problem of time lags. Many economic actions can take a long time to take effect. This can cause problems of instability and an inability of the economy to achieve social efficiency.

In the meantime, there will be further changes in the conditions of demand and supply. Thus the economy is in a constant state of disequilibrium and the long run never comes. As firms and consumers respond to market signals and move towards equilibrium, so the equilibrium position moves and the social optimum is never achieved.

Whenever monopoly/monopsony power exists, the problem is made worse as firms or unions put up barriers to the entry of new firms or factors of production.

Protecting people's interests

Dependants. People do not always make their own economic decisions. They are often dependent on decisions made by others. Parents make decisions on behalf of their children; partners on each other's behalf; younger adults on behalf of old people; managers on behalf of shareholders; etc. This is the principal–agent issue that we looked at in section 8.1.

A free market will respond to these decisions, however good or bad they may be, and whether or not they are in the interests of the dependant. Thus the government may feel it necessary to protect dependants.

?

Give examples of how the government intervenes to protect the interests of dependants from bad economic decisions taken on their behalf.

Poor economic decision making by individuals on their own behalf. The government may feel that people need protecting from poor economic decisions that they make on their *own* behalf. It may feel that, in a free market, people will consume too many harmful things. Thus if the government wants to discourage smoking and drinking, it can put taxes on tobacco and alcohol. In more extreme cases, it could make various activities illegal: activities such as prostitution, certain types of gambling, and the sale and consumption of drugs.

On the other hand, the government may feel that people consume too little of things that are good for them: things such as education, preventative health care and sports facilities. Such goods are known as **merit goods**. The

Definition

Merit goods Goods that the government feels people will underconsume and which therefore ought to be subsidised or provided free.

government could either provide them free or subsidise their production.

 How do merit goods differ from public goods?

Other objectives

As we saw in Chapter 10, one of the major criticisms of the free market is the problem of *inequality*. The Pareto criterion gives no guidance, however, as to the most desirable distribution of income. A redistribution of income will benefit some and make others worse off. Thus Pareto optimality can be achieved for *any* distribution of income. Pareto optimality merely represents the efficient allocation of resources for any *given* distribution of income.

In addition to social efficiency and greater equality, we can identify other social goals: goals such as moral behaviour (however defined), enlightenment, social consciousness, co-operation, the development of culture, fulfilment, freedom from exploitation, and freedom to own, purchase and inherit property. The unfettered free market may not be very successful in achieving social efficiency. It may be even less successful in achieving many other social goals.

Finally, the free market is unlikely to achieve simultaneously the *macroeconomic objectives* of rapid economic growth, full employment, stable prices and a balance of international payments. These problems, and methods of government intervention that may be used to deal with them, are examined in later chapters.

Conclusions

It is not within the scope of economics to make judgements as to the relative importance of social goals. Economics can only consider means to achieving stated goals. First, therefore, the goals have to be clearly stated by the policy makers. Second, they have to be quantifiable so that different policies can be compared as to their relative effectiveness in achieving the particular goal. Certain goals, such as growth in national income, changes in the distribution of income and greater efficiency, are relatively easy to quantify. Others, such as enlightenment, are virtually impossible to quantify. For this reason, economics tends to concentrate on the means to achieving a relatively narrow range of goals. The danger is that, by concentrating on a limited number of goals, economists may well influence the policy makers – the government, local authorities, various pressure groups, etc. – into doing the same, and thus into neglecting other perhaps important social goals.

Different objectives are likely to conflict. For example, economic growth may conflict with greater equality. In the case of such 'trade-offs', all the economist can do is to demonstrate the effects of a given policy, and leave the policy makers to decide whether the benefits in terms of one goal outweigh the costs in terms of another goal.

 Summarise the economic policies of the major political parties. (If it is near an election, you could refer to their manifestos.) How far can an economist go in assessing these policies?

Section summary

1. Real-world markets will fail to achieve Pareto optimality. What is more, there are objectives other than social efficiency, and real-world markets may fail to achieve these too.

2. Externalities are spillover costs or benefits. Whenever there are external costs, the market will (other things being equal) lead to a level of production and consumption *above* the socially efficient level. Whenever there are external benefits, the market will (other things being equal) lead to a level of production and consumption *below* the socially efficient level.

3. Public goods will be underprovided by the market. The problem is that they have large external benefits relative to private benefits, and without government intervention it would not be possible to prevent people having a 'free ride' and thereby escape contributing to their cost of production.

4. Common resources are likely to be overused, since people do not take into account the effect of their use of such resources on other people.

5. Monopoly power will (other things being equal) lead to a level of output below the socially efficient level. It will lead to a deadweight welfare loss: a loss of consumer plus producer surplus.

6. Ignorance and uncertainty may prevent people from consuming or producing at the levels they would otherwise choose. Information, however, may sometimes be provided (at a price) by the market.

7. Markets may respond sluggishly to changes in demand and supply. The time lags in adjustment can lead to a permanent state of disequilibrium and to problems of instability.

8. In a free market there may be inadequate provision for dependants and an inadequate output of merit goods; there are likely to be macroeconomic problems and problems of inequality and poverty; finally, there may be a whole series of social, moral, attitudinal and aesthetic problems arising from a market system.

9. These being normative questions, the economist cannot make ultimate pronouncements on the rights and wrongs of the market. The economist can, however, point out the consequences of the market and of various government policies, and also the trade-offs that exist between different objectives.

BOX 11.3　SHOULD HEALTH-CARE PROVISION BE LEFT TO THE MARKET?

CASE STUDIES AND APPLICATIONS

A case of multiple market failures

In the UK, the National Health Service provides free hospital treatment, a free general practitioner service, and free prescriptions for certain categories of people. Their marginal cost to the patient is thus zero. Of course, these services use resources and they thus have to be paid for out of taxes.

But why are these services not sold directly to the patient, thereby saving the taxpayer money? There are, in fact, a number of reasons why the market would fail to provide the optimum amount of health care.

Difficulty of affording treatment

This is a problem connected with the distribution of income. Because income is unequally distributed, some people will be able to afford better treatment than others, and the poorest people may not be able to afford treatment at all. On grounds of equity, therefore, it is argued that health care should be provided free – at least for poor people.

The concept of equity that is usually applied to health care is that of treatment according to medical need rather than according to the ability to pay.

Does this argument also apply to food and other basic goods?

Difficulty of predicting one's future medical needs

If you were suddenly taken ill and required a major operation, it could be very expensive indeed for you if you had to pay. On the other hand, you may go through life requiring very little if any medical treatment. In other words, there is great uncertainty about your future medical needs. As a result it would be very difficult to plan your finances and budget for possible future medical expenses if you had to pay for treatment. Medical insurance is a possible solution to this problem, but there is still a problem of equity. Would the chronically sick or very old be able to obtain cover, and if so, would they be able to afford the premiums?

Externalities

Health care generates a number of benefits *external* to the patient. If you are cured of an infectious disease, for example, it is not just you who benefits but also others, since you will not infect them. In addition if you have a job you will be able to get back to work, thus reducing the disruption there. These external benefits of health care could be quite large.

If sick people have to pay the cost of their treatment, they may decide not to be treated – especially if they are poor. They may not take into account the effect that their illness has on other people. The market, by equating *private* benefits and costs, would produce too little health care.

Patient ignorance

Markets only function well to serve consumer wishes if the consumer has the information to make informed decisions. For many products that we buy, we have a pretty good idea how much we will like them. In the case of health care, however, 'consumers' (i.e. patients) may have very poor knowledge. If you have a pain in your chest, it may be simple muscular strain, or it may be a symptom of heart disease. You rely on the doctor (the *supplier* of the treatment) to give you the information: to diagnose your condition. Two problems could arise here with a market system of allocating health care.

The first is that unscrupulous doctors might advise more expensive treatment than is necessary; they might even have an agreement with certain drugs companies that they will try to persuade you to buy an expensive branded product rather than an identical cheaper version.

The second is that patients suffering from the early stages of a serious disease might not consult their doctor until the symptoms become acute, by which time it might be too late to treat the disease, or very expensive to do so. With a free health service, however, a person is likely to receive an earlier diagnosis of serious conditions.

Oligopoly

If doctors and hospitals operated in the free market as profit maximisers, it is unlikely that competition would drive down their prices. Instead they might collude to fix standard prices for treatment, so as to protect their incomes. Even if doctors did compete openly, it is unlikely that consumers would have enough information to enable them to 'shop around' for the best value.

We have to be careful: to argue that the market system will fail to provide an optimal allocation of health-care resources does not in itself prove that *free provision* is the best alternative. For example, with no charge for GP appointments it is likely that some patients will consult their doctors over trivial complaints.

In the USA there is much more reliance on *private medical insurance* with only very poor people getting free treatment. Alternatively, the government may simply *subsidise* health care, so as to make it cheaper rather than free. This is the case with prescriptions and dental treatment in the UK, where many people have to pay part of the cost of treatment. Also, the government can *regulate* the behaviour of the providers of health care, to prevent exploitation of the patient. Thus only people with certain qualifications are allowed to operate as doctors, nurses, pharmacists, etc.

1. If health care is provided free, the demand is likely to be high. How is this high demand dealt with? Is this a good way of dealing with it?
2. Go through each of the market failings identified in this box. In each case, consider what alternative policies are open to a government to tackle them. What are the advantages and disadvantages of these alternatives?

TC 3 p24
KI 4 p10
KI 29 p313
KI 23 p217

11.3 FORMS OF GOVERNMENT INTERVENTION

Faced with all the problems of the free market, what is a government to do?

There are several policy instruments that a government can use. At one extreme, it can totally replace the market by providing goods and services itself. At the other extreme, it can merely seek to persuade producers, consumers or workers to act differently. Between the two extremes, the government has a number of instruments that it can use to change the way markets operate. These include taxes, subsidies, laws and regulatory bodies.

Before looking at different forms of government intervention and their relative merits, it is first necessary to look at a general problem concerned with all forms of intervention. This is known as the *problem of the second best*.

In an ideal free market, where there are no market failures of any sort (the 'first-best' world), there would be no need for government intervention at all. If in this world there did then arise just one failure, in theory its correction would be simple. Say a monopoly arose, or some externality (e.g. pollution) was produced by a particular firm, with the result that the marginal social cost was no longer equal to the marginal social benefit. In theory, the government should simply intervene to restore production to the point where $MSC = MSB$. This is known as the *first-best solution*.

Of course, the real world is not like this. It is riddled with imperfections. What this means is that, if one imperfection is 'corrected' (i.e. by making $MSB = MSC$), it might aggravate problems elsewhere. For example, if an airport like Gatwick banned night-time flights so as not to disturb the sleep of local residents, the airlines might simply use Heathrow instead. This simply passes the buck. It now imposes an additional cost on those people living near Heathrow.

Give some examples of how correcting problems in one part of the economy will create problems elsewhere.

As the first-best solution of a perfectly efficient, distortion-free world is obviously not possible, the *second-best solution* needs to be adopted. Essentially this involves seeking the best compromises. This means attempting to minimise the *overall* distortionary effects of the policy measure. Some second-best *rules* can be applied in certain cases. We will examine these in the following sections as we look at specific policy measures.

Taxes and subsidies

A policy instrument particularly favoured by many economists is that of taxes and subsidies. They can be used for two main microeconomic purposes: (a) to promote greater social efficiency by altering the composition of production and consumption: and (b) to redistribute incomes. We examined their use for the second purpose in Chapter 10. Here we examine their use to achieve greater social efficiency.

When there are imperfections in the market (such as externalities or monopoly power), Pareto optimality will not be achieved. Taxes and subsidies can be used to correct these imperfections. Essentially the approach is to tax those goods or activities where the market produces too much, and subsidise those where the market produces too little.

Taxes and subsidies to correct externalities

Assume that a chemical works emits smoke from a chimney and thus pollutes the atmosphere. This creates external costs for the people who breathe in the smoke. The marginal social cost of producing the chemicals thus exceeds the marginal private cost to the firm: $MSC > MC$.

The first-best world. In Figure 11.9, the firm is producing in an otherwise perfect world. It produces Q_1 where $P = MC$ (its profit-maximising output), but in doing so takes no account of the external pollution costs it imposes on society. If the government imposes a tax on production equal to the marginal pollution cost, it will effectively 'internalise' the externality. The firm will have to pay an amount equal to the external cost it creates. It will therefore now maximise profits at Q_2, which is the socially optimum output where $MSB = MSC$. In the first-best world, then, the optimum tax is equal to the marginal external cost.

By analogy, if a firm produced an external benefit, then in the first-best world it ought to be given a subsidy equal to that marginal external benefit.

Note that a tax or subsidy ought to be directed as closely as possible to the source of the externality. For example, if

Definitions

Problem of the second best The difficulty of working out the best way of correcting a specific market distortion if distortions in other parts of the market continue to exist.

First-best solution The solution of correcting a specific market distortion by ensuring that the whole economy operates under conditions of social efficiency (Pareto optimality).

Second-best solution The solution to a specific market distortion that recognises distortions elsewhere and seeks to minimise the overall distortionary effects to the economy of tackling this specific distortion.

Figure 11.9 Using taxes to correct a market distortion: the first-best world

a firm trains labour, and that creates a benefit to society, then ideally it ought to be given a subsidy for each person trained, rather than a general output subsidy. After all, an output subsidy not only encourages the firm to train more people (the desired effect), but also encourages it to use more capital and raw materials (an undesired side-effect). This is a general maxim of welfare economics: *a distortion should be corrected at source if side-effect problems are to be avoided.*

Second-best tax and subsidy policies. In reality, the government must tackle imperfections in a world that has many other imperfections. Figure 11.10 shows a firm that both produces an external cost ($MSC > MC$) and *also* has monopoly power. It will maximise profits at Q_1 where $MC = MR$ (point x).

The socially efficient level of output in this case is Q_2, where MSB equals MSC. To persuade the monopolist to produce at this level, a tax of $a - b$ must be imposed (since at point a, $MR = MC + tax$). This tax is *less* than the full

amount of the externality because of the problem of monopoly power. Were the monopolist to be charged a tax *equal* to the externality (so that its $MC + tax$ curve was equal to the MSC curve), it would maximise profits at point y, at a price of P_3 and an output of Q_3. This would not be socially efficient, since MSB would now be *above MSC*.

Taxes to correct for monopoly

So far we have considered the use of taxes to correct for externalities. Taxes can also be used to regulate the behaviour of monopolies and oligopolies.

If the government wishes to tackle the problem of excessive monopoly profits, it can impose a *lump-sum* tax on the monopolist. The 'windfall tax', imposed in the UK in 1997 by the incoming Labour government on the profits of various privatised utilities, is an example of such a tax. The use of a lump-sum tax is illustrated in Figure 11.11.

Being of a fixed amount, a lump-sum tax is a fixed cost to the firm. It does not affect the firm's marginal cost. It shifts the AC curve upwards.

Profits continue to be maximised where $MC = MR$, at an output of Q_1 and a price of P_1. But profits are reduced from areas 1 + 2 to area 1 alone. Area 2 now represents the amount of tax paid to the government. If the lump-sum tax were large enough to make the $AC +$ lump-sum tax curve cross the demand curve at point a, *all* the supernormal profits would be taken as tax.

If the government also wants to increase the monopolist's output to the socially efficient level of Q_2, and wants it to charge a price of P_2, it could do this with a careful combination of a per-unit subsidy (which will shift both the AC and the MC curves downwards) and a lump-sum tax. The required level of subsidy will be that which shifts the MC curve downwards to the point where it intersects MR at output Q_2. Then a lump-sum tax would be imposed that would be big enough to shift the AC curve back up again so that it crosses the demand curve at point b.

KI 28
p313

KI 26
p306

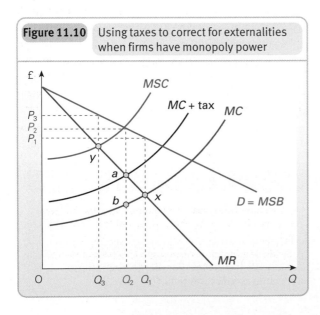

Figure 11.10 Using taxes to correct for externalities when firms have monopoly power

Figure 11.11 Using a lump-sum tax to reduce monopoly profits

BOX 11.4   DEADWEIGHT LOSS FROM TAXES ON GOODS AND SERVICES

The excess burden of taxes

Taxation can be used to correct market failures, but taxes can have adverse effects themselves. One such effect is the deadweight loss that results when taxes are imposed on goods and services (see page 294).

The diagram shows the demand and supply of a particular good. Equilibrium is initially at a price of P_1 and a level of sales of Q_1 (i.e. where $D = S$). Now an excise tax is imposed on the good. The supply curve shifts upwards by the amount of the tax, to $S + tax$. Equilibrium price rises to P_2 and equilibrium quantity falls to Q_2. Producers receive an after-tax price of $P_2 - tax$.

Consumer surplus falls from areas $1 + 2 + 3$, to area 1 (the green area). Producer surplus falls from areas $4 + 5 + 6$ to area 6 (the blue area). Does this mean,

therefore, that total surplus falls by areas $2 + 3 + 4 + 5$? The answer is no, because there is a gain to the government from the tax revenue (and hence a gain to the population from the resulting government expenditure). The revenue from the tax is known as the **government surplus**. It is given by areas $2 + 4$ (the pink area).

But, even after including government surplus, there is still a fall in total surplus of areas $3 + 5$. This is the deadweight loss of the tax. It is sometimes known as the **excess burden**.

Does this loss of total surplus from taxation imply that taxes on goods are always a 'bad thing'? The answer is no. This conclusion would follow only in a 'first-best' world where there were no market failures: where competition was perfect, where there were no externalities and where income distribution was optimum. In such a world, the loss of surplus from imposing a tax on a good would represent a reduction in welfare.

In the real world of imperfect markets and inequality, taxes can do more good than harm. As we have shown in this section, they can help to correct for externalities; and as we showed in the previous chapter, they can be used as a means of redistributing incomes. Nevertheless, the excess burden of taxes is something that ideally ought to be considered when weighing up the desirability of imposing taxes on goods and services, or of increasing their rate.

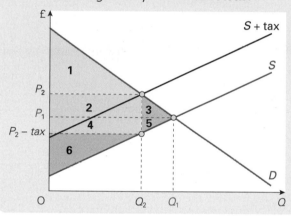

Deadweight loss from an indirect tax

1. *How far can an economist contribute to this normative debate over the desirability of an excise tax?*
2. *What is the excess burden of a lump-sum tax? (For a clue, see Figure 11.11.)*

What could we say about the necessary subsidy if the MR curve crossed the horizontal axis to the left of point b?

Advantages of taxes and subsidies

Many economists favour the tax/subsidy solution to market imperfections (especially the problem of externalities) because it still allows the market to operate. It forces firms to take on board the full social costs and benefits of their actions; this is often described as *internalising the externality*. Furthermore, once the policy is in place, taxes and subsidies can be adjusted according to the magnitude of the problem.

Moreover, if firms are taxed for polluting, they are encouraged to find cleaner ways of producing. The tax acts as an incentive over the longer run to reduce pollution. Likewise, by subsidising *good* practices, firms are given the incentive to adopt more good practices.

The most suitable situation for imposing a pollution tax is when there is a clearly measurable emission, like a particular chemical waste. The government can then impose a tax per litre or per tonne of that waste.

Disadvantages of taxes and subsidies

Infeasibility of using different tax and subsidy rates. Each firm produces different levels and types of externality and operates under different degrees of imperfect competition. It would be administratively very difficult and expensive to charge every offending firm its own particular tax rate (or grant every relevant firm its own particular rate of subsidy). Even in the case of pollution where it is possible to measure a firm's emissions, there would still have to be a different tax rate for each pollutant and even for each environment, depending on its ability to absorb the pollutant.

Definitions

Government surplus (from a tax on a good) The total tax revenue earned by the government from sales of a good.

Excess burden (of a tax on a good) The amount by which the loss in consumer plus producer surplus exceeds the government surplus.

Lack of knowledge. Even if a government did decide to charge a tax equal to each offending firm's marginal external costs, it would still have the problem of measuring those costs and apportioning blame. The damage to lakes and forests from acid rain has been a major concern since the beginning of the 1980s. But just how serious is that damage? What is its current monetary cost? How long lasting is the damage? Just what and who are to blame? These questions cannot be answered precisely. It is thus impossible to fix the 'correct' pollution tax on, say, a particular coal-fired power station.

1. Why is it easier to use taxes and subsidies to tackle the problem of car exhaust pollution than to tackle the problem of peak-time traffic congestion in cities?
2. If the precise environmental costs of CFCs in fridges were known, would the tax solution be a suitable remedy for the problem?

Changes in property rights

One cause of market failure is the limited nature of property rights. If someone dumps a load of rubble in your garden, you can insist that it is removed. If, however, someone dumps a load of rubble in their *own* garden, which is next door to yours, what can you do? You can still see it from your window. It is still an eyesore. But you have no property rights over the next-door garden.

Property rights define who owns property, to what uses it can be put, the rights other people have over it and how it may be transferred. By *extending* these rights, individuals may be able to prevent other people from imposing costs on them or charge them for doing so.

The socially efficient level of charge would be one that was equal to the marginal external cost (and would have the same effect as the government charging a tax on the firm of that amount: see Figure 11.9). The **Coase theorem**[1] states that in an otherwise perfectly competitive market, the socially efficient charge *will* be levied. But why?

Let us take the case of river pollution by a chemical works that imposes a cost on people fishing in the river. If property rights to the river were now given to the fishing community, they could impose a charge on the chemical works per unit of output. If they charged *less* than the marginal external cost, they would suffer more from the

last unit (in terms of lost fish) than they were being compensated. If they charged *more*, and thereby caused the firm to cut back its output below the socially efficient level, they would be sacrificing receiving charges that would be greater than the marginal suffering. It will be in the sufferers' best interests, therefore, to charge an amount *equal* to the marginal externality.

If the sufferers had no property rights, show how it would still be in their interests to 'bribe' the firm to produce the socially efficient level of output.

In most instances, however, this type of solution is totally impractical. It is impractical when *many* people are *slightly* inconvenienced, especially if there are many culprits imposing the costs. For example, if I were disturbed by noisy lorries passing by my house, it would not be practical to negotiate with every haulage company involved. What if I wanted to ban the lorries from the street but my next-door neighbour wanted to charge them 10p per journey? Who gets their way?

The extension of private property rights becomes more practical where the culprits are few in number, are easily identifiable and impose clearly defined costs. Thus a noise abatement Act could be passed which allowed me to prevent my neighbours from playing noisy radios, having noisy parties or otherwise disturbing the peace in my home. The onus would be on me to report them. Or I could agree not to report them if they paid me adequate compensation.

But even in cases where only a few people are involved, there may still be the problem of litigation. Justice may not be free, and thus there is a conflict with equity. The rich can afford 'better' justice. They can employ top lawyers. Thus even if I have a right to sue a large company for dumping toxic waste near me, I may not have the legal muscle to win.

Finally, the extension of private property rights may favour the rich (who tend to have more property) at the expense of the poor. Ramblers may get great pleasure from strolling across a great country estate, along public rights of way. If the owner's property rights were now extended to exclude the ramblers, would this be a social gain?

Of course, equity considerations can also be dealt with by altering property rights, but in a different way. *Public* property, like parks, open spaces, libraries and historic buildings, could be extended. Also, the property of the rich could be redistributed to the poor. Here it is less a question of the rights that ownership confers, and more a question of altering the ownership itself.

1. To what extent could property rights (either public or private) be successfully extended and invoked to curb the problem of industrial pollution (a) of the atmosphere; (b) of rivers; (c) by the dumping of toxic waste; (d) by the erection of ugly buildings; (e) by the creation of high levels of noise?
2. What protection do private property rights in the real world give to sufferers of noise (a) from neighbours; (b) from traffic; (c) from transistor radios at the seaside?

Definition

Coase theorem By sufferers from externalities doing deals with perpetrators (by levying charges or offering bribes), the externality will be 'internalised' and the socially efficient level of output will be achieved.

---

[1] Named after Ronald Coase, who developed the theory. See his 'The problem of social cost', *Journal of Law and Economics*, 1960.

Laws prohibiting or regulating undesirable structures or behaviour

Laws are frequently used to correct market imperfections. This section examines three of the most common cases.

Laws prohibiting or regulating behaviour that imposes external costs

Laws can be applied both to individuals and to firms. In the case of individuals, it is illegal to drive when drunk. Drunk driving imposes costs on others in the form of accidents and death. Another example is the banning of smoking in public places.

In the case of firms, various polluting activities can be banned or restricted; safety standards can be imposed in the place of work; building houses or factories may be prohibited in green-belt areas.

In the case of common resources, restrictions can be placed on their use. For example, in the case of fishing grounds, governments can limit the size of fleets, impose quotas on catches or specify the types of net to be used. In extreme cases, they could ban fishing altogether for a period of time to allow fish stocks to recover. In order to be able to enforce restrictions, many governments have extended their 'territorial waters' to 200 miles from their coast.

Advantages of legal restrictions

- They are simple and clear to understand and are often relatively easy to administer. Inspectors or the police can conduct spot checks to see that the law is being obeyed.
- When the danger is very great, it might be much safer to ban various practices altogether rather than to rely on taxes or on individuals attempting to assert their property rights through the civil courts.
- When a decision needs to be taken quickly, it might be possible to invoke emergency action. For example, in a city like Athens or Los Angeles it would be simpler to ban or restrict the use of private cars during a chemical smog emergency than to tax their use (see Box 12.6).

Disadvantages of legal restrictions. The main problem is that legal restrictions tend to be a rather blunt weapon. If, for example, a firm were required to reduce the effluent of a toxic chemical to 20 tonnes per week, it would have no incentive to reduce it further. With a tax on the effluent, however, the more the firm reduced the effluent, the less tax it would pay. Thus with a system of taxes there is a *continuing* incentive to cut pollution.

Laws to prevent or regulate monopolies and oligopolies

Laws affecting structure. Various mergers or takeovers could be made illegal. The criterion would probably have to be the level of market concentration that results. For example, the law could set a limit of 60 per cent of the market to be controlled by the five largest firms. Or it could require that merging firms have less than a certain percentage share of the market.

Laws affecting behaviour. Firms could be prohibited from engaging in various types of oligopolistic collusion, or various monopolistic practices. For example, manufacturers could be prevented from fixing the prices that retailers must charge, or from refusing to supply certain retailers.

Use of the law to regulate monopolies and oligopolies in the UK and the EU is examined in Chapter 13.

How suitable are legal restrictions in the following cases? (a) ensuring adequate vehicle safety; (b) reducing traffic congestion; (c) preventing the abuse of monopoly power; (d) ensuring that mergers are in the public interest; (e) ensuring that firms charge a price equal to marginal cost.

Laws to prevent firms from exploiting people's ignorance

Given that consumers have imperfect information, consumer protection laws can make it illegal for firms to sell shoddy or dangerous goods, or to make false or misleading claims about their products.

The problem is that the firms most likely to exploit the consumer are often the ones that are most elusive when it comes to prosecuting them.

Regulatory bodies

A more subtle approach than banning or restricting various activities involves the use of regulatory bodies.

Having identified possible cases where action might be required (e.g. potential cases of pollution or the abuse of monopoly power), the regulatory body would probably conduct an investigation and then prepare a report containing its findings and recommendations. It might also have the power to enforce its decisions, or this might be up to some higher authority.

An example of such a body is the Competition Commission, the work of which is examined in section 13.1. Other examples are the bodies set up to regulate the privatised utilities: e.g. Ofwat, the Office of Water Services. These are examined in section 13.2.

The advantage of this approach is that a case-by-case method can be used and, as a result, the most appropriate solution adopted. However, investigations may be expensive and time-consuming, only a few cases may be examined, and offending firms may make various promises of good behaviour which, owing to a lack of follow-up by the regulatory body, may not in fact be carried out.

What other forms of intervention are likely to be necessary to back up the work of regulatory bodies?

Price controls

Price controls could be used to prevent a monopoly or oligopoly from charging excessive prices. Currently, sections of various privatised industries such as telecommunications, water and electricity are not allowed to raise their prices by more than a certain percentage below the rate of inflation (see section 13.2).

Price controls could also be used with the objective of redistributing incomes. Prices could be fixed either above or below equilibrium. Thus (high) minimum farm prices can be used to protect the incomes of farmers, and minimum wage legislation can help those on low incomes. On the consumption side, (low) maximum rents can help poor people afford housing, and price ceilings on food or other essentials during a war or other emergency can allow poor people to afford such items. However, as was argued in section 2.4, the problem with price controls is that they cause shortages (in the case of low prices) or surpluses (high prices).

Provision of information

When ignorance is a reason for market failure, the direct provision of information by the government or one of its agencies may help to correct that failure. An example is the information on jobs provided by job centres to those looking for work. This helps the labour market to work better and increases the elasticity of supply of labour.

Another example is the provision of consumer information – for example, on the effects of smoking, or of eating certain foodstuffs. Another is the provision of government statistics on prices, costs, employment, sales trends, etc. This enables firms to plan with greater certainty.

> *In what way is the provision of information a public good? Do all the examples above come into the category of public goods? Give some other examples of information that is a public good. (Clue: do not confuse a public good with something merely provided by the government, which could also be provided by the private sector.)*

The direct provision of goods and services

In the case of public goods and services, such as streets, pavements, seaside illumination and national defence, the market may completely fail to provide. In this case, the government must take over the role of provision. Central government, local government or some other public agency could provide these goods and services directly. Alternatively, they could pay private firms to do so.

But just what quantity of the public good should be provided? How can the level of public demand or public 'need' be identified? Should any charge at all be made to consumers for each unit consumed?

With a pure public good, once it is provided the marginal cost of supplying one more consumer is zero.

Take the case of a lighthouse. Once it is constructed and in operation, there is no extra cost of providing the service to additional passing ships. Even if it were *possible* to charge ships each time they make use of it, it would not be socially desirable. Assuming no external costs, MSC is zero. Thus $MSB = MSC$ at a price of zero. Zero is thus the socially efficient price.

But what about the construction of a new public good, like a new road or a new lighthouse? How can a rational decision be made by the government as to whether it should go ahead? This time the marginal cost is not zero: extra roads and lighthouses cost money to build. The solution is to identify all the costs and benefits to society from the project, and to weigh them up. This is where cost–benefit analysis comes in – the subject of section 11.4.

The government could also provide goods and services directly which are *not* public goods. Examples include health and education. There are four reasons why such things are provided free or well below cost.

Social justice. Society may feel that these things should not be provided according to ability to pay. Rather, as *merit goods*, they should be provided according to need.

Large positive externalities. People other than the consumer may benefit substantially. If a person decides to get treatment for an infectious disease, other people benefit by not being infected. A free health service thus helps to combat the spread of disease.

Dependants. If education were not free, and if the quality of education depended on the amount spent, and if parents could choose how much or little to buy, then the quality of children's education would depend not just on their parents' income, but also on how much they cared. A government may choose to provide such things free in order to protect children from 'bad' parents. A similar argument is used for providing free prescriptions and dental treatment for all children.

Ignorance. Consumers may not realise how much they will benefit. If they had to pay, they might choose (unwisely) to go without. Providing health care free may persuade people to consult their doctors before a complaint becomes serious.

Public ownership

This is different from direct provision, in that the goods and services produced by publicly owned (nationalised) industries are sold in the market. The costs and benefits of public ownership are examined in detail in section 13.2.

Section summary

1. If there were a distortion in just one part of the economy, the 'first-best' solution would be possible. This would be to correct that one distortion. In the real world, where there are many distortions, the first-best solution will not be possible. The second-best solution will be to seek the best compromise that minimises the *relative* distortions between the industry in question and other parts of the economy.

2. Taxes and subsidies are one means of correcting market distortions. In the first-best world, externalities can be corrected by imposing tax rates equal to the size of marginal external costs, and granting rates of subsidy equal to marginal external benefits. In the second-best world, taxes and subsidies can be used to correct externalities that create *relative* distortions between this industry and others, or externalities that exist along with other distortions within this industry.

3. Taxes and subsidies can also be used to affect monopoly price, output and profit. Subsidies can be used to persuade a monopolist to increase output to the competitive level. Lump-sum taxes can be used to reduce monopoly profits without affecting price or output.

4. Taxes and subsidies have the advantages of 'internalising' externalities and of providing

incentives to reduce external costs. On the other hand, they may be impractical to use when different rates are required for each case, or when it is impossible to know the full effects of the activities that the taxes or subsidies are being used to correct.

5. An extension of property rights may allow individuals to prevent others from imposing costs on them. This is not practical, however, when many people are affected to a small degree, or where several people are affected but differ in their attitudes towards what they want doing about the 'problem'.

6. Laws can be used to tackle various market failures. Legal controls are often simpler and easier to operate than taxes, and are safer when the danger is potentially great. However, they tend to be rather a blunt weapon.

7. Regulatory bodies can be set up to monitor and control activities that are against the public interest (e.g. anti-competitive behaviour of oligopolists).

8. The government may provide information in cases where the private sector fails to provide an adequate level. It may also provide goods and services directly. These could be either public goods or other goods where the government feels that provision by the market is inadequate.

*11.4 COST–BENEFIT ANALYSIS

Cost–benefit analysis (CBA) is a technique used to help governments decide whether to go ahead with various projects such as a new motorway, a bypass, an underground line, a hospital, a health-care programme, a dam, and so on. The analysis seeks to establish whether the benefits to society from the project outweigh the costs, in which case the project should go ahead; or whether the costs outweigh the benefits, in which case it should not.

CBAs are usually commissioned either by a government department or by a local authority. Unlike the techniques of project evaluation used by private firms, which take into account only *private monetary* costs and benefits, CBA takes into account *externalities* and private *non-monetary* costs and benefits as well. Thus a cost–benefit study of a proposed new road might attempt to assess the external costs of noise to local residents and destruction of wildlife as well as the direct costs and benefits to the travellers.

Definition

Cost–benefit analysis The identification, measurement and weighing up of the costs and benefits of a project in order to decide whether or not it should go ahead.

The procedure

The procedure at first sight seems fairly straightforward.

- All costs and benefits are identified. These include all private monetary and non-monetary costs and benefits and all externalities.

- A monetary value is assigned to each cost and benefit. This is essential if costs and benefits are to be added up: a common unit of measurement must be used. As might be expected, assigning monetary values to externalities like noise, pollution and the quality of life is fraught with difficulties!

- Account is taken of the likelihood of a cost or benefit occurring. The simplest way of doing this is to multiply the monetary value of a cost or benefit by the probability of its occurrence. So if there were a 60 per cent chance of a cost of £100 occurring, it would be valued at £60.

- Account is taken of the timing of the costs and benefits. £100 of benefits received today would be regarded as more desirable than having to wait, say, ten years to receive the £100. Likewise it is a greater sacrifice to pay £100 today than to have to pay it within ten years. Thus future costs and benefits must be reduced in value to take this into account. Discounting techniques (similar to those we examined in section 9.3: see pages 261–2) are used for this purpose.

KI 4
p10

- Some account may also be taken of the distribution of the costs and benefits. Is it considered fair that, although some people will gain from the project, others will lose? Will the losers be compensated in any way?
- A recommendation is then made by weighing up the costs and benefits. In the simplest terms, if the benefits exceed the costs, it will be recommended that the project goes ahead.
- Each of these stages involves a number of difficulties. These are examined in the following sections.

Identifying the costs and benefits

Identifying costs and benefits is relatively easy, although there are some problems in predicting what types of external effect are likely to occur.

Costs

KI 2
p8

Direct (private) monetary costs. These include all the construction costs and the operating and maintenance costs.

External costs. These fall into two categories:

- *Monetary costs*, such as the loss of profits to competitors. Thus in the case of a CBA of a tunnel under a river, external monetary costs would include the loss of profits to ferry operators.
- *Non-monetary costs*, such as pollution, spoiling the landscape, noise and various other forms of inconvenience to local residents. In some projects, such as a tunnel, these costs will be largely confined to the construction phase. With other projects, however, like a new airport, there may be considerable externalities resulting from its operation (e.g. noise). These non-monetary externalities are usually the most difficult costs to identify.

Benefits

Direct (private) monetary benefits. These are also easy to identify. They consist of the revenues received from the users of the project. The direct monetary benefits of a toll bridge, for example, are the tolls paid.

Private non-monetary benefits. These are the benefits to consumers over and above what they actually pay: in other words, the consumer surplus. For example, if a bridge had a toll of 50p, and yet a person was prepared to pay £2 if necessary to avoid the long trip round the estuary, then the person's consumer surplus is £1.50. Total consumer surplus is thus the area between the demand curve (which shows what people are willing to pay) and the price charged. This is illustrated in Figure 11.12.

KI 29
p313

External benefits. These are the benefits to the nonusers of the project. For example, the Victoria Underground line CBA identified external benefits to road users in central

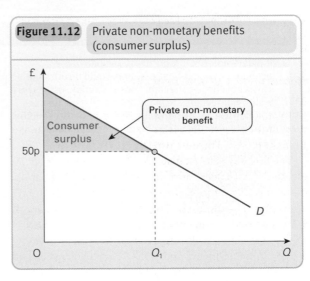

Figure 11.12 Private non-monetary benefits (consumer surplus)

London. The roads would become less congested as people used the new Underground line. Usually these benefits are non-monetary benefits, but sometimes they may result in direct financial gain (e.g. higher profits to companies from reduced transport costs on less crowded roads).

Measuring the costs and benefits

Identifying costs and benefits may be relatively easy: measuring them is another matter. Difficulties in measurement depend on the type of cost and benefit. There are four types.

Direct private monetary costs and benefits

These would seem to be the simplest to measure. Normally the simple financial costs and revenues are used. In the case of a new Underground line, for example, such costs would include excavation, construction and capital costs (such as new rolling stock) and the operating costs (such as labour, electricity and maintenance). Revenues would be the fares paid by travellers. There are two problems, nevertheless:

- What *will* these financial costs and revenues be? It is all very well using current prices, but prices rise over time, and at different and unpredictable rates. Also, it is difficult to forecast demand and hence revenues. There is thus a large element of *uncertainty*.
- The prices will often be distorted by the existence of monopoly power. Should this be taken into account? In an otherwise perfect world (the first-best situation), the answer would be yes. But in the real world, where price distortions exist throughout the economy, actual prices should normally be used. In the case of a proposed Undergound line, for example, it makes sense to use market prices, given that market prices are paid by car drivers and by users of taxis and buses (the alternatives to using the Underground). Thus the second-best solution is to use actual market prices *unless* there is a price distortion that applies *only* to the specific project.

What price should be used when there is such a distortion?

Non-monetary private benefits: consumer surplus

Consumer surplus is a private benefit – it accrues to the users of the project – but is not part of the money earned from the project. There are two ways of estimating it.

The first way is to estimate the demand curve and then estimate the shaded area in Figure 11.12. Estimating demand is very difficult, since it depends on the price and availability of substitutes. The demand for the Channel Tunnel depends on the price, frequency and convenience of ferry crossings. It also depends on the overall level of activity in the economy and perhaps the world generally. Thus estimates of air traffic (essential information when deciding whether to build a new airport) have often been proved wrong as the world economy has grown more rapidly or less rapidly than previously forecast.

Another problem is that the consumer surplus gained from the project (e.g. the Channel Tunnel) may replace the albeit smaller consumer surplus from a competing service (e.g. cross-Channel ferries). In this case, the non-monetary private benefit is merely the *additional* consumer surplus of those who switch, but still the *full* consumer surplus of those who would not otherwise have crossed the Channel. This makes calculation less straightforward.

An alternative approach is to focus on specific non-monetary benefits to consumers. This approach is more useful when the service is to be provided free and thus no estimate of a demand curve can be made. Assume that a new motorway saves 20 000 hours of travelling time per week. (This, of course, will first have to be estimated, and again a prediction will have to be made of the number of people using the motorway.) How is this 20 000 hours to be evaluated? In the case of businesspeople and lorry drivers, the average hourly wage rate will be used to estimate the value of each labour hour saved. In the case of leisure time, there is less agreement on how to value an hour saved. Usually it is simply assumed to be some fraction of the average hourly wage. This method is somewhat arbitrary, however, and a better approach, though probably impractical, would be to attempt to measure how the travellers themselves evaluate their time.

Another way of measuring time saved would be to see how much money people would be prepared to spend to save travelling time. For example, how much extra would people be prepared to pay for a taxi that saved, say, ten minutes over the bus journey? This method, however, has to take account of the fact that taxis may be more desirable for other reasons too, such as comfort.

 How would you attempt to value time that you yourself save (a) getting to work; (b) going on holiday; (c) going out in the evening?

Monetary externalities

These would normally be counted at face value. Thus the external monetary costs of a new Underground line would include the loss of profits to taxi and bus companies. The external monetary benefits of a new motorway would include the profits to be made by the owners of the motorway service stations.

Non-monetary externalities

These are likely to be the hardest to measure. The general principle employed is to try to find out how much people would be prepared to pay to obtain the benefits or avoid the costs, if they were able to do so. There are two approaches here.

Ask people (questionnaires). Take the case of noise from an airport or motorway. People could be asked how much they would need to be compensated. There are two problems with this:

- *Ignorance.* People will not know just how much they will suffer *until* the airport or motorway is built.
- *Dishonesty.* People will tend to exaggerate the compensation they would need. After all, if compensation is actually going to be paid, people will want to get as much as possible. But even if it is not, the more people exaggerate the costs to themselves, the more likely it is that they can get the project stopped.

These problems can be lessened if people are questioned who have already experienced a similar project elsewhere. They have less to gain from being dishonest.

Make inferences from people's behaviour. Take the case of noise again. In similar projects elsewhere, how have people actually reacted? How much have they spent on double glazing or other noise insulation? How much financial loss have they been prepared to suffer to move somewhere quieter? What needs to be measured, however, is not just the financial cost, but also the loss of consumer surplus. The Roskill Commission in 1968 examined the siting of a third London airport. It attempted to evaluate noise costs, and looked at the difference in value of house prices round Gatwick compared with elsewhere. A problem with this approach is in finding cases elsewhere that are directly comparable. Were the four potential sites for the third London airport directly comparable with Gatwick?

Another example of externalities would be a reduction in accidents from a safer road. How is this to be measured? Obviously there are the monetary benefits from reduced medical expenditures. But how would you value a life saved? This question is examined in Box 11.5.

 How would you evaluate (a) the external effects of building a reservoir in an area of outstanding natural beauty; (b) the external effects of acid rain pollution from a power station?

TC 1
p8

---

*BOX 11.5   **WHAT PRICE A HUMAN LIFE?**   EXPLORING ECONOMICS

A difficult question for cost–benefit analysis

Many projects involve saving lives, whether they be new hospitals or new transport systems. This is obviously a major benefit, but how is a life to be evaluated?

Some people argue 'You can't put a price on a human life: life is priceless.' But just what are they saying here? Are they saying that life has an *infinite* value? If so, this project must be carried out *whatever* the costs, and even if other benefits from it were zero! Clearly, when evaluating lives saved from the project, a value less than infinity must be given.

Other people might argue that human life cannot be treated like other costs and benefits and put into mathematical calculations. But what are these people saying? That the question of lives saved should be excluded from the cost–benefit study? If so, the implication is that life has a *zero* value! Again this is clearly not the case.

So if a value somewhere between zero and infinity should be used, what should it be?

Some economists have suggested that a life be valued in terms of a person's future earning potential. But this implies that the only value of a person is as a factor of production! Would the life of a disabled person, for example, who is unable to work and draws state benefit, be given a *negative* value? Again this is clearly not the solution.

Can any inferences be drawn from people's behaviour?

How much are people prepared to spend on safety: on making their car roadworthy, on buying crash helmets, etc.? This approach too has serious drawbacks. People are wishful thinkers. They obviously do not want to be killed, but simply believe that accidents happen to other people, not to them.

Then again, there are the problems of estimating the effects on other people: on family and friends. Can the amount that people are willing to spend on life assurance be a guide here? Again, people are wishful thinkers. Also, it is not the family and friends who buy the assurance; it is the victim, who may not take the effect on others fully into account.

In 2008, the UK Health and Safety Executive put a value of £1 512 800 on a life saved from a road safety project. This was based partly on the (discounted) average value of individuals' lost output for the rest of their lives (£520 700), partly on emergency services and hospital costs (£900) and partly on the human cost based on people's willingness to pay (if they had to) for the enjoyment of life over and above the consumption of goods and services plus costs to family and friends (£991 200). It thus ignored benefits to family and friends, let alone the benefits from safer roads to people now being able to cycle or let their children walk to school, etc. If these are taken into account, it is easy to arrive at a value closer to £2 million.

1. *Can you think of any other ways of getting a more 'rational' evaluation of human life? Would the person's age make any difference?*
2. *If you had to decide whether more money from a hospital's budget were to be spent on hip replacements (which do not save lives, but do dramatically improve the quality of the patient's life), or on heart transplants (which do save lives, but are expensive), how would you set about making a rational decision?*

Risk and uncertainty

KI 11
p75

Taking account of *risk* is relatively straightforward. The value of a cost or benefit is simply multiplied by the probability of its occurrence.

The problem is that *risk* is less frequent than *uncertainty*. As was explained in section 4.2, in the case of uncertainty all that is known is that an outcome *might* occur. The likelihood of its occurring, however, is uncertain.

How then can uncertainty be taken into account? The best approach is to use **sensitivity analysis**. Let us consider two cases.

Definition

Sensitivity analysis Where a range of possible values of uncertain costs and benefits are given to see whether the project's desirability is sensitive to these different values.

Individual uncertain outcomes

A range of possible values can be given to an uncertain item in the CBA: for example, damage from pollution. Table 11.1 illustrates two possible cases.

The lowest estimate for pollution damage is £10 million; the highest is £50 million. In case A, given a very high

Table 11.1   Effect of different estimates of the costs of production on the viability of a project

	Total costs other than pollution (£m)	Total pollution cost (£m)	Total benefits (£m)	Net benefits (total benefits – total costs) (£m)
	100	10	200	90
Case A	100	20	200	80
	100	50	200	50
	140	10	160	10
Case B	140	20	160	0
	140	50	160	−30

margin of benefits over *other* costs, the project's desirability is *not* sensitive to different values for pollution damage. Even with the highest value (£50 million), the project still yields a net benefit.

In case B, however, the project's desirability *is* sensitive to pollution damage. If the damage exceeds £20 million, the project becomes undesirable. In this case, the government will have to decide whether it is prepared to take the gamble.

A number of uncertain outcomes

When there are several uncertain outcomes the typical approach is to do three cost–benefit calculations: the most optimistic (where all the best possible outcomes are estimated), the most pessimistic (where all the worst possible outcomes are estimated), and the most likely (where all the middle-of-the-range outcomes are estimated). This approach can give a good guide to just how 'borderline' the project is.

Discounting future costs and benefits

As we saw in section 9.3, discounting is a procedure for giving a present value to costs and benefits that will not occur until some time in the future.

Discounting in cost–benefit analysis

The procedure is as follows:

- Work out the costs and benefits for each year of the life of the project.
- Subtract the costs from the benefits for each year, to give a net benefit for each year.
- Discount each year's net benefit to give it a present value.
- Add up all of these present values. This gives a *net present value (NPV)*.
- If the *NPV* is greater than zero, the benefits exceed the costs: the project is worthwhile.

Maths Case 11.2 in MyEconLab gives a worked example.

Choosing the discount rate

Apart from the problems of measuring the costs and benefits, there is the problem of choosing the rate of interest/ discount.

If it were a private-sector project, the firm would probably choose the market rate of interest as its rate of discount. This is the rate that it would have to pay to borrow money to finance the project.

In the case of CBA, however, it is argued that the government ought to use a **social rate of discount**. This rate should reflect society's preference for present benefits over future benefits. But just what is this rate? If a high rate is chosen, then future net benefits will be discounted more, and projects with a long life will appear less attractive than projects yielding a quick return. Since the government has

a responsibility to future generations and not just to the present one, it is argued that a relatively low discount rate should be chosen.

> *Imagine that a specific public project yields a return of 13 per cent (after taking into account all social costs and benefits), whereas a 15 per cent private return could typically be earned by projects in the private sector. How would you justify diverting resources from the private sector to this project?*

Inevitably, the choice of discount rate is arbitrary. As a result, the analysis will normally be conducted using two or three alternative discount rates to see whether the outcome is sensitive to the choice of discount rate. If it is, then again the project will be seen as borderline.

CBA and the distribution of costs and benefits

Virtually all projects involve gainers and losers. For example, the majority may gain from the construction of a new motorway, but not those whose homes lie alongside it. So how is the distribution of costs and benefits to be taken into account?

The strict Pareto criterion

According to the strict Pareto criterion, a project is unequivocally desirable only if there are some gains and *no one* is made worse off. But are there likely to be any projects that fulfil this criterion? If there are always losers then let us think about a situation where the losers are compensated. Thus we can now state that a project would be accepted only if the gainers *fully* compensated the losers, with the gainers still being better off after doing so.

In practice, this never happens. Often compensation is simply not paid. Even when it is, the recipients rarely feel as well off as before, and there will still be many who do not get compensation. Also, the compensation is usually paid not by the project users, but by the general taxpayer (who will thus be *worse* off).

The Hicks–Kaldor criterion

To get round this problem, J. R. Hicks and N. Kaldor suggested an alternative criterion. This states that a project is desirable if it leads to a *potential* Pareto improvement: in other words, if the gainers could *in principle* fully compensate the losers and still have a net gain, even though in practice they do not pay any compensation at all.

> **Definition**
>
> **Social rate of discount** A rate of discount that reflects society's preferences for present benefits over future ones.

*BOX 11.6	MEETING THE KYOTO PROTOCOL

The costs and benefits of lowering the sulphur content of petrol and diesel

In signing up to the Kyoto Protocol environmental treaty (see Box 12.4), the EU committed itself to reducing carbon dioxide emissions and other greenhouse gases by up to 8 per cent of 1990 levels by 2012. How best might such reductions be achieved? What strategy would achieve the benefits from lower carbon dioxide emissions at least cost?

One investigation conducted for the EU to assess such questions[1] aimed to evaluate the costs and benefits of lowering the sulphur content of petrol and diesel to less than 10 parts per million (ppm) from its level at the time of 50 ppm. If sulphur levels in petrol were reduced, reductions would be achieved in emissions of carbon dioxide, nitrogen oxides and volatile organic compounds, with resulting improvements in environmental quality. In addition, cars designed to run on low-sulphur fuels (all new cars coming into the EU market from 2006) are more fuel-efficient and thus consume less fuel. Offsetting such gains in environmental quality and fuel efficiency is the fact that producing sulphur-free fuel requires more energy and hence the generation of more carbon dioxide, the very thing the policy is seeking to reduce! In addition, existing refineries had to be adapted to process such fuel. This has resulted in additional investment costs. Operating costs too tend to be higher.

In order to evaluate these costs and benefits, the study identified five alternative scenarios for reducing sulphur content. These varied in terms of time period and type of vehicle:

1. Main scenario 2005: 2005, introduction of sulphur-free petrol[2] and diesel to new vehicles. 2011, 100 per cent sulphur-free fuel made compulsory.
2. Main scenario 2007: identical to scenario 1, only sulphur-free fuel introduced two years later.
3. Phased-in scenario 2007: sulphur-free fuel introduced for new vehicles alone (since only new vehicle types will be able to derive an improvement in fuel efficiency from sulphur-free fuels).
4. 100 per cent switch for cars in 2007: sulphur-free fuel compulsory for all cars in 2007.

5. Phased in for cars from 2007: sulphur-free fuel introduced for cars alone at a rate determined by new car growth.

Emission reductions. Although precise emissions reductions were not identified, it was estimated that enhanced fuel efficiency, and hence reduced fuel consumption, would see vehicle emissions fall by an average of 3 per cent. Diesel vehicle emissions would fall by an estimated 2 per cent.

Additional refinery emissions and costs. As the production of sulphur-free fuel is more energy-intensive, additional carbon dioxide emissions are inevitable. The report concluded that if all fuel was refined to 10 ppm, the additional emissions from refineries would increase by 4.6 million tonnes of carbon dioxide.

The additional investment and running costs of the refineries were estimated at 0.2 euro cents per litre (0.25 euro cents for EU south)[3] for petrol, and 0.45 euro cents per litre (0.65 euro cents for EU south) for diesel. This would represent a 1–2 per cent increase in costs. However, given the fact that approximately 75 per cent of the price of fuel to the consumer is made up of tax, the price increase borne by the consumer was likely to be very small.

The findings. For all the scenarios considered, the benefits (financial and air quality) were greater than the costs, and hence there would be a positive effect on reducing carbon dioxide emissions (see Table (a)).

Comparing the main scenarios from 2005 and 2007, the 2005 scenario produces a far more desirable outcome. The earlier start for gaining fuel cost savings and the higher number of vehicles benefiting from the use of sulphur-free fuel explain the higher *NPV* and the larger reduction in carbon dioxide emissions found in the 2005 scenario (see Tables (b) and (c)).

However, when the use of sulphur-free fuel is phased in as new vehicles are sold, the 2007 scenarios become a

(a) Summary results of the scenarios

	Reduction of CO_2 during 2008–12		Reduction in CO_2 2013–20		Net present value (4%) (€ billion)
	Total mt CO_2	Per annum mt CO_2	Total mt CO_2	Per annum mt CO_2	
Main scenario; introduction in 2005	12.9	2.6	50.8	6.3	2.7
Main scenario; introduction in 2007	9.2	1.8	44.5	5.6	1.1
Phased-in scenario (all vehicles) from 2007	15.8	3.2	58.8	7.3	2.8
Cars-only scenario in 2007	7.8	1.6	63.1	7.9	2.6
Phased-in scenario (cars only) from 2007	11.4	2.3	41.9	5.2	3.0

Note: Net present values (calculated using a 4% real discount rate) include net financial and air quality benefits.

Source: *The costs and benefits of lowering the sulphur content of petrol and diesel to less than 10 ppm* (Commission of the European Communities, DG for Environment, 2001), Table 9.

lot more favourable (scenarios 3 and 5). As drivers swap to new vehicles using sulphur-free fuel, the gain from fuel efficiency consistently outweighs the increase in refining costs.

The use of cost–benefit analysis thus demonstrated the best strategy for introducing low-sulphur fuel. A phased-in use of sulphur-free fuel would generate a higher *NPV* than the compulsory introduction of the fuel for all vehicles at a specified point in time.

 Why is this type of cost–benefit analysis simpler to conduct than ones assessing the desirability of a new road or airport?

[1] *The costs and benefits of lowering the sulphur content of petrol and diesel to less than 10 ppm* (EU Directorate-General Environment, 2001).
[2] The term 'sulphur-free fuel' in the report refers to low-sulphur fuel with less than 10 ppm of sulphur.
[3] The differences in costs between north and south Europe are due to the quality of fuel used in refining and its sulphur content.

(b) 'Main scenario 2005' – costs, benefits and emissions reductions

	2005	2012	2020
CO_2 emissions changes			
Change in CO_2 emissions in refineries, (kT)	215.7	5348.3	5404.3
CO_2 change from cars (3% petrol 2% diesel), (kT)	−562.8	−8241.6	−14960.5
Net change (−=decrease in CO_2 emissions)	−347.1	−2893.2	−9556.2
Costs and benefits, € million			
Increase in refining costs (average per year)	−39.0	−816.9	−831.4
Savings due to lower fuel consumption (average)	54.1	795.5	1441.2
Benefits from better air quality	0.0	221.1	3.7
Net benefits (− depicts net costs)	15.1	199.7	613.5
Net present value (4%), € million	2673.5		
Changes in air-related emissions			
NOx, kilotonnes	0	−28.5	−0.5
VOC, kilotonnes	0	−10.6	−0.2
CO, kilotonnes	0	−135.9	−4.7
PM, tonnes	0	−280.8	−8.0

Note: All costs are without VAT or excise duties. For emissions, negative signs indicate reductions; for benefits, negative signs indicate net costs. The above analysis has assumed a phased introduction of zero-sulphur fuels in 2005.
Source: The costs and benefits of lowering the sulphur content of petrol and diesel to less than 10 ppm (Commission of the European Communities, DG for Environment, 2001), Table 4.

(c) 'Main scenario 2007' – costs, benefits and emissions reductions

	2007	2012	2020
CO_2 emissions changes			
Change in CO_2 emissions in refineries, (kT)	407.0	5348.3	5404.3
CO_2 change from cars (3% petrol 2% diesel), (kT)	−1245.9	−6850.0	−13574.9
Net change (−=decrease in CO_2 emissions)	−838.9	−1501.7	−8170.6
Costs and benefits, € million			
Increase in refining costs (average per year)	−75.4	−995.0	−1019.0
Savings due to lower fuel consumption (average)	120.5	661.6	1309.1
Benefits from better air quality	0.0	304.1	18.3
Net benefits (− depicts net costs)	45.2	−29.3	308.4
Net present value (4%), € million	1061.2		
Changes in air-related emissions			
NOx, kilotonnes	0	−39.0	−2.5
VOC, kilotonnes	0	−14.4	−0.9
CO, kilotonnes	0	−176.8	−9.9
PM, tonnes	0	−366.7	−11.8

Note: All costs are without VAT or excise duties. For emissions, negative signs indicate reductions; for benefits, negative signs indicate net costs. The above analysis has assumed a phased introduction of zero-sulphur fuels from 1 January 2007.
Source: The costs and benefits of lowering the sulphur content of petrol and diesel to less than 10 ppm (Commission of the European Communities, DG for Environment, 2001), Table 5.

This criterion is what lies behind conventional CBA. If the benefits of a project are greater than the costs, then in principle the losers could be fully compensated with some net benefits left over.

KI 3
p10

But what is the justification for using this test? The losers, after all, will still lose. Its advocates argue that questions of *efficiency* should be kept separate from questions of *equity*. Projects, they argue, should be judged on efficiency grounds. They are efficient if their benefits exceed their costs. Questions of fairness in distribution, on the other hand, should be dealt with through the general system of taxation and welfare.

KI 4
p10

This is a 'useful' argument because it lets the proponents of the project off the hook. Nevertheless the problem still remains that some people will lose. People do not like living near a new motorway, airport or power station. These people cannot expect to receive special welfare benefits from general taxation.

Thus other economists have argued that more specific account should be taken of distributional effects when *measuring* costs and benefits.

Taking specific account of distributional consequences

One way this could be done would be to give a higher weighting to the costs of individual, as opposed to corporate, losers. The justification is simple. The pain for one person of losing £10 000 is greater than the collective pain of 10 000 people losing just £1 each. Just how much higher this weighting should be, however, is a matter of judgement, not of precise calculation.

Another way distribution can be taken into account is to give a higher weighting to the costs incurred by poor people than to those incurred by rich people. For example, assume that a new airport is built. As a result, house prices nearby fall by 10 per cent. A rich person's house price falls from £400 000 to £360 000 – a loss of £40 000. A poor person's house price falls from £50 000 to £45 000 – a loss of £5000. Is the loss to the rich person eight times as painful as that to the poor person? Probably not. It is argued, therefore, that the poorer people are, the higher the weighting that should be given to each £1 lost. Just what this weighting should be, however, is controversial.

Section summary

1. Cost–benefit analysis (CBA) can help a government decide whether or not to go ahead with a particular public project, or which of alternative projects to choose. CBA involves a number of stages.

2. All costs and benefits must be identified. These include the direct costs of constructing and operating the project, the direct monetary benefits to the operators and the consumer surplus of the users. They also include external costs and benefits to non-users.

3. Direct monetary costs and benefits are relatively easy to measure. Nevertheless there is still uncertainty about their *future* values. Also, there is a problem if prices are distorted.

4. Non-monetary private benefit (consumer surplus) is difficult to estimate because of the difficulty of estimating the shape and position of the demand curve. The alternative approach is to focus on specific non-monetary benefits, such as journey time saved, and then to evaluate how much people would be prepared to pay for them if they could.

5. Monetary externalities would normally be counted at face value. Non-monetary externalities are much more

difficult to estimate. The approach is to try to estimate the value that consumers would put on them in a market environment. Questionnaire techniques could be used, or inferences could be drawn from people's actual behaviour elsewhere.

6. Figures would then have to be adjusted for risk and uncertainty.

7. Discounting techniques would then have to be used to reduce future benefits and costs to a present value.

8. The study may also take distributional questions into account. The Hicks–Kaldor criterion suggests a compensation test for deciding whether a project is desirable. But given that in practice full compensation would be unlikely, the distributional questions may need to be taken into account more specifically.

9. Having adjusted the costs and benefits for risk and uncertainty, timing and distributional effects, a recommendation to go ahead with the project will probably be given if its net present value *(NPV)* is positive: in other words, if the discounted social benefits exceed the discounted social costs.

11.5 GOVERNMENT FAILURE AND THE CASE FOR THE MARKET

TC 6
p52

Government intervention in the market can itself lead to problems. The case for non-intervention (laissez-faire) or very limited intervention is not that the market is the *perfect* means of achieving given social goals, but rather that the problems created by intervention are greater than the problems overcome by that intervention.

Drawbacks of government intervention

Shortages and surpluses. If the government intervenes by fixing prices at levels other than the equilibrium, this will create either shortages or surpluses (see section 2.4).

If the price is fixed *below* the equilibrium, there will be a shortage. For example, if the rent of council houses is fixed below the equilibrium in order to provide cheap housing for poor people, demand will exceed supply. In the case of such shortages the government will have to adopt a system of waiting lists, or rationing, or giving certain people preferential treatment. Alternatively it will have to allow allocation to be on a first-come, first-served basis or allow queues to develop. Underground markets are also likely to develop (see page 54 and Box 2.4).

If the price is fixed *above* the equilibrium price, there will be a surplus. Such surpluses are wasteful, and high prices may protect inefficient producers. (The problem of food surpluses in the EU was examined in section 3.5.)

 What are the possible arguments in favour of fixing prices (a) below and (b) above the equilibrium? Are there any means of achieving the same social goals without fixing prices?

 Poor information. The government may not know the full costs and benefits of its policies. It may genuinely wish to pursue the interests of consumers or any other group, and yet may be unaware of people's wishes or misinterpret their behaviour.

Bureaucracy and inefficiency. Government intervention involves administrative costs. The more wide-reaching and detailed the intervention, the greater the number of people and material resources that will be involved. These resources may be used wastefully.

 Lack of market incentives. If government intervention removes market forces or cushions their effect (by the use of subsidies, welfare provisions, guaranteed prices or wages, etc.), it may remove certain useful incentives. Subsidies may allow inefficient firms to survive. Welfare payments may discourage people from working. The market may be imperfect, but it does tend to encourage efficiency by allowing the efficient to receive greater rewards.

Shifts in government policy. Industrial performance may suffer if government intervention changes too frequently. It makes it difficult for firms to plan if they cannot predict tax rates, subsidies, price and wage controls, etc.

Lack of freedom for the individual. Government intervention may involve a loss of freedom for individuals to make economic choices. The argument is not just that the pursuit of individual gain is seen to lead to the social good, but that it is desirable in itself that individuals should be as free as possible to pursue their own interests with the minimum of government interference, and with that minimum being largely confined to the maintenance of laws consistent with the protection of life, liberty and property.

 Go through the above arguments and give a reply to the criticisms made of government intervention.

Advantages of the free market

Although markets in the real world are not perfect, even imperfect markets can be argued to have positive advantages over government provision or even government regulation.

Automatic adjustments. Government intervention requires administration. A free-market economy, on the other hand, leads to the automatic, albeit imperfect, adjustment to demand and supply changes.

Even under oligopoly, it is claimed, the competition between firms will be enough to encourage firms to produce goods that are desirable to consumers and at not excessively high prices, and will encourage more efficient production methods. Cases of pure monopoly with total barriers to entry are extremely rare.

Dynamic advantages of the free market. The chances of making high monopoly/oligopoly profits will encourage capitalists to invest in new products and new techniques. Prices may be high initially, but new firms will sooner or later break into the market and competition will ensue. If the government tries to correct the misallocation of resources under monopoly/oligopoly either by regulating monopoly power or by nationalisation, any resulting benefits could be outweighed by a loss in innovation and growth. This is one of the major arguments put forward by the neo-Austrian libertarian school – a school that passionately advocates the free market (see Box 11.7).

 Are there any features of free-market capitalism that would discourage innovation?

A high degree of competition even under monopoly/oligopoly. Even though an industry at first sight may seem to be highly monopolistic, competitive forces may still work for the following reasons.

- A fear that excessively high profits might encourage firms to attempt to break into the industry (assuming that the market is contestable).
- Competition from closely related industries (e.g. coach services for rail services, or electricity for gas).
- The threat of foreign competition. Additional competition was one of the main purposes behind the Single European Act which led to the abolition of trade barriers within the EU in 1993 (see section 24.4).
- Countervailing powers. Large powerful producers often sell to large powerful buyers. For example, the power of

---

BOX 11.7 **MISES, HAYEK AND THE MONT PELERIN SOCIETY**

The birth of post-war libertarianism

After the Second World War, governments in the western world were anxious to avoid a return to the high levels of unemployment and poverty experienced in the 1930s. The free market was seen to have failed. Governments, it was therefore argued, should take on the responsibility for correcting or counteracting these failings. This would involve various measures such as planning, nationalisation, the restriction of monopoly power, controls on prices, the macroeconomic management of the economy and the provision of a welfare state.

But this new spirit of intervention deeply troubled a group of economists and other social scientists who saw it leading to an erosion of freedom. In 1947 this group met in a hotel in the Swiss Alps. There they formed the Mont Pelerin Society: a society pledged to warn against the dangers of socialism and to advocate the freedom for individuals to make their own economic choices.

Two of the most influential figures in the society were the Austrians Ludwig von Mises (1881–1973) and Friedrich von Hayek (1899–1992). They were the intellectual descendants of the nineteenth-century 'Austrian school'. Carl Menger, the originator of the school, had (along with Jevons and Walras (see Box 4.2)) emphasised the importance of individuals' marginal utility as the basis of demand. The Austrian school of economists was famous for its stress on individual choice as the basis for rational economic calculation and also for its advocacy of the free market.

Mises and Hayek (the 'neo-Austrians' as they became known) provided both a critique of socialism and an advocacy of the free market. There were two main strands to their arguments.

The impossibility of rational calculation under socialism

In his famous book *Socialism* (1922), Mises argued that centrally planned socialism was logically incapable of achieving a rational allocation of resources. Given that scarcity is the fundamental economic problem, all

societies, whether capitalist or socialist, will have to make choices. But rational choices must involve weighing up the costs and benefits of alternatives. Mises argued that this cannot be done in a centrally planned economy. The reason is that costs and benefits can be measured only in terms of money prices, prices which reflect demand and supply. But such prices can be established only in a market economy.

In a centrally planned economy, prices will be set by the state and no state will have sufficient information on demand and supply to set rational prices. Prices under centrally planned socialism will thus inevitably be arbitrary. Also, with no market for land or capital these factors may not be given a price at all. The use of land and capital, therefore, may be highly wasteful.

Many democratic socialists criticised Mises' arguments that rational prices *logically* cannot be established under socialism. In a centrally planned economy, the state can in theory, if it chooses, set prices so as to balance supply and demand. It can, if it chooses, set an interest rate for capital and a rent for land, even if capital and land are owned by the state. And certainly in a mixed-market socialist economy, prices will merely reflect the forces of demand and supply that have been modified by the state in accordance with its various social goals.

Hayek modified Mises' arguments somewhat. He conceded that some imperfect form of pricing system could be established under socialism, even under centrally planned socialism. Hayek's point was that such a system would inevitably be inferior to capitalism. The problem was one of imperfect information under socialism.

Calculation of costs and benefits requires knowledge. But that knowledge is dispersed amongst the millions of consumers and producers throughout the economy. Each consumer possesses unique information about his or her own tastes; each manager or worker possesses unique information about his or her own job. No government could hope to have this knowledge. Planning will

---

detergent manufacturers to drive up the price of washing powder is countered by the power of supermarket chains to drive down the price at which they purchase it. Thus power is to some extent neutralised.

• The competition for corporate control (see pages 178–9).

Should there be more or less intervention in the market?

No firm conclusions can be drawn in the debate between those who favour more and those who favour less government intervention, for the following reasons:

• Many normative issues are involved that cannot be settled by economic analysis. For example, it could be argued that freedom to set up in business and freedom from government regulation are desirable *for their own*

sake. As a fundamental ethical point of view, this can be disputed, but not disproved.

• In principle, the issue of whether a government ought to intervene in any situation could be settled by weighing up the costs and benefits of that intervention. Such costs and benefits, however, even if they could be identified, are extremely difficult, if not impossible, to measure, especially when the costs are borne by different people from those who receive the benefits and when externalities are involved.

• Often the effect of more or less intervention simply cannot be predicted: there are too many uncertainties.

Nevertheless, economists can make a considerable contribution to analysing problems of the market and the effects of government intervention. Chapters 12 and 13 illustrate this by examining specific problem areas.

inevitably, therefore, be based on highly imperfect information.

The market, by contrast, is a way of co-ordinating this dispersed information: it co-ordinates all the individual decisions of suppliers and demanders, decisions based on individuals' own information. And it does it all without the need for an army of bureaucrats.

> The economic problem of society is thus not merely a problem of how to allocate 'given' resources – if 'given' is taken tox mean given to a single mind which deliberately solves the problem set by these 'data'. It is rather a problem of how to secure the best use of resources known to any of the members of society, for ends whose relative importance only these individuals know. Or, to put it briefly, it is a problem of the utilization of knowledge not given to anyone in its totality.[1]

Lack of dynamic incentives under socialism

A planned socialist economy will, according to Mises and Hayek, lack the incentives for people to take risks. Even a 'market socialist' society, where prices are set so as to equate demand and supply, will still lack the crucial motivating force of the possibility of large personal economic gains. Under capitalism, by contrast, a firm that becomes more efficient or launches a new or improved product can gain huge profits. The prospect of such profits is a powerful motivator.

> Without the striving of entrepreneurs (including the shareholders) for profit, of the landlords for rent, of the capitalists for interest and the labourers for wages, the successful functioning of the whole mechanism is not to be thought of. It is only the prospect of profit which directs production into those channels in which the demands of the consumer are best satisfied at least cost. If the prospect of profit disappears the mechanism of the market loses its mainspring, for it is only this prospect which sets it in motion and

maintains it in operation. The market is thus the focal point of the capitalist order of society; it is the essence of capitalism. Only under capitalism, therefore, is it possible; it cannot be 'artificially' imitated under socialism.[2]

In addition to these economic criticisms of socialism, Mises and Hayek saw government intervention as leading down the road towards totalitarianism. The more governments intervened to correct the 'failings' of the market, the more this tended to erode people's liberties. But the more people saw the government intervening to help one group of people, the more help they would demand from the government for themselves. Thus inexorably the role of the state would grow and grow, and with it the size of the state bureaucracy.

In the early years after the war, the Mont Pelerin Society had little influence on government policy. Government intervention and the welfare state were politically popular.

In the late 1970s, however, the society, along with other similar libertarian groups, gained increasing influence as a new breed of politicians emerged who were wedded to the free market and were looking for an intellectual backing for their beliefs.

Libertarian thinkers such as Hayek and Milton Friedman (see Person Profiles in MyEconLab) had a profound effect on many right-wing politicians, and considerably influenced the economic programmes of the Thatcher, Reagan and both Bush (Snr and Jnr) administrations.

 Do the arguments of Mises and Hayek necessarily infer that a free market is the most desirable alternative to centrally planned socialism?

[1] F. von Hayek, 'The price system as a mechanism for using knowledge', *American Economic Review*, September, 1945, p. 519.
[2] L. von Mises, *Socialism. An Economic and Sociological Analysis* (Jonathan Cape, 1936), p. 138.

Section summary

1. Government intervention in the market may lead to shortages or surpluses; it may be based on poor information; it may be costly in terms of administration; it may stifle incentives; it may be disruptive if government policies change too frequently; it may remove certain liberties.

2. By contrast, a free market leads to automatic adjustments to changes in economic conditions; the prospect of monopoly/oligopoly profits may stimulate risk taking and hence research and

development and innovation; there may still be a high degree of actual or potential competition under monopoly and oligopoly.

3. It is impossible to draw firm conclusions about the 'optimum' level of government intervention. This is partly due to the normative nature of the question, partly due to the difficulties of measuring costs and benefits of intervention/non-intervention, and partly due to the difficulties of predicting the effects of government policies, especially over the longer term.

END OF CHAPTER QUESTIONS

1. Assume that a firm discharges waste into a river. As a result, the marginal social costs *(MSC)* are greater than the firm's marginal (private) costs *(MC)*. The following table shows how *MC*, *MSC*, *AR* and *MR* vary with output.

Output	1	2	3	4	5	6	7	8
MC (£)	23	21	23	25	27	30	35	42
MSC (£)	35	34	38	42	46	52	60	72
TR (£)	60	102	138	168	195	219	238	252
AR (£)	60	51	46	42	39	36.5	34	31.5
MR (£)	60	42	36	30	27	24	19	14

(a) How much will the firm produce if it seeks to maximise profits?

(b) What is the socially efficient level of output (assuming no externalities on the demand side)?

(c) How much is the marginal external cost at this level of output?

(d) What size tax would be necessary for the firm to reduce its output to the socially efficient level?

(e) Why is the tax less than the marginal externality?

(f) Why might it be equitable to impose a lump-sum tax on this firm?

(g) Why will a lump-sum tax not affect the firm's output (assuming that in the long run the firm can still make at least normal profit)?

2. Why might it be argued that a redistribution of consumption, while not involving a Pareto improvement, could still be desirable?

3. Assume that a country had no state education at all. For what reasons might the private education system not provide the optimal allocation of resources to and within education?

4. Why might it be better to ban certain activities that cause environmental damage rather than to tax them?

5. Distinguish between publicly provided goods, public goods and merit goods.

6. Consider the advantages and disadvantages of extending property rights so that everyone would have the right to prevent people imposing any costs on them whatsoever (or charging them to do so).

7. Should all investment be subject to a social cost–benefit appraisal?

8. Make out a case for (a) increasing and (b) decreasing the role of the government in the allocation of resources.

Online resources

Additional case studies in MyEconLab

11.1 **Can the market provide adequate protection for the environment?** This explains why markets generally fail to take into account environmental externalities.

11.2 **Catastrophic risk.** This examines how a cost–benefit study could put a monetary value on a remote chance of a catastrophe happening (such as an explosion at a nuclear power station).

11.3 **Evaluating the cost of aircraft noise.** This case study looks at the method used by the Roskill Commission, which in the 1960s investigated the siting of a third major London airport.

11.4 **CBA of the Glasgow canal project.** A cost–benefit study carried out in the late 1980s of the restoration of the Glasgow canal system.

11.5 **Public choice theory.** This examines how economists have attempted to extend their analysis of markets to the field of political decision making.

Maths Case 11.1 Calculating deadweight welfare loss. A worked example.

Maths Case 11.2 Calculating net present value. The use of discounting techniques in CBA.

Websites relevant to this chapter

See sites listed at the end of Chapter 13 on page 384.

Environmental Policy

CHAPTER MAP

12.1 Economics of the environment 342
The environmental problem 342
An optimum use of the environment 345
Market failures 346

12.2 Policies to tackle pollution and its effects 347
Market-based policies 347
Non-market-based policies 348
Tradable permits 350
How much can we rely on governments? 354

12.3 The economics of traffic congestion 356
The existing system of allocating road space 357
Identifying a socially efficient level of road usage (short run) 359
Identifying a socially optimum level of road space (long run) 360

12.4 Urban transport policies 361
Direct provision (supply-side solutions) 361
Regulation and legislation 362
Changing market signals 363
Conclusions 365

Just how far should things be left to the market in practice? Just how much should a government intervene? These are clearly normative questions, and the answers to them will depend on a person's politics. Conservative politicians have traditionally tended to favour a lesser degree of intervention to ensure the 'efficient' working of the market. Socialist politicians, on the other hand, prefer a much greater degree of intervention, to ensure not only that the inefficiencies of the market are corrected, but also that questions of 'fairness' and 'equality' are taken into account.

In the final two chapters of section D we examine some topics that illustrate well the possible strengths and weaknesses of both the market and government intervention. In Chapter 12 we look closely at the environment, an area where the existence of externalities results in substantial market failure. We start by considering the broader environmental issues and then turn to alternative policies for dealing with pollution and urban traffic congestion.

As we shall see, the economist's approach is to focus on both the costs and the benefits of various policies and how these costs and benefits can be weighed up. Scientists may be the ones to tell us the physical consequences of our actions, such as the degree of global warming that might result from CO_2 emissions. But it is economists who can assess the implications for various policies to deal with the problems.

12.1 ECONOMICS OF THE ENVIRONMENT

Scarcely a day goes by without some environmental issue or other featuring in the news: another warning about global warming, a company fined for illegally dumping waste, a drought or flood blamed on pollution, traffic gridlock in our major cities, smog in tropical countries caused by forest fires.

Ask virtually anyone if they would like a cleaner and more attractive environment and the answer would be yes. Ask them, however, what we as taxpayers or consumers should be prepared to pay for such improvements and there would be much more disagreement. The point is that environmental improvement normally comes at a cost: whether that is a cost in cleaning up waste or pollution, or a cost in terms of the higher price we might need to pay for 'green' products, such as organic foods, low-emission cars and electricity from renewable sources.

Economists are concerned with choices, and rational choices involve weighing up costs and benefits. Increasingly, people are recognising that such costs and benefits ought to include the effects on the environment: the effects on the planet we share with each other and with future generations.

The environmental problem

Why do people misuse the environment? To answer this we have to understand the nature of the economic relationship between humans and the natural world. We all benefit from the environment in three ways: as an amenity to be enjoyed, as a source of primary products (food, raw materials and other resources) and as a place where we can dump waste.

The relationship between these uses of the environment and the rest of the economy is shown in Figure 12.1. These three uses, however, tend to conflict with each other.

- The use of the environment as a productive resource reduces its amenity value. Fields given over to intensive agriculture, with hedges and woods removed, spoil the beauty of the countryside and lead to a decline in animal and plant species. Mines and quarries are ugly. Commercial forestry is often at the expense of traditional broad-leaved forests.
- Similarly, the use of the environment as a dump for waste reduces its amenity value. The environment becomes dirtier and uglier.

 What are the conflicts between using the environment as a productive resource and as a dump?

These conflicts have always existed, but are they getting worse? Let us examine the arguments.

Population pressures and limited resources

As we saw in Box 5.1, as more and more people crowd on to the fixed supply of world land, so diminishing returns to labour will occur. If food output per head is to remain constant, let alone increase, land must be made to yield

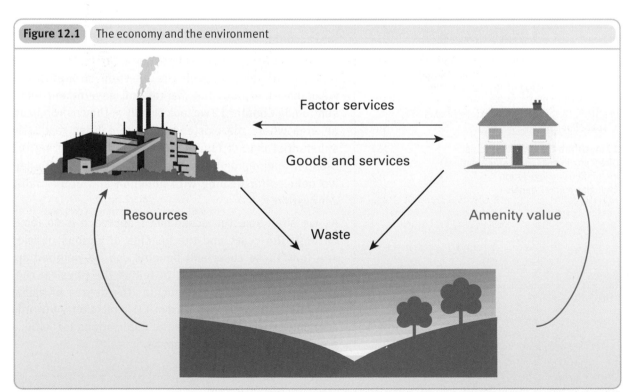

Figure 12.1 The economy and the environment

Factor services

Goods and services

Resources

Waste

Amenity value

more and more. The answer has been to use increasing amounts of fertiliser and pesticides. Likewise, if the increasing world population is to have higher levels of material consumption, this will generate increased demands for natural resources, many of which are non-renewable and generate more pollution. With the rapid growth of countries such as China and India, the pressures on the environment are likely to grow sharply.

The environment is able to absorb most types of waste up to certain levels of emission. Beyond such levels, however, environmental damage is likely to accelerate. Other things being equal, as population and waste grow, so environmental degradation is likely to grow at a faster rate.

Cause for optimism?

Despite population pressures, there are various factors that are helping to reduce environmental degradation.

Technological developments. Many newer industrial processes are cleaner and make a more efficient use of resources, leading to less waste and a slowdown in the rate of extraction of various minerals and fossil fuels. What is more, the production of less waste, or the recycling of waste, is often in the commercial interests of firms: it allows them to cut costs. For example, in 2007 companies in the UK spent in excess of £500 million on initiatives to increase energy efficiency. This is projected to produce cost savings of

around £1 billion. Firms thus have an incentive both to use such technology and also to research into cleaner and more resource-efficient techniques. Similarly, in a competitive market firms have an incentive to produce products that save consumers money, such as fuel-efficient cars, domestic boilers, fires, cookers and electrical appliances.

Increased price of non-renewable resources. As we saw in Box 9.10 (see page 269), as resources become scarcer, so their prices rise. This encourages people to use less of them, either by using more efficient technology or by switching to renewable alternatives as they become available.

Public opinion. As knowledge about environmental damage has grown, so too has pressure from public opinion to do something about it. Many firms see the opportunity to gain commercially from having a 'green image' and to publicise their positive attitude towards corporate social responsibility. In addition governments see electoral advantage in policies to create a cleaner, greener environment.

Despite these developments, however, many aspects of environmental degradation continue to worsen.

The OECD *Environmental Outlook* has identified the main environmental issues for the next twenty years, and uses a traffic-light system to classify them as serious (red light), moderate (amber light) or satisfactory (green light): see Table 12.1.

Table 12.1	The OECD environmental 'traffic signals'		
Pressures on the environment	• Industrial point source pollution • Some air pollutants (lead, CFCs, CO, SO$_x$)	• Water use • Toxic emissions from industry • Hazardous waste generation • Energy production and use	• Agricultural pollution • Overfishing • Greenhouse gas emissions • Motor vehicle and aviation air pollution emissions • Municipal waste generation
State of the environment	• Forest coverage in OECD regions	• Surface water quality • Forest quality in OECD regions • Ozone layer integrity	• Biodiversity • Tropical forest coverage • Fish stocks • Groundwater quality • Urban air quality • Climate change • Chemicals in the environment
Responses	• 'Green' purchasing • 'Green' agriculture • Protected areas • Resource efficiency • Energy efficiency	• Biotechnology • Forest plantations • Aquaculture • Energy and transport technologies • Waste management	

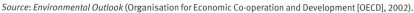

Source: Environmental Outlook (Organisation for Economic Co-operation and Development [OECD], 2002).

BOX 12.1   A STERN WARNING   CASE STUDIES AND APPLICATIONS

It's much cheaper to act now on global warming than to wait

The analysis of global warming is not just for climate scientists. Economists have a major part to play in examining its causes and consequences and the possible solutions. And these solutions are likely to have a major impact on business.

Perhaps the most influential study of climate change in recent times has been the Stern Review. This was an independent review, commissioned by the UK Chancellor of the Exchequer, and headed by Sir Nicholas Stern, head of the Government Economic Service and former chief economist of the World Bank. Here was an economist using the methods of economics to analyse perhaps the most serious problem facing the world.

> Climate change presents a unique challenge for economics: it is the greatest and widest-ranging market failure ever seen. The economic analysis must therefore be global, deal with long time horizons, have the economics of risk and uncertainty at centre stage, and examine the possibility of major, non-marginal change. To meet these requirements, the Review draws on ideas and techniques from most of the important areas of economics, including many recent advances.[1]

First the bad news . . .

According to the Stern Report, if no action is taken, global temperatures will rise by some 2–3°C within the next fifty years. As a result the world economy will shrink by up to 20 per cent – and that would be just the average. The economies of the countries most seriously affected by floods, drought and crop failure could shrink by considerably more. These tend to be the poorest countries, least able to bear the costs of these changes.

Rising sea levels could displace some 200 million people; droughts could create tens or even hundreds of millions of 'climate refugees'. 'Ecosystems will be particularly vulnerable to climate change, with around 15–40% of species potentially facing extinction after only 2°C of warming.'[2]

. . . Then the good

If action is taken now, these consequences could be averted – and at relatively low cost. According to the Stern Report, a sacrifice of just 1 per cent of global GDP (global income) could, if correctly targeted, be enough to stabilise greenhouse gases to an equivalent of 500–550 ppm of CO_2 – a level generally considered to be sustainable. To achieve this, action would need to be taken to cut emissions from their various sources (see the chart). This would involve a mixture of four things:

- Reducing consumer demand for emissions-intensive goods and services;

Greenhouse gas emissions in 2000, by source

Total emissions in 2000: 42 GtCO₂e.

Energy emissions are mostly CO_2 (some non-CO_2 in industry and other energy related).

Non-energy emissions are CO_2 (land use) and non-CO_2 (agriculture and waste).

Source: *Stern Review on the Economics of Climate Change*, Office of Climate Change (OCC) (Stern Review, 2006), Executive Summary, Figure 1 based on data drawn from World Resources Institute *Climate Analysis Indicators Tool* (CAIT) on-line database version 3.0.)

- Increased efficiency, which can save both money and emissions;
- Action on non-energy emissions, such as avoiding deforestation;
- Switching to lower-carbon technologies for power, heat and transport.

What policies did Sir Nicholas recommend to achieve these four objectives? Essentially the answer is to alter incentives. This could involve taxing polluting activities; subsidising green alternatives, including the development of green technology; establishing a price for carbon through trading carbon (see section on tradable permits on pages 350–4 below) and regulating its production; and encouraging behavioural change through education, better labelling of products, imposing minimum standards for building and encouraging public debate.

We consider some of these alternatives in this chapter.

1. *Would it be in the interests of a business to reduce its carbon emissions if this involved it in increased costs?*
2. *How is the concept of 'opportunity cost' relevant in analysing the impact of business decisions on the environment?*

[1] *Stern Review on the Economics of Climate Change* (TSO, 2006), Executive Summary.
[2] *Ibid.*

An optimum use of the environment

If the current levels of pollution and environmental degradation are too high, then can we identify an optimum use of the environment? To do this, we have to go back to first principles of efficiency and also look at the ethics of our relationship with the natural world and at our attitudes towards *sustainability*.

Different approaches to sustainability

We can identify four different approaches to the environment and sustainability.

The free-market approach. At the one extreme, we could regard the world as there purely for ourselves: a resource that belongs to individual property owners to do with as they choose, or a 'common asset', such as the air and seas, for individuals to use for their own benefit. In this view of the world, we are entitled simply to weigh up the marginal costs and benefits to ourselves of any activity. Sustainability is achieved in this free-market world only to the extent that resource prices rise as they become scarce and to the extent that environmentally friendly technologies are in firms' (or consumers') private interests.

The social efficiency approach. A somewhat less extreme version of this view is one that takes the social costs and benefits of using the environment into account: i.e. the costs and benefits not only to the direct producer or consumer, but to people in general. Here we would apply the standard rules for social efficiency: that if marginal social benefit exceeds marginal social cost, we should do more of the activity, and if marginal social cost exceeds marginal social benefit, we should do less. Even though this approach does take into account environmental externalities (such as pollution), these environmental costs are costs only to the extent that they adversely affect *human beings*.

Within this general approach, however, more explicit account can be taken of sustainability, by including the costs of our use of the environment today to *future* generations. For example, we could take into account the effects of climate change not just on ourselves, but on our children and their descendants. Depending on people's views on 'inter-generational' equity, a higher or lower weighting could be given to future (as opposed to present) costs and benefits (see page 333 on the choice of a social discount rate).

The conservationist approach. Many environmentalists argue that our responsibilities should not be limited to each other, or even to future generations, but should include the environment for its own sake. Such a view would involve downplaying the relative importance of material consumption and economic growth, and putting greater emphasis on the maintenance of ecosystems. Growth in consumption would be ethically acceptable only if it led to no (or only very minor) environmental degradation. Maintenance of the environment is thus seen as an ethical *constraint* on human activity.

The Gaia approach. The strongest approach to sustainability involves a fundamentally different ethical standpoint. Here the Earth itself, and its various natural species of animals and plants, have moral rights. According to this **Gaia philosophy**, people are seen as mere custodians of the planet: the planet does not belong to them, any more than a dog belongs to the fleas on its back! This view of the environment is similar to that held by some indigenous peoples living in marginal areas, such as the Aborigines in Australia and the San (Bushmen) of the Kalahari, and to various other 'hunter-gatherer' peoples in developing countries. Their ethic is that the land they leave their descendants should be as good as, if not better than, the land they inherited from their ancestors. Conservation is a 'prime directive'. This approach to the environment has been dubbed the 'deep green' approach.

Making optimum decisions concerning the environment

Choice between these four approaches is essentially normative, and therefore we cannot as economists stand in judgement between them. When anti-road protesters debate with commuters wanting a new bypass to be built across a site of outstanding natural beauty, there is little common ground between them. There is even less common ground between a multinational logging company and indigenous rainforest dwellers.

Nevertheless, economists can help in identifying optimum decisions *within* a given set of values. Most environmental economists adopt an approach that is consistent with the social efficiency view, and which can be easily modified to fit the conservationist view. The main area for disagreement within this approach is over the *value* to be put on specific environmental costs and benefits.

Let us take the case of the production of a good that yields benefits to consumers, but which involves pollution to the environment. What is the optimum level of output of the good? The choices are illustrated in Figure 12.2.

The line $MC_{pollution}$ shows the amount of pollution from each additional unit of the good. Up to level of activity Q_1 there is no pollution: the environment can cope with the

---

Definitions

Sustainability The ability of the environment to survive its use for economic activity.

Gaia philosophy The respect for the rights of the environment to remain unharmed by human activity. Humans should live in harmony with the planet and other species. We have a duty to be stewards of the natural environment, so that it can continue to be a self-maintaining and self-regulating system.

| **Figure 12.2** | Optimum level of an activity that involves pollution |

Output of good

waste generated. The curve gets steeper as output increases because the environment is increasingly unable to cope with the waste. The costs of pollution therefore accelerate.

The line $MB - MC$ shows the net marginal private benefit from the good (i.e. its private profitability). The curve slopes downwards for two reasons: marginal benefit falls as more of the good is consumed (the principle of diminishing marginal utility); marginal cost rises (diminishing marginal returns). It is privately profitable to produce extra units of the good up to Q_4. Total private gain is maximised at this output.

An otherwise perfect free market will produce Q_4 units of output, with a pollution cost of P_4. The *socially* efficient level of output, however, is Q_3, with the lower pollution cost, P_3. (We are assuming that there are no other externalities.) Here the marginal net private benefit is equal to the marginal external cost of the pollution (i.e. where there is a zero net *social* benefit: where $MSB = MSC$). Identifying this socially efficient level of output is not easy in practice, since it requires us to *measure* pollution costs, and that is fraught with problems. These problems were considered in section 11.4.

A more conservationist approach could be to set a maximum pollution cost of, say, P_2. This would reduce the optimum output to Q_2. A Gaian approach would be to restrict output to Q_1 in order to prevent any pollution. Of course, as we move towards 'greener' approaches, so it becomes more important to look for less polluting methods for producing this good (causing the $MC_{\text{pollution}}$ curve to shift downwards), and for alternative goods that involve less pollution (thus reducing the need to consume this good).

Market failures

What is clear from all the attitudes towards sustainability, other than the free-market one, is that the market system will fail to provide adequate protection for the environment. In fact, the market fails for various reasons.

The environment as a common resource. The air, the seas and many other parts of the environment are not privately owned. They are a global 'commons', and thus have the characteristic of 'non-excludability' (see pages 316–7). Many of the 'services' provided by the environment do not have a price, so there is no economic incentive to economise on their use. Yet most environmental resources are *scarce*: there is 'rivalry' in their use. At a zero price, these resources will be overused.

Externalities. One of the major problems of the environment being a public good is that of externalities. When people pollute the environment, the costs are borne mainly by others. The greater these external costs, the lower will be the socially efficient level of output (Q_3 in Figure 12.2). Because no one owns the environment, there is no one to enforce property rights over it. If a company pollutes the air that I breathe, I cannot stop it, because the air does not belong to me.

Ignorance. There have been many cases of people causing environmental damage without realising it, especially when the effects build up over a long time. Take the case of aerosols. It was not until the 1980s that scientists connected their use to ozone depletion. Even when the problems are known to scientists, consumers may not appreciate the full environmental costs of their actions. So even if people would like to be more 'environmentally friendly' in their activities, they might not have the knowledge to be so.

Inter-generational problems. The environmentally harmful effects of many activities are long-term, whereas the benefits are immediate. Thus consumers and firms are frequently prepared to continue with various practices and leave future generations to worry about their environmental consequences. The problem, then, is a reflection of the importance that people attach to the present relative to the future.

> **?** *Look through the categories of possible market failings in section 11.2 on pages 313–21. Are there any others, in addition to the four we have just identified, that will result in a socially inefficient use of the environment?*

Section summary

1. The environment benefits humans in three ways: as an amenity, as a source of primary products and as a dump for waste.

2. Given the increasing population pressures and the demands for economic growth, the pressures on the environment are likely to grow. These pressures can be lessened, however, with the use of cleaner technology, a more efficient use of natural resources and 'greener' behaviour of consumers, firms and governments.

3. The concept of an 'optimum' use of the environment depends on people's attitudes towards sustainability. These attitudes vary from regarding the environment simply as a resource for human use at the one extreme

to seeing the environment as having moral rights at the other.

4. Under the social efficiency approach to sustainability, the optimum output of a good is where the marginal external environmental cost is equal to the marginal net benefit to users (assuming no other externalities).

5. The market fails to achieve a socially efficient use of the environment because large parts of the environment are a common resource, because production or consumption often generates environmental externalities, because of ignorance of the environmental effects of our actions, and because of a lack of concern for future generations.

12.2 POLICIES TO TACKLE POLLUTION AND ITS EFFECTS

Policies to tackle pollution fall into three broad categories: (a) those that attempt to work through the market by changing property rights or by changing market signals (e.g. through the use of taxes or subsidies); (b) those that involve the use of laws, regulations and other forms of non-market-based intervention; (c) those that attempt to combine the two approaches, the main example being that of 'cap and trade' – this is where the government gives firms permits to emit up to a certain limit (regulation) but then lets them trade these permits with each other (market-based).

Market-based policies

The policies that a government adopts to reduce pollution will depend on its attitudes towards sustainability: on how 'green' it is.

If governments adopt a social efficiency approach to sustainability, environmental problems are seen to be the result of prices not reflecting marginal social costs and benefits. In this section, we look at ways in which markets can be adjusted so that they do achieve social efficiency.

Extending private property rights

If those suffering from pollution are granted property rights, they can charge the polluters for the right to pollute. According to the Coase theorem (see page 326), this would result in the socially efficient level of output being achieved.

We can use Figure 12.2 to illustrate the Coase theorem. If output is initially less than Q_3, the marginal profit to the polluter will exceed the marginal pollution cost to the sufferer. In this case, if the sufferers impose a charge on the polluter that is greater than the sufferers' marginal pollution cost but less than the polluter's marginal profit, both

sides will benefit from more of the good being produced. Such a situation can continue up to Q_3. Beyond Q_3, the marginal pollution cost exceeds the marginal profit. There is no charge that would compensate for the victim's suffering and leave enough over for the polluter to make a profit. Equilibrium output is therefore at Q_3, the socially efficient output.

Similarly, if the polluting *firm* is given the right to pollute, victims could offer a payment to persuade it not to pollute. The victims would be prepared to pay only up to the cost to them of the pollution. The firm would cut back production only provided the payment was at least as great as the loss in profit. This would be the case at levels of output above Q_3. Once output falls below Q_3, the maximum payment that the victim would be prepared to pay would be less than the minimum that the firm would be prepared to accept. Again, equilibrium would be at Q_3.

Extending private property rights in this way is normally impractical whenever there are many polluters and many victims. But the principle of the victims paying polluters to reduce pollution is sometimes followed by governments. Thus, under Article 11 of the 1997 Kyoto Protocol, the developed countries agreed to provide financial assistance to the developing countries to help them reduce greenhouse gas emissions.

In addition, there are sometimes direct environmental gains to be made from extending private property rights to individuals. In many developing countries, tenant farmers or squatters in urban slums have no incentive to invest in the land where they work or live. Give such people secure property rights, however, and they are more likely to take care of the property. For example, farmers are much more likely to plant trees if they know they have the right to the wood or fruit several years later.

Figure 12.3 An emissions charge

Level of emission

Charging for use of the environment (as a resource or a dump)

One way of 'pricing the environment' is for the government to impose **environmental charges** on consumers or firms. Thus *emissions charges* could be levied on firms discharging waste. Another example is the use of *user charges* to households for sewage disposal or rubbish collection. If a social efficiency approach to sustainability is taken, the optimum level of environmental use would be where the marginal social benefits and costs of that use were equal. This is illustrated in Figure 12.3, which shows the emission of toxic waste into a river by a chemical plant.

It is assumed that all the benefits from emitting the waste into the river accrue to the firm (i.e. there is no external benefit). Marginal private and marginal social benefits are thus the same ($MB = MSB$). The curve slopes downwards because, with a downward-sloping demand curve for the good, higher output will have a lower marginal benefit, and so too will the waste associated with it.

But what about the marginal costs? Without charges, the marginal private cost of using the river for emitting the waste is zero. The pollution of the river, however, imposes an external cost on those living by the river or using it for fishing or water supply. The marginal external cost rises as the river becomes less and less able to cope with increased levels of emission. As there is no private cost, the marginal social cost is the same as the marginal external cost.

Without a charge, the firm will emit L_1, since this is where its private marginal cost (= 0) equals its private

marginal benefit. The socially efficient level of emission is L_2 and the socially efficient level of emission charge, therefore, is P_2.

If these charges are to achieve a reduction in pollution, they must be a charge *per unit* of emissions or resource use (as in Figure 12.3). *Fixed total* charges, by contrast, such as water rates or council tax, will *not* encourage households to cut back on water use or domestic refuse, since this will not save them any money: such charges have a *marginal* rate of zero. If the firm in Figure 12.3 were charged a fixed total pollution fee, it would still choose to emit L_1 waste.

Environmental ('green') taxes and subsidies

Rather than charging for environmental use, a tax could be imposed on the output (or consumption) of a *good*, wherever external environmental costs are generated. Such taxes are known as **green taxes**. In this case, the good already has a price: the tax has the effect of increasing the price. To achieve a socially efficient output, the rate of tax should be equal to the marginal external cost. The alternative is to subsidise activities that reduce pollution (such as the installation of loft insulation). Here the rate of subsidy should be equal to the marginal external benefit.

Figure 11.9 (on page 324) showed the optimum rate of pollution tax in an otherwise perfect market. In terms of Figure 12.2, this rate of tax would be P_3: i.e. equal to the marginal pollution cost at the socially optimum output Q_3. The tax, by adding to private costs, shifts the $MB - MC$ line downwards so that it crosses the horizontal axis at Q_3. Profit is maximised where $MB - MC = 0$: at Q_3.

Although green taxes and subsidies are theoretically a means of achieving social efficiency, they do have serious limitations (see Box 12.2).

 Draw a diagram like Figure 12.2, only this time assume that the activity has the effect of reducing pollution, with the result that the $MC_{pollution}$ curve lies below the horizontal axis, sloping downwards. Identify the socially optimal level of the activity. What would be the level of subsidy required to achieve this level of activity?

Non-market-based policies

Command-and-control systems (laws and regulations)

The traditional way of tackling pollution has been to set maximum permitted levels of emission or resource use, or minimum acceptable levels of environmental quality, and then to fine firms contravening these limits. Measures of

---

Definitions

Environmental charges Charges for using natural resources (e.g. water or national parks), or for using the environment as a dump for waste (e.g. factory emissions or sewage).

Green tax A tax on output designed to charge for the adverse effects of production on the environment. The socially efficient level of a green tax is equal to the marginal environmental cost of production.

this type are known as ***command-and-control (CAC) systems***. Clearly, there have to be inspectors to monitor the amount of pollution, and the fines have to be large enough to deter firms from exceeding the limit.

Virtually all countries have environmental regulations of one sort or another. For example, the EU has over 200 items of legislation covering areas such as air and water pollution, noise, the marketing and use of dangerous chemicals, waste management, the environmental impacts of new projects (such as power stations, roads and quarries), recycling, depletion of the ozone layer and global warming.

Typically, there are three approaches to devising CAC systems.[1]

- ***Technology-based standards***. The focus could be on the amount of pollution generated, irrespective of its environmental impact. As technology for reducing pollutants improves, so tougher standards could be imposed, based on the 'best available technology' (as long as the cost were not excessive). Thus car manufacturers could be required to ensure that new car engines meet lower CO_2 emission levels as the technology enabled them to do so.
- ***Ambient-based standards***. Here the focus is on the environmental impact. For example, standards could be set for air or water purity. Depending on the location and the number of polluters in that area, a given standard would be achieved with different levels of discharge. If the object is a cleaner environment, this approach is more efficient than technology-based standards.
- ***Social-impact standards***. Here the focus is on the effect on people. Thus tougher standards would be imposed in densely populated areas. Whether this approach is more efficient than that of ambient-based standards depends on the approach to sustainability. If the objective is to achieve social efficiency, human-impact standards are preferable. If the objective is to protect the environment for its own sake (a deeper green approach), ambient standards would be preferable.

Assessing CAC systems. Given the uncertainty over the environmental impacts of pollutants, especially over the longer term, it is often better to play safe and set tough emissions or ambient standards. These could always be relaxed at a later stage if the effects turn out not to be so damaging, but it might be too late to reverse damage if the effects turn out to be more serious. Taxes may be a more sophisticated means of reaching a socially efficient output, but CAC methods are usually more straightforward to devise, easier to understand by firms and easier to implement.

Voluntary agreements

Rather than imposing laws and regulations, the government can seek to enter into voluntary agreements (VAs) with firms for them to cut pollution. Such agreements may involve a formal contract, and hence be legally binding, or they may be looser commitments by firms. VAs will be helped if (a) companies believe that this will improve their image with customers and hence improve sales; (b) there is an underlying threat by the government of introducing laws and regulations should voluntary agreements fail.

Firms often prefer VAs to regulations, because they can negotiate such agreements to suit their own particular circumstances and build them into their planning. The result is that the firms may be able to meet environmental objectives at lower cost. This clearly helps their competitive position.

The effectiveness of VAs depends on how tightly specified the agreements are and how easy they are for government inspectors to monitor. It also depends on the goodwill of firms. Without it, firms may well try to draw up agreements in a way that allows them to get around having to cut emissions as much as was intended by the government.

Education

People's attitudes are very important in determining the environmental consequences of their actions. Fortunately for the environment, people are not always out simply to maximise their own self-interest. If they were, then why do people often buy more expensive 'green' products, such as environmentally friendly detergents? The answer is that many people like to do their own little bit, however small, towards protecting the environment. There is evidence that attitudes have changed markedly over the last few years. See Box 12.3 for more detail on this.

This is where education can come in. If children, and adults for that matter, were made more aware of

---

[1] See R. K. Turner, D. Pearce and I. Bateman, *Environmental Economics* (Harvester Wheatsheaf, 1994), p. 198.

Definitions

Command-and-control (CAC) systems The use of laws or regulations backed up by inspections and penalties (such as fines) for non-compliance.

Technology-based standards Pollution control that requires firms' emissions to reflect the levels that could be achieved from using the best available pollution control technology.

Ambient-based standards Pollution control that requires firms to meet minimum standards for the environment (e.g. air or water quality).

Social-impact standards Pollution control that focuses on the effects on people (e.g. on health or happiness).

BOX 12.2	GREEN TAXES

Are they the perfect answer to the problem of pollution?

Increasingly countries are introducing 'green' taxes in order to discourage pollution as goods are produced, consumed or disposed of. The table shows the range of green taxes used around the world and the chart shows green tax revenues as a percentage of GDP in various countries. As can be seen, they are higher than average in Scandinavian countries, reflecting the strength of their environmental concerns. They are lowest in the USA. By far the largest green tax revenues come from fuel taxes. Fuel taxes are relatively high in the UK and so, therefore, are green tax revenues.

There are various problems, however, with using the tax weapon in the fight against pollution.

Identifying the socially efficient tax rate.   It will be difficult to identify the $MC_{pollution}$ curve for each firm (see Figure 12.2), given that each one is likely to produce different amounts of pollutants for any given level of output. Even if two firms produce identical amounts of pollutants, the environmental damage might be quite different, because the ability of the environment to cope with it will differ between the two locations. Also, the number of people suffering will differ (a factor that is very important when considering the human impact of

pollution). What is more, the harmful effects are likely to build up over time, and predicting these effects is fraught with difficulty.

Problems of demand inelasticity.   The less elastic the demand for the product, the less effective will a tax be in cutting production and hence in cutting pollution. Thus taxes on petrol would have to be very high indeed to make significant reductions in the consumption of petrol and hence significant reductions in the exhaust gases that contribute towards global warming and acid rain.

Problems with international trade.   If a country imposes pollution taxes on its industries, its products will become less competitive in world trade. To compensate for this, it may be necessary to give the industries tax rebates for exports. Also, taxes would have to be imposed on imports of competitors' products from countries where there is no equivalent green tax.

Effects on employment.   Reduced output in the industries affected by green taxes will lead to a reduction in employment. If, however, the effect was to encourage investment in new cleaner technology, employment

Types of environmental taxes and charges

Motor fuels	*Other goods*	*Air transport*
Leaded/unleaded	Batteries	Noise charges
Diesel (quality differential)	Plastic carrier bags	Aviation fuels
Carbon/energy taxation	Glass containers	
Sulphur tax	Drink cans	*Water*
	Tyres	Water charges
Other energy products	CFCs/halons	Sewage charges
Carbon/energy tax	Disposable razors/cameras	Water effluent charges
Sulphur tax or charge	Lubricant oil charge	Manure charges
NO_2 charge	Oil pollutant charge	
Methane charge	Solvents	*Direct tax provisions*
		Tax relief on green investment
Agricultural inputs	*Waste disposal*	Taxation on free company cars
Fertilisers	Municipal waste charges	Employer-paid commuting expenses
Pesticides	Waste-disposal charges	taxable
Manure	Hazardous waste charges	Employer-paid parking expenses taxable
	Landfill tax or charges	Commuter use of public transport tax
Vehicle-related taxation	Duties on waste water	deductible
Sales tax depends on car size		
Road tax depends on car size		

environmental issues and the consequences of their actions, then people's consumption habits could change and more pressure would be put on firms to improve their 'green credentials'.

Tradable permits

A policy measure that has grown in popularity in recent years is that of **tradable permits**, also known as a 'cap-

---

Definition

Tradable permits Each firm is given a permit to produce a given level of pollution. If less than the permitted amount is produced, the firm is given a credit. This can then be sold to another firm, allowing it to exceed its original limit.

might not fall. Furthermore, employment opportunities could be generated elsewhere, if the extra revenues from the green taxes were spent on alternative products (e.g. buses and trains rather than cars).

Redistributive effects.   Many green taxes are regressive. The poor spend a higher proportion of their income on domestic fuel than the rich. A 'carbon tax' on such fuel therefore has the effect of redistributing incomes away from the poor. The poor also spend a larger proportion of their income on food than the rich do. Taxes on agriculture, designed to reduce the intensive use of fertilisers and pesticides, also tend to hit the poor proportionately more than the rich.

Not all green taxes, however, are regressive. The rich spend a higher proportion of their income on motoring than the poor (see Figure 12.4 on page 357). Thus petrol and other motoring taxes could have a progressive effect.

Despite these problems, such taxes can still move output closer to the socially efficient level. What is more, they do have the major advantage of providing a continuing incentive to firms to find cleaner methods of production and thereby save more on their tax bills.

 Is it a good idea to use the revenues from green taxes to subsidise green alternatives (e.g. using petrol taxes for subsidising rail transport)? Consider the implications for wider tax policy in your answer.

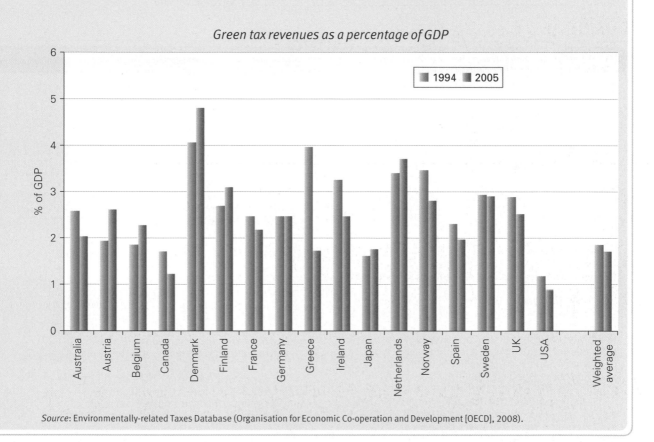

Green tax revenues as a percentage of GDP

Source: Environmentally-related Taxes Database (Organisation for Economic Co-operation and Development [OECD], 2008).

and-trade' system. This is a combination of command-and-control and market-based systems.

A maximum permitted level of emission is set for a given pollutant for a given factory, and the firm is given a permit to emit up to this amount. If it emits less than this amount, it is given a credit for the difference, which it can then use in another of its factories, or sell to other firms. These other firms are then permitted to go that amount

over their permitted level. Thus the overall level of emissions is set by CAC methods, whereas their distribution is determined by the market.

Take the example of firms A and B, which are currently producing twelve units of a pollutant each. Now assume that a standard is set permitting them to produce only ten units each. If firm A managed to reduce the pollutant to eight units, it would be given a credit for two units. It could

BOX 12.3 ARE WE ALL GREEN NOW?

Changing attitudes to the environmental agenda

It wasn't very long ago that concern about the environment and a willingness to take sustainability seriously were seen as eccentric. For every scientist predicting the potentially serious results of climate change, there seemed to be another suggesting that humanity's impact on the planet was of little consequence. However, while it would be complacent to suggest that all individuals and businesses are fully signed up to the green agenda, there are signs that over the past few years there has been a fundamental change in attitudes.

Individuals' attitudes and behaviour

Following a 2007 survey[1] the Office for National Statistics reported a definite change in both behaviour and attitude to the environment. Three-quarters of those surveyed said

that they felt that if most people in the UK recycled more, cut down on car use or flew less, it would have a medium or major impact on the UK's contribution to climate change. In the survey the environment was rated the fourth most important issue for government to address. Surveys undertaken in 2001 and 1996 suggested that individuals were previously less convinced about the impact that their own behaviour could have on climate change.

If we look further at the statistics, it seems that that these changing attitudes are in part feeding through to some areas of household behaviour. By 2007/8 households were recycling 33 per cent of rubbish compared with 23 per cent in 2004/5 and there were marked increases in the use of public transport, particularly in the south-east. Of course some of these behavioural changes will

BOX 12.4 SELLING THE ENVIRONMENT

The market-led solution of the Kyoto Protocol

In 1997, a draft accord to reduce greenhouse gas emissions was agreed by most nations of the world at the UN international climate change conference in Kyoto, Japan. It was based on principles established in a framework convention signed in 1992. The 'Kyoto Protocol' is an agreement to reduce greenhouse gas emissions by an average of 5.2 per cent (based on 1990 levels) by the year 2012.

To become a legally binding treaty, it had to be signed and ratified by nations accounting for at least 55 per cent of greenhouse gas emissions from industrialised countries. Because the Bush administration decided not to ratify the agreement, and given that the USA accounts for some 36 per cent of such emissions, the 55 per cent target could be met only if Russia signed, which it eventually did in November 2004.

The treaty came into force on 16 February 2005, having been ratified by 141 countries. This has since increased to a total of 181 countries and of these, 39 industrialised countries have agreed to emissions reductions. A big boost was given in 2007, when the incoming Labor government in Australia agreed to ratify the treaty, overturning the previous government's opposition to it.

Each of the industrialised countries has its own agreed emissions-reduction target. The UK's target is a reduction of 12.5 per cent from 1990 levels, Germany's is 21 per cent, that of the EU as a whole is 8 per cent and Japan's is 6 per cent, as is Canada's. Australia's target is a ceiling of an 8 per cent increase.

Market-based systems

The agreement, although not originally envisaged in this way, involves the climate being turned into a market, where the right to pollute can be bought and sold through a system of emissions credits. These credits can be earned by reducing emission levels below those agreed or by creating conditions that help to minimise the impact of greenhouse gases on global warming: for example, by planting a forest (which absorbs carbon).

Within the Kyoto Protocol there are three distinct market-based mechanisms:

- Emissions trading;
- Joint Implementation (JI);
- Clean Development Mechanism (CDM).

Emissions trading. The countries that have ratified the Kyoto Protocol are allowed to trade amongst themselves rights to emit six greenhouse gases. If a country reduces emissions below its agreed limit, it will be able to sell the additional reduction as a credit. So if a country is finding it difficult to cut emissions, it will be able to buy these credits within some kind of marketplace. (As you will see in Box 12.5, CO_2 emissions trading began within the EU in January 2005.)

Joint implementation. Under Article 6 of the protocol, an industrialised country can earn credits by investing in projects that reduce emissions in other industrialised countries (primarily former Soviet countries). These credits, in this case called 'emission reduction units' (ERUs), then reduce its own requirement to cut emissions.

Clean Development Mechanism. This is similar to the joint implementation process above, but involves a country or company from the industrialised world earning credits, in this case called 'certified emissions reductions' (CERs), by investing in emissions reduction schemes in *developing* countries. For example, a typical CDM or JI project might involve installing solar panels, planting forests, or investing in a factory producing energy-efficient light bulbs.

Assessing the Kyoto Protocol

While the use of such market mechanisms may make it easier to meet the Kyoto targets, many claim that the targets are much too low. The Intergovernmental Panel on Climate Change (a UN-appointed panel of 2500 of the world's leading scientists) estimates that a 60 to 80 per cent cut in greenhouse gas emissions from 1990 levels will ultimately be needed to avert serious climate disruption. In the light of this, a 5.2 per cent reduction, which will probably not be met anyway, seems minuscule.

CASE STUDIES AND APPLICATIONS

reflect new policies; for example, many local authorities have adopted rubbish collection systems that encourage recycling, while London has introduced a congestion charge. However, we might argue that changing attitudes have enabled those policies to be put in place.

Businesses

Past attitudes of business toward the environment have been summarised as falling into two camps: a few firms were interested in 'saving the planet', while the majority felt that this conflicted with profit maximisation. Two things have challenged the approach of the majority. First, in an era of real increases in commodity prices, and particularly of higher energy costs, a responsible attitude towards the environment and profit maximisation both suggest similar

strategies; firms are investing in new technologies that will reduce long-term energy consumption, and sustainability has become a crucial plank of corporate social responsibility. Second, changes in public attitudes have opened up a new approach for astute businesses: if consumers are themselves becoming environmentally aware, this presents business with opportunities for new approaches to marketing and innovation.

Examine why we have seen substantial increases in air travel over the last three years, despite the reported change in attitudes.

[1] *2007 Survey of Public Attitudes and Behaviours Toward the Environment* (DEFRA, August 2007).

CASE STUDIES AND APPLICATIONS

There is also the danger that businesses, rather than cutting greenhouse gas emissions, will simply buy credits offered for sale on the open market, many of which will not be earned from reducing current emissions. For example, Russia has CO_2 emissions considerably below its 1990 level and as such has a massive emissions credit for sale. However, such credit is not the result of Russian environmental policy, but rather the consequence of the collapse and closure of large sections of Russian industry and the replacing of old dirty factories with much more profitable ones. In other words, the reductions would have taken place anyway. The EU has consistently argued that, to ensure that some real gains are made, no more than 50 per cent of the emissions reduction should be achieved through these market-based mechanisms.

One of the biggest problems with the Kyoto treaty is that developing countries are not obliged to cut their emissions, although they do have to monitor and report the levels. Instead, recognising that developed nations have benefited from 150 years of industrial activity, the Protocol places a greater onus on those nations under the principle of 'common but differentiated responsibilities'.

However, China's increasing emissions have been the subject of much criticism in a period during which it has built an average of one coal-fired power station every week. In 2007 it responded to concerns by unveiling a climate change plan and promising to put the issue at the heart of its energy policies. Despite this, as countries such as China and India continue with their rapid industrialisation, often using relatively dirty technology, emissions are likely to increase rapidly. Finally, the USA, under the Bush administration, having opted out of the Kyoto Protocol, clearly weakened the effectiveness of the treaty.

George W. Bush and the Kyoto Protocol

So did the Bush administration take any measures to cut greenhouse gases? In its 'clear skies and global climate change initiative', launched in February 2002, the USA stated that its aim was to cut the growth in greenhouse gas emissions relative to the growth in the economy. There would be tax incentives to encourage renewable energy schemes and fuel efficiency schemes, but corporations

would not be obliged to meet any CO_2 targets. The effect would still be one of a *growth* in greenhouse gases. By 2012, US CO_2 emissions would be some 25 per cent above 1990 levels: not the 7 per cent below that the Clinton administration had agreed at Kyoto in 1997!

Towards the end of the Bush presidency, there was some limited movement on the US approach to the issue. A Climate Security Act was introduced to the US Senate in 2007 for consideration. This Bill was designed to reduce the amount of greenhouse gases emitted in the USA. If passed, it would have created a national cap-and-trade scheme equivalent to that operating in the EU (see Box 12.5). However, the Bill was eventually killed off by Republicans concerned about the economic impact of the proposed reductions in emissions.

Despite this lack of political willpower in the Bush administration, elsewhere in the USA action was being taken. From January 2007 eight north-eastern states became involved in a regional cap-and-trade programme, while California has committed to reducing emissions by 25 per cent by 2020.

The Bali roadmap

In December 2007, a UN climate change convention took place in Bali. Recognising that the Kyoto agreement made insufficient demands on countries and that it only covered the period to 2012, delegates agreed on a roadmap to making much deeper cuts in emissions.

A final agreement would be reached at a UN summit in December 2009 in Denmark. This agreement would specify the reductions in emissions of countries beyond 2012. For developed countries, the commitments would be measurable, reportable and verifiable. There would also be targets for developing countries, but these would be achieved with the support of developed countries through investment in new, greener technologies.

Explain who are likely to be the 'winners' and 'losers' as a result of talks on carbon dioxide emissions. Use the concepts of game theory to illustrate your argument.

then sell this to firm B, enabling B to continue emitting twelve units. The effect would still be a total reduction of four units between the two firms. However, the trade in pollution permits allows pollution reduction to be concentrated where it can be achieved at lowest cost. In our example, if it cost firm B more to reduce its pollution than firm A, the permits could be sold from A to B at a price that was profitable to both (i.e. at a price above the cost of emission reduction to A, but below the cost of emission reduction to B).

The principle of tradable permits can be used as the basis of international agreements on pollution reduction. Each country could be required to achieve a certain percentage reduction in a pollutant (e.g. CO_2 or SO_2), but any country exceeding its reduction could sell its right to these emissions to other (presumably richer) countries.

A similar principle can be adopted for using natural resources. Thus fish quotas could be assigned to fishing boats or fleets or countries. Any parts of these quotas not used could then be sold.

How are the permitted pollution levels (or fish quotas) to be decided? The way that seems to be the most acceptable is to base them on firms' *current* levels, with any subsequent reduction in total permitted pollution being achieved by requiring firms to reduce their emissions by the *same* percentage. This approach is known as **grandfathering**. The main problem with this approach is that it could be seen as unfair by those firms that are already using cleaner technology. Why should they be required to make the same reductions as firms using dirty technology?

In the EU, a carbon Emissions Trading Scheme (ETS) has been in place since January 2005. This scheme is examined in Box 12.5.

Assessing the system of tradable permits

The main advantage of tradable permits is that they combine the simplicity of CAC methods with the benefits of achieving pollution reduction in the most efficient way. There is also the advantage that firms have a financial incentive to cut pollution. This might then make it easier for governments to impose tougher standards (i.e. impose lower permitted levels of emission).

There are, however, various problems with tradable permits. One is the possibility that trade will lead to pollution being concentrated in certain geographical areas. Another is that it may reduce the pressure on dirtier factories (or countries) to cut their emissions. Finally, the system will lead to significant cuts in pollution only if the permitted

levels are low. Once the system is in place, the government might then feel that the pressure is off to *reduce* the permitted levels.

 What determines the size of the administrative costs of a system of tradable permits? For what reasons might green taxes be cheaper to administer than a system of tradable permits?

How much can we rely on governments?

If governments are to be relied upon to set the optimum green taxes or regulations, several conditions must be met.

First, they must have the will to protect the environment. But governments are accountable to their electorates and must often appease various pressure groups, such as representatives of big business. In the USA, for example, there has been great resistance to cuts in greenhouse gases from the automobile, power and various other industries, many of which have powerful representation in Congress. So there must be the political will in a country if significant environmental improvements are to be made. One of the problems here is that many of the environmental effects of our actions today will be on future generations; but governments are elected by today's generation, and today's generation may not be prepared to make the necessary sacrifices. This brings us back to the importance of education.

Second, it must be possible to identify just what the optimum is. This requires a clear set of objectives concerning sustainability and any conflicts between human and ecological objectives. It also requires a knowledge of just what are the environmental effects of various activities, such as the emission of CO_2 into the atmosphere, and that is something on which scientists disagree.

Finally, there is the problem that many environmental issues are global and not just local or national. Many require concerted action by governments around the world. The history of international agreements on environmental issues, however, is one plagued with difficulties between countries, which seem more concerned with their own national interests. To understand the difficulties of reaching international agreements, we can draw on game theory (see section 7.3, pages 201–5).

Game theory and international agreements

Assume that the world would benefit from a reduction in greenhouse gases and that these benefits would exceed the costs of having to cut back on activities (such as motoring or the generation of electricity) that release such gases into the atmosphere. What would be in the interests of an *individual* country, such as the USA? Its optimum solution would be for *other* countries to cut their emissions, while maintaining its own levels. This *maximax* approach would yield most of the benefits to the USA and none of the costs. However, when *all* countries refuse to cut emissions, no one gains! This is an example of the *prisoners' dilemma* (see Box 7.4, page 203), and is illustrated in Table 12.2.

Definition

Grandfathering Where each firm's emission permit is based on its current levels of emission (e.g. permitted levels for all firms could be 80 per cent of their current levels).

| BOX 12.5 | **TRADING OUR WAY OUT OF CLIMATE CHANGE** | **CASE STUDIES AND APPLICATIONS** |

The EU carbon trading system

In the EU, a carbon Emissions Trading Scheme (ETS) started in January 2005. It created a market in carbon with the intention of providing incentives to companies to reduce their emissions of CO_2 and thus to contribute to the EU's approach to meeting its targets under the Kyoto Treaty (see Box 12.4).

Trading Periods 1 and 2

The first phase of the scheme ran from January 2005 until December 2007. Around 12 000 industrial plants were allocated CO_2 emissions allowances, or credits, by their respective governments. These installations were collectively responsible for around 40 per cent of the EU's CO_2 emissions each year.

Companies that exceeded their limits could purchase credits to cover the difference, while those that reduced their emissions were able to sell their surplus credits for a profit. Companies were able to trade directly with each other or via brokers operating throughout Europe.

At the end of December 2007 all existing allowances became invalid and the second Trading Period began, to last until the end of 2012. Although this will run under the same general principles as Trading Period 1, it also allows companies to use JI and CDM credits earned under the Kyoto Protocol's project-based mechanisms (see Box 12.4). In other words, companies could offset emissions in the EU against emission reductions they achieve in countries outside the EU.

Assessing the ETS

The introduction of the world's largest market-based policy to address climate change has been welcomed by many economists and policy makers. However, others have raised concerns about both the operation of the scheme and its likely impact on overall emissions.

Some of these concerns are valid. For example, there is evidence that not all countries across the EU have been operating the scheme in the same way. Some countries, including the UK, have set tough targets based on past emissions, while others have set more generous forward-looking limits, raising questions about the equity of the scheme. Furthermore, while the allocation of permits for a whole Trading Period does provide certainty for firms, it also reduces the ability of the scheme to be responsive to changing conditions.

What matters crucially for the reduction of pollution is the total number of credits permitted. And this is where the major criticism lies: that allocation has been far too generous. This was compounded by a lack of willingness to prosecute those infringing the rules. The result of all this was that in Trading Period 1 emissions across the EU actually rose, by 1.9 per cent, and carbon prices fell – from a peak of around €30 per tonne of carbon in 2006 to a minuscule €0.02 per tonne by the end of Trading Period 1.

But this is not a criticism of the system of trading, only of the limits set. As long as the demand for permits exceeds the supply at a zero price and as long as the scheme enables free trade in carbon across the EU, then firms will have an incentive to reduce their emissions and sell permits to others. However, the lower the price, the less the incentive.

In Trading Period 2 the cap on emissions was tightened by 7 per cent (although this percentage varies from country to country). As a result, the price rose again – to around €20 per tone at the end of 2008. A problem, however, in the current trading period is that the credits earned through CDM and JI may be from new investments that would have taken place anyway. These 'bogus' credits then permit companies to carry on emitting in the EU.

It is hoped by 2012 to extend the scheme to airline and shipping emissions, although road transport will remain outside the scheme. But the proposed cuts are less than in other industries. In the case of aviation, the figure is 3 per cent from 2004/6 levels. But this is 90 per cent higher than 1990, the base year used for the 8 per cent cut in emissions from the other sectors.

Proposals for change

In January 2008 the European Commission proposed various changes to the scheme. These included centralised allocation of allowances rather than allocation by national governments, progressively replacing the free allocation of allowances by the auctioning of them, with at least 20 per cent of the revenues earmarked for measures to combat climate change (reaching full auctioning by 2020) and the inclusion of other greenhouse gases.

In December 2009, the EU agreed to a '20/20/20' package to tackle climate change. This would involve cutting greenhouse gases by 20 per cent by 2020 compared with 1990 levels, raising the use of renewable energy sources to 20 per cent of total energy usage and cutting energy consumption by 20 per cent. Much of the emissions reductions would be achieved by tighter caps under the ETS, with binding national targets for non-ETS sectors, such as agriculture, transport, buildings and services. However, over half of the reductions could be achieved by international carbon trading, where permits could be bought from abroad: e.g. under the Clean Development Mechanism (see Box 12.4).

 Consider a situation where all firms are of identical size and each is allocated credits that allows it to produce 10 per cent less than its current emissions. How would this compare with a situation where permits are allocated to 90 per cent of firms only? Consider both efficiency and equity in your answer.

Assume that there is an international agreement (as at the Kyoto summit in December 1997) to cut emissions. If all countries stick to the agreement, the outcome is cell A: a moderate gain to all. What should Congress do? Whatever other countries do (all stick to the agreement, some stick to it, none stick to it), it will be in the USA's interests *not* to stick to it: this is the dominant strategy – a lesson that George W. Bush seemed quick to learn! Cell D is preferable to Cell A; E is preferable to B; F is preferable to C. But when *all* countries reason like this, the world ends up in Cell F, with no cut in pollution. Cell F is worse for all countries than Cell A!

Table 12.2 Outcomes for countries from strategies of pollution reduction

USA's strategy	Other countries' strategy		
	All cut pollution	Some cut pollution	None cut pollution
Cut pollution	A Moderate net gain for all	B Small loss for USA; gain for countries not cutting pollution	C Large loss for USA; slight gain for other countries
Don't cut pollution	D High gain for USA; small gain for other countries	E Fairly high gain for USA; loss for other countries	F No gain for any country

Only if countries believe that the other countries will (a) ratify the agreement and (b) stick to it once it is ratified will the agreement be likely to succeed. This requires trust on all sides as well as the ability to monitor the outcomes.

The other major problem area concerns equity. Most countries will feel that they are being asked to do too much and that others are being asked to do too little. Developed countries will want to adopt a grandfathering approach. The starting point with this approach would be current levels of pollution. Every country would then be required to make the same percentage cut. Developing countries, on the other hand, will want the bulk of the cuts, if not all of them, to be made by the developed countries. After all, the rich countries produce much higher levels of pollutants per capita than do the poor countries, and curbing growth in developing countries would have a far more serious impact on levels of absolute poverty.

KI 4
p10

 How does an international negotiation 'game' differ from the prisoners' dilemma game?

Section summary

1. One approach to protecting the environment is to use the market. This can be done by extending private property rights. In many cases, however, this approach is impractical. Another approach is to impose charges for using the environment or taxes per unit of output. The problem with these methods is in identifying the appropriate charges or tax rates, since these will vary according to the environmental impact.

2. Another approach is to use command-and-control systems, such as making certain practices illegal or putting limits on discharges. This is a less sophisticated alternative to taxes or charges, but it is safer when the environmental costs of certain actions are unknown. Other alternatives to market-based approaches include voluntary agreements and education.

3. Tradable permits are a mix of command-and-control and market-based systems. Firms are given permits to emit a certain level of pollution and then these can be traded. A firm that can relatively cheaply reduce its pollution below its permitted level can sell this credit to another firm that finds it more costly to do so. The system is an efficient and administratively cheap way of limiting pollution to a designated level. It can, however, lead to pollution being concentrated in certain areas and can reduce the pressure on firms to find cleaner methods of production.

4. Although governments can make a major contribution to reducing pollution, government action is unlikely to lead to the perfect outcome (however defined). Governments may be more concerned with short-run political considerations and will not have perfect information. What is more, given that many environmental effects spill over national borders, governments may 'play games' internationally to try to reduce the costs to their country of any international action to protect the environment.

12.3 THE ECONOMICS OF TRAFFIC CONGESTION

Traffic congestion is a problem that faces all countries, especially in the large cities and at certain peak times. This problem has grown at an alarming rate as our lives have become increasingly dominated by the motor car. Sitting in a traffic jam is both time-wasting and frustrating.

And it is not only the motorist that suffers. Congested streets make life less pleasant for the pedestrian, and increased traffic leads to increased accidents and significant problems of pollution. Between 1970 and 2007 road traffic in Great Britain rose by 156 per cent, whereas the length of public roads rose by only 23 per cent (albeit some roads were widened). Most passenger and freight transport is by road. In 2007, 92 per cent of passenger kilometres and 64 per cent of freight tonnage kilometres in Great Britain were by road, whereas rail accounted for a mere 7 per cent of passenger traffic and 8 per cent of freight tonnage. Of

Table 12.3	Passenger transport in Great Britain: percentage of passenger kilometres					
Year	Cars	Motor cycles	Buses and coaches	Bicycles	Rail	Air (UK)
1956	37.1	3.3	36.3	6.5	16.3	0.2
1966	68.3	1.9	18.2	1.6	9.5	0.5
1976	77.0	1.5	12.8	1.1	7.3	0.5
1986	82.2	1.4	8.3	1.1	6.5	0.7
1996	86.5	0.6	6.0	0.6	5.4	0.9
2006	84.5	0.7	6.2	0.6	6.8	1.2

Source: Transport Statistics of Great Britain 2007 (Department for Transport, 2007).

road passenger kilometres, 96 per cent was by car in 2007, and this proportion has been growing. Motoring costs now amount to some 12 per cent of household expenditure (depending on the price of fuel). Table 12.3 shows the growth of passenger car transport relative to other modes, although he rail and air passenger transport proportions have increased in recent years.

But should the government do anything about the problem? Is traffic congestion a price worth paying for the benefits we gain from using cars? Or are there things that can be done to ease the problem without greatly inconveniencing the traveller?

We will look later in this section at various schemes and at their relative costs and benefits. But first it is necessary to examine the existing system of allocating road space to see the extent to which it meets or fails to meet society's transport objectives. This will enable us to identify the problems that the government must address. (Our discussion will focus on the motor car and passenger transport, but clearly lorries are another major source of congestion, and any comprehensive policy to deal with traffic congestion must also examine freight transport.)

The existing system of allocating road space

The allocation of road space depends on both demand and supply. Demand is by individuals who base their decisions on largely private considerations. Supply, by contrast, is usually by central government or local authorities. Let us examine each in turn.

Demand for road space (by car users)

The demand for road space can be seen largely as a *derived* demand. What people want is not the car journey for its own sake, but to get to their destination. The greater the benefit they gain at their destination, the greater the benefit they gain from using their car to get there.

The demand for road space, like the demand for other goods and services, has a number of determinants. If congestion is to be reduced, it is important to know how

responsive demand is to a change in any of these: it is important to consider the various elasticities of demand.

Price. This is the *marginal cost* to the motorist of a journey. It includes petrol, oil, maintenance, depreciation and any toll charges.

 Are there any costs associated with motoring that would not be included as marginal costs? Explain why.

The price elasticity of demand for motoring tends to be relatively low. There can be a substantial rise in the price of petrol, for example, and there will be only a modest fall in traffic.

Recent estimates of the short-run price elasticity of demand for road fuel in industrialised countries typically range from −0.15 to −0.28. Long-run elasticities are somewhat higher, but are still generally inelastic.[1]

The low price elasticity of demand suggests that schemes to tackle traffic congestion that merely involve raising the costs of motoring will have only limited success.

In addition to monetary costs, there are also the time costs of travel. The opportunity cost of sitting in your car is the next best alternative activity you could have been pursuing – relaxing, working, sleeping or whatever. Congestion, by increasing the duration of the journey, increases the opportunity cost.

Income. As incomes rise, car ownership and usage increase substantially. Demand for road space is elastic with respect to income.

Figure 12.4 shows motoring costs as a percentage of UK household expenditure by quintile groups of household

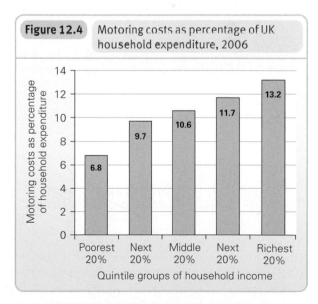

Figure 12.4 Motoring costs as percentage of UK household expenditure, 2006

Source: Family Spending 2007 (National Statistics, 2008).

---

[1] See *Environmentally Related Taxes in OECD Countries: Issues and Strategies* (OECD, 2001), pp. 99–103.

income. The higher the household income, the higher the percentage of income spent on motoring. Clearly, the income elasticity of demand is significantly greater than 1.

This is also reflected in international statistics of car ownership. Figure 12.5 shows the growth of car ownership between 1980 and 2006 in selected European countries. As national incomes have risen, so has the proportion of car ownership. People see car transport as a 'luxury good' compared with alternatives such as public transport, walking or cycling. Also, the growth of suburbs has meant that many people travel longer distances to work.

The implication of this is that, if countries continue to experience economic growth, car ownership and usage are likely to increase substantially: a conclusion in line with most forecasts.

Price of substitutes. If bus and train fares came down, people might switch from travelling by car. The cross-price elasticity, however, is likely to be relatively low, given that most people regard these alternatives as a poor substitute for travelling in their own car. Cars are seen as more comfortable and convenient.

The 'price' of substitutes also includes the time taken to travel by these alternatives. The quicker a train journey is compared with a car journey, the lower will be its time cost to the traveller and thus the more people will switch from car to rail.

Price of complements. Demand for road space will depend on the price of cars. The higher the price of cars, the fewer people will own cars and thus the fewer cars there will be on the road.

 Is the cross-price elasticity of demand for road space with respect to the price of cars likely to be high or low?

Demand will also depend on the price of complementary services, such as parking. A rise in car parking charges will reduce the demand for car journeys. But here again the cross elasticity is likely to be relatively low. In most cases, the motorist will either pay the higher charge or park elsewhere, such as in side streets.

 Go through each of the determinants we have identified so far and show how the respective elasticity of demand makes the problem of traffic congestion difficult to tackle.

Tastes/utility. Another factor explaining the preference of many people for travelling by car is the pleasure they gain from it compared with alternative modes of transport. Car ownership is regarded by many people as highly desirable, and once accustomed to travelling in their own car, most people are highly reluctant to give it up.

One important feature of the demand for road space is that it fluctuates. There will be periods of peak demand, such as during the rush hour or at holiday weekends. At such times, roads can get totally jammed. At other times, however, the same roads may be virtually empty.

Supply of road space
The supply of road space can be examined in two contexts: the short run and the long run.

The short run. In the short run, as we have seen, the supply of road space is constant. When there is no congestion, supply is more than enough to satisfy demand. There is

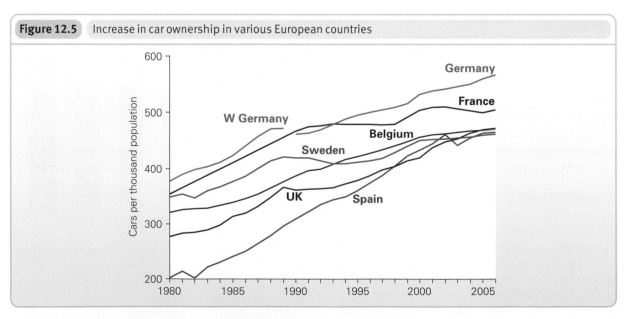

Figure 12.5 Increase in car ownership in various European countries

Source: Based on data in *Energy and Transport in Figures* (Commission of the European Communities, 2007).

spare road capacity. At times of congestion, there is pressure on this fixed supply. Maximum supply for any given road is reached at the point where there is the maximum flow of vehicles per minute along the road.

The long run. In the long run, the authorities can build new roads or improve existing ones. This will require an assessment of the costs and benefits of such schemes.

Identifying a socially efficient level of road usage (short run)

The existing system of *government* provision of roads and *private* ownership of cars is unlikely to lead to an optimum allocation of road space. So how do we set about identifying just what the social optimum is?

In the short run, the supply of road space is fixed. The question of the short-run optimum allocation of road space, therefore, is one of the optimum *usage* of existing road space. It is a question of *consumption* rather than supply. For this reason we must focus on the road user, rather than on road provision.

A socially efficient level of consumption occurs where the marginal social benefit of consumption equals its marginal social cost (*MSB = MSC*). So what are the marginal social benefits and costs of using a car?

Marginal social benefit of road usage

Marginal social benefit equals marginal private benefit plus externalities. Marginal private benefit is the direct benefit to the car user and is reflected in the demand for car journeys, the determinants of which we examined above. External benefits are few. The one major exception occurs when drivers give lifts to other people.

Marginal social cost of road usage

Marginal social cost equals marginal private cost plus externalities. Marginal private costs to the motorist include the costs of petrol, wear and tear, tolls, etc. They also include

the time costs of travel. There may also be substantial external costs. These include the following.

Congestion costs: time. When a person uses a car on a congested road, it will add to the congestion. This will therefore slow down the traffic even more and increase the journey time of other car users.

This is illustrated in Table 12.4 (which uses imaginary figures). Column (1) shows the number of cars travelling along a given road per minute. Column (2) shows the time taken for each car and thus can be seen as the marginal time cost to a motorist of making this journey. It is thus the *private* marginal time cost. With up to three cars per minute there is no congestion and therefore the traffic flows freely, each car taking 5 minutes to complete the journey. As traffic increases beyond this, however, the road becomes progressively more congested, and thus journey times increase. It is not just the additional cars that are forced to travel more slowly, but *all* the cars on the road. The extra cars thus impose a congestion cost on existing users of the road. By the time seven cars per minute are entering the road, journey time has increased to 16 minutes.

Column (3) shows the sum of the journey times of all the motorists on the road. For example, with six cars on the road, each taking 11 minutes, total journey time for all six is 66 minutes. Column (4) shows the increase in total journey time as one more car enters the road. Thus when the seventh car enters the road, total journey time increases from 66 to 112 minutes: an increase of 46 minutes. This is the additional cost to *all* road users: in other words, the marginal *social* cost. But of these 46 minutes, 16 are the private marginal costs incurred by the extra motorist. Only the remaining 30 minutes are *external* costs imposed on other road users. These external costs are shown in column (5).

Complete Table 12.4 up to 9 cars per minute, assuming that the journey time increases to 24 minutes for the eighth car and 35 minutes for the ninth car.

Table 12.4   Time taken to travel between two points along a given road

Traffic density (cars entering road per minute) (1)	Journey time per car (marginal private time cost: in minutes) (2)	Total journey time for all cars (total time cost: in minutes) (3) = (1) × (2)	Extra total journey time as traffic increases by one more car (marginal social time cost: in minutes) (4) = Δ(3)	Additional time cost imposed on other road users by one more car (marginal external time cost: in minutes) (5) = (4) − (2)
1	5	5	5	0
2	5	10	5	0
3	5	15	5	0
4	6	24	9	3
5	8	40	16	8
6	11	66	26	15
7	16	112	46	30

Time costs can be converted into money costs if we know the value of people's time. If time were valued at 10p per minute, the congestion costs (external costs) imposed by the seventh car would be £3 (i.e. 30 minutes × 10p per minute). Case Study 12.4 in MyEconLab examines the method used in the UK for estimating the value of time (in the context of evaluating new road schemes).

Congestion costs: monetary. Congestion increases fuel consumption, and the stopping and starting increases the costs of wear and tear. When a motorist adds to congestion, therefore, there will be additional monetary costs imposed on other motorists. A table similar to Table 12.4 could be drawn to illustrate this.

Environmental costs. When motorists use a road, they reduce the quality of the environment for others. Cars emit fumes and create noise. This is bad enough for pedestrians and other car users, but can be particularly distressing for people living along the road. Driving can cause accidents, a problem that increases as drivers become more impatient as a result of delays. Also, as we saw in section 12.1, exhaust gases contribute to global warming and acid rain.

The socially efficient level of road usage

The point where the marginal social benefit of car use is equal to the marginal social cost can be illustrated on a diagram. In Figure 12.6, costs and benefits are shown on the vertical axis and are measured in money terms. Thus any non-monetary costs or benefits (such as time costs) must be given a monetary value. The horizontal axis measures road usage in terms of cars per minute passing a specified point on the road.

For simplicity it is assumed that there are no external benefits from car use and that therefore marginal private and marginal social benefits are the same. The *MSB* curve is shown as downward sloping. The reason for this is that different road users put a different value on this particular journey. If the marginal (private) cost of making the journey were high, only those for whom the journey had a high marginal benefit would travel along the road. If the marginal cost of making the journey fell, more people would make the journey: people choosing to make the journey at the point at which the marginal cost of using their car had fallen to the level of their marginal benefit. Thus the greater the number of cars in any given time period, the lower the marginal benefit.

The marginal (private) cost curve (*MC*) is likely to be constant up to the level of traffic flow at which congestion begins to occur. This is shown as point *a* in Figure 12.6. Beyond this point, marginal cost is likely to rise as time costs increase and as fuel consumption rises.

The marginal *social* cost curve (*MSC*) is drawn above the marginal private cost curve. The vertical difference between the two represents the external costs. Up to point *b*, external costs are simply the environmental costs. Beyond point *b*, there are also external congestion costs, since additional road users slow down the journey of *other* road users. These external costs get progressively greater as the volume of traffic increases (as column (5) of Table 12.4 illustrated).

The actual level of traffic flow will be at Q_1, where marginal private costs and benefits are equal (point *e*). The socially efficient level of traffic flow, however, will be at the lower level of Q_2, where marginal social costs and benefits are equal (point *d*). In other words, the existing system of allocating road space is likely to lead to an excessive level of road usage.

Identifying a socially optimum level of road space (long run)

In the long run, the supply of road space is not fixed. The authorities must therefore assess what new road schemes (if any) to adopt. This will involve the use of some form of *cost–benefit analysis* (see section 11.4).

The socially efficient level of construction will be where the marginal social benefit from construction is equal to the marginal social cost. This means that schemes should be adopted as long as their marginal social benefit exceeds their marginal social cost.

But how are these costs and benefits assessed in practice? Case Study 12.4 in MyEconLab examines the procedure used in the UK.

KI 27
p310

KI 29
p313

KI 27
p310

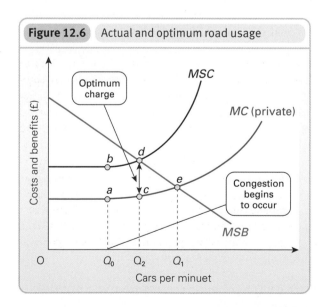

Figure 12.6 Actual and optimum road usage

Optimum charge

MSC

MC (private)

Congestion begins to occur

MSB

Costs and benefits (£)

b *d* *a* *c* *e*

O Q_0 Q_2 Q_1

Cars per minuet

Section summary

1. Increased car ownership and car usage have led to a growing problem of traffic congestion.

2. The allocation of road space depends on demand and supply. Demand depends on the price to motorists of using their cars, incomes, the cost of alternative means of transport, the price of cars and complementary services (such as parking), and the comfort and convenience of car transport. The price and cross-price elasticities of demand for car usage tend to be low: many people are unwilling to switch to alternative modes of transport. The income elasticity, on the other hand, is high. The demand for cars and car usage grows rapidly as incomes grow.

3. The short-run supply of road space is fixed. The long-run supply depends on government road construction programmes.

4. The existing system of government provision of roads and private ownership of cars is unlikely to lead to the optimum allocation of road space.

5. In the short run, with road space fixed, allocation depends on the private decisions of motorists. The problem is that motorists create two types of external cost: pollution costs and congestion costs. Thus $MSC > MC$. Because of these externalities, the actual use of road space (where $MB = MC$) is likely to be greater than the optimum (where $MSB = MSC$).

6. In the long run, the socially efficient amount of road space will be where $LRMSB = LRMSC$. New road schemes should be adopted as long as their $LRMSB > LRMSC$. Governments must therefore conduct some form of cost–benefit analysis in order to estimate these costs and benefits.

12.4 URBAN TRANSPORT POLICIES

We now turn to look at different solutions to traffic congestion. These can be grouped into three broad types: direct provision, regulation and legislation, and changing market signals.

Direct provision (supply-side solutions)

The road solution

One obvious solution to traffic congestion is to build more roads. There are serious problems, however, with this approach.

The objective of equity. The first problem concerns *equity*. After all, social efficiency is not the only possible economic objective. For example, when an urban motorway is built, those living beside it will suffer from noise and fumes. Motorway users gain, but the local residents lose. The question is whether this is fair.

The more the government tries to appeal to the car user by building more and better roads, the fewer will be the people who use public transport, and thus the more will public transport decline. Those without cars lose, and these tend to be from the most vulnerable groups – poor, elderly and disabled people, and children.

Building more roads may lead to a *potential* Pareto improvement: in other words, if the gainers had fully to compensate the losers (e.g. through taxes or tolls), they would still have a net gain. The problem is that such compensation is rarely if ever paid. There is thus no actual Pareto improvement.

Congestion may not be solved. Increasing the amount of road space may encourage more people to use cars.

A good example is the London orbital motorway, the M25. In planning the motorway, not only did the government underestimate the general rate of traffic growth, but it also underestimated the direct effect it would have in encouraging people to use the motorway rather than using some alternative route, or some alternative means of transport, or even not making the journey at all. It also underestimated the effect it would have in encouraging people to live further from their place of work and to commute along the motorway. The result is that there is now serious congestion on the motorway.

Thus new roads may simply generate extra traffic, with little overall effect on congestion.

The environmental impact of new roads. New roads lead to the loss of agricultural land, the destruction of many natural habitats, noise, the splitting of communities and disruption to local residents. To the extent that they encourage a growth in traffic, they add to atmospheric pollution and a depletion of oil reserves. It is thus important to take account of these costs when assessing new road schemes. The problem, however, is that these environmental costs are frequently ignored, or only considered as an afterthought and not taken seriously. Part of the problem is that they are difficult to assess, and part is that there is often a strong road lobby which persuades politicians to ignore or play down environmental considerations.

Government or local authority provision of public transport

An alternative supply-side solution is to increase the provision of public transport. If, for example, a local authority ran a local bus service and decided to invest in additional

TC 5
p50

KI 4
p10

BOX 12.6 RESTRICTING CAR ACCESS TO ATHENS

A solution to local atmospheric pollution?

Athens lies in a bowl-shaped valley. When there are light winds, a humid atmosphere and sunshine, the levels of atmospheric pollution can soar to dangerous heights. The major cause of this chemical smog (the 'néfos') is the emission of exhaust fumes.

The solution that the Greeks have adopted is one of restricting the use of vehicles in the city. The restrictions are of two levels of severity. The more severe ones apply on Mondays to Fridays when there is a chemical smog emergency, typically two or three times a month; the less severe ones apply on all other Mondays to Fridays.

The city is divided into an inner zone and an outer zone. The levels of various pollutants (such as nitrogen dioxide and ozone) are constantly monitored by the city authorities, and when they reach certain critical levels a smog emergency is declared on radio, on television and in the press.

During an emergency, all cars and half the taxis are banned from use in the inner zone. On even-numbered dates, only taxis with an even-numbered registration can operate in the inner zone; on odd-numbered dates, only those with an odd-numbered registration can operate. In the outer zone, all taxis can operate, with the odd/even number plate system applying to cars. The police check on cars entering the zones and turn away those not allowed. The drivers of cars being used illegally in the zones are fined.

When an emergency is not in force, restrictions apply only to the inner zone. The even-numbered/odd-numbered registration restrictions apply to cars, but not to taxis or to cars with foreign number plates.

The measures are successful in one respect: very few cars are driven illegally in the zones (and it is not possible to have two numberplates for the same car!). But many commuters have resorted to owning two cars: one with an even-numbered plate and one with an odd-numbered one. The authorities even help in this by allowing people to request an even or odd-numbered registration!

 Compare the relative advantages and disadvantages of these measures with those of charging people to come into the zones. Consider both the efficiency and equity aspects of the policy.

In recent years, stimulated by hosting the Olympics in 2004, public transport has improved, with a large expansion of the metro system. Only with a more integrated transport system and tougher controls on emissions can Athens' serious pollution be significantly reduced.

---

buses, open up new routes and operate a low-fare policy, these services might encourage people to switch from using their cars.

To be effective, this would have to be an attractive alternative. Many people would switch only if the buses were frequent, cheap, comfortable and reliable, and if there were enough routes to take people close to where they wanted to go.

 What other types of transport could be directly provided by the government or a local authority?

A policy that has proved popular with many local authorities is to adopt park-and-ride schemes. Here the authority provides free or cheap out-of-town parking and cheap bus services from the car park to the town centre. These schemes are likely to be most effective when used in combination with charges for private cars entering the inner city.

Regulation and legislation

An alternative strategy is to restrict car use by various forms of regulation and legislation.

Restricting car access

One approach involves reducing car access to areas that are subject to high levels of congestion. The following measures are widely used: bus and cycle lanes, 'high occupancy vehicle lanes' (confined to cars with two or more occupants), pedestrian-only areas and no entry to side streets from main roads.

There is a serious problem, however, with these measures. They tend not to solve the problem of congestion, but merely to divert it. Bus lanes tend to make the car lanes more congested; no entry to side streets tends to make the main roads more congested; and pedestrian-only areas often make the roads round these areas more congested, with drivers adopting side streets as 'rat-runs'.

Parking restrictions

An alternative to restricting road access is to restrict parking. If cars are not allowed to park along congested streets, this will improve the traffic flow. Also, if parking is difficult, this will discourage people from using their cars to come into city centres.

Apart from being unpopular with people who want to park, there are some serious drawbacks with parking restrictions:

- People may well 'park in orbit', driving round and round looking for a parking space, and in the meantime adding to congestion.
- People may park illegally. This may add to rather than reduce congestion, and may create a safety hazard.
- People may feel forced to park down side streets in residential areas, thereby causing a nuisance for residents.

TC 5 p50

Changing market signals

The solution favoured by many economists is to use the price mechanism. As we have seen, one of the causes of traffic congestion is that road users do not pay the full marginal social costs of using the roads. If they could be forced to do so, a social optimum usage of road space could be achieved.

In Figure 12.6 (page 360) this would involve imposing a charge on motorists of *d–c*. By 'internalising' the congestion and environmental externalities in this way, traffic flow will be reduced to the social optimum of Q$_2$.

So how can these external costs be charged to the motorist? There are several possible ways.

Extending existing taxes

Three major types of tax are levied on the motorist: fuel tax, taxes on new cars and car licences. Could increasing these taxes lead to the optimum level of road use being achieved?

Increasing the rates of new car tax and car licences may have *some* effect on reducing the total level of car ownership, but will probably have little effect on car use. The problem is that these taxes do not increase the *marginal* cost of car use. They are fixed costs. Once you have paid these taxes, there is no extra to pay for each extra journey you make. They do not discourage you from using your car.

Unlike the other two, fuel taxes are a marginal cost of car use. The more you use your car, the more fuel you use and the more fuel tax you pay. They are also mildly related to the level of congestion, since fuel consumption tends to increase as congestion increases. Nevertheless, they are not ideal. The problem is that *all* motorists would pay an increase in fuel tax, even those travelling on uncongested roads. To have a significant effect on congestion, there would have to be a very large increase in fuel taxes and this would be very unfair on those who are not causing congestion, especially those who have to travel long distances. Also, as the fuel protests in recent years have shown, increasing fuel taxes could make the government very unpopular.

 Would a tax on car tyres be a good way of restricting car usage?

Introducing new taxes

An alternative to extending existing taxes is to introduce new ones. One that has received much attention in recent times has been the taxing of car parking spaces, particularly those provided by businesses for their employees. The problem with taxing car parking, however, is similar to that of restricting car parking places: people may simply try to park on neighbouring streets, and may spend longer driving around trying to find a space (thereby adding to congestion in the process).

Road pricing

Taxes are inevitably an indirect means of tackling congestion. Charging people for using roads, on the other hand, where the size of the charge reflects the marginal social cost, is a direct means of achieving an efficient use of road space. The higher the congestion, the higher should be the charge. This would encourage people not only to look for alternative means of transport, but also to travel, wherever possible, at off-peak times.

Variable tolls. Tolls are used in many countries, and could be adapted to reflect marginal social costs.

One obvious problem, however, is that, even with automatic tolls, there can be considerable tailbacks from the booths at peak times. Another problem is that they may simply encourage people to use minor roads into cities, thereby causing congestion on these roads. Cities have networks of streets and thus in most cases it is not difficult to avoid the tolls. Finally, if the tolls are charged to people *entering* the city, they will not affect *local* commuters. But it is these short-distance commuters *within* the city who are most likely to be able to find some alternative means of transport (including walking!), and who thus could make a substantial contribution to reducing congestion.

Area charges. One simple and practical means of charging people to use congested streets is the area charge. People would have to pay (normally by the day) for using their car in a city centre. Earlier versions of this scheme involved people having to purchase and display a ticket on their car, rather like a 'pay-and-display' parking system.

More recently, electronic versions have been developed. The London Congestion Charge is an example. Car drivers must pay £8 per day to enter the inner London area (or 'congestion zone') any time between 7.00 and 18.00, Monday to Friday. Payment can be made by various means, including post, Internet, telephone, mobile phone SMS text message and at various shops and petrol stations. Payment can be in advance or up to midnight on the day of travel, or up to midnight the next day for an extra £2. Cars entering the congestion zone have their numberplate recorded by camera and a computer check then leads to a fine of £120 being sent to those who have not paid.

The London congestion charging system has reduced traffic in the zone by nearly 20 per cent and has significantly increased the rate of traffic flow. The charge is not a marginal one, however, in the sense that it does not vary with the degree of congestion or the amount of time spent or distance travelled by a motorist within the zone. This is an intrinsic problem of area charges. Nevertheless, their simplicity makes the system easy to understand and relatively cheap to operate.

In 2007 proposals were drawn up for a 'CO$_2$ charge' to be applied to vehicles in London. Those that emitted the highest levels of CO$_2$ would have faced a daily charge of £25. However, the plans were withdrawn by the incoming

| BOX 12.7 | ROAD PRICING IN SINGAPORE | CASE STUDIES AND APPLICATIONS |

Part of an integrated transport policy

It takes only one hour to drive from one end of Singapore to the other. Yet the average Singaporean driver travels an estimated 18 600 km per year, more than the average US driver, and over 50 per cent more than the average Japanese driver. But despite very high levels of traffic density, Singapore suffers much less than many of its neighbours from traffic congestion. Part of the reason is that it has an integrated transport policy. This includes the following:

- Restricting the number of new car licences, and allowing their price to rise to the corresponding equilibrium. This makes cars in Singapore among the most expensive in the world.

- A 111-kilometre long mass rail transit (MRT) system with subsidised fares. Trains are comfortable, clean and frequent. Stations are air-conditioned.

- A programme of building new estates near MRT stations.

- Cheap, frequent buses, serving all parts of the island.

- A modest expansion of expressways.

But it is in respect to road usage that the Singaporean authorities have been most innovative.

The first innovation came in 1975. The city centre was made a restricted zone. Motorists who wished to enter this zone had to buy a ticket (an 'area licence') at any one of 33 entry points. Police were stationed at these entry points to check that cars had paid and displayed.

Then in 1990 a quota system for new cars was established. The government decides the total number of cars that the country should have, and issues just enough licences each month to maintain that total. These licences (or 'Certificates of Entitlement') are for ten years and are offered at auction. Their market price varies from around £10 000 to £30 000.

A problem with the licences is that they are a once-and-for-all payment, which does not vary with the amount that people use their car. In other words, their marginal cost (for additional miles driven) is zero. Many people feel that,

having paid such a high price for their licence, they ought to use their car as much as possible in order to get value for money!

With traffic congestion steadily worsening, it was recognised that something more had to be done. Either the Area Licensing Scheme had to be widened, or some other form of charging had to be adopted. The decision was taken to introduce electronic road pricing (ERP). This alternative would not only save on police labour costs, but enable charge rates to be varied according to levels of congestion, times of the day, and locality.

Since 1998 all vehicles in Singapore have been fitted with an in-vehicle unit (IU). Every journey made requires the driver to insert a smart card containing pre-paid units into the IU. On specified roads, overhead gantries read the IU and deduct the appropriate charge from the card. If a car does not have sufficient funds on its smart card, the car's details are relayed to a control centre and a fine is imposed. The system has the benefit of operating on three-lane highways and does not require traffic to slow down.

The ERP system operates on roads subject to congestion and charges can vary every 5 or 20 minutes according to predicted traffic flows. Rates are published in advance but are reviewed every three months. The system is thus very flexible to allow traffic to be kept at the desired level.

The system was expensive to set up, however. Cheaper schemes have been adopted elsewhere, for example in Norway and parts of the USA. These operate by funnelling traffic into a single lane in order to register the car, but they have the disadvantage of slowing the traffic down.

One message is clear from the Singapore solution. Road pricing alone is not enough. Unless there are fast, comfortable and affordable public transport alternatives, the demand for cars will be highly price inelastic. People have to get to work!

 Explain how, by varying the charge debited from the smart card according to the time of day or level of congestion, a socially optimal level of road use can be achieved.

---

mayor, Boris Johnson, following his election in May 2008. Environmental campaigners were outspoken in their criticisms, seeing this as a missed opportunity.

Variable electronic road pricing. The scheme most favoured by many economists and traffic planners is that of variable electronic road pricing. It is the scheme that can most directly relate the price that the motorist is charged to the specific level of marginal social cost. The greater the congestion, the greater the charge imposed on the motorist. Ideally, the charge would be equal to the marginal congestion cost plus any marginal environmental costs additional to those created on non-charged roads.

Various systems have been adopted in various parts of the world, or are under consideration. One involves devices in the road which record the numberplates of cars as

they pass. Alternatively, cars may be required to be fitted with sensors. Charges are registered to cars on a central computer. Each car owner then receives a bill at regular intervals, in much the same way as with telephone bills. Several cities around the world, including Barcelona, Dallas, Orlando, Lisbon, Oklahoma City and Oslo, are already operating such schemes.

Another system involves having a device installed in the car into which a 'smart card' (like a telephone or photo-copying card) is inserted. The cards have to be purchased and contain a certain number of units. Beacons or over-head gantries automatically deduct units from the smart cards at times of congestion. If the card is empty, the number of the car is recorded and the driver fined. Such a system was introduced in 1997 on Stockholm's ring road, and in 1998 in Singapore (see Box 12.7).

With both these systems, the rate can easily be varied electronically according to the level of congestion (and pollution). The rates could be in bands and the current bands displayed by the roadside and/or broadcast on local radio so that motorists knew what they were being charged.

The most sophisticated scheme, still under development, involves equipping all vehicles with a receiver. Their position is located by satellites, which then send this information to a dashboard unit, which deducts charges according to location, distance travelled, time of day and type of vehicle. The charges can operate through either smart cards or central computerised billing. It is likely that such schemes would initially be confined to lorries.

Despite the enthusiasm for such schemes amongst economists, there are nevertheless various problems associated with them:

- Estimates of the level of external costs are difficult to make.
- Motorists have to be informed in advance what the charges will be, so that they can plan the timing of their journeys.
- There may be political resistance. Politicians may therefore be reluctant to introduce road pricing for fear of losing popular support.
- If demand is relatively inelastic, the charges might have to be very high to have a significant effect on congestion.
- The costs of installing road-pricing equipment could be very high.
- If road pricing were introduced only in certain areas, shoppers and businesses would tend to move to areas without the charge.
- A new industry in electronic evasion may spring up!

Subsidising alternative means of transport

An alternative to charging for the use of cars is to subsidise the price of alternatives, such as buses and trains. But cheaper fares alone may not be enough. The government may also have to invest directly in or subsidise an *improved* public transport service: more frequent services, more routes, more comfortable buses and trains.

Subsidising public transport need not be seen as an alternative to road pricing: it can be seen as complementary. If road pricing is to persuade people not to travel by car, the alternatives must be attractive. Unless public transport is seen by the traveller as a close substitute for cars, the elasticity of demand for car use is likely to remain low. This problem is recognised by the UK government, which in the 2000 Transport Act encourages local authorities to use various forms of road pricing and charges on businesses for employee car parking spaces (the Workplace Parking Levy) on condition that the revenues generated are ploughed back into improved public transport. All local authorities have had to produce five-year Local Transport Plans covering all forms of transport. These include targets for traffic reduction and increases in the use of public transport.

Subsidising public transport can also be justified on grounds of equity. It benefits poorer members of society who cannot afford to travel by car.

 Which is preferable: general subsidies for public transport, or cheap fare policies for specific groups (such as children, students and pensioners)?

Conclusions

It is unlikely that any one policy can provide the complete solution. Certain policies or mixes of policies are better suited to some situations than others. It is important for governments to learn from experiences both within their own country and in others, in order to find the optimum solution to each specific problem.

Section summary

1. There are various types of solution to traffic congestion. These include direct provision by the government or local authorities (of additional road space or better public transport); regulation and legislation (such as restricting car access – by the use of bus and cycle lanes, no entry to side streets and pedestrian-only areas – and various forms of parking restrictions); changing market signals (by the use of taxes, by road pricing, and by subsidising alternative means of transport).

2. Problems associated with building additional roads include the decline of public transport, attracting additional traffic on to the roads, and environmental costs.

3. The main problem with restricting car access is that it tends merely to divert congestion elsewhere. The main problem with parking restrictions is that they may actually increase congestion.

4. Increasing taxes is effective in reducing congestion only if it increases the marginal cost of motoring. Even when it does, as in the case of additional fuel tax, the additional cost is only indirectly related to congestion costs, since it applies to all motorists and not just those causing congestion.

5. Road pricing is the preferred solution of many economists. By the use of electronic devices, motorists can be charged whenever they add to congestion. This should encourage less essential road users to travel at off-peak times or to use alternative modes of transport, while those who gain a high utility from car transport can still use their cars, but at a price. Variable tolls and area charges are alternative forms of congestion pricing, but are generally less effective than the use of variable electronic road pricing.

6. If road pricing is to be effective, there must be attractive substitutes available. A comprehensive policy, therefore, should include subsidising efficient public transport. The revenues required for this could be obtained from road pricing.

END OF CHAPTER QUESTIONS

1. Assume that as traffic density increases along a given stretch of road, there comes a point when traffic begins to slow down. The following table gives the times taken for a car to travel the stretch of road (in minutes) according to the number of cars entering the road per minute.

Cars entering the road	5	6	7	8	9	10	11
Journey time		10	10	11	13	16	22	30

   (a) Copy out the table and add the following rows: (i) total journey time for all cars; (ii) extra journey time as traffic increases by one more car (marginal social time cost); (iii) additional time cost imposed on other road users for each additional car entering the road (marginal external time cost). (See Table 12.4.)

   (b) Assume that time is valued at 10p per minute. On a graph, plot the marginal private time cost (journey time) and the marginal social time cost.

   (c) Assume that electronic road pricing is introduced. What charge should be levied when traffic density reaches (i) 6 cars per minute; (ii) 8 cars per minute; (iii) 11 cars per minute?

   (d) What additional information would you need in order to work out the socially efficient traffic density on this particular stretch of road?

2. Assume that there are several chemical firms in an industry, each one producing different levels of an effluent, whose damage to the environment depends on the location of the firm. Compare the relative merits of using green taxes, tradable permits and controls as means of achieving the socially optimum levels of effluent from these firms.

3. Make out a case from a deep green perspective for rejecting the 'social efficiency' approach to the environment.

4. Why might efforts to address the issue of global warming be hampered by a lack of understanding of probability amongst the general public?

5. The USA is the world's largest emitter of CO_2, and China is the second largest. What issues arise from this in the formulation of a global policy to reduce CO_2 emissions?

6. Make out a case for adopting a policy of individual tradable carbon permits, allocated to all citizens within a country. Could such a policy be extended globally?

7. Compare the relative merits of increased road fuel taxes, electronic road pricing and tolls as means of reducing urban traffic congestion. Why is the price inelasticity of demand for private car transport a problem here, whichever of the three policies is adopted? What could be done to increase the price elasticity of demand?

8. Why is the price inelasticity of demand for private car transport a problem when formulating a policy for the reduction of traffic congestion? What could be done to change the price elasticity of demand in a desirable direction?

9. How would you set about measuring the external costs of road transport?

10. From 1 April 2008, the UK government introduced free off-peak bus travel for the over-60s in England and Wales. What is the likely impact of this policy on car usage? Is there a case for extending the policy to (a) bus travel for pensioners at all times of the day, as is the case in Scotland; (b) bus travel for all?

Online resources

Additional case studies in MyEconLab

12.1 **Perverse subsidies**. An examination of the use of subsidies around the world that are harmful to the environment.

12.2 **Selling the environment**. This looks at the proposals made at international climate conferences to use market-based solutions to global warming.

12.3 **Environmental auditing**. Are businesses becoming greener? A growing number of firms are subjecting themselves to an 'environmental audit' to judge just how 'green' they are.

12.4 **Evaluating new road schemes**. The system used in the UK of assessing the costs and benefits of proposed new roads.

Websites relevant to this chapter

See sites listed at the end of Chapter 13 on page 384.

Government Policy towards Business

CHAPTER MAP

13.1 Competition policy   **368**
Competition, monopoly and the public interest   368
The targets of competition policy   368
Oligopolistic collusion: restrictive practice policy   369
Competition policy in the European Union   369
UK competition policy   370
Assessment of competition policy   373

13.2 Privatisation and regulation   **375**
Nationalisation and privatisation   375
How desirable is privatisation?   375
Regulation: identifying the short-run optimum
  price and output   377
Regulation: identifying the long-run optimum
  price and output   378
Regulation in the UK   378
Increasing competition in the privatised
  industries   382

In this chapter we continue our examination of government policy to tackle market imperfections. The focus here is on the problem of market power. We examine various policies the government or its agencies can use to prevent firms abusing a monopolistic or oligopolistic position.

In section 13.1 we examine 'competition policy'. We will see that the targets of such policy include the abuse of monopoly power, the problem of oligopolistic collusion, and mergers that will result in the firm having a dominant position in the market.

Then in section 13.2, we look at privatisation and the extent to which privatised industries should be regulated to prevent them abusing their market power. We also consider whether it is possible to introduce enough competition into these industries to make regulation unnecessary.

The relationship between government and business is always likely to be complex. Governments face the twin pressures of having to ensure consumer protection while needing a dynamic and profitable business environment that will ensure high levels of employment, output and growth. In this chapter we see the conflicts that can arise as a consequence.

13.1 COMPETITION POLICY

Competition, monopoly and the public interest

Most markets in the real world are imperfect, with firms having varying degrees of market power. But will this power be against the public interest? This question has been addressed by successive governments in framing legislation to deal with monopolies and oligopolies.

It might be thought that market power is always 'a bad thing', certainly as far as the consumer is concerned. After all, it enables firms to make supernormal profit, thereby 'exploiting' the consumer. The greater the firm's power, the higher will prices be relative to the costs of production. Also, a lack of competition removes the incentive to become more efficient.

But market power is not necessarily a bad thing. Firms may not fully exploit their position of power – perhaps for fear that very high profits would eventually lead to other firms overcoming entry barriers, or perhaps because they are not aggressive profit maximisers. Even if they do make large supernormal profits, they may still charge a lower price than more competitive sectors of the industry because of their economies of scale. Finally, they may use their profits for research and development and for capital investment. The consumer might then benefit from new or improved products at lower prices.

Competition policy could seek to ban various *structures*. For example, it could ban mergers leading to market share of more than a certain amount. Most countries, however, prefer to focus on whether the *practices* of particular monopolists or oligopolists are anti-competitive. Some of these practices may be made illegal, such as price fixing by oligopolists; others may be assessed on a case-by-case basis to determine whether or not they should be permitted. Such an approach does not presume that the mere *possession* of power is against the public interest, but rather that certain uses of that power may be.

 Try to formulate a definition of 'the public interest'.

The targets of competition policy

There are three possible targets of competition policy.

Abuse of the existing power of monopolies and oligopolies: monopoly policy

Monopoly policy seeks to prevent firms from abusing their economic power. Although it is referred to as 'monopoly' policy, it also applies to many large oligopolists acting on their own. The approach has been to weigh up the gains and losses to the public of individual firms' behaviour.

As we saw in Figure 6.10 (on page 176), faced with the same cost curves as an industry under perfect competition, a monopoly will charge a higher price, produce a lower output and make a larger profit. On the other hand, a monopolist may achieve substantial economies of scale, with the result that its price is *below* the competitive price (see Figure 6.11 on page 178). It may also use a proportion of its profits for investment and for research and development (R&D). This may result in better products and/or lower prices.

Thus the government (or regulatory authority, if separate from the government) has to work out, if it insisted on a reduction in price, whether R&D and other investment would thereby suffer, and whether the consumer would lose in the long run.

The growth of power through mergers and acquisitions: merger policy

The aim of merger policy is to monitor mergers and prevent those that are considered to be against the public interest. The gains and losses to the public must be weighed up, and the authorities must then decide whether or not a prospective merger should be allowed to proceed.

On the plus side, the merged firms may be able to *rationalise*. Horizontal mergers in particular may allow economies of scale to be gained. It may be possible to concentrate production on fewer sites, with a more intensive utilisation of capital and labour. Also, a more efficient use may be made of transport fleets, with distribution in greater bulk. Savings may be made in warehousing costs too.

There may also be some scope for rationalisation with vertical mergers. It may be possible to concentrate various stages in the production process on one site, with consequent savings in transport and handling costs.

Then there are cost savings that apply to all types of merger: horizontal, vertical and conglomerate. One of two head offices may be closed down. Greater financial strength may allow the merged firm to drive down the prices charged by its suppliers. The combined profits may allow larger-scale investment and R&D. Finally, if two relatively small firms merge, their increased market power may allow them to compete more effectively against large firms.

On the negative side, mergers lead to a greater concentration of economic power, which could be used against the consumer's interests. This is particularly true of horizontal mergers, which will result in fewer firms for the consumer to choose from. But even conglomerate mergers can lead to certain anti-competitive activities. In particular, a conglomerate can use large profits gained in one market where it already has monopoly power to *cross-subsidise* prices in a competitive market, thereby driving out competitors.

What are the possible disadvantages of vertical mergers?

What is more, rationalisation may lead to redundancies. While this may be a potential Pareto gain, it is unlikely that the redundant will be fully compensated by the gainers.

In deciding how tough to be with mergers, the government must consider how this will affect firms' behaviour. If the government has a liberal policy towards mergers, the competition for ownership and control of other companies may force firms to be more efficient. If the managers of a firm are afraid that it will be taken over, they will need to ensure that the firm is economically strong and that it is perceived by shareholders to be more profitable than it would be under alternative ownership. This competition for corporate control (see pages 178–9) may lead to lower costs and thereby benefit the consumer. It may, however, make firms even more keen to exploit any monopoly power they have, either in their battle for other firms, or in the battle to persuade shareholders not to vote for being taken over.

Government policy towards this market for corporate control will need to ensure that mergers and the possibility of mergers encourage competition rather than reducing it.

Oligopolistic collusion: restrictive practice policy

In most countries, the approach towards cases of oligopolistic collusion, known as **restrictive practices**, tends to be tougher. After all, the firms are combining to exploit their joint power to make bigger profits. They could do this by jointly trying to keep out new entrants; or they could agree to keep prices high and/or restrict output; or they could divide up the market between them, agreeing not to 'poach' on each other's territory. For example, two or more supermarket chains could agree to open only one supermarket in each district.

Banning formal cartels is easy. Preventing tacit collusion is another matter. It may be very difficult to prove that firms are making informal agreements behind closed doors.

Competition policy in the European Union

Relevant EU legislation is contained in Articles 81 and 82 of the Amsterdam Treaty and in additional regulations

covering mergers, which came into force in 1990 and were amended in 2004.

Article 81 is concerned with restrictive practices and Article 82 with the abuse of market power. The articles mainly concern firms trading between EU members and do not cover monopolies or oligopolies operating solely within a member country. The policy is implemented by the European Commission. If any firm appears to be breaking the provisions of either article, the Commission can refer it to the European Court of Justice.

EU restrictive practices policy

Article 81 covers *agreements* between firms, *joint decisions*, and concerted *practices* that prevent, restrict or distort competition. In other words, it covers all types of oligopolistic collusion that are against the interests of consumers.

Article 81 is designed to prevent not oligopolistic *structures* (i.e. the simple existence of co-operation between firms), but rather collusive *behaviour*. No matter what form collusion takes, if the European Commission finds that firms are committing anti-competitive *practices*, they will be banned from doing so and possibly fined (up to 10 per cent of annual turnover), although firms do have the right of appeal to the European Court of Justice.

Practices considered anti-competitive include firms colluding to do any of the following:

- Fix prices (i.e. above competitive levels).
- Limit production, markets, technical development or investment.
- Share out markets or sources of supply.
- Charge discriminatory prices or operate discriminatory trading conditions, such as to benefit the colluding parties and disadvantage others.
- Make other firms that sign contracts with any of the colluding firms accept unfavourable obligations which, by their nature, have no connection with the subject of such contracts.

In recent years, the Commission has adopted a tough stance and has fined many firms. Case Study 6.4 in MyEconLab looks at the case of Microsoft, a firm whose abuse of its monopoly position has been the subject of ongoing investigations by both the US and EU authorities.

EU monopoly policy

Article 82 relates to the abuse of market power and has also been extended to cover mergers. As with Article 81, it is the *behaviour* of firms that is the target of the legislation. The following are cited as examples of the abuse of market power. As you can see, they are very similar to those in Article 81.

- Charging unfairly high prices to consumers, or paying unfairly low prices to suppliers.
- Limiting production, markets or technical developments to the detriment of consumers.

Definitions

Cross-subsidise To use profits in one market to subsidise prices in another.

Restrictive practices Where two or more firms agree to adopt common practices to restrict competition.

- Using price discrimination or other discriminatory practices to the detriment of certain parties.
- Making other firms that sign contracts accept unfavourable obligations which, by their nature, have no connection with the subject of such contracts.

Under Article 82, such practices can be banned and firms can be fined where they are found to have abused a dominant position. A firm need not have some specified minimum market share before Article 82 can be invoked. Instead, if firms are able to conduct anti-competitive practices, it is simply assumed that they must be in a position of market power. This approach is sensible, given the difficulties of identifying the boundaries of a market, either in terms of geography or in terms of type of product.

EU merger policy

The 1990 merger control measures tightened up the legislation in Article 82. They cover mergers where combined worldwide annual sales exceed €5 billion; where EU sales of at least two of the companies exceed €250 million; and where at least one of the companies conducts no more than two-thirds of its EU-wide business in a single member state.

Relevant mergers must be notified to the Commission, which must then conduct preliminary investigations (Phase 1). A decision must then be made, normally within 25 working days, whether to conduct a formal investigation (Phase 2) or to let the merger proceed. A formal investigation must normally be completed within a further 90 working days (or 110 days in complex cases).

The process of EU merger control is thus very rapid and administratively inexpensive. The regulations are also potentially quite tough. Mergers are disallowed if they result in 'a concentration which would significantly impede effective competition, in particular by the creation or strengthening of a dominant position'.

But the regulations are also flexible, since they recognise that mergers *may* be in the interests of consumers if they result in cost reductions. In such cases they are permitted.

The merger investigation process is now overseen by a Chief Competition Economist and a panel which scrutinises the investigating team's conclusions. One concern of this panel is that the Commission, in being willing to show flexibility, is not too easily persuaded by firms so that it imposes conditions that are too lax and that rely too much on the firms' co-operation. Indeed, in the first 19 years of the merger control measures, 3917 mergers were notified, but only 185 proceeded to Phase 2 and only 20 were prohibited. In many cases (too many, claim critics), the Commission accepted the undertakings of firms.

There is considerable disagreement in the EU between those who want to encourage competition *within* the EU and those who want to see European companies being world leaders. For them, the ability to compete in *world* markets normally requires that companies are large, which may well imply having monopoly power within the EU.

 To what extent is Article 82 consistent with both these points of view?

UK competition policy

There have been substantial changes to UK competition policy since the first legislation was introduced in 1948. The current approach is based on the 1998 Competition Act and the 2002 Enterprise Act.

The Competition Act brought UK policy in line with EU policy, detailed above. The Act has two key sets (or 'chapters') of prohibitions. Chapter I prohibits various restrictive practices, and mirrors EU Article 81. Chapter II prohibits various abuses of monopoly power, and mirrors Article 82. The Enterprise Act strengthened the Competition Act and introduced new measures for the control of mergers.

Under the two Acts, the body charged with ensuring that the prohibitions are carried out is the Office of Fair Trading (OFT). The OFT can investigate any firms suspected of engaging in one or more of the prohibited practices. Its officers have the power to enter and search premises, and can require the production and explanation of documents. Where the OFT decides that an infringement of one of the prohibitions has occurred, it can direct the offending firms to modify their behaviour or cease their practices altogether. Companies in breach of a prohibition are liable to fines of up to 10 per cent of their annual UK turnover. Third parties adversely affected by such breaches can seek compensation through the courts.

The Competition Act also set up a Competition Commission (CC) to which the OFT can refer cases for further investigation. The CC is charged with determining whether the structure of an industry or the practices of firms within it are detrimental to competition.

If a case is referred to the Competition Commission, the CC will carry out an investigation to establish whether competition is adversely affected. If it finds that it is, it will decide on the appropriate remedies, such as prohibiting various practices.

UK restrictive practices policy

Under the 2002 Enterprise Act, it is a *criminal* offence to engage in cartel agreements (i.e. horizontal, rather than vertical, collusive agreements between firms), irrespective of whether there are appreciable effects on competition. Convicted offenders may receive a prison sentence of up to five years and/or an unlimited fine. Prosecutions may be brought by the Serious Fraud Office or the OFT. Under the Act, the OFT can enter premises, seize documents and require people to answer questions or provide information.

But what practices constitute 'cartel agreements'? These involve one or more of the following agreements by firms: price fixing; limiting supply, perhaps by each firm agreeing to an output quota; sharing out markets by geographical area, type or size of customer or nature of outlet (e.g. bus

| BOX 13.1 | A LIFT TO PROFITS? | | CASE STUDIES AND APPLICATIONS |

Record EU fine for operating a lift and escalator cartel

As we have seen, EU competition policy applies to companies operating in two or more EU countries. The policy is implemented by the European Commission and it has the power to levy substantial fines on companies found to be in breach of the legislation.

In February 2007, the Commission imposed a record fine of €992 million on four lift and escalator manufacturers for operating a price-fixing cartel. According to the EU Commission, the companies – ThyssenKrupp of Germany, Otis of the USA, Kone of Finland and Schindler of Switzerland – sought to freeze market share and fix prices. 'Projects that were rigged included lifts and escalators for hospitals, railway stations, shopping centres and commercial buildings.'[1]

The Commission last year passed new fining guidelines that will allow Brussels to further increase the financial pain on abusive companies in all new cases. Officials have argued that the new rules will mean that more companies will be hit with the maximum penalty – a fine equivalent to 10 per cent of their annual global turnover.

The lift cartel operated in Germany, the Netherlands, Belgium and Luxembourg between at least 1995 and 2004. According to the Commission, the groups co-ordinated their bids to ensure that a designated group would win specific contracts.

'[To agree on bids] they usually met in bars and restaurants, they travelled to the countryside or even abroad, and they used pre-paid mobile cards to avoid tracking,' the Commission said.[2]

According to Jonathan Todd of the EU, 'the result of this cartel is that taxpayers, public authorities and property developers have been ripped off big time. These companies ensured that, by rigging the bids [i.e. collusive tendering] and sharing the markets, the prices paid both for the installation and the maintenance were way above what they would have been if there had been a competitive market.'[3]

Neelie Kroes, the EU Competition Commissioner, said that 'the national management of these companies knew what they were doing was wrong, but they tried to conceal their action and went ahead anyway. The damage caused by this cartel will last for many years because it covered not only the initial supply but also the subsequent maintenance of lifts and escalators.'[4]

Of the four companies, ThyssenKrupp was given the largest fine (€480 million), and the biggest ever for a single company, because it was a 'repeat offender'. It had received a previous fine of €3.2 million in 1998 for fixing stainless steel prices. Under guidelines issued in 2006, repeat offenders face an automatic 50 per cent increase in fines.

 What factors determine the likelihood that firms will collude to fix prices – despite the prospect of facing fines of up to 10 per cent of their annual global turnover?

[1] Europa Press release, http://europa.eu/rapid/pressReleasesAction.do?reference=IP/07/209.
[2] 'Brussels imposes €992m fine on lift cartel', *Financial Times*, 22 February 2007.
[3] 'Record EU fine for lift "cartel"', http://news.bbc.co.uk/1/hi/business/6383913.stm.
[4] *Ibid.*

---

companies agreeing not to run services in each other's areas); *collusive tendering* for a contract, where two or more firms put in a tender at secretly agreed (high) prices; or agreements between purchasers (e.g. supermarkets) to keep down prices paid to suppliers (e.g. farmers).

 Are all such agreements necessarily against the interests of consumers?

In the case of other types of agreement, the OFT has the discretion to decide, on a case-by-case basis, whether or not competition is appreciably restricted, and whether, therefore, they should be terminated or the firms should be exempted. Such cases include the following:

- Vertical price-fixing agreements. These are price agreements between purchasing firms and their suppliers. An example of this is *resale price maintenance*. This is where a manufacturer or distributor sets the price for

retailers to charge. It may well distribute a price list to retailers (e.g. a car manufacturer may distribute a price list to car showrooms). Resale price maintenance is a way of preventing competition between retailers driving down retail prices and ultimately the price they pay to the manufacturer. Both manufacturers and retailers, therefore, are likely to gain from resale price maintenance.

Definitions

Collusive tendering Where two or more firms secretly agree on the prices they will tender for a contract. These prices will be above those that would be put in under a genuinely competitive tendering process.

Resale (or retail) price maintenance Where the manufacturer of a product (legally) insists that the product should be sold at a specified retail price.

BOX 13.2   **MORE THAN A COINCIDENCE?**   **CASE STUDIES AND APPLICATIONS**

School fees in the UK

In November 2005 the Office of Fair Trading announced that 50 independent schools had been found guilty of operating a fee-fixing cartel. The OFT found that schools had exchanged details of their planned fee increases between 2001 and 2004, in direct contravention of the 1998 Competition Act. Bursars of all the schools had participated in an annual round-robin message and the OFT found that 'this regular and systematic exchange of confidential information was anti-competitive and resulted in parents being charged higher fees than would otherwise have been the case'.

The investigation took nearly two years and uncovered evidence which showed that schools routinely exchanged both cost and pricing information when preparing fee recommendations to governors. One email, sent with details of over 20 competitor schools' proposed fee increases, contained the message 'Confidential please, so we aren't accused of being a cartel'.

Coincidence or cartel?

Having been found guilty, the schools could have faced large fines, totalling 10 per cent of their turnover. However, for the first time in a case of this nature the OFT negotiated a final settlement, allowing schools to pay a nominal penalty of £10 000 per school and to set up a charitable trust fund, to total £3 million, for the benefit of those who had been pupils at the relevant time.

The schools also had to admit that their participation in the exchange of information distorted competition. However, stepping back from their initial judgement, the OFT did not make any finding about the *effect* of the cartel. This final ruling acknowledged the schools' adamant defence that the sharing of information had not resulted in higher fees; indeed some of the schools involved maintained that the exchange of information resulted in *lower* rather than higher fees.

If this argument is plausible, then what could explain the fact that independent schools' fees rose by almost identical amounts each year? The answer lies in their cost structure; the major input to schools is labour, and wage inflation for teachers will be determined by salaries offered in the (much larger) state sector. In addition, the top schools are likely to have very similar staff/student ratios. The result is that all the independent schools are likely to face very similar increases in wage costs; the schools claimed that this was the cause of the very similar increases in fees. In fact they went further and claimed that sharing good practice actually maximised operational efficiencies, something that is explicitly encouraged by the Charity Commission.

Charitable status

Government scrutiny of independent schools did not end with the OFT investigation. In 2006 the Charities Act was passed and under this Act various organisations, including independent schools and hospitals, lost their automatic right to charitable status. They now have to prove that 'people in poverty' benefit from their services even if they cannot afford their fees. The loss of charitable status would cost the schools £100 million a year in lost tax breaks.

In January 2008 the Charity Commission produced a landmark document which contained a series of recommendations for independent schools. Guidelines were designed to enable the schools to meet the 'public benefit' test to allow them to hold onto their charitable status. Amongst the proposals were suggestions that schools should offer bursaries to fund pupils from low-income households and that they should share facilities and staff with local state schools. In the guidance the Commission suggested that schools should still be able to charge 'reasonable and necessary' fees, but suggested that those keeping fees to a minimum would be more likely to benefit the public.

 What costs, other than wages, would independent schools face? Would these costs support the schools' claim that identical fee increases are driven by identical costs, rather than by collusion?

- Agreements to exchange information that could have the effect of reducing competition. For example, if producers exchange information on their price intentions, it is a way of allowing price leadership, a form of tacit collusion, to continue.

 What problems are likely to arise in identifying which firms' practices are anti-competitive? Should the OFT take firms' assurances into account when deciding whether to grant an exemption?

UK monopoly policy

Under the Chapter II prohibition of the 1998 Competition Act, it is illegal for a dominant firm to exercise its market power in such a way as to reduce competition. Any sus-pected case is investigated by the OFT, which uses a two-stage process in deciding whether an abuse has taken place.

The first stage is to establish whether a firm has a position of dominance. The firm does not literally have to be a monopoly. 'Dominance' normally involves the firm having at least a 40 per cent share of the market (national or local, whichever is appropriate), although this figure will vary from industry to industry. Also, dominance depends on the barriers to entry to new competitors. The higher the barriers to the entry of new firms, the less contestable will be the market (see pages 179–83), and the more dominant a firm is likely to be for any given current market share.

If the firm *is* deemed to be dominant, the second stage involves the OFT deciding whether the firm's practices constitute an abuse of its position. As with restrictive practices,

Chapter II follows EU legislation. It specifies the same four types of market abuse as does EU Article 82 (see above). Within these four categories, the OFT identifies the following practices as being overtly anti-competitive:

- Charging excessively high prices. These are prices above those that the firm would charge if it faced effective competition. One sign of excessively high prices is abnormally high rates of profit.
- Price discrimination. This is regarded as an abuse only to the extent that the higher prices are excessive or the lower prices are used to exclude competitors.
- Predatory pricing. This is where prices are set at loss-making levels, so as to drive competitors out of business (see page 210). The test is to look at the dominant firm's price in relation to its average costs. If its price is below average variable cost, predation would be assumed. If its price is above average variable cost, but below average total cost, then the Director-General would need to establish whether the reason was to eliminate a competitor.
- *Vertical restraints*. This is where a supplying firm imposes conditions on a purchasing firm (or vice versa). For example, a manufacturer may impose rules on retailers about displaying the product or the provision of after-sales service, or it may refuse to supply certain outlets (as with perfume manufacturers refusing to supply discount chains such as Superdrug). Another example is *tie-in sales*. This is where a firm controlling the supply of a first product insists that its customers buy a second product from it rather than from its rivals.

The simple *existence* of any of these practices may not constitute an abuse. The OFT has to decide whether their *effect* is to restrict competition. If the case is not straightforward, the OFT can refer it to the Competition Commission (CC). The CC will then carry out a detailed investigation to establish whether competition is restricted or distorted. If it is, the CC will rule what actions must be taken to remedy the situation.

UK merger policy

Merger policy is covered by the 2002 Enterprise Act. It seeks to prevent mergers that are likely to result in a substantial lessening of competition.

A merger or takeover will be investigated by the OFT if the target company has a turnover of £70 million or more,

or if the merger results in the new company having a market share of 25 per cent or more. The OFT conducts a preliminary investigation to see whether competition is likely to be threatened. If it is, and if there is unlikely to be any substantial compensating benefit to consumers, the OFT refers the case to the Competition Commission.

If reference is made to the CC, it conducts a detailed investigation to establish whether the merger is likely to lead to a significant reduction in competition. If so, it can prohibit the merger. Alternatively, it can require the merged firm to behave in certain ways in order to protect consumers' interests. In such cases, the OFT then monitors the firm to ensure that it is abiding by the CC's conditions. CC investigations must normally be completed within 24 weeks.

The 2002 Act tightened up merger legislation. In the past, the vast majority of mergers were not referred to the CC (or its predecessor, the Monopolies and Mergers Commission). Yet studies had shown that mergers were generally *not* in the public interest. Mergers had contributed to a growing degree of market concentration in the UK and few benefits from cost reduction and research had occurred. The 2002 Act sought to rectify this problem.

Between 2005 and 2008 a number of mergers were referred to the CC; these included the merger of Heinz and HP Foods, the purchase of 115 Morrisons stores by Somerfield, and Sky's purchase of a 17.9 per cent stake in ITV.

However, in the autumn of 2008, following the announcement that a merger was proposed between Lloyds TSB and the troubled bank HBOS, the government said that it would overrule any objections raised by the competition authorities. This highlights the fact that governments may sometimes prefer to take a pragmatic view of competition policy, particularly in times of economic crisis.

 If anti-monopoly legislation is effective enough, is there ever any need to prevent mergers from going ahead?

Assessment of competition policy

With UK competition legislation having been brought in line with EU legislation, it is possible to consider the two together.

It is generally agreed by commentators that it is correct for the policy to concentrate on anti-competitive *practices* and their *effects* rather than simply on the existence of agreements or on the size of a firm's market share. After all, economic power is a problem only when it is abused. When, by contrast, it enables firms to achieve economies of scale, or more finance for investment, the result can be of benefit to consumers. In other words, the assumption that structure determines conduct and performance (see

---

Definitions

Vertical restraints Conditions imposed by one firm on another which is either its supplier or its customer.

Tie-in sales Where a firm is only prepared to sell a first product on the condition that its customers buy a second product from it.

BOX 13.3 WHAT PRICE FOR PEACE OF MIND?

Exploiting monopoly power in the sale of extended warranties on electrical goods

If you go into Currys, Comet, PC World or virtually any other high street retailer to buy an electrical good, such as a DVD player, a fridge or a computer, the sales assistant will probably be very keen to sell you an extended warranty (EW). These EWs are typically for three to five years and sometimes merely extend the product's guarantee against breakdown beyond its normal one- or two-year expiry date. Sometimes they go further and provide cover against other risks, such as accidental damage or theft.

These EWs are highly profitable for the retailer. In 2002 they accounted for approximately 40 per cent of Dixons' profits and 80 per cent of Comet's. It's hardly surprising that retailers are very keen to sell them to you!

In 2002 the Office of Fair Trading (OFT) published a report on EWs and concluded that 'there is insufficient competition and information to ensure that consumers get good value, and that many electrical retailers may make considerable profits on the sale of EWs'.

> Research conducted by the OFT indicates that customers can feel pressurised to rush to a decision to buy an extended warranty when they buy their new appliance. A high percentage of consumers had not thought about buying an extended warranty before they arrive at the store.
>
> Buyers should think whether extended warranties offer them value for money. OFT research found that the average washing machine repair costs between £45 to £65. So if a five-year extended warranty costs £150 on a £300 washing machine, it would need to break down four times for a consumer to benefit.
>
> A recent *Which?* report highlights that modern domestic appliances are generally reliable. It found that 81 per cent of washing machines didn't break down at all in the first six years. . . .
>
> Some sales staff are paid commission on each extended warranty they sell, so may be keen for a customer to sign on the dotted line.[1]

The OFT was concerned that retailers were using their market power at the point of sale and benefiting from consumers' ignorance. It decided, therefore, to refer the case to the Competition Commission (CC), which published its report in December 2003.

The CC report found that there was a 'complex monopoly'[2] in the market, worth £900 million per year,

which was working against the public interest. It concluded that there had been an abuse of monopoly power, stating:

> Were this market fully competitive such that the top five EW retailers' returns were no greater than their cost of capital,[3] we estimate that EW prices would have been, on average, up to one-third lower. . . .
>
> Many of the practices that we have identified during the course of our investigation operate or may be expected to operate against the public interest. They result in lack of choice, excessive prices, insufficient information, insufficient competition at point of sale, limited but not insignificant sales pressure, some terms which could be disadvantageous, and lack of information about the scope of protection under service-backed schemes.[4]

Despite these findings, the Competition Commission did not recommend banning shops from bundling warranties with electrical goods at the point of sale, despite many of the EWs being 'unfair and uncompetitive'. Instead, it recommended that retailers should display prices for EWs alongside the price of the goods, both in shops and in advertisements. It also recommended that the shops should provide information about customers' rights and that customers should get a full refund on the EW if they cancelled within 45 days.

The government minister, the Secretary of State for Trade and Industry, accepted these findings and ruled that they should be implemented – which they were in April 2005.

1. *What features of the market for EWs distort competition?*
2. *To what extent will the ruling by the government make the market for EWs competitive?*

[1] OFT News Release, PN 68/02, October 2002.

[2] A complex monopoly is where several companies separately (i.e. not collusively) are in a position to exploit a particular market advantage to the detriment of the consumer.

[3] A measure of 'normal profit'.

[4] Summary to *Extended Warranties on Domestic Electrical Goods: A Report on the Supply of Extended Warranties on Domestic Electrical Goods within the UK*, Competition Commission, Dec. 2003 (http://www.competition-commission.org.uk/rep_pub/reports/2003/485xwars.htm summary).

---

page 164) is not necessarily true, and certainly it is not necessarily true that market power is always bad and competitive industries are always good.

Also, most commentators favour the system of certain practices being *prohibited*, with fines applicable to the first offence. This acts as an important deterrent to anti-competitive behaviour.

A problem with any policy to deal with collusion is the difficulty in rooting it out. When firms do all their deals

'behind closed doors' and are careful not to keep records or give clues, then collusion can be very hard to spot. The cases that have come to light, such as that of collusive tendering between firms supplying ready-mixed concrete, may be just the tip of an iceberg.

If two or more firms were charging similar prices, what types of evidence would you look for to prove that this was collusion rather than coincidence?

Section summary

1. Competition policy in most countries recognises that monopolies, mergers and restrictive practices can bring both costs and benefits to the consumer. Generally, though, restrictive practices tend to be more damaging to consumers' interests than simple monopoly power or mergers.

2. European Union legislation applies to firms trading between EU countries. Article 81 applies to restrictive practices. Article 82 applies to dominant firms. There are also separate merger control provisions.

3. UK legislation is covered largely by the 1998 Competition Act and the 2002 Enterprise Act. The Chapter I prohibition of the 1998 Act applies to restrictive practices and is similar to EU Article 81.

The Chapter II prohibition applies to dominant firms and is similar to Article 82. The 2002 Act made certain cartel agreements a criminal offence and required mergers over a certain size to be investigated by the Office of Fair Trading, with possible reference to the Competition Commission. Both the OFT and the CC were made independent of government.

4. The focus of both EU and UK legislation is on anti-competitive practices rather than on the simple existence of agreements between firms or market dominance. Practices that are found after investigation to be detrimental to competition are prohibited and heavy fines can be imposed, even for a first offence.

13.2 PRIVATISATION AND REGULATION

Nationalisation and privatisation

One solution to market failure, advocated by some on the political left, is nationalisation. If industries are not being run in the public interest by the private sector, then bring them into public ownership. This way, so the argument goes, the market failures can be corrected. Problems of monopoly power, externalities, inequality, etc. can be dealt with directly if these industries are run with the public interest, rather than private gain, at heart.

Most nationalisation in the UK took place under the Labour government of 1945–51, when coal, railways, gas and steel were nationalised. The Labour Party at the time saw nationalisation not just as a means of correcting market failures, but as something that was morally desirable. It was seen to be much fairer and less divisive to have a society based on common ownership of the means of production than one where people were divided into separate classes, workers and capitalists. This policy reflected the views of a population which had been through a long and hard war from 1939 to 1945; they were not prepared to return to the unequal society that had survived the end of the First World War and the hard economic times of the 1920s and 1930s.

By the mid 1970s, however, it became increasingly clear that the nationalised industries were inefficient and also a source of much industrial unrest. A change of policy was introduced from the early 1980s, when Conservative governments under Margaret Thatcher and then John Major engaged in an extensive programme of 'privatisation', returning virtually all of the **nationalised industries**, including telecommunications, gas, water, steel, electricity and the railways, to the private sector. By 1997, the year the Conservatives left office, the only nationalised industry remaining in the UK was the Post Office.

Other countries have followed similar programmes of privatisation in what has become a worldwide phenomenon. Privatisation has been seen by many governments as a means of revitalising inefficient industries and as a golden opportunity to raise revenues to ease budgetary problems.

In 2008, however, many governments returned to the use of nationalisation. This involved the full or part nationalisation of banks which were at risk of going bankrupt. The use of nationalisation in this *macro*economic context of national or international economic crises is examined in section 23.4.

How desirable is privatisation?

Arguments for privatisation

Market forces. The first argument is that privatisation will expose these industries to market forces, from which will flow the benefits of greater efficiency, faster growth and greater responsiveness to the wishes of the consumer. There are three parts to this argument.

- Greater competition in the goods market. If privatisation involves splitting an industry into competing parts (for example, separate power stations competing to sell electricity to different electricity distribution companies), the resulting competition may drive costs and prices down.
- Greater competition for finance. After privatisation a company has to finance investment through the market: it must issue shares or borrow from financial

Definition

Nationalised industries State-owned industries that produce goods or services that are sold in the market.

institutions. In doing so, it will be competing for funds with other companies, and thus must be seen as capable of using these funds profitably.

- Accountability to shareholders. Shareholders want a good return on their shares and will thus put pressure on the privatised company to perform well. If the company does not make sufficient profits, shareholders will sell their shares. The share price will fall and the company will be in danger of being taken over. The market for corporate control thus provides incentives for private firms to be efficient. There has been considerable takeover activity in the water and electricity industries, with most of the 12 regional electricity companies and several of the water companies being taken over, often by non-UK companies.

Reduced government interference. In nationalised industries, managers may frequently be required to adjust their targets for political reasons. At one time they may have to keep prices low as part of a government drive against inflation. At another they may have to raise their prices substantially in order to raise extra revenue for the government and help finance tax cuts. At another they may find their investment programmes cut as part of a government economy drive.

Privatisation frees the company from these constraints and allows it to make more rational economic decisions and plan future investments with greater certainty.

Financing tax cuts. The privatisation issue of shares earns money directly for the government and thus reduces the amount it needs to borrow. Effectively, then, the government can use the proceeds of privatisation to finance tax cuts.

There is a danger here, however, that in order to raise the maximum revenue the government will want to make the industries as potentially profitable as possible. This may involve selling them as monopolies. But this, of course, would probably be against the interests of the consumer.

Potential problems with privatisation

The markets in which privatised industries operate are unlikely to be perfect. What is more, the process of privatisation itself can create problems.

Natural monopolies. The market forces argument for privatisation largely breaks down if a public monopoly is simply replaced by a private monopoly, as in the case of the water companies. Critics of privatisation argue that at least a public-sector monopoly is not out to maximise profits and thereby exploit the consumer.

Some industries have such great economies of scale that there is only room for one firm in the industry. They are natural monopolies. The best examples of *natural monopolies* are the various grids that exist in the privatised utilities: the national electricity grid, the national gas pipe network, the network of railway lines. These grids account for a relatively high proportion of the total costs of these industries.

Figure 13.1 Natural monopoly

> One firm producing Q_1 would produce at $LRAC_1$

> Two equal-sized firms producing Q_1 between them would each produce at $LRAC_2$

The more intensively the electricity and gas grids are used, however, the lower their cost will become per unit of fuel supplied. Similarly with railways: the relatively high costs of providing track and signalling, etc. will become smaller per passenger, the more passengers use the railway.

In the short run, these costs are fixed. Average fixed costs must necessarily decline as more is produced: overheads are being spread over a greater output.

In the long run, when new (electricity, gas, railway) lines can be built, these costs become variable. It is still likely, however, that the costs per unit of output will decline, the higher the output becomes. A pylon carrying ten lines does not cost five times as much as one carrying two. This means that long-run average costs fall as more is produced.

In Figure 13.1, assume that the total industry output is Q_1. With just one company in the industry, long-run average cost is therefore $LRAC_1$. Now assume that the industry is split into two equal-sized companies, each with its own grid. If total output remains at Q_1, the two firms will produce Q_2 each at the higher long-run average cost of $LRAC_2$.

It is potentially more efficient, therefore, to have a single monopoly supplier whenever there is a natural monopoly. It avoids wasteful duplication.

The problem is that the monopoly producer in a free market could use its power to drive up prices. The long-run profit-maximising position is illustrated in Figure 13.2. The monopolist produces Q_m at a price P_m and at a cost of $LRAC_m$. There is a misallocation of resources.

If, however, the industry remained nationalised, or if it was privatised but regulated, it could be run as a monopoly and thus achieve the full economies of scale. And yet it could be directed to set a price that just covered costs (including normal profits), and thus make no more profit than a highly competitive industry. In Figure 13.2, it would produce Q_n at a price of P_n. We examine regulation later in this section.

Planning and the co-ordination of industry. Road use and road construction affect the demand for railways and vice versa.

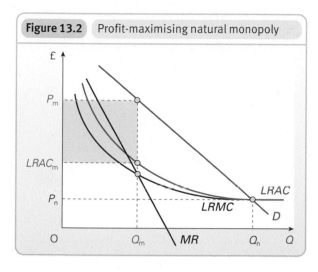

Figure 13.2 Profit-maximising natural monopoly

Critics argue that only the most glaring examples of externalities and injustice can be taken into account, given that the whole ethos of a private company is different from that of a nationalised one: private profit rather than public service is the goal. Externalities, they argue, are extremely widespread and need to be taken into account by the industry itself and not just by an occasionally intervening government.

KI 22
p216

In assessing these arguments, a lot depends on the toughness of government legislation and the attitudes and powers of regulatory agencies after privatisation.

 To what extent can the problems with privatisation be seen as arguments in favour of nationalisation?

Regulation: identifying the short-run optimum price and output

Privatised industries, if left free to operate in the market, will have monopoly power; they will create externalities; and they will be unlikely to take into account questions of fairness. An answer to these problems is for the government or some independent agency to regulate their behaviour so that they produce at the socially optimum price and output.

Exactly what this optimum is depends on what problems need to be taken into account. Take three cases. In the first, the privatised industry is a monopoly (perhaps it is a natural monopoly), but there are no other problems. In the second case, there are also externalities to be considered, and in the third, questions of fairness too.

The privatised industry is a monopoly
The 'first-best' situation: $P = MC$. Assume that all other firms in the economy are operating under perfect competition, and thus producing where $P = MC$. This is the imaginary 'first-best' situation. If this were so, the privatised company should be required to follow the same pricing rule: $P = MC$. As we saw in section 11.1, this will give the Pareto optimal output, where total consumer plus producer surplus is maximised (see pages 305–6).

KI 26
p306

The theory of the 'second best': $P = MC + Z$. Now let us drop the assumption that the rest of the economy operates under perfect competition. If other industries on average are charging a price, say, 10 per cent above MC, then the theory of the second best suggests that the privatised company should also charge a price 10 per cent above MC. At least that way it will not cause a diversion of consumption away from relatively low-cost industries (at the margin) to a relatively high-cost one. The second-best rule is therefore to set $P = MC + Z$, where Z in this case is 10 per cent.

The privatised industry produces externalities
In the first-best situation the privatised industry should produce where price equals marginal *social* (not private)

Decisions in the coal, electricity, gas and oil industries (and to a large extent in the steel industry) all affect each other. If these industries were nationalised, it should make their decisions easier to co-ordinate in the public interest. It could help the sensible planning of the nation's infrastructure. If these industries were under private enterprise, however, either there would be little co-ordination, or alternatively co-ordination might degenerate into oligopolistic collusion, with the consumer losing out. In the extreme case, the same company may have a monopoly in more than one industry. For example, in some regions of the UK, one company runs both buses and trains.

KI 29
p313

Problems of externalities and inequality. Various industries may create substantial external benefits and yet may be privately unprofitable. A railway or an underground line, for example, may considerably ease congestion on the roads, thus benefiting road as well as rail users. Other industries may cause substantial external costs. Nuclear power stations may produce nuclear waste that is costly to dispose of safely, and/or provides hazards for future generations. Coal-fired power stations may pollute the atmosphere and cause acid rain.

For reasons of equity, it can be argued that various transport services should be subsidised in order to keep them going and/or to keep their prices down. For instance, it can be argued that rural bus services should be kept operating at subsidised prices and that certain needy people (e.g. pensioners) should be charged lower prices.

KI 4
p10

Will such externalities and issues of equity be ignored under privatisation? The advocates of privatisation argue that externalities are a relatively minor problem, and anyway can be dealt with by appropriate taxes, subsidies and regulations even if the industry is privatised. Likewise questions of fairness and social justice can be dealt with by subsidies or regulations. A loss-making bus service can be subsidised so that it can be run profitably by a private bus company.

KI 29
p313

cost: $P = MSC$. The second-best solution is to produce where $P = MSC + Z$ (where Z is the average of other industries' price above their MSC).

The difficulty for the regulator in applying these rules in practice is to identify and measure the externalities: not an easy task! (See section 11.4.)

The behaviour of the privatised industry involves questions of fairness

If the government wishes the regulator to insist on a price below MC because it wishes to help certain groups (e.g. pensioners, children, rural dwellers, those below certain incomes), what should this price be?

KI 4
p10

In practice, one of two simple rules could be followed. Either the industry could be required to charge uniform prices, despite higher costs for supplying certain categories of people (this could apply, for example, to rural customers of a privatised postal service); or a simple formula could be used (e.g. half price for pensioners and children). These are often the only practical solutions given the impossibility of identifying the specific needs of individual consumers.

Two further questions arise:

- Should the lower price be subsidised by central or local *government*, or by the privatised company and hence by *other users* of the service (i.e. by them paying *higher* prices)? Justice would suggest that support should come from the community as a whole – the taxpayer – and not just from other users of the service.
- If people require help, should they not be given *general* tax relief or benefits, rather than specifically subsidised services? For example, should pensioners not be paid better pensions, rather than be charged reduced fares on buses?

1. In the case of buses, subsidies are often paid by local authorities to support various loss-making routes. Is this the best way of supporting these services?
2. In the case of postal services, profitable parts of the service cross-subsidise the unprofitable parts. Should this continue if the industry is privatised?

Regulation: identifying the long-run optimum price and output

In the short run, certain factors of production are fixed in supply. For example, electricity output can be increased by using *existing* power stations more fully, but the *number* of power stations is fixed. There will thus be a limit to the amount of electricity that can be generated in the short run. As that limit is approached, the marginal cost of electricity is likely to rise rapidly. For example, oil-fired power stations, which are more costly to operate, will have to be brought on line.

In the long run, all factors are variable. New power stations can be built. The *long*-run marginal costs therefore

Figure 13.3 Short-run and long-run marginal cost pricing

will probably not rise as more is produced. In fact, they may even fall due to economies of scale.

Long-run marginal costs, however, unlike short-run marginal costs, will include the extra capital costs of increasing output. The long-run marginal cost of electricity will thus be all the extra costs of producing one more unit: namely, the extra operating costs (fuel, labour, etc.) *plus* the extra capital costs (power stations, pylons, etc.).

The rule for the optimum long-run price and output is simple. The regulator should require the industry to produce where price equals *long-run* marginal social cost ($LRMSC$). This is illustrated in Figure 13.3.

KI 26
p306

In the short run, optimum price and output are P_S and Q_S where $P =$ (short-run) MSC. This might mean that production is at quite a high cost: existing capital equipment is being stretched and diminishing returns have become serious.

In the long run, then, it will be desirable to increase capacity if $LRMSC < MSC$. Optimum long-run price and output are thus at P_L and Q_L where $P = LRMSC$.

This is the rule for the first-best situation. In the second-best situation, the industry should produce where $P = LRMSC + Z$ (where Z is the average of other industries' price above their $LRMSC$).

If the regulator imposed such rules, would they cause the firm to make a loss if it faced a downward-sloping LRMSC curve? (Clues: Where would the LRAC curve be relative to the LRMC curve? What would be the effect of externalities and the addition of the Z factor on the price?)

Regulation in the UK

To some extent the behaviour of privatised industries may be governed by general monopoly and restrictive practice legislation. For example, in the UK, privatised firms can be investigated by the Office of Fair Trading and if necessary referred to the Competition Commission.

In addition to this, there is a separate regulatory office to oversee the structure and behaviour of each of the privatised utilities. These regulators are as follows: the Office for Gas and Electricity Markets (Ofgem), the Office of Communications (Ofcom) (for telecommunications and broadcasting), the Office of Rail Regulation (ORR) and the Office of Water Services (Ofwat). The regulators set terms under which the industries have to operate. For example, ORR sets the terms under which rail companies have access to the track and stations. The terms set by the regulator can be reviewed by negotiation between the regulator and the industry. If agreement cannot be reached, the Competition Commission acts as an appeal court and its decision is binding.

The regulator for each industry also sets limits to the prices that certain parts of the industry can charge (see Case Study 13.3 in MyEconLab). These parts are those where there is little or no competition: for example, the charges made to electricity and gas retailers by National Grid Transco, the owner of the electricity grid and major gas pipelines.

The price-setting formulae have essentially been of the 'RPI minus X' variety. What this means is that the industries can raise their prices by the rate of increase in the retail price index (RPI) (i.e. by the rate of inflation) *minus* a certain percentage (X) to take account of expected increases in efficiency. Thus if the rate of inflation were 6 per cent, and if the regulator considered that the industry (or firm) could be expected to reduce its costs by 2 per cent ($X = 2\%$), then price rises would be capped at 4 per cent. The $RPI - X$ system is thus an example of **price-cap regulation**. The idea of this system of regulation is that it will force the industry to pass cost savings on to the consumer.

Whether this will result in marginal cost pricing depends on what the price was in the first place. If the price was equal to marginal cost, and if the X factor is the amount by which the regulator expects the MC curve to shift downwards (after taking inflation into account), then the formula could result in marginal cost pricing.

 Why might it equally result in average cost pricing?

Assessing the system of regulation in the UK
The system that has evolved in the UK has various advantages over that employed in the USA and elsewhere, where regulation often focuses on the level of profits (see Case Study 13.4 in MyEconLab).

Definition

Price-cap regulation Where the regulator puts a ceiling on the amount by which a firm can raise its price.

- It is a *discretionary* system, with the regulator able to judge individual examples of the behaviour of the industry on their own merits. The regulator has a detailed knowledge of the industry which would not be available to government ministers or other bodies such as the Office of Fair Trading. The regulator could thus be argued to be the best person to decide on whether the industry is acting in the public interest.
- The system is *flexible*, since it allows for the licence and price formulae to be changed as circumstances change.
- The 'RPI minus X' formula provides an *incentive* for the privatised firms to be as efficient as possible. If they can lower their costs by more than X, they will, in theory, be able to make larger profits and keep them. If, on the other hand, they do not succeed in reducing costs sufficiently, they will make a loss. There is thus a continuing pressure on them to cut costs. (In the US system, where *profits* rather than *prices* are regulated, there is little incentive to increase efficiency, since any cost reductions must be passed on to the consumer in lower prices, and do not, therefore, result in higher profits.)

There are, however, some inherent problems with the way in which regulation operates in the UK:

- The 'RPI minus X' formula was designed to provide an incentive for firms to cut costs. But if X is too low, firms might make excessive profits. Frequently, regulators have underestimated the scope for cost reductions resulting from new technology and reorganisation, and have thus initially set X too low. As a result, instead of X remaining constant for five years, as intended, new higher values for X have been set after only one or two years. Alternatively, one-off price cuts have been ordered, as happened when the water companies were required by Ofwat to cut prices by an average of 10 per cent in 2000. In either case, this can then lead to the same problem as with the US system. The incentive for the industry to cut costs will be removed. What is the point of being more efficient if the regulator is merely going to take away the extra profits?
- With *RPI minus X* effectively reducing firms' profits, concerns have been expressed that the amount of investment may decline and also the quality of service provided to consumers. This has led to calls for regulation to be supplemented by strict 'quality of service' requirements.
- Regulation is becoming increasingly complex. This makes it difficult for the industries to plan and may lead to a growth of 'short-termism'. One of the claimed advantages of privatisation was to give greater independence to the industries from short-term government interference and allow them to plan for the longer term. In practice, one type of interference may have been replaced by another.
- As regulation becomes more detailed and complex, and as the regulator becomes more and more involved in the

BOX 13.4 **SELLING POWER TO THE PEOPLE**

Attempts to introduce competition into the electricity industry

The electricity industry in England and Wales

Competition is generally seen as better than regulation as a means of protecting consumers' interests. The electricity industry provides a good case study of ways to introduce competition into a privatised industry.

The industry before privatisation

Under nationalisation, the industry in England and Wales was organised as a monopoly with the Central Electricity Generating Board (CEGB) supplying 99 per cent of all electricity. It operated the power stations and transmitted the electricity round the country via the national grid. However, the CEGB did not sell electricity directly to the consumer; rather it sold it to twelve regional boards, which in turn supplied it to the consumer.

Privatisation of the industry

Non-nuclear generation in England and Wales was privatised in 1990 as two companies: National Power (with just over 50 per cent of capacity) and PowerGen (with nearly 30 per cent). It was not until 1996, however, that nuclear power stations were privatised.

The twelve regional boards were privatised in 1991 as separate regional electricity companies (RECs), which were responsible for local distribution and supply to consumers. They would also be permitted to build their own power stations if they chose. The RECs jointly owned the national grid, but it was run independently. It was eventually sold as a separate company in 1996.

The diagram shows the structure of the industry. Electricity is produced by the *generators* (the power stations). The electricity is *transmitted* along the power lines of the National Grid Company plc (NGC) to different parts of the country. It is then transmitted locally by the *distributors* (the twelve distribution companies), which initially were also the *suppliers* of electricity to the customers (homes, local authorities and businesses).

An Office of Electricity Regulation (OFFER) was set up to control prices in parts of the industry where there was no competition. The control was of the *RPI – X* variety (see page 379). For example, the charges paid by the generators and the suppliers to the transmission company are regulated. OFFER was later merged with the gas regulator to become the Office of Gas and Electricity Markets (Ofgem).

It was hoped, however, that the new structure would allow a growth in competition, thereby making regulation increasingly unnecessary. So what was the nature of this competition? After all, National Power had over half of the generating capacity; the National Grid Company had a natural monopoly of electricity transmission; and the twelve RECs had a natural monopoly of distribution in each of their areas.

Competition was possible at two levels: at the *wholesale* level, with generators competing with each other to sell to suppliers; and at the *retail* level, with suppliers competing to sell to customers. Let us examine each of these markets in turn.

Competition in the wholesale market for electricity: NETA and BETTA

Since 2001 in England and Wales electricity has been traded in the wholesale market under the New Electricity Trading Arrangements (NETA). In April 2005, this system was extended to Scotland and renamed the British Electricity Trading and Transmission Arrangements (BETTA). Participants in the market include generators, suppliers, large commercial consumers of electricity and traders (i.e. dealers).

In this market, bulk electricity is traded 'forward' in bilateral contracts between individual buyers and sellers. A forward contract means that a price is agreed today for an amount of electricity to be traded over a particular period in the future, which could be as soon as the next day or could be three or more years hence. The long forward contracts are to allow generators to plan to build extra capacity.

Of course, the future price will be based on anticipated demand, and demand in practice may not turn out as anticipated. To allow for this, NGC operates a 'central balancing mechanism'. This is a system of buying and selling additional electricity where necessary to ensure that demand actually balances supply second by second. It is also a system to sort out who owes what to whom when there is a surplus. In practice, only about 2 per cent of electricity has to be traded under the balancing mechanisms; the remainder is traded in the forward contracts.

With more than 200 participants in BETTA, the system is highly competitive. In the first few months of NETA's operation, wholesale prices fell by some 20–25 per cent. In December 2007 a report by Oxford Economic Research Associates found that the UK has the most competitive energy market both in the EU and in the G7.[1]

Competition in the retail market for electricity

All customers, whether domestic or business, can choose their supplier, thereby putting suppliers into competition. This competition was introduced in stages, with larger consumers being the first to be able to 'shop around'. It was not until 1999, however, that the choice of supplier was open to all customers.

But how are consumers able to choose? Suppliers purchase electricity through BETTA. The local distribution company is then obliged to transmit this electricity on behalf of suppliers at the same (regulated) price that it charges itself as a supplier. Thus any supplier can use the same cables. There have been several new entrants into the supplier market, including various gas companies diversifying into electricity supply.

By 2001, 38 per cent of customers had switched suppliers at least once and the former regional monopoly suppliers now had only 70 per cent of the market. In the light of this, and of the fact that switching was seen as easy by 80 per cent of customers, Ofgem announced that competition was sufficiently developed to allow all regulation of the retail market to be removed by April 2002. Indeed, by 2008, 80 per cent of customers had switched at least once and the former suppliers' market share had been reduced below 50 per cent.

Competition between suppliers is likely to go further still, thanks to the development of new technology. 'Smart meters' could eventually be installed in homes to allow customers to switch automatically between suppliers depending on which one was offering the lowest price! The meters would read price information that was transmitted down the electricity cable.

What of the future?

The electricity industry, like other privatised utilities, is complex. Parts, such as the national grid and distribution through local cables, are a natural monopoly. Here regulation is essential. But other parts, such as generation and supply, are potentially competitive. Is it right for these parts to be deregulated?

A danger for competition lies in mergers. These mergers may be horizontal. Generators could merge. So far, however, the number of generators has continued to increase, thanks partly to the regulator requiring National Power and PowerGen to sell power stations. Suppliers could merge. Indeed, it is predicted that, over the next few years, the number of suppliers could be reduced to four or five. Clearly, if the number of firms at any level of the industry is too low, there is a severe danger of collusion or a simple abuse of market power. Here the regulator would have to behave like the OFT and prevent anti-competitive behaviour.

Mergers could be vertical. Generators could merge with distributors or suppliers. In 1998, PowerGen acquired East Midlands Electricity, the third largest supplier. A similar threat comes from the fact that the new gas-fired power stations are mainly owned by the regional electricity companies, which might buy electricity from themselves at inflated prices, which are then passed on to their customers. The regulator warned that a vertically integrated industry, where contracts between separate companies were replaced by internal arrangements within a single company, would be much harder to control.

Does vertical integration matter if consumers still have a choice of suppliers and if generators are still competing with each other?

[1] *Energy market competition in the EU and G7* (Oxera, 2007).

detailed running of the industry, so managers and regulators will become increasingly involved in a game of strategy: each trying to outwit the other. Information will become distorted and time and energy will be wasted in playing this game of cat and mouse.

• Alternatively, there is the danger of *regulatory capture*. As regulators become more and more involved in their industry and get to know the senior managers at a personal level, so they are increasingly likely to see the managers' point of view and will thus become less tough. This, it is argued, has happened in the USA. Commentators do not believe that it has happened yet in the UK: the regulators are generally independently minded. But it remains a potential danger.

• The regulators could instead be 'captured' by the government. Rather than being totally independent, there to serve the interests of the consumer, they might bend to pressures from the government to do things that might help the government win the next election.

One way in which the dangers of ineffective or over-intrusive regulation can be avoided is to replace regulation with competition wherever this is possible. Indeed, one of the major concerns of the regulators has been to do just this. (See Box 13.4 for ways in which competition has been increased in the electricity industry.)

Increasing competition in the privatised industries

Where natural monopoly exists, competition is impossible in a free market. Of course, the industry *could* be broken up by the government, with firms prohibited from owning more than a certain percentage of the industry. But this would lead to higher costs of production. Firms would be operating further back up a downward-sloping long-run average cost curve.

But many parts of the privatised industries are *not* natural monopolies. Generally, it is only the *grid* that is a natural monopoly. In the case of gas and water, it is the pipelines. It would be wasteful to duplicate these. In the case of electricity, it is the power lines: the national grid and the local power lines. In the case of the railways, it is the track.

Other parts of these industries, however, have generally been opened up to competition (with the exception of water). Thus there are now many producers and sellers of electricity and gas. This is possible because they are given access, by law, to the national and local electricity grids and gas pipelines. The telecommunications market, too, has become more competitive with the growth of mobile phones and lines supplied by cable operators.

To help the opening up of competition, regulators have sometimes restricted the behaviour of the established firms (like BT or British Gas), to prevent them using their dominance in the market as a barrier to entry of new firms. For example, British Gas since 1995 has had to limit its share of the industrial gas market to 40 per cent.

As competition has been introduced into these industries, so price-cap regulation has been progressively abandoned. The intention is ultimately to confine price regulation to the operation of the grids: the parts that are natural monopolies.

Even for the parts where there *is* a natural monopoly, they could be made *contestable* monopolies. One way of doing this is by granting operators a licence for a specific period of time. This is known as *franchising*. This has been the approach used for the railways (see Case Study 13.5 in MyEconLab). Once a company has been granted a franchise, it has the monopoly of passenger rail services over specific routes. But the awarding of the franchise can be highly competitive, with rival companies putting in competitive bids, in terms of both price (or, in the case of many of the train operating companies, the level of government subsidy required) and the quality of service.

Another approach is to give all companies equal access to the relevant grid. For example, regional electricity companies have to charge the same price for using their local power lines to both rival companies and themselves.

But despite attempts to introduce competition into the privatised industries, they are still dominated by giant companies. Even if they are no longer strictly monopolies, they still have considerable market power. Competition is far from being perfect! The scope for price leadership or other forms of oligopolistic collusion is great. Thus although regulation through the price formula has been progressively abandoned as elements of competition have been introduced, the regulators have retained a role similar to that of the OFT: namely, to prevent collusion and the abuse of monopoly power. The companies, however, do have the right of appeal to the Competition Commission.

Definitions

Regulatory capture Where the regulator is persuaded to operate in the industry's interests rather than those of the consumer.

Franchising Where a firm is granted the licence to operate a given part of an industry for a specified length of time.

Section summary

1. From around 1983 the Conservative government in the UK embarked on a large programme of privatisation. Many other countries have followed suit.

2. The economic arguments for privatisation include: greater competition, not only in the goods market but in the market for finance and for corporate control; reduced government interference; and raising revenue to finance tax cuts.

3. The economic arguments against privatisation of utilities include the following: the firms are likely to have monopoly power because their grids are natural monopolies; it makes overall planning and co-ordination of the transport and power sectors more difficult; and the industries produce substantial externalities and raise questions of fairness in distribution.

4. Regulators could require firms to charge the socially efficient price. In the first-best world, this will be where price equals marginal social cost. In the real world, this is not the case given that prices elsewhere are not equal to marginal social costs. Ideally, prices should still *reflect* marginal social costs, but there are difficulties in identifying and measuring social costs.

5. In the long run, the optimum price and output will be where price equals long-run marginal social cost. If $LRMSC < MSC$, it will be desirable to invest in additional capacity.

6. Regulation in the UK has involved setting up regulatory offices for the major privatised utilities. These generally operate informally, using negotiation and bargaining to persuade the industries to behave in the public interest. They also set the terms under which firms can operate (e.g. access rights to the respective grid).

7. As far as prices are concerned, the industries are required to abide by an '*RPI* minus X' formula. This forces them to pass potential cost reductions on to the consumer. At the same time, they are allowed to retain any additional profits gained from cost reductions greater than X. This provides them with an incentive to achieve even greater increases in efficiency.

8. Many parts of the privatised industries are not natural monopolies. In these parts, competition may be a more effective means of pursuing the public interest. Various attempts have been made to make the privatised industries more competitive, often at the instigation of the regulator. Nevertheless, considerable market power remains in the hands of many privatised firms, and thus regulators need to be able to retain the ability to prevent the abuse of monopoly power.

END OF CHAPTER QUESTIONS

1. Should governments or regulators always attempt to eliminate the supernormal profits of monopolists/oligopolists?

2. Compare the relative merits of banning certain types of market *structure* with banning certain types of market *behaviour*.

3. Consider the argument that whether an industry is in the public sector or private sector has far less bearing on its performance than the degree of competition it faces.

4. If two or more firms are charging similar prices, does this imply that collusion is taking place? What evidence would you need to determine the existence of collusion?

5. There exists a view that the UK is too small an economy to benefit from competition in many industries, with firms failing to reach minimum efficient scale. What does this imply for competition policy?

6. Should regulators of utilities that have been privatised into several separate companies allow (a) horizontal mergers (within the industry); (b) vertical mergers; (c) mergers with firms in other industries?

7. Summarise the relative benefits to consumers of (a) privatising a nationalised industry, (b) keeping it in the public sector but introducing competition.

8. If an industry regulator adopts an $RPI - X$ formula for price regulation, is it desirable that the value of X should be adjusted as soon as cost conditions change?

9. Examine the case for public ownership of an industry where a natural monopoly exists.

10. Price-cap regulation was abandoned in the gas and electricity industries because the regulator (Ofgem) felt that there was sufficient competition. Consider whether this was a wise decision.

Online resources

Additional case studies in MyEconLab

13.1 **Cartels set in concrete, steel and cardboard.** This examines some of the best-known Europe-wide cartels of recent years.

13.2 **Taking your vitamins – at a price.** An examination of a global vitamins cartel and the action taken against it by the EU.

13.3 **Price-cap regulation in the UK.** How *RPI – X* regulation has been applied to the various privatised industries.

13.4 **Regulation US-style.** This examines rate-of-return regulation: an alternative to price-cap regulation.

13.5 **The right track to reform?** How successful has rail privatisation been in the UK?

13.6 **Privatisation in transition economies.** This extended case study examines state ownership under former communist countries of the USSR and how the transition of these countries to market economies involved a process of privatisation.

13.7 **Forms of privatisation in transition countries.** This focuses on how different types of privatisation are likely to affect the way industries are run.

Websites relevant to Chapters 11–13

Numbers and sections refer to websites listed in the Web Appendix and hotlinked from this book's website at **www.pearsoned.co.uk/sloman**.

- For news articles relevant to this and the previous chapter, see the *Economics News Articles* link from the book's website.

- For general news on market failures and government intervention, see websites in section A, and particularly A1–5, 18, 19, 24, 31. See also links to newspapers in A38, 39, 43 and 44; and see A41 and 42 for links to economics news articles from newspapers worldwide.

- Sites I7 and 11 contain links to *Competition and monopoly*, *Policy and regulation* and *Transport* in the *Microeconomics* section; they also have an *Industry and commerce* section. Site I4 has links to *Environmental* and *Environmental Economics* in the *EconDirectory* section. Site I17 has several sections of links in the *Issues in Society* section.

- UK and EU departments relevant to competition policy can be found at sites E10; G7, 8.

- UK regulatory bodies can be found at sites E4, 11, 15, 16, 18, 19, 22, 25, 29.

- For information on taxes and subsidies, see E30, 36; G13. For use of green taxes (Box 12.2), see H5; G11; E2, 14, 30.

- For information on health and the economics of health care (Box 11.3), see E8; H9. See also links in I8 and 17.

- For sites favouring the free market, see C17; D34. See also C18 for the development of ideas on the market and government intervention.

- For the economics of the environment, see links in I4, 7, 11, 17. For policy on the environment and transport, see E2, 7, 11, 14, 21, 29; G10, 11. See also H11.

- For student resources relevant to these three chapters, see sites C1–7, 9, 10, 19.

- For a simulation on tackling traffic congestion, see site D3.

Foundations of Macroeconomics

14   The National Economy   387

15   Macroeconomic Issues and Analysis: An Overview   415

Why do economies sometimes grow rapidly, while at other times they suffer from recession? Why, if people want to work, do they sometimes find themselves unemployed? Why do economies experience inflation (rising prices), and does it matter if they do? Why do exchange rates change and what will be the impact of such changes on imports and exports? These macroeconomic issues affect all countries, and economists are called on to try to find explanations and solutions.

In the next two chapters we will be looking at these issues and giving you a preliminary insight into the causes of these problems and what governments can do to tackle them.

The National Economy

CHAPTER MAP

14.1 The scope of macroeconomics   388
The major macroeconomic issues   388
Government macroeconomic policy   389

14.2 The circular flow of income   390
The inner flow, withdrawals and injections 391
Relationship between withdrawals and
  injections   392
The circular flow of income and the four
  macroeconomic objectives   392
Equilibrium in the circular flow   393

14.3 Measuring national income and
      output   393
Three ways of measuring GDP   394
Taking account of inflation   394
Taking account of population   394
Taking account of exchange rates   394
Do GDP statistics give a good indication of a
  country's standard of living?   395

14.4 Short-term economic growth and
      the business cycle   398
Actual and potential growth   398
Economic growth and the business cycle   400
The business cycle in practice   400
Causes of fluctuations in actual growth   401

14.5 Long-term economic growth   403
Causes of long-term growth   403
Policies to achieve growth   408
Postscript: The role of investment   408

Appendix: Calculating GDP   409
The product method of measuring GDP   409
The income method of measuring GDP   411
The expenditure method of measuring GDP   412
From GDP to national income   413
Households' disposable income   413

We turn now to macroeconomics. This will be the subject of the second half of this book. As we have already seen, microeconomics focuses on individual markets. It studies the demand for and supply of, for example, oranges, DVDs, petrol and haircuts; bricklayers, doctors, office accommodation and computers. It examines the choices people make between goods, and what determines their relative prices and the relative quantities produced.

In macroeconomics we take a much broader view. We examine the economy as a whole. We still examine demand and supply, but now it is the total level of spending in the economy and the total level of production. In other words, we examine aggregate demand and aggregate supply.

We still examine output, employment and prices, but now it is national output and its rate of growth, national employment and unemployment, and the general level of prices and their rate of increase (i.e. the rate of inflation).

In this chapter, we identify the major macroeconomic objectives and have a preliminary look at how they are related. Then we focus on national income and output. We look at how they are measured and what causes them to grow over time.

14.1 THE SCOPE OF MACROECONOMICS

The major macroeconomic issues

Economic growth

Governments try to achieve high *rates of economic growth* over the long term: in other words, growth that is sustained over the years and is not just a temporary phenomenon. To this end, governments also try to achieve *stable* growth, avoiding both recessions and excessive short-term growth that cannot be sustained (although governments are nevertheless sometimes happy to give the economy an excessive boost as an election draws near!). As we shall see in later chapters, governments around the world were not very successful in preventing a recession in 2008/9.

> **KEY IDEA 32**
> Economies suffer from inherent instability. As a result, economic growth and other macroeconomic indicators tend to fluctuate.

Table 14.1 shows the average annual growth in output between 1960 and 2009 for selected countries. As you can see, the differences between countries are quite substantial.

> **Definition**
>
> **Rate of economic growth** The percentage increase in national output, normally expressed over a 12-month period.

'Newly industrialised countries', such as Malaysia, Singapore and China, have experienced particularly rapid rates of economic growth.

There are also big differences between the growth rates of individual countries in different periods. Look, for example, at the figures for Japan. From being an 'economic miracle' in the 1960s, Japan by the 1990s had become a laggard, with a growth rate well below the OECD average.

Unemployment

Reducing unemployment is another major macroeconomic aim of governments, not only for the sake of the unemployed themselves, but also because it represents a waste of human resources and because unemployment benefits are a drain on government revenues.

Unemployment in the 1980s and early 1990s was significantly higher than in the 1960s and 1970s (see Table 14.1). Then, in the late 1990s and early 2000s, it fell in some countries, such as the UK and USA. In others, such as Germany and France, it remained stubbornly high.

We take a preliminary look at the nature and causes of unemployment in Chapter 15.

Inflation

By inflation we mean a general rise in prices throughout the economy. Government policy here is to keep inflation both low and stable. One of the most important reasons

---

Table 14.1 Economic growth (average % per annum), unemployment (average %) and inflation (average % per annum)

	France	Germany	Japan	UK	USA	EU (12)[a]	OECD[b]	Brazil	Malaysia	Singapore	China
Growth											
1960–9	5.6	4.4	10.4	2.9	4.3	5.8	5.5	5.9	6.5	9.5	3.0
1970–9	4.1	3.1	5.4	2.4	3.3	3.8	3.7	8.5	7.7	9.2	7.4
1980–9	2.3	2.0	3.7	2.4	3.1	2.3	2.9	3.0	5.9	7.5	9.8
1990–9	1.9	2.3	1.5	2.1	3.1	2.2	2.5	1.6	7.2	7.6	10.0
2000–9	1.5	1.0	1.1	2.0	2.0	1.6	1.9	3.5	5.0	4.9	9.6
Unemployment											
1960–9	1.5	0.9	1.3	2.2	4.1	2.5	2.5	n.a.	n.a.	n.a.	n.a.
1970–9	3.7	2.3	1.7	4.5	6.1	4.0	4.3	n.a.	n.a.	3.6	n.a.
1980–9	8.9	7.0	2.5	10.2	7.3	9.3	7.2	3.9	7.2	3.7	2.6
1990–9	11.1	8.1	3.1	8.1	5.8	10.5	7.0	6.9	3.3	2.8	2.8
2000–9	9.1	8.7	4.6	5.4	5.4	8.4	6.6	9.8	3.6	3.5	4.1
Inflation											
1960–9	3.8	3.2	5.5	3.8	2.4	3.7	3.1	46.1	0.8	1.2	n.a.
1970–9	8.9	5.0	9.1	12.6	7.1	9.5	9.2	30.6	5.5	5.9	n.a.
1980–9	7.4	2.9	2.5	7.4	5.6	6.5	8.9	354.5	3.7	2.8	7.5
1990–9	1.9	2.4	1.2	3.7	3.0	2.9	4.4	843.3	3.7	1.9	7.8
2000–9	1.9	1.7	−0.6	2.1	2.5	2.2	2.4	6.5	2.2	1.6	1.9

[a] EU12 = the 12 original countries adopting the euro.
[b] The Organisation for Economic Co-operation and Development: an organisation of 30 major industrialised countries (excluding Russia, but including Korea, Mexico and Turkey).
Note: Year 2009 figures forecast.

for this is that it will aid the process of economic decision making. For example, businesses will be able to set prices and wage rates, and make investment decisions with far more confidence.

In recent years we have become used to *inflation rates* of around 2 or 3 per cent, but it was not long ago that inflation in most developed countries was in double figures. Even though inflation started to rise in many countries in 2008, figures remained much lower than in the past; in 1975, UK inflation reached 24 per cent. With the recession of 2008/9, inflation fell in most countries, becoming negative ('deflation') in some.

In most developed countries, governments have a particular target for the rate of inflation. In the UK the target is 2 per cent. The Bank of England then adjusts interest rates to try to keep inflation on target (we see how this works in Chapter 20).

The balance of payments and the exchange rate

The final issue has to do with the country's foreign trade and its economic relationships with other countries.

A country's *balance of payments account* records all transactions between the residents of that country and the rest of the world. These transactions enter as either debit items or credit items. The debit items include all payments *to* other countries: these include the country's purchases of imports, the investments it makes abroad and the interest and dividends paid to people abroad who have invested in the country. The credit items include all receipts *from* other countries: these include the sales of exports, inflows of investment into the country and earnings of interest and dividends from abroad.

The sale of exports and any other receipts earn foreign currency. The purchase of imports or any other payments abroad use up foreign currency. If we start to spend more foreign currency than we earn, one of two things must happen. Both are likely to be a problem.

- The balance of payments will go into deficit. In other words, there will be a shortfall of foreign currencies. The government will therefore have to borrow money from abroad, or draw on its foreign currency reserves to make up the shortfall. This is a problem because, if it goes on too long, overseas debts will mount up, along with the interest that must be paid; and/or reserves will begin to run low.

- The exchange rate will fall. The *exchange rate* is the rate at which one currency exchanges for another. For example, the exchange rate of the pound into the dollar might be £1 = $1.50.

If the government does nothing to correct the balance of payments deficit, then the exchange rate must fall. (We will show just why this is so in section 15.4.) A falling exchange rate is a problem because it pushes up the price of imports and may fuel inflation. Also, if the exchange rate fluctuates, this can cause great uncertainty for traders and can damage international trade and economic growth.

What are the underlying causes of balance of payments problems? How do the balance of payments and the exchange rate relate to the other macroeconomic issues? What are the best policies for governments to adopt? We take an initial look at these questions in Chapter 15 and then examine them in more detail in Chapters 25 and 26.

Government macroeconomic policy

From the above four issues we can identify four macroeconomic policy objectives that governments typically pursue:

- High and stable economic growth.
- Low unemployment.
- Low inflation.
- The avoidance of balance of payments deficits and excessive exchange rate fluctuations.

Unfortunately, these policy objectives may conflict. For example, a policy designed to accelerate the rate of economic growth may result in a higher rate of inflation and a balance of payments deficit. Governments are thus often faced with awkward policy choices.

KEY IDEA 33

Societies face trade-offs between economic objectives. For example, the goal of faster growth may conflict with that of greater equality; the goal of lower unemployment may conflict with that of lower inflation (at least in the short run). This is an example of opportunity cost: the cost of achieving one objective may be achieving less of another. The existence of trade-offs means that policy makers must make choices.

Definitions

Rate of inflation The percentage increase in prices over a 12-month period.

Balance of payments account A record of the country's transactions with the rest of the world. It shows the country's payments to or deposits in other countries (debits) and its receipts or deposits from other countries

(credits). It also shows the balance between these debits and credits under various headings.

Exchange rate The rate at which one national currency exchanges for another. The rate is expressed as the amount of one currency that is necessary to purchase *one unit* of another currency (e.g. €1.20 = £1).

Section summary

1. Macroeconomics, like microeconomics, looks at issues such as output, employment and prices; but it looks at them in the context of the whole economy.

2. The four main macroeconomic goals that are generally of most concern to governments are economic growth, reducing unemployment, reducing inflation, and avoiding balance of payments and exchange rate problems.

3. Unfortunately, these goals are likely to conflict. Governments may thus be faced with difficult policy choices.

14.2 THE CIRCULAR FLOW OF INCOME

One way in which the four objectives are linked is through their relationship with *aggregate demand* (*AD*). This is the total spending on goods and services made within the country ('domestically produced goods and services'). This spending consists of four elements. The first is *consumer spending on domestically produced goods and services* (C_d), (i.e. total consumer expenditure on all products (*C*) minus expenditure on imports (*M*)). The other three elements are: investment expenditure by firms (*I*), government spending (*G*) and the expenditure by residents abroad on this country's exports (*X*). Thus:[1]

$$AD = C_d + I + G + X$$

or, put another way:

$$AD = C + I + G + X - M$$

To show how the four objectives are related to aggregate demand, we can use a simple model of the economy. This is the circular flow of income, and is shown in Figure 14.1. It is an extension of the model that we looked at back in Chapter 1 (pages 14–15).

In the diagram, the economy is divided into two major groups: *firms* and *households*. Each group has two roles. Firms are producers of goods and services; they are also the

---

[1] We assume, for simplicity, in this first equation that all investment, government expenditure and export expenditure is on domestic products. If, however, any part of these three went on imports, we would have to subtract this imported element (as we did with consumption). We would then have to write $AD = C_d + I_d + G_d + X_d$.

Definitions

Aggregate demand Total spending on goods and services produced in the economy. It consists of four elements, consumer expenditure (*C*), investment (*I*), government expenditure (*G*) and the expenditure on exports (*X*), less any expenditure on foreign goods and services (*M*). Thus $AD = C + I + G + X - M$, or $C_d + I + G + X$.

Consumption of domestically produced goods and services (C_d) The direct flow of money payments from households to firms.

Figure 14.1 The circular flow of income

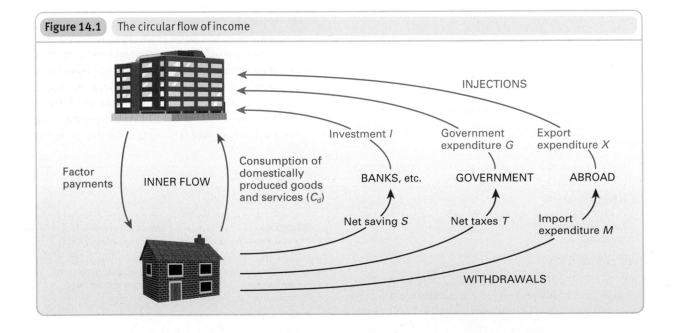

employers of labour and other factors of production. Households (which include all individuals) are the consumers of goods and services; they are also the suppliers of labour and various other factors of production. In the diagram there is an inner flow and various outer flows of incomes between these two groups.

Before we look at the various parts of the diagram, a word of warning. Do not confuse *money* and *income*. Money is a *stock* concept. At any given time, there is a certain quantity of money in the economy (e.g. £100 billion). But that does not tell us the level of national *income*. Income is a *flow* concept (as is expenditure). It is measured as so much *per period of time*. The relationship between money and income depends on how rapidly the money *circulates*: its 'velocity of circulation'. (We will examine this concept in detail later on: see page 458.) If there is £100 billion of money in the economy and each £1 on average is paid out as income five times per year, then annual national income will be £5 billion.

The inner flow, withdrawals and injections

The inner flow

Firms pay money to households in the form of wages and salaries, dividends on shares, interest and rent. These payments are in return for the services of the factors of production – labour, capital and land – that are supplied by households. Thus on the left-hand side of the diagram, money flows directly from firms to households as 'factor payments'.

Households, in turn, pay money to domestic firms when they consume domestically produced goods and services (C_d). This is shown on the right-hand side of the inner flow. There is thus a circular flow of payments from firms to households to firms and so on.

If households spend *all* their incomes on buying domestic goods and services, and if firms pay out *all* this income they receive as factor payments to domestic households, and if the velocity of circulation does not change, the flow will continue at the same level indefinitely. The money just goes round and round at the same speed and incomes remain unchanged.

 Would this argument still hold if prices rose?

In the real world, of course, it is not as simple as this. Not all income gets passed on round the inner flow; some is *withdrawn*. At the same time, incomes are injected into the flow from outside. Let us examine these withdrawals and injections.

Withdrawals (W)

Only part of the incomes received by households will be spent on the goods and services of domestic firms. The remainder will be withdrawn from the inner flow. Likewise only part of the incomes generated by firms will be paid to UK households. The remainder of this will also be withdrawn. There are three forms of **withdrawals** (or *'leakages'* as they are sometimes called).

Net saving (S).   Saving is income that households choose not to spend but to put aside for the future. Savings are normally deposited in financial institutions such as banks and building societies. This is shown in the bottom centre of the diagram. Money flows from households to 'banks, etc.'. What we are seeking to measure here, however, is the net flow from households to the banking sector. We therefore have to subtract from saving any borrowing or drawing on past savings by households to arrive at the *net* saving flow. Of course, if household borrowing exceeded saving, the net flow would be in the other direction: it would be negative.

Net taxes (T).   When people pay taxes (to either central or local government), this represents a withdrawal of money from the inner flow in much the same way as saving; only, in this case, people have no choice. Some taxes, such as income tax and employees' national insurance contributions, are paid out of household incomes. Others, such as VAT and excise duties, are paid out of consumer expenditure. Others, such as corporation tax, are paid out of firms' incomes before being received by households as dividends on shares. (For simplicity, however, taxes are shown in Figure 14.1 as leaving the circular flow at just one point.)

When, however, people receive *benefits* from the government, such as unemployment benefits, child benefit and pensions, the money flows the other way. Benefits are thus equivalent to a 'negative tax'. These benefits are known as **transfer payments**. They transfer money from one group of people (taxpayers) to others (the recipients).

In the model, 'net taxes' (T) represents the *net* flow to the government from households and firms. It consists of total taxes minus benefits.

Import expenditure (M).   Not all consumption is of totally home-produced goods. Households spend some of their incomes on imported goods and services, or on goods and services using imported components. Although the money that consumers spend on such goods initially flows to domestic retailers, it will eventually find its way abroad, either when the retailers or wholesalers themselves import

> ### Definitions
>
> **Withdrawals (W) (or leakages)** Incomes of households or firms that are not passed on round the inner flow. Withdrawals equal net saving (S) plus net taxes (T) plus import expenditure (M): $W = S + T + M$.
>
> **Transfer payments** Moneys transferred from one person or group to another (e.g. from the government to individuals) without production taking place.

KI 24
p260

them, or when domestic manufacturers purchase imported inputs to make their products. This expenditure on imports constitutes the third withdrawal from the inner flow. This money flows abroad.

Total withdrawals are simply the sum of net saving, net taxes and the expenditure on imports:

$$W = S + T + M$$

Injections (J)

Only part of the demand for firms' output arises from consumers' expenditure. The remainder comes from other sources outside the inner flow. These additional components of aggregate demand are known as *injections* (*J*). There are three types of injection.

Investment (I).   This is the money that firms spend after obtaining it from various financial institutions – either past savings or loans, or through a new issue of shares. They may invest in plant and equipment or may simply spend the money on building up stocks of inputs, semi-finished or finished goods.

Government expenditure (G).   When the government spends money on goods and services produced by firms, this counts as an injection. Examples of such government expenditure include spending on roads, hospitals and schools. (Note that government expenditure in this model does not include state benefits. These transfer payments, as we saw above, are the equivalent of negative taxes and have the effect of reducing the *T* component of withdrawals.)

Export expenditure (X).   Money flows into the circular flow from abroad when residents abroad buy our exports of goods and services.[1]

Total injections are thus the sum of investment, government expenditure and exports:

$$J = I + G + X$$

The relationship between withdrawals and injections

There are indirect links between saving and investment, taxation and government expenditure, and imports and exports, via financial institutions, the government (central and local) and foreign countries respectively. If more money is saved, there will be more available for banks and

other financial institutions to lend out. If tax receipts are higher, the government may be more keen to increase its expenditure. Finally, if imports increase, incomes of people abroad will increase, which will enable them to purchase more of our exports.

These links, however, do not guarantee that $S = I$ or $G = T$ or $M = X$. Firms may wish to invest (*I*) more or less than people wish to save (*S*); governments can spend (*G*) more than they receive in taxes (*T*) or vice versa; and exports (*X*) can exceed imports (*M*) or vice versa.

A major point here is that the decisions to save and invest are made by different people, and thus they plan to save and invest different amounts. Likewise the demand for imports may not equal the demand for exports. As far as the government is concerned, it may choose not to make *T* = *G*. It may choose not to spend all its tax revenues: to run a 'budget surplus' (*T* > *G*). Or it may choose to spend more than it receives in taxes – to run a budget deficit (*G* > *T*) – by borrowing or printing money to make up the difference.

Thus planned injections (*J*) may not equal planned withdrawals (*W*).

Are the following net injections, net withdrawals or neither? If there is uncertainty, explain your assumptions.
(a) Firms are forced to take a cut in profits in order to give a pay rise.
(b) Firms spend money on research.
(c) The government increases personal tax allowances.
(d) The general public invests more money in banks and building societies.
(e) UK investors earn higher dividends on overseas investments.
(f) The government purchases US military aircraft.
(g) People draw on their savings to finance holidays abroad.
(h) People draw on their savings to finance holidays in the UK.
(i) The government runs a budget deficit (spends more than it receives in tax revenues) and finances it by borrowing from the public.
(j) The government runs a budget deficit and finances it by printing more money.

The circular flow of income and the four macroeconomic objectives

If planned injections are not equal to planned withdrawals, what will be the consequences? If, for example, injections exceed withdrawals, the level of expenditure will rise: there

---

[1] Note that *X* would not include investment in the UK by foreign companies (i.e. credits on the financial account of the balance of payments). Foreign 'investment' involves the acquisition of assets in the UK and thus represents an income to the previous owners of these assets. It therefore represents an inflow from abroad to the household sector and thus has the effect of reducing *M*.

Definition

Injections (J) Expenditure on the production of domestic firms coming from outside the inner flow of the circular flow of income. Injections equal investment (*I*) plus government expenditure (*G*) plus expenditure on exports (*X*).

will be a rise in aggregate demand. This extra spending will increase firms' sales and thus encourage them to produce more. Total output in the economy will rise. Thus firms will pay out more in wages, salaries, profits, rent and interest. In other words, national income will rise.

The rise in aggregate demand will have the following effects upon the four macroeconomic objectives:

- There will be economic growth. The greater the initial excess of injections over withdrawals, the bigger will be the rise in national income.
- Unemployment will fall as firms take on more workers to meet the extra demand for output.
- Inflation will tend to rise. The greater the rise in aggregate demand relative to the capacity of firms to produce, the more will firms find it difficult to meet the extra demand, and the more likely they will be to raise prices.
- The exports and imports part of the balance of payments will tend to deteriorate. The higher demand sucks more imports into the country, and higher domestic inflation makes exports less competitive and imports relatively cheaper compared with home-produced goods. Thus imports will tend to rise and exports will tend to fall.

 Now consider the situation where there is an initial excess of withdrawals over injections. What effect will there be on the four objectives?

Equilibrium in the circular flow

When injections do not equal withdrawals, a state of disequilibrium will exist. This will set in train a process to bring the economy back to a state of equilibrium where injections are equal to withdrawals.

To illustrate this, let us again consider the situation where injections exceed withdrawals. Perhaps there has been a rise in business confidence so that investment has risen. Or perhaps there has been a tax cut so that withdrawals have fallen. As we have seen, the excess of injections over withdrawals will lead to a rise in national income.

But as national income rises, so households will not only spend more on domestic goods (C_d), but also save more (S), pay more taxes (T) and buy more imports (M). In other words, withdrawals will rise. This will continue until they have risen to equal injections. At that point, national income will stop rising, and so will withdrawals. Equilibrium has been reached.

Section summary

1. The circular flow of income model depicts the flows of money round the economy. The inner flow shows the direct flows between firms and households. Money flows from firms to households in the form of factor payments, and back again as consumer expenditure on domestically produced goods and services.

2. Not all incomes get passed on directly round the inner flow. Some is withdrawn in the form of net saving, some is paid in net taxes, and some goes abroad as expenditure on imports.

3. Likewise, not all expenditure on domestic firms is by domestic consumers. Some is injected from outside the inner flow in the form of investment expenditure, government expenditure and expenditure on the country's exports.

4. Planned injections and withdrawals are unlikely to be the same.

5. If injections exceed withdrawals, national income will rise, unemployment will tend to fall, inflation will tend to rise, imports will tend to rise and exports fall. The reverse will happen if withdrawals exceed injections.

6. If injections exceed withdrawals, the rise in national income will lead to a rise in withdrawals. This will continue until $W = J$. At this point, the circular flow will be in equilibrium.

14.3 MEASURING NATIONAL INCOME AND OUTPUT

The circular flow of income is very useful as a model for understanding the working of an economy. It shows how national income can increase or decrease as a result of changes in the various flows. But just how do we measure national income or output? The measure we use is called *gross domestic product (GDP)*.

This section shows how GDP is calculated. It also looks at difficulties in interpreting GDP statistics. Can the figures be meaningfully used to compare one country's standard of living with another? The appendix to this chapter goes into more detail on the precise way in which the statistics for GDP are derived.

Definition

Gross domestic product (GDP) The value of output produced within the country over a 12-month period.

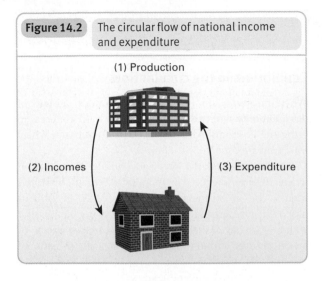

Figure 14.2 The circular flow of national income and expenditure

(1) Production

(2) Incomes

(3) Expenditure

The three ways of measuring GDP

GDP can be calculated in three different ways, which should all result in the same figure. These three methods are illustrated in the simplified circular flow of income shown in Figure 14.2.

The first method of measuring GDP is to add up the value of all the goods and services produced in the country, industry by industry. In other words, we focus on firms and add up all their production. This first method is known as the *product method*.

The production of goods and services generates incomes for households in the form of wages and salaries, profits, rent and interest. The second method of measuring GDP, therefore, is to add up all these incomes. This is known as the *income method*.

The third method focuses on the expenditures necessary to purchase the nation's production. In this simple model of the circular flow of income, with no injections or withdrawals, whatever is produced is sold. The value of what is sold must therefore be the value of what is produced. The *expenditure method* measures this sales value.

Because of the way the calculations are made, the three methods of calculating GDP *must* yield the same result. In other words,

national product = national income = national expenditure

In the appendix to this chapter, we look at each of the three methods in turn, and examine the various factors that have to be taken into account to ensure that the figures are accurate.

Taking account of inflation

If we are to make a sensible comparison of one year's national income with another, we must take inflation into account. For example, if this year national income is 10 per cent higher than last year, but at the same time prices are

also 10 per cent higher, then the average person will be no better off at all. There has been no *real* increase in income (see discussion in Appendix 1 at the end of the book on page A:6).

An important distinction here is between **nominal GDP** and **real GDP**. *Nominal* GDP, sometimes called 'money GDP', measures GDP in the prices ruling at the time and thus takes no account of inflation. *Real* GDP, however, measures GDP in the prices that ruled in some particular year – the *base year*. Thus we could measure each year's GDP in, say, 2000 prices. This would enable us to see how much *real* GDP had changed from one year to another. In other words, it would eliminate increases in money GDP that were merely due to an increase in prices.

The official statistics give both nominal and real figures. Case Study 14.1 in MyEconLab shows in more detail how real GDP figures are calculated.

Taking account of population: the use of per-capita measures

The figures we have been looking at up to now are *total* GDP figures. Although they are useful for showing how big the total output or income of one country is compared with another, we are often more interested in output or income *per head*. Luxembourg obviously has a much lower total national income than the UK, but it has a higher GDP per head. China is often referred to as being the third largest economy in the world and as likely to overtake the USA by 2040. But these are total figures. GDP per capita in China is only 11 per cent of that of the USA (see Figure 27.1 on page 764). Even by 2040 it will still be only a small fraction.

Other per-capita measures are sometimes useful. For example, measuring GDP per head of the *employed* population allows us to compare how much the average worker produces. A country may have a relatively high GDP per head of population, but also have a large proportion of people at work. Its output per worker will therefore not be so high.

 By what would we need to divide GDP in order to get a measure of labour productivity per hour?

Taking account of exchange rates: the use of PPP measures

There is a big problem with comparing GDP figures of different countries. They are measured in the local currency and thus have to be converted into a common currency

---

Definitions

Nominal GDP GDP measured at current prices.

Real GDP GDP after allowing for inflation: i.e., GDP measured in constant prices, i.e., in terms of the prices ruling in some base year.

THRESHOLD CONCEPT 12

THE DISTINCTION BETWEEN REAL AND NOMINAL VALUES

THINKING LIKE AN ECONOMIST

Which would you rather have: (a) a pay rise of 5 per cent when inflation is 2 per cent, or (b) a pay rise of 10 per cent when inflation is 9 per cent? Which debt would you rather have: (a) one where the interest rate is 10 per cent and inflation is 8 per cent, or (b) one where the interest rate is 5 per cent and the inflation rate is 1 per cent?

To answer these questions, you need to distinguish between real and nominal values. **Nominal values** are measured in current prices and take no account of inflation. Thus in the questions above, the nominal pay rises are (a) 5 per cent and (b) 10 per cent; the nominal interest rates are (a) 10 per cent and (b) 5 per cent. In each case it might seem that you are better off with alternative (b).

But if you opted for answers (b), you would be wrong. Once you take inflation into account, you would be better off in each case with alternative (a). What we need to do is to use **real values**. Real values take account of inflation. Thus in the first question, although the nominal pay rise in alternative (a) is 5 per cent, the real pay rise is only 3 per cent, since 2 of the 5 per cent is absorbed by higher prices. You are only 3 per cent better off in terms of what you can buy. In alternative (b) the real pay rise is only 1 per cent, since 9 of the 10 per cent is absorbed by higher prices. Thus in real terms, alternative (a) is better.

In the second question, although in alternative (a) you are paying 10 per cent in nominal terms, your debt is being reduced in real terms by 8 per cent and thus you are paying a real rate of interest of only 2 per cent. In alternative (b), although the nominal rate of interest is only 5 per cent, your debt is being eroded by inflation by only 1 per cent. The real rate of interest is thus 4 per cent. Again, in real terms, you are better off with alternative (a).

The distinction between real and nominal values is a threshold concept, as understanding the distinction is fundamental to assessing statistics about the economy. Often politicians will switch between real and nominal values depending on which are most favourable to them. Thus a government wishing to show how strong economic growth has been will tend to use nominal growth figures. On the other hand, the opposition will tend to refer to real growth figures, as these will be lower (assuming a positive inflation rate).

It's easy to make the mistake of using nominal figures when we should really be using real ones. This is known as 'money illusion': the belief that a rise in money terms represents a real rise.

 When comparing two countries' GDP growth rates, does it matter if we use nominal figures, provided we use them for both countries?

(e.g. dollars or euros) at the current exchange rate. But the exchange rate may be a poor indicator of the purchasing power of the currency at home. For example, £1 may exchange for, say, 200 yen. But will £1 in the UK buy the same amount of goods as ¥200 in Japan? The answer is almost certainly no.

To compensate for this, GDP can be converted into a common currency at a ***purchasing-power parity rate***. This is a rate of exchange that would allow a given amount of money in one country to buy the same amount of goods in another country after exchanging it into the currency of the other country. The European Commission publishes PPP rates against the euro for all EU currencies and for the US dollar and Japanese yen. The OECD also publishes PPP rates against the US dollar for all OECD currencies. Using such rates to measure GDP gives the ***purchasing-power standard (PPS) GDP***.

Box 14.1 compares GDP with PPS GDP for various countries.

Do GDP statistics give a good indication of a country's standard of living?

If we take into account both inflation and the size of the population, and use figures for *real* per-capita PPS GDP, will this give us a good indication of a country's standard of living? The figures *do* give quite a good indication of the level of production of goods and the incomes generated from it, provided we are clear about the distinctions between the different measures. But when we come to ask the more general question of whether the figures give a good indication of the welfare or happiness of the country's citizens, then there are serious problems in relying exclusively on GDP statistics.

Problems of measuring national output

The main problem here is that the output of some goods and services goes unrecorded and thus the GDP figures will understate the nation's output. There are two reasons why items are not recorded.

Non-marketed items. If you employ a decorator to paint your living room, this will be recorded in the GDP statistics.

Definitions

Purchasing-power parity (PPP) exchange rate An exchange rate corrected to take into account the purchasing power of a currency. $1 would buy the same in each country after conversion into its currency at the PPP rate.

Purchasing-power standard (PPS) GDP GDP measured at a country's PPP exchange rate.

BOX 14.1	WHICH COUNTRY IS BETTER OFF?	CASE STUDIES AND APPLICATIONS

Comparing national income statistics

Using PPS GDP figures can give a quite different picture of the relative incomes in different countries than using simple GDP figures. The table shows the GDP per head and PPS GDP per head in various countries. The figures are expressed as a percentage of the average of the EU-15 countries (i.e. those that were members prior to the entry of 10 new members in May 2004).

Thus in 2007, Denmark had a GDP per head 43.4 per cent higher than the EU-15 average. But, because of higher Danish prices, the average person in Denmark could buy only 11.4 per cent more goods and services. By contrast, GDP per head in the Czech Republic was only 42.7 per cent of the EU-15 average, but because of lower Czech prices the average person there could buy 72.7 per cent as much as the average citizen of the EU-15 countries.

 Referring to the figures in the table, which countries' actual exchange rates would seem to understate the purchasing power of their currency?

GDP per head as a percentage of the EU-15 average, 2007

	GDP per head	GDP (PPS) per head
Luxembourg	259.2	253.8
Ireland	147.0	131.0
Denmark	143.4	111.4
Sweden	124.9	110.8
Netherlands	117.5	117.8
UK	114.5	105.8
USA	114.4	138.6
Germany	101.3	102.3
France	101.0	98.1
Italy	89.0	91.0
Japan	86.1	102.0
Spain	80.5	93.5
Greece	70.6	88.2
Portugal	52.8	66.1
Czech Republic	42.7	72.7
Poland	27.7	48.8

Source: Statistical Annex of the European Economy (Commission of the European Communities, 2007).

If, however, you paint the room yourself, it will not. Similarly, if a nanny is employed by parents to look after their children, this childcare will form part of GDP. If, however, a parent stays at home to look after the children, it will not. The exclusion of these 'do-it-yourself' and other home-based activities means that the GDP statistics understate the true level of production in the economy. If over time there is an *increase* in the amount of do-it-yourself activities that people perform, the figures will also understate the *rate of growth* of national output. On the other hand, if in more and more families both partners go out to work and employ people to look after their children, this will overstate the rate of growth in output. The childcare that was previously unrecorded now enters into the GDP statistics.

 If we were trying to get a 'true' measure of national production, which of the following activities would you include: (a) washing-up; (b) planting flowers in the garden; (c) playing an educational game with children in the family; (d) playing any game with children in the family; (e) cooking your own supper; (f) cooking supper for the whole family; (g) reading a novel for pleasure; (h) reading a textbook as part of studying; (i) studying holiday brochures?

Is there a measurement problem if you get pleasure from the do-it-yourself activity itself as well as from its outcome?

The 'underground' economy. The underground economy consists of illegal and hence undeclared transactions. These could be transactions where the goods or services are themselves illegal, as with drugs, guns and prostitution. Alternatively, they could be transactions that are illegal only in that they are not declared for tax purposes. For example, to avoid paying VAT, a garage may be prepared

to repair your car slightly more cheaply if you pay cash. Another example is that of 'moonlighting', where people do extra work outside their normal job and do not declare the income for tax purposes. For example, an electrician employed by a building contractor during the day may rewire people's houses in the evenings, again for cash. Unemployed people may do casual jobs that they do not declare, to avoid losing benefits.

Problems of using GDP statistics to measure welfare

GDP is essentially an indicator of a nation's *production*. But production may be a poor indicator of society's well-being for the following reasons.

Production does not equal consumption. Production is desirable only to the extent that it enables us to *consume* more. If GDP rises as a result of a rise in *investment*, this will not lead to an increase in *current* living standards. It will, of course, help to raise *future* consumption.

The same applies if GDP rises as a result of an increase in exports. Unless there is a resulting increase in imports, it will be consumers abroad that benefit, not domestic consumers.

Production has human costs. If production increases, this may be due to technological advance. If, however, it increases as a result of people having to work harder or longer hours, its net benefit will be less. Leisure is a desirable good, and so too are pleasant working conditions, but these items are not included in the GDP figures.

GDP ignores externalities. The rapid growth in industrial society is recorded in GDP statistics. What the statistics

BOX 14.2 HOW BIG IS THE UNDERGROUND ECONOMY?

The factors that determine its size

Estimates of the size of the underground economy vary enormously from country to country. Clearly it is impossible to get precise estimates because, by their very nature, the details are largely hidden from the authorities. Nevertheless economists have tried to identify the factors that determine the size of the underground economy.

The first determinant is the level of taxes and regulations. The greater their level, the greater the incentive for people to evade the system and 'go underground'.

The second is the determination of the authorities to catch up with evaders, and the severity of the punishments for those found out.

A third is the size of the service sector relative to the manufacturing sector. It is harder for the authorities to detect the illicit activities of motor mechanics, builders and window cleaners than the output of cars, bricks and soap.

Another determinant is the proportion of the population that is self-employed. It is much easier for the self-employed to evade taxes than it is for people receiving a wage where taxes are deducted at source.

Some indication of the size of the underground economy is given by the demand for cash in the economy, since most underground transactions are conducted in cash. It was estimated that eurozone residents, prior to the adoption of euro notes and coins in January 2002, had over €180 billion in old-currency cash – equivalent to 2.6 per cent of eurozone GDP. In order to persuade people to put such money in legitimate accounts, France and Spain ruled that between December 2001 and June 2002 banks only had to report cash deposits of over €10 000.

1. *Is the size of the underground economy likely to increase or decrease as the level of unemployment rises?*
2. *What impact would you expect a relaxation of immigration controls to have on the size of the underground economy?*
3. *If the amount of cash used in the economy falls, does this mean that the size of the underground economy must have fallen?*

---

do not record are the environmental side-effects: the polluted air and rivers, the ozone depletion, the problem of global warming. If these external costs were taken into account, the *net* benefits of industrial production might be much less.

Name some external benefits that are not included in GDP statistics.

The production of certain 'bads' leads to an increase in GDP. Some of the undesirable effects of growth may actually *increase* GDP! Take the examples of crime, stress-related illness and environmental damage. Faster growth may lead to more of all three. But increased crime leads to more expenditure on security; increased stress leads to more expenditure on health care; and increased environmental damage leads to more expenditure on environmental clean-up. These expenditures *add* to GDP. Thus, rather than reducing GDP, crime, stress and environmental damage actually increase it!

Total GDP figures ignore the distribution of income. If some people gain and others lose, we cannot say that there has been an unambiguous increase in welfare. A typical feature of many rapidly growing countries is that some people grow very rich while others are left behind. The result is a growing inequality. If this is seen as undesirable, then clearly total GDP statistics are an inadequate measure of welfare.

Conclusions

If a country's citizens put a high priority on a clean environment, a relaxed way of life, greater self-sufficiency, a less materialistic outlook, more giving rather than selling, and greater equality, then such a country will probably have a lower GDP than a similarly endowed country where the pursuit of wealth is given high priority. Clearly, we cannot conclude that the first country will have a lower level of well-being. However, this does not mean that we should reject GDP statistics as a means of judging economic performance. While GDP statistics are not a good measure of economic welfare, they are an effective measure of *output* or *income*, and should be seen in that context.

Section summary

1. National income is usually expressed in terms of gross domestic product. This is simply the value of domestic production over the course of the year. It can be measured by the product, expenditure or income methods.

2. Real national income takes account of inflation by being expressed in the prices of some base year.

3. In order to compare living standards of different countries, national income has to be expressed per capita and at purchasing-power parity exchange rates.

4. Even if it is, there are still problems in using national income statistics for comparative purposes. Certain items will not be included: items such as non-marketed products, services in the family and activities in the underground economy. Moreover, the statistics include certain 'bads' and ignore externalities, and they also ignore questions of the distribution of income.

The distinction between actual and potential growth

Before examining the causes of economic growth, it is essential to distinguish between *actual* and *potential* economic growth. People frequently confuse the two.

Actual growth is the percentage annual increase in national output: the rate of growth in real GDP. When statistics on growth rates are published, it is actual growth they are referring to.

Potential growth is the speed at which the economy *could* grow. It is the percentage annual increase in the economy's *capacity* to produce: the rate of growth in *potential output*.

Potential output (i.e. potential GDP) is the level of output when the economy is operating at 'normal capacity utilisation'. This allows for firms having a planned degree of spare capacity to meet unexpected demand or for hold-ups in supply. It also allows for some unemployment as

Definitions

Actual growth The percentage annual increase in national output actually produced.

Potential growth The percentage annual increase in the capacity of the economy to produce.

Potential output The sustainable level of output that could be produced in the economy: i.e. one that involves a 'normal' level of capacity utilisation and does not result in rising inflation.

BOX 14.3 **OUTPUT GAPS**

A measure of excess or deficient demand

If the economy grows, how fast and for how long can it grow before it runs into inflationary problems? On the other hand, what minimum rate must be achieved to avoid rising unemployment?

To answer these questions, economists have developed the concept of 'output gaps'.[1] As we have seen, the output gap is the difference between actual output and potential output.

If actual output is below potential output (the gap is negative), there will be a higher than normal level of unemployment as firms are operating below their normal level of capacity utilisation. There will, however, be a downward pressure on inflation, resulting from a lower than normal level of demand for labour and other resources. If actual output is above potential output (the gap is positive), there will be excess demand and a rise in inflation.

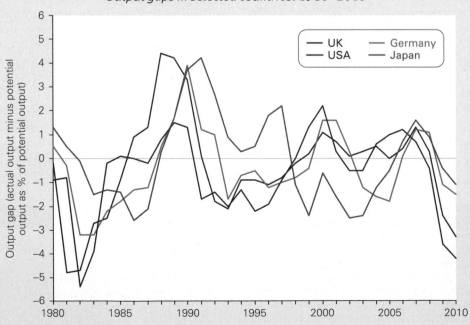

Output gaps in selected countries: 1980–2010

Note: Years 2009 and 2010 based on forecasts.
Source: Based on data in *Economic Outlook* (Organisation for Economic Co-operation and Development [OECD], various years).

people move from job to job. Potential output is thus somewhat below full-capacity output, which is the absolute maximum that could be produced with firms working flat out.

The difference between actual and potential output is known as the *output gap*. Thus if actual output exceeds potential output, the output gap is positive: the economy is operating above normal capacity utilisation. If actual output is below potential output, the output gap is negative: the economy is operating below normal capacity utilisation.

> ### Definition
>
> **Output gap** The difference between actual and potential output. When actual output exceeds potential output, the gap is positive. When actual output is less than potential output, the gap is negative.

Box 14.3 looks at the output gap since 1980 for four major industrial economies.

Two of the major factors contributing to potential economic growth are:

- An increase in resources – natural resources, labour or capital.
- An increase in the efficiency with which these resources are used, through advances in technology, improved labour skills or improved organisation.

If the actual growth rate is less than the potential growth rate, there will be an increase in spare capacity and probably an increase in unemployment: the output gap will become more negative (or less positive). To close a negative output gap, the actual growth rate would temporarily have to exceed the potential growth rate. In the long run, however, the actual growth rate will be limited to the potential growth rate.

Generally, the gap will be negative in a recession and positive in a boom. In other words, output gaps follow the course of the business cycle.

The diagram shows output gaps for four countries from 1980 to 2009. As you can see, there was a large positive output gap in the UK in the late 1980s. This corresponded to a rapid rise in output and inflation and a fall in unemployment. You can also see that there was a large negative output gap in Japan in the early 2000s. This corresponded to a deep recession, high unemployment and inflation just below zero (i.e. a slight decline in prices).

Over the long term, the actual rate of economic growth will be approximately the same as the potential rate. In other words, over the years, the average output gap will tend towards zero.

But how do we measure the output gap? There are two possible methods.

Measuring trend growth

The simplest way of calculating the output gap is by assuming that it averages zero over the long term. This means that potential output is given by the dashed line in Figure 14.3, which shows output trend: the sum of the areas where actual output is above potential output equal the sum of the areas where it is below. To measure the output gap at any particular point in time, we simply see how much actual output diverges from trend output.

A key assumption of this method is that the potential level of output grows steadily. This is, in fact, a major weakness of this method. Technological innovations tend to come in waves, generating surges in an economy's potential output. Rates of innovation, in turn, depend upon how flexible the economy is in adapting to such new technologies and how much investment takes place in

equipment using this technology and in training labour in the necessary skills.

Business surveys

An alternative way to measure the output gap is to ask businesses directly. However, survey-based evidence can provide only a broad guide to rates of capacity utilisation and whether there is deficient or excess demand. Survey evidence tends to focus on specific sectors, which might, or might not, be indicative of the capacity position of the economy as a whole.

Evidence for the UK

The trend growth rate in the UK was about 2.4 per cent per year over the full economic cycle to 2008 (i.e. from 1991, the equivalent point in the previous cycle).

Until the recession of 2008/9, growth rates had been relatively stable since 1992 compared with previous cycles. The slowdown in 2001/2 was relatively mild. In fact, Gordon Brown was claiming in the early 2000s that 'boom and bust' were things of the past. During this period, therefore, output gaps, both positive and negative, were smaller than in the 1980s (or the 1970s for that matter).

Until the recession of 2008/9, it was argued that the greater stability in the UK economy created a climate that encouraged a long-term increase in investment and hence a long-term increase in potential growth. Whether that climate will be resumed in the future will have to be seen.

 Under what circumstances would potential output (i.e. a zero output gap) move further away from the full-capacity output ceiling shown in Figure 14.3?

[1] See C. Giorno et al., 'Potential output, output gaps and structural budget balances', *OECD Economic Studies*, no. 24, 1995: 1.

There are thus two major policy issues concerned with economic growth: the short-run issue of ensuring that actual growth is such as to keep actual output as close as possible to potential output; and the long-run issue of what determines the rate of potential economic growth.

Economic growth and the business cycle

Although growth in potential output varies to some extent over the years – depending on the rate of advance of technology, the level of investment and the discovery of new raw materials – it nevertheless tends to be much more steady than the growth in actual output.

Actual growth tends to fluctuate. In some years, countries will experience high rates of economic growth: the country experiences a boom. In other years, economic growth is low or even negative: the country experiences a slowdown or recession.[1] This cycle of booms and recessions is known as the **business cycle** or **trade cycle**.

There are four 'phases' of the business cycle. They are illustrated in Figure 14.3.

1. *The upturn*. In this phase, a contracting or stagnant economy begins to recover, and growth in actual output resumes.
2. *The expansion*. During this phase, there is rapid economic growth: the economy is booming. A fuller use is made of resources, and the gap between actual and potential output narrows.
3. *The peaking out*. During this phase, growth slows down or even ceases.
4. *The slowdown, recession or slump*. During this phase, there is little or no growth or even a decline in output. Increasing slack develops in the economy.

A word of caution: do not confuse a high *level* of output with a high rate of *growth* in output. The level of output is highest in phase 3. The rate of growth in output is highest in phase 2 (i.e. where the curve is steepest).

 Figure 14.3 shows a decline in actual output in recession. Redraw the diagram, only this time show a mere slowing down of growth in phase 4.

Long-term output trend

A line can be drawn showing the trend of national output over time (i.e. ignoring the cyclical fluctuations around the trend). This is shown as the dashed line in Figure 14.3. If, over time, firms on average operate with a 'normal' degree of capacity utilisation, the trend output line will be the same as the potential output line. Also, if the average level of capacity that is unutilised stays constant from one cycle to another, the trend line will have the same slope as the full-capacity output line. In other words, the trend (or

potential) rate of growth will be the same as the rate of growth of capacity.

If, however, the level of unutilised capacity changes from one cycle to another, then the trend line will have a different slope from the full-capacity output line. For example, if unemployment and unused industrial capacity *rise* from one peak to another, or from one trough to another, the trend line will move further away from the full-capacity output line (i.e. it will be less steep).

 If the average percentage (as opposed to the average level) of capacity that was unutilised remained constant, would the trend line have the same slope as the potential output line?

The business cycle in practice

The business cycle illustrated in Figure 14.3 is a 'stylised' cycle. It is nice and smooth and regular. Drawing it this way allows us to make a clear distinction between each of the four phases. In practice, however, business cycles are highly irregular. They are irregular in two ways:

- *The length of the phases*. Some booms are short-lived, lasting only a few months or so. Others are much longer, lasting perhaps several years. Likewise some recessions are short while others are long.
- *The magnitude of the phases*. Sometimes in phase 2 there is a very high rate of economic growth, perhaps 4 per cent per annum or more. On other occasions in phase 2 growth is much gentler. Sometimes in phase 4 there is a recession, with an actual decline in output. On other

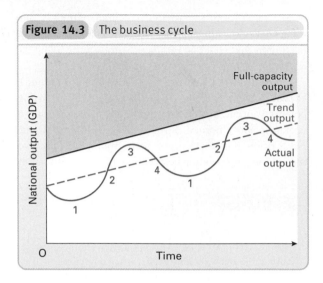

Figure 14.3 The business cycle

Definition

Business cycle or **trade cycle** The periodic fluctuations of national output round its long-term trend.

---

[1] In official statistics, a recession is defined as when an economy experiences falling national output (negative growth) for two or more quarters.

Figure 14.4 Growth rates in selected industrial countries, 1970–2010

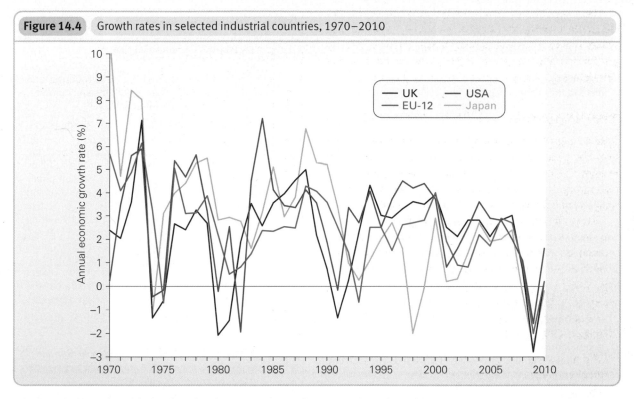

Note: Years 2009 and 2010 figures based on forecasts; EU-12 = the 12 original members of the eurozone.
Source: Based on data in *Economic Outlook* (Organisation for Economic Co-operation and Development [OECD], various years).

occasions, phase 4 is merely a 'pause', with growth simply being low.

Nevertheless, despite the irregularity of the fluctuations, cycles are still clearly discernible, especially if we plot *growth* on the vertical axis rather than the *level* of output. This is done in Figure 14.4, which shows the business cycles in selected industrial economies from 1970 to 2010. As you can see, all four suffered a recession or slowdown in the mid 1970s, the early 1980s, the early 1990s and the early and late 2000s, and a boom in the early 1970s, the late 1970s, the late 1980s and, except in the case of Japan, the late 1990s.

But despite this broad similarity in their experience, there were nevertheless significant differences in the magnitude and timing of their individual cycles. For example, the UK and the USA went into recession in the early 1990s two years before the other three countries. Also, the recession of 2001–2 was more severe in Japan and the eurozone than in the UK and the USA.

Causes of fluctuations in actual growth

The major determinants of variations in the rate of actual growth in the *short run* are variations in the growth of aggregate demand. As we saw in section 14.2, aggregate

demand is total spending on the goods and services produced in the economy:

$$AD = C + I + G + X - M$$

A rapid rise in aggregate demand will create shortages. This will tend to stimulate firms to increase output, thus reducing slack in the economy. Likewise, a reduction in aggregate demand will leave firms with increased stocks of unsold goods. They will therefore tend to reduce output.

Aggregate demand and actual output, therefore, fluctuate together in the short run. A boom is associated with a rapid rise in aggregate demand: the faster the rise in aggregate demand, the higher the short-run growth rate. A recession, by contrast, is associated with a reduction in aggregate demand.

A rapid rise in aggregate demand, however, is not enough to ensure a continuing high level of growth over a *number* of years. Without a corresponding expansion of potential output, rises in actual output must eventually come to an end as spare capacity is used up.

In the long run, therefore, there are two determinants of actual growth:

- The growth in aggregate demand. This determines whether potential output will be realised.
- The growth in potential output.

SHORT-TERM GROWTH IN A COUNTRY'S OUTPUT TENDS TO FLUCTUATE

Countries rarely experience stable economic growth. Instead they experience business cycles. Periods of rapid economic growth are followed by periods of low growth or even a fall in output (negative growth).

Sometimes these cycles can be the result of government policy: raising taxes in a recession in order to compensate for falling tax revenues caused by lower incomes and lower expenditure. The higher taxation dampens consumer demand and causes firms to cut back on production to match the fall in sales.

Usually, however, economic fluctuations are simply the result of the workings of a market system. Some economists see the problem as rooted in fluctuations in aggregate demand. Consumer spending fluctuates; firms' investment fluctuates; export sales fluctuate. What is more, these various elements interact with each other. A rise in consumer expenditure can stimulate firms to invest in order to build up capacity to meet the extra demand. This, in turn, generates more employment in the capital goods industries and extra incomes for their employees. This further stimulates consumer demand. We examine these explanations in section 18.4.

Some economists see the problem as rooted in fluctuations in aggregate supply. These 'real-business-cycle' economists

argue that technological changes can boost output and employment and that these changes often come in waves. We look at these explanations in section 22.3.

But whatever the cause, it is vital to recognise the fundamental instability in market economies. This is what makes the business cycle a threshold concept. Analysing the causes and paths of business cycles occupies many macroeconomists. Their analysis leads to various policy conclusions. Some argue that it is best for the government or central bank to try to stabilise the cycle by active intervention: boosting aggregate demand (e.g. by cutting taxes, raising government expenditure or cutting interest rates) when the economy is experiencing low or negative growth, and dampening aggregate demand when the economy is experiencing unsustainably high growth. Others argue that it is best not to intervene, but to ride out the fluctuations, arguing that attempting to manage aggregate demand often makes things worse.

1. *If people believe that the economy is about to go into recession (i.e. that real GDP will fall), how may their actions aggravate the problem?*
2. *Why will some people suffer more than others from a recession?*

BOX 14.4 **IS STABILITY ALWAYS DESIRABLE?**

Should firms sometimes be given a short, sharp shock?

Governments around the world aim for *stable* economic growth; they try to prevent the ups and downs of the business cycle. Gordon Brown, in his ten years as Chancellor of the Exchequer, claimed to have 'put and end to boom and bust'. But why is stability desirable?

The first reason is that a stable economic environment allows firms to plan with more certainty and thus encourages investment. Instability, by contrast, makes firms cautious and unwilling to make long-term commitments, such as building a new factory; investment becomes more risky. Investment is thus lower and so too, as a result, is long-term economic growth.

The second reason is that some people suffer in times of recession. True, for most people, recessions are relatively minor affairs, as long as they have a job and their pay is little affected. But some firms go out of business; some people lose their jobs. Personal lives are devastated, resulting in stress at the best and the break-up of relationships, depression, crime and suicide at worst. In other words, the effects of recessions are unequally spread.

The third reason concerns perception. Governments are often judged as successes or failures according to the state of the economy, and recessions are seen as a failure – whether or not the recession was caused by global factors largely beyond the scope of the government. Stable growth is thus a high policy priority for all governments.

When bad is good

But recessions can have benefits. If the economy is stable, firms may simply prefer to carry on doing what they have done before. If competition is strong, or where there is a risk of a takeover, this may not be possible. But when competition is weak, many firms can remain inefficient and still make reasonable profits.

When times are tough, however, firms may have to take a much closer look at how their business is operated and find new more efficient methods of production or new and better products. If they cannot, they may not survive. A recession, therefore, may be a useful means of getting rid of inefficient firms and releasing resources – labour, office space, raw materials, equipment, etc. – for the creation of new firms.

If the market is where the fittest survive, bad times are when you need to be fit – or rapidly become so.

1. *If, over a ten-year period, your income stayed constant at £20 000 per year, would you consider yourself to be better or worse off than if your income averaged £20 000 over the period but fluctuated from £5000 to £35 000 per year?*
2. *Explain whether a more risky business environment encourages higher or lower growth in potential output.*

KI 11
p75

KI 4
p10

KI 3
p10

Section summary

1. Actual growth must be distinguished from potential growth. The actual growth rate is the percentage annual increase in the output that is actually produced, whereas potential growth is the percentage annual increase in the capacity of the economy to produce (whether or not this capacity is utilised).

2. Actual growth will fluctuate with the course of the business cycle. The cycle can be broken down into four phases: the upturn, the expansion, the peaking out,

and the slowdown or recession. In practice, the length and magnitude of these phases will vary: the cycle is thus irregular.

3. Actual growth is determined by potential growth and by the level of aggregate demand. If actual output is below potential output, actual growth can temporarily exceed potential growth, if aggregate demand is rising sufficiently. In the long term, however, actual output can grow only as fast as potential output will permit.

14.5 LONG-TERM ECONOMIC GROWTH

For growth to be sustained over the long term, there must be an increase in *potential* output. In other words, the country's capacity to produce must increase. In this section we see what determines this capacity and why some countries grow faster than others over the long term. What we are concerned with here, therefore, is the *supply* side of the economy, rather than the level of aggregate demand.

Causes of long-term growth

There are two main determinants of potential output: (a) the amount of resources available and (b) their productivity. If supply potential is to grow, then either (a) or (b) or both must grow.

Increases in the quantity of resources: capital, labour, land and raw materials

Capital. The nation's output depends on its stock of capital (K). An increase in this stock will increase output. If we ignore the problem of machines wearing out or becoming obsolete and needing replacing, then the stock of capital will increase by the amount of investment: $\Delta K = I$.

But by how much will this investment raise output? This depends on the productivity of this new capital: on the *marginal efficiency of capital* (see page 262). Let us define the nation's marginal efficiency of capital (*MEC*) as the annual extra income (ΔY) yielded by an increase in the capital stock, relative to the cost of that extra capital (ΔK).

$$MEC = \frac{\Delta Y}{\Delta K} = \frac{\Delta Y}{I}$$

Thus if £100 million of extra capital yielded an annual income of £25 million, the marginal efficiency of capital would be £25 million/£100 million = $^1/_4$.

The rate of growth will depend on the fraction (i) of national income devoted to new investment (i.e. investment over and above what is necessary to replace worn-out equipment). The higher this rate of new investment, the higher will be the potential growth rate.

The relationship between the investment rate and the potential growth rate (g_p) is given by the simple formula

$$g_p = i \times MEC$$

Thus if 20 per cent of national income went in new investment (i), and if each £1 of new investment yielded 25p of extra income per year ($MEC = ^1/_4$), then the growth rate would be 5 per cent.

A simple example will demonstrate this. If national income is £100 billion, then £20 billion will be invested (i = 20 per cent). This will lead to extra annual output of £5 billion ($MEC = ^1/_4$). Thus national income grows to £105 billion: a growth of 5 per cent.

But what determines the rate of investment? There are a number of determinants. These include the confidence of businesspeople about the future demand for their products, the profitability of business, the tax regime, the rate of growth in the economy and the rate of interest. We will examine these determinants in section 17.1.

Over the long term, if investment is to increase, then people must *save* more in order to finance that extra investment. Put another way, people must be prepared to consume less in order to allow more resources to be diverted into producing capital goods: factories, machines, etc.

Labour. If there is an increase in the working population, there will be an increase in potential output. This increase in working population may result from a higher 'participation rate': a larger proportion of the total population in work or seeking work. Examples include a greater proportion of women with children deciding to rejoin the labour market, people retiring later and people working part time deciding to work longer hours.

Alternatively, a rise in the working population may be the result of an increase in total population. There is a problem here, however. If a rise in total population does not result in a greater *proportion* of the population working, output *per head* of population may not rise at all. In practice, many developed countries are faced with a growing

THINKING LIKE AN ECONOMIST

THRESHOLD CONCEPT 14 — LONG-TERM GROWTH IN A COUNTRY'S OUTPUT DEPENDS ON A GROWTH IN THE QUANTITY AND/OR PRODUCTIVITY OF ITS RESOURCES

In the short term, economic growth is likely to be influenced by changes in aggregate demand. If the economy is in recession, an expansion in aggregate demand will help to bring the economy out of recession and move it closer to full employment.

Actual output, however, cannot continue growing faster than potential output over the longer term. Firms will start reaching capacity and actual growth will then have to slow. The rate of potential growth thus places a limit to the rate of actual growth over the longer term.

What then determines the rate of growth in potential output? The answer lies on the supply side. It depends on the rate of growth of factors of production. There are two key elements here. The first is growth in the simple quantity of factors: growth in the size of the workforce, of the available land and raw materials, and of the stock of capital. The second is productivity growth. This involves elements such as growth in the educational attainments and skills of the workforce, growth in technology, and growth in the efficiency with which resources are used.

To recognise the importance of resources and their productivity in determining long-term growth is a threshold concept. It helps in understanding the importance of designing appropriate supply-side policies: policies that focus on increasing aggregate supply rather than managing aggregate demand. It is easy to worry too much about the short term.

This is not to say that the short term should be neglected. The famous economist John Maynard Keynes argued that it was fundamentally important to focus on aggregate demand and the short term to avoid severe economic fluctuations, with the twin problems of high unemployment in recessions and high inflation in periods of unsustainably high growth. He used the famous phrase 'In the long term we're all dead.'

But although we all have to die sometime, we may have many years left to reap the benefits of appropriate supply-side policy. And even if we don't, our children will.

1. *Give some examples of supply-side policy (see Chapter 23 for some ideas if you are stuck).*
2. *If there is an increase in aggregate supply, will this result in an increase in potential growth?*

---

proportion of their population above retirement age, and thus a potential *fall* in output per head of population.

Land and raw materials. The scope for generating growth here is usually very limited. Land is virtually fixed in quantity. Land reclamation schemes and the opening up of marginal land can add only tiny amounts to national output. Even if new raw materials (e.g. oil) are discovered, this will result only in *short-term* growth, while the rate of extraction is building up. Once the rate of extraction is at a maximum, economic growth will cease. Output will simply remain at the new higher level, until eventually the raw materials begin to run out. Output will then fall back again.

KI 17
p125

The problem of diminishing returns. If a single factor of production increases in supply while others remain fixed, diminishing returns will set in. For example, if the quantity of capital increases with no increase in other factors of production, diminishing returns to capital will set in. The rate of return on capital will fall.

Unless *all* factors of production increase, therefore, the rate of growth is likely to slow down. It is not enough that labour and capital increase if there is a limited supply of land and raw materials. This was the worry of the classical economists of the nineteenth century, who were pessimistic about the future prospects for growth (see Box 14.5).

Then there is the problem of the environment. If a rise in labour and capital leads to a more *intensive* use of land and natural resources, the resulting growth in output may be environmentally unsustainable.

The solution to the problem of diminishing returns is an increase in the *productivity* of resources.

Increases in the productivity of resources

TC 14
p404

Technological improvements can increase the marginal productivity of capital. Much of the investment in new machines is not just in extra machines, but in superior machines producing a higher rate of return. Modern computers can do the work of many people and have replaced many machines that were cumbersome and expensive to build. Improved methods of transport have reduced the costs of moving goods and materials. Improved communications (such as email and the Internet) have reduced the costs of transmitting information. The high-tech world of today would seem a wonderland to someone of a hundred years ago.

As a result of technical progress, the productivity of capital has tended to increase, not decrease, over time. Similarly, as a result of new skills, improved education and training, and better health, the productivity of labour has also tended to increase over time.

But technical progress on its own is not enough. There must also be the institutions and attitudes that encourage *innovation*. In other words, the inventions must be exploited.

For what reasons might the productivity of land increase over time?

BOX 14.5	THEORIES OF GROWTH		EXPLORING ECONOMICS

From dismal economics to the economics of optimism

The classical theory of growth

The classical economists of the nineteenth century were very pessimistic about the prospects for economic growth. They saw the rate of growth petering out as diminishing returns to both labour and capital led to low wages and a falling rate of profit. The only gainers would be landlords, who, given the fixed supply of land, would receive higher and higher rents as the demand for scarce land rose.

Long-run stationary state in the classical model

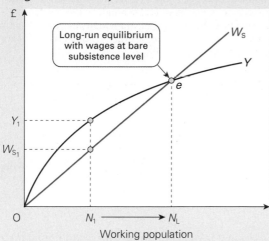

The classical position can be shown graphically. The size of the working population is plotted on the horizontal axis. If it is assumed that there is a basic minimum 'subsistence' wage that workers must earn in order to survive, then the line W_S traces out the total subsistence wage bill. It is a straight line because a doubling in the number of workers would lead to a doubling of the subsistence wage bill.

The line Y shows the total level of income that will be generated as more workers are employed, after subtracting rents to landlords. In other words, it is total wages plus profits. It gets less and less steep due to diminishing returns to labour and capital given the fixed supply of land.

As long as Y is above W_S (say, at a population of N_1), firms can make a profit. They will try to expand and will thus take on more labour.

Initially this will bid up the wage and will thus erode the level of profits. But the higher wages will encourage the population to expand. This increased supply of labour will compete wages back down to the subsistence level and will thus allow some recovery in profits. But profits will not be as high as they were before because, with an increase in workers, the gap between Y and W_S will have narrowed.

Firms will continue to expand and the population will continue to grow until point e is reached. At that point, even with wages at bare subsistence level, no profit can be made. Growth will cease. The economy will be in a long-run stationary state.

No wonder economics became dubbed 'the dismal science'.

New growth theory

Economists today are more optimistic about the prospects for economic growth. This is partly based on a simple appeal to the evidence. Despite a rapid growth in world population, most countries have experienced sustained economic growth. Over the past hundred years the industrialised countries have seen per-capita growth rates averaging from just over 1 per cent to nearly 3 per cent per annum. This has resulted in per-capita real incomes many times higher than in the nineteenth century.

This worldwide experience of economic growth has stimulated the development of new growth theories. These stress two features:

- The development and spread of new technology. The rapid advances in science and technology have massively increased the productivity of factors of production. What is more, new inventions and innovations stimulate other people, often in other countries, to copy, adapt and improve on them in order to stay competitive. Growth through technical progress stimulates more growth.
- The positive externalities of investment. If one firm invests in training in order to raise labour productivity, other firms will benefit from the improved stock of 'human capital'. There will be better-trained labour that can now be hired by other firms. Similarly, if one firm invests in research and development, the benefits can spill over to other firms (once any patents have expired). These spillover benefits to other firms can be seen as the positive externalities of investment.

New growth theories seek to analyse the process of the spread of technology and how it can be influenced.

Given that technological progress allows the spectre of diminishing returns to be banished, or at least indefinitely postponed, it is no wonder that many economists are more optimistic about growth. Nevertheless, there are still serious grounds for concern.

- If the benefits of investment spill over to other firms (i.e. if there are positive externalities), the free market will lead to too little investment: firms considering investing will take into account only the benefits to themselves, not those to other firms. There is thus an important role for governments to encourage or provide training, research and capital investment. (We consider such policies in Chapter 23.)
- Potential growth may not translate into actual growth. A potentially growing economy may be languishing in a deep recession.
- There may be serious costs of economic growth: see Box 14.6.

 Can growth go on for ever, given that certain resources are finite in supply?

KI 29
p313

| BOX 14.6 | THE COSTS OF ECONOMIC GROWTH |

Is more necessarily better?

KI 1
p5

For many developing countries, economic growth is a necessity if they are to remove mass poverty. When the majority of their population is underfed and poorly housed, with inadequate health care and little access to education, few would quarrel with the need for an increase in productive potential. The main query is whether the benefits of economic growth will flow to the mass of the population, or whether they will be confined to the few who are already relatively well off.

For developed countries, the case for economic growth is less clear cut. Economic growth is usually measured in terms of the growth in GDP. The problem is that there are many 'goods' and 'bads' that are not included in GDP (see Box 14.7). Economic growth, therefore, is not the same as growth in a nation's welfare.

So, what are the benefits and costs of economic growth?

The benefits of growth

It leads to increased levels of consumption. Provided economic growth outstrips population growth, it will lead to higher real income per head. This can lead to higher levels of consumption of goods and services. If human welfare is related to the level of consumption, then growth provides an obvious gain to society.

It can help avoid other macroeconomic problems. People aspire to higher living standards. Without a growth in productive potential, people's demands for rising incomes are likely to lead to higher inflation, balance of payments crises (as more imports are purchased), industrial disputes, etc. Growth in productive potential helps to meet these aspirations and avoid macroeconomic crises.

It can make it easier to redistribute incomes to the poor. If incomes rise, the government can redistribute incomes from the rich to the poor without the rich losing. For example, as people's incomes rise, they automatically pay more taxes. These extra revenues for the government can be spent on programmes to alleviate poverty. Without a continuing rise in national income, the scope for helping the poor is much more limited.

Society may feel that it can afford to care more for the environment. As people grow richer, they may become less preoccupied with their own private consumption and more concerned to live in a clean environment. The regulation of pollution tends to be tougher in developed countries than in the developing world.

The costs of growth

In practice, more consumption may not make people happier; economies may be no less crisis-riven; income may not be redistributed more equally; the environment may not be better protected. More than this, some people argue that growth may worsen these problems and create additional problems besides.

It has current opportunity costs. To achieve faster growth, firms will probably need to invest more. This will require financing. The finance can come from more saving, higher retained profits or higher taxes. Either way, there must be a cut in consumption. In the short run, therefore, higher growth leads to less consumption, not more.

In the diagram, assume that consumption is currently at a level of C_1. Its growth over time is shown by the line

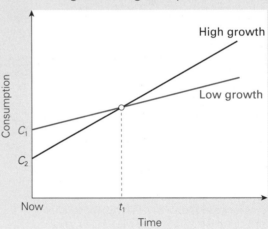

High and low growth paths

out from C_1. Now assume that the government pursues a policy of higher growth. Consumption has to fall to finance the extra investment. Consumption falls to, say, C_2. The growth in consumption is now shown by the line out from C_2. Not until time t_1 is reached (which may be several years into the future) does consumption overtake the levels that it would have reached with the previous lower growth rate.

It may simply generate extra demands. 'The more people have, the more they want.' If this is so, more consumption may not increase people's utility at all. (Diagrammatically, indifference curves may move outwards as fast as, or even faster than, consumers' budget lines: see section 4.3.) It is often observed that happiness depends on relative rather than absolute incomes. Thus as developed countries get richer their citizens do not get happier.

It has social effects. Many people claim that an excessive pursuit of material growth by a country can lead to a more greedy, more selfish and less caring society. As society becomes more industrialised, violence, crime, loneliness, stress-related diseases, suicides, divorce and other social problems are likely to rise.

By contrast, a life that is less materialistic may be more fulfilling. The term 'gross national happiness' was coined by King Jigme Singye of Bhutan. He argued that his people, although poor in materialistic terms, have a high quality of life living in harmony with their environment according to Buddhist philosophy.

It has environmental costs. A richer society may be more concerned for the environment, but it is also likely to do more damage to it. The higher the level of consumption, the higher is likely to be the level of pollution and waste. What is more, many of the environmental costs are likely to be underestimated due to a lack of scientific knowledge. Acid rain and the depletion of the ozone layer have been two examples.

It uses non-renewable resources. If growth involves using a greater amount of resources, rather than using the same amount of resources more efficiently, certain non-renewable resources will run out more rapidly. Unless viable alternatives can be found for various

minerals and fossil fuels, present growth may lead to shortages for future generations (see Box 9.10).

It has effects on the distribution of income. While some people may gain from a higher standard of living, others are likely to lose. If the means to higher growth are greater incentives (such as cuts in higher rates of income tax), then the rich might get richer, with little or no benefit 'trickling down' to the poor.

Growth involves changes in production, both in terms of the goods produced and in terms of the techniques used and the skills required. The more rapid the rate of growth, the more rapid the rate of change. People may find that their skills are no longer relevant. Their jobs may be replaced by machines. People may thus find themselves unemployed and need to retrain, or they may be forced to take low-paid, unskilled work.

Conclusion

So should countries pursue growth? The answer depends on (a) just what costs and benefits are involved, (b) what weighting people attach to them, and (c) how opposing views are to be reconciled.

A problem is that the question of the desirability of economic growth is a normative one. It involves a judgement about what a 'desirable' society should look like.

A simpler point, however, is that the electorate seems to want economic growth. As long as that is so, governments will tend to pursue policies to achieve growth. That is why we need to study the causes of growth and the policies that governments can pursue.

One thing the government can do is to view the problem as one of constrained optimisation. It sets constraints: levels of environmental protection, minimum wages, maximum rates of depletion of non-renewable resources, etc. It then seeks policies that will maximise growth, while keeping within these constraints.

1. *Is a constrained optimisation approach a practical solution to the possible costs of economic growth?*
2. *Are worries about the consequences of economic growth a 'luxury' that only rich countries can afford?*

KI 4
p10

KI 6
p27

*LOOKING AT THE MATHS

Assuming that the quantity of land is fixed, economic growth (g) results from three main sources: the rate of growth in the labour force ($\Delta L/L$), the rate of growth in the stock of capital ($\Delta K/K$) and the rate of growth in overall productivity in the economy or 'total factor productivity' ($\Delta TFP/TFP$). Thus

$$g = \frac{\Delta Y}{Y} = a\frac{\Delta L}{L} + b\frac{\Delta K}{K} + \frac{\Delta TFP}{TFP} \qquad (1)$$

where a is the elasticity of national income (Y) with respect to labour. In other words, a is the percentage increase in national income that would result from a 1 per cent increase in the labour force. Similarly, b is the elasticity of national income with respect to capital: i.e. the percentage increase in national income from a 1 per cent increase in the capital stock.[1] If there are constant returns to scale, then

$$a + b = 1$$

In other words, an increase in both labour and capital of x per cent would lead to an x per cent increase in national income.

If the capital stock is held constant and the labour force increases, there will be diminishing returns to labour. This implies that

$$a < 1$$

and that the value of a gets less as the ratio of labour to capital increases. Similarly, if capital per head of the labour force increases, there will be diminishing returns to capital. This implies that

$$b < 1$$

and that the value of b gets less as the capital/labour ratio increases. In industrialised countries in the 2000s the value of b is typically between 0.2 and 0.4, implying that a 10 per cent increase in the capital stock will increase national income by between 2 and 4 per cent. The value of a is typically between 0.6 and 0.8.

What about total factor productivity? Note that there is no 'c' term attached to $\Delta TFP/TFP$. What this means is that a total factor productivity increase of y per cent will lead to an increase in national income of y per cent for any given quantity of labour and capital. If we know the value of g, a, $\Delta L/L$, b and $\Delta K/K$, we can work out the rate of growth in total factor productivity. Rearranging equation (1) gives

$$\frac{\Delta TFP}{TFP} = g - \left(a\frac{\Delta L}{L} + b\frac{\Delta K}{K} \right) \qquad (2)$$

Case study 14.4 in MyEconLab examines how equation (1) can be used for growth accounting: a system of measuring the contribution of increases in factor inputs to economic growth. It also looks at the evidence for the UK.

---

[1] The term b is the elasticity of Y with respect to changes in K, i.e.,

$$b = \frac{\Delta Y}{\Delta K} \cdot \frac{K}{Y} = MEC \cdot \frac{K}{Y}$$

But, from equation (1), growth from a rise in capital alone is given by

$$g = b\frac{\Delta K}{K} = MEC \cdot \frac{K}{Y} \cdot \frac{\Delta K}{K}$$

Cancelling out the K terms gives

$$g = \frac{\Delta K}{Y} \times MEC = i \times MEC$$

which is the formula for the growth rate that we established on page 403.

The effects of actual growth on potential growth

Some economists argue that potential growth is not influenced by actual growth. It depends largely on growth in factor productivity, and that in turn depends on scientific and technical advance. Such advances, they argue, are independent of the state of the economy.

Other economists, however, argue that actual growth *stimulates* investment and the development of new technology. For these economists, therefore, it is vital for the achievement of high long-term growth rates that the economy experiences continuous and stable growth in actual output. Recessions breed pessimism and a lack of investment, a lack of research and a lack of innovation (see Box 14.4 on page 402).

Policies to achieve growth

How can governments increase a country's growth rate? Policies differ in two ways.

First, they may focus on the demand side or the supply side of the economy. In other words, they may attempt to create sufficient *aggregate demand* to ensure that firms wish to invest and that potential output is realised. Alternatively they may seek to increase *aggregate supply* by concentrating on measures to increase potential output: measures to encourage research and development, innovation and training.

Second, they may be market-orientated or interventionist policies. Many economists and politicians, especially those on the political right, believe that the best environment for encouraging economic growth is one where private enterprise is allowed to flourish: where entrepreneurs are able to reap substantial rewards from investment in new techniques and new products. Such economists, therefore, advocate policies designed to free up the market. Others, however, argue that a free market will be subject to considerable cyclical fluctuations. The resulting uncertainty will discourage investment. These economists, therefore, tend to advocate active intervention by the government to reduce these fluctuations.

We focus on demand-side policies in Chapter 20 and on supply-side policies in Chapter 23. In each case we look at both interventionist and market-orientated policies.

Postscript: The role of investment

Investment plays a dual role in economic growth. It is a component of aggregate demand and thus helps determine the level of actual output. It is also probably the major determinant of potential output, since investment both increases the capital stock and also leads to the development of new technology. It is important, therefore, that when investment rises, the resulting rise in aggregate demand matches the resulting rise in aggregate supply. There is a problem of timing here, however. Generally the effects on aggregate demand happen more quickly than those on aggregate supply.

Section summary

1. Growth in potential output is determined by the rate of increase in the quantity of resources: capital, labour, land and raw materials; and by the productivity of resources. The productivity of capital can be increased by technological improvements and a more efficient use of the capital stock; the productivity of labour can be increased by better education, training, motivation and organisation.

2. Whether governments can best achieve rapid growth through market-orientated or interventionist policies is highly controversial.

3. Investment plays a key role in determining growth, since it affects both aggregate demand and aggregate supply.

APPENDIX: CALCULATING GDP

As explained in section 14.3, there are three ways of estimating GDP. In this appendix, we discuss each method in more detail. We also look at some alternative measures of national income.

The product method of measuring GDP

This approach simply involves adding up the value of everything produced in the country during the year: the output of cars, timber, lollipops, shirts, etc.; and all the myriad of services such as football matches, haircuts, bus rides and insurance services. In the national accounts these figures are grouped together into broad categories such as manufacturing, construction and distribution. The figures for the UK economy for 2007 are shown in Figure A14.1.

When we add up the output of various firms, we must be careful to avoid *double counting*. For example, if a manufacturer sells a television to a retailer for £200 and the retailer sells it to the consumer for £300, how much has this television contributed to GDP? The answer is *not* £500. We do not add the £200 received by the manufacturer to the £300 received by the retailer: that would be double counting. Instead we either just count the final value (£300) or the *value added* at each stage (£200 by the manufacturer + £100 by the retailer).

The sum of all the values added at each of the stages of production by all the various industries in the economy is known as *gross value added at basic prices (GVA)*.

Some qualifications

Stocks (or inventories). We must be careful only to include the values added in the *particular year in question*. A problem here is that some goods start being produced *before* the year

Definition

Gross value added at basic prices (GVA) The sum of all the values added by all industries in the economy over a year. The figures exclude taxes on products (such as VAT) and include subsidies on products.

Figure A14.1 UK GDP by product-based measure, 2007

	Percentage of GVA
Agriculture, forestry and fishing £8910m	0.7
Mining, energy and water supply £51 127m	4.1
Manufacturing £157 728m	12.6
Construction £79 623m	6.4
Wholesale and retail trade; repairs £142 402m	11.4
Hotels and restaurants £36 645m	2.9
Transport and communication £85 326m	6.8
Financial intermediation (Banking, finance, insurance, etc.) £95 398m	7.6
Letting of property (business and dwellings) £302 605m	24.3
Public administration and defence £64 012m	5.1
Education, health and social work £159 794m	12.8
Other services £64 151m	5.1
Gross value added (GVA) at basic prices £1 247 721m	100.0
Taxes on products £158 704m *Less* subsidies on products –£5 383m	
Total GDP (at market prices) £1 401 042m	

Source: *United Kingdom National Accounts: The Blue Book – 2008 Edition* (National Statistics, 2008).

begins. Thus when we come to work out GDP, we must ignore the values that had previously been added to stocks of raw materials and goods. Similarly, other goods are only sold to the consumer *after* the end of the year. Nevertheless

BOX 14.7	WHEN HIGHER GDP CAN LEAD TO LOWER WELFARE

The use of ISEW: the index of sustainable economic welfare

GDP is not a complete measure of economic welfare; nor is it meant to be. So is there any alternative that takes other factors into account and gives a more complete picture of the level of human well-being?

One measure that is popular among environmental groups is the index of sustainable economic welfare (ISEW).[1] This starts with consumption, as measured in GDP, and then makes various adjustments to account for factors that GDP ignores. These include:

- Inequality: the greater the inequality, the more the figure for consumption is reduced. This is based on the assumption of a diminishing marginal utility of income, such that an additional pound is worth less to a rich person than to a poor person.
- Household production (such as childcare, care for the elderly or infirm, housework and various do-it-yourself activities). These 'services of household labour' add to welfare and are thus entered as a positive figure.

- Defensive expenditures. This is spending to offset the adverse environmental effects of economic growth (e.g. asthma treatment for sufferers whose condition arises from air pollution). Such expenditures are taken out of the calculations.
- 'Bads' (such as commuting costs). The monetary expense entailed is entered as a negative figure (to cancel out its measurement in GDP as a positive figure) and then an additional negative element is included for the stress incurred.
- Environmental costs. Pollution is entered as a negative figure.
- Resource depletion and damage. This too is given a negative figure, in just the same way that depreciation of capital is given a negative figure when working out net national income.

The table shows the calculation of ISEW for the UK for three years: 1950, 1973 and 1996. As you can see,

Contributions to the index of sustainable economic welfare (ISEW) (£ per capita, 1990 prices)

	1950	1973	1996
Consumer expenditure	2435	4067	6402
Adjustment for inequality	−201	−316	−917
Services of household labour	948	1470	2368
Public expenditure on health and education	89	192	365
Difference between consumer expenditure on and services from goods	−206	−446	−1160
Defensive private expenditures on health and education	−14	−25	−109
Costs of commuting	−52	−127	−207
Costs of personal pollution control	–	−8	−58
Costs of car accidents	−30	−43	−36
Costs of water and air pollution	−504	−537	−376
Costs of noise pollution	−36	−36	−39
Costs of loss of habitat and farmlands	−35	−64	−88
Depletion of non-renewable resources	−332	−920	−1812
Long-term environmental damage	−292	−718	−1321
Ozone depletion costs	−8	−209	−621
Net capital growth	–	382	1
Change in net international position	37	52	−41
Per capita ISEW	*1799*	*2713*	*2349*
Per capita GDP	*3507*	*6151*	*8890*

Source: An Index of Sustainable Economic Welfare for the UK 1950–96, Centre for Environmental Strategy, University of Surrey (Jackson, T., Marks, N., Ralls, J. and Stymne, S., 1997).

we must still count the values that have been added during *this* year to these stocks of partially finished goods.

A final problem concerned with stocks is that they may increase in value simply due to increased prices. This is known as **stock (or inventory) appreciation**. Since there has been no real increase in output, stock appreciation must be deducted from value added.

Government services. The output of private industry is sold on the market and can thus be easily valued. This is not the case with most of the services provided by the government. Such services (e.g. health and education) should be valued in terms of what they cost to provide.

Ownership of dwellings. When a landlord rents out a flat, this service is valued as the rent that the tenant pays. But owner-occupiers living in their own property do not pay rent and yet they are 'consuming' a similar 'service'. Here a rental value for owner-occupation is 'imputed'. In other

Definition

Stock (or inventory) appreciation The increase in monetary value of stocks due to increased prices. Since this does not represent increased output, it is not included in GDP.

household labour makes a substantial addition to GDP, but this is more than offset by inequality and various adverse environmental effects, especially the depletion of resources and long-term environmental damage.

The net effect is to make the UK's 1996 ISEW per capita only just over a quarter of GDP per capita (at constant prices). What is of perhaps more concern is that, while GDP per capita rose by nearly 50 per cent between 1973 and 1996, ISEW per capita actually fell (by 13.4 per cent). We may be materially richer, but if our lives are more stressful, if our environment is more polluted and if the gap between rich and poor has widened, it is easy to see how we could, in a real sense, be worse off than in the 1970s.

According to the 'threshold hypothesis', economic growth leads to a real improvement in the quality of life up to a certain point. Beyond that, however, further growth actually reduces the quality of life. The diagram shows this effect for three countries: the UK, the USA and the Netherlands. In each case, the maximum achieved ISEW is given a value of 100. Welfare peaked for the USA in the late 1960s, and for the UK and the Netherlands in about 1980.

Not surprisingly, ISEW has come in for considerable criticism. The most important criticism concerns the measurement of environmental effects, especially the long-term ones. For example, there is considerable debate as to the precise amount of global warming that results from the burning of fossil fuels, and the precise damage caused by a given amount of global warming. But as the advocates of the use of ISEW point out, not to count environmental effects is to give them a precise value: namely, zero! Surely, as Herman Daly argues, it is better to be roughly right than precisely wrong.

 Make out a case against using ISEW. How would an advocate of he use of ISEW reply to your points?

[1] This measure was developed in the USA by Herman Daly, John Cobb and Clifford Cobb. See H. Daly and J. Cobb, *For the Common Good* (Beacon Press, Boston, MA, 1989).

ISEW 1950–96 (maximum = 100)

Source: *Quality of Life Briefing*, New Economics Foundation/Friends of the Earth (Mayo, E., MacGillivray, A. and McLaren, D., 1998).

words, a figure corresponding to a rent is included in the GDP statistics under the 'letting of property' heading.

Taxes and subsidies on products. Taxes paid on goods and services (such as VAT) and any subsidies on products are *excluded* from gross value added (GVA), since they are not part of the value added in production. Nevertheless the way GDP is measured throughout the EU and most other countries of the world is at *market prices*: i.e. at the prices actually paid at each stage of production. Thus **GDP at market prices** (sometimes referred to simply as GDP) is GVA *plus* taxes on products *minus* subsidies on products.

The income method of measuring GDP

The second approach focuses on the incomes generated from the production of goods and services. This must be the same as the sum of all values added, since value added is simply

Definition

GDP (at market prices) The value of output (or income or expenditure) in terms of the prices actually paid. GDP = GVA + Taxes on products – Subsidies on products.

the difference between a firm's revenue from sales and the costs of its purchases from other firms. This difference is made up of wages and salaries, rent, interest and profit: the incomes earned by those involved in the production process.

Since GDP is the sum of all values added, it must also be the sum of all incomes generated: the sum of wages and salaries, rent, interest and profit.

 If a retailer buys a product from a wholesaler for £80 and sells it to a consumer for £100, then the £20 of value that has been added will go partly in wages, partly in rent and partly in profits. Thus £20 of income has been generated at the retail stage. But the good actually contributes a total of £100 to GDP. Where, then, is the remaining £80 worth of income recorded?

Figure A14.2 shows how these incomes are grouped together in the official statistics. By far the largest category is 'compensation of employees': in other words, wages and salaries. As you can see, the total in Figure A14.2 is the same as in Figure A14.1, although the components are quite different. In other words, GDP is the same whether calculated by the product or the income method.

Some qualifications

Stock (inventory) appreciation. As in the case of the product approach, any gain in profits from inventory appreciation must be deducted, since they do not arise from a real increase in output.

Transfer payments. GDP includes only those incomes that arise from the production of goods and services. We do not, therefore, include *transfer payments* such as social security benefits, pensions and gifts.

Direct taxes. We count people's income *before* the payment of income and corporation taxes, since it is this *gross* (pretax) income that arises from the production of goods and services.

Taxes and subsidies on products. As with the product approach, if we are working out GVA, we measure incomes before the payment of taxes on products or the receipt of subsidies on products, since it is these pre-tax-and-subsidy incomes that arise from the value added by production. When working out GDP, however, we add in these taxes and subtract these subsidies to arrive at a *market price* valuation.

The expenditure method of measuring GDP

The final approach to calculating GDP is to add up all expenditure on final output (which will be at market prices). This will include the following:

- Consumer expenditure (*C*). This includes all expenditure on goods and services by households and by non-profit institutions serving households (NPISH) (e.g. clubs and societies).

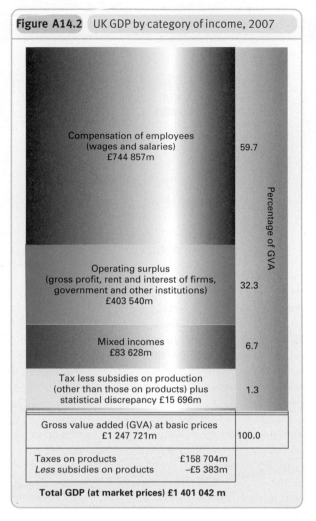

Figure A14.2 UK GDP by category of income, 2007

Source: *United Kingdom National Accounts: The Blue Book – 2008 Edition* (National Statistics, 2008).

- Government expenditure (*G*). This includes central and local government expenditure on final goods and services. Note that it includes non-marketed services (such as health and education), but excludes transfer payments, such as pensions and social security payments.
- Investment expenditure (*I*). This includes investment in capital, such as buildings and machinery. It also includes the value of any increase (+) or decrease (−) in inventories, whether of raw materials, semi-finished goods or finished goods.
- Exports of goods and services (*X*).

We then have to *subtract* imports of goods and services (*M*) from the total in order to leave just the expenditure on *domestic* product. In other words, we subtract the part of consumer expenditure, government expenditure and investment that goes on imports. We also subtract the imported component (e.g. raw materials) from exports.

$$\text{GDP (at market prices)} = C + G + I + X - M$$

Table A14.1 shows the calculation of the 2007 UK GDP by the expenditure approach.

Table A14.1	UK GDP at market prices by category of expenditure, 2007	
	£ million	**% of GDP**
Consumption expenditure of households and NPISH (*C*)	893 414	63.8
Government final consumption (*G*)	296 900	21.2
Gross capital formation (*I*)	257 513	18.4
Exports of goods and services (*X*)	368 337	26.3
Imports of goods and services (*M*)	−415 817	−29.7
Statistical discrepancy	695	0.0
GDP at market prices	1 401 042	100.0

Source: *United Kingdom National Accounts: The Blue Book – 2008 Edition* (National Statistics, 2008).

From GDP to national income

Gross national income

Some of the incomes earned in this country will go abroad. These include wages, interest, profit and rent earned in this country by foreign residents and remitted abroad, and taxes on production paid to foreign governments and institutions (e.g. the EU). On the other hand, some of the incomes earned by domestic residents will come from abroad. Again, these can be in the form of wages, interest, profit or rent, or in the form of subsidies received from governments or institutions abroad. Gross *domestic* product, however, is concerned only with incomes generated *within* the country, irrespective of ownership. If, then, we are to take 'net income from abroad' into account (i.e. these inflows minus outflows), we need a new measure. This is *gross national income (GNY)*.[1] It is defined as follows:

GNY at market prices = GDP at market prices
+ Net income from abroad

Thus GDP focuses on the value of domestic production, whereas GNY focuses on the value of incomes earned by domestic residents.

Net national income

The measures we have used so far ignore the fact that each year some of the country's capital equipment wears out or becomes obsolete: in other words, they ignore capital depreciation. If we subtract from gross national income an allowance for *depreciation* (or 'capital consumption' as

Definitions

Gross national income (GNY) GDP plus net income from abroad.

Depreciation The decline in value of capital equipment due to age or wear and tear.

Net national income (NNY) GNY minus depreciation.

Households' disposable income The income available for households to spend: i.e. personal incomes after deducting taxes on incomes and adding benefits.

Table A14.2	UK GDP, GNY and NNY at market prices, 2007
	£ million
Gross domestic product (GDP)	**1 401 042**
Plus net income from abroad	6 818
Gross national income (GNY)	**1 407 860**
Less capital consumption (depreciation)	158 143
Net national income (NNY)	**1 249 717**

Source: *UK National Income and Expenditure* (National Statistics, 2008).

it is called in the official statistics), we get *net national income (NNY)*.

NNY at market prices = GNY at market prices – Depreciation

Table A14.2 shows the 2007 GDP, GNY and NNY figures for the UK.

Although NNY gives a truer picture of a nation's income than GNY, economists tend to use the gross figures because depreciation is hard to estimate accurately.

Households' disposable income

Finally, we come to a measure that is useful for analysing consumer behaviour. This is called *households' disposable income*. It measures the income that people have available for spending (or saving): i.e. after any deductions for income tax, national insurance, etc. have been made. It is the best measure to use if we want to see how changes in household income affect consumption.

How do we get from GNY at market prices to households' disposable income? As GNY measures the incomes that firms receive from production[2] (plus net income from abroad), we must deduct that part of their income that is *not* distributed to households. This means that we must deduct taxes that firms pay – taxes on goods and services (such as VAT), taxes on profits (such as corporation tax) and any other taxes – and add in any subsidies they receive. We must then subtract allowances for depreciation and any undistributed profits. This gives us the gross income that households receive from firms in the form of wages, salaries, rent, interest and distributed profits.

To get from this to what is available for households to spend, we must subtract the money that households pay in income taxes and national insurance contributions, but add all benefits to households, such as pensions and child benefit: in other words, we must *include* transfer payments.

Households' disposable income = GNY at market prices
– Taxes paid by firms + Subsidies received by firms
– Depreciation – Undistributed profits – Personal taxes
+ Benefits

[1] In the official statistics, this is referred to as *GNI*. We use *Y* to stand for income, however, to avoid confusion with investment.
[2] We also include income from any public-sector production of goods or services (e.g. health and education) and production by non-profit institutions serving households.

Section summary

1. The product method measures the values added in all parts of the economy. Care must be taken in the evaluation of stocks, government services and the ownership of dwellings.

2. The income method measures all the incomes generated from domestic production: wages and salaries, rent, interest and profit. Transfer payments are not included, nor is stock appreciation.

3. The expenditure method adds up all the categories of expenditure: consumer expenditure, government expenditure, investment and exports. We then have to deduct the element of each that goes on imports in order to arrive at expenditure on domestic products. Thus $GDP = C + G + I + X - M$.

4. GDP at market prices measures what consumers pay for output (including taxes and subsidies on what they buy). Gross value added (GVA) measures what factors of production actually receive. GVA, therefore, is GDP at market prices minus taxes on products plus subsidies on products.

5. Gross national income (GNY) takes account of incomes earned from abroad (+) and incomes earned by people abroad from this country (−). Thus GNY = GDP plus net income from abroad.

6. Net national income (NNY) takes account of depreciation of capital. Thus NNY = GNY − Depreciation.

7. Personal disposable income is a measure of household income after the deduction of income taxes and the addition of benefits.

END OF CHAPTER QUESTIONS

1. The following table shows index numbers for real GDP (national output) for various countries (2004 = 100).

	2004	2005	2006	2007	2008	2009*
USA	100.0	102.9	105.8	107.9	109.4	107.7
Japan	100.0	101.9	104.3	106.5	107.0	104.3
Germany	100.0	100.8	103.8	106.4	107.9	105.2
France	100.0	101.9	104.1	106.4	107.4	105.3
UK	100.0	102.1	105.0	108.1	109.0	106.0

*Forecast figures.
Sources: various.

(a) Work out the growth rate for each country for each year from 2005 to 2009.

(b) Plot the figures on a graph. Describe the pattern that emerges.

2. Explain how equilibrium would be restored in the circular flow of income if there were a fall in investment.

3. Explain the circumstances under which an increase in pensions and child benefit would (a) increase national income; (b) leave national income unaffected; (c) decrease national income.

4. For what reasons might GDP be a poor indicator of (i) the level of development of a country; (ii) its rate of economic development?

5. Will the rate of actual growth have any effect on the rate of potential growth?

6. For what possible reasons may one country experience a persistently faster rate of economic growth than another?

7. Why will investment affect both actual (short-term) growth and the long-term growth in potential output? What will be the implications if these two effects differ in magnitude?

8. Explain how you would derive a figure for households' disposable income if you were starting from a figure for GDP.

Online resources

Additional case studies in MyEconLab

14.1 **The GDP deflator.** An examination of how GDP figures are corrected to take inflation into account.

14.2 **Taking into account the redistributive effects of growth.** This case shows how figures for economic growth can be adjusted to allow for the fact that poor people's income growth would otherwise count for far less than rich people's.

14.3 **Simon Kuznets and the system of national income accounting.** This looks at the work of Simon Kuznets, who devised the system of national income accounting that is used around the world. It describes some of the patterns of economic growth that he identified.

14.4 **Growth accounting.** This case study identifies various factors that contribute to economic growth and shows how their contribution can be measured.

Websites relevant to this chapter

See sites listed at the end of Chapter 15 on page 450.

Macroeconomic Issues and Analysis: An Overview

CHAPTER MAP

15.1 **Unemployment**   **416**
The meaning of 'unemployment'   416
Official measures of unemployment   417
The duration of unemployment   417
The composition of unemployment   419
Unemployment and the labour market   420
Disequilibrium unemployment   421
Equilibrium unemployment   423

15.2 **Aggregate demand and supply and**
the level of prices   **425**
The aggregate demand curve   425
The aggregate supply curve   427
Equilibrium   427

15.3 **Inflation**   **428**
The costs of inflation   429
Causes of inflation   432
Policies to tackle inflation   435

15.4 **The balance of payments and**
exchange rates   **439**
The balance of payments account   439
Assessing the balance of payments figures   442
Exchange rates   442
The determination of the rate of exchange in
a free market   443
Exchange rates and the balance of payments   445
Managing the exchange rate   445

15.5 **Postscript to Part E: The relationship**
between the four macroeconomic
objectives   **447**
Aggregate demand and the short-term
relationship between the four objectives   447
The long-term relationship between the
objectives   448

In the previous chapter we examined economic growth. In this chapter we turn to the other three key macroeconomic issues of unemployment, inflation and the balance of payments. We give an overview of these problems: how they are measured and their effects on society. We also have a first look at the causes of these problems. This helps prepare the ground for the analyses in later chapters.

We saw in Chapter 14 that macroeconomics deals with economic problems in the aggregate (i.e. for the whole economy). An important tool for analysing these aggregate problems is *aggregate demand and supply analysis*. We look at this analysis in section 15.2. This is then the basis for our analysis of inflation in section 15.3.

Part E has been laying the foundations of macroeconomics. The final section of this chapter brings the threads together. It examines the relationship between the four macroeconomic objectives in both the short run and the long run: something that will be explored in more detail in Part F.

15.1 UNEMPLOYMENT

Unemployment fluctuates with the business cycle. In recessions, such as those experienced by most countries in the early 1980s, the early 1990s and the early and late 2000s, unemployment tends to rise. In boom years, such as the late 1980s, late 1990s and mid 2000s, it tends to fall. Figure 15.1 shows these cyclical movements in unemployment for selected countries.

As well as experiencing fluctuations in unemployment, most countries have experienced long-term changes in average unemployment rates. This is illustrated in Table 15.1, which shows average unemployment in the UK, the EU countries that were members before 2004 and the USA for five unemployment cycles (minimum to minimum). Average unemployment rates in the 1980s and 1990s were higher than in the 1970s, and average rates in the 1970s were, in turn, higher than in the 1950s and 1960s. In certain countries, such as the UK and the USA, the late 1990s and early 2000s saw a long-term fall in unemployment.

This section gives an overview of the problem of unemployment: how it is measured and what its costs are. Then we look at the range of possible causes of unemployment. We explore these causes and the policies for tackling unemployment in more detail as the book progresses.

The meaning of 'unemployment'

Unemployment can be expressed either as a number (e.g. 1.6 million) or as a percentage (e.g. 6 per cent). But just who should be included in the statistics? Should it be everyone without a job? The answer is clearly no, since we would not want to include children and pensioners. We would probably also want to exclude those who were not looking for work, such as parents choosing to stay at home to look after children.

The most usual definition that economists use for the **number unemployed** is: *those of working age who are without work, but who are available for work at current wage rates*. If the figure is to be expressed as a percentage, then it is a

Table 15.1	Average unemployment for given cycles (%)		
Period	**UK**	**EU-15**	**USA**
1964–73	3.0	2.7	4.6
1974–9	5.0	4.7	5.8
1980–90	9.4	8.3	7.1
1991–2001	7.6	9.0	5.5
2002–7	5.0	7.7	5.3

Definition

Number unemployed (economist's definition) Those of working age who are without work, but who are available for work at current wage rates.

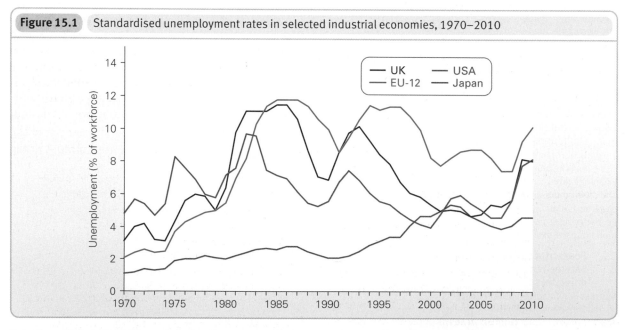

| Figure 15.1 | Standardised unemployment rates in selected industrial economies, 1970–2010 |

Note: Years 2009 and 2010 figures based on forecasts; EU-12 = the 12 original members of the eurozone.
Source: Based on data in *Economic Outlook* (Organisation for Economic Co-operation and Development [OECD], various years).

percentage of the total **labour force**. The labour force is defined as *those in employment plus those unemployed*. Thus if 25 million people were employed and 1.5 million people were unemployed, the **unemployment rate** would be

$$\frac{1.5}{25 + 1.5} \times 100 = 5.7\%$$

Official measures of unemployment

Claimant unemployment

Two common measures of unemployment are used in official statistics. The first is **claimant unemployment**. This is simply a measure of all those in receipt of unemployment-related benefits. In the UK claimants receive the 'jobseeker's allowance'.

Claimant statistics have the advantage of being very easy to collect. However, they exclude all those of working age who are available for work at current wage rates, but who are *not* eligible for benefits. If the government changes the eligibility conditions so that fewer people are eligible, this will reduce the number of claimants and hence the official number unemployed, even if there has been no change in the numbers with or without work.

The following categories of people are ineligible for benefits and are thus not included in claimant unemployment:

- People returning to the workforce (e.g. after raising children).
- Those who are on government training schemes (e.g. school leavers without jobs).
- People over 55. If such people are out of work, the benefit they receive is not regarded as 'unemployment-related'.
- Those in receipt of 'employment and support allowance' (previously called incapacity benefit) but who nevertheless would be available for work of certain types.
- People seeking part-time work, rather than full-time work, for example students.

The claimant statistics in the UK thus understate the true level of unemployment.

Standardised unemployment rates

Recognising the weaknesses of the claimant statistics, the UK government since 1998 has used the **standardised unemployment rate** as the main measure of unemployment. In this measure, the unemployed are defined as people of working age who are without work, available to start work within two weeks and *actively seeking employment* or waiting to take up an appointment.

This is the measure used by the International Labour Organisation (ILO) and the Organisation for Economic Co-operation and Development (OECD), two international organisations that publish unemployment statistics for many countries. The figures are compiled from the results of national labour force *surveys*. A representative cross-section of the population is asked whether they are employed, unemployed (using the above definition) or economically inactive. From their replies, national rates of unemployment can be extrapolated. In the UK, the Labour Force Survey is conducted quarterly.

But is the standardised unemployment rate likely to be higher or lower than the claimant unemployment rate? The standardised rate is likely to be higher to the extent that it includes people seeking work who are nevertheless not entitled to claim benefits, but lower to the extent that it excludes those who are claiming benefits and yet who are not actively seeking work. Clearly, the tougher the benefit regulations, the lower the claimant rate will be relative to the standardised rate. In spring 2008, claimant unemployment in the UK was 0.811 million (2.5 per cent), while standardised unemployment was 1.619 million (5.2 per cent).

 How does the ILO/OECD definition differ from the economist's definition? What is the significance of the phrase 'available for work at current wage rates' in the economist's definition?

The duration of unemployment

A few of the unemployed may never have had a job and maybe never will. For most, however, unemployment lasts only a certain period. For some it may be just a few days while they are between jobs. For others it may be a few months. For others – the long-term unemployed – it could be several years. Table 15.2 shows the composition of standardised unemployment by duration.

What determines the average duration of unemployment? There are three important factors here.

The number unemployed (the size of the stock of unemployment). Unemployment is a 'stock' concept (see Box 9.9). It measures a *quantity* (i.e. the number unemployed) at a particular *point in time*. The higher the stock of unemployment, the longer will tend to be the duration of unemployment. There will be more people competing for vacant jobs.

Definitions

Labour force The number employed plus the number unemployed.

Unemployment rate The number unemployed expressed as a percentage of the labour force.

Claimant unemployment Those in receipt of unemployment-related benefits.

Standardised unemployment rate The measure of the unemployment rate used by the ILO and the OECD. The unemployed are defined as persons of working age who are without work, are available to start work within two weeks and either have actively looked for work in the last four weeks or are waiting to take up an appointment.

Table 15.2 UK unemployment (ILO) by duration: spring quarters (Mar–May)

	Up to 6 months	Over 6 and up to 12 months	Over 12 months	Total
1993 (thousands)	1156	576	1267	2999
(%)	(38.6)	(19.2)	(42.2)	(100.0)
1999 (thousands)	1025	269	503	1797
(%)	(57.0)	(15.0)	(28.0)	(100.0)
2008 (thousands)	955	262	401	1618
(%)	(59.0)	(16.2)	(24.8)	(100.0)

Source: *Economic and Labour Market Review* (National Statistics, various years).

The rate of inflow and outflow from the stock of unemployment. The people making up the unemployment total are constantly changing. Each week some people are made redundant or quit their jobs. They represent an inflow to the stock of unemployment. Other people find jobs and thus represent an outflow from the stock of unemployment. The various inflows and outflows are shown in Figure 15.2.

Unemployment is often referred to as 'the pool of unemployment'. This is quite a good analogy. If the water flowing into a pool exceeds the water flowing out, the level of water in the pool will rise. Similarly, if the inflow of people into unemployment exceeds the outflow, the level of unemployment will rise.

The duration of unemployment will depend on the *rate* of inflow and outflow. The rate is expressed as the number of people per period of time. Table 15.3 shows the inflows and outflows in selected years.

Note the magnitude of the flows. In each of the years, the outflows (and inflows) exceed the total number unemployed. The bigger the flows are relative to the total

number unemployed, the less will be the average duration of unemployment. This is because people move into and out of the pool more quickly, and hence their average stay will be shorter.

1. *If the number unemployed exceeded the total annual outflow, what could we conclude about the average duration of unemployment?*
2. *Make a list of the various inflows to and outflows from employment from and to (a) unemployment; (b) outside the workforce.*

The phase of the business cycle. The duration of unemployment will also depend on the phase of the business cycle. At the onset of a recession, unemployment will rise, but as yet the average length of unemployment is likely to have been relatively short. Once a recession has lasted for a period of time, however, people will on average have been out of work longer, and this long-term unemployment is likely to persist even when the economy is pulling out of recession.

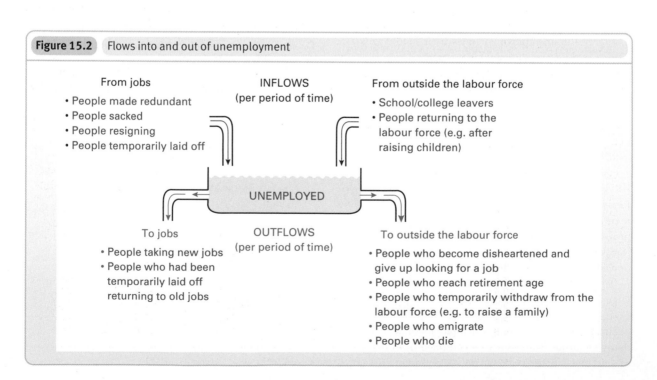

Figure 15.2 Flows into and out of unemployment

Table 15.3	UK (claimant) unemployment flows (millions)										
	1980	**1984**	**1986**	**1990**	**1992**	**1995**	**1998**	**2000**	**2002**	**2004**	**2007**
Inflow	3.85	4.50	4.49	3.51	4.51	3.62	3.08	2.85	2.74	2.42	2.48
Outflow	3.21	4.40	4.88	3.31	4.09	3.84	3.17	2.99	2.76	2.50	2.60
Total level of unemployment	1.66	3.16	3.29	1.65	2.74	2.29	1.35	1.09	0.95	0.85	0.86

Source: Economic and Labour Market Review (National Statistics, various years).

*LOOKING AT THE MATHS

The duration of unemployment (D_u) will equal the stock of unemployment (U) as a proportion of the outflow (F) from unemployment.

$$D_u = \frac{U}{F}$$

Thus the bigger the stock of unemployment relative to the outflow from it, the longer will unemployment last. Taking the figures for 1992:

$$D_u = \frac{2.74}{4.09} = 0.67$$

Thus the average duration of unemployment was 0.67 years or 245 days. By contrast, in 2000, the average duration was $1.09/2.99 = 0.36$ years or 133 days.

The composition of unemployment

Unemployment rates vary enormously between countries and between different groups within countries.

Geographical differences. Table 15.4 illustrates the considerable differences in unemployment rates between countries. Compare the unemployment rates in Ireland and Spain! Countries have very different labour markets, very different policies on unemployment, training schemes, redundancy, etc., and very different attitudes of firms towards their workers. Also, countries may not be at precisely the same phase of their respective business cycles.

Unemployment also varies substantially within a country from one area to another. Most countries have some regions that are more prosperous than others. In the UK, unemployment in the north of England, Scotland and Northern Ireland is higher than in the south of England. For example, in the second quarter of 2008, unemployment was 7.3 per cent in the north-east of England and only 3.9 per cent in the south-west.

But geographical differences in unemployment are not just a regional problem. In many countries, inner-city unemployment is very much higher than suburban or rural unemployment, and, as a result, most developed countries have schemes to attract employment to the inner cities. In June 2008, claimant unemployment in Tower Hamlets in London was 5.0 per cent, whereas in West Oxfordshire it was 0.6 per cent.

Differences in unemployment rates between women and men. In many countries, female unemployment has traditionally been higher than male unemployment. Causes have included differences in education and training, discrimination by employers, more casual or seasonally-related employment among women and other social factors. In many countries, however, the position has changed in recent years. As you can see, in five of the countries in Table 15.4 male unemployment rates are higher than female rates. The main reason is the decline in many of the

Table 15.4	Standardised unemployment rates in different sections of the labour market, Q2 2008					
Country	**Total (all ages)**	**Women (all ages)**	**Men (all ages)**	**Total under 25 years old**	**Women under 25 years old**	**Men under 25 years old**
Belgium	6.6	7.2	6.1	15.7	17.2	14.5
Germany	7.5	7.4	7.5	10.3	9.5	11.0
France	7.2	7.6	6.8	16.7	16.0	17.3
Ireland	5.5	4.4	6.4	11.1	8.4	13.5
Japan	4.0	3.9	4.1	7.1	6.4	7.8
Netherlands	2.8	3.0	2.6	5.2	5.2	5.1
Spain	10.4	12.3	9.1	23.9	25.9	22.2
UK	5.1	4.7	5.5	13.3	10.8	15.4
USA	5.2	5.1	5.4	12.7	11.6	13.8
EU-15	6.8	7.4	6.3	14.5	14.4	14.9

Source: Eurostat, Statistics in Focus (http://epp.eurostat.ec.europa.eu), (Commission of the European Communities, 2008).

| BOX 15.1 | THE COSTS OF UNEMPLOYMENT | EXPLORING ECONOMICS |

Who loses and by how much?

The most obvious cost of unemployment is to the unemployed themselves. There is the direct financial cost of the loss in their earnings. Then there are the personal costs of being unemployed. The longer people are unemployed, the more dispirited they may become. Their self-esteem is likely to fall, and they are more likely to succumb to stress-related illness.

Beyond the unemployed themselves, there are the costs to their family and friends. Personal relations can become strained, and there may be an increase in domestic violence and the number of families splitting up.

Then there are the broader costs to the economy. Unemployment represents a loss of output. In other words, actual output is below potential output. Apart from the loss of disposable income to the unemployed themselves, this underutilisation of resources leads to lower incomes for other people too:

- The government loses tax revenues, since the unemployed pay no income tax and national insurance, and, given that the unemployed spend less, they pay less VAT and excise duties. The government also incurs administrative costs associated with the running of benefit offices. It may also have to spend extra on health care, the social services and the police.
- Firms lose the profits that could have been made if there had been full employment.
- Other workers lose any additional wages they could have earned from higher national output.

What is more, the longer people remain unemployed, the more deskilled they tend to become, thereby reducing potential as well as actual income.

Why have the costs to the government of unemployment benefits not been included as a cost to the economy?

Finally, there is some evidence that higher unemployment leads to increased crime and vandalism. This obviously imposes a cost on the sufferers.

The costs of unemployment are to some extent offset by benefits. If workers voluntarily quit their jobs to look for better ones, then they must reckon that the benefits of a better job more than compensate for their temporary loss of income. From the nation's point of view, a workforce that is prepared to quit jobs and spend a short time unemployed will be a more adaptable, more mobile workforce – one that is responsive to changing economic circumstances. Such a workforce will lead to greater allocative efficiency in the short run and more rapid economic growth over the longer run.

Long-term involuntary unemployment is quite another matter. The costs clearly outweigh any benefits, both for the individuals involved and for the economy as a whole. A demotivated, deskilled pool of long-term unemployed is a serious economic and social problem.

Which of the above costs would be recorded as a reduction in GDP?

---

older industries, such as coal and steel, which employed mainly men.

Differences in unemployment rates between different age groups. Table 15.4 also shows that unemployment rates in the under-25 age group are higher than the average, and substantially so in many countries. There are various explanations for this, including the suitability (or unsuitability) of the qualifications of school leavers, the attitudes of employers to young people, and the greater willingness of young people to spend time unemployed looking for a better job or waiting to start a further or higher education course. The difference in rates is less in Germany, which has a well-established apprenticeship system.

Differences in unemployment rates between different ethnic groups. In many countries, members of ethnic minorities suffer from higher unemployment rates than the average. In the UK, the unemployment rate for Afro-Caribbeans is 2.5 times greater than that for whites. For those of Pakistani and Bangladeshi origin, it is three times greater. Explanations are complex, but include differences in educational opportunities, a higher proportion of younger

people, a greater sense of alienation among the unemployed, and the attitudes and prejudices of employers.

Unemployment and the labour market

We now turn to the causes of unemployment. These causes fall into two broad categories: *equilibrium* unemployment and *disequilibrium* unemployment. To make clear the distinction between the two, it is necessary to look at how the labour market works.

Figure 15.3 shows the **aggregate demand** for labour and **aggregate supply** of labour: that is, the total demand and supply of labour in the whole economy. The *real* average

---

Definitions

Aggregate demand for labour curve A curve showing the total demand for labour in the economy at different average real wage rates.

Aggregate supply of labour curve A curve showing the total number of people willing and able to work at different average real wage rates.

Figure 15.3 Disequilibrium unemployment

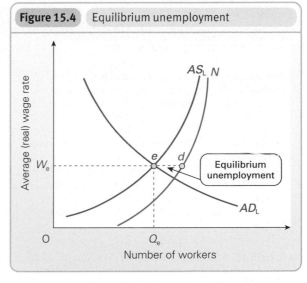

Figure 15.4 Equilibrium unemployment

wage rate is plotted on the vertical axis. This is the average wage rate expressed in terms of its purchasing power: in other words, after taking prices into account.

The aggregate supply of labour curve (AS_L) shows the number of workers *willing to accept jobs* at each wage rate. This curve is relatively inelastic, since the size of the labour force at any one time cannot change significantly. Nevertheless it is not totally inelastic because (a) a higher wage rate will encourage some people to enter the labour market (e.g. parents raising children), and (b) the unemployed will be more willing to accept job offers rather than continuing to search for a better-paid job.

The aggregate demand for labour curve (AD_L) slopes downwards. The higher the wage rate, the more will firms attempt to economise on labour and to substitute other factors of production for labour.

The labour market is in equilibrium at a wage of W_e – where the demand for labour equals the supply.

If the wage rate were above W_e, the labour market would be in a state of disequilibrium. At a wage rate of W_1, there is an excess supply of labour of $a - b$. This is called *disequilibrium unemployment*.

For disequilibrium unemployment to occur, two conditions must hold:

- The aggregate supply of labour must exceed the aggregate demand.
- There must be a 'stickiness' in wages. In other words, the wage rate must not immediately fall to W_e, the market-clearing wage.

Even when the labour market *is* in equilibrium, however, not everyone looking for work will be employed. Some people will hold out, hoping to find a better job. This is illustrated in Figure 15.4.

The curve N shows the total number in the labour force. The horizontal difference between it and the aggregate supply of labour curve (AS_L) represents the excess of people looking for work over those actually willing to accept jobs.

Q_e represents the equilibrium level of employment and the distance $d - e$ represents the *equilibrium level of unemployment*. This is sometimes known as the *natural level of unemployment*.

Note that the AS_L curve gets closer to the N curve at higher wages. The reason for this is that the unemployed will be more willing to accept jobs, the higher the wages they are offered.

Figure 15.5 shows both equilibrium *and* disequilibrium unemployment. At a wage of W_1, disequilibrium unemployment is $a - b$; equilibrium unemployment is $c - a$; thus total unemployment is $c - b$.

But what are the causes of disequilibrium unemployment? What are the causes of equilibrium unemployment? We will examine each in turn.

Disequilibrium unemployment

There are three possible causes of disequilibrium unemployment.

Real-wage unemployment
Real-wage unemployment occurs when trade unions use their monopoly power to drive wages above the market-

KI 8 p43

Definitions

Disequilibrium unemployment Unemployment resulting from real wage rates in the economy being above the equilibrium level.

Equilibrium ('natural') unemployment The difference between those who would like employment at the current wage rate and those willing and able to take a job.

Real-wage unemployment Disequilibrium unemployment caused by real wages being driven up above the market-clearing level.

Figure 15.5 Equilibrium and disequilibrium unemployment

clearing level. It could also be caused by the government setting the national minimum wage too high. In Figure 15.3, the wage rate is driven up above W_e.

Excessive real wage rates were blamed by the Conservative governments under Thatcher and Major for the high unemployment of the 1980s and 1990s. The possibility of higher real-wage unemployment was also one of the reasons for their rejection of a national minimum wage.

One effect of high real wage rates, however, may help to reduce real-wage unemployment. The extra wages paid to those who are still employed could lead to extra *consumer* expenditure. This addition to aggregate demand would in turn lead to firms demanding more labour, as they attempted to increase output to meet the extra demand. In Figure 15.3, the AD_L curve will shift to the right, thereby reducing the gap $a - b$.

If the higher consumer expenditure and higher wages subsequently led to higher prices, what would happen to (a) real wages; (b) unemployment (assuming no further response from unions)?

Demand-deficient or cyclical unemployment

Demand-deficient or **cyclical unemployment** is associated with economic recessions. As the economy moves into recession, consumer demand falls. Firms find that they are unable to sell their current level of output. For a time they may be prepared to build up stocks of unsold goods, but sooner or later they will start to cut back on production and cut back on the amount of labour they employ. The deeper

Definition

Demand-deficient or **cyclical unemployment**
Disequilibrium unemployment caused by a fall in aggregate demand with no corresponding fall in the real wage rate.

the recession becomes and the longer it lasts, the higher will demand-deficient unemployment become.

As the economy recovers and begins to grow again, so demand-deficient unemployment will start to fall again. Because demand-deficient unemployment fluctuates with the business cycle, it is sometimes referred to as 'cyclical unemployment'. Figure 15.1 (on page 416) showed the fluctuations in unemployment in various industrial countries. If you compare this figure with the figure in Box 14.3 (on page 398), you can see how unemployment tends to rise in recessions and fall in booms.

Demand-deficient unemployment is also referred to as 'Keynesian unemployment', after John Maynard Keynes (see Person Profile in MyEconLab), who saw a deficiency of aggregate demand as the cause of the high unemployment between the two world wars. Today, many economists are known as 'Keynesian'. Although there are many strands of Keynesian thinking, these economists all see aggregate demand as important in determining a nation's output and employment.

Demand-deficient unemployment is illustrated in Figure 15.6. Assume initially that the economy is at the peak of the business cycle. The aggregate demand for and supply of labour are equal at the current wage rate of W_1. There is no disequilibrium unemployment. Now assume that the economy moves into recession. Consumer demand falls and as a result firms demand less labour. The demand for labour shifts to AD_{L_2}. If there is a resistance to wage cuts, such that the real wage rate remains fixed at W_1, there will now be disequilibrium unemployment of $Q_1 - Q_2$.

Some Keynesians specifically focus on the reluctance of real wage rates to fall from W_1 to W_2. This downward 'stickiness' in real wage rates may be the result of unions seeking to protect the living standards of their members (even though there are non-members out of work), or of firms worried about the demotivating effects of cutting the real

Figure 15.6 Demand-deficient unemployment

wages of their workers. Sometimes it is simply that wage rates have been agreed through a process of collective bargaining for the following year or more, where the agreement includes an inflation-proofing element to ensure that they are *real* wage rates. For such economists, the problem of demand-deficient unemployment would be solved if there could somehow be a fall in real wage rates.

For other Keynesian economists, however, the problem is much more fundamental than a downward stickiness in real wages. For them the problem is that the low level of aggregate demand causes an *equilibrium* in the *goods* market at an output that is too low to generate full employment. Firms' supply is low (below the full-employment level of supply) because aggregate demand is low.

This low-level equilibrium in the goods market, and the corresponding disequilibrium in the labour market, may *persist*. This is the result of a lack of confidence on the part of firms. After all, why should firms produce more and take on more workers, if they believe that the recession will persist and that they will therefore not sell any more? The economy remains trapped in a low-output equilibrium.

In such cases, a fall in real wages would not cure the unemployment. In fact, it might even make the problem worse. In Figure 15.6, even if the average wage rate were to fall to W_2, demand-deficient unemployment would still persist. The reason is that this general cut in wages throughout the economy would reduce workers' incomes and hence reduce their *consumption of goods*. As the aggregate demand for goods fell, there would be a further reduction in demand for labour: the aggregate demand for labour curve would shift to the left again – to the left of AD_{L_2}. By the time the wage had fallen to W_2, W_2 would no longer be the equilibrium wage. There would still be demand-deficient unemployment.

If this analysis is correct, that is, if a reduction in wages will reduce the aggregate demand for goods, what assumption must we make about the relative proportions of wages and profits that are spent (given that a reduction in real wage rates will lead to a corresponding increase in rates of profit)?

Growth in the labour supply

If labour supply rises with no corresponding increase in the demand for labour, the equilibrium real wage rate will fall. If the real wage rate is 'sticky' downwards, disequilibrium unemployment will occur.

On a diagram similar to Figure 15.6, illustrate how a growth in labour supply can cause disequilibrium unemployment.

This tends not to be such a serious cause of unemployment as demand deficiency, since the supply of labour changes relatively slowly. Nevertheless there is a problem of providing jobs for school leavers each year with the sudden influx of new workers on to the labour market.

From 2004, with the accession of eastern European countries to the EU, there were significant flows of migrants from eastern to western Europe. Does such immigration create disequilibrium unemployment?

Equilibrium unemployment (or natural unemployment)

Although there may be overall *macro*economic equilibrium, with the *aggregate* demand for labour equal to the *aggregate* supply, and thus no disequilibrium unemployment, at a *micro*economic level supply and demand may not match. There may be excess demand for labour (vacancies) in some markets and excess supply (unemployment) in others. There may be vacancies for computer technicians and unemployment in the steel industry, but unemployed steel workers cannot immediately become computer technicians. This is when equilibrium unemployment will occur.

There are various types of equilibrium unemployment.

Frictional (search) unemployment

Frictional (search) unemployment occurs when people leave their jobs, either voluntarily or because they are sacked or made redundant, and are unemployed for a period of time while they are looking for a new job. They may not get the first job they apply for, despite a vacancy existing and despite their being suitably qualified.

The problem is that information is imperfect. Employers are not fully informed about what labour is available; workers are not fully informed about what jobs are available and what they entail. Both employers and workers, therefore, have to search: employers searching for the right labour and workers searching for the right jobs.

The longer people search for a job, the better the wage offers they are likely to be made. This is illustrated in Figure 15.7 by the curve W_o. It shows the highest wage offer that the typical worker will have received since being unemployed

When they first start looking for a job, people may have high expectations of getting a good wage. The longer they are unemployed, however, the more anxious they are likely to be to get a job, and therefore the lower will be the wage they are prepared to accept. The curve W_a shows the wage that is acceptable to the typical worker.

KI 15
p106

TC 9
p105

Why are W_o and W_a drawn as curves rather than straight lines?

Definition

Frictional (search) unemployment Unemployment that occurs as a result of imperfect information in the labour market. It often takes time for workers to find jobs (even though there are vacancies) and in the meantime they are unemployed.

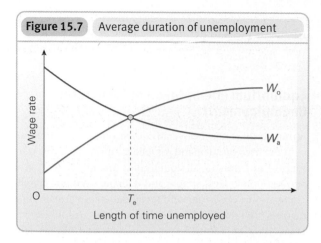

Figure 15.7 Average duration of unemployment

The average duration of unemployment will be T_e. That is, workers will remain unemployed until they find a job at an acceptable wage.

One obvious remedy for frictional unemployment is to provide better job information through government job centres, private employment agencies, or local and national newspapers. This would have the effect of making the curve W_o reach its peak earlier, and thus of shifting the intersection of W_o and W_a to the left.

Another much more controversial remedy is for the government to reduce the level of unemployment benefit. This will make the unemployed more desperate to get a job and thus prepared to accept a lower wage. It will therefore have the effect of shifting the W_a curve downwards and again of shifting the intersection of W_o and W_a to the left.

Structural unemployment

Structural unemployment occurs where the structure of the economy changes. Employment in some industries may expand while in others it contracts. There are two main reasons for this.

A change in the pattern of demand. Some industries experience declining demand. This may be due to a change in consumer tastes as certain goods go out of fashion; or it may be due to competition from other industries. For example, consumer demand may shift away from coal and to other fuels. This will lead to structural unemployment in mining areas.

A change in the methods of production (technological unemployment). New techniques of production often allow the same level of output to be produced with fewer workers (see Case Study 15.2 in MyEconLab). This is known as 'labour-saving technical progress'. Unless output expands sufficiently to absorb the surplus labour, people will be made redundant. This creates **technological unemployment**. An example is the loss of jobs in the banking industry caused by the increase in the number of cash machines and by the development of telephone and Internet banking.

Structural unemployment often occurs in particular regions of the country. When it does, it is referred to as **regional unemployment**. Regional unemployment is due to the concentration of particular industries in particular areas. For example, the collapse in the South Wales coalmining industry led to high unemployment in the Welsh valleys.

The level of structural unemployment will depend on three factors:

- The degree of regional concentration of industry. The more that industries are concentrated in particular regions, the greater will be the level of structural unemployment if particular industries decline.
- The speed of change of demand and supply in the economy. The more rapid the rate of technological change or the shift in consumer tastes, the more rapid will be the rate of redundancies.
- The immobility of labour. The less able or willing workers are to move to a new job, the higher will be the level of structural unemployment. Remember from Chapter 9 the distinction we made between geographical and occupational immobility. Geographical immobility is a particular problem with regional unemployment. Occupational immobility is a particular problem with technological unemployment where old skills are no longer required.

There are two broad approaches to tackling structural unemployment: *market-orientated* and *interventionist*.

A market-orientated approach involves encouraging people to look more actively for jobs, if necessary in other parts of the country. It involves encouraging people to adopt a more willing attitude towards retraining, and if necessary to accept some reduction in wages.

An interventionist approach involves direct government action to match jobs to the unemployed. Two examples are providing grants to firms to set up in areas of high unemployment (regional policy), and government-funded training schemes.

Policies to tackle structural unemployment are examined in detail in sections 23.2 and 23.3.

Definitions

Structural unemployment Unemployment that arises from changes in the pattern of demand or supply in the economy. People made redundant in one part of the economy cannot immediately take up jobs in other parts (even though there are vacancies).

Technological unemployment Structural unemployment that occurs as a result of the introduction of labour-saving technology.

Regional unemployment Structural unemployment occurring in specific regions of the country.

Seasonal unemployment

Seasonal unemployment occurs when the demand for certain types of labour fluctuates with the seasons of the year. This problem is particularly severe in holiday areas, such as Cornwall, where unemployment can reach very high levels in the winter months. Policies for tackling seasonal unemployment are similar to those for structural unemployment.

Section summary

1. Who should be counted as 'unemployed' is a matter for some disagreement. The two most common measures of unemployment are claimant unemployment (those claiming unemployment-related benefits) and ILO/OECD standardised unemployment (those available for work and actively seeking work or waiting to take up an appointment).

2. The 'stock' of unemployment will grow if the inflow of people into unemployment exceeds the outflow (to jobs or out of the labour market altogether). The more rapid these flows, the shorter the average duration of unemployment.

3. In most countries, unemployment is unevenly distributed across geographical regions, between women and men, between age groups and between different ethnic groups.

4. The costs of unemployment include the financial and other personal costs to the unemployed person, the costs to relatives and friends, and the costs to society at large in terms of lost tax revenues, lost profits and lost wages to other workers, and in terms of social disruption.

5. Unemployment can be divided into disequilibrium and equilibrium unemployment.

6. Disequilibrium unemployment occurs when real wage rates are above the level that will equate the aggregate demand and supply of labour. It can be caused by unions or government pushing up wages (real-wage unemployment), by a fall in aggregate demand but a downward 'stickiness' in real wages (demand-deficient unemployment), or by an increase in the supply of labour with again a downward stickiness in wages.

7. In the case of demand-deficient unemployment, the disequilibrium in the labour market may correspond to a low-output equilibrium in the goods market. A fall in real wage rates may be insufficient to remove the deficiency of demand in the labour market.

8. Equilibrium unemployment occurs when there are people unable or unwilling to fill job vacancies. This may be due to poor information in the labour market and hence a time lag before people find suitable jobs (frictional unemployment), to a changing pattern of demand or supply in the economy and hence a mismatching of labour with jobs (structural unemployment – specific types being technological and regional unemployment), or to seasonal fluctuations in the demand for labour.

15.2 AGGREGATE DEMAND AND SUPPLY AND THE LEVEL OF PRICES

Before we examine the causes of inflation (the rate of increase in prices), we need to look at how the *level* of prices in the economy is determined. It is determined by the interaction of aggregate demand and aggregate supply. The analysis is similar to that of demand and supply in individual markets, although, as we shall see in later chapters, there are some crucial differences. Figure 15.8 shows an aggregate demand and an aggregate supply curve. As with demand and supply curves for individual goods, we plot price on the vertical axis, except that now it is the *general* price level; and we plot quantity on the horizontal axis, except that now it is the *total quantity of national output* (GDP).

Let us examine each curve in turn.

Definition

Seasonal unemployment Unemployment associated with industries or regions where the demand for labour is lower at certain times of the year.

The aggregate demand curve

Remember what we said about aggregate demand in Chapter 14. It is the total level of spending in the economy and consists of four elements: consumer spending (*C*), private investment (*I*), government expenditure on goods and services (*G*) and expenditure on exports (*X*) less expenditure on imports (*M*). Thus:

$$AD = C + I + G + X - M$$

The aggregate demand curve shows how much national output (GDP) will be demanded at each level of prices. But why does the *AD* curve slope downwards? Why will people demand less as prices rise? There are two effects that can cause this: income effects and substitution effects.

Income effects

For many people, when prices rise, their wages will not rise in line, at least not in the short run. There will therefore tend to be a redistribution of income away from wage earners (and hence consumers) and to those charging the

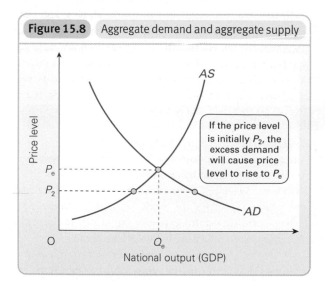

Figure 15.8 Aggregate demand and aggregate supply

If the price level is initially P_2, the excess demand will cause price level to rise to P_e

Price level — AS, AD, P_e, P_2, O, Q_e, National output (GDP)

to buy imports (which are *not* part of aggregate demand). Thus higher domestic prices will lead to a fall in aggregate demand (i.e. cause the *AD* curve to be downward sloping).

The second is known as the **real balance effect**. If prices rise, the value (i.e. the purchasing power) of people's balances in their bank and building society accounts will fall. But many people will be reluctant to reduce the real value of their balances (i.e. their savings) too much, and will thus probably cut back on their spending also. This desire by people to protect the real value of their savings will thus also cause aggregate demand to fall.

The third reason why people may switch away from spending concerns changes in *interest rates*. With higher prices to pay by consumers, and higher wages to pay by firms, there will tend to be a greater demand for *money*. With a given supply of money in the economy, there will now be a shortage of money. As a result, banks will tend to raise interest rates (we examine this process in Chapter 20). These higher rates of interest will have a dampening effect on spending: after all, the higher the interest rates people have to pay, the more expensive it is to buy things on credit. Again, aggregate demand is likely to fall.

The shape of the aggregate demand curve

We have seen that both the income and substitution effects of a rise in the general price level will cause the aggregate demand for goods and services to fall. Thus the *AD* curve is downward sloping. The bigger the income and substitution effects, the more elastic will the curve be.

Shifts in the aggregate demand curve

The aggregate demand curve can shift inwards (to the right) or outwards (to the left), in exactly the same way as the demand curve for an individual good. A rightward shift represents an increase in aggregate demand, whatever the price level; a leftward shift represents a decrease in aggregate demand, whatever the price level.

A shift in the aggregate demand curve will occur if, for any given price level, there is a change in any of its components – consumption, investment, government expenditure or exports minus imports. Thus if the government decides to spend more, or if consumers spend more as a result of lower taxes, or if business confidence increases so that firms decide to invest more, the *AD* curve will shift to the right.

higher prices – namely, firms. Thus for consumers there has been an *income effect* of the higher prices. The rise in prices leads to a cut in real incomes and thus people will spend less. Aggregate demand will fall. The *AD* curve will be downward sloping, as in Figure 15.8.

To some extent this will be offset by a rise in profits, but it is unlikely that much of the additional profits will be spent by firms on investment, especially if they see consumer expenditure falling; and any increase in dividends to shareholders will take a time before it is paid, and then may simply be saved rather than spent. To summarise: if prices rise more than wages, the redistribution from wages to profits is likely to lead to a fall in aggregate demand.

Clearly, this income effect will not operate if wages rise in line with prices. Real incomes of wage earners will be unaffected. In practice, as we shall see at several places in this book, in the short run wages do lag behind prices.

An income effect is also likely to occur as a result of progressive taxes. As prices and incomes rise, so people will find that they are paying a larger proportion of their incomes in taxes. As a result, they cannot afford to buy so much.

Substitution effects

In the *micro*economic situation, if the price of one good rises, people will switch to alternative goods. This is the substitution effect of that price rise and helps to explain why the demand curve for a particular good will be downward sloping. But how can there be a substitution effect at a *macro*economic level? If prices in general go up, what can people substitute for spending? There are in fact three ways in which people can switch to alternatives.

The first, and most obvious, concerns *imports and exports*. Higher prices for our country's goods will discourage foreign residents from buying our exports (which are part of aggregate demand) and encourage domestic residents

Definition

Real balance effect As the price level rises, so the value of people's money balances will fall. They will therefore spend less in order to increase their money balances and go some way to protecting their real value.

The aggregate supply curve

The aggregate supply (AS) curve shows the amount of goods and services that firms are willing to supply at each level of prices. To keep things simple, let us focus on the short-run AS curve. When constructing this curve, we assume that various other things remain constant. These include wage rates and other input prices, technology and the total supply of factors of production (labour, land and capital).[1]

Why do we assume that wage rates and other input prices are constant? Wage rates are frequently determined by a process of collective bargaining and, once agreed, will typically be set for a whole year, if not two. Even if they are not determined by collective bargaining, wage rates often change relatively infrequently. So too with the price of other inputs: except in perfect, or near perfect markets (such as the market for various raw materials), firms supplying capital equipment and other inputs tend to change their prices relatively infrequently. They do not immediately raise them when there is an increase in demand or lower them when demand falls. Thus there is a 'stickiness' in both wage rates and the price of many inputs.

The short-run aggregate supply curve slopes upwards, as shown in Figure 15.8. In other words, the higher the level of prices, the more will be produced. The reason is simple. Because we are holding wages and other input prices constant, then as the prices of their products rise, firms' profitability at each level of output will be higher than before. This will encourage them to produce more.

But what *limits* the increase in aggregate supply in response to an increase in prices? In other words, why is the aggregate supply curve not horizontal? There are two main reasons:

KI 17 p125

- Diminishing returns. With some factors of production fixed in supply, notably capital equipment, firms experience a diminishing marginal physical product from their other factors, and hence have an upward-sloping marginal cost curve. In microeconomic analysis the upward-sloping cost curves of firms explain why the supply curves of individual goods and services slope upwards. Here in macroeconomics we are adding the supply curves of all goods and services and thus the aggregate supply curve also slopes upwards.
- Growing shortages of certain variable factors. As firms collectively produce more, even inputs that can be varied may increasingly become in short supply. Skilled labour may be harder to find, and certain raw materials may be harder to obtain.

Thus rising costs explain the upward-sloping aggregate supply curve. The more steeply costs rise as production increases, the less elastic will the aggregate supply curve be. It is likely that, as the level of national output increases and firms reach full-capacity working, so marginal costs will rise faster. The aggregate supply curve will thus tend to get steeper (as shown in Figure 15.8).

Shifts in the aggregate supply curve

The aggregate supply curve will shift if there is a change in any of the variables that are held constant when we plot the curve. Several of these variables, notably technology, the labour force and the stock of capital, change only slowly – normally shifting the curve gradually to the right. This represents an increase in potential output.

By contrast, wage rates and other input prices can change significantly in the short run, and are thus the major causes of shifts in the short-run supply curve. For example, a general rise in wage rates throughout the economy reduces the amount that firms wish to produce at any level of prices. The aggregate supply curve shifts to the left. A similar effect will occur if other costs, such as oil prices or indirect taxes, increase.

Equilibrium

Equilibrium in the macroeconomy occurs when aggregate demand and aggregate supply are equal. In Figure 15.8, this is at the price level P_e and national output (GDP) of Q_e. To demonstrate this, consider what would happen if aggregate demand exceeded aggregate supply: for example, at P_2 in Figure 15.8. The resulting shortages throughout the economy would drive up prices. This would encourage firms to produce more: there would be a movement up *along* the AS curve. At the same time, the increase in prices would reduce the level of aggregate demand: that is, there would also be a movement back up *along* the AD curve. The shortage would be eliminated when price had risen to P_e.

TC 4 p44

Shifts in the AD or AS curves

If the AD or AS curve shifts, there will be a movement along the other curve to the new point of equilibrium. For example, if there is a cut in income taxes and a corresponding increase in consumer demand, the AD curve will shift to the right. This will result in a movement up along the AS curve to the new equilibrium point: in other words, to a new higher level of national output and a higher price level. The more elastic the AS curve, the more will output rise relative to prices. We will consider the shape of the AS curve in more detail in later chapters, and especially Chapter 21.

---

[1] Long-run AS curves assume that these things *will* change: that they will be affected by changes in aggregate demand and the price level. We will look at long-run aggregate supply curves in later chapters.

Section summary

1. An aggregate demand curve shows the relationship between aggregate demand ($C+I+G+X-M$) and the price level. The curve is downward sloping because of income and substitution effects.

2. If a rise in the price level causes wage rises to lag behind or causes a rise in the proportion of income paid in income tax, then consumers will respond to the resulting fall in their real incomes by cutting consumption. This is the income effect.

3. If a rise in the price level causes (a) imports to rise or exports to fall, or (b) people to spend less in order to maintain the value of their bank balances, or (c) people to spend less and save more because of a rise in interest rates, these too will result in a fall in the level of aggregate demand. These are all substitution effects.

4. If the determinant of any component of aggregate demand (other than the price level) changes, the aggregate demand will shift.

5. The (short-run) aggregate supply curve is upward sloping. This reflects the fact that at higher prices, firms will find it profitable to supply more. The curve will be more elastic, the less rapidly diminishing returns set in and the more elastic the supply of variable factors.

6. The aggregate supply curve will shift to the left (upwards) if wage rates or other costs rise independently of a rise in aggregate demand.

7. Equilibrium in the economy occurs when aggregate demand equals aggregate supply. A rise in the price level will occur if there is a rightward shift in the aggregate demand curve or a leftward shift in the aggregate supply curve.

15.3 INFLATION

The rate of inflation measures the annual percentage increase in prices. The most usual measure is that of *consumer* prices. The UK government publishes a consumer prices index (CPI) each month, and the rate of inflation is the percentage increase in that index over the previous 12 months. This index is used throughout the EU, where it generally goes under its full title of the harmonised index of consumer prices (HICP). The HICP covers virtually 100 per cent of consumer spending (including cross-border spending) and uses sophisticated weights for each item (see Appendix A, page A:6–7 for an analysis of weighting in indices).

Figure 15.9 shows the rates of inflation for the USA, Japan, the UK and the 12 original members of the eurozone. As you can see, inflation was particularly severe between 1973 and 1983, and relatively low in the mid 1980s and since the mid 1990s, but edging up in the late 2000s. Although most countries have followed a similar pattern over time, the average rates of inflation have differed substantially from one country to another. These differences, however, have tended to narrow in recent years as barriers to international trade and capital movements have been reduced and as increasing numbers of countries have directed their macroeconomic policy towards achieving target rates of inflation of around 2 per cent (see Table 15.5).

| Table 15.5 | \multicolumn{4}{l}{Inflation rates for selected countries (average % per annum)} |

Country	1971–80	1981–90	1991–2000	2001–9
Belgium	6.8	4.2	1.8	2.3
France	9.8	6.4	1.4	1.8
Germany	5.2	2.6	1.8	1.6
Italy	14.8	10.0	4.2	2.6
Japan	8.8	2.2	0.3	−0.6
Netherlands	7.3	2.3	2.6	2.5
Spain	15.0	9.2	4.2	3.2
Sweden	9.6	8.0	3.3	1.6
UK	13.3	6.2	3.2	2.2
USA	7.0	4.5	2.2	2.4
EU-12	9.5	6.2	2.7	2.2

Source: Based on data in *Statistical Annex of the European Economy* (Commission of the European Communities, various years).

*LOOKING AT THE MATHS

The inflation rate (π) is calculated from the following formula:

$$\pi_t = \frac{P_t - P_{t-1}}{P_{t-1}} \times 100$$

where P_t is the price index for year t and P_{t-1} is the price index for the previous year. Thus if the price index for year 1 is 140.0 and that for year 2 is 149.1, then inflation in year 2 is

$$\pi = \frac{149.1 - 140.0}{140.0} \times 100 = 6.5\%$$

It is also possible to give the rates of inflation for other prices. For example, indices are published for commodity prices, for food prices, for house prices, for import prices, for prices after taking taxes into account and so on. Their

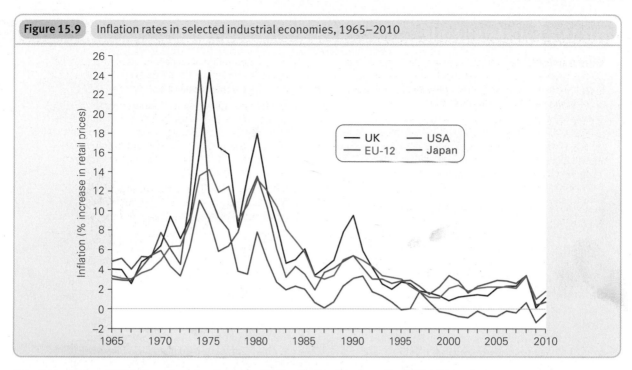

Figure 15.9 Inflation rates in selected industrial economies, 1965–2010

Note: Years 2009 and 2010 figures based on forecasts; EU-12 = the 12 original members of the eurozone.
Source: Based on data in *Economic Outlook* (Organisation for Economic Co-operation and Development [OECD], various years).

respective rates of inflation are simply their annual percentage increases. Likewise it is possible to give the rate of inflation of wage rates ('wage inflation').

Before we proceed, a word of caution: be careful not to confuse a rise or fall in *inflation* with a rise or fall in *prices*. A rise in inflation means a *faster* increase in prices. A fall in inflation means a *slower* increase in prices (but still an increase as long as inflation is positive). (See Box A1.1 on page A:11.)

The costs of inflation

A lack of growth is obviously a problem if people want higher living standards. Unemployment is obviously a problem, both for the unemployed themselves and also for society, which suffers a loss in output and has to support the unemployed. But why is inflation a problem? If prices go up by 10 per cent, does it really matter? Provided your wages kept up with prices, you would have no cut in your living standards.

If people could correctly anticipate the rate of inflation and fully adjust prices and incomes to take account of it, then the costs of inflation would indeed be relatively small. For us as consumers, they would simply be the relatively minor inconvenience of having to adjust our notions of what a 'fair' price is for each item when we go shopping. For firms, they would again be the relatively minor costs of having to change price labels, or prices in catalogues or on menus, or adjust slot machines. These are known as *menu costs*.

In reality, people frequently make mistakes when predicting the rate of inflation and are not able to adapt fully to it. This leads to the following problems, which are likely to be more serious the higher the rate of inflation becomes and the more the rate fluctuates.

Redistribution. Inflation redistributes income away from those on fixed incomes and those in a weak bargaining position, to those who can use their economic power to gain large pay, rent or profit increases. It redistributes wealth to those with assets (e.g. property) that rise in value particularly rapidly during periods of inflation, and away from those with types of savings that pay rates of interest below the rate of inflation and hence whose value is eroded by inflation. Pensioners may be particularly badly hit by rapid inflation.

1. *Do you personally gain or lose from inflation? Why?*
2. *Make a list of those who are most likely to gain and those who are most likely to lose from inflation.*

Uncertainty and lack of investment. Inflation tends to cause uncertainty among the business community, especially when the rate of inflation fluctuates. (Generally, the higher

Definition

Menu costs of inflation The costs associated with having to adjust price lists or labels.

BOX 15.2 HYPERINFLATION

When prices go crazy

In recent years in the UK, along with most other countries of the world, we have come to expect relatively stable prices (see Figure 15.9). If the rate of inflation were to rise to anywhere near the levels reached in the mid 1970s (24 per cent) or the early 1980s (18 per cent), it would be looked upon as a clear sign of economic failure.

But such rates are mild compared with those experienced by many other countries in the past. Inflation in Brazil peaked at 1200 per cent in 1993, in Russia at 2500 per cent in 1992 and in Ukraine at 10 000 per cent in 1993. But even these cases of hyperinflation are mild compared with those experienced by certain European countries in the early 1920s and by Serbia in the 1990s and Zimbabwe in recent years.

Germany 1921–3

Several countries experienced hyperinflation after the First World War. In Austria and Hungary prices were several thousand times their pre-war level. In Poland they were over 2 million times higher, and in the USSR several billion times higher.

But even these staggering rates of inflation seem insignificant beside those of Germany. Following the chaos of the war, the German government resorted to printing money, not only to meet its domestic spending requirements in rebuilding a war-ravaged economy, but also to finance the crippling war reparations imposed on it by the allies in the Treaty of Versailles.

From mid 1921 the rate of monetary increase soared and inflation soared with it. By autumn 1923 the annual rate of inflation had reached a mind-boggling 7 000 000 000 000 per cent! As price increases accelerated, people became reluctant to accept money: before they knew it, the money would be worthless. People thus rushed to spend their money as quickly as possible. But this in turn further drove up prices.

For many Germans the effect was devastating. People's life savings were wiped out. Others whose wages were not quickly adjusted found their real incomes plummeting. Many were thrown out of work as businesses, especially those with money assets, went bankrupt. Poverty and destitution were widespread.

By the end of 1923 the German currency was literally worthless. In 1924, therefore, it was replaced by a new currency – one whose supply was kept tightly controlled by the government.

Serbia 1993–5

After the break-up of Yugoslavia in 1992, the economy of the remaining part of Yugoslavia (Serbia and Montenegro) collapsed. The government relied more and more on printing money to finance public expenditure. Prices soared.

The government attempted to control the inflation by imposing price controls. But these simply made production unprofitable and output fell further. The economy nosedived. Unemployment exceeded 30 per cent.

In October 1993, the government created a new currency, the new dinar, worth one million old dinars.

(a) *Yugoslavian banknote, 1994*

Source: Copyright © National Bank of Serbia, Treasury Department.

In other words, six zeros were knocked off the currency. But this did not solve the problem. Between October 1993 and January 1994, prices rose by 5 quadrillion per cent (5 and fifteen zeros). Normal life could not function. Shops ran out of produce; savings were wiped out; barter replaced normal market activity.

> Many Yugoslavian businesses refused to take the Yugoslavian currency, and the German Deutsche Mark effectively became the currency of Yugoslavia. But government organisations, government employees and pensioners still got paid in Yugoslavian dinars so there was still an active exchange in dinars. On November 12, 1993 the exchange rate was 1 DM = 1 million new dinars. . . . By December 15th it was 1 DM = 3.7 billion new dinars. The average *daily* rate of inflation was *nearly 100 per cent*. At the end of December the exchange rate was 1 DM = 3 trillion new dinars.[1]

At the beginning of January 1994 a 'new new dinar' was introduced, worth 1 billion new dinars. On 24 January this was replaced by a 'novi dinar' pegged 1 to 1 against the Deutsche Mark. This was worth approximately 13 million new new dinars. The novi dinar remained pegged to the Deutsche Mark and inflation was quickly eliminated.

Zimbabwe 2004–8

The most recent example of hyperinflation is that in Zimbabwe. By mid 2008, the official annual inflation had reached over 11 million per cent (see table). Unofficially, it was closer to 20 million per cent.

(b) *Zimbabwe banknote, 2008*

Source: Reserve Bank of Zimbabwe.

Inflation in Zimbabwe

	Rate of inflation (% annual rate)
2000	57
2001	105
2002	174
2003	585
2004	158
2005	503
2006 Q1	773
2006 Q2	1 147
2006 Q3	1 071
2006 Q4	1 164
2007 Q1	1 883
2007 Q2	5 394
2007 Q3	7 415
2007 Q4	40 911
2008 Q1	165 000
2008 Q2	11 250 000
2008 Q3	231 000 000
2008 Q4	6.5×10^{108}

Source: Based on data in International Financial Statistics (IFS) database. (International Monetary Fund [IMF]); and various newspaper sources.

The economy had been in turmoil for some time as white farms were seized as part of the policy of land redistribution, squatter settlements in Harare were demolished and many rural homes were destroyed. As with Serbia, the government printed money to finance its expenditure.

As inflation soared, people rushed to spend their money before inflation made it virtually worthless. Producers, on the other hand, found that the money they received could not cover their costs. Production fell and businesses closed. There was little to buy in the shops. There were chronic shortages of food, medicine and other basics, and electricity and running water were frequently cut. Unemployment was over 80 per cent.

'I just come here to keep my job,' said the cashier at a TM supermarket in Harare, where a tin of baked beans cost – at least for the next few hours – a mere 256bn Zimbabwe dollars (worth about US$1 at the current exchange rate). 'It's just ridiculous. We put the prices up several times a day. The salary I was paid at the start of this month cannot even pay for my bus fare here this morning. I am struggling.' . . .

Harare is fast becoming a city of unemployed, impoverished zillionaires – struggling to spend thick wads of banknotes in empty supermarkets before the cash becomes worthless, and increasingly dependent on funds sent home by the millions of Zimbabweans who have already fled abroad.

In the subdued, seemingly half-empty capital, people wait in long queues outside banks to withdraw a maximum of a 100bn dollars a day. In bars, the price of beer goes up between rounds. Many people are reduced to eating one meal a day. Adults leave hungry children at home and walk for hours to work because they cannot afford the bus fare, while the newspapers advertise lotto prizes of a quadrillion dollars.[2]

Again, as with Serbia, the response of the central bank was to introduce a 'new' currency with fewer zeros. In July 2008, the government had introduced the 100 billion dollar note (with an issue and expiry date, and hence termed a 'cheque' – see picture). On 1 August, 10 zeros were knocked off the currency, making one of the new 100 billion dollar notes worth only 10 new Zimbabwean dollars – initially about 1 US dollar, but within a few days a tiny fraction of a US cent.

In the same month, the central bank (the Reserve bank of Zimbabwe (RBZ)) abandoned issuing inflation statistics.

A report released by the Cato Institute in June 2008 – *Zimbabwe, From Hyperinflation to Growth* – said the RBZ's money machine was the source of the hyperinflation. 'The government spends, and the RBZ finances the spending by printing money. The RBZ has no ability, in practice, to resist the government's demands for cash . . . To stop hyperinflation, Zimbabwe needs to immediately adopt a different monetary system,' the report said.[3]

In January 2009, the RBZ issued the world's first 100 trillion dollar note. Inflation at the time was estimated to be 6.5 quindecillion novemdecillion percent – 65 followed by 107 zeros! People, not surprisingly if they could, were trading in other currencies, such as the US dollar or the South African rand.

The RBZ had already endorsed semi-official dollarisation in September 2008 by introducing 'Foreign Exchange Licensed Warehouses and Shops' when some 1000 retail outlets and 250 wholesalers were permitted to trade in foreign currency.

In a statement released earlier in January 2009, the Zimbabwe Congress of Trade Unions (ZCTU) demanded that 'all workers should be paid in foreign currency, given the fact that shops are now selling their goods in foreign currency - even those that have not been licensed to do so.'[4]

Using another country's currency would involve abandoning control of monetary policy, and that was something the Zimbabwean authorities would not do. Also, you would no longer have the president's head on the currency.

Issuing a new Zimbabwe dollar rigidly pegged to the South African rand would be an alternative to complete abandonment of the domestic currency. This would be similar to the policy adopted by Serbia in 1994. Also, this policy would not be new to the region; the currencies of Namibia, Lesotho and Swaziland are pegged to the rand.

When confronted by hyperinflation, governments frequently seek to blame anyone but themselves. The Serbian government in 1994 blamed international sanctions against the country. The Zimbabwean government in 2008 did exactly the same.

1. *Would restricting the growth in the money supply be enough to cure hyperinflation?*
2. *Look through the costs of inflation identified on pages 429–32 and assess how serious each of them is likely to be in a period of hyperinflation.*

[1] Thayer Watkins, *The Worst Episode of Hyperinflation in History: Yugoslavia 1993–94* (http://www.rogershermansociety.org/yugoslavia.htm).
[2] BBC News (http://news.bbc.co.uk/1/hi/world/africa/7528974.stm).
[3] Integrated Regional Information Networks (UN Office for the Co-ordination of Humanitarian Affairs), http://www.irinnews.org/Report.aspx?ReportId=82500
[4] *ibid.*

the rate of inflation, the more it fluctuates.) If it is difficult for firms to predict their costs and revenues, they may be discouraged from investing. This will reduce the rate of economic growth. On the other hand, as will be explained below, policies to reduce the rate of inflation may themselves reduce the rate of economic growth, especially in the short run. This may then provide the government with a policy dilemma.

Balance of payments. Inflation is likely to worsen the balance of trade. If a country suffers from relatively high inflation, its exports will become less competitive in world markets. At the same time, imports will become relatively cheaper than home-produced goods. Thus exports will fall and imports will rise. As a result, the balance of trade will deteriorate and/or the exchange rate will fall. Both of these effects can cause problems. This is examined in more detail in section 15.4.

Resources. Extra resources are likely to be used to cope with the effects of inflation. Accountants and other financial experts may have to be employed by companies to help them cope with the uncertainties caused by inflation.

The costs of inflation may be relatively mild if inflation is kept to single figures. They can be very serious, however, if inflation gets out of hand. If inflation develops into 'hyperinflation', with prices rising perhaps by several hundred per cent or even thousands per cent per year, the whole basis of the market economy will be undermined. Firms constantly raise prices in an attempt to cover their soaring costs. Workers demand huge pay increases in an attempt to stay ahead of the rocketing cost of living. Thus prices and wages chase each other in an ever-rising inflationary spiral. People will no longer want to save money. Instead they will spend it as quickly as possible before its value falls any further. People may even resort to barter in an attempt to avoid using money altogether.

Box 15.2 looks at three of the most severe case of hyperinflation ever: Germany in the early 1920s, Serbia in the 1990s and Zimbabwe much more recently.

Causes of inflation

Demand-pull inflation

Demand-pull inflation is caused by continuing rises in aggregate demand. In Figure 15.10, the *AD* curve shifts to the right (and continues doing so). Firms will respond to a rise in demand partly by raising prices and partly by increasing output (there is a move up along the *AS* curve). Just how much they raise prices depends on how much their costs rise as a result of increasing output. In other words, it will depend on the shape of the *AS* curve.

The aggregate supply curve will tend to become steeper as the economy approaches the peak of the business cycle. In other words, the closer actual output gets to potential output, and the less slack there is in the economy, the more

Figure 15.10 Demand-pull inflation

will firms respond to a rise in demand by raising their prices.

Sometimes there may be a *single* increase in demand (or a 'demand shock'). This could be due, for example, to an increased level of government expenditure. The effect is to give a *single* rise in the price level. Although this causes inflation in the short run, once the effect has taken place inflation will fall back to zero. For inflation to persist, however, there must be *continuing* rightward shifts in the *AD* curve, and thus continuing rises in the price level. If inflation is to rise, these rightward shifts must get *faster*.

Demand-pull inflation is typically associated with a booming economy. Many economists therefore argue that it is the counterpart of demand-deficient unemployment. When the economy is in recession, demand-deficient unemployment is high, but demand-pull inflation is low. When, on the other hand, the economy is near the peak of the business cycle, demand-pull inflation is high, but demand-deficient unemployment is low.

Cost-push inflation

Cost-push inflation is associated with continuing rises in costs and hence continuing leftward (upward) shifts in the *AS* curve. Such shifts occur when costs of production rise *independently* of aggregate demand.

If firms face a rise in costs, they will respond partly by raising prices and passing the costs on to the consumer, and partly by cutting back on production. This is illustrated in Figure 15.11. There is a leftward shift in the aggregate

Definitions

Demand-pull inflation Inflation caused by persistent rises in aggregate demand.

Cost-push inflation Inflation caused by persistent rises in costs of production (independently of demand).

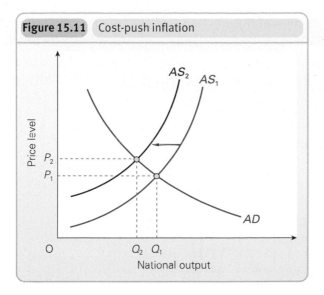

Figure 15.11   Cost-push inflation

As with demand-pull inflation, we must distinguish between *single* shifts in the aggregate supply curve (known as 'supply shocks') and *continuing* shifts. If there is a single leftward shift in aggregate supply, there will be a single rise in the price level. For example, if the government raises the excise duty on oil, there will be a single rise in oil prices and hence in industry's fuel costs. This will cause *temporary* inflation while the price rise is passed on through the economy. Once this has occurred, prices will stabilise at the new level and the rate of inflation will fall back to zero again. If cost-push inflation is to continue over a number of years, therefore, the aggregate supply curve must *continually* shift to the left. If cost-push inflation is to *rise*, these shifts must get *faster*.

Rises in costs may originate from a number of different sources, such as trade unions pushing up wages, firms with monopoly power raising prices in order to increase their profits, or increases in international commodity prices. With the process of globalisation and increased international competition, cost-push pressures have tended to decrease in recent years. One major exception has been the oil shocks that have occurred from time to time. For example, the near tripling of oil prices from $51 per barrel in Jan 2007 to over $141 per barrel in July 2008 put upward pressure on costs and prices around the world.

Temporary supply shocks can come from bad harvests. Longer-term supply-side problems can come from the depletion of natural resources, such as the gradual running-down of North Sea oil, pollution of the seas and hence a decline in incomes for nations with large fishing industries, and, perhaps the most devastating of all, the problem of 'desertification' in sub-Saharan Africa.

supply curve: from AS_1 to AS_2. This causes the price level to rise to P_2 and the level of output to *fall* to Q_2.

Just how much firms raise prices and cut back on production depends on the shape of the aggregate demand curve. The less elastic the AD curve, the less will sales fall as a result of any price rise, and hence the more will firms be able to pass on the rise in their costs to consumers as higher prices.

Note that the effect on output and employment is the opposite of demand-pull inflation. With demand-pull inflation, output and hence employment tends to rise. With cost-push inflation, however, output and employment tends to fall.

BOX 15.3   **COST-PUSH ILLUSION**   **EXPLORING ECONOMICS**

When rising costs are not cost-push inflation

It is easy to get confused between demand-pull and cost-push inflation.

Frequently, inflationary pressures *seem* to come from the cost side. Shopkeepers blame their price rises on the rise in their costs – the wholesale prices they have to pay. The wholesalers blame their price rises on a rise in *their* costs – the prices they are charged by the various manufacturers. The manufacturers in turn blame rising raw material costs, rising wage rates, rising rents and so on. Everyone blames their price rises on the rise in their costs.

But why have these costs risen?

It could well be due to a rise in aggregate *demand*! Wages may go up because of falling unemployment and a shortage of labour. Firms *have* to pay higher wages in order to recruit or maintain enough labour. Rents may rise because of the upsurge in demand. So too with raw materials: higher demand may pull up their prices too.

What we have then is a 'cost-push illusion'. Costs rise, it is true, but they rise because of an increase in demand.

So when does genuine cost-push inflation occur? This occurs when costs of production rise independently of demand. This will normally involve an increased use of monopoly power: unions becoming more powerful or militant and thus driving up wages; firms using their monopoly/oligopoly power to push up prices; commodity producers such as the OPEC countries forming cartels to push up their prices; the government using its power to raise indirect taxes (such as VAT).

In many cases, these cost-push or 'supply-side' shocks are one-off events and after an initial rise in prices, prices settle at the new higher level. There is thus only a temporary inflationary effect while these cost rises work through the economy.

 If consumer demand rises and firms respond by raising prices, is this necessarily an example of demand-pull inflation? Could there be such a thing as demand-pull illusion? (Clue: why might consumer demand have risen?)

BOX 15.4   IS INFLATION DEAD?

Or is it just sleeping and beginning to stir?

'What's the big fuss about inflation?' That might seem to be a justified question today, when inflation rates around the world are so much lower than in the 1990s (see chart).

Indeed, having some inflation, provided that it is relatively modest, could even be seen to be an advantage. This is because wages and prices are often 'sticky' downwards: unions are not prepared to accept wage cuts; firms are often unwilling to cut prices. Having a modest amount of inflation allows *relative* prices and wages in different parts of the economy to be adjusted up *and* down, in line with changes in demand and supply. Where demand has risen (or supply fallen), prices and wages can rise. Where demand has fallen (or supply risen), prices and wages can be held steady. There will be an overall rise in prices and wages in the economy (a modest inflation) and yet *relative* prices and wages will have adjusted.

So why be concerned about inflation, given that it is so low and, at such levels, can be useful? The reason *why* it has been so low for many years now is that it has been made the main target of macroeconomic policy in many countries. For example, in the UK, the Bank of England tries to keep inflation at 2 per cent, as does the European Central Bank (ECB) in the euro area. In both cases, interest rates are adjusted up or down to keep inflation on target. If inflation is predicted to go above its target level, interest rates are raised. The resulting higher cost of borrowing

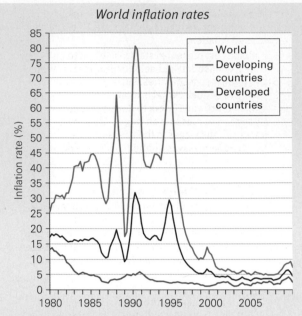

World inflation rates

Source: Based on data in International Financial Statistics (IFS) database (International Monetary Fund [IMF]).

The interaction of demand-pull and cost-push inflation

Demand-pull and cost-push inflation can occur together, since wage and price rises can be caused both by increases in aggregate demand and by independent causes pushing up costs. Even when an inflationary process *starts* as either demand-pull or cost-push, it is often difficult to separate the two. An initial cost-push inflation may encourage the government to expand aggregate demand to offset rises in unemployment. Alternatively, an initial demand-pull inflation may strengthen the power of certain groups, which then use this power to drive up costs.

Either way, the result is likely to be continuing rightward shifts in the *AD* curve and leftward shifts in the *AS* curve. Prices will carry on rising. This is illustrated in Figure 15.12.

Structural (demand-shift) inflation

When the *pattern* of demand (or supply) changes in the economy, certain industries will experience increased demand and others decreased demand. If prices and wage rates are inflexible downwards in the contracting industries, and prices and wage rates rise in the expanding indus-

Figure 15.12   The interaction of demand-pull and cost-push inflation

tries, the overall price and wage level will rise. The problem will be made worse, the less elastic is supply to these shifts.

Thus a more rapid structural change in the economy can lead to both increased structural unemployment and

EXPLORING ECONOMICS

dampens consumer expenditure and investment by firms. The resulting lower aggregate demand leads to a fall in demand-pull inflation.

But what if cost pressures start to rise? Up to 2007, the process of globalisation had helped to *suppress* inflation. Imports from low-cost countries, such as China and India, had driven prices down. What is more, outsourcing call-centre, back-office and IT work to developing countries had put downward pressure on wages. This downward effect on prices and wages in the USA and other developed economies was dubbed the 'China price' effect.

The inflation giant stirs

By 2007, however, the China price effect was beginning to turn upwards. The huge increase in demand for raw materials by China and India had seen a surge in the price of oil, metals and minerals. By mid 2008, the annual rate of commodity price inflation was 26 per cent, with oil up by almost 80 per cent.

At the same time, global food prices were rising as a result of growth in demand from many developing countries. Global food price inflation was almost 50 per cent by mid 2008. Food supplies were unable to keep up with demand because of poor harvests in Australia and other countries, the switching of land from growing food to growing crops for biofuels, and the increased use of land for producing meat rather than grains.

. . . and then goes back to sleep

With the global banking crisis of 2008 and the decline in the availability of credit, so the world economy slowed down rapidly from mid 2008. Within a few months the worry about rising inflation had turned to a worry about global recession. Now the spectre was one of *deflation* – falling prices.

If prices fall, and are predicted to go on falling, people will hold back from spending: why buy an item like a car or television now, when, by waiting, you could get it cheaper later? This speculation is destabilising, as it causes firms to cut prices further in order to sell their products. Then people cut down on spending even more, pushing the economy deeper into recession.

The priority of governments and central banks had thus rapidly shifted from controlling inflation to boosting the economy to combat recession. But, once the world economy recovered, it was likely that inflationary pressures would begin to rise again. Targeting inflation would, once again, be necessary to prevent the inflation giant from stirring.

But could we have higher growth and lower unemployment if we were prepared to accept a higher rate of inflation? Or is low inflation a means to achieving these other goals? We shall consider these questions in the following chapters.

 How is the policy of targeting inflation likely to affect the expected rate of inflation?

---

increased structural inflation. An example of this problem was the so-called north–south divide in the UK during the boom of the second half of the 1980s. The north experienced high structural unemployment as old industries declined, while the south experienced excess demand. This excess demand in the south, among other things, led to rapid house price inflation, and rapid increases in incomes for various groups of workers and firms. With many prices and wages being set *nationally*, the inflation in the south then 'spilt over' into the north.

 With the eurozone classed as a single economy with a single inflation rate, explain whether the above problems apply between the different countries using the euro.

Expectations and inflation

 Workers and firms take account of the *expected* rate of inflation when making decisions.

Imagine that a union and an employer are negotiating a wage increase. Let us assume that both sides expect a rate of inflation of 5 per cent. The union will be happy to receive a wage rise somewhat above 5 per cent. That way the mem-

bers would be getting a *real* rise in incomes. The employers will be happy to pay a wage rise somewhat below 5 per cent. After all, they can put their price up by 5 per cent, knowing that their rivals will do approximately the same. The actual wage rise that the two sides agree on will thus be somewhere around 5 per cent.

Now let us assume that the expected rate of inflation is 10 per cent. Both sides will now negotiate around this benchmark, with the outcome being somewhere round about 10 per cent. Thus the higher the expected rate of inflation, the higher will be the level of pay settlements and price rises, and hence the higher will be the resulting actual rate of inflation.

Just how expectations impact on inflation depends on how they are formed. We examine some models of expectations in Chapter 21.

Policies to tackle inflation

We will be examining a number of different anti-inflationary policies in later chapters. These policies can be directed towards the control of either aggregate demand or aggregate

BOX 15.5	THE PHILLIPS CURVE

Is higher inflation the price for lower unemployment?

If inflation tends to be higher when the economy is booming and if unemployment tends to be higher in recessions, does this mean that there is a 'trade-off' between inflation and unemployment: that lower unemployment tends to be associated with higher inflation, and lower inflation with higher unemployment? Such a trade-off was observed by the New Zealand economist Bill Phillips (see Person Profile in MyEconLab), and was illustrated by the famous *Phillips curve*.

The original Phillips curve

In 1958, Phillips showed the statistical relationship between wage inflation and unemployment in the UK from 1861 to 1957. With wage inflation (ω) on the vertical axis and the unemployment rate (U) on the horizontal axis, a scatter of points was obtained. Each point represented the observation for a particular year. The curve that best fitted the scatter has become known as the 'Phillips curve'. It is illustrated in Figure (a) and shows an inverse relationship between inflation and unemployment.[1]

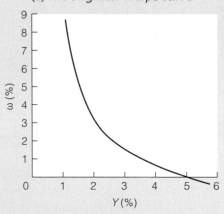

(a) *The original Phillips curve*

Given that wage increases over the period were approximately 2 per cent above price increases (made possible because of increases in labour productivity), a similar-shaped, but lower curve could be plotted showing the relationship between *price* inflation and unemployment.

The curve has often been used to illustrate the effects of changes in aggregate demand. When aggregate demand rose (relative to potential output), inflation rose and unemployment fell: there was an upward movement along the curve. When aggregate demand fell, there was a downward movement along the curve.

There was also a second reason given for the inverse relationship. If wages rose, the unemployed might have believed that the higher wages they were offered represented a *real* wage increase. That is, they might not have realised that the higher wages would be 'eaten up' by price increases: they might have suffered from *money illusion*. They would thus have accepted jobs more readily. The average duration of unemployment therefore

fell. This is a reduction in *frictional* unemployment and is illustrated by an upward shift in the W_o curve in Figure 15.7 (on page 424).

The Phillips curve was bowed in to the origin. The usual explanation for this is that, as aggregate demand expanded, at first there would be plenty of surplus labour, which could meet the extra demand without the need to raise wages very much. But as labour became increasingly scarce, firms would find they had to offer increasingly higher wages to obtain the labour they required, and the position of trade unions would be increasingly strengthened.

The *position* of the Phillips curve depended on *non-demand* factors causing inflation and unemployment: frictional and structural unemployment; and cost-push, structural and expectations-generated inflation. If any of these non-demand factors changed so as to raise inflation or unemployment, the curve would shift outwards to the right. The relative stability of the curve over the hundred years or so observed by Phillips suggested that these non-demand factors had changed little.

The Phillips curve seemed to present governments with a simple policy choice. They could trade off inflation against unemployment. Lower unemployment could be bought at the cost of higher inflation, and vice versa. Unfortunately, the experience since the late 1960s has suggested that no such simple relationship exists beyond the short run.

The breakdown of the Phillips curve

From about 1966 the Phillips curve relationship seemed to break down. The UK, and many other countries in the western world too, began to experience growing unemployment *and* higher rates of inflation.

Figure (b) shows price inflation (π) and (standardised) unemployment in the UK from 1955 to 2009. From 1955 to 1966 a curve similar to the Phillips curve can be fitted through the data (diagram (i)). From 1967 to the early 1990s, however, no simple picture emerges. Certainly the original Phillips curve could no longer fit the data; but whether the curve shifted to the right and then back again somewhat (the broken lines), or whether the relationship broke down completely, or whether there was some quite different relationship between inflation and unemployment, is not clear by simply looking at the data. In fact, in recent years, as inflation has been targeted, the 'curve' would seem to have become a virtually horizontal straight line!

Definitions

Phillips curve A curve showing the relationship between (price) inflation and unemployment. The original Phillips curve plotted wage inflation against unemployment for the years 1861–1957.

Money illusion When people believe that a money wage or price increase represents a real increase: in other words, they ignore or underestimate inflation.

KI 33
p389

TC 12
p395

(b) The breakdown of the Phillips curve
(i) 1955–66

(ii) 1967–2009

Possible Phillips curves?

Note: Year 2009 data based on forecasts.

Over the years, there has been much debate among economists about the relationship between inflation and unemployment. The controversy will be examined in later chapters and particularly in Chapter 21. One thing does seem clear, however: the relationship is different in the short run and the long run.

 Assume that there is a trade-off between unemployment and inflation, traced out by a 'Phillips curve'. What could cause a leftward shift in this curve?

[1] Phillips' estimated equation was $\omega = -0.9 + 9.638U^{-1.394}$.

supply, and hence are referred to as *demand-side* and *supply-side policies* respectively.

Demand-side policies

There are two types of demand-side policy:

Fiscal policy. **Fiscal policy** involves altering the level of government expenditure and/or rates of tax. Aggregate demand can be reduced by cutting government expenditure (one of the four elements in aggregate demand) or by raising taxes and hence reducing consumer expenditure. These are both examples of **contractionary** (or **deflationary**) fiscal policy.

(Fiscal policy could also be used to *boost* aggregate demand if there were a problem of demand-deficient unemployment. In this case, the government would raise government expenditure and/or cut taxes. This is called **expansionary** (or **reflationary**) fiscal policy.)

Monetary policy. **Monetary policy** involves altering the supply of money in the economy or manipulating the rate of interest. The central bank (the Bank of England in the UK) can reduce aggregate demand (a *contractionary* monetary policy) by putting up interest rates and thus making borrowing more expensive, or by acting to reduce the supply of money available through the banking system. If people borrow less, they will spend less.

Supply-side policies

The aim here is to reduce the rate of increase in costs. This will help reduce leftward (upward) shifts in the aggregate supply curve. This can be done either (1) by restraining monopoly influences on prices and incomes (e.g. by policies to restrict the activities of trade unions, or policies to restrict mergers and takeovers), or (2) by designing policies to increase productivity (e.g. giving various tax incentives, encouraging various types of research and development, giving grants to firms to invest in up-to-date equipment or in the training of labour).

We will examine all these various policies as the book progresses. As we shall see, just as economists sometimes disagree on the precise causes of inflation, so too they sometimes disagree on the most appropriate cures.

Section summary

1. Inflation redistributes incomes from the economically weak to the economically powerful; it causes uncertainty in the business community and as a result reduces investment; it tends to lead to balance of payments problems and/or a fall in the exchange rate; it leads to resources being used to offset its effects. The costs of inflation can be very great indeed in the case of hyperinflation.

2. Demand-pull inflation occurs as a result of increases in aggregate demand. This can be due to monetary or non-monetary causes.

3. Cost-push inflation occurs when there are increases in the costs of production independent of rises in aggregate demand. If there is a single supply-side shock, the inflation will peter out. For cost-push inflation to persist, there must be continuous increases in costs.

4. Cost-push and demand-pull inflation can interact to form spiralling inflation.

5. Inflation can also be caused by shifts in the pattern of demand in the economy, with prices rising in sectors of increasing demand but being reluctant to fall in sectors of declining demand.

6. Expectations play a crucial role in determining the level of inflation. The higher people expect inflation to be, the higher it will be.

7. Policies to tackle inflation can be either demand-side policies (fiscal or monetary) or supply-side policies (to reduce monopoly power or increase productivity).

Definitions

Demand-side policies Policies designed to affect aggregate demand: fiscal policy and monetary policy.

Supply-side policies Policies designed to affect aggregate supply: policies to affect costs or productivity.

Fiscal policy Policy to affect aggregate demand by altering the balance between government expenditure and taxation.

Contractionary (or deflationary) policy Fiscal or monetary policy designed to reduce the rate of growth of aggregate demand.

Expansionary (or reflationary) policy Fiscal or monetary policy designed to increase the rate of growth of aggregate demand.

Monetary policy Policy to affect aggregate demand by altering the supply or cost of money (rate of interest).

15.4 THE BALANCE OF PAYMENTS AND EXCHANGE RATES

The balance of payments account

All countries trade with and have financial dealings with the rest of the world. In other words, all countries are **open economies**. The flows of money between residents of a country and the rest of the world are recorded in the country's balance of payments account.

Receipts of money from abroad are regarded as *credits* and are entered in the accounts with a positive sign. *Outflows* of money from the country are regarded as *debits* and are entered with a negative sign.

There are three main parts of the balance of payments account: the *current account*, the *capital account* and the *financial account*. Each part is then subdivided. We shall look at each part in turn, and take the UK as an example. Table 15.6 gives a summary of the UK balance of payments for 1997 and 2007.

The current account

The **current account** records payments for imports and exports of goods and services, plus incomes flowing into and out of the country, plus net transfers of money into and out of the country. It is normally split into four subdivisions.

The trade in goods account. This records imports and exports of physical goods (previously known as 'visibles'). Exports result in an inflow of money and are therefore a credit item. Imports result in an outflow of money and are therefore a debit item. The balance of these is called the **balance on trade in goods** or **balance of visible trade** or **merchandise balance**. A *surplus* is when exports exceed imports. A *deficit* is when imports exceed exports.

The trade in services account. This records imports and exports of services (such as transport, tourism and insurance).

Table 15.6   UK balance of payments (£ millions)

	1997		2007	
CURRENT ACCOUNT				
1. Trade in goods				
(a) Exports of goods	+171 923		+220 797	
(b) Imports of goods	−184 265		−310 312	
Balance on trade in goods	−12 342		−89 515	
2. Trade in services				
(a) Exports of services	+61 104		+139 156	
(b) Imports of services	−47 686		−100 825	
Balance on trade in services	+13 418		+38 331	
Balance on trade in goods and services		+1 076		−51 184
3. Net income flows (wages and investment income)		+3 905		+5 302
4. Net current transfers (government and private)		−5 918		−13 793
Current account balance		**−937**		**−59 675**
CAPITAL ACCOUNT				
5. Net capital transfers, etc.		+982		+2 528
Capital account balance		**+982**		**+2 528**
FINANCIAL ACCOUNT				
6. Investment (direct and portfolio)				
(a) Net investment in UK from abroad	+49 609		+322 266	
(b) Net UK investment abroad	−90 246		−281 115	
Balance of direct and portfolio investment		−40 637		+41 151
7. Other financial flows (mainly short-term)				
(a) Net deposits in UK from abroad and borrowing from abroad by UK residents	+200 352		+784 083	
(b) Net deposits abroad by UK residents and UK lending to overseas residents	−167 151		−765 722	
Balance of other financial flows		+33 201		+18 361
8. Reserves (drawing on + adding to −)		+2 380		−1 191
Financial account balance		**−5 056**		**+58 321**
TOTAL OF ALL THREE ACCOUNTS		−5 011		+1 174
9. Net errors and omissions		+5 011		−1 174
		0		0

Source: UK Economic Accounts (National Statistics, 2008).

Figure 15.13 Current account balance as percentage of GDP in selected countries, 1970–2009

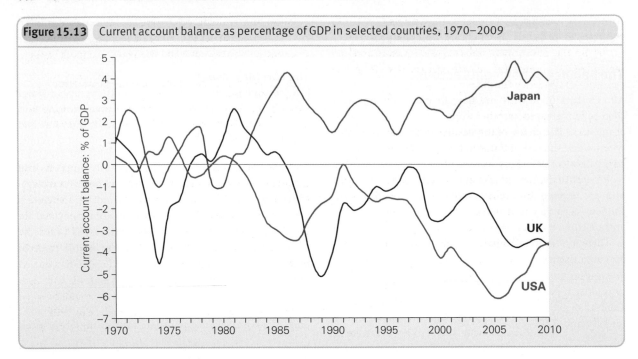

Note: Years 2009 and 2010 figures based on forecasts.
Source: Based on data in *Economic Outlook* (Office for Economic Co-operation and Development [OECD], various years).

Thus the purchase of a foreign holiday would be a debit, since it represents an outflow of money, whereas the purchase by an overseas resident of a UK insurance policy would be a credit to the UK services account. The balance of these is called the *services balance*.

The balance of both the goods and services accounts together is known as the **balance on trade in goods and services** or simply the **balance of trade**.

Income flows. These consist of wages, interest and profits flowing into and out of the country. For example, dividends earned by a foreign resident from shares in a UK company would be an outflow of money (a debit item).

Current transfers of money. These include government contributions to and receipts from the EU and international organisations, and international transfers of money by private individuals and firms. Transfers out of the country are

debits. Transfers into the country (e.g. money sent from Greece to a Greek student studying in the UK) would be a credit item.

The **current account balance** is the overall balance of all the above four subdivisions. A *current account surplus* is where credits exceed debits. A *current account deficit* is where debits exceed credits. Figure 15.13 shows the current account balances of the UK, the USA and Japan as a proportion of their GDP (national output).

 Why is the US current balance approximately a 'mirror image' of the Japanese current balance?

The capital account

The **capital account** records the flows of funds, into the country (credits) and out of the country (debits), associated

Definitions

Open economy One that trades with and has financial dealings with other countries.

Current account of the balance of payments The record of a country's imports and exports of goods and services, plus incomes and transfers of money to and from abroad.

Balance on trade in goods or balance of visible trade or merchandise balance Exports of goods minus imports of goods.

Balance on trade in goods and services or balance of trade Exports of goods and services minus imports of goods and services.

Balance of payments on current account The balance on trade in goods and services plus net investment incomes and current transfers.

Capital account of the balance of payments The record of the transfers of capital to and from abroad.

with the acquisition or disposal of fixed assets (e.g. land), the transfer of funds by migrants, and the payment of grants by the government for overseas projects and the receipt of EU money for capital projects (e.g. from the Agricultural Guidance Fund).

The financial account[1]

The **financial account** of the balance of payments records cross-border changes in the holding of shares, property, bank deposits and loans, government securities, etc. In other words, unlike the current account, which is concerned with money incomes, the financial account is concerned with the purchase and sale of assets.

Investment (direct and portfolio). This account covers primarily long-term investment.

- Direct investment. If a foreign company invests money from abroad in one of its branches or associated companies in the UK, this represents an inflow of money when the investment is made and is thus a credit item. (Any subsequent profit from this investment that flows abroad will be recorded as an *investment income outflow* on the current account.) Investment abroad by UK companies represents an outflow of money when the investment is made. It is thus a debit item.

   Note that what we are talking about here is the acquisition or sale of assets: e.g. a factory or farm, or the takeover of a whole firm, not the imports or exports of equipment.

- Portfolio investment. This is changes in the holding of paper assets, such as company shares. Thus if a UK resident buys shares in an overseas company, this is an outflow of funds and is hence a debit item.

Other financial flows. These consist primarily of various types of short-term monetary movement between the UK and the rest of the world. Deposits by overseas residents in banks in the UK and loans to the UK from abroad are credit items, since they represent an inflow of money. Deposits by UK residents in overseas banks and loans by UK banks to overseas residents are debit items. They represent an outflow of money.

[1] Prior to October 1998, this account was called the 'capital account'. The account that is *now* called the capital account used to be included in the transfers section of the current account. This potentially confusing change of names was adopted in order to bring the UK accounts in line with the system used by the International Monetary Fund (IMF), the EU and most individual countries.

Definition

Financial account of the balance of payments The record of the flows of money into and out of the country for the purposes of investment or as deposits in banks and other financial institutions.

Short-term monetary flows are common between international financial centres to take advantage of differences in countries' interest rates and changes in exchange rates.

1. *Why may inflows of short-term deposits create a problem?*
2. *Where would interest payments on short-term foreign deposits in UK banks be entered on the balance of payments account?*

Note that in the financial account, credits and debits are recorded *net*. For example, UK investment abroad consists of the net acquisition of assets abroad (i.e. the purchase less the sale of assets abroad). Similarly, foreign investment in the UK consists of the purchase less the sale of UK assets by foreign residents. Note that in either case the flow could be in the opposite direction. For example, if UK residents purchased fewer assets abroad than they sold, this item would be a net credit, not a debit (there would be a net return of money to the UK). This was the case in 1994.

By recording financial account items net, the flows seem misleadingly modest. For example, if UK residents deposited an extra £100bn in banks abroad but drew out £99bn, this would be recorded as a mere £1bn net outflow on the other financial flows account. In fact, *total* financial account flows vastly exceed current plus capital account flows.

Flows to and from the reserves. The UK, like all other countries, holds reserves of gold and foreign currencies. From time to time the Bank of England (acting as the government's agent) will sell some of these reserves to purchase sterling on the foreign exchange market. It does this normally as a means of supporting the rate of exchange (see below). Drawing on reserves represents a *credit* item in the balance of payments accounts: money drawn from the reserves represents an *inflow* to the balance of payments (albeit an outflow from the reserves account). The reserves can thus be used to support a deficit elsewhere in the balance of payments.

Conversely, if there is a surplus elsewhere in the balance of payments, the Bank of England can use it to build up the reserves. Building up the reserves counts as a debit item in the balance of payments, since it represents an outflow from it (to the reserves).

When all the components of the balance of payments account are taken together, the balance of payments should exactly balance: credits should equal debits. As we shall see below, if they were not equal, the rate of exchange would have to adjust until they were, or the government would have to intervene to make them equal.

When the statistics are compiled, however, a number of errors are likely to occur. As a result, there will not be a balance. To 'correct' for this, a *net errors and omissions* item is included in the accounts. This ensures that there will be an exact balance. The main reason for the errors is that the statistics are obtained from a number of sources, and there are often delays before items are recorded and sometimes omissions too.

Assessing the balance of payments figures

It is often regarded as being undesirable for the combined current, capital and investment accounts to be in deficit. If they were in deficit, this would have to be covered by borrowing from abroad or attracting deposits from abroad. This might necessitate paying high rates of interest. It also leads to the danger that people abroad might at some time in the future suddenly withdraw their money from the UK and cause a 'run on the pound'. An alternative would be to draw on reserves. But this too causes problems. If the reserves are run down too rapidly, it may cause a crisis of confidence, and again a run on the pound. Also, of course, reserves are limited and hence there is a limit to the extent to which they can be used to pay for a balance of payments deficit.

It is also often regarded as undesirable for a country to have a *current account* deficit, even if it is matched by a surplus on the other two accounts. Although this will bring the short-term benefit of a greater level of consumption through imports, and hence a temporarily higher living standard, the excess of imports over exports is being financed by foreign investment in the UK. This will lead to greater outflows of interest and dividends in the future. On the other hand, inward investment may lead to increased production and hence possibly increased incomes for UK residents.

 With reference to the above, provide an assessment of the UK balance of payments in each of the years illustrated in Table 15.6.

What causes deficits to occur on the various parts of the balance of payments? The answer has to do with the demand for and supply of sterling on the foreign exchange market. Thus before we can answer the question, we must examine this market and in particular the role of the rate of exchange.

Exchange rates

An exchange rate is the rate at which one currency trades for another on the foreign exchange market.

If you go abroad, you will need to exchange your pounds into euros, dollars, Swiss francs or whatever. You will get the money at the exchange rate in operation at the time that you draw it from a cash machine abroad or from a bank: for example, €1.28 to the pound, or $1.56 to the pound. It is similar for firms. If an importer wants to buy, say, some machinery from Japan, it will require yen to pay the Japanese supplier. It will thus ask the foreign exchange section of a bank to quote it a rate of exchange of the pound into yen. Similarly, if you want to buy some foreign stocks and shares, or if companies based in the UK want to invest abroad, sterling will have to be exchanged into the appropriate foreign currency.

Likewise, if Americans want to come on holiday to the UK or to buy UK assets, or American firms want to import UK goods or to invest in the UK, they will require sterling. They will get it at an exchange rate such as £1 = $1.56. This means that they will have to pay $1.56 to obtain £1 worth of UK goods or assets.

Exchange rates are quoted between each of the major currencies of the world. These exchange rates are constantly changing. Minute by minute, dealers in the foreign exchange dealing rooms of the banks are adjusting the rates of exchange. They charge commission when they exchange currencies. It is important for them, therefore, to ensure that they are not left with a large amount of any currency unsold. What they need to do is to balance the supply and demand of each currency: to balance the amount they purchase to the amount they sell. To do this, they will need to adjust the price of each currency, namely the exchange rate, in line with changes in supply and demand.

Not only are there day-to-day fluctuations in exchange rates, but also there are long-term changes in them. Table 15.7 shows the average exchange rate between the pound and various currencies for selected years from 1960 to 2008.

One of the problems in assessing what is happening to a particular currency is that its rate of exchange may rise against some currencies (weak currencies) and fall against others (strong currencies). In order to gain an overall picture of its fluctuations, therefore, it is best to look at a weighted average exchange rate against all other currencies. This is known as the ***exchange rate index***. The last column in Table 15.7 shows the sterling exchange rate index based on 1990 = 100.

The weight given to each currency in the index depends on the percentage of UK trade in goods and services done with that country. The weights are revised annually. Table 15.8 gives the 2007 weights of the various currencies that make up the sterling index.

Note that all the exchange rates must be consistent with each other. For example, if £1 exchanged for $1.60 or 200 yen, then $1.60 would have to exchange for 200 yen directly (i.e. $1 = 125 yen), otherwise people could make money by moving around in a circle between the three currencies in a process known as ***arbitrage***.

Definitions

Exchange rate index A weighted average exchange rate expressed as an index, where the value of the index is 100 in a given base year. The weights of the different currencies in the index add up to 1.

Arbitrage Buying an asset in a market where it has a lower price and selling it again in another market where it has a higher price and thereby making a profit.

Table 15.7   Sterling exchange rates: 1960–2008

	US dollar	Japanese yen	French franc	German mark	Italian lira	Euro[a]	Sterling exchange rate index (2005 = 100)
1960	2.80	1008	13.82	11.76	1747	–	–
1970	2.40	858	13.33	8.78	1500	–	–
1975	2.22	658	9.50	5.45	1447	(1.70)	–
1980	2.33	526	9.83	4.23	1992	(1.62)	115.6
1985	1.30	307	11.55	3.78	2463	(1.71)	100.1
1990	1.79	257	9.69	2.88	2133	(1.37)	96.5
1992	1.77	224	9.32	2.75	2163	(1.33)	94.1
1994	1.53	156	8.49	2.48	2467	(1.27)	86.1
1996	1.56	170	7.99	2.35	2408	(1.21)	83.8
1998	1.66	217	9.77	2.91	2876	(1.49)	100.0
2000	1.52	163	(10.77)	(3.21)	(3180)	1.64	101.1
2001	1.44	175	(10.55)	(3.15)	(3115)	1.61	99.5
2002	1.50	188	–	–	–	1.59	100.6
2003	1.63	189	–	–	–	1.45	96.9
2004	1.83	198	–	–	–	1.47	101.6
2005	1.82	200	–	–	–	1.47	100.0
2006	1.84	214	–	–	–	1.47	101.2
2007	2.00	236	–	–	–	1.46	103.5
2008	1.85	192	–	–	–	1.26	91.0

[a] The euro was introduced in 1999, with euro notes and coins circulating from January 2002. The exchange rates of the former eurozone currencies with the euro were fixed between 1999 and their disappearance in 2002. Their exchange rates with sterling during this period are the rates implied by the euro exchange rate with sterling. The euro figures in brackets prior to 1999 are projections backwards in time using synthetic data values (i.e. based on the weighted average exchange rates of the currencies that made up the euro).
Source: Based on data in the Bank of England Interactive Database (Bank of England).

Table 15.8   The weights of foreign currencies in the sterling exchange rate index

Country	Weight (%)
Eurozone	54.0
USA	16.5
Germany	(13.0)
France	(8.9)
Netherlands	(6.6)
Spain	(5.8)
Ireland	(5.7)
China	5.6
Belgium	(5.4)
Italy	(5.0)
Japan	4.7
Switzerland	3.0
Sweden	2.3
Singapore	1.7
Canada	1.6
India	1.6
South Korea	1.5
Australia	1.4
Denmark	1.4
Turkey	1.4
South Africa	1.2
Hong Kong	1.1
Norway	1.0
Austria	(0.9)
Finland	(0.9)
Greece	(0.9)
Portugal	(0.9)
Total	**100.0**

Note that the countries in brackets use the euro and hence are included in the eurozone weights.
Source: Based on data in the Bank of England Interactive Database (Bank of England).

 How did the pound 'fare' compared with the dollar and the yen from 1960 to 2008 and with the lira from 1960 to 2001? What conclusions can be drawn about the relative movements of these three currencies?

The determination of the rate of exchange in a free market

In a free foreign exchange market, the rate of exchange is determined by demand and supply. This is known as a *floating exchange rate*, and is illustrated in Figure 15.14.

For simplicity, assume that there are just two countries: the UK and the USA. When UK importers wish to buy goods from the USA, or when UK residents wish to invest in the USA, they will *supply* pounds on the foreign exchange market in order to obtain dollars. The higher the exchange rate, the more dollars they will obtain for their pounds. This will effectively make American goods cheaper to buy, and investment more profitable. Thus the *higher* the exchange rate, the *more* pounds will be supplied. The supply curve of pounds, therefore, typically slopes upwards.

When US residents wish to purchase UK goods or to invest in the UK, they will require pounds. They *demand*

TC 4
p44

Definition

Floating exchange rate When the government does not intervene in the foreign exchange markets, but simply allows the exchange rate to be freely determined by demand and supply.

Figure 15.14 Determination of the rate of exchange

Figure 15.15 Floating exchange rates: movement to a new equilibrium

pounds by selling dollars on the foreign exchange market. The lower the $ price of the pound (the exchange rate), the cheaper it will be for them to obtain UK goods and assets, and hence the more pounds they are likely to demand. The demand curve for pounds, therefore, typically slopes downwards.

The equilibrium exchange rate is where the demand for pounds equals the supply. In Figure 15.14 this is at an exchange rate of £1 = $1.60. But what is the mechanism that equates demand and supply?

If the current exchange rate were above the equilibrium, the supply of pounds being offered to the banks would exceed the demand. For example, in Figure 15.14 if the exchange rate were $1.80, there would be an excess supply of pounds of *a – b*. The banks, wishing to make money by *exchanging* currency, would have to lower the exchange rate in order to encourage a greater demand for pounds and reduce the excessive supply. They would continue lowering the rate until demand equalled supply.

Similarly, if the rate were below the equilibrium, say at $1.40, there would be a shortage of pounds of *c – d*. The banks would find themselves with too few pounds to meet all the demand. At the same time, they would have an excess supply of dollars. The banks would thus raise the exchange rate until demand equalled supply.

In practice, the process of reaching equilibrium is extremely rapid. The foreign exchange dealers in the banks are continually adjusting the rate as new customers make new demands for currencies. What is more, the banks have to watch each other closely since they are constantly in competition with each other and thus have to keep their rates in line. The dealers receive minute-by-minute updates on their computer screens of the rates being offered round the world.

Shifts in the currency demand and supply curves

Any shift in the demand or supply curves will cause the exchange rate to change. This is illustrated in Figure 15.15, which shows the euro/sterling exchange rate. If the

demand and supply curves shift from D_1 and S_1 to D_2 and S_2 respectively, the exchange rate will fall from €1.40 to €1.20. A fall in the exchange rate is called a ***depreciation***. A rise in the exchange rate is called an ***appreciation***.

But why should the demand and supply curves shift? The following are the major possible causes of a depreciation:

- *A fall in domestic interest rates*. UK rates would now be less competitive for savers and other depositors. More UK residents would be likely to deposit their money abroad (the supply of sterling would rise), and fewer people abroad would deposit their money in the UK (the demand for sterling would fall).
- *Higher inflation in the domestic economy than abroad*. UK exports will become less competitive. The demand for sterling will fall. At the same time, imports will become relatively cheaper for UK consumers. The supply of sterling will rise.
- *A rise in domestic incomes relative to incomes abroad*. If UK incomes rise, the demand for imports, and hence the supply of sterling, will rise. If incomes in other countries fall, the demand for UK exports, and hence the demand for sterling, will fall.
- *Relative investment prospects improving abroad*. If investment prospects become brighter abroad than in the UK, perhaps because of better incentives abroad, or because of worries about an impending recession in the UK, again the demand for sterling will fall and the supply of sterling will rise.
- *Speculation that the exchange rate will fall*. If businesses involved in importing and exporting, and also banks

Definitions

Depreciation A fall in the free-market exchange rate of the domestic currency with foreign currencies.

Appreciation A rise in the free-market exchange rate of the domestic currency with foreign currencies.

| BOX 15.6 | DEALING IN FOREIGN EXCHANGE | CASE STUDIES AND APPLICATIONS |

A daily juggling act

Imagine that a large car importer in the UK wants to import 5000 cars from Japan costing ¥15 billion. What does it do?

It will probably contact a number of banks' foreign exchange dealing rooms in London and ask them for exchange rate quotes. It thus puts all the banks in competition with each other. Each bank will want to get the business and thereby obtain the commission on the deal. To do this it must offer a higher rate than the other banks, since the higher the ¥/£ exchange rate, the more yen the firm will get for its money. (For an importer a rate of, say, ¥200 to £1 is better than a rate of, say, ¥180.)

Now it is highly unlikely that any of the banks will have a spare ¥15 billion. But a bank cannot say to the importer 'Sorry, you will have to wait before we can agree to sell them to you.' Instead the bank will offer a deal and then, if the firm agrees, the bank will have to set about obtaining the ¥15 billion. To do this, it must offer to obtain pounds for Japanese who are *supplying* yen at a sufficiently *low*

¥/£ exchange rate. (The lower the ¥/£ exchange rate, the fewer yen the Japanese will have to pay to obtain pounds.)

The banks' dealers thus find themselves in the delicate position of wanting to offer a *high* enough exchange rate to the car importer in order to gain its business, but a *low* enough exchange rate in order to obtain the required amount of yen. The dealers are thus constantly having to adjust the rates of exchange in order to balance the demand and supply of each currency.

In general, the more of any foreign currency that dealers are asked to supply (by being offered sterling), the lower will be the exchange rate they will offer. In other words, a higher supply of sterling pushes down the foreign currency price of sterling (see Figure 15.15).

 Assume that an American firm wants to import Scotch whisky from the UK. Describe how foreign exchange dealers will respond.

KI 8
p43

---

and other foreign exchange dealers, think that the exchange rate is about to fall, they will sell pounds *now* before the rate does fall. The supply of sterling will thus rise. People thinking of buying pounds will wait until the rate does fall and hence, in the meantime, the demand for sterling will fall. Speculation thus helps to bring about the very effect people had anticipated (see pages 72–5).

KI 10
p71

- *Longer-term changes in international trading patterns.* Over time the pattern of imports and exports is likely to change as (a) consumer tastes change, (b) the nature and quality of goods change and (c) the costs of production change. If, as a result, UK goods become less competitive than, say, German or Japanese goods, the demand for sterling will fall and the supply will rise. These shifts, of course, are gradual, taking place over many years.

 Go through each of the above reasons for shifts in the demand for and supply of sterling and consider what would cause an appreciation of the pound.

Exchange rates and the balance of payments

KI 5
p21

In a free foreign exchange market, the balance of payments will *automatically* balance. But why?

The credit side of the balance of payments constitutes the demand for sterling. For example, when people abroad buy UK exports or assets, they will demand sterling in order to pay for them. The debit side constitutes the supply of sterling. For example, when UK residents buy foreign goods or assets, the importers of them will require foreign currency to pay for them. They will thus supply pounds. A floating exchange rate ensures that the demand for pounds always equals the supply. It thus also ensures that the

credits on the balance of payments are equal to the debits: that the balance of payments balances.

This does not mean that each part of the balance of payments account will separately balance, but simply that any current account deficit must be matched by a capital plus financial account surplus and vice versa.

For example, suppose initially that each part of the balance of payments *did* separately balance. Then let us assume that interest rates rise. This will encourage larger short-term financial inflows as people abroad are attracted to deposit money in the UK: the demand for sterling would shift to the right (e.g. from D_2 to D_1 in Figure 15.15). It will also cause smaller short-term financial outflows as UK residents keep more of their money in the country: the supply of sterling shifts to the left (e.g. from S_2 to S_1 in Figure 15.15). The financial account will go into surplus. The exchange rate will appreciate.

As the exchange rate rises, this will cause imports to be cheaper and exports to be more expensive. The current account will move into deficit. There is a movement up along the new demand and supply curves until a new equilibrium is reached. At this point, any financial account surplus is matched by an equal current (plus capital) account deficit.

Managing the exchange rate

The government may be unwilling to let the country's currency float freely. Frequent shifts in the demand and supply curves would cause frequent changes in the exchange rate. This, in turn, might cause uncertainty for businesses, which might curtail their trade and investment.

The government may thus ask the central bank (the Bank of England in the case of the UK) to intervene in the foreign exchange market. But what can it do? The answer to this will depend on the government's objectives. It may simply want to reduce short-term movements in the exchange rate that take it away from its longer-term equilibrium rate, or it may want to prevent longer-term, more fundamental shifts in the rate.

Reducing short-term fluctuations

Assume, for example, that the government believes that an exchange rate of €1.40 to the pound is approximately the long-term equilibrium rate. Short-term leftward shifts in the demand for sterling and rightward shifts in the supply, however, are causing the exchange rate to fall below this level (see Figure 15.15). What can be done? There are three possibilities.

Using reserves. The Bank of England can sell gold and foreign currencies from the reserves to buy pounds. This will shift the demand for sterling back to the right.

With the growth in short-term international financial flows over the past thirty years, however, it has become increasingly difficult for individual central banks to influence rates by buying and selling currencies. Today some $4 trillion a day is traded in foreign exchange markets. Central bank reserves are nowhere near large enough to offset concerted selling of their currency. The combined actions of several central banks, however, may be sufficient. For example, combined action in 2000 by the central banks of the eurozone, the USA, Japan and the UK helped to prevent further falls in the euro, which, at the time, was depreciating against the US dollar.

Borrowing from abroad. In extreme circumstances, the government could negotiate a foreign currency loan from other countries or from an international agency such as the International Monetary Fund. The Bank of England can then use these moneys to buy pounds on the foreign exchange market, thus again shifting the demand for sterling back to the right.

Raising interest rates. If the Bank of England raises interest rates, it encourages people to deposit money in the UK and encourages UK residents to keep their money in the country. The demand for sterling increases and the supply of sterling decreases. Changing interest rates for the purpose of influencing exchange rates may not be possible, however, if interest rate changes in the opposite direction are required to keep inflation on target. We examine such policy conflicts in Chapters 20 and 25.

Maintaining a fixed rate of exchange over the longer term

Governments may choose to maintain a fixed rate over a number of months or even years. Indeed, from 1945 to 1972 the whole world operated under such a system. Countries used to 'peg' (i.e. fix) their currencies against the US dollar. This meant, therefore, that every currency was fixed with respect to every other currency (see pages 729–30).

But how can a government maintain an exchange rate that is persistently above the equilibrium? How can it resist the downward pressure on the exchange rate? After all, it cannot *order* dealers to keep the rate up: the dealers would run out of foreign currency. It cannot go on and on using its reserves to support the rate: the reserves would begin to run out. It will probably not want to go on borrowing from abroad and building up large international debts.

So what can it do? It must attempt to shift the demand and supply curves back again, so that they once more intersect at the fixed exchange rate. The following are possible methods it can use.

Deflation. This is where the government deliberately curtails aggregate demand by either fiscal policy or monetary policy or both.

Deflationary fiscal policy involves raising taxes and/or reducing government expenditure. Deflationary monetary policy involves reducing the supply of money and raising interest rates. Note that in this case we are not just talking about the temporary raising of interest rates to prevent a short-term outflow of money from the country, but the use of higher interest rates to reduce borrowing and hence dampen aggregate demand.

A reduction in aggregate demand works in two ways:

- It reduces the level of consumer spending. This directly cuts imports, since there is reduced spending on Japanese electronics, German cars, Spanish holidays and so on. The supply of sterling coming onto the foreign exchange market thus decreases.
- It reduces the rate of inflation. This makes UK goods more competitive abroad, thus increasing the demand for sterling. It also cuts back on imports as UK consumers switch to the now more competitive home-produced goods. The supply of sterling falls.

Supply-side policies. This is where the government attempts to increase the long-term competitiveness of UK goods by encouraging reductions in the costs of production and/or improvements in the quality of UK goods. For example, the government may attempt to improve the quantity and quality of training and R&D (see Chapter 23, pages 664–7).

Controls on imports and/or foreign exchange dealing. This is where the government restricts the outflow of money, either by restricting people's access to foreign exchange, or by the use of tariffs and quotas. Tariffs are another word for customs duties. As taxes on imports, they raise their price and hence reduce their consumption. Quotas are quantitative restrictions on various imports.

 What problems might arise if the government were to adopt this third method of maintaining a fixed exchange rate?

Section summary

1. The balance of payments account records all payments to and receipts from foreign countries. The current account records payments for imports and exports, plus incomes and transfers of money to and from abroad. The capital account records all transfers of capital to and from abroad. The financial account records inflows and outflows of money for investment and as deposits in banks and other financial institutions; it also includes dealings in the country's foreign exchange reserves.

2. The whole account must balance, but surpluses or deficits can be recorded on any specific part of the account.

3. It is generally regarded as undesirable to have persistent current account deficits.

4. The rate of exchange is the rate at which one currency exchanges for another. Rates of exchange are determined by demand and supply in the foreign exchange market. Demand for the domestic currency consists of all the credit items in the balance of payments account. Supply consists of all the debit items.

5. The exchange rate will depreciate (fall) if the demand for the domestic currency falls and/or the supply increases. These shifts can be caused by increases in domestic prices or incomes relative to foreign ones, reductions in domestic interest rates relative to foreign ones, worsening investment prospects at home compared with abroad, or the belief by speculators that the exchange rate will fall. The opposite in each case would cause an appreciation (rise).

6. The government can attempt to prevent the rate of exchange from falling by central bank purchases of the domestic currency in the foreign exchange market, either by selling foreign currency reserves or by using foreign loans. Alternatively, the central bank can raise interest rates. The reverse actions can be taken to prevent the rate from rising.

7. In the longer term, the government can prevent the rate from falling by pursuing deflationary policies or supply-side policies to increase the competitiveness of the country's exports, or by imposing import controls.

15.5 POSTSCRIPT TO PART E: THE RELATIONSHIP BETWEEN THE FOUR MACROECONOMIC OBJECTIVES

Aggregate demand and the short-term relationship between the four objectives

In the short term (up to about two years), the four objectives of faster growth in output, lower unemployment, lower inflation and the avoidance of excessive current account balance of payments deficits are all related. They all depend on aggregate demand, and all vary with the course of the business cycle. This is illustrated in Figure 15.16.

In the expansionary phase of the business cycle (phase 2), aggregate demand grows rapidly. The gap between actual and potential output narrows. There is relatively rapid growth in output, and (demand-deficient) unemployment falls. Thus two of the problems are getting better. On the other hand, the other two problems become worse. The growing shortages lead to higher (demand-pull) inflation and larger current account balance of payments deficits as the extra demand 'sucks in' more imports and as higher prices make UK goods less competitive internationally. As a result, unless there is a compensating rise in interest rates, the equilibrium exchange rate is likely to fall, which will raise the price of imports, thus further stoking up inflation. This will probably increase inflationary expectations.

At the peak of the cycle (phase 3), unemployment is probably at its lowest and output at its highest (for the time being). But growth has already ceased or at least slowed down. Inflation and balance of payments problems are probably acute.

As the economy moves into phase 4, the recession, the reverse process to that of phase 2 happens. Falling aggregate demand makes growth negative and demand-deficient unemployment higher, but inflation is likely to slow down and the current account balance of payments to improve. These two improvements may take some time to occur, however.

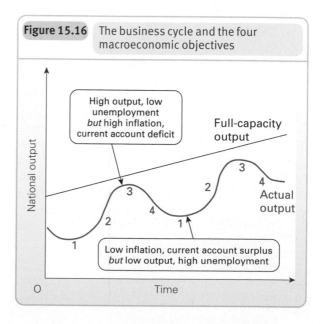

Figure 15.16   The business cycle and the four macroeconomic objectives

---

BOX 15.7 **THE POLITICAL BUSINESS CYCLE (PART I)[1]**

Getting things looking right on the night

Any government standing for re-election would like the economy to look as healthy as possible. It can then claim to the electorate that its economic policies have been a success.

Governments are able to engineer booms and recessions by the use of demand-side policies (fiscal and monetary). For example, by cutting taxes and/or increasing government expenditure, and by cutting interest rates, they can generate a period of economic expansion.

But how is this of any use politically, if the improvement in two of the objectives is at the cost of a deterioration in the other two? That would not help the government's election prospects.

The answer is that there is one point in the business cycle where *all four* objectives are likely to be looking good. This 'window of opportunity' for the government is in the middle of phase 2 – the period of rapid expansion. At this point, growth is at its highest and unemployment is *falling* most rapidly. In fact, falling unemployment is probably more popular with the electorate than simply a *low level* of unemployment. Two million unemployed but falling rapidly will probably win more votes than one million and rising rapidly!

But what about the other two objectives? Surely, in the middle of phase 2, inflation and the balance of payments will be deteriorating? The answer is that they will probably not yet have become a serious problem. Inflation takes a time to build up. It will probably only really start to rise rapidly as the peak of the business cycle is approached and shortages and bottlenecks occur. As far as the balance of payments is concerned, this tends to become a serious *political* issue only when the current account deficit gets really severe, or if the exchange rate starts to plummet. In the middle of phase 2, it is unlikely that this stage will yet have been reached.

By careful economic management, then, the government can get the four objectives to look good

at the time of the election. Of course, economic management is not perfect and policies may take a longer (or shorter) time to work than the government had anticipated. Things are made easier for governments in countries like the UK, however, where the government can choose when to call an election. It is less easy in countries like the USA, where elections are at fixed times.

Once a government has won an election, it can then deflate the economy in order to remove inflationary pressures and improve the balance of payments. A recession is likely to follow. This will probably be highly unpopular with the electorate. But no matter: the government, having created sufficient slack in the economy, can then reflate the economy again in time for the next general election!

It is thus possible to observe *political* business cycles. Recessions in the past tended to follow elections. Rapid growth tended to precede elections.

From the mid 1990s, however, the likelihood of a political business cycle was reduced. In 1997, the Labour government, as soon as it was elected, granted independence to the Bank of England in setting interest rates and gave it a clear mandate to achieve a target rate of inflation (see sections 20.4 and 20.5). This meant that the government could no longer use monetary policy for political purposes.

From 1997 the Chancellor also set limits for the size of government borrowing and hence for the balance between government expenditure and taxation (see Box 20.3). This made it much more difficult, although not impossible, to use fiscal policy for political purposes. With the recession of 2008/9, however, these limits were abandoned (see Box 20.3 on page 572). Whether this would be reflected in victory in the next election, you will have to see.

[1] See Box 21.4 on page 625 for part II.

Governments are thus faced with a dilemma. If they reflate the economy through fiscal and/or monetary policy, they will make two of the objectives (growth and unemployment) better, but the other two (inflation and the current account of the balance of payments) worse. If they deflate the economy, it is the other way round: inflation and the current account of the balance of payments will improve, but unemployment will rise and growth or even output will fall.

Is there any point in the business cycle where all four objectives are looking reasonable? If so, that would be the time when it would be wise for a government to call a general election! (See Box 15.7.)

 What is likely to happen to the exchange rate during phase 2 if the government (a) seeks to maintain a stable rate of interest; (b) raises the rate of interest in order to dampen the growth in aggregate demand?

The long-term relationship between the objectives

In the long run, the relationship between the objectives is much less straightforward. Over the long term, they can all get better or all get worse. Table 15.9 illustrates this. It looks at the four indicators in five-year periods.

 1. *Was there any five-year period when all four indicators were better than in the previous five years?*
2. *Which macroeconomic problem(s) has/have generally been less severe since the early 1990s than in the 1980s?*
3. *Why could the world as a whole not experience the problem of a current account balance of payments deficit?*

Faster long-run economic growth will require a faster increase in the rate of growth of *potential* output, matched by a sufficient growth in aggregate demand. But how can such an increase be achieved? Is it enough to rely on

Table 15.9   UK macroeconomic indicators: 1959–2008

	Inflation[a]	Unemployment[b]	Growth[c]	Current account balance[d]
1959–63	2.3	1.9	3.5	+0.1
1964–8	4.1	1.9	3.2	−0.7
1969–73	8.7	3.0	3.4	+0.4
1974–8	22.1	4.3	1.2	−1.5
1979–83	14.0	8.6	0.8	+1.3
1984–8	4.7	10.7	3.6	−0.8
1989–93	5.7	8.5	0.4	−2.5
1994–8	2.1	7.8	3.3	−0.8
1999–2003	1.2	5.3	2.6	−2.2
2004–8	2.5	5.1	2.5	−3.1

[a] Average annual percentage increase in consumer prices.
[b] Average percentage standardised unemployment.
[c] Average annual growth rate in real GDP at market prices.
[d] Average annual current account deficit (−) or surplus (+) as % of GDP.
Sources: Various.

supply-side policy, and if so, should the focus be on freeing up the market and relying on market incentives; or should the government be much more interventionist and spend more money, for example on training schemes or on the country's transport infrastructure by building more roads or improving the rail system? Or does the government also need to manage the level of aggregate demand so as to create a more stable economy, thereby encouraging more investment and hence an expansion of the economy's capacity to produce?

Then there is the question of unemployment. In the short run, as we have seen, it fluctuates with the business cycle. In the long run, however, to achieve lower unemployment it may not be enough merely to have a more rapidly growing economy. It may also be necessary to tackle underlying structural and frictional problems in the economy: to achieve a more flexible labour force, responsive to changes in the demand for products and skills. This may require government investment in education and training.

But will a reduction in unemployment in the long run also lead to higher inflation? Is there anything resembling a Phillips curve in the long run, and if so, can it be shifted to the left so as to permit both lower unemployment and lower inflation?

Finally there is the question of the balance of payments. Although the size of the current account deficit fluctuates with the business cycle, the underlying deficit may get larger or smaller over the long run. What determines long-run movements in the balance of payments? To what extent does it depend on the competitiveness of the country's exports, and to what extent does this depend on the exchange rate?

As the book progresses we will be looking at the relationship between the four objectives. Over the years there has been considerable debate among economists over these relationships. The next chapter gives an overview of these debates. It helps to put in context the current state of macroeconomics: where economists have reached agreement and where they still disagree.

Section summary

1. In the short run, the four macroeconomic objectives are related to aggregate demand and the business cycle. In the boom phase, growth is high and unemployment is falling, but inflation is rising and the current account of the balance of payments is moving into deficit. In the recession, the reverse is the case.

2. In the long run, the relationship between the four objectives is less straightforward. Nevertheless, improvements on the supply side of the economy can lead to improvements in all four objectives.

END OF CHAPTER QUESTIONS

1. The following table shows the UK consumer prices index (CPI) for the years 2002 to 2008, based on 2005 = 100.

Year	2002	2003	2004	2005	2006	2007	2008
CPI	95.4	96.7	98.0	100.0	102.3	104.7	108.5

Work out the rate of inflation for each of the years 2003 to 2008.

2. At what phase of the business cycle is the average *duration* of unemployment likely to be the highest? Explain.

3. Explain whether it would be desirable to have zero unemployment.

4. Consider the most appropriate policy for tackling each of the different types of unemployment.

5. Do any groups of people gain from inflation?

6. If everyone's incomes rose in line with inflation, would it matter if inflation were 100 per cent or even 1000 per cent per annum?

7. Imagine that you had to determine whether a particular period of inflation was demand-pull, or cost-push, or a combination of the two. What information would you require in order to conduct your analysis?

8. The following are the items in the UK's 2003 balance of payments.

	£ billions
Exports of goods	187.8
Imports of goods	235.1
Exports of services	89.7
Imports of services	75.1
Net income to/from abroad	+22.1
Net current transfers	−9.9
Capital transfers to the UK	2.7
Capital transfers from the UK	1.5
Overseas investment in UK	101.0
UK investment overseas	66.8
Other financial inflows	253.3
Other financial outflows	271.6
Reserves	+1.6

Calculate the following: (a) the balance on trade in goods; (b) the balance of trade; (c) the balance of payments on current account; (d) the capital account balance; (e) the financial account balance; (f) the balancing item.

9. Explain how the current account of the balance of payments is likely to vary with the course of the business cycle.

10. The overall balance of payments must always balance. If this is the case, why might a deficit on one part of the balance of payments be seen as a problem?

11. List some factors that could cause an increase in the credit items of the balance of payments and a decrease in the debit items. What would be the effect on the exchange rate (assuming that it is freely floating)? What effect would these exchange rate movements have on the balance of payments?

12. What policy measures could the government adopt to prevent the exchange rate movements in question 11?

Online resources

Additional case studies in MyEconLab

15.1 **Do people volunteer to be unemployed?** Is it useful to make the distinction, often made, between voluntary and involuntary unemployment?

15.2 **Technology and employment.** Does technological progress create or destroy jobs?

15.3 **A high exchange rate.** This case looks at whether a high exchange rate is necessarily bad news for exporters.

15.4 **Disinflation.** The experience of Europe and Japan.

WEBSITES RELEVANT TO CHAPTERS 14 AND 15

Numbers and sections refer to websites listed in the Web Appendix and hotlinked from this book's website at **www.pearsoned.co.uk/sloman**.

- For news articles relevant to this and the previous chapter, see the *Economics News Articles* link from the book's website.

- For general news on macroeconomic issues, both national and international, see websites in section A, and particularly A1–5, 7–9, 20–25, 31. See also links to newspapers worldwide in A38, 39, 43 and 44, and the news search feature in Google at A41. See also A42 for links to economics news articles from newspapers worldwide.

- For macroeconomic data, see links in B1 or 2; also see B4 and 12. For UK data, see B3 and 34. For EU data, see G1 > *The Statistical Annex*. For US data, see *Current economic indicators* in B5 and the *Data* section of B17. For international data, see B15, 21, 24, 31, 33, 35 and especially 36. For links to datasets, see B28, 33 and 36; I14.

- For national income statistics for the UK (Appendix), see B1, 1. *National Statistics* > the fourth link > *Economy* > *United Kingdom Economic Accounts* and *United Kingdom National Accounts – the Blue Book*.

- For data on UK unemployment, see B1, 1. *National Statistics* > the fourth link > *Labour Market* > *Labour Market Trends*. For international data on unemployment, see G1; H3 and 5.

- For international data on balance of payments and exchange rates, see *World Economic Outlook* in H4 and *OECD Economic Outlook* in B21 (also in section 6 of B1). See also the trade topic in I14.

- For details of individual countries' balance of payments, see B32.

- For UK data on balance of payments, see B1, 1. *National Statistics* > the fourth link > *Economy* > *United Kingdom Balance of Payments – the Pink Book*. See also B3, 34; F2. For EU data, see G1 > *The Statistical Annex* > *Foreign trade and current balance*.

- For exchange rates, see A3; B34; F2, 6, 8.

- For student resources relevant to Chapters 14 and 15, see sites C1–7, 9, 10, 19. See also the simulation *The trade balance and the exchange rate* in site D3.

Macroeconomics

16 The Roots of Modern Macroeconomics   453

17 Short-run Macroeconomic Equilibrium   474

18 Money and Interest Rates   502

19 The Relationship between the Money and Goods Markets   535

20 Fiscal and Monetary Policy   561

21 Aggregate Supply, Unemployment and Inflation   611

22 Long-term Economic Growth   638

23 Supply-side Policies   650

We now build on the foundations of the last two chapters. We will see why economies grow over the longer term but why they fluctuate in the short term and what governments can do to prevent these fluctuations.

In Chapter 16, to help understand the context of modern macroeconomics, we sketch out how the subject has developed over the past hundred years. In the following three chapters, we look at what determines the level of national income and the role that money plays in the process. Then, in Chapter 20, we look at government policy to stabilise the economy. In Chapter 21 we look at the relationship between inflation and unemployment. Finally, in Chapters 22 and 23, we turn to the long run and ask how economies can sustain faster growth.

The Roots of Modern Macroeconomics

CHAPTER MAP

16.1 Setting the scene: three key issues   **454**
Issue 1: the flexibility of prices and wages   454
Issue 2: the flexibility of aggregate supply   455
Issue 3: the role of expectations in the working
    of the market   455
Policy implications   456

16.2 Classical macroeconomics   **456**
The classical analysis of output and employment   457
The classical analysis of prices and inflation   458
The classical response to the Great Depression   459

16.3 The Keynesian revolution   **462**
Keynes' rejection of classical macroeconomics   462
Keynes' analysis of employment and inflation   463
The Keynesian policies of the 1950s and 1960s   464

16.4 The monetarist–Keynesian debate   **466**
The monetarist counter-revolution   466
The Keynesian response   467

**16.5 The current position: an emerging
     consensus?**   **469**
A range of views   469
A mainstream consensus?   471

This chapter is optional. It looks at how the subject of macroeconomics has developed over the past hundred years. As the world economy has experienced various upheavals, such as the mass unemployment of the Great Depression of the 1930s, rapid inflation in the 1970s and recessions in the early 1980s and early 1990s, so economists have sought to analyse them and to provide solutions. Many 'battles' have been fought by opposing camps of economists, each seeking to provide the 'correct' analysis and each advocating particular policies to deal with the problems – policies that have ranged from highly interventionist to highly laissez-faire.

Although it is not necessary to have read this chapter to understand the following chapters, you will get a better feel for macroeconomic theories by understanding this historical context. After all, it was to help understand real problems, and to provide practical solutions to them, that many of the theories we shall be examining later in the book developed.

In this chapter we will be tracing events from the 1920s to the present day and seeing how economists wrestled with the problems. We shall also be seeing how politicians adopted the policies advocated by different schools of economic thought – with varying degrees of success. The unfolding of this story allows us to see how the different theories have developed. It also helps us to understand where there is now a general consensus among economists and where controversies remain.

Macroeconomics as a separate branch of economics had its birth with the mass unemployment experienced in the 1920s and 1930s. The old 'classical theories' of the time, which essentially said that free markets would provide a healthy economy with full employment, could not provide solutions to the problem. Their analysis seemed totally at odds with the facts.

A new analysis of the economy – one that *did* offer solutions to mass unemployment – was put forward by the economist John Maynard Keynes. His book *The General Theory of Employment, Interest and Money*, published in 1936, saw the dawn of 'Keynesian economics'. Keynes advocated active intervention by governments, in particular through the use of fiscal policy. By carefully managing aggregate demand, the government could prevent mass unemployment on the one hand, or an 'overheated' economy with unsustainable growth and high inflation on the other.

After the Second World War, governments around the world adopted Keynesian demand-management policies; and they seemed to be successful. The 1950s and 1960s were a period of low inflation, low unemployment and relatively high economic growth (see Table 15.9 on page 449). Macroeconomists were largely concerned with refining Keynesian economics.

In the 1970s, however, the macroeconomic consensus broke down as both inflation and unemployment rose and growth slowed down. Macroeconomics became highly controversial. Different 'schools of thought' had their own explanations of what was going wrong, and each had its own solutions to the problems.

Then, as the macroeconomic environment generally improved in the 1990s, so increasingly common ground re-emerged. Today there is broad agreement among many macroeconomists over the causes of macroeconomic problems and the appropriate policies to deal with them. There is not total agreement, however. We will be identifying the areas where disagreement remains.

16.1 SETTING THE SCENE: THREE KEY ISSUES

Most of the debate in macroeconomics has centred on the working of the market mechanism: just how well or how badly it achieves the various macroeconomic objectives. There have been three major areas of disagreement: (a) how flexible are wages and prices, (b) how flexible is aggregate supply and (c) what is the role of expectations? We examine each in turn.

Issue 1: the flexibility of prices and wages

Generally, the political right has tended to ally with those economists who argue that prices and wages are relatively flexible. Markets tend to clear, they say, and clear fairly quickly.

Disequilibrium unemployment is likely to be fairly small, according to their view, and normally only a temporary, short-run phenomenon. Any long-term unemployment, therefore, will be equilibrium (or 'natural') unemployment. To cure this, they argue, encouragement must be given to the free play of market forces: to a rapid response of both firms and labour to changes in market demand and supply, to a more rapid dissemination of information on job vacancies, and generally to greater labour mobility, both geographical and occupational.

There are some on the political right, however, who argue that in the short run wages may not be perfectly flexible. This occurs when unions attempt to keep wages above the equilibrium. In this case, disequilibrium unemployment may continue for a while. The solution here, they argue, is to curb the power of unions so that wage flexibility can be restored and disequilibrium unemployment cured.

The political centre and left have tended to ally with economists who reject the assumption of highly flexible wages and prices. If there is a deficiency of demand for labour in the economy, for example during a recession, there will be a resistance from unions to cuts in real wages and certainly to cuts in money wages. Any cuts that do occur will be insufficient to eliminate the disequilibrium, and will anyway serve only to reduce aggregate demand further, so that workers have less money to spend. The demand curve in Figure 15.6 (see page 422) would shift further to the left.

The prices of goods may also be inflexible in response to changes in demand. As industry became more concentrated and more monopolistic over the years, firms, it is argued, became less likely to respond to a general fall in demand by cutting prices. Instead, they were likely to build up stocks if they thought the recession was temporary, or cut production and hence employment if they thought the recession would persist. It is also argued that many firms use cost-plus methods of pricing. If wages are inflexible downwards, and if they form a major element of costs, prices will also be inflexible downwards.

Thus according to those who criticise the right, markets cannot be relied upon automatically to correct disequilibria and hence cure disequilibrium unemployment.

 Why are real wages likely to be more flexible downwards than money wages?

The process of globalisation has helped to offset the growth in market power in many industries in recent years.

Competition from China and India, for example, has made prices in many markets more flexible. In other markets, particularly in the service sector, international competition is less relevant and in others, global giants, such as Microsoft, Monsanto, Boeing and GlaxoSmithKline, have considerable price-setting power.

Issue 2: the flexibility of aggregate supply

The question here is, how responsive is national output (i.e. aggregate supply), and hence also employment, to a change in aggregate demand?

The arguments centre on the nature of the aggregate supply curve (*AS*). Three different *AS* curves are shown in Figure 16.1. In each of the three cases, it is assumed that the government raises aggregate demand through the use of fiscal and/or monetary policy. Aggregate demand shifts from AD_1 to AD_2. The effect on prices and output will depend on the shape of the *AS* curve.

TC 7
p68

Some economists, generally supported by the political right, argue that output is not determined by aggregate demand (except perhaps in the very short run). Instead, the rise in aggregate demand will simply lead to a rise in prices. They therefore envisage an *AS* curve like that in Figure 16.1(a). If the government wants to expand aggregate supply and get more rapid economic growth, it is no good, they argue, concentrating on demand. Instead, governments should concentrate directly on supply by encouraging enterprise and competition, and generally by encouraging markets to operate more freely. For this reason, this approach is often labelled ***supply-side economics***.

Their critics, however, argue that a rise in aggregate demand will lead to a rise in output. In the extreme case where actual output is well below potential output, prices will not rise at all. In this case, the *AS* curve is like that in Figure 16.1(b). Output will rise to Y_2 with the price level remaining at *P*.

Others argue that both prices and output will rise. In this case, the short-term curve will be like that in Figure 16.1(c). If there is plenty of slack in the economy – idle machines, unemployed labour, etc. – output will rise a lot and prices only a little. But as slack is taken up, the *AS* curve becomes steeper. Firms, finding it increasingly difficult to raise output in the short run, simply respond to a rise in demand by raising prices.

In recent years, some consensus has emerged. Most economists now maintain that the short-run *AS* curve is similar to that in Figure 16.1(c), but that in the long run, given time for prices and wages to adjust, the curve is much steeper, if not vertical. Any increase in aggregate demand will simply result in higher prices.

There is not total agreement, however. Some Keynesian economists argue that the long-run effects of an increase in aggregate demand could be a higher level of investment and hence higher capacity and thus a higher aggregate supply. In such a case, the long-run *AS* curve would be much flatter.

 Would it be possible for a short-run AS curve to be horizontal (as in Figure 9.16(b)) at all levels of output?

Issue 3: the role of expectations in the working of the market

TC 9
p105

How quickly and how fully will individuals and firms anticipate changes in prices and changes in output? How are

Definition

Supply-side economics An approach that focuses directly on aggregate supply and how to shift the aggregate supply curve outwards.

Figure 16.1   Different aggregate supply curves

(a) Aggregate supply independent of aggregate demand

(b) Aggregate supply totally dependent on aggregate demand

(c) Aggregate supply becoming less and less responsive to aggregate demand as full employment is reached their expectations formed, and how accurate are they? What effect do these expectations have? This has been the third major controversial topic.

The political right tended to ally with those economists who argue that people's expectations adjust rapidly and fully to changing economic circumstances. They emphasise the role of expectations of *price* changes.

If aggregate demand expands, they argue, people will expect higher prices. Workers will realise that the apparently higher wages they are offered are an illusion. The higher wages are 'eaten up' by higher prices. Thus workers are not encouraged to work longer hours, and unemployed workers are not encouraged to take on employment more readily. Likewise the higher prices that firms can charge are necessary to cover higher wages and other costs, and are not a reflection of higher real demand. Firms thus soon realise that any apparent increased demand for their products is an illusion. Their price rises will fully absorb the extra spending in money terms. There will be no increase in sales, and hence no increase in output and employment.

Thus, they argue, increased aggregate demand merely fuels inflation and can do no more than give a very temporary boost to output and employment. If anything, the higher inflation could damage business confidence and thus worsen long-term output and employment growth by discouraging investment.

Those who criticise this view argue that the formation of expectations is more complex than this. Whether people expect an increase in demand to be fully matched by inflation depends on the current state of the economy and how any increase in demand is introduced.

If there is a lot of slack in the economy (if unemployment is very high and there are many idle resources) and if an increase in demand is in the form, say, of direct government spending on production (on roads, hospitals, sewers and other infrastructure) then output and employment may quickly rise. Here the effect of expectations may be beneficial. Rather than expecting inflation from the increased demand, firms may expect faster growth and an expansion of markets. As a result, they may choose to invest, and this in turn will produce further growth in output and employment.

Views on expectations, therefore, parallel views on aggregate supply. The right argues that a boost to demand will not produce extra output and employment: aggregate supply is inelastic (as in Figure 16.1(a)) and therefore the higher demand will merely fuel expectations of inflation. Their critics argue that a boost to demand will increase aggregate supply and employment. Firms will expect this and therefore produce more.

 If firms believe the aggregate supply curve to be moderately elastic, what effect will this belief have on the outcome of an increase in aggregate demand?

Policy implications

Generally, then, the economists supported by the political right tend to favour a policy of laissez-faire. Any intervention by government to boost demand will merely be inflationary and will thus damage long-term growth and employment. At most, governments should intervene to remove hindrances to the free and efficient operation of markets.

Economists supported by the political centre and left have tended to argue that disequilibrium unemployment may persist for several years and may be very high. The answer is to boost demand, thereby increasing aggregate supply and employment. They also argue that infrastructure investment by the government can make a significant difference in directly boosting aggregate supply.

Section summary

1. There has been considerable debate among economists and politicians over the years about how the market mechanism works at a macroeconomic level.

2. The right has tended to argue (a) that prices and wages are relatively flexible, (b) that aggregate supply is determined independently of aggregate demand and (c) that people's price and wage expectations adjust rapidly to shifts in aggregate demand so as to wipe out any output effect.

3. The centre and left to varying degrees has argued (a) that prices and wages are inflexible downwards, (b) that aggregate supply is relatively elastic when there is slack in the economy and (c) that positive expectations of output and employment can make investment and aggregate supply responsive to changes in aggregate demand.

16.2 CLASSICAL MACROECONOMICS

The classical economists of the early nineteenth century held a pessimistic view of the long-term prospects for economic growth (see Boxes 5.1 and 14.5). Population growth combined with the law of diminishing returns would undermine any benefits from improved technology or the discovery of new sources of raw materials. What is more, there was little the government could do to improve these prospects. In fact governments, they argued, by interfering with competition and the functioning of the market would be likely to make things worse. They therefore advocated a policy of laissez-faire and free trade.

The classical school continued into the twentieth century. By then, its predictions about economic growth had become less pessimistic. After all, the Victorian years had been ones of rapid industrialisation and growth, with a massive expansion of Britain's overseas trade. This growing optimism had, if anything, strengthened the advocacy of laissez-faire. In the early years of the twentieth century, then, most economists, most politicians and virtually all bankers and businesspeople were relatively confident in the power of the free market to provide growing output and low unemployment.

The main role for the government was to provide 'sound finance' (i.e. not to print too much money), so as to maintain stable prices.

The classical analysis of output and employment

The classical theory predicted that, in the long run, equilibrium in the economy would be at virtually full employment. In the long run, any unemployment would be merely *frictional* unemployment: namely, people in the process of changing jobs.

There were two important elements in the classical theory.

The free-market economy works to equate demand and supply in all markets

This element of classical theory assumes flexible prices: of goods and services, of labour (i.e. wage rates) and of money (i.e. the rate of interest).

The classical economists argued that flexible prices would ensure that saving equalled investment ($S = I$) and that imports equalled exports ($M = X$). From this it follows that, if the government were to 'balance its budget' and make taxation equal to government expenditure ($T = G$), then total withdrawals would equal total injections ($W = J$).[1]

$$\left. \begin{array}{l} S = 1 \\ M = X \\ T = G \end{array} \right\} \rightarrow W = J$$

But why should flexible prices ensure that $S = I$ and $M = X$? The reasoning of the classical economists was as follows.

$S = I$. This would be brought about by flexible rates of interest (r) in the **market for loanable funds**. When firms want to invest in new plant and equipment, they will require finance. Investment demand, therefore, represents

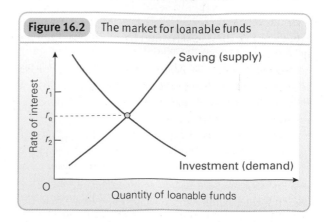

Figure 16.2 The market for loanable funds

a demand for loanable funds from financial institutions (an outflow). The higher the rate of interest, the more expensive will borrowing be, and hence the less will be the demand for investment. The investment schedule will therefore be downward sloping with respect to r. This is illustrated in Figure 16.2.

Saving represents a supply of loanable funds (an inflow). The saving schedule will be upward sloping. The higher the rate of interest, the more people will be attracted to save: that is, the more they will deposit in financial institutions.

Equilibrium will be at r_e, where $S = I$. If the rate of interest were above r_e, say at r_1, financial institutions would be accumulating funds. They would have to lower the rate of interest to attract sufficient borrowers. If the rate of interest were below r_e, say at r_2, financial institutions would find their funds were reducing. They would raise the rate of interest.

Assuming that rates of interest are initially above the equilibrium and that one particular financial institution chooses not to reduce its rate of interest, what will happen? What will be the elasticity of supply of loanable funds to an individual institution?

$M = X$. This would be brought about by flexible UK prices and wages. Before 1914, and from 1925 to 1931, the UK was on the *gold standard*. This was a *fixed* exchange rate system in which each participating country's currency was valued at a certain fixed amount of gold.

If a country had a balance of payments deficit ($M > X$), this had to be paid for in gold from its reserves. A country was then supposed to respond to this outflow of gold by reducing the amount of money in the economy and hence reducing total expenditure. This would create surpluses in

Definitions

Market for loanable funds The market for loans from and deposits into the banking system.

Gold standard The system whereby countries' exchange rates were fixed in terms of a certain amount of gold and whereby balance of payments deficits were paid in gold.

---

[1] The classical economists did not use the terms 'withdrawals' and 'injections': these are modern terms. Nevertheless, their analysis implied an automatic equation of W and J if markets cleared and the government balanced its budget.

the goods and labour markets, which would, in turn, lead to a fall in prices and wages. This fall in the prices of UK goods would increase the sale of exports and reduce the consumption of the now relatively expensive imports. This whole process would continue until the balance of payments deficit was eliminated: until $M = X$.

What would have happened if countries in deficit had not responded to an outflow of gold by reducing total expenditure?

(Note that, under a system of freely floating exchange rates, it is the flexibility in exchange rates, rather than the prices of goods and factors, that will ensure $M = X$.)

Provided the government balanced its budget ($T = G$), therefore, flexibility in the various markets would ensure that withdrawals equalled injections.

Say's law

J.-B. Say was a French economist of the early nineteenth century (see Person Profile in MyEconLab). *Say's law* states that *supply creates its own demand*. What this means is that the production of goods and services will generate expenditures sufficient to ensure that they are sold. There will be no deficiency of demand and no need to lay off workers. There will be full employment. The justification for the law is as follows.

When firms produce goods, they pay out money either directly to other firms, or as factor payments to households. The income that households receive is then partly paid back to firms in the form of consumption expenditure (C_d): the inner flow of the circular flow of income.

But any withdrawals by firms or households are also fully paid back to firms in the form of injections, since $S = I$, $M = X$ and $T = G$. Thus all the incomes generated by firms' supply will be transformed into demand for their products, either directly in the form of consumption, or indirectly via withdrawals and then injections. There will thus be no deficiency of demand.

Of course, although aggregate demand might equal aggregate supply, consumers may shift their demand away from some industries in favour of others. Structural unemployment (a form of equilibrium unemployment) may then occur. But then wages would fall in the declining industries

and rise in the expanding industries. This would help to eliminate the structural unemployment.

The reduction in structural unemployment will be quicker (a) the more flexible are wages and (b) the more willing and able are workers to move to industries and towns where jobs are available (labour mobility). In other words, the better markets work, the lower will be the level of equilibrium unemployment.

The classical analysis of prices and inflation

The classical economists based their analysis of inflation on the *quantity theory of money*. In its simplest form, it states that the general level of prices (P) in the economy depends on the supply of money (M):[1]

$$P = f(M)$$

The greater the quantity of money, the higher the level of prices. Under this theory, inflation is simply caused by a rise in money supply.

To understand the reasoning behind the quantity theory of money, we need to examine the *equation of exchange*. This comes in various versions (see Case Study 16.1 in MyEconLab), but the one most useful for our purposes is the simple identity between national expenditure and national income. This identity may be expressed as follows:

$$MV = PY$$

M, as we have already seen, is the supply of money in the economy. V is the *velocity of circulation*. This is the number of times per year a pound is spent on buying goods and services that make up GDP. Suppose that each pound's worth of money is typically spent five times per year on such goods and services, and that money supply was £20 billion. This would mean that total expenditure on GDP ($M \times V$) was £100 billion.

P, again as we have already seen, is the general level of prices. Let us define it more precisely as the price index based on some specific year (e.g. 1995), where the index in

---

[1] In the quantity theory of money the letter M is used to refer to money supply, whereas in the circular flow of income it is used to refer to the expenditure on imports. Naturally this is potentially confusing, but unfortunately it is normal practice to use the letter M in both ways. To avoid any such confusion we will always specify which is being referred to. Elsewhere, however, you will just have to judge from the context! (There is the same problem with the letter P, which can refer either to price or to product.)

Definitions

Say's law Supply creates its own demand. In other words, the production of goods will generate sufficient demand to ensure that they are sold.

Quantity theory of money The price level (P) is directly related to the quantity of money in the economy (M).

Equation of exchange $MV = PY$. The total level of spending on GDP (MV) equals the total value of goods and services produced (PY) that go to make up GDP.

Velocity of circulation The average number of times annually that money is spent on goods and services that make up GDP.

KI 32
p388

the base year is assumed to be 1.00 (not 100) (see page A:00). *Y* is the real value of national income (i.e. GDP expressed in the prices of the base year). $P \times Y$, therefore, is simply the 'nominal' value of GDP (i.e. GDP expressed in *current* prices, rather than those of the base year). Thus if GDP in real terms (*Y*) (i.e. measured in base-year prices) were £80 billion and if the current price index (*P*) were 1.25, then nominal GDP ($P \times Y$) would be £100 billion.

Thus both *MV* and *PY* are equal to GDP and must, therefore, by definition be equal to each other.

The classical economists argued that both *V* and *Y* were determined independently of the money supply: i.e. a change in the money supply would *not* be expected to lead to a change in *V* or *Y*. The velocity of circulation (*V*), they claimed, was determined by the frequency with which people were paid (e.g. weekly or monthly), the nature of the banking system and other institutional arrangements for holding money. As far as *Y* was concerned, Say's law would ensure that the real value of output (*Y*) was maintained at the full-employment level.

With *V* and *Y* as 'constants' with respect to *M*, therefore, the quantity theory must hold:

$$P = f(M)$$

Increases in money supply simply lead to inflation.

 Assuming that Y rises each year as a result of increases in productivity, can money supply rise without causing inflation? Would this destroy the validity of the quantity theory?

The classical response to the Great Depression

The classical economists had predicted that there would be virtual full employment. Any unemployment would simply be the frictional unemployment of people being 'between jobs'. Before the First World War their predictions were not far from the truth. Between the wars, however, Britain experienced a prolonged recession of unparalleled severity.

Throughout this 'Great Depression' unemployment was very much higher than before the war, reaching over 22 per cent in the winter of 1932–3 with 3 million people unemployed. However, the depression eliminated inflation. In every year from 1921 to 1934 prices either were constant or fell (see Figure 16.3).

Part of the cause of the Depression was the decision in 1925 by Winston Churchill, the Chancellor of the Exchequer, to return to the gold standard at the pre-war rate of $4.86. But with many export markets lost in the war and a rapid rise in imports for rebuilding the economy, the balance of payments was in severe deficit. To correct this deficit required severely deflationary policies. The aim was to drive wage rates down, reduce costs and restore the competitiveness of exports. The result, however, was a severe recession.

But while in Britain output slumped and unemployment soared, most of the rest of the industrialised world initially experienced a boom. But in 1929, after a decade of rapid growth and a huge rise in share values, Wall Street crashed. This sent the US economy plunging into deep recession, with the rest of the world following suit. As the world economy slumped, so did international trade. With a collapse of its exports, Britain dived even deeper into depression. Eventually, in 1932, Britain was forced to leave the gold standard and allow the pound to depreciate. (Case Study 16.3 in MyEconLab looks at the bitter experience of the return to the gold standard in 1925 and its aftermath.)

The deflationary policies of the 1920s seemed to be directly responsible for increasing unemployment. Many critics argued that the government ought deliberately to *expand* aggregate demand. However, the Treasury and other classical economists rejected the analysis that unemployment was caused by a lack of demand; they also rejected policies of reflation (e.g. increased government expenditure).

The classical Treasury view on unemployment

Would deflation of demand not lead to unemployment? According to the Treasury view, unemployment would

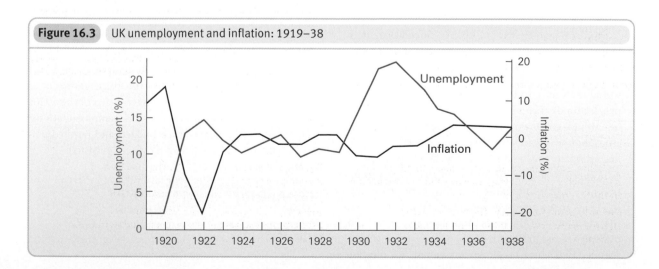

Figure 16.3 UK unemployment and inflation: 1919–38

| BOX 16.1 | BALANCE THE BUDGET AT ALL COSTS | | EXPLORING ECONOMICS |

Fiscal policy in the early 1930s

The budget must be balanced. All government expenditure should be financed from taxation. This was orthodox opinion in the 1920s.

But as unemployment increased during the Great Depression, spending on unemployment benefits (the most rapidly growing item of government expenditure) threatened the balanced budget principle. Other spending had to be cut to restore balance. The result was more unemployment, and hence the payment of more unemployment benefits.

Treasury officials and classical economists called for cuts in unemployment benefits. The May Committee, set up to investigate the budgetary problem, recommended a 20 per cent reduction. Even the Labour government, elected on a mandate to tackle the unemployment problem, proposed a 10 per cent reduction in 1931. This contributed to its subsequent collapse.

Philip Snowdon, Labour's Chancellor of the Exchequer, remarked in 1931 how pensioners had returned their pension books and children sent in their savings to help the nation balance its budget. And yet, as Keynes argued, it was not saving that was necessary to cure the unemployment, but spending. Government deficits were *desirable*. Attempts to balance the budget merely deflated the economy further and deepened the problem of unemployment.

occur only if labour markets *failed to clear*: if real wage costs did not fall sufficiently.

The Treasury concluded that people should be encouraged to take wage cuts. This would also help to reduce prices and restore export demand, thus correcting the balance of payments. People should also be encouraged to save. This would, via flexible interest rates, lead to more investment and hence a growth in output and demand for labour.

The classical Treasury view on public works

In the 1920s and 1930s, some politicians and economists argued that unemployment could be reduced if the government pursued a programme of public works: building roads, hospitals, houses, etc. The Treasury view was that this would not work and could have costly side-effects.

A programme of public works could be funded in three ways: from extra taxation, from extra government borrowing or by printing extra money. *None* of these three ways would, according to the classical Treasury view, solve the unemployment problem.

- *Extra taxation* would merely have the effect of reducing the money that consumers would spend on private industry. Extra public-sector demand would thus be offset by a fall in private-sector demand.
- If the government *borrowed more*, it would have to offer higher interest rates in order to persuade people to buy the additional government securities. The private sector would then have to offer higher interest rates, to compete for funds. As interest rates went up, private borrowing would go down. Thus public investment would *crowd out* private investment (see Box 16.2).
- According to the quantity theory of money, *printing extra money* would simply lead to inflation. The assumption here is that the aggregate supply 'curve' is vertical. In Figure 16.4 a rise in aggregate demand from AD_1 to AD_2 (as a result of the extra money supply) would simply lead to a rise in the price level from P_1 to P_2. National output (and hence employment) would not increase.

| **Figure 16.4** | The effect of printing extra money: the classical analysis |

It would remain constant at Y_1. A re-emergence of inflation, which had been eliminated in the early 1920s, would further erode the competitiveness of British goods, jeopardising the return to the gold standard at the pre-war exchange rate.

Treasury orthodoxy insisted, therefore, that government should attempt to balance its budget, even if this meant cutting welfare benefits to the rising numbers of unemployed (see Box 16.1). The governments of the 1920s and early 1930s followed these classical recommendations. They attempted to balance their budgets and rejected policies of reflation. Yet mass unemployment persisted.

Definition

Crowding out Where increased public expenditure diverts money or resources away from the private sector.

| BOX 16.2 | THE CROWDING-OUT EFFECT | | EXPLORING ECONOMICS |

When public expenditure replaces private

Critics of the use of government expenditure to stimulate output and employment often refer to the problem of *crowding out*. In its starkest form, the argument goes like this.

There is no point in the government embarking on a programme of public works to bring the economy out of recession. If it attempts to spend more, it can do so only by reducing private expenditure. The effect on total spending will be zero. This crowding out can take two main forms.

Resource crowding out

This is when the government uses resources such as labour and raw materials that would otherwise be used by the private sector. If the economy is operating near full capacity, then if resources are used by the government, they cannot at the same time be used by private companies.

The argument is far less convincing, however, if there is slack in the economy. If the government merely mobilises otherwise *idle* resources, there need be no reduction in private-sector output. In fact, if private-sector firms have spare capacity, they will respond to the higher demand by producing more themselves: aggregate demand will stimulate extra production.

Financial crowding out

This occurs when extra government spending diverts *funds* from private-sector firms and thus deprives them of the finance necessary for investment.

If the government spends more (without raising taxes or printing more money), it will have to borrow more and will therefore have to offer higher rates of interest. Private companies will then have to offer higher rates of interest themselves in order to attract funds. Alternatively, if they borrow from banks, and banks have less funds, the banks will charge them higher interest rates. Higher interest rates will discourage firms from borrowing and hence discourage investment.

The weakness with this argument is that it assumes that the supply of money is fixed. If the government spends more but *increases* the amount of money in the economy, it need not deprive the private sector of finance. Interest rates will not be bid up.

But would that not be inflationary? Not if there are idle resources and hence the extra money can be spent on extra output. Only if *resource* crowding out takes place would it be inflationary.

 Could resource crowding out take place at less than full employment?

Section summary

1. The classical analysis of output and employment is based on the assumption that markets clear. More specifically, it assumes that there are flexible wages, flexible prices and flexible rates of interest. The result will be that demand and supply are equated in the labour market, in the goods market and in the market for loanable funds.

2. Given that markets will clear, Say's law will operate. This law states that supply creates its own demand. In other words, the production of goods and services will generate incomes for households, which in turn will generate consumption expenditure, ensuring that the goods are sold. If any incomes are not directly spent on domestic goods, flexible prices will help to ensure that any money withdrawn is reinjected. Flexible interest rates will ensure that investment equals saving, and flexible prices and wages will ensure that exports equal imports. Provided the government balances its budget, withdrawals will equal injections and Say's law will hold.

3. The classical economists based their analysis of prices on the quantity theory of money. This states that the level of prices is directly related to the quantity of money (M) in the economy. Their position can be demonstrated using the equation of exchange:

$$MV = PY$$

where V is the velocity of circulation, P is the price index and Y is real national income expressed in the prices of the base year. The classical economists assumed that V and Y were not affected by changes in the money supply and could thus be regarded as 'constants'. From this it follows that

$$P = f(M)$$

Increases in the money supply simply lead to inflation.

4. In 1925 Britain returned to the gold standard system of fixed exchange rates at the pre-war rate. But given the massive balance of payments deficit at this rate, it had to pursue tough deflationary policies. The result was mass unemployment.

5. The classical economists saw the remedy to the problem as lying in reductions in wages and prices. According to the classical theory, this would allow Say's law to operate and full employment to be restored. They rejected public works as the solution, arguing that it would lead to crowding out if financed by borrowing, and to inflation if financed by printing money.

16.3 THE KEYNESIAN REVOLUTION

Keynes' rejection of classical macroeconomics

The main critic of classical macroeconomics was John Maynard Keynes (see Person Profile in MyEconLab). In his major work, *The General Theory of Employment, Interest and Money* (1936), he rejected the classical assumption that markets would clear. Disequilibrium could persist and mass unemployment could continue. There are two crucial markets in which disequilibrium could persist.

The labour market

Workers would resist wage cuts. Wages were thus 'sticky' downwards. In a recession, when the demand for labour is low, wages might not fall far or fast enough to clear the labour market.

In Figure 16.5 the recession has caused the aggregate demand for labour to shift to AD_{L_2}. If the real wage rate were to remain at W_1, the supply and demand for labour would no longer be in equilibrium. There would exist disequilibrium (demand-deficient) unemployment. But even if wage cuts could be introduced, as advocated by classical economists, Keynes rejected that as the solution to demand deficiency. Workers are also consumers. A cut in workers' wages would mean less consumer spending. Firms would respond to this by reducing their demand for labour. Thus a lowering of wage rates below W_1 would lead to a leftward shift in the AD_L curve, and this would more than offset the reduction in wages. Wage rates would not fall fast enough to clear the market. Disequilibrium would worsen. The recession would deepen.

Employers might well find that labour was cheaper to employ, but if demand for their product was falling, they would hardly be likely to take on more labour.

The market for loanable funds

Keynes also rejected the classical solution of increased saving as a means of stimulating investment and growth. Again the problem was one of market disequilibrium.

An increase in saving will cause a disequilibrium in the market for loanable funds. The rate of interest will fall from r_1 to r_2 in Figure 16.6. But an increase in saving means a fall in consumption. As a result, firms will sell less and will thus be discouraged from investing. The investment demand curve will shift to the left. The rate of interest will have to fall *below* r_2 to clear the market.

The demand for investment, according to Keynes, depends very much on business confidence in the future. A slide into recession could shatter such confidence. The resulting fall in investment would deepen the recession.

The problem of disequilibrium in the market for loanable funds is made worse, according to Keynes, because neither saving nor investment is very responsive to changes in interest rates, and thus very large changes in interest rates would be necessary if equilibrium were ever to be restored after any shift in the saving or investment curves.

Keynes also rejected the simple quantity theory of money. Increases in money supply will not necessarily lead merely to rises in prices. If there is a lot of slack in the economy, with high unemployment, idle machines and idle resources,

Figure 16.5 The problem of demand deficiency in the labour market

Figure 16.6 Disequilibrium in the market for loanable funds

BOX 16.3   WILL WAGE CUTS CURE UNEMPLOYMENT?

EXPLORING ECONOMICS

Keynes' dismissal of the classical remedy

In *The General Theory of Employment, Interest and Money*, Keynes rejects the classical argument that unemployment is due to excessive wages. In Chapter 2 he argues:

> [T]he contention that the unemployment which characterises a depression is due to a refusal by labour to accept a reduction of money wages is not clearly supported by the facts. It is not very plausible to assert that unemployment in the United States in 1932 was due either to labour obstinately refusing to accept a reduction of money wages or to its obstinately demanding a real wage beyond what the productivity of the economic machine was capable of furnishing. Wide variations are experienced in the volume of employment without any apparent change either in the minimum real demands of labour or in its productivity. Labour is not more truculent in the depression than in the boom – far from it. Nor is its physical productivity less. These facts from experience are a *prima facie* ground for questioning the classical analysis.[1]

[1] J. M. Keynes, *The General Theory of Employment, Interest and Money* (Macmillan, 1967), p. 9

an increased spending of money may lead to substantial increases in real income (Y) and leave prices (P) little affected.

Demonstrate this argument on an aggregate demand and supply diagram.

If the government were to cut money supply in an attempt to reduce prices, the major effect might be to reduce output and employment instead. In terms of the quantity equation, a reduction in M may lead to a reduction in output and hence real income Y rather than a reduction in P.

All these arguments meant a rejection of Say's law. Far from supply creating demand and thus ensuring full employment, Keynes argued that it was *demand that created supply*. If aggregate demand rose, firms would respond to the extra demand by producing more and employing more people. But a fall in demand would lead to less output and rising unemployment.

Keynes' central point was that an unregulated market economy *could not ensure sufficient demand*. Governments should therefore abandon laissez-faire, and should intervene to *control* aggregate demand.

Keynes' analysis of employment and inflation

Keynes' analysis of unemployment can be explained most simply in terms of the circular flow of income (see Figure 16.7). Keynes himself did not use this exact model, but it clearly explains the essence of his argument.

If injections (J) do not equal withdrawals (W), a state of disequilibrium exists. What will bring them back into equilibrium, however, is not a change in prices (of labour or of loanable funds), but rather a change in *national income* and *employment*.

Start with a state of equilibrium, where injections equal withdrawals, but with substantial unemployed resources (as was the case in the Great Depression). If there is now a rise in injections – for example, a rise in government

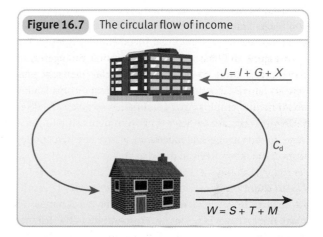

Figure 16.7   The circular flow of income

expenditure – aggregate demand ($C_d + J$) will be higher. Firms will respond to this increased demand by using more labour and other resources and thus paying out more incomes (Y) to households. Household consumption will rise and so firms will sell more.

Firms will respond by producing more, and thus using more labour and other resources. Household incomes will rise again. Consumption and hence production will rise again, and so on. There will thus be a multiplied rise in incomes and employment. This is known as the ***multiplier effect*** and is an example of the 'principle of cumulative causation'.

> **KEY IDEA 34**
>
> **The principle of cumulative causation.** An initial event can cause an ultimate effect that is much larger.

Definition

Multiplier effect An initial increase in aggregate demand of £xm leads to an eventual rise in national income that is greater than £xm.

The process, however, does not go on for ever. Each time household incomes rise, households save more, pay more taxes and buy more imports. In other words, withdrawals rise. When withdrawals have risen to match the increased injections, equilibrium will be restored and national income and employment will stop rising. The process can be summarised as follows:

$$J > W \rightarrow Y \uparrow \rightarrow W \uparrow until\ J = W$$

Similarly, an initial fall in injections (or rise in withdrawals) will lead to a multiplied fall in national income and employment:

$$J < W \rightarrow Y \downarrow \rightarrow W \downarrow until\ J = W$$

Thus equilibrium in the circular flow of income can be at *any* level of output and employment.

If aggregate demand is too low, there will be a recession and high unemployment. In Figure 16.8 it is assumed that there is some level of national income and output (Y_F) at which there would be full employment of resources. This represents a limit to output. If aggregate demand were initially at AD_1, equilibrium would be at Y_1, considerably below the full-employment potential.

In this case, argued Keynes, governments should intervene to boost aggregate demand. There are two policy instruments that they can use.

Fiscal policy

Remember how we defined fiscal policy in Chapter 15 (page 438). It is where the government alters the balance between government expenditure (G) and taxation (T), and thereby alters the balance between injections and withdrawals. In this way, it controls aggregate demand. Faced with a recession, it should raise G and/or lower T. In other words, the government should run a budget deficit rather than a balanced budget. There will then be a multiplier effect:

$$G \uparrow or\ T \downarrow \rightarrow J > W \rightarrow Y \uparrow \rightarrow W \uparrow until\ J = W$$

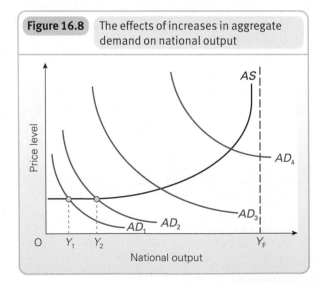

Figure 16.8	The effects of increases in aggregate demand on national output

If the eventual rise in aggregate demand were to, say, AD_2 in Figure 16.8, output would rise to Y_2.

Monetary policy

This is where the central bank alters the supply of money in the economy and/or manipulates interest rates. If it were to raise money supply, there would be more available in the economy for spending, interest rates would fall and aggregate demand would rise. Keynes argued that this was a less reliable policy than fiscal policy, since some of the extra money could be used for speculating in paper assets rather than spending on real goods and services. The details of how the central bank controls money supply and interest rates and the effects of such actions on the economy are examined in later chapters.

It is most effective if both fiscal and monetary policies are used simultaneously. For example, if the government undertook a programme of public works (fiscal policy) and financed it through increases in money supply (monetary policy), there would be no crowding out. There would be a significant rise in output and employment.

 What would be the classical economists' criticisms of this argument?

If aggregate demand rises too much, however, inflation becomes a problem. (This was the case during the Second World War, with the high expenditure on the war effort.) As Y_F is approached, with more and more firms reaching full capacity and with fewer and fewer idle resources, so additional increases in aggregate demand lead more and more to higher prices rather than higher output. This can be seen in Figure 16.8 as aggregate demand rises from AD_2 to AD_3 to AD_4.

 Might the AS curve shift to the right in the meantime? If it did, how would this influence the effects of the rises in aggregate demand?

Governments faced with the resulting demand-pull inflation should, according to Keynes, use *contractionary* fiscal and monetary policies to reduce demand. Contractionary fiscal policy would involve reducing government expenditure and/or raising taxes. Contractionary monetary policy would involve reducing the rate of growth of money supply and/or raising interest rates. Keynes argued that here too fiscal policy was the more reliable, but again that the best solution was to combine both policies.

The Keynesian policies of the 1950s and 1960s

During the 1920s and 1930s, UK governments of all parties adopted the classical Treasury view of balanced budgets. By the end of the Second World War, the consensus had changed. From 1945 up to the mid 1970s, both Conservative and Labour governments pursued Keynesian ***demand-management policies*** in an attempt to stabilise the economy and avoid excess or deficient demand.

When the economy began to grow too fast, with rising inflation and balance of payments deficits, the government adopted *deflationary* (contractionary) fiscal and monetary policies. When inflation and the balance of payments were sufficiently improved, but probably with recession looming, threatening rising unemployment and little or no growth, governments adopted *reflationary* (expansionary) fiscal and monetary policies (see Case Study 16.5 in MyEconLab). This succession of deflationary and reflationary policies to counteract the effect of the business cycle became known as ***stop–go policies***.

During the 1950s and 1960s, inflation in the UK averaged just 3.8 per cent and unemployment a mere 1.7 per cent (see Case Study 16.6 in MyEconLab). Similarly low rates of inflation and unemployment were experienced in other industrialised countries. Nevertheless, from the mid 1960s onwards there was increasing criticism of short-term demand-management policies. Criticisms included the following:

- The policies were not very successful in stabilising the economy. Fluctuations still existed. Some economists even claimed that demand-management policies made fluctuations worse. The main reason given was the time it took for policies to be adopted and to work. If time lags are long enough, a deflationary policy may begin to work only when the economy has already turned down into recession. Likewise a reflationary policy may begin to work only when the economy is already booming, thus further fuelling inflation.

- The UK's long-term growth at around 2.8 per cent per annum was appreciably lower than that of other industrialised countries. Some of the blame for this was attributed to an over-concentration on short-term policies of stabilisation, and a neglect of underlying structural problems in the economy.

- Persistent balance of payments problems meant that governments often had to pursue deflationary policies even when the economy was running below capacity and unemployment was rising. (At the time, there was a virtually fixed rate of exchange and thus *depreciation* of the exchange rate was not a means of correcting balance of payments deficits. Only in extreme circumstances could the exchange rate be 'devalued': i.e. fixed at a new lower rate. This is explained in Chapter 25, page 714.)

- The simple Phillips curve relationship between inflation and unemployment was breaking down. If reflationary policies were the cure for unemployment and deflationary policies were the cure for inflation, what policies should be pursued when both inflation *and* unemployment were rising?

- The most fundamental criticism of all came from a group of economists called 'monetarists'. They rejected Keynesianism as a whole, with its concentration on demand. They returned to the earlier classical analysis, with its concentration on supply, and extended it to take account of the increasingly important role of price expectations in explaining 'stagflation' – the problem of slow growth and rising unemployment (i.e. stagnation) and rising inflation at the same time (see the next section).

From the mid 1970s onwards, the Keynesian/monetarist split between economists was reflected in the political parties. The Conservative leadership in the UK embraced monetarism, whereas the other political parties continued to embrace variants of Keynesianism.

Definitions

Demand-management policies Demand-side policies (fiscal and/or monetary) designed to smooth out the fluctuations in the business cycle.

Stop–go policies Alternate deflationary and reflationary policies to tackle the currently most pressing of the four problems that fluctuate with the business cycle.

Section summary

1. Keynes rejected the classical assumption that all markets would clear. Disequilibrium could persist in the labour market. A fall in aggregate demand would not simply lead to a fall in wages and prices and a restoration of the full-employment equilibrium. Instead there would be demand-deficient unemployment: as demand fell, there would be less demand for labour.

2. Disequilibrium could also persist in the market for loanable funds. As aggregate demand fell, and with it business confidence, so the demand for loanable funds for investment would shrink. Reductions in interest rates would be insufficient to clear the market for loanable funds.

3. Keynes also rejected the simple quantity theory. If there is slack in the economy, an expansion of the money supply can lead to an increase in *output* rather than an increase in prices.

4. Keynes argued that there would be a multiplier effect from changes in injections or withdrawals. A rise in investment, for example, would cause a multiplied rise in national income, as additional expenditures flowed round and round the circular flow, stimulating more and more production and thus generating more and more real income.

5. If the economy is operating below full employment, the government can use fiscal and/or monetary policies to boost aggregate demand and thereby take up the slack in the economy. Excessive aggregate demand, however, causes inflation. Deflationary fiscal and monetary policies can be used to remove this excess demand.

6. Keynesianism became the orthodoxy of the 1950s and 1960s. Governments used fiscal (and to a lesser extent monetary) policies to manage the level of aggregate demand.

7. After the mid 1960s, however, there was growing criticism of Keynesian demand management. The economy still fluctuated and the various macroeconomic problems seemed to be getting worse.

16.4 THE MONETARIST–KEYNESIAN DEBATE

The monetarist counter-revolution

The most powerful criticisms of the Keynesian conventional wisdom came from monetarists, whose chief advocate was Milton Friedman, Professor of Economics at Chicago University (see Person Profile in MyEconLab). Monetarists returned to the old classical theory as the basis for their analysis, and extended it to take account of the growing problem of *stagflation*.

At the heart of monetarism is the quantity theory of money. Friedman examined the historical relationship between money supply and prices, and concluded that inflation was 'always and everywhere a monetary phenomenon'. If money supply over the long run rises faster than the potential output of the economy, inflation will be the inevitable result.

Monetarists argued that over the long run, in the equation $MV = PY$, *both* V and Y are independently determined and are not, therefore, affected by changes in M. Any change in money supply (M), therefore, will only affect prices (P). Whether or not monetarists were correct in arguing that V and Y are not affected by changes in M will be examined in later chapters.

Monetarists drew two important conclusions from their analysis.

- The rising inflation from the mid 1960s onwards was entirely due to the growth in money supply increasingly outstripping the growth in output. If money supply rises, they argued, then the resulting rise in aggregate demand will lead not only to rising prices but also, for a few months, to higher output and employment. But soon people's expectations will adjust. Workers and firms come to expect higher wages and prices. Their actions then ensure that wages and prices *are* higher. Thus after one to two years the extra demand is fully taken up in inflation, and so output and employment fall back again. Then governments are tempted to raise money supply and aggregate demand again in a further attempt to get unemployment down. The effect of this over several years is for inflation simply to get higher and higher.
- Reducing the rate of growth of money supply will reduce inflation without leading to long-run increases in unemployment. It *will* lead to temporary increases in unemployment, they argued, as the demand for goods and labour fall. But once price and wage inflation have

adjusted down to this new level of demand, disequilibrium unemployment will be eliminated. This process will be hindered and high unemployment is likely to persist if workers persist in demanding excessive wage increases, or if firms and workers continue to expect high inflation rates.

Monetarists argued that inflation is damaging to the economy because it creates uncertainty for businesspeople and therefore reduces investment, and also because it reduces the country's competitiveness in international trade. They saw it as essential, therefore, for governments to keep a tight control over money supply and advocated the setting of money supply *targets*. Modest and well-publicised targets should help to reduce the *expected* rate of inflation. The UK government from the late 1970s to the mid 1980s set targets for the growth of money supply, and such targets were central to the Thatcher government's 'medium-term financial strategy'.

Apart from controlling the money supply, governments, according to monetarists, should intervene in the economy as little as possible, save to remove hindrances to the efficient functioning of the market (like various restrictive practices of unions). This way, they argued, aggregate supply would be encouraged to grow as firms and workers responded to market incentives. Monetarist 'supply-side policy', therefore, was essentially one of encouraging free enterprise.

A vertical long-run Phillips curve

Monetarist analysis implied that the long-run Phillips curve (see Figure 16.9 and Box 15.5) is vertical at the equilibrium rate of unemployment (called the 'natural rate' by

Definition

Stagflation A term used in the 1970s to refer to the combination of stagnation (low growth and high unemployment) and high inflation.

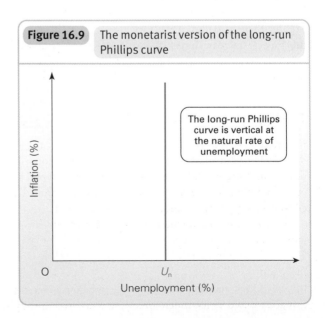

Figure 16.9 The monetarist version of the long-run Phillips curve

The long-run Phillips curve is vertical at the natural rate of unemployment monetarists). In the *short run*, higher aggregate demand will reduce unemployment below the natural level, but in the long run, once expectations have adjusted, all the extra demand is absorbed in higher inflation. Unemployment thus rises back to the natural rate.

If unemployment is to be reduced in the long run, therefore, this vertical Phillips curve must be shifted to the left. This will be achieved by a reduction in the natural (equilibrium) rate of unemployment (U_n), *not* by an increase in demand. To reduce the natural rate, argued the monetarists, supply-side policies would be needed.

 Give some examples of supply-side policies that would help to reduce the natural rate of unemployment.

Government policies

Governments up to the late 1970s responded to rising unemployment by boosting aggregate demand (the balance of payments permitting). This, however, as the monetarists predicted, led only to more inflation, fuelled by rising expectations of inflation.

When governments eventually did curb the growth in aggregate demand, as the Thatcher government did after 1979, it took time for expectations to adjust downwards. In the meantime, there was a further temporary rise in unemployment due to wage rises being slow to moderate.

Nevertheless the pursuit of these policies did, according to monetarists, lead to a dramatic fall in the rate of inflation, and eventually the rise in unemployment was reversed.

The other crucial aspect of government policy in the 1980s, in both the UK and the USA, and increasingly in other countries, was increased reliance on the market. Policies of privatisation and deregulation were pursued; union power was curbed; and tax rates were cut. Controls over the financial system were reduced, as we shall see in Chapter 18, with banks given much more freedom to expand their activities. This 'supply-side' revolution was designed to increase incentives to work, to invest and to innovate. We explore these market-orientated supply-side policies in Chapter 23.

The Keynesian response

Keynesians agreed with monetarists on one point. If demand is expanded too fast and for too long, inflation will result – and there will be a certain amount of unemployment of labour (and other resources too) that cannot be eliminated simply by expanding aggregate demand.

In other respects, Keynesians differed markedly from monetarists.

Inflation

Inflation, they claimed, was not just a problem of excess demand (caused by too much money). It was also caused by increased cost-push pressures: the increasing concentration of economic power in large multinational companies and large trade unions, and the large oil price increases of 1973/4 and 1978/9.

Also, workers had come to expect real wage increases each year, which could simply not be met from real increases in national income. The problem here for the long term was not so much the expectations of price increases, but rather the expectations of increases in real living standards.

Unemployment

Keynesians blamed a deficiency of aggregate demand for the massive rise in unemployment in the 1980s. Aggregate supply was highly elastic downwards in response to a reduction in aggregate demand. Firms responded to falling demand by producing less and employing fewer people. This was further aggravated by firms running down stocks to try to reduce costs and maintain profits.

Expectations are relevant here. But, when aggregate demand is reduced, it is not so much the expectation of lower inflation that reduces inflation (as monetarists claim); rather it is the expectation of lower sales that reduces production, investment and employment. The problem is not merely a short-term difficulty that markets will soon correct. Unless the government adopts a deliberate policy of reflation, the problem may continue. Business confidence may not return. Mass unemployment and recession may persist.

But why, when the world economy boomed in the late 1980s, did unemployment not return to the low levels of the 1970s? In the late 1980s there was little or no deficiency of demand, and yet unemployment fell only slightly. Now the problem was not one of stagflation (a stagnant economy with high inflation). Now the problem was one of a booming economy but with persistently high unemployment. Keynesians typically offered two explanations of the persistence of unemployment.

Structural problems. The 1980s saw an acceleration in the decline of certain industries, a large-scale shift away from labour-intensive processes in manufacturing, an information technology revolution, a programme of privatisation, a more openly competitive world economy and campaigns by both governments and firms against overstaffing. The result was a large increase in equilibrium (structural) unemployment.

Hysteresis. The huge rise in unemployment in the early 1980s throughout the industrialised world, although largely caused by a lack of demand, could not simply be reversed by a rise in demand. The recession had itself *caused* higher levels of unemployment to become embedded in the economy.

Many people had become deskilled and firms had become more cautious about taking on workers, preferring to manage with a smaller, more efficient workforce. What is more, people who remained employed (the *insiders*) were often able, through their unions or close relationships with their employers, or because of the possession of specific skills, to secure wage increases for themselves, and prevent the unemployed (the *outsiders*) from competing wages down. The insiders preferred to secure higher wages for themselves, rather than to have a larger number employed but with everyone on lower wages.

This continuation of high unemployment is known as *hysteresis*. This term, used in physics, refers to the lagging or persistence of an effect, even when the initial cause has been removed. In our context, it refers to the persistence of unemployment even when the initial demand deficiency no longer exists.

Keynesian criticisms of monetarism

Keynesians criticised monetarists for putting too much reliance on markets. The problems of inflation, unemployment and industrial decline were much too deep-seated and complex to be rectified by a simple reliance on controlling the money supply and then leaving private enterprise and labour to respond to unregulated market forces.

Free markets are often highly imperfect and will not lead to an optimum allocation of resources. What is more, markets frequently reflect short-term speculative movements of demand and supply, and do not give a clear indication of long-term costs and benefits. In particular, the stock market, the money market and the foreign exchange market can respond quite violently to short-term pressures. Such fluctuations can be very damaging to investment. For example, violent swings in exchange rates, as experienced between the euro and the dollar in the early 2000s (see Box 25.5), can dissuade firms from making long-term investment decisions to develop export markets. A sudden rise in exchange rates may make it impossible to compete abroad, even though at a lower exchange rate an exporter could have made a large profit.

The fluctuations inherent in free markets cause uncertainty about future demand, supply and prices. This uncertainty reduces investment and hence reduces growth. Government, therefore, should intervene much more to stimulate growth and investment.

Keynesian policy proposals

Keynesians generally favour a much more interventionist approach to policy than do monetarists. The following policies are typical of those favoured by Keynesians.

Maintaining a high and stable level of aggregate demand. A substantial increase in demand may be necessary initially if unemployment levels are very high. The best way of achieving this is for the government to increase its expenditure on public works such as roads and housing, since these projects have a relatively low import content and therefore increased expenditure does not lead to balance of payments problems. Thereafter the government should maintain a high and stable demand, by appropriate demand-management policies. This should keep unemployment down and set the environment for long-term investment and growth.

Stabilising exchange rates. To reduce uncertainties, the central bank should intervene in foreign exchange markets to prevent excessive short-term fluctuations in exchange rates. This might involve international co-operation between central banks. More stable rates will encourage investment and growth.

Greater co-operation between government and industry. To promote long-term growth and to avoid the uncertainties of the market, the government should work much more closely with industry. This might involve the government helping to co-ordinate the plans of interdependent sectors of industry (such as the power and transport industries) and channelling finance to the more promising industries.

Structural policies. To reduce structural unemployment the government should pursue regional and urban policies through grants, tax relief and direct infrastructure investment in areas of high unemployment. This, it is argued, will encourage firms to move to such areas. Also, the government should pursue retraining policies to encourage greater occupational mobility of labour.

Definitions

Insiders Those in employment who can use their privileged position (either as members of unions or because of specific skills) to secure pay rises despite an excess supply of labour (unemployment).

Outsiders Those out of work or employed on a casual, part-time or short-term basis, who have little or no power to influence wages or employment.

Hysteresis The persistence of an effect even when the initial cause has ceased to operate. In economics, it refers to the persistence of unemployment even when the demand deficiency that caused it no longer exists.

Section summary

1. Monetarists argued that there is a close correlation between the rate of growth of the money supply and the rate of inflation. Increases in money supply cause increases in aggregate demand, which in turn cause inflation. Along with the classical economists, they argued that output and employment are determined independently of money supply (at least in the long run). This means that a deflationary policy to cure inflation will *not* in the long run cause a fall in output or a rise in unemployment.

2. Monetarists thus argued that the long-run Phillips curve is vertical. Its position along the horizontal axis will depend on the level of equilibrium or 'natural' unemployment.

3. Keynesians rejected the notion of a totally vertical Phillips curve, but did accept that demand-side policies alone cannot cure unemployment completely. Keynesians blamed the combination of high inflation and high unemployment on a number of factors, each of which has the effect of shifting the Phillips curve to the right. These factors include cost-push and demand-shift pressures on inflation, and government attempts to cure inflation by continually pursuing deflationary policies.

4. Unemployment caused initially by a recession (a deficiency of demand) may persist even when the economy is recovering. This 'hysteresis' may be due to the deskilling of labour, a decline in firms' capacity, insiders preventing outsiders from bidding down the wage rate, or firms being cautious about taking on extra labour when the recovery does come.

5. Keynesians argued that markets do not clear rapidly and that in the meantime expectations of output and employment changes can have major effects on investment plans.

6. Whereas monetarists generally favoured policies of freeing up markets (within the framework of strict government control over money supply), Keynesians favoured a much more interventionist approach by the government. Central to this is the control of aggregate demand so as to retain actual income as close as possible to its potential level.

16.5 THE CURRENT POSITION: AN EMERGING CONSENSUS?

A range of views

From the monetarist–Keynesian debates of the 1970s and 1980s has emerged a degree of consensus among many economists that draws on insights from both schools. This is not to suggest, however, that all economists agree. In fact, a whole range of views can be identified.

One simple way of classifying these differing views is to see them falling along a spectrum. At the one end are those who see the free market as working well and who generally blame macroeconomic problems on excessive government intervention. At the other are those who see the free market as fundamentally flawed. Let us identify different views along this spectrum, starting with the pro-free-market end.

The new classical/rational expectations school

The **new classical school** is like an extreme form of monetarism. New classicists maintain that markets clear very quickly and expectations adjust virtually instantaneously to new situations. These expectations are based on firms' and workers' rational assessment of what is happening in the economy and in their particular sector of it. They may be wrong, but they are just as likely to overpredict as to underpredict the rate of inflation and hence the equilibrium price in their particular market. On average, they will guess it about right.

Expanding money supply will virtually instantaneously lead to higher expectations of inflation. Therefore it can only cause inflation; it cannot reduce unemployment. The short-run Phillips curve is vertical, as is the long-run one. Likewise tight monetary policy reduces inflation; it does not increase unemployment. Rising unemployment is entirely due to a rise in the natural rate of unemployment.

If changes in aggregate demand cannot affect output and employment, how do the new classical economists explain the business cycle of booms and recessions? The answer they give is that these cyclical changes in output and employment are the result of shifts in the aggregate *supply* curve. These in turn are the result of cycles in technological progress and labour productivity. The theory is therefore known as **real business cycle theory**. We examine this in section 21.3.

KI 10
p71

Definitions

New classical school A body of economists who believe that markets are highly competitive and clear very rapidly; any expansion of demand will feed through virtually instantaneously into higher prices, giving a vertical short-run as well as a vertical long-run Phillips curve.

Real business cycle theory The new classical theory which explains cyclical fluctuations in terms of shifts in aggregate supply, rather than aggregate demand.

This school favours laissez-faire (i.e. free-market) policies and is part of what is often called the 'radical right'.

Moderate monetarists/centre-right analysis

Many economists reject the new classical notion of a vertical short-run aggregate supply curve and vertical short-run Phillips curve, but still maintain that markets adjust fairly quickly – perhaps within one or two years.

A rise in money supply and hence aggregate demand will lead to a temporary reduction in unemployment, but as expectations of inflation (and hence of wage increases) adjust upwards, so eventually the whole of the rise in aggregate demand will be swallowed up in higher prices. *Real* aggregate demand falls back to its original level and hence the level of unemployment rises back to its original level too. Thus the short-run Phillips curve is downward sloping, but the long-run curve is vertical.

If the economy is faced with high inflation, a sudden tight monetary policy may temporarily lead to a recession. Thus sudden extreme policies should be avoided. Instead there should be a gradual reduction in the growth of the money supply.

Any temporary demand-deficient unemployment will be reduced if workers can be encouraged to take reductions in real wages. Ultimately, though, any policies to make long-term reductions in unemployment must be aimed at the supply side of the economy: reducing the natural rate of unemployment by increasing labour mobility and getting markets to work better.

This analysis has resulted in the modern approach by governments and central banks of targeting the rate of inflation as the core focus of monetary policy. Adhering to this policy rule, it is argued, creates the stable environment necessary for the market to flourish: expectations will adjust to the target rate of inflation (assuming central banks are successful in sticking to the target) and firms will be able to plan with more confidence. Investment is thereby encouraged and this, in turn, encourages a growth in potential output. In other words, sticking to the targets creates the best environment for the expansion of aggregate *supply*.

Moderate Keynesians

Moderate Keynesians argue that economies will probably eventually pull out of recession even if governments do not boost demand. There will be a natural upturn in the business cycle. Firms' confidence will begin to return and investment will start to increase. Nevertheless a recession can be deep and long-lived and the recovery slow and faltering. Thus moderate Keynesians argue for active intervention by government to boost demand.

As the world plunged into recession in 2008, so governments in many countries adopted Keynesian policy recommendations. Both monetary and fiscal policies were used to boost flagging aggregate demand. Central banks cut interest rates to nearly zero in an attempt to encourage borrowing and therefore spending. Alongside this, huge fiscal stimulus

packages were adopted by governments, involving substantial tax cuts and large increases in public expenditure. The US fiscal package adopted by President Obama in 2009 was $787 billion – a massive 5.7 per cent of GDP.

Once an economy has recovered from recession and is back to near full employment, the government must still continue to control aggregate demand to prevent fluctuations in output and employment. Keynesians generally advocate the use of anti-cyclical demand management policy.

Most moderate Keynesians blame the persistence of recessions on the reluctance of real wages to fall so as to clear the labour market and eliminate demand-deficient unemployment. In recent years **new Keynesians**, as they are called, have attempted to discover the reasons for the downward stickiness in real wages during a recession. These include the following:

- The worry of employers about demotivating their workforce, and thus causing efficiency to suffer. This is known as the *efficiency wage theory*.
- The power of *insiders* to resist real wage cuts.
- The power of firms under *imperfect competition* to maintain their prices. Firms may prefer to respond to a fall in demand by cutting output rather than cutting (real) prices, especially if they believe that their rivals will do the same. In such cases, they are not under the same pressure to cut real wage rates. Instead, they prefer to cut employment.

Extreme Keynesians

Extreme Keynesians argue that there is no automatic mechanism to eliminate demand-deficient unemployment even in the long run.

Not only are real wage rates sticky downwards, but also any reductions in real wage rates that do take place will further reduce consumer demand. The amount of money circulating will automatically fall as banks lend out less and less in response to falling demand. Firms are unlikely to borrow for investment, since they have no confidence in their market. Expectations are likely to remain pessimistic.

Under these circumstances, the government must intervene to expand demand. By raising government expenditure and cutting taxes, the nation must spend its way out of recession. It may be necessary to use import controls to prevent any resulting balance of payments problems.

Definition

New Keynesians Economists who seek to explain the downward stickiness of real wages and the resulting persistence of unemployment. They argue that governments may have to expand aggregate demand when demand-deficient unemployment is persistent.

After the economy has pulled out of recession, it is still important for the government to maintain a high level of demand. Not only will this maintain low unemployment and keep actual national income close to potential national income, it will also provide the most favourable environment for research and development, innovations and investment generally. Thus *potential* national income will grow more rapidly.

Some Keynesians in this group are known as **post-Keynesians**. They highlight some of the key features of Keynes' *General Theory* to explain why economies are not self-correcting. In particular, they stress the importance of what Keynes called 'animal spirits', or what is today known as business expectations or business confidence. The mood of the country's business community is fundamental in determining investment and output. Without appropriate demand-management policy, this mood can remain depressed into the long term.

Post-Keynesians and other 'heterodox economists' also challenge most of the microeconomic assumptions on which other more 'mainstream' macroeconomic theories are based. Firms are not cold, rational profit maximisers, making calm calculations based on marginal analysis. Instead, firms make output decisions largely in response to anticipated demand, again based on their *confidence* in their market. The result is that anticipated demand changes are likely to lead to *output* and *employment* changes, not price changes.

Finally, post-Keynesians tend to focus on a country's *institutions* and *culture* to explain how firms and consumers respond to economic stimuli. In other words, they try to base their explanations and policies on real-world institutional and behavioural information rather than on abstract models.

The radical left

Some economists make a far more fundamental attack on the market economy. Most Keynesians, although they see a free market as leading to serious problems, nevertheless argue that government intervention can rectify these problems. Those on the radical left disagree. They see the market economy as so flawed that mere intervention will not solve its problems. Instead the market economy needs to be *replaced* by an alternative system such as state planning and/or worker control of industry. Marxist economists see the problem of capitalism to be so severe that ultimately there will be a revolution and it will be overthrown.

Definition

Post-Keynesians Economists who stress the importance of institutional and behavioural factors, and the role of business confidence in explaining the state of the economy. They argue that firms are more likely to respond to changes in demand by changing output rather than prices.

The fact that there are so many different views as to how the macroeconomy functions makes it impossible to do justice to them all in an introductory book. Nevertheless it is hoped that you will get some insight into the major schools of thought and why they advocate the policies they do.

 Two economists disagree over the best way of tackling the problem of unemployment. For what reasons might they disagree? Are these reasons positive or normative?

A mainstream consensus?

Although there are many areas of disagreement in macroeconomics, some general points of agreement have emerged in recent years, at least among the majority of economists.

- In the short run, changes in aggregate demand will have a major effect on output and employment. If there is a collapse in demand, as in 2008, governments and/or central banks should intervene through expansionary fiscal and/or monetary policies. Only a few extreme new classical economists would disagree with this proposition.

- In the long run, changes in aggregate demand will have much less effect on output and employment and much more effect on prices. In fact, many economists say that there will be *no* effect at all on output and employment, and that the whole effect will be on prices. There is still a substantial body of Keynesians, however, especially post-Keynesians, who argue that changes in aggregate demand *will* have substantial effects on long-term output and employment via changes in investment and hence in potential output.

- There is no simple long-run trade-off between inflation and unemployment. There is still disagreement, however, as to whether there is no relationship between them at all (i.e. the long-run Phillips curve is vertical), or whether they are connected indirectly via the long term effects of changes in aggregate demand on investment, etc.

- Expectations have an important effect on the economy. There is still disagreement, however, as to whether it is people's expectations of price changes or of output changes that are more important.

- Excessive growth in the money supply will lead to inflation. Some economists argue that the quantity theory of money holds in the long run (i.e. that inflation is *entirely* due to increases in the money supply). Others argue that the relationship is more general. Nevertheless, the consensus is that governments should avoid allowing the money supply to grow too rapidly.

- Controlling inflation through control of the money supply, however, is difficult, since money supply itself is not easy to control. Even if it were possible to control money supply, there is a time lag between changes in money supply and the resulting changes in inflation. This makes a precise control of inflation by this means very difficult. Most economists, therefore, argue that it is easier to control inflation by controlling interest rates, since this directly affects aggregate demand. Most central banks around the world today therefore use interest rate changes to achieve a target rate of inflation.

- Macroeconomic policy should not focus exclusively on the demand side. Long-term growth depends primarily on changes in supply (i.e. in potential output). It is important, therefore, for governments to develop an effective supply-side policy if they want to achieve faster economic growth. There is still disagreement, however, over the forms that supply-side policy should take: should it focus on freeing up the market, or should it focus on various forms of government intervention to compensate for market deficiencies?

- Governments' ability to control their country's macroeconomic destiny is being increasingly eroded by the process of globalisation. As countries become more and more interdependent, and as capital moves more and more freely around the globe, so there is a growing need for co-ordinated policies between governments to tackle problems of global recessions or excessive exchange rate fluctuations. This lesson was brought home in 2008, when it became obvious that most countries were experiencing a collapse in aggregate demand following the banking crisis and the credit crunch. Leaders discussed common policy approaches at several international summits, including both bank rescue packages and expansionary fiscal and monetary policies.

It is perhaps too soon to say that there is now a macroeconomic consensus, but at least the areas of disagreement have been refined.

As the book progresses, we will be looking at the various areas of agreement and disagreement in more detail. We shall pull most of the arguments together in Chapter 21.

Section summary

1. There are many shades of opinion among the different groups of economists, from extreme new classical economists who advocate almost complete laissez-faire to the extreme left where economists advocate the virtual abandonment of markets. In between comes a whole spectrum of opinions and theories about the relative effectiveness of markets and the government in achieving the various macroeconomic goals.

2. Despite these disagreements, most economists would agree on the following points: changes in aggregate demand have a direct effect on output and employment in the short run, but either no effect or a far less certain effect in the long run; there is no simple long-run trade-off between inflation and unemployment; expectations have an important effect on the economy; excessive growth in the money supply causes inflation; it is easier to achieve inflation targets by controlling interest rates than by controlling money supply; changes on the supply side of the economy are the major determinant of long-term growth; globalisation reduces individual countries' ability to control their economies.

END OF CHAPTER QUESTIONS

1. In a given economy, the supply of money is £10 billion; the velocity of circulation of money (spent on final goods and services) is 3; and the price index is 2.00.

    (a) What is the level of real national income?

    (b) How much have prices risen (in percentage terms) since the base year?

    (c) Assume that money supply increases by 10 per cent and that the velocity of circulation remains constant. By what percentage will prices rise if

        (i) there is no increase in real national income;

        (ii) real national income increases by 10 per cent;

        (iii) real national income increases by 5 per cent?

2. In what way will the nature of aggregate supply influence the effect of a change in aggregate demand on prices and real national income?

3. Criticise the classical theory that higher government spending will necessarily crowd out private spending.

4. Criticise the use of increasing government expenditure as a means of reducing unemployment.

5. In what way may short-term demand-management policies help to stabilise the economy? What problems occur in the use of such policies?

6. What explanations can you give for the increase in *both* unemployment and inflation in the 1970s?

7. What is meant by *hysteresis* when applied to unemployment? How do you account for this phenomenon in the 1980s?

8. What will cause people to expect higher rates of inflation? How will expectations of inflation affect the actual rate of inflation?

Online resources

Additional case studies in MyEconLab

16.1 **The equation of exchange.** This examines two more versions that are commonly used: the Fisher version and the Cambridge version.

16.2 **Money and inflation in ancient Rome.** A very early case study of the quantity theory of money: how the minting of extra coins by the Romans caused prices to rise.

16.3 **The Great Depression and the return to the gold standard.** A time of great hardship and sacrifice.

16.4 **Classical 'remedies' for unemployment.** How the policies advocated by the classical economists to cure unemployment would, according to Keynes, make the problem worse.

16.5 **A little bit less of this and a little bit more of that.** Fine tuning in 1959 and 1960.

16.6 **'You've never had it so good.'** The claim in 1957 by Harold Macmillan, the British Conservative Prime Minister, that governments were now able to manage the economy so as to give growing prosperity.

Websites relevant to this chapter

See sites listed at the end of Chapter 17 on page 501.

Short-run Macroeconomic Equilibrium

CHAPTER MAP

17.1 Background to the theory   475
Aggregate demand and national income   475
The Keynesian 45° line diagram   475
Consumption   476
Withdrawals   478
Injections   482

17.2 The determination of national income 486
Equilibrium national income   486
The multiplier: *W* and *J* approach   486
The multiplier: *Y* and *E* approach   489
*The multiplier: some qualifications   490
The relationship between the 45° line diagram
    and the *AD/AS* diagram   491

**17.3 The simple Keynesian analysis of
            unemployment and inflation   492**
'Full-employment' national income   492
The deflationary gap   492
The inflationary gap   493
Unemployment and inflation at the same time   494
The relationship between the AD/AS diagram
    and the 45° line diagram   494

**17.4 The Keynesian analysis of the
            business cycle   495**
Instability of investment: the accelerator   496
The multiplier/accelerator interaction   497
Fluctuations in stocks   497
Determinants of the course of the business cycle   499

In this chapter we look at the determination of national income, employment and inflation in the short run: i.e. over a period of up to two years. The analysis is based on the model developed by Keynesians. Although many economists argue that this is not appropriate for analysing the performance of the macroeconomy over the longer term, most agree that the analysis is essentially true over the short term.

The model assumes that aggregate demand determines the level of economic activity in the economy. In other words, the nation's production and employment depend on the amount of spending. Too little spending will lead to unemployment. More spending will stimulate firms to produce more and employ more people. Too much spending, however, will cause inflation. This chapter examines this relationship between aggregate demand and national income (GDP), employment and inflation.

One important simplifying assumption is made: *the rate of interest is fixed*. This allows us for the time being to ignore what is happening to the amount of *money* in the economy. A fixed interest rate effectively means that the supply of money will passively rise or fall as aggregate demand rises or falls. In other words, if spending rises and hence the demand for money from the banking system also rises, there will be a corresponding increase in the amount of money made available and hence no need for interest rates to rise. In subsequent chapters, we will drop this assumption and take specific account of the role of money in the economy.

17.1 BACKGROUND TO THE THEORY

The relationship between aggregate demand and national income

This chapter explains what determines the level of national income (GDP) in the short run. It is based on the model developed by John Maynard Keynes, back in the 1930s.

The basic explanation is quite simple: the level of production in the economy depends on the level of aggregate demand. If people buy more, firms will produce more in response to this, providing they have spare capacity. If people buy less, firms will cut down their production and lay off workers. But just *how much* will national income rise or fall as aggregate demand changes? We will answer this as the chapter progresses.

First, let us return to the circular flow of income that we looked at in Chapter 14. This is illustrated in Figure 17.1. Looking at the bottom of the diagram, the consumption of domestically produced goods (C_d) and the three withdrawals (W) – net saving (S), net taxes (T) and spending on imports (M) – all depend on the level of national income (Y). In fact, in the model, national income must always equal consumption of domestic goods plus withdrawals: there is nothing else people can do with their incomes!

$$Y \equiv C_d + W$$

Moving now to the top part of Figure 17.1, total spending in the economy on the goods and services of domestic firms is what we have already defined as aggregate demand (AD). In the Keynesian model that we are examining in this chapter, it is normally referred to as *aggregate expenditure* (*E*). (This is useful to distinguish it from the AD and AS model that we looked at in Chapter 15.) Aggregate expenditure consists of C_d plus the three injections (J): investment in the domestic economy (I), government expenditure in the domestic economy (G) and expenditure from abroad on the country's exports (X).

$$AD \equiv E \equiv C_d + J$$

In equilibrium, withdrawals equal injections. (We demonstrated this in Chapter 14.) Since national income (Y) is simply withdrawals plus C_d, and aggregate expenditure (E) is simply injections plus C_d, it follows that in equilibrium national income must equal aggregate expenditure. To summarise:

$$W = J$$
$$\therefore C_d + W = C_d + J$$
$$\therefore Y = E \ (= AD)$$

Whenever aggregate expenditure ($C_d + J$) exceeds national income ($C_d + W$), injections will exceed withdrawals. Firms will respond to the extra demand by producing more and hence employing more factors of production. National income will thus rise. But as national income rises, so too will saving, imports and the amount paid in taxes: in other words, withdrawals will rise. Withdrawals will go on rising until they equal injections: until a new equilibrium has been reached. To summarise:

$$J > W \rightarrow Y \uparrow \rightarrow W \uparrow \text{until } W = J$$

But *how much* will national income rise when aggregate demand (expenditure) rises? What will the new equilibrium level of national income be? To answer this question we must examine the relationship between national income and the component parts of the circular flow of income: consumption, withdrawals and injections. This relationship is shown in the Keynesian '45° line diagram'.

Introducing the Keynesian 45° line diagram

In this model, it is assumed that the levels of consumption and withdrawals are determined by the level of national income. Since national income is part of the model, we say that consumption and withdrawals are *endogenous*. This means that they vary with one of the other components of the model (i.e. income). Injections, however, are assumed to be *exogenous*: they are determined independently of

---

Figure 17.1 A simplified circular flow of income model

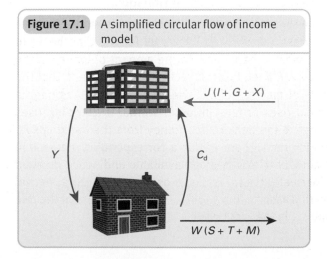

Definitions

Aggregate expenditure (*E*) Aggregate demand in the Keynesian model: i.e. $C_d + J$.

Endogenous variable A variable whose value is determined by the model of which it is part.

Exogenous variable A variable whose value is determined independently of the model of which it is part.

Figure 17.2 The 45° line

Figure 17.3 The consumption function

what is going on in the model; they do *not* depend on the level of national income.

We will justify these assumptions later. First we must look at how the diagram is constructed, and at the significance of the 45° line, which is shown in Figure 17.2. We plot real national income (i.e. national income matched by output) on the horizontal axis, and the various component parts of the circular flow (C_d, W and J) on the vertical axis. If the two axes are plotted to the same scale, then at every point on the 45° line the items on each axis are equal.

But what items on the vertical axis will always equal national income (Y), which is plotted on the horizontal axis? The answer is $C_d + W$, since, by definition, $Y = C_d + W$. For example, if Y were £100 billion, then $C_d + W$ must also be £100 billion (see Figure 17.2).

We turn now to look at each of the components of the circular flow and see how they fit into the 45° line diagram.

Consumption

We will need to distinguish total consumption (C) from that part of consumption that goes purely on the output of domestically produced goods (C_d). C_d excludes expenditure taxes (e.g. VAT) and expenditure on imports.

We start by looking at *total* consumption.

The consumption function

As national income increases, so does consumption. The reason is simple: if people earn more, they can afford to spend more. The relationship between consumption and income is expressed by the *consumption function*:

$$C = f(Y)$$

It can be shown graphically on the 45° line diagram (see Figure 17.3 which is based on Table 17.1). The consumption function slopes upwards. This illustrates that, as

Table 17.1 $C = f(Y)$

National income (£bn)	Consumption (£bn)
0	10
10	18
20	26
30	34
40	42
50	50
60	58
70	66
80	74
90	82
100	90
110	98

national income rises, so does consumption. To keep the analysis simple, the consumption function is drawn as a straight line.

At very low levels of income, the consumption function will lie above the 45° line. When people are very poor, they may be forced to spend more than they earn merely to survive. They usually do this by borrowing or drawing on savings. Above a certain level of income, however (£50 billion in Figure 17.3), the consumption function will lie below the 45° line. People will spend less than they earn. The remainder will go on saving and taxes.

Definition

Consumption function The relationship between consumption and national income. It can be expressed algebraically or graphically.

The higher the level of national income, the smaller the proportion that will be consumed: people can afford to save proportionately more, and will have to pay proportionately more in taxes. It follows that the slope of the consumption function is less than that of the 45° line.

The marginal propensity to consume. The slope of the consumption function is given by the **marginal propensity to consume**. This is the proportion of any increase in national income that goes on consumption.[1] In Table 17.1, for each £10 billion rise in national income there is an £8 billion rise in consumption. Thus the marginal propensity to consume is £8 billion/£10 billion = 8/10 or 4/5 or 0.8. The formula is

$$mpc = \Delta C / \Delta Y$$

In Figure 17.3, the consumption function is a straight line: it has a *constant* slope, and hence the *mpc* is also constant.

 It is possible that as people get richer they will spend a smaller and smaller fraction of each rise in income (and save a larger fraction). Why might this be so? What effect will it have on the shape of the consumption function?

The other determinants of consumption

Of course, people's incomes are not the only determinants of the amount they consume. There are several other determinants.

Assets held. The more wealth people have, whether as savings, as shares or as property, the more they are likely to spend out of current income.

Taxation. The higher the level of income taxes, the less will people have left to spend out of their gross income: consumption depends on **disposable income**.

 Expectations of future prices and incomes. If people expect prices to rise, they tend to buy durable goods such as

furniture and cars before this happens. Similarly, if people expect a rise in their *incomes*, they are likely to spend more now. If, on the other hand, they are uncertain about their future income prospects, or fear unemployment, they are likely to be cautious in their spending.

The distribution of income. The poor have a higher *mpc* than the rich, with very little left over to save. A redistribution of national income from the poor to the rich will therefore tend to reduce the total level of consumption in the economy.

Tastes and attitudes. If people have a 'buy now, pay later' mentality, or a craving for consumer goods, they are likely to have a higher level of consumption than if their tastes are more frugal. The more 'consumerist' and materialistic a nation becomes, the higher will its consumption be for any given level of income.

The age of durables. If people's car, carpets, clothes, etc. are getting old, they will tend to have a high level of 'replacement' consumption, particularly after a recession when they had cut back on their consumption of durables. Conversely, as the economy reaches the peak of the boom, people are likely to spend less on durables as they have probably already bought the items they want.

Movements along and shifts in the consumption function

The effect on consumption of a change in national income is shown by a movement *along* the consumption function. A change in any of the other determinants is shown by a *shift* in the consumption function.

 What effect will the following have on the mpc: (a) the rate of income tax rises; (b) the economy begins to recover from recession; (c) people anticipate that the rate of inflation is about to rise; (d) the government redistributes income from the rich to the poor? In each case sketch what would happen to the consumption function.

Long-run and short-run consumption functions

The long-run consumption function is likely to be steeper than the short-run one (see Figure 17.4).

In the short run, people may be slow to respond to a rise in income. Perhaps they are cautious about whether their higher income will last, or are slow to change their consumption habits. In the short run, then, people may

---

[1] The *mpc* is normally defined as the proportion of a rise in *disposable* national income that goes on consumption, where disposable income is income *after taxes*. By defining it the way we have done (i.e. as the proportion of *gross* income that goes in consumption), the analysis is simpler. The conclusions remain the same.

KI 10 p71

Definitions

Marginal propensity to consume The proportion of a rise in national income that goes on consumption:

$$mpc = \Delta C / \Delta Y.$$

Disposable income Household income after the deduction of taxes and the addition of benefits.

Figure 17.4 Long-run and short-run consumption functions

---

have a relatively low *mpc*. In the long run, however, people have time to adjust their consumption patterns.

Assuming that national income rises over time, the long-run consumption function will be intersected by a series of short-run ones. Each year's short-run function will be above the previous year's.

 Which is likely to show the greater variation from one person to another at any given level of income: the short-run mpc or the long-run mpc?

Consumption of domestically produced goods (C_d)

The parts of consumption that go on imports and indirect taxes constitute withdrawals from the circular flow of income and thus do not contribute to aggregate demand. We shall concentrate on the part of consumption that *does*: namely, the consumption of domestic product (C_d). The C_d function lies below the C function, as in Figure 17.5. The gap between them constitutes imports of consumer goods and indirect taxes.

---

*LOOKING AT THE MATHS

Let us examine the relationship between C and C_d a bit more closely. When people make consumption decisions, this is largely based on their *disposable* income (Y_{dis}), where disposable income is income after the payment of income taxes and the receipt of benefits. We use the term 'net income taxes (T_Y)' to refer to income taxes minus benefits. Thus

$$Y_{dis} = Y - T_Y$$

Also, people tend not to distinguish between domestic goods and imports when they make consumption decisions. Let us then focus on total consumption (C), not just the consumption of domestic products (C_d).

To get a better understanding of people's consumption behaviour, we could express the marginal propensity to consume *all products* (domestic and imported) relative to *disposable* income. Let us call this term *mpc'* (rather than *mpc* or *mpc_d*) where

$$mpc' = \frac{\Delta C}{\Delta Y_{dis}} = \frac{\Delta C}{\Delta Y - \Delta T_Y} \tag{1}$$

Note that the consumption term C refers to consumers' total consumption expenditure, not the net amount received by domestic firms (C_d). To get from C to C_d, we would have to subtract the amount spent on imports (M) and the amount paid in indirect taxes, such as VAT and excise duties, (T_E). Thus

$$C_d = C - M - T_E \text{ or } C = C_d + M + T_E$$

Thus

$$\Delta C = \Delta C_d + \Delta M + \Delta T_E \tag{2}$$

Substituting equation (2) in equation (1) gives

$$mpc' = \frac{\Delta C_d + \Delta T_E + \Delta M}{\Delta Y - \Delta T_Y} \tag{3}$$

Contrast this with the *mpc_d*, where

$$mpc_d = \frac{\Delta C_d}{\Delta Y} \tag{4}$$

Figure 17.5 The consumption of domestic product

Withdrawals

All three withdrawals – net saving, net taxes and import expenditure – depend on the level of national income. They are thus all *endogenously* determined within the model.

Net saving

As with consumption, the major determinant of net saving (i.e. saving minus consumer borrowing and drawing on past savings) is income. As income increases, and a decreasing fraction of it goes on consumption, so an increasing fraction of it will be saved. The rich can afford to save a larger proportion of their income than the poor.

KI 24
p260

The proportion of an increase in national income that is saved is given by the **marginal propensity to save** (mps).

$$mps = \Delta S / \Delta Y$$

Other determinants of saving. To a large extent these are the same as the other determinants of consumption, since most things that encourage people to spend more will thereby encourage them to save less.

It might be easy to get the impression that saving is merely what is left over after consumption has taken place. In fact, for many people the decision to save is a very positive one. They might be saving up for something they are eager to buy but cannot afford at the moment, or saving for retirement. Indeed, people may be encouraged to save *more* by various factors, such as changes in pension provisions or new government-sponsored saving schemes.

 Go through each of the determinants of consumption that were listed in the previous section and consider how they will affect saving. Are there any determinants of consumption that will not cause saving to rise if consumption is caused to fall?

Net taxes

As national income increases, so the amount paid in tax will also increase. The **marginal tax propensity** (mpt) is the proportion of an increase in national income paid in taxes:[1]

$$mpt = \Delta T / \Delta Y$$

The *mpt* depends on tax rates. In a simple world where there was only one type of tax, which was charged at a constant rate – for example, an income tax of 22 per cent – the *mpt* would be given directly by the tax rate. In this example, for each extra pound earned, 22p would be paid in income tax. The $mpt = \Delta T / \Delta Y = 22/100 = 0.22$. In practice, of course, there are many types of tax charged at many different rates, and thus working out the *mpt* is more complicated.

In most countries, the *mpt* rises as national income rises. This is because income tax is progressive. At higher incomes, people pay a higher marginal rate of income tax. In the UK

---

[1] We have defined net taxes as taxes minus benefits (i.e. the net flow from the household sector to the government). For our purposes, then, the *mpt* is the proportion of any rise in income going in taxes and reduced benefits.

---

*BOX 17.1   USING CALCULUS TO DERIVE THE MPC   EXPLORING ECONOMICS

The consumption function can be expressed as an equation. For example, the consumption function of Table 17.1 and Figure 17.3 is given by the equation:

$$C = 10 + 0.8Y \qquad (1)$$

 Try using this equation to derive the figures in Table 17.1.

From this equation we can derive an equation for *mpc*. It is found by differentiating the consumption function. Remember from previous calculus boxes what it is we are doing when we differentiate an equation. We are finding its rate of change. Thus by differentiating the consumption function, we are finding the rate of change of consumption with respect to income. But this is what we mean by the *mpc*.

The difference between using differentiation and the formula $\Delta C / \Delta Y$ is that with the former we are looking at the *mpc* at a single point on the consumption function. With the $\Delta C / \Delta Y$ formula we were looking at the *mpc* between two points.

Differentiating equation (1) gives

$$mpc = dC/dY = 0.8 \qquad (2)$$

Note that, since the consumption function is a straight line in this case, the *mpc* (which measures the slope of the consumption function) is constant.

What would we do to find the *mpc* of a non-linear (curved) consumption function? The procedure is the same.

Assume that the consumption function is given by the following equation:

$$C = 20 + 0.9Y - 0.001Y^2 \qquad (3)$$

 First of all, try constructing a table like Table 17.1 and then graph the consumption function that it gives. What is it about equation (3) that gives the graph its particular shape?

The *mpc* is given by dC/dY:

$$mpc = 0.9 - 0.002Y$$

 1. *What are the values of mpc at incomes of (a) 20; (b) 100?*
2. *What happens to the value of mpc as national income increases? Is this what you would expect by examining the shape of the consumption function?*

Definitions

Marginal propensity to save The proportion of an increase in national income saved: $mps = \Delta S / \Delta Y$.

Marginal tax propensity The proportion of an increase in national income paid in tax: $mpt = \Delta T / \Delta Y$.

and many other countries, however, income tax became much less progressive in the 1980s and 1990s, but the *mpt* remained roughly the same because of rises in indirect taxes.

Imports

The higher the level of national income, the higher will be the amount spent on imports. The **marginal propensity to import** (*mpm*) is the proportion of a rise in national income that goes on imports:

$$mpm = \Delta M / \Delta Y$$

Note that we only count that part of the expenditure on imports that actually goes abroad. Amounts retained by the retailer, the wholesaler and the importer, and amounts paid in indirect taxes are excluded.

Whether the *mpm* rises or falls as national income rises depends on the nature of a country's imports. If a country imports predominantly basic goods, which have a relatively low income elasticity of demand, the rate of increase in their consumption would tail off rapidly as incomes increase. The *mpm* for such a country would thus also rapidly decrease.

If, however, a country's imports were mainly of luxury goods, they would account for an increasing proportion of any rise in national income: the *mpm* would rise.

 If a country imports a whole range of goods whose average income elasticity of demand is the same as for home-produced goods, will the mpm rise or fall as national income rises?

The determinants of the level of imports. Apart from national income, there are a number of other determinants of the level of imports:

Definition

Marginal propensity to import The proportion of an increase in national income that is spent on imports: $mpm = \Delta M / \Delta Y$.

BOX 17.2 | CONSUMPTION AND SAVING IN PRACTICE

Consumer spending follows a regular cyclical pattern each year, reaching its peak in the fourth quarter as Christmas approaches. The graph shows the levels of UK personal disposable income and total consumer expenditure (i.e. consumption before indirect taxes and imports have been deducted) from 1997 Q1 to 2008 Q3. The annual cyclical pattern can clearly be seen, with consumption actually falling in quarter 1 of each year. The gap between consumer expenditure and disposable income represents that fraction of disposable income that is saved. Where consumer expenditure exceeds disposable income, as it has in several quarters in recent years, this represents 'dissaving': i.e. negative saving.

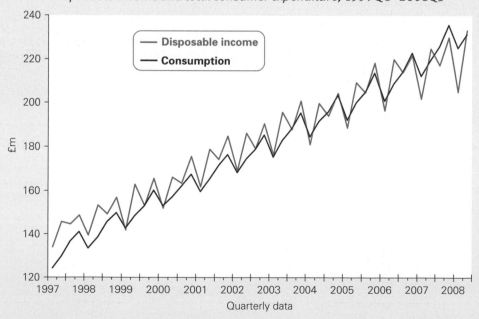

UK disposable income and total consumer expenditure, 1997Q1–2008Q3

Source: Financial Statistics (National Statistics, various years).

- *Relative prices*. If the prices of home-produced goods go up relative to the prices of imports, the level of imports will rise. The rate of exchange is a major influence here. The higher the rate of exchange, the cheaper will imports be and hence the more will be spent on them.
- *Tastes*. If consumer tastes shift towards foreign goods and services, imports will rise. For example, it might become more popular to go abroad for your holidays.
- *Relative quality*. If the quality of foreign goods and services increases relative to that of domestic goods and services, imports will rise.
- *The determinants of consumption*. Since imports of goods and services are part of *total* consumption (as opposed to C_d), the various determinants of consumption that we looked at on page 477 will also be determinants of imports.

The total withdrawals function

Remember that withdrawals consist of the three elements: net saving, net taxes and imports, all of which rise as national income rises. A withdrawals function along with the corresponding consumption of domestic goods function is shown in Figure 17.6.

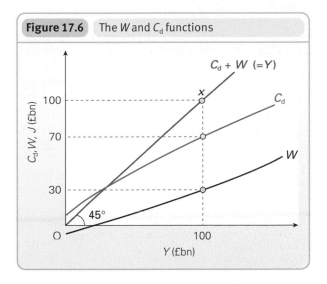

Figure 17.6 The W and C_d functions

CASE STUDIES AND APPLICATIONS

As well as there being a clear annual pattern for consumption and saving, patterns can also be observed over the years. For example, saving ratios tend to fluctuate with the business cycle. In booms the saving ratio tends to fall, especially if real interest rates are low and people are keen to spend, perhaps anticipating rising inflation. This can be seen in the boom of the late 1990s.

The table below shows that there are marked differences in saving ratios between countries. This is partly a reflection of national attitudes towards saving and spending, and partly a reflection of the encouragement given to saving by government and financial institutions.

Some of the changes in saving ratios reflect long-term trends. For example, Italy's and the USA's saving ratios have shown a long-term decline, as traditional beliefs in

the 'virtues' of saving have gradually been eroded. A similar decline in the saving ratio has emerged more recently in the UK (see graph), with more and more people being prepared to 'live on credit'. Other changes reflect changes in government policy. For example, Sweden after 1990 was concerned to prevent its exchange rate falling relative to EU currencies. This involved pursuing a policy of high interest rates, which had the effect of encouraging saving and discouraging borrowing (negative saving).

Comparing the saving ratios in France and New Zealand, what do the differences imply for the balance between government expenditure and taxation if both countries want to achieve similar rates of investment and want to maintain a balance between imports and exports?

Household saving (% of household disposable income)

	1987–91	1992–6	1997–2001	2002–6	2007–9[a]
Australia	7.9	5.4	2.6	−1.6	2.1
Belgium	16.1	18.6	14.4	14.0	10.6
France	7.4	10.2	11.0	10.6	12.4
Germany	13.2	11.8	10.1	10.9	10.8
Italy	23.8	19.7	11.4	10.7	6.8
Japan	13.8	12.4	9.6	5.5	2.8
Netherlands	13.5	14.3	10.4	10.3	6.9
New Zealand	2.6	−1.8	−4.4	−6.6	−6.7
Sweden	−0.1	9.4	4.1	8.3	8.0
UK	7.2	10.2	6.4	6.5	1.3
USA	7.1	5.4	2.9	1.2	1.2

[a] Year 2009 figures forecast.

Source: Based on data in *Economic Outlook* (Organisation for Economic Co-operation and Development [OECD], various years).

Note the relationship between the C_d and W curves. The steeper the slope of the one, the flatter the slope of the other. The reason for this is that C_d and W add up to total national income (Y):

$$Y = C_d + W$$

Since the 45° line measures $C_d + W$, the distance between the C_d function and the 45° line must equal withdrawals. Thus at point x, where national income is £100 billion and C_d is £70 billion, W must be £30 billion – the gap between C_d and the 45° line.

The marginal propensity to withdraw

The formula for the **marginal propensity to withdraw** (*mpw*) is as we would expect:

$$mpw = \Delta W / \Delta Y$$

The *mpw* is the slope of the withdrawals function. Note that, since $W = S + T + M$, *mpw* must equal *mps* + *mpt* + *mpm*. For example, if for any rise in national income, 1/10 were saved, 2/10 paid in net taxes, and 2/10 spent on imports, then 5/10 must be withdrawn.

Note also that, since $C_d + W = Y$, *mpc*$_d$ + *mpw* must add up to 1. For example, if the country spends, say, 3/5 of any rise in income on domestically produced goods, the remaining 2/5 must go on withdrawals.

 If the slope of the C_d function is 3/4, what is the slope of the W function?

Injections

In simple Keynesian theory, injections are assumed not to depend on the level of national income: they are *exogenously* determined. This means that the injections function is drawn as a horizontal straight line. Injections will be at a given level irrespective of the level of national income. The injections function is the vertical addition of the investment, government expenditure and export functions, each of which is a horizontal straight line.

The assumption that injections are independent of national income makes the theory simpler. (It is possible to drop this assumption, however, without destroying the theory.) But is the assumption sufficiently realistic? Let us examine each of the injections in turn.

Investment

There are four major determinants of investment.

Increased consumer demand. Investment is to provide extra capacity. This will only be necessary, therefore, if consumer demand increases. The bigger the increase in consumer demand, the more investment will be needed.

You might think that, since consumer demand depends on the level of national income, investment must too, and that therefore our assumption that investment is independent of national income is wrong. But we are not saying that investment depends on the *level* of consumer demand; rather it depends on *how much it has risen*. If income and consumer demand are high but *constant*, there will be no point in firms expanding their capacity: no point in investing.

The relationship between investment and *increased* consumer demand is examined by the 'accelerator theory'. We will look at this theory in section 17.4.

Expectations. Since investment is made in order to produce output for the future, investment must depend on firms' expectations about future market conditions.

The cost and efficiency of capital equipment. If the cost of capital equipment goes down or machines become more efficient, the return on investment will increase. Firms will invest more. Technological progress is an important determinant here.

The rate of interest. The higher the rate of interest, the more expensive it will be for firms to finance investment, and hence the less profitable will the investment be. Just how responsive total investment in the economy is to changes in interest rates is a highly controversial issue and we will return to it later.

So if these are the main determinants of investment, does it mean that investment is totally independent of the level of national income? Not quite. Replacement of worn-out or outdated equipment *will* depend on the level of national income. The higher the current level of national income, the greater will be the stock of capital and therefore the more will need replacing each year. It is also possible that, if the level of national income is high and firms' profits are

---

Definition

Marginal propensity to withdraw The proportion of an increase in national income that is withdrawn from the circular flow: $mpw = \Delta W / \Delta Y$, where $mpw = mps + mpt + mpm$.

high, they will be able to *afford* more investment. However, it is not a gross distortion of reality to assume that investment and the level of national income are independent, at least in the short run.

Government expenditure

Government expenditure in any year is independent of the level of national income. The reason is as follows. In the months preceding the Budget each year, spending departments make submissions about their needs in the coming year. These are discussed with the Treasury and a sum is allocated to each department. That then (excepting any unforeseen events) fixes government expenditure on goods and services for the following financial year.

Thus, again, for our purposes we can take government expenditure as independent of national income in the short term. Even if tax revenues turn out to be more or less than expected, this will not influence that year's government spending. The government can end up running either a budget surplus ($T > G$) or a budget deficit ($G > T$).

Over the longer term, however, government expenditure *will* depend on national income. The higher the level of national income, the higher is the amount of tax revenue that the government receives, and hence the more it can afford to spend. The governments of richer nations clearly spend much more than those of developing countries.

Exports

Exports are sold to people abroad, and thus depend largely on *their* incomes, not on incomes at home. Nevertheless, there are two indirect links between a country's national income and its exports:

- Via other countries' circular flows of income. If domestic incomes rise, more will be spent on imports. But this will cause a rise in other countries' incomes and lead them to buy more imports, part of which will be this country's exports.
- Via the exchange rate. A rise in domestic incomes will lead to a rise in imports. Other things being equal, this will lead to a depreciation in the exchange rate. This will make it cheaper for people in other countries to buy this country's exports. Export sales will rise.

However, it is useful in simple Keynesian models to assume that exports are determined independently of domestic national income.

Note that, although the injections function is assumed to be constant with respect to income and is drawn as a horizontal straight line, this does not mean that it will be constant *over time*. Investment can suddenly rise or virtually collapse as the confidence of businesspeople changes. Exports can change too with shifts in the exchange rate or with speculation. The injections line, then, is constantly shifting up and down.

Section summary

1. In the simple Keynesian model, equilibrium national income is where withdrawals equal injections, and where national income equals the total expenditure on domestic products: where $W = J$ and where $Y = E$.

2. The relationships between national income and the various components of the circular flow of income can be shown on a 45° line diagram. In the diagram, C, C_d and W are endogenous variables. Each one rises as income rises. The relationships can also be expressed in terms of marginal propensities. The marginal propensity is given by $\Delta V/\Delta Y$ (where V is the variable in question).

3. Apart from being determined by national income, consumption is determined by wealth, taxation, the availability and cost of credit, expectations about future prices and incomes, the distribution of income, tastes and attitudes, and the average age of durables. Consumption of domestic product (C_d) is total consumption minus imports of goods and services and minus indirect taxes and plus subsidies on goods and services.

4. Like consumption, withdrawals (S, T and M) vary with national income. Net saving is also determined by the various factors that determine consumption: if these factors cause consumption to rise, then, except in the

case of a cut in income taxes, they will cause saving to fall and vice versa. Net tax revenues, apart from being dependent on incomes, depend on the rates of tax and benefits that the government sets and how progressive or regressive they are. Imports depend on the relative prices and quality of domestic and foreign goods, total consumption and tastes.

5. In the simple Keynesian model, injections are assumed to be exogenous variables. They are therefore drawn as a horizontal straight line in the 45° line diagram. In practice, there will be *some* relationship between injections and national income. Replacement investment depends to some extent on the level of output; government expenditure depends to some extent on the level of tax revenues; and exports depend on exchange rates and foreign incomes, both of which will depend on the level of imports. Nevertheless, in the short run it is reasonable to assume that injections are independent of national income.

6. The determinants of investment include the rate of interest, the size of increases in consumer demand, the cost and efficiency of capital equipment, and expectations about prices, consumer demand, interest rates and other costs.

BOX 17.3   BUSINESS EXPECTATIONS AND THEIR EFFECT ON INVESTMENT

Recent European experience

In the boom years of the late 1980s, business optimism was widespread throughout Europe. Investment was correspondingly high, and with it there was a high rate of economic growth.

Surveys of European business expectations in the early 1990s, however, told a very different story. Pessimism was rife. Europe was in the grip of a recession, and output was falling (see Table (a)). Along with this decline in output and deteriorating levels of business and consumer confidence, there was a significant fall in investment.

Table (b) gives the indicator of industrial confidence in various EU countries and the indicator for the EU as a whole is plotted in Figure (a). The indicator shows the percentage excess of confident over pessimistic replies to business questionnaires: a negative figure means that there was a higher percentage of pessimistic responses. You can see that the indicator was strongly negative in 1993.

Not only was the total level of investment falling, but the proportion of that investment used to expand capacity was also falling. By contrast, the proportion of investment devoted to rationalisation schemes had risen. Firms were increasingly having to look for ways of cutting their costs through restructuring their operations. One of the consequences of this was a growth in structural unemployment (as well as in demand-deficient unemployment).

After 1993, pessimism began to decrease, and by the last quarter of 1994 the average EU industrial confidence indicator became positive. From 1995 to 2000, the indicator was mainly positive, as the European economy experienced growth rates averaging 2.6 per cent. Investment grew rapidly. Notice how the industrial confidence indicator mirrored the rate of economic growth. For example, both the rate of growth and the confidence indicator fell in 1996.

But then, in 2001, with the world economy slowing down and the 11 September attack on the World Trade Center in New York, industrial confidence plummeted, and so did investment, only to recover again as economic growth and business confidence returned.

In 2007/8, however, with rising oil and food prices, with less credit available (the 'credit crunch') and talk of an impending recession, industrial confidence began to fall once more. Then as recession became a reality and turned out to be much worse than had been forecast, so confidence took a nosedive.

Another useful indicator of the state of the economy is the degree of industrial capacity utilisation. The lower this is, the greater the slack in the economy. Figure (b) shows the percentage capacity utilisation in manufacturing industry in the EU. You can see how this mirrors industrial confidence (and hence economic growth).

If the economy expands and firms respond by investing, there will be a time lag before this can be

(a) *Macroeconomic indicators for the EU-15 countries*

	1989	1990	1991	1992	1993	1994	1995	1996	1998	2000	2001	2002	2003	2004	2005	2006	2007	2008
GDP growth (%)	3.5	3.0	1.8	1.1	−0.4	2.8	2.4	1.6	2.9	3.8	1.9	1.1	1.2	2.3	1.7	2.8	2.6	1.0
Investment (% change)	6.9	3.6	−0.6	−0.4	−5.8	2.8	2.8	1.9	7.1	4.7	0.8	−0.6	1.3	3.0	3.0	5.6	4.7	2.0
Unemployment (%)	7.8	7.3	7.8	8.9	10.1	10.5	10.1	10.2	9.3	7.7	7.2	7.6	7.9	8.0	8.1	7.7	7.0	7.3

Note: EU-15 = the 15 members of the EU prior to its expansion in 2004.
Source: Based on data in *Statistical Annex of the European Economy* (Commission of the European Communities, 2007).

(b) *Industrial confidence indicator*

Country	1989	1991	1993	1995	1996	1998	2000	2001	2002	2003	2004	2005	2006	2007	2008
Belgium	0	−15	−29	−9	−18	−8	2	−14	−12	−15	−3	−9	2	1	−8
Denmark	4	−8	−12	5	−8	−1	6	−2	−4	−6	4	0	8	5	−8
France	8	−20	−35	−2	−18	5	12	−4	−9	−9	−3	−8	−2	2	−11
Germany	5	0	−34	−6	−21	−5	−2	−15	−18	−17	−8	−10	4	7	−8
Ireland	10	−9	−13	7	−1	3	10	−8	−7	−9	−4	−4	4	3	−12
Italy	8	−13	−17	6	−12	0	12	−3	−3	−4	−2	−5	5	3	−9
Netherlands	1	−5	−10	2	−2	2	4	−4	−3	−8	−3	−2	4	5	−1
UK	−2	−32	−11	3	−5	−16	−7	−15	−15	−17	−2	−10	−6	3	−11
EU	4	−14	−26	−1	−14	−3	4	−9	−11	−11	−4	−7	1	5	−9

Source: Based on data in *Business and Consumer Surveys* (Commission of the European Communities, 2008).

(a) *Indicator of industrial confidence in the EU*

(b) *Indicator of the percentage of industrial capacity utilisation in the EU*

Source: Based on data from *Business and Consumer Surveys* (Commission of the European Communities, 2007).

reflected in increased industrial capacity, since capital takes some time to build and/or install. In the meantime, the percentage utilisation of capacity could expand very rapidly, as existing slack is taken up. Then, as new capacity comes on line, the percentage capacity utilisation figure could rapidly cease rising, or even fall, depending on the rate of growth of consumer demand.

1. *How is the existence of surveys of business confidence likely to affect firms' expectations and actions?*
2. *Why, if the growth in output slows down (but is still positive), is investment likely to fall (i.e. the growth in investment be negative)? If you look at Table (a), you will see that this happened in 1991 and 1992 and in 2002. (We will examine this question in section 17.4 when we look at the accelerator theory.)*

17.2 THE DETERMINATION OF NATIONAL INCOME

Equilibrium national income

We can now put the various functions together on one diagram. This is done in Figure 17.7. Note that there is a new line on the diagram that we have not looked at so far. This is the aggregate expenditure (i.e. the aggregate demand) function. We defined aggregate expenditure as $C_d + J$. Graphically, then, the E function is simply the C_d function shifted upwards by the amount of J.

Equilibrium national income can be found in either of two ways.

$W = J$

Withdrawals equal injections at point x in Figure 17.7. Equilibrium national income is thus Y_e. If national income were below this level, say at Y_1, injections would exceed withdrawals (by an amount $a - b$). This additional net expenditure injected into the economy would encourage firms to produce more and hence cause national income to rise. But as people's incomes rose, so they would save more, pay more taxes and buy more imports. In other words, withdrawals would rise. There would be a movement up along the W function. This process would continue until $W = J$ at point x.

If, on the other hand, national income were at Y_2, withdrawals would exceed injections (by an amount $c - d$). This deficiency of demand would cause production and hence national income to fall. As it did so, there would be a movement down along the W function until again point x was reached.

$Y = E$

If $W = J$, then $C_d + W = C_d + J$. In other words, another way of describing equilibrium is where national income ($Y \equiv C_d + W$) equals aggregate expenditure ($E \equiv C_d + J$).

This is shown at point z in Figure 17.7. This is where the expenditure function ($C_d + J$) crosses the 45° line ($C_d + W$).

If aggregate expenditure exceeded national income, say at Y_1, there would be excess demand in the economy (of $e - f$). In other words, people would be buying more than was currently being produced. Firms would find their stocks dwindling and would therefore increase their level of production. In doing so, they would employ more factors of production. National income would thus rise. As it did so, consumption and hence aggregate expenditure would rise. There would be a movement up along the expenditure function. But because not all the extra income would be consumed (i.e. some would be withdrawn), expenditure would rise less quickly than income (the E line is flatter than the Y line). As income rises towards Y_e, the gap between Y and E gets smaller. Once point z is reached, $Y = E$. There is then no further tendency for income to rise.

If national income exceeded national expenditure, at say Y_2, there would be insufficient demand for the goods and services currently being produced. Firms would find their stocks of unsold goods building up. They would thus respond by producing less and employing fewer factors of production. National income would thus fall and go on falling until Y_e was reached.

 Why is it the case that $a - b = e - f$, and $c - d = g - h$?

The multiplier: the withdrawals and injections approach

When injections rise (and continue at the higher level), this will cause national income to rise. But by how much?

In fact, national income will rise by *more* than injections: Y rises by a *multiple* of the rise in J.

$$\Delta Y > \Delta J$$

The number of times that the increase in income (ΔY) is greater than the increase in injections (ΔJ) is known as the *multiplier* (k).

$$k = \Delta Y / \Delta J$$

Thus if a £10 billion rise in injections caused a £30 billion rise in national income, the multiplier would be 3.

KI 34
p463

Figure 17.7 Equilibrium national income

Definition

(Injections) multiplier The number of times by which a rise in income exceeds the rise in injections that caused it: $k = \Delta Y / \Delta J$.

What causes the multiplier effect? The answer is that, when extra spending is injected into the economy, it will then stimulate further spending, which in turn will stimulate yet more spending and so on. For example, if firms decide to invest more, this will lead to more people being employed and hence more incomes being paid to households. Households will then spend part of this increased income on domestically produced goods (the remainder will be withdrawn). This increased consumption will encourage firms to produce more goods to meet the demand. Firms will thus employ more people and other factors of production. This leads to even more incomes being paid out to households. Consumption will thus increase yet again. And so the process continues.

The multiplier is an example of an important principle in economics: that of *cumulative causation* (see page 463). This is the last of our fifteen threshold concepts.

Note that in this simple Keynesian theory we are assuming that prices are constant (i.e. that there is no inflation) and hence that any increase in income is a *real* increase in income matched by extra production. So when we talk about extra injections into the economy causing extra

TC 12
p395

spending, it is the extra *output* that this spending generates that we are concerned with. If the multiplier were 3, for example, this would mean that an injection of £1 of expenditure into the economy would lead to an increase in *output* of £3.

But even if there were limitless resources, an increase in injections would not cause national income to go on rising for ever: the multiplier is not infinite. Each time people receive extra income, they will save some of it, pay some of it in taxes and spend some of it on imports: in other words, withdrawals will rise. Eventually, as income goes on rising, all the extra injections will have leaked away into the three withdrawals. At that point, the multiplier process will have ceased; a new equilibrium will have been reached.

What determines the size of the multiplier? This can be shown graphically using either withdrawals and injections or income and expenditure. The income/expenditure approach will be examined shortly. For now we will use the withdrawals/injections approach. This is illustrated in Figure 17.8.

Assume that injections rise from J_1 to J_2. Equilibrium will move from point a to point b. Income will thus rise from Y_{e_1} to Y_{e_2}. The multiplier is therefore

$$\frac{Y_{e_2} - Y_{e_1}}{J_2 - J_1} \left(\text{i.e. } \frac{\Delta Y}{\Delta J} \right)$$

It can be seen that the size of the multiplier depends on the slope of the W function. Remember that the slope of

---

Definition

Principle of cumulative causation An initial event can cause an ultimate effect that is much larger.

THRESHOLD CONCEPT 15   **CUMULATIVE CAUSATION**   THINKING LIKE AN ECONOMIST

Economic effects can snowball

Once an economy starts to expand, growth is likely to gather pace. Once it starts slowing down, this can gather pace too and end up in a recession. There are many other examples in economics of things getting 'onto a roll'. A rising stock market is likely to breed confidence in investors and encourage them to buy. This 'destabilising speculation' (see pages 73–4) will then lead to further rises in share prices. A fall in stock market prices can lead to panic selling of shares. The booming stock market of the late 1990s and the falls in the early 2000s are good examples of this.

This phenomenon of things building on themselves is known as 'cumulative causation' and occurs throughout market economies. It is a *threshold concept* because it helps us to understand the built-in instability in many parts of the economy and in many economic situations.

Central to explaining cumulative causation is people's psychology. Good news creates confidence and this optimism causes people to behave in ways that build on the good news. Bad news creates pessimism and this leads to people behaving cautiously, which tends to reinforce the bad news.

Take two regions of an economy: an expanding region and a declining region. The expansion of the first region encourages workers to move there in search of jobs. The

optimism in the area causes long-term investment as firms have confidence in an expanding market. This encourages house building and other forms of investment in infrastructure and services. And so the region thrives. Meanwhile the declining region suffers from deprivation as unemployment rises. This encourages people to move away and businesses to close. There is a further decline in jobs and further migration from the region.

Cumulative causation does not just occur at a macro level. If a company is successful, it is likely to find raising extra finance easier; it may be able to use its power more effectively to out-compete rivals. Giant companies, such as Microsoft, can gain all sorts of economies of scale, including network economies (see Case Study 6.4 in MyEconLab), all of which help the process of building their power base. Success breeds success.

1. *How might cumulative causation work at the level of an individual firm that is losing market share?*
2. *Are there any market forces that work against cumulative causation? For instance, how might markets help to arrest the decline of a depressed region of the economy and slow down the expansion of a booming region*

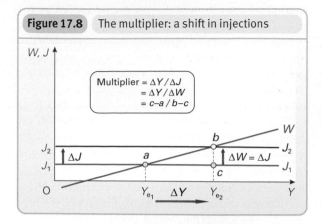

Figure 17.8 The multiplier: a shift in injections

the W function is given by the marginal propensity to withdraw ($\Delta W/\Delta Y$). The less steep the line (and hence the lower the *mpw*), the bigger will be the rise in national income: the bigger will be the multiplier.

> ? Try this simple test of the above argument. Draw a series of W lines of different slopes, all crossing the J line at the same point. Now draw a second J line above the first. Mark the original equilibrium and all the new ones corresponding to each of the W lines. It should be quite obvious that the flatter the W line is, the more Y will have increased.

The point here is that the less is withdrawn each time extra income is generated, the more will be recirculated and hence the bigger will be the rise in national income. The size of the multiplier thus varies inversely with the size of the *mpw*. The bigger the *mpw*, the smaller the multiplier; the smaller the *mpw*, the bigger the multiplier. In fact, the **multiplier formula** simply gives the multiplier as the inverse of the *mpw*:

$$k = 1/mpw$$

or alternatively, since $mpw + mpc_d = 1$ and thus $mpw = 1 - mpc_d$,

$$k = 1/(1 - mpc_d)$$

Thus if the *mpw* were $^1/_4$ (and hence the mpc_d were $^3/_4$), the multiplier would be 4. So if J increased by £10 billion, Y would increase by £40 billion.

But why is the multiplier given by the formula $1/mpw$? This can be illustrated by referring to Figure 17.8. The *mpw* is the slope of the W line. In the diagram, this is given by the amount $(b - c)/(c - a)$. The multiplier is defined as

$\Delta Y/\Delta J$. In the diagram, this is the amount $(c - a)/(b - c)$. But this is merely the inverse of the *mpw*. Thus the multiplier equals $1/mpw$.[1]

*LOOKING AT THE MATHS

The multiplier can be expressed as the first derivative of national income with respect to injections.

$$k = \frac{dY}{dJ}$$

Since in equilibrium $J = W$, it is also the first derivative of income with respect to withdrawals. Thus

$$k = \frac{dY}{dW}$$

The marginal propensity to withdraw (i.e. the slope of the withdrawals curve) is found by differentiating the withdrawals function:

$$mpw = \frac{dW}{dY} = \frac{1}{k}$$

Thus

$$k = \frac{1}{mpw}$$

The algebra of the multiplier is explored in MyEconLab in Maths Case 17.1, which does not use calculus, and Maths Case 17.2, which does.

A shift in withdrawals

A multiplied rise in income can also be caused by a fall in withdrawals. This is illustrated in Figure 17.9.

The withdrawals function shifts from W_1 to W_2. This means that, at the old equilibrium of Y_{e_1}, injections now exceed withdrawals by an amount $a - b$. This will cause national income to rise until a new equilibrium is reached

Figure 17.9 The multiplier: a shift in withdrawals

Definition

(Injections) multiplier formula The formula for the multiplier: $k = 1/mpw$ or $1/(1 - mpc_d)$.

[1] In some elementary textbooks, the formula for the multiplier is given as $1/mps$. The reason for this is that it is assumed (for simplicity) that there is only one withdrawal, namely saving, and only one injection, namely investment. As soon as this assumption is dropped, $1/mps$ becomes the wrong formula.

at Y_{e_2} where $J = W_2$. Thus a downward shift of the withdrawals function of $a - b(\Delta W)$ causes a rise in national income of $c - a(\Delta Y)$. The multiplier in this case is given by $\Delta Y/\Delta W$: in other words, $(c - a)/(a - b)$. Note that the multiplier is based on the *initial* fall in withdrawals. Once the multiplier effect has worked through, withdrawals will have risen back to equal injections at point c.

 Why is the 'withdrawals multiplier' strictly speaking a negative figure?

The multiplier: the income and expenditure approach

The multiplier can also be demonstrated using the income/expenditure approach. Assume in Figure 17.10 that the aggregate expenditure function shifts to E_2. This could be due either to a rise in one or more of the three injections, or to a rise in the consumption of domestically produced goods (and hence a fall in withdrawals). Equilibrium national income will rise from Y_{e_1} to Y_{e_2}.

What is the size of the multiplier? The initial rise in expenditure was $b - a$. The resulting rise in income is $c - a$. The multiplier is thus $(c - a)/(b - a)$.

The effect is illustrated in Table 17.2. Consumption of domestic product (C_d) is shown in column 2 for various

levels of national income (Y). For every £100 billion rise in Y, C_d rises by £80 billion. Thus the $mpc_d = 0.8$. Assume initially that injections equal £100 billion at all levels of national income. Aggregate expenditure (column 4) equals $C_d + J$. Equilibrium national income is £700 billion. This is where $Y = E$.

Now assume that injections rise by £20 billion to £120 billion. Aggregate expenditure is now shown in the final column and is £20 billion higher than before at each level of national income (Y). At the original equilibrium national income (£700 billion), aggregate expenditure is now £720 billion. This excess of E over Y of £20 billion will generate extra incomes and continue doing so as long as E remains above Y. Equilibrium is reached at £800 billion, where once more $Y = E$. The initial rise in aggregate expenditure of £20 billion (from £700bn to £720bn) has led to an eventual rise in both national income and aggregate expenditure of £100 billion. The multiplier is thus 5 (i.e. £100bn/£20bn). But this is equal to $1/(1 - 0.8)$ or $1/(1 - mpc_d)$.

 1. *What determines the slope of the E function?*
2. *How does the slope of the E function affect the size of the multiplier? (Try drawing diagrams with E functions of different slopes and see what happens when they shift.)*

The multiplier: a numerical illustration

The multiplier effect does not work instantaneously. When there is an increase in injections, whether investment, government expenditure or exports, it takes time before this brings about the full multiplied rise in national income.

Consider the following example. Let us assume for simplicity that the *mpw* is $^1/_2$. This will give an mpc_d of $^1/_2$ also. Let us also assume that investment (an injection) rises by £160 million and stays at the new higher level. Table 17.3 shows what will happen.

As firms purchase more machines and construct more factories, the incomes of those who produce machines and those who work in the construction industry will increase by £160 million. When this extra income is received by households, whether as wages or profits, half will be withdrawn ($mpw = ^1/_2$) and half will be spent on the goods and services of domestic firms. This increase in consumption

Figure 17.10 The multiplier: a shift in the expenditure function

Multiplier = $\Delta Y/\Delta J$
= $c - a/b - a$

Table 17.2 The effect of an increase in aggregate expenditure (£ billions)

Y	C_d	J (old)	E (old)	J (new)	E (new)
500	440	100	540	120	560
600	520	100	620	120	640
700	600	100	**700**	120	720
800	680	100	780	120	**800**
900	760	100	860	120	880

Table 17.3 The multiplier 'round'

Round	ΔJ(£m)	ΔY(£m)	ΔC_d(£m)	ΔW(£m)
1	160	160	80	80
2	–	80	40	40
3	–	40	20	20
4	–	20	10	10
5	–	10	5	5
6	–	5	.	.
.		.	.	.
$1 \rightarrow \infty$		320	160	160

thus generates additional incomes for firms of £80 million over and above the initial £160 million (which is still being generated in each time period). When this additional £80 million of incomes is received by households (round 2), again half will be withdrawn and half will go on consumption of domestic product. This increases national income by a further £40 million (round 3). And so each time we go around the circular flow of income, national income increases, but by only half as much as the previous time ($mpc_d = \frac{1}{2}$).

If we add up the additional income generated in each round (assuming the process goes on indefinitely), the total will be £320 million: twice the rise in injections. The multiplier is 2.

The bigger the mpc_d (and hence the smaller the mpw), the more will expenditure rise each time national income rises, and hence the bigger will be the multiplier.

*The multiplier: some qualifications

(This section examines the multiplier formula in more detail. You may omit it without affecting the flow of the argument.)

Some possible errors can easily be made in calculating the value of the multiplier. These often arise from a confusion over the meaning of terms.

The marginal propensity to consume domestic product

Remember the formula for the multiplier:

$$k = 1/(1 - mpc_d)$$

It is important to realise just what is meant by the mpc_d. It is the proportion of a rise in households' gross (i.e. pre-tax-and-benefit) income that actually accrues to domestic firms. It thus excludes that part of consumption that is spent on imports and that part which is paid to the government in VAT and other indirect taxes.

Up to now we have also been basing the mpc on gross income. As Case Study 17.1 in MyEconLab shows, however, the mpc is often based on *disposable* (i.e. post-tax-and-

Table 17.4 Calculating the mpc_d

(£m)	ΔY	$-$	ΔT_Y	$=$	ΔY_{dis}		
	100		20		80		

(£m)	ΔY_{dis}	$-$	ΔS	$=$	ΔC		
	80		10		70		

(£m)	ΔC	$-$	ΔT_E	$-$	ΔM	$=$	ΔC_d
	70		7		13		50

benefit) income. After all, when consumers decide how much to spend, it is their disposable income rather than their gross income that they will consider. So how do we derive the mpc_d (based on gross income) from the mpc based on disposable income (mpc')? To do this, we must use the following formula:

$$mpc_d = mpc'(1 - t_E)(1 - t_Y) - mpm$$

where t_Y is the marginal rate of income tax, and t_E is the marginal rate of expenditure tax.

To illustrate this formula consider the following effects of an increase in national income of £100 million. It is assumed that $t_Y = 20$ per cent, $t_E = 10$ per cent and $mpc = 7/8$. It is also assumed that the mps (from gross income) = 1/10 and the mpm (from gross income) = 13/100. Table 17.4 sets out the figures.

Gross income rises by £100 million. Of this, £20 million is taken in income tax ($t_Y = 20$ per cent). This leaves a rise in disposable income of £80 million. Of this, £10 million is saved ($mps = 1/10$) and £70 million is spent. Of this, £7 million goes in expenditure taxes ($t_E = 10$ per cent) and £13 million leaks abroad ($mpm = 13/100$). This leaves £50 million that goes on the consumption of domestic product ($mpc_d = 50/100 = \frac{1}{2}$). Substituting these figures in the above formula gives:

$$\begin{aligned} mpc_d &= mpc(1 - t_E)(1 - t_Y) - mpm \\ &= \tfrac{7}{8}(1 - \tfrac{1}{10})(1 - \tfrac{2}{10}) - \tfrac{13}{100} \\ &= (\tfrac{7}{8} \times \tfrac{9}{10} \times \tfrac{8}{10}) - \tfrac{13}{100} \\ &= \tfrac{63}{100} - \tfrac{13}{100} = \tfrac{50}{100} = \tfrac{1}{2} \end{aligned}$$

BOX 17.4	**DERIVING THE MULTIPLIER FORMULA**	**EXPLORING ECONOMICS**

An algebraic proof

The formula for the multiplier can be derived using simple algebra. First of all, remember how we defined the multiplier:

$$k \equiv \Delta Y/\Delta J \qquad (1)$$

and the marginal propensity to withdraw:

$$mpw \equiv \Delta W/\Delta Y \qquad (2)$$

If we now take the inverse of equation (2), we get

$$1/mpw \equiv \Delta Y/\Delta W \qquad (3)$$

But in equilibrium we know that $W = J$. Hence any change in injections must be matched by a change in withdrawals and vice versa, to ensure that withdrawals and injections remain equal. Thus

$$\Delta W = \Delta J \qquad (4)$$

Substituting equation (4) in equation (3) gives

$$1/mpw = \Delta Y/\Delta J \, (= k)$$

i.e. the multiplier equals $1/mpw$.

Note that the mpc_d, mps, mpm and mpt are all based on the rise in *gross* income, not disposable income. They are 50/100, 10/100, 13/100 and 27/100 respectively.

Maths Case 17.3 in MyEconLab derives the multiplier formula when the propensities to consume, save and import are all based on *disposable* as opposed to gross income.

Assume that the rate of income tax is 15 per cent, the rate of expenditure tax is $12\frac{1}{2}$ per cent, the mps is $\frac{1}{20}$, the mpm is $\frac{1}{8}$ and the mpc (from disposable income) is $\frac{16}{17}$. What is the mpc_d? Construct a table like Table 17.4 assuming again that national income rises by £100 million.

The effects of changes in injections and withdrawals on other injections and withdrawals

In order to work out the size of a multiplied rise or fall in income, it is necessary to know first the size of the initial *total* change in injections and/or withdrawals. The trouble is that a change in one injection or withdrawal can affect others. For example, a rise in income taxes will reduce not only consumption, but also saving, imports and the revenue from indirect taxes. Thus the total rise in withdrawals will be *less* than the rise in income taxes.

Give some other examples of changes in one injection or withdrawal that can affect others.

The relationship between the 45° line diagram and the aggregate demand and supply diagram

We have used two diagrams to show the determination of equilibrium national income: the aggregate demand and supply diagram and the 45° line diagram. The first shows aggregate demand dependent on the price level. The second shows aggregate demand (i.e. aggregate expenditure (*E*)) dependent on the level of national income. Figure 17.11 shows the multiplier effect simultaneously on the two diagrams. Initially, equilibrium is at Y_{e_1} where aggregate

Figure 17.11 Showing the multiplier effect on the 45° line and *AD/AS* diagrams

demand equals aggregate supply and where the aggregate expenditure line crosses the 45° line.

Now assume that there is an autonomous increase in expenditure. For example, increased business confidence results in increased investment. In Figure 17.11(b), the *E* line shifts to E_2. There is a multiplied rise in income to Y_{e_2}. In Figure 17.11(a), the aggregate supply curve is drawn as a horizontal straight line between Y_{e_1} and Y_{e_2}. This means that an increase in aggregate demand from AD_1 to AD_2 will raise income to Y_{e_2} with no increase in prices.

But what if the economy is approaching full employment? Surely we cannot expect the multiplier process to work in the same way as when there is plenty of slack in the economy? In this case, the aggregate supply curve will be upward sloping. This means that an increase in aggregate demand will raise prices and not just output. How do we analyse this with the 45° line diagram? We examine this in the next section.

TC 15 p487

Section summary

1. Equilibrium national income can be shown on the 45° line diagram at the point where $W = J$ and $Y = E$.

2. If there is an increase in injections (or a reduction in withdrawals), there will be a multiplied rise in national income. The multiplier is defined as $\Delta Y/\Delta J$.

3. The size of the multiplier depends on the marginal propensity to withdraw (*mpw*). The smaller the *mpw*, the less will be withdrawn each time incomes are generated round the circular flow, and thus the more will go round again as *additional* demand for domestic product. The multiplier formula is $k = 1/mpw$ or $1/(1 - mpc_d)$.

*4. When working out the size of the multiplier, you must be careful to identify clearly the mpc_d (which is based on *gross* income and only includes expenditure that actually accrues to domestic firms) and not to confuse it with the *mpc* based on *disposable* income (which includes consumption of imports and the payment of indirect taxes). It is also necessary to identify the *full* changes in injections and withdrawals on which any multiplier effect is based.

5. The multiplier effect can also be illustrated on an aggregate demand and supply diagram.

BOX 17.5 **THE PARADOX OF THRIFT**

EXPLORING ECONOMICS

When prudence is folly

The classical economists argued that saving was a national virtue. More saving would lead via lower interest rates to more investment and faster growth. Keynes was at pains to show the opposite. Saving, far from being a national virtue, could be a national vice.

Remember the fallacy of composition (see Box 3.7 on page 84). Just because something is good for an individual, it does not follow that it is good for society as a whole. This fallacy applies to saving. If individuals save more, they will increase their consumption possibilities in the future. If society saves more, however, this may *reduce* its future income and consumption. As people save more, they will spend less. Firms will thus produce less. There will thus be a multiplied *fall* in income. The phenomenon of higher saving leading to *lower* national income is known as 'the paradox of thrift'.

But this is not all. Far from the extra saving encouraging more investment, the lower consumption will *discourage* firms from investing. If investment falls, the *J* line will shift downwards. There will then be a further multiplied fall in national income. (This response of investment to changes in consumer demand is examined in section 17.4 under the 'accelerator theory'.)

The paradox of thrift had in fact been recognised before Keynes, and Keynes himself referred to various complaints about 'underconsumption' that had been made back In the sixteenth and seventeenth centuries:

> In 1598 Laffemas . . . denounced the objectors to the use of French silks on the grounds that all purchasers of French luxury goods created a livelihood for the poor, whereas the miser caused them to die in distress. In 1662 Petty justified 'entertainments, magnificent shews, triumphal arches, etc.', on the ground that their costs flowed back into the pockets of brewers, bakers, tailors, shoemakers and so forth . . . In 1695 Cary argued that if everybody spent more, all would obtain larger incomes 'and might then live more plentifully'.[1]

But despite these early recognitions of the danger of underconsumption, the belief that saving would increase the prosperity of the nation was central to classical economic thought.

 Is an increase in saving ever desirable?

---

[1] J. M. Keynes, *The General Theory of Employment, Interest and Money* (Macmillan, 1967), pp. 358–9.

17.3 THE SIMPLE KEYNESIAN ANALYSIS OF UNEMPLOYMENT AND INFLATION

'Full-employment' national income

The simple Keynesian theory assumes that there is a maximum level of national output, and hence real income, that can be obtained at any one time. If the equilibrium level of income is at this level, there will be no deficiency of aggregate demand and hence no disequilibrium unemployment. This level of income is referred to as the *full-employment level of national income*. (In practice, there would still be some unemployment at this level because of equilibrium unemployment – structural, frictional and seasonal.)

Governments of the 1950s, 1960s and early 1970s aimed to achieve this full-employment income (Y_F), if inflation and the balance of payments permitted. To do this, they attempted to manipulate the level of aggregate demand.

This approach was also adopted by the George W. Bush administration in the USA in 2001 and again in 2007/8, when attempts were made to stimulate aggregate demand through the use of fiscal and monetary policy in order to stimulate the US economy and prevent it falling into recession. These policies were then used in earnest in late 2008 and in 2009 by many countries around the world to combat a deepening recession. For example, the incoming Obama administration introduced a massive stimulus package of $787 billion (5.7 per cent of US GDP).

The deflationary gap

If the equilibrium level of national income (Y_e) is below the full-employment level (Y_F), there will be excess capacity in the economy and hence demand-deficient unemployment.

There will be what is known as a *deflationary* or *recessionary gap*. This is illustrated in Figure 17.12.

Definitions

Full-employment level of national income The level of national income at which there is no deficiency of demand.

Deflationary or recessionary gap The shortfall of national expenditure below national income (and injections below withdrawals) at the full-employment level of national income.

Figure 17.12 The deflationary (recessionary) gap

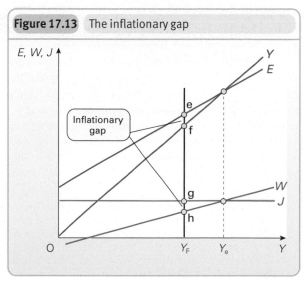

Figure 17.13 The inflationary gap

The full-employment level of national income (Y_F) is represented by the vertical line. The equilibrium level of national income is Y_e, where $W = J$ and $Y = E$. The deflationary gap is $a - b$: namely, the amount that the E line is below the 45° line at the full-employment level of income (Y_F). It is also $c - d$: the amount that injections fall short of withdrawals at the full-employment level of income.

Note that the size of the deflationary gap is *less* than the amount by which Y_e falls short of Y_F. This provides another illustration of the multiplier. If injections were raised by $c - d$, income would rise by $Y_F - Y_e$. The multiplier is thus given by

$$\frac{Y_F - Y_e}{c - d}$$

In this simple Keynesian model, then, the cure for demand-deficient unemployment is to close the deflationary gap. This could be achieved by an expansionary *fiscal* policy of increasing government expenditure or lowering taxes, or by an expansionary *monetary* policy of reducing interest rates and increasing the amount of money in the economy, thereby encouraging extra consumption and investment. Either way, if the deflationary gap is successfully closed, there will be a multiplied rise in income of $Y_F - Y_e$. Equilibrium national income will be restored to the full-employment level.

The inflationary gap

If, at the full-employment level of income, aggregate expenditure exceeds national income, there will be a problem of *excess* demand. Y_e will be above Y_F. The problem is that Y_F represents a real ceiling to output. In the short run, real national income *cannot* expand beyond this point.[1] Y_e cannot be reached. The result will therefore be demand-pull inflation.[2]

This situation involves an ***inflationary gap***. This is the amount by which aggregate expenditure exceeds national income or injections exceed withdrawals at the full-employment level of national income. This is illustrated by the gaps $e - f$ and $g - h$ in Figure 17.13.

To eliminate this inflation, the inflationary gap must be closed by either raising withdrawals or lowering injections or some combination of the two until Y_e equals Y_F. This can be done by a deliberate government policy of deflation. This could be either a contractionary *fiscal* policy of lowering government expenditure or raising taxes, or a contractionary *monetary* policy of raising interest rates and reducing the amount of money in the economy.

Even if the government does not actively pursue a deflationary policy, the inflationary gap may still close automatically. If the rich are better able than the poor to defend themselves against inflation, there will be a redistribution from the poor to the rich. But the rich tend to have a higher marginal propensity to save than the poor. Thus saving will rise and consumption will fall. This will swing the W line up and the E line down, thus narrowing the inflationary gap.

[1] Except with increased overtime working. In this simple model, we assume that this is not possible.

[2] Note that the horizontal axis in the 45° line diagram represents *real* national income. If incomes were to rise by, say, 10 per cent but prices also rose by 10 per cent, real income would not have risen at all. People could not buy any more than before. In such a case, there will have been no rightward movement along the horizontal axis.

Definition

Inflationary gap The excess of national expenditure over income (and injections over withdrawals) at the full-employment level of national income.

Inflation will also tend to worsen the balance of payments. Higher money incomes at home will lead to more imports being purchased. Higher domestic prices will lead to fewer exports being sold and more imports being bought in preference to the now dearer home-produced goods. The effect of this will be to shift the W line up and the J and E lines down, thus helping to close the inflationary gap.

Finally, as money incomes go up, people will tend to find themselves paying higher rates of tax (unless the government increases tax bands and allowances in line with inflation). This will shift the W line up and the E line down.

The present level of a country's exports is £12 billion; investment is £2 billion; government expenditure is £4 billion; total consumer spending (not C_d) is £36 billion; imports are £12 billion; and expenditure taxes are £2 billion. The economy is currently in equilibrium. It is estimated that an income of £50 billion is necessary to generate full employment. The mps is 0.1, the mpt is 0.05 and the mpm is 0.1.
(a) Is there an inflationary or deflationary gap in this situation?
(b) What is the size of the gap? (Don't confuse this with the difference between Y_e and Y_F.)
(c) What would be the appropriate government policies to close this gap?

Unemployment and inflation at the same time

The simple analysis of the preceding pages implies that the aggregate supply curve looks like AS_1 in Figure 17.14. Up to Y_F, output and employment can rise with no rise in prices at all. The deflationary gap is being closed. At Y_F no further rises in output are possible. Any further rise in aggregate demand is entirely reflected in higher prices. An inflationary gap opens. In other words, this implies that either inflation *or* unemployment can occur, but not both simultaneously.

Two important qualifications need to be made to this analysis to explain the occurrence of both unemployment *and* inflation at the same time.

First, there are *other* types of inflation and unemployment not caused by an excess or deficiency of aggregate demand: for example, cost-push and expectations-generated inflation; frictional and structural unemployment.

Thus, even if a government could manipulate national income so as to get Y_e and Y_F to coincide, this would not eliminate all inflation and unemployment – only demand-pull inflation and demand-deficient unemployment. Keynesians argue, therefore, that governments should use a whole package of policies, each tailored to the specific type of problem. But certainly one of the most important of these policies will be the management of aggregate demand.

Second, not all firms operate with the same degree of slack. Thus a rise in aggregate demand can lead to *both* a reduction in unemployment *and* a rise in prices: some firms responding to the rise in demand by taking up slack and hence increasing output; other firms, having little or no slack, responding by raising prices; others doing both. Similarly, labour markets have different degrees of slack and therefore the rise in demand will lead to various mixes of higher wages and lower unemployment. Thus the AS curve will look like AS_2 in Figure 17.14.

How does the above argument about firms' responses to a rise in demand relate to the shape of their marginal cost curves?

These types of argument were used to justify a belief in a downward-sloping Phillips curve (see Box 15.5) by the majority of economists and politicians in the 1960s and into the 1970s. A modified version of these arguments is still used today by Keynesian economists. This is examined in more detail in Chapter 21.

The problem is that if there is a trade-off between unemployment and inflation, demand management policies used to make one of the objectives better will succeed only in making the other one worse. It then becomes a matter of political judgement which of the objectives is the right one to direct demand management policies towards. Is *inflation* public enemy number one, or is it *unemployment*?

KI 33
p389

The relationship between the *AD/AS* diagram and the 45° line diagram

Now that we have introduced the argument that inflation can begin to occur *before* the full-employment level of income is reached, how does this affect the relationship between our two models: the *AD/AS* model and the 45° line model? This is examined in Figure 17.15. Initial equilibrium is at Y_{e_1} in both parts of the diagram, where $AD_1 = AS$ and where E_1 crosses the 45° line.

Now let us assume that there is a rise in aggregate demand. The E line shifts initially to E_2 in diagram (b). If this rise in demand were to lead to a full multiplied rise in real income, equilibrium income would rise to Y_{e_2}. But we are now assuming that inflation can occur *before* the full-employment level of income is reached. In other

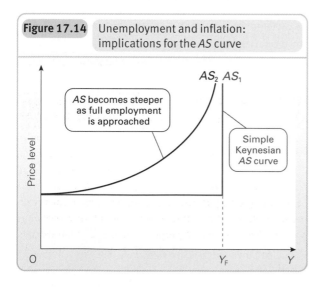

Figure 17.14 Unemployment and inflation: implications for the *AS* curve

Figure 17.15 Allowing for inflation in the 45° line and *AD/AS* diagrams

words, we are assuming that the *AS* curve is upward sloping (not horizontal as it was in Figure 17.11).

In diagram (a), the rise in aggregate demand has shifted the *AD* curve from AD_1 to AD_2. Part of this increase in demand is reflected in higher prices – the price level rises to P_2 – and only *part* is reflected in higher output. Equilibrium real income therefore rises only to Y_{e_3} and not Y_{e_2}. In other words, it does not rise by the full extent of the multiplier.

In diagram (b), the effect of the higher prices is to reduce the real value of expenditure (*E*). In other words, a given amount of money buys fewer goods. If there is no compensating increase in money supply (which would shift the *AD* curve further to the right in diagram (a)), the *E* line must fall to the point where it intersects the 45° line at a real income of Y_{e_3}: the *E* line must fall to E_3.

What is the mechanism that drives down the expenditure function from E_2 to E_3?

- The shortage of money drives up interest rates. This reduces investment and encourages saving.
- Higher prices reduce the real value of people's savings. They may therefore save more to compensate for this.
- Higher prices of domestic goods reduce exports and increase imports.
- Given the progressive nature of the tax system, higher money incomes lead to increased taxes.
- Inflation is likely to redistribute income from the poor to the rich, who have a higher *mps*.

 If money supply did increase sufficiently for the E line to remain at E_2, what would be the position of the new AD curve?

TC 12 p395

Section summary

1. If equilibrium national income (Y_e) is below the full-employment level of national income (Y_F), there will be a deflationary (recessionary) gap. This gap is equal to $Y - E$ or $W - J$ at Y_F. This gap can be closed by expansionary fiscal or monetary policy, which will then cause a multiplied rise in national income (up to a level of Y_F) and will eliminate demand-deficient unemployment.

2. If equilibrium national income exceeds the full-employment level of income, the inability of output to expand to meet this excess demand will lead to demand-pull inflation. This excess demand gives an inflationary gap, which is equal to $E - Y$ or $J - W$ at Y_F. This gap can be closed by deflationary policies.

3. This simple analysis tends to imply that the *AS* curve is horizontal up to Y_F and then vertical. In practice, the *AS* curve is likely to be upward sloping but getting steeper as full employment is approached and as bottlenecks increasingly occur.

4. An initial rise in aggregate demand (and an upward shift in the *E* curve) will be eroded to the extent that inflation reduces the real value of this demand: the *E* curve will shift back downwards again somewhat, unless there is a further boost to demand.

17.4 THE KEYNESIAN ANALYSIS OF THE BUSINESS CYCLE

TC 13 p402

Keynesians blame fluctuations in output and employment on fluctuations in aggregate demand. Theirs is therefore a 'demand-side' explanation of the business cycle. In the upturn (phase 1), aggregate demand starts to rise. It rises rapidly in the expansionary phase (phase 2). It then slows down and may start to fall in the peaking-out phase (phase 3). It then falls or remains relatively stagnant in the recession (phase 4) (see Figure 14.3 on page 400).

Keynesians seek to explain why aggregate demand fluctuates, and then to devise appropriate stabilisation policies to iron out these fluctuations. A more stable economy, they argue, provides a better climate for investment. With more investment, *potential* output grows more rapidly. This, given appropriate demand management policy, then allows a faster growth in actual output to be maintained.

Instability of investment: the accelerator

One of the major factors contributing to the ups and downs of the business cycle is the instability of investment.

When an economy begins to recover from a recession, investment can rise very rapidly. When the growth of the economy slows down, however, investment can fall dramatically, and during a recession it can all but disappear. Since investment is an injection into the circular flow of income, these changes in investment will cause multiplied changes in income and thus heighten a boom or deepen a recession.

The theory that relates investment to *changes* in national income is called the **accelerator theory**. The term 'accelerator' is used because a relatively modest rise in national income can cause a much larger percentage rise in investment.

When there is no change in income and hence no change in consumption, the only investment needed is a relatively small amount of replacement investment for machines that are wearing out or have become obsolete. When income and consumption increase, however, there will have to be *new* investment in order to increase production capacity. This is called **induced investment** (I_i). Once this has taken place, investment will fall back to mere replacement investment (I_r) unless there is a further rise in income and consumption.

Thus induced investment depends on *changes* in national income (ΔY):

$$I_i = \alpha \Delta Y$$

where α is the amount by which induced investment depends on changes in national income, and is known as the **accelerator coefficient**. Thus if a £1 million *rise* in

national income caused the *level* of induced investment to be £2 million, the accelerator coefficient would be 2.

The size of α depends on the economy's **marginal capital/output ratio** ($\Delta K/\Delta Y$). If an increase in the country's capital stock of £2 million (i.e. an investment of £2 million) is required to produce £1 million extra national output, the marginal capital/output ratio would be 2. Other things being equal, the accelerator coefficient and the marginal capital/output ratio will therefore be the same.

 How is it that the cost of an investment to a firm will exceed the value of the output that the investment will yield? Surely that would make the investment unprofitable? (Clue: the increase in output refers to output over a specific time period, usually a year.)

The following example (see Table 17.5) illustrates some important features of the accelerator. It looks at the investment decisions made by a firm in response to changes in the demand for its product. The firm is taken as representative of firms throughout the economy. The example is based on various assumptions:

- The firm's machines last exactly ten years and then need replacing.
- At the start of the example, the firm has ten machines in place, one 10 years old, one 9 years old, one 8 years old, one 7, one 6 and so on. Thus one machine needs replacing each year.
- Machines produce exactly 100 units of output per year. This figure cannot be varied.
- The firm always adjusts its output and its stock of machinery to match consumer demand.

Table 17.5 The accelerator effect

				Year			
	0	**1**	**2**	**3**	**4**	**5**	**6**
Quantity demanded by consumers (sales)	1000	1000	2000	3000	3500	3500	3400
Number of machines required	10	10	20	30	35	35	34
Induced investment (I_i) (extra machines)		0	10	10	5	0	0
Replacement investment (I_r)		1	1	1	1	1	0
Total investment ($I_i + I_r$)		1	11	11	6	1	0

KI 32
p388

Definitions

Accelerator theory The level of investment depends on the rate of change of national income, and as a result tends to be subject to substantial fluctuations.

Induced investment Investment that firms make to enable them to meet extra consumer demand.

Accelerator coefficient The level of induced investment as a proportion of a rise in national income: $\alpha = I_i/\Delta Y$.

Marginal capital/output ratio The amount of extra capital (in money terms) required to produce a £1 increase in national output. Since $I_i = \Delta K$, the marginal apital/output ratio $\Delta K/\Delta Y$ equals the accelerator coefficient (α).

The example shows what happens to the firm's investment over a six-year period when there is first a substantial rise in consumer demand, then a levelling off and then a slight fall. It illustrates the following features of the accelerator.

- *Investment will rise when the growth of national income (and hence consumer demand) is rising* ($\Delta Y_{t+1} > \Delta Y_t$). Years 1 to 2 illustrate this (see Table 17.5). The rise in consumer demand is zero in year 1 and 1000 units in year 2. Investment rises from one to eleven machines. The growth in investment may be considerably greater than the growth in consumer demand, giving a large accelerator effect. Between years 1 and 2, consumer demand doubles but investment goes up by a massive *eleven* times!
- *Investment will be constant even when national income is growing, if the increase in income this year is the same as last year* ($\Delta Y_{t+1} = \Delta Y_t$). In years 2 to 3, consumer demand continues to rise by 1000 units, but investment is constant at eleven machines.
- *Investment will fall even if national income is still growing, if the rate of growth is slowing down* ($\Delta Y_{t+1} > \Delta Y_t$). In years 3 to 4, consumer demand rises by 500 units (rather than 1000 units as in the previous year). Investment falls from eleven to six machines.
- *If national income is constant, investment will be confined to replacement investment only*. In years 4 to 5, investment falls to the one machine requiring replacement.
- *If national income falls, even if only slightly, investment can be wiped out altogether*. In years 5 to 6, even though demand has fallen by only 1/35, investment will fall to zero. Not even the machine that is wearing out will be replaced.

In practice, the accelerator will not be as dramatic and clear cut as this. The effect will be extremely difficult to predict for the following reasons:

- Many firms may have spare capacity and/or carry stocks. This will enable them to meet extra demand without having to invest.

- The willingness of firms to invest will depend on their confidence in *future* demand (see Box 17.3). Firms are not going to rush out and spend large amounts of money on machines that will last many years if it is quite likely that demand will fall back again the following year.
- Firms may make their investment plans a long time in advance and may be unable to change them quickly.
- Even if firms do decide to invest more, the producer goods industries may not have the capacity to meet a sudden surge in demand for machines.
- Machines do not as a rule suddenly wear out. A firm could thus delay replacing machines and keep the old ones for a bit longer if it was uncertain about its future level of demand.

All these points tend to reduce the magnitude of the accelerator and to make it very difficult to predict. Nevertheless the effect still exists. Firms still take note of changes in consumer demand when deciding how much to invest.

Box 17.6 shows how, from 1975 to 2008, fluctuations in investment were far more severe than fluctuations in national income. This tends to suggest that there was a substantial accelerator effect operating during the period.

The multiplier/accelerator interaction

If there is an initial change in injections or withdrawals, then theoretically this will set off a chain reaction between the multiplier and the accelerator. For example, if there is a rise in government expenditure, this will lead to a multiplied rise in national income. But this *rise* in national income will set off an accelerator effect: firms will respond to the rise in income and the resulting rise in consumer demand by investing more. But this rise in investment constitutes a further rise in injections and thus will lead to a second multiplied rise in income. If this rise in income is larger than the first, there will then be a second rise in investment (the accelerator), which in turn will cause a third rise in income (the multiplier). And so the process continues indefinitely.

But does this lead to an exploding rise in national income? Will a single rise in injections cause national income to go on rising for ever? The answer is no, for two reasons. The first is that national income, in real terms, cannot go on rising faster than the growth in potential output. It will bump up against the ceiling of full employment, whether of labour or of other resources.

A second reason is that, if investment is to go on rising, it is not enough that national income should merely go on *rising*: instead, national income must *rise faster and faster*. Once the growth in national income slows down, investment will begin to fall, and then the whole process will be reversed. A fall in investment will lead to a fall in national income, which will lead to a massive fall in investment. The multiplier/accelerator interaction is shown more formally in Table 17.6. A numerical example is given in Case Study 17.3 in MyEconLab.

Fluctuations in stocks

Firms hold stocks (inventories) of finished goods. These stocks tend to fluctuate with the course of the business cycle, and these fluctuations in stocks themselves contribute to fluctuations in output.

Imagine an economy that is recovering from a recession. At first, firms may be cautious about increasing production. Doing so may involve taking on more labour or making additional investment. Firms may not want to make these commitments if the recovery could soon peter out. They may, therefore, run down their stocks rather than increase output. Initially the recovery from recession will be slow.

BOX 17.6 **HAS THERE BEEN AN ACCELERATOR EFFECT OVER THE PAST THIRTY YEARS?**

Investment is highly volatile. It is subject to far more violent swings than national income. If we look at the period from 1975 to 2008, the maximum annual rise in GDP was 5.6 per cent and the maximum fall was 3.8 per cent. By contrast, the maximum annual rise in investment was 21.1 per cent and the maximum fall was 13.5 per cent.

If we focus on *manufacturing* investment, the swings were even greater. The maximum annual rise in manufacturing investment in plant and machinery was 20 per cent and the maximum fall was 28 per cent, and in new buildings and works the maximum annual rise was a massive 59 per cent and the maximum fall was 39 per cent.

These figures are consistent with the accelerator theory, which argues that the *level* of investment depends on the *rate of change* of national income. A relatively small percentage change in national income can give a much bigger percentage change in investment.

The ups and downs in GDP and investment do not completely match because there are additional factors that determine investment other than simple changes in national income. These factors include interest rates, exchange rates and business expectations of future demand.

1. *Can you identify any time lags in the graph? Why might there be time lags?*
2. *Why does investment in construction and producer goods industries tend to fluctuate more than investment in retailing and the service industries?*

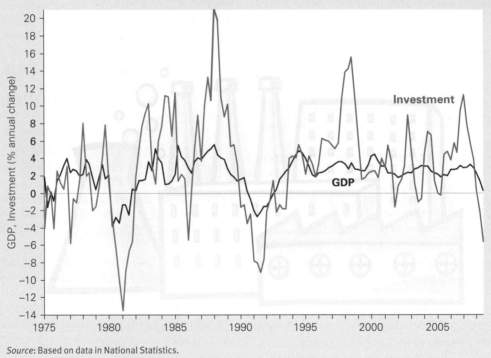

Fluctuations in UK real GDP and investment, 1975–2008

Source: Based on data in National Statistics.

Table 17.6 The multiplier/accelerator interaction

Period t	$I\uparrow \rightarrow Y\uparrow$	(Multiplier)
Period $t+1$	$Y\uparrow \rightarrow I\uparrow$	(Accelerator)
	$I\uparrow \rightarrow Y\uparrow$	(Multiplier)
Period $t+2$	If $\uparrow Y_{t+1} > \uparrow Y_t$ then $I\uparrow$	
	If $\uparrow Y_{t+1} = \uparrow Y_t$ then I stays the same	(Accelerator)
	If $\downarrow Y_{t+1} < \uparrow Y_t$ then $I\downarrow$	
	This in turn will have a multiplied upward effect, no effect, or a multiplied downward effect respectively on national income.	
Period $t+3$	This will then lead to a further accelerator effect and so on . . .	

If the recovery does continue, however, firms will start to gain more confidence and will increase production. Also, they will find that their stocks have got rather low and will need building up. This gives a further boost to production, and for a time the growth in output will exceed the growth in demand. This extra growth in output will then, via the multiplier, lead to a further increase in demand.

Once stocks have been built up again, the growth in output will slow down to match the growth in demand. This slowing down in output will, via the accelerator and multiplier, contribute to the ending of the expansionary phase of the business cycle.

As the economy slows down, firms will find their stocks building up. Unless they cut back on production immediately, this increase in stocks cushions the effect of falling demand on output and employment.

If the recession continues, however, firms will be unwilling to go on building up stocks. But as firms attempt to reduce their stocks back to the desired level, production will fall *below* the level of sales, despite the fact that sales themselves are lower. This could lead to a dramatic fall in output and, via the multiplier, to an even bigger fall in sales.

Eventually, once stocks have been run down to the minimum, production will have to rise again to match the level of sales. This will contribute to a recovery and the whole cycle will start again.

Determinants of the course of the business cycle

We are now in a position to paint a more complete Keynesian picture of the business cycle. We need to answer two key questions: (a) why do booms and recessions last for several months or even years, and (b) why do they eventually come to an end – what determines their turning points? Let us examine each in turn.

Why do booms and recessions persist?

Time lags. It takes time for changes in injections and withdrawals to be fully reflected in changes in national income, output and employment. The multiplier process takes time. Moreover, consumers, firms and government may not all respond immediately to new situations.

'Bandwagon' effects. Once the economy starts expanding, expectations become buoyant. People think ahead and adjust their expenditure behaviour: they consume and invest more *now*. Likewise in a recession, a mood of pessimism may set in. The effect is cumulative. The multiplier and accelerator interact: they feed on each other.

Why do booms and recessions come to an end?

Ceilings and floors. Actual output can go on growing more rapidly than potential output only as long as there is slack in the economy. As full employment is approached and as more and more firms reach full capacity, so a ceiling to output will be reached.

At the other extreme, there is a basic minimum level of consumption that people tend to maintain. During a recession, people may not buy many luxury and durable goods, but they will continue to buy food and other basic goods. There is thus a floor to consumption.

The industries supplying these basic goods will need to maintain their level of replacement investment. Also, there will always be some minimum investment demand as firms feel the need to install the latest equipment. There is thus a floor to investment too.

Echo effects. Durable consumer goods and capital equipment may last several years, but eventually they will need replacing. The replacement of goods and capital purchased in a previous boom may help to bring a recession to an end.

The accelerator. For investment to continue rising, consumer demand must rise at a *faster and faster* rate. If this does not happen, investment will fall back and the boom will break.

Random shocks. National or international political, social, institutional or natural events can affect the mood and attitudes of firms, governments and consumers, or the conditions under which they operate, and thus affect aggregate demand. Changes in world oil prices, a war, an election or a banking crisis are all examples.

Changes in government policy. In a boom, a government may become most worried by inflation and balance of payments deficits and thus pursue contractionary policies. In a recession, it may become most worried by unemployment and lack of growth and thus pursue expansionary policies. These government policies, if successful, will bring about a turning point in the cycle.

Keynesians argue that governments should attempt to reduce cyclical fluctuations by using active stabilisation policies. A more stable economy will encourage investment and allow a faster growth in output to be maintained. The policy traditionally favoured by Keynesians is *fiscal policy*. This is the subject of Chapter 20.

An analysis of the factors contributing to each of the four phases of the business cycle is given in Case Study 17.5 in MyEconLab.

Section summary

1. Keynesians explain cyclical fluctuations in the economy by examining the causes of fluctuations in the level of *aggregate demand*.

2. A major part of the Keynesian explanation of the business cycle is the instability of investment. The accelerator theory explains this instability. It relates the level of investment to *changes* in national income and consumer demand. An initial increase in consumer demand can result in a very large percentage increase in investment; but as soon as the rise in consumer demand begins to level off, investment will fall; and even a slight fall in consumer demand can reduce investment to virtually zero.

3. The accelerator effect will be dampened by the carrying of stocks, the cautiousness of firms, forward planning by firms and the inability of producer goods industries to supply the capital equipment.

4. The interaction of the multiplier and accelerator will cause cycles.

5. Keynesians identify other causes of cyclical fluctuations, such as cycles in the holding of stocks, time lags, 'bandwagon' effects, ceilings and floors to output, echo effects, swings in government policy and random shocks.

END OF CHAPTER QUESTIONS

1. An economy is currently in equilibrium. The following figures refer to elements in its national income accounts.

	£ billions
Consumption (total)	60
Investment	5
Government expenditure	8
Imports	10
Exports	7

(a) What is the current equilibrium level of national income?

(b) What is the level of injections?

(c) What is the level of withdrawals?

(d) Assuming that tax revenues are £7 billion, how much is the level of saving?

(e) If national income now rose to £80 billion and, as a result, the consumption of domestically produced goods rose to £58 billion, what is the mpc_d?

(f) What is the value of the multiplier?

(g) Given an initial level of national income of £80 billion, now assume that spending on exports rises by £4 billion, spending on investment rises by £1 billion, whilst government expenditure falls by £2 billion. By how much will national income change?

(h) Given this new level of national income, assume that full employment is achieved at a national income of £100 billion. Is there an inflationary or a deflationary gap?

(i) What is the size of this gap?

2. What is the relationship between the *mpc*, the mpc_d and the *mpw*?

3. Why will the short-run consumption function be different from the long-run consumption function?

4. Construct a table similar to Table 17.3 (on page 489), only this time assume that the mpc_d is 3/4. Show that national income will increase by £640 million.

5. Assume that the multiplier has a value of 3. Now assume that the government decides to increase aggregate demand in an attempt to reduce unemployment. It raises government expenditure by £100 million with no increase in taxes. Firms, anticipating a rise in their sales, increase investment by £200 million, of which £50 million consists of purchases of foreign machinery. How much will national income rise? (Assume *ceteris paribus*.)

6. What factors could explain why some countries have a higher multiplier than others?

7. How can the interaction of the multiplier and the accelerator explain cyclical fluctuations in national income?

8. Why is it difficult to predict the size of the accelerator?

Online resources

Additional case studies in MyEconLab

17.1 **Keynes' views on the consumption function**. An analysis of how the assumptions made by Keynes affect the shape of the consumption function.

17.2 **The relationship between income and consumption**. This examines three different theories of the consumption function – the absolute income hypothesis, the relative income hypothesis and the permanent income hypothesis. Each one is based on different assumptions about consumer behaviour.

17.3 **The multiplier/accelerator interaction**. A numerical example showing how the interaction of the multiplier and accelerator can cause cycles in economic activity.

17.4 **Heavenly cycles**. An examination of the claim by Jevons in the late nineteenth century that the business cycle depends on the sunspot cycle!

17.5 **The phases of the business cycle**. A demand-side analysis of the factors contributing to each of the four phases.

Maths Case 17.1 Calculating the value of the multiplier. Examining the algebra.

Maths Case 17.2 Calulating the value of the multiplier. Using calculus.

Maths Case 17.3 Calculating the value of the multiplier with marginal propensities based on disposable income. Examining the algebra.

Websites relevant to chapters 16 and 17

Numbers and sections refer to websites listed in the Web Appendix and hotlinked from this book's website at **www.pearsoned.co.uk/sloman**.

- For news articles relevant to this and the previous chapter, see the *Economics News Articles* link from the book's website.

- For general news on national economies and the international economy, see websites in section A, and particularly A1–5. See also links to newspapers worldwide in A38, 39, 43 and 44, and the news search feature in Google at A41. See also links to economics news in A42.

- For information on the development of ideas, see C12, 18; also see links under *Methodology and History of Economic Thought* in C14; links to economists in I4 and 17. See also sites I7 and 11 > *Economic Systems and Theories > History of Economic Thought*.

- For data on economic growth, employment and the business cycle, see links in B1 or 2; also see B4 and 12. For UK data, see B3, 34 and 36. For EU data, see G1 > *The Statistical Annex*. For US data, see *Current economic indicators* in B5 and the *Data* section of B17. For international data, see B15, 21, 24, 31, 33 and 35. For links to datasets, see B28; I14.

- For a model of the economy (based on the Treasury model), see *The Virtual Economy* (site D1). In addition to the model, where you can devise your own Budget, there are worksheets and outlines of theories and the work of famous economists. See also *The Virtual Chancellor* (D10).

- For student resources relevant to this chapter, see sites C1–7, 9, 10, 19.

18 Chapter

Money and Interest Rates

CHAPTER MAP

18.1 The meaning and functions of money   503
The functions of money   503
What should count as money?   504

18.2 The financial system   504
The role of the financial sector   504
The banking system   505
Deposit taking and lending   506
Liquidity and profitability   509
The central bank   511
The role of the money market   515

18.3 The supply of money   520
Definitions of the money supply   520
The creation of credit: the simplest case   520
The creation of credit: the real world   522
What causes money supply to rise?   524
The flow-of-funds equation   525
The relationship between money supply and
    the rate of interest   526

18.4 The demand for money   527
The motives for holding money   527
The transactions plus precautionary demand
    for money: L_1 528
The speculative (or assets) demand for money: L_2 529
The total demand for money: $L_1 + L_2$ 530

18.5 Equilibrium   531
Equilibrium in the money market   531
Equilibrium in the foreign exchange market   532

In this chapter and the next, we are going to look at the special role that money plays in the economy. Changes in the amount of money can have a powerful effect on all the major macroeconomic indicators, such as inflation, unemployment, economic growth, interest rates, exchange rates and the balance of payments.

But why do changes in the money supply affect the economy? The answer is that the supply of money and the demand for money between them determine the *rate of interest,* and this has a crucial impact on aggregate demand and the performance of the economy generally. In section 18.5 we shall see just how this process works.

First we define what is meant by money and examine its functions. Then in sections 18.2 and 18.3 we look at the operation of the financial sector of the economy and its role in determining the supply of money. This sector has come in for considerable scrutiny in recent times following the banking turmoil associated with the 'credit crunch' of 2007–9.

We then turn to look at the demand for money. Here we are not asking how much money people would like. The answer to that would probably be 'as much as possible'! What we are asking is: how much of people's assets do they want to hold in the form of money?

Finally, we put supply and demand together to see how free-market interest rates are determined. In Chapter 20 we will see how the central bank intervenes in money markets to alter interest rates.

18.1 THE MEANING AND FUNCTIONS OF MONEY

Before going any further we must define precisely what we mean by 'money' – not as easy a task as it sounds. Money is more than just notes and coin. In fact the main component of a country's money supply is not cash, but deposits in banks and other financial institutions. Only a very small proportion of these deposits is kept by the banks in their safes or tills in the form of cash. The bulk of the deposits appear merely as bookkeeping entries in the banks' accounts.

This may sound very worrying. Will a bank have enough cash to meet its customers' demands? The answer in the vast majority of cases is yes. Only a small fraction of a bank's total deposits will be withdrawn at any one time, and banks always seek to ensure that they have the ability to meet their customers' demands. The chances of banks running out of cash are very low indeed. The only circumstance where this could become possible is if people lost confidence in a bank and started to withdraw money in what is known as a 'run on the bank'. This happened with the Northern Rock Bank in 2008. But in these circumstances the central bank or government would intervene to protect people's deposits by making more cash available to the bank or, in the last resort, by nationalising the bank (as happened with Northern Rock).

What is more, the bulk of all but very small transactions are not conducted in cash at all. By the use of cheques, credit cards and debit cards, most money is simply transferred from the purchaser's to the seller's bank account without the need for first withdrawing it in cash.

What items should be included in the definition of money? To answer this we need to identify the *functions* of money.

The functions of money

The main purpose of money is for buying and selling goods, services and assets: i.e. as a 'medium of exchange'.

It also has three other important functions. Let us examine each in turn.

A medium of exchange

In a subsistence economy, where individuals make their own clothes, grow their own food, provide their own entertainments, etc., people do not need money. If people want to exchange any goods, they will do so by barter. In other words, they will do swaps with other people.

The complexities of a modern developed economy, however, make barter totally impractical for most purposes (see Case Study 18.1 in MyEconLab). What is necessary is a ***medium of exchange*** that is generally acceptable as a means of payment for goods and services and as a means of payment for labour and other factor services. 'Money' is any such medium.

To be a suitable physical means of exchange, money must be light enough to carry around, must come in a number of denominations, large and small, and must not be easy to forge (the attributes of money are explored in Case Study 18.2 in MyEconLab). Alternatively, money must be in a form that enables it to be transferred *indirectly* through some acceptable mechanism. For example, money in the form of bookkeeping entries in bank accounts can be transferred from one account to another by the use of such mechanisms as debit cards and direct debits.

A means of storing wealth

People need a means whereby the fruits of *today's* labour can be used to purchase goods and services in the *future*.

> **Definition**
>
> **Medium of exchange** Something that is acceptable in exchange for goods and services.

KI 24
p260

BOX 18.1 MONEY SUPPLY, NATIONAL INCOME AND NATIONAL WEALTH   *EXPLORING ECONOMICS*

Don't confuse the supply of money with the money value of national income. National income is a *flow* concept. It measures the value of the nation's output per year. Money supply, by contrast, is a *stock* concept. At any one point in time, there is a given amount of money in the economy.

But what if the money supply increases? Will the national income increase by that amount? No, because the extra money will usually be spent more than once per year on final goods and services. The rise in national income would thus be greater than the rise in money supply. On the other hand, some of the extra spending may simply result in higher prices. *Real* national income

will rise by less than national income measured at current prices.

So if money supply is not the same as national *income*, is it the same as national *wealth*? After all, wealth is a stock concept. Again the answer is no. The nation's wealth consists of its *real* assets: land, buildings, capital equipment, works of art, etc. People may well hold part of their wealth in the form of money, it is true, but this is not wealth as far as the nation is concerned: if it were, the government could make us all wealthier by simply printing more money! Money represents wealth to the individual only to the extent that it represents a claim on *real* goods and services. It has nothing to do with national wealth.

People need to be able to store their wealth: they want a means of saving. Money is one such medium in which to hold wealth. It can be saved.

A means of evaluation

Money allows the value of goods, services or assets to be compared. The value of goods is expressed in terms of prices, and prices are expressed in money terms. Money also allows dissimilar things, such as a person's wealth or a company's assets, to be added up. Similarly, a country's GDP is expressed in money terms. Money thus serves as a 'unit of account'.

 Why may money prices give a poor indication of the value of goods and services?

A means of establishing the value of future claims and payments

People often want to agree *today* the price of some *future* payment. For example, workers and managers will want to agree the wage rate for the coming year. Firms will want to sign contracts with their suppliers specifying the price of raw materials and other supplies. Money prices are the most convenient means of measuring future claims.

What should count as money?

What items, then, should be included in the definition of money? Unfortunately, there is no sharp borderline between money and non-money.

Cash (notes and coin) obviously counts as money. It readily meets all the functions of money. Goods (fridges, cars and cabbages) do not count as money. But what about various financial assets, such as bank accounts, building society accounts and stocks and shares? Do they count as money? The answer is: it depends on how narrowly money is defined. The narrowest definition of money includes just cash (i.e. notes and coins). Broader definitions include various types of bank account, and broader definitions still include various financial assets as well. We examine the different definitions in the UK and the eurozone in Box 18.4 on page 521.

 In terms of the broad definition of money, would a deposit account passbook count as money?

In order to understand the significance of different measures of the money supply and the ways in which money supply can be controlled, it is first necessary to look at the various types of account in which money can be held and at the various financial institutions involved.

Section summary

1. Money's main function is as a medium of exchange. In addition, it is a means of storing wealth, a means of evaluation and a means of establishing the value of future claims and payments.

2. What counts as money depends on how narrowly it is defined. All definitions include cash, but they vary according to what other financial assets are included.

18.2 THE FINANCIAL SYSTEM

The role of the financial sector

Banks and other financial institutions are known as **financial intermediaries**. They all have the common function of providing a link between those who wish to lend and those who wish to borrow. In other words, they act as the mechanism whereby the supply of funds is matched to the demand for funds. In this process, they provide five important services.

Definition

Financial intermediaries The general name for financial institutions (banks, building societies, etc.) which act as a means of channelling funds from depositors to borrowers.

Expert advice

Financial intermediaries can advise their customers on financial matters: on the best way of investing their funds and on alternative ways of obtaining finance. This should help to encourage the flow of savings and the efficient use of them.

Expertise in channelling funds

Financial intermediaries have the specialist knowledge to be able to channel funds to those areas that yield the highest return. They also have the expertise to assess risks and to refuse loans for projects considered too risky or to charge a risk premium to others. This all encourages the flow of saving as it gives savers the confidence that their savings will earn a good rate of interest. Financial intermediaries also help to ensure that projects that are potentially profitable will be able to obtain finance. They help to increase allocative efficiency.

Maturity transformation

Many people and firms want to borrow money for long periods of time, and yet many depositors want to be able to withdraw their deposits on demand or at short notice. If people had to rely on borrowing directly from other people, there would be a problem here: the lenders would not be prepared to lend for a long enough period. If you had £100 000 of savings, would you be prepared to lend it to a friend to buy a house if the friend was going to take 25 years to pay it back? Even if there was no risk whatsoever of your friend defaulting, most people would be totally unwilling to tie up their savings for so long.

This is where a bank or building society comes in. It borrows money from a vast number of small savers, who are able to withdraw their money on demand or at short notice. It then lends the money to house purchasers for a long period of time by granting mortgages (typically these are paid back over 20 to 30 years). This process whereby financial intermediaries lend for longer periods of time than they borrow is known as **maturity transformation**. They are able to do this because with a large number of depositors it is highly unlikely that they would all want to withdraw their deposits at the same time. On any one day, although some people will be withdrawing money, others will be making new deposits.

Risk transformation

You may be unwilling to lend money directly to another person in case they do not pay up. You are unwilling to take the risk. Financial intermediaries, however, by lending to large numbers of people, are willing to risk the odd case of default. They can absorb the loss because of the interest they earn on all the other loans. This spreading of risks is known as **risk transformation**. What is more, financial intermediaries may have the expertise to be able to assess just how risky a loan is.

Which of the above are examples of economies of scale?

Transmission of funds

In addition to channelling funds from depositors to borrowers, certain financial institutions have another import-ant function. This is to provide a means of transmitting payments. Thus by the use of debit cards, credit cards, Internet and telephone banking, cheques, direct debits, etc., money can be transferred from one person or institution to another without having to rely on cash.

The banking system

Types of bank

By far the largest element of money supply is bank deposits. It is not surprising, then, that banks play an absolutely crucial role in the monetary system. Banking can be divided into two main types: *retail banking* and *wholesale banking*. Most banks today conduct both types of business and are thus known as 'universal banks'.

Retail banking. **Retail banking** is the business conducted by the familiar high street banks, such as Barclays, Lloyds TSB, HSBC, Royal Bank of Scotland and NatWest (part of the RBS group). They operate bank accounts for individuals and businesses, attracting deposits and granting loans at published rates of interest. Some of these accounts are accessed through the banks' branches and some via telephone or Internet banking.

Wholesale banking. The other major type of banking is **wholesale banking**. This involves receiving large deposits from and making large loans to companies or other banks and financial institutions; these are known as **wholesale deposits and loans**.

As far as companies are concerned, these may be for short periods of time to account for the non-matching of a firm's payments and receipts from its business, or they may be for longer periods of time, for various investment purposes. As these wholesale deposits and loans are very large sums of money, banks compete against each other for them and negotiate individual terms with the firm to suit the firm's particular requirements. The rates of interest negotiated will reflect the current market rates of interest and the terms of the particular loan/deposit. Very large loans to firms are often divided ('syndicated') among several banks.

In the past, there were many independent wholesale banks, known as *investment banks*. These included famous names such as Morgan Stanley, Rothschild, S G Hambros

---

Definitions

Maturity transformation The transformation of deposits into loans of a longer maturity.

Risk transformation The process whereby banks can spread the risks of lending by having a large number of borrowers.

Retail banking Branch, telephone, postal and Internet banking for individuals and businesses at published rates of interest and charges. Retail banking involves the operation of extensive branch networks.

Wholesale banking Where banks deal in large-scale deposits and loans, mainly with companies and other banks and financial institutions. Interest rates and charges may be negotiable.

Wholesale deposits and loans Large-scale deposits and loans made by and to firms at negotiated interest rates.

and Goldman Sachs. With the worldwide financial crisis of 2008, however, most of the independent investment banks merged with universal banks. Today, most wholesale banking is conducted in a division of the major universal banks.

Banks also lend and borrow wholesale funds to and from each other. Banks that are short of funds borrow large sums from others with surplus funds, thus ensuring that the banking sector as a whole does not have funds surplus to its requirements. The rate at which they lend to each other is known as the IBOR (inter-bank offered rate). The IBOR has a major influence on the other rates that banks charge. In the eurozone, the IBOR is known as Euribor. In the UK, it is known as the LIBOR (where 'L' stands for 'London'). As inter-bank loans can be anything from overnight to 12 months, the IBOR will vary from one length of loan to another.

Building societies

These UK institutions specialise in granting loans (mortgages) for house purchase. They compete for the savings of the general public through a network of high street branches. Unlike banks, they are not public limited companies, their 'shares' being the deposits made by their investors. In recent years, many of the building societies have converted to banks (including all the really large building societies except the Nationwide).

In the past, there was a clear distinction between banks and building societies. Today, however, they have become much more similar, with building societies now offering current account facilities and cash machines, and retail banks granting mortgages. As with the merging of retail and wholesale banks, this is all part of a trend away from the narrow specialisation of the past and towards the offering of a wider and wider range of services. This has been helped by a process of *financial deregulation*.

Deposit taking and lending

Banks are in the business of deposit taking and lending. To understand this, we must distinguish between banks' *liabilities* and *assets*. The total liabilities and assets for the UK banks are set out in a balance sheet in Table 18.1.

Liabilities

Customers' deposits in banks (and other deposit-taking institutions such as building societies) are **liabilities** to these institutions. This means simply that the customers have the claim on these deposits and thus the institutions are liable to meet the claims.

There are four major types of deposit: sight deposits, time deposits, certificates of deposit and 'repos'.

Table 18.1	Balance sheet of UK banks: November 2008					
Sterling liabilities	**£bn**	**%**	**Sterling assets**	**£bn**	**%**
Sight deposits		(31.0)	Notes and coin	9.2	(0.3)
UK banks, etc.	103.1		Balances with Bank of England		(1.4)
UK public sector	8.9		Reserve balances	40.8	
UK private sector	749.7		Cash ratio deposits	2.0	
Non-residents	128.4		Market loans		(15.2)
Time deposits		(36.0)	UK banks	175.3	
UK banks, etc.	82.3		UK banks' CDs, etc.	52.6	
UK public sector	51.2		UK building societies	3.9	
UK private sector	645.8		Non-residents	243.3	
Non-residents	373.5		Bills of exchange	52.6	(1.7)
Certificates of deposit (CDs)	240.3	(7.5)	Reverse repos	272.7	(8.7)
Repos	383.8	(12.0)	Investments	333.2	(10.6)
Sterling capital & other funds	310.0	(9.7)	Advances	1816.3	(58.1)
Other	121.1	(3.8)	Other	126.1	(4.0)
Total sterling liabilities	**3198.2**	(100.0)	**Total sterling assets**	**3127.9**	(100.0)
Liabilities in other currencies	4645.7		Assets in other currencies	4715.9	
Total liabilities	7843.9		Total assets	7843.9	

Note: The latest data can be accessed from www.bankofengland.co.uk/mfsd/iadb/NewIntermed.asp.
Source: Based on data in *Bankstats* (Bank of England), Table B1.2.

Definitions

Financial deregulation The removal of or reduction in legal rules and regulations governing the activities of financial institutions.

Liabilities All legal claims for payment that outsiders have on an institution.

Sight deposits. **Sight deposits** are any deposits that can be withdrawn on demand by the depositor without penalty. In the past, sight accounts did not pay interest. Today, however, there are many sight accounts that do. In fact, there is quite aggressive competition nowadays between banks to offer apparently very attractive interest rates on such accounts, although these are often on balances up to a relatively small amount.

The most familiar form of sight deposits are current accounts at banks. Depositors are issued with cheque books and/or debit cards (e.g. Visa/Delta or Switch/Maestro) that enable them to spend the money directly without first having to go to the bank and draw the money out in cash. In the case of debit cards, the person's account is electronically debited when the purchase is made and the card is 'swiped' across the machine and the pin entered. This process is known as EFTPOS (electronic funds transfer at point of sale).

An important feature of current accounts is that banks often allow customers to be overdrawn. That is, they can draw on their account and make payments to other people in excess of the amount of money they have deposited.

Time deposits. **Time deposits** require notice of withdrawal. However, they normally pay a higher rate of interest than sight accounts. With some types of account, a depositor can withdraw a certain amount of money on demand, but there will be a penalty of so many days' lost interest. They are not cheque-book or debit-card accounts, although some allow customers to use cash cards. The most familiar form of time deposits are the deposit and savings accounts in banks and the various savings accounts in building societies. No overdraft facilities exist with time deposits.

A substantial proportion of time deposits are from the *banking sector*: i.e. other banks and other financial institutions. Inter-bank lending has grown over the years as money markets have become deregulated and as deposits are moved from one currency to another to take advantage of different rates of interest between different countries. A large proportion of overseas deposits are from foreign banks.

As we shall see below, however, inter-bank lending virtually dried up in 2008. Banks became increasingly fearful that if they lent money to other banks, the other banks might default on payment. The reason was that many banks held assets based on mortgages granted to people unable to pay. As these assets fell in value, so banks became less and less able to raise enough money to pay back inter-bank loans.

Certificates of deposit. **Certificates of deposit** are certificates issued by banks to customers (usually firms) for large deposits of a fixed term (e.g. £100 000 for 18 months). They can be sold by one customer to another, and thus provide a means whereby the holders can get money quickly if they need it without the banks that have issued the CDs having to supply the money. (This makes them relatively 'liquid' to the depositor but 'illiquid' to the bank: we examine this below.) The use of CDs has grown rapidly in recent years. Their use by firms has meant that, at a wholesale level, sight accounts have become *less* popular.

Sale and repurchase agreements (repos). If banks have a temporary shortage of funds, they can sell some of their financial assets to other banks or to the central bank – the Bank of England in the UK and the European Central Bank in the eurozone (see below) – and later repurchase them on some agreed date, typically a fortnight later. These **sale and repurchase agreements (repos)** are in effect a form of loan – the bank borrowing for a period of time using some of its financial assets as the security for the loan. One of the major assets to use in this way are government bonds, normally called 'gilt-edged securities' or simply 'gilts' (see below). Sale and repurchase agreements involving gilts are known as *gilt repos*. As we shall see in section 20.2, gilt repos play a vital role in the operation of monetary policy.

Capital and other funds. This consists largely of the share capital in banks. Since shareholders cannot take their money out of banks, it provides a source of funding to meet sudden increases in withdrawals from depositors and to cover bad debts. As we shall see below, it is vital that banks have sufficient capital.

Assets

A bank's financial **assets** are its claims on others. There are three main categories of assets.

Definitions

Sight deposits Deposits that can be withdrawn on demand without penalty.

Time deposits Deposits that require notice of withdrawal or where a penalty is charged for withdrawals on demand.

Certificates of deposit (CDs) Certificates issued by banks for fixed-term interest-bearing deposits. They can be resold by the owner to another party.

Sale and repurchase agreements (repos) An agreement between two financial institutions whereby one in effect borrows from another by selling its assets, agreeing to buy them back (repurchase them) at a fixed price and on a fixed date.

Assets Possessions, or claims held on others.

Cash and reserve balances in the central bank (Bank of England in the UK, ECB in the eurozone). Banks need to hold a certain amount of their assets as cash. This is largely used to meet the day-to-day demands of customers. They also keep 'reserve balances' in the central bank. In the UK these earn interest at the Bank of England's repo rate (or 'Bank Rate' as it is called), if kept within an agreed target range. These are like the banks' own current accounts and are used for clearing purposes (i.e. for settling the day-to-day payments between banks). They can be withdrawn in cash on demand. With inter-bank lending being seen as too risky during the crisis of 2008, many banks resorted to depositing surplus cash in the Bank of England, even though Bank Rate was lower than the LIBOR.

In the UK, banks and building societies are also required to deposit a small fraction of their assets as 'cash ratio deposits' with the Bank of England. These cannot be drawn on demand and earn no interest.

As you can see from Table 18.1, cash and balances in the Bank of England account for a very small proportion of banks' assets. The vast majority of banks' assets are in the form of various types of loan – to individuals and firms, to other financial institutions and to the government. These are 'assets' because they represent claims that the banks have on other people. Loans can be grouped into two types: short and long term.

Short-term loans. These are in the form of *market loans, bills of exchange* or *reverse repos*. The market for these various types of loan is known as the **money market**.

- **Market loans** are made primarily to other banks or financial institutions. This inter-bank lending consists of (a) money lent 'at call' (i.e. reclaimable on demand or at 24 hours' notice); (b) money lent for periods up to one year, but typically a few weeks; (c) CDs (i.e. certificates of deposits made in other banks or building societies).
- **Bills of exchange** are loans either to companies (**commercial bills**) or to the government (**Treasury bills**). These are, in effect, an IOU, with the company issuing them (in the case of commercial bills), or the Bank of England on behalf of the government (in the case of

Treasury bills), promising to pay the holder a specified sum on a particular date (the 'maturity date'), typically three months later. Since bills do not pay interest, they are sold below their face value (at a 'discount') but redeemed on maturity at the face value. This enables the purchaser, in this case the bank, to earn a return.

The price paid for bills will depend on demand and supply. For example, the more Treasury bills that the Bank of England offers for sale at its weekly tender of bills (i.e. the higher the supply), the lower will be their equilibrium price, and hence the higher will be their rate of return (i.e. their rate of interest, or 'rate of discount').

Normally, a bank will buy *commercial* bills only if they have been first 'accepted' by another financial institution (typically an investment bank). This means that the investment bank will redeem the bill (i.e. pay up) on the maturity date, if the firm issuing the bill defaults on payment. Of course the investment bank charges for this insurance (or 'underwriting'). Bills that have been accepted in this way are known as **bank bills**.

- **Reverse repos**. When a sale and repurchase agreement is made, the financial institution *purchasing* the assets (e.g. gilts) is, in effect, giving a short-term loan. The other party agrees to buy back the assets (i.e. pay back the loan) on a set date. The assets temporarily held by the bank making the loan are known as 'reverse repos'. Reverse repos are typically for one week, but can be for as little as overnight or as long as one year.

Longer-term loans. These consist primarily of loans to customers, both personal customers and businesses. These loans, also known as *advances*, are of four main types: fixed-term (repayable in instalments over a set number of years – typically, six months to five years), overdrafts (often for an unspecified term), outstanding balances on credit-card accounts, and mortgages (typically for 25 years).

Banks also make *investments*. These are partly in government bonds (gilts), which are effectively loans to the government. The government sells bonds, which then pay a fixed sum each year as interest. Once issued, they can then be bought and sold on the stock exchange. Banks are

---

Definitions

Money market The market for short-term loans and deposits.

Market loans Short-term loans (e.g. money at call and short notice).

Bills of exchange Certificates promising to repay a stated amount on a certain date, typically three months from the issue of the bill. Bills pay no interest as such, but are sold at a discount and redeemed at face value, thereby earning a rate of discount for the purchaser.

Commercial bills Bills of exchange issued by firms.

Treasury bills Bills of exchange issued by the Bank of England on behalf of the government. They are a means whereby the government raises short-term finance.

Bank bills Bills that have been accepted by another financial institution and hence insured against default.

Reverse repos Gilts or other assets that are purchased under a sale and repurchase agreement. They become an asset to the purchaser.

normally only prepared to buy bonds that have less than five years to maturity (the date when the government redeems the bonds). Banks also invest in various subsidiary financial institutions and in building societies.

Liquidity and profitability

As we have seen, banks keep a range of liabilities and assets. The balance of items in this range is influenced by three important considerations: profitability, liquidity and capital adequacy.

Profitability

Profits are made by lending money out at a higher rate of interest than that paid to depositors. The average interest rate received by banks on their assets is greater than that paid by them on their liabilities.

Liquidity

The *liquidity* of an asset is the ease with which it can be converted into cash without loss. Cash itself, by definition, is perfectly liquid.

Some assets, such as money lent at call to other financial institutions, are highly liquid. Although not actually cash, these assets can be converted into cash virtually on demand with no financial penalty. Other short-term inter-bank lending is also very liquid. The only issue here is one of confidence that the money will actually be repaid. This was a worry in the financial crisis of autumn 2008, when many banks stopped lending to each other on the inter-bank market for fear that the borrowing bank might become insolvent.

Other assets, such as gilts, can be converted into cash straight away by selling them on the Stock Exchange, but with the possibility of some financial loss, given that their market price fluctuates. Such assets, therefore, are not as liquid as money at call.

Other assets are much less liquid. Personal loans to the general public or mortgages for house purchase can be redeemed by the bank only as each instalment is paid. Other advances for fixed periods are repaid only at the end of that period.

Banks must always be able to meet the demands of their customers for withdrawals of money. To do this, they must hold sufficient cash or other assets that can be readily turned into cash. In other words, banks must maintain sufficient liquidity.

1. If a bank buys a £500 000 Treasury bill at the start of its 91-day life for £480 000, at roughly what price could it sell it to another financial institution after 45 days? Why is it not possible to predict the precise price when the bill is first purchased?
2. Suppose there were a sudden surge in demand for cash from the general public. Would the existence of inter-bank market loans help to meet the demand in any way?

Capital adequacy

Banks must have sufficient capital (i.e. funds) to allow them to meet all demands from depositors and to cover losses if borrowers default on payment. Capital adequacy is a measure of a bank's capital relative to its assets, where the assets are weighted according to the degree of risk. The more risky the assets, the greater the amount of capital that will be required.

A measure of capital adequacy is given by the *capital adequacy ratio (CAR)*. This is given by the following formula:

$$CAR = \frac{\text{Tier 1 capital} + \text{Tier 2 capital}}{\text{Risk-weighted assets}}$$

Tier 1 capital includes bank reserves (from retained profits) and ordinary share capital, where dividends to shareholders vary with the amount of profit the bank makes. Such capital thus places no burden on banks in times of losses as no dividend need be paid. What is more, unlike depositors, shareholders cannot ask for their money back. Tier 2 capital consists largely of preference shares. These pay a fixed rate of interest and thus do continue to place a burden on the bank even when losses are made (unless the bank goes out of business).

Risk-weighted assets are the value of assets, where each type of asset is multiplied by a risk factor. Under the internationally agreed Basel II accord, cash and government bonds have a risk factor of zero and are thus not included. Inter-bank lending between the major banks has a risk factor of 0.2 and is thus included at only 20 per cent of its value; residential mortgages have a risk factor of 0.35; personal loans, credit-card debt and overdrafts have a risk factor of 1; loans to companies carry a risk factor of 0.2, 0.5, 1 or 1.5, depending on the credit rating of the company. Thus the greater the average risk factor of a bank's assets, the greater will be the value of its risk-weighted assets, and the lower will be its CAR.

Definitions

Liquidity The ease with which an asset can be converted into cash without loss.

Capital adequacy ratio (CAR) The ratio of a bank's capital (reserves and shares) to its risk-weighted assets. Under the Basel II Accord, a bank's CAR should be a minimum of 8 per cent.

The greater the CAR, the greater the capital adequacy of a bank. Under Basel II, banks are required to have a CAR of at least 8 per cent (i.e. 0.08). They are also required to hold a ratio of Tier 1 capital to risk-weighted assets of at least 4 per cent.

In times of lack of confidence of investors and/or of recession, more borrowers are likely to default on payment and thus a higher CAR may be necessary if the bank is to avoid becoming insolvent. Also, in such times, borrowing companies or other banks may have their credit rating downgraded, giving them a higher risk factor, thereby reducing the bank's CAR. This was the problem in 2008. Many banks needed an injection of capital (i.e. the sale of more shares) either from the private sector or the government, in order to maintain a high enough CAR to satisfy investors.

The balance between profitability and liquidity

Profitability is the major aim of banks and most other financial institutions. However, the aims of profitability and liquidity tend to conflict. In general, the more liquid an asset, the less profitable it is, and vice versa. Personal and business loans to customers are profitable to banks, but highly illiquid. Cash is totally liquid, but earns no profit. Thus financial institutions like to hold a range of assets with varying degrees of liquidity and profitability.

For reasons of *profitability*, the banks will want to 'borrow short' (at low rates of interest, as are generally paid on current accounts) and 'lend long' (at higher rates of interest, as are normal on personal loans). The difference in the average maturity of loans and deposits is known as the **maturity gap**. In general terms, the larger the maturity gap between loans and deposits, the greater the profitability. For reasons of *liquidity*, however, banks will want a relatively small gap: if there is a sudden withdrawal of deposits, banks will need to be able to call in enough loans.

The ratio of an institution's liquid assets to total assets is known as its **liquidity ratio**. For example, if a bank had £100 million of assets, of which £10 million were liquid and £90 million were illiquid, the bank would have a 10 per cent liquidity ratio. If a financial institution's liquidity ratio is too high, it will make too little profit. If the ratio is too low, there will be the risk that customers' demands may not be able to be met: this would cause a crisis of confidence and possible closure. Institutions thus have to make a judgement as to what liquidity ratio is best – one that is neither too high nor too low.

Balances in the central bank, short-term loans (i.e. those listed above) and government bonds with less than 12 months to maturity would normally be regarded as liquid assets.

Over the years, banks had reduced their liquidity ratios (i.e. the ratio of liquid assets to total assets). This was not a problem as long as banks could always finance lending to customers by borrowing on the inter-bank market. In 2008, however, banks became increasingly worried about bad debt. They thus felt the need to increase their liquidity ratios and hence cut back on lending and chose to keep a higher proportion of deposits in liquid form. In the UK, for example, banks substantially increased their level of reserves in the Bank of England.

 Why are government bonds that still have 11 months to run regarded as liquid, whereas overdrafts granted for a few weeks are not?

Secondary marketing and securitisation

As we have seen, one way of reconciling the two conflicting aims of liquidity and profitability is for financial institutions to hold a mixture of liquid and illiquid assets. Another way is through the *secondary marketing* of assets. This is where holders of assets sell them to someone else before the maturity date. This allows banks to close the maturity gap for *liquidity* purposes, but maintain the gap for *profitability* purposes.

Certificates of deposit (CDs) are a good example of secondary marketing. CDs are issued for fixed-period deposits in a bank (e.g. one year) at an agreed interest rate. The bank does not have to repay the deposit until the year is up. CDs are thus illiquid liabilities for the bank, and they allow it to increase the proportion of illiquid assets without having a dangerously high maturity gap. But the holder of the CD in the meantime can sell it to someone else (through a broker). It is thus liquid to the holder. Because CDs are liquid to the holder, they can be issued at a relatively *low* rate of interest and thus allow the bank to increase its profitability.

Another example of secondary marketing is when a financial institution sells some of its assets to another financial institution. The advantage to the first institution is that it gains liquidity. The advantage to the second one is that it gains profitable assets. The most common method for the sale of assets has been through a process known as *securitisation*.

Definitions

Maturity gap The difference in the average maturity of loans and deposits.

Liquidity ratio The proportion of a bank's total assets held in liquid form.

Secondary marketing Where assets are sold before maturity to another institution or individual. The possibility of secondary marketing encourages people or institutions to buy assets/grant loans in the primary market, knowing that they can sell them if necessary in the secondary market. The sale of existing shares and bonds on the stock market is an example of secondary marketing.

Securitisation Where future cash flows (e.g. from interest rate or mortgage payments) are turned into marketable securities, such as bonds. The sellers (e.g. banks) get cash immediately rather than having to wait and can use it to fund loans to customers. The buyers make a profit by buying below the discounted value of the future income. Such bonds can be very risky, however, as the future cash flows may be less than anticipated.

Figure 18.1 Securitisation chain

Securitisation occurs when a financial institution pools some of its assets, such as residential mortgages, and sells them to an intermediary known as a *special purpose vehicle (SPV)*. SPVs are legal entities created by the financial institution. In turn, the SPV funds its purchase of the assets by issuing bonds to investors (noteholders). These bonds are known as *collateralised debt obligations* (CDOs). Through this process, the financial institution removes the assets from its own balance sheets and so frees up capital for further advances. However, it continues to generate a return on its former assets by receiving a fee from the SPV for the servicing. In this way, it retains its relationships with its customers despite ceasing to own the assets. Indeed customers are very unlikely to be aware that their advance has been securitised.

The securitisation chain is illustrated in Figure 18.1. The financial institution looking to sell its assets is referred to as the 'originator' or the 'originator-lender'. Working from left to right, we see that the originator-lender sells its assets to another financial institution, the SPV, which then bundles assets together into CDOs and sells them to investors (e.g. banks or pension funds) as bonds. Now working from right to left, we see that by purchasing the bonds issued by the SPV, the investors provide the funds for the SPV's purchase of the lender's assets. The SPV is then able to use the proceeds from the bond sales (CDOs proceeds) to provide the originator-lender with liquidity.

The effect of secondary marketing is to reduce the liquidity ratio that banks feel they need to keep. It has the effect of increasing their maturity gap.

Dangers of secondary marketing. There are dangers to the banking system, however, from secondary marketing. To the extent that banks individually feel that they can operate with a lower liquidity ratio, so this will lead to a lower national liquidity ratio. This may lead to an excessive expansion of credit (illiquid assets) in times of economic boom.

Also, there is an increased danger of banking collapse. If one bank fails, this will have a knock-on effect on those banks which have purchased its assets. In the specific case of securitisation, the strength of the chain is potentially weakened if individual financial institutions move into riskier market segments, such as *sub-prime* residential mortgage markets. Should the income streams of the originator's assets dry up – for instance, if individuals default on their loans – then the impact is felt by the whole of the chain. In other words, institutions and investors are exposed to the risks of the originator's lending strategy.

The issue of securitisation and its impact on the liquidity of the financial system from 2006 is considered in Box 18.2.

The central bank

The Bank of England is the UK's central bank. The European Central Bank (ECB) is the central bank for the countries using the euro. The Federal Reserve Bank of America (the Fed) is the USA's central bank. All countries with their own currency have a central bank, and the central banks fulfil two vital roles in the economy.

The first is to oversee the whole monetary system and ensure that banks and other financial institutions operate as stably and as efficiently as possible.

The second is to act as the government's agent, both as its banker and in carrying out monetary policy. The Bank of England traditionally worked in very close liaison with the Treasury, and there used to be regular meetings between the Governor of the Bank of England and the Chancellor of the Exchequer. Although the Bank may have disagreed with Treasury policy, it always carried it out. With the election of the Labour government in 1997, however, the Bank of England was given independence to decide the course of monetary policy. In particular, this meant that the Bank of England and not the government would now decide interest rates.

Another example of an independent central bank is the European Central Bank, which operates the monetary policy

---

Definitions

Special purpose vehicle (SPV) Legal entity created by financial institutions for conducting specific financial functions, such as bundling assets together into fixed-interest bonds and selling them.

Collateralised debt obligations (CDOs) These are a type of security consisting of a bundle of fixed-income assets, such as corporate bonds, mortgage debt and credit-card debt.

Sub-prime debt Debt where there is a high risk of default by the borrower (e.g. mortgage holders who are on low incomes facing higher interest rates and falling house prices).

BOX 18.2 RESIDENTIAL MORTGAGES AND SECURITISATION

Was this the cause of the credit crunch?

The conflict between profitability and liquidity may have sown the seeds for the credit crunch that affected economies across the globe in the second half of the 2000s.

To understand this, consider the size of the 'advances' item in the banking sector's balance sheet – nearly 60 per cent of the value of sterling assets (see Table 18.1). The vast majority of these are to households. Advances secured against property have, in recent times, accounted for around 80 per cent by value of all household advances. *Residential mortgages* involve institutions lending long.

The number of residential mortgages rose as both the size of the housing stock and the proportion of owner-occupiers grew. Figures from the Department of Communities and Local Government show that the owner-occupation rate rose from 50 per cent in 1971 to 70 per cent in 2006.

But what further fuelled the growth in the *value* of residential mortgages was the long-term increase in house prices from 1996–2008 (see Box 2.2 on pages 46–7). While UK house prices are volatile, the trend has been for them to grow more quickly than consumer prices and so for the real price of housing to rise.

Securitisation of mortgages

One way in which individual institutions can achieve the necessary liquidity to expand the size of their mortgage lending (illiquid assets) is through *securitisation*. Securitisation has grown especially rapidly in the UK and the USA. In the UK this is particularly true amongst banks; building societies have historically made greater use of retail deposits to fund advances. Figures from the Bank of England show that the value of the securitisation of secured lending to individuals (e.g. mortgage debt) plus

loan transfers (a disposal of assets without the issue of bonds by an SPV) increased from just over £0.25 billion in 1997 to £102.5 billion in 2008 (see chart).

Securitisation is akin to financial re-engineering. It provides the originator-lenders with liquidity and enables them to engage in further lending opportunities. It provides the SPV with the opportunity to issue profitable securities. The increase in securitisation suggests that there has been a strong demand amongst investors for these securities. The attraction of these fixed-income products for the noteholders is the potential for higher returns than on similarly-rated products. However, investors have no recourse should people with mortgages fall into arrears or, worse still, default on their mortgages.

Risks and the sub-prime market

The securitisation of assets is not without risks for all those in the securitisation chain and consequently for the financial system as a whole.

The pooling of advances in itself *reduces* the cash-flow risk facing investors. However, there is a **moral hazard** problem here (see page 108). The pooling of the risks may encourage originator-lenders to lower their credit criteria by offering higher income multiples (advances relative to annual household incomes) or higher loan-to-value ratios (advances relative to the price of housing).

Towards the end of 2006 the USA witnessed an increase in the number of defaults by households on residential mortgages. This was a particular problem in the sub-prime market – higher-risk households with poor credit ratings. Similarly, the number falling behind with their payments rose. This was on the back of rising interest rates.

---

for the eurozone countries. Similarly, the Fed is independent of both the President and Congress, and its chairman is generally regarded as having great power in determining the country's economic policy. Although the degree of independence of central banks from government varies considerably around the world, there has been a general move in recent years to make central banks more independent.

If the UK were to adopt the euro, there would be a much reduced role for the Bank of England. At present, however, within its two broad roles, it has a number of different functions. Although we will consider the case of the Bank of England, the same principles apply to other central banks.

It issues notes

The Bank of England is the sole issuer of banknotes in England and Wales. (In Scotland and Northern Ireland, retail banks issue notes.) The issue of notes is done through the Issue Department, which organises their printing. This is one of two departments of the Bank of England. The other is the Banking Department. Table 18.2 shows the bal-

ance sheets of these two departments on 6 August 2008. The balance sheet of the Issue Department shows the outstanding value of the banknote issue and the assets that back this issue. As you can see from the balance sheet for the Issue Department, the note issue is largely backed by a mixture of short-term and long-term repos. The Ways and Means advance is the UK central government's overdraft facility at the Bank.

The amount of banknotes issued by the Bank of England depends largely on the demand for notes from the general public. If people draw more cash from their bank accounts,

Definition

Moral hazard The temptation to take more risks when you know that someone else will cover the risks if you get into difficulties. In the case of banks taking risks, the 'someone else' may be another bank, the central bank or the government.

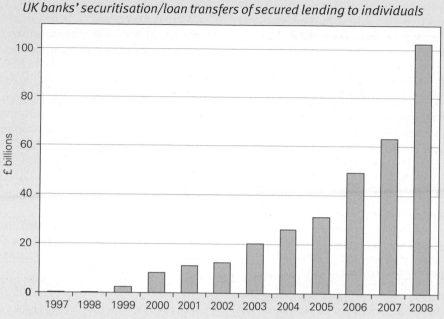

UK banks' securitisation/loan transfers of secured lending to individuals

Source: Based on data in *Bankstats* (Bank of England), Table A5.7.

These problems in the US sub-prime market are commonly seen as the catalyst for the liquidity problem that beset financial systems in 2007 and 2008. Where these assets have been securitised, investors, largely other financial institutions, suffer from the contagion arising from arrears and defaults.

Securitisation also internationalised the contagion. Investors are global, so that advances, such as a US family's residential mortgage, can cross national borders. This resulted in institutions writing off debts, a deterioration of their balance sheets, the collapse in the demand for securitised assets and the drying-up of liquidity.

 Does securitisation necessarily involve a moral hazard problem?

Table 18.2 Balance sheet of the Bank of England: 26 November 2008

Liabilities	£m	Assets	£m
Issue Department			
Notes in circulation	44 524	Short-term sterling reverse repo and other assets	29 310
Notes in Banking Department	0	Longer-term sterling reverse repo	10 446
		Bonds and other securities	4 399
		Ways and Means advance	370
	44 524		44 524
Banking Department			
Reserve balances	43 797	Longer-term sterling reverse repo	134 768
Short term open market operations	60 450	Bonds and other securities	6 959
Cash ratio deposits	2 280	Other assets	82 108
Foreign currency public securities	5 226		
Other liabilities	112 080		
	223 834		223 834

Source: Based on data in *Bankstats* (Bank of England), Table B1.1.1.

the banks will have to draw more cash from their balances in the Bank of England. These balances are held in the Banking Department. The Banking Department will thus have to acquire more notes from the Issue Department, which will simply print more in exchange for extra government or other securities supplied by the Banking Department. Thus the amount of notes in circulation is always more at Christmas time.

It acts as a bank

To the government. It keeps the two major government accounts: the 'Exchequer' and the 'National Loans Fund'. Taxation and government spending pass through the Exchequer. Government borrowing and lending pass through the National Loans Fund. The government tends to keep its deposits in the Bank of England (the *public deposits* item in the balance sheet) to a minimum. If the deposits begin to build up (from taxation), the government will probably spend them on paying back government debt. If, on the other hand, it runs short of money, it will simply borrow more.

To banks. Banks' deposits in the Bank of England consist of reserve balances and cash ratio deposits (see Table 18.1). As we have seen, the reserve balances are used for clearing purposes between the banks and to provide them with a source of liquidity. Banks undertake to hold a target level of reserves over any given month. If the average balance over the month is within ±1 per cent of a bank's chosen target, the bank is paid at Bank Rate. In times of uncertainty, banks may choose to hold greater reserve balances.

In addition, under its Operational Standing Facilities system, the Bank of England is prepared to lend to banks, on demand, through reverse repos[1] at 0.25 percentage points above Bank Rate or to receive extra deposits at 0.25 percentage points below Bank Rate.

To overseas central banks. These are deposits of sterling (or euros in the case of the ECB) made by overseas authorities as part of their official reserves and/or for purposes of intervening in the foreign exchange market in order to influence the exchange rate of their currency.

It manages the government's borrowing programme

Whenever the government runs a budget deficit (i.e. spends more than it receives in tax and other revenues), it will have to finance that deficit by borrowing. It can borrow by issuing bonds (gilts), National Savings certificates or Treasury bills. The Bank of England organises this borrowing. Even when the government runs a budget surplus, the Bank of England will still have to manage the national debt (the accumulated borrowing from the past). The reason is that old bonds will be maturing and new issues of bonds will probably be necessary to replace them.

When an old issue of bonds is approaching maturity, the Bank of England will probably enter the market to buy them back over a number of weeks or months, rather than waiting till the maturity date and then suddenly releasing a large amount of liquidity into the economy.

When a new issue of bonds is made, the Bank of England will set a minimum price somewhat below the £100 face value and then invite tenders for these bonds above or at the minimum price. It will allocate them in descending order from the highest-priced bid to the lowest. Any unsold bonds (known as 'tap stock') will then be released onto the market in an orderly way at a price set by the Bank of England. Any temporary shortfall of money for the government is met by issuing Treasury bills.

The issuing of bonds and bills will also depend on the operation of monetary policy. This is examined in Chapter 20.

It provides liquidity, as necessary, to banks

It attempts to ensure that there is always an adequate supply of liquidity to meet the legitimate demands of depositors in banks. As we shall see below, it does this through the discount and repo markets. In the crisis of 2008/9, the Bank of England, along with other central banks around the world, supplied massive amounts of extra liquidity in an attempt to combat the decline in inter-bank lending (see Box 18.3).

The Bank of England also operates a Discount Window Facility, whereby it allows banks to borrow gilts for up to a year against a wide range of assets as collateral. These gilts could then be sold on the money markets to provide banks with extra liquidity.

It oversees the activities of banks and other financial institutions

It advises banks on good banking practice. It discusses government policy with them and reports back to the government. It requires all recognised banks to maintain adequate liquidity: this is called **prudential control**.

Since May 1997, the Bank of England has ceased to be responsible for the detailed supervision of banks' activities. This responsibility has passed to the Financial Services Authority (FSA). As we shall see below, however, in 2007/8 many banks experienced a large rise in bad debts (much of it securitised 'sub-prime' mortgage debt) and a considerable shortage of liquidity. This raised the question of whether the FSA, or the Bank of England for that matter, was sufficiently watchful of banks' liquidity and the risks of liquidity shortage. Some commentators argued that a much tighter form of prudential control should have been imposed.

This was one of the major issues discussed at the summit of leaders of twenty of the world's largest economies (the

---

[1] Note that a repo to a bank (the borrower) is a reverse repo to the Bank of England (the lender).

> **Definition**
>
> **Prudential control** The insistence by the Bank of England that recognised banks maintain adequate liquidity.

'G20') in November 2008. It was agreed that much greater international co-ordination of bank regulation and surveillance was necessary to ensure that banks maintained sufficient liquidity and capital and were not overexposed to risky assets, such as sub-prime mortgage debt.

It operates the government's monetary and exchange rate policy

Monetary policy. The Bank of England's Monetary Policy Committee (MPC) sets Bank Rate at its monthly meetings. This nine-member committee consists of four experts appointed by the Chancellor of the Exchequer and four senior members of the Bank of England, plus the Governor in the chair. By careful management of the issue and re-purchasing of gilts and Treasury bills, the Bank of England then keeps interest rates in line with the level decided by the MPC. It also, in the process, influences the size of the money supply. Details of this are given in Chapter 20.

Exchange rate policy. The Bank of England manages the country's gold and foreign currency reserves on behalf of the Treasury. This is done through the **exchange equalisation account**. The Treasury sets the Bank an annual Remit for the management of the account (for example, setting a limit on changes in the level of reserves). By buying and selling foreign currencies on the foreign exchange market, the Bank of England can affect the exchange rate. For example, if there were a sudden selling of sterling (due, say, to bad trade figures and a resulting fear that the pound would depreciate), the Bank of England could help to prevent the pound from falling by using reserves to buy up pounds on the foreign exchange market. Intervention in the foreign exchange market is examined in detail in Chapter 25.

1. *Would it be possible for an economy to function without a central bank?*
2. *What effect would a substantial increase in the sale of government bonds and Treasury bills have on interest rates?*

The role of the money market

It is through the money market that a central bank exercises control of the economy. The market deals in short-term lending and borrowing.

We take the case of the London money market, which is normally divided into the 'discount' and 'repo' markets and the 'parallel' or 'complementary' markets.

The discount and repo markets

The markets for bills of exchange (the discount market) and for repos play a crucial role in ensuring that banks have sufficient liquidity to meet all their needs.

Assume that bank customers start drawing out more cash. As a result, banks find themselves short of liquid assets. What can they do? The answer is that they borrow from the Bank of England. There are two ways in which this can be done.

The first is to enter into a repo agreement, whereby the Bank of England buys gilts from the banks (thereby supplying them with money) on the condition that the banks buy the gilts back at a fixed price and on a fixed date, typically two weeks later. The repurchase price will be above the sale price. The difference is the equivalent of the interest that the banks are being charged for having what amounts to a loan from the Bank of England. The repurchase price (and hence the 'repo rate') is set by the Bank of England to reflect the Bank Rate chosen by the MPC (see section 20.2).

The second method is to sell Treasury bills back to the Bank of England before they have reached maturity (i.e. before the three months are up). This process is known as **rediscounting**. The Bank of England will pay a price below the face value, thus effectively charging interest to the banks. Again, the price is set so that the 'rediscount rate' reflects the Bank Rate.

In being prepared to rediscount bills or provide money through gilt repos, the Bank of England is thus the ultimate guarantor of sufficient liquidity in the monetary system and is known as the **lender of last resort**.

It is not uncommon for banks to need to acquire liquidity in this way. This shortage of liquidity allows the Bank of England to control interest rates. If the banks are forced to obtain liquidity from the Bank of England, they will be borrowing at the Bank of England's *chosen rate* (i.e. the repo rate). The banks will then have to gear their other rates to it, and other institutions will gear their rates to those of the banks. The way in which the Bank of England creates a shortage of liquidity and the way in which it forces through changes in interest rates are examined in section 20.2 and Box 20.4.

The Bank of England manages liquidity not only in order to achieve the rate of interest set by the MPC each month but also to ensure the *stability* of the financial system. Box 18.3 details the timeline of responses by the Bank of England to the stresses in the money markets from summer 2007.

The parallel money markets

The parallel money markets include the following:

- The inter-bank market (wholesale loans from one bank to another over periods from one day to up to several months). Inter-bank lending has traditionally been a major source of liquidity. Banks with surplus liquidity lend to other banks, which then use this as the basis for loans to individuals and companies. As we shall see

---

Definitions

Exchange equalisation account The gold and foreign exchange reserves account in the Bank of England.

Rediscounting bills of exchange Buying bills before they reach maturity.

Lender of last resort The role of the Bank of England as the guarantor of sufficient liquidity in the monetary system.

BOX 18.3 | TACKLING THE CREDIT CRUNCH

Doing whatever it takes?

A central bank manages liquidity to influence interest rates *and* to ensure stability of the financial system. From summer 2007, central banks, including the ECB, the Federal Reserve and the Bank of England, became increasingly pro-active in injecting liquidity into the financial system so as to underpin the lending activities of financial institutions.

But why were financial institutions short of liquidity? As we saw in Box 18.2, they were forced to write off bad debts, particularly those emanating from the securitisation of sub-prime residential mortgages. The deterioration in the balance sheets of banks meant that there was less surplus capital to fund advances.

The impact on the UK's inter-bank market is illustrated in chart (a). It depicts the one-month LIBOR, which is the rate at which institutions lend to each other for one month (see above, page 506), and the differential (or 'spread') between the LIBOR and Bank Rate (the Bank of England's repo rate and the rate it pays on banks' reserves). The spread of the LIBOR over the Bank Rate jumped to 0.75 percentage points in August 2007 and, though falling back a little, was still frequently pushing 0.5 percentage points through 2008.

Then with the crisis of October 2008, the spread widened considerably to 1.6 percentage points. Despite a cut in the Bank Rate from 5 to 4.5 per cent, the LIBOR actually rose (see chart (a)). This upward pressure on the spread is consistent with a shortage of surplus funds and fears by potential lenders that borrowing banks might go bust, leaving any unsecured debt unpaid.

Considerable media attention was focused on the impact of the credit crunch on households and firms. The attention on the housing and mortgage markets was particularly stark. Chart (b) shows the spread of the average mortgage rate over the Bank of England Bank Rate. Compared with the spread for the LIBOR, that for the mortgage rate is consistently positive. But, as with the LIBOR spread, we see the spread for mortgage rates rise in the latter part of 2007, rising to $2^1/_4$ percentage points over Bank Rate in February and April 2008.

Supplying liquidity through repos

The Bank of England provides liquidity to banks via 'open-market operations' (see Chapter 20, page 577). This involves the use of repos. The Bank of England offers funds for a fixed term against eligible collateral of a financial institution (such as government bonds – gilt repos).

In normal circumstances these repo operations are predominantly very short-term, examples being overnight 'fine-tuning' repo operations. But, as we have seen, in the period from summer 2007 circumstances ceased to be 'normal'. In response to the liquidity shortage, the Bank of England increased the maturity of its repo operations and expanded the type of collateral it was willing to lend against. It also increased the number of institutions it was prepared to lend to. For instance, on 18 March 2008 the Bank offered £10 billion in 3-month repos (much longer than the typical 1 to 14 days) and on 15 April 2008 it offered another £15 billion.[1]

(a) *LIBOR and Bank Rate*

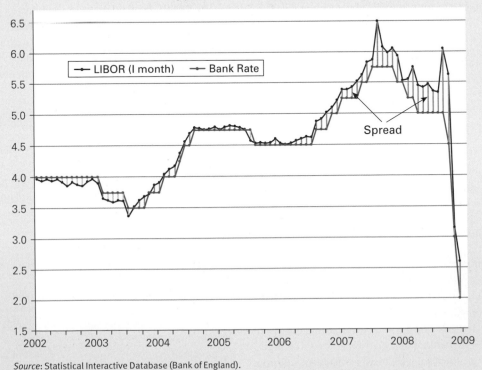

Source: Statistical Interactive Database (Bank of England).

This, however, was still not enough and on 21 April 2008 it introduced a 'Special Liquidity Scheme'. This enabled banks to swap high-quality but illiquid assets, such as mortgages and credit-card debt (but not sub-prime debt), for special one-year Treasury Bills that could then be exchanged for cash in the money markets. Banks could renew the swaps annually for up to three years. Responsibility for losses on their loans, however, stayed with the banks.[2] By September 2008, some £100 billion had been made available to banks under the scheme.

Bailing out banks under threat

As the credit crisis deepened during 2008, it became obvious that the measures of central banks around the world to supply extra liquidity were totally insufficient to tackle the problem. At the heart of the issue was a lack of trust between banks. With the securitisation of sub-prime debt, banks feared that many of other banks' assets were 'toxic'. In other words, these assets were becoming increasingly worthless as their market value plummeted. Why should bank A lend to bank B, if bank B might not be able to pay back the loan?

But this only made the problem worse. As inter-bank lending dried up, so banks with a high proportion of sub-prime assets looked increasingly vulnerable. As fear of bankruptcy spread, so several banks had to be bailed out by their respective governments.

Northern Rock in the UK was the first to be rescued. It was particularly vulnerable as it had financed mortgages of up to 120 per cent from borrowing on the inter-bank

market. After two unsuccessful bids to take over the bank and then with a run on the bank, with customers queuing to withdraw their money, the government was forced to take it into public ownership in February 2008. Deposits are now guaranteed by the Treasury.

Then, in the autumn of 2008, more banks around the world were bailed out by their respective governments: Bradford & Bingley in the UK, Fortis in the Benelux countries, the Belgian-French bank Dexia, the mortgage giants Freddie Mac and Fannie Mae in the USA, and the three main Icelandic banks.

In addition, governments felt it increasingly necessary to buy up toxic debts from banks. In the USA, after much debate, Congress accepted the Paulson Plan. This committed a staggering $700 billion to buy up banks' bad debt in return for a government stake in the banks. The US government would raise the money by selling Treasury securities on international markets.

But even this was insufficient to restore confidence and governments turned to even more drastic measures. The UK led the way with a three-pronged bailout package in October 2008.

Britain's three-pronged rescue plan

The rescue plan for the banking system was announced on 8 October 2008. It involved making an additional £400 billion available to banks in the UK (the same amount as the Paulson Plan for a country only one-fifth of the size of the USA). There were three elements of the plan:

(b) *Spread of average mortgage rate over Bank Rate*

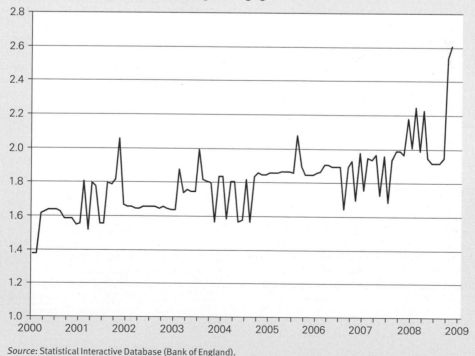

Source: Statistical Interactive Database (Bank of England).

- *Extra capital.* A total of up to £50 billion of extra capital would be provided to the seven largest banks and the largest building society as the government and FSA felt necessary. This was to tackle their growing capital inadequacy as the riskiness of their assets increased. The new capital was to be in the form of new shares.

  Five days later, after negotiations with the government and the FSA, it was announced that the Royal Bank of Scotland would raise £20 billion. This would have to be largely from the government, giving the government a 58 per cent stake in the bank. HBOS and Lloyds TSB, soon to be merged into the Lloyds Banking Group, would raise a combined £17 billion, again largely from the government, giving the government a 43 per cent stake. A new government body, the UK Financial Investments (UKFI), was created to manage the public shareholdings in banks. Other banks agreed to raise additional *private* capital to meet the government's requirements. For example, Barclays would raise an additional £6.6 billion.

  The net result was a significant increase in banks' capital ratios. For example, RBS's Tier 1 ratio rose by 4 percentage points. All banks would have a Tier 1 ratio of at least 9 per cent, giving them a considerable margin above the Basel II minimum capital adequacy ratio.

- *Additional liquidity.* An additional £100 billion was made available under the Special Liquidity Scheme (see above). What is more, riskier assets would be acceptable for swapping for Treasury Bills than previously. Also banks could exchange higher-risk assets for the low-risk ones *already* deposited with the Bank of England under the scheme. These low-risk assets could then be sold on the money markets. Also, as we have seen, under a new Discount Window Facility, banks could borrow gilts for up to 30 days against a wide range of assets. These gilts could be sold to provide short-term liquidity.

- *Guaranteeing loans on the inter-bank market.* Under the Credit Guarantee Scheme, £250 billion was made available for loan guarantees for new inter-bank lending. In other words, if bank A lends to bank B and bank B then defaults, the government would pay bank A. The hope was that this would 'kick-start' inter-bank lending.

The scale of this rescue plan was totally unprecedented and amounted to a partial nationalisation of some of Britain's biggest banks. In return for this support, banks had to agree to start lending to each other and to their customers again and to curb the pay and bonuses of their top executives, which in some cases had been several million pounds per year.

Developments elsewhere

A few days later, European leaders announced a similar rescue package for eurozone banks, worth €1.5 trillion. National governments would provide extra capital by buying preference shares; they would also guarantee inter-bank lending until the end of 2009. In addition they announced that no major bank would be allowed to fail.

The next day, the USA also announced a similar plan: $250 billion of the $700 billion from the Paulson plan would be used to buy preference shares in America's nine largest banks; the US Treasury would guarantee new inter-bank lending; it would also act as buyer of last resort for old commercial debt.

Subsequent events

Over the next few months the scale of bank losses turned out to be even worse than first thought. Also, as the recession deepened, banks were reluctant to restore lending for fear of incurring further bad debt (i.e. assets, such as loans and securitised bonds, which could not be redeemed in full – if at all). But increasing lending was vital to prevent a further collapse in aggregate demand. Thus governments had to take additional measures.

For example, in January 2009, the UK government announced a new rescue plan. The main element was an Asset Protection Scheme. This involved the government insuring banks against losses. Banks had to agree with the government the amount they expected to lose from bad debt and then the government, for a fee, would insure banks against 90 per cent of additional losses from this debt. In return for taking out the insurance, banks would have to agree to resume normal lending to both businesses and individuals. It was very difficult, however, to measure the value of risky assets, as the market in such assets had virtually collapsed.

The Credit Guarantee Scheme for new inter-bank lending was extended from April to December 2009. Once loans were made they could then be renewed in a rolling programme up to April 2014. In addition, the government would guarantee various high-quality asset-backed securities, including mortgages and corporate and consumer debt. This was a further attempt to encourage inter-bank lending. Also the Bank of England would extend the Discount Window Facility so that gilts could be borrowed for up to 1 year (as opposed to 30 days previously). This would give banks increased access to longer-term liquidity.

In February 2009 the government had once more to come to the rescue of RBS. It provided £19 billion of extra capital in exchange for £6.5 billion of ordinary shares, thereby increasing its stake in the bank from 58 to 70 per cent. It also agreed to guarantee £325 billion of RBS's assets against default under the Asset Protection Scheme. In return, RBS would have to increase lending by £25 billion over the following 12 months.

Then in March 2009, the government was forced again to come to the rescue of the Lloyds Banking Group, suffering from the bad debt inherited from HBOS. The government increased its stake in Lloyds from 43 to 65 per cent and agreed to guarantee £260 billion of assets under the Asset Protection Scheme. In return, Lloyds had to agree to increase its lending by £14 billion in 2009.

This comprehensive programme of support for bank lending was mirrored in various aspects in other countries around the world, all concerned to combat the drying up of credit and to lessen the depth of the oncoming recession.

1 Why may supplying extra liquidity to banks not necessarily be successful in averting a slowdown in borrowing and spending?

2 Why is there a potential 'moral hazard' in supporting failing banks? How could the terms of a bailout help to reduce this moral hazard?

[1] Further details of the Bank's open-market operations in managing the stability of the financial system during the liquidity crisis can be found in the Bank's *Financial Stability Report* at http://www.bankofengland.co.uk/publications/fsr/index.htm.

[2] See http://www.bankofengland.co.uk/markets/sls/.

below, during the financial crisis of 2008, inter-bank lending virtually ceased as banks became worried that the bank they were lending to might default.

- The market for certificates of deposit.
- The inter-companies deposit market (short-term loans from one company to another arranged through the market).
- The foreign currencies market (dealings in foreign currencies deposited short-term in London).
- The finance house market (short-term borrowing to finance hire purchase).
- The building society market (wholesale borrowing by the building societies).
- The commercial paper market (borrowing in sterling by companies, banks and other financial institutions by the issue of short-term (less than one year) 'promissory notes'. (These, like bills of exchange, are sold at a discount and redeemed at their face value, but in the interim can be traded on the market at any time.)

The parallel markets have grown in size and importance in recent years. The main reasons for this have been (a) the opening-up of markets to international dealing, given the abolition of exchange controls in 1979, (b) the deregulation of banking and money market dealing and (c) the volatility of interest rates and exchange rates, and thus the desire of banks to keep funds in a form that can be readily switched from one form of deposit to another, or from one currency to another. The main areas of growth have been in inter-bank deposits, certificates of deposit and the foreign currency markets.

Although the Bank of England has not traditionally dealt directly in the parallel markets and has not provided 'last-resort' lending facilities, it nevertheless closely monitors the various money market rates of interest and if necessary seeks to influence them, through its dealings in the discount and repo markets.

In October 2008, at the height of the credit crisis, the Bank of England announced that it would guarantee loans on the inter-bank market. With banks worried that other banks might default on loans, inter-bank lending had all but dried up. By removing the risk of default for lenders, the Bank of England was hoping to encourage banks to start lending to each other again (see Box 18.3).

 Why should Bank of England determination of the rate of interest in the discount and repo markets also influence rates of interest in the parallel markets?

Section summary

1. Central to the financial system are the retail and wholesale arms of banks. Between them they provide the following important functions: giving expert advice, channelling capital to areas of highest return, maturity transformation, risk transformation and the transmission of payments. Some of these banks had to be rescued by the government in 2008 – they were too important to the health of the economy to be allowed to fail.

2. Banks' liabilities include both sight and time deposits. They also include certificates of deposit and repos. Their assets include: notes and coin, balances with the Bank of England, market loans, bills of exchange (Treasury bills and commercial bills), reverse repos, advances to customers (the biggest item – including overdrafts, personal loans, credit-card debt and mortgages) and investments (government bonds and inter-bank investments). In recent years they have increasingly included securitised assets.

3. Banks aim to make profits, but they must also have a sufficient capital base and maintain sufficient liquidity. Liquid assets, however, tend to be relatively unprofitable and profitable assets tend to be relatively illiquid. Banks therefore need to keep a balance of profitability and liquidity in their range of assets.

4. The Bank of England is the UK's central bank. It issues notes; it acts as banker to the government, to banks and to various overseas central banks; it manages the government's borrowing programme; it ensures sufficient liquidity for the financial sector; it operates the country's monetary and exchange rate policy.

5. The money market is the market in short-term deposits and loans. It consists of the discount and repo markets and the parallel money markets.

6. The Bank of England operates in the repo and discount markets. By buying (rediscounting) bills and through gilt repos, it provides liquidity to the banks at the rate of interest chosen by the Monetary Policy Committee (Bank Rate). It is always prepared to lend in this way in order to ensure adequate liquidity in the economy. To supplement this process, the Bank of England introduced a Special Liquidity Scheme in 2008 as inter-bank lending declined during the credit crunch.

7. The parallel money markets consist of various markets in short-term finance between various financial institutions.

18.3 THE SUPPLY OF MONEY

Definitions of the money supply

If money supply is to be monitored and possibly controlled, it is obviously necessary to measure it. But what should be included in the measure? Here we need to distinguish between the *monetary base* and *broad money*.

The **monetary base** (or 'high-powered money') consists of cash (notes and coin) in circulation outside the central bank. Thus, in the eurozone, the monetary base is given by cash (euros) in circulation outside the ECB.[1]

But the monetary base gives us a very poor indication of the effective money supply, since it excludes the most important source of liquidity for spending: namely, bank deposits. The problem is which deposits to include. We need to answer three questions:

- Should we include just sight deposits, or time deposits as well?
- Should we include just retail deposits, or wholesale deposits as well?
- Should we include just bank deposits, or building society (savings institution) deposits as well?

In the past there has been a whole range of measures, each including different combinations of these accounts. However, financial deregulation, the abolition of foreign exchange controls and the development of computer technology have led to huge changes in the financial sector throughout the world. This has led to a blurring of the distinctions between different types of account. It has also made it very easy to switch deposits from one type of account to another. For these reasons, the most usual measure that countries use for money supply is **broad money**, which in most cases includes both time and sight deposits, retail and wholesale deposits, and bank and building society (savings institution) deposits.

In the UK this measure of broad money is known as *M4*. In most other European countries and the USA it is known as *M3*. There are, however, minor differences between countries in what is included. (Official UK and eurozone measures of money supply are given in Box 18.4.)

As we have seen, bank deposits of one form or another constitute by far the largest component of (broad) money supply. To understand how money supply expands and contracts, and how it can be controlled, it is thus necessary to understand what determines the size of bank deposits.

Banks can themselves expand the amount of bank deposits, and hence the money supply, by a process known as 'credit creation'.

The creation of credit: the simplest case

To illustrate this process in its simplest form, assume that banks have just one type of liability – deposits – and two types of asset – balances with the central bank (to achieve liquidity) and advances to customers (to earn profit).

Banks want to achieve profitability while maintaining sufficient liquidity. Assume that they believe that sufficient liquidity will be achieved if 10 per cent of their assets are held as balances with the central bank. The remaining 90 per cent will then be in advances to customers. In other words, the banks operate a 10 per cent liquidity ratio.

Assume initially that the combined balance sheet of the banks is as shown in Table 18.3. Total deposits are £100 billion, of which £10 billion (10 per cent) are kept in balances with the central bank. The remaining £90 billion (90 per cent) are lent to customers.

Now assume that the government spends more money – £10 billion, say, on roads or hospitals. It pays for this with cheques drawn on its account with the central bank. The people receiving the cheques deposit them in their banks. Banks return these cheques to the central bank and their balances correspondingly increase by £10 billion. The combined banks' balance sheet now is shown in Table 18.4.

But this is not the end of the story. Banks now have surplus liquidity. With their balances in the central bank having increased to £20 billion, they now have a liquidity ratio of 20/110, or 18.2 per cent. If they are to return to a 10 per cent liquidity ratio, they need only retain £11 billion as balances at the central bank (£11 billion/£110 billion = 10 per cent). The remaining £9 billion they can lend to customers.

Table 18.3	Banks' original balance sheet		
Liabilities	**£bn**	**Assets**	**£bn**
Deposits	100	Balances with the central bank	10
		Advances	90
Total	100	Total	100

[1] Before 2006, there used to be a measure of narrow money called 'M0'. This included cash in circulation outside the Bank of England and banks' non-interest-bearing 'operational balances' in the Bank of England, with these balances accounting for a tiny proportion of the whole. Since 2006, the Bank of England has allowed banks to hold interest-bearing reserve accounts, which are much larger than the former operational balances. The Bank of England thus decided to discontinue M0 as a measure and focus on cash in circulation as its measure of narrow money.

Definitions

Monetary base Notes and coin outside the central bank.

Broad money Cash in circulation plus retail and wholesale bank and building society deposits.

TC 15
p487

BOX 18.4 UK AND EUROZONE MONETARY AGGREGATES

CASE STUDIES AND APPLICATIONS

How long is a piece of string?

UK measures

There are two main measures of the money supply in the UK: cash in circulation (i.e. outside the Bank of England) and M4. Cash in circulation is referred to as the 'monetary base' or 'narrow money' and M4 is referred to as 'broad money' or simply as 'the money supply'. In addition, there is a measure called 'Retail deposits and cash in M4' (previously known as M2). This measure excludes wholesale deposits.

The definitions are as follows:

Cash in circulation. This is all cash held outside the Bank of England: in other words by individuals, firms, banks and the public sector.

Retail deposits and cash in M4. Cash in circulation with the public (but not cash in banks and building societies) + private-sector *retail* sterling deposits in banks and building societies.

M4. Retail deposits and cash in M4 + private-sector wholesale sterling deposits in banks and building societies + sterling certificates of deposit.

Table (a) gives the figures for these aggregates for the end of December 2008.

(a) *UK monetary aggregates, end December 2008 (not seasonally adjusted)*

	£ million
Cash in circulation (i.e. outside the Bank of England)[a]	54 399
− Cash in banks and cash held outside the country[a b]	−9 531
+ Private-sector retail bank and building society deposits	1 077 872
= **Retail deposits and cash in M4**	**1 122 740**
+ Private-sector wholesale bank and building society deposits + CDs	827 097
= **M4**	**1 949 837**

[a] Cash in circulation is calculated mid-month and thus the figure slightly understates the end-month value.

[b] Row 4 minus rows 3 and 1.

Source: Based on data in Monetary and Financial Statistics, *Bankstats*, January (Bank of England 2009), Tables A1.1.1 and A2.2.1.

 Why is cash in banks and building societies not included in M4?

Eurozone measures

Although the ECB uses three measures of the money supply, they are different from those used by the Bank of England. The narrowest definition (M1) includes overnight deposits (i.e. call money) as well as cash, and is thus much broader than the UK's narrow money measure. The broadest eurozone measure (M3) is again broader than the UK's broadest measure (M4), since the eurozone measure includes various other moderately liquid assets. The definitions of the three eurozone aggregates are:

M1. Cash in circulation with the public + overnight deposits.

M2. M1 + deposits with agreed maturity up to two years + deposits redeemable up to three months' notice.

M3. M2 + repos + money-market funds and paper + debt securities with residual maturity up to two years.

Table (b) gives the figures for UK money supply for each of these three ECB measures – again, for the end of December 2008.

(b) *UK money supply using ECB measures: end December 2008 (not seasonally adjusted)*

	£ million
Currency in circulation	45 577
+ Overnight deposits	983 487
= **M1**	**1 029 063**
+ Deposits with agreed maturity up to 2 years	222 665
+ Deposits redeemable up to 3 months' notice	624 565
= **M2**	**1 876 293**
+ Repos	207 683
+ Money market funds and paper	85 262
+ **M3**	**2 169 238**

Source: Monetary and Financial Statistics, *Bankstats*, January (Bank of England 2009), Table A2.3.

 What are the benefits of including these additional items in the broad measure of money supply?

Table 18.4 The initial effect of an additional deposit of £10 billion

Liabilities	£bn	Assets	£bn
Deposits (old)	100	Balances with the central bank (old)	10
Deposits (new)	10	Balances with the central bank (new)	10
		Advances	90
Total	110	Total	110

Table 18.5	The full effect of an additional deposit of £10 billion			
Liabilities	**£bn**	**Assets**		**£bn**
Deposits (old)	100	Balances with the central bank (old)		10
Deposits (new: initial)	10	Balances with the central bank (new)		10
(new: subsequent)	90	Advances (old)		90
		Advances (new)		90
Total	200	Total		200

Assume now that customers spend this £9 billion in shops and the shopkeepers deposit the cheques in *their* bank accounts. When the cheques are cleared, the balances in the central bank of the *customers'* banks will duly be debited by £9 billion, but the balances in the central bank of the *shopkeepers'* banks will be credited by £9 billion, *leaving overall balances in the central bank unaltered.* There is still a surplus of £9 billion over what is required to maintain the 10 per cent liquidity ratio. The new deposits of £9 billion in the shopkeepers' banks, backed by balances in the central bank, can thus be used as the basis for *further* loans. Ten per cent (i.e. £0.9 billion) must be kept back in the central bank, but the remaining 90 per cent (i.e. £8.1 billion) can be lent out again.

When the money is spent and the cheques are cleared, this £8.1 billion will still remain as surplus balances in the central bank and can therefore be used as the basis for yet more loans. Again, 10 per cent must be retained and the remaining 90 per cent can be lent out. This process goes on and on until eventually the position is as shown in Table 18.5.

The initial increase in balances with the central bank of £10 billion has allowed banks to create new advances (and hence deposits) of £90 billion, making a total increase in money supply of £100 billion.

TC 15
p487

This effect is known as the **bank deposits multiplier**. In this simple example with a liquidity ratio of 1/10 (i.e. 10 per cent), the bank deposits multiplier is 10. An initial increase in deposits of £10 billion allowed total deposits to rise by £100 billion. In this simple world, therefore, the bank deposits multiplier is the inverse of the liquidity ratio (l).

Bank deposits multiplier = $1/l$

?   *If banks choose to operate a 20 per cent liquidity ratio and receive extra cash deposits of £10 million,*
   (a) How much credit will ultimately be created?
   (b) By how much will total deposits have expanded?
   (c) What is the size of the bank deposits multiplier?

Definition

Bank deposits multiplier The number of times greater the expansion of bank deposits is than the additional liquidity in banks that causes it: 1/l (the inverse of the liquidity ratio).

*LOOKING AT THE MATHS

The process of credit creation can be expressed mathematically as the sum of an infinite series. If a is the proportion of any deposit that is lent by banks, where $a = 1 - l$, then total deposits will expand by

$$D_T = D_0(1 + a + a^2 + a^3 + \ldots)$$
$$= D_0(1/1 - a)$$
$$= D_0(1/l) \qquad \text{(1)}$$

Thus if there were an initial additional deposit (D_0) of £100 and if $a = 0.8$, giving a liquidity ratio (l) of 0.2, total deposits would expand by £100 × 1/0.2 = £500. The bank deposits multiplier is 5.

Proof of equation (1) is given in Maths Case 18.1 in MyEconLab.

Note that the maths of the bank deposits multiplier is very similar to that of the Keynesian expenditure multiplier of section 17.2 (see Maths Case 17.1 in MyEconLab). The economics, however, is quite different. The Keynesian multiplier is concerned with the effects of increased demand on real national output. The bank deposits multiplier is simply concerned with money creation.

TC 12
p395

The creation of credit: the real world

In practice, the creation of credit is not as simple as this. There are three major complications.

Banks' liquidity ratio may vary

Banks may choose a different liquidity ratio. At certain times, banks may decide that it is prudent to hold a bigger proportion of liquid assets. For example, if banks are worried about increased risks of default on loans, they may choose to hold a higher liquidity ratio to ensure that they have enough to meet customers' needs. This was the case in 2008 when many banks became less willing to lend to other banks for fear of the other banks' assets containing sub-prime debt. Banks, as a result, hoarded cash and became more cautious about granting loans.

On the other hand, there may be an upsurge in consumer demand for credit. Banks may be very keen to grant additional loans and thus make more profits, even though they have acquired no additional assets. They may simply go ahead and expand credit, and accept a lower liquidity ratio.

Customers may not want to take up the credit on offer. Banks may wish to make additional loans, but customers may not want to borrow. There may be insufficient demand. But will the banks not then lower their interest rates, thus encouraging people to borrow? Possibly; but if they lower the rate they charge to borrowers, they must also lower the rate they pay to depositors. But then depositors may switch to other institutions such as building societies.

 How will an increased mobility of savings and other capital between institutions affect this argument?

Banks may not operate a simple liquidity ratio

The fact that banks hold a number of fairly liquid assets, such as short-term loans to other banks on the inter-bank market, bills of exchange and certificates of deposit, makes it difficult to identify a simple liquidity ratio. For example, if banks use £1 million in cash to purchase £1 million of bills, can we assume that the liquidity ratio has remained exactly the same? In other words, can we assume that *near money* assets, such as bills, are just as liquid as cash? If we assume that they are not, then has the liquidity ratio fallen? If so, by how much?

Banks do not see a clear-cut dividing line between liquid and non-liquid assets. They try to maintain a rough balance across the liquidity range, but the precise composition of assets will vary as interest rates on the various assets vary, and as the demands for liquidity vary.

In practice, therefore, the size of the bank deposits multiplier will vary and is thus difficult to predict in advance.

 Is the following statement true: 'The greater the number of types of asset that are counted as being liquid, the smaller will be the bank deposits multiplier'?

Some of the extra cash may be withdrawn by the public

If extra cash comes into the banking system, and as a result extra deposits are created, part of them may be held by households and non-bank firms (known in this context as the *non-bank private sector*) as cash *outside* the banks. In other words, some of the extra cash leaks out of the banking system. This will result in an overall multiplier effect that is smaller than the full bank deposits multiplier. This overall multiplier is known as the *money multiplier*. It is

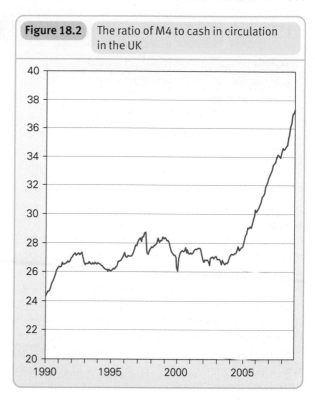

Figure 18.2 The ratio of M4 to cash in circulation in the UK

Source: Based on data in Statistical Interactive Database (Bank of England).

defined as the rise in total money supply expressed as a proportion of the rise in the monetary base that caused it: $\Delta M_s / \Delta M_b$ (where M_s is total broad money supply and M_b is the monetary base). The precise value will, of course, depend on how the broad money supply and the monetary base are defined. In the UK, the money multiplier is usually given by $\Delta M4 / \Delta$cash in circulation. In the eurozone it is given by $\Delta M3 / \Delta$currency. Box 18.5 shows how the money multiplier is calculated.

The money multiplier in the UK

The UK money multiplier grew rapidly after 2004. An indication of this is given by the ratio of the *level* of M4 to the *level* of cash in circulation. This is plotted in Figure 18.2. From the mid 1990s to the mid 2000s, the value of this ratio was between 26 and 29. It then increased markedly. In other words, for a given monetary base (i.e. cash in circulation), much more credit was created. The effect of this was to give a bigger money multiplier: in other words, for a given *change* in cash in circulation, there would be a bigger *change* in M4 than previously.

But why did M4 increase in this way relative to the monetary base? The next section looks at factors determining the money supply.

 Which would you expect to fluctuate more, the money multiplier ($\Delta M4 / \Delta$cash), or the simple ratio, M4/cash, illustrated in Figure 18.2?

Definitions

Near money Highly liquid assets (other than cash).

Non-bank private sector Households and non-bank firms. In other words, everyone in the country other than banks and the government (central and local).

Money multiplier The number of times greater the expansion of money supply is than the expansion of the monetary base that caused it: $\Delta M_s / \Delta M_b$.

The money multiplier (m) is the rise in total money supply (ΔM_s) divided by the rise in the monetary base (ΔM_b):

$$m = \Delta M_s / \Delta M_b \qquad (1)$$

The total money supply (M_s) consists of deposits in banks and building societies (D) plus cash held by the public (C). Thus a rise in money supply would be given by

$$\Delta M_s = \Delta D + \Delta C \qquad (2)$$

The monetary base (M_b) consists of bank and building society reserves (R) plus cash held by the public (C). Thus a rise in the monetary base would be given by

$$\Delta M_b = \Delta R + \Delta C \qquad (3)$$

Thus, by substituting equations (2) and (3) into equation (1), the money multiplier is given by

$$m = \frac{\Delta D + \Delta C}{\Delta R + \Delta C} \qquad (4)$$

Assume now that banks wish to hold a given fraction (r) of any rise in deposits in the form of reserves, i.e.

$$r = \Delta R / \Delta D \qquad (5)$$

and that the public wishes to hold a given fraction (c) of any rise in its deposits as cash, i.e.

$$c = \Delta C / \Delta D \qquad (6)$$

If we now divide the top and bottom of equation (4) by ΔD, we get

$$m = \frac{\Delta D / \Delta D + \Delta C / \Delta D}{\Delta R / \Delta D + \Delta C / \Delta D} = \frac{1 + c}{r + c} \qquad (7)$$

Thus if c were 0.2 and r were 0.1, the money multiplier would be

$$(1 + 0.2) / (0.1 + 0.2) = 1.2 / 0.3 = 4$$

i.e.

$$\Delta M_s = 4 \times \Delta M_b$$

1. If c were 0.1 and r were 0.01, by how much would money supply expand if the monetary base rose by £1 million?
2. Money supply (M4) includes wholesale as well as retail deposits. Given that firms will wish to keep only a very small fraction of a rise in wholesale deposits in cash (if any at all), how will a change in the balance of wholesale and retail deposits affect the value of c and hence of the money multiplier?

What causes money supply to rise?

There are four sets of circumstances in which the money supply can rise.

Banks choose to hold a lower liquidity ratio

If banks collectively choose to hold a lower liquidity ratio, they will have surplus liquidity. The banks have tended to choose a lower liquidity ratio over time because of the increasing use of direct debits and debit-card and credit-card transactions.

Surplus liquidity can be used to expand advances, which will lead to a multiplied rise in broad money supply (e.g. M4).

An important trend in recent years has been the growth in *inter-bank lending*. Table 18.1 showed that short-term loans to other banks (including overseas banks) are now the largest element in banks' liquid assets. These assets may be used by a bank as the basis for expanding loans and thereby starting a chain of credit creation. But although these assets are liquid to an *individual bank*, they do not add to the liquidity of the banking system *as a whole*. By using them for credit creation, the banking system is operating with a lower *overall* liquidity ratio.

This was a major element in the banking crisis of 2008. By operating with a collectively low liquidity ratio, banks were vulnerable to people defaulting on debt, such as mortgages. The problem was compounded by the holding of sub-prime debt in the form of securitised assets. Realising the vulnerability of other banks, banks became increasingly unwilling to lend to each other. The resulting decline in inter-bank lending reduced the amount of credit created.

What effects do debit cards and cash machines (ATMs) have on (a) banks' prudent liquidity ratios; (b) the size of the bank deposits multiplier?

The non-bank private sector chooses to hold less cash

Households and firms may choose to hold less cash. Again, the reason may be a greater use of cards, direct debits, etc. (see Box 18.6). This means that a greater proportion of the cash base will be held as deposits in banks rather than in people's wallets, purses or safes outside banks. The extra cash deposits allow banks to create more credit.

The above two reasons for an expansion of broad money supply (M4) are because more credit is being created for a given monetary base. As Figure 18.2 showed, the ratio of M4 to cash rose substantially after 2003. The other two reasons for an expansion of money supply are reasons why the monetary base itself might expand.

An inflow of funds from abroad

If the government intervenes in the foreign exchange market to maintain a rate of exchange *below* the equilibrium, there will be an excess demand for sterling (see Figure 15.14 on page 444). To maintain the exchange rate at this level, the Bank of England has to buy up the excess foreign currencies on offer with *extra* pounds, thereby building up the foreign currency reserves. When this sterling is used to pay for UK exports and is then deposited back in the banks by the exporters, credit will be created on the basis of it, leading to a *multiplied* increase in money supply.

The money supply will also expand if depositors of *sterling* in banks overseas then switch these deposits to banks in the UK. This is a *direct* increase in the money supply. In an open economy like the UK, movements of sterling and other currencies into and out of the country can be very large, leading to large fluctuations in the money supply.

A public-sector deficit

The public-sector net cash requirement (PSNCR) is the difference between public-sector expenditure and public-sector receipts. To meet this deficit, the government has to borrow money by selling interest-bearing securities (Treasury bills and gilts). In general, the bigger the PSNCR, the greater will be the growth in the money supply. Just how the money supply will be affected, however, depends on who buys the securities.

Such securities could be sold to the Bank of England. In this case, the Bank of England credits the government's account to the value of the securities it has purchased. When the government spends the money, it draws on its account with the Bank of England. When the recipients of this money pay it into their bank accounts, these additional balances will then become the basis for credit creation. There will be a multiplied expansion of the money supply.

Similarly, if the government borrows through additional Treasury bills, and if these are purchased by the banking sector, there will be a multiplied expansion of the money supply. The reason is that, although banks' balances at the central bank will go down when the banks purchase the bills, they will go up again when the government spends the money. In addition, the banks will now have additional liquid assets (bills), which can be used as the basis for credit creation.

If, however, the government securities are purchased by the non-bank private sector the money supply will remain unchanged. When people buy the bonds or bills, they will draw money from their banks. When the government spends the money, it will be redeposited in banks. There is no increase in money supply. It is just a case of existing money changing hands.

The government could attempt to minimise the boost to money supply by financing the PSNCR through the sale of gilts, since, even if these were partly purchased by the banks, they could not be used as the basis for credit creation.

Note that if there is a public-sector *surplus* (a negative PSNCR), this will either reduce the money supply or have no effect, depending on what the government does with the surplus. The fact that there is a surplus means that the public sector is spending less than it receives in taxes, etc. The initial effect, therefore, is to reduce the money in the economy: it is being 'retired' in the central bank.

If, however, the government then uses this money to buy back securities from the non-bank private sector, the money will merely return to the economy, and there will be no net effect on money supply.

If the government borrows but does not spend the proceeds, what effect will this have on the money supply if it borrows from
(a) the banking sector;
(b) the non-bank private sector?

The flow-of-funds equation

All these effects on money supply can be summarised using a ***flow-of-funds equation***. This shows the components of a *change* in money supply (ΔM_s). The following flow-of-funds equation is the one most commonly used in the UK, that for M4. It consists of four items (or 'counterparts' as they are known):

ΔM4	equals	PSNCR	(Item 1)
	minus	Sales of public-sector debt to (or *plus* purchases of public-sector debt from) the non-bank private sector	(Item 2)
	plus	Banks' and building societies' sterling lending to the UK private sector	(Item 3)
	plus	External effect	(Item 4)

Public-sector borrowing (item 1) will lead to a direct increase in the money supply, but not if it is funded by selling bonds and bills to the non-bank private sector. Such sales (item 2) have therefore to be subtracted from the PSNCR. But conversely, if the government buys back old bonds from the non-bank private sector, this will further increase the money supply.

The initial increase in liquidity from the sale of government securities to the banking sector is given by item 1. This increase in their liquidity will enable banks to create credit. To the extent that this extra lending is to the UK private sector (item 3), money supply will increase, and by a multiple of the initial increase in liquidity (item 1). Bank lending may also increase (item 3) even if there is no increase in liquidity or even a reduction in liquidity (item 1 is zero or negative), if banks respond to increases in the demand for loans by accepting a lower liquidity ratio, or if, through securitisation and other forms of secondary marketing, individual banks gain extra liquidity from each other, even though there is no total increase in liquidity in the banking system. Item 3 will be reduced if banks choose to hold more capital.

Finally, if there is a net inflow of funds from abroad (item 4), this too will increase the money supply.

The flow-of-funds equation that we have just described is a simplified version of the one actually used in official statistics to analyse the components of changes in M4. The

---

Definition

Flow-of-funds equation The various items making up an increase (or decrease) in money supply.

Table 18.6 Counterparts to changes in M4 (£m)

	PSNCR (+) (Public-sector net cash requirement) (1)	Sales (−)/purchases (+) of public-sector debt to/from non-bank private sector (2)	Banks' and building societies' sterling lending to UK private sector (less increases in bank's capital) (3)	External effect: inflows (+)/ outflows (−) (4)	Total ∆M4
2000	−37 525	+13 536	+80 279	+10 689	=+66 979
2004	+41 150	−26 298	+86 000	−4 249	=+96 603
2007	+32 343	−2 673	+233 549	−80 528	=+182 691

Source: Based on data from www.statistics.gov.uk (National Statistics).

equation can easily be modified to show changes in retail deposits in M4 or the eurozone measure of M3.

Table 18.6 shows the components of changes in M4 for 2000, 2004 and 2007. It is interesting to compare 2007 with 2000. In 2007 there was a large public-sector deficit (PSNCR) (item 1), which therefore had the effect of increasing the money supply. The effect was compounded by a very large increase in bank lending (item 3) but was offset somewhat by sales of government stock (item 2) and a substantial outflow of funds abroad (item 4). By contrast, in 2000 there was a large public-sector surplus (a negative PSNCR), which, other things being equal, would have reduced the money supply. But as you can see quite clearly from the table, other things were not equal: there was quite a large increase in bank lending (item 3), compounded by the use of some of the public-sector surplus to purchase government stock (item 2) and a moderate inflow of funds from abroad (item 4).

The relationship between money supply and the rate of interest

Simple monetary theory often assumes that the supply of money is totally independent of interest rates. This is illustrated in Figure 18.3. The money supply is *exogenous*. It is assumed to be determined by the government or central bank ('the authorities'): what the authorities choose it to be, or what they allow it to be by their choice of the level and method of financing the PSNCR.

In practice, however, even if narrow money were to be tightly controlled by the central bank (which it is not), it would be very hard to have a precise control of broad money. More complex models, therefore, and especially Keynesian

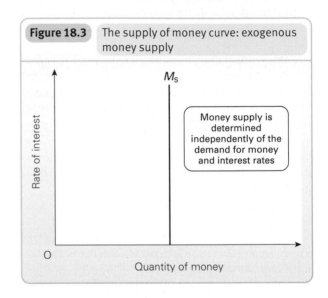

Figure 18.3 The supply of money curve: exogenous money supply

M_S

Rate of interest

Quantity of money

Money supply is determined independently of the demand for money and interest rates

models, assume that money supply is *endogenous*: that it depends on the demand for money. The argument is that higher money demand will result in higher interest rates and in higher levels of money supplied. The result is an upward sloping money supply curve, as in Figure 18.4. The reasons for this are as follows:

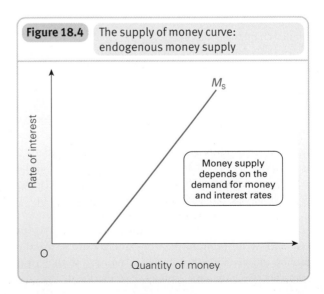

Figure 18.4 The supply of money curve: endogenous money supply

M_S

Rate of interest

Quantity of money

Money supply depends on the demand for money and interest rates

Definitions

Exogenous money supply Money supply that does not depend on the demand for money but is set by the authorities.

Endogenous money supply Money supply that is determined (at least in part) by the demand for money.

- Increases in money supply may occur as a result of banks expanding credit in response to the demand for credit. This assumes that banks have surplus liquidity in the first place, or are happy to operate with lower liquidity, or can increase liquidity through secondary marketing of otherwise illiquid assets, or can obtain liquidity from the central bank through repos. Higher demand for credit will drive up interest rates, making it more profitable for banks to supply more credit.

- Higher interest rates may encourage depositors to switch their deposits from sight accounts (earning little or no interest) to time accounts. Since money is less likely to be withdrawn quickly from time accounts, banks may feel the need to hold less liquidity, and therefore may

decide to increase credit, thus expanding the money supply.

- Higher interest rates attract deposits from overseas. This increases the money supply to the extent that the Bank of England does not allow the exchange rate to appreciate in response.

To summarise: an increase in demand for money raises interest rates, which in turn increases the quantity of money supplied (see sections 18.4 and 18.5): a movement along an upward-sloping money supply curve.

Some economists go further still. They argue that not only is money supply endogenous, but the 'curve' is effectively horizontal; money supply expands passively to match the demand for money.

Section summary

1. Money supply can be defined in a number of different ways, depending on what items are included. A useful distinction is between narrow money and broad money. Narrow money includes just cash, and possibly banks' balances at the central bank. Broad money also includes deposits in banks and possibly various other short-term deposits in the money market. In the UK, M4 is the preferred measure of broad money. In the eurozone it is M3.

2. Bank deposits are a major proportion of broad money supply. The expansion of bank deposits is the major element in the expansion of the money supply.

3. Bank deposits expand through a process of credit creation. If banks' liquid assets increase, they can be used as a base for increasing loans. When the loans are redeposited in banks, they form the base for yet more loans, and thus a process of multiple credit expansion takes place. The ratio of the increase of deposits to an expansion of banks' liquidity base is called the 'bank deposits multiplier'. It is the inverse of the liquidity ratio.

4. In practice, it is difficult to predict the precise amount by which money supply will expand if there is an

increase in cash. The reasons are that banks may choose to hold a different liquidity ratio; customers may not take up all the credit on offer; there may be no simple liquidity ratio given the range of near money assets; and some of the extra cash may leak away into extra cash holdings by the public.

5. Money supply will rise if (a) banks choose to hold a lower liquidity ratio and thus create more credit for an existing amount of liquidity; (b) people choose to hold less cash outside the banks; (c) there is a net inflow of funds from abroad; (d) the government runs a PSNCR and finances it by borrowing from the banking sector or from abroad.

6. The flow-of-funds equation shows the components of any change in money supply. A rise in money supply equals the PSNCR *minus* sales of public-sector debt to the non-bank private sector, *plus* banks' lending to the private sector (less increases in banks' capital), *plus* inflows of money from abroad.

7. Simple monetary theory assumes that the supply of money is independent of interest rates. In practice, a rise in interest rates (in response to a higher demand for money) will often lead to an increase in money supply.

18.4 THE DEMAND FOR MONEY

The motives for holding money

The demand for money refers to the desire to *hold* money: to keep your wealth in the form of money, rather than spending it on goods and services or using it to purchase financial assets such as bonds or shares. It is usual to distinguish three reasons why people want to hold their assets in the form of money. Note that we are talking here about broad money: M4 in the UK.

The transactions motive

Since money is a medium of exchange, it is required for conducting transactions. But since people receive money

only at intervals (e.g. weekly or monthly) and not continuously, they require to hold balances of money in cash or in current accounts.

The precautionary motive

Unforeseen circumstances can arise, such as a car breakdown. Thus individuals often hold some additional money as a precaution. Firms too keep precautionary balances because of uncertainties about the timing of their receipts and payments. If a large customer is late in making payment, a firm may be unable to pay its suppliers unless it has spare liquidity.

BOX 18.6 ARE THE DAYS OF CASH NUMBERED? CASE STUDIES AND APPLICATIONS

EFTPOS versus ATMs

Banking is becoming increasingly automated, with computer debiting and crediting of accounts replacing the moving around of pieces of paper. What was once done by a bank clerk is often now done by computer.

One possible outcome of this replacement of labour by computers is the gradual elimination of cash from the economy – or so some commentators have claimed.

The most dramatic example of computerisation in recent years has been EFTPOS (electronic funds transfer at the point of sale). This is where you pay for goods in the shops by means of a credit or debit card. When the card is swiped across the machine and the amount entered, your card is then automatically debited and the shop's account credited.

The advantage of this system is that it does away with the processing by hand of pieces of paper. In particular, it does away with the need for (a) credit-card slips when used in conjunction with credit cards and (b) cheques. Both cheques and credit-card slips have to be physically moved around and then read and processed by *people*. If cards were to become more extensively used for *small* transactions, they could well reduce the need for cash.

So are we moving towards a cashless society? Probably not. Cash is still the simplest and most efficient way of paying for a host of items, from a bus ticket to a newspaper to a packet of mints. What is more, another

technical innovation is moving us in the direction of using *more* cash, not less! This is the cash machine – or *ATM* (automated teller machine), to give it its official title. The spread of cash machines to virtually every bank and building society branch and to many larger stores and supermarkets has been rapid in recent years. The sheer simplicity of obtaining cash at all hours from these machines, not only from current accounts but also on credit cards, is obviously a huge encouragement to the use of cash.

So are we using more cash or less cash? The evidence suggests that, until recent years, there was a gradual decline in cash in circulation as a proportion of GDP. It fell from just over 5 per cent of GDP in 1980 to just over 3 per cent in the mid 1990s. Since then it has risen slightly. Between 2000 and 2008 it varied between 3.3 and 3.5 per cent.

But although the effects of EFTPOS and ATMs may be quite different in terms of the use of cash, they both have the same advantage to banks: they reduce the need for bank staff and thereby reduce costs.

 Under what circumstances are cheques more efficient than cash and vice versa? Would you get the same answer from everyone involved in transactions: individuals, firms and banks?

The speculative or assets motive

TC 9
p105

Certain firms and individuals who wish to purchase financial assets, such as bonds, shares or other securities, may prefer to wait if they feel that their price is likely to fall. In the meantime, they will hold money balances instead. This speculative demand can be quite high when the price of securities is considered certain to fall. Money when used for this purpose is a means of temporarily storing wealth.

Similarly, people who will require foreign currency at some time in the future (people such as importers, holiday-makers, or those thinking of investing abroad or in foreign securities) may prefer to wait before exchanging pounds into the relevant foreign currencies if they believe that the sterling price of these currencies is likely to fall (the pound is likely to *appreciate*).

The transactions plus precautionary demand for money: L_1

The transactions plus precautionary demand for money is termed L_1. 'L' stands for **liquidity preference**: that is, the desire to hold assets in liquid form. Money balances held for these two purposes are called **active balances**: money to be used as a medium of exchange. What determines the size of L_1?

The major determinant of L_1 is *nominal national income* (i.e. national income at current prices). The bigger people's

money income, the greater their expenditure and the bigger their demand for active balances. The *frequency with which people are paid* also affects L_1. The less frequently they are paid, the greater the level of money balances they will require to tide them over until the next payment.

 Will students in receipt of a grant or an allowance who are paid once per term have a high or a low transactions demand for money relative to their income?

The *rate of interest* has some effect on L_1, albeit rather small (see Figure 18.5). At high rates of interest, people may choose to spend less and save more of their income, e.g. by buying shares. The effect is likely to be bigger on the precautionary demand: a higher interest rate may encourage people to risk tying up their money. Firms' active balances are more likely to be sensitive to changes in r than those of individuals.

Other determinants of L_1 include the season of the year: people require more money balances at Christmas, for

---

Definitions

Liquidity preference The demand for holding assets in the form of money.

Active balances Money held for transactions and precautionary purposes.

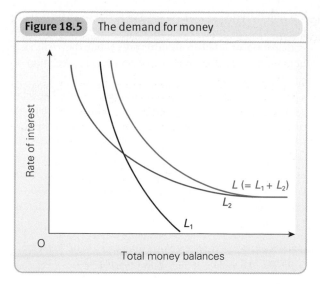

Figure 18.5 The demand for money

Rate of interest (vertical axis) / *Total money balances* (horizontal axis)

$L (= L_1 + L_2)$
L_2
L_1
O

example. Also, any other factors that affect consumption will affect L_1.

The increased use of credit cards in recent years has reduced both the transactions and precautionary demands. Paying once a month for goods requires less money on average than paying separately for each item purchased. Moreover, the possession of a credit card reduces or even eliminates the need to hold precautionary balances for many people. On the other hand, the increased availability of cash machines, the convenience of debit cards and the ability to earn interest on current accounts have all encouraged people to hold more money in bank accounts. The net effect has been an increase in the demand for (broad) money.

The speculative (or assets) demand for money: L_2

The speculative demand for money balances is termed L_2. Money balances held for this purpose are called **idle balances**.

People who possess wealth, whether they are wealthy or simply small savers, have to decide the best form in which to hold that wealth. Do they keep it in cash in a piggy bank, or in a current account in a real bank; or do they put it in some interest-bearing time account; or do they buy stocks and shares or government bonds; or do they buy some physical asset such as a car or property?

In making these decisions, people will have to weigh up the relative advantages and disadvantages of the various alternative assets. Assets can be compared according to two criteria: *liquidity* and the *possibility of earning income*. Just as

TC 1
p8

Definition

Idle balances Money held for speculative purposes: money held in anticipation of a fall in asset prices.

we saw in the case of a bank's assets, these two criteria tend to conflict. The more liquid an asset is, the lower is likely to be the income earned from holding it. Thus cash is totally liquid to the holder: it can be used to buy other assets (or spent on goods) instantly, but it earns no interest. Stocks and shares, on the other hand, are not very liquid since they cannot be sold instantly *at a guaranteed price*. (They *can* be sold pretty well instantly, but if share prices are depressed, a considerable loss may be incurred in so doing. In other words, they are a *risky* means of holding wealth.) But stocks and shares have the *potential* of earning quite a high income for the holder, not only in terms of the dividends paid out of the firms' profits, but also in terms of the capital gain from any increase in the shares' prices.

KI 11
p75

 Buying something like a car is at the other end of the spectrum from holding cash. A car is highly illiquid, but yields a high return to the owner. In what form is this 'return'?

There are three major determinants of the speculative demand for money. Let us examine each in turn.

KI 10
p71

The rate of interest (or rate of return) on assets

The higher the rate of return on assets, such as shares and bonds, the greater the opportunity cost of holding money and therefore the lower the speculative demand for money.

The rate of return on assets varies inversely with their price. Take the case of a government bond (which pays a fixed sum of money throughout its life). Assume that the government issued a £100 bond at a time when interest rates were 10 per cent. Thus the bond must pay £10 per year. Although the government will not redeem bonds until their maturity date, which could well be 20 years from when they were issued, holders can sell bonds at any time on the stock market. Their market price will reflect market rates of interest. Assume, for example, that interest rates fall to 5 per cent. What will happen to the market price of the bond paying £10 per year? It will be driven up to £200. At that price, the £10 per year is worth the current market rate of 5 per cent. Thus the market price of bonds varies inversely with the rate of interest.

Expectations of changes in the prices of securities and other assets

If people believe that share prices are about to rise rapidly on the stock market, they will buy shares and hold smaller speculative balances of money. If they think that share prices will fall, they will sell them and hold money instead. Some clever (or lucky) individuals anticipated the 2000–3 stock market decline. They sold shares and 'went liquid'. Some people made a similar move in the stock market decline of 2007–8.

As we have just seen, if the market price of securities is high, the rate of interest (i.e. the rate of return) on these securities will be low. Potential purchasers of these securities will probably wait until their prices fall and the rate of interest rises. Similarly, existing holders of securities will probably sell them while the price is high, hoping to buy them back again when the price falls, thus making a capital gain. *In the meantime, therefore, large speculative balances of money will be held. L_2 is high.*

If, on the other hand, the rate of interest is high, then L_2 is likely to be low. To take advantage of the high rate of return on securities, people buy them now instead of holding on to their money.

 Would the demand for securities be low if their price was high, but was expected to go on rising?

The relationship between L_2 and the rate of interest (r) is again shown in Figure 18.4. The inverse relationship between r and L_2 gives a downward-sloping curve.

Speculative demand and the exchange rate

In an open economy like the UK where large-scale movements of currencies across the foreign exchanges take place, expectations about changes in the exchange rate are a major determinant of the speculative demand for money.

If people believe that the pound is likely to appreciate, they will want to hold sterling until it does appreciate. For example, if the current exchange rate is £1 = $1.50 and speculators believe that it will shortly rise to £1 = $1.75, then if they are correct they will make a 25c per £1 profit by holding sterling. The more quickly is the exchange rate expected to rise, the more will people want to hold sterling (as money). If, however, people believe that it will be a slow rise over time, they will want to buy sterling assets (such as UK government bonds) rather than money, since such assets will also earn the holder a rate of interest.

Conversely, if people believe that the exchange rate is likely to fall in the near future, they will economise on their holdings of sterling, preferring to hold their liquid assets in some other currency – the one most likely to appreciate against other currencies.

Graphically, changes in expectations about the exchange rate will have the effect of shifting the L_2 curve in Figure 18.5.

There is a further complication here. Expectations about changes in the exchange rate will themselves be influenced by the interest rate (relative to overseas interest rates). If the UK rate of interest goes up, people will want to deposit their money in the UK. This will increase the demand for sterling on the foreign exchange market: there will be a short-term financial inflow into the UK (the financial account of the balance of payments will go into surplus). The effect will be to drive up the exchange rate. Thus if people believe that the UK rate of interest will rise, they will *also* believe that the rate of exchange will appreciate, and they will want to hold larger speculative balances of sterling.

The introduction of the 'foreign exchange dimension' into our analysis will have two effects on the L_2 curve. First, the curve will become more elastic. If the rate of interest is low and is thought likely to rise, the speculative demand is likely to be *very* high. Not only will people hold money in anticipation of a fall in security prices, but they will also hold money (sterling) in anticipation of an appreciation of the exchange rate.

Second, the curve will become more unstable. Expectations of changes in the exchange rate do not just depend on current domestic interest rates. They depend on the current and anticipated future state of the balance of trade, the rate of inflation, the current and anticipated levels of interest rates in other major trading countries, the price of oil, and so on. If any of these cause people to expect a lower exchange rate, the speculative demand for money will fall: L_2 will shift to the left.

 Which way is the L_2 curve likely to shift in the following cases?
(a) The balance of trade moves into deficit.
(b) People anticipate that foreign interest rates are likely to rise substantially relative to domestic ones.
(c) The domestic rate of inflation falls below that of other major trading countries.
(d) People believe that the pound is about to depreciate.

The total demand for money: $L_1 + L_2$

Figure 18.5 also shows the total demand for money balances (L). This is found by the horizontal addition of curves L_1 and L_2. This curve is known as the 'liquidity preference curve' or simply the demand for money curve.

Any factor, other than a change in interest rates, that causes the demand for money to rise will shift the L curve to the right. For example, a rise in national income will cause L_1 to increase, and thus L will shift to the right.

Additional effects of expectations

We have talked about expectations and their importance in determining the speculative demand for money. In particular, we have looked at (a) the effect of interest rates on people's anticipations of future security prices and (b) the effect of expectations about exchange rate movements. There are two other ways in which expectations can influence the demand for money, and make it more unstable.

Expectations about prices. If people expect *prices* to rise, they may reduce their money balances and purchase goods and assets now, before prices do rise. This will tend to shift L to the left. (Note, though, that once prices *have* risen, people will need more money to conduct the same amount of transactions.)

Expectations of interest rate levels over the longer term. If people come to expect that interest rates will normally be higher than they used to be, then any given interest rate will seem lower relative to the 'normal' rate than it used to be. People will be more inclined to hold speculative balances of money in anticipation of a rise in interest rates. This will tend to shift L upwards.

*LOOKING AT THE MATHS

The demand for money (L) can be expressed by the following function:

$$L = L_1 + L_2$$
$$= l_1(PY, f, i) + l_2(i, er^e)$$
$$= l_1(PY, f, (r + \pi^e)) + l_2((r + \pi^e), er^e) \tag{1}$$

This states that L_1 is a function l_1 of nominal national income (i.e. real national income (Y) multiplied by the price index (P)), the frequency with which people are paid (f) and the (nominal) rate of interest (i), which equals the real rate of interest (r) on alternative assets to money plus the expected rate of inflation (π^e). L_2 is a function of the nominal rate of interest (i) and the expected value of the exchange rate er^e.

The advantage of specifying a relationship in this way is that it gives a simple way of representing a situation where something depends on a number of determinants. It is a convenient shorthand. Indeed, a more complex function could easily be specified where the demand for money depends on a longer list of variables. The one above, however, identifies the main determinants. By putting plus and minus signs under each of the terms, we could also identify whether the relationship with each of the determinants is a positive or negative one (i.e. whether the respective partial derivative is positive or negative). Equation (1) could thus be written

$$L = l_1(PY, f, i) + l_2(i, er^e) \tag{2}$$
$$\quad + \quad - - \quad - +$$

This merely states that the demand for money will rise as PY and er^e rise and f and i fall.

In an era of uncertainty about inflation, interest rates and exchange rates, people's expectations will be hard to predict. They will be volatile and susceptible to rumours and political events. In such circumstances, the L curve itself will be hard to predict and will be subject to considerable shifts. Generally, it is likely that the greater the uncertainty, the greater will be the preference for liquidity, and the greater the risk of tying wealth up in illiquid assets.

Section summary

1. The three motives for holding money are the transactions, precautionary and speculative (or assets) motives.

2. The transactions-plus-precautionary demand for money (L_1) depends primarily on the level of nominal national income, the frequency with which people are paid and institutional arrangements (such as the use of credit or debit cards). It also depends to some degree on the rate of interest.

3. The speculative demand for money (l_2) depends on the rate of return on assets and on anticipations about future movements in security prices (and hence their rate of return) and future movements in exchange rates. If security prices are anticipated to fall or the exchange rate to rise, people will hold more money balances.

4. The demand for money is also influenced by expectations of price changes and the levels of interest rates over the longer term.

18.5 EQUILIBRIUM

Equilibrium in the money market

Equilibrium in the money market is where the demand for money (L) is equal to the supply of money (M_s). This equilibrium is achieved through changes in the rate of interest.

In Figure 18.6, equilibrium is achieved with a rate of interest r_e and a quantity of money M_e. If the rate of interest were above r_e, people would have money balances surplus to their needs. They would use these to buy shares, bonds and other assets. This would drive up the price of these assets and drive down the rate of interest.

As the rate of interest fell, so there would be a contraction of the money supply (a movement down along the M_s curve) and an increase in the demand for money balances, especially speculative balances (a movement down along the liquidity preference curve). The interest rate would go on falling until it reached r_e. Equilibrium would then be achieved.

Similarly, if the rate of interest were below r_e, people would have insufficient money balances. They would sell securities, thus lowering their prices and raising the rate of interest until it reached r_e.

A shift in either the M_s or the L curve will lead to a new equilibrium quantity of money and rate of interest at the new intersection of the curves. For example, a rise in the supply of money will cause the rate of interest to fall.

Figure 18.6   Equilibrium in the money market

In practice, there is no *one* single rate of interest. Different assets have different rates of interest. Table 18.7 gives examples of the rates of interest on various assets in the UK in June 2008.

Equilibrium in the money markets, therefore, will be where demand and supply of *each type* of financial asset separately balance. If, for example, there were excess demand for short-term loans (such as one-month inter-bank lending) and excess supply of money to invest in long-term assets (such as bonds), short-term rates of interest would rise relative to long-term rates. Generally, however, different interest rates tend to move roughly together as the overall demand for money and other liquid assets

(or their supply) changes. Thus interest rates may generally rise or generally fall.

Equilibrium in the foreign exchange market

Changes in the money supply also affect the foreign exchange market. In a free foreign exchange market, equilibrium will be achieved by changes in the exchange rate. Assume that the money supply increases. This has three direct effects:

- *Part* of the excess money balances will be used to purchase foreign assets. This will therefore lead to an increase in the supply of domestic currency coming on to the foreign exchange markets.
- The excess supply of money in the domestic money market will push down the rate of interest. This will reduce the return on domestic assets below that on foreign assets. This, like the first effect, will lead to an increased demand for foreign assets and thus an increased supply of the domestic currency on the foreign exchange market. It will also reduce the demand for domestic assets by those outside the country, and thus reduce the demand for the domestic currency.
- Speculators will anticipate that the higher supply of the domestic currency will cause the exchange rate to depreciate. They will therefore sell domestic currency and buy foreign currencies before the expected depreciation takes place.

The effect of all three is to cause the exchange rate to depreciate.

 Trace through the effects on the foreign exchange market of a fall in the money supply.

Table 18.7   Selected rates of interest: June 2008 (end of month)

Asset	Period of loan	Rate of interest (% per annum)
Call money	Overnight	5.25
Gilt repos	2 weeks	5.12
Inter-bank loans	1 month	5.47
Treasury bills	3 months	5.24
Long-dated government bonds	20 years	5.03
Bank and building society mortgages	Variable (25 years typical)	6.92
Ordinary shares (dividend yield of FTSE 100)	–	4.20
(Banks' base rate = Bank Rate)	–	5.00

Source: *Bankstats* (Bank of England).

*LOOKING AT THE MATHS

Equilibrium in the money market is where demand and supply of money are equal. From Box 18.5, the money supply (M_s) equals the monetary base (M_b) multiplied by the money multiplier:

$$M_s = M_b \left(\frac{1+c}{rs+c} \right)$$

Note that this is the more complex version of the money multiplier that we examined in Box 18.5, not the simple bank deposits multiplier developed in the text.

From the 'Looking at the maths' panel on page 530, the demand for money (L) is given by

$$L = l_1(PY, f, (r+\pi^e)) + l_2((r+\pi^e), er^e)$$

Thus, in equilibrium,

$$M_s = L$$

i.e.

$$M_b \left(\frac{1+c}{rs+c} \right) = l_1(PY, f, (r+\pi^e)) + l_2((r+\pi^e), er^e) \qquad (1)$$

At first sight, this equation looks quite daunting, but what we have done is to bring together money supply and demand, each of which has been separately derived in a set of simple stages. In one single equation (equation (1)) we have completed a jigsaw made up of several simple parts.

Section summary

1. Equilibrium in the money market is where the supply of money is equal to the demand. Equilibrium will be achieved through changes in the rate of interest.

2. A rise in money supply causes money supply to exceed money demand. This causes interest rates to fall and a movement down along both the supply of money curve and the demand for money curve until money supply is equal to money demand.

3. Equilibrium in the foreign exchange market is where the demand and supply of a currency are equal. A rise in money supply causes interest rates to fall. The rise in money supply plus the fall in interest rates causes an increased supply of domestic currency to come on to the foreign exchange market and a reduced demand for the domestic currency. This causes the exchange rate to depreciate.

END OF CHAPTER QUESTIONS

1. Imagine that the banking system receives additional deposits of £100 million and that all the individual banks wish to retain their current liquidity ratio of 20 per cent.

   (a) How much will banks choose to lend out initially?

   (b) What will happen to banks' liabilities when the money that is lent out is spent and the recipients of it deposit it in their bank accounts?

   (c) How much of these latest deposits will be lent out by the banks?

   (d) By how much will *total* deposits (liabilities) eventually have risen, assuming that none of the additional liquidity is held outside the banking sector?

   (e) How much of these are matched by (i) liquid assets; (ii) illiquid assets?

   (f) What is the size of the bank deposits multiplier?

   (g) If one half of any additional liquidity is held *outside* the banking sector, by how much less will deposits have risen compared with (d) above?

2. What is meant by the terms *narrow money* and *broad money*? Does broad money fulfil all the functions of money?

3. How does money aid the specialisation and division of labour?

4. What enables banks safely to engage in both maturity transformation and risk transformation?

5. Why do banks hold a range of assets of varying degrees of liquidity and profitability?

6. What is meant by the securitisation of assets? How might this be (a) beneficial and (b) harmful to banks and the economy?

7. What were the causes of the credit crunch and the banking crisis of 2008?

8. If the government reduces the size of its public-sector net cash requirement, why might the money supply nevertheless increase more rapidly?

9. Why might the relationship between the demand for money and the rate of interest be an unstable one?

10. What effects will the following have on the equilibrium rate of interest? (You should consider which way the demand and/or supply curves of money shift.)

    (a) Banks find that they have a higher liquidity ratio than they need.

    (b) A rise in incomes.

    (c) A growing belief that interest rates will rise from their current level.

Online resources

Additional case studies in MyEconLab

18.1 **Barter: its use in Russia in the 1990s.** When barter was used as an alternative to money.

18.2 **The attributes of money.** What distinguishes it from other assets?

18.3 **From coins to bank deposit money.** This case traces the evolution of modern money.

18.4 **Changes in the banking industry.** Is bigger better?

18.5 **Gresham's law.** This examines the famous law that 'bad money drives good money out of circulation'.

18.6 **German banking.** This case compares the tradition of German banks with that of UK retail banks. Although the banks have become more similar in recent years, German banks have a much closer relationship with industry.

18.7 **Making money grow.** A light-hearted illustration of the process of credit creation.

Maths Case 18.1 Calculating the value of the bank multiplier. Looking at the algebra.

Websites relevant to this chapter

See sites listed at the end of Chapter 19 on page 560.

The Relationship between the Money and Goods Markets

CHAPTER MAP

19.1 The effects of monetary changes on national income 536
The quantity theory of money 536
The interest rate transmission mechanism 536
The exchange rate transmission mechanism 539
Portfolio balance: a more direct transmission mechanism 541
How stable is the velocity of circulation? 543

19.2 The monetary effects of changes in the goods market 544
The monetary effects of an increase in injections 544
Crowding out 545
Is money supply exogenous or endogenous? 546

*19.3 ISLM analysis: the integration of the goods and money market models 548
The goods and money markets 548
The IS curve 548
The LM curve 550
Equilibrium 551
Full effects of changes in the goods and money markets 552
Deriving an AD curve from the ISLM model 554

19.4 Taking inflation into account 556
Keeping inflation down 556
Aggregate demand and supply plotted against inflation 556
Response to changes in aggregate demand and supply 558

In Chapter 17 we saw how equilibrium national output was determined. In other words, we looked at macroeconomic equilibrium in goods markets. In Chapter 18 we saw how equilibrium was determined in the money market. In this chapter we combine the analysis of the two chapters.

In section 19.1 we examine how changes in money supply affect real national income. In other words, we see how changes in money markets are transmitted through to goods markets: how monetary changes affect real output. Then, in section 19.2, we look at things the other way round. We examine the effects on money markets and interest rates of changes in the goods market. For example, if aggregate demand increases and firms start to produce extra goods, to what extent will money markets act as a constraint on this process?

Then, in section 19.3, we combine goods and money market analysis into one model: the ISLM model. This helps us to see how the two markets interact and how an overall macroeconomic equilibrium is determined.

Finally we look at the interaction of goods and money markets when the central bank targets the rate of inflation: a common practice around the world today.

Although economists agree on many things, there is no complete agreement in macroeconomics. The debates between Keynesians (of various types), monetarists and new classicists (see section 16.5) have evolved, but have not been settled. As we go through this chapter, we will see the places where economists agree, and where they still differ.

19.1   THE EFFECTS OF MONETARY CHANGES ON NATIONAL INCOME

In this section we examine the impact on the economy of changes in money supply and interest rates: how they affect aggregate demand and how this, in turn, affects national income. A simple way of understanding the issues is in terms of the *quantity theory of money*.

The quantity theory of money

In section 16.2 (pages 458–9), we looked at the following version of the quantity equation:

$$MV = PY$$

In case you did not study Chapter 16, let us state the theory again. First a definition of the terms: M is the supply of money; V is the income velocity of circulation (the number of times money is spent per year on national output (GDP)); P is the price index (where the index = 1 in the base year); and Y is the real value of national income (= national output) for the year in question (i.e. GDP measured in base-year prices).

MV is the total spending on national output. For example, if total money supply was £100 billion and each pound was spent on average five times per year on national output, then total spending on national output (MV) would equal £500 billion for that year. MV is thus simply (nominal) aggregate demand, since total spending on national output consists of the four elements of aggregate demand: consumer spending (C), investment expenditure (I), government spending (G), and expenditure on exports less expenditure on imports ($X - M$), all measured in current prices.

PY is the money value of national output: in other words, GDP measured at *current* prices. For example, if real national income (i.e. in base-year prices) was £200 billion, and the price index was 2.5 (in other words, prices were $2^{1}/_{2}$ times higher than in the base year), then the value of national output in current prices would be £500 billion.

Because of the way we have defined the terms, MV must equal PY. A simple way of looking at this is that MV and PY are both ways of measuring GDP. MV measures it in terms of national expenditure. PY measures it in terms of the value of what is produced.

The effect of a change in money supply

If money supply (M) changes, how will it affect the other three elements of the quantity equation? Will a rise in money supply simply lead to a rise in prices (P), or will there be a rise in real national income (Y): i.e. a rise in real GDP? What will happen to the velocity of circulation? Can we assume that it will remain constant, or will it change?

Clearly the relationship between money supply and prices depends on what happens to V and Y. What happens

to them has been the subject of considerable debate between economists over the years. Keynesians have generally had different views from monetarists and new classical economists.

Essentially there are two issues. In this chapter we look at the first one: the variability of V. If V is constant, a change in money supply (M) will directly affect nominal aggregate demand (MV) and hence nominal national income (PY). If, however, V varies, a change in M may have a much less predictable effect on PY.

The second issue is examined in Chapter 21. This concerns the variability of Y. Will a rise in aggregate demand lead to increased employment and output (Y), or will it simply lead to higher prices (P), or some combination of the two?

1. If V is constant, will (a) a £10 million rise in M give a £10 million rise in MV; (b) a 10 per cent rise in M give a 10 per cent rise in MV?
2. If both V and Y are constant, will (a) a £10 million rise in M lead to a £10 million rise in P; (b) a 10 per cent rise in M lead to a 10 per cent rise in P?

The interest rate transmission mechanism

There are two ways in which a rise in money supply causes a rise in aggregate demand. The first is via changes in interest rates – known as the **interest rate transmission mechanism**. The second is via changes in the exchange rate – known as the **exchange rate transmission mechanism**. These are illustrated in Figure 19.1.

The interest rate transmission mechanism is illustrated in the top part of Figure 19.1. This is graphed in Figure 19.2. It is a three-stage process.

- Figure 19.2(a) shows the money market. A rise in money supply from M to M' leads to a surplus of money at r_1, and hence a fall in the rate of interest from r_1 to r_2.
- Figure 19.2(b) shows the relationship between investment (I) and the rate of interest. A fall in the rate of interest from r_1 to r_2 leads to a rise in investment (and any other interest-sensitive expenditures) from I_1 to I_2. Note that it also encourages consumers to spend, since borrowing through credit cards and personal loans is now cheaper. At the same time, it discourages saving.

Definitions

Interest rate transmission mechanism How a change in money supply affects aggregate demand via a change in interest rates.

Exchange rate transmission mechanism How a change in money supply affects aggregate demand via a change in exchange rates.

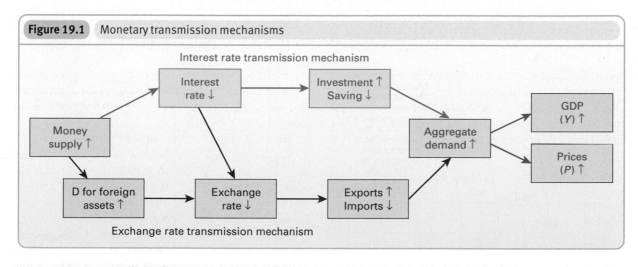

Figure 19.1 Monetary transmission mechanisms

Interest rate transmission mechanism

Exchange rate transmission mechanism

Figure 19.2 Effect of a rise in money supply: the interest rate transmission mechanism

(a) Stage 1: $M_s \uparrow \rightarrow r \downarrow$

(b) Stage 2: $r \downarrow \rightarrow I \uparrow$

(c) Stage 3: $I \uparrow \rightarrow J \uparrow \rightarrow Y \uparrow$

- Figure 19.2(c) is the Keynesian withdrawals and injections diagram. A rise in investment leads to a multiplied rise in national income (from Y_1 to Y_2). If saving fell, there would also be a downward shift in the W line.

The rise in income will be less than that shown in Figure 19.2(c), however, since any rise in income will lead to a rise in the transactions demand for money, L_1. L will shift to the right in Figure 19.2(a), and thus r will not fall as much as illustrated. Thus investment (Figure 19.2(b)) and national income (Figure 19.2(c)) will not rise as much as illustrated either.

The overall effect of a change in money supply on national income will depend on the size of the effect in each of the three stages. This will depend on the shapes of the curves in each of the three diagrams and whether they are likely to shift. The effect will be bigger

- the less elastic the liquidity preference curve (L): this will cause a bigger change in the rate of interest;
- the more interest-elastic the investment curve (I): this will cause a bigger change in investment;
- the lower the marginal propensity to withdraw (*mpw*), and hence the flatter the withdrawals function: this will

cause a bigger multiplied change in national income and aggregate demand.

The problem is that stages 1 and 2 may be both weak and unreliable, especially in the short run. This problem is stressed by Keynesians.

Problems with stage 1: the money–interest link

An interest-elastic demand for money. According to Keynesians, the speculative demand for money is highly responsive to changes in interest rates. If people believe that the rate of interest will rise, and thus the price of bonds and other securities will fall, few people will want to buy them. Instead there will be a very high demand for liquid assets (money and near money). The demand for money will therefore be very elastic in response to changes in interest rates. This was a problem in 2008/9 when central banks around the world increased money supply in an attempt to offset the credit crunch. Many banks, firms and individuals preferred to increase the liquidity of their asset holdings rather than buy bonds, shares or houses.

In such circumstances, the demand-for-money curve (the liquidity preference curve, L) will be relatively flat and

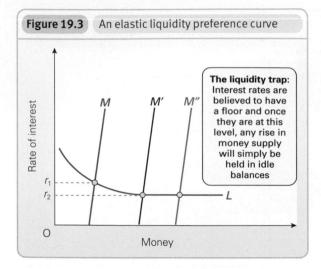

Figure 19.3 An elastic liquidity preference curve

The liquidity trap: Interest rates are believed to have a floor and once they are at this level, any rise in money supply will simply be held in idle balances

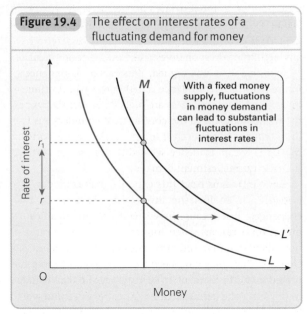

Figure 19.4 The effect on interest rates of a fluctuating demand for money

With a fixed money supply, fluctuations in money demand can lead to substantial fluctuations in interest rates

may even be infinitely elastic at some minimum interest rate. This is the point where everyone believes interest rates will rise, and therefore no one wants to buy bonds. Everyone wants to hold their assets in liquid form.

With a very gently sloping L curve (as in Figure 19.3), a rise in money supply from M to M' will lead to only a small fall in the rate of interest from r_1 to r_2. Once people believe that the rate of interest will not go any lower, any further rise in money supply will have no effect on r. The additional money will be lost in what Keynes called the **liquidity trap**. People simply hold the additional money as idle balances.

Keynes himself saw the liquidity trap as merely a special case: the case where the economy is in deep recession. In such a case, an expansion of money supply would have no effect on the economy. In more normal times, an expansion of money supply would be likely to have *some* effect on interest rates. Nevertheless, the problem could be severe in times of recession. The Japanese economy suffered from a prolonged recession from the early 1990s to the early 2000s (see Case Study 20.6 in MyEconLab). The government and central bank expanded the money supply, but people seemed unwilling to spend. They preferred to hold idle balances. What is more, with interest rates already being virtually zero, there was little incentive to buy bonds or other assets. Thus any extra money was simply kept in idle balances – lost in the liquidity trap.

KI 32
p388

An unstable demand for money. A more serious problem for most countries is that the liquidity preference curve (L) is *unstable*. People hold speculative balances when they

anticipate that interest rates will rise (security prices will fall). But it is not just the current interest rate that affects people's expectations of the future direction of interest rates. Many factors could affect such expectations:

- Changes in foreign interest rates. Domestic interest rates would have to follow suit if the authorities wished to maintain a stable exchange rate.
- Changes in exchange rates. With a falling exchange rate, the authorities may raise interest rates to prevent it depreciating further.
- Statements of government intentions on economic policy.
- Good or bad industrial news. With good news, people tend to buy shares.
- Newly published figures on inflation or money supply. If inflation or the growth in money supply is higher than anticipated, people will expect a rise in interest rates in anticipation of a tighter monetary policy.

Thus the L curve can be highly volatile. With an unstable demand for money, it is difficult to predict the effect on various interest rates of a change in money supply.

A policy of *targeting* money supply can be criticised for similar reasons. A volatile demand for money can cause severe fluctuations in interest rates if the supply of money is kept constant (see Figure 19.4). These fluctuations will cause further uncertainty and further shifts in the speculative demand for money. Targeting the money supply can therefore add to the volatility of the velocity of circulation (V).

Problems with stage 2: the interest rate–investment link

An interest-inelastic investment demand. In the 1950s and 1960s, many Keynesians argued that investment was

KI 9
p67

Definition

Liquidity trap The absorption of any additional money supply into idle balances at very low rates of interest, leaving aggregate demand unchanged.

unresponsive to interest rate changes: that the *I* curve in Figure 19.2(b) was steep. In these circumstances, a very large change in interest rates would be necessary to have any significant effect on investment and aggregate demand.

TC 9
p105

Investment, it was argued, depends on confidence in future markets. If confidence is high, firms will continue to invest even if interest rates are high. They can always pass the higher costs on to the consumer. If confidence is low, firms will not invest even if interest rates are low and borrowing is cheap. Evidence seemed to confirm the interest inelasticity of investment demand.

Few Keynesians hold this extreme position today. The evidence for an inelastic investment demand has been challenged. Just because investment was not significantly higher on occasions when interest rates were low, it does not follow that investment is unresponsive to interest rate changes. There may have been changes in *other* factors that helped to *curb* investment: in other words, the *I* curve shifted to the left. For example, a fall in consumer demand would both cause the low interest rate *and* discourage investment.

Figure 19.5 shows a steep investment demand curve. If the rate of interest falls from r_1 to r_2, there is only a small rise in investment from I_1 to I_2. Now draw a much more elastic I curve passing through point a. Assume that this is the true I curve. Show how the rate of interest could still fall to r_2 and investment still only rise to I_2 if this curve were to shift.

Even if fixed investment in plant and machinery is not very interest sensitive, other components of aggregate demand may well be: for example, investment in stocks, consumer demand financed through credit cards, bank loans or hire purchase, and the demand for houses financed through mortgages.

KI 32
p388

An unstable investment demand. Today the major worry about the interest–investment link is not that the investment curve is inelastic, but rather that it shifts erratically with the confidence of investors.

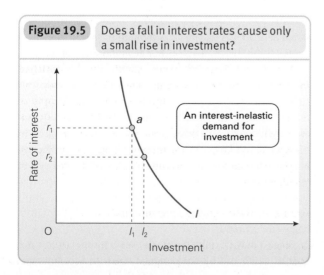

Figure 19.5 Does a fall in interest rates cause only a small rise in investment?

An interest-inelastic demand for investment

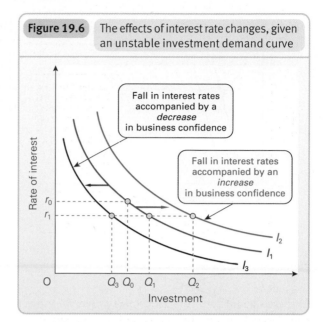

Figure 19.6 The effects of interest rate changes, given an unstable investment demand curve

Fall in interest rates accompanied by a *decrease* in business confidence

Fall in interest rates accompanied by an *increase* in business confidence

Assume in Figure 19.6 that the initial investment demand curve is given by I_1. Now assume that the central bank reduces interest rates from r_0 to r_1. Other things being equal, the level of investment will rise from Q_0 to Q_1. If, however, firms believe that the economy will now pull out of recession, their confidence will increase. The investment curve will shift to I_2 and investment will increase quite markedly to Q_2. If, on the other hand, firms believe that inflation will now rise, which in turn will later force the central bank to raise interest rates again, their confidence may well decrease. The investment curve will shift to I_3 and the level of investment will actually fall to Q_3.

Monetary policy is likely to be effective, therefore, only if people have confidence in its effectiveness. This *psychological* effect can be quite powerful. It demands considerable *political* skill, however, to manipulate it.

For example, in October 2008, with growing concerns around the world that there would be a serious global recession, central banks in the USA, the UK, the eurozone and several other countries all cut interest rates on the same day. As we saw in section 18.2, there were also concerted attempts around the world to inject extra liquidity into the banking system. But crucial to these policy decisions was the attempt to reassure people that the measures would work. Politicians stressed that they were on top of things and that they would do whatever it took to sort out the problem. They knew that getting confidence to return was vital to the success of the policies.

The exchange rate transmission mechanism

The second transmission mechanism is the exchange rate transmission mechanism. This is illustrated in the bottom half of Figure 19.1 on page 537 and graphed in Figure 19.7. This mechanism backs up the interest rate mechanism. It

KI 5
p21

Figure 19.7 The exchange rate transmission mechanism

(a) Stage 1: $M_s \uparrow \rightarrow r \downarrow$

(b) Stage 2: $r \downarrow \rightarrow S \uparrow, D \downarrow \rightarrow er \downarrow$

(c) Stage 3: $er \downarrow \rightarrow X \uparrow, M \downarrow$

(d) Stage 4: $X \uparrow, M \downarrow \rightarrow Y \uparrow$

includes the exchange rate as an intermediate variable between changes in the money supply and changes in aggregate demand. There are four stages in this exchange rate transmission mechanism (see Figure 19.7):

- In Figure 19.7(a), a rise in money supply causes a fall in domestic interest rates from r_1 to r_2.
- In Figure 19.7(b), the fall in domestic interest rates leads to an increased outflow of short-term finance from the country as people demand more foreign assets instead. These will also be a reduced inflow, as depositors seek to take advantage of relatively higher interest rates abroad. The supply of the domestic currency on the foreign exchange market rises from S_1 to S_2 and the demand falls from D_1 to D_2. This causes a depreciation of the exchange rate from er_1 to er_2 (assuming the authorities allow it). There is a second factor contributing to the rightward shift in the supply curve: the use of part of the increased money supply to buy foreign assets directly. What is more, the depreciation in the exchange rate may be speeded up or amplified by speculation.
- In Figure 19.7(c), the depreciation of the exchange rate causes a rise in demand for exports (X), since they are now cheaper for people abroad to buy (there is a movement down along the X curve). It also causes a fall in demand for imports (M), since they are now more expensive (there is a movement up along the M curve). Note that the rise in exports and fall in imports gives

a current account balance of payments surplus. This is matched by the financial account deficit resulting from the lower interest rate encouraging people to buy foreign assets and people abroad buying fewer of this country's assets.

- In Figure 19.7(d), the rise in exports (an injection) and a fall in imports (a withdrawal) will cause a multiplied rise in national income.

Stage 1 will tend to be more powerful than in a closed economy. The liquidity preference curve will tend to be less elastic because, as interest rates fall, people may fear a depreciation of sterling and switch to holding other currencies. Just how strong stage 1 will be depends on *how much* people think the exchange rate will depreciate.

Stage 2 is likely to be very strong indeed. Given the openness of international financial markets, international financial flows can be enormous in response to interest rate changes. Only a relatively small change in interest rates is necessary to cause a relatively large financial flow. Monetarists and new classical economists stress the importance of this effect. Any fall in interest rates, they argue, will have such a strong effect on international financial flows and the exchange rate that the rise in money supply will be relatively quickly and fully transmitted through to aggregate demand.

Stage 3 may be quite strong in the long run. Given time, both the demand by consumers abroad for this country's

TC 7
p68

BOX 19.1   **CHOOSING THE EXCHANGE RATE OR THE MONEY SUPPLY**   *EXPLORING ECONOMICS*

You can't choose both

If the government expands the money supply, then interest rates will fall and aggregate demand will tend to rise. With a floating exchange rate, this will cause the currency to depreciate.

But what if the government attempts to maintain a fixed exchange rate? To do this it must keep interest rates comparable with world rates. This means that it is no longer free to choose the level of money supply. The money supply has become endogenous.

The government can't have it both ways. It can choose the level of the money supply (providing it has the

techniques to do so) and let interest rates and the exchange rate be what they will. Or it can choose the exchange rate, but this will then determine the necessary rate of interest and hence the supply of money. These issues are explored in Chapter 25.

Can the government choose both the exchange rate and the money supply if it is prepared to use the reserves to support the exchange rate?

---

exports and the domestic demand for imports may be quite elastic. In the short run, the effect may be rather limited. However, the size of the effect depends on people's expectations of exchange rate movements. If people think that the exchange rate will fall further, importers will buy *now* before the rate does fall. Exporters, on the other hand, will hold back as long as possible before shipping their exports. These actions will tend to push the exchange rate down. But such speculation is very difficult to predict as it depends on often highly volatile expectations.

 If importers and exporters believe that the exchange rate has 'bottomed out', what will they do?

Stage 4 is the familiar multiplier, only this time triggered by a change in imports and exports.

Note that, as with the interest rate transmission mechanism, the full effect will not be as large as that illustrated. This is because the increased national income will cause an increased *transactions* demand for money. This will shift the *L* curve to the right in Figure 19.7(a), and thus lead to a smaller fall in the rate of interest than that illustrated. The overall effect can be quite strong, but the precise magnitude is usually highly unpredictable.

The effects of changes in money supply will depend also on just how free the exchange rate is. If the government intervenes to 'peg' (i.e. fix) the exchange rate or to prevent excessive fluctuations, the transmission mechanism will not work in the way described. Alternative exchange rate systems (or 'regimes', as they are called) are examined in Chapter 25.

Portfolio balance: a more direct transmission mechanism

Monetarists stress a more direct transmission mechanism. If money supply increases, people will have more money than they require to hold. They will spend this surplus.

Much of this spending will go on goods and services, thereby directly increasing aggregate demand:

$$M_s \uparrow \rightarrow M_s > M_d \rightarrow AD \uparrow$$

The theoretical underpinning for this is given by the *theory of* **portfolio balance**. People have a number of ways of holding their wealth: as money, or as financial assets such as bills, bonds and shares, or as physical assets such as houses, cars and televisions. In other words, people hold a whole portfolio of assets of varying degrees of liquidity – from cash to central heating.

If money supply expands, people will find themselves holding more money than they require: their portfolios are unnecessarily liquid. Some of this money will be used to purchase financial assets, and some to purchase *goods and services*. As more assets are purchased, this will drive up their price. This will effectively reduce their 'yield'. For bonds and other financial assets, this means a reduction in their rate of interest. For goods and services, this means a reduction in their marginal utility/price ratio: a higher level of consumption will reduce their marginal utility and drive up their price. The process will stop when a balance has been restored in people's portfolios. In the meantime, there will have been extra consumption and hence a rise in aggregate demand.

 Do you think that this is an accurate description of how people behave when they acquire extra money?

This mechanism has been criticised by Keynesians. Just how is the extra money injected into people's portfolios in the first place? There are two possible means in the short term.

Definition

Portfolio balance The balance of assets, according to their liquidity, that people choose to hold in their portfolios.

BOX 19.2	THE STABILITY OF THE VELOCITY OF CIRCULATION

What is the evidence?

How stable is the velocity of circulation (*V*) in practice? Does the evidence support the monetarist case that it is relatively stable or the Keynesian case that it fluctuates unpredictably, at least in the short run? Unfortunately, the facts do not unequivocally support either side.

The evidence

How has *V* behaved over time? To answer this we need to measure *V*. A simple way of doing this is to use the formula $V = PY/M$ (rearranging the terms in the quantity equation $MV = PY$). Thus we need to measure *PY* and *M*.

PY is simply the money value of national output: in other words, GDP at current prices. The value of *M* (and hence *V*) will depend on which measure of the money supply we use.

The diagram shows how the velocities of circulation in the UK of both broad money (M4) and narrow money (notes and coin) have changed over the years.

The long run

As far as broad money is concerned, long-term increases in its velocity from 1973 to 1979 are explained by the

Velocities of circulation for narrow and broad money

Extra government expenditure or tax cuts financed by an increased money supply. This will lead to people receiving more money from the government, but what is causing the rise in aggregate demand? It could be argued that it is the extra government expenditure or the rise in people's disposable *incomes* that has directly caused the rise in aggregate demand, not the rise in people's money balances.

The use of monetary techniques. As we shall see in the next chapter, the central bank may release extra money into the economy by buying back bills and bonds (since they will pay for them with extra money). But the resulting extra money in portfolios has not involved any increase in wealth. People have more money, but fewer bonds and bills. Even if they buy more shares or physical assets with the extra money, this will largely merely offset the lower bond and bill holding.

Alternatively, the central bank can make more funds available to the banking sector as loans. But whether this extra liquidity will result in extra credit depends on the demand for credit, which in recession may fall as people try to rein in their spending.

In the *short run*, therefore, the direct mechanism may be weak. The subsequent effects, however, when the banks use their newly acquired balances to grant loans and hence initiate a process of credit creation, will be stronger.

Portfolio balance and the interest rate mechanism

The holding of a range of assets in people's portfolios can strengthen the interest rate transmission mechanism by making the liquidity preference curve less elastic (curve *L* in Figure 19.2(a) is relatively steep). The reason is that speculative balances of money may now have a much smaller role. But why?

A reduction in the rate of interest (*r*) following an increase in the money supply may well make bond holding less attractive, but this does not mean that the extra money will be mainly held in idle balances. Again, it can be used to purchase other assets such as property. Idle balances may expand only slightly.

TC 7
p68

CASE STUDIES AND APPLICATIONS

increase in money substitutes and credit cards, and thus smaller holdings of money balances. The decrease after 1980 is explained by falling inflation and nominal interest rates, with people being increasingly prepared to hold money in sight accounts; by the growth in wholesale deposits (which earn interest); and by people putting a larger proportion of their savings into bank and building society accounts, attracted by higher real interest rates and new types of high-interest instant-access account. As the pace of these changes slowed down, so the fall in velocity became much more gentle after 1990.

As far as narrow money is concerned, its velocity more than doubled between 1974 and 1993. One reason for this was the increased use of credit and debit cards, which reduced the amount of cash people need to hold. The growth of cash machines has also reduced the need to hold so much cash, given that many people can easily obtain more at any time. The relatively smaller amount of cash thus circulates faster. But, as with broad money, these changes in the velocity of narrow money ceased in the early 1990s and since 1993 it has fallen slightly. Part of the reason has been a slowing down in the growth of credit and debit cards, and part has been lower inflation, which has reduced the opportunity cost of holding cash.

The point made by monetarists is that these changes are predictable and gradual and do not, therefore, undermine the close relationship between *M* and *PY*.

The short run

Evidence shows that the velocity of circulation is relatively stable in the short run, especially in recent years. However, this is largely because changes in money supply have not been used to manipulate aggregate demand and hence national income. If they had been, the attempt

might well have been unsuccessful, in which case *V* would have fluctuated.

The direction of causality

Monetary and real changes often work together – especially in the long run. An expansionary fiscal policy over a number of years will increase the PSNCR, which in turn will lead to an increase in money supply (*M*). If the fiscal policy increases nominal national income (*PY*), *V* may well as a result remain constant. But it does not follow from this that it was the growth in *M* that *caused* the growth in *PY*. On the few occasions when fiscal and monetary policy work in opposite directions, the evidence is unclear as to which has the bigger effect – especially as the time period is rarely long enough for the full effects to be identified.

What we are concerned about here is the direction of causality. Changes in aggregate demand may go together with changes in money supply. But is it higher money supply causing higher aggregate demand, or the other way round, or the two simply occurring simultaneously?

Monetarists argue that increases in money supply cause aggregate demand to expand (with a lag of perhaps a few months). For them money supply is exogenous: determined independently by the central bank. Keynesians, by contrast, argue that higher aggregate demand causes an increased demand for bank loans, and banks are only too happy to create the necessary credit, thus expanding the money supply. For them, money supply is endogenous.

 Why might it be difficult to establish the direction of causality from the evidence?

 Redraw the three diagrams of Figure 19.2 with a steeper L curve. Show how an increase in money supply will have a larger effect on national income.

How stable is the velocity of circulation?

Short-run variability of V

Most economists agree that there is some variability of the velocity of circulation (*V*) in the short run if the money supply is changed. To the extent that interest rates and yields do fall with an expansion of the money supply, people may well hold somewhat larger money balances: after all, the interest sacrificed by not holding bonds etc. has been reduced. If people hold relatively more money, the velocity of circulation is thereby reduced, thus reducing the effect on aggregate demand. Furthermore, the direct mechanism may take time to operate. In the meantime, *V* will fall.

Also, the demand for money can shift unpredictably in the short run with changing expectations of prices, interest rates and exchange rates. Thus *V* is unpredictable in the

short run, and so is the effect of monetary policy on aggregate demand. For these reasons, changing the money supply may not be an effective means of short-run demand management.

Long-run stability of V

The main claim of monetarists is that the velocity of circulation (*V*) is relatively stable over the longer run, and any changes that do occur are the predictable outcome of institutional changes, such as the increased use of credit cards (see Box 19.2).

One explanation of why *V* remains relatively stable in the long run, despite an increase in money supply, is that sufficient time has elapsed for the direct mechanism to have worked fully through.

Another explanation is the effect on inflation and consequently on interest rates. This works as follows.

Assume an initial increase in money supply. Interest rates fall. *V* falls. But if money supply goes on rising and hence expenditure goes on rising, inflation will rise. This

TC 9
p105

KI 31
p320

will drive up *nominal* interest rates (even though *real* interest rates will stay low). But in choosing whether to hold money or to buy assets, it is the *nominal* rate of interest that people look at, since that is the opportunity cost of holding money. Thus people economise on money balances and V rises back again.

In extreme cases V will even rise to levels higher than before. This is likely if people start speculating that prices will rise further. People will rush to buy goods and assets before their prices rise further. This action will help to push the prices up even more. This form of destabilising speculation took place in the hyperinflation of Germany in the 1920s and recently in Zimbabwe, as people spent their money as quickly as possible (see Box 15.2).

With a predictable V in the longer run, monetarists have claimed that monetary policy is the essential means of controlling long-term aggregate demand. For this reason, they have favoured a longer-term approach to monetary policy, including targets for the growth of the money supply (see page 594).

Today, most governments adopt a policy of setting a target for the rate of inflation. This involves the central bank controlling aggregate demand by choosing an appropriate rate of interest. In these circumstances, the money supply must be *passively* adjusted to ensure that the chosen rate of interest is the equilibrium rate. This means expanding the money supply in line with the increase in real national income (Y) and the targeted increase in the price level (P).

We explore inflation targeting and its effects in section 19.4. We explore the operation of monetary policy in section 20.2.

Section summary

1. The quantity equation $MV = PY$ can be used to analyse the possible relationship between money and prices. Whether and how much increases in money supply (M) affect the price level (P) depends on whether the velocity of circulation (V) and the level of real national income (Y) are independent of money supply (M).

2. The interest rate transmission mechanism works as follows: (a) a rise in money supply causes money supply to exceed money demand; interest rates fall; (b) this causes investment to rise; (c) this causes a multiplied rise in national income; but (d) as national income rises, so the transactions demand for money rises, thus preventing quite such a large fall in interest rates.

3. The effect will be weak if the demand-for-money curve (L) is elastic and the investment demand curve is inelastic. The effects may also be unreliable because of an unstable and possibly inelastic investment demand.

4. The exchange rate transmission mechanism works as follows: (a) a rise in money supply causes interest rates to fall; (b) the rise in money supply plus the fall in interest rates causes an increased supply of domestic currency to come on to the foreign exchange market; this causes the exchange rate to fall; (c) this causes increased exports and reduced imports, and hence a multiplied rise in national income.

5. According to the theory of portfolio balance, if people have an increase in money in their portfolios, they will attempt to restore portfolio balance by purchasing assets, including goods. Thus an increase in money supply is transmitted directly into an increase in aggregate demand.

6. The demand for money is more stable in the long run than in the short run. This leads to a greater long-run stability in V (unless it changes as a result of other factors, such as institutional arrangements for the handling of money).

19.2 THE MONETARY EFFECTS OF CHANGES IN THE GOODS MARKET

If there is an expansion in one of the components of aggregate demand (C, I, G or $X - M$), what will be the monetary effects? Will the current level of money supply act as a constraint on the growth in national income? In other words, will an expansion of one component of aggregate demand, such as government expenditure, be at the expense of another component, such as investment?

The monetary effects of an increase in injections

Let us assume that business confidence grows and that, as a result, the level of investment increases. Let us also assume that there is a given quantity of money in the economy.

Will the rise in investment lead to a full multiplier effect on national income?

The effect of the rise in investment is illustrated in Figure 19.8. In Figure 19.8(a), the rise in investment leads to a rise in injections to J_2. Other things being equal, national income would rise to Y_2. But this increase in national income also leads to a rise in the transactions demand for money. In Figure 19.8(b), the demand-for-money curve shifts from L to L'.

If the central bank does not wish to allow money supply to rise, the higher demand for money will force it to raise interest rates to r_2. The effect of the higher interest rates is to reduce the level of investment. The overall rise in injections will be smaller than the rise from J_1 to J_2. Also net

Figure 19.8 The monetary effects of a rise in injections

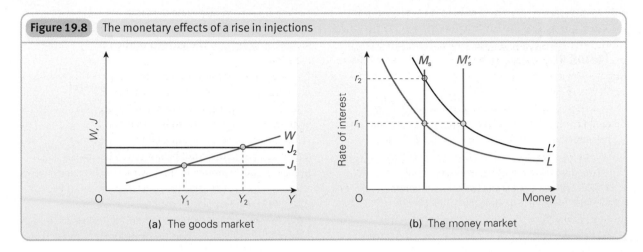

(a) The goods market   (b) The money market

saving (i.e. saving minus borrowing) will rise as the higher interest rate acts as both an incentive for households to save and a disincentive for them to borrow. This causes an upward shift in the W curve. The result is that national income will not rise as far as Y_2. In the extreme case, there would be no rise in national income at all.

If, however, the central bank responded to the increase in investment by expanding the money supply to M'_s, there would be no change in the rate of interest and hence no dampening effect on either investment or consumption.

Assume that the government cuts its expenditure and thereby runs a public-sector surplus.
(a) What will this do initially to equilibrium national income?
(b) What will it do to the demand for money and initially to interest rates?
(c) Under what circumstances will it lead to
   (i) a decrease in money supply;
   (ii) no change in money supply?
(d) What effect will (i) and (ii) have on the rate of interest compared with its original level?

Crowding out

Another example of the monetary constraints on expansion in the goods market is the phenomenon known as *financial crowding out*. This is where an increase in public-sector spending reduces private-sector spending (see Box 16.2 on page 461).

To illustrate the effects, assume that previously the government has had a balanced budget, but that now it chooses to expand the level of government expenditure without raising additional taxes. As a result, it runs a bud-

Definition

Financial crowding out Where an increase in government borrowing diverts money away from the private sector.

get deficit ($G > T$). But this deficit will have to be financed by borrowing. The resulting public-sector net cash requirement will lead to an increase in the money supply if it is financed by borrowing from the central bank through the issue of bonds (gilts), or by the sale of Treasury bills to the banking sector. Alternatively, if it is financed by selling bills or bonds outside the banking sector, there will be no increase in the money supply.

The effect can once more be shown in Figure 19.8. The rise in government expenditure will cause injections to rise to J_2 and, other things being equal, national income will rise to Y_2. But, as with the case of increased investment, this increase in national income will lead to a rise in the demand for money. In Figure 19.8(b), the demand-for-money curve shifts from L to L'. If the PSNCR is financed in such a way as to allow money supply to expand to M'_s, there will be no change in the interest rate and no crowding-out effect. If, however, the money supply is not allowed to expand, interest rates will rise to r_2. This in turn will reduce investment: crowding out will occur. Injections will fall back again below J_2. In the extreme case, injections could even fall back to J_1 and thus national income return to Y_1. Here crowding out is total.

The extent of crowding out

Just how much crowding out will occur when there is an expansionary fiscal policy, but when money supply is *not* allowed to expand, depends on two things.

The responsiveness (elasticity) of the demand for money to a change in interest rates. If the demand is relatively *elastic* (as in Figure 19.9(a)), the increase in demand, represented by a *horizontal* shift in the liquidity preference curve from L to L', will lead to only a small rise in interest rates. If, however, the demand is relatively inelastic (as in Figure 19.9(b)), the same horizontal shift will lead to a bigger rise in interest rates.

As we saw in section 19.1, Keynesians generally see the liquidity preference curve as being more elastic than do

---

BOX 19.3   **CROWDING OUT IN AN OPEN ECONOMY**   EXPLORING ECONOMICS

Taking exchange rate effects into account

Will fiscal policy be crowded out in an open economy with floating exchange rates? Assume that the government increases its expenditure but does not allow the money supply to expand: a case of pure fiscal policy. What will happen?

- The increased government expenditure will increase the demand for money (see Figure 19.8(b)).
- This will drive up interest rates – the amount depending on the elasticity of the liquidity preference curve.
- This will lead to an inflow of finance from abroad, which in turn will lead to an appreciation of the exchange rate.

- The higher exchange rate will reduce the level of exports (an injection) and increase the level of imports (a withdrawal). This will add to the degree of crowding out.

Thus in an open economy with floating exchange rates, an expansionary fiscal policy will be crowded out not only by higher interest rates, but also by a higher exchange rate.

 We have argued that the short-term inflow of finance following a rise in the rate of interest will drive up the exchange rate. Are there any effects of expansionary fiscal policy on the demand for imports (and hence on the current account) that will go some way to offsetting this?

Figure 19.9   Different views on the demand for money

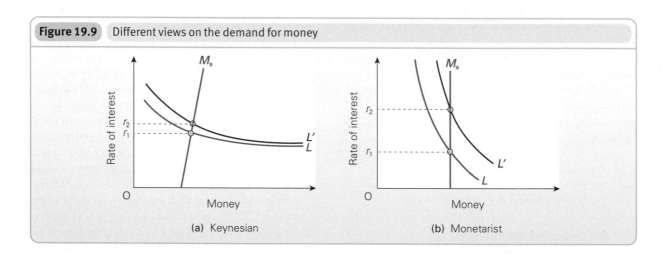

(a) Keynesian   (b) Monetarist

---

monetarists. Thus, unlike monetarists and new classical economists, they argue that a rise in money demand normally leads to only a relatively modest rise in interest rates.

The responsiveness (elasticity) of investment to a change in interest rates. Keynesians argue that investment is relatively *unresponsive* to changes in interest rates. Businesspeople are much more likely to be affected by the state of the market for their product than by interest rates. Thus in Figure 19.10(a), there is only a small fall in investment. Monetarists and new classical economists argue that investment is relatively *responsive* to changes in interest rates. Thus in Figure 19.10(b), there is a bigger fall in investment.

In the Keynesian case, therefore, the rise in demand for money arising from an expansionary fiscal policy will have only a small effect on interest rates and an even smaller effect on investment. Little or no crowding out takes place. In fact, the expansion of demand might cause an increase in investment through the accelerator effect (see pages 496–7).

Monetarists argue that interest rates will rise significantly and that there will be a severe effect on investment. Crowding out is substantial. For this reason, they argue that, if money supply is to be kept under control to prevent inflation rising, it is vital for governments to reduce the size of their budget deficit. They argue that, in the long run, crowding out is total, given the long-run stability of the velocity of circulation.

Is money supply exogenous or endogenous?

Money supply is *exogenous* (independently determined) if it can be fixed by the authorities and if it does not vary with aggregate demand and interest rates. The money supply 'curve' would be vertical, as in Figure 19.9(b). It would shift only if the government or central bank *chose* to alter the money supply.

Money supply is *endogenous* (determined within the model) if it is determined by aggregate demand and hence the demand for money: banks expanding or contracting credit in response to customer demand. In such a case, the

Figure 19.10 Different views on the demand for investment

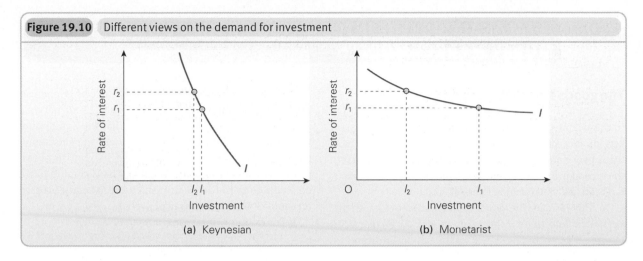

(a) Keynesian

(b) Monetarist

money supply curve would be upward sloping or even horizontal. The more that money supply expands in response to an increase in aggregate demand, the more gently upward sloping the money supply curve would be.

The more elastic the money supply curve, the less will money act as a constraint on expansion in the goods market, and the less will a rise in government expenditure crowd out private expenditure. In other words, the less will interest rates rise in response to a rise in the demand for money.

The extreme monetarist position is that money supply is wholly exogenous. The extreme Keynesian position is that money supply is wholly endogenous. Money simply passively expands to meet the demand for money.

In reality, money supply is partly exogenous and partly endogenous. The authorities are able to influence money supply, but banks and other financial institutions have considerable scope for creating credit in response to demand. If control of the money supply is adopted as the basis for policy, the authorities must reduce the endogenous element to a minimum.

As we shall see in the next chapter, the authorities in many countries recognise the difficulties in controlling the money supply directly. They therefore influence the supply of money indirectly by controlling interest rates and hence the demand for money.

Sometimes, however, in extreme circumstances, the authorities may attempt to control money supply directly. Thus in 2008/9, central banks in several countries, including the USA, the eurozone, the UK and Japan, injected large amounts of liquidity into the financial system in an attempt to stimulate bank lending in the face of the credit crunch. Money supply had been falling as banks, finding that many of their assets were less liquid than they thought or finding that some of their customers were defaulting on loans, created less credit. The idea of the central banks making considerably more liquid funds available to banks was that the banks could use this additional liquidity as the basis for additional credit. Just how much credit would be created, however, and thus how much broad money would expand, was nevertheless very uncertain.

Section summary

1. Changes in injections or withdrawals will have monetary implications. If there is a rise in investment with no change in the money supply, the increased demand for money will drive up interest rates and reduce both investment and consumption. The resulting rise in income will be smaller.

2. Similarly, if there is a fiscal expansion and *no* change in the money supply, the increased demand for money will again drive up the interest rate. This will to some extent crowd out private expenditure and thus reduce the effectiveness of the fiscal policy.

3. The extent of crowding out will depend on the shape of the liquidity preference curve and the investment demand curve. The less elastic the demand for money,

and the more elastic the investment demand, the more crowding out will take place, and the less effective will fiscal policy be.

4. If there is a rise in aggregate demand, money supply may rise in response to this. The more elastic the supply of money curve, the less crowding out will take place.

5. Money supply is not totally exogenous. This makes it hard for the authorities to control it precisely. Generally, therefore, central banks try to control *interest rates* and attempt to alter liquidity to back this up. Sometimes, however, they may take more deliberate steps to inject extra liquidity into the financial system.

The goods and money markets

In this chapter, we have shown that there are two key markets in the economy at macroeconomic level, and that these two markets interact. The first is the goods market; the second is the money market. Each of these two markets has been analysed by using a model.

In the case of the goods market, the model is the Keynesian injections/withdrawals model. Any change in injections or withdrawals will cause national income to change. For example, a rise in government expenditure shifts the J line upwards and causes a rise in equilibrium national income. In other words, an increase in the demand for goods and services causes a (multiplied) rise in the output of goods and services (assuming that there are sufficient idle resources).

In the case of the money market, the model is the one showing the demand for money (L) and the supply of money (M) and their effect on the rate of interest. A change in the supply or demand for money will cause the equilibrium rate of interest to change. Monetary policy operates directly in this market, either by affecting the supply of money or by operating on interest rates.

What we have shown in this chapter is that the two markets *interact*: that changes in one market cause changes in the other. Take the case of an increase in investment: it has a direct effect in the goods markets, but also an indirect effect in money markets. We illustrated this in Figure 19.8. The goods market effect was shown in Figure 19.8(a). The rise in injections led to a multiplied rise in income to Y_2. The money market effect was shown in Figure 19.8(b). The rise in income led to a rise in the transactions demand for money and a resulting rise in interest rates to r_2. This in turn had an effect back in the goods market, with a higher interest rate dampening investment and consumption somewhat and reducing the final rise in income.

The effect of a rise in money supply in the two markets was shown in Figures 19.1, 19.2 and 19.7 (on pages 537 and 540). The rise in money supply reduces interest rates. This then, via an increase in investment (or a reduction in the exchange rate and a resulting increase in exports and a reduction in imports), leads to a multiplied rise in income in the goods market. This in turn has an effect back in the money market, with a higher income leading to a higher demand for money, thus limiting the fall in interest rates.

The trouble with our analysis so far is that we have needed at least two diagrams. What we are going to look at in this section is a model which *combines* these two markets, which means that we will need only one diagram. The model is known as the *ISLM model*.

The model allows us to examine the effects of changes originating in one of the two markets on *both* national income *and* interest rates: it shows what the equilibrium will be in both the goods and the money markets simultaneously. The model, as its name suggests, consists of two curves: an *IS* curve and an *LM* curve. The *IS* curve is based on equilibrium in the goods market; the *LM* curve is based on equilibrium in the money market.

Let us examine these two curves in turn.

The *IS* curve

Deriving the IS curve

To explain how the *IS* curve is derived, let us examine Figure 19.11, which as you can see is in two parts. The top part shows the familiar Keynesian injections and withdrawals diagram, only in this case, for simplicity, we are assuming that saving is the only withdrawal from the circular flow of income, and investment the only injection. Thus in equilibrium $I = S$ (i.e. $J = W$). The bottom part of Figure 19.11 shows the *IS* curve. This shows all the various combinations of interest rates (r) and national income (Y) at which $I = S$.

Let us assume that initially interest rates are at r_1. Both investment and saving are affected by interest rates, and thus, other things being equal, an interest rate of r_1 will give particular investment and saving schedules. Let us say that, in the top part of Figure 19.11, these are shown by the curves I_1 and S_1. Equilibrium national income will be where $I = S$, i.e. at Y_1. Thus in the lower part of Figure 19.11, an interest rate of r_1 will give a level of national income of Y_1. Thus point a is one point on the *IS* curve. At an interest rate of r_1 the goods market will be in equilibrium at an income of Y_1.

Now what will happen if the rate of interest changes? Let us assume that it falls to r_2. This will cause a rise in investment and a fall in saving. A rise in investment is shown in the top part of Figure 19.11 by a shift in the investment line to I_2. Likewise a fall in saving is shown by a shift in the saving curve to S_2. This will lead to a multiplied rise in income to Y_2 (where $I_2 = S_2$). This corresponds to point b in the lower diagram, which therefore gives a second point on the *IS* curve.

Definition

ISLM **model** A model showing simultaneous equilibrium in the goods market ($I = S$) and the money market ($L = M$).

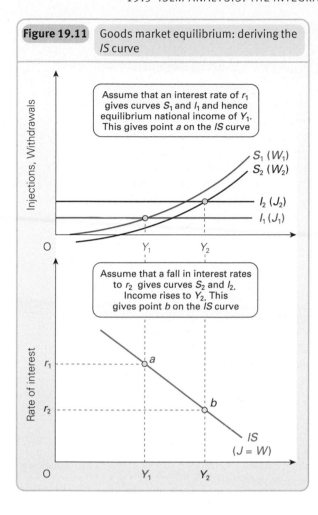

Figure 19.11 Goods market equilibrium: deriving the *IS* curve

Assume that an interest rate of r_1 gives curves S_1 and I_1 and hence equilibrium national income of Y_1. This gives point *a* on the *IS* curve

Assume that a fall in interest rates to r_2 gives curves S_2 and I_2. Income rises to Y_2. This gives point *b* on the *IS* curve

curve. The flatter the curve, the bigger the multiplier. The larger the value of the multiplier, the bigger will be the effect on national income of any rise in investment and fall in saving, and the more elastic therefore will be the *IS* curve. Thus the flatter the *S* curve in the top part of Figure 19.11, the flatter the *IS* curve in the bottom part.

 In a complete model where there were three injections (I, G and X) and three withdrawals (S, T and M), what else would determine the shape of the 'JW' curve?

Keynesians argue that the *IS* curve is likely to be fairly inelastic. The reason they give is that investment is not very responsive to changes in interest rates: the demand-for-investment curve in Figure 19.2(b) on page 537 is relatively inelastic. Saving also, claim Keynesians, is unresponsive to interest rate changes. The effect of this is that there will only be a relatively small shift in the *I* and *S* curves in response to a change in interest rates, and thus only a relatively small change in national income.

Monetarists, by contrast, argue that investment and saving are relatively responsive to changes in interest rates and that therefore the *IS* curve is relatively elastic.

Shifts in the IS curve

A change in interest rates will cause a movement *along* the *IS* curve. As we saw in Figure 19.11, a reduction in interest rates from r_1 to r_2 causes a movement *along* the *IS* curve from point *a* to point *b*.

A change in any *other* determinant of investment or saving, however, will *shift* the whole curve. The reason is that it will change the equilibrium level of national income at any given rate of interest.

An increase in investment, other than as a result of a fall in interest rates, will shift the *IS* curve to the *right*. This could happen, for example, if there were an increase in business confidence. A rise in business confidence *at the current interest rate* will cause an upward shift of the *I* curve in the top part of Figure 19.11, which will cause a multiplied rise in income. Thus in the lower part of Figure 19.11 a higher equilibrium income is now associated with each level of the interest rate: the *IS* curve has shifted to the right. Likewise, for any given interest rate, a fall in saving, and hence a rise in consumption, would also shift the *IS* curve to the right.

In a complete model (with three injections and three withdrawals), where the *IS* curve was a '*J* = *W*' curve rather than a simple '*I* = *S*' curve, similar shifts would result from changes in other injections or withdrawals. Thus an expansionary fiscal policy that increased government expenditure (*G*) or cut taxes (*T*) would shift the '*IS*' curve (i.e. the *JW* curve) to the right.

Thus *lower* interest rates are associated with *higher* national income, if equilibrium is to be maintained in the goods market (*I* = *S*).

The elasticity of the IS curve

KI 9
p67

The elasticity of the *IS* curve (i.e. the responsiveness of national income to changes in interest rates) depends on two factors.[1]

The responsiveness of investment and saving to interest rate changes. The more investment and saving respond to a change in the rate of interest, the bigger will be the vertical shift in the *I* and *S* curves in the top part of Figure 19.11, and thus the bigger will be the effect on national income. The bigger the effect on national income, the more elastic will be the *IS* curve.

KI 34
p463

The size of the multiplier. This is given by 1/*mps* (i.e. 1/*mpw* in the full model). The *mps* is given by the slope of the *S*

 In a complete JW model, what else would cause the JW curve (a) to shift to the right; (b) to shift to the left?

---

[1] Note that, as with demand and supply curves, the elasticity of the *IS* curve will vary along its length. Therefore we should really talk about the elasticity at a particular point on the curve, or between two points.

Figure 19.12   Money market equilibrium: deriving the *LM* curve

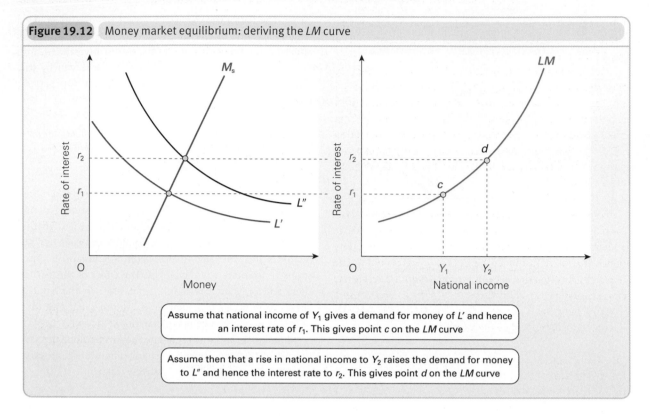

Assume that national income of Y_1 gives a demand for money of L' and hence an interest rate of r_1. This gives point *c* on the *LM* curve

Assume then that a rise in national income to Y_2 raises the demand for money to L'' and hence the interest rate to r_2. This gives point *d* on the *LM* curve

The *LM* curve

The *IS* curve is concerned with equilibrium in the goods market. The *LM* curve is concerned with equilibrium in the money market. The *LM* curve shows all the various combinations of interest rates and national income at which the demand for money (*L*) equals the supply (*M*).

Deriving the *LM* curve

To explain how the *LM* curve is derived, we again use a diagram in two parts (see Figure 19.12), only this time they are side by side (the reason being that we use the same *vertical* axis (*r*) this time, whereas in Figure 19.11 we used the same horizontal axis (*Y*)). The left-hand part of Figure 19.12 is the familiar money market diagram, showing a liquidity preference (demand for money) curve (*L*) and a supply of money curve (*M*).

At any given level of national income, there will be a particular level of transactions-plus-precautionary demand for money, and hence a given overall demand-for-money curve (*L*). Let us assume that, when national income is at a level of Y_1 in the right-hand part of Figure 19.12, the demand-for-money curve is L'. With the given money supply curve M_s, the equilibrium rate of interest will be r_1. Thus point *c* is one point on the *LM* curve. At a level of national income Y_1, the money market will be in equilibrium at a rate of interest of r_1. (Note that we are assuming that the money supply curve is not totally exogenous; in other words, the curve is upward sloping. In simple

ISLM models, the money supply curve is (unrealistically) assumed to be vertical.)

Now what will happen if the level of national income changes? Let us assume that national income rises to Y_2. The effect is to increase the transactions-plus-precautionary demand for money. The *L* curve shifts to the right: to, say, L''. This will cause the rate of interest to rise to the new equilibrium level of r_2. This therefore gives us a second point on the *LM* curve (point *d*).

Thus *higher* national income leads to a greater demand for money and hence *higher* interest rates if equilibrium is to be maintained in the money market. The *LM* curve is therefore upward sloping.

The elasticity of the *LM* curve

The elasticity of the *LM* curve (i.e. the responsiveness of interest rate changes to a change in national income)[1] again depends on two factors.

The responsiveness of the demand for money to changes in national income. The greater the marginal propensity to consume, the more will the transactions demand for money rise as national income rises, and thus the more

---

[1] Note this time that the rate of interest is the dependent variable and the level of national income is the independent variable. Thus the more elastic is the *LM* curve (i.e. the more responsive interest rates are to changes in national income), the *steeper* it will be.

the *L* curve will shift to the right. Hence the more the equilibrium interest rate will rise, and the steeper will be the *LM* curve.

The endogeneity of money will lessen this effect. In the case of an upward-sloping money supply curve (as in Figure 19.12), the less steep it is, the more will money supply expand in response to a rise in the demand for money and the less will interest rates rise. Hence the flatter will be the *LM* curve. Where money supply simply expands passively to meet any rise in demand, the *LM* curve will be horizontal.

The responsiveness of the demand for money to changes in interest rates. The more the demand for money responds to a change in interest rates, the flatter will be the liquidity preference curve in the left-hand part of Figure 19.12. The flatter the *L* curve, the less will the equilibrium interest rate change for any given horizontal shift in the *L* curve (arising from a change in *Y*). The less the equilibrium interest rate changes, the flatter will be the *LM* curve.

The Keynesian and monetarist views on the shape of the *LM* curve reflect the respective views on the elasticity of the *L* curve. Keynesians argue that the *L* curve is likely to be relatively flat given the responsiveness of the speculative demand for money to changes in interest rates and the endogeneity of money. They thus argue that the *LM* curve is correspondingly flat (depending, of course, on the scales of the axes). Monetarists, on the other hand, argue that the *LM* curve is relatively steep. This is because they see the demand for money as insensitive to changes in interest rates and the supply of money as being exogenous.

Shifts in the LM curve

A change in national income will cause a movement *along* the *LM* curve to a new interest rate. Thus in Figure 19.12 a rise in national income from Y_1 to Y_2 leads to a movement along the *L* curve from point *c* to point *d* and hence a rise in the rate of interest from r_1 to r_2.

A change in any *other* determinant of the demand and supply of money will *shift* the whole curve. The reason is that it will change the equilibrium level of interest associated with any given level of national income.

An increase in the demand for money, other than as a result of a rise in income, will shift the *L* curve to the *right*. This could be due to people being paid less frequently, or a greater use of cash, or increased speculation that the price of securities will fall. This increased demand for money will raise the equilibrium rate of interest at the current level of national income. The *LM* curve will shift upwards.

An increased supply of money by the authorities will shift the M_s curve to the right. This will lower the rate of interest (in the left-hand part of Figure 19.12). This will shift the *LM* curve downwards: a lower rate of interest will be associated with any given level of national income.

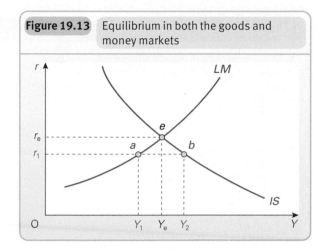

Figure 19.13 Equilibrium in both the goods and money markets

Draw a diagram like Figure 19.12, only with just one L curve. Assume that the current level of national income is Y_1. Now assume that the supply of money decreases. Show the effect on
(a) the rate of interest;
(b) the position of the LM curve.

Equilibrium

The *IS* curve shows all the combinations of the rate of interest (*r*) and national income (*Y*) at which the *goods* market is in equilibrium. The *LM* curve shows all the combinations of *r* and *Y* at which the *money* market is in equilibrium. *Both* markets will be in equilibrium where the curves intersect. This is at r_e and Y_e in Figure 19.13.

But what would happen if both markets were not simultaneously in equilibrium? How would equilibrium be achieved?

Let us suppose that the current level of national income is Y_1. This will create a demand for money that will lead to an equilibrium interest rate of r_1 (point *a* on the *LM* curve). But at this low interest rate, the desired level of investment and saving would generate an income of Y_2 (point *b* on the *IS* curve). Thus national income will rise. But as national income rises, there will be a movement up along the *LM* curve from point *a*, since the higher income will generate a higher demand for money and hence push up interest rates. And as interest rates rise, so the desired level of investment will fall and the desired level of saving will rise so as to reduce the equilibrium level of national income below Y_2. There will be a movement back up along the *IS* curve from point *b*. Once the interest rate has risen to r_e, the actual level of income will be at the equilibrium level (i.e. *on* the *IS* curve). Both markets will now be in equilibrium.

Assume that national income is initially at Y_2 in Figure 19.13. Describe the process whereby equilibrium in both markets will be achieved.

KI 8
p43

KI 5
p21

*LOOKING AT THE MATHS

Equilibrium in the *ISLM* model is where the two functions, *IS* and *LM*, are equal. The simplest mathematical representation of this is where both *IS* and *LM* are simple linear (i.e. straight-line) functions. The *IS* function could be expressed as

$$r = a - bY \qquad (1)$$

In other words, the higher the real rate of interest (*r*), the lower will be the level of aggregate demand and hence national income (*Y*).[1] This is consistent with a downward-sloping *IS* curve.

The *LM* function can be written as

$$r = g + hY \qquad (2)$$

In other words, the higher the level of real national income (and hence the higher the demand for money), the higher will be the real rate of interest. This is consistent with an upward-sloping *LM* curve.

We can then solve for *Y* by setting the two equations equal. Thus:

$$a - bY = g + hY$$

i.e.

$$bY + hY = a - g$$

giving

$$Y = \frac{a - g}{h + b}$$

More complex IS and LM functions

In practice, neither function is likely to be linear. Both *IS* and *LM* are likely to be curves rather than straight lines. To understand why, we need to look at the other determinants of *Y* in the case of the *IS* curve and of *r* in the case of the *LM* curve. Let us first examine the *IS* function.

Real national income consists of five elements:

$$Y = C + I + G + X - M \qquad (3)$$

or

$$Y = C(Y, T, r, \pi^e) + I(r, \pi^e, \Delta Y) + G + X(er) - M(Y, T, r, \pi^e er) \qquad (3a)$$

Equation (3a) is simply an expansion of equation (3) listing the key determinants of each of the variables in equation (3), where *T* is taxes, π^e is expected inflation and *er* is the exchange rate. Investment being a function of changes in national income (ΔY) is the accelerator effect. Thus an *IS* function could be expressed as

$$Y = IS(r, T, \pi^e, \Delta Y, G, er)$$
$$\quad\; - - + \; + \; + \; - \qquad (4)$$

All the variables in this function are contained in equation (3a). It is highly likely that the relationship between *Y* and most, if not all, these variables is non-linear (i.e. contains squared or higher power terms).

The sign under each of the variables indicates the direction in which *Y* changes when the variable changes. For example, the negative sign under the *T* term means that a rise in taxes would lead to a *fall* in *Y*. Put another way, the sign indicates the sign of the partial derivative of *Y* with respect to each variable. For example, the positive sign under the expected inflation term (π^e) means that when you differentiate *Y* with respect to π^e, you end up with a positive number. This simply means that a rise in π^e leads to a *rise* in *Y*.

Note that a change in *r* would lead to a movement along the *IS* curve. A change in any of the other determinants in equation (4) would shift the curve. A rise in any of the determinants with a positive sign would result in a rightward shift in the curve; a rise in any of the determinants with a negative sign would result in a leftward shift.

Turning to the *LM* function, this can be expressed as

$$r = LM(Y, \frac{M_s}{P}, \pi^e, er^e, f)$$
$$\quad\; + - \; + + \; - \qquad (5)$$

where M_s / P is the real money supply, π^e is the expected rate of inflation, er^e is the expected exchange rate and *f* is the frequency with which people are paid. The *LM* curve assumes equilibrium in the money market. It therefore represents all the combinations of *r* and *Y* where the real demand for money is equal to the real supply. The real supply of money is given by the term M_s / P and the real demand for money depends on the other terms in equation (5) (see page 530).

A rise in *Y* would cause a movement up along the *LM* curve. A rise in any of the other determinants would shift the curve: upwards in the case of the determinants with a positive sign; downwards in the case of those with a negative sign.

As with the *IS* function, it is highly likely that the relationship between *r* and most, if not all, the variables in the *LM* function is likely to be non-linear.

Maths Case 19.1 in MyEconLab shows how equilibrium in the *ISLM* model can be derived from specific *IS* and *LM* functions.

[1] Note that although equation (1) shows *r* as a function of *Y*, the model in fact has *Y* as the dependent variable. In other words, *r* determines *Y*. We express equation (1) this way to make it consistent with equation (2), where *r* is the dependent variable.

TC 12
p395

Full effects of changes in the goods and money markets

ISLM analysis can be used to examine the full effects of changes in the goods market. Such changes are illustrated by a shift in the *IS* curve. Likewise, the full effects of changes in the money market can be illustrated by a shift in the *LM* curve.

KI 5
p21

Changes in the goods market

Assume that business confidence rises and firms decide to increase their investment. The rise in injections leads to a rightward shift in the *IS* curve. This is illustrated in Figure 19.14(a). It is assumed that there is no exogenous increase in the money supply and that, therefore, the *LM* curve does not shift. Income rises to Y_2, but interest rates also rise (to r_2).

Figure 19.14   *ISLM* analysis of changes in the goods and money markets

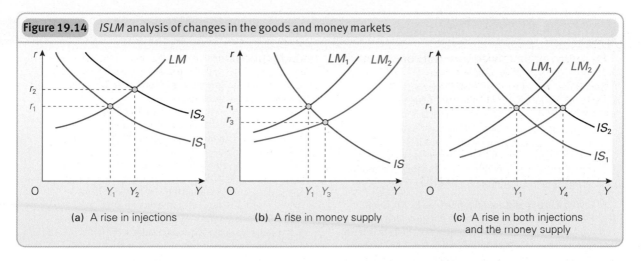

(a) A rise in injections

(b) A rise in money supply

(c) A rise in both injections and the money supply

The rise in the rate of interest to r_2 restricts the rise in national income, since the higher interest rate dampens both investment and consumption. The net rise in injections is less than the original rise in investment. The steeper the *LM* curve, the less will national income rise.

If, however, money supply is expanded passively to meet the extra demand for money, then interest rates will not have to rise. This is illustrated in Figure 19.14(c). The rightward shift in the *IS* curve is matched by a downward shift in the *LM* curve. The rate of interest remains at r_1 and there is a full multiplied rise in national income to Y_4.

Changes in the money market

Assume that there is an increase in money supply. The *LM* curve shifts downwards. This is illustrated in Figure 19.14(b). Interest rates fall and this encourages an increase in borrowing and hence an increase in investment and consumption. This is shown by a movement down along the *IS* curve. National income rises. Equilibrium is reached at a rate of interest of r_3 and a national income of Y_3.

The fall in the rate of interest means that some of the extra money is absorbed in idle balances and is not all used to finance additional expenditure and this reduces the resulting increased national income. The effect on national income also depends on the elasticity of the *IS* curve. The steeper the *IS* curve, the less will national income rise. This will be the case when investment is relatively insensitive to cuts in interest rates.

If, however, the rise in money supply is accompanied by an autonomous rise in injections (for example, a rise in government expenditure), then the effect can be much bigger. If the downward shift in the *LM* curve is matched by a rightward shift in the *IS* curve, then the effect is once more illustrated in Figure 19.14(c).

To summarise: the effect on national income of a change in either market depends on the slope of the *IS* and *LM* curves.

- The effect of a shift in the *IS* curve will be bigger, the flatter the *LM* curve and the steeper the *IS* curve are.

When *LM* is relatively flat, a rightward shift in *IS* will lead to only a small rise in the rate of interest (*r*). If *IS* is steep, this rise in *r* will lead to only a small curtailing of investment. In these two circumstances, the dampening effect on investment and consumption is limited. There will be a large increase in national income (*Y*).

- The effect of a shift in the *LM* curve will be bigger when the liquidity preference curve (*L*) (e.g. in Figure 19.12(a))

Figure 19.15   Deriving the *AD* curve from an *ISLM* diagram

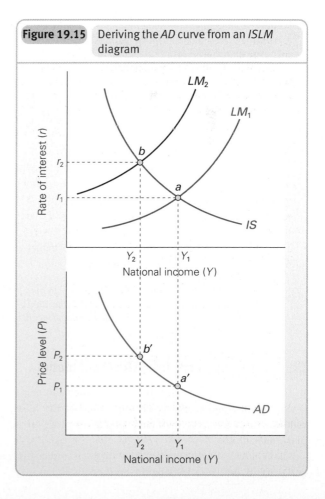

Rate of interest (*r*)

National income (*Y*)

Price level (*P*)

National income (*Y*)

*BOX 19.4   ENVIRONMENTALLY SUSTAINABLE MACROECONOMIC EQUILIBRIUM

Introducing an environmental constraint into the ISLM model[1]

In Box 14.7 we saw that economic growth, as conventionally measured using GDP figures, is not necessarily desirable. One reason for this is that economic growth can damage the environment.

Can we amend macroeconomic models to take the environment into account? The answer is yes. Here we show how it could be incorporated into the *ISLM* model.

We start with two simple propositions:

- *Using current technology, there will be a maximum level of national income that is environmentally sustainable.* If national income rises above this level, environmental degradation will occur. A higher level of national income *could* be sustained, however, if a cleaner technology were used.
- *Generally, more capital-intensive techniques are cleaner than more labour-intensive techniques.* This is mainly because capital-intensive techniques tend to be more modern and make a less wasteful use of resources, or have tighter environmental safeguards (e.g. emission levels) built into the technology. Generally, then, by using capital-intensive techniques, a higher level of national income can be sustained. One major factor that will encourage the use of more capital-intensive technology is a lower rate of interest (since the rate of interest represents the price of capital).

We can illustrate these two propositions graphically. The *EE* line in Figure (a) shows the various combinations of the maximum level of national income and interest rates that are environmentally sustainable. Any point on the line or to the left of it would be environmentally sustainable. Any point to the right of it would represent

(a)

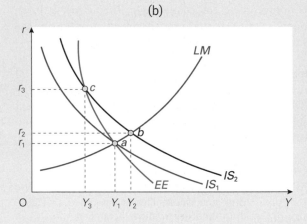
(b)

is steep and the *IS* curve is relatively flat. When *L* is steep, there will be a relatively large downward shift in the *LM* curve for any given increase in the money supply and hence a relatively large fall in *r*. When *IS* is relatively flat, this fall in *r* will lead to a relatively large increase in investment and hence *Y*.

- The effect of a shift in either curve will be bigger if matched by a similar shift in the other curve.

 On a diagram similar to Figure 19.13, trace through the effects of (a) a fall in investment and (b) a fall in the money supply. On what does the size of the fall in national income depend?

Deriving an *AD* curve from the *ISLM* model

In section 15.2, we saw why the aggregate demand curve is downward sloping. Now we have looked at the *ISLM* model, we can give a more formal explanation of the shape of the *AD* curve.

Figure 19.15 shows both an *ISLM* diagram and an *AD* curve. In the top part of the figure, both goods and money

markets are in equilibrium at point *a* (the point where the *IS* and *LM* curves cross). National income is Y_1 and the rate of interest is r_1. Turning to the bottom part, let us assume that with national income at Y_1, the price level happens to be P_1. The aggregate demand curve thus passes through point *a'*.

Now let us assume that the price level rises to P_2. The effect of the higher price is to raise the demand for (nominal) money balances: after all, people will need bigger money balances if they are to pay higher prices for goods. The higher demand for money balances will raise the equilibrium rate of interest at the current level of national income. In the top diagram, the *LM* curve will shift upwards. Assuming that the *LM* curve shifts to LM_2, equilibrium will now be at point *b*. National income will fall to Y_2. Thus a rise in the price level to P_2 has caused national income to fall to Y_2. In the bottom diagram, the *AD* curve must now pass through point *b'*.

If the *IS* curve shifts, or if the *LM* curve shifts other than as a result of a change in the price level, the *AD* curve must shift. For example, if investment rises, the *IS* curve will shift

TC 12
p395

EXPLORING ECONOMICS

an environmentally unsustainable level of national income: it would cause environmental degradation to occur. Why is the curve negatively sloped? This shows that a lower rate of interest, by encouraging the use of more capital-intensive (i.e. cleaner) technology, would allow a higher level of environmentally sustainable national income.

We can now superimpose this line on an *ISLM* diagram. This is done in Figure (b), and we assume that the initial level of national income (Y_1), given by the point where the IS_1 and *LM* curves cross, is on the *EE* line (point *a*): i.e. is just environmentally sustainable.

If there is now an expansionary fiscal policy, the *IS* curve will shift to the right. This is illustrated by a shift in the *IS* curve from IS_1 to IS_2. The new equilibrium is at point *b*. But this is not environmentally sustainable. In fact, to restore sustainability, given the new *IS* curve, there would have to be a movement to point *c*. This would necessitate shifting the *LM* curve to the left through a contractionary monetary policy. The result, however, would be a *lower* level of national income than originally.

Going back to point a, show how an expansionary monetary policy (combined with a contractionary fiscal policy) would allow a higher level of environmentally sustainable national income.

If national income does rise into the environmentally unsustainable region, what will happen? Are there any forces that will restore sustainability? In fact there are forces pulling in opposite directions.

On the one hand, if current levels of national income cause environmental degradation, there will be political pressures to protect the environment, perhaps through controls or through market instruments, such as green taxes. Either way, firms will have the incentive to adopt greener technology and consumers will have the incentive to switch to greener products. The *EE* curve will shift to the right.

On the other hand, if the economy is currently to the right of *EE*, the environmental degradation will reduce the *future* capacity of the environment to absorb pollution. This will have the effect of shifting the *EE* curve to the left. The further to the right of the *EE* line the current position is, the faster will the *EE* line shift to the left.

Whether the *EE* line will actually shift to the right or left depends on which of these two forces is the stronger. Clearly, (a) the greener governments are and the more active their environmental policies and (b) the less far to the right of the *EE* line the current position is, the more likely the *EE* curve is to shift to the right: the more likely is the environment to be able to cope with economic growth.

1. *What will determine the slope of the EE curve?*
2. *Draw an IS-LM-EE diagram with the EE curve flatter than the IS curve. Now illustrate the effect of an expansionary fiscal policy. Given this fiscal expansion, illustrate by a shift in the LM curve the monetary policy that would be necessary to restore sustainability. Is national income now higher or lower than it was originally?*

[1] This box is based on A. Heyes, 'A proposal for the greening of textbook macro: "IS-LM-EE"' (Royal Holloway College, University of London working paper, 1998).

---

to the right. National income will rise for any given price level, and hence the *AD* curve must shift to the right. To summarise: rightward shifts in the *IS* or *LM* curve will lead to rightward shifts in the *AD* curve.

1. *Trace through the effects of a fall in the price level to show how a further point on the AD curve can be derived.*
2. *Explain what could cause a downward shift in the LM curve and how this would affect the AD curve.*

Section summary

1. The *ISLM* model allows equilibrium to be shown in both goods and money markets simultaneously. The model shows the relationship between national income and interest rates.

2. Equilibrium in the goods market is shown by the *IS* curve. This shows all the combinations of the rate of interest and national income where investment (*I*) equals saving (*S*) (or, in a complete Keynesian model, where injections equal withdrawals). As the rate of interest rises, so investment will fall and saving will rise: thus equilibrium national income will fall. The *IS* curve is thus downward sloping.

3. A change in interest rates will cause a movement along the *IS* curve. A change in anything else that affects national income (i.e. a change in injections or withdrawals other than as a result of a change in interest rates) will cause a shift in the *IS* curve.

4. Equilibrium in the money market is shown by the *LM* curve. This shows all the combinations of national income and the rate of interest where the demand for money (*L*) equals the supply (*M*). As national income rises, so the demand for money will rise: thus the equilibrium rate of interest in the money market will rise. The *LM* curve is thus upward sloping.

5. A change in national income will cause a movement along the *LM* curve. A change in anything else that affects interest rates (i.e. a change in the demand or supply of money other than as a result of a change in national income) will shift the *LM* curve.

6. Simultaneous equilibrium in both goods and money markets (i.e. the equilibrium national income *and* the equilibrium rate of interest) is where *IS = LM*.

7. A change in injections or withdrawals will shift the *IS* curve. A rise in injections will shift it to the right. This will cause a rise in both national income and the rate of interest. The rise in income will be bigger and the rise in the rate of interest smaller, the steeper the *IS* curve and the flatter the *LM* curve.

8. A rise in money supply will shift the *LM* curve downwards. This will cause a fall in interest rates and a rise in national income. The rise in national income will be larger, the flatter the *IS* curve and the steeper the liquidity preference curve (*L*) and hence the bigger the downward shift in the *LM* curve for any given increase in the money supply.

9. An *AD* curve can be derived from an *ISLM* diagram. A higher price level will shift the *LM* curve upwards. This will lead to a lower level of national income. The higher price level and lower national income gives a new point on the *AD* curve.

19.4 TAKING INFLATION INTO ACCOUNT

Keeping inflation down

Since the early 1990s, most developed countries have experienced relatively low inflation. Inflation rates of between 0 and 3 per cent are typical of those experienced today. The average inflation rate for the G7[1] countries from 1997 to 2009 was just 1.5 per cent and for the OECD countries as a whole it was 2.7 per cent.

Part of the reason for this is the process of globalisation. Trade barriers between countries have been reduced; international price comparisons have been made easier through the Internet; competition legislation around the world has been tightened; labour markets have become more flexible, and the power of labour to drive up wages has declined. This all bears down on inflation. Labour markets are increasingly competitive and companies are increasingly wary about raising prices for fear of losing market share.

The other major reason for low inflation is the deliberate policy of targeting a low rate of inflation. As we shall see in section 20.5, using interest rates to achieve a target rate of inflation has become the prime focus of monetary policy in many countries (including the UK) and an important element in monetary policy in many others. In both the UK and the eurozone, the target inflation rate is 2 per cent.

If inflation is forecast to be above target in the medium term (two years in the UK), the central bank raises real interest rates (i.e. interest rates after taking the higher inflation into account) so as to dampen aggregate demand and thereby reduce inflation. If inflation is forecast to be below target, the central bank lowers real interest rates, thereby boosting aggregate demand and pushing inflation back up to target.

Such policies have been generally successful (although with rising food and commodity prices in the late 2000s,

inflation rates around the world were generally above target). What is more, as inflation targets are met, so this feeds through into people's expectations. People expect inflation to be at approximately its target level and hence wage and price setting reflect this. As a result, inflation remains at its target level.

In a world of inflation targets, how are the relationship between the goods and money markets affected? What will be the effect of a change in aggregate demand? In this section, we explore these questions.

Aggregate demand and supply plotted against inflation

To illustrate the impact of changes in aggregate demand or supply in an economy with inflation targets, we can use a variant of the aggregate demand and supply model. This new version is illustrated in Figures 19.16 and 19.17.

In this version, the horizontal axis, as before, measures real national income (*Y*). The vertical axis, however, measures the *rate of inflation*, not the *level* of prices. The aggregate demand and supply curves are labelled *ADI* and *ASI* to distinguish them from the curves in the normal aggregate demand and supply diagram. We also add a line showing the target rate of inflation.

Before we look at the properties of the model, let us examine each of the three lines in turn. The first two are illustrated in Figure 19.16.

The inflation target line

This is simply a horizontal line at the target rate of inflation (π_{target}). If inflation is above target, real interest rates will be raised by the central bank. If it is below target, real interest rates will be cut.

If the government or central bank changes the target, the line will shift to the new target rate.

[1] The Group of Seven countries are Canada, France, Germany, Italy, Japan, the UK and the USA.

Figure 19.16 *AD plotted against inflation*

be a movement up the curve as the central bank raises the real rate of interest and this causes real income to fall. When *inflation* begins to fall in response to the higher rate of interest, there will be a movement back down the curve again.

The position of the ADI curve. A given *ADI* curve represents a given monetary policy. The particular *ADI* curve in Figure 19.16 intersects with the inflation target line at a real income of Y_1. This means that if inflation is on target, real national income will be Y_1. The central bank will need to consider whether this is consistent with long-term equilibrium in the economy: in other words, whether Y_1 is the *potential* level of national output, i.e. the level of income with a zero output gap (see Box 14.3 on page 398). If it is, then the monetary policy it has chosen is appropriate.

A shift in the ADI curve. Any factor that causes aggregate demand to change, other than the central bank responding to inflation being off target, will cause the *ADI* curve to shift. A rightward shift represents an increase in aggregate demand. A leftward shift represents a decrease.

Examples of a rightward shift include cuts in tax rates, an increase in government expenditure and a rise in consumer or business confidence. The *ADI* curve will also shift to the right if the government or central bank sets a higher target rate of inflation. The reason is that this will lead to lower interest rates at every level of inflation.

The curve will also shift if the central bank changes its monetary policy, such that it no longer wants Y_1 to be the equilibrium level of national income. For example, if Y_1 in Figure 19.16 were below the potential level, and there was therefore demand-deficient unemployment, the central bank would want to reduce real interest rates in order to achieve a higher level of aggregate demand at the target rate of inflation. This will shift the *ADI* curve to the right. In other words, each level of inflation along this new *ADI* curve would correspond to a lower real rate of interest (i) and hence a higher level of aggregate demand.

But what determines the level of Y? This is determined by the interaction of aggregate demand and aggregate supply. To show this we introduce a third line: the *ASI* curve.

The aggregate supply/inflation curve
The *ASI* curve, like the normal *AS* curve, is upward sloping. In the short run it will be relatively flat. In the long run it will be relatively steep, if not vertical at the potential level of national income. The curve illustrated in Figure 19.17 is the short-run *ASI* curve. But why is it shaped this way? Why will a higher rate of inflation lead to higher real national income?

Assume that the economy is currently generating a real national income of Y_1 and that inflation is on target (π_{target}). Equilibrium is at point *a*. Assume also that Y_1 represents the long-run potential level of output.

The aggregate demand/inflation curve
As with the normal *AD* curve, the *ADI* curve is downward sloping. In other words, a higher rate of inflation leads to a lower level of (real) aggregate demand. But why?

The reason is simple. It consists of a two-stage process.

1. If the rate of inflation (π) goes above the target level, the central bank will raise the *real* rate of interest (i). In other words it will raise the nominal rate *more* than the rise in inflation. Thus if inflation goes up from a targeted 2 per cent to 3 per cent, the nominal interest rate must rise by more than 1 percentage point in order to achieve a rise in the real interest rate.
2. The higher real rate of interest will then reduce (real) aggregate demand (*AD*), through both the interest rate mechanism and the exchange rate mechanism (see pages 536–42).

To summarise:

$$\pi \uparrow \to i \uparrow \to AD \downarrow$$

Similarly, a fall in the rate of inflation will cause the central bank to lower the real rate of interest. This will then lead to an increase in aggregate demand.

The slope of the ADI curve. The slope of the *ADI* curve depends on the strength of the two stages. The curve will be relatively flat

- the more real interest rates respond to a change in inflation. Interest rate changes will be larger, the faster the central bank wants to get inflation back to its target level and the less concerned it is about cutting back on aggregate demand and hence output and employment;
- the more responsive investment, consumption and exports (i.e. the components of aggregate demand) are to a change in interest rates.

A movement along the ADI curve. This will be caused by a change in the rate of inflation. If inflation rises, there will

Figure 19.17 *AD* and *AS* plotted against inflation

Now assume that consumer confidence rises, and that, as a result, the *ADI* curve shifts to ADI_2. Firms will respond to the higher aggregate demand partly by raising prices more than the current (i.e. target) rate of inflation and partly by increasing output: there is a movement along the *ASI* curve. Equilibrium moves to point *b*, where *ADI* = *ASI*.

But why will firms raise output as well as prices? The reason is that wage rises lag behind price rises. This is because of the time it takes to negotiate new wage rates and the fact that people were probably anticipating that inflation would stay at its target level. The higher prices now charged by firms will generate bigger profit margins for them, and thus they will be willing to supply more.

Over time, however, if the higher demand persists, wage rises would get higher. This would be the result of firms trying to obtain more labour to meet the higher demand and of unions seeking wage increases to compensate for the higher rate of inflation. Thus, assuming no increase in productivity, the *ASI* curve would shift upwards and continue doing so until real national income returned to the potential level Y_1. The long-run *ASI* curve would be vertical through point *a*.

Response to changes in aggregate demand and supply

A rise in aggregate demand
Assume, in Figure 19.17, that there has been a rise in real aggregate demand and that the *ADI* curve has shifted to ADI_2. Assume also that Y_1 is the potential level of national output. If inflation remained at its target level, the economy would move to point *c*, with national income increasing to Y_3. But as firms respond partly by increasing prices more rapidly, equilibrium is reached at point *b*. In other words, there has been a movement up along the *ASI* curve from point *a* to point *b* and back up along the new *ADI* curve from point *c* to point *b*. This movement along curve

ADI_2 is the result of the higher interest rates imposed by the central bank in response to inflation rising to π_2.

But equilibrium at point *b* is above the target rate. This is unsustainable, even in the short run. One of two things must happen. The first option is for the central bank (or government) to accept a higher target rate of inflation: i.e. π_2. But if it does this, real income can only remain above its potential level in the short run. Soon, higher prices will feed through into higher wages and back into higher prices, and so on. The *ASI* curve will shift upwards.

The second option – the only effective option in the long run – is for the central bank to reduce aggregate demand back to ADI_1. This will mean changing monetary policy, such that a higher real rate of interest is chosen for each rate of inflation. This tighter monetary policy shifts the *ADI* curve to the left.

In other words, if the central bank is adhering strictly to an inflation target, any rise in real aggregate demand can have only a temporary effect, since the higher inflation that results will force the central bank to bring aggregate demand back down again.

The one exception to this would be if the higher aggregate demand encouraged firms to invest more. When the effects of this on aggregate supply began to be felt in terms of higher output, the short-term *ASI* curve itself would shift to the right, leading to a new equilibrium to the right of point *a*. In such a case, there would have been a long-term increase in output, even though the central bank was sticking to an inflation target.

Using a graph similar to Figure 19.17, trace through the effect of a reduction in aggregate demand.

A rise in aggregate supply
Assume now that aggregate supply rises. This could be a temporary 'supply shock', such as a cut in oil prices or a good harvest, or it could be a permanent increase caused, say, by technical progress. Let us take each in turn.

A temporary supply shock. In Figure 19.18, initial equilibrium is at point *a*, with curves ADI_1 and ASI_1 intersecting at the target rate of inflation. The rise in aggregate supply causes the *ASI* curve temporarily to shift from ASI_1 to ASI_2. Inflation thus falls below the target rate. As a result, the central bank reduces the real rate of interest (i). The effect is to increase aggregate demand. This is shown by a movement *along* curve ADI_1 from point *a* to point *d*. Inflation has fallen to π_3 and real national income has risen to Y_4. Since this is only a temporary increase in aggregate supply, the central bank will not change its monetary policy. The *ADI* curve, therefore, will not shift.

As the supply shock subsides, aggregate supply will fall again. The *ASI* curve will shift back from ASI_2 to ASI_1, causing inflation to rise again. The result is a move back up the ADI_1 curve from point *d* to point *a*.

KI 31
p320

Figure 19.18 The effects of an increase in aggregate supply

1. Trace through the effect of an adverse supply shock, such as a rise in oil prices.
2. What determines the amount that national income fluctuates when there is a temporary shift in the ASI curve?

A permanent increase in aggregate supply. Now assume that ASI_2 represents a permanent shift. As before, the reduction

in inflation causes the central bank to reduce interest rates. If there is no change in monetary policy, there would be simply be, once more, a movement from point *a* to point *d* with inflation now at π_3.

Once the central bank realises that the rise in aggregate supply is permanent, it will want to move to equilibrium at point *e*. To do this it will have to *change* its monetary policy and adopt a lower real interest rate at each rate of inflation. This will shift the *ADI* curve to ADI_2. If it does this, equilibrium will be restored at the target rate of inflation. Y_5 will be the new sustainable level of real national income.

In other words, the central bank, by maintaining an inflation target, will allow aggregate demand to expand sufficiently to accommodate the full rise in aggregate supply.

In the next chapter we explore policies to control aggregate demand. In the final section of that chapter (section 20.5), we look at whether it is best for a central bank to target inflation or whether it should adopt an alternative target. We also look at the more general issue of whether governments ought to set targets and stick to them, or whether they should allow themselves more discretion in managing the economy.

Section summary

1. Today, most countries have low rates of inflation compared with the past. Part of the reason for this is the deliberate targeting of low inflation by governments and central banks.

2. The effects of adhering to an inflation target can be illustrated in a modified version of the aggregate demand and supply diagram. Inflation, rather than the price level, is plotted on the vertical axis. The aggregate demand curve in this diagram (labelled *ADI*) is downward sloping. This is because higher inflation encourages the central bank to raise interest rates and this leads to a fall in real national income.

3. The aggregate supply (*ASI*) curve in the short run is upward sloping. This is because wage rises lag behind price rises and thus firms are encouraged to supply more in response to a rise in demand knowing that their profits will increase.

4. If aggregate demand rises, the *ADI* curve will shift to the right. Inflation will rise above its target level. This is shown by a movement up the *ASI* curve and back up the new *ADI* curve to the new intersection point (as in Figure 19.17). The movement up the new *ADI* curve is in response to the higher interest rate now set by the

central bank as it attempts to bring inflation back down to its target level.

5. Since the new equilibrium is above the target rate of inflation, the central bank must change to a tighter monetary policy and raise the real rate of interest. This shifts the *ADI* curve back to the left, and equilibrium is restored at its original level. The rise in aggregate demand (unless accompanied by a rightward shift in aggregate supply) has had only a temporary effect on real national income.

6. A rise in aggregate supply (unless merely a temporary supply shock) will have a permanent effect on real national income. A rightward shift in aggregate supply will lead to an initial equilibrium at a rate of inflation below target and some rise in real national income as the rate of interest is reduced (as in Figure 19.18). The equilibrium is now below the target rate of inflation. The central bank must therefore change to a looser monetary policy and reduce the real rate of interest. This will shift the *ADI* curve to the right, causing a further rise in real national income that now fully reflects the rise in aggregate supply.

END OF CHAPTER QUESTIONS

1. Using one or more diagrams like Figures 19.2, 19.7, 19.8, 19.9 and 19.10, illustrate the following:

   (a) The effect of a contraction in the money supply on national income. Refer to both the interest rate and exchange rate transmission mechanisms and show how the shapes of the curves affect the outcome.

   (b) The effect of a fall in investment on national income. Again show how the shapes of the curves affect the outcome. Specify your assumptions about the effects on the *supply* of money.

2. Controlling the money supply is sometimes advocated as an appropriate policy for controlling inflation. What implications do different assumptions about the relationships between *M* and *V*, and *M* and *Y*, in the equation *MV* = *PY* have for the effectiveness of this policy?

3. Why may an expansion of the money supply have a relatively small effect on national income? Why may any effect be hard to predict?

4. Why does the exchange rate transmission mechanism strengthen the interest rate transmission mechanism?

5. Explain how the holding of a range of assets in people's portfolios may help to create a more direct link between changes in money supply and changes in aggregate demand.

6. Explain how financial crowding out can reduce the effectiveness of fiscal policy. What determines the magnitude of crowding out?

*7. What determines the shape of the *IS* and *LM* curves?

*8. Under what circumstances will (a) a rise in investment and (b) a rise in money supply cause a large rise in national income?

*9. Using *ISLM* analysis, explain what would cause the aggregate demand curve to be steep.

10. What would cause (a) a steep *ADI* curve; (b) a gently sloping *ADI* curve? Compare the short-run and long-run effects of (i) a temporary adverse supply shock and (ii) a permanent supply reduction under each of (a) and (b).

11. Under what circumstances would a rightward shift in the *ADI* curve lead to a *permanent* increase in real national income?

Online resources

Additional case studies in MyEconLab

19.1   Crowding out. This case looks at a different version of crowding out from that analysed in section 19.2.

Maths Case 19.1 Using *IS* and *LM* equations to find the equilibrium national income and interest rate. Using the algebra in a worked example.

Websites relevant to Chapters 18 and 19

Numbers and sections refer to websites listed in the Web Appendix and hotlinked from this book's website at **www.pearsoned.co.uk/sloman**.

- For news articles relevant to this and the previous chapter, see the *Economics News Articles* link from the book's website.

- For general news on money and banking, see websites in section A, and particularly A1–5, 7–9, 20–22, 25, 26, 31, 36. See also links to economic and financial news in A42.

- For monetary and financial data (including data for money supply and interest rates), see section F and particularly F2. Note that you can link to central banks worldwide from site F17. See also the links in B1 or 2.

- For monetary targeting in the UK, see F1 and E30. For monetary targeting in the eurozone, see F6 and 5.

- For links to sites on money and monetary policy, see the *Financial Economics* sections in I4, 7, 11, 17.

- For student resources relevant to Chapters 18 and 19, see sites C1–7, 9, 10, 12, 13, 19. See also '2nd floor – economic policy' in site D1. See also site D11 (*The virtual bank of Biz/ed*).

Fiscal and Monetary Policy

Both fiscal and monetary policy can be used to control aggregate demand. Excessive growth in aggregate demand can cause unsustainable short-term growth and higher rates of inflation. Too little aggregate demand can result in a recession, with negative growth and rising unemployment.

Fiscal policy seeks to control aggregate demand by altering the balance between government expenditure (an injection into the circular flow of income) and taxation (a withdrawal). Monetary policy seeks to control aggregate demand by directly controlling the money supply or by altering the rate of interest and then backing this up by any necessary change in money supply. A reduction in interest rates will encourage more borrowing and hence raise aggregate demand. A rise in interest rates will dampen aggregate demand.

The first two sections of this chapter examine fiscal and monetary policy in turn: how they work and how effective they are. The third (optional) section shows how *ISLM* analysis can be used to compare the relative effectiveness of the two policies.

Increasingly attention has focused on the longer-term impact of monetary and fiscal policy. Therefore, in the final two sections look at how the policies have been used in the UK and around the world and at whether governments should adopt fixed targets for policy (e.g. inflation targets) or whether they should adjust policies according to circumstances.

CHAPTER MAP

20.1 Fiscal policy	**562**
Government finances: some terminology	562
The government's 'fiscal stance'	563
Automatic fiscal stabilisers	565
The effectiveness of automatic stabilisers	565
Discretionary fiscal policy	565
The effectiveness of discretionary fiscal policy	567
Problems of magnitude	568
Problems of timing	569
Fiscal rules	571
20.2 Monetary policy	**574**
The policy setting	574
Control of the money supply over the medium and long term	574
The operation of monetary policy in the short term	576
Techniques to control the money supply	576
Techniques to control interest rates	584
Using monetary policy	587
*20.3 *ISLM* analysis of fiscal and monetary policy	**589**
The Keynesian position	590
The monetarist position	590
20.4 Fiscal and monetary policy in the UK	**591**
Attitudes towards demand management	591
Demand management in the 1950s and 1960s	592
The demise of fine tuning in the 1970s	593
Monetarism under Thatcher	595
A return to discretionary policies after 1985	596
Targeting the exchange rate	596
Targeting inflation	597
Policy of the Labour government (1997–)	598
20.5 Rules versus discretion	**601**
The case for rules	601
The case for discretion	601
Conclusions	608

Fiscal policy has two possible roles as far as controlling aggregate demand is concerned. The first is to remove any severe deflationary or inflationary gaps. In other words, expansionary fiscal policy could be used to prevent an economy experiencing a severe or prolonged recession, such as that experienced in the Great Depression of the 1930s or in east and south-east Asia, Russia and Brazil in the late 1990s. It has also been used for this purpose in Japan in recent years (see Case Study 20.6 in MyEconLab), in the USA in 2001/2 and in 2007/8 (see Box 20.1) and around the world in 2008 when substantial tax cuts and increased government expenditure were used by many countries, including the UK (see Box 20.3), to combat the onset of recession. Likewise, deflationary fiscal policy could be used to prevent rampant inflation, such as that experienced in the 1970s. To summarise: this first role is to prevent the occurrence of *fundamental* disequilibrium in the economy.

The second role is to smooth out the fluctuations in the economy associated with the business cycle. This involves reducing government expenditure or raising taxes when the economy begins to boom. This will dampen down the expansion and prevent 'overheating' of the economy, with its attendant problems of rising inflation and a deteriorating current account balance of payments. Conversely if a recession looms, the government should cut taxes or raise government expenditure in order to boost the economy. If these stabilisation policies are successful, they will amount merely to 'fine tuning'. Problems of excess or deficient demand will never be allowed to get severe. Any movement of aggregate demand away from a steady growth path would be quickly 'nipped in the bud'.

Fiscal policy can also be used to influence aggregate *supply*. For example, government can increase its expenditure on infrastructure, or give tax incentives for investment. These supply-side policies are considered in Chapter 23.

Before we look at just how fiscal policy can be used, it is important to understand some of the terminology of government spending and taxation.

Government finances: some terminology

Central government

Central government deficits and surpluses. Since an expansionary fiscal policy involves raising government expenditure and/or lowering taxes, this has the effect of either increasing the **budget deficit** or reducing the **budget surplus**. A budget deficit in any one year is where central government's expenditure (including benefits) exceeds its revenue from taxation. A budget surplus is where tax revenues exceed central government expenditure.

For most of the last fifty years, governments around the world have run budget deficits. In recent years, however, many countries, the UK included, made substantial efforts to reduce their budget deficits, and some achieved budget surpluses for periods of time. The position changed dramatically in 2008/9, however, as governments around the world increased their expenditure and cuts taxes in an attempt to stave off recession.

To finance a deficit, the government will have to borrow (e.g. through the issue of bonds (gilts) or Treasury bills). As we saw in section 18.3, this will lead to an increase in the money supply to the extent that the borrowing is from the banking sector. The purchase of bonds or Treasury bills by the (non-bank) private sector, however, will not lead to an increase in the money supply.

The national debt. The budget deficit refers to the debt that the government incurs in one year. If the government runs persistent deficits over many years, these debts will accumulate. The accumulated debt is known as the **national debt**. Note that the national debt is *not* the same thing as the country's overseas debt. In the case of the UK, only a relatively small fraction of national debt is owed overseas. The bulk of it is owed to UK residents. In other words, the government finances its budget deficits largely by borrowing at home and not from abroad.

General government

'General government' includes central and local government. Thus we can refer to **general government deficits and surpluses** and **general government debt**. Table 20.1 shows government deficits/surpluses and debt for selected countries averaged over three five-year periods. They are expressed as a proportion of GDP.

As you can see, all of them experienced deficits in the first period. But, with the exception of Japan, all experienced a reduction of these deficits in the second period and two countries experienced a surplus. Seven of the countries, however, experienced an increase in deficits or a reduction

---

Definitions

Budget deficit The excess of central government's spending over its tax receipts.

Budget surplus The excess of central government's tax receipts over its spending.

National debt The accumulated budget deficits (less surpluses) over the years: the total amount of government borrowing.

General government deficit (or surplus) The combined deficit (or surplus) of central and local government.

General government debt The combined accumulated debt of central and local government.

Table 20.1   General government deficits/surpluses and debt as percentage of GDP

Country	General government deficits (−) or surpluses (+)			General government debt		
	Average 1991–5	Average 1996–2000	Average 2001–8	Average 1991–5	Average 1996–2000	Average 2001–8
Belgium	−6.5	−1.3	−0.3	139.2	125.2	93.7
France	−4.7	−2.6	−2.9	51.2	68.3	62.6
Germany	−2.9	−1.7	−2.5	46.6	61.6	64.0
Greece	−11.2	−4.0	−4.3	99.3	108.9	97.6
Ireland	−2.5	+2.1	+0.7	90.8	55.8	29.1
Italy	−9.9	−3.1	−3.1	127.6	131.0	105.2
Japan	−1.6	−5.8	−5.0	75.0	113.2	168.2
Netherlands	−3.5	−0.2	−0.6	91.6	79.6	49.2
Sweden	−7.4	+1.1	+1.4	74.9	76.9	47.9
UK	−6.0	−0.3	−2.6	44.7	50.9	41.1
USA	−4.5	0.0	−3.5	73.8	66.9	61.3
Euro area	−5.2	−2.1	−2.0	70.9	80.8	68.2

Source: Based on data in *Statistical Annex of the European Economy* (Commission of the European Communities, 2007), various tables.

in surpluses in the latest period. All the countries were forecast to experience a substantial increase in deficits, and hence debt, from 2008 as governments borrowed more to finance extra spending and/or tax cuts to combat recession.

The whole public sector

To get a more complete view of public finances, we would need to look at the deficit or surplus of the entire public sector: namely, central government, local government and public corporations.

Total public expenditure.   First we need to distinguish between *current* and *capital expenditures*. Current expenditures include items such as wages and salaries of public-sector staff, administration and the payments of welfare benefits. Capital expenditures give rise to a stream of benefits *over time*. Examples include expenditure on roads, hospitals and schools.

We must also distinguish between *final expenditure* on goods and services, and *transfers*. This distinction recognises that the public sector directly adds to the economy's aggregate demand through its spending on goods and services, including the wages of public-sector workers, but also that it redistributes incomes between individuals and firms. Transfers include subsidies and benefit payments, such as payments to the unemployed.

Between 2000 and 2008, the UK's public expenditure was typically split 94 to 6 per cent between current and capital expenditure, and 58 to 42 per cent between final expenditure and transfers.

The PSNCR.   If the public sector spends more than it earns (through taxes and the revenues of public corporations, etc.), the amount of this deficit is known as the *public-sector net cash requirement (PSNCR)* (previously known as the *'public-sector borrowing requirement'*). It is defined as public-sector expenditure minus public-sector receipts. The

reason for the name 'public-sector net cash requirement' is simple. If the public sector runs a deficit in the current year of, say, £1 billion, then it will have to borrow £1 billion in money this year in order to finance it.

If the public sector runs a surplus (a negative PSNCR), it will be able to repay some of the public-sector debts that have accumulated from previous years. Table 20.2 shows the PSNCR for selected years from 1984 to 2008. As you can see, in most years it has been positive (i.e. the public sector was running a deficit and had to borrow).

Public-sector deficits and surpluses and the government's 'fiscal stance'

The government's *fiscal stance* refers to whether it is pursuing an expansionary or contractionary fiscal policy. Does the fact that there was a public-sector deficit in the UK right from 1971 to 1986 mean that the government's fiscal

Definitions

Current expenditure Recurrent spending on goods and factor payments.

Capital expenditure Investment expenditure; expenditure on assets.

Final expenditure Expenditure on goods and services. This is included in GDP and is part of aggregate demand.

Transfers Transfers of money from taxpayers to recipients of benefits and subsidies. They are not an injection into the circular flow but are the equivalent of a negative tax (i.e. a negative withdrawal).

Public-sector net cash requirement (PSNCR) or **public-sector borrowing requirement** The (annual) deficit of the public sector, and thus the amount that the public sector must borrow.

Fiscal stance How expansionary or contractionary the Budget is.

Table 20.2 UK public-sector deficits (+)/surpluses (−): selected years, 1984–2008

Year	1984	1986	1988	1990	1992	1994	1996	1998	2000	2001	2002	2003	2004	2005	2006	2007	2008
PSNCR (£bn)	10.3	2.3	−12.1	−1.7	28.4	39.3	24.7	−6.3	−37.1	−2.0	19.1	37.2	42.2	41.1	33.4	32.3	56.6
% of GDP	3.2	0.7	−2.6	−0.3	4.6	5.7	3.2	−0.7	−3.8	−0.2	1.8	3.3	3.5	3.3	2.5	2.3	4.0

Source: National Statistics.

stance was expansionary throughout this period? Would the mere existence of a surplus mean that the stance was contractionary? The answer is no. Whether the economy expands or contracts depends on the balance of *total* injections and *total* withdrawals.

What we need to focus on is *changes* in the size of the deficit or surplus. If the deficit this year is lower than last year, then (*ceteris paribus*) aggregate demand will be lower this year than last. The reason is that either government expenditure (an injection) must have fallen, or tax revenues (a withdrawal) must have increased, or a combination of the two.

The fiscal stance and the state of the economy

Another problem is that the size of the deficit or surplus is not entirely due to deliberate government policy. It may not give a very good guide, therefore, to government intentions. The size of the deficit or surplus is influenced by the state of the economy. If the economy is booming with people earning high incomes, the amount paid in taxes will be high. In a booming economy the level of unemployment will be low. Thus the amount paid out in unemployment benefits will also be low. The combined effect of increased tax revenues and reduced benefits is to give a public-sector surplus (or a reduced deficit). By contrast, if the economy were depressed, tax revenues would be low and the amount paid in benefits would be high. The public-sector deficit would thus be high.

This relationship between the budget deficit or surplus and the state of the economy is illustrated in Figure 20.1. The tax revenue function is upward sloping. Its slope depends on tax rates. The government expenditure function (which in this diagram includes transfer payments on benefits) is drawn as downward sloping, showing that at higher levels of income and employment less is paid out in benefits. As can be clearly seen, there is only one level of income (Y_1) where there is a public-sector financial balance. Below this level of income there will be a public-sector deficit. Above this level there will be a surplus. The further income is from Y_1, the bigger will be the deficit or surplus. This is illustrated in Table 20.1. During the boom that was experienced in Europe and North America between 1996 and 2000, deficits fell. Japan, by contrast, was experiencing a prolonged recession. Its deficit rose, partly as a result of falling tax revenues and partly from a deliberately expansionary fiscal policy (see Case Study 20.6 in MyEconLab).

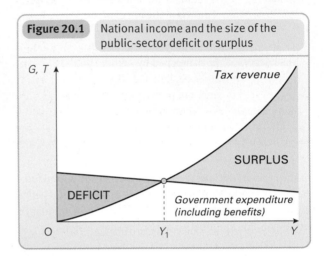

Figure 20.1 National income and the size of the public-sector deficit or surplus

To conclude, the size of the deficit or surplus is a poor guide to the stance of fiscal policy. A large deficit *may* be due to a deliberate policy of increasing aggregate demand, but it may be due simply to the fact that the economy is depressed.

The structural balance

The public-sector deficit or surplus that would arise if the economy were producing at the potential level of national income (see Box 14.3 on page 398) is termed the **structural deficit or surplus**. Remember that the potential level of national income is where there is no excess or deficiency of aggregate demand. In Figure 20.1, if potential national income were below the intersection point of the two lines, there would be structural deficit.

If the economy is producing above or below the potential level of national income, there will be a cyclical component of the public-sector deficit or surplus. Thus the government could aim for a *structural* balance ($G = T$ at the potential level of national income), but be prepared to accept a deficit if the economy was in a recession, or a surplus if it was experiencing a boom.

Definition

Structural deficit (or surplus) The public-sector deficit (or surplus) that would occur if the economy were operating at the potential level of national income: i.e. one where there is a zero output gap.

Automatic fiscal stabilisers

We saw from Figure 20.1 that the size of the public-sector surplus or deficit will automatically vary according to the level of national income. The effect of this will be to reduce the level of fluctuations in national income without the government having to take any deliberate action.

Taxes whose revenues rise as national income rises and benefits that fall as national income rises are called *automatic stabilisers*. They have the effect of reducing the size of the multiplier, reducing both upward and downward movements of national income. Thus, in theory, the business cycle should be dampened by such built-in stabilisers. The more taxes rise or benefits fall, the bigger will be the *mpt* (the net marginal tax propensity). Remember that we defined this as the proportion of any rise in income going in taxes and reduced benefits. The bigger the *mpt*, the smaller will be the multiplier and the greater will be the stabilising effect.

Draw an injections and withdrawals diagram, with a fairly shallow W curve. Mark the equilibrium level of national income. Now draw a second steeper W curve passing through the same point. This second W curve would correspond to the case where tax rates were higher. Assuming now that there has been an increase in injections, draw a second J line above the first. Mark the new equilibrium level of national income with each of the two W curves. You can see that national income rises less with the steeper W curve. The higher tax rates are having a dampening effect on the multiplier.

The effectiveness of automatic stabilisers

Automatic stabilisers have the obvious advantage that they act instantly as soon as aggregate demand fluctuates. By contrast, it may take some time before the government can institute discretionary changes in taxes or government expenditure, especially if forecasting is unreliable.

Nevertheless automatic stabilisers can never be the complete answer to the problem of fluctuations. Their effect is merely to reduce the multiplier – to reduce the severity of fluctuations, not to eliminate them altogether.

In addition, they tend to suffer two specific drawbacks: adverse effects on aggregate supply and the problem of 'fiscal drag'. Let us examine each in turn.

Adverse supply-side effects

TC 5
p50

High tax rates may discourage effort and initiative. The higher the marginal tax rate (*mpt*), the greater the stability provided by the tax system. But the higher tax rates are, the more likely they are to create a disincentive to work and to invest. For example, steeply progressive income taxes may discourage workers from doing overtime or seeking promotion. A higher marginal rate of income tax is equivalent to a higher marginal cost of working. People may prefer to work less and substitute leisure for income. The substitution effect of more progressive taxes may thus outweigh the

income effect. These issues were examined in detail in section 10.2 (see pages 294–6).

High unemployment benefits may increase equilibrium unemployment. High unemployment benefits, by reducing the hardship of being unemployed, may encourage people to spend longer looking for the 'right' job rather than taking the first job offered. This has the effect of increasing unemployment and thus of shifting the Phillips curve to the right. This is because a longer average period of job search represents a higher level of *friction* in the economy and thus a higher *natural* (or *equilibrium*) level of unemployment.

High income-related benefits may create a poverty trap. The higher the level of income-related benefits and the more steeply they taper off, the greater will be the problem of the 'poverty trap'. What is the point in unemployed people seeking jobs, or people in very low-paid jobs seeking better ones, if as a result they lose their benefits and end up being little or no better off than before? The more that people are discouraged in this way, the lower will be the level of aggregate supply. (The question of the poverty trap was also examined in Chapter 10 (see pages 297–8).)

The problem of fiscal drag

Automatic stabilisers help to reduce upward and downward movements in national income. This is fine if the current level of income is the *desirable* level. But suppose that there is currently a deep recession in the economy, with mass unemployment. Who would want to stabilise the economy at this level?

In these circumstances, if the economy began to recover, the automatic stabilisers would act as a drag on the expansion. This is known as *fiscal drag*. By reducing the size of the multiplier, the automatic stabilisers reduce the magnitude of the recovery. Similarly, they act as a drag on discretionary policy: the more powerful the automatic stabilisers are, the bigger the change in *G* or *T* that would be necessary to achieve a given change in national income.

Discretionary fiscal policy

Automatic stabilisers cannot prevent fluctuations. They merely reduce their magnitude. If there is a fundamental disequilibrium in the economy or substantial fluctuations in other injections and withdrawals, the government may choose to *alter* the level of government expenditure or the

---

Definitions

Automatic fiscal stabilisers Tax revenues that rise and government expenditure that falls as national income rises. The more they change with income, the bigger the stabilising effect on national income.

Fiscal drag The tendency of automatic fiscal stabilisers to reduce the recovery of an economy from recession.

CASE STUDIES AND APPLICATIONS

BOX 20.1   MANAGING THE US ECONOMY

To fiscally stimulate or not to fiscally stimulate, that is the question

Response to the slowdown in 2001

Since the start of 2001, the US Federal Reserve, led by Alan Greenspan, had been fighting a sharp slowdown in the US economy. Interest rates had been cut seven times from their level of 6.5 per cent at the beginning of the year to 3.5 per cent in August. By September 2001, the economy seemed to be starting to recover.

The terrorist attacks on 11 September brought this modest recovery to an abrupt halt. At this point, many analysts were suggesting that it might be necessary to lower rates close to zero in order to kick-start the economy. Even then the success of such a strategy was not guaranteed.

At this point, it was decided that a measure of discretionary fiscal policy was required in order to help reduce pressure on the Federal Reserve and its use of interest rates to pump-prime the economy.

Following a meeting at the end of September 2001, Alan Greenspan advised Congress that a fiscal stimulus of $100 billion, or almost 1 per cent of US GDP, was advisable. The Stimulus Bill proposed cutting personal taxation from 27 to 25 per cent, and offering tax exemption to business for new investment. The Democrats were opposed to the personal tax cuts, which would go largely to the rich. A compromise was reached in March 2002 when a stimulus package of $51 billion passed into law, consisting mainly of tax incentives to business.

Such was the delay in passing the Stimulus Bill that recovery began to occur without it. With continued reductions in interest rates, which by December 2001 had been cut eleven times and, at 1.75 per cent, were at the lowest level since the presidency of John F. Kennedy in the 1960s, the economy seemed to be bouncing back. Economic growth was 1.6 per cent in 2002, 2.5 per cent in 2003 and 3.6 per cent in 2004.

But it was not just the Stimulus Bill and the interest rate cuts that were boosting the economy. Fiscal policy generally was becoming more and more expansionary as the size of the budget deficit increased. Tax cuts totalling over $650 billion were given between 2001 and 2004 (71.7 per cent of which went to the richest 20 per cent, 26.4 per cent to the richest 1 per cent and just 0.2 per cent to the poorest 20 per cent). In 2000, there was a budget surplus of 2.4 per cent of GDP. By 2004, the total tax cuts during the period had transformed this into a deficit of 3.6 per cent.

Another dose of medicine

In 2007, the US economy once more seemed to be heading for recession. As we saw in Box 18.2 on pages 572–3, many large mortgages had been given to people with low credit ratings (sub-prime mortgages) when interest rates had been low. With interest rates rising steeply from 2004 to 2006, many people defaulted on their mortgages and other debt. Banks found themselves in a liquidity crisis as many held large amounts of securitised assets containing sub-prime debt. They cut back on loans in what became known as the 'credit crunch'.

By the end of 2007, the US economy seemed to be heading for recession and by the final quarter or the year, annual economic growth had become negative (−0.2 per cent). In January 2008, President Bush announced an emergency $154 billion stimulus package of tax rebates, worth 1.1 per cent of GDP. The effect was to boost consumer spending, and recession seemed to have been averted. By the second quarter of 2008, the economy was growing at an annual rate of 3.3 per cent.

But the effect was short-lived. Once the tax rebates had been spent, the growth in consumer spending ceased. By the end of 2008, GDP was declining; the country was in recession.

Shortly after coming into office in 2009, President Obama signed into law a major fiscal stimulus package, worth $787 billion – the American Recovery and Investment Act. This was in addition to monetary policies designed to increase the flow of credit (see Box 20.5). The aim of the fiscal stimulus was to create 3.6 million jobs and reverse the collapse in aggregate demand that had followed the credit crunch. The package included $212 billion in tax cuts for individuals and business, but the main feature was targeted increases in government expenditure to improve infrastructure: doubling the production of renewable energy, modernising some 75 per cent of government buildings to save energy, and large-scale investment in schools, colleges and public universities, in nationwide broadband, in science, research and technology.

The measures would bring the US budget deficit for 2009 to between $1.2 and $1.6 trillion, or between 8 and 11 per cent of GDP. This compared with a forecast 2.9 per cent for Germany, 3.8 per cent for Italy, 6.2 per cent for Spain and 8.8 per cent for the UK.

Whether such measures would work to revive the economy would depend on their effects on consumer behaviour and business confidence. Would the tax cuts, for example, encourage people to go out and spend? Or would people simply save the tax cuts for fear of losing their jobs in the deepening recession? What would be the multiplier and accelerator effects of the increased government expenditure? Would it stimulate further consumer spending and hence increased investment, or would the effects be offset by falling consumer expenditure and thus reduced investment as firms cut back on capacity?

 Which is likely to give a bigger boost to aggregate demand: tax cuts of a given amount targeted to (a) the rich, or (b) the poor?

rates of taxation. This is known as *discretionary fiscal policy*. It involves *shifting* the *J* and *W* lines.

In the UK, changes in taxation and some changes in government expenditure are announced by the Chancellor of the Exchequer in the Budget (which usually takes place in March). Some of these changes apply to the coming financial year (April to March); some apply to the next financial year or even the one after that.

Since Budgets are normally held only once per year, 'fine tuning' aggregate demand on a week-by-week or month-by-month basis is left to monetary policy – to changes in interest rates (see section 20.2). Very occasionally, however, changes are made between Budgets. Thus in September 2008 the government raised the threshold above which stamp duty must be paid on house purchase in an attempt to help first-time buyers. Then, in the Pre-Budget Report of November 2008, as recession deepened, VAT was cut and planned public-sector projects were brought forward (see Box 20.3).

Note that discretionary changes in taxation or government expenditure, as well as being used to alter the level of aggregate demand (fiscal policy), are also used for other purposes, including the following:

- Altering aggregate supply. Examples include tax incentives to encourage people to work more, or increased government expenditure on training or on transport infrastructure (e.g. roads and railways). We look at such 'supply-side policies' in Chapter 23.
- Altering the distribution of income. As Chapter 10 explained, taxation and benefits are the government's major means of redistributing incomes from the rich to the poor.

Let us now compare the relative effects of changing government expenditure and changing taxes. Will a £100 million increase in government expenditure have the same effect as a £100 million cut in taxes? Will the multiplier be the same in each case?

Discretionary fiscal policy: changing G

If government expenditure on goods and services (roads, health care, education, etc.) is raised, this will create a full multiplied rise in national income. The reason is that all the money gets spent and thus all of it goes to boosting aggregate demand.

 Show the effect of an increase in government expenditure by using (a) the injections and withdrawals diagram; (b) the income/expenditure diagram (see Figures 17.8 and 17.10 on pages 488 and 489).

Definition

Discretionary fiscal policy Deliberate changes in tax rates or the level of government expenditure in order to influence the level of aggregate demand.

Discretionary fiscal policy: changing T

Cutting taxes by £1 million will have a smaller effect on national income than raising government expenditure on goods and services by £1 million. The reason is that cutting taxes increases people's *disposable* incomes, of which only *part* will be spent. Part will be withdrawn into extra savings, imports and other taxes. In other words, not all the tax cuts will be passed on round the circular flow of income as extra expenditure.

The proportion of the cut in taxes that will be withdrawn is given by the *mpw*, and the proportion that will circulate round the flow is given by the mpc_d. Thus if the mpc_d were 4/5, the tax multiplier would only be 4/5 of the normal multiplier.[1] If the mpc_d were 2/3, the tax multiplier would only be 2/3 of the normal multiplier, and so on. The formula for the tax multiplier (k_t) becomes

$$k_t = mpc_d \times k$$

Thus if the normal multiplier were 5 (given an mpc_d of 4/5), the tax multiplier would be 4/5 × 5 = 4. If the normal multiplier were 4 (given an mpc_d of 3/4), the tax multiplier would be 3/4 × 4 = 3, and so on. It should be obvious from this that the tax multiplier is always 1 less than the normal multiplier:

$$k_t = k - 1$$

Since the tax multiplier is smaller than the government expenditure multiplier, to achieve a given rise in income through tax cuts would therefore require a bigger budget deficit than if it were achieved through increased government expenditure. In other words, the required tax cut would be bigger than the required government expenditure increase.

 Why will the multiplier effect of government transfer payments such as child benefit, pensions and social security be less than the full multiplier effect given by government expenditure on goods and services? Will this 'transfer payments multiplier' be the same as the tax multiplier? (Clue: will the recipients of such benefits have the same mpc_d as the average person?)

The effectiveness of discretionary fiscal policy

How successful will discretionary fiscal policy be? Can it 'fine tune' demand? Can it achieve the level of national income that the government would like it to achieve?

There are two main problem areas with discretionary fiscal policy. The first concerns the *magnitude* of the effects. If *G* or *T* is changed, how much will *total* injections and withdrawals change? What will be the size of the multiplier? How much will a change in aggregate demand affect output and employment, and how much will it affect prices?

---

[1] Strictly speaking, the tax multiplier is negative, since a *rise* in taxes causes a *fall* in national income.

Figure 20.2   The monetary effects of a rise in injections

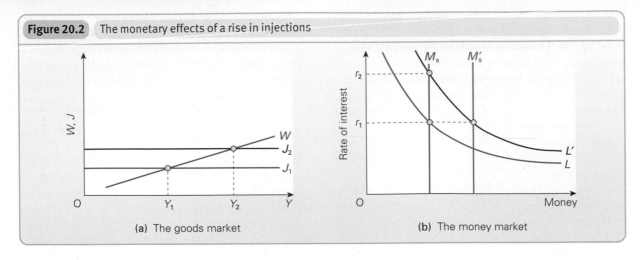

(a) The goods market

(b) The money market

KI 31
p320

The second concerns the *timing* of the effects. How quickly can policy be changed and how quickly will the changes affect the economy?

Problems of magnitude

TC 15
p487

Before changing government expenditure or taxation, the government will need to calculate the effect of any such change on national income, employment and inflation. Predicting these effects, however, is often very unreliable for a number of reasons.

Predicting the effect of changes in government expenditure

A rise in government expenditure of £x may lead to a rise in total injections (relative to withdrawals) that is smaller than £x. This will occur if the rise in government expenditure *replaces* a certain amount of private expenditure. For example, a rise in expenditure on state education may dissuade some parents from sending their children to private schools. Similarly an improvement in the National Health Service may lead to fewer people paying for private treatment.

Crowding out. If the government relies on **pure fiscal policy** – that is, if it does not finance an increase in the budget deficit by increasing the money supply – it will have to borrow the money from the non-bank private sector. It will thus be competing with the private sector for finance and will have to offer higher interest rates. This will force the private sector also to offer higher interest rates, which may discourage firms from investing and individuals from buying on credit. Thus government borrowing *crowds out*

Definition

Pure fiscal policy Fiscal policy that does not involve any change in money supply.

private borrowing. In the extreme case, the fall in consumption and investment may completely offset the rise in government expenditure, with the result that aggregate demand does not rise at all.

Figure 20.2 illustrates the extent of crowding out. (It is the same as Figure 19.8 on page 545.) The rise in government expenditure shifts the injections line from J_1 to J_2 in Figure 20.2(a). The full multiplier effect of this would be a rise in national income to Y_2. However, the increased government expenditure leads to an increased demand for money. In Figure 20.2(b), the liquidity preference curve shifts to L'. This raises the interest rate to r_2. Note that we are assuming that the money supply is purely exogenous – i.e. does not vary with the demand for money – and that, therefore, the money supply 'curve' is a vertical straight line (M_s).

The higher rate of interest reduces investment. The injections line falls below J_2, and, as a result, national income does not rise as far as Y_2. The amount by which actual income falls short of Y_2 measures the extent of crowding out.

The amount of crowding out from pure fiscal policy depends on three things:

- The shape of the L curve. The flatter the curve, the less will interest rates rise. A greater amount of liquidity will be released from idle balances and there will be a bigger increase in the velocity of circulation.
- Whether money supply is exogenous. If the extra demand for money leads to banks creating extra credit, the money supply curve will be upward sloping, not vertical. The more money is created, the flatter will be the M_s curve, the less interest rates will rise and the less will be the crowding out.
- The responsiveness of investment (and consumption) to a change in interest rates. The more responsive investment is to a rise in interest rates, the more will the J curve shift downwards and the bigger will be the crowding-out effect.

If the fiscal policy is not *pure* fiscal policy, if the extra government borrowing is financed by borrowing from the banking sector, then the supply of money curve will shift to the right. If it were to shift as far as M'_s, the rate of interest would remain at r_1 and there would be no crowding out.

How do people's expectations influence the extent of crowding out?

Predicting the effect of changes in taxes

A cut in taxes, by raising people's real disposable income, increases not only the amount they spend but also the amount they save. The problem is that it is not easy to predict the relative size of these two increases. In part it depends on whether people feel that the cut in tax is only temporary, in which case they may simply save the extra disposable income, or permanent, in which case they may adjust their consumption upwards.

Do theories of the long-run and short-run consumption function help us to understand consumer reactions to a change in taxes? (See section 17.1 and Case Studies 17.1 and 17.2 in MyEconLab.)

Predicting the resulting multiplied effect on national income

Even if the government *could* predict the net initial effect on injections and withdrawals, the extent to which national income will change is still hard to predict for the following reasons:

- The size of the *multiplier* may be difficult to predict. This is because the mpc_d and *mpw* may fluctuate. For example, the amount of a rise in income that households save or consume will depend on their expectations about future price and income changes.
- Induced investment through the *accelerator* (see pages 496–7) is also extremely difficult to predict. It may be that a relatively small fiscal stimulus will be all that is necessary to restore business confidence, and that induced investment will rise substantially. In such a case, fiscal policy can be seen as a 'pump primer'. It is used to *start* the process of recovery, and then the *continuation* of the recovery is left to the market. But for pump priming to work, businesspeople must *believe* that it will work. Business confidence can change very rapidly and in ways that could not have been foreseen a few months earlier.
- Multiplier/accelerator interactions. If the initial multiplier and accelerator effects are difficult to estimate, their interaction will be virtually impossible to estimate. Small divergences in investment from what was initially predicted will become magnified as time progresses.

Random shocks

Forecasts cannot take into account the unpredictable, such as the attack on the World Trade Center in New York in September 2001. Even events that, with hindsight, should have been predicted, such as the banking crisis of 2007–9, often are not. Unfortunately, unpredictable or unpredicted events do occur and may seriously undermine the government's fiscal policy.

Give some examples of these random shocks.

Problems of timing

Fiscal policy can involve considerable time lags. If these are long enough, fiscal policy could even be *de*stabilising. Expansionary policies taken to cure a recession may not come into effect until the economy has *already* recovered and is experiencing a boom. Under these circumstances, expansionary policies are quite inappropriate: they simply worsen the problems of overheating. Similarly, contractionary policies taken to prevent excessive expansion may not take effect until the economy has already peaked and is plunging into recession. The contractionary policies only deepen the recession.

This problem is illustrated in Figure 20.3. Path (a) shows the course of the business cycle without government

KI 31
p320

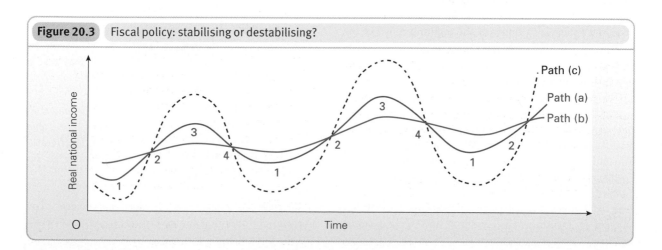

Figure 20.3 Fiscal policy: stabilising or destabilising?

BOX 20.2   **RIDING A SWITCHBACK**

EXPLORING
EOCNOMICS

A parable for Chancellors

Imagine that you are driving a car along a straight but undulating road. These undulations are not regular: some of the hills are steep, some are gentle; some are long, some are short.

You are given the instruction that you must keep the car going at a constant speed. To do this, you will need to accelerate going up the hills and brake going down them.

There is a serious problem, however. The car is no ordinary car. It has the following distinctly unusual features:

- The front windscreen and side windows are blacked out, so you cannot see where you are going! All you can see is where you have been by looking in your rear-view mirror.
- The brake and accelerator pedals both work with a considerable and unpredictable delay.
- The car's suspension is so good that you cannot feel whether you are going up or downhill. You can only judge this by looking in your mirror.
- Finally (you are relieved to know), the car has a special sensor and automatic steering that keep it in the correct lane.

As you are going along, you see that the road behind you is higher, and you realise that you are going downhill. The car gets faster and faster. You brake – but nothing happens. In your zeal to slow the car down, you put your foot down on the brake as hard as you can.

When the brake eventually does come on, it comes on very strongly. By this time, the car has already reached the bottom of the hill. As yet, however, you do not realise this and are still braking. But now the car is going up the next hill with the brakes still on. Looking in your mirror, you eventually realise this. You take your foot off the brake and start accelerating. But the pedals do not respond. The car is still slowing down rapidly, and you only just manage to reach the top of the hill.

Then, as you start going down the other side, the brakes eventually come off and the accelerator comes on . . .

This famous parable – first told by Frank Paish, Professor of Economics at the LSE, some 35 years ago – demonstrates how 'stabilising' activity can in fact be destabilising. When applied to fiscal policy, long and uncertain time lags can mean that the government can end up stimulating the economy in a boom and contracting it in a slump.

So what should be done? One alternative, of course, would be to try to reduce the time lags and to improve forecasting. But failing this, the best policy may be to do nothing: to take a 'steady as you go' or 'fixed throttle' approach to running the economy. Going back to the car analogy, a fixed throttle will not prevent the car from going faster downhill and slower uphill, but at least it will not make the speed even more irregular.

 What would a fixed throttle approach to fiscal policy involve?

KI 31
p320

---

intervention. Ideally, with no time lags, the economy should be dampened in stage 2 and stimulated in stage 4. This would make the resulting course of the business cycle more like path (b), or even, if the policy were perfectly stabilising, a straight line.

With time lags, however, contractionary policies taken in stage 2 may not come into effect until stage 4, and expansionary policies taken in stage 4 may not come into effect until stage 2. In this case, the resulting course of the business cycle will be more like path (c). Quite obviously, in these circumstances 'stabilising' fiscal policy actually makes the economy less stable.

There are five possible lags associated with fiscal policy.

Time lag to recognition.   Since the business cycle can be irregular and forecasting unreliable, governments may be unwilling to take action until they are convinced that the problem is serious.

Time lag between recognition and action.   Most significant changes in government expenditure have to be planned well in advance. The government cannot increase spending on motorways overnight or suddenly start building new hospitals. As far as taxes are concerned, these can normally be changed only at the time of the Budget, and will not be instituted until the new financial year or at some other point in the future. As Budgets normally occur annually, there could be a considerable time lag if the problems are recognised a long time before the Budget.

Time lag between action and changes taking effect.   A change in tax rates may not immediately affect tax payments, as some taxes are paid in arrears and new rates may take a time to apply.

Time lag between changes in government expenditure and taxation and the resulting change in national income, prices and employment.   The multiplier round takes time. Accelerator effects take time. The multiplier and accelerator go on interacting. It all takes time.

Consumption may respond slowly to changes in taxation.   The short-run consumption function tends to be flatter than the long-run function.

If the fluctuations in aggregate demand can be forecast, and if the lengths of the time lags are known, then all is not lost. At least the fiscal measures can be taken early and their delayed effects can be taken into account.

Fiscal rules

Given the problems of pursuing active fiscal policy, many governments in recent years took a much more passive approach. Instead of the policy being changed as the economy changes, a rule would be set for the level of public finances. This rule would then be applied year after year, with taxes and government expenditure being planned to meet that rule. For example, a target could be set for the PSNCR, with government expenditure and taxes being adjusted to keep the PSNCR at or within its target level. Fiscal (and monetary) rules are examined in more detail in section 20.5.

The approach to fiscal policy in the UK

From 1998, the UK government set targets for government expenditure, not for just one year, but for a three-year period. Did this mean, therefore, that fiscal policy as a means of adjusting aggregate demand has been abandoned? In one sense, this was the case. The Labour government was committed to following its 'golden rule', whereby public-sector receipts should cover all *current* (as opposed to capital) spending, averaged over the course of the business cycle (see Box 20.3).

But despite this apparent rejection of short-term discretionary fiscal adjustments, there was still a role for automatic fiscal stabilisers, with deficits rising in a recession and falling in a boom. There was also still the possibility, within the golden rule, of financing additional investment by borrowing, thereby providing a stimulus to a sluggish economy.

The golden rule also permitted increased government expenditure (or tax cuts) if there was a budget surplus. Thus in the 2001 Budget the Chancellor announced spending increases of 3.7 per cent per year for three years. The effect was to provide a stimulus to the economy just at a time when the world economy was slowing down. This helped to make the slowdown in UK economic growth in the period 2001–3 much less severe than in many other countries.

But a rule cannot cope with severe disruption to the global economy, such as occurred in the credit crunch of 2008. As we shall see in section 20.5, countries around the world resorted to discretionary fiscal policy to boost aggregate demand. They abandoned fiscal rules – at least temporarily.

Section summary

1. The government's fiscal policy influences the size of the budget deficit or surplus and the size of the PSNCR. The size of these alone, however, is a poor guide to the government's fiscal stance. A large deficit, for example, may simply be due to the fact that the economy is in recession and therefore tax receipts are low. A better guide is whether the change in the deficit or surplus will be expansionary or contractionary.

2. Automatic fiscal stabilisers are tax revenues that rise, and benefits that fall, as national income rises. They have the effect of reducing the size of the multiplier and thus reducing cyclical upswings and downswings.

3. Automatic stabilisers take effect as soon as aggregate demand fluctuates, but they can never remove fluctuations completely. They also create disincentives and act as a drag on recovery from recession.

4. Discretionary fiscal policy is where the government deliberately changes taxes or government expenditure in order to alter the level of aggregate demand. Changes in government expenditure on goods and services have a full multiplier effect. Changes in taxes and benefits, however, have a smaller multiplier effect. The tax multiplier has a value 1 less than the full multiplier.

5. There are problems in predicting the magnitude of the effects of discretionary fiscal policy. Expansionary fiscal policy can act as a pump primer and stimulate increased private expenditure, or it can crowd out private expenditure. The extent to which it acts as a pump primer depends crucially on business confidence – something that is very difficult to predict beyond a few weeks or months. The extent of crowding out depends on monetary conditions and the government's monetary policy.

6. There are five possible time lags involved with fiscal policy: the time lag before the problem is diagnosed, the lag between diagnosis and new measures being announced, the lag between announcement and implementation, the lag while the multiplier and accelerator work themselves out, and the lag before consumption fully responds to new economic circumstances.

7. In recent years, many governments preferred a more passive approach towards fiscal policy. Targets were set for one or more measures of the public-sector finances, and then taxes and government expenditure were adjusted so as to keep to the target.

8. Nevertheless, in extreme circumstances, as occurred in 2008/9, governments were prepared to abandon rules and give a fiscal stimulus to their economies.

BOX 20.3   FOLLOWING THE GOLDEN RULE

Fiscal policy in a straitjacket?

If the government persistently runs a budget deficit, the national debt will rise. If it rises faster than GDP, it will account for a growing proportion of GDP. There is then likely to be an increasing problem of 'servicing' this debt: i.e. paying the interest on it. The government could find itself having to borrow more and more to meet the interest payments, and so the national debt could rise faster still. As the government borrows more and more, so it has to pay higher interest rates to attract finances. If it is successful in this, borrowing and hence investment by the private sector could be crowded out (see page 568).

Recognising these problems, many governments in recent years have attempted to reduce their debts.

Preparing for the euro

In signing the Maastricht Treaty in 1992, the EU countries agreed that to be eligible to join the single currency (i.e. the euro), they should have sustainable deficits and debts. This was interpreted as follows: the general government deficit should be no more than 3 per cent of GDP and general government debt should be no more than 60 per cent of GDP, or should at least be falling towards that level at a satisfactory pace.

But in the mid 1990s, several of the countries that were subsequently to join the euro had deficits and debts substantially above these levels (see Table 20.1). Getting them down proved a painful business. Government expenditure had to be cut and taxes increased. These fiscal measures unfortunately, proved to be powerful! Unemployment rose and growth remained low.

The EU Stability and Growth Pact

In June 1997, at the European Council in Amsterdam, the EU countries agreed that governments adopting the euro should seek to balance their budgets (or even aim for a surplus) averaged over the course of the business cycle, and that deficits should not exceed 3 per cent of GDP in

any one year. A country's deficit is permitted to exceed 3 per cent only if its GDP has declined by at least 2 per cent (or 0.75 per cent with special permission from the Council of Ministers). Otherwise, countries with deficits exceeding 3 per cent are required to make deposits of money with the European Central Bank. These then become fines if the excessive budget deficit is not eliminated within two years.

There are two main aims of targeting a zero budget deficit over the business cycle. The first is to allow automatic stabilisers to work without 'bumping into' the 3 per cent deficit ceiling in years when economies are slowing. The second is to allow a reduction in government debts as a proportion of GDP (assuming that GDP grows on average at around 2–3 per cent per year).

But was the pact flexible enough? From 2002, both Germany and France breached the 3 per cent ceiling (see Figure (a)). This was partly the result of slow growth and rising unemployment, and hence falling tax revenue and rising benefit payments. Not surprisingly, both countries were reluctant to cut government expenditure to bring the deficit in line for fear of dampening an already sluggish economy. Despite various promises by the two countries to rein in expenditure, they continued to have deficits in excess of 3 per cent. It is interesting to note that the general government deficits in the USA and Japan in 2003 were 4.8 per cent and 7.9 per cent of GDP respectively, and both countries were adopting *expansionary* fiscal policy.

Eventually, in March 2005 a deal was reached between European finance ministers. This allowed Germany to exclude reunification costs and France to exclude military and aid costs from the calculation of government expenditure. This compromise brought the deficits of the two countries below the 3 per cent ceiling and allowed them to escape having to adopt tighter fiscal policy.

As you can see from Figure (a), until 2008 deficits had been kept below the 3 per cent ceiling, although both

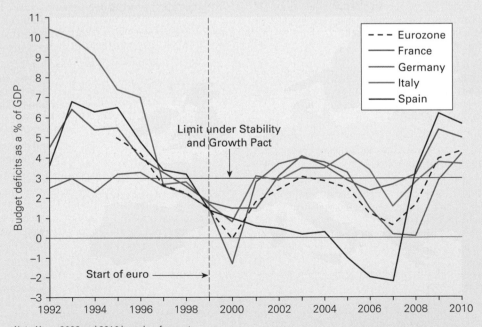

(a) *Keeping budget deficits within the 3% ceiling?*

Note: Years 2009 and 2010 based on forecasts.
Source: Based on data in *Statistical Annex of the European Economy* (Commission of the European Communities).

France and Italy were perilously close to it in 2008 as their economies slowed down.

In November 2008, however, the European Commission announced a €200 billion fiscal stimulus plan, mainly in the form of increased public expenditure. €170 of the money would come from member governments and €30 from the EU, amounting to a total of 1.2 per cent of EU GDP. The money would be for a range of projects, such as job training, help to small businesses, developing green energy technologies and energy efficiency. Most member governments quickly followed by announcing how their specific plans would accord with the overall plan.

The measures would push most eurozone countries' budget deficits well above the 3 per cent ceiling (see Figure (a)). But since the recession in EU countries was predicted to deepen in 2009, with GDP forecast to decline by 1.9 per cent in the eurozone as a whole, and by 2.3 per cent in Germany, 1.8 per cent in France and 2 per cent in Italy, this was not seen to breach the Stability and Growth Pact rules.

Labour's golden rule

The Labour government in the UK adopted a similar approach to that of the Stability and Growth Pact. Under its 'golden rule', the government pledged that over the economic cycle, it would borrow only to invest (e.g. in roads, hospitals and schools) and not to fund current spending (e.g. on wages, administration and benefits). Investment was exempted from the zero borrowing rule because it contributes towards the growth of GDP. In addition, under its 'sustainable investment rule', the government also set itself the target of maintaining a stable public-sector debt/GDP ratio below 40 per cent.

To allow the golden rule to operate, government departments were set three-year spending limits and each had separate current and capital (investment) budgets.

As with the Stability and Growth Pact, the argument was that by using an averaging rule over the cycle, automatic stabilisers would be allowed to work. Deficits of receipts over current spending can occur when the economy is in recession or when growth is sluggish (as in 2001–3), helping to stimulate the economy. As can be seen from Figure (b), the golden rule was met over the cycle 1997/8 to 2006/7.

In 2008, however, the golden rule had to be suspended. As the UK, along with many other countries, plunged into recession in the aftermath of the credit crunch, the government decided to use discretionary fiscal policy to boost the economy.

In the Pre-Budget Report of November 2008, amongst other measures the government introduced a 13-month cut in VAT from 17.5 per cent to 15 per cent. It also brought forward from 2010/11 £3 billion of capital spending on projects such as motorways, new social housing, schools and energy efficiency. The projected effects on government borrowing of these measures, plus those of the automatic fiscal stabilisers as the economy slowed, is shown in Figure (b). The current deficit for 2009/10 was projected by the Treasury to be some 4.5 per cent of GDP. Public-sector debt was also set to breach the 40 per cent of GDP ceiling, reaching 57.4 per cent by 2013/14.

The hope, however, was that, as the economy recovered and the government was able to raise taxes again, the golden rule could be resumed once more.

 What effects will an increase in government investment expenditure have on public-sector debt (a) in the short run; (b) in the long run?

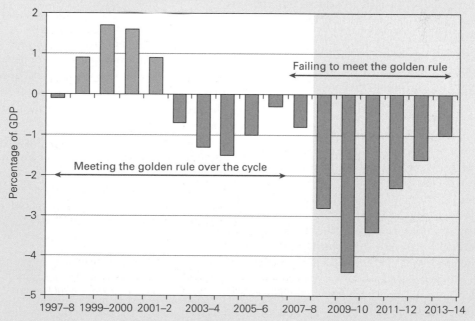

(b) *Cyclically adjusted surplus on UK current budget*

Source: Pre-Budget Report 2008 (HM Treasury, 2008).

20.2 MONETARY POLICY

Each month the Bank of England's Monetary Policy Committee (MPC) meets to set Bank Rate. The event gets considerable media coverage. Pundits, for two or three days before the meeting, try to predict what the MPC will do and economists give their 'considered' opinions about what the MPC *ought* to do.

The fact is that changes in interest rates have gained a central significance in macroeconomic policy. And it is not just in the UK. Whether it is the European Central Bank setting interest rates for the eurozone countries, or the Federal Reserve Bank setting US interest rates, or any other central bank around the world choosing what the level of interest rates should be, monetary policy is seen as having a major influence on a whole range of macroeconomic indicators.

But is monetary policy just the setting of interest rates? In reality, it involves the central bank intervening in the money market to ensure that the interest rate announced is also the *equilibrium* interest rate.

The policy setting

In framing its monetary policy, the government must decide on what the goals of the policy are. Is the aim simply to control inflation, or does the government wish also to affect output and employment, or does it want to control the exchange rate?

The government also has to decide the role of the central bank in carrying out monetary policy. There are three possible approaches.

In the first, the government both sets the policy and decides the measures necessary to achieve it. Here the government would set the interest rate, with the central bank simply influencing money markets to achieve this rate. This first approach was used in the UK before 1997.

The second approach is for the government to set the policy *targets*, but for the central bank to be given independence in deciding interest rates. This is the approach adopted in the UK today. The government has set a target rate of inflation of 2 per cent, but then the MPC is free to choose the rate of interest.

The third approach is for the central bank to be given independence not only in carrying out policy, but in setting the policy targets itself. The ECB, within the statutory objective of maintaining price stability over the medium term, has decided on the target of keeping inflation below, but close to 2 per cent over the medium term.

Finally, there is the question of whether the government or central bank should take a long-term or short-term perspective. Should it adopt a target for inflation or money supply growth and stick to it come what may? Or should it adjust its policy as circumstances change and attempt to 'fine tune' the economy?

We will be looking primarily at *short-term* monetary policy: that is, policy used to keep to a set target for infla-

tion or money supply growth, or policy used to smooth out fluctuations in the business cycle. It is important first, however, to take a longer-term perspective. Governments generally want to prevent an excessive growth in the money supply over the longer term. Likewise they want to ensure that money supply grows enough and that there is not a shortage of credit, such as that during the credit crunch. If money supply grows too rapidly, then inflation is likely to be high; if money supply grows too slowly, or even falls, then recession is likely to result.

Control of the money supply over the medium and long term

There are two major sources of monetary growth: (a) banks choosing to hold a lower liquidity ratio (probably in response to an increase in the demand for loans); (b) public-sector borrowing financed by borrowing from the banking sector. If the government wishes to restrict monetary growth over the longer term, it could attempt to control either or both of these.

Banks' liquidity ratio

The central bank could impose a statutory **minimum reserve ratio** on the banks, *above* the level that banks would otherwise choose to hold. Such ratios come in various forms. The simplest is where the banks are required to hold a given minimum percentage of deposits in the form of cash or deposits with the central bank. Other versions are where they are required to hold a given minimum percentage of certain specified types of deposit in the form of various liquid assets. This was the system used in the UK up to 1981. Various types of liquid asset had to add up to at least 12.5 per cent of certain 'eligible liabilities'.

The effect of a minimum reserve ratio is to prevent banks choosing to reduce their cash or liquidity ratio and creating more credit. This was a popular approach of governments in many countries in the past. Some countries imposed very high ratios indeed in their attempt to slow down the growth in the money supply.

Minimum reserve ratios also have the effect of reducing the bank deposits multiplier, since, for any expansion of the monetary base, *less* credit can be created. For example, if banks would otherwise choose a 10 per cent cash ratio, and if the central bank imposes a 20 per cent cash ratio, the bank deposits multiplier is reduced from 10 (= $1/\frac{1}{10}$) to 5 (= $1/\frac{1}{5}$).

Definition

Minimum reserve ratio A minimum ratio of cash (or other specified liquid assets) to deposits (either total or selected) that the central bank requires banks to hold.

A major problem with imposing restrictions of this kind is that banks may find ways of getting round them. After all, normally banks would like to lend and customers would like to borrow. It is very difficult to regulate and police every single part of countries' complex financial systems.

Nevertheless, attitudes changed substantially after the excessive lending of the mid 2000s. The expansion of credit had been based on 'liquidity' achieved through secondary marketing between financial institutions and the growth of securitised assets containing sub-prime debt (see pages 510–11 and Box 18.2). After the credit crunch and the need for central banks or governments to rescue ailing banks, such as Northern Rock and later the Royal Bank of Scotland in the UK and many other banks around the world, there were calls for greater regulation of banks to ensure that they had sufficient capital and operated with sufficient liquidity and that they were not exposed to excessive risk of default. As we saw in Box 18.3 on page 516, a number of measures were taken.

Public-sector deficits

In section 18.3, we showed how government borrowing tends to lead to an increase in money supply. To prevent this, the public-sector net cash requirement (PSNCR) must be financed by selling *bonds* (as opposed to bills, which could well be taken up by the banking sector, thereby increasing money supply). However, to sell extra bonds the government will have to offer higher interest rates. This will have a knock-on effect on private-sector interest rates. The government borrowing will thus crowd out private-sector borrowing and investment.

If governments wish to reduce monetary growth and yet avoid financial crowding out, they must therefore reduce the level of the PSNCR. Monetarism, which reached its high point in the 1980s, advocated governments making reductions in the PSNCR (as a proportion of national income) the central part of their medium- and longer-term monetary strategy. Not only would this help to restrict monetary growth, but, if it involved cutting government expenditure (as opposed to increasing taxes), it would also increase the size of the private sector relative to the public sector – and it was the private sector that monetarists saw as the main source of long-term growth in output and employment.

In the UK, the Conservative government's medium-term financial strategy, introduced in 1980, attempted to do just this (see section 20.4). As well as setting targets for the growth of money supply, it also set targets for the PSNCR as a percentage of GDP.

How could long-term monetary growth come about if the government persistently ran a public-sector surplus (a negative PSNCR)?

Once inflation is at or near its target level, longer-term control of the monetary base is largely a matter of ensuring that government borrowing is kept in check (see Box 20.3). Keeping bank lending under control is achieved by *short-term* measures to keep inflation at its target rate (see below).

In the early years, however, when a government is embarking on a policy of bringing inflation down there can be serious problems. When the Thatcher government in 1980 adopted a policy of medium-term monetary control, inflation was 18 per cent.

The higher the initial rate of inflation, and the more rapidly the government wishes to reduce it, the bigger the problems can be. The government must cut the PSNCR, but this will be a contractionary *fiscal* policy. This could lead to a recession, given that inflation may be slow to fall.

Adverse effects of automatic stabilisers. In a recession, automatic fiscal stabilisers come into force that will tend to push the PSNCR back up again. Lower incomes and lower expenditure will mean that less taxes are paid. At the same time, higher unemployment will involve increased government expenditure on unemployment benefits. This was a major problem in the UK in the early 1980s, and again in the early 1990s, when the severe recession turned a public-sector surplus of £12 billion in 1988 into a massive deficit of £43 billion by 1993. Attempts to cut the size of the PSNCR by tax increases (e.g. VAT on domestic fuel) and cuts in government expenditure served only to prolong the recession.

It is for this reason that, under the Stability and Growth Pact (see Box 20.3), eurozone countries are required to aim for a zero government deficit over the business cycle, so that in times of economic slowdown the deficit will not exceed 3 per cent (the limit set for deficits under the Pact).

Similarly, in the UK, the Labour government adopted the 'golden rule' of fiscal policy. This is that, over the course of the business cycle, the government will borrow only to invest. In other words, leaving investment aside, there is a long-term target for government borrowing of zero.

Long-term monetary control and inflation

Although there are issues with achieving long-term control of the money supply, there is widespread agreement that it is important to do so. The argument is that *increasing* the money supply cannot increase output in the long run; all that will happen is an increase in prices.

It is widely agreed that in the long run – after all adjustments in the economy have worked through – a change in the quantity of money in the economy will be reflected in a change in the general level of prices. But it will not induce permanent changes in real variables such as real output or unemployment.

This general principle, referred to as the **long-run neutrality of money**, underlies all standard macro-

---

Definition

Long-run neutrality of money Changes in money supply over the long run will only affect prices and not real output or employment.

economic thinking. Real income or the level of employment are, in the long term, essentially determined by real factors, such as technology, population growth or the preferences of economic agents.[1]

If inflation is to be kept under control, therefore, it is important to control the supply of money. And if long-term control is to be achieved, it is also important not to allow excessive expansion (or contraction) of the money supply in the short term too. But what instruments does a central bank have at its disposal? We examine these next.

The operation of monetary policy in the short term

Inflation may be off target. Alternatively, the government (or central bank) may wish to alter its monetary policy. Assume, for example, that it wishes to operate a tighter monetary policy in order to reduce aggregate demand and inflation. What can it do?

For any given supply of money (M_s) there will be a particular equilibrium rate of interest at any one time: where the supply of money (M_s) equals the demand for money (L). This is shown as r_1 in Figure 20.4.

Thus to operate a tighter monetary policy, the authorities can do the following:

- Reduce money supply and accept whatever equilibrium interest rate results. Thus if money supply is reduced to Q_2 in Figure 20.4, a new higher rate of interest, r_2, will result.
- First raise interest rates to r_2 and then manipulate the money supply to reduce it to Q_2. The more endogenous the money supply is, the more this will occur automatically through banks adjusting credit to match the lower demand at the higher rate of interest and the less the central bank will have to take deliberate action to reduce liquidity.

There is another possibility. This is to keep interest rates low (at r_1), but also reduce money supply to a level of Q_2. The trouble here is that the authorities cannot both control the money supply *and* keep interest rates down without running into the problem of disequilibrium. Since the demand for money now exceeds the supply by $Q_1 - Q_2$, some form of credit rationing would have to be applied.

Credit rationing was widely used in the past, especially during the 1960s. The aim was to keep interest rates low, so as not to discourage investment, but to restrict credit to more risky business customers and/or to consumers. In the UK the Bank of England could order banks to abide by such a policy, although in practice it always relied on persuasion. The government also, from time to time, imposed restrictions on hire-purchase credit, by specifying minimum deposits or maximum repayment periods.

[1] European Central Bank, http://www.ecb.int/mopo/intro/role/html/index. en.html.

Figure 20.4   The demand for and supply of money

Such policies were progressively abandoned around the world from the early 1980s. They were seen to stifle competition and prevent efficient banks from expanding. Hire-purchase controls could badly hit certain industries (e.g. cars and other consumer durables), whose products are bought largely on hire-purchase credit. What is more, with the deregulation and globalisation of financial markets up to 2007, it had become very difficult to ration credit. If one financial institution was controlled, borrowers could simply go elsewhere.

With the excessive lending in sub-prime markets that had triggered the credit crunch of 2007–9, however, there were calls around the world for tighter controls over bank lending. But this was different from credit rationing as we have defined it. In other words, tighter controls would be used to prevent reckless behaviour by banks, rather than to achieve a particular level of money at a lower rate of interest.

We thus focus on the two major approaches to monetary policy: (a) controlling the money supply and (b) controlling interest rates.

Techniques to control the money supply

There are two broad approaches to controlling the money supply.

The first is alter the level of liquidity in the banking system, on which credit is created. Suppose, for example, that banks operate a rigid 10 per cent cash ratio and have just two types of asset: cash and advances. Suppose also that the authorities are able to reduce cash in banks by £1 million. With a bank multiplier of 10 (= 1/cash ratio), advances must be reduced by £9 million, and hence (broad) money supply by £10 million (see Table 20.3).

 If banks operated a rigid 5 per cent cash ratio and the government reduced cash in banks by £1 million, how much must credit contract? What is the bank deposits multiplier?

Table 20.3	Reducing the money supply		
Liabilities		**Assets**	
Deposits	£10m↓	Cash	£1m ↓
		Advances	£9m ↓

The second approach is to alter the size of the bank deposits multiplier, by altering the ratio of reserves to deposits. Thus if the bank deposits multiplier can be reduced, credit will have to be reduced for any given reserve base.

Before they can actually apply techniques of monetary control, the authorities must make two preliminary decisions:

- Should a statutory minimum reserve or a minimum liquidity ratio be imposed on the banks, or should the banks be allowed to choose whatever ratios they consider to be prudent?
- Should the authorities attempt to control a range of liquid assets, or should they focus on controlling just the monetary base?

There are four techniques that a central bank could use to control the money supply. Assume in each case that the central bank wishes to reduce money supply.

Open-market operations

Open-market operations are the most widely used of the four techniques around the world. They alter the monetary base (cash in circulation outside the central bank). This then affects the amount of credit that banks can create and hence the level of broad money (M4 in the UK).

Open-market operations involve the sale or purchase by the central bank of government securities (bonds or bills) in the open market. These sales or purchases are *not* in response to changes in the PSNCR, and are best understood in the context of an unchanged PSNCR

If the central bank wishes to *reduce* the money supply, it sells more securities. When people buy these securities, they pay for them by drawing on their accounts in banks. Thus banks' balances with the central bank are reduced. If this brings bank reserves below their prudent ratio (or statutory ratio, if one is in force), banks will reduce advances. There will be a multiple contraction of credit and hence of (broad) money supply. (Details of how open-market operations work in the UK are given in Box 20.4.)

The effect will be limited if the extra securities are bills (as opposed to bonds) and if some are purchased by banks.

The reduction in one liquid asset (balances with the central bank) will be offset to some extent by an increase in another liquid asset (bills). Open-market operations are more likely to be effective in reducing the money supply, therefore, when conducted in the bond market.

1. Explain how open-market operations could be used to increase the money supply.
2. Why would it be difficult for a central bank to predict the precise effect on money supply of open-market operations?

Reduced central bank lending to the banks

The central bank in most countries is prepared to provide extra money to banks (through rediscounting bills, gilt repos or straight loans). If banks obtain less money in this way, they will have to cut back on lending. Less credit will be created and broad money supply will thereby be reduced.

Whether or not banks *choose* to obtain extra money from the central bank depends on (a) the rate of interest charged by the central bank (i.e. its discount rate, repo rate or lending rate); and (b) its willingness to lend (or repurchase securities).

In some countries, it is the policy of the central bank to keep its interest rate to banks *below* market rates, thereby encouraging banks to borrow (or sell back securities) whenever such facilities are available. By controlling the amount of money it is willing to provide at these low rates, the central bank can control the monetary base and hence the amount of credit that banks can create.

In other countries, such as the UK and the eurozone countries, it is not so much the amount of money made available that is controlled, but rather the rate of interest (or discount). The higher this rate is relative to other market rates, the less will banks be willing to borrow, and the lower, therefore, will be the monetary base. Raising this rate, therefore, has the effect of reducing the money supply.

In some countries, central banks operate two rates: a main repo rate (or 'refinancing rate') on a set amount of money that the central bank wants to be made available, and a higher rate (a penal rate) used for 'last-resort' lending to banks short of liquidity. The European Central Bank operates such a system (see Box 20.6). Its higher rate is known as the 'marginal lending facility rate'.

In response to the credit crunch of 2007/8, central banks in several countries extended their willingness to lend to banks. As we saw in Box 18.3 on pages 516–8, under its 'Special Liquidity Scheme', the Bank of England was willing to swap, on a temporary basis, banks' mortgage and other debt (an illiquid asset) for special 12-month Treasury Bills (a liquid asset). The Bank was effectively lending Treasury Bills against the security of mortgage and other debt. Normally banks could sell these mortgage assets on the money markets as a means of raising finance. With the credit crunch, however, such markets dried up as lenders became more cautious.

KI 5
p21

Definition

Open-market operations The sale (or purchase) by the authorities of government securities in the open market in order to reduce (or increase) money supply.

CASE STUDIES AND APPLICATIONS

BOX 20.4 THE OPERATION OF MONETARY POLICY IN THE UK

What goes on at Threadneedle Street?

The Bank of England (the 'Bank') does not normally attempt to control money supply directly. Instead it seeks to control interest rates by conducting open-market operations (OMOs) through short-term and longer-term repos and through the outright purchase of high-quality bonds, These operations, as we shall see, determine short-term interest rates, which then have a knock-on effect on longer-term rates, as returns on different forms of assets must remain competitive with each other.

Let us assume that the Monetary Policy Committee (MPC) of the Bank of England forecasts that inflation will fall below target resulting from a low level of aggregate demand. At its monthly meeting, therefore, it decides to reduce interest rates. What does the Bank do?

The first thing is that it will announce a cut in Bank Rate. But it must do more than this. It must back up the announcement by using OMOs to ensure that its announced interest rate is the equilibrium rate.

Short-term open-market operations

Central to the process is banks' reserves with the Bank of England. Banks are paid at Bank Rate on these reserves. The Bank of England conducts short-term OMOs every week (on a Thursday) at Bank Rate. In other words, if banks start running short of reserves, as they may well do if lower interest rates encourage customers to spend more from their accounts, they can borrow at Bank Rate through short-term repos (with a one-week maturity).

The size of the weekly OMO is adjusted to help banks maintain reserves at the target level and reflect variations in the amount of cash withdrawn or deposited in banks. Fluctuations in banknotes in circulation, and hence in banks' reserves, are accepted *within* the week as the reserve target is a weekly *average*.

Although there is usually a shortage of liquidity in the banking system, in some weeks there may be a surplus. To prevent this driving market interest rates down too far, the Bank will invite banks to bid for outright purchase of short-dated Treasury bills (i.e. ones part-way through their life) at prices set by the Bank to reflect Bank Rate: i.e. in this case, at prices *lower* than the market would otherwise set. At such prices, the Bank has no difficulty in selling them and hence in 'mopping up' the surplus liquidity.

At the end of the monthly period between MPC interest rate decisions, the Bank of England conducts a 'fine-tuning' OMO. This is conducted on a Wednesday – the day before the MPC decision on interest rates. The idea is to ensure that banks meet their reserve targets as closely as possible. This OMO could expand or contract liquidity as appropriate.

Longer-term open-market operations

Normally once per month – on a Tuesday at 10am mid-month – the Bank of England conducts longer-term OMOs. This involves repos at 3-, 6-, 9- and 12-month maturities. In other words, the Bank of England lends money to banks to provide longer-term liquidity.

The rate of interest is market determined. Banks bid for the money and the funds are offered to the successful bidders. The bigger the demand for these funds by banks and the lower the supply by the Bank of England, the higher will be the interest rate that banks must pay. By adjusting the supply, therefore, the Bank of England can influence longer-term interest rates.

Since 2006, the Bank of England has also been willing to make outright purchases of gilts and high-quality foreign-currency government bonds. This was used as a means of offsetting the drying up of liquidity in the credit crunch of 2007–9. Such purchases are normally made monthly on a Monday.

In January 2009, as part of a second bank rescue plan (see Box 18.3) the Treasury agreed that the Bank of England could purchase up to £50 billion of high-quality assets, such as government and corporate bonds and assets backed under the Credit Guarantee Scheme. These open-market purchases would have the effect of injecting extra narrow money into the economy. This massively extended the scope of OMOs to boost liquidity in the economy. This deliberate injection of additional narrow money is known as 'quantitative easing' and is examined in Box 20.9.

 Assume that the Bank of England wants to raise interest rates. Trace through the process by which it achieves this.

Funding

Rather than focusing on controlling the monetary base (as in the case of the above two techniques), an alternative is for the central bank to attempt to alter the overall liquidity position of the banks. An example of this approach is a change, by the central bank, in the balance of *funding* the national debt. To reduce money supply the central bank issues more bonds and fewer bills. Banks' balances with the central bank will be little affected, but to the extent that banks hold fewer bills, there will be a reduction in their liquidity and hence a reduction in the amount of credit created. Funding is thus the conversion of one type of government debt (liquid) into another (illiquid).

Definition

Funding (in monetary policy) Where the authorities alter the balance of bills and bonds for any given level of government borrowing.

Table 20.4	Effect of raising the minimum reserve ratio from 10% to 20%						

Initial position: 10% reserve ratio				New position: 20% reserve ratio			
Liabilities		**Assets**		**Liabilities**		**Assets**	
Deposits	£100bn	Reserve assets	£10bn	Deposits	£50bn	Reserve assets	£10bn
		Advances, etc.	£90bn			Advances, etc.	£40bn
Total	£100bn	Total	£100bn	Total	£50bn	Total	£50bn

 If the Bank of England issues £1 million of extra bonds and buys back £1 million of Treasury bills, will there automatically be a reduction in credit by a set multiple of £1 million?

Variable minimum reserve ratios

If banks are required to maintain a statutory minimum reserve ratio and if the central bank is free to alter this ratio, it can use it as a means of controlling the money supply. It does this by affecting not the monetary base, but the size of the bank multiplier.

Assume that there are just two types of asset: cash and advances, and that banks are required to maintain a minimum 10 per cent cash ratio (a ratio above that which the banks would have chosen for reasons of prudence). The bank multiplier is thus 10 (= $1/\frac{1}{10}$). Assume that banks' total assets are £100 billion, of which £10 billion are cash reserves and £90 billion are advances. This is illustrated in the first part of Table 20.4.

Now assume that the central bank raises the minimum reserve ratio to 20 per cent. Banks still have £10 billion cash reserves, and so they have to reduce their advances to £40 billion (giving total assets of £50 billion, of which the £10 million cash is the required 20 per cent). This is shown in the second part of Table 20.4. The bank multiplier has been reduced to 5 (= $1/\frac{1}{5}$).

In the past, central banks that imposed minimum reserve ratios on the banks tended to vary them in this way as a means of altering the money supply for any given monetary base. For example, several of the EU countries used this technique before joining the euro. Increasingly, countries that still have minimum reserve ratios are relying on open-market operations or direct lending to banks, rather than on varying the ratio. This is the case with the ECB, which has a fixed reserve ratio of 2 per cent. The USA, however, still uses variable minimum reserve ratios in this way (see Box 20.5).[1]

Difficulties in controlling money supply

The authorities may experience considerable difficulties in controlling the money supply (M4 in the UK). Difficulties occur whether they focus on doing this via control of narrow money – the 'monetary base' – or whether they attempt to control a wider range of liquid assets.

Problems with monetary base control. Assume that the authorities seek to control narrow money: i.e. notes and coin. This could be done by imposing a statutory cash ratio on banks. Assume that a statutory ratio of 10 per cent is imposed. Then provided the authorities control the supply of cash by, say, open-market operations, it would seem that they can thereby control the creation of credit and hence deposits. There would be a bank multiplier of 10. For every £1 million decrease in cash held by the banks, money supply would fall by £10 million. There are serious problems, however, with this form of **monetary base control**:

- Banks could hold cash in excess of the statutory minimum. For a time, therefore, they could respond to any restriction of cash by the authorities by simply reducing their cash ratio towards the minimum, rather than having to reduce credit.
- Unless cash ratios were imposed on every single financial institution, the control of certain institutions' lending would merely shift business to other uncontrolled institutions, including overseas ones. Banks operate in a global market. Thus UK banks can do business with UK borrowers using money markets abroad, thereby diverting potentially profitable business away from London. This is an example of Goodhart's law (see Box 20.7).
- Alternatively, if those banks subject to statutory cash requirements were short of cash, they could attract cash away from the uncontrolled institutions.

[1] In one sense, it could be argued that the imposition of a minimum reserve ratio is a *form* of credit rationing. It restricts the ability of banks to expand credit as much as they would like for the amount of reserves they hold. In Figure 20.4, however, higher minimum reserves would still shift the *supply* curve, given that this curve measures broad money and not the monetary base. It is for this reason that we considered minimum reserve ratios under the heading of 'techniques to control the money supply'.

Definition

Monetary base control Monetary policy that focuses on controlling the monetary base (as opposed to broad liquidity).

How the 'Fed' works

The central bank in the USA is called the Federal Reserve System (or 'Fed'). It was set up in 1913 and consists of twelve regional Federal Reserve Banks, each of which is responsible for distributing currency and regulating banks in its region. But despite its apparent regional nature, it is still a national system. The Federal Reserve Board, based in Washington, decides on monetary policy and then the Federal Open Market Committee (FOMC) decides how to carry it out. The FOMC meets eight times a year. The Fed is independent of both the President and the Congress, and its chairman is generally regarded as having great power in determining the country's economic policy.

Its macroeconomic objectives include low inflation, sustainable economic growth, low unemployment and moderate long-term interest rates. Of course, these objectives may well conflict from time to time. In such a case, an assessment has to be made of which is the most pressing problem.

When there is no threat of rising inflation, the Fed may use monetary policy aggressively to pursue these other goals. Thus, from January to December 2001, with the US economy moving into recession, the FOMC cut interest rates ten times. In January the rate was 6 per cent; by December it was down to 1.75 per cent.

Even when inflation is rising, the Fed may still cut interest rates if the economy is slowing. With the onset of the credit crunch of 2007/8, the Fed cut rates several times. In August 2007, the rate was 5.25 per cent. By August 2008 it had been cut to 2 per cent, even though inflation was rising (see Figure (a) in Box 20.11). Then as inflation fell and recession deepened, rates were cut again to stand at between 0 and 0.25 per cent by December 2008.

To carry out its objectives, the FOMC has traditionally had three policy instruments. The most important one is open-market operations. These are conducted through the Federal Reserve Bank of New York, which buys and sells Treasury bills and government bonds. For example, if the FOMC wishes to reduce money supply, the New York Fed will sell more of these securities. The purchasers, whether they be banks, corporations or individuals, will pay for them with cheques drawn on bank accounts. When these cheques are cleared, banks' reserves with the Fed will be reduced and hence there will be a multiple contraction of credit.

The second policy instrument is the discount rate. Known as the 'federal funds rate', this is the rate of interest at which the Fed is willing to lend to banks, thereby providing them with liquidity on which they can create credit. This is known as 'lending through the discount window'. If this rate is raised, banks are discouraged from borrowing, and credit is thereby squeezed. Since 1995, the FOMC has published its target federal funds rate. Sometimes this rate merely mirrors other market rates and is not, therefore, an active instrument of policy. On other occasions, however, the Fed changes it ahead of other market rates in order to signal its intentions to tighten (or loosen) monetary policy.[1]

The final instrument is variable minimum reserves. Banks are legally required to hold a certain minimum percentage of various assets in the form of non-interest-bearing reserves. These percentages vary from around 10 per cent for sight accounts to zero for personal savings accounts. The Fed can vary these percentages within set limits. Thus it could raise the minimum reserve ratio to as high as 14 per cent on sight accounts ('checking accounts'). Given that any change in the reserve ratio causes a multiplied effect on advances, changes are made only occasionally and by a small amount.

Response to the credit crunch

With the credit crunch of 2007/8 and the difficulties of banks in obtaining finance from the inter-bank market, the Fed extended its activities. It made considerable liquidity available to banks by swapping Treasury bills for hard-to-trade securities, such as mortgage-backed bonds and other securitised assets, including those backed by student loans. It also extended the period of its short-term loans through the discount window and was now willing to lend not only to retail banks but to investment banks and mortgage lenders too.

Then in October 2008, as part of a $700 billion rescue package for ailing banks, the US government bought shares in banks to provide extra capital and encourage bank lending.

This was backed up in early 2009 by the Fed, which embarked on an aggressive policy of increasing the money supply. This involved using open-market operations to purchase some $600 billion of mortgage and other private-sector debt associated with the mortgage lenders Fannie Mae and Freddie Mac, which had recently been nationalised to save them from collapse. The hope was to stimulate mortgage lending and thereby help to revive the collapsed housing market. The Fed was also willing to lend to the secondary market in credit-card debt and both consumer and business debt in an attempt to revive lending and boost aggregate demand.

This willingness of the Fed or the US government to bail out financial institutions that are in difficulties raises the problem of moral hazard (see page 512). If banks know that the authorities will always come to their rescue, they may make more risky loans and generally be less prudent in their activities.

Also, putting the avoidance of recession ahead of controlling inflation might lead to a rise in inflationary expectations. This would then feed through into higher actual inflation through higher wage demands and firms being more willing to raise prices.

 In what ways is the Fed's operation of monetary policy (a) similar to and (b) different from the Bank of England's?

[1] For details of the Fed's interest rate policy, see http://www.federalreserve.gov/fomc/fundsrate.htm.

The switching of business away from controlled banks is known as *disintermediation*. To avoid this problem and to allow the greatest freedom of competition between financial institutions, the alternative is to use monetary base control with no *statutory* cash ratio.

But two major problems with monetary base control, with or without a statutory cash ratio, are the most serious of all. The first is that central banks *are always prepared to increase the monetary base, through repos or rediscounting, if it is demanded*. This makes it virtually impossible to have a precise control of the monetary base.

The second is the size and variability of the money multiplier. As we saw in section 18.3 (page 523), the money multiplier is the number of times greater the rise in (broad) money supply is than the rise in the monetary base (i.e. $\Delta M4/\Delta cash$ in the UK). In the mid 2000s, the money multiplier in the UK was around 28 and highly variable. In other words, controlling the monetary base would have a highly unpredictable effect on the money supply (M4).

For these reasons, the support for monetary base control has waned in recent years.

> 1. *Trace through the effects of a squeeze on the monetary base from an initial reduction in cash to banks' liquidity being restored through gilt repos. Will this restoration of liquidity by the central bank totally nullify the initial effect of reducing the supply of cash? (Clue: what is likely to happen to the rate of interest?)*
> 2. *Given the difficulties of monetary base control, would you expect cash in circulation and broader measures of the money supply, such as M4, to rise and fall by the same percentage as each other?*

Problems with controlling broad money supply. One solution to the problems of monetary base control would be for the authorities to attempt to control broader money supply directly. In the UK, targets for the growth in broad money were an important part of monetary policy from 1976 to 1985. The UK has not targeted money supply growth since the 1980s, however. The European Central Bank has a 'reference value' of 4.5 per cent for M3 growth of the euro (see Box 18.4 on page 521 for a definition of M3). This, however, is only a guideline and not a strict target.

How would such a policy work? Assume that the authorities want to operate a tight monetary policy. They sell bonds on the open market. Banks, now short of cash, obtain money from the central bank through rediscounting bills or through repos. Thus although the central bank has been obliged to restore the amount of cash it had withdrawn from the system, there has been a decrease in bills and short-term bonds held by the banks. Banks' *overall*

liquidity has thus been reduced. Such measures could be backed up by funding.

But, as with monetary base control, there are problems with attempting to control broad money supply. Banks may be prepared to reduce their liquidity ratio. This is likely if they already have surplus liquidity, or if their customers are prepared to switch from sight to time accounts (for which banks require fewer cash reserves). This will involve offering higher interest rates on time accounts, and hence charging higher interest rates on bank loans. But if the demand for loans is relatively insensitive to interest rate changes, this will have little effect on credit or on overall deposits.

The use of open-market operations or funding to reduce money supply involves selling more bonds. But if potential purchasers believe interest rates will rise in the future (highly likely when the government is attempting to operate a tighter monetary policy), they will hold off buying bonds now and may even attempt to sell bonds before bond prices fall. Thus the authorities may be forced into a large immediate increase in bond interest rates.

In circumstances where the central bank wants to *increase* broad money, the problem can be even more serious. Purchasing bonds may increase liquidity in the banking sector, but (a) people may not want to borrow if the economy is going into recession and people are trying to cut back on spending; (b) banks may be reluctant to lend, preferring to keep the extra liquidity in reserve as a precaution against people defaulting on debts.

Perhaps the biggest problem is the effect on interest rates.

The effect on interest rates. A policy of controlling money supply can lead to severe fluctuations in interest rates. This can cause great uncertainty for business and can be very damaging to long-term investment and growth.

The problem is more acute if the overall demand for money is inelastic and is subject to fluctuations. In Figure 20.5, with money supply controlled at M_s, even a fairly

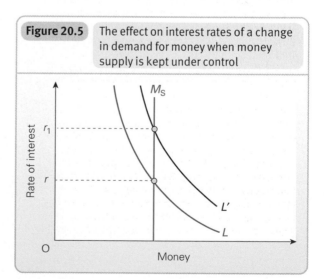

Figure 20.5 The effect on interest rates of a change in demand for money when money supply is kept under control

TC 15
p487

TC 9
p105

Definition

Disintermediation The diversion of business away from financial institutions that are subject to controls.

BOX 20.6 **MONETARY POLICY IN THE EUROZONE**

The role of the ECB

The European Central Bank (ECB) is based in Frankfurt and is charged with operating the monetary policy of those EU countries that have adopted the euro. Although the ECB has the overall responsibility for the eurozone's monetary policy, the central banks of the individual countries, such as the Bank of France and Germany's Bundesbank, were abolished. They are responsible for distributing euros and for carrying out the ECB's policy with respect to institutions in their own countries. The whole system of the ECB and the national central banks is known as the European System of Central Banks (ESCB).

In operating the monetary policy of a 'euro economy' roughly the size of the USA, and in being independent from national governments, the ECB's power is enormous and is equivalent to that of the Fed (see Box 20.5). So what is the structure of this giant on the European stage, and how does it operate?

The structure of the ECB

The ECB has two major decision-making bodies: the Governing Council and the Executive Board.[1]

- The Governing Council consists of the members of the Executive Board and the governors of the central banks of each of the eurozone countries. The Council's role is to set the main targets of monetary policy and to take an oversight of the success (or otherwise) of that policy.
- The Executive Board consists of a president, a vice-president and four other members. Each serves for an eight-year, non-renewable term. The Executive Board is responsible for implementing the decisions of the Governing Council and for preparing policies for the Council's consideration. Each member of the Executive Board has a responsibility for some particular aspect of monetary policy.

The targets of monetary policy

The overall responsibility of the ECB is to achieve price stability in the eurozone. The target is a rate of inflation below, but close to, 2 per cent over the medium term. It is a weighted average rate for all the members of the eurozone, not a rate that has to be met by every member individually.

The ECB also sets a reference value for the annual growth of M3, the broad measure of the money supply (see Box 18.4 on page 521). This was set at 4.5 per cent at the launch of the euro in 1999 and was still the same in 2008. The reference value is not a rigid target, but is used as a guide to whether monetary policy is consistent with long-run price stability.

> It is a concept which, we trust, is useful over the medium to longer term, because it allows the central banks to be reminded of the fundamental principle that over sufficiently long-term horizons, the rate of monetary growth must be consistent with the price stability objective.[2]

In setting the reference value, three things are taken into account: the target for inflation, assumptions about the rate of growth of GDP (assumed to have a trend growth rate of 2 to 2.5 per cent per year) and the velocity of circulation of M3 (assumed to be declining at a rate of between 0.5 and 1 per cent per year). The reference value is reviewed in December each year.

On the basis of its inflation target and M3 reference value, the ECB then sets the rates of interest. In January 2009, the rates were as follows: 2 per cent for the main 'refinancing operations' of the ESCB (i.e. the minimum rate of interest at which liquidity is offered once per week to 'monetary financial institutions' (MFIs) by the ESCB); a 'marginal lending' rate of 3 per cent (for providing overnight support to the MFIs); and a 'deposit rate' of 1 per cent (the rate paid to MFIs for depositing overnight surplus liquidity with the ESCB).

Interest rates are set by the Governing Council by simple majority. In the event of a tie, the president has the casting vote.

The operation of monetary policy

The ECB sets a minimum reserve ratio. It argues that this gives greater stability to the system and reduces the need for day-to-day intervention by the ECB. The ECB argues that, if there were no minimum reserves, with banks free to use as much of their reserves with the ESCB as they chose, then they would do so if there were an upsurge in demand from customers. After all, the banks know that they can always borrow from the ESCB to meet any liquidity requirements. In such a situation, the ECB would be forced to rely much more on open-market operations to prevent excessive lending by banks to their customers, and hence excessive borrowing from the ESCB, and this would mean much greater fluctuations in interest rates.

> Without the use of a minimum reserve system, the ESCB would be faced with a relatively high volatility of money market rates, which would require the frequent use of open market operations for fine-tuning purposes. Such a situation would have clear disadvantages in practical terms and could undermine the operational efficiency of monetary policy, as central bank signals may become blurred if markets have difficulty distinguishing policy signals from technical adjustments.[3]

The minimum reserve ratio is not designed to be used to make changes in monetary policy. In other words, it is not used as a variable minimum reserves ratio, and for this reason it is set at a low level. Since 1999 the ratio has been 2 per cent of key liquid and relatively liquid assets.

The main instrument for keeping the ECB's desired interest rate as the equilibrium rate is open-market operations in government bonds and other recognised assets, mainly in the form of repos. These repo operations are conducted by the national central banks, which must ensure that the repo rate does not rise above the marginal overnight lending rate or below the deposit rate.

The ECB uses four types of open-market operations:

- *Main refinancing operations*. These are short-term repos with a maturity of one week. They take place weekly and are used to maintain liquidity consistent with the chosen ECB interest rate.
- *Longer-term refinancing operations*. These take place monthly and have a maturity of three months. They are to provide additional longer-term liquidity to banks as required at rates determined by the market, not the ECB.
- *Fine-tuning operations*. These can be short-term sales or purchases of short-term assets. They are designed to combat unexpected changes in liquidity and hence to keep money market rates at the ECB's chosen rate.

- *Structural operations*. These are used as necessary to adjust the amount of liquidity in the eurozone. They can involve either the purchase or sale of various assets.

ECB independence

The ECB is one of the most independent central banks in the world. It has very little formal accountability to elected politicians. Although its president can be called before the European Parliament, the Parliament has virtually no powers to influence the ECB's actions. Also, its deliberations are secret. Unlike those of the Bank of England's Monetary Policy Committee, the minutes of the Council meetings are not published.

There is one area, however, where the ECB's power is limited by politicians and this concerns the exchange rate of the euro. Under the Maastricht Treaty, EU finance ministers have the responsibility for deciding on exchange rate policy (even though the ECB is charged with carrying it out). If the finance ministers want to stop the exchange rate of the euro rising, in order to prevent putting EU exporters at a competitive disadvantage, this will put pressure on the ECB to lower interest rates, which might run directly counter to its desire to meet its inflation and money supply targets. This is an example of the principle of 'targets and instruments'. If you have only one instrument (the rate of interest), it cannot be used to achieve two targets (the exchange rate and inflation) if these two targets are in conflict (see Box 20.8).

More details of monetary policy in the eurozone and the role of the ECB are give in Case Study 20.7 in MyEconLab.

 What are the arguments for and against publishing the minutes of the meetings of the ECB's Governing Council and Executive Board?

---

[1] See http://www.ecb.int/ecb/orga/decisions/govc/html/index.en.html.
[2] Jean-Claude Trichet, President of the ECB, at a press conference in Dublin, 10 May 2007.
[3] 'The use of a minimum reserve system by the European System of Central Banks in Stage Three', http://www.ecb.int/press/pr/date/1998/html/pr981013r3.en.html.

Figure 20.6 Central bank operations in the gilt repo and bill markets to affect interest rates

If banks are short of liquidity they sell gilts through gilt repos

D_2 by central bank

D_1 by central bank

S of gilts by banks

(a) The central bank alters the repo rate at which it is prepared to buy gilts

S_1 by central bank S_2 by central bank D by banks

If banks have surplus liquidity, they buy bills

(b) The central bank sells more bills

moderate increase in demand from L to L' leads to a large rise in interest rates from r to r_1.

And yet, if the authorities are committed to controlling money supply, they will have to accept that equilibrium interest rates may well fluctuate in this way.

Because of the above difficulties in controlling the money supply directly, countries have become increasingly reliant on controlling interest rates (backed up, normally, by open-market operations).

Techniques to control interest rates

The approach to monetary control today in many countries is to focus directly on interest rates. Normally an interest rate change will be announced, and then open-market operations will be conducted by the central bank to ensure that the money supply is adjusted so as to make the announced interest rate the *equilibrium* one. Thus, in Figure 20.4, the central bank might announce a rise in interest rates from r_1 to r_2 and then conduct open-market operations to ensure that the money supply is reduced from Q_1 to Q_2.

In the UK, since the Bank of England was made independent in 1997, interest rate changes have been made by the Bank's Monetary Policy Committee (MPC) at its monthly meetings. These are then backed up through the Bank's operations in the gilt repo and discount markets. Similarly, in the eurozone, the ECB's Governing Council sets interest rates at its fortnightly meetings.

Let us assume that the central bank decides to raise interest rates. What does it do? In general, it will seek to keep banks short of liquidity. This will happen automatically on any day when tax payments by banks' customers exceed the money they receive from government expenditure. This excess is effectively withdrawn from banks and ends up in the government's account at the central bank. Even

when this does not occur, sales of bills by the central bank will effectively keep the banking system short of liquidity.

This 'shortage' can then be used as a way of forcing through interest rate changes. Banks will obtain the necessary liquidity from the central bank through gilt repos or by selling it back bills. The central bank can *choose the rate of interest to charge* (i.e. the gilt repo rate or the bill rediscount rate). This will then have a knock-on effect on other interest rates throughout the banking system.

The effects can be illustrated in Figure 20.6, both parts of which assume that the central bank wishes to raise the interest rate (the repo or discount rate) from r_1 to r_2.

In Figure 20.6(a), it is assumed that banks are short of liquidity and are seeking to sell gilts to the central bank on a repo basis. It is assumed that the central bank will supply as much cash (i.e. demand as many gilts through repos) as banks choose, but only at the central bank's chosen repo rate. The demand for gilts is thus perfectly elastic at the central bank's repo rate. The supply curve of gilts by the banks represents their demand for cash from the central bank, and hence is *downward* sloping: the lower the repo rate, the cheaper it is for the banks to obtain cash. If the central bank raises the repo rate to r_2, banks will supply fewer gilts (i.e. demand less cash from the central bank). If there is less liquidity in the banking system, the money supply will fall.

In the event of banks having a surplus of liquidity, Figure 20.6(b) applies. Here banks are seeking to use their surplus liquidity to *buy* bills from the central bank. Their demand curve is *upward* sloping: the higher the rate of discount (i.e. the lower the price that banks have to pay for bills), the more the banks will demand. In this case, the central bank can raise the rate of discount by offering more bills for sale. By increasing the supply of bills from S_1 to S_2, it can increase the equilibrium rate from r_1 to r_2.

KI 5
p21

In both cases, the central bank will first decide on the repo rate (or discount rate) and then adjust the supply or demand of gilts or bills to ensure that the chosen rate is the equilibrium rate (see Boxes 20.4, 20.5 and 20.6 for details of how the Bank of England, the Fed and the ECB do this in practice).

A change in the repo rate will then have a knock-on effect on other interest rates. For example, in the UK, banks normally automatically adjust their base rates (to which they gear their other rates) when the Bank of England announces a change in the Bank Rate (i.e. the repo rate). Thus a 0.25 percentage point rise in Bank Rate will normally mean a 0.25 percentage point rise in banks' deposit rates, overdraft rates, etc.

Changes in Bank Rate, however, will not necessarily have an *identical* effect on other interest rates. Banks are often slow to adjust mortgage rates. Inter-bank rates also may not follow Bank Rate changes precisely. During the height of the credit crunch in 2008, the LIBOR diverged considerably from Bank Rate (see chart (a) in Box 18.3 on page 516).

Problems with controlling interest rates

Even though central bank adjustment of the repo rate is the current preferred method of monetary control in most countries, it is not without its difficulties. The problems centre on the nature of the demand for loans. If this demand is (a) unresponsive to interest rate changes or (b) unstable because it can be significantly affected by other determinants (e.g. anticipated income or foreign interest rates), it will be very difficult to control by controlling the rate of interest.

TC 7
p68

Problem of an inelastic demand for loans. If the demand for loans is inelastic, as in Figure 20.7, any attempt to reduce demand (e.g. from Q_1 to Q_2) will involve large rises in inter-est rates (r_1 to r_2). The problem will be compounded if the demand curve shifts to the right, due, say, to a consumer spending boom. High interest rates lead to the following problems:

- They may discourage long-term investment (as opposed to current consumption) and hence long-term growth.
- They add to the costs of production, to the costs of house purchase and generally to the cost of living. They are thus cost inflationary.
- They are politically unpopular, since the general public do not like paying higher interest rates on overdrafts, credit cards and mortgages.
- The necessary bond issue to restrain liquidity will commit the government to paying high rates on these bonds for the next twenty years or so.
- High interest rates encourage inflows of money from abroad. This makes it even more difficult to restrain bank lending.
- Inflows of money from abroad drive up the exchange rate. This can be very damaging for export industries and industries competing with imports. Many firms in the UK suffered badly between 1998 and 2007 from a high exchange rates (see Table 15.7 on page 443) induced partly by higher interest rates than those in the eurozone.

Evidence suggests that the demand for loans may indeed be quite inelastic, especially in the short run. Although investment plans may be curtailed by high interest rates, borrowing to finance current expenditure by many firms cannot easily be curtailed. Similarly, while householders may be discouraged from taking on new mortgages, they may find it difficult to reduce current expenditure as a means of reducing their credit card debt. What is more, although high interest rates may discourage many firms from taking out long-term fixed-interest loans, some firms may merely switch to shorter-term variable-interest loans.

Problem of an unstable demand. Accurate monetary control requires the authorities to be able to predict the demand curve for money. Only then can they set the appropriate level of interest rates. Unfortunately, the demand curve may shift unpredictably, making control very difficult. The major reason is *speculation*:

KI 32
p388

- If people think interest rates will rise and bond prices fall, in the meantime they will demand to hold their assets in liquid form. The demand for money will rise.
- If people think exchange rates will rise, they will demand sterling while it is still relatively cheap. The demand for money will rise.
- If people think inflation will rise, the transactions demand for money may rise. People spend now while prices are still relatively low.
- If people think the economy is going to grow faster, the demand for loans will increase as firms seek to increase their investment.

Figure 20.7 An inelastic demand for loans

A large rise in interest rates (to r_2) will be necessary to reduce the demand for loans to Q_2

D for loans

BOX 20.7 | GOODHART'S LAW

EXPLORING ECONOMICS

'To control is to distort'

'If you want to tackle a problem, it's best to get to the root of it.'

This is a message that economists are constantly preaching. If you merely treat the symptoms of a problem rather than its underlying causes, the problem may simply manifest itself in some other form. What is more, the symptoms (or lack of them, if the treatment makes them go away) will now be a poor indicator of the problem. Let's illustrate this with a medical example.

Assume that you suffer from deteriorating eyesight. As a result, you get increasingly bad headaches. The worse the headaches become, the worse it suggests your eyesight is getting. The headaches are thus a symptom of the problem and an indicator of the problem's magnitude. So what do you do? One approach is to treat the symptoms. You regularly take painkillers and the headaches go away. But you haven't treated the underlying problem – by getting stronger glasses, or perhaps even having eye surgery – all you have done is to treat the symptoms. As a result, headaches (or rather the lack of them) are now a poor indicator of your eyesight.

If you control the indicator rather than the underlying problem, the indicator ceases to be a good indicator. 'To control [the indicator] is to distort [its use as an indicator].' This is **Goodhart's law** and it has many applications in economics, especially when targets are set by the government. Let us take the example of a money supply target.

KEY IDEA 35 Goodhart's law: Controlling a symptom (i.e. an indicator) of a problem will not cure the problem. Instead, the indicator will merely cease to be a good indicator of the problem.

Money as an indicator of aggregate demand

Monetarists argue that the level of money supply determines the level of nominal aggregate demand and prices. They therefore argue in favour of setting targets for the growth of money supply. Critics, however, argue that the level of money supply is only an indicator of the level of nominal aggregate demand (and a poor one at that). As soon as you start to control money supply, they say, the relationship between them breaks down. If, for example, you restrict the amount of money and yet people still want to borrow, money will simply circulate faster (the velocity of circulation (V) will rise), and hence aggregate demand may not decline.

The choice of money supply target

If targets for the growth of money supply are to be set, which measure of money supply should be chosen? Goodhart's law suggests that whichever measure is chosen it will, by virtue of its choice, become a poor indicator. If the government targets cash in circulation and directs its policy to reducing the amount of notes and coin in the economy, banks may try to reduce their customers' demand for cash by, say, increasing the charges for cash advances on credit cards. As a result, cash may well be constrained, but M4 may well go on rising.

The choice of institutions

If bank advances are a good indicator of aggregate demand, the government may choose to control bank lending. But as soon as it does so, bank lending will become a poor indicator. If people's demand for loans is still high and bank loans are becoming difficult to obtain, people will simply go elsewhere to borrow money. If you regulate part of the financial system, you are likely to end up merely diverting business to other parts which are unregulated.

1. Give some everyday examples of Goodhart's law.
2. How may the use of targets in the health service (such as getting waiting lists down) provide an example of Goodhart's Law?

TC 9
p105

It is very difficult for the authorities to predict what people's speculation will be. Speculation depends largely on world political events, rumour and 'random shocks'.

If the demand curve shifts very much, and if it is inelastic, monetary control will be very difficult. Furthermore, the authorities will have to make frequent and sizeable adjustments to interest rates. These fluctuations can be very damaging to business confidence and may discourage long-term investment.

Definition

Goodhart's law Controlling a symptom of a problem or only one part of the problem will not cure the problem: it will simply mean that the part that is being controlled now becomes a poor indicator of the problem.

Why does an unstable demand for money make it difficult to control the supply of money?

The net result of an inelastic and unstable demand for money is that substantial interest rate changes may be necessary to bring about the required change in aggregate demand. An example occurred in 2001, when the US Federal Reserve, seeing the economy moving rapidly into recession, had to cut interest rates several times. At the beginning of 2001, the US 'federal funds rate' was 6 per cent. By the end of the year it had been reduced to 1.75 per cent (see Box 20.5).

Similar moves were made to prevent recession arising from the credit crunch. In August 2007, the rate was 5.25 per cent. By December 2008, the Fed had cut it to between 0 and 0.25 per cent. But even this was not enough to give

BOX 20.8   USING INTEREST RATES TO CONTROL *BOTH* AGGREGATE DEMAND *AND* THE EXCHANGE RATE

EXPLORING ECONOMICS

A problem of one instrument and two targets

Assume that the central bank is worried about excessive growth in the money supply and rising inflation. It thus decides to raise interest rates. One effect of these higher interest rates is to attract deposits into the country (causing a financial account surplus) and thus drive up the exchange rate. This makes imports cheaper and exports less competitive. This will result in a current account deficit, which will match the financial (plus capital) account surplus.

Now let us assume that the central bank becomes worried about the damaging effect on exports and wants to reduce the exchange rate. If it uses interest rates as the means of achieving this, it will have to lower them: lower interest rates will cause deposits to flow out of the country, and this will cause the rate of exchange to depreciate.

But there is a dilemma here. The central bank wants high interest rates to contain inflation, but low interest rates to help exporters. If interest rates are the only policy instrument, one objective will have to be sacrificed for the other.

Another example, but this time the reverse case, was when the UK was forced out of the 'exchange rate mechanism' (ERM) in September 1992. As we shall see in section 26.2, the ERM was a system of semi-fixed exchange rates between European currencies. The UK joined the ERM in 1990 at a relatively high rate of exchange. In its attempt to stay in the ERM and prevent speculation driving down the exchange rate, it had to keep interest rates at very high levels. But the economy was deep in recession and a lower interest rate would have helped to stimulate investment and aggregate demand generally. On this occasion the government wanted high interest rates to support the exchange rate, but low interest rates to revive the economy. Once the country had left the ERM and the pound was allowed to float, interest rates were reduced. There was no longer any conflict.

These examples illustrate a rule in economic policy: you must have at least as many instruments as targets. If you have two targets (e.g. low inflation and a low exchange rate), you must have at least two policy instruments (e.g. interest rates and one other).

1. *Give some other examples of the impossibility of using one policy instrument to achieve two policy objectives simultaneously.*
2. *If the central bank wanted to achieve a lower rate of inflation and also a higher exchange rate, could it under these circumstances rely simply on the one policy instrument of interest rates?*

a sufficient boost to lending and borrowing. The Fed had to resort to a large expansion of money supply by extraordinary means: a policy known as 'quantitative easing' (see Box 20.9).

Using monetary policy

It is impossible to use monetary policy as a precise means of controlling aggregate demand. It is especially weak when it is pulling against the expectations of firms and consumers, and when it is implemented too late. However, if the authorities operate a tight monetary policy firmly enough and long enough, they should eventually be able to reduce lending and aggregate demand. But there will inevitably be time lags and imprecision in the process.

An expansionary monetary policy is even less reliable. If the economy is in recession, no matter how low interest rates are driven, people cannot be forced to borrow if they do not wish to. Firms will not borrow to invest if they predict a continuing recession.

A particular difficulty in using interest rate reductions to expand the economy arises if the repo rate is nearly zero but this is still not enough to stimulate the economy. The problem is that (nominal) interest rates cannot be negative, for clearly nobody would be willing to lend in these circumstances. Japan was in such a situation in the early 2000s. It was caught in the 'liquidity trap' (see pages 537–8).

Despite these problems, largely of a short-term nature, changing interest rates can be quite effective in the medium term. After all, they can be changed very rapidly. There are not the time lags of implementation that there are with various forms of fiscal policy. Indeed, since the early 1990s, most governments or central banks have used interest rate changes as the major means of keeping inflation and/or aggregate demand under control.

In the UK, the eurozone and many other countries, the government or central bank sets a target for the rate of inflation for the medium term. In the UK, the target is 2 per cent CPI inflation in two years' time plus or minus 1 per cent. In the eurozone, the target is a rate of CPI inflation[1] below, but close to, 2 per cent over the medium term (where the precise period is unspecified). If forecasts suggest that inflation is going to be off-target, interest rate changes are announced, and then appropriate open-market operations are conducted to support the new interest rate. The use of such targets is examined in section 20.4.

One important effect of changing interest rates in this very public way is that it sends a clear message to people that inflation *will* be kept under control. People will therefore be more likely to adjust their expectations accordingly and keep their borrowing in check.

KI 10
p71

Definition

Quantitative easing A deliberate attempt by the central bank to increase the money supply by buying large quantities of securities through open-market operations. These securities could be securitised mortgage and other private sector debt or government bonds.

---

[1] In the eurozone the CPI is known as the 'harmonised index of consumer prices (HICP)'.

BOX 20.9 | **QUANTITATIVE EASING**

CASE STUDIES AND APPLICATIONS

Rethinking monetary policy in hard times

As the economies of the world slid into recession in 2008, central banks became more and more worried that the traditional instrument of monetary policy – controlling interest rates – was insufficient to ward off a slump in demand.

Running out of options?

Interest rates had been cut at an unprecedented rate. Typically central banks have changed interest rates by just a quarter of a percentage point at a time. But in November 2008 the Bank of England cut Bank Rate from 4.5 to 3 per cent and in December to 2 per cent and then by half a percentage point each month to stand at 0.5 per cent by March 2009. The ECB too was making large cuts: from 3.25 to 2.5 per cent in December, to 2 per cent in January and to 1.5 per cent in March.

It was clear that central banks were reaching the end of the road for interest rate cuts. The Fed was the first to be in this position. It had cut the target federal funds rate (the overnight rate at which the Fed lends to banks) from 2 to 1.5 per cent in October, to 1 per cent in November and to a range between 0 and 0.25 per cent in December. But you cannot cut nominal rates below zero – otherwise you would be paying people to borrow money, which would be like giving people free money.

The problem was that there was an acute lack of willingness of banks to lend and firms and consumers to borrow as people saw the oncoming recession. Banks were more cautious about mortgage lending as the prices of houses fell and unemployment rose, and more cautious about lending to business as the recession deepened. Firms did not want to invest and consumers tried to rein in debt. So the cuts in interest rates were not having enough effect on aggregate demand.

Increasing the money supply

So what were central banks to do? The answer was to increase money supply directly, in a process known as *quantitative easing*. This involves an aggressive version of open-market operations, where the central bank buys up a range of assets, such as securitised mortgage debt and long-term government bonds. The effect is to pump large amounts of additional cash into the economy in the hope of stimulating demand and, through the process of credit creation, to boost broad money too.

In the USA, in December 2008, at the same time as the federal funds rate was cut to a range of 0 to 0.25 per cent, the Fed embarked on large-scale quantitative easing. It began buying hundreds of billions of dollars worth of mortgage-backed securities on the open market and planned also to buy large quantities of long-term government debt. The Federal Open Market Committee (the interest rate setting body in the USA) said that, 'The focus of the committee's policy going forward will be to support the functioning of financial markets and stimulate the economy through open-market operations and other measures that sustain the size of the Federal Reserve's balance sheet at a high level.'

The result was that considerable quantities of new money were injected into the system. This also had the effect of reducing interest rates on the assets purchased by the Fed, thereby stimulating aggregate demand.

In the UK, in January 2009, the Bank of England was given powers by the Treasury to buy up to £50 billion of high-quality assets, such as government and corporate bonds, commercial paper and various viable securitised assets. The aim was directly to increase money supply. In addition, the Monetary Policy Committee was given the power to use asset purchases as an additional means of meeting the inflation target.

In March, the Bank of England used these powers to buy £7 billion of government bonds from various banks, thereby increasing the monetary base by £7 billion. This was just the start of a process of considerable quantitative easing.

The danger of this approach is that in the short run little credit creation may take place. People need to have the confidence to borrow. In the equation $MV = PY$, the rise in (narrow) money supply (M) may be largely offset by a fall in the velocity of circulation (V) (see pages 536–8). There is also the danger that if this policy is conducted for too long, the growth in money supply may then prove to be excessive, resulting in inflation rising above the target level. It would thus be important for central banks to foresee this and turn the monetary 'tap' off in time.

 Would it be appropriate to define the policy of quantitative easing as 'monetarist'?

Section summary

1. Control of the growth in the money supply over the longer term will normally involve governments attempting to restrict the size of the PSNCR. Whilst this is relatively easy once inflation has been brought under control, it can lead to serious problems if inflation is initially high. Increases in taxes and cuts in government expenditure are not only politically unpopular, but could also result in a recession.

2. In the short term, the authorities can use monetary policy to restrict the growth in aggregate demand in one of two major ways: (a) reducing money supply directly; (b) reducing the demand for money by raising interest rates.

3. The money supply can be reduced directly by using open-market operations. This involves the central bank selling more government securities and thereby reducing banks' reserves when their customers pay for them from their bank accounts. Alternatively, the central bank can reduce the amount of lending or rediscounting it is prepared to do (other than as a last-resort measure). Rather than controlling the monetary base in either of these two ways, the central bank could

use funding. This involves increasing the sale of bonds relative to bills, thereby reducing banks' liquid assets. Finally, it could operate a system of variable minimum reserve ratios. Increasing these would force banks to cut back the amount of credit they create.

4. Controlling either the monetary base or broad liquidity in the short term, however, is difficult given that central banks are always prepared to provide liquidity to the banks on demand. Even if the authorities are successful in controlling the money supply, there then arises the problem of severe fluctuations in interest rates if the demand for money fluctuates and is relatively inelastic.

5. The current method of control in the UK and many other countries involves the central bank influencing interest rates by its operations in the gilt repo and discount markets. The central bank keeps banks short of liquidity and then supplies them with liquidity, largely through gilt repos, at its chosen interest rate (gilt repo rate). This then has a knock-on effect on interest rates throughout the economy.

6. With an inelastic demand for loans, however, changes in interest rates may have to be very large to bring the required changes in monetary growth. High interest rates are politically unpopular and discriminate against those with high borrowing commitments. They also drive up the exchange rate, which can damage exports. Controlling aggregate demand through interest rates is made even more difficult by fluctuations in the demand for money. These fluctuations are made more severe by speculation against changes in interest rates, exchange rates, the rate of inflation, etc.

7. It is impossible to use monetary policy as a precise means of controlling aggregate demand in the short term. Nevertheless, controlling interest rates is a rapid way of responding to changing forecasts, and can be an important signal to markets that inflation will be kept under control, especially when, as in the UK and the eurozone, there is a firm target for the rate of inflation.

*20.3 ISLM ANALYSIS OF FISCAL AND MONETARY POLICY

ISLM analysis can be used to examine the effects of fiscal and monetary policy, taking both goods and money market effects into account simultaneously.

Assume that the economy is in recession and that the government wishes to raise the level of national income. Figure 20.8 illustrates the policy alternatives.

Figure 20.8(a) shows the effect of an increase in government expenditure (G) or a cut in taxes (T), but with no increase in money supply. The *IS* curve shifts to the right. Income rises to Y_2, but interest rates also rise (to r_2). Thus some crowding out occurs.

Figure 20.8(b) shows the effect of an increase in money supply. The *LM* curve shifts downwards. Interest rates fall to r_3 and this encourages an increase in investment. As a result of this, income rises to Y_3.

Figure 20.8(c) shows what happens when the government finances higher government expenditure or lower taxes by increasing the money supply. There is no rise in interest rates, and thus no crowding out. National income rises by a greater amount than in (a) or (b), to Y_4.

The effectiveness of fiscal and monetary policy

The effectiveness of fiscal and monetary policy depends on the slope of the two curves. Fiscal policy is more effective the flatter the *LM* curve and the steeper the *IS* curve. When *LM* is relatively flat, a rightward shift in *IS* will lead to only a small rise in the rate of interest (r). If *IS* is relatively steep, this rise in r will lead to only a small curtailing of investment. In these two circumstances, crowding out is minimised. There will be a large increase in national income (Y).

Figure 20.8 *ISLM* analysis of fiscal and monetary policy

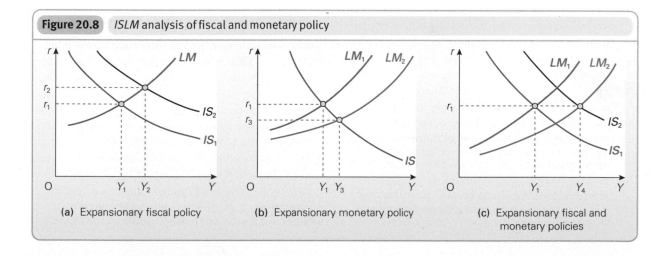

(a) Expansionary fiscal policy

(b) Expansionary monetary policy

(c) Expansionary fiscal and monetary policies

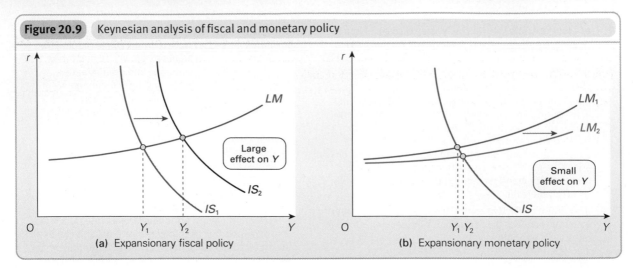

Figure 20.9 Keynesian analysis of fiscal and monetary policy

(a) Expansionary fiscal policy

(b) Expansionary monetary policy

Monetary policy, by contrast, is most effective when the *LM* curve is relatively steep and the *IS* curve is relatively flat. When *LM* is relatively steep, a rightward shift in *LM* will lead to a relatively large fall in *r*. When *IS* is relatively flat, a fall in *r* will lead to a relatively large increase in investment and hence *Y*.

Fiscal and monetary policies will be most effective when applied simultaneously, as in Figure 20.8(c).

The Keynesian position

Keynesian analysis has traditionally made the following assumptions:

- *The LM curve is relatively flat.* This is because the liquidity preference curve (*L*) is relatively flat, due to the important role of the speculative demand for money (see Figure 19.9(a) on page 546).
- *The IS curve is relatively steep.* This is because the investment demand curve is relatively inelastic, due to the unresponsiveness of investment to changes in interest rates (see Figure 19.10(a) on page 547). Also, saving is relatively unresponsive to interest rate changes.

Under these circumstances, fiscal policy is more effective than monetary policy in controlling aggregate demand. Figure 20.9(a) shows a bigger increase in national income with expansionary fiscal policy, than does Figure 20.9(b) with expansionary monetary policy. Monetary policy is weak because increases in money supply lead to substantially increased holdings of idle balances and hence only a small fall in interest rates and a small downward shift in the *LM* curve.

 According to Keynesians, which will have a bigger effect on national income and employment: (unforeseen) fluctuations in investment or (unforeseen) fluctuations in the money supply?

If money supply is endogenous, fiscal policy will be more effective still. A relatively elastic supply of money curve in the left-hand diagram of Figure 19.12 (on page 550) will give an even shallower *LM* curve.

Keynesians also stress that the *IS* curve tends to be *unstable* (for example, as investment fluctuates with business confidence). Fluctuations in a steep *IS* curve will lead to substantial fluctuations in national income (*Y*). To avoid this, argue Keynesians, active demand management (fiscal) policy will be required.

The monetarist position

Monetarist analysis has traditionally made the following assumptions:

- *The LM curve is relatively steep.* This is because the *L* curve is relatively steep (see Figure 19.9(b)), due to the relatively small role of speculative balances of money, and the general interest inelasticity of the demand for money.
- *The IS curve is relatively shallow.* This is because the *I* curve is relatively shallow (see Figure 19.10(b)), due to the wide range of interest-sensitive expenditures.

Under these circumstances, monetary policy is more effective than fiscal policy. Figure 20.10(b) shows a bigger increase in income with expansionary monetary policy than does Figure 20.10(a) with expansionary fiscal policy.

According to these assumptions, fiscal policy is weak because of crowding out. This is illustrated in Figure 20.10(a) by the steepness of the *LM* curve. The increased transactions demand resulting from a rise in income will lead to a large rise in interest rates. The reason is that there are few speculative holdings of money, and therefore a large rise in interest rates will be necessary to release sufficient money balances to meet the new higher transactions demand.

Figure 20.10   Monetarist analysis of fiscal and monetary policy

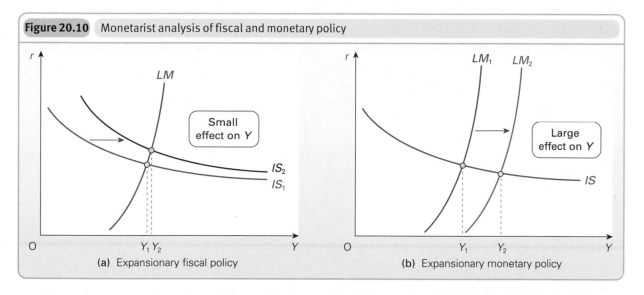

(a) Expansionary fiscal policy

(b) Expansionary monetary policy

Section summary

1. Fiscal policy shifts the *IS* curve. An expansionary fiscal policy shifts it to the right. This causes a rise in both national income and the rate of interest. The rise in income will be bigger and the rise in the rate of interest smaller, the steeper the *IS* curve and the flatter the *LM* curve.

2. Keynesians argue that fiscal policy is relatively effective and that there will be relatively little crowding out because the *IS* curve is relatively steep (due to an inelastic investment demand schedule) and the *LM* curve is relatively shallow (due to an elastic liquidity preference curve).

3. Monetarists argue the opposite: that fiscal policy is relatively ineffective and that there will be substantial crowding out because the *IS* curve is relatively shallow (due to the wide range of interest-sensitive expenditures) and the

   LM curve is relatively steep (due to the small role of speculative balances).

4. Monetary policy shifts the *LM* curve. An expansionary monetary policy shifts it downwards. This causes a fall in interest rates and a rise in national income. The rise in national income will be larger, the flatter the *IS* curve and the steeper the liquidity preference curve (*L*) and hence the bigger the downward shift in the *LM* curve for any given increase in the money supply. This means that monetarists argue that monetary policy is relatively effective, whereas Keynesians argue that it is relatively ineffective.

5. Fiscal and monetary policy operating together will have the most powerful effect. An expansionary fiscal policy accompanied by a rise in money supply can lead to an increase in national income with no rise in interest rates and thus no crowding out, irrespective of the shapes of the *IS* and *LM* curves.

20.4 FISCAL AND MONETARY POLICY IN THE UK

This historical section is optional and may be omitted without loss of continuity, or you may prefer to look just at the final part of this section dealing with the most recent period.

Attitudes towards demand management

The history of demand management in the UK since the 1950s has mirrored debates between different schools of thought. Economists and politicians calling themselves 'Keynesian' advocated active fiscal policy as a means of stabilising aggregate demand. Others, calling themselves

'monetarist', argued in favour of using monetary policy rather than fiscal policy as a means of controlling inflation, seeing inflation as purely the consequence of excessive growth in the money supply.

Debates over the control of demand have shifted ground somewhat in recent years. There is now less debate over the relative merits of fiscal and monetary policy. There is general agreement that a *combination* of fiscal and monetary policies will have a more powerful effect on demand than either used separately.

The debate today is much more concerned with whether the government ought to pursue an active demand man-

Figure 20.11 UK macroeconomic performance, 1920–2010

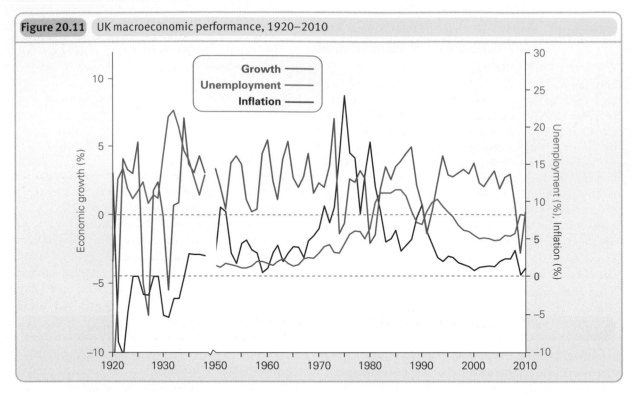

Note: Years 2009 and 2010 figures based on forecasts.

agement policy at all, or whether it ought merely to adhere to a set of policy rules.

Those in the Keynesian tradition prefer discretionary policy – changing policy as circumstances change. Those in the monetarist tradition prefer to set firm rules (e.g. targets for inflation, the PSNCR or growth in the money supply) and then stick to them. We examine the current debate in section 20.5. For the remainder of this section we will see how fiscal and monetary policies have evolved over the past sixty years.

Keynesian demand management in the 1950s and 1960s

During the 1950s and 1960s, both Labour and Conservative governments in the UK embraced Keynesian ideas. They pursued active demand management policies in an attempt to smooth out cyclical fluctuations and to keep national income as close as possible to the full-employment level.

The main policy instrument was changes in tax rates. But use was also made of government expenditure changes. Monetary policy was generally thought to be ineffective, because of both the insensitivity of demand to interest rate changes, and the difficulties in controlling overall liquidity through open-market operations. In the 1960s, however, increasing use was made of credit rationing to back up fiscal policy and to keep interest rates down.

The overall performance of the economy

Economic performance during the 1950s and 1960s compares very favourably with the periods both before and after (see Figure 20.11 and Table 20.5).

Unemployment was considerably lower in the 1950s and 1960s than either before or after. *Inflation*, although averaging 4 per cent, and thus above the negative rates of the interwar years, was nevertheless very modest compared with later years. *Growth* in the 1950s and 1960s was at a higher level than in the periods before or up to the mid 1980s. Also there was no deep or prolonged recession like those of the early 1920s, the early 1930s, 1979–82 and 1990–3.

However, there were still fluctuations in the economy, albeit of shorter duration and lower intensity than before or since. Also, although growth was relatively high by UK

Table 20.5 UK macroeconomic performance, 1921–2008

	Unemployment (% of labour force)[a]	Inflation (% increase in RPI)[b]	Growth (% increase in real GDP)[b]
1921–38	13.4	−1.5	2.1
1950–69	1.6	4.0	2.8
1970–99	7.6	8.0	2.0
2000–8	5.2	3.1	2.6

[a] Average.
[b] Average annual.

standards, it was significantly lower than in West Germany, France and Japan.

The balance of payments

Throughout the 1950s and 1960s, the UK was operating on a fixed exchange rate system. The exchange rate was pegged at $2.80 to the pound from 1949 until 1967 when it was devalued to $2.40. A fixed exchange rate constrained the government in its demand management policy. If the economy expanded too fast, the balance of payments went into deficit. The government would then pursue a deflationary policy, both to reduce the demand for imports directly, and to reduce inflation in order to increase the competitiveness of UK goods. If the balance of payments went into surplus, the government would reflate the economy. As a result of this, demand management was often referred to as **stop–go policy**. The most common weapon used in times of balance of payments crisis was Bank Rate. This was the rate of interest set by the Bank of England, to which all the banks had to gear their rates. Bank Rate rose quite steeply on several occasions.

During the 1960s, however, the maintenance of balance of payments equilibrium and of growth at full employment became increasingly incompatible objectives. Stop–go policy was thus perceived as swinging from one objective (correction of balance of payments deficits with 'stop' policy) to the other (stimulating growth and employment with 'go' policy). The underlying problem was that UK goods were becoming increasingly uncompetitive in world markets, due to a decline in the relative quality of UK goods and their higher relative prices.

Under a fixed exchange rate system there was therefore a long-term tendency for the balance of payments to deteriorate, and for governments to deflate. Eventually in 1967, with mounting pressure on sterling, the UK was forced to devalue the pound.

Monetarist criticisms of the policies of the 1950s and 1960s

Monetarists made two major criticisms of the Keynesian policies pursued during the 1950s and 1960s. First, they actually served to make the economy more unstable for the following reasons:

- Forecasting was bad. Frequently, the forecasters failed to foresee exogenous changes to demand, or wrongly predicted the magnitude and timing of their effects.
- Governments as a result were hesitant to take action until the economy was clearly either booming (or in balance of payments crisis) or in recession.
- When governments did take action, they tended to overreact in their attempt to speed up the correction of the problem.

Second, inflation was kept fairly low in this period *despite* attempts to fine tune the economy. The reason for this was the fixed exchange rate, which forced govern-

ments to deflate whenever inflation threatened the balance of payments. If there had been no such constraint, Keynesian governments would have pursued much more expansionist policies, which would have driven up the rate of inflation.

 Would a floating exchange rate have imposed no constraint at all on expansionist policies?

The Keynesian response

In reply, Keynesians argued that the economy was relatively stable, and that there was a good record of achieving the various macroeconomic objectives.

However, they admitted that if there had been more flexibility in the exchange rate, or at least an earlier devaluation, this would have reduced the need for stop–go measures. There could then have been a more sustained expansion of the economy. This in turn would have boosted business confidence, increased investment and thereby increased long-term growth potential.

Provided demand was prevented from expanding too rapidly, any tendency for inflation to increase would be more due to cost-push or structural factors. These would be much better dealt with by using interventionist supply-side policies, such as **prices and incomes policy** to prevent cost-push inflation, and selective investment grants and infrastructure projects to relieve bottlenecks.

Finally, improvements in forecasting techniques and the swifter implementation of policies would help to reduce time lags and allow finer tuning.

 Answer these points from a monetarist perspective.

The demise of fine tuning in the 1970s: the problem of stagflation

Fine tuning became impossible in the 1970s because of the rising problem of **stagflation**: a combination of stagnation (low growth and high unemployment) and high inflation (see Figure 20.11). Demand management policies were still used, but they could no longer achieve an acceptable

---

Definitions

Stop–go policies Alternate deflationary and reflationary policies.

Prices and incomes policy When the government seeks to restrain price and wage increases. This may be in the form of a voluntary agreement with firms and/or unions, or there may be statutory limits imposed.

Stagflation A term used in the 1970s to refer to the combination of stagnation (low growth and high unemployment) and high inflation.

combination of inflation and unemployment. The Phillips curve had broken down.

Economists are not agreed on the precise causes of this stagflation, but there were a number of possible contributing factors.

The approach to monetary control. In an attempt to move to a more market-based form of monetary control, all ceilings on bank credit were abandoned and the liquidity ratio that banks were required to hold was reduced. The effect was to make it much more difficult to prevent an expansion of credit and there was a mushrooming of new banks and credit institutions.

Highly reflationary budgets in 1972 and 1973. The Heath government (1970–4) was committed to a rapid rate of economic growth. This was to be achieved by sharply expansionary fiscal policy. The effect was a rapid increase in the PSNCR. This, combined with more lax monetary control, led to a very rapid growth in money supply in 1972 and 1973 (see Table 20.6). Growth in nominal aggregate demand could only in small part be met by increased output and employment.

Statutory controls over wages and prices, first introduced in November 1972, kept price rises in check for a while. But with a miners' strike being seen as a direct challenge to this prices and incomes policy, the government called an election in February 1974 and was defeated. The incoming Labour government abolished the prices and incomes policy, but this allowed the pent-up demand to feed straight through into price and wage increases. Inflation soared. By 1975 price inflation was nearly 25 per cent and wage inflation was over 30 per cent.

The adoption of floating exchange rates. In June 1972 a fixed exchange rate with the dollar was abandoned. A floating pound reduced the need to pursue deflationary policies in response to a balance of payments deficit. Instead the exchange rate could be allowed to depreciate. This removed a major constraint on the growth in money supply. This applied not just in the UK but throughout the world as countries moved over to floating exchange rates.

Oil prices. Between 1973 and 1974 the price of oil rose from $3 to $12 per barrel, and between 1978 and 1980 it rose from $13 to $31 per barrel. This not only raised costs and thus caused cost-push inflation, but also caused recessions in 1975 and 1979–81 as governments throughout the world deflated in response to the inflation and balance of payments crises.

Domestically generated cost-push pressures. Cost-push inflationary pressures increased as a result of the following: growing union power and militancy; the desire for real wage increases each year in excess of the economy's real growth; the increasing monopoly power of firms, as increased mergers led to a growth in industrial concentration; and low productivity growth and hence a lack of price competitiveness of UK goods.

Increased import penetration and a decline in the UK's share of world exports. Increasing competition from foreign imports and a lack of quality in UK goods led to a poor balance of payments, low growth, structural unemployment, and inflation caused by a falling exchange rate (necessary to restore price competitiveness of UK exports).

Table 20.6	Selected monetary indicators, 1969–2004				
	Change in M4 (%) (1)	PSNCR (£bn) (2)	Inflation[a] (%) (3)	Nominal interest rate[b] (%) (4)	Real interest rate (4−3) (5)
1969	5.1	−0.5	5.4	9.1	3.7
1970	11.5	−0.1	6.4	9.2	2.8
1971	16.0	1.3	9.4	8.9	−0.5
1972	23.7	2.0	7.1	9.0	1.9
1973	22.3	4.1	9.2	10.7	1.5
1974	11.1	6.5	16.0	14.8	−1.2
1975	12.4	10.2	24.2	14.4	−9.8
1976	11.2	8.9	16.5	14.4	−2.1
1977	14.7	5.4	15.8	12.7	−3.2
1978	15.0	8.3	8.3	12.5	4.2
1979	14.1	12.6	13.4	13.0	−0.4
1980	17.2	11.8	18.0	13.8	−4.2
1981	20.9	10.5	11.9	14.7	2.8
1982	12.1	4.9	8.6	12.9	4.3
1983	12.7	11.6	4.6	10.8	6.2
1984	13.2	10.3	5.0	10.4	5.4
1985	13.0	7.5	6.1	10.5	4.4
1986	15.6	2.3	3.4	9.9	6.5
1987	16.7	−1.4	4.2	9.5	5.3
1988	17.2	−12.1	4.9	9.4	4.5
1989	18.0	−9.3	7.8	9.6	1.8
1990	11.8	−1.7	9.5	11.1	1.6
1991	5.9	6.9	5.9	9.9	4.0
1992	3.5	28.4	3.7	9.1	5.4
1993	4.6	43.0	1.6	7.9	6.3
1994	4.7	39.3	2.4	8.1	5.7
1995	9.9	35.4	3.5	8.3	4.8
1996	9.5	24.7	2.4	8.1	5.7
1997	11.9	12.0	3.1	7.1	4.0
1998	8.3	−6.3	3.4	5.5	2.1
1999	4.2	−3.2	1.5	4.7	3.2
2000	8.2	−37.1	3.0	4.7	1.7
2001	6.7	−2.0	1.8	4.8	3.0
2002	7.3	19.1	1.7	4.8	3.1
2003	7.3	37.2	2.9	4.6	1.7
2004	9.3	42.2	3.0	4.8	1.8
2005	12.8	41.1	2.8	4.4	1.6
2006	12.7	33.4	3.2	4.3	1.1
2007	11.9	32.3	4.3	4.7	0.4
2008	16.4	56.6	4.0	4.7	0.7

[a] Based on the retail price index (RPI), the main measure of consumer prices inflation prior to 2003.
[b] Annual average on 20-year bonds.
Source: From www.statistics.gov.uk (National Statistics).

Technological change. The microchip revolution and other labour-displacing technology created unemployment. There was insufficient aggregate demand to create new jobs elsewhere.

Expectations of inflation. High and volatile inflation rates fuelled expectations of high inflation, which then made inflation worse.

> *Go through each of the above causes of the stagflation of the 1970s and early 1980s and consider whether there were any policies that the government could realistically have adopted to deal with it.*

The response to stagflation

Several of these problems were problems of cost and supply, rather than excess or deficient demand. It was increasingly realised that, in addition to fiscal and monetary policies, there would have to be significant 'supply-side' policies.

The Keynesian response was to recommend supplementing demand management with interventionist supply-side policies, such as prices and incomes policy, regional policy, import restrictions and retraining policies (see section 23.1).

The Labour government of 1974–9 responded to the rise in both inflation and unemployment by reintroducing prices and incomes policy in the summer of 1975 (see Case Study 23.3 in MyEconLab). Inflation began to fall in 1976 and growth re-emerged. The government let the exchange rate fall to help stimulate the demand for exports, but the falling pound caused speculation and a sterling crisis in late 1976. The government was forced to borrow from the International Monetary Fund to support the pound, and in return had to pursue tough monetary and fiscal policies, including, for the first time, setting targets for the growth in money supply.

This accorded with the views of monetarists, who recommended abandoning discretionary demand management of the stop–go variety altogether, and moving to a 'steady-as-you-go' policy of sticking to monetary targets. In addition, they advocated the use of market-orientated supply-side policies such as tax reform, union reform, the abandonment (or non-introduction) of minimum wage rates, and lower unemployment benefits (see section 23.3).

From 1976 to 1979 growth was steady at between 2.5 and 3 per cent, unemployment was steady at between 5 and 5.5 per cent, and inflation was falling. But growing resentment at incomes restraint led to the 'winter of discontent' of 1978–9, when several groups of workers attempted to defy the incomes policy. The government lost the 1979 election.

Monetarism under Thatcher

With the election of the Conservatives in 1979, the UK for the first time had a government committed to monetarist policies.

On the supply side, the government pursued policies to free up the market. The prices and incomes policy was abandoned; legislation was introduced to curb trade union power; foreign exchange controls were lifted; the standard rate of income tax was cut from 33 per cent to 30 per cent (with VAT being raised to compensate for the loss of revenue); the government made it clear that it would not bail out 'lame duck' industries; and later on, it pursued a comprehensive policy of privatisation.

On the demand side, the use of discretionary demand management to fine tune the economy was totally abandoned. Instead, each year progressively descending targets were adopted for money supply growth for the following four years. This was known as the 'medium-term financial strategy' (MTFS). These targets, combined with statements that inflation was 'public enemy number one', were designed to reduce people's expectations of inflation, and hence the level of wage settlements. Money supply was to be kept on target in the short term by changes in interest rates, brought about by Bank of England operations in the discount market. All other forms of monetary control were abandoned. Foreign exchange controls were abolished in 1979, as were all forms of credit rationing; statutory reserve requirements were abolished in 1981.

In the medium term, the achieving of money supply targets would require a progressive reduction in the PSNCR as a proportion of GDP (if crowding out was to be avoided). Indeed, targeted reductions in the PSNCR were part of the medium-term financial strategy. Thus tight monetary policy was backed up by tight fiscal policy. In the public mind, the government's monetarist policy became synonymous with 'cuts'.

Demand-side policies in the early 1980s

1979–81. The abandoning of incomes policy, the rise in oil prices from 1979 to 1981 and a rise in VAT from 7 per cent to 15 per cent led to a rise in inflation from 8.3 per cent in 1978 to 18 per cent in 1980. At the same time, fiscal and monetary policy had a highly deflationary effect. Interest rates rose rapidly, reaching 17 per cent in late 1979. The high interest rates, plus an improving balance of payments due to North Sea oil, led to a rapid rise in the exchange rate, fuelled by speculation of further rises.

The combination of low demand, high interest rates, a high exchange rate and rapidly rising costs led to a severe recession – the deepest since the 1930s. Unemployment rocketed from just over 5 per cent in 1979 to nearly 10 per cent in 1981.

1982–5. The continuing tight monetary policy with high real interest rates allowed only a slow recovery from recession. Recovery was, however, helped somewhat by a fall in the exchange rate between 1981 and 1985. This was in part a response to the strength of the dollar, which was due to high US interest rates resulting from a large and growing US budget deficit. Growth re-emerged from 1982 and inflation fell back to around 5 per cent. The growth in demand, how-ever, was insufficient to prevent the continuing rise in unemployment, which reached 11.2 per cent in 1985.

Exogenous factors such as consumer and business expectations made it difficult to keep money supply on tar-get, but there was a relatively consistent attempt to pursue a steady-as-you-go demand management policy. Rules had replaced discretion (see section 20.5).

Assessing the monetarist experiment

Was the government able to carry through its monetarist intentions? On the plus side, after an initial upsurge (1979–81) the growth of money supply was reduced and inflation fell (see Table 20.6). But despite this there were a number of problems.

- The PSNCR proved very difficult to control and was above target in several years.
- From 1983 onwards, the recorded level of the PSNCR was artificially reduced by the sale of public-sector assets (British Telecom, British Gas, etc.). This allowed the government to pursue a more expansionary fiscal policy while *appearing* to maintain a tight monetary policy.
- The growth in money supply was also above target in several years despite a wide target range. The eventual reduction in its growth after 1981 was achieved at the cost of very high real interest rates (see Table 20.6).
- The government was forced to raise the target ranges for PSNCR and money supply in 1982, despite its commit-ment in the MTFS to a progressive lowering of them.
- Although it eventually managed to get its chosen mea-sure of the money supply (M3) under control, other measures of money supply went on growing – an exam-ple of Goodhart's law.

- Allowing sterling to float more freely brought problems. High interest rates and North Sea oil caused the pound to soar in 1980, reaching $2.45 at the peak, with conse-quent damage to the export sector. But the government was afraid of intervening to lower the exchange rate because that would have increased the money supply (through reducing interest rates or having a net inflow of funds from abroad).
- The opposite problem was faced in January/February 1985, when the pound fell dramatically against a strong US dollar (reaching $1.04 at the lowest point). As the pound approached $1, the government felt obliged to intervene and interest rates were raised dramatically.

Despite all these difficulties, the government consist-ently saw inflation as 'public enemy number one', and the means of getting it down was a tight monetary policy and adherence to monetary targets.

A return to discretionary policies after 1985

As the 1980s progressed, although monetary targets were almost being achieved, their importance was waning.

With unemployment over 3 million, the government was putting less emphasis on the desirability of a generally tight monetary policy and instead was becoming more pragmatic.

With the effective abandonment of money supply tar-gets after 1985, demand management policy reverted to a more traditional stop–go pattern. Discretion seemed to be replacing rules.

The period from 1985 to 1988 can be summarised as a period of unbalanced fiscal and monetary policy. Monetary policy was expansionary. With inflation still relatively low after the recession, interest rates were lowered to stimulate economic growth, reduce unemployment and prevent fur-ther rises in the exchange rate (and the consequent damage to exports). Fiscal policy, on the other hand, remained rela-tively tight. Although the government made several cuts in tax rates, the now rapid growth in incomes caused tax *revenues* to increase. At the same time, the government continued to try to reduce its expenditure as a proportion of national income. The net result was that a public-sector deficit of over £11.6 billion in 1983 was turned into a sur-plus of £12.1 billion by 1988.

This resulted in an imbalance in the impact of the policy. The extra money was spent largely on property and consumer durables (a large proportion of which were imported). House prices soared as mortgages were easy to obtain. Car sales boomed, as did the sales of electrical goods, furniture and foreign holidays.

Monetary policy was relatively expansionary through-out the world, and part of the extra money went into stocks and shares. The resulting increase in share prices was faster than the increase in profits and dividends. Eventually, in October 1987, 'the bubble burst' and share prices crashed. To avoid a collapse of confidence by firms and a plunge into recession, monetary policy was further relaxed. Aggregate demand grew more rapidly. Unemployment fell more rapidly and output grew more rapidly; but inflation began to rise and the balance of payments on current account plunged into a record deficit (see Figure 15.13 on page 440).

In response to this crisis, interest rates were raised sev-eral times in the last part of 1988 and during 1989. Banks' base rate rose from 7.5 per cent in May 1988 to 15 per cent by October 1989, and then remained at this level until October 1990 when the UK joined the exchange rate mech-anism (ERM) of the European Monetary System (see section 26.2). It was clear that the government was pursuing a stop–go monetary policy, depending on how bad were the problems of inflation, the balance of payments and a depreciating exchange rate.

 In what way was the stop–go policy of the late 1980s different from the stop–go policies pursued during the 1950s and 1960s?

Targeting the exchange rate

Shadowing the German mark

Targets were not completely abandoned after 1985. There was a growing belief that, with closer links being forged with Europe, and with the desirability of a stable exchange rate between the pound and other European currencies, the exchange rate ought to be targeted. But as we saw in Box 20.8, the problem with effectively having only one instrument (interest rates) was that the government could not use it at one and the same time to control both the level of aggregate demand (and hence inflation) *and* the rate of exchange. In 1988, high interest rates were required to control the rapidly expanding credit, but low interest rates were required to prevent the exchange rate from rising above its target level of around £1 = 3.00 German marks, a rise that would be damaging to exports. The debate, however, resolved itself. With a *falling* pound in 1989, high interest rates were desirable for both exchange rate and counter-inflationary reasons.

 Will targeting the exchange rate help to reduce inflation? Does it depend on the rate of inflation in the countries to whose currencies the pound is fixed?

Fiscal policy was largely confined to the role of improving the *supply* side of the economy. This would be achieved by reducing the size of the public sector (which was seen by the government to be less productive than the private sector), and by giving tax cuts to improve incentives. So did fiscal policy have no demand management role at all? It did, but only to the extent that the amount of tax cuts was influenced by demand considerations.

ERM membership: 1990–2

In October 1990 the UK joined the European *exchange rate mechanism (ERM)*. This was a system, set up in 1979, of semi-fixed exchange rates. Participating EU countries' currencies were allowed to fluctuate against each other only within set bands (see section 26.2 for more details). The requirement to keep the pound within an exchange rate band of approximately 2.78–3.13 marks meant that there was now effectively an exchange rate target. But with essentially only one instrument of macroeconomic policy, namely the rate of interest, all other macroeconomic goals had to be subordinated to this target.

In this fixed exchange rate system, UK interest rates were governed largely by those of the other countries within the system. The reunification of Germany had involved a large expansion of German money supply. In response, the Bundesbank (the German central bank), in

order to prevent inflation rising, raised interest rates. To maintain sterling's value within the ERM, the UK government therefore had to pursue a high interest rate policy too. At first this was appropriate as the UK inflation rate was over 10 per cent.

Within a few months, however, it was clear that the UK was plunging into recession. On domestic grounds alone, lower interest rates would have been desirable. But by mid 1991 the pound was again under pressure in the ERM and so monetary policy had to be kept tight. Inflation was now falling rapidly, but interest rates were reduced only slightly. This meant that *real* interest rates had risen (see Table 20.6). In the 12 months after joining the ERM, UK inflation fell by 6 percentage points whereas nominal interest rates fell by only 4 percentage points. There was thus a growing policy conflict between the *external* requirement of maintaining the exchange rate and the internal requirement of reflating a depressed domestic economy.

Throughout 1991 and the first part of 1992, the government stuck resolutely to maintaining sterling's value in the ERM. Ministers justified this as being the best means of continuing the fight against inflation. But, as we shall see in section 26.2, this rate was becoming increasingly untenable as speculators became convinced that interest rates would have to fall and that sterling, as a result, would have to be devalued. Eventually, on 'Black Wednesday', 16 September 1992, after a 5 percentage point rise in interest rates was insufficient to stop the speculation, the UK left the ERM and the pound was allowed to float.

A return to domestic-orientated policies: targeting inflation

With the need to defend the value of the pound removed, the government could focus once more on the domestic situation. Within four months, interest rates had been reduced by 4 percentage points. This loosening of monetary policy gave a welcome boost to the economy, which was still only just beginning to pull out of recession.

The government was not worried that this would lead to an unwelcome growth in money supply and inflation. Indeed, the control of inflation was now to be the main objective of monetary policy. An initial target rate of inflation of 1–4 per cent was set, to be backed up by 'monitoring ranges' of 0–4 per cent for M0 (the measure of narrow money used at that time) and 3–9 per cent for M4 until 1997, by which time inflation should be between 1 and 2.5 per cent.

Targeting inflation was based on the belief in the long-run neutrality of money (see page 575): that monetary policy cannot influence *real* variables such as output and employment in the long run. It can only influence inflation. It is better, therefore, to focus on achieving low inflation in order to provide the best environment for businesses to thrive. But to achieve an inflation target meant doing two things.

Definition

ERM (the exchange rate mechanism) A system of semi-fixed exchange rates used by most of the EU countries prior to adoption of the euro. Members' currencies were allowed to fluctuate against each other only within agreed bands. Collectively, they floated against all other currencies.

First, given the time lags between changing interest rates and their effect on inflation, interest rates would have to be changed in response to inflation *forecasts*, rather than the current rate of inflation. Second, people would have to be made to believe that the government could and would achieve the target. To this end, a number of steps were taken:

KI 15
p106

- The Bank of England published inflation forecasts, which the government publicly used to assess whether policy was on target.
- The Chancellor and the Governor of the Bank of England met monthly to consider the necessary interest rate policy to keep inflation within the target range. The Bank would then determine the *timing* of any agreed changes.
- Minutes of these meetings were published six weeks later, in order to give transparency to the process.
- Each time interest rates were changed, a press notice would be issued explaining the reasons. The idea here was to show the government's commitment to keeping to the target.

Was the policy a success? Inflation remained within the target bands, and the government claimed that this was the result of the policy. In fact, the reduction in inflation from 1992 to 1994 was the lagged result of the tight monetary conditions during the previous two years when the UK was in the ERM. Indeed, the government *reduced* interest rates several times between September 1992 and February 1994. After 1994, however, the policy *did* help to keep inflation down, with the government raising interest rates whenever inflationary forecasts were adverse.

As far as fiscal policy was concerned, with the PSNCR in 1993 being a massive £43 billion (see Table 20.6), there was a serious problem that, if monetary growth were kept in check, government borrowing would crowd out private-sector growth. The government thus saw the need to get a 'better' balance between fiscal and monetary policy. It therefore announced a series of tax increases to be phased in over the coming years. It also stated its intention to examine ways of reducing government expenditure.

If tax increases are 'phased in' as an economy recovers from recession, how will this affect the magnitude and timing of the recovery?

Policy of the Labour government (1997–)

Fiscal policy

In 1997, the incoming Labour government confirmed its election commitment to stick to the previous government's expenditure targets for two years and to continue bringing down the PSNCR. That, plus a reluctance to raise taxes, initially prevented it from spending money on various social programmes advocated by many of its supporters.

Given, however, that the economy grew by over 3 per cent in 1997, the PSNCR fell rapidly (see Table 20.6), and that enabled the government to plan for a *growth* in government expenditure from 1999 onwards. The plans, announced in 1998 in the government's Comprehensive Spending Review, set targets for government expenditure, not for just one year, but for a three-year period.

Did this mean, therefore, that fiscal policy as a means of adjusting aggregate demand had been abandoned? In one sense, this was the case. The government was now committed to following its 'golden rule' (see Box 20.3), whereby public-sector receipts should cover all current spending, averaged over the course of the business cycle. In fact, in supporting sticking to the golden rule, the Chancellor explicitly rejected Keynesian fine tuning:

> In today's deregulated, liberalised financial markets, the Keynesian fine tuning of the past, which worked in relatively sheltered, closed national economies and which tried to exploit a supposed long-term trade-off between inflation and unemployment, will simply not work.[1]

But despite this apparent rejection of short-term discretionary fiscal adjustments, there is still a role for *automatic* fiscal stabilisers, with deficits rising in a recession and falling in a boom. There is also still the possibility, within the golden rule, of financing additional *investment* by borrowing, thereby providing a stimulus to a sluggish economy.

The golden rule also permitted increased government expenditure (or tax cuts) if there was a budget surplus. Thus in the 2001 Budget, the government announced spending increases of 3.7 per cent per year for three years and also modest tax cuts. The effect was to turn a forecast surplus of £16 billion in 2000/1 into a forecast deficit of £10 billion by 2003/4 (when the economy was predicted to be mid-cycle). But this was in line with the golden rule, which permits borrowing against capital spending – and that was planned to be £18 billion by 2003/4.

As it turned out, the fiscal stimulus in the 2001 Budget was timely, as the world economy was slowing down, with the slowdown hastened by the attack on the World Trade Center in New York in September of that year.

But the government's forecast of the size of the public-sector deficit turned out to be a considerable underestimate. By 2004, it had risen to £41.9 billion and many economists cast doubt as to whether the golden rule could be maintained. In the 2005 Budget, however, the government was still maintaining that the current budget would be in surplus when averaged over the cycle 1998/9 to 2005/6 (see Figure (b) in Box 20.3 on pages 572–3).

Monetary policy

As far as monetary policy was concerned, the Labour government continued its predecessor's approach of targeting

[1] Extract from the Chancellor's Mansion House speech, 11 June 1998.

inflation. The target rate was set initially at 2.5 per cent for RPI inflation. (This was changed to 2 per cent for CPI inflation[1] in December 2003.) Unlike its predecessor, however, the government decided to make the Bank of England independent. Indeed, this was the first action taken by the Chancellor when the government came to power.

But why did the government give up its right to set interest rates? First, there is the political advantage of taking 'blame' away from the government if interest rates need to be raised in order to prevent inflation rising above its target. Second, an independent central bank, free to set interest rates in order to achieve a clear target, is more likely to be consistent in pursuit of this objective than a government concerned about its popularity. Then there is the question of transparency in decision making.

> If inflation is more than 1 percentage point higher or lower than the target, an open letter will be sent by the Governor to the Chancellor so that the public is fully informed as to why the divergence has occurred; the policy action being taken to deal with it; the period within which inflation is expected to return to the target; and how this approach meets the government's monetary policy objectives. Monetary policy decision-making is now among the most transparent and accountable in the world.[2]

Transparency is enhanced by the publication of the minutes of the monthly meetings of the Bank's Monetary Policy Committee (MPC), at which interest rates are set. One of the main purposes of transparency is to convince people of the seriousness with which the Bank of England will adhere to its targets. This, it is hoped, will keep people's *expectations* of inflation low: the lower expected inflation is, the lower will be the actual rate of inflation. (We will explore the relationship between expected and actual inflation in the next chapter.)

As it turned out, inflation targeting was successful in its prime purpose: keeping inflation at or near its target. For the whole period from 1997 to April 2008, the chosen measure of inflation never diverged by more than 1.1 percentage point from the target. In the light of the history of macroeconomic management over the last 60 years, this would seem remarkable.

A rules-based approach to demand-side policy?

With monetary policy geared to an inflation target and fiscal policy geared to following the golden rule, there seemed to be little scope for discretionary demand management policy. Rules appeared to have replaced discretion.

When there are ever more rapid financial flows across the world that are unpredictable and uncertain, the answer is to ensure stability through establishing the right long-term policy objectives and to build credibility in the policy through well-understood procedural rules that are followed for fiscal and monetary policy.[3]

There was, however, a new form of fine tuning: the frequent adjustment of interest rates, not to smooth out the business cycle, but to make sure that the inflation rule is adhered to. Nevertheless, with automatic fiscal stabilisers still operating, and with interest rate changes to stabilise inflation also having the effect of stabilising aggregate demand, cyclical fluctuations had become less pronounced – at least until 2007. In the 12 years to 2007, annual economic growth did not fall below 1.8 per cent or rise above 3.8 per cent.

Growing problems in 2008

In 2007/8, the government was faced with a possible return of stagflation. World food and other commodity prices were rising rapidly (see Box 15.4 on pages 434–5). This supply-side shock meant that inflation rose. By September 2008, annual CPI inflation had reached 5.2 per cent and RPI inflation had reached 5.0 per cent. Food price inflation was over 10 per cent.

At the same time, the credit crunch that started in the USA spread like a contagion around the world. Growth rates fell. In the UK annual growth was zero by mid 2008. The housing market was in rapid decline, with prices falling by over 10 per cent (see Box 2.2) and sales by 50 per cent.

Monetary policy. Both the Bank of England and the government were faced with a dilemma. To meet its inflation target, the Bank of England was under pressure to raise the Bank Rate. To avert a recession it was under pressure to cut it. The result was that for several months it kept it unchanged. Eventually, with confidence in the banking system plummeting and inter-bank markets virtually frozen, the Bank of England (along with several other central banks) cut its interest rate by 0.5 per cent. In addition, as we saw in Box 18.3 on pages 576–8, massive amounts of liquidity and capital were pumped into the banking system to stimulate lending and hence aggregate demand.

From October 2008, however, the price level (both CPI and RPI) started falling and hence monthly inflation became negative, with annual inflation falling rapidly. The Bank of England predicted that inflation would considerably undershoot its target and that the economy would contract in 2009 (see the Figures in Box 20.12 on page 606). It thus reduced Bank Rate substantially. In September 2008, Bank Rate was 4.25 per cent; by March 2009, it was just 0.5 per cent.

---

[1] The consumer prices index (CPI) is the measure used in the eurozone (known there as the harmonised index of consumer prices (HICP)) and gives a slightly lower inflation rate than the retail prices index (RPI). Thus the former 2.5 per cent target is equivalent to the current 2 per cent target.

[2] *The Government's Overall Economic Strategy* (http://www.hm-treasury.gov.uk/pub/html/erinfo/overview/1rgoes.html).

[3] Extract from the Chancellor's Mansion House speech, 11 June 1998.

Fiscal policy. The government was also under pressure to give a fiscal stimulus, as in the USA (see Box 20.1 on page 566). But with the current budget already in deficit, the government was in danger of breaching its golden rule (see Box 20.3 on pages 572–3) and thus would seem to have had very limited scope for increased expenditure or tax cuts to stimulate aggregate demand.

But the problem was seen to be too serious to stick to rules for rules' sake. The golden rule would have to be abandoned – at least temporarily. Thus a £20 billion package of tax cuts and increased government expenditure was announced in the Pre-Budget Report in late November. This was forecast to bring the deficit on the current budget to a record 4.4 per cent of GDP by 2009–10 (see Figure (b) in Box 20.3 on page 573) and the overall budget deficit to 9 per cent of GDP. The boost consisted of a cut in VAT from 17.5 to 15 per cent for 13 months. In addition £3 billion of government expenditure on upgrading motorways, refurbishing schools and council houses would be brought forward to speed up the process.

The Chancellor also announced that taxes would increase from 2011 to pay for the measures. Income tax would increase from 40 to 45 per cent for those earning over $150 000 and national insurance would go up by 0.5 per cent. In other words, the golden rule was to be temporarily abandoned, but reinstated from 2014 when, it was hoped, the economy would be growing strongly again.

So should governments and central banks stick to rules, come what may? Or should they have the discretion to break them when economic (or political) circumstances change? We examine the arguments in the final section of this chapter.

1. *From 1998 to 2007 the exchange rate of sterling was very high (see Table 15.7 on page 443). This was largely the result of the MPC keeping interest rates above those in other countries in order to try to keep inflation down to its target. What are the arguments for and against a discretionary rise in the inflation target in such circumstances?*
2. *Why do 'ever more rapid financial flows across the world that are unpredictable and uncertain' make Keynesian discretionary fiscal (and monetary policy) less suitable?*

Section summary

1. In the 1950s and 1960s, both Labour and Conservative governments pursued active demand management policies. The dominating constraints on these policies were the balance of payments and electoral considerations. Demand management was little more than stop–go policy dictated by the state of the balance of payments and the need to win elections.

2. The period of the 1950s and 1960s was one of relative economic success. But whether this was due to the pursuit of Keynesian demand management policies or to other factors such as a buoyant world economy and economic optimism is a matter of debate.

3. In the 1970s, stagflation became a major problem due to a number of factors, including expansionary fiscal and monetary policies in the early 1970s, the adoption of floating exchange rates, a large rise in oil prices, growing domestically generated cost-push pressures, a decline in the competitiveness of UK exports, technological change and increasingly pessimistic expectations.

4. As a result of the dilemma of rising inflation and rising unemployment, government policy swung violently from a 'dash for growth' in the early 1970s, to two sets of prices and incomes policies, to a tight monetary policy towards the end of the decade.

5. The Conservative government in the 1980s initially pursued a tight monetary policy and targeted the PSNCR and the growth in the money supply. The exchange rate rose and the economy plunged into a deep recession.

6. Then, after 1985, targets for monetary growth were abandoned and for a time targeting the exchange rate became the main focus of monetary policy. But with only one instrument (interest rates) there was a conflict between keeping exchange rates down and controlling inflation. This conflict disappeared after 1988 when high interest rates were required both for keeping inflation down and for preventing a fall in the exchange rate.

7. The UK joined the ERM in October 1990 and the conflict between domestic and exchange rate policy soon re-emerged. The economy was moving rapidly into recession, but the government was unable to make substantial cuts in interest rates because of the need to defend the value of the pound. Eventually in September 1992, with huge speculation against sterling, the UK was forced to leave the ERM.

8. After 1992, there was a return to using interest rates to manage domestic demand in line with inflation targets. There was mounting concern, however, about the size of the PSNCR, and fiscal policy was tightened until the PSNCR had been sufficiently reduced.

9. The Labour government elected in 1997 made the Bank of England independent. The Bank now targets a 2 per cent rate of inflation, and adjusts interest rates in order to meet that target. The government set a golden rule to balance its current (as opposed to capital) budget over the course of the business cycle. There seemed to be little scope for discretionary demand-management policy.

10. This became a serious problem in 2008 with rising inflation and falling growth. For several months the Bank of England felt unable to cut interest rates and the government was unable to provide a substantial fiscal boost for fear of breaching its golden rule.

11. In November 2008, however, the government temporarily abandoned its golden rule and gave a fiscal boost to the economy to combat the slide into recession.

20.5 RULES VERSUS DISCRETION

Central to debates over the control of aggregate demand is the question of rules versus discretion. Should monetary (and fiscal) rules be adhered to, or should governments exercise the discretion to change the policies as economic circumstances change?

The case for rules

There are two important arguments against discretionary policy.

- *Political behaviour.* The first concerns the motivation of government. Politicians may attempt to manipulate the economy for their own political purposes – such as the desire to be re-elected. As we saw in Box 15.7 on the political business cycle (see page 448), the government, if not constrained by rules, may over-stimulate the economy some time before an election so that growth is strong at election time. After the election, the government strongly dampens the economy to deal with the higher inflation which is now beginning to accelerate, and to create enough slack for another boost in time for the next election.

  A less extreme version is where governments from time to time use monetary and fiscal policy to try to boost their popularity. The manipulation of the instruments is not necessarily systematic or regular in the way that the political business cycle model implies. Nonetheless, the manipulation is intended to court short-term favour with the public and may store up problems for the economy and, in the case of fiscal policy, for the public finances.

  When politicians behave in this way, they may lose *credibility* concerning sound economic management. This can lead to higher inflationary expectations, uncertainty and lower long-term investment. Trade unions are likely to bargain for increases in wages that protect their purchasing power should government loosen its policy stance to try and boost its popularity. Models of politically motivated decision making suggest that, whilst inflation on average will be higher, unemployment will be no lower.

- *Time lags with discretionary policy.* Both fiscal and monetary policies can involve long and variable time lags, which can make the policy at best ineffective and at worst destabilising. Taking the measures *before* the problem arises, and thus lessening the problem of lags, is no answer since forecasting tends to be unreliable.

By contrast, by setting and sticking to rules, and then not interfering further, the government can provide a sound monetary framework in which there is maximum freedom for individual initiative and enterprise, and in which firms are not cushioned from market forces and are therefore encouraged to be efficient. By the government setting a target for a steady reduction in the growth of money supply, or a target for the rate of inflation, and then resolutely sticking to it, people's expectations of inflation will be reduced, thereby making the target easier to achieve.

This sound and stable monetary environment, with no likelihood of sudden contractionary or expansionary fiscal or monetary policy, will encourage firms to take a longer-term perspective and to plan ahead. This could then lead to increased capital investment and long-term growth.

The optimum situation is for all the major countries to adhere to mutually consistent rules, so that their economies do not get out of line. This will create more stable exchange rates and provide the climate for world growth (we explore this issue in section 26.1).

Advocates of this point of view in the 1970s and 1980s were the monetarists, but in recent years support for the setting of targets has become widespread. As we have seen, in both the UK and the eurozone countries, targets are set for both inflation and public-sector deficits.

Would it be desirable for all countries to stick to the same targets?

The case for discretion

Keynesians reject the argument that rules provide the environment for high and stable growth. Demand, argue Keynesians, is subject to many and sometimes violent exogenous shocks: e.g. changes in expectations, domestic political events (such as an impending election), financial market effects (such as the credit crunch), world economic factors (such as the world economic recession of 2008–9) or world political events (such as a war). The resulting shifts in injections or withdrawals cause the economy to deviate from a stable full-employment growth path.

Any change in injections or withdrawals will lead to a cumulative effect on national income via the multiplier and accelerator and via changing expectations. These endogenous effects take time and interact with each other, and so a process of expansion or contraction can last many months before a turning point is eventually reached.

Since the exogenous changes in demand occur at irregular intervals and are of different magnitudes, the economy is likely to experience cycles of irregular duration and of varying intensity.

Given that the economy is inherently unstable and is buffeted around by various exogenous shocks, Keynesians argue that the government needs actively to intervene to stabilise the economy. Otherwise, the uncertainty caused

BOX 20.10 INFLATION TARGETING

The fashion of the age

More and more countries are turning to inflation targeting as their main macroeconomic policy. The table gives the targets for a selection of countries (as of 2008).

Part of the reason is the apparent failure of discretionary macroeconomic policies. Discretionary fiscal and monetary policies suffer from time lags, from being used for short-term political purposes and from failing to straighten out the business cycle. But if discretionary policies have seemed not to work, why choose an inflation target rather than a target for the money supply or the exchange rate?

Money supply targets were adopted by many countries in the 1980s, including the UK, and this policy too was largely a failure. Money supply targets proved very difficult to achieve. As we have seen, money supply depends on the amount of credit banks create, and this is not easy for the authorities to control. Then, even if money supply is controlled, this does not necessarily mean that aggregate demand will be controlled: the velocity of circulation may change. Nevertheless, many countries do still target the money supply, although in most cases it is not the main target. In a study of 91 countries by the Bank of England in 1999, of the 55 that targeted inflation, 31 also targeted the money supply (see Case Study 20.12 in MyEconLab).

Exchange rate targets, as we shall see in Chapter 25, may have serious disadvantages if the equilibrium exchange rate is not the one that is being targeted. The main instrument for keeping the exchange rate on target is the rate of interest. But, as we saw in Box 20.8 (on page 586), if the rate of interest is being used to achieve an exchange rate target, it cannot be used for other purposes, such as controlling aggregate demand or inflation. Raising interest rates to achieve an exchange rate target may lead to a recession.

Inflation targets have proved relatively easy to achieve. There may be problems at first, if the actual rate of inflation is way above the target level. The high rates of interest necessary to bring inflation down may cause a recession. But once inflation has been brought down and the objective is then simply to maintain it at the target level, most countries have been relatively successful. And the more successful they are, the more people will expect this success to be maintained, which in turn will help to ensure this success.

So, have there been any problems with inflation targeting? Ironically, one of the main problems lay in its success. With worldwide inflation having fallen, and with global trade and competition helping to keep prices down, there was now less of a link between inflation and the business cycle. Booms no longer seemed to generate the inflation they once did. Gearing interest rate policy to maintaining low inflation could still see economies experiencing unsustainable booms, followed by recessions. Inflation may be controlled, but the business cycle may not be.

Then there is the more recent problem of rising world inflation resulting from the rapid growth in China and India. The resulting rise in food and commodity prices has pushed up inflation around the world. Too strict an adherence to an inflation target could see higher interest rates and countries pushed into recession. This was a problem in the UK in the first part of 2008. Despite signs of an impeding recession, high inflation persuaded the Bank of England to maintain Bank Rate at 5 per cent from April right through to October. Only when inflation was predicted to fall rapidly was the Monetary Policy Committee willing to cut interest rates. By then GDP was already falling.

 Why may there be problems in targeting (a) both inflation and money supply; (b) both inflation and the exchange rate?

Inflation targets

Country	Inflation target (%)	Details
Australia	2–3	Average over the business cycle
Brazil	4.5	Tolerance band of ±2 percentage points
Canada	2	Tolerance band of ±1 percentage point
Chile	3	2 year horizon; tolerance band of ±1 percentage point
Czech Republic	3	Until 2010; tolerance band of ±1 percentage point
Eurozone	<2 but close to it	Average for eurozone as a whole; over medium term
Hungary	3	Tolerance band of ±1 percentage point; over medium term
Iceland	2.5	Tolerance band of ±1.5 percentage points
Israel	1–3	
Mexico	3	Tolerance band of ±1 percentage point
New Zealand	1–3	On average over the medium term
Norway	2.5	Over 1–3 years
Peru	2	Tolerance band of ±1 percentage point
Poland	2.5	Tolerance band of ±1 percentage point
South Africa	3–6	
South Korea	3	Tolerance band of ±0.5 of a percentage point; 3-year average
Sweden	2	1–2-year horizon; tolerance band of ±1 percentage point
Switzerland	<2 but close to it	
Thailand	0–3.5	
UK	2	2-year horizon; tolerance band of ±1 percentage point

Source: Various bank websites. See www.bis.org/cbanks.htm.

by unpredictable fluctuations will be very damaging to investment and hence to long-term growth in potential output (quite apart from the short-term effects of recessions on actual output and employment).

If demand fluctuates in the way Keynesians claim, and if the policy of having a money supply or inflation rule is adhered to, interest rates must fluctuate. But excessive fluctuations in interest rates will discourage long-term business planning and investment. What is more, the government may find it difficult to keep to its targets. This too may cause uncertainty and instability.

Difficulties with the choice of target

If the government is to adopt a target, which one should it choose? If a money supply measure is to be chosen, which one? They frequently do not grow at the same rate. What is more, the adoption of one measure as the target may lead to distortions as people switch the form of their holdings of liquidity and wealth (Goodhart's law).

If an inflation target is chosen, then again Goodhart's Law is likely to apply. Inflation may become a poor indicator of the state of the economy. If people believe that the central bank will be successful in achieving its inflation target, then those expectations will feed into their inflationary expectations, and not surprisingly the target will be met.

But that target rate of inflation may now be consistent with both a buoyant and a depressed economy. In other words, the Phillips curve may become *horizontal*. Similarly, in terms of Figure 19.18 (on page 559), the *ASI* curve will be horizontal (at least up to near full capacity in the economy). Shifts in the *ADI* curve will simply lead to changes in real national income. An example occurred in 2001/2 when the UK economy slowed down considerably and yet there was virtually no change in the rate of inflation. Thus achieving an inflation target may not tackle the much more serious problem of creating stable economic growth and an environment which will therefore encourage long-term investment.

In extreme cases, as occurred in 2008, the economy may slow down rapidly and yet cost-push factors cause inflation to rise. Targeting inflation in these circumstances will demand *higher* interest rates, which will help to deepen the recession.

Use of a Taylor rule

For this reason, many economists have advocated the use of a **Taylor rule**,[1] rather than a simple inflation target. A Taylor rule takes *two* objectives into account – (1) inflation

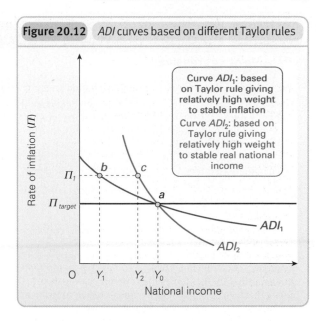

Figure 20.12 *ADI* curves based on different Taylor rules

Curve ADI_1: based on Taylor rule giving relatively high weight to stable inflation

Curve ADI_2: based on Taylor rule giving relatively high weight to stable real national income

and (2) either real national income or unemployment – and seeks to get the optimum degree of stability of the two. The degree of importance attached to each of the two objectives can be decided by the government or central bank. The central bank adjusts interest rates when either the rate of inflation diverges from its target or the level of real national income (or unemployment) diverges from its potential (or natural) level.

Take the case where inflation is above its target level. The central bank following a Taylor rule will raise the rate of interest. It knows, however, that this will reduce real national income. This, therefore, limits the amount that the central bank is prepared to raise the rate of interest. The more weight it attaches to stabilising inflation, the more it will raise the rate of interest. The more weight it attaches to stabilising real national income, the less it will raise the rate of interest.

This is illustrated in Figure 20.12. It shows two aggregate demand curves plotted against inflation (see Figure 19.16 on page 557). Assume that the economy is currently at point *a*, with inflation on target and real national income at Y_0, which happens to be the potential level. Now assume that inflation rises to π_1. As this is above the target level, the central bank raises the rate of interest. This causes real

---

[1] Named after John Taylor, from Stanford University, who proposed that for every 1 per cent that GDP rises above potential (sustainable) GDP, real interest rates should be raised by 0.5 percentage points, and that for every 1 per cent that inflation rises above its target level, real interest rates should be raised by 0.5 percentage points (i.e. nominal rates should be raised by 1.5 percentage points).

Definition

Taylor rule A rule adopted by a central bank for setting the rate of interest. It will raise the interest rate if (a) inflation is above target or (b) real national income is above the potential level (or unemployment is below the natural rate). The rule states how much interest rates will be changed in each case.

| BOX 20.11 | INTEREST RATE RESPONSES AND THE FINANCIAL CRISIS OF 2007/8 |

Passive or aggressive?

The Federal Reserve, the European Central Bank (ECB) and the Bank of England are examples of independent central banks. In each case the responsibility for setting interest rates has been delegated to a decision-making board of the central bank. However, the policy remit of each of these banks is different. We consider here how this may have influenced interest rate decisions in the period from 2005 and, in particular, in the aftermath of the liquidity crisis that hit financial systems across the world from summer 2007.

In the USA the goals of monetary policy are set down in the Federal Reserve Act, originally proposed in 1913. The Federal Open Market Committee (FOMC) has eight regularly scheduled meetings each year. It is charged with ensuring that there is long-run economic growth so as to achieve the goals of maximum employment, stable prices and moderate long-term interest rates.

The ECB's independence is laid down in the institutional framework for the single monetary policy. Its aim is to promote price stability. For operational purposes the ECB has a target rate of inflation below, but close to, 2 per cent over the medium term. It is a weighted average across the eurozone. At the end of the first of two monthly meetings the Governing Council takes its interest rate decision.

The 1998 Bank of England Act gave the Bank independence in setting interest rates. The Bank's

Monetary Policy Committee meets at the beginning of each month to decide on interest rates. The Bank is charged to deliver price stability, but operationally it has a symmetrical target around a 2 per cent inflation rate. Interest rates are set to meet this target 24 months hence. If current inflation exceeds or undershoots this target by more than one percentage point then the Governor is forced to write an open letter to the Chancellor of the Exchequer explaining the reasons for it and the Bank's intended response. Subject to delivering price stability, monetary policy should also support the government's economic objectives, including growth and employment.

Different policy responses?

The goals set for the Federal Reserve are broader than those of its two European counterparts. This would be expected to impact on the relationship between interest rates and inflation observed across the three central banks. For more detail on alternative policy rules see Box 20.12.

Chart (a) displays the annual rates of consumer price inflation for the USA, the eurozone and the UK from 2005. The US rate of inflation was consistently higher than those in the UK and the eurozone throughout 2005 and into the autumn of 2006. During much of this period the Federal Reserve was raising interest rates. This can be observed in

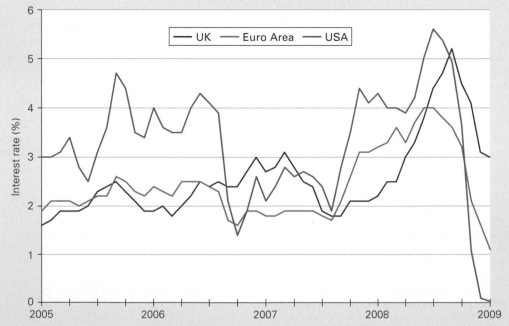

(a) *Annual rates of consumer price inflation*

Sources: Federal Reserve; ECB; Bank of England; Bureau of Labor Studies; National Statistics.

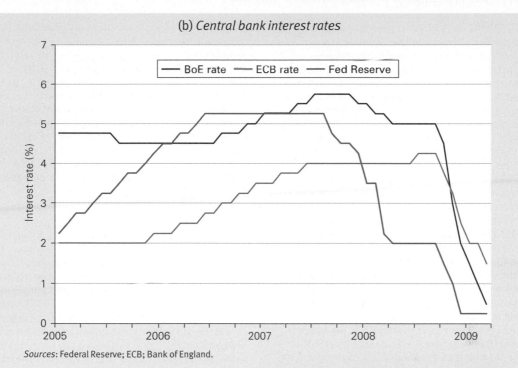

(b) *Central bank interest rates*

Sources: Federal Reserve; ECB; Bank of England.

Chart (b), which plots the interest rates set by the decision-making boards of the three central banks: the Fed increased rates from 2.25 per cent at the start of 2005 to 5.25 per cent by June 2006.

The Fed kept interest rates at 5.25 per cent until the liquidity crisis hit global financial systems in late summer 2007. Interestingly, its broader policy remit appears to have enabled it to respond more aggressively to the impact of financial instability on the macroeconomy. The responses of the ECB and the Bank of England were constrained by their policy remits and, specifically, their inflation rate targets. This was because inflationary pressures were emerging at around the same time as the liquidity crisis was biting. These emanated largely from the supply side, with increases in the cost of raw materials, energy and fuel. Therefore, the ECB and the Bank of England felt unable to cut rates. They were concerned about easing the brake on aggregate demand and further fuelling inflation, both directly and through raising inflation expectations.

The European Central Bank looks to have been especially concerned to suppress inflation. It raised interest rates from 4.75 to 5 per cent in June 2007 and maintained them at this level until July 2008, when it raised them again to 5.25 per cent. In sharp contrast, the Fed Rate fell from 5.25 per cent in August 2007 to 2 per cent by April 2008.

The Bank of England's interest rate policy from the time of the liquidity crisis was to tread carefully in the presence of inflation rate fears. It eased rates in December 2007 from 5.75 to 5.5 per cent and to 5.25 per cent in

February and 5 per cent in April 2008. But it was not until inflation started to fall and GDP was falling that it lowered interest rates substantially: from 5 to 4.5 per cent in October, to 3 per cent in November (falling below the ECB rate for the first time), and then by half a percentage point each month to stand at 0.5 per cent by March 2009.

Our economic commentary demonstrates that different independent central banks can be quite different beasts. Of course, each is reacting to its own economic reality. But the policy goals of the decision-making boards are very important. This is vividly demonstrated in the aftermath of the global financial uncertainties and inflation rate pressures in late summer 2007. The interest rate decisions of three of the most powerful and important central banks in the world were quite distinctive. While the Fed cut rates aggressively, the Bank of England, and the ECB in particular, were more passive.

Such distinctive responses undoubtedly raise questions about the rights and wrongs of alternative policy rules. Is it better to stick to a firm inflation target, like the ECB? Or is it better to allow central banks to have more discretion to take a number of economic indicators into account, as is the case with the Fed?

 In which of the following circumstances are the three central banks more likely to respond in a similar way: (a) rising demand-pull inflation; (b) rising cost-push inflation? Explain.

*BOX 20.12 | **HOW DO INFLATION TARGETS WORK IN PRACTICE?**

A Taylor rule or a forward-looking inflation-only rule?

A Taylor rule

Central banks typically try to keep inflation to a predetermined target level. If inflation rises above the target level, the central bank will raise the rate of interest.

The trouble is that this will also reduce real national income. Thus some countries, including the USA, take real national income (i.e. national output) specifically into account when setting interest rates. Adopting a Taylor rule is a way of doing this. A general form of the Taylor rule can be written as follows:

$$i = i^* + a(\pi - \pi^*) + by$$

where i is the real rate of interest set by the central bank; i^* is the real rate of interest consistent with long-run equilibrium in the economy; π is the current rate of inflation; π^* is the target rate of inflation, and so $a(\pi - \pi^*)$ is the divergence of actual inflation from the target rate weighted by an amount a; y is the percentage deviation of real national income from its potential level and b is the weight attached to this.

What this equation says is that if inflation goes above its target (i.e. $(\pi - \pi^*)$ is positive), or if real national income rises above its potential level (i.e. y is positive), the central bank will raise the real rate of interest, the amount depending on the values of a and b respectively.

The greater the importance attached by the central bank to getting inflation back to target and the less

concerned it is about fluctuations in real national income, the greater will be the value of a and the less the value of b. The more, therefore, it will raise the rate of interest when inflation goes above target, and the flatter, therefore, will be the *ADI* curve in Figure 20.12.

Conversely, the more concerned the bank is about stabilising real national income and is prepared to see inflation deviate from its target, the greater will be the value of b and the less of a. The steeper, therefore, will be the *ADI* curve.

Another version has been developed by Lars Svensson, from Princeton University, who is now a deputy governor of the Swedish central bank.

He supposes that the central bank wants to minimise the weighted sum of the square of the inflation gap and the square of the output gap. The relative weight given to the output gap is denoted by the Greek letter lambda. The higher lambda is, the more the central bank worries about output and the longer it is prepared to take to return inflation to target. Set lambda equal to nought, and the bank could not give a jot about output: it is run by 'inflation nutters', in the phrase of Mr King. Set lambda equal to infinity, and inflation becomes irrelevant.

The question is, how explicit can central banks be? Mr Svensson thinks that they should publish lambda if they can. Most other central banks think that although

Fan chart of CPI inflation and GDP growth projections (made in 2008 Q4, based on market interest rate expectations)

(a) CPI inflation

(b) Real GDP growth

Source: Inflation Report, November (Bank of England, 2008).

lambdas are useful theoretical devices, publishing them is unrealistic. For one thing, it gives the impression that the central bank knows more about the world, or even about its own reaction function, than it really does. For another, the weight banks give to output gaps may change over time –they may set a lower lambda, for instance, when they want to establish a reputation as inflation fighters.[1]

The Bank of England rule

The Bank of England uses a rule that is apparently simpler than the Taylor rule, but in some respects is more sophisticated. The Bank of England targets inflation alone; in this sense the rule is more simple. But the inflation figure on which it bases its interest rate decisions is the forecast rate of inflation, not the current rate; in this sense it is more sophisticated.

The Bank of England publishes a quarterly Inflation Report, which contains projections for inflation for the next three years. These projections assume that interest rates follow market expectations. They form the basis for the Monetary Policy Committee's monthly deliberations. If the projected inflation in 24 months' time is off target, the MPC will change interest rates accordingly.

Two key projections of the MPC are given in the Bank of England's Inflation Report, which is published each quarter. These are shown in the diagram. They are known as 'fan charts'. The first plots the forecast range of inflation. The second plots the forecast range of real GDP growth. In each case, the darkest central band represents a 10 per cent likelihood, as does each of the eight subsequent pairs of lighter areas out from the central band. Thus inflation or GDP growth are considered to have a 90 per cent probability of being within the fan. The bands get wider as the time horizon is extended, indicating increasing uncertainty about the outcome. Also, the less reliable the MPC considers the forecasts on which it bases its projections, the wider will be the fan.

The dashed line indicates the two-year target point. Thus in quarter 4 of 2008, the 2 per cent inflation target was for quarter 4 of 2010. As you can see from the chart, although inflation was predicted to rise to around 5 per cent in late 2008, in two years' time the average forecast rate with no change in policy was around 1 per cent – under the target of 2 per cent.

Although projections are made for GDP growth, these are to help inform the forecast for inflation. GDP growth is not itself an explicit target.

The inflation target rule can be written as follows:

$$i_t = a(\pi_{t+j}^e - \pi^*) + bx_t$$

where i_t is the real rate of interest (i) set by the central bank at the current time (t); π_{t+j}^e is the forecast rate of inflation (π^e) at some future point in time ($t+j$).

In the Bank of England's case, j is eight quarters (i.e. two years in the future); π^* is the target rate of inflation, and so $a(\pi_{t+j}^e - \pi^*)$ is the forecast divergence of the inflation rate from target weighted by an amount a; x_t is a set of other variables that the policy makers would like to be taken into account when setting interest rates, weighted by an amount b. These other variables could include expected inflation before and after time $t+j$ and the predicted speed of response of inflation to changes in interest rates. They could also include the percentage divergence of real income from the potential level if policy makers wanted to include this (making the Bank of England rule more like a forward-looking Taylor rule).

Comparing the two rules

The first main difference between the two rules is that the Bank of England rule is based on forecasts. To the extent that these forecasts are accurate, this is a strength of the rule as it allows decisions to be made that can pre-empt changes in inflation and help to prevent them. Thus in late 2008, interest rates were cut several times. Bank Rate was 5 per cent in September; by March 2009 it was a mere 0.5 per cent, despite CPI inflation remaining well above 2 per cent throughout this period (see the two charts in Box 20.11). This was because forecast inflation for two years' time was well below 2 per cent and a recession was imminent.

By contrast, under the simple Taylor rule, interest rate decisions are based on the latest figures of actual inflation, which will already be out of date when they are published. There is thus likely to be a considerable time lag before inflation adjusts. Inflation is therefore likely to be far less stable than following a forward-looking rule.

On the other hand, the Bank of England rule does require inflation forecasts to be accurate if inflation is to be kept on target. Forecasts cannot predict the unpredictable, such as the 11 September 2001 attack on the World Trade Center and its dampening effect on aggregate demand. Likewise, supply-side shocks, such as oil price changes, are difficult to predict with any accuracy.

The second main difference is the explicit incorporation of national income deviations into a Taylor rule. Given the instability of economic growth, the result has been much greater interest rate fluctuations in the USA than in the UK and the eurozone (see chart (b) in Box 20.11).

 If people believe that the central bank will be successful in keeping inflation on target, does it matter which of the above two rules is used? Explain.

national income to fall and is represented by a movement up along the *ADI* curve.

If the central bank puts a high weight on controlling inflation rather than on stabilising real national income, the curve will be relatively shallow, like ADI_1 in Figure 20.12. The bank will be prepared to raise interest rates a lot and, as a result, see real national income fall a lot in the short term.

If, however, it puts a relatively high weight on stabilising real national income, the curve will be relatively steep, like ADI_2. The bank will not be prepared to see real national income fall very much and will thus only raise interest rates modestly.

Thus the central bank has to trade off inflation stability against real income stability. Its Taylor rule shows its optimum trade-off and is illustrated by the slope of the *ADI* curve.

The Taylor rule is explored in more detail in Box 20.12 and is compared with the rule followed by the Bank of England of having an inflation target based on forecast inflation (rather than current inflation).

Difficulties with the target level

When a target is first set, the short-term costs of achieving it may be too high. If expectations are slow to adjust downward and inflation remains high, then adherence to a tight monetary or inflation rule may lead to a very deep and unacceptable recession. This was a criticism made by many economists of monetarist policies between 1979 and 1982.

When a target has been in force for some time, it may cease to be the appropriate one. Economic circumstances might change. For example, a faster growth in productivity or a large increase in oil revenues may increase potential growth and thus warrant a faster growth in money supply. Or an extended period of relatively low inflation may warrant a lower inflation target. The government must at least have the discretion to *change* the rules, even if only occasionally. But if rules should not be stuck to religiously, does

this mean that the government can engage in fine tuning? Keynesians today recognise that fine tuning may not be possible; nevertheless, significant and persistent excess or deficient demand *can* be corrected by demand management policy. For example, the actions taken in the USA by the Federal Reserve Bank in 2001 and again in 2007/8 to cut interest rates substantially, and by the US government to increase its expenditure and to cut taxes, helped to stave off even deeper recessions in 2001/2 and 2008/9.

Improvements in forecasting, a willingness of governments to act quickly and the use of quick-acting policies can all help to increase the effectiveness of discretionary demand management.

 Under what circumstances would adherence to money supply targets lead to (a) more stable interest rates and (b) less stable interest rates than pursuing discretionary demand management policy?

Conclusions

The resolution of this debate will depend on the following factors:

- The confidence of people in the effectiveness of either discretionary policies or rules: the greater the confidence, the more successful is either policy likely to be.
- The degree of self-stabilisation of the economy (in the case of rules), or conversely the degree of inherent instability of the economy (in the case of discretion).
- The size and frequency of exogenous shocks to demand: the greater they are, the greater the case for discretionary policy.
- In the case of rules, the ability and determination of governments to stick to the rules and the belief by the public that they will be effective.
- In the case of discretionary policy, the ability of governments to adopt and execute policies of the correct magnitude, the speed with which such policies can be effected and the accuracy of forecasting.

Section summary

1. The case against discretionary policy is that it involves unpredictable time lags that can make the policy destabilising. Also, the government may ignore the long-run adverse consequences of policies designed for short-run political gain.

2. The case in favour of rules is that they help to reduce inflationary expectations and thus create a stable environment for investment and growth.

3. The case against sticking to money supply or inflation rules is that they may cause severe fluctuations in

interest rates and thus create a less stable economic environment for business planning. Given the changing economic environment in which we live, rules adopted in the past may no longer be suitable for the present.

4. Although perfect fine tuning may not be possible, Keynesians argue that the government must have the discretion to change its policy as circumstances demand.

END OF CHAPTER QUESTIONS

1. The following table shows part of a country's national expenditure schedule (in £ billions):

National income (Y)	100	120	140	160	180	200	220
National expenditure (E)	115	130	145	160	175	190	205

   (a) What is the government expenditure multiplier?

   (b) What is the tax multiplier?

   Assume that full employment is achieved at a level of national income of £200 billion.

   (c) Is there an inflationary or a deflationary gap, and what is its size?

   (d) By how much would government expenditure have to be changed in order to close this gap (assuming no shift in other injections or withdrawals)?

   (e) Alternatively, by how much would taxes have to be changed in order to close the gap (again assuming no shift in other injections or withdrawals)?

   (f) Alternatively, assuming that there were initially a balanced budget, and that the government wanted to maintain a balanced budget, by how much would both government expenditure and taxes have to be changed in order to close the gap?

2. What are the problems of relying on automatic fiscal stabilisers to ensure a stable economy at full employment?

3. Does it matter if a country has a large national debt as a proportion of its national income?

4. If the government is running a budget deficit, does this mean that national income will increase?

5. What factors determine the effectiveness of discretionary fiscal policy?

6. Why is it difficult to use fiscal policy to 'fine tune' the economy?

7. Assume that a bank has the following simplified balance sheet, and is operating at its desired liquidity ratio:

Liabilities	(£m)	Assets	(£m)
Deposits	100	Balances with central bank	10
		Advances	90
	100		100

   Now assume that the central bank repurchases £5 million of government bonds on the open market. Assume that the people who sell the bonds all have their accounts with this bank and keep a constant amount of cash outside the bank.

   (a) Draw up the new balance sheet directly after the purchase of the bonds.

   (b) Now draw up the eventual balance sheet after all credit creation has taken place.

   (c) Would there be a similar effect if the central bank rediscounted £5 billion of Treasury bills?

   (d) How would such open-market operations affect the rate of interest?

8. Is it possible for the government to target the money supply over the longer term without targeting the PSNCR?

9. What are the mechanics whereby the central bank raises the rate of interest?

10. What is Goodhart's law? How is it relevant to (a) monetary policy; (b) using assignment grades to assess a student's ability; (c) paying workers according to the amount of output they produce; (d) awarding local authority contracts to cleaning or refuse disposal companies on the basis of tendered prices?

11. 'It is easier to control the monetary base than broader money, but it is less relevant to do so.' Do you agree with this statement?

*12. Using diagrams like Figures 20.9 and 20.10, compare Keynesian and monetarist analyses of contractionary fiscal and monetary policy.

13. Is there a compromise between purely discretionary policy and adhering to strict targets?

14. Compare the relative merits of targeting (a) the money supply; (b) the exchange rate; (c) the rate of inflation.

Online resources

Additional case studies in MyEconLab

20.1 **The national debt.** This explores the question of whether it matters if a country has a high national debt.

20.2 **Fine tuning in 1959 and 1960.** This looks at two Budgets in the era of Keynesian 'fine tuning'.

20.3 **Trends in public expenditure.** This case examines attempts to control public expenditure in the UK and relates them to the crowding-out debate.

20.4 **Injections against the contagion.** The use of discretionary fiscal policy in the late 1990s.

20.5 **Any more G and T?** Does the Code for Fiscal Stability mean that the UK government balances its books? An examination of the evidence.

20.6 **Discretionary fiscal policy in Japan.** Attempts by successive Japanese governments since 1992 to bring the economy out of recession though expansionary fiscal policy.

20.7 **Monetary policy in the eurozone.** This is a more detailed examination of the role of monetary policy and the ECB than that contained in Box 20.6.

20.8 **Credit and the business cycle.** This case traces cycles in the growth of credit and relates them to the business cycle. It also looks at some of the implications of the growth in credit.

20.9 **Effective monetary policy versus banking efficiency and stability.** This case examines potential conflicts between banking stability, efficiency and the effective operation of monetary policy.

20.10 **Should central banks be independent of government?** An examination of the arguments for and against independent central banks.

20.11 **Managing the macroeconomy.** This considers whether there have been conflicts of objectives in recent UK macroeconomic policy.

20.12 **Monetary targeting: its use around the world.** An expanded version of Box 20.10.

Websites relevant to this chapter

Numbers and sections refer to websites listed in the Web Appendix and hotlinked from this book's website at **www.pearsoned.co.uk/sloman**.

- For news articles relevant to this chapter, see the *Economics News Articles* link from the book's website.
- For general news on fiscal and monetary policies, see websites in section A, and particularly A1–5. See also links to newspapers worldwide in A38, 39 and 43, and the news search feature in Google at A41. See also links to economics news in A42.
- For information on UK fiscal policy and government borrowing, see sites E30, 36; F2. See also sites A1–8 at Budget time. For fiscal policy in the eurozone, see *Public Finances in EMU* in H1.
- For a model of the economy (based on the Treasury model), see *The Virtual Economy* (site D1). In addition to the model, where you can devise your own Budget, there are worksheets and outlines of theories and the work of famous economists.
- Sites I7 and 11 contain links to fiscal policy: go to *Macroeconomics > Macroeconomic Policy > Taxes and Taxation*.
- For monetary policy in the UK, see F1 and E30. For monetary policy in the eurozone, see F6 and 5. For monetary policy in the USA, see F8. For monetary policy in other countries, see the respective central bank site in section F.
- For links to sites on money and monetary policy, see the *Financial Economics* sections in I4, 7, 11, 17.
- For demand-side policy in the UK, see the latest Budget Report (e.g. section on maintaining macroeconomic stability) at site E30.
- For inflation targeting in the UK and eurozone, see sites F1 and 6.
- For student resources relevant to this chapter, see sites C1–7, 9, 10, 12, 13, 19. See also '2nd floor – economic policy' in site D1. Also see sites D10 (*The Virtual Chancellor*) and D11 (*The Virtual Bank of Biz/ed*).

Aggregate Supply, Unemployment and Inflation

CHAPTER MAP

21.1 Aggregate supply   **612**
Short-run aggregate supply   612
Long-run aggregate supply   613
The classical model of labour markets   614
Keynesian models of labour markets   615
Aggregate demand and supply, and inflation   616

21.2 The expectations-augmented
       Phillips curve   **619**
Adaptive expectations   620
The accelerationist theory   620
The long-run Phillips curve and the natural
    rate of unemployment   621
The effects of contractionary policy   621
Explanations of stagflation   622
Evidence   623
Policy implications   625
Limitations of the adaptive expectations
    hypothesis   626

21.3 Inflation and unemployment:
       the new classical position   **626**
AS and the Phillips curve: correct expectations   628
AS and the Phillips curve: incorrect expectations   628
Policy implications   630
Real business cycles   630

21.4 Inflation and unemployment:
       the modern Keynesian position   **632**
Modern developments of the Keynesian model   632
Changes in equilibrium unemployment   632
Persistence of demand-deficient unemployment   633
The incorporation of expectations   633
The Keynesian criticism of non-intervention   635

21.5 Postscript: Common ground among
       economists?   **636**

In the previous chapter, we focused on ways of managing aggregate demand. But what will be the effects of changes in aggregate demand on output, employment and prices? The answer depends on the responsiveness of aggregate supply.

We begin this chapter by examining what determines this responsiveness: in other words, we examine what determines the shape of the aggregate supply curve. As we shall see, there are different views on this. Also, the effect will be different in the long run from the short run.

Then we turn to the relationship between inflation and unemployment. Again, what is crucial here is the response of aggregate supply to a change in aggregate demand, in this case reflected in the shape of the Phillips curve. If aggregate supply responds to changes in aggregate demand, then a rise in aggregate demand should lead to a fall in unemployment, but will probably lead to a rise in inflation.

We examine three different views on the relationship between inflation and unemployment. One thing is clear: a simple Phillips curve does not exist beyond the short term.

21.1 AGGREGATE SUPPLY

The effect of an increase in aggregate demand on output, employment and prices is a crucial issue in macroeconomic policy and is at the heart of macroeconomic debate. The debate hinges on the shape of the aggregate supply curve and how it varies with time.

The extreme Keynesian and new classical positions are shown in Figure 21.1. Extreme Keynesians argue that up to full employment (Y_F), the aggregate supply (AS) curve is *horizontal*, at least in the short run. A rise in aggregate demand from AD_1 to AD_2 will raise output from Y_1 to Y_2, but there will be *no effect on prices* until full employment is reached. In this model, aggregate supply up to the full-employment level is determined entirely by the level of aggregate demand. But there is no guarantee that aggregate demand will intersect aggregate supply at full employment. Therefore governments should manage aggregate demand by appropriate fiscal and monetary policies to ensure production at Y_F.

Many economists argue that the aggregate supply curve is *vertical*, in the long run. New classicists argue that it is vertical in the short run too. Any rise in aggregate demand will have *no effect on output and employment*. It will merely lead to higher prices. Thus it is essential to keep (nominal) demand under control if *prices* are to be kept under control. To raise output and employment, however, will require supply-side policies: to shift the AS curve to the right.

If AS is somewhere between these two extremes, an increase in AD will have some effect on prices and some effect on output and employment (see Figure 21.1(c)).

Just what is the shape of the AS curve in practice, and what implications follow for policies to cure inflation and unemployment? How do economists differ in their answers to these questions? These are the topics for this chapter. First we must distinguish between short-run and long-run aggregate supply curves.

1. *In the extreme Keynesian model, is there any point in supply-side policies?*
2. *In the new classical model, is there any point in using supply-side policies to tackle inflation?*

Short-run aggregate supply

To understand the shape of the short-run AS curve, it is necessary to look at its microeconomic foundations. How will *individual* firms and industries respond to a rise in demand? What shape will their individual supply curves be?

In the short run, we assume that firms respond to the rise in demand for their product without considering the effects of a general rise in demand on their suppliers or on the economy as a whole. We also assume that the prices of inputs, including wage rates, are constant.

In the case of a profit-maximising firm under monopoly or monopolistic competition, there will be a rise in price and a rise in output. In Figure 21.2, profit-maximising output rises from where $MC = MR_1$ to where $MC = MR_2$. Just how much price changes compared with output depends on the slope of the marginal cost (MC) curve.

The nearer the firm is to full capacity, the steeper the MC curve is likely to be. Here the firm is likely to find diminishing returns setting in rapidly, and it is also likely to have to use more overtime with correspondingly higher unit labour costs. If, however, the firm is operating well below capacity, it can probably supply more with little or no increase in price. Its MC curve may thus be horizontal at lower levels of output.

Under oligopoly, where there is a tendency for prices to be more stable, firms may respond to an increase in demand without raising prices, even if their costs rise somewhat.

When there is a general rise in demand in the economy, the *aggregate* supply response in the short run can be seen

Figure 21.1 Contrasting views on the aggregate supply curve

(a) Extreme Keynesian

(b) New classical

(c) A moderate view of the short-run AS curve

Figure 21.2 Short-run response of a profit-maximising firm to a rise in demand

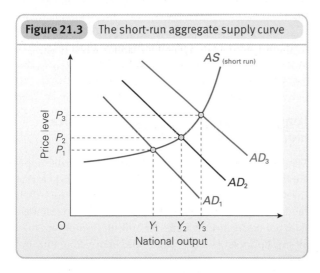

Figure 21.3 The short-run aggregate supply curve

as simply the sum of the responses of all the individual firms. The short-run *AS* curve will look something like that in Figure 21.3. If there is generally plenty of spare capacity, a rise in aggregate demand (e.g. from AD_1 to AD_2) will have a big effect on output and only a small effect on prices. However, as more and more firms find their costs rising as they get nearer to full capacity, so the *AS* curve becomes steeper. Further increases in aggregate demand (e.g. from AD_2 to AD_3) will have bigger effects on prices and smaller effects on output. A general rise in prices, of course, means that individual firms were mistaken in assuming that a rise in price from P_1 to P_2 in Figure 21.2 was a *real* price rise (i.e. relative to prices elsewhere).

Long-run aggregate supply

Three important factors affect the *AS* curve in the long run.

The interdependence of firms

A rise in aggregate demand will lead firms throughout the economy to raise their prices (in accordance with the short-run *AS* curve). But as raw material and intermediate

Figure 21.4 The long-run aggregate supply curve when firms are interdependent

good producers raise their prices, this will raise the costs of production further up the line. A rise in the price of steel will raise the costs of producing cars and washing machines. At the same time, workers, experiencing a rise in demand for labour, and seeing the prices of goods rising, will demand higher wages. Firms will be relatively willing to grant these wage demands, since they are experiencing buoyant demand. The effect of all this is to raise firms' costs, and hence their prices. As prices rise for any given level of output, the short-run *AS* curve shifts upwards.

These long-run effects of a rise in aggregate demand are shown in Figure 21.4. Aggregate demand shifts to AD_1. The economy moves from point *a* to point *b* along the short-run *AS* curve (AS_1). As costs rise and are passed on throughout the economy, the short-run *AS* curve shifts to AS_2, and the economy moves to point *c*. Thus the long-run *AS* curve passing through points *a* and *c* is steeper than the short-run *AS* curve. A rise in aggregate demand will therefore have a smaller effect on output and a bigger effect on prices in the long run than in the short run.

 Under what circumstances would this interdependence of firms give a vertical long-run AS curve?

Investment

With a rise in demand, firms may be encouraged to invest in new plant and machinery (the accelerator effect). In so doing, they may well be able to increase output significantly in the long run with little or no increase in their prices. Their long-run *MC* curves are much flatter than their short-run *MC* curves.

In Figure 21.5, the short-run *AS* curve shifts to the right. Equilibrium moves from point *a* to *b* to *d*. In this case, the

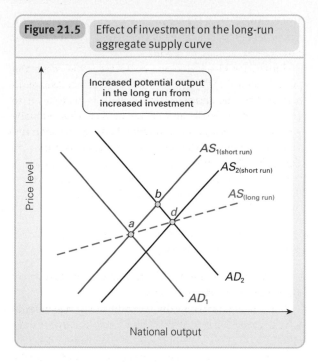

Figure 21.5 Effect of investment on the long-run aggregate supply curve

If there is a fall in aggregate demand, the above three factors will operate in reverse; and again they will affect aggregate supply in different ways:

- The general reduction in costs will lead to the short-run *AS* curve shifting downwards (to the right).
- A fall in investment may lead to a decline in the capital stock and a leftward shift in the short-run *AS* curve.
- People may expect a recession and falling output (*AS* shifts to the left), or merely that prices will fall (*AS* shifts downwards to the right).

Depending on the relative strength of these three factors, the long-run *AS* curve could be shallow, steep or vertical. A fall in *AD* could thus lead to a deep recession with little effect on prices, or there could be little or no long-run reduction in output, but a significant reduction in prices.

Different economists put very different emphases on the three factors, and as a result draw very different conclusions about the shape of the long-run *AS* curve. Central to the debate is their analysis of labour markets and the link between the aggregate demand and supply of goods and the aggregate demand and supply of labour.

long-run *AS* curve joining points *a* and *d* is much more elastic than that in Figure 21.4. There is a relatively large increase in output and a relatively small increase in price.

The long-run *AS* curve will be flatter and possibly even downward sloping if the investment involves the introduction of new cost-reducing technology, or if firms generally experience economies of scale. It will be steeper if the extra investment causes significant shortages of materials, machinery or labour. This is more likely when the economy is already operating near its full-capacity output.

1. *Will the shape of the long-run AS curve here depend on just how the 'long' run is defined?*
2. *If a shift in the aggregate demand curve from AD to AD₁ in Figure 21.5 causes a movement from point a to point d in the long run, would a shift in aggregate demand from AD₁ to AD cause a movement from point d back to point a in the long run?*

Expectations

The effect of a rise in aggregate demand on output and prices will depend crucially on what effect people *expect* it

TC 9
p105

will have.

If firms believe that it will lead to rapid economic growth, they will invest. The short-run *AS* curve will shift to the right.

If, on the other hand, people expect that a rise in demand will simply lead to higher prices, firms will not invest. Workers will demand higher wages to compensate for the higher costs of living. Firms will grant wage rises, knowing that they can pass on the rise in labour costs to the consumer. In these circumstances, the short-run *AS* curve will shift upwards (to the left).

Long-run aggregate supply: the classical model of labour markets

Many economists argue that the long-run aggregate supply curve is vertical. (The extreme new classical position is that the short-run aggregate supply curve is vertical too.) Their model is based on the 'classical' assumptions that real wage rates are flexible in the long run and that people are fully aware of price and wage changes, and hence do not believe that a given percentage pay increase will make them better off when prices are rising by the same percentage (i.e. they do not suffer from ***money illusion***).

TC 12
p395

Figure 21.6 shows the aggregate demand and supply of labour. It is very similar to the diagram we looked at back on pages 421 and 422. On the vertical axis we measure the average *real* wage rate (W/P): i.e. the wage rate after adjusting for prices. The aggregate demand for labour curve (AD_L) slopes downwards. This is merely an extension of the microeconomic demand for labour curve (see section 9.1) and is based on the assumption of diminishing returns to labour. For a given capital stock, the more people are employed, the lower their marginal productivity. Thus firms take on more labour only if there is a fall in the real wage rate to compensate them for the lower output produced by the additional workers.

KI 17
p125

A higher real wage rate encourages more people to enter the labour market. For example, more married women may

Definition

Money illusion The belief that a *money* change in wages or prices represents a *real* change.

Figure 21.6 The aggregate labour market

seek employment. The total number in the labour force (N) rises. The curve gets steeper as the limit of the potential labour force is reached.

There will, however, be some frictional and structural unemployment. Some workers will be searching for better jobs and others will have the wrong qualifications or live in the wrong location. The number of workers willing and able to accept jobs, therefore – the *effective aggregate supply of labour* (AS_L) – will be less than the total labour force.

The equilibrium real wage will be W_e, where $AD_L = AS_L$, with Q_e workers employed. There is no disequilibrium unemployment at this real wage rate, but there is some equilibrium or **natural unemployment** (i.e. frictional plus structural unemployment), shown by $(b - a)$.

With flexible prices and wage rates in the long run, *real wage rates will also be flexible in the long run*. This will ensure that long-run employment is kept at Q_e. Assume that aggregate demand (for goods) rises. Prices rise. This causes the real wage to fall below W_e, say to W_1 in Figure 21.6. But at this real wage rate there is an excess demand for labour of $d - c$. This will drive up the money wage rate until the *real* wage rate has returned to W_e. Thus equilibrium employment is at Q_e irrespective of changes in aggregate demand. Q_e would change only if there were some *exogenous* shift in the AD_L or AS_L curve (e.g. a growth in the working population would cause N and AS_L to shift to the right; a growth in labour productivity would cause AD_L to shift to the right).

Assume that there is a fall in aggregate demand (for goods). Trace through the short-run and long-run effect on employment.

With long-run employment being at Q_e (the natural rate) irrespective of what happens to prices and *money* wages, the long-run aggregate supply curve will be vertical

at the **natural level of output**. This is just another name for the *potential level of output*: i.e. where there is a zero output gap (see Box 14.3, on page 398).

Some new classical economists argue that wage and price flexibility is very great, especially with increased numbers of part-time and short-term jobs. This flexibility is so great that both goods and labour markets clear virtually instantaneously, and the distinction between the short run and the long run breaks down. In such circumstances, the arguments above apply to the short run as well as to the long run. The effect is to give a vertical short-run aggregate supply curve as well as a vertical long-run one.

Long-run aggregate supply: Keynesian models of labour markets

Keynesian models of long-run aggregate supply take a very different view of labour markets.

Many labour markets exhibit considerable wage inflexibility. Employers bargain with unions and usually set wage rates for a whole year. If there is a fall in consumer demand, firms usually respond *not* by cutting wages, but rather by laying off workers, or by instituting early retirement, or by not replacing workers when they leave. In the short run, therefore, wages in many sectors of the economy are insensitive to a fall in demand.

In Figure 21.7, assume initially that with aggregate demand for labour at AD_{L_1}, the labour market is in equilibrium. The only unemployment is equilibrium unemployment of $b - a$. If there is a fall in the aggregate demand for goods, with prices sticky in the short run, the production of goods goes down, but real wage rates are little affected. The effect on the labour market is felt, therefore, by a fall in the aggregate demand for labour to AD_{L_2}, reflecting the lower demand for goods. But with wages sticky downwards, the real wage rate does not fall either. Instead, firms reduce employment from Q_1 to Q_2. There is now demand-deficient unemployment of $a - c$. *Total* unemployment is $b - c$.

This gives a short-run aggregate supply (of goods) curve that is highly elastic below the current wage. A fall in aggregate demand will lead to a large fall in output and only a small fall in prices. The flatter are firms' marginal cost curves, the smaller will be the fall in prices.

Definitions

Natural level of unemployment The level of equilibrium unemployment in monetarist analysis measured as the difference between the (vertical) long-run gross labour supply (N) and the (vertical) long-run effective labour supply (AS_L).

Natural level of output The level of output in monetarist analysis where the vertical long-run aggregate supply curve cuts the horizontal axis.

KI 31
p320

KI 10
p71

TC 12
p395

Figure 21.7 Short-run response to a fall in the aggregate demand for labour: sticky wages

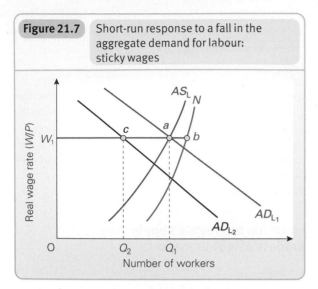

As the recession persists, those previously laid off may not be readily re-employable, especially if they have been out of work for some time and have become deskilled and demoralised. The aggregate supply of labour curve has shifted to the left, perhaps as far as AS_{L_2}. In such a case, there would now no longer be an excess supply of labour that firms regard as 'employable' ($AD_{L_2} = AS_{L_2}$). There is no downward pressure on real wages: a long-run equilibrium has been reached. The implication of this is that the long-run aggregate supply (of goods) curve is *not* vertical. A leftward shift in aggregate demand has led to a long-run fall in output.

Assume now that the government pursues a reflationary policy, and that the aggregate demand for labour shifts back to AD_{L_1}. There will be a move up along AS_{L_2} to point d. Unemployment is now $e - d$, higher than the original level of $c - a$.

Expectations of output. If aggregate demand falls and the economy moves into recession, business confidence will fall and so will investment. The capital stock will therefore fall. This will reduce aggregate supply. Unless confidence quickly returns, and there is no guarantee that it will, the recession may be long-lived. The reduction in aggregate supply will be *long*-term.

The reduction in the capital stock will magnify the leftward shift in the aggregate demand for labour and increase the level of unemployment.

But what about the *long* run? Clearly it depends on how long the long run is. Many Keynesians argue that prices and especially wages exhibit a degree of inflexibility over quite a long period of time, and over this period of time, therefore, the aggregate supply curve would not be vertical. What is more, Keynesians argue that the long-run AS curve is unlikely to be vertical for a number of other reasons.

Hysteresis. As you may have seen on pages 467–8, *hysteresis* refers to the lagging or persistence of an effect, even when the initial cause has been removed. In other words, an equilibrium position depends on the path taken to arrive there. In this context, hysteresis would be where long-run aggregate supply depends on what has been happening to aggregate demand and supply in the short run. Assume that the economy goes into recession, with a corresponding rise in demand-deficient unemployment and a fall in output. In Figure 21.8, aggregate demand has fallen from AD_{L_1} to AD_{L_2}. Demand-deficient unemployment is $a - b$ (the short-run effect).

Long-run money illusion. The problem of demand deficiency will be compounded if there is long-run money illusion. Assume again that there is a fall in aggregate demand. Workers may be reluctant to accept a reduction in money wages, not appreciating that there is a corresponding fall in prices, thus leaving real wages unaffected. Thus real wages may be forced up, compounding the problem of disequilibrium unemployment.

Aggregate demand and supply, and inflation

Aggregate demand and supply analysis can be used to distinguish between demand-pull and cost-push inflation.

Demand-pull inflation

Assume that aggregate demand rises. In Figure 21.9(a), there is some increase in output, and the price level rises from P_0 to P_1. If demand goes on rising, so that the AD curve goes on shifting to the right, the price level will go on rising and there will be demand-pull inflation. There will be a movement from point a to b to c in Figure 21.9(b).

But sooner or later the short-run aggregate *supply* curve will start shifting. If the effects of rising costs and rising price expectations offset any stimulus to investment, the short-run AS curve will shift upwards. This will lead to a falling back of output but a further rise in prices as the economy moves to point d. If the government responds by

Figure 21.8 The effect on wages and employment of a recovery from recession

Figure 21.9 Demand-pull inflation

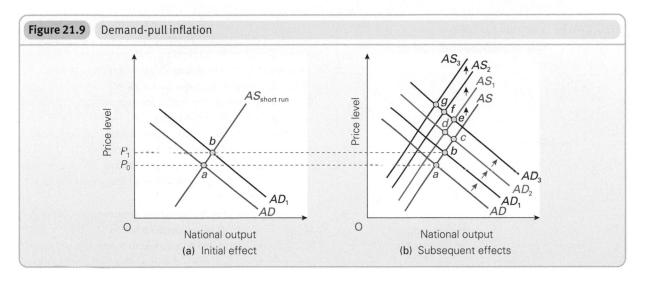

(a) Initial effect

(b) Subsequent effects

giving a further boost to demand in order to keep expansion going, there will be a movement outward again to point e, but a further rise in prices. Then the AS curve will probably continue shifting upwards and the economy will move to point f.

If the government now makes the control of inflation its main policy objective, it may stop any further increases in aggregate demand. Aggregate supply may continue shifting upwards for a while as cost increases and expectations feed through. The economy moves to point g. In the extreme case, point g may be vertically above point a: the long-run aggregate supply curve is vertical. The only effect of the shift in AD to AD_3 has been inflation.

Note that, although costs in Figure 21.9(b) have increased and hence the AS curves have shifted upwards, this is not *cost-push* inflation because the rise in costs is the result of the rise in *demand*.

 If point g is vertically above point a, does this mean that the long-run AS curve is vertical? Are there any circumstances where point g might be to the left of point a?

Cost-push inflation

Assume that there is some exogenous increase in costs: a sharp increase in world oil prices, or an increase in wages due to increased trade union activity, or firms raising prices to cover the costs of a rise in interest rates. In Figure 21.10(a), the short-run AS curve shifts to AS_1. Prices rise to P_1 and there is a fall in national output.

If these increases in costs continue for some time, the AS curve will go on shifting upwards. Price rises will continue and there is cost-push inflation. The economy will move from point a to b to c in Figure 21.10(b). Continuous upward shifts in the AS curve are particularly likely if there is a continuing struggle between different groups (e.g. unions and employers' organisations) for a larger share of national income.

After a time, aggregate demand is likely to rise. This may be due to the government using expansionary fiscal and monetary policies to halt the falling output and employment. Or it may be due to money supply expanding endogenously as workers and firms need larger money balances to allow for increasingly costly transactions.

BOX 21.1   COST-PUSH INFLATION AND SUPPLY SHOCKS

It is important to distinguish a *single* supply shock, such as a rise in oil prices or an increase in VAT or excise duties, from a continuing upward pressure on costs, such as workers continually demanding increases in real wages above the level of labour productivity, or firms continually using their monopoly power to increase the real value of profits.

A single supply shock will give a *single* upward movement in the AS curve. Prices will move to a new higher equilibrium. Cost-push inflation in this case is a *temporary* phenomenon. Once the new higher price level

has been reached, the cost-push inflation disappears. If, however, there is a continuous upward pressure on costs, cost-push inflation is likely to continue. It will get worse if the cost pressure intensifies.

 Give some examples of single shocks and continuing changes on the demand side. Does the existence of multiplier and accelerator effects make the distinction between single shocks and continuing effects more difficult to make on the demand side than on the supply side?

Figure 21.10 Cost-push inflation

(a) Initial effect

(b) Subsequent effects

---

*BOX 21.2 **ANALYSING DEMAND-PULL AND COST-PUSH INFLATION USING THE *ADI/ASI* MODEL**

EXPLORING ECONOMICS

Types of inflation under a policy of inflation targeting

We can use the *ADI/ASI* model to analyse the implications of demand-pull and cost-push pressures under a policy of inflation targeting. The diagram below is similar to Figure 19.18 (on page 559). Assume that the central bank operates with an inflation target of π_{target} and that the economy is currently in equilibrium at point *a* with aggregate demand and supply given by ADI_1 and ASI_1 respectively. Real national income is at the potential (or 'natural') level of Y_1.

Demand-pull inflation

If there is a rise in aggregate demand to ADI_2, this will result in demand-pull pressures on inflation. The government or central bank could respond in either of two ways.

- Fiscal or monetary policy could be tightened to shift the *ADI* curve back to ADI_1, thereby maintaining inflation at the target level.

Demand-pull and cost-push inflation

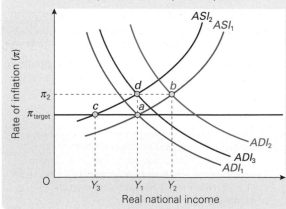

- A new higher inflation target could be adopted (e.g. π_2), allowing an equilibrium at point *b*. Note, however, that if the potential level of income remains at Y_1, Y_2 will not be sustainable. In the long run, the *ASI* curve will drift upwards, pushing inflation above the new higher target level. A tighter monetary policy (ADI_3) would then be needed to bring national income back down to the potential level, Y_1.

Cost-push inflation

If costs now rise faster than the rate of inflation (a *real* rise in costs), the *ASI* line will shift upwards (e.g. to ASI_2). Again, the government or central bank could respond in either of two ways.

- The central bank could stick to its target and adopt a tighter monetary policy. In this case the *ADI* curve will shift to the left to give an equilibrium at point *c* at the target rate of inflation. The potential level of output is now at the lower level of Y_3.

- The central bank could be given a higher target rate of inflation (π_2) to prevent real income falling. It will thus expand aggregate demand and the *ADI* line will shift to ADI_3. Equilibrium would now be at point *d*. The problem with this second approach is that if there has been a long-term reduction in potential output to Y_3, there will be further upward pressure on inflation: the *ASI* curve will continue shifting upwards as long as real national income remains above Y_3. It will only be possible to keep to the target rate of inflation, at any level, if *ADI* is allowed to fall so that it intersects with *ASI* at Y_3.

 If cost-push pressures reduce the potential level of real national income (e.g. from Y_1 to Y_3 in the diagram), why do demand-pull pressures not increase the potential level of real national income (e.g. from Y_1 to Y_2 in the diagram)?

Aggregate demand shifts to AD_1 and there is a movement to point d. There may be a further increase in costs and a movement to point e, and then a further increase in aggregate demand and so on.

Note again that, although demand has increased, this is not *demand-pull* inflation because the rise in demand is the result of the upward pressure on *costs*.

What causes inflation in practice?

Inflation targeting, with the use of interest-rate changes to achieve the target, implies that inflation is generally of the demand-pull variety. Forecasts of inflation (e.g. by the Bank of England) tend to concentrate on various factors affecting aggregate demand, such as the size of the PSNCR and business and consumer confidence. In most cases, changes in inflation are indeed caused by changes in the rate of growth of aggregate demand.

There are, however, occasions when there are exogenous changes in costs. In the short run, these can be shocks such as a rise in oil or other commodity prices or a period of industrial unrest. In the longer term, technological changes can affect the rate of growth of aggregate supply. If this slows down, then for any given rate of growth in aggregate demand, there will be a higher rate of inflation. This rise in inflation could be described as 'cost push'. Under a policy of inflation targeting, however, the response to this problem would be one of slowing down the rate of growth in aggregate demand to match the slower growth in aggregate supply. In other words, a higher interest rate would be needed to achieve the target rate of inflation.

One of the key determinants of inflation is people's expectations. The higher inflation is expected to be, the higher it will be. In the remainder of the chapter we look at just how expectations affect inflation and how they affect the relationship between inflation and unemployment. In doing so we will look at theories that develop the old Phillips curve (see Box 15.5).

Section summary

1. The short-run aggregate supply curve depends on firms' short-run marginal cost curves. The more rapidly costs rise as output increases, the less elastic will the *AS* curve be.

2. The long-run *AS* curve will be less elastic (a) the more that cost increases are passed on from one part of the economy to another, (b) the less that increases in aggregate demand stimulate cost-reducing investment and (c) the more that people expect prices to rise as a result of the increase in demand.

3. Classical assumptions imply that the long-run aggregate supply curve is vertical. The key assumptions here are flexible prices and wages, and an absence of money illusion.

4. Keynesians argue that the long-run supply curve will not be vertical. It will be more elastic the greater the problem of hysteresis, the more that firms react to changes in aggregate demand by changing the level of investment and hence the size of the capital stock, and the greater the degree of long-run money illusion.

5. Demand-pull inflation occurs where there is a continuous rightward shift in the *AD* curve. Cost-push inflation occurs where there is a continuous upward shift in the *AS* curve. In practice, it is difficult to separate demand-pull and cost-push inflation as there are often exogenous and endogenous factors affecting both demand and costs simultaneously.

21.2 THE EXPECTATIONS-AUGMENTED PHILLIPS CURVE

A major contribution to the theory of unemployment and inflation was made by Milton Friedman (see Person Profile in MyEconLab) and others in the late 1960s. They incorporated people's expectations about the future level of prices into the Phillips curve. In its simplest form, this *expectations-augmented Phillips curve* may be expressed as

$$\pi = f(1/U) + \pi^e + \kappa \qquad (1)$$

This states that the rate of price inflation (π) depends on three things.

- First, it is a function (f) of the inverse of unemployment ($1/U$). This is simply the normal Phillips curve relationship. A rise in aggregate demand will lead to a fall in unemployment (a rise in $1/U$) and a rise in inflation: e.g. a movement from point a to point b in Figure 21.11.
- Second, the expected rate of inflation π^e must be added to the inflation that would result simply from the level of excess demand represented by ($1/U$).

Definition

Expectations-augmented Phillips curve A (short-run) Phillips curve whose position depends on the expected rate of inflation.

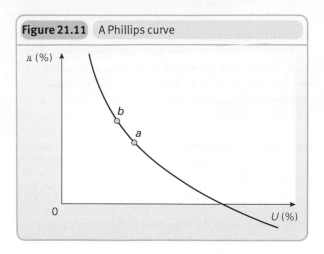

Figure 21.11 A Phillips curve

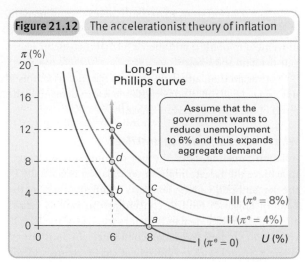

Figure 21.12 The accelerationist theory of inflation

Assume that the government wants to reduce unemployment to 6% and thus expands aggregate demand

- Third, if there are any exogenous cost pressures on inflation (κ) (such as increases in international commodity prices), this must be added too.

Thus if people expected a 3 per cent inflation rate ($\pi^e = 3\%$) and if excess demand were causing demand-pull inflation of 2 per cent ($f(1/U) = 2\%$) and exogenous increases in costs were adding another 1 per cent to inflation ($\kappa = 1\%$), actual inflation would be $3 + 2 + 1 = 6$ per cent.

The model is developed in the framework of market clearing. Wages are not sticky downwards, at least not in the long run. There can be no long-run disequilibrium unemployment: no long-run deficiency of demand.

Adaptive expectations

KI 10
p71

What determines the expected rate of inflation (π^e)? In the model we are developing it depends on inflation rates *in the past*. This is known as the ***adaptive expectations hypothesis***. What this means is that people learn from experience. If last year they underpredicted the rate of inflation, then this year they will adapt: they will revise their expectations of inflation upwards.

In its simplest form, the adaptive expectations hypothesis assumes that the expected rate of inflation this year (π^e_t) will be the rate that inflation actually was last year (π_{t-1}):

$$\pi^e_t = \pi_{t-1} \tag{2}$$

To keep the analysis straightforward, we will stick to this simple version of the adaptive expectations hypothesis.

The accelerationist theory

Let us trace the course of inflation and expectations over a number of years in an imaginary economy. To keep the analysis simple, assume there is no growth in the economy and no exogenous cost pressures on inflation ($\kappa = 0$ in equation (1)).

Table 21.1 The accelerationist theory of inflation and inflationary expectations

Year	Point on graph	π	=	$f(1/U)$	+	π^e
1	a	0	=	0	+	0
2	b	4	=	4	+	0
3	c	4	=	0	+	4
4	d	8	=	4	+	4
5	e	12	=	4	+	8

Year 1. Assume that at the outset, in year 1, there is no inflation of any sort; that none is expected; that $AD = AS$; and that equilibrium unemployment is 8 per cent. The economy will be at point *a* in Figure 21.12 and Table 21.1.

Year 2. Now assume that the government expands aggregate demand in order to reduce unemployment. Unemployment falls to 6 per cent. The economy moves to point *b* along curve I. Inflation has risen to 4 per cent, but people, basing their expectations of inflation on year 1, still expect a zero inflation. There is therefore no shift as yet in the Phillips curve. Curve I corresponds to an expected rate of inflation of zero. (See Case Study 21.1 in MyEconLab for an explanation of why the short-run Phillips curve slopes downwards.)

Year 3. People now revise their expectations of inflation to the level of year 2. The Phillips curve shifts up by

Definition

Adaptive expectations hypothesis The theory that people base their expectations of inflation on past inflation rates.

TC 12
p395

4 percentage points to position II. If *nominal* aggregate demand (i.e. demand purely in monetary terms, irrespective of the level of prices) continues to rise at the same rate, the whole of the increase will now be absorbed in higher prices. *Real* aggregate demand will fall back to its previous level and the economy will move to point *c*. Unemployment will return to 8 per cent. There is no *demand-pull* inflation now ($f(1/U) = 0$), but inflation is still 4 per cent due to expectations ($\pi^e = 4$ per cent).

Year 4. Assume now that the government expands *real* aggregate demand again so as to reduce unemployment once more to 6 per cent. This time it must expand *nominal* aggregate demand by *more* than it did in year 2, because this time, as well as reducing unemployment, it also has to validate the 4 per cent expected inflation. The economy moves to point *d* along curve II. Inflation is now 8 per cent.

Year 5. *Expected* inflation is now 8 per cent (the level of actual inflation in year 4). The Phillips curve shifts up to position III. If at the same time the government tries to keep unemployment at 6 per cent, it must expand nominal aggregate demand 4 per cent faster in order to validate the 8 per cent expected inflation. The economy moves to point *e* along curve III. Inflation is now 12 per cent.

Year 6 onwards. To keep unemployment at 6 per cent, the government must continue to increase nominal aggregate demand by 4 per cent more than the previous year. As the expected inflation rate goes on rising, the Phillips curve will go on shifting up each year.

Thus in order to keep unemployment below the initial equilibrium rate, price rises must go on *accelerating* each year. For this reason, the adaptive expectations theory of the Phillips curve is sometimes known as the *accelerationist theory*.

The more the government reduces unemployment, the greater the rise in inflation that year, and the more the rise in expectations the following year and each subsequent year; and hence the more rapidly will price rises accelerate. Thus the true longer-term trade-off is between unemployment and the rate of *increase* in inflation.

Definitions

Accelerationist theory The theory that unemployment can be reduced below the natural rate only at the cost of accelerating inflation.

Natural rate of unemployment or **non-accelerating-inflation rate of unemployment (NAIRU)** The rate of unemployment consistent with a constant rate of inflation: the rate of unemployment at which the vertical long-run Phillips curve cuts the horizontal axis.

$$\Delta\pi = f(1/U) \qquad\qquad (3)$$

($\Delta\pi$ may be written $\dot{\pi}$.)

Note that the upward shift in the Phillips curve will be less rapid if expectations do not fully adjust to the previous year's inflation rate. The upward shift will be more rapid if expectations adjust to the rate of *increase* in inflation last year ($\Delta\pi_{t-1}$).

Construct a table like Table 21.1, only this time assume that the government wishes to reduce unemployment to 5 per cent. Assume that every year from year 1 onwards the government is prepared to expand aggregate demand by whatever it takes to do this. If this expansion of demand gives $f(1/U) = 7$ per cent, fill in the table for the first six years. Do you think that after a couple of years people might begin to base their expectations differently?

The long-run Phillips curve and the natural rate of unemployment

As long as there are demand-pull pressures ($f(1/U) > 0$), inflation will rise as the expected rate of inflation (π^e) rises. In the long run, therefore, the Phillips curve will be *vertical* at the rate of unemployment where real aggregate demand equals *real* aggregate supply. This is the *equilibrium* rate of unemployment. Monetarists refer to it as the **natural rate** (U_n). It is sometimes also known as the **non-accelerating-inflation rate of unemployment (NAIRU)**.[1] In Figure 21.12, $U_n = 8$ per cent.

KI 8
p43

The implication for government policy is that expansionary monetary and fiscal policy can reduce unemployment below U_n only in the *short* run. In the long run, the effect will be purely inflationary.

What will determine the speed at which inflation accelerates?

The effects of contractionary policy

Let us now move on a few years from Table 21.1. Assume that the economy has returned to the natural rate of unemployment: $f(1/U) = 0$. The economy is therefore on the long-run Phillips curve. But, due to past excess demand, the expected rate of inflation is 20 per cent. The economy is thus at point *j* on short-run Phillips curve X in Figure 21.13.

The government now decides to make the control of inflation its main priority. It therefore reduces the growth of nominal aggregate demand *below* the rate of inflation. Real aggregate demand falls. Let us assume that there is a

---

[1] Strictly speaking, the NAIRU is theoretically different from the natural rate in that it is based on the assumption of imperfect competition, price and wage stickiness and hysteresis: in other words, on Keynesian assumptions. The NAIRU is thus merely the rate of unemployment at which inflation is constant. We look at the NAIRU in section 21.4.

Figure 21.13 The effects of deflation

2 per cent downward pressure on inflation: $f(1/U) = -2$. Inflation thus falls to 18 per cent. But unemployment rises, let us assume, from 8 per cent to 13 per cent. The economy moves along curve X to point k.

The following year the expected rate of inflation will fall to 18 per cent to match, and if real demand is still being deflated by the same amount ($f(1/U) = -2$), actual inflation will fall to 16 per cent. The economy moves to point l on curve XI.

If the government maintains unemployment at 13 per cent, inflation will continue to fall by 2 per cent a year. After ten years of unemployment at 13 per cent, the economy could return to point a, with unemployment falling back to U_n.

Construct a table like Table 21.1, only this time assume that in year 1 the economy is in recession with high unemployment, but also high inflation due to high inflationary expectations as a result of past excess demand. Assume that in year 1, $\pi = 30$ per cent, $f(1/U) = -6$ per cent and $\pi^e = 36$ per cent. Continue the table for as many years as it takes for inflation to be 'squeezed out' of the economy (assuming that the government keeps aggregate demand at a low enough level to maintain $f(1/U) = -6$ per cent throughout).

How quickly can inflation be eliminated?

The short-run Phillips curve may be relatively shallow to the right of U_n. The more sticky downwards wages and prices are in the short run, the shallower the curve will be. Thus to get a relatively rapid fall in inflation, unemployment may have to be very high indeed.

According to the adaptive expectations model, there are two alternative routes to eliminating inflation.

The quick route. This involves a *severe* contraction. Unemployment rises to very high rates and the economy is plunged into a deep recession. However, the short-run Phillips curve shifts down fairly rapidly as the expected rate of inflation (π^e) falls quite quickly. Inflation may be squeezed out of the economy within two or three years. This approach could be called the 'short, sharp shock'.

The slow route. This involves a *mild* contraction. Unemployment rises perhaps one or two percentage points above the natural rate. Inflation falls only slightly in the first year, and thus π^e falls only slowly the next year and each subsequent year. Although less painful, this approach may take many years to eliminate inflation.

Explanations of stagflation

In the 1970s, many countries experienced 'stagflation' – a simultaneous rise in unemployment and inflation. Monetarists used the adaptive expectations model to explain why this occurred. The explanation involved clockwise loops and rightward shifts in the long-run Phillips curve.

Clockwise Phillips loops

Consider a ten-year cycle. This is illustrated in Figure 21.14. The economy starts at position a in year 0. There is no inflation and the economy is at the natural rate of unemployment. The government pursues an expansionary policy over the next three years in order to reduce unemployment. The economy moves up through points b, c and d.

---

*BOX 21.3 **BASING EXPECTATIONS ON THE PAST** **EXPLORING ECONOMICS**

More sophisticated adaptive expectations models

More complex adaptive expectations models assume that π^e is a weighted average of past rates of inflation:

$$\pi^e_t = a\pi_{t-1} + b\pi_{t-2} + c\pi_{t-3} \ldots + m\pi_{t-n} \quad \text{(1)}$$

where $a + b + c \ldots + m = 1$, and where $a > b > c$, etc.

In other words, people will base their expectations of inflation on the actual inflation rates over the last few years, but with last year's inflation having a bigger influence on people's expectations than the previous year's and so on.

In times of rapidly *accelerating* inflation, people may adjust their expectations of inflation upward by the amount that inflation *rose* last year ($\Delta\pi_{t-1}$). This gives:

$$\Delta\pi^e_t = \Delta\pi_{t-1} \quad \text{(2)}$$

Under what circumstances will term a in equation (1) be large relative to terms b, c etc.?

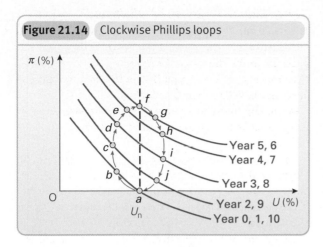

Figure 21.14 Clockwise Phillips loops

Under what circumstances would a Phillips loop be (a) tall and thin; (b) short and wide?

Rightward shifts in the long-run Phillips curve

If frictional or structural unemployment rises (due, say, to increased unemployment benefits), U_n will increase. The long-run Phillips curve will shift to the right.

Assume that the economy was initially on the long-run Phillips curve with $U_n = 8$ per cent and a stable inflation rate of 5 per cent. U_n now rises to 12 per cent. The government uses demand-management policy to keep the rise in unemployment to only 10 per cent. But this is now *below* U_n and thus inflation will increase. Thus both inflation *and* unemployment have risen.

The government then starts worrying about inflation. It allows unemployment to rise somewhat, but as it is still below U_n there is still demand-pull inflation. The economy moves to point *e*. The government now allows unemployment to rise to U_n, but the Phillips curve still shifts up as expectations catch up with last year's inflation. The economy moves from point *e* to point *f*.

Thereafter the government allows unemployment to rise further, and the economy eventually returns to point *a*, via points *g*, *h*, *i* and *j*. The economy has thus moved through a clockwise loop.

Stagflation is easy to see. From points *d* to *f*, both unemployment *and* inflation are rising. What is more, several points are to the 'north-east' of other earlier points. For example, point *g* is north-east of point *c*. In other words, inflation *and* unemployment in year 6 (point *g*) are worse than in year 2 (point *c*).

Evidence

The evidence for the UK since 1967 is consistent with the adaptive expectations model. (But note that it is consistent with other explanations too!) In Figure 21.15 loops can clearly be seen up to around 1993, when inflation targeting began (see sections 19.4 and 20.5). At the same time, U_n would seem to have increased from about 4.5 per cent in the mid 1970s to around 11 per cent in the mid 1980s, and to have fallen to about 8 per cent in the late 1980s/early 1990s and to about 5 per cent in the mid 2000s.

Since the mid 1990s, hitting the inflation target has been the central aim of monetary policy and people have grown to believe that the target will be achieved. Figure 21.16 shows expected inflation and actual inflation from 1990 to 2008. As you can see, for the first few years, expected inflation was between 1 and 2 percentage points

Figure 21.15 The path of inflation and unemployment in the UK

Note: Year 2009 figures based on forecasts.
Source: Data from Times Series Data (National Statistics, various years).

Figure 21.16 Inflation performance and expectations

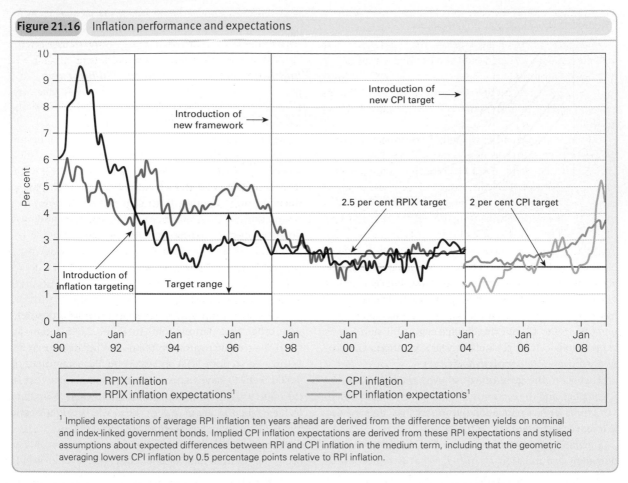

Source: *Pre-Budget Report 2008* (HM Treasury, 2008), Chart 2.4.

above actual inflation, but since 1998 expectations have turned out to be pretty well correct.

So, does this mean that the Phillips curve has now become horizontal, as Figure 21.16 would seem to imply? The answer is that it depends on policy. As long as inflation is successfully kept on target and people believe that it will remain so, the path of inflation and unemployment will be a horizontal straight line. Movements left and right along the line will depend on what happens to unemployment.

If, however, shocks to the world economy, such as the rapid rises in food, oil and other commodity prices in 2007/8, cause a rise in inflation, then confidence in the central bank's ability to maintain inflation at the target rate may be shaken. Both inflation and unemployment may rise.

Even if the central bank does succeed in achieving the target rate of inflation, in the short term, unemployment will fluctuate with the business cycle. Thus there may be movements left or right from one year to the next depending on the level of economic activity. Such fluctuations in unemployment are consistent with a stable inflation rate, provided that the fluctuations are mild and are not enough to alter people's expectations of inflation. Thus there was a very slight rise in unemployment, from 5.1 to 5.2 per cent,

from 2001 to 2002 as the economic growth slowed slightly and a fall again to 4.8 per cent in 2004 as growth picked up somewhat.

Over the medium term (3 to 6 years), there may be a left-ward movement if the economy starts in recession and then the output gap is gradually closed through a process of steady economic growth (growth that avoids 'boom and bust'). Demand-deficient unemployment will be gradually eliminated. Thus between 1993 (the trough of the reces-sion) and 1999, the output gap was closed from −2.1 to 0.2 (see the diagram in Box 14.3 on page 398). Provided the process is gradual, inflation can stay on target.

Over the longer term, movements left (or right) will depend on what happens to equilibrium unemployment. A reduction in equilibrium unemployment will result in a leftward movement. Evidence suggests that since the mid 1980s there has been a significant reduction in equilibrium unemployment from around 11 per cent to around 5 per cent. The precise amount, however, is not certain as it is subject to measurement errors.

What if inflation targeting were abandoned?

If inflation targeting were abandoned and aggregate demand expanded rapidly, perhaps through tax cuts or a cut in interest rates, the short-run Phillips curve could re-emerge. A rapid expansion of aggregate demand would both reduce unemployment below the equilibrium rate and raise inflation. There would be a positive output gap.

This position could not be sustained, however, as inflationary expectations would rise and the short-run Phillips curve would begin shifting upwards (as in Figure 21.12 on page 620).

With rising food and commodity prices in 2007/8, combined with a slowing economy, the Bank of England was faced with a dilemma. Should it continue rigidly targeting inflation, which would mean raising interest rates, or should it increase aggregate demand in an attempt to avoid recession, which would mean cutting interest rates? If, as in the USA, it had taken the course of substantially cutting interest rates, it could have undermined its credibility in keeping inflation under control as its overriding objective. Inflation expectations would have risen. As it was, as Figure 21.16 shows, they were beginning to edge up and were around 3 per cent in 2008 (1 percentage point above the target).

If the effect of the credit crunch and rising world commodity prices were to increase the equilibrium level of unemployment, attempts to keep unemployment down by interest rate cuts would have sparked an acceleration of inflation.

As it turned out, inflation fell in late 2008 and the output gap rose substantially; inflation was forecast to fall well below the target rate at the 24-month horizon. The Bank of England was thus able to cut interest rates to boost aggregate demand without compromising its inflation target. You will have to see whether it was willing to raise interest rates again some time later, once forecasts of inflation rose above 2 per cent.

 How would you explain the apparent re-emergence of a Phillips loop after 2004?

Policy implications

The implications of the expectations-augmented Phillips curve are that monetary or fiscal policy can have no *long-run* effect on unemployment. They can only be used to influence the inflation rate. Ultimately, monetary and fiscal policies merely move the economy up or down the vertical long-run Phillips curve. An expansionary policy, for example, could only ever bring a *temporary* reduction in unemployment below U_n.

To reduce unemployment permanently, *supply-side* policies should be used. These could either be market-orientated policies of removing impediments to the working of the market (see section 23.3) or interventionist policies, such as improving education and training or the country's transport and communications infrastructure (see section 23.4). By reducing frictional and/or structural unemployment, such policies will shift the long-run Phillips curve back to the left.

BOX 21.4 | **THE POLITICAL BUSINESS CYCLE (PART II)**[1]   **CASE STUDIES AND APPLICATIONS**

The art of looping the loop

Imagine that a politically naïve government has been fulfilling election promises to reduce unemployment, cut taxes and increase welfare spending. In Figure 21.14 this is shown by a move from points *a* to *b* to *c*.

To its dismay, by the time the next election comes, inflation is accelerating and unemployment is rising again. The economy is moving from point *d* to *e* to *f*. You would hardly be surprised to learn that it loses the election!

But now suppose a much more politically adroit government is elected. What does it do? The answer is that it does politically unpopular things at first, so that before the next election it can do nice things and curry favour with the electorate.

The first thing it does is to have a tough Budget. 'We are having to clear up the economic mess left by the last government.' It thus engineers a recession and begins to squeeze down inflationary expectations. The economy moves from point *f* to *g* to *h*.

But people have very short memories (despite opposition attempts to remind them). After a couple of years of misery, the government announces that the economy has 'begun to turn the corner'. Things are looking up. Inflation has fallen and unemployment has stopped rising. The economy has moved from point *h* to *i* to *j*.

'Thanks to prudent management of the economy', claims the Chancellor, 'I am now in a position to reduce taxes and to allow modest increases in government expenditure.' Unemployment falls rapidly; the economy grows rapidly; the economy moves from point *j* to *a* to *b*.

The government's popularity soars; the pre-election 'give-away' Budget is swallowed by the electorate who trustingly believe that similar ones will follow if the government is returned to office. The government wins the election.

Then comes the nasty medicine again. But who will be blamed this time?

 1. *Why might a government sometimes 'get it wrong' and find itself at the wrong part of the Phillips loop at the time of an election?*

2. *Which electoral system would most favour a government being re-elected: the US fixed-term system with presidents being elected every four years, or the UK system where the government can choose to hold an election any time within five years of the last one?*

[1] See Box 15.7 on p. 448 for part I.

Limitations of the adaptive expectations hypothesis

The adaptive expectations hypothesis suffers from a serious flaw: it assumes that people base their expectations on the past. So if inflation is on an upward trend, the future of inflation will always be underestimated. Similarly, inflation will always be overestimated if it is on a downward trend. Thus people will normally be wrong.

But people will soon realise that it is not rational to base their expectations blindly on the past. They will look at the *current* situation and what is likely to affect inflation. Thus, it is argued, adaptive expectations cannot be a rational basis of behaviour. An alternative view of price expectations was subsequently developed. We look at it in the next section.

Section summary

1. A refinement of the simple Phillips curve involves the incorporation of people's expectations about the rate of inflation. This gives an expectations-augmented Phillips curve. One explanation of how people form these expectations is given by the adaptive expectations hypothesis. In its simplest form, the hypothesis states that the expected rate of inflation this year is what it actually was last year: $\pi^e_t = \pi_{t-1}$.

2. If there is excess demand in the economy, producing upward pressure on wages and prices, initially unemployment will fall. The reason is that workers and firms will believe that wage and price increases represent *real* wage and price increases respectively. Thus workers are prepared to take jobs more readily and firms choose to produce more. But as people's expectations adapt upwards to these higher wages and prices, so ever-increasing rises in nominal aggregate demand will be necessary to maintain unemployment below the natural rate. Price and wage rises will accelerate: i.e. inflation will rise.

3. The Phillips curve, according to this analysis, is thus vertical at the natural rate of unemployment.

4. If an economy suffering from high inflation is deflated, initially unemployment will rise above the natural rate.

But as expectations adapt downwards, so the short-run Phillips curve will shift downwards and inflation will fall. Eventually the economy will return to zero inflation at the natural rate of unemployment.

5. This position can be reached more quickly if the government deflates sharply, but then in the short run the rate of unemployment may rise substantially above the natural rate.

6. Stagflation can be explained in this model either by a movement from 9 o'clock to 12 o'clock round a clockwise Phillips loop, or by a rightward shift in the vertical Phillips curve combined with a mild expansionary policy.

7. Evidence shows that the effects of inflation targeting on expectations has made the time-path of the Phillips curve horizontal at the target rate of inflation. This does not mean, however, that a vertical long-run Phillips curve would not soon become apparent if inflation targeting were abandoned.

8. The weakness of the adaptive expectations hypothesis is that people do not just base expectations of inflation on the past. They are also likely to base them on *current* events and conditions.

21.3 ## INFLATION AND UNEMPLOYMENT: THE NEW CLASSICAL POSITION

Economists of the *new classical school* (see page 469) go further than the monetarist theory described above. They argue that even the short-run Phillips curve is vertical: that there is *no* trade-off between unemployment and inflation, even in the short run. They base their arguments on two key assumptions:

- Prices and wages are flexible, and thus markets clear very rapidly.
- Expectations are 'rational', but are based on imperfect information.

Flexible wages and prices

New classical economists assume that markets clear virtually instantaneously. This is likely, they argue, in modern

economies with flexible labour markets (see Box 9.8 on pages 254–5) and facing global competition. There is thus no disequilibrium unemployment, even in the short run. All unemployment, therefore, is *equilibrium* unemployment, or 'voluntary unemployment' as new classical economists tend to call it. Increases in unemployment are therefore due to an increase in the natural level of unemployment, as people choose not to take jobs because of a lack of incentives to do so.

Rational expectations

The analysis of the previous section was based on *adaptive* expectations. Expectations of inflation are based on *past* information and therefore take a time to catch up with

---

BOX 21.5 **THE RATIONAL EXPECTATIONS REVOLUTION**

Trying to 'unfool' the economics profession

The rational expectations revolution swept through the economics profession in the 1970s in a way that no other set of ideas had done since Keynes. Although largely associated with the free-market, non-interventionist wing of economics, the rational expectations revolution has been far more wide-reaching. Even economists implacably opposed to the free market have nevertheless incorporated rational expectations into their models.

The rational expectations revolution is founded on a very simple idea. People base their expectations of the future on the information they have available. They don't just look at the past, they also look at current information, including what the government is saying and doing and what various commentators have to say.

The new classical economists use rational expectations in the following context. If the *long-run* Phillips curve is vertical, so that an expansionary policy will in the end merely lead to inflation, it will be difficult for the government to fool people that this will not happen. If employers, unions, city financiers, economic advisers, journalists, etc. all expect this to happen, then it will: and it will happen in the *short run*. Why should firms produce more in response to a rise in demand if their costs are going to rise by just as much? Why should higher wages attract workers to move jobs, if wages everywhere are going up? Why should firms and unions not seek price and wage rises fully in line with the expected inflation?

But can the government not surprise people? The point here is that 'surprising' people really only means 'fooling'

them – making them believe that an expansionary policy really *will* reduce unemployment. But why should the public be fooled? Why should people believe smooth-talking government ministers rather than the whole host of critics of the government, from the opposition, to economic commentators, to the next-door neighbour?

The rational expectations school revised the old saying 'You can't fool all the people all the time' to 'You can hardly fool the people at all'. And if that is so, argue the new classical economists, unemployment can only momentarily be brought below its natural level.

Two of the most famous rational expectations economists are Robert Lucas and Thomas Sargent. Robert Lucas, like Milton Friedman and many other famous conservative economists, has his academic base in the University of Chicago, where he has been a professor since 1974. In 1995, like Milton Friedman in 1976, Lucas was awarded the Nobel prize in economics. Tom Sargent is professor of Economics at New York University and senior fellow at the Hoover Institution of Stanford University.

In recent years, they have gone beyond the simple context of the new classical world of perfect markets with instant market clearing, and have considered the role of rational expectations when markets are distorted. In this context, government policy *can* be effective. For example, supply-side policies can be directed to removing market distortions.

---

changes in aggregate demand. Thus, for a short time, a rise in aggregate demand will raise output and employment above the natural level, while prices and wages are still relatively low.

The new classical analysis is based on **rational expectations**. Rational expectations are not based on past rates of inflation. Instead they are based on the current state of the economy and the current policies being pursued by the government. Workers and firms look at the information available to them – at the various forecasts that are published, at various economic indicators and the assessments of them by various commentators, at government pronouncements, and so on. From this information they predict

the rate of inflation as well as they can. It is in this sense that the expectations are 'rational': people use their reason to assess the future on the basis of current information.

But forecasters frequently get it wrong, and so do economic commentators! And the government does not always do what it says it will. Thus workers and firms base their expectations on *imperfect information*. Other versions assume that they may make very poor use of information. But either way, people frequently forecast incorrectly. The crucial point about the rational expectations theory, however, is that these errors in prediction are *random*. People's predictions of inflation are just as likely to be too high as too low.[1]

TC 9 p105

Definition

Rational expectations Expectations based on the *current* situation. These expectations are based on the information people have to hand. While this information may be imperfect and therefore people will make errors, these errors will be random.

---

[1] The rational expectations hypothesis can be stated as:

$$\pi_t = \pi_t^e + \epsilon_t \left(\sum_{t=1}^{t=\infty} \right) (\epsilon = 0)$$

In other words, the rate of inflation for any time period (π_t) will be the rate that people expected in that time period (π_t^e) plus an error term (ϵ_t). This error term may be quite large but is equally likely to be positive or negative. Thus when you sum (Σ) the error terms over the years (strictly speaking, to infinity), the positive and negative values will cancel each other out and the sum will therefore be zero.

Figure 21.17 The effects of an increase in aggregate demand

(a) Adaptive expectations

(b) Ratinal expectations

Aggregate supply and the Phillips curve when expectations are correct

If people are correct in their expectations, and if the long-run aggregate supply and Phillips curves are vertical, so too will be the short-run curves. In the *adaptive* expectations model, the short-run *AS* curve is upward sloping (and the short-run Phillips curve downward sloping) only because expectations lag behind any changes in aggregate demand. Once expectations have adapted, the effect is felt purely in terms of price changes. Output and employment stay at the natural level in the long run.

In the new classical (rational expectations) model, there is *no* lag in expectations. If their information is correct, people will rationally predict that output and employment will stay at the natural level. They predict that any change in *nominal* aggregate demand will be reflected purely in terms of changes in prices, and that real aggregate demand will remain the same. If real aggregate demand remains the same, so will the demand for and supply of labour and the demand for and supply of goods. Thus, even in the *short* run, output and employment will stay at the natural level.

Let us see how the adaptive expectations and the rational expectations models analyse the effects of an increase in aggregate demand. Figure 21.17 uses simple aggregate demand and supply curves. Figure 21.17(a) gives the adaptive expectations analysis. Figure 21.17(b) gives the rational expectations analysis.

In both diagrams, there is an initial equilibrium at point *a*. This is a long-run equilibrium, where aggregate demand (AD_1) equals long-run aggregate supply ($LRAS$). Price is stable and is at the level of P_1. The short-run supply curve with P_1 as the *expected* price level is given by $SRAS_1$. Note that this is upward sloping in *both* diagrams because it shows how much will be supplied *if* (and only if) people expect price to remain at P_1.

Now assume that the government raises aggregate demand to AD_2. What will happen to prices and output?

In Figure 21.17(a), people base their expectations of prices on the past. In other words, at first they expect the price level to stay at P_1. The economy thus moves to point *b*, where $AD_2 = SRAS_1$. Output rises to Q_2 and the price level rises to P_2. Then over time, as price expectations rise, the short-run aggregate supply curve shifts upwards, eventually reaching $SRAS_2$. Long-run equilibrium is thus at point *c*, where $AD_2 = LRAS$. In the short run, therefore, if the government expands aggregate demand, there will be a rise in output and employment. It is only in the long run that the effect is confined to higher prices. The actual length of time it takes to reach point *c* will depend on how quickly expectations adjust upwards.

In Figure 21.17(b), people correctly anticipate the full price effects of any increase in aggregate demand. The short-run aggregate supply curve based on a particular price (e.g. $SRAS_1$ based on a price level P_1) cannot be moved along. The moment aggregate demand shifts to the right, people will correctly anticipate a rise in the price level. Thus the moment the economy begins to move up along $SRAS_1$ from point *a*, the whole $SRAS$ curve will shift upwards. As a result, the economy moves *directly* to point *c*. Thus the *actual* short-run supply curve is vertical and, assuming expectations are correct, will be identical to the long-run 'curve'.

> ? Show these effects of an increase in aggregate demand from both the adaptive expectations and rational expectations points of view, only this time show the effects on Phillips curves.

Aggregate supply and the Phillips curve when expectations are incorrect

Although over the years people's expectations are assumed to be correct on average, it is more than likely that in any one year they will be wrong. What implication does this have for output and employment?

| BOX 21.6 | FORECASTING THE WEATHER | CASE STUDIES AND APPLICATIONS |

An example of rational expectations

'What's the weather going to be like tomorrow?' If you are thinking of having a picnic, you will want to know the answer before deciding.

So what do you do? You could base your assessment on past information. Yesterday was fine; so was the previous day. Today is glorious. So, you think to yourself, it's a good bet that tomorrow will be fine too. If, on the other hand, the weather has been very changeable recently, you may feel that it's wiser not to take the risk. These 'forecasts' are examples of *adaptive* expectations: your forecasts are based on the actual weather over the last few days.

But would you really base such a crucial decision as to whether or not to have a picnic on something so unreliable? Wouldn't you rather take on board more information to help you make up your mind?

The first thing that might come to mind is the old saying that a British summer is three fine days and a thunderstorm. We've just had the three fine days, you think to yourself, so perhaps we'd better stay at home tomorrow.

Or, being a bit more scientific about it, you turn on the weather forecast. Seeing loads of sunshine symbols all over the map, you decide to take a chance.

Basing your expectations in this way on current information (including even seeing whether there is a red sky that night) is an example of *rational* expectations.

So you go on your picnic and, guess what, it rains! 'I bet if we had decided to stay at home, it would have been fine', you grumble, as you eat your soggy sandwiches.

What you are acknowledging is that your decision was made on *imperfect* information. But the decision was still rational. It was still the best decision you could have made on the information available to you.

Weather forecasters make mistakes. But they are just as likely to get it wrong in predicting a sunny day as in predicting a wet day. It is still rational to base your decisions on their forecasts provided they are reasonably accurate.

 Under what circumstances might weather forecasters have a tendency to err on the side of pessimism or optimism? If you knew this tendency, how would this affect your decisions about picnics, hanging out the washing or watering the garden?

The goods market

Assume that aggregate demand increases but that firms *under*predict the resulting rate of inflation: $\pi^e < \pi$. Firms do not realise that the increased expenditure on their product will be offset by an increase in costs. As a result, as profit maximisers, they decide to produce more. Thus if the government catches people unawares and unexpectedly boosts demand, then output will rise as firms, underpredicting the rate of inflation, believe that *real* demand has risen.

But in a rational expectations framework, this is just luck on the government's side. Firms might just as well have thought the government would give an even bigger boost to aggregate demand than it actually did. In this case, firms would have *over*predicted the rate of inflation, and as a result would have cut their output, believing that real demand had fallen. (A graphical analysis of these arguments is given in Case Study 21.3 in MyEconLab.)

The labour market

Let us assume that the government raises aggregate demand more than people expect, so that people underpredict the rate of inflation: $\pi^e < \pi$.

This means that workers will believe that they are getting a higher real wage (W/P) than they really are: $(W/P)^e > W/P$. They will supply more labour. In Figure 21.18, the labour supply curve shifts from AS_{L_1} to AS_{L_2}. Employment rises above the natural level Q_1 (where expectations are correct), to Q_2. If only labour (and not firms) underpredict the rate

Figure 21.18 Effects in the labour market of an underprediction of inflation

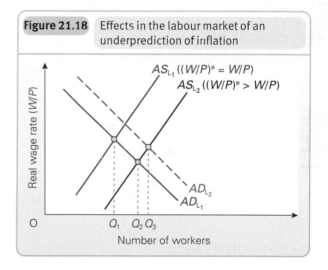

of inflation, this rise in employment to Q_2 is the only short-run effect.

If, however, firms underpredict the rate of inflation too, the effect on employment will be more complicated. On the one level, as explained above, firms will want to produce more, and thus the demand for labour will tend to increase. For example, it might shift to AD_{L_2} in Figure 21.18, and thus employment would rise to Q_3. On the other hand, given that they are underpredicting the rate of inflation, they will believe that any given level of money

Figure 21.19   Short-run Phillips curves

wages (W) represents a higher level of *real* wages $(W/P)^e$ than it really does (W/P). They will tend, therefore, to employ fewer people at each wage rate, and the demand curve will shift to the left. Thus, depending on which way the demand curve shifts, firms could employ more or less labour than Q_2.

If people *over*predict the rate of inflation, employment will fall as workers believe that their real wage is lower than it really is and therefore work less; and output may well fall as firms believe their product's relative price has fallen.

Thus output and employment can vary from their natural level when people make errors in their predictions of inflation. But the short-run *AS* and Phillips curves will still be vertical because these errors are random. Errors in prediction simply shift the curves. This is shown in Figure 21.19. Underprediction of inflation shifts the short-run Phillips curve to the left (and the *AS* curve to the right) as unemployment temporarily falls below the natural level (and output rises above its natural level). Overprediction of inflation shifts the Phillips curve to the right (and the *AS* curve to the left). The average position for the short-run Phillips curve will be at U_n.

 Should the government therefore simply give up as far as curing unemployment is concerned? (For the answer, see below.)

Policy implications

If the new classical analysis is correct, anticipated changes in aggregate demand will have no effect on output and employment. *Un*anticipated changes in aggregate demand will have some effect, but only for as long as it takes people to realise their mistake and for their wages and prices to be corrected. Given rational expectations, people can be fooled in this way only by luck. There is no way that a government can *systematically* use demand management policy to keep output and employment above the natural level.

The new classical economists therefore totally reject Keynesian demand management policy, even in the short

run. Monetary policy should be used to control inflation, but neither fiscal nor monetary policy can be used to increase output and employment. Similarly, there is no fear of a deflationary monetary policy reducing output and employment and leading to a recession. The reduction in aggregate demand will simply lead to lower inflation. Output and unemployment will remain at the natural level.

Thus for new classicists, the problems of inflation and unemployment are totally separate. Inflation is caused by excessive growth in the money supply and should be controlled by monetary policy. Unemployment will be at the natural rate and should be reduced by supply-side policies designed to increase the incentives to work.

To prevent unanticipated changes in aggregate demand and thus to prevent unemployment deviating from its natural level, new classical economists advocate the announcement of clear monetary rules and then sticking to them.

 1. *If the government announced that it would, come what may, reduce the growth of money supply to zero next year, what (according to new classical economists) would happen? How might their answer be criticised?*
2. *For what reasons would a new classical economist support the policy of the Bank of England publishing its inflation forecasts and the minutes of the deliberations of the Monetary Policy Committee?*

Real business cycles

If unemployment and output fluctuate only *randomly* from the natural level, and then only in the short run, how can the new classical economists explain booms and recessions? How can they explain the business cycle?

Their answer, unlike that of Keynesians, lies not in fluctuations in aggregate demand, but rather in shifts in aggregate *supply*. In a recession, the vertical short- and long-run aggregate supply curves will shift to the left (output falls) and the vertical short- and long-run Phillips curves will shift to the right (unemployment rises). The reverse happens in a boom. Since the new classical theory of cyclical fluctuations focuses on supply, it is known as *real business cycle theory*.

But what makes aggregate supply shift in the first place, and why, after an initial shift, will the aggregate supply curve *go on* shifting, causing a recession or boom to continue?

The initial shift in aggregate supply could come from a structural change: say, a shift in demand from older manufacturing industries to new service industries. Because of

KI 16
p124

> ### Definition
>
> **Real business cycle theory**   The new classical theory which explains cyclical fluctuations in terms of shifts in aggregate supply, rather than aggregate demand.

BOX 21.7   **THE BOY WHO CRIED 'WOLF'**   CASE STUDIES AND APPLICATIONS

A government had better mean what it says

Do you remember the parable of the boy who cried 'Wolf!'?

There was once this little village on the edge of the forest. The villagers used to keep chickens, but, when no one was around, wolves would come out of the forest and carry off the chickens. So one of the boys in the village was given the job of keeping a lookout for wolves.

One day for a joke the boy called out 'Wolf, wolf! I see a wolf!' even though there was none. All the villagers came rushing out of their houses or back from the fields to catch the wolf. As you might expect, they were very angry to find that it was a false alarm.

The next day, thinking that this was great fun, the boy played the same trick again. Everyone came rushing out, and they were even more angry to find that they had been fooled again. But the boy just grinned.

The next day, when everyone was away in the fields, a wolf stalked into the village. The boy, spotting the animal, cried out 'Wolf, wolf! I see a wolf!' But the people in the fields said to each other 'We're not going to be fooled this time. We've had enough of his practical jokes.' And so they carried on working. Meanwhile, back in the village, the wolf was killing all the chickens.

You can probably guess what the villagers said when they returned in the evening to find just a large pile of feathers.

A government says 'We will take tough action to bring the rate of inflation down to 2 per cent.' Now of course this might be a 'joke' in the sense that the government doesn't really expect to succeed or even seriously to try, but is merely attempting to persuade unions to curb their wage demands. But if unions *believe* in both the government's intentions and its ability to succeed, the 'joke' may pay off. Some unions may well moderate their pay demands.

But some may not. What is more, the government may decide to give tax cuts to boost its popularity and stimulate growth, knowing that union pay demands are generally quite moderate. As a result, inflation soars.

But can the government get away with it a second or third time? It's like the boy who cried 'Wolf!' After a time, people will simply not believe the government. If they see the government boosting aggregate demand, they will say to themselves, 'Here comes inflation. We'd better demand higher wages to compensate.'

 Does this parable support the adaptive or the rational expectations hypothesis?

---

the immobility of labour, not all those laid off in the older industries will find work in the new industries. Structural unemployment (part of equilibrium unemployment) rises and output falls.

Alternatively, the initial shift in aggregate supply could come from a change in technology. For example, a technological breakthrough in telecommunications could shift aggregate supply to the right. Or it could come from an oil price increase, shifting aggregate supply to the left.

The persistence of supply-side effects

But why, when a shift occurs, does the effect persist? Why is there not a single rise or fall in aggregate supply? There are two main reasons. The first is that several changes may take months to complete. For example, a decline in demand for certain older industries, perhaps caused by growing competition from abroad, does not take place overnight. Likewise, a technological breakthrough does not affect all industries simultaneously.

The second reason is that these changes affect the profitability of investment. If investment rises, this will increase firms' capacity and aggregate supply will shift to the right. If investment falls (as a result, say, of the election of a government less sympathetic to industry), aggregate supply will shift to the left. In other words, investment is

causing changes in output not through its effect on aggregate *demand* (through the multiplier), but rather through its effect on aggregate *supply*.

Turning points

So far we have seen how the theory of real business cycles explains persistent rises or falls in aggregate supply. But how does it explain *turning points*? Why do recessions and booms come to an end? The most likely explanation is that once a shock has worked its way through, aggregate supply will stop shifting. If there is then any shock in the other direction, aggregate supply will start moving back again. For example, after a period of recession, an eventual rise in business confidence will cause investment to rise and hence aggregate supply to shift back to the right. Since these 'reverse shocks' are likely to occur at irregular intervals, they can help to explain why real-world business cycles are themselves irregular.

 Assume that there are two shocks. The first causes aggregate supply to shift to the left. The second, occurring several months later, has the opposite effect on aggregate supply. Show that if both these effects persist for some time, but gradually fade away, the economy will experience a recession that will bottom out and be followed in smooth succession by a recovery.

Section summary

1. The new classical theory assumes flexible prices and wages in the short run as well as in the long run. It also assumes that people base their expectations of inflation on a rational assessment of the *current* situation.

2. People may predict wrongly, but they are equally likely to underpredict or to overpredict. On average, over the years, they will predict correctly.

3. The rational expectations theory implies that not only the long-run but also the short-run *AS* and Phillips curves will be vertical. If people correctly predict the rate of inflation, they will correctly predict that any increase in nominal aggregate demand will simply be reflected in higher prices. Total output and employment will remain the same: at the natural level.

4. If people underpredict the rate of inflation, they will believe that there has been a *real* increase in aggregate demand, and thus output and employment will increase. But they are just as likely to overpredict the rate of inflation, in which case they will believe that real aggregate demand has fallen. The result is that output and employment will fall.

5. When the government adopts fiscal and monetary policies, people will rationally predict their effects. Given that people's predictions are equally likely to err on either side, fiscal and monetary policies are useless as means of controlling output and employment.

6. With a vertical aggregate supply curve, cyclical fluctuations must arise from shifts in aggregate supply, not shifts in aggregate demand. Real business cycle theory thus focuses on aggregate supply shocks, which then persist for a period of time. Eventually their effect will peter out, and supply shocks in the other direction can lead to turning points in the cycle.

21.4 INFLATION AND UNEMPLOYMENT: THE MODERN KEYNESIAN POSITION

Keynesians in the 1950s and early 1960s looked to aggregate demand to explain inflation and unemployment. Their approach was typically that of the inflationary/deflationary gap model (see pages 492–4). Although they recognised the existence of some cost-push inflation and some equilibrium unemployment, these factors were seen as relatively constant. As a result, there was thought to be a relatively stable inverse relationship between inflation and unemployment, as depicted by the Phillips curve. Governments could trade off inflation against unemployment by manipulating aggregate demand.

Modern developments of the Keynesian model

Keynesians still see aggregate demand as playing the crucial role in determining the level of inflation, output and employment. They still argue that the free market works inefficiently: it frequently fails to clear; price signals are distorted by economic power; most wages and many prices are 'sticky'; and most important, the free market is unlikely to settle at full employment.

They still argue, therefore, that it is vital for governments to intervene actively to prevent either a slump in demand or an overexpansion of demand.

Nevertheless the Keynesian position has undergone some major modifications in recent years. This has been in response to apparent shifts in the Phillips curve and the inability of the traditional Keynesian model to explain it.

The breakdown of the Phillips curve in the 1970s and the growing problem of 'stagflation' (see pages 592–4) led many Keynesians to focus on cost-push causes of inflation. These causes included increased power and militancy of trade unions, a growing concentration of monopoly power in industry, and rising oil and other commodity prices. The effect was to push the short-run Phillips curve outwards.

Later, with a decline in industrial unrest in the 1990s and a growth of international competition keeping prices down, the Phillips curve apparently shifted inwards again. Keynesians attributed this partly to a *decline* in cost-push inflation. (These cost-push explanations are examined in Case Study 21.4 in MyEconLab.)

More recently, Keynesian analysis has incorporated three major modifications:

- An increased importance attached to equilibrium unemployment.
- A rationale for the persistence of demand-deficient unemployment.
- The incorporation of the theory of expectations: either adaptive or rational.

Changes in equilibrium unemployment

Changes in structural unemployment

Most Keynesians include growth in equilibrium unemployment (NAIRU) as part of the explanation of the apparent rightward shift in the Phillips curve in the 1970s and

1980s. In particular, Keynesians highlight the considerable structural rigidities that existed in the economy in a period of rapid industrial change. The changes include the following:

- Dramatic changes in technology. The microchip revolution, for example, made many traditional jobs obsolete.
- Competition from abroad. The introduction of new products from abroad, often of superior quality to domestic goods, or produced at lower costs, had led to the decline of many older industries: e.g. the textile industry.
- Shifts in demand away from the products of older labour-intensive industries to new 'high-tech' capital-intensive products.

Keynesians argue that the free market simply could not cope with these changes without a large rise in structural/technological unemployment. Labour was not sufficiently mobile – either geographically or occupationally – to move to areas where there were labour shortages or into jobs where there were skill shortages. A particular problem here was the lack of investment in education and training, with the result that the labour force was not sufficiently flexible to respond to changes in demand for labour.

> 1. What effect did these developments have on (a) the Phillips curve; (b) the aggregate supply curve?
> 2. What policy implications follow from these arguments?

In recent years, structural unemployment has fallen as labour markets have become more flexible and as various government supply-side policies have had effect (see Chapter 23).

Hysteresis

If a recession causes a rise in unemployment which is not then fully reversed when the economy recovers, there is a problem of hysteresis (see page 616).

The recessions of the early 1980s and early 1990s led to a growing number of people becoming both deskilled and demotivated. Many people in their forties and fifties who had lost their jobs were seen as too old by prospective employers. Many young people, unable to obtain jobs, became resigned to 'life on social security' or to doing no more than casual work. What is more, many firms, in an attempt to cut costs, cut down on training programmes. In these circumstances, a rise in aggregate demand would not simply enable the long-term unemployed to be employed again. The effect was a rightward shift in the Phillips curve: a rise in the NAIRU. To reverse this, argue Keynesians, the government should have embarked on a radical programme of retraining.

Recessions also cause a lack of investment. The reduction in their capital stock means that many firms cannot respond to a recovery in demand by making significant increases in output and taking on many more workers. Instead they are more likely to raise prices. Unemployment

may thus fall only modestly and yet inflation may rise substantially. The NAIRU increased: the Phillips curve shifted to the right.

With the growth of the economy continuous from 1993–2008, so gradually long-term unemployment fell as people left the labour market (e.g. through retirement) or retrained; long-term unemployment in the UK (those unemployed for more than a year) fell from 1.24 million in 1993 to 0.75 million by 1997 and to 0.28 million by 2004. The NAIRU decreased.

The persistence of demand-deficient unemployment

If there is demand-deficient unemployment, why will there not be a long-run fall in real wage rates so as to eliminate the surplus labour? Keynesians give two major explanations for the persistence of real wage rates above equilibrium.

- *Efficiency wages.* The argument here is that wage rates fulfil two functions. The first is the traditional one of balancing the demand and supply of labour. To this Keynesians add the function of motivating workers. If real wage rates are reduced when there is a surplus of labour (demand-deficient unemployment), then those workers already in employment may become dispirited and work less hard. If, on the other hand, firms keep wage rates up, then by maintaining a well-motivated workforce, by cutting down on labour turnover and by finding it easier to attract well-qualified labour, firms may find that their costs are reduced: a higher real wage rate is thus more profitable for them. The maximum-profit real wage rate (the *efficiency wage rate*: see pages 251–5) is likely to be above the market-clearing real wage rate. Demand-deficient unemployment is likely to persist.
- *Insider power.* If those still in employment (the insiders) are members of unions while those out of work (the outsiders) are not, or if the insiders have special skills or knowledge that give them bargaining power with employers while the outsiders have no influence, then there is no mechanism whereby the surplus labour – the outsiders – can drive down the real wage rate and eliminate the demand-deficient unemployment.

These two features help to explain why real wage rates did not fall during the recessions of the early 1980s and early 1990s.

The incorporation of expectations

Some Keynesians incorporate adaptive expectations into their models. Others incorporate rational expectations. Either way, their models differ from new classical models in two important respects:

- Prices and wages are not perfectly flexible. Markets are characterised by various rigidities.

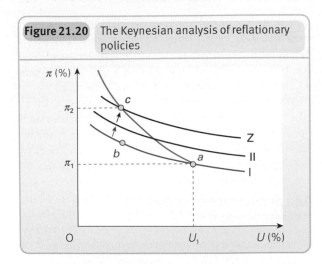

Figure 21.20 The Keynesian analysis of reflationary policies

- If U_1 includes a considerable number of long-term unemployed, then the expansion of demand may be *initially* inflationary, since many of the newly employed will require some retraining (a costly exercise). But as these newly employed workers become more productive, their lower labour costs may offset any further upward pressure on wages from the expansion of demand. At the same time, the higher investment may embody new, more productive, techniques that will also help to prevent further acceleration in costs. These factors occurred in the 1990s as the economy recovered from recession.

It is quite likely that these effects can prevent any further rises in inflation. Inflation can become stable at, say, π_2, with the economy operating at point *c*. The short-run Phillips curve settles at position Z. There is thus a long-run downward-sloping Phillips curve passing through points *a* and *c*.

 Would it in theory be possible for this long-run Phillips curve to be horizontal or even upward sloping over part of its length?

If expectations are formed rationally rather than adaptively, there will merely be a quicker movement to this long-run equilibrium. If people rationally predict that the effect of government policy will be to move the economy to point *c*, then their predictions will bring this about. All rational expectations do is to bring the long run about much sooner! The theory of rational expectations on its own does not provide support specifically for either the new classical or the Keynesian position.

The lesson here for governments, however expectations are formed, is that a sustained, but moderate, increase in aggregate demand can lead to a sustained growth in aggregate supply. What should be avoided is an excessive and unsustainable expansion of aggregate demand, as occurred in the late 1980s in the UK and in the late 1990s in the USA. This will lead to a boom, only to be followed by a 'bust' and a consequent recession.

- Expectations influence *output* and *employment* decisions, not just pricing decisions.

Price and wage rigidities are likely to be greater downwards than upwards. It is thus necessary to separate the analysis of a decrease in aggregate demand from that of an increase.

Expansion of aggregate demand

Unless the economy is at full employment or very close to it, Keynesians argue that an expansion of demand *will* lead to an increase in output and employment, even in the long run after expectations have fully adjusted.

In Figure 21.20, assume that the economy has a fairly high level of unemployment (U_1) but at the same time some cost inflation. Inflation is constant at π_1, with expectations of inflation at π_1 also. The economy is at point *a*.

Now assume that the economy begins to recover. Aggregate demand rises. As there is plenty of slack in the economy, output can rise and unemployment fall. The economy moves to point *b* on short-run Phillips curve I. The rise in inflation will feed through into expectations. The short-run Phillips curve will shift upwards. With adaptive expectations, it will initially shift up, say, to curve II.

But will the short-run Phillips curve not go on shifting upwards as long as there is any upward pressure on inflation? Keynesians reject this argument for two reasons:

- If there is a gradual but sustained expansion of aggregate demand, firms, seeing the economy expanding and seeing their orders growing, will start to invest more and make longer-term plans for expanding their labour force. People will generally *expect* a higher level of output, and this optimism will cause that higher level of output to be produced. In other words, expectations will affect output and employment as well as prices. The Phillips curve will shift downwards to the left, offsetting (partially, wholly or more than wholly) the upward shift from higher inflationary expectations.

Contraction of aggregate demand

Many Keynesians argue that the short-run Phillips curve is kinked at the current level of real aggregate demand. A reduction in real aggregate demand will have only a slight effect on inflation, since real wages are sticky downwards. Unions may well prefer to negotiate a reduction in employment levels, preferably by natural wastage (i.e. not replacing people when they leave), rather than accept a reduction in real wages. Thus in Figure 21.21, to the right of point *a*, the short-run Phillips curve is very shallow.

As long as this curve is not totally horizontal to the right of *a*, the introduction of expectations into the analysis will cause the short-run curve to shift downwards over time (if unemployment is kept above U_1) as people come to expect a lower rate of inflation.

Figure 21.21 The Keynesian analysis of deflationary policies

they are attempting to 'catch up' with other workers, then even if they rationally predict the correct amount by which inflation will fall, inflation will fall only slowly. People will rationally predict the *resistance* to wage restraint, and sure enough, therefore, inflation will fall only slowly.

The worst scenario is when the government, in its attempt to eliminate inflation, keeps unemployment high for a number of years. As the core of long-term unemployed workers grows, an increasing number of workers become deskilled and therefore effectively unemployable. The effective labour supply is reduced, and firms find there is no longer a surplus of employable labour *despite* high unemployment. A long-term equilibrium is reached at, say, point *e* with still substantial inflation. The *long*-run Phillips curve too may thus be relatively shallow to the right of point *a*.

With *adaptive* expectations, however, the curve could shift downwards very slowly indeed. If a movement from point *a* to point *d* represents only a 1 per cent reduction in inflation, and if it takes, say, two years for this to be fully reflected in expectations, then if unemployment is kept at U_2, inflation will reduce (i.e. the curve shift downwards) by only 0.5 per cent a year. This may be totally unacceptable politically if inflation is already at very high levels, and if U_2 is also very high.

Even with *rational* expectations the response may be too slow. If there is a resistance from unions to receiving increases in wages below the current rate of inflation, or if

The Keynesian criticism of non-intervention

Keynesians are therefore highly critical of the new classical conclusion that governments should not intervene other than to restrain the growth of money supply. High unemployment may persist for many years and become deeply entrenched in the economy if there is no deliberate government policy of creating a steady expansion of demand.

 Why is it important in the Keynesian analysis for there to be a steady expansion of demand?

Section summary

1. Modern Keynesians incorporate expectations into their analysis of inflation and unemployment. They also see an important role for cost-push factors and changes in equilibrium unemployment in explaining the position of the Phillips curve.

2. A growth in equilibrium unemployment in the 1970s and 1980s was caused by rapid changes in technology, greater competition from abroad and more rapid changes in demand patterns. It was also due to the persistence of unemployment beyond the recessions of the early 1980s and early 1990s, because of a deskilling of labour during the recessions (an example of hysteresis). The effect of increased equilibrium unemployment was to shift the Phillips curve to the right.

3. Demand-deficient unemployment may persist because real wage rates may be sticky downwards, even into the longer term. This stickiness may be the result of efficiency real wage rates being above market-clearing

real wage rates and/or outsiders not being able to influence wage bargains struck between employers and insiders.

4. If expectations are incorporated into Keynesian analysis, the Phillips curve will become steeper in the long run (and steeper in the short run too in the case of rational expectations). It will not become vertical, however, since people will expect changes in aggregate demand to affect output and employment as well as prices.

5. If people expect a more rapid rise in aggregate demand to be sustained, firms will invest more, thereby reducing unemployment in the long run and not just increasing the rate of inflation. The long-run Phillips curve will be downward sloping.

6. The short- and long-run Phillips curves may be kinked. Reductions in real aggregate demand may have only a slight effect on inflation if real wage rates are sticky downwards.

21.5 POSTSCRIPT: COMMON GROUND AMONG ECONOMISTS?

Whilst there is some disagreement among economists over the nature of the aggregate supply and Phillips curves, and hence over the effects of changes in aggregate demand, it is important not to get the impression that economists disagree over everything. There is, in fact, quite a lot of common ground among the majority of economists over the issues that we have examined in this chapter.

If you look back to pages 471–2, we identified several areas where there is a high measure of agreement among economists. Let us restate three of these areas in the light of the theories we have covered in this chapter.

In the short run, changes in aggregate demand will have a major effect on output and employment. With the exception of extreme new classical economists, who argue that markets clear instantly and that expectations are formed rationally, all other economists would accept that the short-run aggregate supply curve is upward sloping, albeit getting steeper as full-capacity output is approached. Similarly, they would argue that the short-run Phillips curve is downward sloping. There are two major implications of this analysis:

- Reductions in aggregate demand can cause reductions in output and increases in unemployment. In other words, too little spending will cause a recession.
- An expansion of aggregate demand by the government (whether achieved by fiscal or monetary policy, or both) will help to pull an economy out of a recession. There may be considerable time lags, however, before the economy responds fully to such expansionary policies.

In the long run, changes in aggregate demand will have much less effect on output and employment and much more effect on prices. As we have seen, new classical economists and others argue that both the long-run aggregate supply curve and the long-run Phillips curve are vertical. Most Keynesian economists, while arguing that these curves are not vertical, would still see them as less elastic than the short-run curves. Nevertheless, many Keynesians argue that changes in aggregate demand, if steady, *will* have substantial effects on long-term output and employment via changes in investment and hence in potential output (see Figure 21.5 on page 614).

Expectations have important effects on the economy. In fact, they are crucial in determining the success of government policy on unemployment and inflation. Whatever people expect to happen, their actions will tend to make it happen.

If people believe that an expansion of money supply will merely lead to inflation (the monetarist and new classical position), then it will. Firms and workers will adjust their prices and wage rates upwards. Firms will make no plans to expand output and will not take on any more labour. If, however, people believe that an expansion of demand will lead to higher output and employment (the Keynesian position), then, via the accelerator mechanism, it will.

Similarly, just how successful a deflationary policy is in curing inflation depends in large measure on people's expectations (but, as explained above, it also depends on the downward stickiness of real wages). If people believe that a deflationary policy will cause a recession, firms will stop investing and will cut their workforce. If they believe that it will cure inflation and restore firms' competitiveness abroad, firms may increase investment.

To manage the economy successfully, therefore, the government must convince people that its policies will work. This is as much a job of public relations as of pulling the right economic levers.

1. If constant criticism of governments in the media makes people highly cynical about any government's ability to manage the economy, what effect will this have on the performance of the economy?
2. Suppose that, as part of the national curriculum, everyone in the country had to study economics up to the age of 16. Suppose also that the reporting of economic events by the media became more thorough (and interesting!). What effects would these developments have on the government's ability to manage the economy? How would your answer differ if you were a Keynesian from if you were a new classicist?

The causes of longer-term growth. One other area where there is considerable agreement among economists concerns the causes of longer-term growth. Although demand-side policy may be important for ensuring that economies achieve their potential output, only by increasing that potential itself can growth be sustained. To achieve higher rates of economic growth over the long term, therefore, the government should focus on means of getting potential output to grow more rapidly, and this requires an appropriate supply-side policy.

Chapter 22 examines long-term growth and Chapter 23 discusses various types of supply-side policy open to governments.

END OF CHAPTER QUESTIONS

1. Assume that inflation depends on two things: the level of aggregate demand, indicated by the inverse of unemployment $(1/U)$, and the expected rate of inflation (π_t^e). Assume that the rate of inflation (π_t) is given by the equation

   $$\pi_t = (48/U - 6) + \pi_t^e$$

   Assume initially (year 0) that the actual and expected rate of inflation is zero.

   (a) What is the current (natural) rate of unemployment?

   (b) Now assume in year 1 that the government wishes to reduce unemployment to 4 per cent and continues to expand aggregate demand by as much as is necessary to achieve this. Fill in the rows for years 0 to 4 in the following table. It is assumed for simplicity that the expected rate of inflation in a given year (π_t^e) is equal to the actual rate of inflation in the previous year (π_{t-1}).

Year	U	$48/U - 6$	+	π^e	=	π
0	...	...	+	...	=	...
1	...	...	+	...	=	...
2	...	...	+	...	=	...
3	...	...	+	...	=	...
4	...	...	+	...	=	...
5	...	...	+	...	=	...
6	...	...	+	...	=	...
7	...	...	+	...	=	...

   (c) Now assume in year 5 that the government, worried about rising inflation, reduces aggregate demand sufficiently to reduce inflation by 3 per cent in that year. What must the rate of unemployment be raised to in that year?

   (d) Assuming that unemployment stays at this high level, continue the table for years 5 to 7.

2. For what reasons might the long-run aggregate supply curve be (a) vertical; (b) upward sloping; (c) downward sloping?

3. How would you attempt to assess whether a particular period of inflation was the result of cost-push or demand-pull pressures?

4. What is the difference between adaptive expectations and rational expectations?

5. How can adaptive expectations of inflation result in clockwise Phillips loops? Why would these loops not be completely regular?

6. What implications would a vertical short-run aggregate supply curve have for the effects of demand management policy?

7. For what reasons may the NAIRU increase?

8. Given the Keynesian explanation for the persistence of high levels of unemployment after the recessions of the early 1980s and early 1990s, what policies would you advocate to reduce unemployment in the years following a recession?

Online resources

Additional case studies in MyEconLab

21.1 **Explaining the shape of the short-run Phillips curve.** This shows how money illusion on the part of workers can explain why the Phillips curve is downward sloping.

21.2 **The quantity theory of money restated.** An examination of how the vertical long-run *AS* curve in the adaptive expectations model can be used to justify the quantity theory of money.

21.3 **Getting predictions wrong.** How incorrect predictions can lead to a rise or fall in output in the new classical model.

21.4 **Cost-push factors in Keynesian analysis.** How Keynesians incorporated cost-push inflation into their analysis of shifts in the Phillips curve.

Websites relevant to this chapter

See sites listed at the end of Chapter 23 on page 668.

Long-term Economic Growth

CHAPTER MAP

**22.1 Long-run economic growth in
industrialised countries** **639**
Growth over the decades 639
Comparing the growth performance of different
countries 640
The causes of economic growth 641

**22.2 Economic growth without
technological progress** **642**
Capital accumulation 642
A model of economic growth 642
An optimum rate of saving? 643
An increase in the workforce 644

**22.3 Economic growth with technological
progress** **645**
The effect of technological progress in output 645
Endogenous growth theory 648

In this chapter we turn our attention to the determinants of long-run economic growth. All developed countries have experienced economic growth over the past sixty years, but rates have differed significantly from one country to another. We look at some of these differences in section 22.1.

If an economy is to achieve sustained economic growth over the longer term, there must be a sustained increase in potential output. This means that there has to be a continuous rightward shift in aggregate supply.

The main ingredient in long-term economic growth is a growth in labour productivity. This, in turn, depends on two major factors: a growth in the amount of capital that workers use, and technological progress. We can see these two elements if we look around us. Take a modern car factory, with its high-tech robot-driven equipment: it is no surprise that workers' productivity is much higher than it was, say, thirty years ago. Take a modern office, with powerful computers: again it is no surprise that today's office staff are much more productive than their counterparts of years gone past.

In section 22.2 we look at the effects of an increase in the rate of capital investment when there is no change in technology. As we shall see, the effect will simply be growth to a new higher level of national income, not a permanently higher rate of economic growth.

If economic growth is to be higher over the long term, therefore, there must be an increase in the rate of technological progress. We look at how this affects economic growth in section 22.3. We also examine what determines the rate of invention, technological development and the use of new technology. It is important to understand this if the government is to develop appropriate supply-side policies – the subject of Chapter 23.

22.1 LONG-RUN ECONOMIC GROWTH IN INDUSTRIALISED COUNTRIES

Quite naturally, governments and individuals are concerned with the ups and downs of the business cycle. How does this year's economic performance compare with last year's? Are the various macroeconomic indicators such as growth, unemployment and inflation getting better or worse?

When we step back, however, and look at the longer span of history, these short-term fluctuations take on less significance. What we see is that economies tend to experience long-term economic growth, not long-term economic decline. Measured in terms of income per head (after adjusting for inflation), all developed nations are considerably richer today than they were fifty years ago.

The picture, however, is not one of universal improvement. People are not necessarily happier; there are many stresses in modern living; the environment is in many respects more polluted; inequality has increased in most countries, especially over the past twenty years; for many people work is more demanding and the working day is longer than in the past; there is more crime and more insecurity. If you look back to Boxes 14.6 and 14.7, you will see that 'more' is not always 'better'.

Nevertheless, most people *want* more consumer goods; they want higher incomes. In this chapter, we examine what causes long-term economic growth, and how it can be

increased. We leave you to judge whether a materially richer society is a better society.

Growth over the decades

Most developed countries experienced recessions in the early 1980s, the early 1990s and the early and late 2000s. Some experienced a minor recession in the mid 1970s. But these periods have been the exception. For the rest of the time since 1950, most countries have experienced sustained economic growth. Figure 22.1 shows UK GDP from 1950 to 2009. As you can see, the fluctuations in output appear minor compared with the long-term growth in output.

Such growth cannot be explained by a closing of the gap between actual and potential output: by an expansion of aggregate demand leading to a fuller use of resources. Instead, the explanation lies on the supply side. Countries' economic *capacity* has increased. There has been a growth in the average output per worker. Table 22.1 shows the average annual growth in output per employed person for several developed countries for the four decades from 1961 to 2010. The effect of an average annual growth in output of just 2 or 3 per cent builds up over the years to a substantial rise in output. Table 22.2 shows how many

KI 2
p8

| **Figure 22.1** | UK GDP at market prices (2003 = 100) |

Note: Years 2009 and 2010 based on forecasts.
Source: From Times Series Data (National Statistics, various years).

Table 22.1	Average annual percentage growth rate in GDP per person employed					
	1961–70	**1971–80**	**1981–90**	**1991–2000**	**2001–10**[b]	**1961–2010**[b]
France	4.9	2.8	2.2	1.8	0.8	2.5
Germany[a]	4.2	2.6	1.3	2.5	1.2	2.4
Ireland	4.2	3.7	3.8	3.3	1.7	3.3
Italy	6.2	2.8	2.2	1.6	0.0	2.6
Japan	8.6	3.7	3.0	1.1	1.5	3.6
Netherlands	3.8	2.7	1.6	1.5	1.1	2.1
Spain	6.7	4.2	1.9	1.1	0.8	2.9
UK	2.5	1.7	1.9	2.2	1.3	1.9
USA	2.3	1.2	1.3	1.7	1.5	1.6

[a] Up to 1991, figures are for West Germany only.
[b] Years 2009 and 2010 figures are forecast.
Source: Based on data in *Statistical Annex of the European Economy* (Commission of the European Communities).

Table 22.2	Output per person employed in 2009 relative to that in 1961
	Output per head in 2009/ output per head in 1961
France	3.2
Germany[a]	3.0
Ireland	4.8
Italy	3.5
Japan	5.3
Netherlands	2.8
Spain	4.0
UK	2.5
USA	2.1

[a] Up to 1991, West Germany only.
Source: Based on data in *Statistical Annex of the European Economy* (Commission of the European Communities).

Table 22.3	Average annual growth rate 2001–9 at constant prices: total and per capita	
	Economic growth	**Economic growth per capita**
Australia	3.2	1.9
Brazil	3.5	2.1
China	9.9	9.3
France	1.6	1.0
Germany	1.2	1.2
India	7.5	5.8
Ireland	4.7	3.0
Italy	0.9	0.5
Japan	1.6	1.5
Malaysia	5.1	3.2
Netherlands	1.8	1.2
Russia	6.6	7.1
Spain	3.1	1.5
UK	2.4	2.0
USA	2.0	1.0

Source: Author's calculations based on data in *World Economic Outlook* (International Monetary Fund [IMF], 2008).

times greater output per person employed in 2009 was compared with that in 1961.

Comparing the growth performance of different countries

As you can see from these two tables, there has been a considerable difference in the rates of growth experienced by the different countries. Japan, Italy, France and West Germany had much higher rates of growth than the UK and USA in the earlier part of the period, but then they experienced a slowdown in growth rates in the later periods. Ireland has had generally high rates of growth throughout. The UK and USA, while experiencing a slowdown in growth in the 1970s, have since experienced faster growth.

If economic growth is to give an indication of an increase in living standards, it has to be measured per head of the population. Table 22.3 shows average annual growth rates from 2001 to 2009, both overall and per capita, for a range of countries. Australia and Spain had faster absolute growth rates than the UK, but after taking into account their more rapid increase in populations, they experienced a lower per capita growth rate. Japan, despite its low absolute rate of growth, had a higher per capita rate of growth

than the USA. Russia, with a decline in its population, experienced higher growth per capita than India.

In general, the richer developed countries have grown at a slower rate than the less rich ones. The result has been a narrowing of the gap. For example, in 1950, GDP per head in the USA (in purchasing-power standard terms) was 2.5 times that in West Germany and 20 times that in Japan. By 2009, GDP per head in the USA was only 4 per cent higher than that in Germany and 20 per cent higher than that in Japan.

This *convergence in GDP per head*, however, has not been universal across the world. Although China, India and various other Asian countries have grown very rapidly, some of

Definition

Convergence in GDP per head The tendency for less rich developed countries to catch up with richer ones. Convergence does not apply to many of the poorer developing countries, however; the gap between them and richer countries has tended to widen.

the poorest developing countries, and especially those in sub-Saharan Africa, have grown at pitifully slow rates, and in some cases GDP per head has declined. We examine the causes of low growth in developing countries in Chapter 27.

Although recent generations have come to expect economic growth, it is a relatively new phenomenon. For most of the last two thousand years, countries have experienced virtually static output per head over the long term. Economic growth has become significant only once countries have undergone an industrial revolution, and it is only with the technological advances of the twentieth and now the twenty-first centuries that long-term growth rates of 2 per cent or more have been achieved.

The causes of economic growth

The sources of economic growth can be grouped into two broad categories:

- An increase in the *quantity* of factors. Here we would include an increase in the workforce or the average number of hours that people work, an increase in raw materials (e.g. discoveries of oil) and an increase in capital. Of these, for most countries, it is an increase in the capital stock, brought about by investment, that is the most important source of growth. The amount of capital per worker – the capital/labour ratio (K/L) – has increased over time and has resulted in a greater output per worker (Y/L).

- An increase in the *productivity* of factors. Here we would include an increase in the skills of workers, a more efficient organisation of inputs by management and more productive capital equipment. Most significant here is technological progress. Developments of computer technology, of new techniques in engineering, of lighter, stronger and cheaper materials, of digital technology in communications and of more efficient motors have all contributed to a massive increase in the productivity of capital. Machines today can produce much more output than machines in the past that cost the same to manufacture.

In the next two sections, we will examine these two sources of growth and focus first on capital accumulation (an increase in the *quantity* of capital) and then on technological progress (an increase in the *productivity* of factors).

---

*LOOKING AT THE MATHS

Since 1961, the UK economy has grown on average by 2.4 per cent per annum. This means that it has doubled in size roughly every 29 years. Over the same period, the Irish economy has grown by an average of 4.9 per cent per annum. As a result, its economy has doubled in size roughly every 14.5 years.

But how do we work out these numbers of years? To do this we use logarithms. To find the number of years, n, that it takes an economy to grow by a factor x (e.g. 2 in the case of a doubling), we divide the log of x by the log of the factor by which the economy is growing each year, g (so $g = 1.024$ for 2.4% and $g = 1.049$ for 4.9%):

$$n = \frac{\log x}{\log g}$$

We can use our calculators to find the logs. Thus, in the case of the UK:

$$n = \frac{\log x}{\log g} = \frac{\log 2}{\log 1.024} = \frac{0.301030}{0.010300} = 29.2$$

and in the case of Ireland:

$$n = \frac{\log x}{\log g} = \frac{\log 2}{\log 1.049} = \frac{0.301030}{0.020775} = 14.5$$

In practice, these figures are only approximate as the two countries' growth rates varied from year to year.

 How long would it take an economy, like China, growing at an annual rate of 10 per cent to (a) double in size; (b) triple in size?

Section summary

1. The determinants of economic growth in the long run lie primarily on the supply side.

2. Most developed countries have experienced average annual rates of economic growth of 2 per cent or more over the last fifty years, but there have been considerable differences between countries.

3. The income gap between developed countries has tended to narrow as the less rich ones have grown faster than the richer ones. Some of the poorest countries of the world, however, have experienced very low rates of growth, with the result that the gap between them and richer countries has widened.

4. The determinants of economic growth can be put into two broad categories: an increase in the quantity of factors and an increase in the productivity of factors.

22.2 ECONOMIC GROWTH WITHOUT TECHNOLOGICAL PROGRESS

Capital accumulation

An increase in capital per worker will generally increase output. In other words, the more equipment that is used by people at work, the more they are likely to produce. But to increase capital requires investment, and that investment requires resources – resources that could have been used for producing consumer goods. Thus more investment means diverting resources away from producing finished goods into producing machines, buildings and other capital equipment. This is the opportunity cost of investment.

If we take a simple circular flow of income model, with saving as the only withdrawal and investment as the only injection, then saving will be equal to investment ($S = I$). An increase in saving, therefore, will enable more investment and more output for the future. Thus sacrifices today, in terms of more saving and less consumption, will mean more output and hence possibly more consumption for the future.

A model of economic growth

In Chapter 14, we looked at a simple growth model (see pages 403–4). This stated that growth depends on the proportion of a rise in income that is saved and hence invested (i) and the marginal efficiency of capital (MEC):

$$g = i \times MEC$$

Thus if 15 per cent of national income is saved and invested ($i = 15\%$) and if a 1 per cent increase in the capital stock ($\Delta K = I$) leads to a $^1/_3$ per cent increase in annual output ($MEC = ^1/_3$), then the rate of growth will be 5 per cent. For example, if national income is £100 billion, £15 billion will be invested ($i = 15\%$), and this will yield extra annual output of £5 billion ($MEC = ^1/_3$). Thus national income has grown by 5 per cent (from £100 billion to £105 billion).

What would be the rate of economic growth if 20 per cent of national income were saved and invested and the marginal efficiency of capital were $^2/_5$?

However, we need to make two qualifications to this simple model. The first is that the marginal efficiency of capital is likely to decline as the amount of capital per worker increases. This is because of diminishing returns to capital. The second is that a proportion of investment has to be used for replacing worn-out or obsolete equipment. The problem here is that, the larger the capital stock, the greater the proportion of investment that will be needed for replacement purposes, and the smaller the proportion that can be used for increasing the size of the capital stock.

Growth to a long-run equilibrium level of national income

Let us now incorporate these two qualifications into a model of growth. This is known as the neoclassical or 'Solow' growth model, after the MIT economics professor and Nobel Prize winner, Robert Solow. In this model, we are assuming for simplicity that the size of the workforce is constant. Any increase in the capital stock, therefore, means an increase in the average amount of capital per worker.

The model is illustrated in Figure 22.2. The size of the capital stock (K) is measured on the horizontal axis; the level of national output (Y) is measured on the vertical axis.

We start by looking at the effects of a growth in the capital stock on national output (i.e. on real national income (Y)). This is shown by the green output curve. As the capital stock increases, so output increases, but at a diminishing rate (the curve gets less and less steep). The reason for this is the law of diminishing returns: in this case, diminishing returns to capital. For example, if, in an office, you start equipping workers with computers, at first output will increase very rapidly. But as more and more workers have their own computer rather than having to share, so the rate of increase in output slows down. When everyone has their own, output is likely to be at a maximum. Any additional computers (of the same specification) will remain unused.

Increased output will mean increased saving and hence increased investment (the amount depending on the level of i). This is shown by the blue investment (I) curve. In this simple model, the vertical distance between the Y and I curves represents consumption ($C = Y - I$).

The magenta (D) line shows the amount of depreciation of capital that takes place, and hence the amount of replacement investment required. The bigger the capital stock, the larger the amount of replacement investment required.

Figure 22.2 Steady-state output

Assume initially that the size of the capital stock is K_0. This will generate an output of Y_0 (point a). This output, in turn, will generate saving and investment of I_0, but of this, D_0 will have to be used for replacement purposes. The difference $(b-c)$ will be available to increase the size of the capital stock. The capital stock will thus increase up to K_1 (point g). At this point, all investment will be required for replacement purposes. Output will therefore cease growing. Y_1 represents the **steady-state level of national income**.

Effect of an increase in the saving rate

In the simple model, $g = i \times MEC$, an increase in the saving rate will increase i and hence the growth rate (g). When we take into account diminishing returns to capital and depreciation, however, an increase in the saving rate will lead to only a temporary increase in output, and to no long-term *growth* at all!

Figure 22.3 Effect of an increase in the rate of saving and investment

---

*LOOKING AT THE MATHS

Steady-state equilibrium in the Solow growth model is achieved where investment (I) equals depreciation (D).

Investment is assumed to be a given fraction (s) of the level of national income Y, where national income is a function of the total capital stock (K): $Y = f(K)$. Thus

$$I = sY$$
$$= s \times f(K) \qquad (1)$$

Depreciation in the model is assumed to be a fixed proportion (d) of the capital stock (K). Thus

$$D = dK \qquad (2)$$

In steady-state equilibrium, given that $I = D$, from equations (1) and (2) we can write

$$s \times f(K) = dK$$

Thus

$$K = \frac{s \times f(K)}{d}$$

Thus if we know the production function ($Y = f(K)$), the saving rate (s) and the depreciation rate (d), we can solve for the steady-state equilibrium value of K and hence also for Y. Maths Case 22.1 in MyEconLab gives a worked example of this.

This is illustrated in Figure 22.3. If the saving rate increases, the investment curve will shift upwards. This is shown by a shift from I_1 to I_2. Investment is now above that which is necessary to maintain the capital stock at K_1. The capital stock will grow, therefore, and so will national income. But this growth is only temporary. Once the capital stock has risen to K_2, all the new higher level of investment will be absorbed in replacing capital ($I = D$ at point n). National income stops rising. Y_2 represents the new steady-state national income.

Does this mean, therefore, that there is no long-term gain from an increase in the saving rate? There *is* a gain, to

the extent that income per worker is now higher (remember that we are assuming a constant labour force), and this higher income will be received not just once, but every year from now on as long as the saving rate remains at the new higher level. There is no increase in the long-term *growth rate*, however. To achieve that, we would have to look to the other determinants of growth.

Human capital and education

The analysis of Figures 22.2 and 22.3 need not be confined to the stock of physical capital: machines, buildings, tools, etc. It can also apply to *human capital*. Human capital, as we saw in Chapter 9, refers to the skills and expertise of workers that have been acquired through education and training. If part of saving is used for investment in education and training, then the productivity of workers will rise, and so will output. In Figures 22.2 and 22.3, therefore, the horizontal axis measures both physical and human capital. An increase in either has the effect of increasing the steady-state level of national income.

 If there were a gradual increase in the saving rate over time, would this lead to sustained economic growth?

An optimum rate of saving?

If an increase in the saving rate does at least lead to a higher level of output, is there an *optimum* level of saving? Clearly we would need to define 'optimum'. One definition would be where *consumption* per head is maximised.

Definition

Steady-state level of national income The long-run equilibrium level of national income. The level at which all investment is used to maintain the existing capital stock at its current level.

Assuming a fixed population and a fixed workforce, higher saving will do two things. First, it will directly decrease consumption, since what is saved is not directly spent. Second, as we have seen, it will lead to higher output and hence higher income. So, with a higher saving rate, consumption will be a smaller proportion, but of a higher income. This implies that there will be some optimum saving rate at which consumption is maximised. This is illustrated in Figure 22.4.

If the saving rate is zero, the capital stock will be zero. Output and consumption will thus be zero (point *a*). As saving rises above zero, so the capital stock will grow, as will output and consumption. At the other extreme, if the saving rate were 100 per cent, although the capital stock would be high, all of the nation's income would go on maintaining that capital stock: there would be no consumption (point *b*). A saving rate somewhere between 0 and 100 per cent, therefore, will give the maximum consumption. In Figure 22.4, this is a rate of *s**, giving a level of consumption of *C** (point *m*). This is sometimes known as the *golden-rule saving rate*.

Evidence suggests that all countries have saving rates below the golden-rule level. Thus increases in saving rates would result in increases in consumption.

 If this is true, why do people not increase their rate of saving?

An increase in the workforce

An increase in the workforce, or in the number of hours worked by the existing workforce, will have the effect of shifting both the *Y* and *I* lines upwards in Figures 22.2 and 22.3. In other words, if a given amount of capital is used by more workers or for longer periods, output and hence saving and investment will increase. As more labour hours are used with any given amount of capital, diminishing returns to labour will set in. Output will grow, but at a diminishing rate. The marginal and average product of labour will fall (see Figure 5.1 on page 128). Thus although national output has risen (the new steady-state income is higher), the output per labour hour is less.

The effect on GDP per head of the population
If the rise in total hours worked is the result of an increased *participation rate* (i.e. a greater proportion of the population wishing to work) or of people working longer hours, then GDP per capita will be higher, even though output per hour worked will be lower. If, however, the increased hours

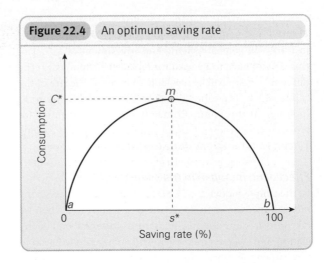

Figure 22.4 An optimum saving rate

worked are the result of an increased *population*, with no increase in the participation rate or number of hours worked per worker, then, because of diminishing returns to labour, output per head of the population will have gone down: GDP per capita will be lower.

 1. *If there were a higher participation rate and GDP per capita rose, would output per worker also have risen?*
2. *If people worked longer hours and, as a result, GDP per capita rose, how would you assess whether the country was 'better off'?*

If, however, there is an increase in both labour *and* capital, GDP per capita need not fall, even with the same number of hours worked per head. There are likely to be constant returns to scale. For example, if country A has double the population and double the capital stock of country B, its GDP is likely to be approximately double, and its GDP per head approximately the same.

What should be clear from the above analysis is that, without technological progress or some other means of increasing output from a given quantity of inputs, long-term growth cannot be sustained.

Definitions

Golden-rule saving rate The rate of saving that maximises the level of long-run consumption.

Participation rate The percentage of the working-age population that is part of the workforce.

KI 17 p125

Section summary

1. An increased saving rate will lead to higher investment and hence to an increase in the capital stock. This, in turn, will lead to a higher level of national income.

2. A larger capital stock, however, will require a higher level of replacement investment. Once this has risen to absorb all the extra investment, national income will stop rising: growth will cease. A steady-state level of national income has been achieved. An increased saving rate will therefore lead only to a rise in output, not to a long-term rise in the rate of growth.

3. An optimum rate of saving could be defined as one where consumption per head is maximised. This is sometimes known as the 'golden-rule saving rate'.

4. An increase in the workforce will lead to higher total output, but unless accompanied by an increase in the capital stock, it will generally lead to a reduction in output per worker.

22.3 ECONOMIC GROWTH WITH TECHNOLOGICAL PROGRESS

The effect of technological progress on output

Technological progress has the effect of increasing the output from a given amount of investment. This is shown in Figure 22.5. Initial investment and income curves are I_1 and Y_1; steady-state income is at a level of Y_1 (point f). A technological advance has the effect of shifting the Y line upwards, say to Y_2. The higher income curve leads to a higher investment curve (for a given *rate* of saving). This is shown by curve I_2. The new long-term equilibrium capital stock is thus K_2, and the new steady-state level of income is Y_2 (point p).

If there is a 'one-off' technological advance, the effect is the one we have just illustrated. Income rises to a higher level, but does not go on rising once the new steady-state level has been reached. But technological progress marches on over time. New inventions are made; new processes are discovered; old ones are improved. In terms of Figure 22.5, the Y curve *goes on* shifting upwards over time. The faster the rate of technological progress, the faster will the Y curve shift upwards and the higher will be the rate of eco-nomic growth. This is illustrated in Figure 22.6, which shows the increase in output over time. The faster the rate of technological progress, the higher the rate of growth of output.

Maths Case 22.2 in MyEconLab explores the algebra of technological progress.

The effect of an increase in the saving rate with a given rate of technological progress

Figure 22.7 shows the combined effects of an increased saving rate and continuing technological progress. The rate of technological progress gives the slope of the **steady-state growth path**. This is the growth path for any given saving rate. The saving rate determines the *position* (as opposed to

Definition

Steady-state growth path The growth path for a given saving rate (where growth results from technological progress).

Figure 22.5 Effect of a technological advance

Figure 22.6 Effect of technological progress on growth rates

| BOX 22.1 | PRODUCTIVITY AND ECONOMIC GROWTH |

The key to a better standard of living?

KI 16
p124

There are four common ways of measuring productivity. The first is output per worker. This is the most straightforward measure to calculate. All that is required is a measure of total output and employment. Chart (a) shows the UK lagging behind the USA and France and on a par with Germany.

The second measure is output per hour worked. This has the advantage that it is not influenced by the *number* of hours worked. So for an economy like the UK, with a very high percentage of part-time workers on the one hand, and long average hours worked by full-time employees on the other, such a measure would be more accurate in gauging worker efficiency. Here the UK lags behind all three countries. This is because of the high number of hours worked in the UK compared with France and Germany.

The third measure is output per person of working age. This is influenced by the employment rate. The higher the proportion of people of working age who are employed, the higher will this measure of productivity be. The UK performs better on this measure than France and Germany because of much higher unemployment in these two countries and a lower participation rate.

The first three measures focus solely on the productivity of labour. In order to account directly for the productivity of both labour *and* capital, we need to consider the growth in *total* factor productivity (*TFP*) looking at the Maths box on page 408). This fourth measure gives output relative to the amount of factors used. Changes in total factor productivity over time provide a good indicator of technological progress. Chart (b) shows the average annual growth in total factor productivity for various countries from 1991 to 2000 and from 2001 to 2007. The UK has experienced relatively fast growth on this measure compared with the other countries.

The importance of productivity

The higher the productivity of its factors of production, the higher will be a country's potential output; and the faster the rate of growth in productivity, the faster is likely to be the country's rate of economic growth. Any government seeking to raise the long-term growth rate in its country, therefore, must find ways of stimulating productivity growth.

On what does the growth of productivity depend? There are seven main determinants:

- Private investment in new physical capital (machinery and buildings) and in R&D.
- Public investment in education, R&D and infrastructure.
- Training and the development of labour skills.
- Innovation and the application of new technology.
- The organisation and management of factors of production.
- The rate of entry of new firms into markets: generally such firms will have higher productivity than existing firms.

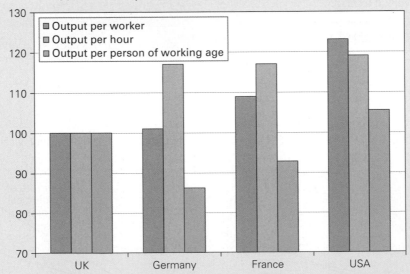

(a) *Productivity in selected countries, 2006 (UK = 100)*

Sources: *Productivity in the UK: 7, Securing long-term prosperity* (HM Treasury); plus various other sources.

- The business environment in which firms operate. Is there competition over the quality and design of products? Is there competitive pressure to reduce costs?

 Identify some policies that a government could pursue to stimulate productivity growth through each of the above means.

But what are the mechanisms whereby productivity growth feeds through into growth of the economy?

- The capacity of the economy to grow will increase as productivity improvements extend potential output.
- Productivity improvements will drive prices downwards, stimulating demand and actual growth.
- With high returns from their investment, investors might be prepared to embark upon new projects and enterprises, stimulating yet further productivity growth and higher output.
- As labour productivity rises, so wages are likely to rise. The higher wages will lead to higher consumption, and hence, via the multiplier and accelerator, to higher output and higher investment, thereby stimulating further advances in productivity.
- In the longer term, businesses experiencing higher productivity growth would expect their lower costs,

and hence enhanced competitiveness, to allow them to gain greater market share. This will encourage further investment and productivity growth.

It is clear that the prosperity of a nation rests upon its ability to improve its productivity. The more successful it is in doing this, the greater will be its rate of economic growth.

For decades the UK has invested a smaller proportion of its national income than most other industrialised nations. Although this rose from an average of 17.1 per cent of GDP in the 1990s to 17.9 per cent between 2005 and 2008, this compares with 18.1 per cent for Germany, 18.5 per cent for the USA, 20.6 per cent for France, 23.3 per cent for Japan, 25.1 per cent for Ireland and 30.4 per cent for Spain (all 2005–8). This helps to explain the comparatively low level of labour productivity illustrated in chart (a).

Nevertheless, despite the lower proportion of national income invested, the productivity gap with the UK's main competitors has narrowed somewhat in recent years thanks to a faster *growth* in productivity (see chart (b)). For an analysis of UK productivity, see Case Study 22.1 in MyEconLab.

 What could explain the differences in productivity between the four countries in chart (a), and why do the differences vary according to which of the three measures is used?

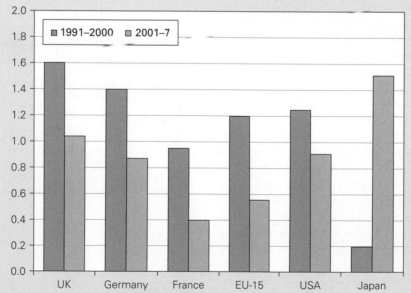

(b) *Total factor productivity growth (average % per annum)*

Source: Author's calculations based on data in *Statistical Annex of the European Economy* (Commission of the European Communities).

| **Figure 22.7** | Effect of an increase in the saving rate, with a given rate of technological progress |

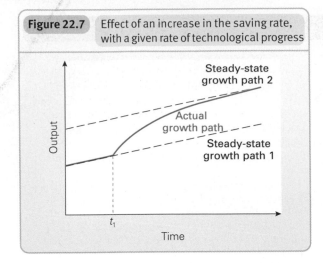

---

slope) of the curve. Assume that the economy is on steady-state growth path 1. Then, at time t_1, there is an increase in the saving rate. This has the effect of increasing output and the economy will move towards steady-state growth path 2. But the full effect does not take place immediately, since new capital equipment takes time to plan and install and then to generate additional income, part of which will be used for more investment. Thus the actual growth path will follow the green line, gradually converging on steady-state growth path 2.

Endogenous growth theory

It should be clear from what we have argued that an increase in technological progress is essential if a country wants to achieve faster rates of growth in the long term. But is this purely in the lap of the scientists and engineers? In the Solow growth model that we have been considering up to now, this is the type of assumption made. In other words, technological progress is simply a 'given': it is exogenously determined.

But cannot governments adopt policies that encourage scientific breakthroughs and technological developments? What can be done to speed up the rate of innovation? Many economists argue that the rate of technological progress *can* be increased if more resources are devoted to research and development and to education and training, and if people are given appropriate incentives to innovate.

Once a discovery is made, its effects will depend on how widely the knowledge is dispersed. The more people can use the new technology and replicate and develop it, the greater will be the resulting increase in output.

What *endogenous growth theory* argues is that the rate of invention and technological development and the rate of diffusion of new technology depend on economic institutions, incentives and the role of government. All this suggests that appropriate policies can increase the rate of technological progress and hence increase the rate of economic growth.

A model of endogenous technological progress

Endogenous growth models argue two things. The first is that technological progress is *dependent* on various economic factors such as the rate of investment in research and development. This could be included as an element in the investment (I) term, i.e.

$$I = I_n + I_c$$

where I_n is investment in research and development of new technology (it could also include investment in training) and I_c is investment in capital that uses current technology. The greater the value of I_n/I_c, the faster will the Y curve shift upwards in Figure 22.2 and the steeper will be the steady-state growth path in Figure 22.7. Any policy, then, that increases the proportion of national income being devoted to R&D and training will increase the long-run rate of economic growth.

The second factor is the responsiveness of Y to I_n. The greater the value of $\Delta Y/I_n$, the greater will be the rate of economic growth: the steeper will be the steady-state growth path.

The values of I_n and $\Delta Y/I_n$ depend on a range of factors, such as attitudes of business and financial institutions, tax incentives, government grants, a research infrastructure (laboratories, the number and skills of researchers, etc.), the degree of competition over the development of new products, and so on. In other words, they depend on structural and institutional factors within the economy and on the role of government.

Government policies to encourage R&D, innovation and risk-taking are known as 'supply-side policies' and are the subject of the next chapter.

KI 22 p216

---

*LOOKING AT THE MATHS

The above endogenous growth model can be expressed algebraically as follows:

$$\Delta Y/Y = v(I_n/Y)$$

This states that the rate of economic growth ($\Delta Y/Y$) depends on the proportion of national income devoted to R&D and training (I_n/Y) by an amount v.

The higher the value of I_n/Y and the higher the value of v, the steeper will be the steady-state growth path.

Definition

Endogenous growth theory A theory that the rate of growth depends on the rate of technological progress and diffusion, both of which depend on institutions, incentives and the role of government.

Section summary

1. A higher long-term rate of growth will normally require a faster rate of technological progress.

2. The rate of technological progress determines the slope of the steady-state growth path (i.e. the rate of steady-state growth). If there is a rise in the saving rate, this will shift the steady-state growth path upwards

(parallel) and the actual growth path will move from the lower to the higher path.

3. Endogenous growth theory argues that the rate technological progress and its rate of diffusion depend on economic institutions and incentives. Supply-side policy could be used to alter these.

END OF CHAPTER QUESTIONS

1. For what reasons do countries experience very different long-run rates of economic growth from each other?

2. Why do developed countries experience a degree of convergence over time? Would you expect there to be total convergence of GDP per head?

3. If increased investment (using current technology) does not lead to increased long-run economic growth, does it bring any benefits?

4. What determines the rate of depreciation? What would happen if the rate of depreciation fell?

5. What is meant by the 'steady-state economic growth path'? What determines its slope?

6. What is the significance of the term 'endogenous' in endogenous growth theory? What, according to this theory, determines the long-run rate of economic growth?

7. Under what circumstances would a higher rate of investment lead to a higher rate of economic growth?

8. What determines the rate of growth in total factor productivity?

Online resources

Additional case studies in MyEconLab

22.1 Productivity performance and the UK economy. A detailed examination of how the UK's productivity compares with that in other countries.

22.2 The USA: is it a 'new economy'? An examination of whether US productivity increases are likely to be sustained.

Maths Case 22.1 Finding the steady-state equilibrium in the Solow model. Using the algebra in worked example.

Maths Case 22.2 The effect of technological progress in the Solow model. Using the algebra in a worked example.

Websites relevant to this chapter

See sites listed at the end of Chapter 23 on page 668.

23 Chapter

Supply-side Policies

CHAPTER MAP

**23.1 Supply-side policies and the
macroeconomy** **651**
Economic growth and supply-side policies 651
Supply-side policies and other macroeconomic
objectives 651

23.2 Approaches to supply-side policy **652**
The new classical approach 652
The Keynesian approach 653
'Third Way' supply-side policies 653
The link between demand-side and supply-side
policies 653

**23.3 Market-orientated supply-side
policies** **654**
Supply-side policies in the 1980s 654
Reducing government expenditure 654
Tax cuts: the effects on labour supply and
employment 654
Tax cuts for business and other incentives 656
Reducing the power of labour 656
Reducing welfare 657
Policies to encourage competition 658
Conclusions 660

23.4 Interventionist supply-side policy **661**
The case against the market 661
The forms of intervention 664
Planning 664
Selective intervention 664
The case against intervention 667

As we saw in Chapter 22, long-run economic growth can only be achieved through an increase in aggregate supply. If growth is to continue and not peter out, this in turn requires an increase in productivity. But how can productivity be increased?

We begin this chapter by drawing out various policy conclusions from the growth models we examined in sections 22.2 and 22.3. They stress the importance of technological progress and innovation. We also examine how developments on the supply side can affect the other macroeconomic objectives of achieving low unemployment and low inflation.

We then focus on the various policy options to increase aggregate supply. In doing this we consider the different approaches to supply-side policy and how they relate to the analysis of the economy. For example, we contrast Keynesian and new classical approaches.

Supply-side policies can be put into two broad categories: market orientated and interventionist. Market-orientated policies focus on 'freeing up' markets and improving market incentives. They involve policies such as tax cuts, privatisation and deregulation. We look at such policies in section 23.3.

Interventionist policies, by contrast, focus on ways of countering the inadequacies of markets through direct government provision of transport infrastructure, training or R&D, or financial support for private provision. We look at this type of policy in section 23.4.

Not surprisingly, the political right argues in favour of 'freeing up' the market; the left argues in favour of intervention.

23.1 SUPPLY-SIDE POLICIES AND THE MACROECONOMY

Economic growth and supply-side policies

As we saw in section 22.1, long-term growth rates vary from country to country. We also saw that even small changes in the long-term growth rate, when compounded over time, can make significant differences to a country's living standards. Then, in sections 22.2 and 22.3, we looked at the neoclassical and endogenous models of economic growth and how they can explain differences in growth rates between countries. Here we consider the implications of these models for *policies* to raise the economy's long-run growth rate.

Governments across the world have increasingly focused on supply-side policies; these are policies designed to increase the potential output of economies and hence long-run aggregate supply. This focus has reflected the resurgence in interest amongst academics in the determinants of growth and, in particular, attempts to gain a better understanding of the sources of productivity increases, such as technological progress and innovation.

The importance of technological progress and innovation

The interest in understanding technological progress stems partly from the conclusions of the neoclassical growth model that we detailed in the previous chapter. According to the model, without technological progress the economy will reach a steady state where economic growth slows to the rate at which the labour input is growing; in other words, growth per hour will cease.

This is not an attractive prospect for countries, such as the UK, where there is no systematic trend for an increase in hours worked. Indeed, if hours per worker fall – as they have in many countries – then without technological progress (which could include more efficient work practices), output *per worker* will fall.

Whilst the neoclassical model identifies the importance of technological progress for enduring growth, it does not offer governments actual policy prescriptions. This void is filled by endogenous growth theory. Endogenous growth models explicitly model technological advancement (see page 648). There is thus interest and debate surrounding endogenous growth models not just amongst academics but amongst policy makers too.

In such models, a major determinant of technological progress is the size and composition of the capital stock. As economies accumulate capital, they are likely to devote more resources to the development and maintenance of capital goods industries. In other words, they are likely to have a larger sector devoted to producing and developing capital goods. This in turn may raise the rate of technological progress and enable further capital accumulation. A virtuous circle is created.

Investment in research and development is encouraged through the use of patents and copyrights. These provide some protection to firms, enabling them to capture more of the benefits from their own ideas and thus providing them with an incentive to create and innovate. Furthermore, the striving for profit and the pursuit of competitive advantage over rivals are incentives that can drive this innovation and creativity.

But there are limits to the ability of firms to exclude other firms from prospering from their own ideas, such as the development of products and processes and of the skills of their workforce. The virtuous circle is thus reinforced by externalities: the spillover of ideas from one firm to another. New ideas cannot be put back into the meta-phorical bottle once its lid is off.

The resurgence of interest in growth theory, particularly with the developments of the endogenous growth literature, has focused attention on policies to foster and promote technological progress. If there is a virtuous circle arising from firms investing and innovating, how are governments best placed to encourage it?

Equally important is the question of how to ensure the greatest possible impact from such investments. For instance, to be able to take full advantage of technical innovations, workers and management need suitable flexibility and an appropriate array of skills. This may require new working practices and new forms of organisation.

Thus supply-side policy to encourage faster economic growth should focus not just on research and development, but also on investment, education and training, industrial organisation, work practices and the whole range of incentives that may be necessary to make optimum use of new techniques.

 Why do Keynesians argue that, even in the long run, demand-side policies will still be required if faster growth in aggregate supply is to be achieved?

Supply-side policies and other macroeconomic objectives

Unemployment

Supply-side policies can also be directed at other macroeconomic objectives. The cure for demand-deficient unemployment may lie on the demand side, but other types of unemployment require supply-side solutions.

Equilibrium unemployment – frictional, structural, etc. – is caused by rigidities or imperfections in the market. There is a mismatching of aggregate supply and demand, and vacancies are not filled despite the existence of unemployment. The problem is that labour is not sufficiently mobile, either occupationally or geographically, to respond to changes in the job market. Labour supply for particular jobs is too inelastic.

Supply-side policies aim to influence labour supply by making workers more responsive to changes in job opportunities. They may also aim to make employers more adaptable and willing to operate within existing labour constraints. Alternatively, they may seek to reduce the monopoly power of unions to drive real wages above the equilibrium.

Inflation and supply-side policies

If inflation is caused by cost-push pressures, supply-side policy can help to reduce it in three ways:

- By reducing the power of unions and/or firms (for example, by the use of anti-monopoly legislation) and thereby encouraging more competition in the supply of labour and/or goods.
- By preventing people from exercising that power by some form of prices and incomes policy. (Such policies were used in the 1970s: see Case Study 23.3 in MyEconLab.)
- By encouraging increases in productivity through retraining, or by investment grants to firms, or by tax incentives, etc.

Section summary

1. The resurgence of interest in growth theory has led policy makers to focus on policies that can sustain increases in productivity and, in particular, promote more rapid technological progress.

2. Demand-side policies (fiscal and monetary) may be suitable for controlling demand-pull inflation or demand-deficient unemployment, but supply-side policies will be needed to control the other types of inflation and unemployment.

23.2 APPROACHES TO SUPPLY-SIDE POLICY

The new classical approach

New classical economists argue that demand-side policy (by which they mean monetary policy) can only control inflation; it cannot affect growth and employment. Supply-side policy is the appropriate policy to increase output and reduce the level of unemployment.

Supply-side policy can be used to shift the aggregate supply curve to the right: to increase the amount that firms wish to supply at any given price. In Figure 23.1, output rises to Q_2 and prices fall to P_2. In the labour market, it can also reduce the natural rate of unemployment, and thus shift the vertical long-run Phillips curve to the left.

New classical economists advocate policies to 'free up' the market: policies that encourage private enterprise, or provide incentives and reward initiative. Section 23.3 examines these *market-orientated supply-side policies*.

This part of the new classical agenda has much in common with the *neo-Austrian/libertarian school* (see

Box 11.7). The argument here is that a free market, with the absolute minimum of government interference, will provide the dynamic environment where entrepreneurs will be willing to take risks and develop new products and new techniques.

Unlike neoclassical economists, who concentrate on the desirability of achieving economic efficiency in competitive markets, the neo-Austrians take a longer-term perspective. They argue that the prospect of monopoly profits is often what provides a major motivation for firms to take risks.

Figure 23.1 Aggregate demand and supply: monetarist analysis

Definitions

Market-orientated supply-side policies Policies to increase aggregate supply by freeing up the market.

Neo-Austrian/libertarian school A school of thought that advocates maximum liberty for economic agents to pursue their own interests and to own property.

Figure 23.2   Aggregate demand and supply: Keynesian analysis

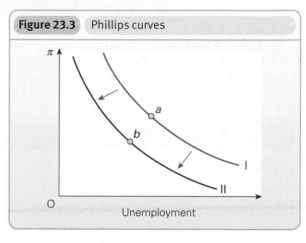

Figure 23.3   Phillips curves

The search to achieve market advantages through new products and new techniques is just as important a part of competition, they argue, as competition in the market for existing goods. Thus private property rights are a key element in neo-Austrian thought: the right to keep the fruits of innovation and investment, with minimum taxation.

The Keynesian approach

Modern Keynesians do not just advocate the management of demand. They too advocate supply-side policies, but generally of a more ***interventionist*** nature (e.g. training schemes, or policies to encourage firms to set up in areas of high unemployment).

The appropriate balance between demand- and supply-side policies depends on the degree of slack in the economy. In Figure 23.2, if output is below Q_1 with aggregate demand below AD_1, the immediate policy requirement is to increase aggregate *demand* rather than aggregate supply. If, however, the economy is approaching full employment with aggregate demand at AD_2 and output at Q_2, the most appropriate policy to increase output is a supply-side policy. This will shift the AS curve to the right (e.g. to AS_2) and raise output (e.g. to Q_3).

Does this mean that Keynesians would advocate using supply-side policies only at times of full employment?

Definition

Interventionist supply-side policies Policies to increase aggregate supply by government intervention to counteract the deficiencies of the market.

Keynesians also advocate supply-side policies to shift the Phillips curve to the left. If successful, such policies could lead simultaneously to lower unemployment and lower inflation. The economy could move from, say, point *a* to point *b* in Figure 23.3.

'Third Way' supply-side policies

With the election of the new Labour government in the UK in 1997, there was much discussion of a 'Third Way' between the unfettered market system advocated by many of those on the right and the interventionist approach advocated by those on the left. The Third Way borrows from the right in advocating incentives, low taxes and free movements of capital. It also borrows from the left in advocating means whereby governments can provide support for individuals in need while improving economic performance by investing in the country's infrastructure, such as its transport and telecommunication systems, and in its social capital, such as schools, libraries and hospitals.

Its main thrust is the concept of helping people to help themselves. Thus unemployment policies should be focused on helping the unemployed become employable, with unemployment benefits linked to the obligation actively to look for work. Growth policies should be a mixture of strengthening market incentives and keeping taxes low, regulation to encourage more competition and prevent monopoly abuse, and providing improved infrastructure and improved education and training.

The link between demand-side and supply-side policies

Policies can have both demand-side and supply-side effects. For example, many supply-side policies involve increased government expenditure, whether on retraining schemes, on research and development projects, or on industrial relocation. They will therefore cause a rise in aggregate demand (unless accompanied by a rise in taxes). Similarly, supply-side policies of tax cuts designed to increase incentives will increase aggregate demand (unless accompanied by a cut in government expenditure). It is thus important to consider the consequences for demand when planning various supply-side policies.

Likewise, demand management policies often have supply-side effects. If a cut in interest rates boosts investment, there will be a multiplied rise in national income: a demand-side effect. But that rise in investment will also create increased productive capacity: a supply-side effect.

Section summary

1. Supply-side policies, if successful, will shift the aggregate supply curve to the right, and possibly shift the Phillips curve downwards/to the left.

2. New classical and neo-Austrian economists favour market-orientated supply-side policies. Keynesians tend to favour interventionist supply-side policies. The Third Way advocates carefully targeted government intervention, regulation, welfare and education programmes to encourage people better to help themselves and markets to work more effectively.

3. Supply-side policies often have demand-side effects, and demand-side policies often have supply-side effects. It is important for governments to take these secondary effects into account when working out their economic strategy.

23.3 MARKET-ORIENTATED SUPPLY-SIDE POLICIES

Supply-side policies in the 1980s

Radical market-orientated supply-side policies were first adopted in the early 1980s by the Thatcher government in the UK and the Reagan administration in the USA. The essence of these policies was to encourage and reward individual enterprise and initiative, and to reduce the role of government; to put more reliance on market forces and competition, and less on government intervention and regulation. The policies were thus associated with the following:

- Reducing government expenditure so as to release more resources for the private sector.
- Reducing taxes so as to increase incentives.
- Reducing the monopoly power of trade unions so as to encourage greater flexibility in both wages and working practices and to allow labour markets to clear.
- Reducing the automatic entitlement to certain welfare benefits so as to encourage greater self-reliance.
- Reducing red tape and other impediments to investment and risk-taking.
- Encouraging competition through policies of deregulation and privatisation.
- Abolishing exchange controls and other impediments to the free movement of capital.

Such policies were increasingly copied by other governments around the world. Today most countries have adopted some or all of the above measures.

Reducing government expenditure

The desire by many governments to cut government expenditure is not just to reduce the PSNCR and hence reduce the growth of money supply; it is also an essential ingredient of their supply-side strategy.

In most countries the size of the public sector, relative to national income, had grown substantially by the 1980s compared with the 1950s and 1960s (see Table 23.1). A major aim of conservative governments throughout the world has been to reverse this trend. The public sector is portrayed as more bureaucratic and less efficient than the private sector. What is more, it is claimed that a growing proportion of public money has been spent on administration and other 'non-productive' activities, rather than on the direct provision of goods and services.

Two things are needed, it is argued: (a) a more efficient use of resources within the public sector and (b) a reduction in the size of the public sector. This would allow private investment to increase with no overall rise in aggregate demand. Thus the supply-side benefits of higher investment could be achieved without the demand-side costs of higher inflation.

In practice, governments have found it very difficult to cut their expenditure without cutting services and the provision of infrastructure.

Why might a recovering economy (and hence a fall in government expenditure on social security benefits) make the government feel even more concerned to make discretionary cuts in government expenditure?

Tax cuts: the effects on labour supply and employment

Cutting the marginal rate of income tax was a major objective of the Thatcher and Major governments (1979–97), as it was of the Reagan administration. In 1979, the standard rate of income tax was 33 per cent, with higher rates rising to 83 per cent. By 1997 the standard rate was only 23 per cent and the top rate was only 40 per cent. The Blair and

Table 23.1	General government expenditure as a percentage of GDP at market prices (average annual)							
	1961–70	**1971–80**	**1981–5**	**1986–90**	**1991–5**	**1996–2000**	**2001–5**	**2006–10**[a]
Belgium	33.7	48.2	60.1	54.2	53.2	50.5	50.2	49.1
Germany	37.0	45.0	46.3	43.9	47.6	48.6	47.6	44.0
France	38.3	44.9	50.3	49.9	53.2	53.1	52.8	52.9
Japan		26.8	34.2	32.7	34.6	39.9	40.1	39.4
Netherlands	39.9	49.7	58.6	56.3	54.3	46.8	46.0	46.2
Sweden		52.8	65.0	58.5	66.3	59.4	55.8	54.1
UK	36.5	45.4	50.1	41.7	44.2	39.4	41.9	46.0
USA	29.1	32.6	35.6	35.8	36.2	33.4	33.7	37.1

[a] Years 2009 and 2010 forecast.
Source: Statistical Annex of the European Economy (Commission of the European Communities, various years).

BOX 23.1 THE SUPPLY-SIDE REVOLUTION IN THE USA

CASE STUDIES AND APPLICATIONS

'Reaganomics'

In both the UK and the USA, the 1980s proved to be years of radical political and economic change. Traditional economic and political practices were replaced by new and often controversial policies, although in theory many of the ideas advocated were based on old principles of laissez-faire capitalism.

In the USA, the era of 'Reaganomics' began in January 1981 when Ronald Reagan became President. With this new administration came a radical shift in policy aimed at directly tackling the supply side of the economy. This policy strategy involved four key strands:

- A reduction in the growth of Federal (central government) spending.
- A reduction in individual and corporate tax rates.
- A reduction in Federal regulations over private enterprise.
- A reduction in inflation through tight monetary policy.

On all four points, President Reagan was to achieve a degree of success. Federal spending growth was reduced even though military spending rocketed. Tax rates fell dramatically. Deregulation was speeded up. Inflation at first was stabilised and then fell sharply.

These supply-side measures were hailed as a great success by Republicans, and followers in both the UK and the USA were quick to advocate an even bigger reduction in the government's role.

Critics remained sceptical and pointed to the costs of Reaganomics. Huge budget deficits plagued the Reagan administration and the Bush Snr, Clinton and Bush Jnr administrations that followed. The massive tax cuts were not matched by an equivalent cut in public expenditure; nor did they produce a sufficiently high rate of economic growth, through which additional tax revenues were to balance the budget. In the 1980s, 'civilian' or welfare spending was cut repeatedly in preference to the huge military budget. This led to increasing social hardship.

And such hardship still existed under George W. Bush, 27 years later, and, with the onset of the credit crunch, was getting worse as many poor people people lost their houses. The emphasis had remained on cutting welfare and tightening requirements to receive state assistance. Critics claim that, even though the numbers on welfare might have fallen over the years, individuals and families remained in poverty, being forced to work for poverty wages as welfare support dwindled. The revolution was far from complete and its benefits to all social groups have been far from even.

Whether the Obama administration will succeed in providing greater support for the poor without jeopardising the 'supply-side revolution' remains to be seen.

Brown governments continued with this policy, so that by 2008 the standard rate was 20 per cent.

Cuts in the marginal rate of income tax are claimed to have five beneficial effects: people work longer hours; more people wish to work; people work more enthusiastically; employment rises; unemployment falls. These are big claims. Are they true?

TC 5 p50

People work longer hours

A cut in the marginal rate of income tax has a *substitution effect* inducing people to work more and also an *income effect* causing people to work less. (At this point, you should review the arguments about the incentive effects of tax

KI 7 p33

cuts: see pages 294–6.) Evidence suggests that the two effects will roughly cancel each other out. Anyway, for many people there is no such choice in the short run. There is no chance of doing overtime or working a shorter week. In the long run, there may be some flexibility in that people can change jobs.

More people wish to work

This applies largely to second income earners in a family, mainly women. A rise in after-tax wages may encourage more women to look for jobs. It may now be worth the cost in terms of transport, childcare, family disruption, etc. The effects of a 1 or 2 per cent cut in income tax rates, however, are likely to be negligible. A more significant effect may be achieved by raising tax allowances. Part-time workers, especially, could end up paying no taxes. Of course, if unemployment is already high, the government will not want to increase the labour force.

People work more enthusiastically

There is little evidence to test this claim. The argument, however, is that people will be more conscientious and will work harder if they can keep more of their pay.

Employment rises

If wages are flexible, total employment will rise. This is illustrated in Figure 23.4. The N curve shows the total labour force. The AS_L curve shows the number of people who are actually qualified and willing to do the specific jobs they are offered at each (after-tax) wage rate. Equilibrium is where the aggregate demand for labour (AD_L) is equal to the labour cost to the employer (i.e. the pre-tax wage rate). Assume an initial income tax per worker of $a - b$. The equilibrium employment will be Q_1. Workers receive an after-tax wage W_1 and thus supply Q_1 labour. Employers' labour cost is the pre-tax wage lc_1. At this wage, they demand Q_1 labour.

If the income tax per worker now falls to $c - d$, equilibrium employment will rise to Q_2. Firms will employ more workers because their labour costs have fallen to lc_2. More workers will take up jobs because their after-tax wages have risen to W_2.

Unemployment falls

One of the causes of natural (equilibrium) unemployment highlighted by new classical economists is the cushioning provided by unemployment benefit. If income tax rates are cut, there will be a bigger difference between after-tax wage rates and unemployment benefit. More people will be motivated to 'get on their bikes' and look for work.

In Figure 23.4, the horizontal gap between N and AS_L represents equilibrium unemployment. With a cut in income tax per worker from $a - b$ to $c - d$, equilibrium unemployment will fall from $e - b$ to $f - d$.

 What would happen to the AS_L curve and the level of unemployment if unemployment benefits were increased?

Despite the cuts in marginal rates of income tax in many countries, it has been commonplace for these to be offset by significant increases in other taxes. For example, in the UK, VAT stood at only 8 per cent in 1979; in 2008[1] it was 17.5 per cent. The marginal rate of national insurance contributions was 6.5 per cent in 1979; in 2009 it was 11 per cent. The net effect was that taxes as a proportion of GDP rose from 34.7 per cent in 1979 to 36.8 per cent in 2008.

 Does this mean that there were no positive incentive effects from the Conservative government's tax measures?

To the extent that tax cuts do succeed in increasing take-home pay, there is a danger of 'sucking in' imports. In the UK, there is a high income elasticity of demand for imports. Extra consumer incomes may be spent on Japanese MP3 players, foreign cars, holidays abroad and so on. Tax cuts can therefore have a serious effect on the current account of the balance of payments.

Tax cuts for business and other investment incentives

A number of financial incentives can be given to encourage investment. Selective intervention in the form of grants for specific industries or firms is best classified as an interventionist policy and will be examined later in this chapter. Market-orientated policies seek to reduce the general level of taxation on profits, or to give greater tax relief to investment.

A cut in corporation tax (the tax on business profits) will increase after-tax profits. This will leave more funds for ploughing back into investment. Also, the higher after-tax return on investment will encourage more investment to take place. In 1983 the main rate of corporation tax in the UK stood at 52 per cent. A series of reductions have taken place since then, and in 2009 the rate was 28 per cent for large companies and 21 per cent for small companies.

An alternative policy would be to increase investment allowances. Investment allowances are the system whereby the cost of investment can be offset against pre-tax profit, thereby reducing a firm's tax liability.

Reducing the power of labour

In Figure 23.5, if the power of unions to push wage rates up to W_1 were removed, then (assuming no change in the

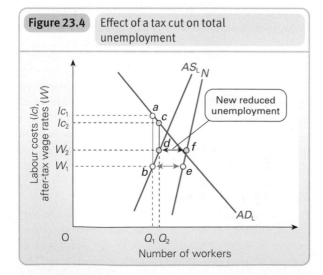

| **Figure 23.4** | Effect of a tax cut on total unemployment |

[1] The rate was cut to 15 per cent in December 2008 for 13 months as part of the government's fiscal stimulus package.

Figure 23.5 Effect of reducing the power of labour

Figure 23.6 The effects of a cut in benefits on the number unemployed

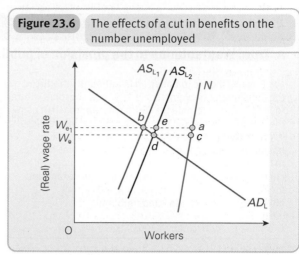

demand curve for labour) wage rates would fall to W_e. Disequilibrium unemployment $(Q_2 - Q_1)$ would disappear. Employment would rise from Q_1 to Q_e.

Equilibrium unemployment, however, will rise somewhat as the gap between gross and effective labour supply widens. With the reduction in wage rates, some people may now prefer to remain on unemployment benefits.

If labour costs to employers are reduced, their profits will probably rise. This could encourage and enable more investment and hence economic growth. If the monopoly power of labour is reduced, then cost-push inflation will also be reduced.

The Thatcher government took a number of measures to weaken the power of labour. These included restrictions on union closed shops, restrictions on secondary picketing, financial assistance for union ballots, and enforced secret ballots on strike proposals (see Chapter 9). It set a lead in resisting strikes in the public sector. Unlike previous Labour governments, it did not consult with union leaders over questions of economic policy. It was publicly very critical of trade union militancy and blamed the unions for many of the UK's economic ills. As a result, unions lost a lot of political standing and influence.

As labour markets have become more flexible, with increased part-time working and short-term contracts, and as the process of globalisation has exposed more companies to international competition, so the power of labour has been further eroded in many sectors of the economy.

 Is the number of working days lost through disputes a good indication of (a) union power; (b) union militancy?

Reducing welfare

New classical economists claim that a major cause of unemployment is the small difference between the welfare benefits of the unemployed and the take-home pay of the employed. This causes voluntary unemployment (i.e.

frictional unemployment). People are caught in a 'poverty trap': if they take a job, they lose their benefits (see pages 296–7).

A dramatic solution to this problem would be to cut unemployment benefits. Unlike policies to encourage investment, this supply-side policy would have a very rapid effect. It would shift the effective labour supply curve to the right. In Figure 23.6, equilibrium unemployment would fall from $a - b$ to $c - d$ if real wage rates were flexible downwards; or from $a - b$ to $a - e$ if they were not flexible. In the case of non-flexible real wage rates, the reduction in equilibrium unemployment would be offset by a rise in disequilibrium unemployment $(e - b)$.

Because workers would now be prepared to accept a lower wage, the average length of job search by the unemployed would be reduced. In Figure 23.7, the average duration of unemployment would fall from T_1 to T_2 (see pages 423–4).

Figure 23.7 The effects of a cut in benefits on the average duration of unemployment

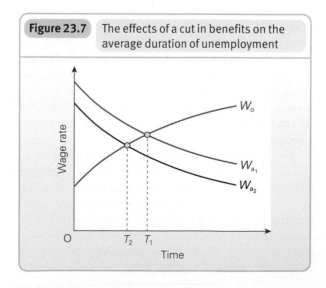

BOX 23.2 | **ASSESSING PFI**

A 'Third Way' solution to the provision of public services

The Private Finance Initiative (PFI), although introduced by the Conservative government in 1992, has become central to the Labour government's 'Third Way' approach of using the private sector to deliver public projects and services. It has become increasingly common for new schools, hospitals, roads, bridges, student accommodation, etc. to be funded and built by private companies under PFI contracts (see table and figure). Well-known examples include the Channel Tunnel rail link and capital investment in the London Underground.

PFI projects: total to March 2008

Department(s)	Number of signed projects	Capital value (£m)
Transport	51	22 634.9
Health	102	10 898.4
Defence	49	8 725.3
Scotland	85	5 378.0
Education and Skills	123	5 175.1
Environment	21	2 006 7
Communities	59	1 719.5
Northern Ireland	32	1 283.3
Work and Pensions	4	1 138.3
HM Revenue & Customs	7	840.0
Home Office	25	818.8
Ministry of Justice	23	736.1
Wales	24	535.2
Culture, Media, Sport	14	262.4
Other	9	653.9
Total	629	62 806.0

The government or local authority decides the service it requires, and then seeks tenders from the private sector for designing, building, financing and running projects to provide these services. The capital costs are borne by the private sector, but then, if the provision of the service is not self-financing, the public sector pays the private firm for providing it. Thus instead of the public sector being an owner of assets and provider of services, it is merely an enabler, buying services from the private sector.

A key aim of PFI is to introduce competition (through the tendering process), private-sector expertise, innovation and the management of risk into the provision of public services.

Under the Private Finance Initiative (PFI) the public sector contracts to purchase services on a long-term basis so as to take advantage of private sector management skills incentivised by having private finance at risk. The private sector has always been involved in the building and maintenance of public infrastructure, but PFI ensures that contractors are bound into long-term maintenance contracts and shoulder responsibility for the quality of the work they do. With PFI, the public sector defines what is required to meet public needs and ensures delivery of the outputs through the contract. Consequently, the private sector can be harnessed to deliver investment in better quality public services while frontline services are retained within the public sector.[1]

Clearly, there are immediate benefits to the public finances from using private, rather than public, funds to finance a project. Later, however, there is potentially an extra burden of having to buy the services from the private provider at a price that includes an element for profit. What is hoped is that the costs to the taxpayer of these profits will be more than offset by gains in efficiency.

Critics, however, claim that PFI projects have resulted in poorer quality of provision and that cost control has often been poor, resulting in a higher burden for the taxpayer in the long term. What is more, many of the projects have turned out to be highly profitable, suggesting that the terms of the original contracts were too lax. Take the case of Carillion. It owns stakes in 18 PFI projects, including the new GCHQ communications centre at Cheltenham and the

---

 Would a cut in benefits affect the W_o curve? If so, with what effect?

In the early 1980s, the gap between take-home pay and welfare benefits to the unemployed did indeed widen. However, over the same period unemployment rose dramatically. Nevertheless, the claim that there was too little incentive for people to work was still a major part of the Thatcher government's explanation of growing unemployment.

A major problem is that with changing requirements for labour skills, many of the redundant workers from the older industries are simply not qualified for new jobs that are created. What is more, the longer people are unemployed, the more demoralised they become. Employers would probably be prepared to pay only very low wage rates to such workers. To persuade these unemployed people to take these low-paid jobs, the welfare benefits would have to be slashed. A 'market' solution to the problem, therefore, may be a very cruel solution. A fairer solution would be an interventionist policy: a policy of retraining labour.

Another alternative is to make the payment of unemployment benefits conditional on the recipient making a concerted effort to find a job. In the jobseeker's allowance scheme introduced in the UK in 1996, claimants must be available for, and actively seeking, work and must complete a Jobseeker's Agreement, which sets out the types of work the person is willing to do, and the plan to find work. Payment can be refused if the claimant refuses to accept the offer of a job.

Policies to encourage competition

If the government can encourage more competition, this should have the effect of increasing national output and

M6 toll road. In 2005, it announced that the net present value of its PFI investments was £83 million. This compared with an investment cost of just £29 million.

There is also the question of what happens if the private company runs into financial difficulties. In 2005, the engineering company Jarvis only just managed to avoid bankruptcy by securing refinancing on all 14 of its PFI deals. This involved selling a large amount of assets and renegotiating loans.

With the credit crunch of 2008/9 many firms operating PFI projects found it difficult to raise finance. In March

2009, the government announced that it would lend up to £2 billion that year to ensure projects worth some £13bn would be able to continue. Such projects included schools, hospital buildings, waste treatment plants and motorway widening.

 Do a news Web search for PFI projects and identify the issues currently surrounding the success or otherwise of PFI.

[1] Financial Statement and Budget Report, Chapter C (HM Treasury, 2005).

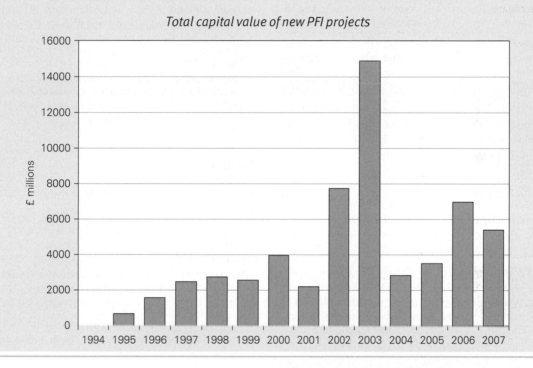

Total capital value of new PFI projects

reducing inflation. Five major types of policy have been pursued under this heading.

Privatisation

If privatisation simply involves the transfer of a natural monopoly to private hands (as with the water companies), the scope for increased competition is limited. However, where there is genuine scope for competition (e.g. in the supply of gas and electricity), privatisation can lead to increased efficiency, more consumer choice and lower prices.

Alternatively, privatisation can involve the introduction of private services into the public sector (e.g. private contractors providing cleaning services in hospitals, or refuse collection for local authorities). Private contractors may compete against each other for the franchise. This may well lower the cost of provision of these services, but the

quality of provision may also suffer unless closely monitored. The effects on unemployment are uncertain. Private contractors may offer lower wages and thus may use more labour. But if they are trying to supply the service at minimum cost, they may employ less labour.

Deregulation

This involves the removal of monopoly rights. In 1979 the National Bus Corporation lost its monopoly of long-distance coach haulage. Private operators were now allowed to compete. This substantially reduced coach fares on a number of routes. In 1986 competition was allowed in providing local bus services (see Case Study 23.1 in MyEconLab).

An example in the private sector was the so-called 'Big Bang' on the Stock Exchange in 1986. Under this, the monopoly power of jobbers to deal in stocks and shares on the Stock Exchange was abolished. In addition,

KI 23
p217

stockbrokers now compete with each other in the commission rates that they charge, and online share dealing has become commonplace.

Introducing market relationships into the public sector

KI 22
p216

This is where the government tries to get different departments or elements within a particular part of the public sector to 'trade' with each other, so as to encourage competition and efficiency.

The process often involves 'devolved budgeting'. For example, under the locally managed schools scheme (LMS), schools have become self-financing. Rather than the local authority meeting the bill for teachers' salaries, the schools have to manage their own budgets. The objective is to encourage them to cut costs, thereby reducing the burden on council tax payers. However, one result is that schools have tended to appoint inexperienced (and hence cheaper) teachers rather than those who can bring the benefits of their years of teaching.

Perhaps the most radical example of devolved budgeting was the introduction by the Thatcher government of an 'internal market' into the National Health Service (NHS). General practitioners were offered the opportunity to control their own budget. The size of the budget was determined by the number of patients and by their age and health profiles. GP fundholders purchased services directly from hospitals and had to cover their drugs bill. The suppliers of treatment, the hospitals, depended for much of their income on attracting the business of GP purchasers. They were thus put in competition with other hospitals.

Advocates of the internal market in the NHS argued that it created greater efficiency through competition. Critics, however, claimed that it led to growing inequalities of service between practices and between hospitals, and increased the administrative costs of the NHS.

The Labour government abolished the NHS internal market and replaced GP fundholding with a system of local primary care trusts, which co-ordinate health-care provision in a particular locality. They also purchase services for patients from hospitals with the objective of giving patients, through their GPs, more choice of where to be treated.

The government also introduced (in 2003) a system of 'foundation trusts'. Hospitals can apply for foundation trust status. If successful, they are given much greater financial autonomy in terms of purchasing, employment and investment decisions. Applications are judged by Monitor, the independent health regulator. By January 2009, there were 113 foundation trusts. Critics argue that funds have been diverted to foundation hospitals away from the less well-performing hospitals where greater funding could help that performance.

The Private Finance Initiative (PFI)

This is where a private company, after a competitive tender, is contracted by a government department or local authority to finance and build a project, such as a new road or a prison. The government then pays the company to maintain and/or run it, or simply rents the assets from the company. The public sector thus becomes a purchaser of services rather than a direct provider itself. The benefits and costs of PFI are explored in Box 23.2.

KI 23
p217

Free trade and free capital movements

The opening-up of international trade and investment is central to a market-orientated supply-side policy. One of the first measures of the Thatcher government (in October 1979) was to remove all exchange controls, thereby permitting the free inflow and outflow of capital, both long-term and short-term. Most other industrialised countries also removed or relaxed exchange controls during the 1980s and early 1990s.

The Single European Act of 1987, which came into force in 1993, was another example of international liberalisation. As we shall see in section 24.4, it was designed to create a 'single market' in the EU: a market without barriers to the movement of goods, services, capital and labour. This has been largely achieved, although some restrictions on trade between member states do still apply.

Conclusions

Although a number of supply-side measures have been taken in many countries during the last twenty years, many of the supply-side *effects* have been the result of changes in demand.

The recessions of the early 1980s and early 1990s caused many firms to fail. Those that survived were often able to do so only by increases in efficiency. Resistance from unions to the introduction of new labour-saving technology was weakened by high unemployment and the fear that, without the new technology, firms might be forced to close.

Similarly, demand had effects on the supply side during periods of expansion, such as the late 1980s and late 1990s. Firms were encouraged to innovate and develop new products to take advantage of buoyant markets.

Even where supply-side changes cannot be traced directly to changes in aggregate demand, they often occur not as a result of government supply-side policy, but as a result of international competition and capital movements, new business practices, new inventions and new products.

Thus, although productivity in the UK and the USA grew more rapidly in the 1980s and 1990s than in the 1970s (see Table 22.1 on page 640), it is not clear to what extent this was the direct result of supply-side *policy*.

 If supply-side measures led to a 'shake out' of labour and a resulting reduction in overstaffing, but also to a rightward shift in the Phillips curve, would you judge the policy as a success?

Section summary

1. Market-orientated supply-side policies aim to increase the rate of growth of aggregate supply by encouraging private enterprise and the freer play of market forces.

2. Reducing government expenditure as a proportion of GDP is a major element of such policies.

3. Tax cuts can be used to encourage more people to take up jobs, and to encourage people to work longer hours and more enthusiastically. They can be used to reduce equilibrium unemployment and encourage employers to take on more workers. Likewise tax cuts for businesses or increased investment allowances may encourage higher investment. The effects of tax cuts depend on how people respond to incentives. For example, people will work longer hours only if the substitution effect outweighs the income effect.

4. Reducing the power of trade unions by legislation could reduce disequilibrium unemployment and cost-push inflation. It could also lead to a redistribution of income to profits, which could increase investment and growth (but possibly lead to greater inequality).

5. A reduction in welfare benefits, especially those related to unemployment, will encourage workers to accept jobs at lower wages and thus decrease equilibrium unemployment.

6. Various policies can be introduced to increase competition. These include privatisation, deregulation, introducing market relationships into the public sector, public–private partnerships and freer international trade and capital movements.

23.4 INTERVENTIONIST SUPPLY-SIDE POLICY

In this section, we look at the limitations of the market in stimulating supply-side improvements. We then look at ways in which the government can intervene to encourage more investment and a faster rate of economic growth. We will also assess the relative effectiveness of different types of interventionist policy.

Many of these policies come under the general heading of *industrial policy*: the government taking an active role to support investment in industry and to halt the decline of the manufacturing sector (see Box 23.5).

The case against the market

The basis of the case for government intervention is that the free market is likely to provide too little research and development, training and investment.

As we argued earlier in Chapter 11 (see page 314), there are potentially large external benefits from research and development. Firms investing in developing and improving products, and especially firms engaged in more general scientific research, may produce results that provide benefits to many other firms and to the wider economy. Thus the social rate of return on investment may be much higher than the private rate of return. Investment that is privately unprofitable for a firm may therefore still be economically desirable for the nation.

Definition

Industrial policies Policies to encourage industrial investment and greater industrial efficiency.

Similarly, investment in training may continue yielding benefits to society that are lost to the firms providing the training when the workers leave.

Investment often involves risks. Firms may be unwilling to take those risks, since the costs of possible failure may be too high. When looked at nationally, however, the benefits of investment might well have substantially outweighed the costs, and thus it would have been socially desirable for firms to have taken the risk. Successes would have outweighed failures.

Imperfections in the capital market

Imperfections in the capital market may result in investment not being financed, even though it is privately profitable. Banks in the UK, unlike banks in France, Germany and Japan, have been reluctant to lend to firms for long-term investment.

Similarly, if firms rely on raising finance by the issue of new shares, this makes them very dependent on the stock market performance of their shares, which depends on current profitability and expected profitability in the near future, not on long-term profitability. Shareholders, who are mainly financial institutions, tend to demand too high a dividend rate from the companies in which they invest. This, in part, is due to competition between financial institutions to attract savers to buy their savings packages. The result is that there is less profit left over for ploughing back into investment. The fear of takeovers (the competition for corporate control) again makes managers overconcerned to keep shareholders happy. Finally, floating successful companies on the Stock Exchange provides a large windfall gain to the original owners. This encourages entrepreneurs to *set up* companies, but discourages them from making *long-term* commitments to them. This all leads to the UK disease of

BOX 23.3 ALTERNATIVE APPROACHES TO TRAINING AND EDUCATION

It is generally recognised by economists and politicians alike that improvements in training and education can yield significant supply-side gains. Indeed, the UK's past failure to invest as much in training as many of its major competitors is seen as a key explanation for the country's poor economic performance until recent years.

Training and economic performance are linked in three main ways:

- *Labour productivity.* In various studies comparing the productivity of UK and German industry, education and training is seen as the principal reason for the productivity gap between the two countries (see Box 22.1).
- *Innovation and change.* A key factor in shaping a firm's willingness to introduce new products or processes will be the adaptability and skills of its workforce. If the firm has to spend a lot of money on retraining, or on attracting skilled workers away from other firms, the costs may prove prohibitive.
- *Costs of production.* A shortage of skilled workers will quickly create labour bottlenecks and cause production costs to increase. This will stifle economic growth.

If training is left to the employer, the benefits will become an externality if the workers leave to work elsewhere. Society has benefited from the training, but the firm has not. The free market, therefore, will provide a less than optimal amount of training. The more mobile the labour force, and the more 'transferable' the skills acquired from training, the more likely it is that workers will leave, and the less willing firms will be to invest in training.

In the UK, there is a high level of labour turnover. What is more, wage differentials between skilled and unskilled workers are narrower than in many other countries, and so there is less incentive for workers to train.

How can increased training be achieved? There are three broad approaches:

- Workers could be encouraged to stay with their employer so that employers would be more willing to invest in training. Externalities would be reduced.
- The government could provide subsidies for training. Alternatively, the government or some other agency could provide education and training directly.
- Firms could co-operate to prevent 'poaching' and set up industry-wide training programmes, perhaps in partnership with the government and unions.

Approaches to training in various countries

As far as the first approach is concerned, most countries have seen a movement towards greater labour mobility. The rise in the 'flexible firm' (see Box 9.8) has involved the employment of fewer permanent workers and more part-time and temporary workers. Some countries, such as Japan and Germany, however, have a generally lower rate of labour turnover than most. In Japan, the relationship between employer and employee has traditionally extended well beyond a simple short-term economic arrangement. Workers give loyalty and commitment to their employers, who in return virtually guarantee long-term employment and provide various fringe benefits (such as housing, childcare, holiday schemes and health care). It is not surprising that Japanese firms invest highly in training.

In the USA, labour turnover is very high and yet there is little in the way of industry-wide training. Instead, the US government hopes, by having a high percentage of young people in further and higher education, that sufficient numbers and quality of workers are available for industry. Approximately 45 per cent of the US population enters higher education with 33 per cent of the population graduating, and only just over 0.2 per cent of GDP is spent on training.

In Germany, the proportion entering higher education is considerably lower (some 28 per cent, with just over 19 per cent of the population graduating), but expenditure on training accounts for 1.6 per cent of GDP. Most young people who do not enter higher education embark on some form of apprenticeship. They attend school for part of the week, and receive work-based training for the rest. The state, unions and employers' associations work closely in determining training provision, and they have developed a set of vocational qualifications based around the apprenticeship system. Given that virtually all firms are involved in training, the 'free-rider' problem of firms poaching labour without themselves paying for training is virtually eliminated. The result is that the German workforce is highly skilled. Many of the skills, however, are highly specific. This is a problem when the demand for particular skills declines and can result in high structural unemployment.

KI 30
p316

The UK approach

In the UK, the Conservative government's attitude towards training was initially influenced by its free-market approach to supply-side policy. Training was to be left largely to employers. However, with growing worries over the UK's 'productivity gap', the government set up Training and Enterprise Councils (TECs) in 1988. The TECs identified regional skills shortages, organised training and financed work-based training schemes.

The TECs were replaced in 2001 by the Learning and Skills Council (LSC). This has a budget of over £9 billion and is responsible for planning and funding training in sixth forms and further education colleges, work-based training for young people aged 16 to 24 ('Apprenticeships' and 'Advanced Apprenticeships'), adult and community learning, the provision of information, advice and guidance for adults, and developing links between education and business.

The LSC operates through 47 local arms, which have responsibility for co-ordinating plans for their area. The LSC also co-ordinates the activities of Centres of Vocational Excellence (CoVEs), which provide specialist vocational training, primarily in FE colleges, and which work closely with employers. It has also administered a series of Employer Training Pilots. These provide free or subsidised training to employees without a level 2 qualification, plus compensation to employers for giving workers time off to train.

In addition, a support service called 'Connexions' offers training and employment advice and support for young people between the ages of 13 and 19.

In 1991, the National Vocational Qualification (NVQ) was launched. Students work for an employer, and receive on-the-job training. They also attend college on an occasional basis. The NVQ is awarded when they have achieved sufficient experience. In addition, the government launched General National Vocational Qualifications (GNVQs). These further-education qualifications were intended to bridge the gap between education and work, by ensuring that education was more relevant to work.

The GNVQ system was modelled on the system in France, where a clear vocational educational route is seen as the key to reducing skills shortages. At the age of 14, French students can choose to pursue academic or vocational education routes. The vocational route provides high-level, broad-based skills (unlike in Germany, where skills tend to be more job-specific).

However, GNVQs compete alongside other well-established vocational qualifications such as City and Guilds and BTEC certificates and diplomas. Such competition led to the withdrawal of the GNVQ by October 2007. The NVQ survives largely because it complements other vocational qualifications, e.g. on apprenticeship schemes.

Another approach adopted by the Labour government in the UK has been to encourage 'lifelong learning'. Measures have included setting up the following.

- A University for Industry, which through its 'Learndirect' brand offers online courses in a range of business, technical and IT subjects.
- Some 700 UK Online centres. These offer access to the Internet, and helpers are on hand to provide basic IT, literacy and numeracy support.
- *Work-based Learning for Adults* in England and Wales and *Training for Work* in Scotland: two schemes to provide work-based training for people aged 25 and over who have been out of work for six months or more, with grants paid to employers.

- Two-year foundation degrees, offered by universities or higher education colleges. These are designed in conjunction with employers to meet various skill shortages. They are taken at the university or an associated college, normally on a part-time basis, and often include work-based study with local employers.

There has been considerable concern in the UK with respect to training and skilling the workforce to levels appropriate for future national prosperity.

In 2005 and 2006 the Government produced two White Papers covering, respectively, skills and further education. The skills White Paper set out a skills strategy for the UK, which continued to reinforce the role of business in shaping vocational qualifications and training. It also established a the National Employer Training Programme – known by its brand name 'Train to Gain' – which was rolled out in England in 2006. Advisers analyse training needs in firms and part funding is available to raise the skill levels of employees.

In addition, the skills White Paper proposed that all young people should continue in learning until they are 18. GCSEs and A-levels are retained but 14 new diplomas are to be developed by 2015. The first four (ICT, Engineering, Health and Social Care, Creative and Media) are due for launch in 2008 and eight more are to follow by 2010. Apprenticeships, which attract around 25 per cent of 14-to-19-year-olds, remain but are to be aligned with the new diplomas.

Critics of the UK strategy have argued that employers still face the threat of having newly trained labour poached; that the regional activities of the LSC fail to account for national, long-term training issues; and that the vocational qualifications framework lacks any coherence. Most importantly, the funding devoted to training is still low compared with most other industrialised countries. They claim that the UK system has the worst features of both the US and the German systems: too little training and too specific training. In reviewing the UK's skills potential, the Leitch Committee stated that the UK had to 'raise its game'[1] (see Case Study 22.1 in MyEconLab).

1. *Governments and educationalists generally regard it as desirable that trainees acquire transferable skills. Why may many employers disagree?*
2. *There are externalities (benefits) when employers provide training. What externalities are there from the undergoing of training by the individual? Do they imply that individuals will choose to receive more or less than the socially optimal amount of training?*

KI 29
p313

---

[1] Leitch Committee (2005), *Skills in the UK: The Long Term Challenge. Interim Report*, HMSO, December.

'short-termism': the obsession with short-term profits and the neglect of investment that yields profits only after a number of years.

Finally, in the case of ailing firms, if the government does not help finance a rescue investment programme, there may be substantial social costs from job losses. The avoidance of these social costs may make the investment socially, if not privately, profitable.

How would the radical right reply to these arguments?

The forms of intervention

Nationalisation

This is the most extreme form of intervention, and one that most countries have in the past rejected, given the world-wide trend of privatisation. Nevertheless, many countries have stopped short of privatising certain key transport and power industries, such as the railways and electricity generation. Having these industries under public ownership may result in higher investment than if they were under private ownership. Thus French governments have invested heavily in the state-owned railway system. This has resulted in fast, efficient rail services, with obvious benefits to rail users and the economy generally.

Nationalisation may also be a suitable solution for rescuing vital industries suffering extreme market turbulence. This was the case in 2008 with many banks. With the credit crunch, over-exposure to risky investments in securitised sub-prime debt, inadequate levels of capital, declining confidence and plummeting share prices, many banks were taken into full or partial public ownership. In the UK, Northern Rock and Bradford & Bingley were fully nationalised, while the government took a majority shareholding in the Royal Bank of Scotland and Lloyds Banking Group.

Direct provision

Improvements in infrastructure – such as a better motorway system – can be of direct benefit to industry. Alternatively, the government could provide factories or equipment to specific firms.

Grants

The government may sponsor research and development in certain industries (e.g. aerospace) or in specific fields (e.g. microprocessors). It may back investment programmes considered to benefit the economy as a whole.

Rationalisation

The government may encourage mergers or other forms of industrial reorganisation that will lead to greater efficiency and/or higher levels of investment. This could be done through government agencies or government departments.

Advice and persuasion

The government may engage in discussions with private firms in order to find ways to improve efficiency and innovation. It may bring firms together to exchange information and create a climate of greater certainty. It may bring firms and unions together to try to create greater industrial harmony.

Information

The government may provide various information services to firms: technical assistance, the results of public research, information on markets, etc.

Planning

The most comprehensive approach to industrial policy is for the government to engage in national economic planning. This is not the 'command planning' of the former Soviet Union, where factories were issued with instructions on what to produce, what inputs to use and how much to invest (see Case Study 13.6 in MyEconLab). Rather, it is 'indicative planning'. Indicative planning works alongside the market. It does not replace it.

In a free market, there are likely to be many uncertainties for firms. Industries are highly interconnected. For example, if the electricity industry plans to expand, it will want to know the likely availability of coal or other fuels. Unless firms can know the plans of other firms, they may be cautious about taking investment decisions.

Indicative planning is where the government consults with industrialists to find out their intentions. It then seeks to co-ordinate the plans of firms, industries and sectors, and to recommend realistic and mutually consistent targets for output and investment. The government could also use persuasion or various financial incentives to obtain a consistent plan. The use of indicative planning in the UK is examined in Case Study 23.6 in MyEconLab.

Today in the UK and most other countries there is no comprehensive indicative planning at national level. Nevertheless, local authorities, regional development agencies (see Case Study 23.10 in MyEconLab) and government departments do consult with industry and with chambers of commerce to improve the flow of information.

What instruments might a government use to 'persuade' firms to abide by a national plan? What are their advantages and disadvantages?

Selective intervention

Conservative governments have never favoured a comprehensive industrial strategy. Nevertheless, governments of both parties have intervened selectively in areas where they have felt that the market has provided inadequate investment.

| BOX 23.4 | UNEMPLOYMENT AND SUPPLY-SIDE POLICIES | CASE STUDIES AND APPLICATIONS |

Two approaches

Although some countries, such as Germany and France, have found that unemployment has remained stubbornly high at around 10 per cent, others have had much more success in reducing unemployment through appropriate supply-side policies.

In 2006, the OECD put countries into four groups according to their policies towards labour markets. The first two groups have been successful in cutting unemployment. The other two have not.

The first group, labelled 'mainly English-speaking' by the OECD (Japan, South Korea and Switzerland are honorary Anglophones), tends to have weaker job protection, less generous unemployment benefits and thinner tax wedges than the average. Its employment rate is comfortably higher than the OECD average; its jobless rate [5.3 per cent] is comfortably lower [than the OECD average of 7.5 per cent]. In the second, 'northern European' group (Scandinavia, the Netherlands, Austria and Ireland), taxes and unemployment benefits are high and workers hard to fire. Yet the average employment rate is a little higher than the first group's and the unemployment rate a little lower [4.8 per cent].

There are two reasons why the second group can match the first. Their product markets are, like those of the first group, fairly loosely regulated, making the whole economy more dynamic. And they spend much more on schemes intended to ensure that the unemployed try hard to find work: in return for high benefits, they must accept that their search for a job will be closely watched and that some work-seeking programmes may be compulsory. That high unemployment benefits are a disincentive to seek work is not in doubt; but it seems that a sufficiently diligent and well-funded employment service can offset their effects. . . .

Countries in the third group – mainly southern European ones, plus France and Germany – tend to pay high benefits too. But they have not offset these with labour-market programmes on the scale of the second group, and their product markets are more protected. [Unemployment in this group averages 9.0 per cent.]

In the last group, which includes the Czech Republic, Poland and Slovakia, benefits are low. But workers are not especially easy to fire; little is spent on pushing the jobless into work; and product markets are more regulated than in any other group. [Unemployment in this group averages 15.1 per cent.][1]

1. *How would you classify the approaches of the first two groups in terms of whether they are 'market-orientated' or 'interventionist'?*
2. *Is there an even more effective approach to reducing unemployment that uses elements of each?*

[1] 'Intricate workings', *The Economist*, 17 June 2006.

Research and development (R&D)

Some 30 per cent of UK R&D is financed by the government, but around half of this has been concentrated in the defence, aerospace and nuclear power industries. As a result, there has been little government sponsorship of research in the majority of industry. Since the mid 1970s, however, there have been a number of government initiatives in the field of information technology. Even so, the amount of government support in this field has been very small compared with Japan, France and the USA. What is more, the amount of support declined between the mid 1980s and the late 1990s.

In 2000, however, the Labour government introduced a system of tax credits for small firms that invest in research and development. This was extended to large firms in 2002. Firms can offset 130 per cent of R&D expenditure (175 per cent in the case of firms with fewer than 500 employees) against profits when working out corporation tax. These tax credits amount to just under 10 per cent of the value of business R&D.

Private-sector R&D is generally lower in the UK than in other major industrialised countries. Of the companies in the top 1250 R&D spenders in the world in 2006, US companies' R&D as a percentage of sales was 4.6 per cent. For Japanese, German and French companies the figures were 3.7, 3.6 and 2.5 per cent respectively, while for UK com-panies it was only 1.9 per cent. Globally the figure was 3.5 per cent (see Case Study 23.2 in MyEconLab).

Industrial reorganisation

UK Labour governments in the past were concerned with encouraging efficiency and investment via rationalisation. For example, the Industrial Reorganisation Corporation (IRC) was set up in 1967 to provide loans to industry, and to arrange and finance mergers, where these were felt to lead to economies of scale and greater scope for investment. It was wound up in 1970 by the incoming Conservative government.

The main industrial reorganisation strategy pursued by the Conservative governments of the 1980s and 1990s was privatisation (see section 13.2 and page 659).

Assistance to small firms

UK governments in recent years have recognised the import-ance of small firms to the economy and have introduced various forms of advisory services, grants and tax conces-sions. For example, small firms pay a 21 per cent rate of corporation tax compared with 28 per cent for larger com-panies. In addition, small firms are subject to fewer plan-ning and other bureaucratic controls than large companies.

Support to small firms in the UK is examined in Case Study 23.7 in MyEconLab.

KI 22
p216

TC 15
p487

BOX 23.5   **A NEW APPROACH TO INDUSTRIAL POLICY**

As with many other areas of economic policy, industrial policy throughout most of the world has undergone a radical reorientation in recent years. The government's role has shifted from one of direct intervention in the form of subsidies and protecting industry from competition, to one of focusing upon the external business environment and the conditions that influence its competitiveness.

The reasons for such a change are both philosophical and structural:

- The rise of the political right in the 1980s led to a shift away from interventionist and towards market-based supply-side policy.
- Growing government debt, and a desire to curb public expenditure, acted as a key incentive to reduce the state's role in industrial affairs. This was argued to be one of the driving forces behind the European privatisation process since the 1980s.
- Industry, during the 1980s, became progressively more global in its outlook. As such, its investment decisions were increasingly being determined by external environmental factors, especially the technology, productivity and labour costs of its international competitors.

The new approach to industrial policy, being widely adopted by many advanced countries, is to focus on improving those factors that shape a nation's competitiveness. This involves shifting away from particular sectors to targeting what are referred to as 'framework conditions for industry'. Policies include the following:

- The promotion of investment in physical and human capital. Human capital in particular, and the existence of a sound skills base, are seen as crucial for attracting global business and ensuring long-run economic growth.
- A reduction in non-wage employment costs, such as employers' social security and pension contributions. Many governments see these costs as too high and as a severe limitation on competitiveness and employment creation.
- The promotion of innovation and the encouragement of greater levels of R&D.
- Support for small and medium-sized enterprises. SMEs have received particular attention due to their crucial role in enhancing innovation, creating employment and contributing to skills development, especially in high-tech areas.
- The improvement of infrastructure. This includes both physical transport, such as roads and railways, and information highways.
- The protection of intellectual property by more effective use of patents and copyright. By reinforcing the law in these areas it is hoped to encourage firms to develop new products and commit themselves to research.

These policies, if they are to be truly effective, are likely to require co-ordination and integration, since they represent a radical departure from traditional industrial policy.

1. *In what senses could these new policies be described as (a) non-interventionist; (b) interventionist?*
2. *Does globalisation, and in particular the global perspective of multinational corporations, make industrial policy in the form of selective subsidies and tax relief more or less likely?*

Training

The government may set up training schemes, or encourage educational institutions to make their courses more vocationally relevant, or introduce new vocational qualifications (such as the GNVQs and NVQs in the UK). Alternatively, the government can provide grants or tax relief to firms which themselves provide training schemes. Alternative approaches to training in the UK, Germany, France and the USA are examined in Box 23.3.

Regional and urban policy

Certain parts of the country suffer from lower economic growth and higher unemployment than others. These can be broad regions, such as the north-east of England or Calabria in southern Italy, or much smaller areas, such as parts of inner cities. These regional and urban problems normally result from structural problems – the main one being the decline of certain industries, such as mining or heavy manufacturing industry, which had previously been concentrated in those areas.

When an area declines, there will be a downward *regional multiplier effect*. The decline in demand and loss of jobs

lead to less money being spent in the local community; transport and other service industries lose custom. The whole region becomes more depressed.

In addition, labour may be geographically immobile. The regional pattern of industrial location may change more rapidly than the labour market can adjust to it. Thus jobs may be lost in the depressed areas more rapidly than people can migrate from them. Unemployment rises. Even when people do leave the area, this can compound the downward multiplier effect as spending further declines.

If the capital market functioned well, this could help to arrest the decline. If wages were lower and land were

---

Definition

Regional multiplier effects When a change in injections into or withdrawals from a particular region causes a multiplied change in income in that region. The regional multiplier (k_r) is given by $1/mpw_r$, where the import component of mpw_r consists of imports into that region either from abroad or from other regions of the economy.

cheaper in the depressed areas, capital would be attracted there. In practice, capital, like labour, is often relatively immobile. *Existing* capital stock is highly immobile. Buildings and most machinery cannot be moved to where the unemployed are! *New* capital is much more mobile. But there may be insufficient new investment, especially during a recession, to halt regional decline, and investors may be put off by the depressed and run-down nature of the area, the lack of suitably qualified labour and lack of infrastructure.

A supply-side response to this problem is for governments or local authorities to provide support for such areas. This can come in various forms, such as giving grants or subsidies for the creation of jobs; expenditure on infrastructure, such as roads and communications, technical colleges, community facilities and housing; the siting of government offices in such areas; the setting up of government agencies to provide advice and support for incoming firms or local community action groups.

Case Study 23.10 in MyEconLab is an extended case study of regional and urban policy in both the UK and the EU.

The case against intervention

New classical economists, monetarists, neo-Austrian economists and others advocating the free market argue the following:

- A poor investment record may be due to managerial inertia and union restrictive practices. Forcing firms and unions to face up to competition in the market may be a better way of encouraging willingness to accept change. Government subsidies may simply allow firms to continue producing inefficiently.
- The government may not make an efficient use of taxpayers' money by giving investment grants. The money may well go to extravagant and unprofitable projects, such as Concorde or the Millennium Dome.
- Private industry's low investment record may be due to a low potential return on investment. If market opportunities were good, firms would invest without the need of government support.
- UK investment has remained low in the past despite interventionist industrial policy.
- If the government is to help industry, it is best to reduce the tax burden generally, so as to increase the return on investment. The microeconomic allocation of investment resources will then still be provided by the market.

 Provide a critique of these arguments.

An example of a 'Third Way' approach to supply-side policy is the UK Labour government's 'welfare to work' policy (see Case Study 23.9 in MyEconLab). This provides benefits and other support to unemployed people and people currently outside the workforce to seek employment. It is interventionist to the extent that it targets support at particular people, but pro-market to the extent that it provides incentives for people to become more occupationally mobile.

Section summary

1. Those in favour of interventionist industrial policy point to failings of the market, such as the externalities involved in investment and training, the imperfections in the capital market and the short-term perspective of decision makers.

2. Intervention can take the form of grants, the encouragement of mergers and other forms of rationalisation, advice and persuasion, the provision of information and the direct provision of infrastructure.

3. Selective intervention can take the form of grants for research and development, encouragement of reorganisation, assistance to small firms and help for training.

END OF CHAPTER QUESTIONS

1. Define *demand-side* and *supply-side* policies. Sometimes it is said that Keynesians advocate demand-side policies and monetarists advocate supply-side policies. Is there any accuracy in this statement?

2. What is the relationship between 'successful' supply-side policies and unemployment in (i) the short run and (ii) the long run, according to (a) Keynesian and (b) monetarist assumptions?

3. Why might market-orientated supply-side policies have undesirable side-effects on aggregate demand?

4. What type of tax cuts are likely to create the greatest (a) incentives, (b) disincentives to effort?

5. Is deindustrialisation necessarily undesirable?

6. In what ways can interventionist industrial policy work *with* the market, rather than against it? What are the arguments for and against such policy?

7. Compare the relative merits of pro-market and interventionist solutions to regional decline.

8. What are the arguments for and against relying entirely on *discretionary* regional and urban policy?

9. Select a European country other than the UK and compare its regional and urban policy with that of the UK.

Online resources

Additional case studies in MyEconLab

23.1 **Deregulating the UK bus industry**. Has this led to greater competition and improved services?

23.2 **The R&D Scoreboard**. An international comparison of spending by companies on R&D.

23.3 **Controlling inflation in the past**. This case study looks at the history of prices and incomes policies in the UK.

23.4 **UK industrial performance**. This examines why the UK has had a poorer investment record than many other industrial countries and why it has suffered a process of 'deindustrialisation'.

23.5 **Technology and economic change**. How to get the benefits from technological advance.

23.6 **Indicative planning in the UK**. Experiments with planning in the 1960s and 1970s.

23.7 **Assistance to small firms in the UK**. An examination of current government measures to assist small firms.

23.8 **Small-firm policy in the EU**. This looks at the range of support available to small and medium-sized firms in the EU.

23.9 **Welfare to work**. An examination of the UK Labour government's policy of providing support to people looking for work.

23.10 **Regional and urban policy**. This extended case study looks at the causes of regional imbalance and urban decay, at various approaches to regional and urban policy and at how regional and urban policy are implemented in the UK and the EU.

Websites relevant to Chapters 21, 22 and 23

Numbers and sections refer to websites listed in the Web Appendix and hotlinked from this book's website at **www.pearsoned.co.uk/sloman**.

- For news articles relevant to these three chapters, see the *Economics News Articles* link from the book's website.

- For general news on unemployment, inflation, economic growth and supply-side policy, see websites in section A, and particularly A1–5. See also links to newspapers worldwide in A38 and 39, and the news search feature in Google at A41. See also links to economics news in A42.

- For data on unemployment, inflation and growth, see links in B1 or 2; also see B4 and 12. For UK data, see B3 and 34. For EU data, see G1 > *The Statistical Annex*. For US data, see *Current economic indicators* in B5 and the *Data* section of B17. For international data, see B15, 21, 24, 31, 33. For links to datasets, see B28; I14.

- For specific data on UK unemployment, see B1, *1. National Statistics* > the fourth link > *Labour Market* > *Labour Market Trends*. For international data on unemployment, see G1; H3 and 5.

- For information on the development of ideas, including information on classical, Keynesian, monetarist, new classical and new Keynesian thought, see C12, 18; also see links under *Methodology and History of Economic Thought* in C14; links to economists in I4 and 17. See also sites I7 and 11 > *Economic Systems and Theories* > *History of Economic Thought*.

- For the current approach to UK supply-side policy, see the latest Budget Report (e.g. sections on productivity and training) at site E30. See also sites E5 and 9.

- For support for a market-orientated approach to supply-side policy, see C17.

- For information on training in the UK and Europe, see sites D7; E5; G5, 14; and E34.

- For information on the support for small business in the UK, see site E38.

- For information on regional policy in the UK, see site E2; and in the EU, see site G12.

- For student resources relevant to these three chapters, see sites C1–7, 9, 10, 19. See also the *Labour market reforms* simulation in D3.

The World Economy

24	International Trade	671
25	The Balance of Payments and Exchange Rates	705
26	Global and Regional Interdependence	742
27	Economic Problems of Developing Countries	761

'Globalisation' is a word frequently used nowadays. But it neatly captures one of the key features of economics today: that it is global in nature. International trade has grown at a much faster rate than the levels of national output in any country. International financial flows have grown faster still. The result is that economies around the globe are intermeshed, and what happens in one country can have profound effects on others.

In Chapters 24 and 25 we look at the two key economic elements in this interdependence: international trade and international finance. Then in Chapter 26 we look at particular aspects of global interdependence. Finally we turn to the poorest countries of the world, whose development depends so much on the economic policies of the rich world.

International Trade

CHAPTER MAP

24.1 The advantages of trade	**672**
The growth of world trade	672
Specialisation as the basis for trade	672
The law of comparative advantage	672
The gains from trade based on comparative advantage	673
International trade and its effect on factor prices	677
Increasing opportunity costs and the limits to specialisation and trade	677
The terms of trade	677
*Intermediate analysis of gains from trade	679
Other reasons for gains from trade	680
The competitive advantage of nations	681
24.2 Arguments for restricting trade	**683**
Methods of restricting trade	683
Arguments in favour of restricting trade	684
Problems with protection	687
The World Trade Organisation	689
24.3 Preferential trading	**692**
Types of preferential trading arrangement	693
The direct effects of a customs union: trade creation and trade diversion	693
Longer-term effects of a customs union	695
Preferential trading in practice	696
24.4 The European Union	**697**
Historical background	697
From customs union to common market	697
The benefits and costs of the single market	698
Completing the internal market	700

Without international trade we would all be much poorer. There would be some items like pineapples, coffee, cotton clothes, foreign holidays and uranium that we would simply have to go without. Then there would be other items like wine and spacecraft that we could produce only very inefficiently. International trade has the potential to benefit all participating countries. This chapter explains why.

Totally free trade, however, may bring problems to countries or to groups of people within those countries. Many people argue strongly for restrictions on trade. Textile workers see their jobs threatened by cheap imported cloth. Car manufacturers worry about falling sales as customers switch to Japanese or other east Asian models. But are people justified in fearing international competition, or are they merely trying to protect some vested interest at the expense of everyone else? Section 24.2 examines these arguments and also looks at world attitudes towards trade restrictions.

A step on the road to freer trade is for countries to enter free-trade agreements with just a limited number of other countries. Examples include the EU and more recently the North American Free Trade Association (NAFTA – the USA, Canada and Mexico). We consider such 'preferential trading systems' in section 24.3. Finally, we look in more detail at the EU and the development of the 'single European market'.

This chapter may be studied after Chapter 11 or Chapter 13 if you prefer.

24.1 THE ADVANTAGES OF TRADE

The growth of world trade

World trade has grown rapidly over the past sixty years and at consistently higher rates than world GDP. Table 24.1 shows exports as a percentage of various countries' GDP. As you can see, in all cases the proportion was higher in 2008 than in 1960, and in some cases considerably higher.

Developed countries dominate world trade (see Figure 24.1). They account for 60 per cent of world exports and 65 per cent of world imports. The top ten trading nations account for 50 per cent of world merchandise exports. The country with the highest share is Germany (9.7%), followed by China (8.9%), the USA (8.5%), Japan (5.2%), France (4.1%), the Netherlands (3.8), Italy (3.6%) and the UK (3.2%).

Table 24.1	Exports of goods and services as percentage of GDP			
	1960	**1980**	**1995**	**2008**
Belgium	37.2	56.5	67.8	89.8
France	14.4	21.0	22.8	26.6
Ireland	29.3	45.5	76.2	81.5
Japan	10.6	13.6	9.2	18.6
Luxembourg	89.0	90.9	106.4	179.7
Sweden	22.4	29.1	39.8	54.4
UK	19.8	27.1	28.2	29.1
USA	5.2	10.2	11.1	13.5
EU-15	19.5	27.0	29.3	40.5

Source: Based on data in *Statistical Annex of the European Economy* (Commission of the European Communities, various years).

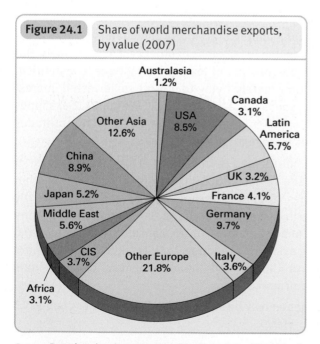

Figure 24.1	Share of world merchandise exports, by value (2007)

Source: Based on data in *International Trade Statistics* (World Trade Organization [WTO], 2008).

Specialisation as the basis for trade

Why do countries trade with each other, and what do they gain from it? The reasons for international trade are really only an extension of the reasons for trade *within* a nation. Rather than people trying to be self-sufficient and do everything for themselves, it makes sense to specialise.

Firms specialise in producing certain goods. This allows them to gain economies of scale and to exploit their entrepreneurial and management skills and the skills of their labour force. It also allows them to benefit from their particular location and from the ownership of any particular capital equipment or other assets they might possess. With the revenues firms earn, they buy in the inputs they need from other firms and the labour they require. Firms thus trade with each other.

Countries also specialise. They produce more than they need of certain goods. What is not consumed domestically is exported. The revenues earned from the exports are used to import goods that are not produced in sufficient amounts at home.

 Why does the USA not specialise as much as General Motors or Texaco? Why does the UK not specialise as much as Tesco? Is the answer to these questions similar to the answer to the questions 'Why does the USA not specialise as much as Luxembourg?' and 'Why does Tesco or Unilever not specialise as much as the local butcher?'?

But which goods should a country specialise in? What should it export and what should it import? The answer is that it should specialise in those goods in which it has a *comparative advantage*. Let us examine what this means.

The law of comparative advantage

Countries have different endowments of factors of production. They differ in population density, labour skills, climate, raw materials, capital equipment, etc. These differences tend to persist because factors are relatively immobile between countries. Obviously land and climate are totally immobile, but even with labour and capital there are more restrictions on their international movement than on their movement within countries. Thus the ability to supply goods differs between countries.

What this means is that the relative cost of producing goods varies from country to country. For example, one country may be able to produce one fridge for the same cost as 6 tonnes of wheat or three compact disc players, whereas another country may be able to produce one fridge for the same cost as only 3 tonnes of wheat or four CD players. It is these differences in relative costs that form the basis of trade.

At this stage, we need to distinguish between *absolute advantage* and *comparative advantage*.

Absolute advantage

When one country can produce a good with less resources than another country, it is said to have an **absolute advantage** in that good. If France can produce wine with less resources than the UK, and the UK can produce gin with less resources than France, then France has an absolute advantage in wine and the UK an absolute advantage in gin. Production of both wine and gin will be maximised by each country specialising and then trading with the other country. Both will gain.

Comparative advantage

The above seems obvious, but trade between two countries can still be beneficial even if one country could produce *all* goods with less resources than the other, providing the *relative* efficiency with which goods can be produced differs between the two countries.

Take the case of a developed country that is absolutely more efficient than a less developed country at producing both wheat and cloth. Assume that with a given amount of resources (labour, land and capital) the alternatives shown in Table 24.2 can be produced in each country.

Despite the developed country having an absolute advantage in both wheat and cloth, the less developed country (LDC) has a **comparative advantage** in wheat, and the developed country has a comparative advantage in cloth.

This is because wheat is relatively cheaper in the LDC: only 1 square metre of cloth has to be sacrificed to produce 2 kilos of wheat, whereas 8 square metres of cloth would

have to be sacrificed in the developed country to produce 4 kilos of wheat (i.e. 2 square metres of cloth for every 1 kilo of wheat). In other words, the opportunity cost of wheat is four times higher in the developed country (8/4 compared with 1/2).

On the other hand, cloth is relatively cheaper in the developed country. Here the opportunity cost of producing 8 square metres of cloth is only 4 kilos of wheat, whereas in the LDC 1 square metre of cloth costs 2 kilos of wheat. Thus the opportunity cost of cloth is four times higher in the LDC (2/1 compared with 4/8).

Draw up a similar table to Table 24.2, only this time assume that the figures are: LDC 6 wheat or 2 cloth; DC 8 wheat or 20 cloth. What are the opportunity cost ratios now?

To summarise: countries have a comparative advantage in those goods that can be produced at a lower opportunity cost than in other countries.

If countries are to gain from trade, they should export those goods in which they have a comparative advantage and import those goods in which they have a comparative disadvantage. From this we can state a **law of comparative advantage** (see KI 36).

> **KEY IDEA 36**
>
> **The law of comparative advantage.** Provided opportunity costs of various goods differ in two countries, both of them can gain from mutual trade if they specialise in producing (and exporting) those goods that have relatively low opportunity costs compared with the other country.

See Case Study 24.1 in MyEconLab for Ricardo's original statement of the law in 1817.

But why do they gain if they specialise according to this law? And just what will that gain be? We will consider these questions next.

The gains from trade based on comparative advantage

Before trade, unless markets are very imperfect, the prices of the two goods are likely to reflect their opportunity costs. For example, in Table 24.2, since the less developed country can produce 2 kilos of wheat for 1 square metre of cloth, the *price* of 2 kilos of wheat will roughly equal the price of 1 square metre of cloth.

Definitions

Absolute advantage A country has an absolute advantage over another in the production of a good if it can produce it with less resources than the other country.

Comparative advantage A country has a comparative advantage over another in the production of a good if it can produce it at a lower opportunity cost: i.e. if it has to forgo less of other goods in order to produce it.

Law of comparative advantage Trade can benefit all countries if they specialise in the goods in which they have a comparative advantage.

Table 24.2	Production possibilities for two countries				
			Kilos of wheat		**Square metres of cloth**
Less developed country	Either		2	or	1
Developed country	Either		4	or	8

KI 36
p673

BOX 24.1   SHARING OUT THE JOBS

A parable of comparative advantage

Imagine that you and a group of friends are fed up with the rat race and decide to set up a self-sufficient community. So you club together and use all your savings to buy an old run-down farmhouse with 30 acres of land and a few farm animals.

You decide to produce all your own food, make your own clothes, renovate the farmhouse, make all the furniture, provide all your own entertainment and set up a little shop to sell the things you make. This should bring in enough income to buy the few items you cannot make yourselves.

The day comes to move in, and that evening everyone gathers to decide how all the jobs are going to be allocated. You quickly decide that it would be foolish for all of you to try to do all the jobs. Obviously it will be more efficient to specialise. This does not necessarily mean that everyone is confined to doing only one job, but it does mean that each of you can concentrate on just a few tasks.

But who is to do which job? The answer would seem to be obvious: you pick the best person for the job. So you go down the list of tasks. Who is to take charge of the renovations? Pat has already renovated a cottage, and is brilliant at bricklaying, plastering, wiring and plumbing. So Pat would seem to be the ideal person. Who is to do the cooking? Everyone agrees on this. Pat makes the best cakes, the best quiches and the best Irish stew. So Pat is

everyone's choice for cook. And what about milking the sheep? 'Pat used to keep sheep', says Tarquin, 'and made wonderful feta cheese.' 'Good old Pat!' exclaims everyone.

It doesn't take long before it becomes obvious that 'clever-clogs' Pat is simply brilliant at everything, from planting winter wheat, to unblocking drains, to doing the accounts, to tie-dyeing. But it is soon realised that, if Pat has to do everything, nothing will get done. Even Chris, who has never done anything except market research, would be better employed milking the sheep than doing nothing at all.

So what's the best way of allocating the jobs so that the work gets done in the most efficient way? Sharon comes up with the solution. 'Everyone should make a list of all the jobs they could possibly do, and then put them in order from the one they are best at to the one they are worst at.'

So this is what everyone does. And then people are allocated the jobs they are *relatively* best at doing. Chris escapes milking the sheep and keeps the accounts instead. And Pat escapes with an eight-hour day!

 If Pat took two minutes to milk the sheep and Tarquin took six, how could it ever be more efficient for Tarquin to do it?

TC 2
p23

Assume, then, that the pre-trade exchange ratios of wheat for cloth are as follows:

LDC	:	2 wheat for 1 cloth
Developed country	:	1 wheat for 2 cloth (i.e. 4 for 8)

Both countries will now gain from trade, provided the exchange ratio is somewhere between 2:1 and 1:2. Assume, for the sake of argument, that it is 1:1, that 1 wheat trades internationally for 1 cloth. How will each country gain?

The LDC gains by exporting wheat and importing cloth. At an exchange ratio of 1:1, it now only has to give up 1 kilo of wheat to obtain a square metre of cloth, whereas before trade it had to give up 2 kilos of wheat.

The developed country gains by exporting cloth and importing wheat. Again at an exchange ratio of 1:1, it now has to give up only 1 square metre of cloth to obtain 1 kilo of wheat, whereas before it had to give up 2 square metres of cloth.

Thus both countries have gained from trade.

The actual exchange ratios will depend on the relative prices of wheat and cloth after trade takes place. These prices will depend on total demand for and supply of the two goods. It may be that the trade exchange ratio is nearer

to the pre-trade exchange ratio of one country than the other. Thus the gains to the two countries need not be equal. (We will examine these issues below.)

1. *Show how each country could gain from trade if the LDC could produce (before trade) 3 wheat for 1 cloth and the developed country could produce (before trade) 2 wheat for 5 cloth, and if the exchange ratio (with trade) was 1 wheat for 2 cloth. Would they both still gain if the exchange ratio was (a) 1 wheat for 1 cloth; (b) 1 wheat for 3 cloth?*
2. *In question 1, which country gained the most from a trade exchange ratio of 1 wheat for 2 cloth?*

Simple graphical analysis of comparative advantage and the gains from trade: constant opportunity cost

The gains from trade can be shown graphically using production possibility curves. Let us continue with the example of the developed and less developed countries that we looked at in Table 24.2, where both countries produce just two goods: wheat and cloth.

For simplicity, assume that the pre-trade opportunity costs of cloth in terms of wheat in the two countries do not vary with output: i.e. there are *constant opportunity costs* of cloth in terms of wheat of 2/1 in the LDC and 1/2 in the

Table 24.3   Pre-trade production possibilities

| | Less developed country | | | Developed country | |
	Wheat (million kg)	Cloth (million m²)		Wheat (million kg)	Cloth (million m²)
a	1000	0	g	500	0
b	800	100	h	400	200
c	600	200	i	300	400
d	400	300	j	200	600
e	200	400	k	100	800
f	0	500	l	0	1000

Figure 24.2   Effect of trade on consumption possibilities

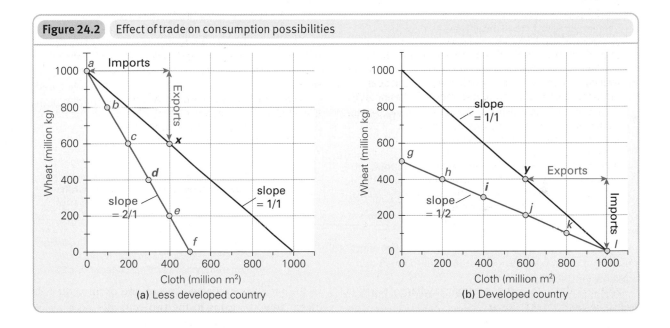

(a) Less developed country

(b) Developed country

developed country. Let us assume that the pre-trade production possibilities are as shown in Table 24.3.[1]

For each 100 extra square metres of cloth that the LDC produces, it has to sacrifice 200 kilos of wheat. For each extra 100 kilos of wheat that the developed country produces, it has to sacrifice 200 square metres of cloth. Straight-line pre-trade production possibility 'curves' can thus be drawn for the two countries with slopes of (minus) 2/1 and (minus) 1/2 respectively. These lines illustrate the various total combinations of the two goods that can be produced and hence consumed. They are shown as the blue lines in Figure 24.2.

Assume that before trade the LDC produces (and consumes) at point *d*: namely, 400 million kilos of wheat and

300 million square metres of cloth; and that the developed country produces at point *i*: namely, 300 million kilos of wheat and 400 million square metres of cloth.

If they now trade, the LDC, having a comparative advantage in wheat, will specialise in it and produce at point *a*. It will produce 1000 million kilos of wheat and no cloth. The developed country will specialise in cloth and produce at point *l*. It will produce 1000 million square metres of cloth and no wheat.

For simplicity, let us assume that trade between the two countries takes place at an exchange ratio of 1:1 (i.e. 1 kilo of wheat for 1 square metre of cloth). This means that the two countries can now *consume* along the red lines in Figure 24.2: at, say, points *x* and *y* respectively. At point *x* the LDC consumes 600 million kilos of wheat (a gain of 200 million kilos over the pre-trade position) and 400 million square metres of cloth (a gain of 100 million square metres over the pre-trade position). At point *y* the developed country consumes 400 million kilos of wheat (a gain of 100 million kilos over the pre-trade position) and

KI 2
p8

---

[1] Note that, for simplicity, it is assumed that the size of the two economies is similar. The LDC can still have an *absolute* disadvantage in both goods, however, because it may take many more resources to produce these goods. For example, it may have a very much larger population than the developed country and hence a very much lower output per person.

Table 24.4 The production and consumption gains from trade

	Less developed country			Developed country			Total	
	Production	Consumption	Imports (−)/ Exports (+)	Production	Consumption	Imports (−)/ Exports (+)	Production	Consumption
No trade								
Wheat (million kg)	400	400	0	300	300	0	700	700
Cloth (million m²)	300	300	0	400	400	0	700	700
With trade								
Wheat (million kg)	1000	600	+400	0	400	−400	1000	1000
Cloth (million m²)	0	400	−400	1000	600	+400	1000	1000

600 million square metres of cloth (a gain of 200 million square metres over the pre-trade position). Thus trade has allowed both countries to increase their consumption of both goods.

To summarise: before trade, the countries could only consume along their production possibility curves (the blue lines); after trade, they can consume along the higher red lines.

Note that in this simple two-country model total production and consumption of the two countries for each of the two goods must be the same, since one country's exports are the other's imports. Thus if the LDC produces at point *a* and consumes at point *x*, the developed country, producing at point *l*, must consume at point *y*. The effects on trade of the two countries consuming at points *x* and *y* are shown in Table 24.4.

As complete specialisation has taken place in our example, the LDC now has to import all its cloth and the developed country has to import all its wheat. Thus, given the exchange ratio of 1:1, the LDC exports 400 million kilos of

wheat in exchange for imports of 400 million square metres of cloth. (These imports and exports are also shown in Figure 24.2.)

The final two columns of Table 24.4 show that trade has increased the total production and consumption of the two countries.

1. *Draw a diagram with the same two countries and with the same production possibilities and exchange ratio as in Figure 24.2. But this time show how much would be imported and exported for each country if, after trade, the LDC consumes 500 million kilos of wheat. Fill the figures in on a table like Table 24.4.*
2. *If the opportunity cost ratio of wheat for cloth is 1/2 in the LDC, why is the slope of the production possibility curve 2/1? Is the slope of the production possibility curve always the reciprocal of the opportunity cost ratio?*
3. *Show (graphically) that, if the (pre-trade) opportunity cost ratios of the two countries were the same, there would be no gain from trade – assuming that the production possibility curves were straight lines and did not shift as a result of trade.*

TC 2 p23

KI 36 p673

KI 4 p10

BOX 24.2 TRADE AS EXPLOITATION? — EXPLORING ECONOMICS

Does free trade exploit cheap labour abroad?

People sometimes question the morality of buying imports from countries where workers are paid 'pittance' wages. 'Is it right', they ask, 'for us to support a system where workers are so exploited?' As is often the case with emotive issues, there is some truth and some misunderstanding in a point of view like this.

First the truth. If a country like the UK trades with a regime that denies human rights, and treats its workers very badly, we may thereby be helping to sustain a corrupt system. We might also be seen to be lending it moral support. In this sense, therefore, trade may not help the cause of the workers in these countries. It is arguments like these that were used to support the imposition of trade sanctions against South Africa in the days of apartheid.

Now the misunderstanding. If we buy goods from countries that pay low wages, we are *not* as a result contributing to their low-wage problem. Quite the reverse. If countries like India export textiles to the West, this will help to *increase* the wages of Indian workers. If India has a comparative advantage in labour-intensive goods, these goods will earn a better price by being exported than by being sold entirely in the domestic Indian market. Provided *some* of the extra revenues go to the workers, they will gain from trade.

Under what circumstances would a gain in revenues by exporting firms not lead to an increase in wage rates?

International trade and its effect on factor prices

Countries tend to have a comparative advantage in goods that are *intensive in their abundant factor*. Canada has abundant land and hence it is cheap. Therefore Canada specialises in grain production since grains are land-intensive. South Asian countries have abundant supplies of labour with low wage rates, and hence specialise in clothing and other labour-intensive goods. Europe, Japan and the USA have relatively abundant and cheap capital, and hence specialise in capital-intensive manufactured goods.

Trade between such countries will tend to lead to greater equality in factor prices. For example, the demand for labour will rise in labour-abundant countries like India if they specialise in labour-intensive goods. This will push up wage rates in these low-wage countries, thereby helping to close the gap between their wage rates and those of the developed world. Without trade, wage rates would tend to be even lower.

Increasing opportunity costs and the limits to specialisation and trade

In practice, countries are likely to experience increasing opportunity costs (and hence have bowed-out production possibility curves). The reason for this is that, as a country increasingly specialises in one good, it has to use resources that are less and less suited to its production and which were more suited to other goods. Thus ever-increasing amounts of the other goods have to be sacrificed. For example, as a country specialises more and more in grain production, it has to use land that is less and less suited to growing grain.

These increasing costs as a country becomes more and more specialised lead to the disappearance of its comparative cost advantage. When this happens, there will be no point in further specialisation. Thus whereas a country like Germany has a comparative advantage in capital-intensive manufactures, it does not produce only manufactures. It would make no sense not to use its fertile lands to produce food or its forests to produce timber. The opportunity costs of diverting all agricultural labour to industry would be very high.

Thus increasing opportunity costs limit the amount of a country's specialisation and hence the amount of its trade. There are also other limits to trade:

- Transport costs may outweigh any comparative advantage. A country may be able to produce bricks more cheaply than other countries, but their weight may make them too expensive to export.
- It may be the factors of production, rather than the goods, that move from country to country. Thus developed countries, rather than exporting finished goods to LDCs, may invest capital in LDCs to enable manu-

factures to be produced there. Also, labour may migrate from low-wage to high-wage countries.
- Governments may restrict trade (see section 24.2).

The terms of trade

What price will our exports fetch abroad? What will we have to pay for imports? The answer to these questions is given by the *terms of trade*.

To simplify matters, suppose there is only one exported good and only one imported good. In this case, the terms of trade are defined as P_x/P_m, where P_x is the price of the exported good and P_m is the price of the imported good. This is the reciprocal of the exchange ratio: for example, if 2x exchange for 1m (an exchange ratio of 2/1), the price of x will be half the price of m. The terms of trade will be 1/2.

1. If 4x exchange for 3m, what are the terms of trade?
2. If the terms of trade are 3, how many units of the imported good could I buy for the money earned by the sale of 1 unit of the exported good? What is the exchange ratio?

In the real world where countries have *many* exports and imports, the **terms of trade** are given by

$$\frac{\text{Average price of exports}}{\text{Average price of imports}}$$

expressed as an index, where price changes are measured against a base year in which the terms of trade are assumed to be 100. Thus if the average price of exports relative to the average price of imports has risen by 20 per cent since the base year, the terms of trade will now be 120. The terms of trade for selected countries are shown in Figure 24.3 (with 2000 as the base year).

If the terms of trade rise (export prices rising relative to import prices), they are said to have 'improved', since fewer exports now have to be sold to purchase any given quantity of imports. Changes in the terms of trade are caused by changes in the demand for and supply of imports and exports, and by changes in the exchange rate.

In Figure 24.3, which countries' terms of trade improved between 1987 and 2007?

The terms of trade and comparative advantage

Assuming there are two goods, x and m, trade can be advantageous to a country as long as the terms of trade P_x/P_m are different from the opportunity cost ratios of the two goods,

---

Definition

Terms of trade The price index of exports divided by the price index of imports and then expressed as a percentage. This means that the terms of trade will be 100 in the base year.

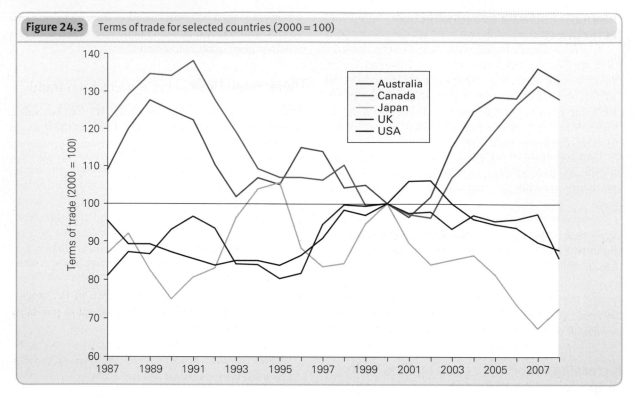

Figure 24.3 Terms of trade for selected countries (2000 = 100)

Source: Based on data in *Economic Outlook* (Organisation for Economic Co-operation and Development [OECD]).

KI 14
p102

TC 11
p310

given by MC_x/MC_m. For example, if the terms of trade were greater than the opportunity cost ratio ($P_x/P_m > MC_x/MC_m$), it would benefit the country to produce more x for export in return for imports of m, since the relative value of producing x (P_x/P_m) is greater than the relative cost (MC_x/MC_m).

With increasing opportunity costs, however, increasing specialisation in x will lead to MC_x rising (and MC_m falling), until $P_x/P_m = MC_x/MC_m$. At this point, there can be no more gain from further specialisation and trade: the maximum gain has been achieved and comparative cost advantages have been exhausted.

The determination of the terms of trade

When countries import and export many goods, the terms of trade will depend on the prices of all the various exports and imports. These prices will depend on the demand and supply of each traded good and their elasticities in the respective countries. Take the case of good g in which country A has a comparative advantage with respect to the rest of the world. This is illustrated in Figure 24.4.

Demand and supply curves of good g can be drawn for both country A and the rest of the world. (The upward-sloping supply curves imply increasing opportunity costs of

Figure 24.4 Determination of the price of an individual traded good

(a) Country A

(b) Rest of the world

production.) Before trade, country A has a low equilibrium price of P_1 and the rest of the world a high equilibrium price of P_2. After trade, price will settle at P_3 in both countries (assuming no transport costs), where total demand by both country A and the rest of the world together equals total supply, and thus where the imports of g into the rest of the world ($d - c$) equal the exports from country A ($b - a$). The position of P_3 relative to P_1 and P_2 will depend on the elasticities of demand and supply.

A similar analysis can be conducted for all the other traded goods – both exports and imports of country A. The resulting prices will allow country A's terms of trade to be calculated.

 Draw a similar diagram to Figure 24.4 showing how the price of an individual good imported into country A is determined.

The analysis is complicated somewhat if different national currencies are involved, since the prices in each country will be expressed in its own currency. Thus to convert one country's prices to another currency will require knowledge of the rate of exchange: e.g. for the USA and the UK it might be $2 = £1. But under a floating exchange rate system, the rate of exchange will depend in part on the demand for and supply of imports and exports. If the rate of exchange depreciates – say, from $2 = £1 to $1.50 = £1 – the UK's terms of trade will worsen. Exports will earn less foreign currency per pound: e.g. £1 worth of exports will now be worth only $1.50 rather than $2. Imports, on the other hand, will be more expensive: e.g. $6 worth of imports previously cost £3; they now cost £4.

 Why will exporters probably welcome a 'deterioration' in the terms of trade?

In a world of many countries and many goods, an individual country's imports and exports may have little effect on world prices. In the extreme case, the country may face prices totally dictated by the external world demand and supply. The country in this case is similar to an individual firm under perfect competition. The country is too small to influence world prices, and thus faces a horizontal demand curve for its exports and a horizontal supply curve for its imports. In foreign currency terms, therefore, the terms of trade are outside its control. Nevertheless, these terms of trade will probably be to its benefit, in the sense that the gains from trade will be virtually entirely received by this small country rather than the rest of the world. It is too small for its trade to depress the world price of its exports or drive up the price of its imports.

In general, a country's gains from trade will be greater the less elastic its own domestic demand and supply of tradable goods are, and the more elastic the demand and supply of other countries. You can see this by examining Figure 24.4. The less elastic the domestic demand and

supply, the bigger will be the effect of trade on prices faced by that country. The more the trade price differs from the pre-trade price, the bigger the gain.

*Intermediate analysis of gains from trade

The analysis of section 11.1 (pages 310–12) can be used to demonstrate the welfare gains from trade and the limits to specialisation under conditions of increasing opportunity cost. A simple two-good model is used, and the pre-trade position is compared with the position with trade.

Pre-trade
Let us make the following simplifying assumptions:

- There are two goods, x and m.
- Country A has a comparative advantage in the production of good x.
- There are increasing opportunity costs in the production of both x and m. Thus the production possibility curve is bowed out.
- Social indifference curves can be drawn, each one showing the various combinations of x and m that give society in country A a particular level of utility.

Figure 24.5 shows the pre-trade position in country A. Production and consumption at P_1C_1 will give the highest possible utility. (All other points on the production possibility curve intersect with lower indifference curves.)

If there is perfect competition, production will indeed be at P_1C_1. There are four steps in establishing this:

- The slope of the production possibility curve ($-\Delta m/\Delta x$) is the marginal rate of transformation (MRT), and equals MC_x/MC_m (see page 312). For example, if the opportunity cost of producing 1 extra unit of x (Δx) was a sacrifice of 2 units of m ($-\Delta m$), then an extra unit of x would cost twice as much as an extra unit of m: i.e. $MC_x/MC_m = 2/1$,

Figure 24.5 Equilibrium before trade

which is the slope of the production possibility curve, $-\Delta m/\Delta x$.

- The slope of each indifference curve ($-\Delta m/\Delta x$) is the marginal rate of substitution in consumption (*MRS*), and equals MU_x/MU_m. For example, if x had three times the marginal utility of m ($MU_x/MU_m = 3$), consumers would be willing to give up 3m for 1x ($-\Delta m/\Delta x = 3$).

- Under perfect competition,

$$\frac{MC_x}{MC_m} = \frac{P_x}{P_m} = \frac{MU_x}{MU_m}$$

- Thus the domestic pre-trade price ratio P_x/P_m under perfect competition must equal the slope of the production possibility curve (MC_x/MC_m) and the slope of the social indifference curve (MU_x/MU_m). This is the case at P_1C_1 in Figure 24.5.

1. If production were at point a in Figure 24.5, describe the process whereby equilibrium at point P_1C_1 would be restored under perfect competition.
2. Why would production be unlikely to take place at P_1C_1 if competition were not perfect?

With trade

If country A has a comparative advantage in good x, the price of x relative to m is likely to be higher in the rest of the world than in country A: i.e. world P_x/P_m > pre-trade domestic P_x/P_m. This is shown in Figure 24.6. The world price ratio is given by the slope of the line *WW*. With this new steeper world price ratio, the optimum production point will be P_2 where *MRT* (the slope of the production possibility curve) = world P_x/P_m (the slope of *WW*).

With production at P_2, the country can by trading consume *anywhere* along this line *WW*. The optimum consumption point will be C_2 where *MRS* (the slope of the indifference curve) = world P_x/P_m (the slope of *WW*). Thus trade has allowed consumption to move from point C_1 on

the lower indifference curve I_1 to point C_2 on the higher indifference curve I_2. There has thus been a gain from trade. Perfect competition will ensure that this gain is realised, since production at P_2 and consumption at C_2 meet the equilibrium condition that

$$\frac{MC_x}{MC_m} = \frac{P_x}{P_m} = \frac{MU_x}{MU_m}$$

How much will be imported and how much will be exported? With production at P_2 and consumption at C_2, country A will import $C_2 - D$ of good m in exchange for exports of $P_2 - D$ of good x.

Similar diagrams to Figure 24.6 can be drawn for other countries. Since they show equilibrium for both imports and exports on the *one* diagram, economists refer to them as *general equilibrium diagrams* (see page 312 for another example).

1. Draw a similar diagram to Figure 24.6, only this time assume that the two goods are good a measured on the vertical axis and good b measured on the horizontal axis. Assume that the country has a comparative advantage in good a. (Note that the world price ratio this time will be shallower than the domestic pre-trade price ratio.) Mark the level of exports of a and imports of b.
2. Is it possible to gain from trade if competition is not perfect?

Other reasons for gains from trade

Decreasing costs

Even if there are no initial comparative cost differences between two countries, it will still benefit both to specialise in industries where economies of scale (either internal or external) can be gained, and then to trade. Once the economies of scale begin to appear, comparative cost differences will also appear, and thus the countries will have gained a comparative advantage in these industries.

A similar argument applies to different models of the same product (e.g. different models of cars or electrical goods). Several countries, by specialising in just one or two models each, can gain the full economies of scale and hence a comparative advantage in their particular model(s). Then, through trade, consumers can gain from having a wider range from which to choose. Much of the specialisation that international trade permits is of this nature.

Figure 24.6 Equilibrium with trade

> ### Definition
>
> **General equilibrium diagrams (in trade theory)**
> Indifference curve/production possibility curve diagrams that show a country's production and consumption of both imports and exports.

The decreasing cost reason for trade is particularly relevant for small countries where the domestic market is not large enough to support large-scale industries. Thus exports form a much higher percentage of GDP in small countries such as Singapore than in large countries such as the USA.

 Would it be possible for a country with a comparative disadvantage in a given product at pre-trade levels of output to obtain a comparative advantage in it by specialising in its production and exporting it?

Differences in demand

Even with no comparative cost differences and no potential economies of scale, trade can benefit both countries if demand conditions differ.

If people in country A like beef more than lamb, and people in country B like lamb more than beef, then rather than A using resources better suited for lamb to produce beef and B using resources better suited for producing beef to produce lamb, it will benefit both to produce beef *and* lamb and to export the one they like less in return for the one they like more.

Increased competition

If a country trades, the competition from imports may stimulate greater efficiency at home. This extra competition may prevent domestic monopolies/oligopolies from charging high prices. It may stimulate greater research and development and the more rapid adoption of new technology. It may lead to a greater variety of products being made available to consumers.

Trade as an 'engine of growth'

In a growing world economy, the demand for a country's exports is likely to grow, especially when these exports have a high income elasticity of demand. This provides a stimulus to growth in the exporting country.

Non-economic advantages

There may be political, social and cultural advantages to be gained by fostering trading links between countries.

The competitive advantage of nations

The theory of comparative advantage shows how countries can gain from trade, but why do countries have a comparative advantage in some goods rather than others?

One explanation is that it depends on the resources that countries have. If a country has plenty of land, then it makes sense to specialise in products that make use of this abundant resource. Thus Canada produces and exports wheat. If a country has a highly skilled workforce and an established research base, then it makes sense to specialise in high-tech products and export these. Thus Germany exports many highly sophisticated manufactured products. By contrast, many developing countries with plentiful but

Figure 24.7 The competitive advantage of nations: Porter's diamond model

Source: *The Competitive Advantage of Nations*, The Free Press (Porter, M. E., 1998), p. 127.

relatively low-skilled workers specialise in primary products or simple manufactured products.

In other words, countries should specialise in goods which make intensive use of their abundant resources. But this still does not give enough detail as to why countries specialise in the precise range of products that they do. Also, why do countries both export and import the *same* products? Why do many countries produce and export cars, but also import many cars?

According to Porter,[1] there are four key determinants of why nations are highly competitive in certain products but less so in others. These are illustrated in a diagram which has become known as the 'Porter diamond' (see Figure 24.7).

Available resources. These include 'given' resources, such as raw materials, population and climate, but also specialised resources that have been developed by humans, such as the skills of the labour force, the amount and type of capital, the transport and communications infrastructure, and the science and technology base. These specialised resources vary in detail from one country to another and give them a competitive advantage in very specific products. Once an industry has started to develop, this may attract further research and development, capital investment and training, all of which are very specific to that industry. This then further builds the country's competitive advantage in that industry. Thus the highly developed engineering skills and equipment in Germany give it a competitive advantage in producing well-engineered cars.

---

[1] Michael E. Porter, *The Competitive Advantage of Nations* (The Free Press, 1998).

Demand conditions in the home market. The more discerning customers are within the country, the more this will drive the development of each firm's products and the more competitive the firm will then become in international markets. The demand for IT solutions within the USA drove the development of the software industry and gave companies such as Microsoft, Intel and Google an international advantage.

Strategy, structure and rivalry of firms. Competition between firms is not just in terms of price. Competitive rivalry extends to all aspects of business strategy, from product design, to marketing, to internal organisation, to production efficiency, to logistics. The very particular competitive conditions within each industry can have a profound effect on the development of firms within that industry and determine whether or not they gain an international competitive advantage. Strategic investments and rivalry gave Japanese electronic companies an international competitive advantage.

Related and supporting industries. Firms are more likely to be successful internationally if there are well-developed supporting industries within the home economy. These may be industries providing specialist equipment or specialist consultancy, or they may simply be other parts of the main value chain, from suppliers of inputs to distributors of the firms' output. The more efficient this value chain, the greater the competitive advantage of firms within the industry.

KEY IDEA 37

The competitive advantage of nations is the ability of countries to compete in the market for exports and with potential importers to their country. The competitiveness of any one industry depends on the availability and quality of resources, demand conditions at home in that industry, the strategies and rivalry of firms within the industry and the quality of supporting industries and infrastructure. It also depends on government policies, and there is also an element of chance.

As the arrows in Figure 24.7 show, the four determinants of competitive advantage are interlinked and influence each other. For example, the nature of related and supporting industries can influence a firm's strategic decision about whether to embark on a process of vertical integration or de-integration. Similarly, the nature of related and supporting industries depends on demand conditions in these industries and the availability of resources.

With each of the four determinants in Figure 24.7, competitive advantage can be stimulated by appropriate government supply-side policies, such as a supportive tax regime, investment in transport and communications infrastructure, investment in education and training, competition policy and sound macroeconomic management of the economy. Also, chance often has a large part to play. Any pharmaceutical company which discovers a cure for AIDS or for various types of cancer will give a significant competitive advantage to the country in which it is based.

Section summary

1. Countries can gain from trade if they specialise in producing those goods in which they have a comparative advantage: i.e. those goods that can be produced at relatively low opportunity costs. This is merely an extension of the argument that gains can be made from the specialisation and division of labour.

2. If two countries trade, then, provided that the trade price ratio of exports and imports is between the pre-trade price ratios of these goods in the two countries, both countries can gain. They can both consume *beyond* their production possibility curves.

3. With increasing opportunity costs there will be a limit to specialisation and trade. As a country increasingly specialises, its (marginal) comparative advantage will eventually disappear. Trade can also be limited by transport costs, factor movements and government intervention.

4. The terms of trade give the price of exports relative to the price of imports. Additional trade can be beneficial if the terms of trade (P_x/P_m) are greater than the relative marginal costs of exports and imports (MC_x/MC_m).

5. A country's terms of trade are determined by the demand and supply of imports and exports and their respective elasticities. This will determine the prices at which goods are traded and affect the rate of exchange. A country's gains from trade will be greater the less elastic its own domestic demand and supply of tradable goods, and the more elastic the demand and supply of other countries.

*6 Trade allows countries to achieve a higher level of utility by consuming on a higher social indifference curve. The maximum gain from trade is achieved by consuming at the point where the world price ratio is tangential to both the production possibility curve and a social indifference curve. This would be achieved under perfect competition.

7. Gains from trade also arise from decreasing costs (economies of scale), differences in demand between countries, increased competition from trade and the transmission of growth from one country to another. There may also be non-economic advantages from trade.

8. Comparative advantage is related to competitive advantage. Countries tend to have a competitive advantage in those industries where specialist resources have been developed, where products have been developed in response to changing consumer demands, where business strategy is conducive and where there is a network of supporting industries and infrastructure.

24.2 ARGUMENTS FOR RESTRICTING TRADE

Most countries have not pursued a policy of totally free trade. Their politicians know that trade involves costs as well as benefits. In this section, we will attempt to identify what these costs are, and whether they are genuine reasons for restricting trade.

Although countries may sometimes contemplate having completely free trade, they usually limit their trade. However, they certainly do not ban it altogether. The sorts of questions that governments pose are (a) should they have freer or more restricted trade and (b) in which sectors should restrictions be tightened or relaxed? Ideally, countries should weigh up the marginal benefits against the marginal costs of altering restrictions, although just *what* benefits and costs should be taken into account, and what weighting should be attached to them, may be highly contentious. For example, should external costs and benefits be considered and should these include *global* externalities?

Methods of restricting trade

Tariffs (customs duties). These are taxes on imports and are usually **ad valorem tariffs**: i.e. a percentage of the price of

> ### Definition
>
> **Ad valorem** **tariffs** Tariffs levied as a percentage of the price of the import.

the import. Tariffs that are used to restrict imports are most effective if demand is elastic (e.g. when there are close domestically produced substitutes). Tariffs can also be used as a means of raising revenue, but in this case they are more effective if demand is inelastic. They can also be used to raise the price of imported goods to prevent 'unfair' competition for domestic producers.

Quotas. These are limits imposed on the quantity of a good that can be imported. Quotas can be imposed by the government, or negotiated with other countries which agree 'voluntarily' to restrict the amount of exports to the first country.

Exchange controls. These include limits on how much foreign exchange can be made available to importers (financial quotas), or to citizens travelling abroad, or for investment. Alternatively, they may take the form of charges for the purchase of foreign currencies.

Import licensing. The imposition of exchange controls or quotas often involves requiring importers to obtain licences. This makes it easier for the government to enforce its restrictions.

Embargoes. These are total government bans on certain imports (e.g. drugs) or exports to certain countries (e.g. to enemies during war).

> **BOX 24.3** | **FREE TRADE AND THE ENVIRONMENT** | CASE STUDIES AND APPLICATIONS
>
> #### Do whales, rainforests and the atmosphere gain from free trade?
>
>
>
> International trade provides an outlet for hardwood from the rainforests, for tiger parts for medicines, for chemicals and other industrial products produced with little regard for safety or environmental standards, and for products produced using electricity generated from low-cost, high-sulphur, highly polluting coal.
>
> The problem is that countries are likely to export goods that they can produce at a relatively low opportunity cost. But these opportunity costs are *private* costs. They do not take into account externalities. This is a powerful argument against free trade based on free-market prices.
>
> Surely, though, the developed countries use taxes, legislation and other means to prevent the abuse of the environment? They may do, but this does not stop them importing products from countries that do not.
>
> In reply, the advocates of free trade argue that it is up to each country to decide its own environmental standards. If a poor country produces a product in a
>
> cheap polluting way, the gains from exporting it may more than offset the environmental damage done.
>
> There is some strength in this argument provided (a) the government of that country has done a proper study of the costs and benefits involved, including the external costs; and (b) the externalities are confined to within the country's borders. Unfortunately, in many cases neither of these conditions holds. Much of the pollution generated from industrial production has global effects (e.g. global warming).
>
> As countries such as China and India take an increasingly large share of world exports of industrial products, so these problems are likely to grow. Both countries have much lower environmental protection standards than those in Europe and North America.
>
> *Should the world community welcome the use of tariffs and other forms of protection by the rich countries against imports of goods from developing countries that have little regard for the environment?*

Administrative barriers. Regulations may be designed to exclude imports: examples include customs delays and excessive paperwork.

Procurement policies. This is where governments favour domestic producers when purchasing equipment (e.g. defence equipment).

Dumping. Alternatively, governments may favour domestic producers by subsidising their exports in a process known as **dumping**. The goods are 'dumped' at artificially low prices in the foreign market.

Arguments in favour of restricting trade

Economic arguments having some general validity

The infant industry argument. Some industries in a country may be in their infancy, but have a potential comparative advantage. This is particularly likely in developing countries. Such industries are too small yet to have gained economies of scale; their workers are inexperienced; they lack back-up facilities, such as communications networks and specialist suppliers. They may have only limited access to finance for expansion. Without protection, these **infant industries** will not survive competition from abroad.

Protection from foreign competition, however, will allow them to expand and become more efficient. Once they have achieved a comparative advantage, the protection can then be removed to enable them to compete internationally.

Similar to the infant industry argument is the *senile industry argument.* This is where industries with a potential comparative advantage have been allowed to run down and can no longer compete effectively. They may have considerable potential, but be simply unable to make enough profit to afford the necessary investment without some temporary protection. This is one of the most powerful arguments used to justify the use of special protection for the automobile and steel industries in the USA.

 How would you set about judging whether an industry had a genuine case for infant/senile industry protection?

To reduce reliance on goods with little dynamic potential. Many developing countries have traditionally exported primaries:

foodstuffs and raw materials. The world demand for these, however, is fairly income inelastic, and thus grows relatively slowly. In such cases, free trade is not an engine of growth. Instead, if it encourages countries' economies to become locked into a pattern of primary production, it may prevent them from expanding in sectors like manufacturing that have a higher income elasticity of demand. There may thus be a valid argument for protecting or promoting manufacturing industry. (We explore these arguments in section 27.2.)

To prevent dumping and other unfair trade practices. A country may engage in dumping by subsidising its exports. The result is that prices may no longer reflect comparative costs. Thus the world would benefit from tariffs being imposed to counteract such practices.

 Does the consumer in the importing country gain or lose from dumping?

It can also be argued that there is a case for retaliating against countries that impose restrictions on your exports. In the *short* run, both countries are likely to be made worse off by a contraction in trade. But if the retaliation persuades the other country to remove its restrictions, it may have a longer-term benefit. In some cases, the mere threat of retaliation may be enough to get another country to remove its protection.

To prevent the establishment of a foreign-based monopoly. Competition from abroad, especially when it involves dumping or predatory pricing (see pages 210 and 373), could drive domestic producers out of business. The foreign company, now having a monopoly of the market, could charge high prices with a resulting misallocation of resources.

All of the above arguments suggest that governments should adopt a 'strategic' approach to trade. **Strategic trade theory** (see Box 24.4) argues that protecting certain industries allows a net gain *in the long run* from increased competition in the market. This argument has been used to justify the huge financial support given to the aircraft manufacturer Airbus, a consortium based in four European countries. The subsidies have allowed it to compete with Boeing, which would otherwise have a monopoly in many

---

Definitions

Dumping Where exports are sold at prices below marginal cost – often as a result of government subsidy.

Infant industry An industry that has a potential comparative advantage, but which is as yet too underdeveloped to be able to realise this potential.

Strategic trade theory The theory that protecting/supporting certain industries can enable them to compete more effectively with large monopolistic rivals abroad. The effect of the protection is to increase long-run competition and may enable the protected firms to exploit a comparative advantage that they could not have done otherwise.

BOX 24.4	STRATEGIC TRADE THEORY	EXPLORING ECONOMICS

An argument for protection?

KI 22
p216

Lester Thurow is professor of management and economics in the Sloan School of Management at the Massachusetts Institute of Technology (MIT). He is also an economics journalist and editor. He is also one of the USA's best-known and most articulate advocates of 'managed trade'.

Thurow (and others) have been worried by the growing penetration of US markets by imports from Japan and Europe and also from China and many other developing countries. Their response is to call for a carefully worked-out strategy of protection for US industries.

The *strategic trade theory* that they support argues that the real world is complex. It is wrong, they claim, to rely on free trade and existing comparative advantage. Particular industries will require particular policies of protection or promotion tailored to their particular needs:

- Some industries will require protection against unfair competition from abroad – not just to protect the industries themselves, but also to protect the consumer from the oligopolistic power that the foreign companies will gain if they succeed in driving the domestic producers out of business.
- Other industries will need special support in the form of subsidies to enable them to modernise and compete effectively with imports.
- New industries may require protection to enable them to get established – to achieve economies of scale and build a comparative advantage.
- If a particular foreign country protects or promotes its *own* industries, it may be desirable to retaliate in order to persuade the country to change its mind.

But, despite the enthusiasm of the strategic trade theorists, their views have come in for concerted criticism from economic liberals. If the USA is protected from cheap imports from Asia, they claim, all that will be achieved is a huge increase in consumer prices. The car, steel, telecommunications and electrical goods industries might find their profits bolstered, but this is hardly likely to encourage them to be more efficient.

Another criticism of managed trade is the difficulty of identifying just which industries need protection, and how much and for how long. Governments do not have perfect knowledge. What is more, the political lobbyists from various interested groups are likely to use all sorts of tactics – legal or illegal – to persuade the government to look favourably on them. In the face of such pressure, will the government remain 'objective'? No, say the liberals.

So how do the strategic trade theorists reply? If it works for China and Japan, they say, it can work for the USA. What is needed is a change in attitudes. Rather than industry looking on the government as either an enemy to be outwitted or a potential benefactor to be wooed, and government looking on industry as a source of votes or tax revenues, both sides should try to develop a partnership – a partnership from which the whole country can gain.

But whether sensible, constructive managed trade is possible in the US democratic system, or the UK for that matter, is a highly debatable point. 'Sensible' managed trade, say the liberals, is just pie in the sky.

Airbus, a consortium based in four European countries, has received massive support from the four governments, in order to enable it to compete with Boeing, which until the rise of Airbus had dominated the world market for aircraft. To what extent are (a) air travellers; (b) citizens of the four countries likely to gain or lose from this protection? (See Case Study 24.9 in MyEconLab.)

---

types of passenger aircraft. Airlines and their passengers worldwide, it is argued, have benefited from the increased competition.

To spread the risks of fluctuating markets. A highly special-ised economy – Zambia with copper, Cuba with sugar – is highly susceptible to world market fluctuations. Greater diversity and greater self-sufficiency can reduce these risks.

To reduce the influence of trade on consumer tastes. It is a mis-take to assume that fixed consumer tastes dictate the pattern of production through trade. Multinational com-panies through their advertising and other forms of sales promotion may influence consumer tastes. Thus some restriction on trade may be justified in order to reduce this 'producer sovereignty'.

In what ways may free trade have harmful cultural effects on developing countries?

To prevent the importation of harmful goods. A country may want to ban or severely curtail the importation of things such as drugs, pornographic literature and live animals.

To take account of externalities. Free trade will tend to reflect private costs. Both imports and exports, however, can involve externalities. The mining of many minerals for export may damage the health of miners; the production of chemicals for export may involve pollution; the importa-tion of juggernaut lorries may lead to structural damage to houses; shipping involves large amounts of CO_2 emissions (some 4–5 per cent of total world emissions) (see Box 24.3).

KI 29
p313

In recent years some politicians and green groups have called for the imposition of 'carbon tariffs'. The rate of tariff would reflect the amount of carbon emitted in the produc-tion of the good being imported. Such tariffs would be hard to implement, however. Assessing and valuing the carbon emitted would be very difficult and could lead to arbitrary tariff rates. Also, domestic goods would have to be subject to similar taxes.

Economic arguments having some validity for specific groups or countries

The arguments considered so far are of general validity: restricting trade for such reasons could be of net benefit to the world. There are other arguments, however, that are used by individual governments for restricting trade, where their country will gain, but at the *expense* of other countries, such that there will be a net loss to the world. Such arguments include the following.

The exploitation of market power. If a country, or a group of countries, has market power in the supply of exports (e.g. South Africa with diamonds, OPEC with oil) or market power in the demand for imports (e.g. the USA or other large wealthy countries), it can exploit this power by intervening in trade.

Let us first take the case of a country, or a group of countries acting as a cartel, which has monopoly power in the sale of a particular export: for example, West African countries in the sale of cocoa. But let us assume that there are many individual producers that are therefore price takers and are thus not in a position to exploit the country's overall market power. In Figure 24.8, these price-taking firms will collectively produce at point *a* where $P = MC$. Market equilibrium is at a trade price of P_1 and an output of Q_1.

The country's profit, however, would be maximised at point *b* where $MC = MR$, with output at the lower level of Q_2. By imposing an export tax of $P_2 - P_3$, therefore, the country can maximise its gain from this export. Producers will receive P_3 and will therefore supply Q_2. Market price will be P_2.

> 1. How much would be the total tax revenue for the government?
> 2. Will the individual producers gain from the export tax?

Now let us take the case of a country that has *monopsony* power in the demand for an import. This is illustrated in Figure 24.9. Without intervention, equilibrium will be at

Figure 24.9 A country with a monopsony demand for an export

point *d* where demand equals supply. Q_1 would be purchased at a price of P_1.

But the marginal cost of imports curve will be *above* the supply curve because, given the country's size, the purchase of additional imports would drive up their price. This means that the cost of additional imports would be the new higher price (given by the supply curve) *plus* the rise in expenditure on the imports that would previously have been purchased at a lower price. The country will maximise its gain from trade at point *f* by importing Q_2, where demand equals marginal cost. Consumption can be reduced to Q_2 if the government imposes a tariff of $P_3 - P_2$. This is known as the **optimum tariff**. The country now only pays P_2 to importers. Consumers have to pay P_3 (i.e. P_2 plus the tariff).

The country gains from such intervention, but only at the expense of the other countries with which it trades.

To protect declining industries. The human costs of sudden industrial closures can be very high. In such circumstances, temporary protection may be warranted to allow industries that have lost comparative advantage to decline more slowly. Such policies will be at the expense of the consumer, who will be denied access to cheaper foreign imports.

To improve the balance of payments. Under certain special circumstances, when other methods of balance of payments correction are unsuitable, there may be a case for resorting to tariffs (see Chapter 25).

Definition

Optimum tariff A tariff that reduces the level of imports to the point where marginal social cost equals marginal social benefit.

Figure 24.8 A country with a monopoly supply of an export

*BOX 24.5 THE OPTIMUM TARIFF OR EXPORT TAX

Using calculus

The size of the optimum export tax depends on the price elasticity of demand (P_{ϵ_d}). You can see this if you imagine rotating the demand and *MR* curves in Figure 24.8. The less elastic the demand curve, the bigger will be the optimum export tax. The formula for the optimum export tax rate is

$$t = 1/P_{\epsilon_d}$$

The proof of this is as follows.

In Figure 24.8, the optimum tax rate is

$$(P_2 - P_3) \div P_2 \qquad (1)$$

From the point of view of the country (as opposed to individual producers) this is simply

$$(P - MR) \div P \qquad (2)$$

Remember from Box 3.3 (on page 65) that price elasticity of demand is given by

$$P_{\epsilon_d} = \frac{-dQ}{dP} \times \frac{P}{Q} \qquad (3)$$

Remember also, from Box 5.9 (on page 158), that

$$MR = \frac{dTR}{dQ} = \frac{d(P \cdot Q)}{dQ} \qquad (4)$$

From the rules of calculus:

$$\frac{d(P \cdot Q)}{dQ} = \frac{dP \cdot Q + dQ \cdot P}{dQ} \qquad (5)$$

$$\therefore \quad P - MR = P - \frac{dP \cdot Q + dQ \cdot P}{dQ} \qquad (6)$$

and

$$\frac{P}{P - MR} = \frac{P}{P - \dfrac{dP \cdot Q + dQ \cdot P}{dQ}} \qquad (7)$$

$$= 1 - \frac{P}{P - \dfrac{dP \cdot Q + dQ \cdot P}{dQ}} \qquad (8)$$

Again from the rules of calculus:

$$= 1 - \left(\frac{dQ \cdot P}{dP \cdot Q} + \frac{dQ \cdot P}{dQ \cdot P} \right) \qquad (9)$$

$$= 1 - \frac{dQ \cdot P}{dP \cdot Q} - 1 \qquad (10)$$

$$= \frac{-dQ \cdot P}{dP \cdot Q} = P_{\epsilon_d} \qquad (11)$$

$\therefore$ from equations (2) and (11):

$$\frac{P - MR}{P} = \text{optimum tax rate} = \frac{1}{P_{\epsilon_d}}$$

 See if you can devise a similar proof to show that the optimal import tariff, where a country has monopsony power, is $1/P_{\epsilon_s}$ (where P_{ϵ_s} is the price elasticity of supply of the import).

'Non-economic' arguments

A country may be prepared to forgo the direct economic advantages of free trade – consumption at a lower opportunity cost – in order to achieve objectives that are often described as 'non-economic':

- It may wish to maintain a degree of self-sufficiency in case trade is cut off in times of war. This may apply particularly to the production of food and armaments.
- It may decide not to trade with certain countries with which it disagrees politically.
- It may wish to preserve traditional ways of life. Rural communities or communities based on old traditional industries may be destroyed by foreign competition.
- It may prefer to retain as diverse a society as possible, rather than one too narrowly based on certain industries.

Pursuing such objectives, however, involves costs. Preserving a traditional way of life, for example, may mean that consumers are denied access to cheaper goods from abroad. Society must therefore weigh up the benefits against the costs of such policies.

 If economics is the study of choices of how to use scarce resources, can these other objectives be legitimately described as 'non-economic'?

Problems with protection

Tariffs and other forms of protection impose a cost on society. This is illustrated in Figure 24.10. It illustrates the case of a good that is partly home produced and partly imported. Domestic demand and supply are given by D_{dom} and S_{dom}. It is assumed that firms in the country produce under perfect competition and that therefore the supply curve is the sum of the firms' marginal cost curves.

Let us assume that the country is too small to affect world prices: it is a price taker. The world price is given, at P_w, and world supply to the country (S_{world}) is perfectly elastic. At P_w, Q_2 is demanded, Q_1 is supplied by domestic suppliers and hence $Q_2 - Q_1$ is imported.

Now a tariff is imposed. This shifts up the world supply curve to the country by the amount of the tariff. Price rises to $P_w + t$. Domestic production increases to Q_3, consumption falls to Q_4, and hence imports fall to $Q_4 - Q_3$.

BOX 24.6 | **GIVING TRADE A BAD NAME** | **EXPLORING ECONOMICS**

Arguments that don't add up

'*Why buy goods from abroad and deny jobs to workers in this country?*' This is typical of the concerns that many people have about an open trade policy. However, these concerns are often based on arguments that do not stand up to close inspection. Here are four of them.

'*Imports should be reduced since they lower the standard of living. The money goes abroad rather than into the domestic economy.*' Imports are consumed and thus add directly to consumer welfare. Also, provided they are matched by exports, there is no net outflow of money. Trade, because of the law of comparative advantage, allows countries to increase their standard of living: to consume beyond their production possibility curve (see Figures 24.2 and 24.6).

'*Protection is needed from cheap foreign labour.*' Importing cheap goods from, say, Indonesia, allows more goods to be consumed. The UK uses less resources by buying these goods through the production and sale of exports than by producing them at home. However, there will be a cost to certain UK workers whose jobs are lost through foreign competition.

'*Protection reduces unemployment.*' At a microeconomic level, protecting industries from foreign competition may allow workers in those industries to retain their jobs. But if foreigners sell fewer goods to the UK, they will not be able to buy so many UK exports. Thus unemployment will rise in UK export industries. Overall unemployment, therefore, is little affected, and in the meantime the benefits from trade to consumers are reduced. Temporary protection given to declining industries, however, may help to reduce structural unemployment.

'*Dumping is always a bad thing, and thus a country should restrict subsidised imports.*' Dumping may well reduce world economic welfare: it goes against the law of comparative advantage. The importing country, however, may well gain from dumping. Provided the dumping is not used to drive domestic producers out of business and establish a foreign monopoly, the consumer gains from lower prices. The losers are the taxpayers in the foreign country and the workers in competing industries in the home country.

 Go through each of these four arguments and provide a reply to the criticisms of them.

Figure 24.10 | The cost of protection

What are the costs of this tariff to the country? Consumers are having to pay a higher price, and hence consumer surplus falls from *ABC* to *ADE*. The cost to consumers in lost consumer surplus is thus *EDBC* (i.e. areas 1 + 2 + 3 + 4). *Part* of this cost, however, is redistributed as a *benefit* to other sections in society. *Firms* face a higher price, and thus gain extra profits (area 1): where profit is given by the area between the price and the *MC* curve. The *government* receives extra revenue from the tariff payments (area 3): i.e. $Q_4 - Q_3 \times$ tariff. These revenues can be used, for example, to reduce taxes.

But *part* of this cost is not recouped elsewhere. It is a net cost to society (areas 2 and 4).

Area 2 represents the extra costs of producing $Q_3 - Q_1$ at home, rather than importing it. If $Q_3 - Q_1$ were still imported, the country would only be paying S_{world}. By producing it at home, however, the costs are given by the domestic supply curve (= *MC*). The difference between *MC* and S_{world} (area 2) is thus the efficiency loss on the production side.

Area 4 represents the loss of consumer surplus by the reduction in consumption from Q_2 to Q_4. Consumers have saved area FBQ_2Q_4 of expenditure, but have sacrificed area DBQ_2Q_4 of utility in so doing – a net loss of area 4.

The government should ideally weigh up such costs against any benefits that are gained from protection.

 In this model, where the country is a price taker and faces a horizontal supply curve (the small country assumption), is any of the cost of the tariff borne by the overseas suppliers?

Apart from these direct costs to the consumer, there are several other problems with protection. Some are direct effects of the protection; others follow from the reactions of other nations.

Protection as 'second best'. Many of the arguments for protection amount merely to arguments for some type of government intervention in the economy. Protection, however, may not be the best way of dealing with the problem, since protection may have undesirable side-effects. There may be a more direct form of intervention that has no side-effects. In such a case, protection will be no more than a *second-best* solution.

For example, using tariffs to protect old inefficient industries from foreign competition may help prevent unemployment in those parts of the economy, but the consumer will suffer from higher prices. A better solution would be to subsidise retraining and investment in those areas of the country in *new efficient* industries – industries with a comparative advantage. In this way, unemployment is avoided, but the consumer does not suffer.

Even if the *existing* industries were to be supported, it would still be better to do this by paying them subsidies than by putting tariffs on imports. This argument can be expressed in terms of Figure 24.10. As we have seen, a tariff imposes costs on the consumer of areas $1 + 2 + 3 + 4$. In the current example, area 2 may be a cost worth paying in order to increase domestic output to Q_3 (and hence reduce unemployment). Areas 1 and 3, as argued above, are merely *redistributed* elsewhere (to firms and the government respectively). But this still leaves area 4. This is a side-effect cost not recouped elsewhere.

A *subsidy*, on the other hand, would not have involved this side-effect cost. In order to raise output to Q_3, a rate of subsidy the same as the tariff rate would have to be given to producers. This would raise the amount they receive per unit to $P_w + t$. They would choose to supply Q_3. The price to the consumer, however, would *remain at the world price P_w*. There would thus be no cost to the consumer. The cost of the subsidy to the taxpayer would be areas $1 + 2$. Area 1 would be redistributed to firms as extra profit. Area 2, as argued above, may be worth paying to achieve the desirable output and employment consequences.

If the aim is to increase output, a *production* subsidy is the best policy. If the aim is to increase employment, an *employment* subsidy is the best policy. In either case, to use *protection* instead would be no more than second best, since it would involve side-effects.

To conclude: the best policy is to tackle the problem directly. Unless the aim is specifically to reduce imports (rather than help domestic industry), protection is an indirect policy, and hence never more than second best.

1. What would be the 'first-best' solution to the problem of an infant industry not being able to compete with imports?
2. Protection to allow the exploitation of monopoly/monopsony power can be seen as a 'first-best' policy for the country concerned. Similarly, the use of tariffs to counteract externalities directly involved in the trade process (e.g. the environmental costs of an oil tanker disaster) could be seen to be a first-best policy. Explain why.

World multiplier effects. If the UK imposes tariffs or other restrictions, imports will be reduced. But these imports are other countries' exports. A reduction in their exports will reduce the level of injections into the 'rest-of-the-world'

economy, and thus lead to a multiplied fall in rest-of-the-world income. This in turn will lead to a reduction in demand for UK exports. This, therefore, tends to undo the benefits of the tariffs.

What determines the size of this world multiplier effect?

Retaliation. If the USA imposes restrictions on, say, imports from the EU, then the EU may impose restrictions on imports from the USA. Any gain to US firms competing with EU imports is offset by a loss to US exporters. What is more, US consumers suffer, since the benefits from comparative advantage have been lost.

The increased use of tariffs and other restrictions can lead to a trade war: each country cutting back on imports from other countries. In the end, everyone loses.

Protection may allow firms to remain inefficient. By removing or reducing foreign competition, protection may reduce firms' incentive to reduce costs. Thus if protection is being given to an infant industry, the government must ensure that the lack of competition does not prevent it 'growing up'. Protection should not be excessive and should be removed as soon as possible.

Bureaucracy. If a government is to avoid giving excessive protection to firms, it should examine each case carefully. This can lead to large administrative costs.

Corruption. Some countries that have an extensive programme of protection suffer from corruption. Home producers want as much protection as possible. Importers want as much freedom as possible. It is very tempting for both groups to bribe officials to give them favourable treatment.

The World Trade Organisation

After the Wall Street crash of 1929 (when prices on the US stock exchange plummeted), the world plunged into the Great Depression (see pages 459–60). Countries found their exports falling dramatically, and many suffered severe balance of payments difficulties. The response of many countries was to restrict imports by the use of tariffs and quotas. Of course, this reduced other countries' exports, which encouraged them to resort to even greater protectionism. The net effect of the Depression and the rise in protectionism was a dramatic fall in world trade. The volume of world trade in manufactures fell by more than a third in the three years following the Wall Street crash. Clearly there was a net economic loss to the world from this decline in trade.

After the Second World War there was a general desire to reduce trade restrictions, so that all countries could gain the maximum benefits from trade. There was no desire to return to the beggar-my-neighbour policies of the 1930s.

In 1947, 23 countries got together and signed the General Agreement on Tariffs and Trade (GATT). By 2009, there were 153 members of its successor organisation, the World Trade Organisation (WTO), which was formed in 1995. Between them, the members of the WTO account for some 96 per cent of world trade. The aims of GATT, and now the WTO, have been to liberalise trade.

WTO rules

The WTO requires its members to operate according to various rules. These include the following:

- Non-discrimination. Under the 'most favoured nations clause', any trade concession that a country makes to one member must be granted to *all* signatories. The only exception is with free-trade areas and customs unions (such as the EU). Here countries are permitted to abolish tariffs between themselves while still maintaining them with the rest of the world.

- Reciprocity. Any nation benefiting from a tariff reduction made by another country must reciprocate by making similar tariff reductions itself.
- The general prohibition of quotas.
- Fair competition. If unfair barriers are erected against a particular country, the WTO can sanction retaliatory action by that country. The country is not allowed, however, to take such action without permission.
- Binding tariffs. Countries cannot raise existing tariffs without negotiating with their trading partners.

Unlike the GATT, the WTO has the power to impose sanctions on countries breaking trade agreements. If there are disputes between member nations, these will be settled by the WTO, and if an offending country continues to impose trade restrictions, permission will be granted for other countries to retaliate.

For example, in March 2002, the Bush administration imposed tariffs on steel imports into the USA in order to protect the ailing US steel industry (see Case Study 24.7 in MyEconLab). The EU and other countries referred the case

---

BOX 24.7 **THE DOHA DEVELOPMENT AGENDA**

A new direction for the WTO?

Globalisation, based on the free play of comparative advantage, economies of scale and innovation, has produced a genuinely radical force, in the true sense of the word. It essentially amplifies and reinforces the strengths, but also the weaknesses, of market capitalism: its efficiency, its instability, and its inequality. If we want globalisation not only to be efficiency-boosting but also fair, we need more international rules and stronger multilateral institutions.[1]

In November 1999, the members of the World Trade Organisation met in Seattle in the USA. What ensued became known as the 'Battle of Seattle' (see Case Study 24.4 in MyEconLab). Anti-globalisation protesters fought with police; the world's developing economies fell out with the world's developed economies; and the very future of the WTO was called into question. The WTO was accused of being a free trader's charter, in which the objective of free trade was allowed to ride roughshod over anything that might stand in its way. Whatever the issue – the environment, the plight of developing countries, the dominance of trade by multinationals – free trade was king.

At Seattle, both the protesters and developing countries argued that things had gone far enough. The WTO must redefine its role, they argued, to respect *all* stakeholders. More radical voices called for the organisation to be scrapped. As Pascal Lamy, the EU Trade Commissioner, made clear in the speech quoted above, rules had to be strengthened, and the WTO had to ensure that the gains from trade were fairer and more sustainable.

The rebuilding process of the WTO began in Doha, Qatar, in November 2001. The meeting between the then

142 members of the WTO concluded with the decision to launch a new round of WTO trade talks, to be called the 'Doha Development Agenda'. As with previous trade rounds, the talks were designed to increase the liberalisation of trade. However, this time such a goal was to be tempered by a policy of strengthening assistance to developing economies.

At Doha it was agreed that the new trade talks would address questions such as:

- Sustainable development and the environment. In the past, international trade agreements always seemed to take precedence over international environmental agreements, even though they are legally equivalent. The hope this time was to achieve greater coherence between various areas of international policy making.
- Trade and development. The Doha round would attempt to address a number of issues of concern to developing countries as they become more integrated into the world's trading system. These included improving access to markets in developed countries and strengthening the special treatment that developing countries received, such as the ability to maintain higher rates of tariff protection.

Other areas identified for discussion include: greater liberalisation of agriculture; rules to govern foreign direct investment; the co-ordination of countries' competition policies; the use and abuse of patents on medicines; and the needs of developing countries.

The talks were originally scheduled for completion by January 2005, but this deadline was extended several times as new talks were arranged and failed to the WTO, which in December 2003 ruled that they were illegal. This ruling made it legitimate for the EU and other countries to impose retaliatory tariffs on US products. President Bush consequently announced that the steel tariffs would be abolished.

 Could US action to protect its steel industry from foreign competition be justified in terms of the interests of the USA as a whole (as opposed to the steel industry in particular)?

The greater power of the WTO has persuaded many countries to bring their disputes to it. In the first 13 years of its existence it had dealt with over 380 disputes (compared with 300 by GATT over the whole of its 48 years).

Trade rounds

Periodically, member countries have met to negotiate reductions in tariffs and other trade restrictions. There have been eight 'rounds' of such negotiations since the signing of GATT in 1947. The last major round to be completed was the Uruguay round, which began in Uruguay in 1986, continued at meetings around the world and culminated in a deal being signed in April 1994. By that time, the average tariff on manufactured products was 4 per cent and falling. In 1947 the figure was nearly 40 per cent. The Uruguay round agreement also involved a programme of phasing in substantial reductions in tariffs and other restrictions up to the year 2002 (see Case Study 24.2 in MyEconLab).

Despite the reduction in tariffs, many countries have still tried to restrict trade by various other means, such as quotas and administrative barriers. Also, barriers have been particularly high on certain non-manufactures. Agricultural protection in particular has come in for sustained criticism by developing countries. High fixed prices and subsidies given to farmers in the EU, the USA and other advanced countries mean that the industrialised world continues to export food to many developing countries that have a comparative advantage in food production! Farmers in developing countries often find it impossible to compete with subsidised food imports from the rich countries.

CASE STUDIES AND APPLICATIONS

to reach agreement. A particular sticking point was the unwillingness of rich countries, and the USA and the EU in particular, to make sufficient reductions in agricultural protection, given the pressure from their domestic farmers. The USA was unwilling to make substantial cuts in agricultural subsidies and the EU in agricultural tariffs.

There was also an unwillingness on the part of large developing countries, such as India and Brazil, to reduce protection to their industrial and service sectors. What is more, there were large divergences in opinion between developing countries on how much they should reduce their own agricultural protection.

Breakdown of the talks

The talks seemed finally to have broken down at a meeting in Geneva in July 2008. Despite the willingness of developing countries to reduce industrial tariffs by more than 50 per cent, and that of the USA and the EU to make deep cuts in agricultural subsidies and tariffs, the talks foundered over the question of agricultural protection for developing countries. This was item 18 on a 'to-do' list of 20 items; items 1 to 17 had already been agreed. China and India wanted to protect poor farmers by retaining the ability to impose temporary tariffs on food imports in the event of a drop in food prices or a surge in imports. The USA objected. When neither side would budge, the talks collapsed.

But even 'success' would not have addressed some thorny issues, such as achieving equal access to rich countries' markets by all banana-producing countries (see Case Study 24.5 in MyEconLab) and protecting cotton producers in developing countries from cheap subsidised cotton grown in the USA. And Africa's interests would not have been properly addressed. In fact, no African country was present in the inner circle of talks at the end.

Many commentators, however, argued that failure was no catastrophe. The gain from total liberalisation of trade would have boosted developing countries' GDP by no more than 1 per cent. And anyway, tariffs were generally falling and were already at an all-time low. But, with the world economy faltering in 2008, there were worries that protectionism would begin to rise again – something that an agreement could have helped. Disillusionment with the WTO could hasten the erection of barriers.

This issue was very much on the minds of the leaders of twenty of the world's largest economies when they met in Washington in November 2008 to find ways of reforming the financial sector and combating recession. The G20 meeting agreed not to increase trade barriers for the next 12 months and to strive for a conclusion of the Doha round. But with leaders anxious not to take risks with their own countries' interests at a time of economic uncertainty, a deal seemed unlikely before the end of 2009 and probably later. By the time you read this, a final agreement may have been reached – or perhaps not!

 Does the process of globalisation mean that the role of the WTO is becoming less and less important?

[1] 'Global policy without democracy' (speech by Pascal Lamy, EU Trade Commissioner, given in 2001).

The most recent round of trade negotiations began in Doha, Qatar, in 2001 (see Box 24.7). The negotiations have focused on both trade liberalisation and measures to encourage development of poorer countries. In particular, the Doha Development Agenda, as it is called, is concerned with measures to make trade fairer so that its benefits are spread more evenly around the world. This would involve improved access for developing countries to markets in the rich world. The Agenda is also concerned with the environmental impacts of trade and development. The negotiations were originally due to be completed in

2005, but, as Box 24.7 explains, deadlines continued to be missed and three years later agreement had still not been reached.

To make matters worse, as the world plunged into recession in 2008/9, concerns grew that countries would resort to protectionism to support their domestic industries. But this was a classic prisoner's dilemma (see pages 201–5 and 354–6). Policies that seemed to be in the interests of countries separately would be to the overall determinant of the world. The Nash equilibrium of such a 'game', therefore, is one where countries are generally worse off.

Section summary

1. Countries use various methods to restrict trade, including tariffs, quotas, exchange controls, import licensing, export taxes, and legal and administrative barriers. Countries may also promote their own industries by subsidies.

2. Reasons for restricting trade that have some validity in a world context include the infant industry argument; the inflexibility of markets in responding to changing comparative advantage, dumping and other unfair trade practices; the danger of the establishment of a foreign-based monopoly; the problems of relying on exporting goods whose market is growing slowly or even declining; the need to spread the risks of fluctuating export prices; and the problems that free trade may adversely affect consumer tastes, may allow the importation of harmful goods and may not take account of externalities.

3. Often, however, the arguments for restricting trade are in the context of one country benefiting even though other countries may lose more. Countries may intervene in trade in order to exploit their monopoly/ monopsony power. In the case of imports, the optimum tariff would be that which would reduce consumption to the level where price was equal to the country's marginal cost. In the case of exports, the optimum export tax would be that which reduced production to the level where the country's marginal revenue was equal to marginal cost. Other 'beggar-my-neighbour' arguments include the protection of declining industries and improving the balance of payments.

4. Finally, a country may have other objectives in restricting trade, such as remaining self-sufficient in certain strategic products, not trading with certain countries of which it disapproves, protecting traditional ways of life or simply retaining a non-specialised economy.

5. In general, trade brings benefits to countries, and protection to achieve one objective may be at a very high opportunity cost. Other things being equal, there will be a net loss in welfare from restricting trade, with any gain in government revenue or profits to firms being outweighed by a loss in consumer surplus. Even if government intervention to protect certain parts of the economy is desirable, restricting trade is unlikely to be a first-best solution to the problem, since it involves side-effect costs. What is more, restricting trade may have adverse world multiplier effects; it may encourage retaliation; it may allow inefficient firms to remain inefficient; it may involve considerable bureaucracy and possibly even corruption.

6. Most countries of the world are members of the WTO and in theory are in favour of moves towards freer trade. The Uruguay round brought significant reductions in trade restrictions, both tariff and non-tariff. Nevertheless, countries have been very unwilling to abandon restrictions if they believe that they can gain from them, even though they might be at the expense of other countries.

24.3 PREFERENTIAL TRADING

The world economy seems to have been increasingly forming into a series of trade blocs, based upon regional groupings of countries: a European region centred on the European Union, an Asian region on Japan, a North American region on the USA and a Latin American region. Such trade blocs are examples of *preferential trading arrangements*. These arrangements involve trade restrictions with the rest of the world, and lower or zero restrictions between the members.

Although trade blocs clearly encourage trade between their members, many countries outside the blocs complain

that they benefit the members at the expense of the rest of the world. For many developing economies, in need of access to the most prosperous nations in the world, this represents a significant check on their ability to grow and develop.

Definition

Preferential trading arrangements A trade agreement whereby trade between the signatories is freer than trade with the rest of the world.

Types of preferential trading arrangement

There are three possible forms of such trading arrangements.

Free-trade areas

A *free-trade area* is where member countries remove tariffs and quotas between themselves, but retain whatever restrictions *each member chooses* with non-member countries. Some provision will have to be made to prevent imports from outside coming into the area via the country with the lowest external tariff.

Customs unions

A *customs union* is like a free-trade area, but in addition members must adopt *common* external tariffs and quotas with non-member countries.

Common markets

A *common market* is where member countries operate as a *single* market. As with a customs union, there are no tariffs and quotas between member countries and there are common external tariffs and quotas. But a common market goes further than this. A full common market includes the following features:

- *A common system of taxation.* In the case of a *perfect* common market, this will involve identical rates of tax in all member countries.
- *A common system of laws and regulations governing production, employment and trade.* For example, in a perfect common market, there would be a *single* set of laws governing issues such as product specification (e.g. permissible artificial additives to foods, or levels of exhaust emissions from cars), the employment and dismissal of labour, mergers and takeovers, and monopolies and restrictive practices.
- *Free movement of labour, capital and materials, and of goods and services.* In a perfect common market, this will involve a total absence of border controls between member states, the freedom of workers to work in any member country and the freedom of firms to expand into any member state.
- *The absence of special treatment by member governments of their own domestic industries.* Governments are large purchasers of goods and services. In a perfect common market, they should buy from whichever companies within the market offer the most competitive deal and not show favouritism towards domestic suppliers: they should operate a *common procurement policy*.

The definition of a common market is sometimes extended to include the following two features of *economic and monetary union:*

- *A fixed exchange rate between the member countries' currencies.* In the extreme case, this would involve a single currency for the whole market.
- *Common macroeconomic policies.* To some extent, this must follow from a fixed exchange rate, but in the extreme case it will involve a single macroeconomic management of the whole market, and hence the abolition of separate fiscal or monetary intervention by individual member states.

We will examine European economic and monetary union in section 26.2.

The direct effects of a customs union: trade creation and trade diversion

By joining a customs union (or free-trade area), a country will find that its trade patterns change. Two such changes can be distinguished: trade creation and trade diversion.

Trade creation

Trade creation is where consumption shifts from a high-cost producer to a low-cost producer. The removal of trade barriers allows greater specialisation according to comparative advantage. Instead of consumers having to pay high prices for domestically produced goods in which the country has a comparative disadvantage, the goods can now be obtained more cheaply from other members of the customs union. In return, the country can export to them goods in which it has a comparative advantage.

For example, suppose that the most efficient producer in the world of good x is France. Assume that, before it joined the EU in 2004, Poland had to pay tariffs on good x from France. After joining the EU, however, it was then able to

KI 36
p673

Definitions

Free trade area A group of countries with no trade barriers between themselves.

Customs union A free-trade area with common external tariffs and quotas.

Common market A customs union where the member countries act as a single market with free movement of labour and capital, common taxes and common trade laws.

Trade creation Where a customs union leads to greater specialisation according to comparative advantage and thus a shift in production from higher-cost to lower-cost sources.

Figure 24.11 Trade creation

Figure 24.12 Trade diversion

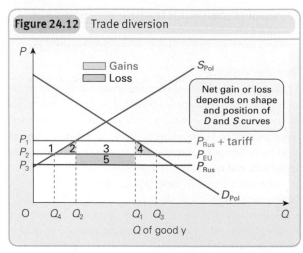

import good x from France without paying tariffs. There was a gain to Polish consumers. This gain is illustrated in Figure 24.11. Curves S_{Pol} and D_{Pol} show the domestic supply and demand curves in Poland. The diagram assumes for simplicity that Poland is a price taker as an importer of good x from France: the EU price is given.

The diagram shows that, before joining the EU, Poland had to pay the EU price *plus* the tariff (i.e. P_1). At P_1 Poland produced Q_2, consumed Q_1 and thus imported $Q_1 - Q_2$. With the removal of tariffs, the price fell to P_2. Consumption increased to Q_3 and production fell to Q_4. Imports thus increased to $Q_3 - Q_4$. Trade had been created.

The gain in welfare from the removal of the tariff is also illustrated in Figure 24.11. A reduction in price from P_1 to P_2 leads to an increase in Polish consumer surplus of areas $1 + 2 + 3 + 4$. On the other hand, there is a loss in profits to domestic producers of good x of area 1 and a loss in tariff revenue to the government of area 3. There is still a net gain, however, of areas $2 + 4$.

The increased consumption of wine in the UK after joining the EU may be seen as trade creation.

Trade diversion

Trade diversion is where consumption shifts from a lower-cost producer outside the customs union to a higher-cost producer within the union.

Assume that the most efficient producer of good y in the world was Russia – outside the EU. Assume that, before membership, Poland paid a similar tariff on good y from any country, and thus imported the product from Russia rather than the EU.

After joining the EU, however, the removal of the tariff made the EU product cheaper, since the tariff remained on the Russian product. Consumption thus switched to a higher-cost producer. There was thus a net loss in world efficiency. As far as Poland was concerned, consumers still gained, since they were paying a lower price than before, but this time the loss in profits to Polish producers plus the loss in tariff revenue to the Polish government might have outweighed these gains, giving a net loss.

These benefits and costs are shown in Figure 24.12. For simplicity it assumes a constant Russian and EU price (i.e. that their supply curves to Poland are infinitely elastic). The domestic supply curve (S_{Pol}) is upward sloping, and is assumed to be equal to marginal cost.

Before joining the EU, Poland was importing good y from Russia at a price P_1 (i.e. the Russian price plus the tariff). Poland thus consumed Q_1, produced Q_2 domestically and imported the remainder, $Q_1 - Q_2$. On joining the EU, it was now able to consume at the EU (tariff-free) price of P_2. (Note that this is above the tariff-free Russian price, P_3). What are the gains and losses to Poland?

Definition

Trade diversion Where a customs union diverts consumption from goods produced at a lower cost outside the union to goods produced at a higher cost (but tariff-free) within the union.

- Consumers' gain: Polish consumer surplus rises by areas 1 + 2 + 3 + 4.
- Producers' loss: Polish producer surplus (profit) falls by area 1.
- Government's loss: previously tariffs of areas 3 + 5 were paid. Now no tariffs are paid. The Polish government thus loses this revenue.

There is thus a net gain of areas 1 + 2 + 3 + 4 minus areas 1 + 3 + 5, i.e. areas 2 + 4 minus area 5. If, however, area 5 is bigger than area 2 + 4, there is a net loss.

When trade *diversion* takes place, therefore, there may still be a net gain, but there may be a net loss. It depends on circumstances.

 Under which of the following circumstances is there likely to be a net gain from trade diversion? (Refer to Figure 24.12.) (a) A small difference between the EU price and the Russian pre-tariff price, and a large difference between the EU price and the Russian price with the tariff, or vice versa. (b) Elastic or inelastic Polish demand and supply curves. (c) The Polish demand and supply curves close together or far apart.

A customs union is more likely to lead to trade diversion rather than trade creation:

- When the union's external tariff is very high. Under these circumstances, the abolition of the tariff within the union is likely to lead to a large reduction in the price of goods imported from other members of the union.
- When there is a relatively small cost difference between goods produced within and outside the union. Here the abolition of even relatively low tariffs within the union will lead to internally produced goods becoming cheaper than externally produced goods.

Longer-term effects of a customs union

The problem with the above analysis is that it assumes *static* demand and supply curves: in other words, supply and demand curves that are unaffected by changes in trading patterns. In reality, if a country joins a customs union, the curves are likely to shift. Membership itself affects demand and supply – perhaps beneficially, perhaps adversely.

Longer-term advantages (economic) include the following:

- Increased market size may allow a country's firms to exploit (*internal*) *economies of scale*. This argument is more important for small countries, which have therefore more to gain from an enlargement of their markets.
- *External economies of scale.* Increased trade may lead to improvements in the infrastructure of the members of the customs union (better roads, railways, financial services, etc.). This in turn could bring bigger long-term benefits from trade between members, and from external trade too, by making the transport and handling of imports and exports cheaper.
- The bargaining power of the whole customs union with the rest of the world may allow member countries to gain *better terms of trade*. This, of course, will necessarily involve a degree of political co-operation between the members.
- *Increased competition* between member countries may stimulate efficiency, encourage investment and reduce monopoly power. Of course, a similar advantage could be gained by the simple removal of tariffs with any competing country.
- Integration may encourage a *more rapid spread of technology*.

Longer-term disadvantages (economic) include the following:

- *Resources may flow from a country* to more efficient members of the customs union, or to the geographical centre of the union (so as to minimise transport costs). This can be a major problem for a *common market* (where there is free movement of labour and capital). The country could become a depressed 'region' of the community, with adverse regional multiplier effects.
- If integration encourages greater co-operation between firms in member countries, it may also encourage *greater oligopolistic collusion*, thus keeping prices to the consumer higher. It may also encourage mergers and takeovers which would increase monopoly power.
- *Diseconomies of scale.* If the union leads to the development of very large companies, they may become bureaucratic and inefficient.
- The *costs of administering* the customs union may be high. This problem is likely to be worse, the more the intervention in the affairs of individual members.

It is extremely difficult to assess these arguments. To decide whether membership has been beneficial to a country requires a prediction of what things would have been like if it had not joined. No *accurate* predictions of this sort can be made, and they can never be tested. Also, many of the advantages and disadvantages are very long-term, and depend on future attitudes, institutions, policies and world events, which again cannot be predicted.

In addition, some of the advantages and disadvantages are distinctly political, such as 'greater political power' or 'loss of sovereignty'.

 How would you set about assessing whether or not a country had made a net long-term gain by joining a customs union? What sort of evidence would you look for?

Preferential trading in practice

Preferential trading has the greatest potential to benefit countries whose domestic market is too small, taken on its own, to enable them to benefit from economies of scale, and where they face substantial barriers to their exports. Most developing countries fall into this category, and as a result many have attempted to form preferential trading arrangements.

Examples in Latin America and the Caribbean include the five-member Central American Common Market (CACM) (part of the broader Central American Integration Association (LAIA)), the four-member Andean Community, and the fifteen-member Caribbean Community (CARICOM). A Southern Common Market (MerCoSur) was formed in 1991, consisting of Argentina, Brazil, Paraguay and Uruguay, and six other South American countries are planned to join. It has a common external tariff and most of its internal trade is free of tariffs.

In 1993, the six original ASEAN nations (Brunei, Indonesia, Malaysia, the Philippines, Singapore and Thailand) agreed to work towards an ASEAN Free Trade Area (AFTA). ASEAN (the Association of South-East Asian Nations) now has ten members (the new ones being Laos, Myanmar, Vietnam and Cambodia) and is dedicated to increased economic co-operation within the region. What progress has been made in achieving AFTA? By 2005 the original six members had reduced internal tariffs to an average of 3.8 per cent and had no tariffs on over 60 per cent of products. Plans are to eliminate all tariffs between these six by 2010 and for the remaining countries by 2015. ASEAN also plans to establish a common market, the ASEAN Economic Community (AEC), by 2020.

In Africa, the Economic Community of West African States (ECOWAS) has been attempting to create a common market between its fifteen members. The West African franc is used in seven of the countries and another six plan to introduce a common currency, the eco. The ultimate goal is to combine the two currency areas and adopt a single currency for all member states.

North American Free Trade Association (NAFTA)

Along with the EU, NAFTA is one of the two most powerful trading blocs in the world. It came into force in 1994 and consists of the USA, Canada and Mexico. These three countries have agreed to abolish tariffs between themselves in the hope that increased trade and co-operation will follow. Tariffs between the USA and Canada were phased out by 1999, and tariffs between Mexico and the other two countries will be by 2009. New non-tariff restrictions will not be permitted either, but many existing ones can remain in force, thus preventing the development of true free trade between the members. Indeed, some industries, such as textiles and agriculture, will continue to have major non-tariff restrictions.

NAFTA members hope that, with a market similar in size to the EU, they will be able to rival the EU's economic power in world trade. Other countries may join in the future, so NAFTA may eventually develop into a Western Hemisphere free-trade association.

NAFTA is, however, at most only a free-trade area and not a common market. Unlike the EU, it does not seek to harmonise laws and regulations, except in very specific areas such as environmental management and labour standards. Member countries are permitted total legal independence, subject to the one proviso that they must treat firms of other member countries equally with their own firms – the principle of 'fair competition'. Nevertheless, NAFTA has encouraged a growth in trade between its members, most of which is trade creation rather than trade diversion.

Case Study 24.8 in MyEconLab looks at the costs and benefits of NAFTA membership to the three countries involved.

Asia-Pacific Economic Co-operation forum (APEC)

The most significant move towards establishing a more widespread regional economic organisation in east Asia appeared with the creation of the Asia-Pacific Economic Association (APEC). APEC links the economies of the Pacific rim, including Asian, Australasian and North and South American countries (nineteen countries, plus Hong Kong and Taiwan). These countries account for some 60 per cent of world GDP and 48 per cent of world trade. At the 1994 meeting of APEC leaders, it was resolved to create a free-trade area across the Pacific by 2010 for the developed industrial countries, and by 2020 for the rest.

Unlike the EU and NAFTA, APEC is likely to remain solely a free-trade area and not to develop into a customs union, let alone a common market. Within the region there exists a wide disparity in GNY per capita, ranging from Japan and the USA at over $34 000 to Vietnam at a mere $500 ($2500 in PPP terms). Such disparities create a wide range of national interests and goals. Countries are unlikely to share common economic problems or concerns. In addition, political differences and conflicts within the region are widespread, reducing the likelihood that any organisational agreement beyond a simple economic one would succeed.

The economic benefits from free trade, however, and the resulting closer regional ties, could be immense. If the whole of the US and Russian economies are included, then APEC accounts for nearly half of world trade – a truly massive trading zone.

The longest established and most comprehensive of preferential trading arrangements is the European Union. The remainder of this chapter is devoted to examining its evolution from a rather imperfect customs union to a common market (though still not perfect).

Section summary

1. Countries may make a partial movement towards free trade by the adoption of a preferential trading system. This involves free trade between the members, but restrictions on trade with the rest of the world. Such a system can be either a simple free-trade area, or a customs union (where there are common restrictions with the rest of the world), or a common market (where in addition there is free movement of capital and labour, and common taxes and trade laws).

2. A preferential trading area can lead to trade creation where production shifts to low-cost producers within the area, or to trade diversion where trade shifts away from lower-cost producers outside the area to higher-cost producers within the area.

3. There is a net welfare gain from trade creation: the gain in consumer surplus outweighs the loss of tariff revenue and the loss of profit to domestic producers.

   With trade diversion, however, these two losses may outweigh the gains to consumers: whether they do depends on the size of the tariffs and on the demand for and supply of the traded goods.

4. Preferential trading may bring dynamic advantages of increased external economies of scale, improved terms of trade from increased bargaining power with the rest of the world, increased efficiency from greater competition between member countries, and a more rapid spread of technology. On the other hand, it can lead to increased regional problems for members, greater oligopolistic collusion and various diseconomies of scale. There may also be large costs of administering the system.

5. There have been several attempts around the world to form preferential trading systems. The two most powerful are the European Union and the North American Free Trade Association (NAFTA).

24.4 THE EUROPEAN UNION

Historical background

The European Economic Community was formed by the signing of the Treaty of Rome in 1957 and came into operation on 1 January 1958.

The original six member countries of the EEC (Belgium, France, Italy, Luxembourg, the Netherlands and West Germany) had already made a move towards integration with the formation of the European Coal and Steel Community in 1952. This had removed all restrictions on trade in coal, steel and iron ore between the six countries. The aim had been to gain economies of scale and allow more effective competition with the USA and other foreign producers.

The EEC extended this principle and aimed eventually to be a full common market with completely free trade between members in all products, and with completely free movement of labour, enterprise and capital.

All internal tariffs between the six members had been abolished and common external tariffs established by 1968. But this still only made the EEC a *customs union*, since a number of restrictions on internal trade remained (legal, administrative, fiscal, etc.). Nevertheless the aim was eventually to create a full common market.

In 1973 the UK, Denmark and Ireland became members. Greece joined in 1981, Spain and Portugal in 1986, and Sweden, Austria and Finland in 1995. Then in May 2004, a further ten countries joined: Cyprus, the Czech Republic, Estonia, Hungary, Latvia, Lithuania, Malta, Poland, Slovakia and Slovenia. With Bulgaria and Romania joining in 2007, the European Union, as it is now called, has 27 members.

From customs union to common market

The EU is clearly a customs union. It has common external tariffs and no internal tariffs. But is it also a common market? For many years, there have been *certain* common economic policies.

The Common Agricultural Policy (CAP). The Union has traditionally set common high prices for farm products. This has involved charging variable import duties to bring foreign food imports up to EU prices and intervention to buy up surpluses of food produced within the EU at these above-equilibrium prices (see section 3.5). Although the main method of support has shifted to providing subsidies (or 'income support') unrelated to current output, this still represents a *common* economic policy.

Regional policy. EU regional policy provides grants to firms and local authorities in relatively deprived regions of the Union (see Case Study 23.10 in MyEconLab).

Competition policy. EU policy here has applied primarily to companies operating in more than one member state (see section 13.1). For example, Article 81 of the Amsterdam Treaty prohibits agreements between firms which will adversely affect competition in trade between member states.

Harmonisation of taxation. VAT is the standard form of indirect tax throughout the EU. However, there are substantial differences in VAT rates between member states (see Box 24.9), as there are with other tax rates.

What would be the economic effects of (a) different rates of VAT, (b) different rates of personal income tax and (c) different rates of company taxation between member states if there were no other barriers to trade or factor movements?

Social policy. In 1989 the European Commission presented a *social charter* to the heads of state. This spelt out a series of worker and social rights that should apply in all member states (see Case Study 24.10 in MyEconLab). These rights were grouped under twelve headings covering areas such as the guarantee of decent levels of income for both the employed and the non-employed, freedom of movement of labour between member countries, freedom to belong to a trade union and equal treatment of men and women in the labour market. However, the charter was only a recommendation and each element had to be approved separately by the European Council of Ministers.

The social chapter of the Maastricht Treaty (1991) attempted to move the Community forward in implementing the details of the social charter in areas such as maximum hours, minimum working conditions, health and safety protection, information and consultation of workers, and equal opportunities.

The UK Conservative government refused to sign this part of the Maastricht Treaty. It maintained that such measures would increase costs of production and make EU goods less competitive in world trade. Critics of the UK position argued that the refusal to adopt minimum working conditions (and also a minimum wage) would make the UK the 'sweatshop' of Europe. One of the first acts of the incoming Labour government in 1997 was to sign up to the social chapter.

Would the adoption of improved working conditions necessarily lead to higher labour costs per unit of output?

Despite these various common policies, in other respects the Community of the 1970s and 1980s was far from a true common market: there were all sorts of non-tariff barriers such as high taxes on wine by non-wine-producing countries, special regulations designed to favour domestic producers, governments giving contracts to domestic producers (e.g. for defence equipment), and so on.

The category often cited by businesses as being the most important single barrier was that of regulations and norms. In some cases, the regulations merely added to the costs of imports. But in the cases of many mechanical engineering

and telecommunications products, technical and health and safety regulations sometimes ruled out foreign imports altogether.

Moves towards a single market

The Single European Act of 1987, however, sought to remove these barriers and to form a genuine common market by the end of 1992 (see Box 24.9).

One of the most crucial aspects of the Act was its acceptance of the principle of **mutual recognition**. This is the principle whereby if a firm or individual is permitted to do something under the rules and regulations of *one* EU country, it must also be permitted to do it in all other EU countries. This means that firms and individuals can choose the country's rules that are least constraining.

Mutual recognition also means that individual governments can no longer devise special rules and regulations that keep out competitors from other EU countries (see Box 24.8). Here was the answer to the dilemma of how to get all EU countries to agree to common sets of rules and regulations. All that was required was that they recognised the rules and regulations applying in each other's countries. However, there was a danger that governments would end up competing against each other to provide the lightest set of regulations in order to attract firms to invest in their country. This could be to the detriment of consumers and workers.

Thus *some* common sets of rules and regulations were still required. One other feature of the Single European Act helped here. This was the institution of *majority* voting in questions of harmonisation of rules and regulations. Previously, unanimous approval had been necessary. This had meant that an individual country could veto the dismantling of barriers. This new system of majority voting, however, does not apply to the harmonisation of taxes.

The benefits and costs of the single market

It is difficult to quantify the benefits and costs of the single market, given that many occur over a long period, and that it is hard to know to what extent the changes that are taking place are the direct result of the single market.

One study conducted in 1998 did, nevertheless, estimate the benefits in terms of increased consumption (see Table 24.5). This found that the benefits to the smaller, lower-income countries, such as Portugal and Greece, were the greatest. Such estimates, however, do depend crucially on the assumptions made and are thus open to substantial error.

Definition

Mutual recognition The EU principle that one country's rules and regulations must apply throughout the EU. If they conflict with those of another country, individuals and firms should be able to choose which to obey.

CASE STUDIES AND APPLICATIONS

BOX 24.8   MUTUAL RECOGNITION: THE CASSIS DE DIJON CASE

Or when is a liqueur not a liqueur?

Crème de Cassis is an alcoholic blackcurrant drink made by the French firm Cassis de Dijon. Added to white wine, it makes the drink kir. It is not just the French who like drinking kir; it is also, among others, the Germans. In this seemingly innocent fact lay the seeds for the dismantling of some of the most serious trade barriers in Europe!

The story starts back in 1978. The West German company Rewe Zentral AG wanted to import Cassis, but found that under West German law it could not. The problem was that Cassis does not contain enough alcohol to be classed as a liqueur, and it also fell outside any other category of alcoholic drink that was permitted by West German law.

But Rewe was not to be put off. It started legal proceedings in Europe to challenge the German law. The basis of Rewe's case was that this law discriminated against non-German companies. After much legal wrangling, the European Court of Justice in Luxembourg ruled that Germany had no right to prevent the importation of a product that was legitimately on sale in another member country (i.e. France). The only exceptions to this ruling would be if the product was barred for reasons of consumer protection, health or fair trade. None of these applied to Cassis, so the Germans can now drink kir to their hearts' content without having to become smugglers.

But what of the implications of the case? These are enormous and were spelt out in the Single European Act: 'the Council may decide that provisions in force in a member state must be recognised as being equivalent to those applied by another'. In other words, individuals and firms can choose which country's sets of regulations suit them the best and then insist that they be applied in *all* member states.

'Mutual recognition' of each other's laws tends to lead to deregulation, as people choose those countries' laws that give them the greatest freedom. This appeals to economic and political liberals. Equally, it worries those who argue that regulations and laws on industrial standards have been instituted for a purpose, and should not be undone just because some other member country has not been wise enough to institute them itself.

How has the Cassis de Dijon ruling affected the balance of power in the EU between (a) individual states and the EU as a whole; (b) governments and the courts?

Table 24.5   Gains from the single market

Countries	Extra consumption as % of GDP
France, Germany, UK, Italy	2–3
Denmark	2–5
Netherlands, Spain	3–4
Belgium, Luxembourg	4–5
Ireland	4–10
Greece	5–16
Portugal	19–20

Source: The competition effects of the single market in Europe, *Economic Policy* (Allen, C., Gasiorek, M. and Smith, A., 1998).

Even though the precise magnitude of the benefits is difficult to estimate, it is possible to identify the *types* of benefit that have resulted, many of which have been substantial.

Trade creation. Costs and prices have fallen as result of a greater exploitation of comparative advantage. Member countries can now specialise further in those goods and services that they can produce at a comparatively low opportunity cost.

Reduction in the direct costs of barriers. This category includes administrative costs, border delays and technical regulations. Their abolition or harmonisation has led in many cases to substantial cost savings.

Economies of scale. With industries based on a Europe-wide scale, many firms can now be large enough, and their plants large enough, to gain the full potential economies of scale (see Box 5.8 on pages 150–1). Yet the whole European market is large enough for there still to be adequate competition. Such gains have varied from industry to industry depending on the minimum efficient scale of a plant or firm. Economies of scale have also been gained from mergers and other forms of industrial restructuring.

Greater competition. Increased competition between firms has led to lower costs, lower prices and a wider range of products available to consumers. This has been particularly so in newly liberalised service sectors such as transport, financial services, telecommunications and broadcasting. In the long run, greater competition can stimulate greater innovation, a greater flow of technical information and the rationalisation of production.

Despite these gains, the single market has not received universal welcome within the EU. Its critics argue that, in a Europe of oligopolies, unequal ownership of resources, rapidly changing technologies and industrial practices, and factor immobility, the removal of internal barriers to trade has merely exaggerated the problems of inequality and economic power. More specifically, the following criticisms are made.

Radical economic change is costly. Substantial economic change is necessary to achieve the full economies of scale and efficiency gains from a single European market. These changes necessarily involve redundancies – from bankruptcies, takeovers, rationalisation and the introduction of new technology. The severity of this structural and technological unemployment depends on (a) the pace of economic change and (b) the mobility of labour – both occupational and geographical. Clearly, the more integrated markets become across the EU, the less the costs of *future* change.

Adverse regional multiplier effects. Firms are likely to locate as near as possible to the 'centre of gravity' of their markets and sources of supply. If, before barriers were removed, a firm's prime market was the UK, it might well have located in the Midlands or the north of England. If, however, with barriers now removed, its market has become Europe as a whole, it may choose to locate in the south of England or in France, Germany or the Benelux countries instead. The creation of a single European market thus tends to attract capital and jobs away from the edges of the Union to its geographical centre.

In an ideal market situation, areas like Cornwall, the south of Italy or Portugal should attract resources from other parts of the Union. Since they are relatively depressed areas, wage rates and land prices are lower. The resulting lower industrial costs should encourage firms to move into the areas. In practice, regional multiplier effects may worsen the problem (see page 666). As capital and labour (and especially young and skilled workers) leave the extremities of the Union, so these regions are likely to become more depressed. If, as a result, their infrastructure is neglected, they then become even less attractive to new investment.

 Has the problem of adverse regional multiplier effects been made better or worse by the adoption of a single European currency? (This issue is explored in section 26.3.) (Clue: without a single currency, how would the devaluation of the drachma (the former Greek currency) have affected a depressed Greek economy?)

The development of monopoly/oligopoly power. The free movement of capital can encourage the development of giant 'Euro-firms' with substantial economic power. Indeed, recent years have seen some very large European mergers (see Box 8.5 on pages 226–7). This can lead to higher, not lower, prices and less choice for the consumer. It all depends on just how effective competition is, and how effective EU competition policy is in preventing monopolistic and collusive practices.

Trade diversion. Just as increased trade creation has been a potential advantage from completing the internal market, so trade diversion has been a possibility too. This is more likely if *external* barriers remain high (or are even increased) and internal barriers are *completely* abolished.

 Is trade diversion more likely or less likely in the following cases? (a) European producers gain monopoly power in world trade. (b) Modern developments in technology and communications reduce the differences in production costs associated with different locations. (c) The development of the internal market produces substantial economies of scale in many industries.

Perhaps the biggest objection raised against the single European market is a political one: the loss of national sovereignty. Governments find it much more difficult to intervene at a microeconomic level in their own economies.

 Why may the newer members of the Union have the most to gain from the single market, but also the most to lose?

Completing the internal market

Despite the reduction in barriers, the internal market is still not 'complete'. In other words, various barriers to trade between member states still remain. Thus, in June 1997, an Action Plan was adopted by the European Council. Its aim was to ensure that all barriers were dismantled by the launch of the euro in January 1999.

To monitor progress, an 'Internal Market Scoreboard' was established. This is published every six months and shows progress towards the total abandonment of any forms of internal trade restrictions (see Box 24.10). It shows the percentage of EU Single Market Directives still to be transposed into national law. In addition to giving each country's 'transposition deficit', the Scoreboard identifies the number of infringements of the internal market that have taken place. The hope is that the 'naming and shaming' of countries will encourage them to make more rapid progress towards totally free trade within the EU.

The Action Plan was largely, though not totally, successful. In 1997, the average transposition deficit of member countries was 6.3 per cent. By 1999, this had fallen to 3.5 per cent and by 2008, to just 1.8 per cent, despite the accession of 12 new members to the EU.

Nevertheless, national governments have continued to introduce *new* technical standards, several of which have had the effect of erecting new barriers to trade. Also, infringements of single market rules by governments have not always been dealt with. The net result is that, although trade is much freer today than in the early 1990s, especially given the transparency of pricing with the euro, there still do exist various barriers, especially to the free movement of goods.

To counteract new barriers, the EU periodically issues new Directives. If this process is more rapid than that of the transposition of existing directives into national law, the transposition deficit increases.

 If there have been clear benefits from the single market programme, why do individual member governments still try to erect barriers, such as new technical standards?

BOX 24.9 FEATURES OF THE SINGLE MARKET

Since 1 January 1993 trade within the EU has operated very much like trade within a country. In theory, it should be no more difficult for a firm in Birmingham to sell its goods in Paris than in London. At the same time, the single market allows free movement of labour and involves the use of common technical standards.

The features of the single market are summed up in two European Commission publications.[1] They are:

- Elimination of border controls on goods within the EU: no more long waits.
- Free movement of people across borders.
- Common security arrangements.
- No import taxes on goods bought in other member states for personal use.
- The right for everyone to live in another member state.
- Recognition of vocational qualifications in other member states: engineers, accountants, medical practitioners, teachers and other professionals able to practise throughout Europe.
- Technical standards brought into line, and product tests and certification agreed across the whole EU.
- Common commercial laws – making it attractive to form Europe-wide companies and to start joint ventures.
- Public contracts to supply equipment and services to state organisations now open to tenders across the EU.

So what does the single market mean for individuals and for businesses?

Individuals

Before 1993, if you were travelling in Europe, you had a 'duty-free allowance'. This meant that you could only take goods up to the value of €600 across borders within the EU without having to pay VAT in the country into which you were importing them. Now you can take as many goods as you like from one EU country to another, provided they are for your own consumption. But to prevent fraud, member states may ask for evidence that the goods have been purchased for the traveller's own consumption if they exceed specified amounts.

Individuals have the right to live and work in any other member state. Qualifications obtained in one member state must be recognised by other member states.

Firms

Before 1993 all goods traded in the EU were subject to VAT at every internal border. This involved some 60 million customs clearance documents at a cost of some €70 per consignment.[2]

This has all now disappeared. Goods can cross from one member state to another without any border controls: in fact, the concepts of 'importing' and 'exporting' within the EU no longer officially exist. All goods sent from one EU country to another will be charged VAT only in the country

of destination. They are exempt from VAT in the country where they are produced.

One of the important requirements for fair competition in the single market is the convergence of tax rates. Although income tax rates, corporate tax rates and excise duties still differ between member states, there has been some narrowing in the range of VAT rates. There is now a lower limit of 15 per cent on the standard rate of VAT. What is more, the member states have agreed to abolish higher rates of VAT on luxury goods, and to have no more than two lower rates of at least 5 per cent on 'socially necessary' goods, such as food and water supply. The table shows VAT rates in 1988 and 2008.

 In what ways would competition be 'unfair' if VAT rates differed widely between member states?

VAT rates (%) in the EU: 1988 and 2008

	1988		2008
	Standard rate	High rates	Standard rate
Austria			20
Belgium	19	25.3	21
Bulgaria			20
Cyprus			15
Czech Republic			19
Denmark	22	–	25
Estonia			18
Finland			22
France	18.6	33.3	19.6
Germany	14	–	19
Greece	18	36	19
Hungary			20
Ireland	25	–	21.5
Italy	18	38	20
Latvia			18
Lithuania			18
Luxembourg	12	–	15
Malta			18
Netherlands	20	–	19
Poland			22
Portugal	16	30	20
Romania			19
Slovakia			19
Slovenia			20
Spain	12	33	16
Sweden			25
UK	15	–	17.5[3]

[1] *A Single Market for Goods* (Commission of the European Communities, 1993); *10 Key Points about the Single European Market* (Commission of the European Communities, 1992).
[2] See *A Single Market for Goods* (Commission of the European Communities, 1993).
[3] Temporarily reduced to 15 per cent from December 2008 to December 2009.

The effect of the new member states

Given the very different nature of the economies of many of the new entrants to the EU, and their lower levels of GDP per head, their potential gain from membership has been substantial. The gains come through trade creation, increased competition, technological transfer and inward investment, both from other EU countries and from outside the EU.

BOX 24.10 THE INTERNAL MARKET SCOREBOARD

CASE STUDIES AND APPLICATIONS

Keeping a tally on progress to a true single market

This success or otherwise of implementing EU internal market directives is measured by the Internal Market Scoreboard, which tracks the transposition (or 'implementation') deficit for each country. This is the percentage of directives that have failed to be implemented into national law by their agreed deadline.

The Scoreboard has been published every six months since 1997 and, in addition to tracking the deficit for each country, also shows the average deficit across all EU countries. The chart shows that the average deficit was falling until May 2002, but then rose somewhat. Part of the problem is that new directives are being issued as existing ones are being implemented.

According to the January 2005 Scoreboard,

Member States persistently fail to transpose Internal Market rules correctly and on time. The transposition deficit for the EU has got significantly worse and now stands at 3.6%. This is a long way from the 1.5% interim target set by successive European Councils. And the real target is, of course, 0% because timely and correct transposition is a legal obligation.

Since then, the transposition deficit has fallen once again, even with the accession of ten new members in 2004 and two more in 2007. An average deficit target of 1 per cent was set in 2007 and, to the surprise of many members, this was reached by 2008. As the July 2008 Scoreboard stated,

Member States have stepped up their efforts considerably to ensure timely transposition of Internal Market legislation. Only one year after the European Heads of State and Government agreed on the future deficit target of 1%, 18 out of 27 Member States are already in line with this target. In addition, 4 Member States meet the 1.5% target. That leaves only

5 Member States to have a transposition deficit above 1.5%

Most Member States have transposition delays in the area of financial services which is also an area where the proportion of directives not yet transposed is the second highest (4.5%). The highest transposition deficit is related to rules on free movement of persons (7.9%). The fragmentation of the Internal Market legislation is still 7% which penalises all Member States, in particular in those sectors with a particularly high fragmentation factor, e.g. the financial services area, where 10% of outstanding directives are not transposed by at least one Member State.

But the issue is not just one of transposing Internal Market rules into national legislation; it is also one of applying the rules correctly. The July 2008 Scoreboard argued that

The number of Internal Market related infringement procedures remains relatively high and it takes too long to resolve them. The efficient handling of infringement procedures depends to a certain extent on Member States themselves, in particular as regards their timely reply to the concerns set out by the Commission in its 'letters of formal notice' and 'reasoned opinions'. . . .

When broken down by sector, infringements relating to the environment, taxation, energy and transport remain the source of most infringement cases.

1. *What value are scoreboards for Member States and the European Commission?*
2. *Why do you think that it is so important that legislation such as that governing the Internal Market is in place in all Member States at the same time?*

Internal Market Scoreboard: average transposition deficit

A study in 2004 concluded that Poland's GDP would rise by 3.4 per cent and Hungary's by almost 7 per cent.[3] Real wages would rise, with those of unskilled workers rising faster than those of skilled workers, in accordance with these countries' comparative advantage. There would also be benefits for the 15 pre-2004 members from increased trade and investment, but these would be relatively minor in comparison to the gains to the new members.

[3] M. Maliszewska, 'Benefits of the Single Market Expansion for current and new member states', *Centrum Analiz Społeczno-Ekonomicznych*, 2004.

In future years, now that the euro is used by at least 15 of the member states, trade within the EU is likely to continue to grow as a proportion of GDP. We examine the benefits and costs of the single currency and the whole process of economic and monetary union in the EU in section 26.2.

To examine the arguments about full monetary union, we need first to look at the question of exchange rate determination and alternative exchange rate systems. This is the subject of the next chapter.

Section summary

1. The European Union is a customs union in that it has common external tariffs and no internal ones. But virtually from the outset it has also had elements of a common market, particularly in the areas of agricultural policy, regional policy, monopoly and restrictive practice policy, and to some extent in the areas of tax harmonisation and social policy.

2. Nevertheless, there have been substantial non-tariff barriers to trade within the EU, such as different tax rates, various regulations over product quality, licensing, state procurement policies, educational qualification requirements, financial barriers, various regulations and norms, and subsidies or tax relief to domestic producers.

3. The Single European Act of 1987 sought to sweep away these restrictions and to establish a genuine free market within the EU: to establish a full common market. Benefits from completing the internal market have included trade creation, cost savings from no longer having to administer barriers, economies of scale for firms now able to operate on a Europe-wide scale, and greater competition leading to reduced costs and prices, greater flows of technical information and more innovation.

4. Critics of the single market point to various changes in industrial structure that have resulted, bringing problems of redundancies and closures. They also point to adverse regional multiplier effects as resources are attracted to the geographical centre of the EU, to possible problems of market power with the development of giant 'Euro-firms', and to the possibilities of trade diversion.

5. The actual costs and benefits of EU membership to the various countries vary with their particular economic circumstances – for example, the extent to which they gain from trade creation, or lose from adverse regional multiplier effects – and with their contributions to and receipts from the EU budget.

6. These cost and benefits in the future will depend on just how completely the barriers to trade are removed, on the extent of monetary union and on any further enlargements to the Union.

END OF CHAPTER QUESTIONS

1. Imagine that two countries, Richland and Poorland, can produce just two goods, computers and coal. Assume that for a given amount of land and capital, the output of these two products requires the following constant amounts of labour:

	Richland	Poorland
1 computer	2	4
100 tonnes of coal	4	5

Assume that each country has 20 million workers.

(a) Draw the production possibility curves for the two countries (on two separate diagrams).

(b) If there is no trade, and in each country 12 million workers produce computers and 8 million workers produce coal, how many computers and tonnes of coal will each country produce? What will be the total production of each product?

(c) What is the opportunity cost of a computer in (i) Richland; (ii) Poorland?

(d) What is the opportunity cost of 100 tonnes of coal in (i) Richland; (ii) Poorland?

(e) Which country has a comparative advantage in which product?

(f) Assuming that price equals marginal cost, which of the following would represent possible exchange ratios?

   (i) 1 computer for 40 tonnes of coal;

   (ii) 2 computers for 140 tonnes of coal;

   (iii) 1 computer for 100 tonnes of coal;

   (iv) 1 computer for 60 tonnes of coal;

   (v) 4 computers for 360 tonnes of coal.

(g) Assume that trade now takes place and that computer exchanges for 65 tonnes of coal. Both countries specialise completely in the product in which they have a comparative advantage. How much does each country produce of its respective product?

   (h) The country producing computers sells 6 million domestically. How many does it export to the other country?

   (i)   How much coal does the other country consume?

   (j)   Construct a table like Table 24.4 to show the no-trade and with-trade positions of each country.

2. If capital moves from developed to less developed countries, and labour moves from less developed to developed countries, what effects will these factor movements have on wage rates and the return on capital in the two types of country?

3. What factors determine a country's terms of trade?

4. Go through each of the arguments for restricting trade (both those of general validity and those having some validity for specific countries) and provide a counter-argument for not restricting trade.

5. If countries are so keen to reduce the barriers to trade, why do many countries frequently attempt to erect barriers?

6. What factors will determine whether a country's joining a customs union will lead to trade creation or trade diversion?

7. Why is it difficult to estimate the magnitude of the benefits of completing the internal market of the EU?

8. Look through the costs and benefits that we identified from the completion of the internal market. Do the same costs and benefits arise from the enlarged EU of 27 members?

Online resources

Additional case studies in MyEconLab

24.1   **David Ricardo and the law of comparative advantage.** The original statement of the law of comparative advantage by David Ricardo back in 1817.

24.2   **The Uruguay round.** An examination of the negotiations that led to substantial cuts in trade barriers.

24.3   **The World Trade Organisation.** This looks at the various opportunities and threats posed by this major international organisation.

24.4   **The Battle of Seattle.** This looks at the protests against the WTO at Seattle in November 1999 and considers the arguments for and against the free trade policies of the WTO.

24.5   **Banana, banana.** The dispute between the USA and the EU over banana imports.

24.6   **Beyond bananas.** Other US/EU trade disputes.

24.7   **Steel barriers.** This examines the use of tariffs by the George W. Bush administration in 2002 to protect the ailing US steel industry.

24.8   **Assessing NAFTA.** Who are the winners and losers from NAFTA?

24.9   **Strategic trade theory.** The case of Airbus.

24.10 **The social dimension of the EU.** The principles of the social charter.

24.11 **The benefits of the single market.** Evidence of achievements and the Single Market Action Plan of 1997.

Websites relevant to this chapter

Numbers and sections refer to websites listed in the Web Appendix and hotlinked from this book's website at **www.pearsoned.co.uk/sloman**.

- For news articles relevant to this chapter, see the *Economics News Articles* link from the book's website.
- For general news on international trade, see websites in section A, and particularly A1–5, 7–9, 24, 25, 31. See also links to newspapers worldwide in A38, 39 43 and 44, and the news search feature in Google at A41. See also links to economics news in A42.
- For international data on imports and exports, see site H16 > *Resources* > *Trade statistics*. See also *World Economic Outlook* in H4 and trade data in B23. See also the trade topic in I14. The ESDS International site (B35) has links to World Bank, IMF, OECD, UN and Eurostat datasets (but you will need an Athens password, available free to all UK higher education students).
- For details of individual countries' structure of imports and exports, see B32.
- For UK data, see B1, 1. *National Statistics* > the fourth link > *Compendia and Reference* > *Annual Abstract* > *External trade and investment*. See also B3 and 34. For EU data, see G1 > *The Statistical Annex* > *Foreign trade and current balance*.
- For discussion papers on trade, see H4 and 7.
- For trade disputes, see H16.
- For various pressure groups critical of the effects of free trade and globalisation, see H12–14.
- For information on various preferential trading arrangements, see H20–22.
- For EU sites, see G1, 3, 7–14, 16–18.
- Sites I7 and 11 contain links to various topics in *International economics* (*International trade*, *International agreements*, *Economic co-operation* and *EU Economics*). Sites I4 and 17 have links to International economics.
- For student resources relevant to this chapter, see sites C1–7, 9, 10, 19

Chapter 25

The Balance of Payments and Exchange Rates

CHAPTER MAP

25.1 Alternative exchange rate regimes   **706**
Policy objectives: internal and external   706
Nominal and real exchange rates   707
Alternative exchange rate regimes   709
Correction under fixed exchange rates   710
Correction under free-floating exchange rates   712
Intermediate exchange rate regimes   714

25.2 Fixed exchange rates   **716**
*Effects of shocks under fixed exchange rates   716
Causes of longer-term balance of payments
      problems under fixed exchange rates   717
Advantages of fixed exchange rates   718
Disadvantages of fixed exchange rates   719

25.3 Free-floating exchange rates   **720**
The freeing of domestic policy   720
Response to shocks under a floating rate   721
Speculation   724
Advantages of a free-floating exchange rate   726
Disadvantages of a free-floating exchange rate   727

25.4 Exchange rate systems in practice   **729**
The adjustable peg system: 1945–73   729
Managed floating   730
Problems with managed floating since 1972   731
The UK experience of managed floating   731
The volatility of exchange rates   735

*Appendix: Open economy *ISLM* analysis   **737**
Analysis under a fixed exchange rate   737
Fiscal policy under fixed exchange rates   737
Monetary policy under fixed exchange rates   738
Analysis under free-floating exchange rates   739
Fiscal policy under floating exchange rates   739
Monetary policy under floating exchange rates   739

We live in a world in which events in one country or group of countries can have profound effects on other countries. Look at what happened in 2007/8. Excessive sub-prime mortgage lending in the USA led to huge losses for many financial institutions. With such debt securitised into bonds held by financial institutions across the world, the credit crunch rapidly became global.

As globalisation has increased, with trade and international financial movements growing much more rapidly than countries' GDP, and becoming much freer at the same time, so countries' vulnerability to balance of payments problems and exchange rate fluctuations has increased.

This chapter explores the relationships between a country's balance of payments and its exchange rate. In particular, we ask whether a country should allow its exchange rate to be determined entirely by market forces, with the possible instability that this brings, or whether it should attempt to fix its exchange rate to another currency (such as the US dollar), or at the very least attempt to reduce exchange rate fluctuations through central bank intervention in the foreign exchange market. We also look at the experience of countries in operating different types of exchange rate system.

25.1 ALTERNATIVE EXCHANGE RATE REGIMES

Policy objectives: internal and external

A country is likely to have various **internal** and **external policy objectives**. *Internal* objectives include such things as economic growth, low unemployment and low inflation. *External* objectives include such things as avoiding current account balance of payments deficits, encouraging international trade and preventing excessive exchange rate fluctuations. Internal and external objectives may come into conflict, however.

A simple illustration of potential conflict is with the objectives of *internal balance* and *external balance*.

Internal balance. **Internal balance** is where the economy is at the potential level of national income: i.e. where the output gap is zero (see Box 14.3 on page 398). This can be expressed in various ways, depending on the model of the economy and the policy objectives being pursued.

Thus, in the simple Keynesian model, internal balance is where the economy is at the *full-employment* level of national income: i.e. where Y_e (equilibrium national income) $= Y_f$ (full-employment national income) (see Chapter 17). In the monetarist and new classical models, it would be where the economy is on the vertical Phillips curve with stable inflation. In the context of inflation targeting, it would be where meeting the inflation target is consistent with achieving potential national income: i.e. where the *ADI* crosses the *ASI* curve at the targeted inflation rate (see Figure 19.18 on page 559).

If there is initially internal balance and then aggregate demand falls, in the short run output will fall below the potential level and disequilibrium unemployment will occur. Internal balance will be destroyed. The stickier wages and prices are, the longer it will take for internal balance to be restored.

External balance. **External balance** is the term for a *balance of payments* equilibrium. In the context of floating exchange rates, it is normally used in the narrow sense of a current account balance, and therefore also a capital plus financial account balance.

In the context of a fixed exchange rate, or an exchange rate target, it is often used more loosely to refer merely to a *total currency flow balance*. This is where the total demand and supply of the currency are equal at the targeted exchange rate with *no need for intervention from the reserves*: in other words, where any current account deficit is matched by a surplus on the other two accounts, and vice versa.

Conflicts between internal and external balance

It may, however, be difficult to achieve internal and external balance simultaneously. This is illustrated in Figure 25.1. Assume in Figure 25.1(b) that the exchange rate is er_1. Currency demand and supply curves are given by D and S_1 and there is no central bank intervention. Thus er_1 is the *equilibrium* exchange rate and there is external balance in the loose sense. Assume also that there is external balance in the narrow sense: i.e. a current account balance.

Let us also assume, however, that there is a recession. This is illustrated in Figure 25.1(a). Equilibrium national income is Y_{e_1}, where W_1 equals J_1. There is a deflationary gap: Y_{e_1} is below the full-employment level, Y_F. There is no *internal* balance.

Now assume that the government expands aggregate demand through fiscal policy in order to close the deflationary gap and restore internal balance. It raises injections to J_2 and reduces withdrawals to W_2. National income rises to Y_{e_2}. But this higher national income leads to an increased demand for imports. The supply of sterling will shift to S_2 in Figure 25.1(b). There is now a current account deficit, which destroys external balance in the narrow sense. If the government maintains the exchange rate at er_1 (by buying sterling from the reserves), external balance will be destroyed in the loose sense too.

External balance in the loose sense could be restored by allowing the exchange rate to depreciate to er_2, so that the demand and supply of sterling are equated at the new lower exchange rate.

But will this also correct the current account deficit and restore external balance in the narrow sense? It will go *some* way to correcting the deficit, as the lower exchange rate will make imports relatively more expensive and exports relatively cheaper. The amount that imports fall and exports rise will depend on their price elasticity of demand.

But there may also be an effect on the financial account. The higher aggregate demand will lead to a higher demand for money. This will drive up interest rates unless money supply is allowed to expand to offset the higher demand for money. If interest rates rise, this will lead to an inflow of

Definitions

Internal policy objectives Objectives relating solely to the domestic economy.

External policy objectives Objectives relating to the economy's international economic relationships.

Internal balance Where the equilibrium level of national income is at the desired level.

External balance Narrow definition: where the current account of the balance of payments is in balance (and thus also the capital plus financial accounts). Loose definition: where there is a total currency flow balance at a given exchange rate.

KI 33
p389

TC 4
p44

TC 7
p68

Figure 25.1   Internal and external balance

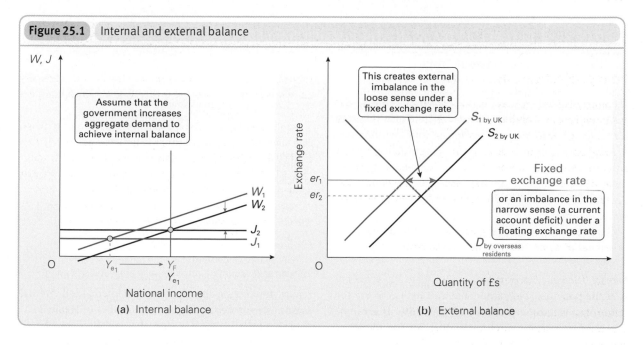

(a) Internal balance

(b) External balance

finance (a financial account surplus). In Figure 25.1(b), the supply curve of sterling would shift to the left and the demand curve to the right. The exchange rate would not fall as far, therefore, as er_2. If the positive effect of higher interest rates on the financial account was bigger than the negative effect of higher imports on the current account, the exchange rate would actually *appreciate*.

Either way, there will be a current account deficit and an equal and opposite financial plus capital account surplus. Narrow external balance has not been restored in the short term. (We explore the long-term current account balance under floating exchange rates in section 25.3.)

Figure 25.2 shows the effect of various 'shocks' that can affect both internal and narrow external balance.

1. *Assume that there is both internal and narrow external balance. Now assume that as a result of inflation being below target, the central bank cuts interest rates. Into which of the four quadrants in Figure 25.2 will the economy move?*
2. *Imagine that there is an inflationary gap, but a current account equilibrium. Describe what will happen if the government raises interest rates in order to close the inflationary gap. Assume first that there is a fixed exchange rate; then assume that there is a floating exchange rate.*

The ability of the economy to correct these imbalances depends on the *exchange rate regime*. We examine altern-

Figure 25.2   Effects on internal and (narrow) external balance

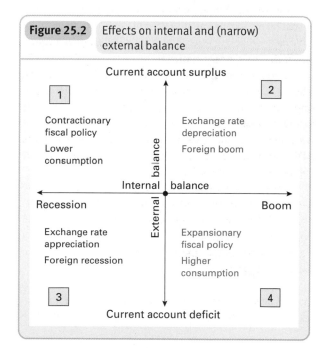

ative exchange rate regimes in the final part of this section, but first we must distinguish between nominal and real exchange rates.

Nominal and real exchange rates

A nominal exchange rate is simply the rate at which one currency exchanges for another. All exchange rates that you see quoted in the newspapers, on television or the Internet, or at travel agents, banks or airports, are nominal rates. Up to this point we have solely considered nominal rates.

Definition

Exchange rate regime The system under which the government allows the exchange rate to be determined.

TC 12
p395

BOX 25.1	BALANCE OF TRADE AND THE PUBLIC FINANCES	EXPLORING ECONOMICS

The relationship between them

We have seen that the external situation can affect the ability of an economy to achieve internal balance (where actual income is at the potential level). But it also impacts on the composition of aggregate demand. This is most readily demonstrated by observing the relationship between the *public sector's budget balance* and *the balance of trade*.

The public sector's budget balance is measured in the UK by the public sector net cash requirement (PSNCR). This concept was introduced in Chapter 20. We saw that it measures the excess of the sector's spending over its receipts. The balance of trade is one of three principal items that comprises the balance of the current account; the other two are net investment income from abroad and net current transfers (see section 15.4). The balance of trade is exports of goods and services minus imports of goods and services ($X - M$).

The relationship between the public finances and the balance of trade can be illustrated by revisiting the circular flow of income that we introduced in Chapter 14. There we saw that actual (as opposed to planned) withdrawals from the circular flow (net saving (S) plus net taxes (T) plus imports (M)) must equal injections (investment (I) plus government expenditure (G) plus exports (X)):

$$S + T + M = I + G + X \qquad (1)$$

The public sector's budget balance is simply the difference between its taxation receipts (net of transfers) and its spending on goods and services, or $T - G$. The balance of trade is the difference between expenditure on exports and imports, or $X - M$. If we rearrange the above condition slightly we find:

$$(T - G) = (X - M) + (I - S) \qquad (2)$$

This tells us that if the public sector runs a budget surplus ($T - G$ is positive), there is a likelihood that the trade balance will be in surplus too. We can see from equation 2 that this will depend on the extent to which investment and saving are equal. In the case that investment and saving are equal then a budget surplus would be exactly matched by a trade surplus, or a budget deficit by an identical trade deficit. This gives rise to the term 'the *twin deficits*'.

The chart plots the UK's public sector's budget balance and its balance of trade; it also plots the whole current account balance of the balance of payments. Each is presented as a percentage of GDP.

First, we see how very close the balance of trade and the current account balance actually are when presented as percentages of GDP. Since 1965 both balances have more often than not been negative, with both averaging very close to –1% of GDP. Second, we also see that the public sector has typically run a deficit, with the balance averaging –2.75 per cent of GDP. The public sector has effectively been acting as a net injector of income.

The size of the net withdrawal from the trade deficit does not quite match the net injection from the public sector. This means that private-sector investment expenditure has been less than private saving ($I < S$). It also reinforces the argument that we examined in Chapter 20 that public-sector deficits can reduce private investment. This is known as *crowding out*. In the UK it would appear that public-sector borrowing has been financed partly through foreign borrowing from running a trade deficit and partly from the private saving that is not used for private investment.

 If the exchange rate depreciated, how would this affect the trade and budget balances?

UK budget and trade balances as percentage of GDP, 1965–2008

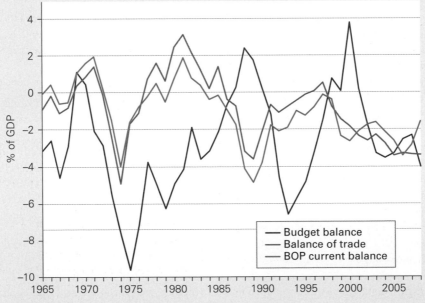

Source: Data from *Economic and Labour Market Review* (National Statistics).

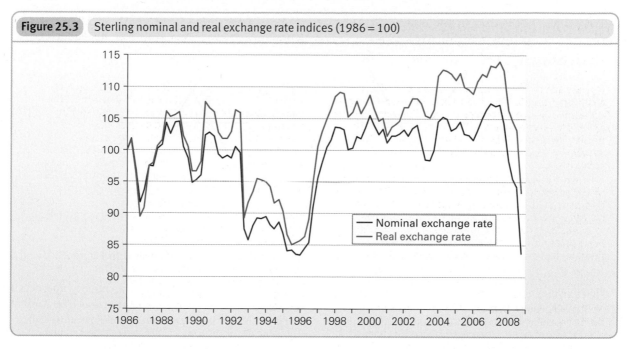

Figure 25.3   Sterling nominal and real exchange rate indices (1986 = 100)

Sources: Based on data in Interactive Database (Bank of England) and *International Statistics* (International Monetary Fund [IMF]), re-based by author to 1986.

The ***real exchange rate*** is the exchange rate index adjusted for changes in the prices of imports (measured in foreign currencies) and exports (measured in domestic prices): in other words, adjusted for the terms of trade. Thus if a country has a higher rate of inflation for its exports than the weighted average inflation of the imports it buys from other countries, its real exchange rate index (RERI) will rise relative to its nominal exchange rate index (NERI).

The real exchange rate index can be defined as:

$$\text{RERI} = \text{NERI} \times P_X / P_M$$

where P_X is the domestic currency price index of exports and P_M is the foreign currencies weighted price index of imports. Thus if (a) a country's inflation is 5 per cent higher than the trade-weighted average of its trading partners (P_X/P_M rises by 5 per cent per year) and (b) its nominal exchange rate depreciates by 5 per cent per year (NERI falls by 5 per cent per year), its real exchange rate index will stay the same.

Take another example: if a country's export prices rise faster than the foreign currency prices of its imports (P_X/P_M rises), its real exchange rate will appreciate relative to its nominal exchange rate.

The real exchange rate thus gives us a better idea of the *quantity* of imports a country can obtain from selling a given quantity of exports. If the real exchange rate rises, the country can get more imports for a given volume of exports.

Figure 25.3 shows the nominal and real exchange rate indices of sterling. As you can see, the real exchange rate has risen over time relative to the nominal exchange rate.

This is because the UK has had a higher rate of inflation than the weighted average of its trading partners.

The real exchange rate also gives a better idea than the nominal exchange rate of how competitive a country is. The lower the real exchange rate, the more competitive will the country's exports be. Figure 25.3 shows that the UK has become less competitive since 1996, thanks not only to a rise in the nominal exchange rate index, but also to higher inflation than its trading partners.

Alternative exchange rate regimes

There are a number of possible exchange rate regimes. They all lie somewhere between two extremes. These two extreme regimes are a ***totally fixed rate*** and a *freely floating rate*.

Definitions

Real exchange rate A country's exchange rate adjusted for changes in the domestic currency prices of its exports relative to the foreign currency prices of its imports. If a country's prices rise (fall) relative to those of its trading partners, its real exchange rate will rise (fall) relative to the nominal exchange rate.

Totally fixed exchange rate Where the government takes whatever measures are necessary to maintain the exchange rate at some stated level.

Freely floating exchange rate Where the exchange rate is determined entirely by the forces of demand and supply in the foreign exchange market with no government intervention whatsoever.

Figure 25.4 Central bank intervention to maintain a fixed exchange rate

(a) Total currency flow deficit

(b) Total currency flow surplus

In the case of a *fixed rate*, the government or central bank will almost certainly have to intervene in the foreign exchange market in order to maintain that rate, and will probably have to take internal policy measures too.

In the case of a *freely floating rate*, there is no government intervention in the foreign exchange market. Exchange rates fluctuate according to market forces – according to changes in the demand for and supply of currencies on the foreign exchange market. Changes in the exchange rate may well affect internal policy objectives, however, and thus cause the government to take various internal policy measures.

> *What adverse internal effects may follow from (a) a depreciation of the exchange rate; (b) an appreciation of the exchange rate?*

Between these extremes there are a number of **intermediate regimes**, where exchange rates are partly left to the market, but where the government intervenes to influence the rate. These intermediate regimes differ according to how much the government intervenes, and thus according to how much flexibility of the exchange rate it is prepared to allow.

Correction under fixed exchange rates

Foreign exchange intervention

Unless the demand for and supply of the domestic currency on the foreign exchange markets are equal at the fixed rate – unless, in other words, there is a total currency flow balance – the central bank will have to intervene in the market and buy or sell the domestic currency to make

up the difference. This is illustrated in Figure 25.4, which looks at the case of the UK.

Figure 25.4(a) shows the case of a currency flow deficit (an excess of pounds) of an amount $a - b$. The Bank of England thus has to purchase these excess pounds by drawing on its foreign exchange reserves, or by borrowing foreign currency from foreign banks.

In Figure 25.4(b), there is a currency flow surplus of $c - d$. In this case, the Bank of England has to supply $c - d$ additional pounds to the market, and will acquire foreign currencies in exchange. It can use these to build up reserves or to pay back foreign loans.

Foreign exchange market intervention and the money supply. Maintaining a fixed exchange rate causes changes in the money supply. If the rate is maintained *above* the equilibrium (Figure 25.5(a)), there is a total currency flow deficit. The Bank of England buys pounds. It thereby withdraws them from circulation and reduces the money supply.

The effect of this reduction in money supply is to raise the equilibrium rate of interest. This attracts financial inflows and improves the financial account. It also dampens aggregate demand, and thus reduces imports and improves the current account. The net effect is to reduce the overall currency flow deficit and thus reduce the gap $a - b$ in Figure 25.4(a). The problem here, of course, is that the lower aggregate demand may well result in a recession.

If the rate is maintained *below* equilibrium (Figure 25.4(b)), there is a total currency flow surplus. The Bank of England supplies additional pounds (which are spent by people abroad on UK exports, etc. and are thus injected into the UK economy). It thereby increases the money supply.

The effect of the increased money supply is to reduce interest rates. This worsens the financial account and, by boosting aggregate demand, increases imports. The currency flow surplus is reduced. The gap $d - c$ narrows.

Sterilisation. If the Bank of England did not want the money supply to alter, it would have to counter these effects with other monetary measures: e.g. open-market operations. Thus when there is a deficit and money supply

> ## Definition
>
> **Intermediate exchange rate regimes** Where the government intervenes to influence movements in the exchange rate.

| BOX 25.2 | THE UK'S BALANCE OF PAYMENTS DEFICIT | CASE STUDIES AND APPLICATIONS |

A cyclical problem or a long-term trend?

In the late 1980s, the UK current account balance of payments moved sharply into deficit, as the diagram shows. In 1989 the current account deficit was 4.9 per cent of GDP – the highest percentage ever recorded. Opinions differed dramatically, however, as to how seriously we should have taken these figures. Not surprisingly, the government claimed that the problem was merely temporary and was not something to cause serious concern. The opposition parties (also not surprisingly) saw the figures as disastrous and a sign that the economy was badly off course.

So who was correct? In fact there was an element of truth in both these claims.

The government was correct to the extent that the severity of the deficit partly reflected the unprecedented boom of the late 1980s. An average growth rate of real GDP of 3.6 per cent between 1984 and 1988 had led to a huge increase in imports. Since the boom could not be sustained, the growth in imports was bound to slow down. Another factor contributing to the deficit was the fall in oil revenues caused by a fall in oil prices. Oil exports fell from £16.1 billion in 1985 to £5.9 billion in 1989. Again, this fall in oil revenues was unlikely to continue once oil prices began to rise again. The current account deficit was also a mirror image of the financial account surplus. This had been caused by a rise in interest rates, used to slow the economy down. As short-term finance flowed into the country to take advantage of the higher interest rate, so this drove the exchange rate up (see Table 15.7 on page 443). The higher exchange rate contributed to the fall in exports and the rise in imports.

But the opposition parties were also correct. The severity of the deficit reflected an underlying weakness of the UK's trading position. If the deficit had been merely a cyclical problem associated with the boom phase of the business cycle, the current account should have gone into *surplus* in the early 1990s as the economy moved into recession. But even in the depths of the recession in 1991, the current account deficit was still nearly 2 per cent of GDP.

The government, however, sought to place a large portion of the blame on a falling demand for exports as the rest of the world began to move into recession.

Subsequent events appeared to support the Conservative government's interpretation. The world economy was recovering in 1994 and the current account deficit virtually disappeared. But then, with a large appreciation of sterling from 1997, and an even larger appreciation of the real exchange rate (see Figure 25.3), the current account started to deteriorate again, as the diagram shows. By 2008, the trade in goods deficit had reached record levels. Optimists claimed that this was, once more, simply a temporary situation, caused by a high exchange rate and low growth in demand in the eurozone. Pessimists again saw it as a sign of a much deeper malaise in the UK exporting sector – that the supply-side reforms of the 1980s, 1990s and early 2000s had made too little difference.

So should we worry about balance of payments deficits? What effect do they have on exchange rates, inflation, growth, unemployment, etc.? What should the government do? These are questions we shall look at in this chapter.

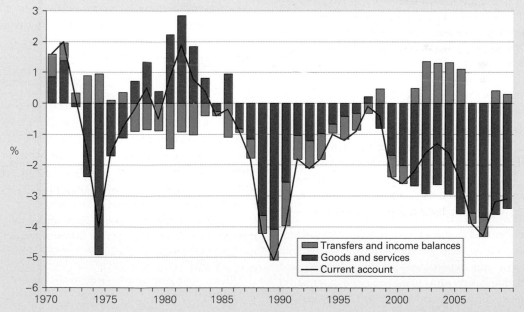

UK balance of payments as a percentage of GDP, 1970–2009

Sources: Based on Time Series Data (National Statistics, various years); Year 2009 figure based on forecast in *Pre-Budget Report* (Bank of England, 2008).

falls, the Bank of England could buy back government bonds from the general public, thereby restoring the money supply to its previous level. This will prevent the economy moving into recession.

This process of countering the effects on money supply of a balance of payments deficit or surplus is known as *sterilisation*.

 Describe the open-market operations necessary to sterilise the monetary effects of a balance of payments surplus. Would this in turn have any effect on the current or financial accounts of the balance of payments?

There is a problem with sterilisation, however. If the money supply is not allowed to change, the currency flow deficit or surplus will persist. In the case of a deficit, a recession may be avoided, but the central bank will have to continue using reserves to support the exchange rate. But reserves are not infinite. Sooner or later they will run out! A recession may be inevitable.

Correcting the disequilibrium

If a balance of payments deficit persists, and reserves continue to dwindle or foreign debts mount, the government will have to tackle the underlying disequilibrium. If the exchange rate is to remain fixed, it must shift the demand and supply curves so that they intersect at the fixed exchange rate.

It can use contractionary fiscal and monetary policies for this purpose. Such policies have two main effects on the current account: an income effect (*expenditure reducing*) and a substitution effect between home and foreign goods (*expenditure switching*).

Expenditure reducing. Contractionary policy reduces national income. This in turn reduces expenditure, including expenditure on imports, shifting the supply of sterling curve to the left in Figure 25.4(a). The bigger the marginal propensity to import, the larger the shift.

There is a possible conflict here, however, between external and internal objectives. The balance of payments may improve, but unemployment is likely to rise and the rate of growth to fall.

 Under what circumstances would (a) contractionary and (b) expansionary policies cause no conflict between internal and external objectives?

Expenditure switching. If contractionary policies reduce the rate of inflation below that of foreign competitors, exports will become relatively cheaper compared with foreign competing goods and imports will become relatively more expensive compared with home-produced alternatives. Some foreign consumers will switch to UK exports. The more elastic the demand, the bigger the switch. Some UK consumers will switch from imports to home-produced goods. Again, the more elastic the demand, the bigger the

switch. Demand in both cases will be more elastic the closer UK goods are as substitutes for foreign goods.

To the extent that contractionary policies result in expenditure switching rather than expenditure reducing, so this reduces the conflict between balance of payments and employment objectives.

Expenditure switching can also be achieved by placing restrictions on imports (tariffs and/or quotas) or the subsidising of exports. But this would conflict with the objective of free trade.

To the extent that fiscal and monetary policies affect interest rates, so this will affect the financial account of the balance of payments. Higher interest rates will increase the demand for sterling and will thus lead to an improvement on the financial account. (The implications of this are explored in section 25.2.)

Correction under free-floating exchange rates

Freely floating exchange rates should automatically and immediately correct any balance of payments deficit or surplus: by depreciation and appreciation respectively. Foreign exchange dealers simply adjust the exchange rate so as to balance their books – in line with demand and supply.

As with fixed rates, an income effect and a substitution effect of the correction process can be distinguished. But the nature of the income and substitution effects of depreciation/appreciation is quite different from that of deflation. It is only the substitution effect that corrects the disequilibrium. The income effect makes the problem *worse*! First the substitution effect: *expenditure switching*.

Expenditure switching (the substitution effect)

The process of adjustment. Assume a higher rate of inflation in the UK than abroad. As domestic prices rise relative to

---

Definitions

Sterilisation Where the government uses open-market operations or other monetary measures to neutralise the effects of balance of payments deficits or surpluses on the money supply.

Expenditure changing (reducing) from a contraction: the income effect Where contractionary policies lead to a reduction in national income and hence a reduction in the demand for imports.

Expenditure switching from a contraction: the substitution effect Where contractionary policies lead to a reduction in inflation and thus cause a switch in expenditure away from imports and towards exports.

Expenditure switching from depreciation: the substitution effect Where a lower exchange rate reduces the price of exports and increases the price of imports. This will increase the sale of exports and reduce the sale of imports.

Figure 25.5 Adjustment of the exchange rate to a shift in demand and supply

Figure 25.6 The income effect (stable prices)

the price of imports, more imports will be purchased. The supply of pounds curve will shift to the right (to S_2 in Figure 25.5). UK exports will now be relatively more expensive for foreigners. Less will be sold. The demand for pounds curve will shift to the left (to D_2).

Foreign exchange dealers will now find themselves with a glut of unsold pounds. They will therefore lower the exchange rate (to er_2 in Figure 25.5). The amount that the exchange rate has to change depends on:

- The amount that the curves shift. Thus large differences in international inflation rates or large differences in international interest rates will cause large shifts in the demand for and supply of currencies, and hence large movements in exchange rates.
- The elasticity of the curves. The less elastic the demand and supply curves of sterling, the greater the change in the exchange rate for any given shift in demand and supply.

But what determines the elasticity of the demand and supply curves? This is examined in Case Study 25.1 in MyEconLab.

Expenditure changing (the income effect)

Depreciation, as well as affecting relative prices, will affect national income. This will cause *expenditure changing*.

We have already established that, as the exchange rate falls, so more exports will be sold and less imports pur-

KI 7
p33

Definition

Expenditure changing (increasing) from depreciation: the income effect Where depreciation, via the substitution effect, will alter the demand for imports and exports, and this, via the multiplier, will affect the level of national income and hence the demand for imports.

chased: this was the substitution effect. But this is only an initial effect.

Exports are an injection into, and imports a withdrawal from, the circular flow of income. There will thus be a multiplied rise in national income. This income effect (expenditure *increasing*) reduces the effectiveness of the depreciation. Two situations can be examined.

A rise in national income and employment, but no change in prices. Assume that there are substantial unemployed resources, so that an increase in aggregate demand will raise output and employment but not prices. As national income rises, so imports rise (thereby tending to offset the initial fall), but exports are unaffected.

This is illustrated by the line $(X - M)_1$ in Figure 25.6. At low levels of national income, spending on imports is low; thus exports (X) exceed imports (M). $X - M$ is positive. As national income and hence imports rise, $X - M$ falls, and after a point becomes negative. Thus the $X - M$ line is downward sloping.

Assume an initial equilibrium national income at Y_1, where national income (Y) equals national expenditure (E_1), but with imports exceeding exports by an amount $a - b$. The exchange rate thus depreciates.

This will cause a substitution effect: exports rise and imports fall. The $X - M$ line therefore shifts upwards. But this in turn causes an income effect. Aggregate demand rises, and the E line shifts upwards.

An eventual internal and external equilibrium is reached at Y_2, where $Y = E_2$ and $(X - M)_2 = 0$.

The positive substitution effect of this depreciation is $c - b$. The negative income effect is $c - a$. The net effect is thus only $a - b$, which is the size of the initial deficit. Had it not been for this negative income effect, a smaller depreciation would have been needed.

At least in this case, the income effect is having a desirable *internal* consequence: reducing unemployment.

A rise in prices. If the economy is near full employment, the rise in aggregate demand from depreciation will make that depreciation even less effective. Not only will the higher demand lead directly to more imports, it will also lead to higher inflation. There will thus be an adverse substitution effect too. This will partially offset the beneficial substitution effect of the depreciation. The higher inflation will have the effect of shifting the $X - M$ line back down again somewhat.

In the extreme case, where money supply expands to accommodate the rise in aggregate demand, $X - M$ may simply return to its original position. The depreciation will fail to correct the balance of payments disequilibrium. In Figure 25.5, the fall in the exchange rate to er_2 will simply lead to a further rightward shift in supply and a leftward shift in demand, until the gap between them is the same as it was at er_1.

To offset the income effect, a government may feel it necessary to back up a currency depreciation with deflationary demand management policies.

Intermediate exchange rate regimes

There are a number of possible intermediate systems between the two extremes of totally fixed and completely free-floating exchange rates.

Adjustable peg. The **adjustable peg** system is towards the fixed end of the spectrum. Exchange rates are fixed (or 'pegged') for a period of time – perhaps several years.

In the short and medium term, therefore, correction is the same as with a totally fixed system. Central banks have to intervene in the foreign exchange market to maintain the rate. If a deficit persists, then deflationary or other policies must be adopted to *shift* the currency demand and supply curves. This will be a problem, however, if there already exist substantial unemployed resources.

In the long term, if a fundamental disequilibrium occurs, the currency can be repegged at a lower or higher rate. Adjusting the peg downwards is known as **devaluation**. Adjusting it upwards is known as **revaluation**.

Alternatively, more frequent smaller adjustments could be made, thus moving the system away from the fixed end of the spectrum.

Managed floating. The **managed floating** system is towards the free-floating end of the spectrum. Exchange rates are not pegged: they are allowed to float. But the central bank intervenes from time to time to prevent excessive exchange rate fluctuations. It is thus a form of 'managed flexibility'.

Under such a system, the central bank does not seek to maintain a long-term or even medium-term disequilibrium

rate. Rather it tries to allow an 'orderly' exchange rate adjustment to major changes in demand and supply, while preventing the violent short-term swings that can occur with a totally free float (swings arising from currency speculation).

To back up the central bank's use of reserves, it may also alter interest rates to prevent exchange rate fluctuations. If, for example, there were a large-scale selling of the domestic currency, the central bank could raise interest rates to counter this effect and prevent the exchange rate from falling.

 How would raising interest rates in this way affect the balance between the current and financial accounts of the balance of payments?

The degree of currency stability sought, and hence the degree of intervention required, will vary from country to country and from government to government. At one extreme, the government may intervene only if exchange rate fluctuations become very severe; at the other extreme, the government may try to maintain the exchange rate at some unofficial target level.

Crawling peg. The **crawling peg** system is midway between managed floating and the adjustable peg system. Instead of making large and infrequent devaluations (or revaluations), the government adjusts the peg by small amounts, but frequently – say, once a month, as the equilibrium exchange rate changes.

Joint float. Under a **joint float** a group of countries have a fixed or adjustable peg system between their *own* currencies, but *jointly float* against all other currencies.

Exchange rate band. With an **exchange rate band** the government sets a lower and an upper limit to the exchange

---

Definitions

Adjustable peg A system whereby exchange rates are fixed for a period of time, but may be devalued (or revalued) if a deficit (or surplus) becomes substantial.

Devaluation Where the government repegs the exchange rate at a lower level.

Revaluation Where the government repegs the exchange rate at a higher level.

Managed floating A system of flexible exchange rates, but where the government intervenes to prevent excessive fluctuations or even to achieve an unofficial target exchange rate.

Crawling peg A system whereby the government allows a gradual adjustment of the exchange rate.

Joint float Where a group of currencies pegged to each other jointly float against other currencies.

Exchange rate band Where a currency is allowed to float between an upper and lower exchange rate, but is not allowed to move outside this band.

Figure 25.7 The crawling peg within exchange rate bands

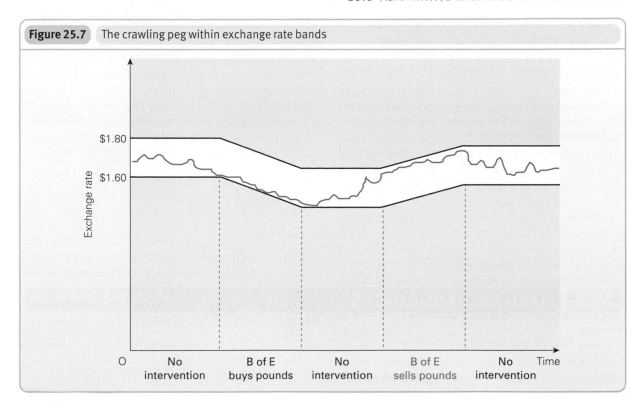

rate: say, £1 = $1.60 and £1 = $1.80. It then allows the exchange rate to fluctuate freely within these limits. It will intervene, however, if the rate hits the floor or the ceiling. Exchange rate bands could be narrow (say ±1 per cent) or wide (say ±15 per cent).

Exchange rate bands can be incorporated in other systems – the band could be adjustable, crawling or fixed. For example, Figure 25.7 illustrates a crawling peg system with an exchange rate band.

The exchange rate mechanism (ERM) of the European Monetary System (EMS) was an example of a joint float against non-member currencies and an adjustably pegged

exchange rate band with member currencies (see section 26.2). The ERM2 system for Denmark, and for new members of the EU prior to adopting the euro, is similar.

All these intermediate systems are attempts to achieve as many as possible of the advantages of both fixed and flexible exchange rates, with as few as possible of the attendant disadvantages. To assess any of these compromise systems, therefore, we must examine the advantages and disadvantages of fixed and flexible exchange rates. We do this in the next two sections.

Section summary

1. There may be a conflict in achieving both internal and external balance simultaneously. The nature of the conflict depends on the exchange rate regime that the country adopts.

2. Nominal exchange rates are simply the rates at which one currency exchanges for another. Real exchange rates take account of differences in inflation rates between import and export prices and are a measure of the competitiveness of a country's exports.

3. Under a fixed exchange rate system, the government will have to intervene whenever the equilibrium exchange rate ceases to coincide with the fixed rate. If the equilibrium rate falls below the fixed rate, the government will have to buy in the domestic currency on the foreign exchange market. This will have the

effect of reducing the money supply. Likewise, selling the domestic currency in order to prevent an appreciation will increase money supply. The government can prevent these changes in money supply by the use of appropriate open-market operations or other monetary measures. This is known as 'sterilisation'. Sterilisation, however, means that the disequilibrium is likely to go uncorrected.

4. If a deficit (or surplus) persists under a fixed rate, the government can attempt to shift the currency demand and supply curves. To cure a deficit, it can use contractionary fiscal or monetary policies. These have two effects. Deflation leads to a fall in national income (the income effect) and hence a fall in the demand for imports. It also leads to a fall in inflation

▶

and hence a switch in demand from foreign goods to home-produced goods (the substitution effect).

5. Correction under free-floating exchange rates also involves an income and a substitution effect. If there is a deficit, the exchange rate will depreciate. This will make imports more expensive and exports cheaper, and hence there will be a substitution effect as imports fall and exports rise.

6. The income effect of a depreciation, however, reduces its effectiveness. The rise in exports and fall in imports (i.e. the substitution effect of a depreciation) will lead to a multiplied rise in national income, which will cause imports to rise back again somewhat. The bigger this income effect, the bigger will be the depreciation necessary to achieve equilibrium in the foreign exchange market. Correction is made more difficult if any depreciation leads to increases in domestic prices and hence to a second substitution effect – only this time an adverse one.

7. There are intermediate exchange rate regimes between the extremes of fixed rates and free-floating rates. The exchange rate may be fixed for a period of time (the adjustable peg); or it may be allowed to change gradually (the crawling peg); or the government may merely intervene to dampen exchange rate fluctuations (managed floating); or the exchange rate may be allowed to fluctuate within a band, where the band in turn may be fixed, adjustable or crawling.

25.2 FIXED EXCHANGE RATES

In this section we examine the causes of balance of payments problems under fixed nominal exchange rates, in both the short run and the long run. First, in an optional section, we look at short-run causes and whether balance will be restored. We then look at longer-run, more fundamental causes of balance of payments problems. Finally, we assess the desirability of fixed exchange rates.

*Effects of shocks under fixed exchange rates

Under fixed exchange rates, it is unlikely that internal and external balance can persist for long without government intervention. Various macroeconomic 'shocks', such as changes in injections or withdrawals, or changes in international interest rates, are constantly occurring. These are likely to destroy either internal or external balance or both. Even with government intervention, it may still be very difficult, if not impossible, to restore both balances. Correction of balance of payments disequilibria will come into conflict with the other macroeconomic goals of growth, full employment and stable prices.

How the economy responds to shocks under fixed exchange rates, and which policy measures are most effective in dealing with the resultant disequilibria, depend on two things: (a) whether the shocks are internal or external; (b) the flexibility of wages and prices, which, in turn, depends on the time period under consideration.

Response to an internal shock
Let us assume that there is a fall in aggregate demand, caused by a fall in consumer demand or investment, or by a rise in saving.

Short-run effect. In the short run, prices and especially wages tend to be relatively inflexible (this is a central assumption of Keynesian analysis). The fall in aggregate demand will lead to a recession. Internal balance will be destroyed. In a closed economy, the central bank would probably reduce interest rates to boost the economy, either to tackle the recession directly or because *forecast* inflation had fallen below its target level.

In an open economy under fixed exchange rates, however, this is not possible. But why?

The lower aggregate demand will lead to a fall in imports, resulting in a *current account* surplus. There is an opposite effect on the *financial account*, however. The reduced aggregate demand will lead to a fall in the demand for money and hence downward pressure on interest rates. If interest rates were allowed to fall, there would be a resulting financial outflow and hence a financial account deficit.

But which would be the larger effect: the current account surplus or the financial account deficit? This depends on the marginal propensity to import (*mpm*) and the mobility of international finance. The higher the *mpm*, the bigger the current account surplus. The higher the international mobility of finance, the bigger the financial outflow and hence the bigger the financial account deficit. In today's world of massive financial flows across the foreign exchanges, international finance is highly, if not perfectly, mobile. If the central bank allows interest rates to fall, the financial account deficit will therefore exceed the current account surplus.

To prevent this happening, interest rates must not be allowed to fall or, at least, must fall only very slightly – just enough for the resulting financial account deficit to match the current account surplus. With hardly any fall in interest rates, money supply must thus be allowed to contract to match the fall in the demand for money.

Thus to maintain the fixed exchange rate (without massively draining reserves) interest rates will be determined by the balance of payments. They cannot be used for domestic purposes, such as targeting inflation, targeting real national income or some combination (e.g. a Taylor rule: see page 608). Internal imbalance will persist in the short run.

Long-run effect. In the long run, there will be much greater, if not perfect, price and wage flexibility. Under new classical assumptions, such flexibility will exist in the short run too. This flexibility will ensure that internal balance is restored. The Phillips curve is vertical at the natural rate of unemployment.

But, with a fixed exchange rate, will it also ensure external balance? Again, let us assume that people decide to spend less and save more. As in the short run, this will lead to a *current account* surplus. This time, however, the effect is much bigger. In the short run, there was little or no price effect (i.e. no substitution effect) since there was little change in inflation. There was only an income effect from reduced imports caused by the recession. In the long run, however, the lower real aggregate demand reduces inflation. Assuming that inflation falls below that of trading partners, the *real* exchange rate falls. This makes exports relatively cheaper and imports relatively more expensive. This causes exports to rise and imports to fall.

The resulting rise in aggregate demand not only helps to eliminate the recession, but also helps to reduce the current account surplus.

Thus, despite a fixed *nominal* exchange rate, wage and price flexibility cause the *real* exchange rate to be flexible. This helps restore overall external balance. Nevertheless, a current account surplus may persist. Indeed, as the surplus is used to buy foreign assets, so, over time, these will yield an income, further crediting the current account.

But what is clear is that, although interest rates are determined by the need to maintain a fixed nominal exchange rate, wage and price flexibility in the long run will eventually restore internal balance. The question is, how long will the long run be? How long will the recession persist? If it is too long, and if interest rates cannot be cut, then can expansionary fiscal policy be used? We examine this in Box 25.3.

Response to an external shock

Assume now that there is a fall in demand for exports.

Short-run effect. The fall in exports causes the *current account* to go into deficit. It also reduces aggregate demand, causing a multiplied fall in national income. This reduces the demand for imports: the larger the *mpm*, the bigger the reduction in imports. Aggregate demand will go on falling until the lower injections are matched by lower withdrawals. But the current account deficit will not be eliminated, since the fall in withdrawals to match the fall in exports consists only partly of lower imports; part will consist of lower saving and lower tax receipts.

The reduction in aggregate demand reduces the transactions demand for money, putting downward pressure on interest rates. This would result in a financial outflow and hence a *financial account* deficit, making the overall currency flow deficit worse. To prevent this happening, the central bank must prevent interest rates from falling by reducing the money supply (through open-market operations). Indeed, given the current account deficit, interest rates may have to be slightly higher than they were originally in order to create a financial account surplus sufficient to offset the current account deficit. This will make the recession worse.

Long-run effect. The reduction in aggregate demand will put downward pressure on domestic inflation. This will help to reduce the *real* exchange rate and hence correct the current account deficit. It will also restore internal balance. Again, however, without fiscal policy, the long run may be some time in coming. The recession may persist.

 Trace through the short-run and long-run internal and external effects (under a fixed exchange rate) of (a) a fall in domestic saving; (b) a rise in the demand for exports.

Causes of longer-term balance of payments problems under fixed exchange rates

With moderately flexible prices, current account balance may eventually be restored after 'one-off' shocks. However, long-term continuing shifts in the demand and supply of imports and exports can make balance of payments problems persist. We will examine four causes of these long-term shifts.

Different rates of inflation between countries. If a country has persistently higher rates of inflation than the countries with which it trades, it will have a growing current account deficit. Exports and import substitutes will become less and less competitive as its *real* exchange rate appreciates.

Different rates of growth between countries. If a country grows faster than the countries with which it trades, its imports will tend to grow faster than its exports.

Income elasticity of demand for imports higher than for exports. If the income elasticity of demand for imports is relatively high, and the income elasticity of demand for exports is relatively low, then as world incomes grow, the country's imports will grow faster than its exports. This has been a particular problem for many developing countries: they import manufactured goods and capital equipment, whose demand grows rapidly, and export primary products – food and raw materials – whose demand, until recent years, has grown relatively slowly (see section 27.2).

Long-term structural changes.

- Trading blocs may emerge, putting up tariff barriers to other countries. Australian and New Zealand exports were adversely affected when the UK joined the EEC.
- Countries may exercise monopoly power to a greater extent than previously. The OPEC oil price increases of 1973/4 and 1978/9 are examples.
- Countries may develop import substitutes. Thus plastics and other synthetics have in many cases substituted for rubber and metals, worsening the balance of payments of traditional primary exporters.
- The nature and quality of a country's products may change. Thus Japan has shifted from producing low-quality simple manufactured goods in the 1950s to producing high-quality sophisticated manufactured goods today. This has helped increase its exports.

To maintain a fixed exchange rate under such circumstances, governments have to take measures to correct the disequilibria. They can use demand-side policies (fiscal and monetary: see Box 25.3), supply-side policies or protectionist policies.

Advantages of fixed exchange rates

Many economists are opposed to fixed exchange rates, for reasons to be examined shortly. Nevertheless, many businesspeople are in favour of relatively rigid exchange rates. The following arguments are used.

Certainty.   With fixed exchange rates, international trade and investment become much less risky, since profits are not affected by movements in the exchange rate.

Little or no speculation.   Provided the rate is *absolutely* fixed – and people believe that it will remain so – there is no point in speculating. For example, between 1999 and 2001, when the old currencies of the eurozone countries were still

---

| BOX 25.3 | THE EFFECTIVENESS OF FISCAL AND MONETARY POLICIES UNDER FIXED EXCHANGE RATES | EXPLORING ECONOMICS |

Monetary policy

Monetary policy is not very effective under fixed exchange rates.

Assume that the central bank, worried by rising inflation, wishes to reduce the growth in nominal aggregate demand. It thus reduces the rate of growth in money supply. This drives up interest rates and causes a fall in real national income.

What effect will this have on the balance of payments? The lower national income reduces expenditure on imports and hence leads to a surplus on the current account. Also, the higher interest rates encourage an inflow of finance and hence a surplus on the financial account too. This balance of payments surplus will *increase* money supply again and reduce interest rates back towards the original level. Aggregate demand will rise back towards its original level. Monetary policy has been ineffective.

But rather than changing the *supply* of money, can the government not directly alter interest rates? The problem here is that, in order to maintain the rate of exchange at the fixed level, the government's room for manoeuvre is very limited. For example, if it raises interest rates, the resulting inflow of finance will cause a balance of payments surplus. The government could, for a period of time, simply build up reserves, but it may not want to do this indefinitely.

The problem is more serious if the economy is in recession and the central bank wants to increase aggregate demand by *reducing* interest rates. The financial outflow will force the central bank to buy in the domestic currency by using its reserves. But it can do this for only so long. Eventually, it will be forced to raise interest rates again in order to stem the drain on the reserves. In today's world, with little in the way of exchange controls and with massive amounts of short-term international liquidity, such flows can be enormous.

This gives the central bank virtually no discretion over changing interest rates. Interest rates will have to be kept at a level so as to maintain the exchange rate. In the case of *perfect* mobility of international finance, interest rates must be kept at world rates. Monetary policy will be totally ineffective.

Fiscal policy

Fiscal policy is much more effective.

Assume that there is a recession and the government wishes to increase aggregate demand. It thus cuts taxes and/or raises government expenditure. This raises national income and increases expenditure on imports. Also, higher inflation raises the real exchange rate. This makes exports less competitive and imports relatively cheaper. The current account moves into deficit.

The increase in aggregate demand will raise the demand for money and hence put upward pressure on interest rates. This will lead to an inflow of finance and a financial account surplus. To prevent this swamping the current account deficit, the central bank must prevent interest rates from rising very much. In the case of an infinitely elastic supply of finance, interest rates must not be allowed to rise at all.

Thus money supply must be allowed to expand to keep interest rates down. This expansion of the money supply thus reinforces the expansionary fiscal policy and prevents crowding out.

Thus a high level of international financial mobility *enhances* the effectiveness of fiscal policy.

 Suppose that under a managed floating system the central bank is worried about high inflation and wants to keep the exchange rate up in order to prevent import prices rising. To tackle the problem of inflation, it raises interest rates. What will happen to the current and financial accounts of the balance of payments?

used, but were totally fixed to the euro, there was no speculation that the German mark, say, would change in value against the French franc or the Dutch guilder.

 When the UK joined the ERM in 1990, it was hoped that this would make speculation pointless. As it turned out, speculation forced the UK to leave the ERM in 1992. Can you reconcile this with the argument that fixed rates discourage speculation?

Automatic correction of monetary errors. If the central bank allows the money supply to expand too fast, the resulting extra demand and lower interest rates will lead to a balance of payments deficit. This will force the central bank to intervene to support the exchange rate. Either it must buy the domestic currency on the foreign exchange market, thereby causing money supply to fall again (unless it sterilises the effect), or it must raise interest rates. Either way this will have the effect of correcting the error.

Preventing governments pursuing 'irresponsible' macroeconomic policies. If a government deliberately and excessively expands aggregate demand – perhaps in an attempt to gain short-term popularity with the electorate – the resulting balance of payments deficit will force it to constrain demand again (unless it resorts to import controls).

Disadvantages of fixed exchange rates

The new classical view
New classicists make two crucial criticisms of fixed rates.

Fixed exchange rates make monetary policy ineffective. Interest rates must be used to ensure that the overall balance of payments balances. As a result, money supply must be allowed to vary with the demand for money in order to keep interest rates at the necessary level. Thus monetary policy cannot be used for domestic purposes (see Box 25.3). Inflation depends on world rates, which may be high and domestically unacceptable. If the central bank tries to reduce inflation by attempting to reduce money supply and raise interest rates, the current and financial accounts will go into surplus. Money supply will thus increase until domestic inflation rises back to world levels.

Fixed rates contradict the objective of having free markets. Why fix the exchange rate, when a simple depreciation or appreciation can correct a disequilibrium? In the new classical world where markets clear, and supply and demand are relatively elastic, why not treat the foreign exchange market like any other, and simply leave it to supply and demand?

The Keynesian view
In the Keynesian world, wages and prices are relatively 'sticky', and demand-deficient unemployment and cost-push inflation may persist. As such, there is no guarantee of achieving both internal and external balance simultan-

eously when exchange rates are fixed. This leads to the following problems.

Balance of payments deficits can lead to a recession. A balance of payments deficit can occur even if there is no excess demand. As we saw above, this could be caused by different rates of growth or different rates of inflation from trading partners, a higher income elasticity of demand for imports than for exports, and so on. If protectionism is to be avoided, and if supply-side policies work only over the long run, the government will be forced to reduce the rate of growth of aggregate demand. This will lead to higher unemployment and possibly a recession.

If wages and prices are sticky downwards, the contraction may have to be severe if a significant improvement in the *current* account is to be made. Here, reliance would have to be placed largely on lower *incomes* reducing the demand for imports. If the deflation is achieved through higher interest rates, however, an improvement on the *financial* account may remove the need for a severe deflation, especially given the high degree of financial mobility that exists nowadays. Nevertheless, the rate of interest may still be higher than that desired for purely internal purposes.

If a country has a *persistent* current account deficit, it may need to have persistently higher interest rates than its competitors and suffer persistently lower growth rates as a result. It will also tend to build up short-term debts, as money is put on deposit in the country to take advantage of the higher interest rates. This can make the problem of speculation much more acute if people come to believe that the fixed rate cannot be maintained (see below).

Competitive deflations leading to world depression. If deficit countries deflated, but surplus countries *reflated*, there would be no overall world deflation or reflation. Countries may be quite happy, however, to run a balance of payments surplus and build up reserves. Countries may thus competitively deflate – all trying to achieve a balance of payments surplus. But this is beggar-my-neighbour policy. Not all countries can have a surplus! Overall the world must be in balance. Such policies lead to general world deflation and a restriction in growth.

Problems of international liquidity. If trade is to expand, there must be an expansion in the supply of currencies acceptable for world trade (dollars, euros, gold, etc.): there must be adequate **international liquidity**. Countries' reserves of these currencies must grow if they are to be

> ### Definition
>
> **International liquidity** The supply of currencies in the world acceptable for financing international trade and investment.

sufficient to maintain a fixed rate at times of balance of payments disequilibrium. Conversely, there must not be excessive international liquidity. Otherwise the extra demand that would result would lead to world inflation. It is important under fixed exchange rates, therefore, to avoid too much or too little international liquidity. The problem is how to maintain adequate control of international liquidity. The supply of dollars, for example, depends largely on US policy, which may be dominated by the US internal economic situation rather than by any concern for the well-being of the international community. Similarly, the supply of euros depends on the policy of the European Central Bank, which is governed by the internal situation in the eurozone countries.

 Why will excessive international liquidity lead to international inflation?

 Speculation. If speculators believe that a fixed rate simply cannot be maintained, speculation is likely to be massive. If there is a huge deficit, there is no chance whatsoever of a

*re*valuation. Either the rate will be devalued or it will remain the same. Speculators will thus sell the domestic currency. After all, it is a pretty good gamble: heads they win (devaluation); tails they don't lose (no devaluation). This speculative selling will worsen the deficit, and may itself force the devaluation. Speculation of this sort had disastrous effects on some south-east Asian currencies in 1997 (see Case Study 25.4 in MyEconLab) and on the Argentinian peso in 2002 (see Case Study 25.6).

 To what extent do Keynesians and new classicists agree about the role of fixed exchange rates?

Postscript

An argument used in favour of fixed rates is that they prevent governments from pursuing inflationary policies. But if getting inflation down is desirable, why do governments not pursue an anti-inflationary policy directly? Today, many governments (or central banks) make inflation targeting the goal of monetary policy. Most, however, have floating exchange rates.

Section summary

1. *Macroeconomic shocks are constantly occurring. Whether internal and external balance will be restored under a fixed exchange rate, following a shock, depends on price and wage flexibility and on the time period.

2. *In the short run there is a degree of wage and price inflexibility. If there is a fall in aggregate demand, the resulting fall in national income will reduce the demand for imports. This will cause a current account surplus. The fall in aggregate demand will also reduce the demand for money and put downward pressure on interest rates. This will cause a financial account deficit. This effect can be large, given the high mobility of international finance. Interest rates are thus constrained by the need for the financial account to balance the current account.

3. *In the long run, with wage and price flexibility, the real exchange rate can change. This will help to restore both internal and external balance.

4. Over the longer term, balance of payments disequilibria under fixed exchange rates can arise from different rates of inflation and growth between

   countries, different income elasticities of demand for imports and exports, and long-term structural changes.

5. Under fixed exchange rates, monetary policy will not be very effective, but fiscal policy will be much more effective.

6. Fixed exchange rates bring the advantage of certainty for the business community, which encourages trade and foreign investment. They also help to prevent governments from pursuing irresponsible macroeconomic policies.

7. Both new classical and Keynesian economists, however, see important disadvantages in fixed exchange rates. New classical economists argue that they make monetary policy totally ineffective, and that they run counter to the efficiency objective of having free markets. Keynesians argue that fixed rates can lead to serious internal imbalance with perhaps a persistent recession; that with competitive deflations a recession can be worldwide; that there may be problems of excessive or insufficient international liquidity; and that speculation could be very severe if people came to believe that a fixed rate was about to break down.

25.3 FREE-FLOATING EXCHANGE RATES

Floating exchange rates and the freeing of domestic policy

With a freely floating exchange rate there can be no overall balance of payments disequilibrium. Foreign exchange dealers will constantly adjust the exchange rate to balance

their books, so that the demand for and supply of any currency are equal.

This, therefore, removes the balance of payments constraint on domestic policy that exists under a fixed exchange rate. No reserves are required, since there is no central bank intervention to support the exchange rate.

The government would seem free to pursue whatever domestic policy it likes. Any resulting effects on the balance of payments are simply and automatically corrected by a depreciation or appreciation of the exchange rate.

In reality, however, things are not quite so simple. Even under a totally free-floating exchange rate, some constraints on domestic policy may be imposed by the effects of these exchange rate movements. For example, a depreciation of the exchange rate increases the price of imports. If the demand for imports is relatively inelastic, this may lead to a higher rate of inflation.

Response to shocks under a floating exchange rate

Internal shocks

Let us assume that there is a rise in aggregate demand that causes inflation. For the moment, however, let us also assume that monetary policy maintains real interest rates at international levels. For simplicity, let us assume that there is no inflation abroad. How will a floating exchange rate system cope with this internal shock of a rise in aggregate demand? The exchange rate will simply depreciate to maintain the competitiveness of exports and import substitutes.

For example, assume an initial exchange rate of £1 = $2. A UK product costing $2 in the USA will earn £1 for the UK exporter. If UK inflation now causes prices to double, the exchange rate will roughly halve. If it falls to £1 = $1, then the same product costing $2 in the USA will now earn £2 for the UK exporter, which in *real* terms is the same amount as before. This is the ***purchasing-power parity theory***. This states that domestic price changes will be offset by (nominal) exchange rate changes, thereby maintaining the same relative prices between countries as before.

 If this is the case, need firms worry about losing competitiveness in world markets if domestic inflation is higher than world inflation?

If we now drop the assumption that real interest rates are maintained at the same level as abroad, the purchasing-power parity theory will break down. Let us assume that the rise in aggregate demand causes a rise in UK real interest rates. This could be either the effect of the higher demand for money pushing up interest rates, or a deliberate act of the central bank to bring inflation back down to the target level.

There are now two effects on the exchange rate. The higher aggregate demand and higher inflation will cause the current account to move into deficit, thereby putting downward pressure on the exchange rate. The higher real interest rates, however, will cause the financial account to move into surplus as depositors choose to hold their money in pounds. This will put upward pressure on the exchange rate. Whether the exchange rate actually falls or rises depends on which of the two effects is the bigger. In today's world of huge international financial flows, the effect on the financial account is likely to be the larger

one: the exchange rate will thus *appreciate*. The greater the interest elasticity of supply of such flows, the greater the appreciation.

But either way, because of the financial account effect, the new equilibrium exchange rate will be above the purchasing-power parity rate. This will adversely affect export industries, since the exchange rate has not fallen sufficiently (if at all) to compensate for their higher sterling price. It will also adversely affect domestic industries that compete with imports, since again the exchange rate has not fallen sufficiently to retain their competitiveness with imports. The current account thus remains in deficit, matched by an equal and opposite financial plus capital account surplus.

This has been the position in the UK for several years. The rate of inflation has been above that of major trading partners; the current account has been persistently in deficit (see Box 25.2) and the capital plus financial account has been persistently in surplus; interest rates have been persistently above interest rates in the USA and the eurozone. The result has been an appreciating real exchange rate (see Figure 25.3).

The carry trade. The problem for current account deficit countries has been made worse in recent years by the growth in the ***carry trade***. This involves international investors taking advantage of nominal interest rate differences between countries.

Current account deficit countries, such as the UK, Australia and New Zealand, have had relatively high interest rates, while current account surplus countries such as Japan and Switzerland have had relatively low ones. It is thus profitable to borrow, say, yen at the low interest rate that obtains in Japan, exchange it into sterling and deposit the money at the higher interest rate available in the UK. If there is no change in the exchange rate between the pound and the yen, the investor makes a profit equal to the difference in the interest rates.

If, however, the higher interest rates in the UK and other deficit countries were simply to compensate investors for the risk of currency depreciation, then there would be no excessive inflow of finance. The benefit of the higher interest rate would be offset by a depreciating currency. But

> ### Definitions
>
> **Purchasing-power parity theory** The theory that the exchange rate will adjust so as to offset differences in countries' inflation rates, with the result that the same quantity of internationally traded goods can be bought at home as abroad with a given amount of the domestic currency.
>
> **Carry trade** Borrowing at low interest rates and then using it to buy assets that earn higher rates. In foreign exchange markets, the carry trade involves borrowing money in a currency of a country where interest rates are low and exchanging it for another currency where the country pays higher interest rates.

the carry trade had the effect of making deficit currencies *appreciate*, thereby further boosting the carry trade by speculation of further exchange rate rises.

Thus the currencies of deficit countries appreciated, making their goods less competitive and worsening their current account deficit. Between 1996 and 2006, the average current account deficits as a percentage of GDP for the USA, the UK and Australia were 4.0, 1.8 and 4.4 respectively. The US dollar appreciated by 9.8 per cent, sterling by 27.7 per cent and the Australian dollar by 3.8 per cent over the same period.

Currencies of surplus countries depreciated, making the their goods more competitive and further boosting their current account surpluses. Between 2004 and 2006, the average current account surpluses as a percentage of GDP for Japan, Switzerland and Sweden were 3.8, 13.8 and 7.3 respectively. Their short-term interest rates averaged a mere 0.1, 1.0 and 2.1 per cent respectively (compared with 3.4, 4.7 and 5.7 per cent for the USA, the UK and Australia). The yen depreciated by 10.4 per cent, the Swiss franc by 2.3 per cent and the Swedish krona by 4.3 per cent over the same period.

With the credit crunch of 2007/8, however, short-term flows of finance declined significantly. This had the effect of reducing the carry trade and its effect on exchange rates. The current account became relatively more significant in determining exchange rates. The currencies of deficit countries, such as the UK and USA, began to depreciate and those of surplus countries, such as Japan and Switzerland, began to appreciate. Between January 2007 and January 2009, the US dollar and sterling depreciated by 5.1 and 27.3 per cent respectively; the yen and the Swiss franc appreciated by 36.2 and 10.0 per cent.

External shocks

Now let us assume that the rest of the world goes into recession (but with no change in international interest rates). The demand for UK exports will fall. This will lead to a depreciation of the exchange rate. This in turn will boost the demand for UK exports and domestic substitutes for imports. This boost to demand again will help to offset the dampening effect of the world recession.

Floating exchange rates thus help to insulate the domestic economy from world economic fluctuations.

| BOX 25.4 | THE PRICE OF A BIG MAC |

The Economist's guide to purchasing-power parity rates

Twice a year *The Economist* publishes its 'hamburger standard' exchange rates for currencies. It is a light-hearted attempt to see if currencies are exchanging at their purchasing-power parity rates. The test is the price at which a 'Big Mac' McDonald's hamburger sells in different countries! According to this simplified version of the purchasing-power parity theory, exchange rates should adjust so that a Big Mac costs the same in dollars everywhere.

The following extracts are from the July 2008 Big Mac report.[1]

Ever since the credit storms first broke last August, the prices of stocks, bonds, gold and other investment assets have been blown this way and that. Currencies have been pushed around too. . . .

Only a handful of currencies are close to their Big Mac PPP. Of the seven currencies that make up the Federal Reserve's major-currency index, only one (the Australian dollar) is within 10% of its fair [i.e. PPP] value. Most of the rest look expensive. The euro is overvalued by a massive 50%. The British pound, Swedish krona, Swiss franc and Canadian dollar are also trading well above their burger benchmark. All are more overvalued against the dollar than a year ago. Only the Japanese yen, undervalued by 27%, could be considered a snip.

If the Big Mac is taken as representative of all goods and services, then the euro would, indeed, have been overvalued by 50 per cent in PPP terms compared with the dollar. In other words, at the market exchange rate of €1 = $1.59, a Big Mac would cost $5.34 in the eurozone: 50 per cent more than the $3.57 price in the USA.

The hamburger standard

	Big Mac price in dollars at current exchange rate	Under (−)/over (+) valuation against the dollar (%)
Norway	7.88	+121
Sweden	6.37	+78
Switzerland	6.36	+78
Denmark	5.95	+67
Eurozone[a]	5.34	+50
Brazil	4.73	+32
UK	4.57	+28
Czech Republic	4.56	+28
Turkey	4.32	+21
Canada	4.08	+14
New Zealand	3.72	+4
Argentina	3.64	+2
USA[b]	3.57	0
Poland	3.45	−3
Australia	3.36	−6
South Korea	3.14	−12
Singapore	2.92	−18
Japan	2.62	−27
Russia	2.54	−29
South Africa	2.24	−37
Indonesia	2.04	−43
Pakistan	1.97	−45
Sri Lanka	1.95	−45
Thailand	1.86	−48
China	1.83	−49
Malaysia	1.70	−52

[a] Weighted average of member countries.
[b] Average of New York, Chicago, San Francisco and Atlanta.

Will there be any cost to the UK economy from a decline in the demand for exports resulting from a world recession?

The path to long-run equilibrium

If there is a single shock, and if there is initially both internal balance and also external balance in the narrow sense (i.e. a current account balance), eventually both internal balance and current account balance will be restored. Current account balance will be restored by a change in the exchange rate that restores purchasing-power parity. This is illustrated in Figure 25.8.

Assume that the country experiences the same long-term rate of inflation as its trading partners and that, therefore, the nominal exchange rate follows the same path as the real exchange rate. Assume also that there are no *long-term* changes to cause an appreciation or depreciation and that, therefore, the long-term equilibrium exchange rate is constant over time. This is shown by the horizontal line at er_L.

Now assume, as before, that there is a rise in aggregate demand and a resulting rise in interest rates. This occurs at time t_1. As the demand for imports rises, the current

Figure 25.8 Exchange rate path to long-run equilibrium after a shock at time t_1

account goes into deficit. Higher interest rates, however, lead to a financial inflow and an immediate appreciation of the exchange rate to er_1. But then, the exchange rate will gradually fall back to its long-run rate as the higher interest rates curb demand and interest rates can thus come back down.

CASE STUDIES AND APPLICATIONS

The table shows the degree of overvaluation or undervaluation in Big Mac PPP terms of a range of currencies. A Big Mac cost an average of just under £2.29 in the UK and $3.57 in the USA. At the exchange rate at the time of £1 = $2.00, this made a Big Mac cost $4.57 in the UK – 28 per cent more than in the USA: in other words, a 28 per cent overvaluation of the pound. For a Big Mac to cost the same in the UK as in the USA, the exchange rate would have to have been £1 = $1.56 ($2.00 is 28% higher than $1.56).

But what about the currencies that are undervalued in the table?

The Singapore dollar is undervalued by 18% and the South Korean won by 12%. The currencies of less well-off Asian countries, such as Indonesia, Malaysia and Thailand, look even cheaper. China's currency is among the most undervalued, though a bit less so than a year ago.

Generally, richer countries' currencies seem to be overvalued and poorer ones' undervalued. The explanation lies in differences in local costs, such as rents and wages. These are higher in rich countries. According to David Parsley, of Vanderbilt University, and Shang-Jin Wei, of the International Monetary Fund, non-traded inputs, such as labour, rent and electricity, account for between 55 and 64 per cent of the price of a Big Mac.[2]

Also, exchange rates can diverge from their PPP values because of factors influencing the *financial account* of the balance of payments: factors such as actual and expected interest rate differentials, investment prospects and speculation about exchange rate movements. Both Brazil and Turkey are relatively poor countries and yet both have

exchange rates above their Big Mac PPP rates. The reason lies in their high interest rates.

Turkey's central bank recently raised its benchmark rate to 16.75%; Brazil's pushed its key rate up to 13% on July 23rd. These rates offer juicy returns for those willing to bear the risks. Those searching for a value meal should look elsewhere.

Nevertheless, despite the limitation of the Big Mac index, it does give some indication of whether a currency is above or below its long-term equilibrium rate.

John Lipsky, number two at the IMF, said this week that the euro is above the fund's medium-term valuation benchmark. China's currency is 'substantially undervalued' in the IMF's view.

1. *If the Chinese yuan is undervalued by 49 per cent in PPP terms against the US dollar and the Norwegian kroner overvalued by 121 per cent, what implications does this have for the interpretation of Chinese, Norwegian and US GDP statistics?*
2. *Why do developing countries' currencies tend to be undervalued relative to those of developed countries (see table)?*
3. *At the time the table was compiled, the Big Mac PPP rate for the Japanese yen was $1 = ¥106.8. What was the market exchange rate?*

[1] *The Economist*, 24 July 2008.
[2] 'A prism into the PPP puzzles: the microfoundations of Big Mac real exchange rates', October 2004. Available at www2.owen.vanderbilt.edu/david.parsley/research.htm.

BOX 25.5 THE EURO/DOLLAR SEESAW

Ups and downs in the currency market

For periods of time, world currency markets can be quite peaceful, with only modest changes in exchange rates. But with the ability to move vast sums of money very rapidly from one part of the world to another and from one currency to another, speculators can suddenly turn this relatively peaceful world into one of extreme turmoil.

In this box we examine the huge swings of the euro against the dollar since the euro's launch in 1999. In Case Study 25.4 in MyEconLab we examine two other examples of currency turmoil, both from the 1990s.

First the down . . .

On 1 January 1999, the euro was launched and exchanged for $1.16. By October 2000 the euro had fallen to $0.85. What was the cause of this 27 per cent depreciation? The main cause was the growing fear that inflationary pressures were increasing in the USA and that, therefore, the Federal Reserve Bank would have to raise interest rates. At the same time, the eurozone economy was growing only slowly and inflation was well below the 2 per cent ceiling set by the ECB. There was thus pressure on the ECB to cut interest rates.

The speculators were not wrong. As the diagram shows, US interest rates rose, and ECB interest rates initially fell, and when eventually they did rise (in October 1999), the gap between US and ECB interest rates soon widened again.

In addition to the differences in interest rates, a lack of confidence in the recovery of the eurozone economy and a continuing confidence in the US economy encouraged investment to flow to the USA. This inflow of finance (and lack of inflow to the eurozone) further pushed up the dollar relative to the euro.

The low value of the euro meant a high value of the pound relative to the euro. This made it very difficult for UK companies exporting to eurozone countries and also for those competing with imports from the eurozone (which had been made cheaper by the fall in the euro).

In October 2000, with the euro trading at around 85¢, the ECB plus the US Federal Reserve Bank, the Bank of England and the Japanese central bank all intervened on the foreign exchange market to buy euros. This arrested the fall, and helped to restore confidence in the euro. People were more willing to hold euros, knowing that central banks would support the currency.

Fluctuations between the euro and the dollar

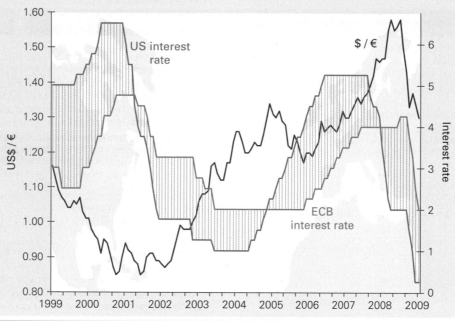

What determines the level of er_1? This exchange rate must be high enough to balance the gain from the higher interest rate against the fact that the exchange rate will be expected to depreciate again back to its long-run equilibrium level er_L. For example, if the interest rate rises by 1 per cent, the exchange rate must rise to the level where people anticipate that it will fall by 1 per cent per year. Only that way will finance stop flowing into the country.

 Describe the exchange rate path if there were a single shock that caused interest rates to fall. What determines the magnitude and speed of changes in the exchange rate in such a scenario?

Speculation

In the real world, shocks are occurring all the time. Also there is considerable uncertainty over the future course of the exchange rate path. What is more, things are made more complicated by the activities of speculators. As soon as any exchange rate change is anticipated, speculators will buy or sell the currency.

Assume, for example, that there is a rise in UK inflation above international rates, but no change in interest rates. This causes a fall in the demand for exports and hence a fall in the demand for sterling (assuming a price elasticity of demand greater than 1), and a rise in imports and

KI 10
p71

CASE STUDIES AND APPLICATIONS

. . . then the up

The position changed completely in 2001. With the US economy slowing rapidly and fears of an impending recession, the Federal Reserve Bank reduced interest rates eleven times during the year: from 6.5 per cent at the beginning of the year to 1.75 per cent at the end (see the chart). Although the ECB also cut interest rates, the cuts were relatively modest: from 4.75 per cent at the beginning of the year to 3.25 per cent at the end. With eurozone interest rates now considerably above US rates, the euro began to rise.

In addition, a massive deficit on the US current account, and a budget deficit nearing 4 per cent of GDP, made foreign investors reluctant to invest in the US economy. In fact, investors were pulling out of the USA. One estimate suggests that European investors alone sold $70 billion of US assets during 2002. The result of all this was a massive depreciation of the dollar and appreciation of the euro, so that by December 2004 the euro had risen to $1.36: a 60 per cent appreciation since July 2001!

In 2004–5, the US economy began to experience strong economic growth once more (an annual average of 3.4 per cent) and consequently the Fed raised interest rates several times, from 1 per cent in early 2004 to 5.25 by June 2006. With growth in the eurozone averaging just 1.8 per cent in 2004–5, the ECB kept interest rates constant at 2 per cent until early 2006. The result was that the euro depreciated against the dollar in 2005. But then the rise of the euro began again as the US growth slowed and eurozone growth rose and people anticipated a narrowing of the gap between US and eurozone interest rates.

In 2007 and 2008, worries about the credit crunch in the USA led the Fed to make substantial cuts in interest rates to stave off recession. In August 2007 the US federal funds rate was 5.25 per cent. It was then reduced on several occasions to stand at between 0 and 0.25 per cent by December 2008. The ECB, in contrast, kept the eurozone rate constant at 4 per cent for the first part of this period and even raised it to 4.25 temporarily in the face of rapidly rising commodity prices. As a result, short-term finance flooded into the eurozone and the euro appreciated again, from $1.37 in mid 2007 to $1.58 in mid 2008.

Eventually, in September 2008, with the eurozone on the edge of recession and predictions that eurozone rates would fall, the euro at last began to fall. It continued to do so as the ECB cut rates, to stand at 1.5 per cent by March 2009.

What is clear from the 10 years of the euro, is that interest-rate volatility and divergences in interest rates between the USA and the eurozone have been a major factor in exchange rate volatility between the euro and the dollar – itself a cause of uncertainty in international trade and finance.

The effects on business in the eurozone

From 2002 to 2008 the euro appreciated by a massive 82 per cent against the dollar. So has a strong euro been bad for European business? With over 22 per cent of the eurozone's GDP determined by export sales (to non-eurozone countries), and a large part of those exports going to the USA, the dollar/euro exchange rate will invariably be significant. The question is, how significant? The investment bank Morgan Stanley estimated that for every 10 per cent rise in the value of the euro against the dollar, European corporate profits fall by 3 per cent.

And it was not just the fact that the euro has been strong. What also worried European businesses was the *speed* at which the euro strengthened against the dollar. The question was whether they could adjust quickly enough to accommodate the rise.

However, the impact of the euro's rise on eurozone business was tempered by a number of factors:

- Companies are increasingly using sophisticated management and operational systems, in which value creation is spread throughout a global value chain. Often procurement systems are priced in dollars.
- Firms hedge their currency risks. Companies typically use forward exchange markets to agree to buy or sell currencies in the future at a price quoted *today* (this, of course, costs them a premium).
- Many European companies (BMW is an example) have located some of their production facilities in the USA and use them to help meet demand in the US market. This helps to insulate them from the effects of the rise in the value of the euro.

The result is that most businesses in the eurozone seem to have accommodated the euro's large and rapid rise.

 Find out what has happened to the euro/dollar exchange rate over the past 12 months. (You can find the data from the Bank of England's Statistical Interactive Database at www.bankofengland.co.uk/statisticsindex.htm). Explain why the exchange rate has moved the way it has.

---

hence a rise in the supply of sterling. This is illustrated in Figures 25.9 and 25.10. The exchange rate depreciates from er_1 to er_2. Speculators seeing the exchange rate falling can react in one of two ways. The first is called *stabilising speculation*; the second is called *destabilising speculation* (see section 3.2).

Stabilising speculation

This occurs when speculators believe that any exchange rate change will soon be reversed.

In our example, speculators may anticipate that the central bank will raise interest rates or take some other measure to reduce inflation. They thus believe that the

exchange rate will appreciate again. As a result, they buy more pounds and sell fewer. But this very act of speculation causes the appreciation they had anticipated.

This is illustrated in Figure 25.9. Inflation has caused the demand for and supply of pounds to shift from D_1 and S_1 to D_2 and S_2, and the exchange rate to fall from er_1 to er_2. Stabilising speculation then shifts the curves back again, to D_3 and S_3, and the exchange rate rises again to er_3.

The action of speculators in this case, therefore, prevents excessively large exchange rate changes. In general, stabilising speculation occurs whenever speculators believe that the exchange rate has 'overreacted' to the current economic situation.

Figure 25.9 Stabilising speculation

People believe that exchange rate change is only temporary

Figure 25.10 Destabilising speculation

People believe that exchange rate change indicates a trend

 Draw a similar diagram to Figure 25.9, showing how an initial appreciation of the exchange rate would similarly be reduced by stabilising speculation.

Destabilising speculation

KI 32 p388

This occurs when speculators believe that exchange rate movements will continue in the same direction.

In our example, speculators may believe that inflation will not be brought under control. They anticipate a continuing fall in the exchange rate and thus sell *now* before the exchange rate falls any further. In Figure 25.10, this speculation causes the demand and supply curves to shift further, to D_3 and S_3, and causes the exchange rate to fall further, to er_3.

Eventually, however, this destabilising speculation could cause **overshooting**, with the exchange rate falling well below the purchasing-power parity rate. At this point speculators, believing that the rate will rise again, will start buying pounds again. This causes the exchange rate to rise.

Obviously, governments prefer stabilising to destabilising speculation. Destabilising speculation can cause severe exchange rate fluctuations. The resulting uncertainty is very damaging to trade. It is very important, therefore, that governments create a climate of confidence. People must believe that the government can prevent economic crises from occurring.

Conclusion

Whatever speculators anticipate will happen to the exchange rate, their actions will help to bring it about. If they

think the sterling exchange rate will fall, they will sell pounds, hence causing it to fall. Thus speculators as a whole will gain. This applies to both stabilising and destabilising speculation.

 If speculators on average gain from their speculation, who loses?

Advantages of a free-floating exchange rate

The advantages and disadvantages of free-floating rates are to a large extent the opposite of those of fixed rates.

Automatic correction. The government simply lets the exchange rate move freely to the equilibrium. In this way, balance of payments disequilibria are automatically and instantaneously corrected without the need for specific government policies – policies that under other systems can be mishandled.

TC 4 p44

No problem of international liquidity and reserves. Since there is no central bank intervention in the foreign exchange market, there is no need to hold reserves. A currency is automatically convertible at the current market exchange rate. International trade is thereby financed.

Insulation from external economic events. A country is not tied to a possibly unacceptably high world inflation rate, as it is under a fixed exchange rate. It can choose its own inflation target. It is also to some extent protected against world economic fluctuations and shocks (see pages 721–3).

Governments are free to choose their domestic policy. Under a fixed rate, a government may have to deflate the economy even when there is high unemployment. Under a floating rate, the government can choose whatever level of domestic demand it considers appropriate, and simply leave exchange rate movements to take care of any balance of payments effect. This is a major advantage, especially when the effectiveness of deflation is reduced by downward wage

Definition

Exchange rate overshooting Where a fall (or rise) in the long-run equilibrium exchange rate causes the actual exchange rate to fall (or rise) by a greater amount before eventually moving back to the new long-run equilibrium level.

and price rigidity, and when competitive deflation between countries may end up causing a world recession.

Disadvantages of a free-floating exchange rate

Despite these advantages, there are still some serious problems with free-floating exchange rates.

Speculation. Short-run instability can be lessened by stabilising speculation, thus making speculation advantageous. If, due to short-run inelasticity of demand, a deficit causes a very large depreciation, speculators will *buy* pounds, knowing that in the long run the exchange rate will appreciate again. Their action therefore helps to lessen the short-run fall in the exchange rate.

Nevertheless, in an uncertain world where there are few restrictions on currency speculation, where the fortunes and policies of governments can change rapidly, and where large amounts of short-term deposits are internationally 'footloose', speculation can be highly destabilising in the short run. Considerable exchange rate overshooting can occur.

An example of such overshooting occurred between August and December 2008 when the pound depreciated 20 per cent against the euro, 27 per cent against the US dollar and 38 per cent against the yen (see Figure 25.11). Speculators were predicting that interest rates in the UK would fall further than in other countries and stay lower for longer. This was because recession was likely to be deeper in the UK, with inflation undershooting the Bank of England's 2 per cent target and perhaps even becoming negative. But the fall in the exchange rate represented considerable overshooting and, after reaching a low of £1 = €1.02 at the end of December 2008, by the end of January it was trading at €1.13.

This is just one example of the violent swings in exchange rates that have occurred in recent years. They even occur under managed floating exchange rate systems where governments have attempted to dampen such fluctuations!

The continuance of exchange rate fluctuations over a number of years is likely to encourage the growth of speculative holdings of currency. This can then cause even larger and more rapid swings in exchange rates.

Uncertainty for traders and investors. The uncertainty caused by currency fluctuations can discourage international trade and investment. To some extent, the problem can be overcome by using the **forward exchange market**. Here traders agree with a bank *today* the rate of exchange for some point in the *future* (say, in six months' time). This allows traders to plan future purchases of imports or sales of exports at a known rate of exchange. Of course, banks charge for this service, since they are taking upon themselves the risks of adverse exchange rate fluctuations.

This will not help long-term investment, however, where decisions are made based on anticipated costs and revenue flows for many years to come. The possibility of

KI 10
p71

KI 32
p388

KI 11
p75

Figure 25.11 Sterling exchange rates

exchange rate appreciation may well discourage firms from investing abroad.

 Why would banks not be prepared to offer a forward exchange rate to a firm for, say, five years from now?

Lack of discipline on the domestic economy. Governments may pursue irresponsibly inflationary policies. Also, unions and firms may well drive up wages and prices, without the same fear of losing overseas markets or of the government imposing deflationary policies. The depreciation resulting from this inflation will itself fuel the inflation by raising the price of imports.

Conclusion

Neither fixed nor free-floating exchange rates are free from problems. For this reason, governments have sought a compromise between the two, the hope being that some intermediate system will gain the benefits of both, while avoiding most of their disadvantages.

One compromise was tried after the Second World War. This was the *adjustable peg.* Another is the system that replaced the adjustable peg in the early 1970s and continues for much of the world today. This is the system of *managed floating.* We examine these systems in the next section.

Definition

Forward exchange market Where contracts are made today for the price at which a currency will be exchanged at some specified future date.

BOX 25.6 **THE EFFECTIVENESS OF MONETARY AND FISCAL POLICIES UNDER FLOATING EXCHANGE RATES**

EXPLORING ECONOMICS

With a floating exchange rate, monetary policy is strong and fiscal policy is weak (the reverse of the case with fixed exchange rates).

Monetary policy

Assume that the economy is in recession and the central bank wishes to increase aggregate demand. It thus reduces interest rates. Three effects follow, each contributing to the effectiveness of the monetary policy.

1. *The expansionary monetary policy directly increases aggregate demand.* The size of the effect here depends on the amount that interest rates change and the elasticity of aggregate demand in response to the changes in interest rates.

2. *The exchange rate depreciates.* Higher aggregate demand increases imports and (via higher prices) reduces exports. This and the lower interest rates reduce the demand for and increase the supply of domestic currency on the foreign exchange market. The exchange rate thus depreciates.

   This reinforces the increase in domestic demand. A lower exchange rate makes exports less expensive again and therefore increases their demand (an injection). Imports become more expensive again and therefore their demand falls (a withdrawal). There is thus a *further* multiplied rise in income.

3. *Speculation may cause initial exchange rate overshooting.* Lower interest rates cause speculative financial outflows in anticipation of the depreciation. This causes the exchange rate to fall below its eventual rate – to overshoot, thus causing a further rise in aggregate demand.

This is only a short-term effect, however, since speculators will stop selling the domestic currency when the rate has gone so low that they feel it must rise again (back towards the purchasing-power parity level) sufficiently fast to offset the lower interest rates they are now getting. The greater the mobility of international finance and the better the information of the speculators, the shorter will the short run be.

Fiscal policy

Fiscal policy is relatively weak under a floating rate. Again let us assume that the objective is to raise aggregate demand to combat a recession. The government thus reduces taxes and/or increases its expenditure. The rise in aggregate demand raises imports and (via higher prices) reduces exports. This effect on the current account of the balance of payments puts downward pressure on the exchange rate.

The higher aggregate demand, however, increases the transactions demand for money and hence *raises* interest rates. These higher interest rates will lead to financial inflows. This will put upward pressure on the exchange rate, which is likely to swamp the downward pressure from the current account deficit. There will therefore be an *appreciation* of the exchange rate. This will increase imports and reduce exports, thus reducing aggregate demand again, and reducing the effectiveness of the fiscal expansion.

 Compare the relative effectiveness of fiscal and monetary policies as means of reducing aggregate demand under a system of floating exchange rates.

Section summary

1. Under a free-floating exchange rate, the balance of payments will automatically be kept in balance by movements in the exchange rate. This removes the *balance of payments* constraint on domestic policy. It does not, however, remove external constraints entirely.

2. According to the purchasing-power parity theory, any changes in domestic prices will simply lead to equivalent changes in the exchange rate, leaving the international competitiveness of home-produced goods unaffected. If, however, internal shocks cause changes in interest rates, there will be a change in the *financial* account balance. This will influence exchange rates and destroy the purchasing-power parity theory. The current account will go out of balance (in an equal and opposite way to the financial account).

3. This problem is made more acute by the carry trade, whereby people borrow money in low-interest-rate (current account surplus) countries and deposit them in high-interest-rate (current account deficit) countries. This causes deficit countries' exchange rates to appreciate, thereby worsening their current account deficit.

4. External shocks will be reflected in changes in exchange rates and will help to insulate the domestic economy from international economic fluctuations.

5. Exchange rate movements are highly influenced by speculation. If speculators believe that an appreciation or depreciation is merely temporary, their activities will help to stabilise the exchange rate. If, however, they believe that an exchange rate movement in either direction will continue, their activities will be destabilising and cause a bigger movement in the exchange rate.

6. The advantages of free-floating exchange rates are that they automatically correct balance of payments disequilibria; they eliminate the need for reserves; and they give governments a greater independence to pursue their chosen domestic policy.

7. On the other hand, a completely free exchange rate can be highly unstable, made worse by destabilising speculation. This may discourage firms from trading and investing abroad. What is more, a flexible exchange rate, by removing the balance of payments constraint on domestic policy, may encourage governments to pursue irresponsible domestic policies for short-term political gain.

25.4 EXCHANGE RATE SYSTEMS IN PRACTICE

The adjustable peg system: 1945–73

After the collapse in 1931 of the fixed exchange rate system of the gold standard (see section 16.2), the huge scale of the initial disequilibria caused wild swings in exchange rates. Many countries resorted to protectionism, given the great uncertainties associated with free trade under fluctuating exchange rates.

The Bretton Woods system

In 1944 the allied countries met at Bretton Woods in the USA to hammer out a new exchange rate system: one that would avoid the chaos of the 1930s and encourage free trade, but that would avoid the rigidity of the gold standard. The compromise they worked out was an adjustable peg system that lasted until 1971.

Under the **Bretton Woods system** there was a totally fixed dollar/gold exchange rate ($35 per ounce of gold). The USA guaranteed that it would freely convert dollars into gold. It was hoped that this would encourage countries to hold dollars as their major reserve currency. After all, if dollars were freely convertible into gold, they were as good as gold. All other countries pegged their exchange rate to the dollar.

To prevent temporary, short-term fluctuations in the exchange rate, central banks *intervened* on the foreign exchange markets using their foreign reserves. This enabled them to maintain the pegged rate within a 1 per cent band.

If the disequilibrium became more serious, governments were supposed to pursue policies of *deflation* or *reflation*. In the meantime, in the case of a deficit, the central bank might have insufficient reserves to maintain the exchange rate. The International Monetary Fund was set up to provide such liquidity. All countries were required to deposit a quota of funds with the IMF, depending on the size of their trade. The IMF would then lend to countries in balance of payments deficit to enable them to maintain their exchange rate. The more a country had to borrow from the IMF, the more the IMF would insist that it pursued appropriate deflationary policies to correct the disequilibrium.

Definitions

Bretton Woods system An adjustable peg system whereby currencies were pegged to the US dollar. The USA maintained convertibility of the dollar into gold at the rate of $35 to an ounce.

J-curve effect Where a devaluation causes the balance of payments first to deteriorate and then to improve. The graph of the balance of payments over time thus looks like a letter J.

If the deficit became severe, countries could *devalue*: the pegged rate could be adjusted (in consultation with the IMF).

 Under this system, how would you expect countries to respond to a balance of payments surplus? Would a revaluation benefit such countries?

Advocates of an adjustable peg system argue that the Bretton Woods arrangement made a significant contribution to the long boom of the 1950s and 1960s.

- Since rates were fixed for a long period of time – perhaps many years – uncertainty was reduced and trade was encouraged.
- Pegged rates, plus the overseeing role of the IMF, prevented governments from pursuing irresponsible policies, and helped to bring about an international harmonisation of policies. They kept world inflation in check.
- If a deficit became severe, countries could devalue. This prevented them being forced into a depression or into adopting protectionist policies. The IMF ensured an orderly process of devaluation.

However, there were two serious weaknesses with the system. These became more and more apparent during the 1960s, and eventually led to the system's downfall.

Problems of adjustment to balance of payments disequilibria

To avoid internal policy being governed by the balance of payments, and to avoid being forced into a depression, countries with a fundamental deficit were supposed to devalue. There were several difficulties here, however.

- Identifying whether a deficit was fundamental. Governments were frequently overoptimistic about the future balance of payments position.
- If devaluation did take place, it could be very disruptive to firms. A devaluation suddenly alters the costs and revenues of importers and exporters by a substantial amount. If a devaluation is felt to be imminent, it can cause great uncertainty and may make them reluctant to take on new trade commitments.

 Would this uncertainty have a similar or a different effect on exporting companies and companies using imported inputs?

- At first a devaluation might make a current account deficit *worse*: the **J-curve effect**. The price elasticities of demand for imports and exports may be low in the short run (see Case Study 25.1 in MyEconLab). Directly after devaluation, few extra exports may be sold, and more will have to be paid for imports that do not have

Figure 25.12 The J-curve effect

immediate substitutes. There is thus an initial deterioration in the balance of trade before it eventually improves. In Figure 25.12, devaluation takes place at time t_1. As you can see, the diagram has a J shape.

For these reasons, countries in deficit tended to put off devaluing until they were forced to by a crisis. The reluctance of countries to devalue caused other problems.

Stop–go policies. Countries had to rely much more on *deflation* as a means of curing deficits. The UK in particular found that, whenever the economy started to grow, the balance of payments went into deficit. This forced the government to curb demand again through fiscal and/or monetary policies.

Speculation. If countries delayed devaluing until a deficit became really severe, an eventual large devaluation became inevitable. This provided a field day for speculators: they could not lose, and there was a high probability of a substantial gain.

Large-scale disruption. The delay in devaluing plus the build-up of speculative pressure could cause the devaluation to be very large when it eventually came. This could be highly disruptive.

Countries' balance of payments deficits could be reduced and adjustment made easier if surplus countries were willing to revalue. There was a reluctance to do this, however, by countries such as Japan. Revaluation was strongly opposed by exporters (and producers of import substitutes), who would find it suddenly more difficult to compete. What is more, there were not the same pressures for surplus countries to revalue as there were for deficit countries to devalue. A lack of reserves can force deficit countries to devalue. Surplus countries, however, may be quite happy to carry on building up reserves.

The USA was not allowed to devalue when in deficit. The onus was on other countries to revalue, which they were reluctant to do. Hence large US deficits persisted. The problem of these deficits was linked to the second major problem area: that of international liquidity.

Problems of international liquidity and the collapse of the system

With an adjustable peg system, there have to be sufficient stocks of internationally acceptable currencies or other liquid assets. This 'international liquidity' is necessary both to finance trade and to provide enough reserves for central banks to support their currencies whenever there is a currency flow deficit. Under the Bretton Woods system, there were three main sources of liquidity: gold, dollars and IMF quotas. But since IMF quotas were only in existing currencies, they were not a source of *additional* liquidity.

As world trade expanded, so deficits (and surpluses) were likely to be larger, and so more reserves were required. But the supply of gold was not expanding fast enough, so countries increasingly held dollars. After all, dollars earned interest. The willingness to hold dollars enabled the USA to run large balance of payments deficits. All the USA needed to do to pay for the deficits was to 'print' more dollars, which other countries were prepared to accept as reserves.

US balance of payments deficits in the 1960s got steadily worse. The financing of the Vietnam War, in particular, deepened the deficit. Dollars flooded out of the USA. World liquidity thus expanded rapidly, fuelling world inflation. Furthermore, the rapid growth in overseas dollar holdings meant that US gold reserves were increasingly inadequate to guarantee convertibility. Some countries, fearful that the USA might eventually be forced to suspend convertibility, chose to exchange dollars for gold. US gold reserves fell, creating a further imbalance and a deepening of the crises.

Despite various attempts to rescue the system, with its overreliance on the dollar, it eventually collapsed. The dollar was devalued against gold by 8 per cent in December 1971. In June 1972 the pound was floated. Over the following year, other countries followed suit, and despite a further dollar devaluation the system was finally abandoned in 1973. By mid 1973 gold was trading at $120 per ounce.

Why would the adjustable peg system have been less suitable in the world of the mid 1970s than it was back in the 1950s?

Managed floating

The world has been on a floating exchange rate system since the breakdown of the Bretton Woods system in the early 1970s. This allows adjustment to be made to the inevitable shifts in demand and supply, shifts that got more extreme in the early 1970s with a quadrupling of oil prices in 1973–4 and rapid changes in world trading patterns. Domestic policy has been largely freed from balance of payments constraints. At the same time, *managed* floating was claimed to allow adjustment to be more gentle, ideally avoiding wild swings in the exchange rate aggravated by speculation.

Some minor currencies remain pegged (but adjustable) to a major currency such as the dollar, but float along with it against other currencies. Other currencies are pegged to each other, but jointly float against the rest of the world. The most notable examples of this have been the currencies of the exchange rate mechanism (ERM) of the European Monetary System (see section 26.2) and now the members of ERM2, mainly the various new members of the EU, such as the Baltic States, as they prepare for membership of the euro.

Some countries allow their currencies to float freely. Most countries, however, from time to time have attempted to stabilise their exchange rate, and have thus been operating a system of 'managed flexibility'.

If the country decides to adopt a managed floating system, how could the central bank prevent the exchange rate from falling? There are two main methods:

- Using reserves or foreign loans to purchase domestic currency on the foreign exchange market.
- Raising interest rates to attract short-term financial inflows.

Problems with managed floating since 1972

Managing the exchange rate involved problems, however. Governments needed to know when to intervene, what exchange rate level they should aim to maintain, and how persistently they should try to maintain that rate in the face of speculative pressure.

Predicting the long-term equilibrium exchange rate
Differing inflation rates between countries will require exchange rate adjustments to maintain purchasing-power parity. It is not correct, however, for governments to assume that this will be the *only* cause of shifts in the long-term equilibrium exchange rate. For example, the 1973–4 and 1979–80 oil crises caused fundamental and unpredictable changes in currency demand and supply. So too did other factors, such as the dismantling of trade barriers within the EU, protectionist measures adopted in different parts of the world, changes in technology and changes in tastes.

It is therefore very difficult for the government to predict what the long-term equilibrium will be, and what proportion of any exchange rate movement is therefore due to long-term and what proportion merely to short-term phenomena.

The growth in speculative financial flows
The OPEC oil price increase in 1973–4 caused huge balance of payments deficits for oil importers. The OPEC countries could not spend all of these surpluses on additional imports since (a) they did not have the capacity to consume such a huge increase in imports and (b) the oil-importing countries did not have the capacity to supply such a huge increase in exports. The surpluses were thus largely invested in short-term dollar (and, to a lesser extent, other major currency) assets. This created a large capacity for short-term loans by western banks. These moneys could be rapidly shifted from one world financial centre to another,

depending on which country had the most favourable interest rates and exchange rates. This created a massive capacity for speculation, and thus made it difficult for countries to control exchange rates by currency sales alone.

 KI 10 p71

Over the years, the scale of speculative flows has continued to increase. Some $4 trillion now passes across the international exchanges every day. Reserves and access to foreign loans are simply inadequate to prevent concerted speculative selling.

To manage the exchange rate, therefore, central banks would have to rely much more on using interest rates.

Conflicts with internal policy
Using interest rates to support the exchange rate has become more and more unpopular as countries have preferred to use interest rates to keep inflation at or below a target level.

KI 33 p389

As a result of these problems, countries have increasingly opted for a system of freely floating exchange rates.

> ? *Would any of these problems be lessened by the world returning to an adjustable peg system? If so, what sort of adjustable peg system would you recommend?*

The UK experience of managed floating

Figure 25.12 shows the fluctuations in UK exchange rates since 1975, with respect to both the dollar and the more important trade-weighted average exchange rate with all other countries. As can be seen, the fluctuations have been large and often violent. Other countries have experienced similar fluctuations. Also, there have been clear long-term trends, as Table 25.1 shows.

But why have exchange rates changed so much? Part of the explanation lies in differences in countries' rates of inflation. This is the purchasing-power parity theory (see page 721). If a country's prices went up by 10 per cent more than the weighted average of its trading partners, its exchange rate would need to depreciate by 10 per cent to compensate. But this provides only part of the explanation. Other causes of exchange rate movements include changes in relative interest rates, various international shocks, longer-term shifts in demand and supply for imports and exports, and speculation.

The first oil crisis and its aftermath: 1973–6
The 1973–4 oil crisis, which followed large world commodity price increases over the previous two years, caused a major shock to the world economy. What were the UK and other industrialised countries to do?

Depreciation could not provide the solution. The demand for oil is highly price inelastic. The price increase had thus already caused a major inflationary shock to the world economy. Depreciation would probably have made things worse. What is more, deflationary policies, or a growth in protectionism, would have caused a major world recession.

Table 25.1	Exchange rate indices, averages for each period (2000 = 100)										
	1970–3	1974–7	1978–81	1982–5	1986–9	1990–3	1994–6	1997–9	2000–2	2003–5	2006–8
USA	108	102	96	121	96	87	84	96	104	88	80
Japan	29	31	40	46	69	72	92	84	92	87	82
Germany	55	68	82	87	100	107	113	108	101	115	124
UK	159	119	114	110	97	92	82	97	100	99	97
Italy	360	259	190	150	140	132	104	106	101	115	124

Source: Based on data in the BIS Effective Exchange Rate Indices (www.bis.org/statistics/eer/index.htm) (Bank for International Settlements).

Figure 25.13 $/£ exchange rate and £ exchange rate index, 1975–2008

The solution seemed to be to borrow: (a) to 'recycle' the oil revenue so as to prevent excessive deflation, and (b) to attempt to maintain reasonably stable exchange rates and avoid competitive depreciation. Until 1975 the UK was reasonably successful in this policy. A substantial proportion of the OPEC surpluses were deposited in the UK, and the government undertook large-scale foreign borrowing. The exchange rate was thus kept up by these financial inflows, and also by using reserves.

From early 1975, however, the exchange rate began falling (see Figure 25.13), despite continued intervention. In 1976 it began to plummet, even though by now inflation was falling and the balance of payments was improving. Destabilising speculation set in. Many of the short-term financial deposits were withdrawn from the UK.

In November 1976, a major loan had to be negotiated with the IMF. The resulting rescue package included an insistence on deflationary measures such as higher interest rates. The exchange rate bottomed out at the end of 1976.

The second oil crisis and the rise of monetarism: 1976–81

The measures of late 1976, helped by the growing importance of North Sea oil, caused renewed confidence in sterling.

Until autumn 1977, the Bank of England intervened to prevent the exchange rate from rising too much. Vast amounts of sterling were sold, and the foreign exchange acquired was used to build up the reserves and to pay off some of the foreign loans of previous years.

Then, from autumn 1977 to autumn 1981, the pound was allowed to float relatively freely. The result was a massive 30 per cent appreciation of the exchange rate (a 53 per cent appreciation in the PPP rate!) from its low point in 1976. There were four main reasons for this:

- The UK's growing oil surplus. North Sea oil was making an increasing contribution to the current account of the balance of payments.
- The 1979–80 oil crisis. Oil rose in price from $13 to $19 per barrel during 1979 and to $31 during 1980. Since the UK was becoming a major oil exporter, and the pound was now a 'petrocurrency', OPEC surpluses were attracted to London.
- The advent of monetarism. From 1977 the money supply was targeted. When the Thatcher government came to power in 1979, these monetarist policies were more rigorously applied. In order to keep to its monetary targets, the government drove up interest rates, with (nominal)

Does PPP hold in the long run?

We can see from Figure 25.3 that the trade-weighted real exchange rate of sterling exhibits considerable volatility as well as rising for some time from the mid 1990s and then falling dramatically in 2008. The significance of movements in the real exchange rate is that it demonstrates that purchasing-power parity (PPP) fails for hold at all times.

For PPP to have held in the long run, differences in countries' inflation rates would need to have been exactly reflected in changes in exchange rates. We can demonstrate that this is not the case for the UK and eight other countries (see chart).

On the horizontal axis is plotted the average annual percentage change in the number of foreign currency units per £1 over the period from 1975 to 2006. Positive values indicate that sterling appreciated, negative values that it depreciated. For instance, sterling appreciated by 1.75 per cent per annum against the New Zealand dollar, but depreciated by 2.5 per cent per annum against the Swiss franc.

On the vertical axis is plotted the inflation differential; this measures the difference between the average annual rate of inflation in the UK and that in each of the other eight countries. Interestingly, there is a positive inflation differential in all eight cases, though that in New Zealand is only 0.1 of a percentage point. This means that the rate of UK inflation was higher than those of all the other countries. Indeed the typical difference between the rate of inflation in the UK and that in Switzerland and Japan was 4.4 and 4.7 percentage points respectively.

If inflation differentials were reflected in exchange rate changes we would expect to see the observations for the eight countries lying along the downward-sloping blue line. This links positive values of the inflation differential with the equivalent percentage depreciation; this would be consistent with PPP holding in the long run. However, it is quite apparent that this is not the case. All our observations lie *above* the blue line. This tells us that that for each inflation differential, sterling has depreciated less or appreciated more than we would have expected. This is the same as saying that the *real* exchange rate of sterling has risen against each country's currency over the period of analysis.

Take Australia as an example. The inflation rate differential with the UK is 1.7 percentage points per annum. The higher rate of inflation in the UK means that the exchange rate would need to *depreciate* by 1.7% per annum to compensate. However, sterling actually *appreciated* by 1.6% per annum.

We see something similar for all the countries in the chart. Even in those cases where a depreciation of sterling is observed, its magnitude is not sufficient to compensate for the higher inflation rates of the UK.

All of this suggests that we need to take into account more than just inflation differentials in understanding exchange rate movements. Other causes of exchange rate movements include changes in relative interest rates, various international shocks, longer-term shifts in demand and supply for imports and exports, and speculation.

 Identify two factors in the UK economy which help to explain the appreciation of the real exchange rate.

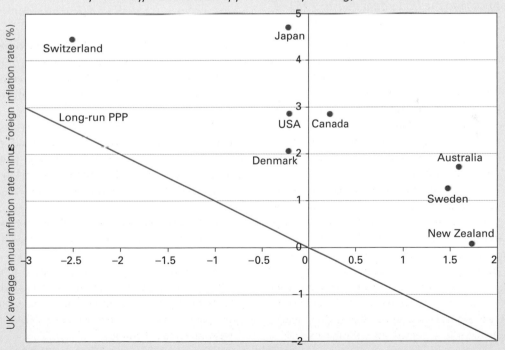

Inflation differentials and appreciation of sterling, 1975–2006

Note: Inflation rates are based on annual changes in the GDP deflator. This is a more broadly-based measure of price changes than consumer price inflation.

Sources: *Financial Statistics* (exchange rates) and United Nations (inflation rates).

short-term interest rates reaching over 17 per cent in late 1979. Interest rates remained considerably higher than in competitor countries. But this simply encouraged further financial inflows. The exchange rate had to rise.

- The recession of 1980–2. These highly deflationary monetary policies caused a deep recession. The resulting decline in the demand for imports further contributed to a rising exchange rate.

The huge appreciation of sterling devastated large parts of UK industry. Many exporters simply could not compete, while imports were so cheap that they drove many firms out of business.

Keynesian critics argued that the government should have adopted a less restrictive fiscal and monetary policy. As far as fiscal policy is concerned, they argued that taxation from oil revenues could have been directly invested in infrastructure. Alternatively, significant tax cuts could have been given. As for monetary policy, they argued that the government should have adopted higher monetary targets. This would have kept interest rates down and lowered the exchange rate.

Keynesians maintained that these policies would not have been inflationary because North Sea oil gave the UK an increase in *potential* income. A rise in aggregate demand to match this would simply have prevented a deflationary gap from opening.

1. *Were there any advantages of the high exchange rate?*
2. *Would there have been a danger of inflation rising if deflationary policies had not been used, even though there was a rise in potential income caused by North Sea oil?*

'Reaganomics' and the US budget deficit: 1981–5

With the election of President Reagan in late 1980, the USA adopted 'Reaganomics'. This had two main features:

- Increasing incentives. The major element in this policy was tax cuts.
- Monetarism. Tight control was to be kept over the growth of the money supply.

His commitment to increasing defence expenditure led to a rapid increase in the overall level of government spending, and the budget deficit increased from $76 billion in 1980 to $212 billion in 1985. The US administration was unwilling to finance the budget deficit by significantly increasing the money supply. The deficit therefore had to be financed largely by borrowing. This pushed interest rates well above those of other countries.

The high interest rates, however, attracted foreign finance to the USA and thus provided a financial account surplus. These financial movements were so large that they caused the dollar to appreciate, despite the current account deficit. This, in turn, worsened the current account deficit.

Other industrialised economies, and especially Japan, experienced the opposite effect. With its lower inflation and lower growth in domestic demand, Japan had a large current account surplus. This was more than offset, however, by a huge outflow of finance, encouraged by low Japanese interest rates. The yen *depreciated* (see Table 25.2).

The high dollar caused grave problems for US exporting industries and industries competing with imports. Large numbers of bankruptcies were suffered in both industry and agriculture. There were growing demands for protectionism, but President Reagan resisted them.

Sterling was particularly vulnerable as many of the OPEC oil revenues deposited in the UK were switched to the USA. As the dollar rose, so the pound fell (see Figure 25.12). Crisis was reached in January/February 1985 with the exchange rate dipping as low as £1 = $1.04 (see Case Study 25.3 in MyEconLab). This drove the main central banks of the world into concerted action to sell dollars, and the dollar started to fall.

Until early 1985, destabilising speculation had worked to drive the dollar up and other currencies, especially the pound, down. After February 1985, speculation went into reverse. With the dollar now falling, people sold dollars and bought other currencies.

1. *Why would the pound not have gone on falling indefinitely?*
2. *Could the UK have done anything to prevent the massive fall in the dollar/pound exchange rate from $2.40 in 1981 to only just above $1.00 in early 1985?*

Mixed fortunes for the pound: 1985–90

After February 1985 sterling at first appreciated. But then, with a falling oil price (which affected sterling as a petrocurrency) and a more relaxed monetary policy in the run-up to the 1987 election, the pound depreciated again.

However, in 1987 the pound began to rise. Oil prices were firmer; inflation had fallen to just over 3 per cent and interest rates were still very high relative to those of other countries. The Chancellor, Nigel Lawson, anxious to avoid repeating the damage to UK industry that was done by the high exchange rate of the early 1980s, was keen to prevent the pound rising. He was also keen to keep the exchange rate pegged as closely as possible to the German mark, hoping to pave the way for the UK joining the ERM (see section 26.2).

But how was he to keep the exchange rate from rising? The answer was to reduce interest rates. Between October 1986 and May 1988 interest rates fell from 11 per cent to 7.5 per cent. For several months the policy of shadowing

Table 25.2	US and Japanese exchange rates, 1980–5 (1980 = 100)					
	1980	**1981**	**1982**	**1983**	**1984**	**1985**
US effective exchange rate (trade-weighted)	100.0	112.7	125.9	133.2	143.7	150.2
Japanese effective exchange rate (trade-weighted)	100.0	102.6	91.0	95.1	95.2	95.4

Source: Based on data in the International Financial Statistics (IFS) database (www.imfstatistics.org) (International Monetary Fund [IMF]).

the mark seemed to work. The exchange rate was effectively pegged; the economy grew and unemployment fell.

Keeping the exchange rate down through reductions in interest rates, plus a policy of reducing income taxes, was causing the economy to expand rapidly. The current account thus moved rapidly into deficit (see Box 25.2) and inflation began to rise sharply. Between 1985 and 1989 an annual current account deficit of £0.6 billion had been transformed into one of £26.3 billion. In mid 1989, with the current account still deteriorating, the exchange rate began to fall.

The weakness of the pound and worries about rising inflation put growing pressure on the government to join the ERM. After all, the ERM countries had managed to secure much lower average rates of inflation than the UK, and there was a strong desire among the business community to be part of this 'low inflation club'. Eventually, in October 1990, Margaret Thatcher decided to join the ERM and sacrifice the monetary independence she had so long cherished. The era of a floating pound had apparently come to an end.

 To what extent was there a conflict after 1988 between using interest rates to affect the rate of inflation and using them to maintain a given exchange rate? Explain under what circumstances there was and was not a conflict.

Sterling in the 1990s and 2000s

 Between October 1990 and September 1992, sterling was in the ERM, at a central rate of £1 = 2.95 German marks, with permitted fluctuations of ±6 per cent against any other ERM currency (we will examine the ERM in section 26.2). As we saw in section 20.4 (pages 595–6), this exchange rate proved unsustainably high and the UK, along with Italy, was forced out of the ERM by a massive wave of speculation. Within two months of this, sterling had depreciated by some 15 per cent.

Since 1992, the UK has adopted a virtually free-floating exchange rate. Between 1992 and 1996, fluctuations in the exchange rate were relatively minor. The government was now targeting inflation, and with inflation coming down, it was at first able to reduce interest rates. But this mirrored reductions in inflation and interest rates in other countries, and thus there was little need for exchange rate changes.

A high sterling exchange rate. By the beginning of 1996, however, speculators began buying pounds, believing that the exchange rate would appreciate. They saw that the economy was now beginning to grow quite rapidly, and was likely to continue doing so, given that an election was coming up. Inflation was thus likely to rise and this would force the government to raise interest rates. Indeed, by mid 1996 interest rates bottomed out. When the new Labour government was elected in 1997 and the Bank of England was made independent, the Bank raised interest rates several times in order to bring inflation down to the target level. The effect was a large-scale appreciation of sterling. Between January 1996 and April 1998, the exchange rate index rose by 24 per cent, and with inflation still above the trade-weighted average of the UK's trading partners, the

real exchange rate index rose even more: by 28 per cent (see Figure 25.3). This clearly made it very difficult for UK exporters and industries competing with imports.

From 1998 to 2007 the pound was well above its purchasing-power parity rate. This was largely the result of UK interest rates being higher than eurozone and Japanese rates, and frequently above US rates too. With the growth of the carry trade in recent years (see pages 721–2), this had helped keep the exchange rate above the PPP rate. The overvaluation of the pound continued to put both the export and import-competing sectors in the UK under great competitive pressure. The current account remained in deficit and in most years deteriorated (see the chart in Box 25.2 on page 711).

Depreciation in 2008. In 2008, at last the pound began depreciating. With the effects of speculation, this then became rapid (see Figure 25.11 on page 727). Worries about recession suggested that the Bank of England would reduce interest rates – as indeed it did: Bank Rate fell from 5 per cent in October 2008 to 1.5 per cent in January 2009.

But other central banks were reducing their rates too (see Figure in Box 20.11), so why would a cut in Bank Rate result in depreciation? There were various reasons for this:

- The cut was greater than in the eurozone.
- There were worries that the recession would be deeper and more prolonged in the UK than elsewhere and that low interest rates would therefore persist for longer than in other countries.
- Investment in the UK was seen as more risky than in other countries, given the importance of the financial services sector in the UK (a sector badly hit by the credit crunch) and the more rapid rise in government borrowing than in many other countries.

The carry trade began to unwind. With the onset of recession, the UK's high current account deficit was no longer seen as a reason to expect relatively high interest rates. Many who had borrowed in yen or other low interest-rate currencies to purchase sterling, now began selling sterling and returning to the original currencies, causing such currencies to appreciate substantially.

With the high level of the exchange rate over many years, and a high degree of volatility too, it is not surprising that large portions of the business community have been in favour of the UK adopting the euro. We shall be looking at the euro in the next chapter.

The volatility of exchange rates

 Exchange rates have become extremely volatile. Currencies can gain or lose several percentage points in the space of a few days. These changes can then make all the difference between profit and loss for trading companies. There are a number of reasons for this volatility:

- Inflation or money supply targets. Central banks may have to make considerable changes to interest rates in order to keep to their targets. These in turn cause exchange rate fluctuations.

- A huge growth in international financial markets. This has encouraged the international transfer of money and capital.
- The abolition of exchange controls in most industrialised countries.
- The growth in information technology. The simple use of a computer can transfer capital and finance internationally in a matter of seconds.
- The preference for liquidity. With the danger of currency fluctuations, companies prefer to keep their financial capital as liquid as possible. They do not want to be locked into assets denominated in a declining currency.
- The growing speculative activities of trading companies. Many large companies have a team of dealers to help manage their liquid assets: to switch them from currency to currency in order to take advantage of market movements.
- The growing speculative activities of banks and other financial institutions.
- The growing belief that rumour and 'jumping on the bandwagon' are more important determinants of cur-

rency buying or selling than cool long-term appraisal. If people *believe* that speculation is likely to be destabilising, their actions will ensure that it is. Many companies involved in international trade and finance have developed a 'speculative mentality'.

- The growing belief that governments are powerless to prevent currency movements. As short-term capital (or 'hot money') grows relative to official reserves, it is increasingly difficult for central banks to stabilise currencies through exchange market intervention.

Although most governments and firms dislike highly volatile exchange rates, few today advocate a return to fixed exchange rates, or a system like the Bretton Woods one. In fact, apart from the Gulf states, very few countries still peg their currencies to the dollar. Even China, which from 1997 to 2005 was pegged to the dollar at $1 = 8.27 yuan, has moved to a managed float based round the weighted average of a basket of currencies. The yuan in early 2009 was trading at 6.8 to the dollar – an appreciation of nearly 18 per cent since 2005.

Despite the preference of most countries for floating exchange rates, suggestions have been made for reducing volatility. We examine some of these in Chapter 26.

Section summary

1. Under the Bretton Woods system (1945–71), currencies were pegged to the US dollar. The rate was supported from countries' reserves and if necessary with loans from the IMF. If there was a moderate disequilibrium, countries were supposed to use deflationary/reflationary policies. If the disequilibrium became severe, they were supposed to devalue/revalue.

2. The system was claimed to bring certainty for business and a constraint on governments pursuing irresponsible fiscal and monetary policies, while avoiding the problem of a recession if a balance of payments deficit became severe.

3. However, it was sometimes difficult to identify whether a deficit was severe enough to warrant a devaluation; a devaluation itself could be very disruptive for firms; and devaluation at first could make the deficit worse (the J-curve effect). If a country was reluctant to devalue, it would have to rely on deflation and a possible recession to tackle a balance of payments deficit.

4. Problems for deficit countries were made worse by an unwillingness of surplus countries to revalue or reflate.

5. Dollars were the main source of international liquidity under the Bretton Woods system. The USA, by creating dollars to pay for balance of payments deficits, caused excessive liquidity. This caused worldwide inflation, a lack of confidence in the USA and an eventual collapse of the system.

6. Since the early 1970s the world has largely been on a managed floating exchange rate system. The degree of intervention varies from country to country and from time to time.

7. In theory, managed floating can give the necessary degree of exchange rate flexibility in a world where shifts in currency demand and supply have become much larger. It can also release domestic policy from being dominated by balance of payments considerations. At the same time, the intervention could (in theory) prevent violent exchange rate fluctuations and allow a more orderly adjustment to new equilibrium exchange rates.

8. Nevertheless, there are problems under managed floating of predicting long-term equilibrium exchange rates. What is more, with the massive growth in 'hot money' since the early 1970s, it has become increasingly difficult for countries on their own to counteract speculation. The main instrument of intervention has become the rate of interest. There may be a conflict, however, in using interest rates both to control exchange rates *and* to control the domestic economy.

9. Sterling exchange rates have shown considerable volatility over the years, with large divergences from the purchasing-power parity rate. For example, the rise in UK interest rates in 1997–8 caused a large appreciation of sterling, much to the consternation of exporters. The cut in interest rates in 2008 was accompanied by an equally large depreciation.

10. The volatility of exchange rates around the world has grown. Reasons include: a growth in international financial markets and a liberalisation of international financial movements combined with easier computer transfer of funds, a growth in speculative activities and a growing belief in the impotence of governments acting on their own to stabilise rates.

*APPENDIX: THE OPEN ECONOMY AND *ISLM* ANALYSIS

In this appendix, we show how the *ISLM* analysis that we examined in section 20.3 can be extended to incorporate the open economy. We will first assume a fixed rate of exchange and then later a free-floating rate.

Analysis under a fixed exchange rate

The BP curve

We start by introducing a third curve, the *BP* (balance of payments) curve. This curve, like the *IS* and *LM* curves, plots a relationship between the rate of interest (*r*) and the level of national income (*Y*). All points along the *BP* curve represent a position of *balance of payments equilibrium*.

The curve slopes upwards from left to right (see Figure 25.14). Increases in the rate of interest (*r*) will cause the financial account to move into surplus as finance is attracted into the country. Increases in national income (*Y*), in contrast, will cause the current account to move into deficit as more imports are purchased. If the overall balance of payments is to stay in equilibrium, current account deficits must be matched by financial (plus capital) account surpluses and vice versa. Thus a rise in *Y* must be accompanied by a rise in *r*, and reductions in *Y* must be accompanied by reductions in *r*. The *BP* curve therefore slopes upwards. Any point below the *BP* line represents a position of overall deficit; any point above the line, a position of surplus.

The slope of the *BP* curve depends on two factors.

The marginal propensity to import (mpm = ΔM/ΔY). The higher the *mpm*, the steeper will be the *BP* curve. The reason is that with a high *mpm* there will be a correspondingly large rise in imports for any given rise in national income. This will cause a large current account deficit. To maintain an overall balance of payments equilibrium, this will require a correspondingly large financial account surplus. This in turn will require a large rise in interest rates. Thus the bigger the *mpm*, the larger the rise in interest rates that will be necessary to restore balance of payments equilibrium, and hence the steeper will be the *BP* curve.

The elasticity of supply of international finance. The greater the elasticity of supply of international finance, the less will be the rise in interest rates necessary to attract an inflow of finance and thereby restore balance of payments equilibrium after a rise in national income, and hence the flatter will be the *BP* curve. In the case of a perfectly elastic supply of international finance, the *BP* curve will be horizontal at the world rate of interest.

KI 9
p67

Equilibrium in the model

If we now put the *BP* curve on an *ISLM* diagram, we have the position shown in Figure 25.15. Point *a* represents full equilibrium. At r_1 and Y_1, investment equals saving (point *a* is on the *IS* curve), the demand for money equals the supply (point *a* is also on the *LM* curve), and finally the balance of payments is in balance (point *a* is also on the *BP* curve).

KI 8
p43

But what is the mechanism that ensures that all three curves intersect at the same point? To answer this question, let us assume that the three curves just happen to intersect at the same point, and then let us examine the effects of changes in fiscal and monetary policies, which shift the *IS* and *LM* curves respectively. Will equilibrium be restored? The answer is yes, via a change in the money supply. Let us examine fiscal and monetary policy changes in turn.

Fiscal policy under fixed exchange rates

An expansionary fiscal policy, i.e. a rise in government spending and/or a reduction in tax, will have the effect of

---

Figure 25.14   The *BP* curve

Figure 25.15   Full equilibrium in the goods, money and foreign exchange markets

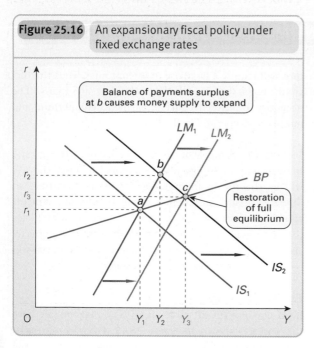

Figure 25.16 An expansionary fiscal policy under fixed exchange rates

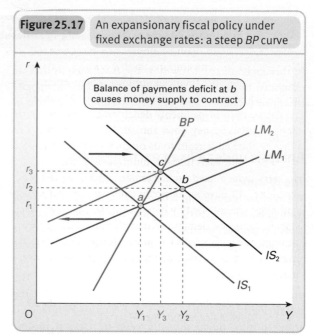

Figure 25.17 An expansionary fiscal policy under fixed exchange rates: a steep *BP* curve

shifting the *IS* curve to the right (e.g. to IS_2 in Figure 25.16). The reason is that for any given rate of interest there will be a higher equilibrium level of national income than before.

This will increase national income, but the extra demand for money that results will drive up interest rates. In a *closed* economy, equilibrium would now be at point *b* (r_2, Y_2), where $IS_2 = LM_1$. But in our open economy model, this equilibrium is *above the BP curve*. There is a balance of payments surplus. The reason for this is that the higher interest rates have caused a financial account surplus that is bigger than the current account deficit that results from the higher national income.

Such a surplus will cause the money supply to rise as funds flow into the country. This will in turn cause the *LM* curve to shift to the right. Equilibrium will finally be achieved at point *c* (r_3, Y_3), where $IS_2 = LM_2 = BP$. Thus under these conditions, the monetary effect of the change in the balance of payments will *reinforce* the fiscal policy and lead to a bigger rise in national income.

 What will be the effect of an expansionary fiscal policy on interest rates and national income if there is a perfectly elastic supply of international finance?

If the *BP* curve were steeper than the *LM* curve, the effect would be somewhat different. (Remember the *BP* curve will be steep if there is a high *mpm* and an inelastic supply of international finance.) This is illustrated in Figure 25.17.

Under these circumstances, an initial rise in national income to Y_2 (where $IS_2 = LM_1$) will cause a balance of payments *deficit* (point *b* is *below the BP curve*). The reason is that this time the current account deficit is bigger than the financial account surplus (due to a large *mpm* and a small inflow of finance). This will reduce the money supply and

cause the *LM* curve to shift to the left. Equilibrium will be achieved at point *c*, where $LM_2 = IS_2 = BP$.

When the *BP* curve is steeper than the *LM* curve, therefore, the monetary effect of the change in the balance of payments will *dampen* the effect of the fiscal policy and lead to a smaller rise in national income.

Monetary policy under fixed exchange rates

An expansionary monetary policy will cause the *LM* curve to shift to the right (e.g. to LM_2 in Figure 25.18). The increased supply of money will drive down the rate of

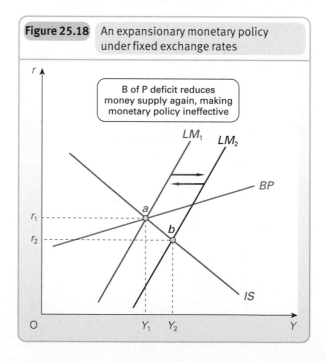

Figure 25.18 An expansionary monetary policy under fixed exchange rates

interest and increase national income. In a closed economy, equilibrium would now be at point *b* (r_2, Y_2), where $LM_2 = IS$. But in an open economy, this extra demand will have sucked in extra imports, and the lower interest rate will have led to net financial outflows. There will be a balance of payments deficit: point *b* is below the *BP* curve.

The balance of payments deficit will cause the money stock to fall as money flows abroad. This will cause the *LM* curve to shift back again to its original position. The economy will return to its initial equilibrium at point *a*.

Thus under a fixed exchange rate regime, monetary policy alone will have *no long-term effect* on national income and employment. Only when accompanied by an expansion in aggregate demand (either through fiscal policy or through an autonomous rise in investment or a fall in savings) will an expansion of money supply lead to higher national income.

1. *Why does this conclusion remain the same if the BP curve is steeper than the LM curve?*
2. *Trace through the effects of a fall in exports (thereby shifting the BP curve).*
3. *Show what will happen if there is (a) a rise in business confidence and a resulting increase in investment; (b) a rise in the demand for money balance (say, for precautionary purposes).*

Analysis under free-floating exchange rates

As the exchange rate changes, the *BP* curve will shift (see Figure 25.19). If the *IS* and *LM* curves intersect *above* the *BP* curve, there will be a balance of payments surplus. This will cause the exchange rate to appreciate. The appreciation will cause the surplus to disappear. This in turn will cause the *BP* curve to shift upwards.

Similarly, if the *IS* and *LM* curves intersect *below* the *BP* curve, the resulting balance of payments deficit will cause a depreciation and a downward shift of the *BP* curve. Thus the *BP* curve will always shift so that it intersects where the *IS* and *LM* curves intersect.

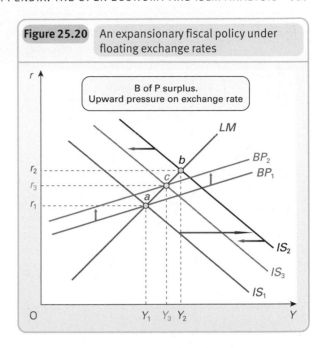

Figure 25.20 An expansionary fiscal policy under floating exchange rates

Fiscal policy under floating exchange rates

Assume that the government pursues a reflationary fiscal policy. The *IS* curve shifts to IS_2 in Figure 25.20.

At point *b*, where the *LM* curve and the new *IS* curve intersect, there is a balance of payments surplus (due to higher financial inflows attracted by the higher rate of interest). This causes the exchange rate to appreciate and the *BP* curve to shift upwards.

But the higher exchange rate will cause a fall in exports and a rise in imports. This fall in aggregate demand will cause the *IS* curve to shift back towards the left. The new equilibrium will be at a point such as *c*. This represents only a modest change from point *a*. Thus under a floating exchange rate the effects of fiscal policy may be rather limited.

The effect will be stronger, however, the steeper the *BP* curve. In Figure 25.21, the *BP* curve is steeper than the *LM* curve. This time a rise in the *IS* curve from IS_1 to IS_2 will lead to a balance of payments *deficit* and hence a *depreciation* of the exchange rate. The *BP* curve will shift *downwards*. The depreciation will cause a rise in exports and a fall in imports. This *rise* in aggregate demand will cause the *IS* curve to shift to the *right*. The new equilibrium will be at point *c*, which is at a higher level of national income, Y_3. Under these circumstances, the balance of payments effect makes fiscal policy stronger.

Under what circumstances would an expansionary fiscal policy have no effect at all on national income?

Monetary policy under floating exchange rates

An expansionary monetary policy will shift the *LM* curve to the right, to LM_2 in Figure 25.22. In a closed economy, equilibrium would now be at point *b*.

Figure 25.19 Movements of the *BP* curve under floating exchange rates

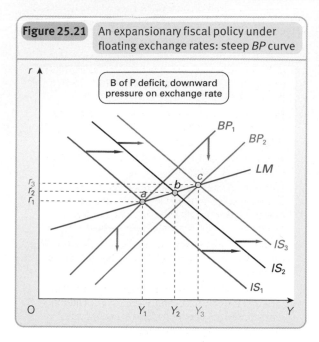

Figure 25.21 An expansionary fiscal policy under floating exchange rates: steep *BP* curve

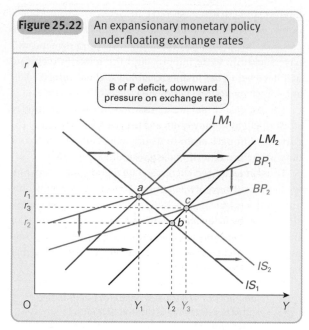

Figure 25.22 An expansionary monetary policy under floating exchange rates

In an open economy under a floating exchange rate, the fall in the rate of interest will cause the exchange rate to depreciate and the *BP* curve to shift downwards. The depreciation will cause exports to rise and imports to fall. This increase in aggregate demand will shift the *IS* curve to the right. The new equilibrium will thus be at point *c*, where $LM_2 = IS_2 = BP_2$. This represents a large change from the initial point *a*.

Thus monetary policy can have a substantial effect on the level of national income under a system of floating exchange rates.

 What will determine the size of the shift in the BP curve in each case?

Section summary

1. A BP curve can be added to an *ISLM* diagram. It shows all the combinations of national income and interest rates at which the balance of payments is in equilibrium. The curve is upward sloping, showing that a rise in national income (causing a current account deficit) will require a rise in interest rates to give a counterbalancing financial account surplus.

2. The lower the *mpm* and the more elastic the supply of international finance, the flatter will be the *BP* curve.

3. Under a fixed exchange rate, the flatter the *BP* curve, the larger will be the effect on national income of an expansionary fiscal policy. Provided the *BP* curve is flatter than the *LM* curve, an expansionary fiscal policy will cause a balance of payments surplus (via its effect of increasing interest rates). The resulting increase in money supply will strengthen the initial effect of the fiscal policy.

4. Monetary policy under fixed exchange rates will have no effect on national income. Any expansion of money

supply will, by depressing interest rates, simply lead to a balance of payments deficit and thus a reduction in the money supply again.

5. Under a floating exchange rate an appreciation will shift the *BP* curve upwards and a depreciation will shift it downwards.

6. If the *BP* curve is flatter than the *LM* curve, fiscal policy under a floating exchange rate will be dampened by the resulting changes in the exchange rate. An expansionary fiscal policy will lead to an appreciation (due to the effects of higher interest rates), which in turn will dampen the rise in aggregate demand.

7. Monetary policy will have a relatively large effect on aggregate demand under floating rates. A rise in money supply will reduce interest rates and raise aggregate demand. This will cause a balance of payments deficit and thus a depreciation. This in turn will lead to a further expansion of aggregate demand.

END OF CHAPTER QUESTIONS

1. Assume a free-floating exchange rate. Draw a diagram like Figure 25.6 (on page 713), only this time show an initial equilibrium national income with a balance of payments surplus.

   (a) Mark the size of the surplus.

   (b) Show the resulting shifts in the $(X - M)$ and the E curves.

   (c) Mark the eventual equilibrium.

   (d) Show the size of the income and substitution effects (of the change in the exchange rate).

   (e) Under what circumstances will the income effect be (i) 'desirable'; (ii) 'undesirable'?

   (f) Could the income effect of the change in the exchange rate ever be larger than the substitution effect?

2. Compare the relative effectiveness of fiscal and monetary policy under (a) fixed; (b) free-floating exchange rates. How is the effectiveness influenced by the elasticity of supply of international finance?

3. What will be the effects on the domestic economy under free-floating exchange rates if there is a rapid expansion in world economic activity? What will determine the size of these effects?

4. For what reasons might the exchange rate diverge from the purchasing-power parity rate over the longer term?

5. Why does exchange rate overshooting occur? What determines its magnitude?

6. Consider the argument that in the modern world of large-scale, short-term international capital movements, the ability of individual countries to affect their exchange rate is very limited.

7. If speculators had better information about future exchange rates, would their actions be more or less stabilising than at present?

*8. Using *ISLMBP* analysis, trace through the effect of (a) a deflationary fiscal policy and (b) a deflationary monetary policy under (i) a fixed exchange rate; (ii) a free-floating exchange rate.

Online resources

Additional case studies in MyEconLab

25.1 The Marshall–Lerner condition. An analysis of the determinants of the elasticities of demand and supply of a currency.

25.2 The gold standard. A historical example of fixed exchange rates.

25.3 The sterling crisis of early 1985. When the pound fell almost to $1.00.

25.4 Currency turmoil in the 1990s. Two examples of speculative attacks on currencies: first on the Mexican peso in 1995; then on the Thai baht in 1997.

25.5 The euro, the US dollar and world currency markets. An analysis of the relationship between the euro and the dollar.

Websites relevant to this chapter

See sites listed at the end of Chapter 26 on p. 759.

Global and Regional Interdependence

CHAPTER MAP

**26.1 Globalisation and the problem of
        instability**   **743**
Interdependence through trade   743
Financial interdependence   744
The need for international policy co-ordination   745
International harmonisation of economic
   policies   746

**26.2 European economic and monetary
        union (EMU)**   **748**
The ERM (exchange rate mechanism)   749
The Maastricht Treaty and the road to the single
   currency   751
The birth of the euro   751
Advantages of the single currency   752
Opposition to EMU   752

**26.3 Achieving greater currency
        stability**   **755**
Controlling exchange transactions   756
Exchange rate target zones   758

One of the major causes of currency fluctuations is the very different conditions existing in different countries and the different policies they pursue. For example, an expansionary fiscal policy plus a tight monetary policy can lead to huge currency appreciation if other countries do not follow suit. This is what happened to the dollar in 1983 and 1984. Conversely, a persistent current account deficit, plus a policy of interest rate reductions in order to stimulate the economy, can lead to large-scale currency depreciation. This happened to sterling after it left the ERM in 1992 and to the dollar in 2007 and to sterling again in 2008.

Changes in exchange rates are then often amplified by speculation. And this problem is becoming worse. As we have seen, approximately $4 trillion per day passes across the foreign exchange markets. The scale of such movements makes any significant speculation simply too great for individual countries to resist. And on some occasions even the concerted action of groups of countries cannot maintain exchange rate stability.

In the first section, we explore the nature of the interdependence of economies and why countries are so vulnerable to international fluctuations. We then look at what can be done to create a greater co-ordination of international economic policies and consider the role of the G7, G8 and G20 countries in this process.

The extreme solution to currency instability is for countries to adopt a common currency. In section 26.2, we look at the euro and how economic and monetary union (EMU) operates. The chapter finishes by looking at some alternative suggestions for reducing currency fluctuations.

26.1 GLOBALISATION AND THE PROBLEM OF INSTABILITY

We live in an interdependent world. Countries are affected by the economic health of other countries and by their governments' policies. Problems in one part of the world can spread like a contagion to other parts, with perhaps no country immune.

There are two major ways in which this process of 'globalisation' affects individual economies. The first is through trade. The second is through financial markets.

Interdependence through trade

So long as nations trade with one another, the domestic economic actions of one nation will have implications for those which trade with it. For example, if the US administration feels that the US economy is growing too fast, it might adopt various contractionary fiscal and monetary measures, such as higher tax rates or interest rates. US consumers will not only consume fewer domestically produced goods, but also reduce their consumption of imported products. But US imports are other countries' exports. A fall in these other countries' exports will lead to a multiplier effect in these countries. Output and employment will fall.

Changes in aggregate demand in one country thus send ripples throughout the global economy. The process whereby changes in imports into (or exports from) one country affect national income in other countries is known as the *international trade multiplier*.

 Assume that the US economy expands. What will determine the size of the multiplier effect on other countries?

The more open an economy, the more vulnerable it will be to changes in the level of economic activity in the rest of the world. This problem will be particularly acute if a nation is heavily dependent on trade with one other nation (e.g. Canada on the USA) or one other region (e.g. Switzerland on the EU).

International trade has been growing as a proportion of countries' national income for many years. This is illustrated in Figure 26.1, which shows the growth in world real exports and in real GDP. You can see that exports have been growing much more rapidly than GDP. From 1948 to 2008 the average annual growth in world output was 3.7 per cent, whereas the figure for world exports was 6.2 per cent. With most nations committed to freer trade, and with the WTO overseeing the dismantling of trade barriers, so international trade is likely to continue growing

Definition

International trade multiplier The effect on national income in country B of a change in exports (or imports) of country A.

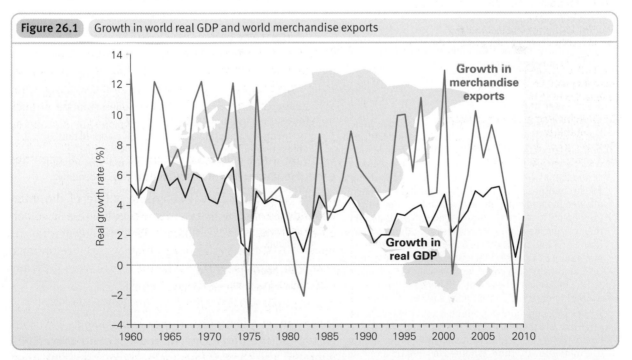

| **Figure 26.1** | Growth in world real GDP and world merchandise exports |

Sources: Based on data in International Trade Statistics (World Trade Organization [WTO]) and *World Economic Outlook* (International Monetary Fund [IMF]).

as a proportion of world GDP. This will increase countries' interdependence and their vulnerability to world trade fluctuations.

Are exports likely to continue growing faster than GDP indefinitely? What will determine the outcome?

Financial interdependence

International trade has grown rapidly over the last thirty years, but international financial flows have grown much more rapidly. The value of banks' holdings of liabilities to foreign residents (individuals and institutions) has been increasing by an average of some 15 per cent per year over the past thirty years. The value of cross-border transactions

in bonds and equities has increased by nearly 30 per cent per year over the same period. Even after taking inflation into account, this is still a very large real rate of increase.

Each day, some $4 trillion of assets are traded across the foreign exchanges. Many of the transactions are short-term financial flows, moving to where interest rates are most favourable or to currencies where the exchange rate is likely to appreciate. This again makes countries interdependent.

Assume that the Federal Reserve Bank in the USA, worried about rising inflation, decides to raise interest rates. What will be the effect on business in America's trading partners? There are three major effects.

- If aggregate demand in America falls, so will its expenditure on imports from firms abroad, thus directly affecting

---

BOX 26.1   GLOBALISATION AND THE US TRADE IMBALANCE

Is the world paying for excessive American expenditure?

The USA has a huge current account deficit. In 2006, it was $811 billion (6.2 per cent of GDP). Although it has fallen somewhat since, it is still around 5 per cent of GDP (see chart).

The current account deficit is offset by an equal and opposite capital-plus-financial account surplus, much of which consists of the purchase of US government bonds and Treasury bills. These massive inflows to the USA represent some 80 per cent of the savings which the rest of the world invests abroad. These financial inflows permitted the current account deficit to deepen.

And yet US interest rates for much of the 2000s have been at historically low levels. Nominal interest rates from mid 2003 to mid 2004 were a mere 1 per cent (see chart in Box 25.5 on pages 724–5) and real rates were −1.3 per cent! Similarly, in 2008, interest rates were very low by comparison with other countries. How is it, then, that with such low interest rates, the USA could maintain such a large financial account surplus?

An answer in Asia

Several Asian currencies, including the Chinese yuan (or 'renminbi'), were pegged to the dollar and had been running large current account surpluses. Instead of letting their currencies appreciate against the dollar, Asian central banks were using their surpluses to buy dollars. These countries saw a triple advantage in this. First, it allowed them to build up reserves and thereby bolster their ability to resist any future speculative attacks on their currencies. Chinese reserves (excluding gold) rose from $168 billion in 2000 to $1530 billion by 2007 – a staggering 811 per cent increase. Over the same period, reserves of all Asian countries rose from $1078 billion to $3865 billion, an increase of 258 per cent. The effect was a huge increase in global liquidity and hence money supply.

Second, and more important, it kept their exchange rates low and thereby helped to keep their exports competitive. This helped to sustain their rapid rates of economic growth. Third, it helped to keep US interest rates down and therefore boost US spending on Asian exports.

In 2005, the Chinese, after much international pressure, agreed to revalue the yuan and would then peg it against a basket of currencies with subsequent further revaluations. But these have averaged less than 5 per cent per annum, considerably below the level necessary to achieve a PPP rate. It remains undervalued by some 40 per cent against the dollar in PPP terms.

Consequences of the imbalance

Can the USA simply continue with a massive current account deficit, financed by the acquisition of equally huge amounts of dollars by the rest of the world, and Asia in particular? Or must there be a correction of the current account imbalance?

A depreciation of the dollar

From mid 2004, US interest rates began to rise – but not fast enough to prevent the dollar's slide on the foreign exchange market. From 2004 to 2008 the effective exchange rate of the dollar depreciated by 20 per cent. Despite this, there has been only a modest reduction in the current account deficit (see chart).

Many commentators, however, have argued that the rate would need to fall significantly more if the deficit was to be reduced to a sustainable size without injecting excessive liquidity into the world economy. This would mean an exchange rate perhaps as high as $1.80 to the euro and $2.30 to the pound, which would have devastating effects on European exports and make sustained European recovery much more difficult.

Overheating in China

A real danger for the Chinese and other Asian economies is that real increases in output may not match the increase in money supply. The result would then be inflation, compounded by rising commodity prices. In 2008, inflation reached 8.7 per cent, the highest for twelve years. From 2000 to 2006, inflation had averaged only 1.2 per cent. China's concern about the inflationary businesses exporting to the USA. With a decline in their exports, aggregate demand in these other countries falls.

- The higher interest rate in the USA will tend to drive up interest rates in other countries. This will depress investment. Again, aggregate demand will tend to fall in these countries.
- The higher interest rate will attract an inflow of funds to the USA from other countries. This will cause the dollar to appreciate relative to other currencies. This will make these other countries' exports to the USA more competitive and imports from the USA relatively more expensive. This will result in an improvement in the current account of the USA's trading partners: their exports rise and imports fall. This represents a *rise* in aggregate demand in these countries – the opposite from the first two effects.

There is a simple conclusion from the above analysis. The larger the financial flows, the more will interest rate changes in one country affect the economies of other countries: the greater will be the financial interdependence.

 What will be the effect on the UK economy if the European Central Bank cuts interest rates?

The need for international policy co-ordination

There is an old saying: 'If America sneezes, the rest of the world catches a cold.' Viruses of a similar nature regularly infect the world economy. A dramatic example has been the credit crunch of 2007/8 resulting from defaults on US

CASE STUDIES AND APPLICATIONS

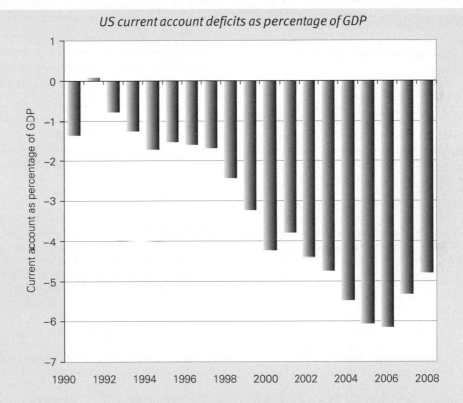

US current account deficits as percentage of GDP

impact of increased money supply resulted in it raising interest rates several times from 2004 onwards, thereby helping to sterilise some of the currency flow surplus. The worry, however, was whether this would cause the rapid Chinese growth to falter.

Potential currency volatility

Perhaps the biggest long-term danger of the huge increase in international liquidity is the potential for large-scale

selling of the dollar and consequent overshooting of the long-term equilibrium exchange rate. Indeed, as Box 25.5 showed, by 2008 the dollar had fallen to a historical low against the euro (the euro was historically high against the dollar).

 Examine the merits for the Chinese of (a) floating the yuan freely; (b) pegging it to a trade-weighted basket of currencies.

sub-prime debt and banks' unwillingness to lend to each other against securitised assets (see Box 18.2) containing such debt. World leaders were seriously worried that the whole world would plunge into recession. What was needed was a co-ordinated policy response from governments and central banks. This came in October 2008 when governments in Britain, Europe, North America and other parts of the world injected some $2 trillion of extra capital into banks.

International business cycles

As a consequence of both trade and financial interdependence, the world economy, like the economy of any individual country, tends to experience periodic fluctuations in economic activity – an *international* business cycle. The implication of this is that countries will tend to share common problems and concerns at the same time. At one time, the most pressing problem may be world inflationary pressures; at another time, it may be a world recession.

In order to avoid 'beggar-my-neighbour' policies, it is better to seek *common* solutions to these common problems: i.e. solutions that are international in scope and design rather than narrowly based on national self-interest. For example, during a world recession, countries are likely to suffer from rising unemployment. Policies that lead to a depreciation of the exchange rate (such as cutting interest rates) will help to stimulate demand by making exports cheaper and imports more expensive. But this will then only worsen the trade balance of other countries, whose aggregate demand will thus fall. The first country is thus tackling its own unemployment at the expense of rising unemployment in other countries.

However, if other nations (which will also be experiencing higher unemployment) can be convinced to co-ordinate their policy actions, an expansionary *international* economic policy will benefit all. In addition to the resulting rise in their imports, all nations will also experience rising export sales.

Even if national policies are not in the strictest sense co-ordinated, discussions between nations regarding the nature and magnitude of the problems they face may help to improve the policy-making process.

 Give some examples of beggar-my-neighbour policies.

International harmonisation of economic policies

The four main underlying causes of exchange rate movements are divergences in *interest rates*, *growth rates*, *inflation rates* and *current account balance of payments*. Table 26.1 shows the variation in the levels of these and other indicators for the seven major industrial countries (the 'Group of 7' or 'G7') – the USA, Japan, Germany, the UK, France, Italy and Canada. Although the divergences between the countries have narrowed somewhat since the early 1990s, they are still considerable.

For many years now, the leaders of these countries have met at an economic summit conference once a year (and more frequently if felt necessary). In more recent years they have been joined by Russia. Top of the agenda in most of these G8 meetings has been how to generate world economic growth without major currency fluctuations. But to achieve this, it is important that there is a **harmonisation** of economic policies between nations. In other words, it is important that all the major countries are pursuing consistent policies aiming at common international goals.

But how can policy harmonisation be achieved? As long as there are significant domestic differences between the

---

Definition

International harmonisation of economic policies Where countries attempt to co-ordinate their macroeconomic policies so as to achieve common goals.

Table 26.1	Average annual difference between highest and lowest values of the G7 countries for various macroeconomic indicators			
	1991–5	**1996–2000**	**2001–5**	**2006–8**
Economic growth (% change in real GDP)	3.5	3.8	2.8	1.4
Output gap (%)	4.3	3.3	3.4	1.5
Unemployment (%)	8.5	7.4	4.6	4.5
Inflation (CPI) (%)	4.1	2.6	3.1	2.9
Short-term nominal interest rate (%)	7.9	6.5	4.5	4.9
Current account (% of GDP)	5.6	5.3	8.1	12.1
General government borrowing (% of GDP)	8.6	7.8	7.6	4.5
General government gross debt (% of GDP)	84	82	114	121
Effective exchange rate[a]	22	6	7	5

[a] Largest percentage relative annual average appreciation of one currency against another.

Source: Based on data in *Economic Outlook* (Organisation of Economic Co-operation and Development [OECD]).

major economies, there is likely to be conflict, not harmony. For example, if one country, say the USA, is worried about the size of its budget deficit, it may be unwilling to respond to world demands for a stimulus to aggregate demand to pull the world economy out of recession. What is more, speculators, seeing differences between countries, are likely to exaggerate them by their actions, causing large changes in exchange rates. The G8 countries have therefore sought to achieve greater *convergence* of their economies. But as Box 26.2 shows, convergence may be a goal of policy, but in practice it has proved elusive.

Referring to Table 26.1, in what respects was there greater convergence between the G7 countries in the period 2006–8 than in the period 2001–5?

Because of a lack of convergence, there are serious difficulties in achieving international policy harmonisation:

- Countries' budget deficits and national debt may differ substantially as a proportion of their national income. This puts very different pressures on the interest rates necessary to service these debts.
- Harmonising rates of monetary growth or inflation targets would involve letting interest rates fluctuate with the demand for money. Without convergence in the demand for money, interest rate fluctuations could be severe.
- Harmonising interest rates would involve abandoning monetary, inflation and exchange rate targets (unless

interest rate 'harmonisation' meant adjusting interest rates so as to maintain monetary or inflation targets or a fixed exchange rate).

- Countries have different internal structural relationships. A lack of convergence here means that countries with higher endemic *cost* inflation would require higher interest rates and higher unemployment if international inflation rates were to be harmonised, or higher inflation if interest rates were to be harmonised.
- Countries have different rates of productivity increase, product development, investment and market penetration. A lack of convergence here means that the growth in exports (relative to imports) will differ for any given level of inflation or growth.
- Countries may be very unwilling to change their domestic policies to fall in line with other countries. They may prefer the other countries to fall in line with them!

If any one of the four – interest rates, growth rates, inflation rates or current account balance of payments – could be harmonised across countries, it is likely that the other three would then not be harmonised.

Total convergence and thus total harmonisation may not be possible. Nevertheless most governments favour some movement in that direction: some is better than none. To achieve this, co-operation is necessary.

Although co-operation is the ideal, in practice discord often tends to dominate international economic relations. The reason is that governments are normally concerned with the economic interests of other countries only if they coincide with those of their own country. This, however, can create a prisoners' dilemma problem (see pages 202 and 354). With each country looking solely after its own interests, the world economy suffers and everyone is worse off.

If total convergence were achieved, would harmonisation of policies follow automatically?

Definition

Convergence of economies When countries achieve similar levels of growth, inflation, budget deficits as a percentage of GDP, balance of payments, etc.

Section summary

1. Changes in aggregate demand in one country will affect the amount of imports purchased and thus the amount of exports sold by other countries and hence their national income. There is thus an international trade multiplier effect.

2. Changes in interest rates in one country will affect financial flows to and from other countries, and hence their exchange rates, interest rates and national income.

3. To prevent problems in one country spilling over to other countries and to stabilise the international business cycle will require co-ordinated policies between nations.

4. Currency fluctuations can be lessened if countries harmonise their economic policies. Ideally this will involve achieving compatible growth rates, inflation rates, balance of payments (as a percentage of GDP) and interest rates. The attempt to harmonise one of these goals, however, may bring conflicts with one of the other goals.

5. Leaders of the G7 or G8 countries meet at least annually to discuss ways of harmonising their policies. Usually, however, domestic issues are more important to the leaders than international ones, and frequently they pursue policies that are not in the interests of the other countries.

BOX 26.2	ATTEMPTS AT HARMONISATION

Meetings of the G8

In recent years, governments of the major industrial nations have tried to come to terms with the ever-growing interdependence of their economies. Economic disruptions in one country (e.g. the sub-prime mortgage crisis in the USA or a unilateral decision by, say, the ECB or Japan to raise interest rates) can have profound effects on the world economy.

G8 meetings

As a result of the potentially highly unstable nature of economic relationships, finance ministers and heads of state of the *Group of Eight* (G8) countries – Canada, France, Germany, Italy, Japan, Russia, the UK and the USA – have met on a regular basis to try to harmonise their policies. But the key problem in this has been the nations' overriding self-interest.

Problems with G8 agreements

There are two major problems with G8 agreements. The first is that they are not binding. If governments are not prepared to give up national sovereignty and submit to international control, they are always likely to put purely national interests first. For example, the USA may unilaterally cut interest rates in order to tackle domestic unemployment, or raise them to tackle inflation. Large and disruptive financial flows can result from such interest rate changes and there can be significant effects on exchange rates. In such cases, the rest of the world may suffer and countries may be forced to adjust their own interest rates.

Thus whilst G8 ministers may say 'the right things', in practice they may do little to implement their recommendations. For example, in the communiqué from the April 2005 meeting, ministers stated that vigorous action was needed to address global imbalances and foster growth. Such actions would include fiscal tightening in the USA and further structural reforms in the EU and Japan. As it turned out, there was little or no resulting change in domestic policy.

The second problem is the lack of international convergence. Successful policy co-ordination requires that serious imbalances in world trade should be kept to a minimum. But such are the size of the US and UK current account deficits and the Japanese and Chinese surpluses that huge pressures are placed on the foreign exchange market, pressures exacerbated by the carry trade (see pages 721–2). These imbalances also create

massive financial flows and great uncertainty. As a result, speculation is likely to be a far more powerful determinant of events than any agreement made by finance ministers. Exchange rates can thus be highly volatile (see Box 25.5).

Response to the south-east Asian crisis

The need to establish greater co-operation was demonstrated by the south-east Asian crisis in 1997–8 (see Case Studies 26.3 and 26.4 in MyEconLab) and the shock waves it sent round the global economy. The fact that the crisis came as a total surprise to governments, international institutions, international financiers and speculators clearly revealed the need to monitor more closely and, when necessary, regulate the world economy.

Following weeks of negotiations with the IMF and World Bank, the finance ministers and central bank governors of the G7 countries (Russia was not then a member) met in October 1998 to agree a package of measures designed to prevent a repeat of the 'Asian contagion' and to restore greater stability to the international financial system. The agreement included the provision of credit facilities, through the IMF and the World Bank, for 'well-run' economies whose currencies were victims of speculative attack. The IMF would have $90 billion for this purpose. It also called for the establishment of closer links between national and international regulatory bodies, to provide more effective regulation of financial markets.

On the central issue of exchange rate regimes, however, the G7 had little to say, merely calling for 'consideration of the elements necessary for the maintenance of sustainable exchange rate regimes in emerging markets, including consistent macroeconomic policies'.

Harmonising attempts to reduce poverty

The Genoa Summit in 2001 was dominated by riots and protests, and it was these that made the news. However, the G8 made significant moves in extending help to the world's poorest countries. The G8's aim was to co-ordinate strategies more effectively over a wide range of development areas: debt relief, trade access, health and education.

At a subsequent meeting in Gleneagles, Scotland in July 2005, the G8 leaders agreed to cancel debts of 18 of the poorest developing countries, mainly in Africa (see page 790), owed to the IMF, the World Bank and the African Development Bank (but not private banks).

26.2 EUROPEAN ECONOMIC AND MONETARY UNION (EMU)

The ultimate way for a group of countries to achieve greater currency stability between themselves is to adopt a single currency and, therefore, to have a common central bank and a common monetary policy – to form an *economic and monetary union (EMU)*. This is what has happened in the EU, with countries coming together to adopt a single

Definition

Economic and monetary union (EMU) The adoption by a group of countries of a single currency with a single central bank and a single monetary policy. In the EU the term applies to the countries that have adopted the euro.

It was also agreed to more than double the amount of aid to Africa by 2010 compared to the level in 2004.

But progress on implementing the agreement was slow, especially on aid. Of the additional $25 billion in aid to Africa committed at Gleneagles, only $4 billion had been delivered by 2008. Total aid actually declined in both 2006 and 2007, by 4.7 and 8.4 per cent respectively.

Words not action

Final communiqués from G8 summits often contain fine words and commitments. In practice few are carried out. For example, at the 2007 summit 329 commitments were made, of which only about a third are being implemented. One of the commitments at that summit was to provide $60 billion to fight AIDS, malaria and TB, but no timetable was set or contributions by individual donor countries specified. Also it was not clear how much of the $60 billion was additional money.

At the 2008 meeting in Japan, there was much discussion of the high price of oil and its impact on the world economy, but there was little agreement on actions that could be taken (such as releasing crude from reserves). Instead, there was a 'call' for more oil extraction and refining. What is more, there was no agreement on concerted action to stave off the effects of the credit crunch on the world economy – something the G8 leaders had failed to predict in 2007 – and nothing to alleviate soaring food prices. 'Strong concern' may have been expressed. But concern is not enough; action is what was needed.

At the same meeting, the leaders agreed to the goal of at least halving greenhouse gas emissions by 2050. But again, there were no specifics on how this could be achieved. Instead the communiqué simply recognised that individual nations 'will need to commit to meaningful mitigation actions to be bound in the international agreement to be negotiated by the end of 2009'.

The G8 will become increasingly irrelevant unless firm agreements on quantifiable actions are made and the actions are then carried out in a clear and transparent way. It will also become increasingly irrelevant unless it is extended to become a G12 or more, to include major global economies such as China, India, Brazil and South Africa.

The 2008 banking crisis . . .

Although it is easy to be cynical about the role of such international 'talking shops', the G7 meeting in October 2008 was significant in helping to shape the worldwide rescue package for banks. Finance ministers and heads of central banks of the G7 countries agreed on a five-point plan.

- No bank would be allowed to fail.
- All banks should have sufficient access to liquidity, for example by central bank guarantees of inter-bank loans.
- Governments would ensure that banks had sufficient capital by buying shares in banks if necessary.
- Depositors' savings would be guaranteed, at least up to a significantly high level.
- Action would be taken to restart the market in mortgages and other securitised assets.

Over the following few days, governments announced how they would put these pledges into action – most following the UK model outlined in Box 18.3 (see pages 516–8).

. . . and plunge into global recession

Another criticism of the G7 and G8 meetings is that they do not involve some of the most important countries in the world, such as China, India and Brazil. A more inclusive form is the G20, formed in 1999. This includes finance ministers and central bank governors of the G8 countries, plus Argentina, Australia, Brazil, China, India, Indonesia, Mexico, Saudi Arabia, South Africa, South Korea, Turkey and the EU as a whole. Together the G20 countries produce some 85 per cent of world GDP.

The G20 countries meet each year, but generally the meetings are again full of fine words resulting in little action. But at a summit in London in April 2009, the fear of a deepening global recession focused minds and a package of measures worth over $1 trillion was agreed to stimulate trade and growth. This included $750 billion for the IMF to help economies in severe difficulties, $250 billion for financing world trade and $100 in extra aid to the poorest countries. There was also agreement to tighten financial regulation and to resist protectionism.

 To what extent can international negotiations over economic policy be seen as a game of strategy? Are there any parallels between the behaviour of countries and the behaviour of oligopolists? (See the section on game theory in Chapter 7, pp. 201–5.)

---

currency – the euro. The euro began in 1999, with notes and coins circulating from 2002. Initially 11 countries joined; by 2009 there were 16 members, with a further two due to join in 2010.

The ERM (exchange rate mechanism)

The forerunner to EMU was the *exchange rate mechanism (ERM)*. This was an adjustable peg system, where members

Definition

Exchange rate mechanism A semi-fixed system whereby participating EU countries allow fluctuations against each other's currencies only within agreed bands. Collectively they float freely against all other currencies.

pegged their exchange rates to each other while floating against the rest of the world. This had two advantages:

- Trade was encouraged between the members. The greater the harmonisation of policies between them, and therefore the less frequent any adjustments of the pegged rates, the more trade was encouraged.
- The combined reserves of all member countries were used to prevent excessive fluctuations of their currencies with the rest of the world.

The ERM came into existence in March 1979 and the majority of the EU countries were members. The UK, however, chose not to join. Spain joined in 1989, the UK in 1990 and Portugal in April 1992. Then in September 1992, the UK and Italy indefinitely suspended their membership of the ERM, but Italy rejoined in November 1996 as part of its bid to join the single European currency. Austria joined in 1995, Finland in 1996 and Greece in 1998. By the time the ERM was replaced by the single currency in 1999, only Sweden and the UK were outside the ERM.

The features of the ERM

Under the system, each currency was given a central exchange rate with each of the other ERM currencies in a grid. However, fluctuations were allowed from the central rate within specified bands. For most countries these bands were set at ±2.25 per cent. The central rates could be adjusted from time to time by agreement, thus making the ERM an 'adjustable peg' system. All the currencies floated jointly with currencies outside the ERM.

If a currency approached the upper or lower limit against *any* other ERM currency, intervention would take place to maintain the currencies within the band. This would take the form of central banks in the ERM selling the strong currency and buying the weak one. It could also involve the weak currency countries raising interest rates and the strong currency countries lowering them.

The ERM in practice

In a system of pegged exchange rates, countries should harmonise their policies to avoid excessive currency misalignments and the need for large devaluations or revaluations. There should be a convergence of their economies: they should be at a similar point on the business cycle and have similar inflation rates and interest rates.

The ERM in the 1980s. In the early 1980s, however, French and Italian inflation rates were persistently higher than German rates. This meant that there had to be several realignments (see Table 26.2). After 1983 realignments became less frequent, and then from 1987 to 1992 they ceased altogether. This was due to a growing convergence of members' internal policies.

By the time the UK joined the ERM in 1990, it was generally seen by its existing members as being a great success. It had created a zone of currency stability in a world of highly unstable exchange rates, and had provided the necessary environment for the establishment of a truly common market by the end of 1992.

Crisis in the ERM. Shortly after the UK joined the ERM, strains began to show. The reunification of Germany involved considerable reconstruction in the eastern part of the country. Financing this reconstruction was causing a growing budget deficit. The Bundesbank (the German central bank) thus felt obliged to maintain high interest rates in order to keep inflation in check. At the same time, the UK was experiencing a massive current account deficit (partly the result of entering the ERM at what many commentators argued was too high an exchange rate). It was thus obliged to raise interest rates in order to protect the pound, despite the fact that the economy was sliding rapidly into recession. The French franc and Italian lira were also perceived to be overvalued, and there were the

Table 26.2	History of the ERM

	Mar 1979	Sept 1979	Nov 1979	Mar 1981	Oct 1981	Feb 1982	June 1982	Mar 1983	July 1985	Apr 1986	Aug 1986	Jan 1987	Jun 1989	Jan 1990	Oct 1990	Apr 1992	Sept 1992	Sept 1992	Nov 1992	Jan 1993	May 1993	Aug 1993	Jan 1995	Mar 1995	Oct 1996	Nov 1996	Mar 1998	Jan 1999	Jan 2001
Belgian franc	En2¼%					−8.5	+1.5	+2.0	+1.0			+2.0										B15%						S	
Danish krone	En2¼%	−2.9	−4.8			−3.0	+2.5	+2.0	+1.0													B15%						B2¼%	
German mark	En2¼%	+2.0			+5.5		+4.25	+5.5	+2.0	+3.0		+3.0										B15%						S	
French franc	En2¼%				−3.0		−5.75	−2.5	+2.0	−3.0												B15%						S	
Irish punt	En2¼%							−3.5	+2.0		−8.0									−10.0		B15%					+3.0	S	
Italian lira	En6%			−6.0	−3.0		−2.75	−2.5	−6.0					B2¼%			−7.0	Ex								−En15%		S	
Dutch guilder	En2¼%				+5.5		+4.25	+3.5	+2.0	+3.0		+3.0										B15%						S	
UK pound															En6%			Ex											
Spanish peseta													En6%				−5.0		−6.0		−8.0	B15%		−7.0				S	
Portuguese escudo																En6%			−6.0		−6.5	B15%		−3.5				S	
Austrian schilling																							−En15%					S	
Finnish markka																									−En15%			S	
Greek drachma																											−En15%		S

− = % devaluation; + = % revaluation; B% = new band; En% = entry band; Ex = exit; S = join single currency.
Source: Statistical Annex of the European Economy (Commission of the European Communities).

first signs of worries as to whether their exchange rates within the ERM could be retained.

At the same time, the US economy was moving into recession and, as a result, US interest rates were cut. This led to a large outflow of capital from the USA. With high German interest rates, much of this capital flowed to Germany. This pushed up the value of the German mark and with it the other ERM currencies. In September 1992, things reached crisis point. First the lira was devalued. Then two days later, on 'Black Wednesday' (16 September), the UK and Italy were forced to suspend their membership of the ERM: the pound and the lira were floated. At the same time, the Spanish peseta was devalued by 5 per cent.

 Under what circumstances may a currency bloc like the ERM (a) help to prevent speculation; (b) aggravate the problem of speculation?

Turmoil returned in the summer of 1993. The French economy was moving into recession and there were calls for cuts in French interest rates. But this was possible only if Germany was prepared to cut its rates too, and it was not. Speculators began to sell francs and it became obvious that the existing franc/mark parity could not be maintained. In an attempt to rescue the ERM, the EU finance ministers agreed to adopt very wide ±15 per cent bands. The result was that the franc and the Danish krone depreciated against the mark.

A return of calm.   The old ERM appeared to be at an end. The new ±15 per cent bands hardly seemed like a 'pegged' system at all. However, the ERM did not die. Within months, the members were again managing to keep fluctuations within a very narrow range (for most of the time, within ±2.5 per cent!).

The Maastricht Treaty and the road to the single currency

The ERM was conceived as a stage on the road to complete economic and monetary union (EMU) of member states. Details of the path towards EMU were finalised in the Maastricht Treaty, which was signed in February 1992. The timetable for EMU involved the adoption of a single currency by 1999 at the latest.

One of the first moves was to establish a European Monetary Institute (EMI). Its role was to co-ordinate monetary policy and encourage greater co-operation between EU central banks. It also monitored the operation of the ERM and prepared the ground for the establishment of a European central bank in time for the launch of the single currency.

Before they could join the single currency, member states were obliged to achieve convergence of their economies. Each country had to meet five convergence criteria:

- Inflation: should be no more than 1.5 per cent above the average inflation rate of the three countries in the EU with the lowest inflation.

- Interest rates: the rate on long-term government bonds should be no more than 2 per cent above the average of the three countries with the lowest inflation rates.
- Budget deficit: should be no more than 3 per cent of GDP at market prices.
- National debt: should be no more than 60 per cent of GDP at market prices.
- Exchange rates: the currency should have been within the normal ERM bands for at least two years with no realignments or excessive intervention.

Before the launch of the single currency, the Council of Ministers had to decide which countries had met the convergence criteria and would thus be eligible to form a ***currency union*** by fixing their currencies permanently to the euro. Their national currencies would effectively disappear.

At the same time, a European System of Central Banks (ESCB) would be created, consisting of a European Central Bank (ECB) and the central banks of the member states. The ECB would be independent: independent from governments and also from EU political institutions. It would operate the monetary policy on behalf of the countries that had adopted the single currency.

The birth of the euro

In March 1998, the European Commission ruled that 11 of the 15 member states were eligible to proceed to EMU in January 1999. The UK and Denmark were to exercise their opt-out, and Sweden and Greece failed to meet one or more of the convergence criteria. (Greece joined the euro in 2001.)

All 11 countries unambiguously met the interest rate and inflation criteria, but doubts were expressed by many 'Eurosceptics' as to whether they all genuinely met the other three criteria.

- *Exchange rates.* Neither Finland nor Italy had been in the ERM for two years and the Irish punt was revalued by 3 per cent on 16 March 1998. However, the Commission regarded these three countries as being sufficiently close to the reference value.
- *Government deficits.* All 11 countries met this criterion, but some countries only managed to achieve a deficit of 3 per cent or below by taking one-off measures, such as a special tax in Italy and counting privatisation receipts in Germany. Yet, under the Stability and Growth Pact, eurozone countries would be required to keep their deficits within the 3 per cent limit (see Box 20.3). The concern was that countries that only just met this

---

Definition

Currency union A group of countries (or regions) using a common currency.

criterion at time of entry would find it difficult to keep within the limit in times of recession or slow growth. This proved to be the case with France and Germany from 2002 to 2005.

- *Government debt.* Only four countries had debts that did not exceed 60 per cent (France, Finland, Luxembourg and the UK). However, the Maastricht Treaty allowed countries to exceed this value as long as the debt was 'sufficiently diminishing and approaching the reference value at a satisfactory pace'. Critics argued that this phrase was interpreted too loosely.

The euro came into being on 1 January 1999, but euro banknotes and coins were not introduced until 1 January 2002. In the meantime, national currencies continued to exist alongside the euro, but at irrevocably fixed rates. The old notes and coins were withdrawn a few weeks after the introduction of euro notes and coins.

Ten new members joined the EU in May 2004, and another two in January 2007. Under the Maastricht Treaty, they should all make preparations for joining the euro by meeting the convergence criteria. Estonia, Lithuania and Slovenia were the first to join ERM2 in June 2004 with Latvia, Cyprus, Malta and Slovakia following in 2005. They adopted the wide band of ±15 per cent against the euro. Slovenia adopted the euro in 2007, Malta and Cyprus in 2008 and Slovakia in 2009.

Advantages of the single currency

EMU has several major advantages.

Elimination of the costs of converting currencies. With separate currencies in each of the EU countries, costs were incurred each time one currency was exchanged into another. The elimination of these costs, however, was probably the least important benefit from the single currency. The European Commission estimated that the effect was to increase the GDP of the countries concerned by an average of only 0.4 per cent. The gains to countries like the UK, which have well-developed financial markets, would be even smaller.

Increased competition and efficiency. Despite the advent of the single market, large price differences remained between member states. Not only does the single currency eliminate the need to convert one currency into another (a barrier to competition), but it brings more transparency in pricing, and puts greater downward pressure on prices in high-cost firms and countries.

Elimination of exchange rate uncertainty (between the members). Removal of exchange rate uncertainty has helped to encourage trade between the eurozone countries. Perhaps more importantly, it has encouraged investment by firms that trade between these countries, given the greater certainty in calculating costs and revenues from such trade.

Increased inward investment. Investment from the rest of the world is attracted to a eurozone of some 326 million inhabitants, where there is no fear of internal currency movements. By contrast, the UK, by not joining, has found that inward investment has been diverted away to countries within the eurozone. From 1990 to 1998, the UK's share of inward investment to EU countries (including from other EU countries) was 21.0 per cent. From 1999 to 2003, it was 12.5 per cent, and it fell throughout this period, from 17.5 per cent in 1999 to 6.5 per cent in 2003 (see Figure 26.2). From 2003 to 2005, however, its share increased substantially as the UK economy grew more strongly than other major economies in the EU. Since then it has fallen again.

Lower inflation and interest rates. A single monetary policy forces convergence in inflation rates (just as inflation rates are very similar between the different regions within a country). With the ECB being independent from short-term political manipulation, this has resulted in a low average inflation rate in the eurozone countries. This, in turn, has helped to convince markets that the euro will be strong relative to other currencies. The result is lower long-term rates of interest. This, in turn, further encourages investment in the eurozone countries, both by member states and by the rest of the world.

Opposition to EMU

Monetary union has been bitterly opposed, however, by certain groups. Many 'Eurosceptics' see within it a surrender of national political and economic sovereignty. The lack of an independent monetary and exchange rate policy is a serious problem, they argue, if an economy is at all out of harmony with the rest of the Union. For example, if countries such as Italy and Spain have higher rates of inflation (due, say, to greater cost-push pressures), then how are they to make their goods competitive with the rest of the Union? With separate currencies these countries could allow their currencies to depreciate. With a single currency, however, they could become depressed 'regions' of Europe, with rising unemployment and all the other problems of depressed regions *within* a country. This might then require significant regional policies – policies that might not be in place or, if they were, would be seen as too interventionist by the political right.

> *How might multiplier effects (the principle of cumulative causation) lead to prosperous regions becoming more prosperous and less prosperous regions falling even further behind?*

The reply given by proponents of EMU is that it is better to tackle the problem of high inflation in such countries by the disciplines of competition from other EU countries, than merely to feed that inflation by keeping separate

Figure 26.2 Inward investment to selected EU countries as percentage of total EU inward investment

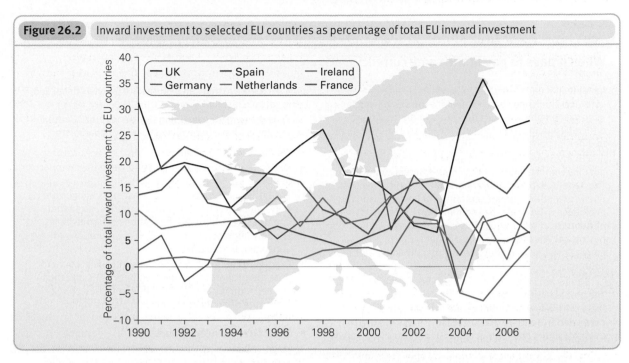

Note: Inward investment is that originating from any other country, including another EU country.
Source: Based on data in Foreign Direct Investment Database (http://stats.unctad.org/fdi) (United Nation Conference on Trade and Development [UNCTAD]).

currencies and allowing repeated devaluations, with all the uncertainty that they bring. What is more, the high-inflation countries tend to be the poorer ones with lower wage levels (albeit faster wage *increases*). With the high mobility of labour and capital that will accompany the development of the single market, resources are likely to be attracted to such countries. This could help to narrow the gap between the richer and poorer member states.

The critics of EMU counter this by arguing that labour is relatively immobile, given cultural and language barriers. Thus an unemployed worker in Wales could not easily move to a job in Turin or Helsinki. What the critics are arguing here is that the EU is not an *optimal currency area* (see Box 26.3).

Perhaps the most serious criticism is that the same rate of interest must apply to all eurozone countries: the 'one-size-fits-all' problem. The trouble is that while one country might require a lower rate of interest in order to ward off recession (as was the case with Germany in 2003–5), another might require a higher one to prevent inflation. As convergence between the member economies increases, however, this problem is likely to lessen.

Another problem for members of a single currency occurs in adjusting to a shock when that shock affects members to different degrees. Such occurrences are known as *asymmetric shocks*. For example, a sudden change in the price of oil would affect an oil-exporting country like the UK differently from oil-importing countries. This problem is more serious, the less the factor mobility between member countries and the less the price flexibility within member countries.

This problem, however, should not be overstated. The divergences between economies are often the result of a lack of harmony between countries in their demand management policies: something that is impossible in the case of monetary policy, and more difficult in the case of fiscal policy, for countries in the eurozone. Also, many of the shocks that face economies today are global and have similar (albeit not identical) effects on all countries. Adjustment to such shocks would often be better with a single co-ordinated policy, something that is much easier with a single currency and a single central bank.

Even when shocks are uniformly felt in the member states, however, there is still the problem that policies

---

Definitions

Optimal currency area The optimal size of a currency area is the one that maximises the benefits from having a single currency relative to the costs. If the area were increased or decreased in size, the costs would rise relative to the benefits.

Asymmetric shocks Shocks (such as an oil price increase or a recession in another part of the world) that have different-sized effects on different industries, regions or countries.

BOX 26.3 OPTIMAL CURRENCY AREAS

When it pays to pay in the same currency

Imagine that each town and village used a different currency. Think how inconvenient it would be having to keep exchanging one currency into another, and how difficult it would be working out the relative value of items in different parts of the country.

Clearly, there are benefits of using a common currency, not only within a country but across different countries. The benefits include greater transparency in pricing, more open competition, greater certainty for investors and the avoidance of having to pay commission when you change one currency into another. There are also the benefits from having a single monetary policy if that is delivered in a more consistent and effective way than by individual countries.

So why not have a single currency for the whole world? The problem is that the bigger a single currency area gets, the more likely the conditions are to diverge in the different parts of the area. Some parts may have high unemployment and require expansionary policies. Others may have low unemployment and suffer from inflationary pressures. They may require *contractionary* policies.

What is more, different members of the currency area may experience quite different shocks to their economies, whether from outside the union (e.g. a fall in the price of one of their major exports) of from inside (e.g. a prolonged strike). These 'asymmetric shocks' would imply that different parts of the currency area should adopt different policies. But with a common monetary policy and hence common interest rates, and with no possibility of devaluation/revaluation of the currency of individual members, the scope for separate economic policies is reduced.

The costs of asymmetric shocks (and hence the costs of a single currency area) will be greater, the less the mobility of labour and capital, the less the flexibility of prices and wage rates, and the fewer the alternative policies there are that can be turned to (such as fiscal and regional policies).

So is the eurozone an optimal currency area? Certainly strong doubts have been raised by many economists.

- Labour is relatively immobile.
- There are structural differences between the member states.
- The transmission effects of interest rate changes are different between the member countries, given that countries have different proportions of borrowing at variable interest rates and different proportions of consumer debt to GDP.
- Exports to countries outside the eurozone account for different proportions of the members' GDP, and thus their economies are affected differently by a change in the rate of exchange of the euro against other currencies.
- Wage rates are relatively inflexible.
- Under the Stability and Growth Pact (see Box 20.3), the scope for using discretionary fiscal policy is curtailed.

This does not necessarily mean, however, that the costs of having a single European currency outweigh the benefits. Also, the problems outlined above should decline over time as the single market develops. Finally, the problem of asymmetric shocks can be exaggerated. European economies are highly diversified; there are often more differences *within* economies than between them. Thus shocks are more likely to affect different industries or localities, rather than whole countries. Changing the exchange rate, if that were still possible, would hardly be an appropriate policy in these circumstances.

 Why is a single currency area likely to move towards becoming an optimal currency area over time?

---

adopted centrally will have different impacts on each country. For example, in the UK, a large proportion of borrowing is at variable interest rates. In Germany, by contrast, much is at fixed rates. Thus if the European central bank were to raise interest rates, the contractionary effects would be felt disproportionately in the UK. Of course, were this balance to change – and there is some evidence that types of borrowing are becoming more uniform across the EU – this problem would diminish.

The problem for economists is that the issue of monetary union is a very emotive one. 'Europhiles' often see monetary union as a vital element in their vision of a united Europe. Many Eurosceptics, however, see EMU as a surrender of sovereignty and a threat to nationhood. In such an environment, a calm assessment of the arguments and evidence is very difficult.

1. *By what means would a depressed country in an economic union with a single currency be able to recover? Would the market provide a satisfactory solution to its problems or would (union) government intervention be necessary, and if so, what form could that intervention take?*
2. *Is greater factor mobility likely to increase or decrease the problem of cumulative causation associated with regional multipliers? (See page 666.)*

The UK Labour government specified five convergence criteria that must be met before it would put the question of UK adoption of the euro to the electorate in a referendum. These are examined in Case Study 26.6 in MyEconLab. Given the strength of feeling against the euro by large sections of the population, such as referendum would seem to be a very long way off.

Section summary

1. One means of achieving greater currency stability is for a group of countries to peg their exchange rates with each other and yet float jointly with the rest of the world. The exchange rate mechanism of the EU (ERM) was an example. Members' currencies were allowed to fluctuate against other member currencies within a band. The band was ±2.25 per cent for the majority of the ERM countries until 1993.

2. The need for realignments seemed to have diminished in the late 1980s as greater convergence was achieved between the members' economies. Growing strains in the system, however, in the early 1990s led to a crisis in September 1992. The UK and Italy left the ERM. There was a further crisis in July 1993 and the bands were widened to ±15 per cent, although in practice fluctuations were kept within ±2.25 per cent for most of the time from 1993 to the start of the euro in 1999.

3. The ERM was seen as an important first stage on the road to complete economic and monetary union.

4. The euro was born on 1 January 1999. Twelve countries adopted it, having at least nominally met the Maastricht convergence criteria. Euro notes and coins were introduced on 1 January 2002, with the notes and coins of the old currencies withdrawn a few weeks later.

5. The advantages claimed for EMU are that it eliminates the costs of converting currencies and the uncertainties associated with possible changes in inter-EU exchange rates. This encourages more investment, both inward and by domestic firms. What is more, a common central bank, independent from domestic governments, provides the stable monetary environment necessary for a convergence of the EU economies and the encouragement of investment and inter-Union trade.

6. Critics claim, however, that it makes adjustment to domestic economic problems more difficult. The loss of independence in policy making is seen by such people to be a major issue, not only because of the loss of political sovereignty, but also because domestic economic concerns may be at variance with those of the Union as a whole. A single monetary policy is claimed to be inappropriate for dealing with asymmetric shocks. What is more, countries and regions at the periphery of the Union may become depressed unless there is an effective regional policy.

26.3 ACHIEVING GREATER CURRENCY STABILITY

One important lesson of recent years is that concerted speculation has become virtually unstoppable. This was made clear by the expulsion of the UK and Italy from the ERM in 1992, the collapse of various south-east Asian currencies and the Russian rouble in 1997–8, and the collapse of the Argentinean peso in early 2002. In comparison with the vast amounts of short-term finance flowing across the foreign exchanges each day, the reserves of central banks seem trivial.

If there is a consensus in the markets that a currency will depreciate, there is little that central banks can do. For example, if there were a 50 per cent chance of a 10 per cent depreciation in the next week, selling that currency now would yield an 'expected' return of just over 5 per cent for the week (i.e. 50% of 10%): equivalent to more than 1200 per cent at an annual rate!

For this reason, many commentators have argued that there are only two types of exchange rate system that can work over the long term. The first is a completely free-floating exchange rate, with no attempt by the central bank to support the exchange rate. With no intervention, there is no problem of a shortage of reserves!

The second is to share a common currency with other countries: to join a common currency area, such as the eurozone, and let the common currency float freely. The country would give up independence in its monetary policy, but at least there would be no problem of exchange rate instability within the currency area. A similar alternative is to adopt a major currency of another country, such as the US dollar or the euro. Many smaller states have done this. For example, Kosovo and Montenegro adopted the German mark and then the euro; and Ecuador has adopted the US dollar.

An attempt by a country to peg its exchange rate is likely to have one of two unfortunate consequences. Either it will end in failure as the country succumbs to a speculative attack, or its monetary policy will have to be totally dedicated to maintaining the exchange rate.

So is there any way of 'beating the speculators' and pursuing a policy of greater exchange rate rigidity? Or must countries outside a currency union be forced to accept freely floating exchange rates, with all the uncertainty for traders that such a regime brings?

This section looks at two possible solutions. The first is to reduce international financial mobility, by putting various types of restriction on foreign exchange transactions. The second is to move to a new type of exchange rate regime that offers the benefits of a degree of rigidity without being susceptible to massive speculative attacks.

Controlling exchange transactions

Until the early 1990s, many countries retained restrictions of various kinds on financial flows. Such restrictions made it more expensive for speculators to gamble on possible exchange rate movements. It is not the case, as some commentators argue, that it is impossible to reimpose controls. Indeed, Malaysia did just that in 1998 when the ringgit was under speculative attack. Many countries in the developing world still retain controls, and the last ERM countries to give them up did so only in 1991. It is true that the complexity of modern financial markets provides the speculator with more opportunity to evade controls, but they will still have the effect of dampening speculation.

In September 1998, the IMF said that controls on inward movements of finance could be a useful tool, especially for countries that were more vulnerable to speculative attack. In its 1998 annual report, it argued that the Asian crisis of 1997–8 was the result not only of a weak banking system, but also of open financial accounts, allowing massive withdrawals of funds.

The aim of financial controls is not to prevent international flows of finance. After all, such flows are an important source of financing investment. Also, if finance moves from countries with a lower marginal productivity of capital to countries where it is higher, this will lead to an efficient allocation of world savings. The aim of financial controls must therefore be to prevent speculative flows that are based on rumour or herd instinct rather than on economic fundamentals.

Types of control

In what ways can movements of short-term finance be controlled? There are various alternatives, each one with strengths and drawbacks.

BOX 26.4	THE TOBIN TAX

A new panacea?

In the mid 1980s, the daily turnover in the world's foreign exchange markets was approximately $150 billion. By 2008, it had risen to a truly massive $4 trillion. But only some 5 per cent of this was used for trade in goods and services.

With the massive growth in speculative flows, it is hardly surprising that this can cause great currency instability and financial crises at times of economic uncertainty. Global financial markets have often been decisive in both triggering and intensifying economic crises. The ERM crisis in 1992, the Mexican peso crisis in 1994, the south-east Asian crisis in 1997, the Russian rouble meltdown in 1998 and the crisis in Argentina in 2001/2 are the most significant in a long list.

The main issue is one of volatility of exchange rates. If currency markets responded to shifts in economic fundamentals, then currency volatility would not be so bad. However, it is increasingly the case that vast quantities of money flow around the global economy on pure speculation, in which the herd instinct often drives speculative waves. Invariably, given the volume of speculative flows, exchange rates overshoot their natural equilibrium, intensifying the distortions created. Such currency movements are a huge destabilising force, not just for individual economies but for the global economy as a whole.

So is there anything countries can do to reduce destabilising speculation? One suggestion is the introduction of a Tobin tax.

The Tobin tax

Writing in 1972, James Tobin proposed a system for reducing exchange rate volatility without fundamentally impeding the operation of the market. This involved the imposition of an international tax of some 0.1 to 0.5 per cent payable on all spot or cash exchange rate transactions. He argued that this would make currency trading more costly and would therefore reduce the volume of destabilising short-term financial flows, which would invariably lead to greater exchange rate stability.

Tobin's original proposal suggested that the tax rate would need to be very low so as not to affect 'normal business'. Even if it was very low, speculators working on small margins would be dissuaded from regular movements of money, given that the tax would need to be paid per transaction. If a tax rate of 0.2 per cent was set, speculators who moved a sum of money once a day would face a yearly tax bill of approximately 50 per cent. An investor working on a weekly movement of money would pay tax of 10 per cent per annum, and a monthly movement of currency would represent a tax of 2.4 per cent for the year. Given that 40 per cent of currency transactions have only a two-day time horizon, and 80 per cent have a time horizon of less than seven days, such a tax would clearly operate to dampen speculative currency movements.

In addition to moderating volatility and speculation, the Tobin tax might yield other benefits. It would, in the face of globalisation, restore to the nation state an element of control over monetary policy. In the face of declining governance over international forces, this might be seen as a positive advantage of the Tobin proposals.

The tax could also generate significant revenue. Estimates range from $150–300 billion annually. Many of the world's leading pressure groups, such as War on Want and Stamp out Poverty, have argued that the revenue from such an international tax could be used to tackle international problems, such as world poverty and environmental degradation. The World Bank estimates that some $225 billion is needed to eliminate the world's

Quantitative controls. Here the authorities would restrict the amount of foreign exchange dealing that could take place. Perhaps financial institutions would be allowed to exchange only a certain percentage of their assets. Developed countries and most developing countries have rejected this approach, however, since it is seen to be far too anti-market.

The exception is the use of special emergency measures to restrict capital movements in times of a currency crisis. According to Article 57 of the Treaty of Amsterdam, the EU Council of Ministers may 'adopt measures on the movement of capital to or from third countries'. Article 59 allows 'safeguard measures' to be taken if 'in exceptional circumstances, movements of capital to or from third countries cause . . . serious difficulties for the operation of economic and monetary union'. Article 60 allows member states to take 'unilateral measures against a third country with regard to capital movements and payments'.

A 'Tobin' tax. This is named after James Tobin, who in 1972 advocated the imposition of a small tax of 0.1 to 0.5 per cent on all foreign exchange transactions, or just on financial account transactions.[1] This would discourage destabilising speculation (by making it more expensive) and would thus impose some 'friction' in the foreign exchange markets, making them less volatile.

Calls for the use of Tobin taxes have become more frequent in recent years (see Box 26.4), and in November 2001 the French National Assembly became the first national legislature to incorporate into law a Tobin tax of up to 0.1 per cent. Belgium followed in 2002. The EU finance ministers ordered the European Commission to undertake

---

[1] J. Tobin, 'A proposal for international monetary reform', *Eastern Economic Journal*, 4(3–4) (1978), pp. 153–9.

EXPLORING ECONOMICS

worst forms of poverty. The revenue from a Tobin tax would, in a relatively short period of time, easily exceed this amount. Even with a worldwide rate as low as 0.005% (the rate recommended by Stamp out Poverty), the tax could still raise some $50 billion per year.

Problems with the Tobin tax

How far would a tax on currency transactions restrict speculative movements of money? The issue here concerns the rate of return investors might get from moving their money. If a currency were to devalue by as little as 3 to 4 per cent, a Tobin tax of 0.2 per cent would do little to deter a speculative transaction based upon such a potential return. Given devaluations of 50 per cent in Thailand and Indonesia following the 1997 crash, and an 82 per cent appreciation of the euro against the dollar from 2002 to 2008, along with severe short-term fluctuations, a 3 to 4 per cent movement in the currency appears rather modest. Raising the rate of the Tobin tax would be no solution, as it would begin to impinge upon 'normal business'.

One response to such a situation has been proposed by a German economist, Paul Bernd Spahn. He suggests that a two-tier system is used. On a day-to-day basis, a minimal tax rate, as originally envisaged by Tobin, is charged against each transaction conducted. However, during periods when exchange rates are highly unstable, a tax surcharge is levied. This would be at a far higher rate, and would only be triggered once a currency moved beyond some predetermined band of exchange rate variation.

A further problem identified with the Tobin tax concerns the costs of its administration. However, given inter-linked computer systems and the progressive centralisation of foreign exchange markets – in terms of marketplaces, traders and currencies – effective administration is becoming easier. Most foreign exchange markets are well monitored already and extending such monitoring to include overseeing tax collection would not be overly problematic.

Another problem is tax avoidance. For example, the Tobin tax is a tax payable on spot exchange rate transactions. This could encourage people to deal more in futures. Foreign exchange futures are a type of 'derivative' that allow people to trade currencies in the future at a price agreed today (see Box 3.4). These would be far more difficult to monitor, since no currency is exchanged at the time of the agreement, and hence more difficult to tax. One solution would be to apply a tax on the notional value of a derivative contract. However, derivatives are an important way through which businesses hedge against future risk. Taxing them might seriously erode their use to a business and damage the derivatives market as a whole, making business more risky.

Even with avoidance, however, supporters of the Tobin tax argue that it is still likely to be successful. The main problem is the one of political will.

Although some countries, such as France, Canada, Belgium and Venezuela, have supported the introduction of a Tobin tax, most of the major economies are opposed to it. With reservations being expressed by the IMF, any concerted international action to control global financial movements will be difficult to put on the agenda, let alone put in place and administer.

George Soros, multi-millionaire currency speculator, has referred to global capital markets as being like a wrecking ball rather than a pendulum, suggesting that such markets are becoming so volatile that they are damaging to all concerned, including speculators. What might lead Soros to such an observation?

a feasibility study of such a tax. In late 2001, the charity War on Want declared that 13 March 2002 would be international 'Tobin tax day'. Ironically, Tobin died on 11 March 2002.

A problem with such a tax is that it would penalise transactions that were for normal trading or investment purposes as well as those for speculative purposes. Another problem is that the tax might have to be quite high to prevent speculation in times of uncertainty, and this would be very damaging to trade and investment. A possibility here would be to impose the tax only at times of exchange market turbulence, or to impose a higher tax at such times. At least a tax is far less distortionary than quantitative controls.

Non-interest-bearing deposits. Here a certain percentage of inflows of finance would have to be deposited with the central bank in a non-interest-bearing account for a set period of time. Chile in the late 1990s used such a system. It required that 30 per cent of all inflows be deposited with Chile's central bank for a year. This clearly amounted to a considerable tax (i.e. in terms of interest sacrificed) and had the effect of discouraging short-term speculative flows. The problem was that it meant that interest rates in Chile had to be higher in order to attract finance.

One objection to all these measures is that they are likely only to dampen speculation, not eliminate it. If speculators believe that currencies are badly out of equilibrium and will be forced to realign, then no taxes on financial movements or artificial controls will be sufficient to stem the flood.

There are two replies to this objection. The first is that, if currencies are badly out of line, exchange rates *should* be adjusted. The second is that merely *dampening* speculation is probably the ideal. Speculation *can* play the valuable role of bringing exchange rates to their long-term equilibrium more quickly. Controls are unlikely to prevent this aspect of speculation: adjustments to economic fundamentals. If they help to lessen the wilder forms of destabilising speculation, so much the better.

Exchange rate target zones

One type of exchange rate regime that has been much discussed in recent years is that proposed by John Williamson, of Washington's Institute for International Economics.[2]

Williamson advocated a form of crawling peg within broad exchange rate bands (see Figure 25.7 on page 715). This would have four major features:

- Wide bands. For example, currencies would be allowed to fluctuate by ±10 per cent of their central parity.
- Central parity set in *real* terms, at the 'fundamental equilibrium exchange rate' (FEER): i.e. a rate that is consistent with long-run balance of payments equilibrium.
- Frequent realignments. In order to stay at the FEER, the central parity would be adjusted frequently (say, monthly) to take account of the country's rate of inflation. If its rate of inflation were 2 per cent per annum above the trade-weighted average of other countries, the central parity would be devalued by 2 per cent per annum. Realignments would also reflect other changes in fundamentals, such as changes in the levels of protection, or major political events, such as German reunification.
- 'Soft buffers'. Governments would not be forced to intervene at the ±10 per cent mark or at some specified fraction of it. In fact, from time to time the rate might be allowed to move outside the bands. The point is that the closer the rate approached the band limits, the greater would be the scale of intervention.

There are two main advantages of this system. First, the exchange rate would stay at roughly the equilibrium level, and therefore the likelihood of large-scale devaluations or revaluations, and with them the opportunities for large-scale speculative gains, would be small. The reason why the narrow-banded ERM broke down in 1992 and 1993 was that the central parities were *not* equilibrium rates.

Second, the wider bands would leave countries freer to follow an independent monetary policy: one that could therefore respond to domestic needs.

The main problem with the system is that it may not allow an independent monetary policy. If the rate of exchange has to be maintained within the zone, monetary policy may sometimes have to be used for that purpose rather than controlling inflation.

Nevertheless, crawling bands have been used relatively successfully by various countries, such as Chile and Israel, over quite long periods of time. What is more, in 1999 Germany's former finance minister, Oskar Lafontaine, argued that they might be appropriate for the euro relative to the dollar and yen. A world with three major currencies, each changing gently against the other two in an orderly way, has a lot to commend it.

1. *Would the Williamson system allow countries to follow a totally independent monetary policy?*
2. *If the euro were in a crawling peg against the dollar, what implications would this have for the ECB in sticking to its inflation target of no more than 2 per cent?*

[2] See, for example, J. Williamson and M. Miller, 'Targets and indicators: a blueprint for the international coordination of economic policy', *Policy Analyses in International Economics*, 22, IIE, 1987.

Section summary

1. Many economists argue that, with the huge flows of short-term finance across the foreign exchanges, governments are forced to adopt one of two extreme forms of exchange rate regime: free floating, or being a member of a currency union.

2. If financial flows could be constrained, however, exchange rates could be stabilised somewhat.

3. Forms of financial control include quantitative controls, a tax on exchange transactions, and non-interest-bearing deposits of a certain percentage of capital inflows with the central bank. Such controls can dampen speculation, but may discourage capital from flowing to where it has a higher marginal productivity.

4. An alternative means of stabilising exchange rates is to have exchange rate target zones. Here exchange rates are allowed to fluctuate within broad bands around a central parity, which is adjusted to the fundamental equilibrium rate in a gradual fashion.

5. The advantage of this system is that, by keeping the exchange rate at roughly its equilibrium level, destabilising speculation is avoided, and yet there is some freedom for governments to pursue an independent monetary policy. Monetary policy, however, may still from time to time have to be used to keep the exchange rate within the bands.

END OF CHAPTER QUESTIONS

1. Under what circumstances does a growth in financial flows make exchange rates less stable?

2. Assume that countries in the eurozone decide to pursue a deflationary fiscal policy. What effect is this likely to have on the UK economy?

3. It is often argued that international convergence of economic indicators is a desirable objective. Does this mean that countries should all seek to achieve the same rate of economic growth, monetary growth, interest rates, budget deficits as a percentage of their GDP, etc.?

4. Did the exchange rate difficulties experienced by countries under the ERM strengthen or weaken the arguments for progressing to a single European currency?

5. Assume that just some of the members of a common market like the EU adopt full economic and monetary union, including a common currency. What are the advantages and disadvantages to those members joining the full EMU and to those not?

6. Is the eurozone an optimal currency area? Explain your answer.

7. How are asymmetric shocks dealt with within a country? To what extent can this process be mirrored within the eurozone?

8. Would the world benefit from the general imposition of controls on the movement of international finance?

Online resources

Additional case studies in MyEconLab

26.1   The new economy. Does globalisation bring economic success?

26.2   High oil prices. What is their effect on the world economy?

26.3   Crisis in south-east Asia. Causes of the severe recession in many south-east Asian countries in 1997/8.

26.4   The 1997/8 crisis in Asia: the role played by the IMF.

26.5   Converging on the euro. Did the 11 countries that adopted the euro in 1999 genuinely meet the convergence criteria?

26.6   The UK Labour government's convergence criteria for euro membership. An examination of the five tests set by the UK government that would have to be passed before the question of euro membership would be put to the electorate in a referendum.

Websites relevant to Chapters 25 and 26

Numbers and sections refer to websites listed in the web appendix and hotlinked from this book's website at **www.pearsoned.co.uk/sloman**.

- For news articles relevant to this and the previous chapter, see the *Economics News Articles* link from the book's website.

▶

- For general news on countries' balance of payments and exchange rates, see websites in section A, and particularly A1–5, 7–9, 20–25, 31. For articles on various aspects of economic development, see A27, 28; I9. See also links to newspapers worldwide in A38, 39, 43 and 44, and the news search feature in Google at A41. See also links to economics news in A42.

- For international data on balance of payments and exchange rates, see *World Economic Outlook* in H4 and *OECD Economic Outlook* in B21 (also in section 6 of B1). See also the trade topic in I14. The ESDS International site (B35) has links to World Bank, IMF, OECD, UN and Eurostat datasets (but you will need an Athens password, available free to all UK higher education students).

- For details of individual countries' balance of payments, see B32.

- For UK data on balance of payments, see B1, *1. National Statistics* > the fourth link > *Economy* > *United Kingdom Balance of Payments – the Pink Book*. See also B3, 34; F2. For EU data, see G1 > *The Statistical Annex* > *Foreign trade and current balance*.

- For exchange rates, see A3; B34; F2, 6, 8.

- For discussion papers on balance of payments and exchange rates, see H4 and 7.

- Sites I7 and 11 contain links to *Balance of payments and exchange rates* in *International economics*.

- For various pressure groups critical of the effects of free trade and globalisation, see H12–14.

- For information on EMU, see sites G1, 2, 3 and 6; F3–6 and 9.

- For student resources relevant to these two chapters, see sites C1–7, 9, 10, 19. See also *The trade balance and the exchange rate* in site D3.

Economic Problems of Developing Countries

CHAPTER MAP

27.1 The problem of underdevelopment   **762**
The gulf between rich and poor countries   762
The meaning of 'development'   762

27.2 International trade and development   **766**
The importance of international trade to
   developing countries   766
Trade strategies   766
Approach 1: Exporting primaries – exploiting
   comparative advantage   767
Approach 2: Import-substituting
   industrialisation (ISI)   769
Approach 3: Exporting manufactures – a
   possible way forward?   772

**27.3 Structural problems within
   developing countries**   **776**
The neglect of agriculture   776
Inappropriate technology   777
Unemployment   779

27.4 The problem of debt   **783**
The oil shocks of the 1970s   783
Coping with debt: rescheduling   784
Dealing with debt: structural reform within the
   developing countries   787
Dealing with debt: debt forgiveness   788

In this final chapter, we turn to the economic problems of the poorer countries of the world. These include all the countries of Africa and Latin America and most of the countries of Asia. More than three-quarters of the world's population lives in these countries. As Theodore Schultz said when accepting the Nobel Prize in Economics in 1979:

> Most of the people of the world are poor, so if we knew the economics of being poor we would know much of the economics that really matters.

We start by looking at the nature and extent of their poverty and the means by which it can be measured. We then look at the trade relations between the poorer countries and the advanced industrialised world. As we shall see, most developing countries are highly dependent for their development, or lack of it, on their relationships with the rich world.

In section 27.3, the focus shifts to some of the internal problems faced by developing countries: problems such as the neglect of agriculture, the use of inappropriate technology and the rise in unemployment. The final section looks at one of the most serious problems facing poorer countries: the problem of huge international debts. We look at the growing calls for the debts of the poorest countries to be cancelled and at the response of the rich countries.

27.1 THE PROBLEM OF UNDERDEVELOPMENT

The gulf between rich and poor countries

The typical family in North America, western Europe, Japan and Australasia has many material comforts: plentiful food to eat; a house or apartment with electricity and running hot and cold water; an inside toilet connected to an underground sewerage system; access to free or affordable health care and education; numerous consumer durables; holidays away from home; visits to the cinema, concerts, sports events, etc. There are some people, it is true, who are very poor. But it is only a small minority that cannot afford the basics of life, such as adequate food, shelter and clothing.

In most of Africa and large parts of Asia and Latin America, the picture is quite different. The majority of people live in poverty. For them life is a daily struggle for survival. Affluence does exist in these countries, but here it is the fortunate few who can afford good food, good housing and the various luxury items that typify life in the industrialised world.

A large proportion of the inhabitants live in the countryside. For many, this means living in a family with many children and working on a small amount of land with too little income to buy adequate agricultural machinery, fertilisers or pesticides. With a rapid growth in population there is less and less land to go round. As land is passed on from generation to generation, it is divided up between the offspring into smaller and smaller plots. Many who cannot make ends meet are forced to sell their land to the local landlords. Then as landless labourers they have to accept very low-paid jobs on the large farms or plantations. Others try to survive by borrowing, hoping to be able to pay off their debts with future crop sales. But often the only source of finance is again the local landlord who charges exorbitant rates of interest. As a result, they end up in a state of 'debt bondage' where they can never pay off their debts, but year in year out have to give part of their crops to the landlord as interest.

Others come to the rapidly growing cities. In the cities, at least there are some jobs. But far more people migrate to the cities than there are jobs available. Thus the number of unemployed in the cities grows inexorably. People are forced to do anything to earn a living: selling wares on street corners, or working as casual labourers, domestic servants or shoe shiners; some resort to prostitution and crime, others merely beg. All round the outskirts of cities throughout the developing world, shanty towns mushroom as the poor flock in from the countryside. Families crowd into one- or two-roomed shacks, often with no electricity, no water and no sanitation. There are schools in these towns, but often parents cannot afford to allow their children to attend. Instead they have to send them out to work to supplement the family's meagre income.

Statistics cannot give the complete picture, but they can give us some indication of the gulf between rich and poor countries. Table 27.1 gives some details.

Some 84 per cent of the world's population lives in developing countries (low- and middle-income countries) but these people earn only 24 per cent of the world's income. In high-income countries, the average GNY[1] per head in 2006 was over $36 000. In low-income countries it was a mere $649. Even in purchasing-power parity terms, the figures were $34 932 and $1860 respectively, and just $1681 for sub-Saharan Africa. What is more, some of the poorest developing countries have the slowest rates of per-capita growth – just 0.5 per cent per annum from 1990 to 2006 for sub-Saharan African countries. The gulf between rich and poor countries can also be seen in other basic indicators, including health, life expectancy and literacy (see Table 27.1).

The meaning of 'development'

Countries want to develop. But just what do we mean by 'development'? Clearly it is a normative concept. Its definition will depend on the goals that the economist assumes societies want to achieve. So how do economists define and measure development?

The basic needs approach
A starting point is to identify the basic needs that people have if they are to be able to realise their potential as human beings. Different economists have identified various lists of requirements, including the following items:

- Adequate food, shelter, warmth and clothing.
- Universal access to education.
- Availability of adequate health care.
- Availability of non-demeaning jobs.
- Sufficient free time to be able to enjoy social interaction.
- Freedom to make one's own economic decisions.
- Freedom to participate in the decisions of government and other bodies that affect one's life.

  What other items might be included as basic needs?

There are four major problems with defining development in terms of a basic list of requirements.

The first is in deciding *what to include*. Any definition of *economic* development would clearly include people's *material* standard of living. But should development include social and political factors such as 'self-esteem', freedom from servitude and freedom of religion?

[1] GNY (gross national income): see appendix to Chapter 14.

Table 27.1   Selected world statistics

	Low-income economies[a]	Sub-Saharan Africa	Lower-middle-income economies[b]	Upper-middle-income economies[c]	High-income economies[d]	All countries
Population (millions, 2006)	2420	781	2276	811	1 031	6538
GNY per capita ($ per annum, 2006)	649	828	2038	5913	36 608	7447
Population growth (average annual %, 1990–2006)	2.1	2.6	1.7	1.0	0.7	1.4
Growth in private consumption per capita (average annual %, 1990–2006)	2.2	0.5	4.4	2.4	1.9	1.5
Growth in exports of goods and services (average annual %, 1990–2006)	9.5	4.6	10.5	6.2	6.0	6.7
Life expectancy at birth (years) (2006)	60	50	71	70	79	68
Number of doctors per 1000 people (1998–2005)	0.5	0.2	1.3	2.4	2.6	1.6
% of population with HIV (2005)	1.7	5.8	0.3	1.7	0.4	1.0
Under-5 mortality per 1000 (2006)	112	157	36	26	7	73
Adult literacy (%, 2005):						
Female	50	50	85	92	98	77
Male	72	69	93	94	99	87
Urban population as % of total population (2006)	30	36	47	75	78	49
Urban population growth (average annual %, 1990–2006)	3.2	4.2	3.1	1.5	1.1	2.2

[a] Those countries with a GNY per head in 2006 of $905 or less.
[b] Those countries with a GNY per head in 2006 of $906–$3595.
[c] Those countries with a GNY per head in 2006 of $3596–$11 115.
[d] Those countries with a GNY per head in 2006 of over $11 115.
Source: World Development Indicators (World Bank, 2005).

The second problem is in *measuring each of the items*. It is possible to measure such things as income per head, literacy rates and mortality rates. It is much more difficult, however, to measure the achievement of social and political objectives such as self-esteem.

The third problem is in arriving at a *single measure* of the level of development. You cannot add the average calorific intake to the number of doctors and nurses to the percentage of homes having various basic amenities such as running water. You can meaningfully add things up only if they are expressed in the same units, or if appropriate *weights* are attached to each of the items. Clearly, the assigning of any such weights would be highly controversial.

The fourth problem is in deciding the importance of the *distribution* of the various items. If, say, the average calorific intake increases, but the poorest sections of the population have less to eat, has the country really experienced an increase in the level of development?

However, many economists argue that the basic needs approach does provide a useful 'checklist' to see whether a country's development is broadly based or confined to just one or two indicators.

 Would it be possible with this basic needs approach to say (a) that one country was more developed than another; (b) that one country was developing faster than another?

Using GNY to measure development

The desire to have a single measure for development and thus to be able to make simple comparisons between countries has led to the universal use of real gross national income (GNY) per capita as the main indicator. It has some major advantages:

- It takes into account virtually all the goods and services produced in a country, and converts them into a single measure by the use of market prices.
- Although markets are by no means perfect, they do reflect the strength of demand and the opportunity costs of supply.
- The rules for the measurement of GNY are universally agreed.
- Virtually all countries compile GNY statistics.
- Although not every item that affects human welfare is included in GNY, a sustained rise in GNY is generally agreed to be a *necessary* condition for a sustained rise in welfare.
- There is a fairly close correlation between the level of per-capita GNY and other indicators such as mortality rates, literacy rates, and calorific and protein intake.

However, there are four fundamental criticisms of relying on simple GNY per capita as an indicator of development.

Many items are excluded. Much of production that does not get bought and sold will escape being recorded. This is a particular problem with rural societies that are largely subsistence-based. People grow their own food, build their own houses, make their own clothes and provide their own entertainment. GNY statistics are therefore likely to *understate* the level of production in these societies.

On the other hand, as these societies 'develop', the size of the market sector is likely to grow. A larger proportion of people's consumption will be of items they have purchased and which therefore do enter into GNY statistics. Thus GNY figures will *overstate* the rate of growth of production and consumption.

As an economy becomes more urbanised, there is likely to be a growth in *external* costs of production and consumption, such as pollution and crime. Traditional ways of life will be destroyed; people may find themselves increasingly in a competitive, uncaring environment. Again the growth in GNY is likely to *overstate* the growth in human welfare.

Market prices may be highly distorted. GNY is based on market prices, but these prices may be distorted. Markets are often highly fragmented, and there is little competition to ensure that prices reflect undistorted marginal costs. Companies often have considerable monopoly power to push up prices of manufactured goods; landlords often have power to push up rents; governments may impose price controls on food; employers with monopsony power may be able to pay very low wages.

KI 29
p313

How would a redistribution of income to the powerful be likely to affect GNY?

Exchange rates may not reflect local purchasing power. GNY statistics are initially compiled in terms of the domestic currency. For purposes of international comparison they then have to be converted into a common currency – usually the US dollar – at the current exchange rate. But exchange rates reflect demand and supply of *traded* goods; they do not reflect the prices of *non-traded* goods. Generally, the price of non-traded goods and services in developing countries will be lower than the price of similar goods and services in advanced countries. The *level* of GNY is therefore likely to *understate* the level of production in poor countries. If, on the other hand, the proportion of traded goods increases over time, the *growth* of GNY will again *overstate* the growth in production.

It is much better, therefore, to estimate GNY using purchasing-power parity exchange rates. Even if this is done, however, massive differences remain in GNY per head between rich and poor countries. This is illustrated in Figure 27.1, which shows GNY per head at PPP exchange rates as a percentage of US GNY per head.

Simple GNY per head ignores the distribution of income. Since the early 1980s, many developing countries have achieved relatively rapid growth in per capita GNY as they have sought overseas investment, privatised their industries and

KI 4
p10

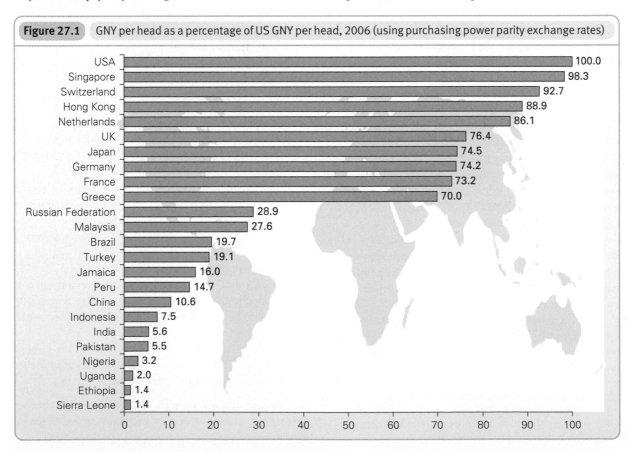

Figure 27.1 GNY per head as a percentage of US GNY per head, 2006 (using purchasing power parity exchange rates)

Country	Value
USA	100.0
Singapore	98.3
Switzerland	92.7
Hong Kong	88.9
Netherlands	86.1
UK	76.4
Japan	74.5
Germany	74.2
France	73.2
Greece	70.0
Russian Federation	28.9
Malaysia	27.6
Brazil	19.7
Turkey	19.1
Jamaica	16.0
Peru	14.7
China	10.6
Indonesia	7.5
India	5.6
Pakistan	5.5
Nigeria	3.2
Uganda	2.0
Ethiopia	1.4
Sierra Leone	1.4

| BOX 27.1 | THE HUMAN DEVELOPMENT INDEX (HDI) | EXPLORING ECONOMICS |

A measure of human welfare?

Since 1990, the United Nations Development Programme (UNDP) has published an annual Human Development Index (HDI). This is an attempt to provide a more broadly-based measure of development than GDP or GNY. HDI is the average of three indices based on three sets of variables: life expectancy at birth, education (a weighted average of adult literacy (two-thirds) and average years of schooling (one-third)), and real GDP per capita, measured in US dollars at purchasing-power parity exchange rates. Countries are then placed in one of three groups according to their HDI: high human development (0.8 to 1.0), medium human development (0.5 to 0.799) and low human development (below 0.5).

For each of the three indices making up the HDI, a sophisticated formula is used. Thus the index for GDP attempts to measure material well-being by building in the assumption of a rapidly diminishing marginal utility of income above average world levels.

The table, based on the 2007/8 Human Development Report, gives the 2005 HDIs for selected countries and their rankings. It also gives rankings for GDP per capita. The final column shows the divergence between the two rankings. A positive number shows that a country has a higher ranking for HDI than GDP per capita. As can be seen, the rankings differ substantially in some cases between the two measures. For some countries, such as Australia, Cuba, Armenia and Tanzania, GDP understates their relative level of human development, whereas for others, such as the USA, Saudi Arabia and South Africa, GDP per capita overstates their relative level of human development. Thus Angola's (PPP) GDP per capita is over three times that of Tanzania and yet its HDI is lower.

The point is that countries with similar levels of national income may use that income quite differently.

Recently, work has been done to adjust HDI figures for various other factors, such as overall income distribution, gender inequalities and inequalities by region or ethnic group. Thus the overall HDI can be adjusted downwards to reflect greater degrees of inequality. Alternatively, separate HDIs can be produced for separate regions or ethnic groups, or for women and men within a country.

1. *For what reasons are HDI and per capita GDP rankings likely to diverge?*
2. *Why do Saudi Arabia and South Africa have such a large negative figure in the final column of the table?*

Human Development Index for selected countries (2005)

Country	HDI ranking	HDI	GDP per head (PPP$)	GDP (PPP$) ranking	GDP (PPP$) rank minus HDI rank
High human development					
Iceland	1	0.968	36 510	5	4
Norway	2	0.968	41 420	3	1
Australia	3	0.962	31 794	16	13
Canada	4	0.961	33 375	10	6
USA	12	0.951	41 890	2	−10
UK	16	0.946	33 238	11	−5
Singapore	25	0.922	29 663	19	−6
Cuba	51	0.838	6 000	94	43
Saudi Arabia	61	0.812	15 711	42	−19
Russia	67	0.802	10 845	58	−9
Brazil	70	0.800	8 402	67	−3
Medium human development					
Venezuela	74	0.792	6 632	88	14
Thailand	78	0.781	8 677	65	−13
China	81	0 777	6 757	86	5
Armenia	83	0.775	4 945	103	20
Turkey	84	0.775	8 407	66	−18
South Africa	121	0 674	11 110	56	−65
India	128	0 619	3 452	117	−11
Pakistan	136	0.551	2 370	128	−8
Low human development					
Nigeria	158	0.470	1 128	162	4
Tanzania	159	0.467	744	174	15
Angola	162	0.446	2 335	129	−33
Malawi	164	0.437	667	177	13
Sierra Leone	177	0.336	806	172	−5

Source: UNDP Human Development Report 2007/2008 (United Nations Development Program, 2007).

cut the levels of public provision. But with a deepening of poverty, a growing inequality in the distribution of income and an increase in unemployment, few would argue that this constitutes genuine 'development'.

Many who have advocated the concentration on GNY and its rate of growth have argued that, while the rich may be the first to benefit from prosperity, gradually the benefits will 'trickle down' to the poor. In practice, the wealth has failed to trickle down in many countries. The rich have got richer while the poor have got poorer.

Given the weaknesses of GNY, but given the desirability of having a single measure of development, various composite indicators have been constructed. The most widely used is the *Human Development Index (HDI)*, which is a combined measure of life expectancy, education and GDP per head at PPP exchange rates. This index is examined in Box 27.1.

Section summary

1. There are a number of ways of categorising countries according to their level of development.

2. The level of development of a country can be defined in terms of the extent to which it meets basic needs for human life. There is no universal agreement, however, about which items should be measured or about how to measure and weight them. Nevertheless, the approach provides a useful indicator of whether development is broadly based and how rapidly the most serious problems of poverty are being tackled.

3. The most widely used measure of development is GNY per head at PPP exchange rates. However, there are serious problems with using GNY: many items may be excluded, especially for a more subsistence-based society; prices may be highly distorted; and the statistics ignore the question of the distribution of income. Another widely used measure is the Human Development Index.

27.2 INTERNATIONAL TRADE AND DEVELOPMENT

The importance of international trade to developing countries

International trade is one of the most contentious issues in development economics. Should countries adopt an open trading policy with few if any barriers to imports? Should governments actively promote trade by subsidising their export sector? Or should they restrict trade and pursue a policy of greater self-sufficiency? These are issues that we will be looking at in this section.

Whether it is desirable that developing countries should adopt policies of more trade or less, trade is still vital. Certain raw materials, capital equipment and intermediate products that are necessary for development can be obtained only from abroad. Others *could* be produced domestically, but only at much higher cost.

Trade strategies

As they develop, countries' policies towards trade typically go through various stages.

Primary outward-looking stage

Traditionally, developing countries have exported primaries – minerals such as copper, cash crops such as coffee, and non-foodstuffs such as cotton – in exchange for manufactured consumer goods. Having little in the way of an

industrial base, if they want to consume manufactured goods, they have to import them.

Secondary inward-looking stage

In seeking rapid economic development, most developing countries drew lessons from the experience of the advanced countries. The main conclusion was that industrialisation was the key to economic success.

But industrialisation required foreign exchange to purchase capital equipment. This led to a policy of *import-substituting industrialisation*, which involved cutting back on non-essential imports and thereby releasing foreign exchange. Tariffs and other restrictions were imposed on those imports for which a domestic substitute existed, or which were regarded as unimportant.

Definition

Human Development Index (HDI) A composite index made up of three elements: an index for life expectancy, an index for school enrolment and adult literacy, and an index for GDP per capita (in PPP$).

Import-substituting industrialisation A strategy of restricting imports of manufactured goods and using the foreign exchange saved to build up domestic substitute industries.

Secondary outward-looking stage

Once an industry had satisfied domestic demand, it had to seek markets abroad if expansion was to continue. What is more, as we shall see, import substitution brought a number of serious problems for developing countries. The answer seemed to be to look outward again, this time to the export of manufactured goods. Many of the most economically successful developing countries (especially Hong Kong, Singapore, South Korea, Taiwan and, more recently, China) have owed their high growth rates to a rapid expansion of manufactured exports.

We will now examine the three stages in more detail.

Approach 1: Exporting primaries – exploiting comparative advantage

The importance of primary exports

Despite moves towards import substitution and secondary export promotion, many developing countries still rely heavily on primary exports. These constituted 72 per cent of total developing country exports in 1970. Although by 2006 this had fallen to 40 per cent for low-income countries and 37 per cent for middle-income countries, it was still much higher than the figure for advanced countries (22 per cent). For the 17 most heavily indebted poor countries, most of them in Africa, the figure was 83 per cent.

The justification for exporting primaries

Three major arguments have traditionally been used for pursuing a policy of exporting primaries. In each case, the arguments have also been used to justify a policy of free or virtually free trade.

Exporting primaries exploits comparative advantage. Traditional trade theory implies that countries should specialise in producing those items in which they have a comparative advantage: i.e. those goods that can be produced at relatively low opportunity costs. For most developing countries, this means that a large proportion of their exports should be primaries.

The reasons for differences in comparative costs were examined by two Swedish economists, Eli Heckscher and Bertil Ohlin. They believed that comparative cost differences arise from differences in factor endowments. The *Heckscher–Ohlin theory* states that *a country should specialise in those goods that are intensive in the country's abundant factor.* The more abundant a factor, the relatively cheaper it is likely to be, and thus the lower will be the opportunity cost of producing goods that are intensive in its use. Thus labour-abundant developing countries should specialise in labour-intensive products. By exporting these products, which will typically be primaries, they can earn the foreign exchange to import goods that use large amounts of capital and other resources that are in short supply.

According to this theory, international trade would lead not only to higher consumption, but also to *factor price*

equalisation: i.e. the erosion of income inequalities between trading nations. For example, if wage rates are low in developing countries, trade will increase the demand for their labour-intensive products and thereby push up wage rates. International trade will also erode income differentials *within* countries. The demand for exports will increase the demand for the relatively cheap factors, and imports will reduce the demand for the relatively expensive ones. Thus the cheap factors will go up in price and the expensive ones will come down.

> 1. What effect will trade have on the price of capital in developing and developed countries?
> 2. It is sometimes claimed that trade with developing countries is unjust because it leads to the importation of goods produced at pitifully low wages. How can the Heckscher–Ohlin theory be used to refute this claim? Is there any validity in the claim? (See Box 24.2.)

Exporting primaries provides a 'vent for surplus'. Trade offers a *vent for surplus*: i.e. a means of putting to use resources that would otherwise not be used. These surpluses will occur where the domestic market is simply not big enough to consume all the available output of a particular good. There is far too little demand within Zambia to consume its potential output of copper. The same applies to Namibian uranium or Peruvian tin.

Exporting primaries provides an 'engine for economic growth'. According to this argument, developing countries benefit from the growth of the economies of the developed world. As industrial expansion takes place in the rich North, this will create additional demand for primaries from the poor South.

Traditional trade theory in the context of development

There are several reasons for questioning whether the above arguments justify a policy of relying on primary exports as the means to development.

Comparative costs change over time. Over time, with the acquisition of new skills and an increase in the capital

---

Definitions

Heckscher–Ohlin version of comparative advantage A country has a comparative advantage in those goods that are intensive in the country's relatively abundant factor.

Factor price equalisation The tendency for international trade to reduce factor price inequalities both between and within countries.

Vent for surplus Where international trade enables a country to exploit resources that would otherwise be unused.

stock, a developing country that once had a comparative advantage in primaries may find that it now has a comparative advantage in certain *manufactured* products, especially those that are more labour-intensive and use raw materials of which the country has a plentiful supply. The market, however, cannot necessarily be relied upon to bring about a smooth transition to producing such products.

Concentrating on primary production may hinder growth. The theory of comparative advantage shows how trade allows a country to consume beyond its production possibility curve (see pages 673–6). As its economy grows, however, this production possibility curve will *shift outwards*. By concentrating on primaries, the curve may shift outwards more slowly than if the country had pursued a policy of industrialisation. In other words, economic growth may be slower from a policy of exporting primaries than from a policy of industrialisation.

The benefits from trade may not accrue to the nationals of the country. If a mine or plantation is owned by a foreign company, it will be the foreign shareholders who get the profits from the sale of exports. In addition, these companies may bring in their own capital and skilled labour from abroad. The benefits gained by the local people will probably be confined to the additional wages they earn. With these companies being in a position of monopsony power, the wages are often very low.

 Why does this argument make GNY a better indicator of development than GDP? (See the appendix to Chapter 14.)

 Trade may lead to less equality. Trade shifts income distribution in favour of those factors of production employed intensively in the export sector. If exports are labour intensive, greater equality will tend to result. But if they are land or raw material intensive, trade will redistribute income in favour of large landowners or mine owners.

 Exporting primary exports may involve external costs. Mining can lead to huge external costs, such as the despoiling of the countryside and damage to the health of miners. Mines and plantations can lead to the destruction of traditional communities and their values.

Trade may adversely influence tastes. The more freely a country trades, the more will people's aspirations for a 'better life' be fuelled. If people cannot afford to buy the goods imported from the affluent world, their frustrations are likely to increase.

These arguments cast doubt on whether a policy of relying on free trade in primary exports is the best way of achieving economic development. Various trends in the international economy have also worked against primary exporters, causing them serious balance of payments problems.

Balance of payments problems: long term

Long-term trends in international trade have caused problems for primary exporting countries in three ways: (a) exports have grown slowly; (b) imports have grown rapidly; (c) until recent years, the terms of trade have moved against them.

Low income elasticity of demand for primary products. As world incomes grow, so a smaller proportion of these incomes is spent on primaries. Since food is a necessity, consumers, especially in rich countries, already consume virtually all they require. A rise in incomes, therefore, tends to be spent more on luxury goods and services, and only slightly more on basic foodstuffs. The exceptions are certain 'luxury' imported foodstuffs such as exotic fruits. In the case of raw materials, as people's incomes grow, they tend to buy more and more expensive products. The extra value of these products, however, arises not from the extra raw materials they might contain, but from their greater sophistication.

This argument has not applied in recent years, however, as the rapid growth of countries such as China and India, where people spend a relatively large proportion of their income on food, led to an increase in world food prices (see Table 27.2). This has been aggravated by poor harvests in many parts of the world and by switching land to growing crops for biofuels instead of food.

Agricultural protection in advanced countries. Faced with the problem of a slowly growing demand for food produced by their own farmers, advanced countries increasingly imposed restrictions on imported food. Reducing these restrictions was one of the main aims of the Doha Development Agenda (the latest round of WTO trade negotiations: see Box 24.7 on pages 690–1).

Technological developments. Synthetic substitutes have in many cases replaced primaries in the making of consumer durables, industrial equipment and clothing. Also, the process of miniaturisation, as microchips have replaced machines, has meant that less and less raw materials have been required to produce any given amount of output.

Rapid growth in imports. There tends to be a high income elasticity of demand for imported manufactures. This is the result partly of better-off people in developing countries being able to afford luxury goods, and partly of the development of new tastes as people are exposed to the products of the developed world – products such as Coca-Cola, Levi jeans, mobile phones and iPods. In fact, the whole process has been dubbed 'Coca-Colanisation'. Because of a lack of domestic substitutes, the price elasticity of demand for manufactured imports is low. This gives market power to the overseas suppliers of these imports, which tends to raise their price relative to exports.

Table 27.2	World primary commodity prices (2000 = 100)					
	1960	**1970**	**1980**	**1990**	**2000**	**2007**
Food	254	199	214	122	100	169
Metals and minerals	174	183	152	127	100	313
All non-fuel commodities	221	184	188	118	100	177
Oil	27	15	122	86	100	252

Source: Data drawn from *World Development Indicators 2005* (World Bank, 2005); *UNCTAD Handbook of Statistics 2008* (United Nations Conference on Trade and Development, 2008).

Deterioration in the terms of trade. The slow growth in demand for primary exports and the rapid growth in demand for manufactured imports led to chronic current account balance of payments problems for primary exporters. This caused their exchange rates to depreciate and hence brought a decline in their terms of trade, where a country's terms of trade are defined as the average price of its exports divided by the average price of its imports (P_x/P_m).

This problem was compounded by adverse movements in international prices of primaries and manufactures. The overall demand for primaries tends to be relatively price inelastic. There is no substitute for food, and in the short run there is often no substitute for minerals. On the other hand, the demand for any *one* primary product, and especially the demand for any one *country's* primary exports, will be very price elastic: there are plenty of other countries producing substitutes. This will encourage countries to produce as much as possible (as long as price remains above marginal cost), but as all countries do the same, the low overall price elasticity will depress primary product prices. Between 1980 and 2000, non-fuel primary product prices fell by 47 per cent (see Table 27.2).

A quite different picture emerged in the 2000s. As the demand for food and raw materials grew rapidly, reflecting the rapid growth of China and various other emerging economies, so primary commodity prices rose sharply. This is shown in the final column of Table 27.2.

With the world recession of 2008/9, however, primary product prices fell again – and sharply so. Primary exporters once more saw a deterioration in their terms of trade. For example, from March 2008 to February 2009 world wheat prices fell by 56 per cent, soybeans by 40 per cent, copper by 63 per cent and aluminium by 58 per cent.

Balance of payments problems: short term

There are also problems for primary exporting countries in the *short term*.

The prices of primary products are subject to large fluctuations. This causes great uncertainty for primary exporters. The current account of the balance of payments fluctuates wildly, which tends to cause large swings in exchange rates or requires massive government intervention to stabilise them.

Price fluctuations are caused partly by the low price elasticity of demand and supply of primaries, which we have just considered. They are also caused by substantial *shifts* in their demand and supply.

The demand for *food* is relatively stable, but that for minerals varies with the business cycle and tends to vary more than the demand for consumer goods. The reason is the *accelerator principle* (see section 17.4). Since the *level* of investment demand depends on the size of *changes* in consumer demand, investment will fluctuate much more than consumer demand. But since many minerals are inputs into *capital* equipment, their demand is also likely to fluctuate more than consumer demand. For example, with the boom in construction in emerging economies in the mid 2000s, the prices of iron ore, copper, nickel and lead shot up.

The supply of minerals is relatively stable. The supply of cash crops, however, varies with the harvest. Many developing countries are subject to drought or flood, which can virtually wipe out their export earnings from the relevant crop.

 If a disastrous harvest of rice were confined to a particular country, would (a) the world price and (b) its own domestic price of rice fluctuate significantly? What would happen to the country's export earnings and the earnings of individual farmers?

With a price-inelastic world demand and supply for primaries, shifts in either curve will lead to substantial fluctuations in world prices. The problem is most serious for countries that rely on just one or two primary products, such as Ghana, which relies on cocoa, and the Congo, which relies on copper. Diversification into other primaries would help to reduce their exposure.

Approach 2: Import-substituting industrialisation (ISI)

Dissatisfaction with relying on primary exporting has led most countries to embark on a process of industrialisation. The newly industrialised countries (NICs), such as China, Malaysia, Brazil and India, are already well advanced along the industrialisation road. Other developing countries have not yet progressed very far, especially the poorest African countries.

The most obvious way for countries to industrialise was to cut back on the imports of manufactures and substitute them with home-produced manufactures. This could not be done overnight: it had to be done in stages, beginning with assembly, then making some of the components, and finally making all, or nearly all, of the inputs into production. Most developing countries have at least started on the

---

A case of import substitution in Brazil

Two major changes in world trade hit Brazil in the 1970s. The first was the fourfold increase in world oil prices. Brazil has very little oil of its own. The second was the slump in the world sugar cane market as a result of northern countries' protection of their sugar beet industries. Brazil was a major cane sugar exporter.

Faced with a resulting large increase in its import bill and a slump in its sugar exports, the Brazilian government came up with an ingenious solution. It could use surplus sugar cane to make alcohol, which could then be used instead of petrol for cars. Farmers were given subsidies to grown sugar cane.

Large distilleries were set up to convert the sugar cane into alcohol. At the same time, cars were produced (e.g. VW Beetles) that could run on alcohol (ethanol) rather than petrol.

Thus by one measure two problems were alleviated. By 1985, more than 90 per cent of cars produced in Brazil were designed to burn alcohol.

Then, with the decline in oil prices from the mid 1980s, the relative cost-efficiency of alcohol-powered cars declined: at times it was cheaper to import oil than to produce alcohol. The government cut subsidies and by 1997 less than 1 per cent of cars produced in Brazil were alcohol-powered.

The story illustrates the danger of basing major schemes on terms of trade existing at a particular time. If these terms of trade subsequently change, the schemes could prove to be uneconomical.

A new dawn for the biofuels industry

A more flexible solution was found in 2003 with the introduction of dual-fuel cars that could run on either alcohol or petrol or a mixture of the two. This gave consumers the chance of using whichever fuel was the cheapest at the time. The popularity of these 'flexi-fuel' cars has given a much-welcomed boost to the sugar cane and ethanol industries. By 2005, 54 per cent of Brazilian cars were dual-fuel, and by 2008 the figure was over 90 per cent.

Although subsidies to the ethanol industry have been abolished, the industry is now well able to survive without. With oil prices over $50 per barrel, ethanol can be produced at half of the cost of petrol.

The environmental benefits of renewable sources of fuel which do not displace food production or the rainforest are clear. However, the conditions for sugar cane workers are some of the toughest in the world.

Given the success of the alcohol programme and the huge savings in oil imports, Brazil has now embarked on another import-substituting drive: to displace diesel fuel with fuel produced from soybeans. Perhaps this 'biodiesel' will become the new dollar saver. But soya-based biodiesel can have very damaging effects on the environment. It is far less energy-efficient than sugar cane as a source of fuel and it absorbs less carbon per hectare as it grows. In fact, given that rainforest is being cleared to grow soya, the net effect is to reduce carbon capture substantially.

 Could a case be made out for a flexible tax on oil imports to ensure that it was always profitable to produce alcohol?

---

first stage. Several of the more advanced developing countries have component-manufacturing industries. Only a few of the larger NICs, such as China, India, Brazil and South Korea, have built extensive capital goods industries.

The method most favoured by policy makers has been *tariff escalation*. Here tariff rates (or other restrictions) increase as one moves from the raw materials to the intermediate product to the finished product stage. Thus finished goods have higher tariffs than intermediate products. This encourages assembly plants, which are protected by high tariffs from imported finished products, and are able to obtain components at a lower tariff rate.

Definition

Tariff escalation The system whereby tariff rates increase the closer a product is to the finished stage of production.

One of the problems with ISI is that countries are desperately short of resources to invest in industry. As a result, a policy of ISI has usually involved encouraging investment by multinational companies. But even without specific 'perks' (e.g. tax concessions, cheap sites, the cutting of red tape), multinationals will still probably be attracted by the protection afforded by the tariffs or quotas.

Adverse effects of import substitution

Some countries, such as South Korea and Taiwan, pursued an inward-looking ISI policy for only a few years. For them it was merely a stage in development, rapidly to be followed by a secondary outward-looking policy. Infant industries were initially given protection, but when they had achieved sufficient economies of scale, the barriers to imports were gradually removed.

The countries that have continued to pursue protectionist ISI policies have generally had a poorer growth record. They have also tended to suffer from other problems, such as a deepening of inequality. The development of the modern industrial sector has often been to the detriment of the traditional sectors and also to the export sector.

The criticisms of ISI are numerous, and include the following.

It has run directly counter to the principle of comparative advantage. Rather than confining ISI to genuine infant industries and then gradually removing the protection, ISI has been applied indiscriminately to a whole range of industries. Countries end up producing goods in which they have a comparative *disadvantage*.

 If a country specialises in a good in which it has a comparative disadvantage, where will it be consuming with respect to its production possibility curve?

 KI 20
p164

It has cushioned inefficient practices and encouraged the establishment of monopolies. Without competition from imports, many of the industries are highly inefficient and wasteful of resources. What is more, in all but the largest or most developed of the developing countries the domestic market for manufactures is small. If a newly established industry is to be large enough to gain the full potential economies of scale, it must be large relative to the market. This means that it will have considerable monopoly power.

It has involved artificially low real interest rates. To encourage capital investment in the import-substituting industries, governments have often intervened to keep interest rates low. This has encouraged the use of capital-intensive technology with a consequent lack of jobs. It has also starved other sectors (such as agriculture) of much-needed finance, and it has discouraged saving.

It has led to urban wages above the market-clearing level. Wage rates in the industrial sector, although still low compared with advanced countries, are often considerably higher than in the traditional sectors.

- They are pushed up by firms seeking to retain labour in which they have invested training.
- Governments, seeking to appease the politically powerful urban industrial working class, have often passed minimum wage laws.
- Trade unions, although less widespread in developing than in advanced countries, are mainly confined to the new industries.

Higher industrial wages again encourage firms to use capital-intensive techniques.

It has involved overvalued exchange rates. Restricting imports tends to lead to an appreciation of the exchange rate. This makes non-restricted imports cheaper. This then discourages the production of domestic goods, such as food and component parts, which compete with those imports. Also, a higher exchange rate discourages exports. Exports tend to be priced in dollars. If the exchange rate appreciates, domestic currency will buy more dollars; or put another way, a dollar will exchange for less domestic currency. Thus exporters will earn less domestic currency as the exchange rate appreciates.

 Why is an overvalued exchange rate likely to encourage the use of capital-intensive technology?

It does not necessarily save on foreign exchange. Many of the new industries are highly dependent on the importation of raw materials, capital equipment and component parts. These imported inputs, unlike imports of finished goods, are often supplied by a single firm, which can thus charge monopoly prices. What is more, a large proportion of the extra incomes generated by these industries tends to be spent on imports by the new urban elites.

Protection has not been applied evenly. Many different tariff rates have often been used in one country: in fact, a policy of tariff escalation demands this. In addition, governments have often used a whole range of other protectionist instruments, such as the licensing of importers, physical and value quotas, and foreign exchange rationing. The result is that protection has been highly uneven.

Economists have developed the concept of *effective protection* to measure the true degree of protection that an industry gets. Effective protection measures the extra domestic value added that protection gives an industry. By *domestic value added* we mean the difference between the world market price of the finished good and the cost of the imported inputs used to make the good.

The effective rate of protection is given by the formula

$$\frac{V^* - V}{V} \times 100$$

where V is the free-trade domestic value added, and V^* is the value added after the imposition of tariffs. There are three variables that determine the rate of effective protection:

- The tariff rate on the finished good (the nominal rate of protection). The higher this is, the higher will be the value of V^* relative to V, and hence the higher will be the effective rate of protection.
- The tariff rate (or rates) on the inputs. The higher these are, the lower will be the value of V^* relative to V, and hence the lower will be the effective rate of protection.

Definition

Effective rate of protection The percentage increase in an industry's domestic value added resulting from protection given to that industry.

- The level of value added as a proportion of the price of the finished good. The higher this is, the lower will be the effective rate of protection (assuming tariff escalation).

 To demonstrate this last point, work out the effective rate of protection in the following three cases:
(a) Free-trade finished good price = £100; free-trade cost of imported inputs = £40.
(b) Free-trade finished good price = £100; free-trade cost of imported inputs = £80.
(c) Free-trade finished good price = £100; free-trade cost of imported inputs = £100.
In each case, assume that a 50 per cent tariff is imposed on the finished good and a 10 per cent tariff on the imported inputs.

In many countries, effective protective rates have varied massively from one industry to another. For example, according to World Bank estimates, in 1980 effective rates of protection in manufacturing ranged from –85 per cent to 219 per cent in Brazil and from –62 per cent to 1119 per cent in Nigeria! Clearly, such huge differences in effective protection imposed massive distortions on the market.

 Under what circumstances could the effective rate of protection be negative?

 Income distribution is made less equal. Additional incomes generated by the modern sector tend to be spent on modern-sector goods and imported goods. Thus there is a multiplier effect *within* the modern sector, but virtually none between the sectors. Also, as we saw above, an over-valued exchange rate leads to a bias against agriculture, and thus further deepens the divide between rich and poor. Finally, the relatively high wages of the modern sector encourage workers to migrate to the towns, where many, failing to get a job, live in dire poverty.

Social, cultural and environmental costs. A policy of ISI often involves imposing an alien set of values. Urban life can be harsh, competitive and materialistic. Moreover, the drive for industrialisation may involve major costs to the environment, as a result of waste products from new industries.

Finally, import substitution is necessarily limited by the size of the domestic market. Once that is saturated, ISI can come to an abrupt halt. At that stage, further expansion can come only from exporting; but if these industries have been overprotected, they will be unable to compete in world markets.

This has been a long list of problems and different economists put different emphases on them. Neoclassical economists stress the problems of market distortions, arguing that ISI leads to great inefficiency. Neo-Marxist economists, on the other hand, stress the problems of *dependency*. Many of the new industries will be owned by multinational companies, which import unsuitable technologies. The countries will then become dependent on imported inputs and foreign sources of capital. (See Case Study 27.2 in MyEconLab.)

Approach 3: Exporting manufactures – a possible way forward?

The countries with the highest rates of economic growth are those that have successfully made the transition to being exporters of manufactures. Table 27.3 gives some examples.

The transition from inward-looking to outward-looking industrialisation

How is a country to move from import substituting to being outward-looking? One approach is to take it industry

> **Definition**
>
> **Dependency** Where the development of a developing country is hampered by its relationships with the industrialised world.

Table 27.3 Growth rates and export performance of selected secondary outward-looking countries

	Average annual growth in real GDP (%)		Share of manufactures in merchandise exports (%)		Average annual growth rate of merchandise exports (%)	
	1960–90	**1991–2009**	**1970**	**2006**	**1960–90**	**1991–2008**
Brazil	5.5	3.0	13	51	14.1	8.0
Malaysia	6.8	6.2	7	74	13.4	10.0
South Korea	8.4	5.4	77	93	30.4	13.9
Singapore	9.2	6.4	28	80	16.3	7.4
Hong Kong	7.9	4.4	96	91	18.3	8.8
China	8.1	10.2	35	92	13.4	17.9
All developing countries	4.3	4.9	27	60	13.6	8.7

Sources: Data drawn from *World Development Indicators 2005* (World Bank, 2005); *UNCTAD Handbook of Statistics 2008* (United Nations Conference on Trade and Development, 2008).

by industry. When an industry has saturated the home market and there is no further scope for import substitution, it should then be encouraged to seek markets overseas. The trouble with this approach is that, if the country is still protecting other industries, there will probably still be an overvalued exchange rate. Thus specific subsidies, tax concessions or other 'perks' would have to be given to this industry to enable it to compete. The country would still be highly interventionist, with all the distortions and misallocation of resources that this tends to bring.

The alternative is to wean the whole economy off protection. Three major things will need doing. There will need to be a devaluation of the currency in order to restore the potential profitability of the export sector. There will also need to be a dismantling of the various protective measures that had biased production towards the home market. Finally, there will probably need to be a removal or relaxing of price controls. But these are things that cannot be done 'at a stroke'. Firms may have to be introduced gradually to the greater forces of competition that an outward-looking trade policy brings. Otherwise there may be massive bankruptcies and a corresponding massive rise in unemployment.

The benefits from a secondary outward-looking policy

The advocates of outward-looking industrialisation make a number of points in its favour.

It conforms more closely to comparative advantage. Countries pursuing an open trade regime will be able to export only goods in which they have a comparative advantage. The resources used in earning a unit of foreign exchange from exports will be less than those used in saving a unit of foreign exchange by replacing imports with home-produced goods. In other words, resources will be used more efficiently.

Economies of scale. If the home market is too small to allow a firm to gain all the potential economies of scale, these can be gained by expanding into the export market.

Increased competition. By having to compete with foreign companies, exporters will be under a greater competitive pressure than industries shielded behind protective barriers. This will encourage (a) resource saving in the short run, both through their better *allocation* and through reductions in X inefficiency (see Box 6.5), and (b) innovation and investment, as firms attempt to adopt the latest technology, often obtained from developed countries.

Increased investment. To the extent that outward-looking policies lead to a greater potential for economic growth, they may attract more foreign capital. To the extent that they involve an increase in interest rates, they will tend to encourage saving. To the extent that they lead to increased incomes, additional saving will be generated, especially given that the *marginal* propensity to save may be quite high. The extra savings can be used to finance extra investment.

It can lead to more employment and a more equal distribution of income. According to the Heckscher–Ohlin theory, the manufactured goods in which a country will have a comparative advantage are those produced by labour-intensive techniques. Export expansion will thus increase the demand for labour relative to capital, and create more employment. The increased demand for labour will tend to lead to a rise in wages relative to profits.

 Will the adoption of labour-intensive techniques necessarily lead to a more equal distribution of income?

It removes many of the costs associated with ISI. Under a policy of ISI, managers may spend a lot of their time lobbying politicians and officials, seeking licences (and sometimes paying bribes to obtain them), adhering to norms and regulations or trying to find ways round them. If an outward-looking policy involves removing all this, managers can turn their attention to producing goods more efficiently.

Drawbacks of an export-orientated industrialisation strategy

The export of manufactures is seen by many developed countries as very threatening to their own industries. Their response has often been to erect trade barriers. These barriers have tended to be highest in the very industries (such as textiles, footwear and processed food) where developing countries have the greatest comparative advantage. Even if the barriers are *currently* low, developing countries may feel that it is too risky to expand their exports of these products for fear of a future rise in barriers. Recognising this problem, the World Trade Organisation is very keen to ensure fair access for developing countries to the markets of the rich world (see Box 24.7 on pages 690–1).

 Consider the arguments from the perspective of an advanced country for and against protecting its industries from imports of manufactures from developing countries.

The successes of developing countries such as China, Malaysia and South Korea in exporting manufactures do not imply that other developing countries will have similar success. As additional developing countries attempt to export their manufactures, they will be facing more and more competition from each other.

Another problem is that, if a more open trade policy involves removing or reducing exchange and capital controls, the country may become more vulnerable to speculative attack. This was one of the major contributing factors to the east Asian crisis of the late 1990s (see Case Study 27.3

BOX 27.3 **THE CHINESE ECONOMIC MIRACLE**

Riding the dragon

'China is amazing. It is capitalism, but at an unprecedented speed.' 'The talent of Chinese software engineers is unbelievable. I can't believe how effective they are.' (Bill Gates, Chairman, Microsoft)

'If your business isn't making money in China, it probably wouldn't make money anywhere else.' (Carlos Ghosn, President, Nissan Motor Company)[1]

On the basis of several indicators, China's economic performance is extraordinary. From 1990 to 2008 annual economic growth averaged 9.9 per cent. Its exports grew by an average of 19.5 per cent (see chart). In 2007 it overtook the USA to become the world's second largest exporter (after Germany; see Figure 24.1 on page 672). In PPP terms, China is the world's second biggest economy after the USA, or third if the eurozone is taken as a single economy.

And as China's economy and exports have boomed, so foreign investment has flooded into the country. In 1990 foreign direct investment (FDI) into China was $3.5 billion. By 2007 the figure had risen to $71.8 billion.

Chinese export-orientated growth has been based on three key factors: specialising in goods in which it has a comparative advantage; having an economy that is favourable to both domestic and inward investment; and having an exchange rate that is undervalued in PPP terms.

Specialisation

China has been industrialising rapidly. With the huge size of the domestic market and with an open policy towards exporting, China has specialised in goods that exploit its diverse but relatively well-trained labour force. Huge industrial complexes have sprung up along the coast from which it is easy to export.

Chinese firms have adapted to changing world markets and to their own changing comparative advantage. Twenty years ago, textiles and clothing were China's main export industry. These relatively labour-intensive industries were ideally suited to exploit the abilities of China's abundant labour. Today textiles and clothing account for a sixth of China's exports. Electronic goods, by contrast, account for more than a third and are growing at a rate three times as fast as textiles. Electronic goods exploit China's increasingly well-trained and well-educated workforce.

Investment

But why are foreign investors attracted to China? Is it simply that the economy is growing rapidly? Clearly that is part of the attraction, but it is more than that. For a start, the Chinese economy is huge. With a population of 1.33 billion and a GDP of $3.9 trillion in 2008, China represents a massive potential market. The government has also

KI 36
p673

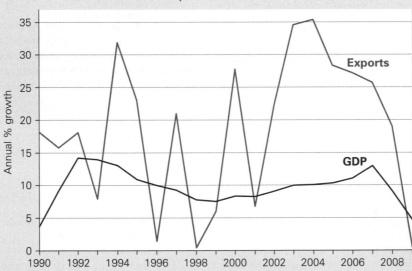

Growth in Chinese export volumes and real GDP (%)

Source: Data drawn from *World Development Indicators* (World Bank); *Asian Development Outlook 2008* (Asian Development Bank, 2008).

invested heavily in improving the country's transport, power and communications infrastructure.

What is more, much of the growth in income in the Chinese economy is concentrated in the hands of the middle class, which now constitutes over 20 per cent of the population and 50 per cent of the urban population. The demand for consumer goods by these middle-class Chinese is very income elastic. As a result, sales of electrical goods, furniture, cars and fashion clothing are growing rapidly. Not only foreign manufacturers, but foreign retailers too are taking advantage of this. For example, Wal-Mart entered China in 1996 and by 2008 had 77 Supercenters in China, sourcing 95 per cent of its merchandise from local suppliers. Carrefour, the French supermarket chain, entered China in 1995 and by 2008 had 118 stores.

But foreign investors are not only attracted by the growing domestic Chinese market. They are also attracted by the opportunity to manufacture high-tech products with a highly skilled workforce.

More and more companies become cutting edge and leapfrog foreign rivals. Whether games consoles, DVD recorders or flat-screen monitors, Chinese factories are grabbing high-tech market share.

'Ten years ago, China was about low cost,' says Infineon's Ulrich Schumacher. 'Now it is at the forefront of technical development. Infineon can develop twice as fast in China as anywhere else.'

'Engineers are working in three shifts, seven days a week,' enthuses Mr Schumacher. 'In Germany that would not be possible: there, engineers don't work on weekends.'

Bill Gates is similarly impressed after his latest visit to Microsoft's research lab in Beijing, one of four in China and Hong Kong. 'The talent of the people there is unbelievable, I can't believe how effective they are,' he says.

All this is worrying news for high-tech workers in industrialised countries, who hoped their skills would give them a competitive advantage in the globalised economy.[2]

An undervalued exchange rate

Despite the booming economy and export sector, and a massive current account surplus against the USA ($162 billion in 2004), the Chinese yuan remained pegged to the US dollar at $1 = 8.28 yuan from 1995 to 2005. This undervaluation of the yuan against the dollar was a major contributing factor in the growth in Chinese exports.

The situation had become even more extreme with other countries. With the fall in the dollar in 2003/4

against the euro yen and sterling, the dollar-pegged yuan thus also fell against these currencies. This made Chinese exports even cheaper in Europe and east Asia, further fuelling the trade imbalance.

The USA for some time had been pressing for a revaluation of the yuan or a floating of the yuan so that it could appreciate. Indeed, in 2005 the US Senate was pushing the Bush administration to adopt a 27.5 per cent tariff on all Chinese imports unless China revalued its currency.

China eventually, in 2005, moved to a pegged exchange rate with a basket of eleven currencies, each currency being weighted in the basket by the amount of trade with China. It also revalued the yuan by 2.1 per cent.

Since then the yuan has appreciated and by 2008 was exchanging at $1 = 6.86 yuan. But it was still considerably undervalued in PPP terms, giving China a strong competitive edge against other developing countries seeking export-led growth. The effect has been a huge current account surplus, running at some 11 per cent of GDP in 2007. This has resulted in massive Chinese purchases of dollars and other currencies. By 2008 China had $1.8 trillion in foreign exchange reserves. The inflows have also allowed China to purchase stakes in many American and European companies and to make substantial investments in various developing countries.

Another issue facing the Chinese authorities is the perceived overheating of the economy. With worries about rising inflation and investment considerably outstripping consumption, the concern is that the boom is becoming unsustainable. The problem is exacerbated by the undervalued yuan. As finance flows into China, this puts upward pressure on the Chinese money supply.

If interest rates are raised or controls on investment tightened, this could cause the investment bubble to burst. The resulting slowing of the economy could then become excessive and lead to a decline in FDI. This could then send shock waves around the world economy, as did the south-east Asian crisis in 1997/8 (see Case Studies 26.3, 26.4 and 27.3 in MyEconLab). The task, then, is how to achieve a slight slowdown in growth to sustainable levels without triggering a crash.

1. *In what ways does a booming Chinese economy benefit the rest of the world?*
2. *Why may the Chinese be reluctant to adopt a freely floating exchange rate?*

[1] 'Is China a goldmine or minefield?', BBC News Online, 19 February 2004 (http://news.bbc.co.uk/1/hi/business/3494069.stm).
[2] *Ibid.*

in MyEonLab). Gripped by currency and stock market speculation, and by banking and company insolvency, many countries of the region found that economic growth had turned into a major recession. The 'miracle' seemed to be over. Nevertheless, the countries with the fewest distortions fared the best during the crisis. Thus Singapore and Taiwan, which are open and relatively flexible, experienced only a slowdown, rather than a recession.

Exporting manufactures may thus be a very risky strategy for the least developed countries, such as many in Africa. Perhaps the best hope for the future may be for a growth in manufacturing trade *between* such developing countries. That way they can gain the benefits of specialisation and economies of scale that trade brings, while at the same time producing for a growing market. The feasibility of this approach depends on whether developing countries can agree to free-trade areas or even customs unions between themselves (see section 24.3). There does, however, seem to be a strong movement in this direction (see page 696).

Section summary

1. Trade is of vital importance for the vast majority of developing countries, and yet most developing countries suffer from chronic balance of trade deficits.

2. Developing countries have traditionally been primary exporters. This has allowed them to exploit their comparative advantage in labour-intensive goods and has provided a market for certain goods that would otherwise have no market at home.

3. However, with a low income elasticity of demand for primary products in developed countries, with the development of synthetic substitutes and with the protection of agriculture in Europe and the USA, the demand for primary exports has, until recent years, grown only slowly. At the same time, the demand for manufactured imports into developing countries has grown rapidly. The result has been a worsening balance of trade problem; and with a price-inelastic demand for both imports and exports, the terms of trade worsened too. There is also the danger that comparative costs may change over time; that most of the benefits from primary exports may accrue to foreign owners of mines and plantations, or to wealthy elites in the domestic population; that mines and plantations can involve substantial environmental and other external costs; and that export earnings can fluctuate, given instabilities in supply and unstable world prices.

4. Import-substituting industrialisation was seen to be the answer to these problems. This was normally achieved in stages, beginning with the finished goods stage and then working back towards the capital goods stage. ISI, it was hoped, would allow countries to benefit from the various dynamic advantages associated with manufacturing.

5. For many countries, however, ISI brought as many, if not more, problems than it solved. It often led to the establishment of inefficient industries, protected from foreign competition and facing little or no competition at home either. It led to considerable market distortions, with tariffs and other forms of protection haphazardly applied and with resulting huge variations in effective rates of protection; to overvalued exchange rates with a resulting bias against exports and the agricultural sector generally; to a deepening of inequalities and to large-scale social and environmental problems as the cities expanded and as poverty and unemployment grew. Finally, the balance of payments was in many cases made worse as the new industries became increasingly dependent on imported inputs and as growing urbanisation caused a growing demand for imported consumer goods.

6. The most rapidly growing of the developing countries are those that have pursued a policy of export-orientated industrialisation. This has allowed them to achieve the benefits of economies of scale and foreign competition. It has allowed them to specialise in goods in which they have a comparative advantage (i.e. labour-intensive goods) and yet which have a relatively high income elasticity of demand. Whether countries that have pursued ISI can successfully turn to an open, export-orientated approach depends to a large extent on the degree of competition they face, not only from rich countries, but also from other developing countries.

27.3 STRUCTURAL PROBLEMS WITHIN DEVELOPING COUNTRIES

The neglect of agriculture

The drive to industrialise by many developing countries has often been highly damaging to agriculture, especially in the poorest countries such as those of sub-Saharan Africa. With a backward and run-down agricultural sector, with little or no rural infrastructure, many countries today face a food crisis of immense proportions. Harrowing scenes of famine and death from countries like Ethiopia and the Sudan have become all too familiar.

Over the years, opinions have gradually changed. It is now realised that the relief of poverty, unemployment and the maldistribution of income can best be achieved by improving productivity and incomes in the rural sector.

No longer is agriculture seen as a sector to be 'squeezed' like an orange. Rather it is seen as a sector that must be developed in harmony with the urban sector. Agricultural output must be increased for the benefit of rural and urban dwellers alike. At the same time, industrial output can be given new markets in the rural sector if rural incomes expand. The following are some of the possible ways forward.

Price reform. The price of food needs to be raised relative to the price of industrial goods. This may be achieved simply through the reduction of protection of manufactured products. Higher relative food prices increase the profitability of agricultural production and enable farmers to afford to invest in irrigation, agricultural implements, land improvement, etc.

A particular problem has come from cheap subsidised food 'dumped' on the markets of developing countries by the EU and the USA. A substantial reduction in such subsidies was one of the major demands by developing countries in the Doha round of trade negotiations (see Box 24.7 on pages 690–1).

Rising world food prices in recent years have provided much-needed help for farmers who make a living selling food. But they have worsened the plight of city dwellers, who naturally demand lower prices. In most developing countries only a minority of households sell more food than they buy.

Devaluation. If the currency is devalued, or allowed to depreciate, this increases the price of food imports and thus makes it easier for domestic food producers to compete. It also increases the profitability of food exports.

Government support for rural infrastructure projects. If food is to be marketed, there must be adequate rural infrastructure. Government road-building schemes and the setting-up of marketing boards can make a dramatic difference to the viability of commercial food production.

The provision of finance. Farmers need access to cheap finance and not to be forced to borrow at sky-high interest rates from local moneylenders. This can be achieved by setting up rural banks specialising in the provision of finance to small farmers. These could be nationalised institutions, or the government could give incentives to private banks to expand into the rural sector.

The adoption of new technologies and practices. There have been rapid advances in agricultural technology in recent years. The development of new fertilisers, pesticides, simple but effective agricultural machinery, and most of all of new high-yielding strains of grain, especially wheat and rice, have helped to transform traditional agriculture in certain developing countries such as India. There has been a *Green Revolution*, hastened in recent years by the production of genetically modified strains of crops.

Other countries, however, and especially those of sub-Saharan Africa, have made little progress in adopting these technologies. This is due partly to an inability to afford the new equipment, chemicals and seeds, partly to the lack of infrastructure to make them available, and partly to their unsuitability to the generally more arid African conditions. When the technologies are adopted, it is often only by large multinationals operating in plantations. For example, companies like Monsanto have been the main developers and users of genetically modified crops.

Governments can help by funding research into the best farming methods and inputs for local conditions. They can also help by providing finance for the adoption of the new methods.

Education and advice. Many farmers are simply unaware of new more efficient farming methods. Training schemes or rural advisers can help here.

Land reform. As population grows, land holdings are divided and subdivided as they are passed from generation to generation. Thus many farmers operate on tiny plots of land that can never yield an adequate income. Increasingly, they get into debt and are forced to mortgage their land to large landowners at high interest rates, or to sell it to them at low prices. The number of landless labourers or farmers in 'debt bondage' therefore grows.

A solution to this problem is the redistribution of land. Clearly, this cannot be done unless there is a government sympathetic to the rural poor and willing to take on the inevitable opposition from the large farmers. Often these large farmers are politically powerful and have the police on their side.

Two of the most successful newly industrialised countries, Taiwan and South Korea, despite having right-wing governments at the time, underwent a radical redistribution of land from rich to poor in the late 1940s and early 1950s. In both countries, the growth of the agricultural sector has been rapid and yet continues to be egalitarian, based as it is on small, but not tiny, peasant holdings. In both countries extreme rural poverty has been virtually eliminated.

The encouragement of rural co-operatives. If small farmers get together and form co-operatives, they may be able to afford to share agricultural equipment such as tractors and harvesters, and undertake irrigation schemes; they may be able to set up input-purchasing and crop-marketing and distribution organisations, and gain easier access to credit. In many countries, national or local governments have actively encouraged such co-operatives by providing subsidies, tax incentives and advice, and by passing favourable legislation.

Inappropriate technology

The technology employed in a country depends on the type of development strategy it is pursuing. Some strategies lead to the adoption of relatively labour-intensive technologies, others to relatively capital-intensive ones.

Neoclassical theory suggests that countries should use techniques that are intensive in their abundant factor. This is simply an extension of the Heckscher–Ohlin theory, only this time it is applied to the choice of techniques rather than to the choice of goods. The theory implies that (labour-abundant) developing countries should adopt labour-intensive techniques; techniques that use relatively more of the cheap factor (labour) and relatively less of the expensive factor (capital).

With the advent of policies of industrialisation, however, came strong arguments for adopting capital-intensive technology. Capital-intensive technologies were seen to be more advanced. These were the technologies that were developed in rich countries, countries with sophisticated research facilities. The argument here was that, despite having a higher capital/labour ratio, these techniques nevertheless had a low capital/output ratio. The equipment might be expensive, but it would yield a very high output and would thus cost less *per unit* of output.

If a modern capital-intensive technique has a higher capital/labour ratio and a lower capital/output ratio than a traditional labour-intensive one, what can we say about its labour/output ratio relative to the traditional technique?

A second argument was that, if multinationals were to be encouraged to invest in developing countries, they had to be allowed to bring with them their own technology – technology that was almost invariably capital-intensive. In other words, the choice was not between more labour-intensive and more capital-intensive techniques, but rather between having *extra* capital (by allowing multinationals to invest) and not having it at all.

A final argument in favour of capital-intensive technology was that it provides a greater level of profit, and that this profit will then be reinvested, thereby causing a faster rate of economic growth.

Given these arguments, many governments of developing countries actively encouraged the use of capital-intensive techniques; some still do. But also there were other features of ISI that unintentionally led to biases in favour of capital-intensive technology. These included the following:

- Wage rates above the market-clearing level, driven up by minimum wage legislation, trade union activity, or firms trying to ensure that workers they had trained were not 'poached' by other firms.
- Low interest rates to encourage investment. The effect of this, plus relatively high wage rates in the expanding industries, is to encourage the substitution of capital for labour.
- An overvalued exchange rate. This lowers the relative price of imported inputs, which under a policy of tariff

escalation have low tariffs. This encourages the use of import-intensive technology, which also tends to be capital-intensive.
- The ignorance of many multinational companies of alternative efficient labour-intensive technology.
- The bias of engineers. It is engineers rather than economists who are often instrumental in deciding which production techniques a firm will use. Engineers tend to be biased in favour of mechanically efficient techniques, which tend to be capital-intensive, rather than economically efficient techniques, which may well be labour-intensive.

What is the difference between mechanical efficiency and economic efficiency?

In recent years, with the criticism of ISI has come the criticism of capital-intensive technologies.

- Capital-intensive equipment may require more maintenance.
- It may have to be imported, and may use a high proportion of imported inputs. This will put a strain on the country's balance of trade. If less domestic inputs are used, there will be less spread effect to other sectors of the economy: there will be a smaller multiplier effect.
- There may be problems of hold-ups, breakdowns and incorrect usage due to problems in obtaining parts and an absence of properly trained maintenance staff.
- Even if the technologies do generate higher profits, there is no guarantee that these will be reinvested. They may simply flow abroad to foreign shareholders, or be spent largely on luxury consumption if the profits initially stay within the country (and a high proportion of luxury goods are imported anyway).
- Capital-intensive techniques often involve large-scale production. There have been many examples of countries opening up plants that are simply too large relative to the market. As a result, they never operate at full capacity, and thus may operate inefficiently.

In addition, capital-intensive technologies have other detrimental effects. As we shall see shortly, they worsen the unemployment problem. Also, as they are large-scale technologies, the firms using them usually locate in the cities. This tends to worsen the problem of **dualism**. Inequality between urban and rural incomes tends to grow; and with

> ### Definition
>
> **Dualism** The division of an economy into a modern (usually urban) sector and a poor traditional (usually rural) sector.

relatively few workers being employed in these industries at relatively high wages, the gap between their wages and those of the urban poor tends to grow also.

The concentration of large-scale plants in cities can cause severe problems of pollution, especially if the government is not very strict in enforcing pollution control.

 Why may governments of developing countries be less strict than developed countries in controlling pollution?

So what can be done to encourage a more appropriate technology? Part of the solution lies in correcting market distortions: there will probably need to be a devaluation of the currency and a rise in interest rates. This would remove two of the key factors favouring capital-intensive industry.

Then there will probably also need to be positive encouragement given to the invention or adoption of *efficient* labour-intensive technologies. This could involve government-sponsored research, information centres to provide details of the various techniques used around the world, education and training schemes for managers and workers, the provision of advice on production, marketing, distribution, etc., and incentives for inventions (such as subsidies or patent protection).

The government could help to encourage small businesses (which typically use more labour-intensive techniques) by, for example, setting up development banks that provide services specifically for small businesses (including farms and other rural businesses), and which grant loans at similar rates to those charged to large firms; encouraging the formation of co-operatives through tax concessions or subsidies, or by reducing the amount of red tape such organisations are likely to encounter; and providing small workshops at low or zero rent.

 What difficulties is a government likely to encounter in encouraging the use of labour-intensive technology?

Unemployment

Imagine the choice of living in a large family in the countryside with too little land to be able to feed you and the other family members, or of seeking your fortune in the city where there are nowhere near enough jobs to go round. It is not much of a choice. But it is the sort of choice that millions of people are forced to make. Open unemployment rates in developing countries are generally much higher than in developed countries: rates in excess of 15 per cent are not uncommon.

But even these high rates grossly understate the true extent of the problem. With the system of extended families, where the family farm or the family trade occupies all the family members, people may not be out looking for jobs and are thus not openly unemployed, but their output is nevertheless very low. There is simply not enough work to occupy them fully. This is the problem of *disguised unemployment*. Then there are those who manage to do a few hours' work each week as casual labourers or as petty traders. These people are *underemployed*. When you add the problem of disguised unemployment and underemployment to the problem of open unemployment, the problem becomes overwhelming.

The causes of the unemployment problem are deep-seated and complex, but four stand out as being particularly important in most developing countries.

Rapid population growth

With reductions in mortality rates (due to improved health care) that have not been matched by equivalent reductions in birth rates, populations in most developing countries have grown rapidly for many years now. The labour force has thus grown rapidly too. The growth in production has simply not been fast enough to create enough jobs for these extra workers.

Capital-intensity bias

As we have seen, import-substituting industrialisation has involved a bias in favour of capital-intensive technology. This has led to the production of goods and to the use of processes that provide only limited employment opportunities. As long as the relative price of capital to labour is kept low, or as long as there is a lack of modern efficient *labour-intensive* techniques available, or as long as multinational companies choose to bring in their own (capital-intensive) technology, so there will continue to be a lack of demand for labour.

Rural–urban migration

Throughout the developing world, people flock from the countryside to the towns and thereby swell the numbers of urban unemployed. Migration accounts for some 55 per cent of urban population growth in developing countries. But, if life in the shanty towns is wretched, what is the point? The point is that for most of the migrants there was no chance at all of getting another job in the countryside, whereas in the towns there is at least some chance. If one in five migrants gets a job, then you might be the lucky one.

The decision to migrate thus depends on four main factors:

Definitions

Disguised unemployment Where the same work could be done by fewer people.

Underemployment Where people who want full-time work are only able to find part-time work.

*BOX 27.4 UNEMPLOYMENT IN DEVELOPING COUNTRIES

Three simple models

In this box we will look at three models that have been developed to explain Third World unemployment.

Limited choice of techniques

The simplest version of this model assumes that there is only one technique available to firms and that just two factors of production are involved – labour and capital. Firms will thus face a right-angled isoquant (see section 5.3). This is illustrated in diagram (a).

Each isoquant shows a particular level of output (Q). Given that there is only one choice of technique, involving a particular combination of labour and capital, then for each amount of capital used a particular amount of labour will be needed – no more and no less. Any extra labour will simply be idle.

For example, if each machine required one operative and if ten machines were available, then ten operatives would be required. An eleventh would add nothing to output. Similarly, if there were ten operatives available, an eleventh machine would be idle.

If, in diagram (a), the total supply of capital were $\bar{K}$, then firms would require L_1 of labour. But if the total labour force were $\bar{L}$, then $\bar{L} - L_1$ workers would be unemployed.

Thus the lack of availability of labour-intensive techniques means that there is not enough capital to employ everyone.

Capital-intensity bias

This model assumes that there are labour-intensive techniques available, but that firms choose not to

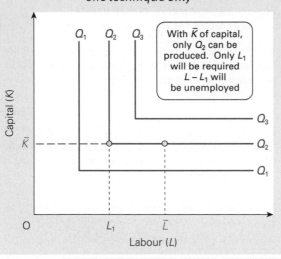

(a) *Limited choice of techniques:
one technique only*

With $\bar{K}$ of capital, only Q_2 can be produced. Only L_1 will be required $L - L_1$ will be unemployed

(b) *Capital intensity bias*

With a lower relative price of capital (given by slope of line CD) or a bias in favour of capital-intensive techniques, less labour will be employed (L_1) and output will be lower (Q_2)

- The income differential between the countryside and the town. The more that jobs in the town pay relative to what the migrant could earn by staying behind, the more the person is likely to migrate. If their decision was to be totally rational, they would also take into account the differences in the cost of living between the two areas.
- The chance of getting a job. The higher the rate of urban unemployment, the less the chance of getting a job and thus the less likely the person is to migrate.
- The 'risk attitude' of the person: in other words, how willing potential migrants are to take the gamble of whether or not they will get a job.
- The degree of misinformation. People may migrate to the towns, attracted by the 'bright lights' of the city and

the belief (probably misplaced) that their prospects are much better there.

What would be the effect on the levels of migration and urban unemployment of the creation of jobs in the towns?

External influences

Most developing countries are highly dependent on international economic forces. If the world economy goes into recession, or world interest rates rise, or protectionist policies are pursued by developed countries, this will have a damaging effect on industry in developing countries. Their exports will fall and unemployment will rise.

use them. Assuming again that there are just the two factors, labour and capital, this time firms will face curved isoquants. In other words, the firm can choose to combine labour and capital in any proportions it chooses. This is illustrated in diagram (b).

Assume that the total supplies of capital and labour are $\bar{K}$ and $\bar{L}$ respectively. With a price ratio given by the slope of the isocost AB, the factor market will clear. All capital and all labour will be employed at point d on isoquant Q_1.

Managers, however, may have a bias in favour of capital-intensive techniques. Alternatively, the price of labour may be above the market-clearing level, or the price of capital may be below the market-clearing level, so that the isocost is steeper than AB (e.g. CD). In either case, if $\bar{K}$ capital is used, less than $\bar{L}$ labour will be employed. With an isocost of CD, only L_1 will be employed. $\bar{L} - L_1$ will be unemployed. There will also be a lower level of output, since production is now on the lower isoquant Q_2.

 If there were three techniques available, what would the isoquant look like? Would it make any difference to the conclusions of this model?

Rural–urban migration

This model assumes that migration depends first on the difference between urban wages (W_u) and rural wages (W_r). The bigger the differential, the more will people wish to migrate. Second, it depends on the likelihood of getting a job. The more likely people are to find a job, the more likely they are to migrate.

These two can be combined in the concept of an expected urban wage (W_u^e). This is the actual average urban wage multiplied by the probability of getting a job. Thus if the average wage were £40 per week,

and if there were a 50 per cent chance of getting a job, the expected urban wage would be £20. If the chance were only 25 per cent, the expected wage would be only £10, and so on. This can be expressed formally as

$$W_u^e = W_u \cdot L_m / L_u$$

where L_m is the total number of workers employed in the urban sector and L_u is the total labour supply (employed and unemployed). Thus L_m/L_u is the employment rate, which can be taken as an indication of the probability of getting a job.

So when will rural workers migrate to the towns? According to the model this will occur when

$$W_u^e > (W_r + \alpha)$$

where α is a term representing the costs of migration. In other words, people will migrate when, after taking the cost of migrating into account, they can expect to earn more in the towns than in the countryside.

But as people migrate, W_r will tend to rise as the supply of rural labour falls, and W_u^e will tend to fall as the new arrivals in the towns increase L_u and thus reduce the likelihood of others getting a job. An equilibrium urban unemployment will be reached when

$$W_u^e = W_r + \alpha$$

At that point, migration will stop.

Thus in this model, urban unemployment will be greater (a) the higher is the level of the actual urban wage (W_u), (b) the lower is the level of the rural wage (W_r) and (c) the lower are the costs of migrating (α).

 If more jobs were created in the towns, how, in the rural–urban migration model, would this affect (a) the level of urban unemployment; (b) the rate of urban unemployment?

There is no simple cure for unemployment in developing countries. Nevertheless, there are certain measures that governments can take which will help to reverse its growth:

- The government can encourage the use of more labour-intensive techniques by adopting the sorts of policy outlined earlier.
- It can help to reverse rural–urban migration by reducing the rural 'push'. This will involve policies of encouraging rural development and thereby providing jobs away from the big towns.
- It can provide jobs directly by embarking on labour-intensive infrastructure construction projects. For example, it can employ gangs of workers to build roads or dig irrigation ditches.

- It can adopt policies that help to reduce the rate of population growth: policies such as educational and propaganda programmes to persuade people to have smaller families, measures to raise the economic and social status of women so that they have a freer choice over family size, and policies directed at tackling extreme poverty so that the very poor do not feel the need to have a large family as an insurance that they will be supported in their old age.

 1. *Is there any potential conflict between the goals of maximising economic growth and maximising either (a) the level of employment or (b) the rate of growth of employment?*
2. *What is the relationship between unemployment and (a) poverty; (b) inequality?*

| BOX 27.5 | THE BUILDING BRICS OF DEVELOPMENT | CASE STUDIES AND APPLICATIONS |

The importance of infrastructure development for emerging economies

A key supply-side constraint on development is poor quality transport, communications and power infrastructure. The most rapidly growing emerging economies have recognised this and have invested heavily in construction, whether through state investment or by encouraging private construction projects.

Infrastructure investment now accounts for a higher proportion of world GDP than at any time in history and over half of such investment is taking place in emerging countries. Some 74 per cent of this is in the four large emerging countries – Brazil, Russia, India and China, the so-called BRICs. According to forecasts by Morgan Stanley, over the period from 2008 to 2017 total infrastructure investment in the BRICs will be some $15.4 trillion (see chart).

Infrastructure investment can yield big economic gains. Building roads or railways immediately boosts output and jobs, but it also helps to spur future growth – provided the money is spent wisely. Better transport helps farmers to get their produce to cities, and manufacturers to export their goods overseas. Countries with the lowest transport costs tend to be more open to foreign trade and so enjoy faster growth. Clean water and sanitation also raise the quality of human capital, thereby lifting labour productivity. The World Bank estimates that a 1% increase in a country's infrastructure stock is associated with a 1% increase in the level of GDP. Other studies have concluded that East Asia's much higher investment in infrastructure explains a large part of its faster growth than Latin America.[1]

What is more, there is a process of cumulative causation between consumption and infrastructure investment. Infrastructure construction boosts incomes and employment. But as people get richer and as more live in towns, so they demand better facilities, such as sealed roads, running water, sanitation, electricity, a good phone network and access to the Internet. All this stimulates the production of these facilities, whether through market forces or through political pressure for public provision.

Forecast infrastructure investment, 2008–17 ($ trillions)

- $1.1tr — Brazil
- $2.2tr — Russia
- $2.8tr — India
- $9.3tr — China
- $2.4tr — Other Asia
- $0.9tr — Middle East
- $3.1tr — Other emerging economies
- Total $21.7tr

 Why might an outward-looking economy experience higher infrastructure investment than an inward-looking one?

Source: Forecast by Morgan Stanley in *The Economist*, 5 June 2008.

[1] 'Economics focus', *The Economist*, 5 June 2008.

Section summary

1. The urban/industrial bias of many development programmes has led to the neglect of agriculture. The effect has been a deepening of rural poverty and a growing inability of the rural sector to feed the towns. Policies to reverse this trend include the raising of food prices, devaluation of the currency, government support for rural infrastructure projects, the provision of lower-interest finance to the rural sector, encouragement for the adoption of new labour-intensive techniques in farming and the use of new high-yielding seeds, land reform and the setting-up of rural co-operatives.

2. Development programmes have often encouraged the use of capital-intensive technology through policies of low interest rates, relatively high urban wages, an overvalued exchange rate or encouraging investment by multinational companies. These capital-intensive technologies were often seen as advantageous in that they yielded higher profits and thus more surplus for reinvestment. Often they were more sophisticated than labour-intensive techniques, and sometimes they had a lower capital/output ratio despite having a higher capital/labour ratio. Nevertheless, labour-intensive techniques may involve less maintenance and less reliance on imported inputs and foreign skilled personnel; the profits generated from them are more likely to be retained within the country; they are likely to create more employment and a more equal spread of the benefits of economic growth; and they may be less polluting.

3. Unemployment is a major problem for most developing countries, both in the countryside and in the ever-growing shanty towns surrounding the cities. The causes are complex, but include rapid population growth, biases towards the use of capital-intensive technology, and a vulnerability to world economic changes. Urban unemployment has grown rapidly as people have migrated from the countryside, attracted by the relatively higher wages, the 'bright lights of the city' and at least the possibility (however remote) of getting a job.

27.4   THE PROBLEM OF DEBT

A serious consequence of the oil shocks of the 1970s and the reactions of the developed world to these shocks was a major debt crisis in developing countries. Attempts to service these debts – to pay interest and instalments on capital repayments – have caused severe strains on the economies of many developing countries. By the early 1980s, the problem had become so severe that many developing countries found it virtually impossible to continue servicing their debt. There was a growing fear that countries would default on payment, thereby precipitating an international banking crisis.

Although today, from the perspective of the rich world, the debt problem is no longer seen as a 'crisis', this is largely because the world financial system has found ways of coping with the debt, and threats of default have subsided. From the perspective of the majority of poor countries, however, the problems are still acute. For many the debts are still mounting and the suffering of their people continues to grow. For others, total debt is falling, but still remains at levels where the costs of servicing it put huge strains on their economies and represent a massive transfer of moneys to the rich world. Table 27.4 shows the growth of debt from 1970 to 2007.

In this final section, we look first at the origins of the debt crisis and then at schemes that have been adopted to cope with it. We then turn finally to look at ways in which the problem of debt can be tackled.

The oil shocks of the 1970s

In 1973–4, oil prices quadrupled and the world went into recession. Oil imports cost much more and export demand was sluggish. The current account deficit of oil-importing developing countries rose from 1.1 per cent of GNY in 1973 to 4.3 per cent in 1975.

It was not difficult to finance these deficits, however. The oil surpluses deposited in commercial banks in the industrialised world provided an important additional source of finance. The banks, flush with money and faced with slack demand in the industrialised world, were very willing to lend. Bank loans to developing countries rose from $3 billion in 1970 to $12 billion in 1975. These flows enabled developing countries to continue with policies of growth.

The world recession was short-lived, and with a recovery in the demand for their exports and with their debts being eroded by high world inflation, developing countries found it relatively easy to service these increased debts (i.e. pay interest and make the necessary capital repayments).

In 1979/80 world oil prices rose again (from $15 to $38 per barrel). This second oil shock, like the first one, caused a large increase in the import bills of developing countries. But the full effects on their economies this time were very much worse, given the debts that had been accumulated in the 1970s and given the policies adopted by the industrialised world after 1979.

Table 27.5 illustrates the worsening debt position after 1979, compared with that in 1974. These are averages for all developing countries. Some fared very much worse than this. For example, in 1984 the ratio of debt service (i.e. interest and capital repayments) to exports was 35 per cent for Kenya, 45 per cent for Brazil and Mexico, and 63 per cent for Bolivia.

But why were things so much worse this time?

- The world recession was deeper and lasted longer (1980–3), and when recovery came, it came very slowly.

Table 27.4   Growth in debt of developing countries (% over period)

	1970–4	1975–9	1980–4	1985–9	1990–4	1994–9	2000–7
All developing countries	101	148	53	33	34	19	42
Low-income countries	91	90	54	66	17	–1	–7
Middle-income countries	105	167	53	26	39	23	49
Sub-Saharan Africa	137	151	49	47	26	–9	–20

Source: Based on data in *Global Development Finance* (World Bank, 2008).

Table 27.5   Debt ratios: average of all developing countries, selected years

	1974	1980	1984	1986	1988	1990	1994	1998	2000	2002	2004	2006
Ratio of debt to GNY (%)	11	21	31	35	36	35	39	41	38	38	33	26
Ratio of debt to exports (%)	80	86	166	231	201	182	170	157	123	120	91	65
Ratio of debt service to exports (%)	12	14	22	28	26	20	17	20	20	19	14	12

Source: Based on data in *Global Development Finance* (World Bank, 2008).

BOX 27.6   ARGENTINA IN CRISIS

Why did it all go so wrong?

In December 2001, the IMF refused a fresh loan of $1.3 billion to Argentina. This triggered a crisis in the country with mass rioting and looting. As the crisis deepened, Argentina announced that it was defaulting on its $166 billion of foreign debt. This hardly came as a surprise, however. For many commentators, it was simply a question of when.

The severity of Argentina's predicament was summed up by a 2001 report from Jubilee Plus, which stated:

> Argentina has to pay $75.3bn in foreign debt payments between now (September 2001) and the first quarter of 2003. This represents 27 per cent of her GDP; and 322 per cent of her annual export earnings. To repay these debts, Argentina has to triple exports; halt all imports and divert one quarter of GDP away from domestic consumption to foreign creditors. As this cannot conceivably be achieved, Argentina is effectively insolvent.[1]

Background to the crisis

Argentina's debt problem stretches back over many decades. Since it joined the IMF in 1956, in 34 of the succeeding years it has had to borrow money. Debt growth began to escalate with the military regimes of the 1970s and early 1980s. Foreign debt increased from $7.8 billion in 1975 to $46 billion in 1984. In more recent times, the rate of increase had declined, but debt continued to grow. In 1991, foreign debt stood at $65 billion; in 2001, it reached $160.2 billion.

In the 1980s, Argentina suffered hyperinflation, as the government simply printed money to pay for its expenditure, and corruption was rife. By the end of the 1980s, prices were rising by some 200 per cent a month. In return for debt rescheduling, the government pursued policies of privatisation and liberalisation, but seemed unable to make significant cuts in the budget deficit.

Then in 1991, the decision was taken to peg the Argentine peso to the dollar at a rate of $1 = 1 peso. This move seemed to work as prices were effectively set in dollars. As the world economy pulled out of the recession of the early 1990s, and as foreign investment flowed into Argentina, it seemed as if things were set fair for the Argentine economy. From 1991 to 1994, economic growth averaged nearly 8 per cent.

Things took a massive turn for the worse in 1998/9, however, as Argentina suffered fallout from the south-east Asian crisis (see Case Studies 26.3, 26.4 and 27.3 in MyEconLab). The crisis had a bad effect on Brazil, with large-scale speculation against the Brazilian currency, the real. In 1999 the real plummeted, but the peso, being linked to the dollar, could not follow suit.

In the face of Argentina's overvalued peso, Brazil and many of its other rivals took the opportunity to capture Argentinian export markets. With declining foreign currency earnings from exports, debt management became progressively more difficult to the point of default.

Between 1998 and 2002, Argentina was in deep recession and debts were increasingly difficult to service. Although new rescheduling arrangements were made, these came with tough demands by the IMF that austerity measures be pursued. As part of these measures, wages were cut. Not surprisingly, the result was a collapse in consumer spending. As unemployment rose (it was estimated at 29 per cent in 2000), reducing the budget deficit became increasingly difficult. In the first half of November 2001, tax receipts dropped by 17 per cent.

Thus, in attempting to control its debt growth, and meet the conditionality imposed by the IMF, Argentina saw a collapse of its economy and a dramatic increase in inequality and poverty.

Developing countries' current account balance of payments deteriorated sharply. This was due both to a marked slowing down in the growth of their exports and to a fall in their export prices.

- The tight monetary policies pursued by the industrialised countries led to a sharp increase in interest rates, and the resulting fall in inflation meant, therefore, that there was a very sharp increase in real interest rates. This greatly increased developing countries' costs of servicing their debts (see Table 27.5).
- The problem was made worse by the growing proportion of debt that was at variable interest rates. This was largely due to the increasing proportion of debt that was in the form of loans from commercial banks.

After 1979, many developing countries found it increasingly difficult to service their debts. Then in 1982 Mexico, followed by several other countries such as Brazil, Bolivia, Zaire and Sudan, declared that it would have to suspend payments. There was now a debt crisis, which threatened not only the debtor countries, but also the world banking system.

Coping with debt: rescheduling

There have been two dimensions to tackling the debt problems of developing countries. The first is to cope with difficulties in servicing their debt. This usually involves some form of rescheduling of the repayments. The second dimension is to deal with the causes of the problem. Here we will focus on rescheduling.

Rescheduling official loans

Official loans are renegotiated through the Paris Club. Industrialised countries are members of the club, which arranges terms for the rescheduling of their loans to developing countries. Agreements normally involve delaying

The default and its aftermath

Argentina's default on its debts in January 2002 was the biggest of its kind in history.

In a series of dramatic measures, the Argentine peso was initially devalued by 29 per cent and then unpegged from the dollar. Over the next three months, the peso depreciated a further 40 per cent. The economy seemed in free-fall. GDP fell by 11 per cent in 2002, and by the end of the year, income per head was 22 per cent below that of 1998. Unemployment was 21 per cent.

Then, however, the economy began to recover, helped by higher (peso) prices for exports resulting from the currency depreciation. In 2003 economic growth was 8.7 per cent; it averaged 8.8 per cent per annum from 2004 to 2008.

> On the streets of Buenos Aires, the change is tangible. Cars and white goods are flying out of the showrooms thanks to cheap credit. Cinemas and restaurants are packed at weekends. Seaside resorts are heavily booked for the southern-hemisphere summer. Unemployment has fallen to 10.2%.[2]

The current account, in deficit from 1991 to 2001, was then in substantial surplus, helped by the depreciation; the surplus averaged 3.5 per cent of GDP from 2003 to 2007. In 2007/8 the surplus was boosted by rising world food prices – Argentina is a major food exporter.

Inflation initially fell from 26 per cent in 2002 to 4.4 per cent in 2004. But then, with the output gap closing and continuing expansionary policies, inflation rose to 11 per cent in 2006 and to 14 per cent in 2008.

But what of the debt? In 2005, Argentina successfully made a huge debt swap (see Box 27.8) with banks and other private creditors. A large proportion of its defaulted debt was in the form of bonds. It offered to swap the old bonds for new peso bonds, but worth only 35 per cent as much (known as a 'hair cut'). By the deadline of 25 February, there was a 76 per cent take-up of the offer: clearly people thought that 35 per cent was better than nothing! At a stroke, bonds originally worth $104 billion now became worth just $36.2 billion. Then in 2006 its debt of nearly $10 billion was repaid to the IMF. Total debt stock as a percentage of GNY fell from 156 per cent in 2002 to 56 per cent in 2007.

After the massive default of 2001, will creditors be willing to lend to Argentina again? Surprising as it may seem, the answer seems to be yes. The strengthening Argentine economy has been attracting foreign capital at only 3 to 4 per cent above rates on US bonds. Investors seem to have a short memory and/or a high level of optimism. From 2002 to 2006 investment as a percentage of GDP rose from 11.0 to 21.4.

Then in September 2008, the government pledged to use some of its foreign currency reserves of $47 billion to pay back the remaining $6.7 billion of defaulted debt still owed to Paris Club creditors. Up to that point, access to overseas credit had been limited because of this unresolved debt. However, Argentina still faces lawsuits from creditors who refused the debt swap in 2005.

One solution proposed to help solve Argentina's weak financial position was that it should have abandoned the peso altogether as its unit of currency, and replaced it with the US dollar. What advantages and drawbacks might such a solution have for the Argentine economy both in the short and the long term?

---

[1] Ann Pettifor, Liana Cisneros and Alejandro Olmos Gaona, *It Takes Two to Tango* (Jubilee Plus report, 2001).
[2] 'Argentina: Tucking in to the good times', *The Economist*, 19 December 2006.

---

the date for repayment of loans currently maturing, or spreading the repayments over a longer period of time. Paris Club agreements are often made in consultation with the IMF, which works out a programme with the debtor country for tackling its underlying economic problems.

The main recipients of official loans are low-income and lower-middle-income countries (the upper-middle-income countries relying largely on commercial bank loans). Between 1982 and 1987, demands by low-income countries for Paris Club renegotiations increased dramatically. By 1987 virtually all the sub-Saharan African countries had sought repeated Paris Club assistance. By 1987 it was becoming clear that the existing arrangements were inadequate for many countries.

Several attempts have been made since the mid 1980s to make rescheduling terms more generous, with longer periods before repayments start, longer to repay when they do start, and lower interest rates. In return, the developing countries have had to undertake various 'structural adjustment programmes' supervised by the IMF (see below).

But despite the apparent advances made by the Paris Club in making its terms more generous, the majority of low-income countries failed to meet the required IMF conditions, and thus failed to have their debts reduced. What is more, individual Paris Club members were often reluctant to reduce debts unless they were first convinced that other members were 'paying their share'. Nevertheless, some creditor countries unilaterally introduced more generous terms and even cancelled some debts.

The net effect of rescheduling, but only very modest debt forgiveness, can be seen in Table 27.5. By the mid 1990s average debt service ratios had fallen from the levels of the mid 1980s and yet the ratio of total debt to GNY was higher. There were thus growing calls for the cancellation of debts (see below).

BOX 27.7   'ECOCIDE'

Debt and the environment

KI 29
p313

Faced with mounting debts and the need to service them, many developing countries have attempted to increase their export earnings. One way of achieving this is through the intensified extraction of minerals and ores or intensified farming, often by multinational corporations. But a consequence of this may be massive environmental damage. Some examples include:

- Long-term degradation of the soil from monoculture and from the increased use of chemical pesticides and fertilisers.
- Overfishing of rivers and seas.
- Chopping down forests for timber.
- Clearing forests for grazing cattle or for growing cash crops.
- 'Desertification', as a lack of forest cover leads to the encroachment of deserts in marginal areas.
- Open-cast mining, with little concern for the direct effect on the environment, or for poisonous waste products tipped into rivers.
- Burning highly polluting low-grade coal for electricity generation.
- Building dams for electricity generation and irrigation which flood large areas of land and destroy communities.

Brazil. An example of a country forced into what has been called 'ecocide' in response to its huge debt burden is Brazil. One of the most environmentally damaging of all Brazilian projects has been the Grande Carajas iron ore project. Proposed in 1980, the Carajas scheme cost some $62 billion and has involved massive deforestation of an area larger than France and Britain together. The Brazilian government has been willing to allow this environmental damage because Carajas is seen as a 'national export project'.

Venezuela. Another example of ecocide has occurred in Venezuela. The country has huge gold reserves – some 12 per cent of the world total. With the fall in oil prices in the 1990s, and hence a fall in revenues for Venezuela, one of the world's leading oil exporters, the Venezuelan authorities sought to exploit the country's gold reserves more aggressively. By 1994, the state had contracted out some 436 sites, covering 12 839 km^2. By 2000, this had risen to 30 000 km^2 (an area the size of Belgium), earning revenue of some $250 million per year.

The extraction of gold, however, has wrought great environmental damage. The richest gold reserves are in the region of Guayana, which makes up part of the Amazon river basin. It is an area rich, and in many respects unique, in its biodiversity. The environmental impact of open-cast mining within the region is already being felt. One of the most serious consequences has been the poisoning of rivers with mercury (used to separate gold from other minerals). In addition to the destruction of the forests and rivers, there are many cases where indigenous peoples have had their human rights violated and have even been murdered to make way for the mines.

Indonesia. The misuse and destruction of rainforests caused dramatic effects in 1997. In large parts of Indonesia (another highly indebted country), it is normal practice to burn land after forests have been felled, either to clear it for crops or for replanting. In 1997, the El Niño effect on ocean currents had caused a major drought and the forest fires got out of hand. As a result, air pollution on a massive scale affected many countries in south-east Asia. Most of Indonesia, Malaysia and Singapore became covered with a haze of dense smoke. The international air pollutant index has a scale on which readings above 500 are considered extremely hazardous. In parts of Malaysia readings of 1200 were recorded – equivalent to smoking a

Rescheduling commercial bank loans

After the declarations by Mexico and other countries of their inability to service their debts, there was fear of an imminent collapse of the world banking system. Banks realised that disaster could be averted only by collective action of the banks to reschedule debts. This has normally involved the creditor banks forming a Bank Advisory Committee (BAC) – a small committee that liaises with the country and the banks concerned. Such arrangements have sometimes been referred to as the 'London Club'. The BAC negotiates a rescheduling agreement with the debtor country. When all creditor banks have approved the agreement, it is signed by each of them.

The approach of banks in the 1980s was to reschedule some of the debts – the minimum necessary to avoid default – and to provide some additional loans in return for debtor countries undertaking structural adjustment (as described below). Additional loans, however, fell well short of the amount that was needed. Banks were unwilling to

supply extra money to deal with current debt-servicing problems when they saw the problem as a long-term one of countries' inability to pay. Nevertheless, banks were increasingly setting aside funds to cover bad debt, and thus the crisis for the banks began to recede.

As banks felt less exposed to default, so they became less worried about it and less concerned to negotiate deals with debtor countries. Many of the more severely indebted countries, however, found their position still deteriorating rapidly. What is more, many of them were finding that the IMF adjustment programmes were too painful (often involving deep cuts in government expenditure) and were therefore abandoning them. Thus in 1989 US Treasury Secretary Nicholas Brady proposed measures to *reduce* debt.

The *Brady Plan* involved the IMF and the World Bank lending funds to debtor countries to enable them to repay debts to banks. In return for this instant source of liquidity, the banks would have to be prepared to accept repayment of less than the full sum (i.e. they would sell the debt back

CASE STUDIES AND
APPLICATIONS

couple of packs of cigarettes a day. Schools and airports were closed, and income from tourism was lost throughout the region.

Biodiesel.   A recent case of ecocide is the production of palm oil as a biofuel. The environmental justification was that the carbon dioxide given off by burning the fuel is offset by the carbon absorbed by growing the oil palm trees. But this has turned out to be only part of the story. The production of the additional palm oil has involved either cutting down rainforest, which, apart from being a much more efficient carbon absorber than oil palm trees, is habitat for many endangered species, or the draining and burning of peat lands, which sends huge amounts of carbon dioxide into the atmosphere.

Changing international attitudes

In recent years, there has been growing international awareness of the scale of the environmental destruction that is taking place. In particular, the rich countries have begun to realise that they too might suffer from this destruction, with its consequences for global warming and the loss of many unique species of plants and animals. Increasingly, international agencies such as the IMF and the World Bank are taking ecological issues into account when considering appropriate development and adjustment programmes.

Many in the developed world now realise that development must be sustainable. It is no good trying to secure 'development' for the current generation if, in the process, the environment is damaged and future generations suffer. This is a message that has been well understood by indigenous peoples for countless generations, especially those living on marginal lands: from the Aborigines of the Australian outback to the tribes of the African bush. It is seen as a moral imperative that the land bequeathed by one's ancestors should be passed on in just as good a state to one's descendants (see page 345).

In 1992 in Rio de Janeiro, the United Nations Conference on Environment and Development (UNCED) put forward a programme for environmentally responsible development. In Agenda 21 it set out various policies that could be carried out by the international community. The policies, which were approved by 178 countries, included: targeting aid to projects that helped improve the environment (such as providing clean water); research into environmentally friendly farming methods; and programmes that help reduce population growth (such as family planning and education).

The test of such sentiments, however, is action. To monitor this, a Commission on Sustainable Development was established in December 1992. In 2003 it set out a programme until 2015. Every two years from 2004 there would be a particular focus for action. For example, in 2004–5 the focus was on water, sanitation and human settlements; in 2006–7, it was on energy for sustainable development, industrial development, air pollution and climate change; in 2008–9 it is on agriculture, rural development, land, drought, desertification and Africa; and in 2010–11 it will be on transport, chemicals, waste management, mining and long-term consumption and production patterns.

1. *If reductions in developing countries' debt are in the environmental interests of the whole world, then why have developed countries not gone much further in reducing or cancelling the debts owed to them?*
2. *Would it be possible to devise a scheme of debt repayments that would both be acceptable to debtor and creditor countries and not damage the environment?*

to the country at a discount). To benefit from such deals, the debtor countries would have to agree to structural adjustment programmes. Several such agreements were negotiated, with countries buying back their debt at discount rates ranging between 44 and 84 per cent. Much of the debt reduction has involved debt swaps of one sort or another (see Box 27.8).

What are the relative advantages and disadvantages to a developing country of rescheduling its debts compared with simply defaulting on them (either temporarily or permanently)?

Dealing with debt: structural reform within the developing countries

Before it is prepared to sanction the rescheduling of debts, the IMF frequently demands that debtor countries under-

take severe market-orientated adjustment programmes. These include the following:

- Tight fiscal and monetary policies to reduce government deficits, reduce interest rates and reduce inflation.
- Supply-side reforms to encourage greater use of the market mechanism and greater incentives for investment.
- A more open trade policy and devaluation of the currency in order to encourage more exports and more competition.

These policies, however, often brought extreme hardship as countries were forced to deflate. Unemployment and poverty increased and growth slowed down or became negative. Even though in the long run some developing countries emerged as more efficient and better able to compete in international trade, in the short run the suffering for many was too great to bear. Popular unrest and resentment against the IMF and the country's government led to riots in many countries and a breakdown of law and order.

A more 'complete' structural adjustment would extend beyond simple market liberalisation and tough monetary policies to much more open access to the markets of the rich countries, to more aid and debt relief being channelled into health and education, and to greater research and development in areas that will benefit poor people (e.g. into efficient labour-intensive technology and into new strains of crops that are suitable for countries' specific climate and soil conditions, and which do not require large amounts of chemicals).

Dealing with debt: debt forgiveness

By the end of the 1990s, the debt burden of many of the poorest countries had become intolerable. Despite portions of their debt being written off under Paris Club terms, the debts of many countries were still rising. Between 1980 and 2000, the debt of sub-Saharan Africa had increased some $3^{1}/_{2}$ times, from $61 billion to $212 billion. Some countries, such as Ethiopia and Mozambique, were spending nearly half their export earnings on merely servicing their debt.

Even with substantial debt rescheduling and some debt cancellation, highly indebted countries were being forced to make savage cuts in government expenditure, much of it on health, education and transport. The consequence was a growth in poverty, hunger, disease and illiteracy. African countries on average were paying four times more to rich countries in debt servicing than they were spending on health and education: it was like a patient giving a blood transfusion to a doctor! The majority of these countries had no chance of 'growing their way out of debt'. The only solution for them was for a more substantial proportion of their debt to be written off.

The heavily indebted poor countries (HIPC) initiative

In 1996 the World Bank and the IMF launched the HIPC initiative. A total of 42 countries, mainly in Africa, were identified as being in need of substantial debt relief. (This number was subsequently reduced to 41.) The object of the initiative was to reduce the debts of such countries to 'sustainable' levels by cancelling debts above 200–250 per cent of GDP (this was reduced to 150 per cent in 1999 and to a lower level still for five countries).

The HIPC process involves countries passing through two stages. In the first stage, eligible countries must demonstrate a track record of 'good performance'. This means that they must satisfy the IMF, the World Bank and the Paris Club that they are undertaking adjustment measures, such as cutting government expenditure and liberalising their markets. It also involves the countries preparing a Poverty Reduction Strategy Paper (PRSP) to show how they will use debt relief to tackle poverty, and especially how they will improve health and education. Once the IMF and the World Bank are satisfied that the country is making sufficient progress, the 'decision point' is reached and the

level of debt relief would be determined. The country would then enter the second stage.

During this second stage, some interim debt relief is provided. Meanwhile the country must establish a 'sound track record' by implementing policies established at the decision point and based on the PRSP. The length of this stage depends on how long it takes the country to implement the policies. At the end of the second stage, the country reaches the 'completion point' and debts are cancelled (as agreed at the decision point) by the various creditors, on a pro rata basis, to bring the debt to the sustainable threshold.

Despite the welcome given to the HIPC initiative back in 1996, it has been heavily criticised on the following grounds:

- The qualifying period is too long. By 2008, only 23 countries had reached the completion point, with another 10 having reached the decision point, with the remaining 8 yet to get even to the decision point. The total amount of relief committed by the end of 2007 was $49 billion. By 2004, total debt of the HIPC countries had reached $145 billion. By 2006, this had fallen to $101 billion. Despite having a previous 'good track record', many countries still had to adhere to the full two-stage process, which could be very lengthy.

- The thresholds have been set too high, with the resulting reduction in debt servicing being quite modest, or in many cases zero. In response to this criticism and calls for creditor countries to do more, the G8 countries agreed at the Gleneagles summit in July 2005 to cancel all remaining debt owed to the World Bank, the IMF and the African Development Bank by HIPC countries once they reached the completion point. For the 23 countries that had reached the completion point by 2008, this amounted to a further $21 billion beyond that agreed at the decision point.

- Countries in arrears to multilateral agencies, such as the World Bank and the IMF, have first to make the back payments due. For some of the poorest countries, particularly those which have suffered civil wars (such as the Republic of Congo), such a requirement is virtually impossible to meet. Individual donor countries have sometimes agreed to partial forgiveness of arrears, but this has generally been insufficient to allow enough funds to be diverted to clear arrears with multilateral agencies.

- The IMF reform programmes have been too harsh. The required reductions in government expenditure lead to deep cuts in basic health and education, and deflationary policies lead to reductions in investment.

- Many of the non-HIPCs are also suffering debts which divert a large percentage of their income from poverty relief. Just because non-HIPCs can manage to service their debts, it does not make it desirable that they should be forced to do so.

BOX 27.8   **SWAPPING DEBT**

A solution to developing countries' debt?

Faced with the inability of many developing countries to service, let alone repay, their debts, many banks have collaborated with debtor countries or companies in ingenious schemes to convert debt into some other form. There are a number of types of these 'debt swaps', as they are called.

Debt-for-equity swaps

Banks sell a certain amount of a country's debt at a discount in the secondary market. The purchaser (a firm or a bank) then swaps the debt with the central bank of the developing country for local currency, which is then used to buy shares in one or more of the country's companies. Sometimes debt–equity swaps are part of a privatisation programme, the debt being swapped for shares in a newly privatised company.

As far as the debtor country is concerned, this has the benefit of both reducing the debt and increasing the amount of investment in domestic companies. It has the drawback, however, of increasing foreign ownership and control in the country.

Debt-for-cash swaps

This is where the banks allow a debtor country to 'buy back' (i.e. repay) its debt at a discount. In order to do this, the developing country will probably have to secure a loan from another source. The developing country gains from achieving a net reduction in its debt. The bank gains by achieving an instant repayment of a percentage of the original debt.

Debt-for-bonds swaps

Here debt is converted into lower-interest-rate or lower-value bonds. The developing country gains by having to pay a lower rate of interest. The bank gains by having a greater certainty of payment. A version of this system was adopted by Argentina in 2005 (see Box 27.6) when it agreed to swap old bonds, on which it had defaulted, for new ones worth only 35 per cent of the old ones, but which would at least be honoured.

Debt-for-export swaps

Under these schemes, banks arrange for developing countries to sell exports that they would otherwise have difficulty in selling (perhaps because of industrial country protection), provided the revenues are used to pay off specific debt. Clearly, the developing country can gain from the development of new export markets, but there is a danger that, by being a form of 'export protection', it could encourage the production of goods in which the country has a comparative disadvantage, and encourage inefficiency in production.

Debt-to-local-debt swaps

This is where external debt is converted into debt in the local currency (usually indexed to the US dollar). The original creditor sells the debt to a company that requires local currency to finance a subsidiary operating in the debtor country. The company benefits from a cheap source of local currency. The country benefits from a reduction in the need for scarce foreign currency.

Debt-for-nature or debt-for-development swaps

In recent years, the process of debt swapping has been applied directly to specific projects. A debt-for-nature swap is where debts are cancelled in return for investment in environmental projects. There are two types of scheme: bilateral and commercial.

In a bilateral swap, a creditor country agrees to cancel debt in return for the debtor country investing a proportion of the amount in environmental projects. In a commercial swap, the debt owed to banks is sold to an international environmental agency at a substantial discount (or sometimes even given away); the agency then agrees to cancel this debt in return for the country funding the agency to carry out various environmental projects. By 2007, the total debt cancelled through debt-for-nature swaps was just over $870 million.

Like debt-for-nature swaps, debt-for-development swaps involve the selling or donating of debt to an international development agency, which then cancels it in return for the country carrying out specific projects in the fields of education, transport infrastructure, health, agriculture, etc.

Most of these types of debt swaps have taken place with HIPC countries. By 2007, of the $15.0 billion of debt reduced by debt-for-development swaps, $11.4 billion involved HIPC countries. But these countries would probably have had such debts cancelled anyway. What is more, the size of such debt swaps has been tiny compared with the total stock of debt, which in 2007 was $3357 billion. But debt-for-development swaps can still make a useful contribution to debt relief.

Despite their limitations, swaps can produce creative and participatory projects. Swaps can be beneficial in terms of local development and small-scale projects. As suggested by some civil society organisations such as Jubilee Peru, swaps that are well conceived and carried out 'can re-energise local development and strengthen poorest communities by promoting projects that respond to local needs. They can also strengthen participative democracy by offering local communities good opportunities.'[1]

 Would the objections of developing countries to debt–equity swaps be largely overcome if foreign ownership were restricted to less than 50 per cent in any company? If such restrictions were imposed, would this be likely to affect the 'price' at which debt is swapped for equity?

[1] Marta Ruiz, *Debt Swaps for Development*, (EURODAD, 2007), p. 26.

According to many charities, such as Oxfam, a much better approach would be to target debt relief directly at poverty reduction, with the resources released being used for investment in fields such as health, education, rural development and basic infrastructure. The focus, they argue, should be on what countries can afford to pay *after* essential spending on poverty relief and human development.

 Imagine that you are an ambassador of a developing country at an international conference. What would you try to persuade the rich countries to do in order to help you and other poor countries overcome the debt problem? How would you set about persuading them that it was in their own interests to help you?

Should all debt be cancelled and aid increased?

In recent years there have been growing calls for the cancellation of debts and a significant increase in aid, especially for the poorest developing countries, many ravaged by war, drought or AIDS. The United Nations has for many years called on wealthy countries to give 0.7 per cent of their GDP in aid. In practice they give only a little over 0.2 per cent.

As we have seen, the G8 meeting in Gleneagles in 2005 agreed to cancel all the remaining debts owed to multilateral agencies such as the World Bank and the IMF by the HIPC countries that had reached the completion point. The combination of this and HIPC has amounted to some $60 billion. This is still, however, only a tiny proportion of the $400 billion of debt owed by low-income countries and the $3350 billion owned by developing countries as a whole. Then there is the plight of many non-HIPC countries, such as Kenya, which could be argued to be in greater need of debt relief than some HIPC countries.

At the summit France, Germany, Italy and the UK also committed themselves to meeting the 0.7 per cent of GDP aid target by 2015. The G8 as a whole agreed to increase aid to Africa by $25 billion a year by 2010 – more than doubling aid compared to 2004. But agreeing was not doing. In 2005, total aid from developed countries amounted to 0.33 per cent of their GDP. By 2007, this had fallen to 0.28 per cent. The figures for France, Germany, Italy and the UK were 0.39, 0.37, 0.19 and 0.36 per cent respectively. The figure for the USA was a mere 0.16 per cent.

The argument against debt cancellation and a substantial increase in aid is that this could represent a 'moral hazard' (see Box 4.5 on page 108). Once the burden of debt had been lifted and aid had been increased, countries might be tempted to squander the money. It might also encourage them to seek further loans, which might again be squandered.

If, however, moneys were paid into national 'Poverty Funds', which could be monitored by civil society, parliament and possibly multilateral agencies, this might help to ensure that the money would be used to fund key poverty-reducing projects, such as health, education, clean water and other basic infrastructure projects. (Case Study 27.6 in MyEconLab examines some of the issues surrounding aid.)

Section summary

1. After the 1973 oil crisis, many developing countries borrowed heavily in order to finance their balance of trade deficits and to maintain a programme of investment. Despite this increase in debt, a combination of low real interest rates, a recovery in the world economy and high international rates of inflation allowed developing countries to sustain moderate rates of economic growth after 1975.

2. After the 1979 oil price rises, however, there was a much deeper world recession than in the mid 1970s, and real interest rates were much higher. Debt increased dramatically, and much of it was at variable interest rates.

3. Although the problem for middle-income countries is now less serious, the situation has deteriorated for many of the poorest countries.

4. Rescheduling can help developing countries to cope with increased debt in the short run. During the 1980s and early 1990s there were several initiatives to encourage rescheduling programmes. Official loans are renegotiated through the Paris Club. This will normally involve some combination of longer repayment periods, grace periods in which payments may be delayed and either lower interest rates or partial cancellation of debts. Commercial bank loans have also frequently been renegotiated through a Bank Advisory Committee of the banks concerned. This has normally involved delaying paying loans for a period of time and the extension of the repayment period. In addition, under the Brady Plan, countries borrowed from the World Bank and other international institutions to buy back their debt from banks at a discount.

5. If the problem is to be tackled, however, then either debts have to be written off – something that banks have been increasingly forced to do – or the developing countries themselves must take harsh corrective measures. The IMF favours 'structural adjustment' policies of deflation and market-orientated supply-side policies. An alternative is to use debt relief and aid to invest in health, education, roads and other infrastructure.

6. In 1996 the World Bank and the IMF launched the HIPC initiative to help reduce the debts of heavily indebted poor countries to sustainable levels. HIPC relief has been criticised, however, for being made conditional on the debtor countries pursuing excessively tough IMF adjustment programmes, for having an excessively long qualifying period and debt sustainability thresholds that are too high, and for delays in its implementation. A better approach might be to target debt relief directly at programmes to help the poor.

END OF CHAPTER QUESTIONS

1. Compare the relative merits of using GNY statistics with those of various basic needs indicators when assessing both the level and the rate of a country's economic development.
2. If a developing country has a comparative advantage in primary products, should the government allow market forces to dictate the pattern of trade?
3. What are the advantages and disadvantages for a developing country of pursuing a policy of ISI?
4. Should all developing countries aim over the long term to become *exporters* of manufactured products?
5. How would you attempt to assess whether the technology used by an industry in a developing country was 'inappropriate'?
6. What policies could be adopted to reduce urban unemployment in developing countries?
7. To what extent was the debt crisis of the early 1980s caused by inappropriate policies that had been pursued by the debtor countries?
8. What are the advantages and disadvantages of debt swapping as a means of reducing the debts of developing countries?

Online resources

Additional case studies in MyEconLab

27.1 Theories of development. This looks at different approaches to the analysis of poverty and development.
27.2 Multinational corporations and developing countries. This examines whether multinational investment is a net benefit to developing countries.
27.3 A miracle gone wrong. Lessons from east Asia.
27.4 Ethical business. An examination of the likelihood of success of companies which trade fairly with developing countries.
27.5 The great escape. This case examines the problem of capital flight from developing countries to rich countries.
27.6 Economic aid. Does aid provide a solution to the debt problem?

Websites relevant to this chapter

Numbers and sections refer to websites listed in the Web Appendix and hotlinked from this book's website at **www.pearsoned.co.uk/sloman**.

- For news articles relevant to this chapter, see the *Economics News Articles* link from the book's website.
- For news on various aspects of economic development, see A27, 28; I9. See also links to newspapers worldwide in A38, 39, 43 and 44, and the news search feature in Google at A41. See also links to economics news in A42.
- For links to a range of development sites, see sites I9 and 10.
- For data on developing countries, see sites B1, 19, 23, 31, 32, 33 and especially 35.
- For data on debt and development, see B24 and 35 (*Global Development Finance*) and B31. Also see the debt section in I14.
- For information on trade and developing countries, see H4, 7, 9, 10, 16, 17.
- For information on debt and developing countries, see H4, 7, 9, 10, 12–14, 17–19.
- Sites I7 and 11 contain links to *Capital flows and aid* and *Trade and trade policy* in *Economic Development*. Site I4 has links to *International economics*, *Development economics* and *Economic development*. Site I17 has links to *Trade policy* and *Development economics*.
- For student resources relevant to this chapter, see sites C1–7, 9, 10, 19. See also *Virtual Developing Country* in *Virtual Worlds* in site C2.

Postscript: The Castaways
or Vote for Caliban

The Pacific Ocean –
A blue demi-globe.
Islands like punctuation marks.

A cruising airliner,
Passengers unwrapping pats of butter.
A hurricane arises,
Tosses the plane into the sea.

Five of them flung onto an island beach,
Survived.

Tom the reporter.
Susan the botanist.
Jim the high-jump champion.
Bill the carpenter.
Mary the eccentric widow.

Tom the reporter sniffed out a stream of drinkable water.
Susan the botanist identified a banana tree.
Jim the high-jump champion jumped up and down and gave them each a bunch.
Bill the carpenter knocked up a table for their banana supper.
Mary the eccentric widow buried the banana skins,
But only after they had asked her twice.

They all gathered sticks and lit a fire.
There was an incredible sunset.

Next morning they held a committee meeting.
Tom, Susan, Jim and Bill
Voted to make the best of things.
Mary, the eccentric widow, abstained.

Tom the reporter killed several dozen wild pigs.
He tanned their skins into parchment
And printed the Island News with the ink of squids.

Susan the botanist developed new strains of banana
Which tasted of chocolate, beefsteak, peanut butter,
Chicken and bootpolish.

Jim the high-jump champion organised organised games
Which he always won easily.
Bill the carpenter constructed a wooden water wheel

And converted the water's energy into electricity.
Using iron ore from the hills, he constructed lampposts.

They all worried about Mary, the eccentric widow,
Her lack of confidence and her –
But there wasn't time to coddle her.

The volcano erupted, but they dug a trench
And diverted the lava into the sea
Where it formed a spectacular pier.
They were attacked by pirates but defeated them
With bamboo bazookas firing
Sea-urchins packed with home-made nitro-glycerine.
They gave the cannibals a dose of their own medicine
And survived an earthquake thanks to their skill in jumping.

Tom had been a court reporter
So he became a magistrate and solved disputes.
Susan the botanist established
A university which also served as a museum.
Jim the high-jump champion
Was put in charge of law enforcement –
Jumped on them when they were bad.
Bill the carpenter built himself a church,
Preached there every Sunday.

But Mary the eccentric widow . . .
Each evening she wandered down the island's main street,
Past the Stock Exchange, the Houses of Parliament,
The prison and the arsenal.
Past the Prospero Souvenir Shop,
Past the Robert Louis Stevenson Movie Studios,
Past the Daniel Defoe Motel
She nervously wandered and sat on the end of the pier of lava.

Breathing heavily,
As if at a loss,
As if at a lover,
She opened her eyes wide
To the usual incredible sunset.

Adrian Mitchell

1. *Had the castaways reduced their problem of scarcity by the end of the poem?*
2. *Could the 'usual incredible sunset' be described as an economic good?*

© Adrian Mitchell. Available in ADRIAN MITCHELL'S GREATEST HITS, 1991.
  Reprinted by permission of PFD on behalf of Adrian Mitchell.

  Educational Health Warning! Adrian Mitchell asks that none of his poems
  be used in connection with any examination whatsoever.

Appendix 1: Some Techniques of Economic Analysis

As you will see if you flick back through the pages, there are many diagrams and tables and several equations. But this does not mean that there are many mathematical techniques that you will have to master in order to study this book. In fact there are relatively few techniques, but they are ones which we use many times in many different contexts. You will find that if you are new to the subject, you will very quickly become familiar with these techniques. If you are not new to the subject, perhaps you could reassure your colleagues who are!

On some university courses, however, you will take mathematics to a higher level. To meet your needs there are a number of optional 'Looking at the Maths' sections scattered throughout the book. These use maths to express arguments that have just been covered in words or diagrams. Most of these 'Looking at the Maths' sections also refer to 'Maths Cases' in MyEconLab. These cases consist of worked examples and also have a question at the end for you to test your understanding of the relevant technique. The answers to these questions are also given in MyEconLab.

But please note that the 'Looking at the Maths' sections are purely optional and will not be suitable for many courses. In such cases you can simply ignore them.

Diagrams as pictures

On many occasions, we use diagrams simply to provide a picture of a relationship. Just as a photograph in a newspaper can often depict an event much more vividly than any verbal account, so too a diagram in economics can often picture a relationship with a vividness and clarity that could never be achieved by words alone.

For example, we may observe that as people's incomes rise, they spend a lot more on entertainment and only a little more on food. We can picture this relationship very nicely by the use of a simple graph.

In Figure A1.1, an individual's income is measured along the horizontal axis and expenditure on food and entertainment is measured up the vertical axis. There are just two lines on this diagram: one showing how the expenditure on entertainment rises as income rises, the other how the expenditure on food rises as income rises. Now we could use a diagram like this to plot actual data. But we may simply be using it as a sketch – as a picture. In this case we do not necessarily need to put figures on the two axes. We are simply showing the relative *shapes* of the two curves. These shapes tell us that the person's expenditure on entertainment rises more quickly than that on

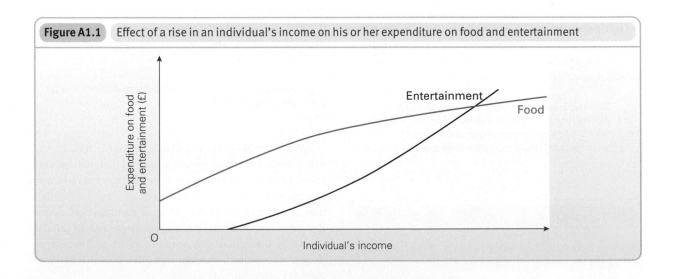

Figure A1.1 Effect of a rise in an individual's income on his or her expenditure on food and entertainment

Table A1.1	UK unemployment, 2004 Q1–2008 Q3																	
	2004				**2005**				**2006**				**2007**				**2008**		
	Q1	Q2	Q3	Q4	Q1	Q2	Q3	Q4	Q1	Q2	Q3	Q4	Q1	Q2	Q3	Q4	Q1	Q2	Q3
Unemployment (millions)	1.43	1.44	1.40	1.42	1.41	1.44	1.44	1.57	1.60	1.69	1.69	1.70	1.70	1.66	1.64	1.60	1.62	1.69	1.83

Source: Based on Time Series Data (National Statistics, 2008).

food, and that above a certain level of income the expenditure on entertainment becomes greater than that on food.

 What else is the diagram telling us?

Representing real-life statistics

In many cases, we will want to depict real-world data. We may want to show, for example, how unemployment has changed over the years in a particular country, or how income is distributed between different groups in the population. In the first we will need to look at *time-series* data. In the second we will look at *cross-section* data.

Time-series data

Table A1.1 shows the level of UK unemployment between the first quarter of 2004 and the third quarter of 2008. A table like this is a common way of representing **time-series data**. It has the advantage of giving the precise figures, and is thus a useful reference if we want to test any theory and see if it predicts accurately.

Notice that in this particular table the figures are given quarterly. Depending on the period of time over which we want to see the movement of a variable, it may be more appropriate to use a different interval of time. For example, if we wanted to see how unemployment had changed over the past fifty years, we might use annual figures or even average figures for longer periods of time. If, however, we wanted to see how unemployment had changed over the course of a year, we would probably use monthly or even weekly figures.

 The table in Box 1.2 shows time-series data for four different variables for four different countries. Would there have been any advantage in giving the figures for each separate year? Would there have been any disadvantage?

Definition

Time-series data Information depicting how a variable (e.g. the price of eggs) changes over time.

Time-series data can also be shown graphically. In fact the data from a table can be plotted directly on to a graph. Figure A1.2 plots the data from Table A1.1. Each dot on the graph corresponds to one figure from the table. The dots are then joined up to form a single line. Thus if you wanted to find the level of unemployment at any time between 2004 Q1 and 2008 Q3, you would simply find the appropriate date on the horizontal axis, read vertically upward to the line you have drawn, then read across to find the level of unemployment.

Although a graph like this cannot give you quite such an accurate measurement of each point as a table does, it gives a much more obvious picture of how the figures have moved over time and whether the changes are getting bigger (the curve getting steeper) or smaller (the curve getting shallower). We can also read off what the likely figure would be for some point *between* two observations.

 What was the level of unemployment midway between quarter 3 and quarter 4 2005?

It is also possible to combine *two* sets of time-series data on one graph to show their relative movements over time. Table A1.2 shows the figures for UK economic growth for the same time period. Figure A1.3 plots these data along with those from Table A1.1. This enables us to get a clear picture of how unemployment and the rate of economic growth moved in relation to each other over the period in question. Note that we use a different vertical scale for the two variables. This is inevitable given that they are measured in different units.

 How would it be possible to show three different lines on the same diagram?

All developed countries publish time-series data for the major macroeconomic variables such as national income, prices, employment and unemployment, interest rates, and imports and exports. Microeconomic data on the distribution of income, the performance of particular industries, the distribution of household expenditure and so on also appear in the official government statistics. Firms, consumers' associations, charities and other organisations also publish microeconomic statistics.

| **Figure A1.2** | UK unemployment, 2004 Q1–2008 Q3 |

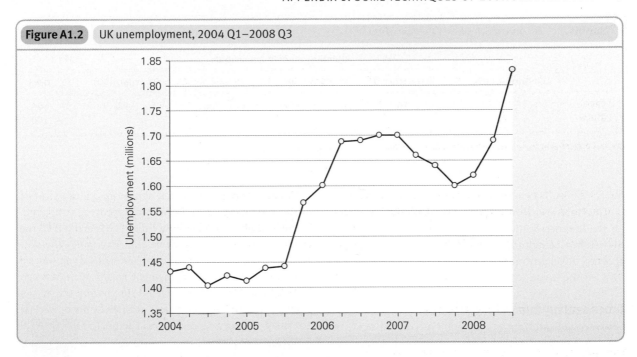

| **Table A1.2** | UK economic growth, 2004 Q1–2008 Q3 (% increase over equivalent quarter in previous year) |

	2004				**2005**				**2006**				**2007**				**2008**		
	Q1	Q2	Q3	Q4	Q1	Q2	Q3	Q4	Q1	Q2	Q3	Q4	Q1	Q2	Q3	Q4	Q1	Q2	Q3
Economic growth (%)	3.1	3.1	2.5	2.3	2.2	1.9	2.1	2.0	2.7	2.7	2.8	3.2	2.9	3.0	3.3	2.9	2.3	1.5	0.3

Source: Based on Time Series Data (National Statistics, 2008).

| **Figure A1.3** | UK unemployment and annual economic growth, 2004 Q1–2008 Q3 |

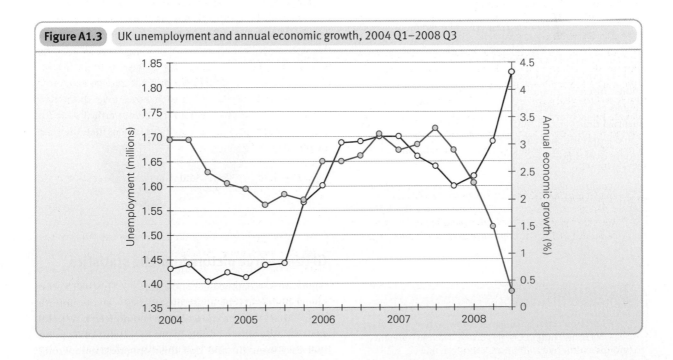

Table A1.3   Income before taxes and benefits

| | Quintile groups of households | | | | | |
	Bottom 20%	Next 20%	Middle 20%	Next 20%	Top 20%	Total
1977	4	10	18	26	42	100
2006/7	3	7	15	24	51	100

Source: The Effects of Taxes and Benefits on Household Income, 2006/07 (National Statistics, 2008).

There are also several sources of data freely available on the Internet. Section B of Appendix 2 gives a number of websites containing datasets. These websites can be accessed directly from the hotlinks section of this book's own website (www.pearsoned.co.uk/sloman).

Cross-section data

Cross-section data show different observations made at the same point in time. For example, they could show the quantities of food and clothing purchased at various levels of household income, or the costs to a firm or industry of producing various quantities of a product.

Table A1.3 gives an example of cross-section data. It shows the distribution of household income in the UK before the deduction of taxes and the addition of benefits. It puts households into five equal-sized groups (or 'quintiles') according to their income. Thus the poorest 20 per cent of households are in one group, the next poorest 20 per cent are in the next and so on. Looking just at the 2006/7 figures, they show that the poorest 20 per cent earned just 3 per cent of total household incomes, whereas the richest 20 per cent earned 51 per cent.

Cross-section data like these are often represented in the form of a chart. Figure A1.4 shows the data as a *bar chart*, and Figure A1.5 as a *pie chart*.

It is possible to represent cross-section data at two or more different points in time, thereby presenting the figures as a time series. In Table A1.3, figures are given for just two time periods. With a more complete time series we could graph the movement of the shares of each of the five groups over time.

 Could bar charts or pie charts be used for representing time-series data?

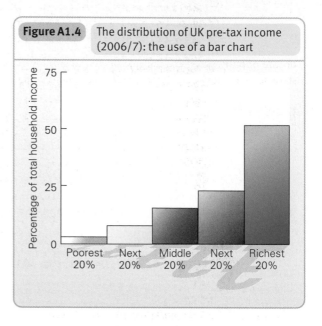

Figure A1.4   The distribution of UK pre-tax income (2006/7): the use of a bar chart

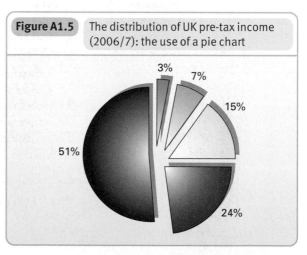

Figure A1.5   The distribution of UK pre-tax income (2006/7): the use of a pie chart

Getting a true picture from the statistics

'There are lies, damned lies and statistics.' This well-known saying highlights the abuse of statistics – abuse, unfortunately, that is commonplace. Have you noticed how politicians always seem to be able to produce statistics to 'prove' that they are right and that their opponents are wrong? And it's not just politicians. Newspapers frequently present

Definition

Cross-section data Information showing how a variable (e.g. the consumption of eggs) differs between different groups or different individuals at a given time.

statistics in the most 'newsworthy' way; companies try to show their performance in the most flattering way; pressure groups fighting for a cause (such as the protection of the environment) again present statistics in the way that best supports their case.

It is not difficult to present data in such a way as to give a grossly distorted picture of a situation. Let us have a look at some of the most common examples.

Selective use of data

This is where people select only those statistics that support their case and ignore those that do not. For example, assume that unemployment has risen but inflation has fallen. The government highlights the inflation statistics to show how successful its policies have been. The opposition parties do the opposite: they concentrate on the unemployment statistics to demonstrate the failure of government policy.

Graphical presentation of data

Two graphs may present exactly the same data and yet convey a quite different impression about them. Figure A1.6 shows how the amount that people buy of a particular foodstuff varies with their income. It is based on the information in Table A1.4.

Diagram (a) shows *exactly the same* information as diagram (b), and yet at a glance it would seem from diagram (a) that people buy a lot more as their incomes rise, whereas from diagram (b) it would seem that people only buy a little more.

Clearly the choice of *scales* for the two axes will determine the shape of the graph.

1. If the vertical scale for Figure A1.2 ran from 0 to 5 million, how would this alter your impression of the degree to which unemployment had changed?
2. What are the advantages and disadvantages of presenting data graphically with the axes starting from zero?

Use of absolute or proportionate values

'People are paying more taxes now than they did when the government came to office', claims the opposition.

'Since coming into office we have cut taxes substantially', claims the government.

So who is right? Do we pay more or less tax? Quite possibly they are both right. If incomes have risen, we probably do pay more tax in total. After all, the more we earn, the greater the sum of money we will be paying in income tax; and the more we spend, the more we will be paying out in VAT. Thus in *absolute* terms we probably are paying more in taxes.

On the other hand, if the government has cut the rates of tax, we may be paying a smaller *proportion* of our income. In other words, a smaller proportion of a larger total can still represent an absolute increase.

Ignoring questions of distribution

'The average person has become better off under this government', claims a minister.

'Poverty has increased steeply under this government', claims the opposition. 'More than half the population are worse off now than when the government came to office.'

Surely, this time one of the claims must be wrong? But again, both could be right. The term 'average' normally

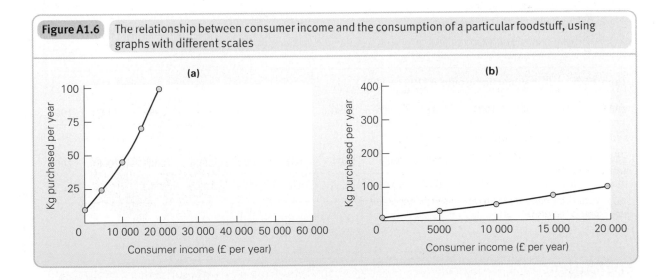

Figure A1.6 The relationship between consumer income and the consumption of a particular foodstuff, using graphs with different scales

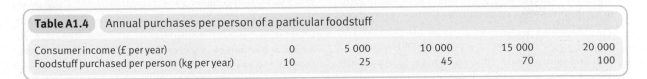

Table A1.4 Annual purchases per person of a particular foodstuff

Consumer income (£ per year)	0	5 000	10 000	15 000	20 000
Foodstuff purchased per person (kg per year)	10	25	45	70	100

refers to the **mean**. The mean income is simply the total national income divided by the number in the population: i.e. income *per head*. If this is what is meant by the average, then the government may well be correct. Income per head may have risen.

If, however, a small number of people have got a lot richer and the rest have got a little poorer, the **median** income will have fallen. The median income is the income of the *middle* person. For example, if the population were 50 million, the median income would be the income of the twenty-five millionth richest person. This person's income may have fallen.

Real or nominal values

'Incomes have risen by 5 per cent this last year', claims the government.

'The standard of living has fallen', claims the opposition.

One of the most common abuses of statistics is deliberately switching between real and nominal figures, depending on what message you want to give your audience. **Nominal** figures are the simple monetary values at the prices ruling at the time. For example, if you earned a wage of £100 per week last year and are earning £105 per week this year, then in nominal terms your wage has risen by 5 per cent.

But what if prices have risen by 8 per cent? Your 5 per cent increase in wages will in fact buy you 3 per cent *less* goods. Your **real** wages have gone down by 3 per cent. In other words, to show how much better or worse off a person or nation is, the nominal figure must be corrected for inflation.

 KEY IDEA 38 The distinction between nominal and real figures. Nominal figures are those using current prices, interest rates, etc. Real figures are figures corrected for inflation.

Thus:

Real growth = Nominal growth – Inflation

1. If a bank paid its depositors 3 per cent interest and inflation was 5 per cent, what would be the real rate of interest?
2. Has your real income gone up or down this last year?

The time chosen for comparison

'Between 1982 and 1990, Britain's real growth rate averaged 3.5 per cent per year', boasted the Conservative government of the time.

'Between 1979 and 1993, Britain could only manage a real growth rate of 1.6 per cent per year', chided the opposition.

Again both were correct, but they had chosen either to include or to ignore the periods from 1979 to 1982 and from 1990 to 1993 when the real growth rate was negative.

Index numbers

Time-series data are often expressed in terms of **index numbers**. Consider the data in Table A1.5. It shows index numbers of manufacturing output in the UK from 1982 to 2007.

One year is selected as the **base year** and this is given the value of 100. In our example this is 2003. The output for other years is then shown by their percentage variation from 100. For 1982 the index number is 73.8. This means that manufacturing output was 26.2 per cent lower in 1982 than in 2003. The index number for 2007 is 103.0. This means that manufacturing output was 3.0 per cent higher in 2007 than in 2003.

 Does this mean that the value of manufacturing output in 2007 was 3.0 per cent higher than 2003 in money terms?

Table A1.5	UK manufacturing output (2003 = 100)											
1982	1983	1984	1985	1986	1987	1988	1989	1990	1991	1992	1993	1994
73.8	75.4	78.2	80.4	81.5	85.4	91.6	95.2	95.1	90.4	90.3	91.6	95.9
1995	1996	1997	1998	1999	2000	2001	2002	2003	2004	2005	2006	2007
97.4	98.1	99.9	100.5	101.4	103.8	102.5	99.8	100.0	102.0	100.8	102.4	103.0

Source: *Economic Trends* (National Statistics, various years).

Definitions

Mean (or arithmetic mean) The sum of the values of each of the members of the sample divided by the total number in the sample.

Median The value of the middle member of the sample.

Nominal values Money values measured at *current* prices.

Real values Money values corrected for inflation.

Index number The value of a variable expressed as 100 plus or minus its percentage deviation from a base year.

Base year (for index numbers) The year whose index number is set at 100.

The use of index numbers allows us to see clearly any upward and downward movements and to make an easy comparison of one year with another. For example, Table A1.5 shows quite clearly that manufacturing output fell from 1989 to 1992 and did not regain its 1989 level until 1994.

Using index numbers to measure percentage changes

To find the annual percentage growth rate in any one year we simply look at the percentage change in the index from the previous year. To work this out we use the following formula:

$$\left(\frac{I_t - I_{t-1}}{I_{t-1}}\right) \times 100$$

where I_t is the index in the year in question and I_{t1} is the index in the previous year.

Thus to find the growth rate in manufacturing output from 1987 to 1988 we first see how much the index has risen $(I_t - I_{t-1})$. The answer is $91.6 - 85.4 = 6.2$. But this does *not* mean that the growth rate is 6.2 per cent. According to our formula, the growth rate is equal to

$$\frac{91.6 - 85.4}{85.4} \times 100$$
$$= 6.2/85.4 \times 100$$
$$= 7.26$$

 What was the growth rate in manufacturing output from (a) 1982 to 1983; (b) 2001 to 2002?

The price index

Perhaps the best known of all price indices is the *consumer prices index (CPI)*. It is an index of the prices of goods and services purchased by the average household. Movements in this index, therefore, show how the cost of living has changed. Annual percentage increases in the CPI are the commonest definition of the rate of inflation. Thus if the CPI went up from 100 to 110 over a 12 month period, we would say that the rate of inflation was 10 per cent.

 If the CPI went up from 150 to 162 over twelve months, what would be the rate of inflation?

The use of weighted averages

The CPI is a *weighted average* of the prices of many items. The index of manufacturing output that we looked at previously was also a weighted average, an average of the output of many individual products.

To illustrate how a weighted average works, consider the case of a weighted average of the output of just three industries, A, B and C. Let us assume that in the base year (year 1) the output of A was £7 million, of B £2 million and of C £1 million, giving a total output of the three industries of £10 million. We now attach weights to the output of each industry to reflect its proportion of total output. Industry A is given a weight of 0.7 because it produces seven-tenths of total output. Industry B is given a weight of 0.2 and industry C a weight of 0.1. We then simply multiply each industry's index by its weight and add up all these figures to give the overall industry index.

The index for each industry in year 1 (the base year) is 100. This means that the weighted average index is also 100. Table A1.6 shows what happens to output in year 2. Industry A's output falls by 10 per cent, giving it an index of 90 in year 2. Industry B's output rises by 10 per cent and industry C's output rises by 30 per cent, giving indices of 110 and 130, respectively. But as you can see from the table, despite the fact that two of the three industries have had a rise in output, the total industry index has *fallen* from 100 to 98. The reason is that industry A is so much larger than the other two that its decline in output outweighs their increase.

Table A1.6 Constructing a weighted average index

Industry	Weight	Year 1		Year 2	
		Index	Index times weight	Index	Index times weight
A	0.7	100	70	90	63
B	0.2	100	20	110	22
C	0.1	100	10	130	13
Total	1.0		100		98

Definitions

Consumer prices index (CPI) An index of the prices of goods bought by a typical household.

Weighted average The average of several items where each item is ascribed a weight according to its importance. The weights must add up to 1.

The consumer prices index is a little more complicated. This is because it is calculated in two stages. First, products are grouped into categories such as food, clothing and services. A weighted average index is worked out for each group. Thus the index for food would be the weighted average of the indices for bread, potatoes, cooking oil, etc. Second, a weight is attached to each of the groups in order to work out an overall index.

Functional relationships

Throughout economics we examine how one economic variable affects another: how the purchases of cars are affected by their price; how consumer expenditure is affected by taxes, or by incomes; how the cost of producing washing machines is affected by the price of steel; how the rate of unemployment is affected by the level of government expenditure. These relationships are called *functional relationships*. We will need to express these relationships in a precise way, preferably in the form of a table or a graph or an equation.

Simple linear functions

These are relationships which produce a straight line when plotted on a graph. Let us take an imaginary example of the relationship between total value added tax receipts in an economy (V) and the level of consumer expenditure (C). This functional relationship can be written as:

$$V = f(C)$$

This is simply shorthand for saying that VAT receipts are a function of (i.e. depend on) the level of consumer expenditure.

If we want to know just *how much* VAT revenue will be at any given level of consumer expenditure, we will need to spell out this functional relationship. Let us do this in each of the three ways.

As a table. Table A1.7 gives a selection of values of C and the corresponding level of V. It is easy to read off from the table the level of VAT receipts at one of the levels of consumer expenditure listed. It is clearly more difficult to work out the level of VAT receipts if consumer expenditure is £23.4 billion or £47.6 billion.

As a graph. Figure A1.7 plots the data from Table A1.7. Each of the dots corresponds to one of the points in the table. By joining the dots up into a single line we can easily

Table A1.7 A VAT function

Consumer expenditure (£bn per year)	VAT receipts (£bn per year)
0	0
10	2
20	4
30	6
40	8
50	10

Figure A1.7 A graph of the VAT function: $V = 0.2C$

read off the value for VAT receipts at some level of consumption other than those listed in the table. A graph also has the advantage of allowing us to see the relationship at a glance.

It is usual to plot the *independent variable* (i.e. the one that does not depend on the other) on the horizontal or *x*-axis, and the *dependent variable* on the vertical or *y*-axis. In our example, VAT receipts *depend* on consumer expenditure. Thus VAT receipts are the dependent variable and consumer expenditure is the independent variable.

As an equation. The data in the table can be expressed in the equation

$$V = 0.2C$$

This would be the equation if the VAT rate were 20 per cent on all goods and services.

An equation has the major advantage of being precise. We could work out *exactly* how much would be paid in VAT at any given level of consumption.

This particular function starts at the origin of the graph (i.e. the bottom left-hand corner). This means that when the value of the independent variable is zero, so too is the value of the dependent variable.

When a graph does not pass through the origin its equation will have the form

$$y = a + bx$$

where y stands for the dependent variable and x for the independent variable, and a and b will have numbers assigned in an actual equation. For example, the equation might be

Definition

Functional relationships The mathematical relationships showing how one variable is affected by one or more others.

Table A1.8 $y = 4 + 2x$

x	y
0	4
1	6
2	8
3	10
4	12
5	14
.	.
.	.

Table A1.9 $y = 4 + 10x - x^2$

x	y
0	4
1	13
2	20
3	25
4	28
5	29
6	28
7	25
.	.

Figure A1.8 $y = 4 + 2x$

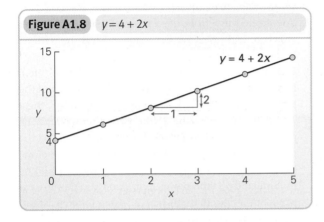

Figure A1.9 $y = 4 + 10x - x^2$

$y = 4 + 2x$

This would give Table A1.8 and Figure A1.8.

Notice two things about the relationship between the equation and the graph:

- The point where the line crosses the vertical axis (at a value of 4) is given by the constant (*a*) term. If the *a* term is negative, the line will cross the vertical axis *below* the horizontal axis.
- The slope of the line is given by the *b* term. The slope is 2/1: for every 1 unit increase in *x* there is a 2 unit increase in *y*.

 On a diagram like Figure A1.8 draw the graphs for the following equations: $y = -3 + 4x$; $y = 15 - 3x$.

Note that in the second equation of the question, the *x* term is negative. This means that *y* and *x* are *inversely related*. As *x* increases, *y* decreases.

Non-linear functions

With these functions the equation involves a squared term (or other power terms). Such functions will give a curved line when plotted on a graph. As an example, consider the following equation:

$y = 4 + 10x - x^2$

Table A1.9 and Figure A1.9 are based on it.

As you can see, *y* rises at a decelerating rate and eventually begins to fall. This is because the negative x^2 term is becoming more and more influential as *x* rises and eventually begins to outweigh the 10*x* term.

 What shaped graph would you get from the equations $y = -6 + 3x + 2x^2$ and $y = 10 - 4x + x^2$? (If you cannot work out the answer, construct a table like Table A1.9 and then plot the figures on a graph.)

*Elementary differentiation

In several starred boxes and *Looking at the Maths* sections we use some elementary calculus. The part of calculus we use is called **differentiation**. This is a technique to enable us to calculate the rate of change of a variable. The purpose of this section is not to explain why differentiation involves the procedures it does, but simply to state the rules that are necessary for our purposes. You will need to consult a maths book if you want to know how these rules are derived.

First, let us see when we would be interested in looking at the rate of change of a variable. Take the case of a firm

Definition

Differentiation A mathematical technique to find the rate of change of one variable with respect to another.

Table A1.10	$C = 20 + 5Q + Q^2$
x	**y**
0	20
1	26
2	34
3	44
4	56
5	70
6	86
7	104
8	124
·	·

Figure A1.10 A total cost function: $C = 20 + 5Q + Q^2$

thinking of expanding. It will want to know how much its costs will increase as its output increases. It will want to know the rate of change of costs with respect to changes in output.

Let us assume that it faces a cost function of the form

$$C = 20 + 5Q + Q^2 \qquad (1)$$

where C is the total cost of production and Q is the quantity produced. Table A1.10 and Figure A1.10 are derived from this equation.

The rate of increase in its costs with respect to increases in output is given by the *slope* of the cost curve in Figure A1.10. The steeper the slope, the more rapidly costs increase. At point a the slope of the curve is 11. This is found by drawing the tangent to the curve and measuring the slope of the tangent. At this point on the curve, what we are saying is that for each one unit increase in output there is an £11 increase in costs. (Obviously as the graph is curved, this rate of increase will vary at different outputs.)

This rate of increase in costs is known as the **marginal cost**. It is the same with other variables that increase with quantity: their rate of increase is known as *marginal*. For example, *marginal revenue* is the rate of increase of sales revenue with respect to output.

We can use the technique of differentiation to derive a marginal from a total equation: in other words, to derive

the slope of the total curve. Let us assume that we have an equation:

$$y = 10 + 6x - 4x^2 + 2x^3 \qquad (2)$$

When we differentiate it, we call the new equation dy/dx: this stands for the rate of increase in y (dy) with respect to the increase in x (dx).

The rules for differentiating a simple equation like equation (2) are very straightforward.

1. You delete the constant term (10). The reason for this is that, being constant, by definition it will not cause an increase in y as x increases, and it is the *increase* in y that we are trying to discover.

2. You delete the x from the x term which has no power attached, and just leave the number. Thus the term $6x$ becomes simply 6.

3. For any term with a power in it (a square, a cube, etc.), its value should be *multiplied* by the power term and the power term reduced by one. Thus in the term $4x^2$, the 4 would be multiplied by 2 (the power term), and the power term would be reduced from 2 to 1 (but x to the power of 1 is simply x). After differentiation, therefore, the term becomes $8x$. In the term $2x^3$, the 2 would be multiplied by 3 (the power term), and the power term would be reduced from 3 to 2. After differentiation, therefore, the term becomes $6x^2$.

Applying these three rules to the equation

$$y = 10 + 6x - 4x^2 + 2x^3 \qquad (2)$$

gives

$$dy/dx = 6 - 8x + 6x^2 \qquad (3)$$

To find the rate of change of y with respect to x at any given value of x, therefore, you simply substitute that value of x into equation (3).

Thus when $x = 4$, $dy/dx = 6 - (8 \times 4) + (6 \times 16) = 70$. In other words, when $x = 4$, for every 1 unit increase in x, y will increase by 70.

Returning to our cost function in equation (1), what is the marginal cost equation? Applying the three rules to the equation

$$C = 20 + 5Q + Q^2 \qquad (1)$$

gives

$$dC/dQ = 5 + 2Q \qquad (4)$$

Thus at an output of 3, the marginal cost (dC/dQ) is $5 + (2 \times 3) = 11$, which is the slope of the tangent to point a.

Definition

Marginal cost The rate of increase in costs with respect to output.

What would be the marginal cost equation if the total cost equation were

$$C = 15 + 20Q - 5Q^2 + Q^3?$$

What would be the marginal cost at an output of 8?

Finding the maximum or minimum point of a curve

The other important use we can make of calculus is to find the maximum or minimum point of a curve. This has a number of important applications. For example, a firm may want to know the minimum point on its average cost curve (a curve which shows how costs per unit of output vary as output increases). Also it is likely to want to know the output at which it will earn maximum profit. Let us examine this particular case.

Assume that the equation for total profit (Π) is:

$$\Pi = -20 + 12Q - Q^2 \tag{5}$$

---

*BOX A1.1   WHEN IS GOOD NEWS REALLY GOOD?   CASE STUDIES AND APPLICATIONS

Are things getting better or merely getting worse more slowly?

From the second quarter of 1990 unemployment rose continuously for many quarters. By the third quarter of 1991 unemployment had increased by some 0.75 million. What good news could the government possibly draw from this?

Governments, always in search of any glimmer of good economic news, proclaimed that unemployment was rising more slowly (in other words, that the rate of increase in unemployment was falling). This was perfectly correct.

To show this, let us assume that N is the number of people out of work. The rate of change of unemployment is therefore given by dN/dt (where t is time). A positive figure for dN/dt represents a rise in unemployment, a negative figure a fall. Its value is given by the slope of the green line in the diagram. From the second quarter of 1990 this figure was positive. Bad news!

But the government sought a rosier interpretation. By using a second-order derivative, d^2N/dt^2, it could show that the rate of increase in unemployment from early 1991 had been falling. The value of this is given by the slope of the red line in the diagram. The government proclaimed that this was evidence that the economy was beginning to recover. Good news!

The use of calculus in this manner is a two-edged sword and such statistical sophistry is open to the political opposition, who could at a later date, if they so wished, claim that a fall in unemployment was bad economic news. Dare they?

 If the opposition were indeed to claim that a fall in unemployment was bad news, what would have to be the value of d^2N/dt^2: positive or negative?

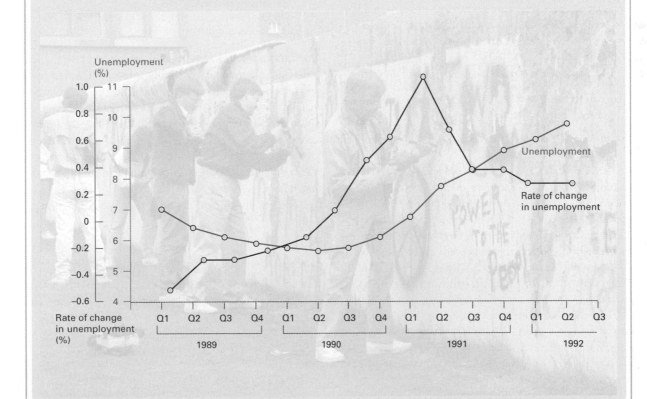

Table A1.11 $\Pi = -20 + 12Q - Q^2$

Q	Π
0	−20
1	−9
2	0
3	7
4	12
5	15
6	16
7	15
8	12
9	7
10	0

Figure A1.11 A total profit function: $\Pi = -20 + 12Q - Q^2$

This gives profit at various outputs as shown in Table A1.11. The corresponding graph is plotted in Figure A1.11.

 What is the meaning of a negative profit?

It can be seen at a glance that profits are maximised at an output of 6 units. But we could have worked this out directly from the profit equation without having to draw up a table or graph. How is this done?

Remember that when we differentiate a curve, the equation we get (known as 'the first derivative') gives us the slope of the curve. You can see that at the point of maximum profit (the top of the curve) its slope is zero: the tangent is horizontal. So all we have to do to find the top of the curve is to differentiate its equation and set it equal to zero.

Given that

$$\Pi = -20 + 12Q - Q^2 \tag{5}$$

then:

$$d\Pi/dQ = 12 - 2Q \tag{6}$$

Setting this equal to zero gives:

$$12 - 2Q = 0$$
$$\therefore \quad 2Q = 12$$
$$\therefore \quad Q = 6$$

Thus profits are maximised at an output of 6 units: the result we obtained from the table and graph.

The second derivative test

There is a problem with this technique, however. How can we tell from equation (6) that we have found the *maximum* rather than the *minimum*? The problem is that *both* the maximum *and* the minimum points of a curve have a zero slope.

The answer is to conduct a **second derivative test**. This involves differentiating the equation a second time. This gives the rate of change of the *slope* of the original curve. If you look at Figure A1.11, as output increases, the tangent moves from being upward sloping, to horizontal, to downward sloping. In other words, the slope is getting less and less. Its rate of change is *negative*. Thus if we differentiate the equation for the slope (i.e. the first derivative), we should get a negative figure.

When we differentiate a second time we get what is called the **second derivative**. It is written d^2y/dx^2.

If we differentiate equation (6):

$$d\Pi/dQ = 12 - 2Q \tag{6}$$

we get:

$$d^2\Pi/dQ^2 = -2 \tag{7}$$

(Note that the rules for differentiating a second time are the same as for the first time.) Given that the second derivative in this case is negative, we have demonstrated that we have indeed found the maximum profit point (at $Q = 6$), and not the minimum.

 Given the following equation for a firm's average cost (AC), i.e. the cost per unit of output (Q):

$$AC = 60 - 16Q + 2Q^2$$

(a) At what output is AC at a minimum?
(b) Use the second derivative test to prove that this is a minimum and not a maximum.

Partial differentiation

Many relationships in economics involve more than two variables. For example, the demand for a product depends not just on its price, but also on income, the price of substitutes, the price of complements, etc. Similarly, a firm's cost of production depends not just on the quantity of output it produces, but also on wage rates, the prices of the various materials it uses, the productivity of its workers and machinery, and so on.

Such relationships can be expressed as a function as follows:

$$y = f(x_1, x_2, x_3, \ldots x_n)$$

where x_1, x_2, etc. are the various determinants of y.

Definitions

Second derivative test If on differentiating an equation a second time the answer is negative (positive), the point is a maximum (minimum).

Second derivative The rate of change of the first derivative, found by differentiating the first derivative.

Let us take a simple example where a firm's total cost (TC) depends on just two things: the quantity produced (Q) and the wage rate (W). The cost function will be of the form

$$TC = f(Q, W)$$

Assume that in the case of a particular firm the function is

$$TC = 20 + 10Q - 4Q^2 + 2Q^3 + 6W \qquad (8)$$

What we are likely to want to know is how this firm's total cost changes as quantity changes, assuming the wage rate is held constant. Alternatively we may wish to know how its total cost changes as the wage rate changes, assuming that output is held constant. To do this we use the technique of **partial differentiation**. This involves the same technique as simple differentiation but applied to just the one variable that is not held constant.

Definitions

Partial differentiation A mathematical technique used with functions containing two or more independent variables. The technique is used to find the rate of change of the dependent variable with respect to a single independent variable assuming that the other independent variables are held constant.

Partial derivative The partial derivative of a function of two or more independent variables is the derivative with respect to just one of those variables, while holding the others constant.

Thus to find the rate of change of costs with respect to quantity in equation (8), we differentiate the equation with respect to Q and ignore the W term. We ignore it as it is held constant and is thus treated like the constant (20) term in the equation. Using the rules of differentiation, the **partial derivative** is thus

$$\frac{\partial TC}{\partial Q} = 10 - 8Q + 6Q^2 \qquad (9)$$

Note that instead of using the symbol 'd' that we used in simple differentiation, we now use the symbol '∂'. Apart from that, the rules for partial differentiation are exactly the same as with simple differentiation.

If we now wanted to see how this firm's costs vary with the wage rate for any given output, then we would partially differentiate equation (8) with respect to W, giving

$$\frac{\partial TC}{\partial W} = 6$$

In other words, for each £1 rise in the wage rate, total cost would rise by £6.

Assume that the demand for a product is given by the following function:

$$Q_D = 1000 - 50P + 2P^2 + 10P_S + P_S^2$$

where Q_D is the quantity demanded, P is the price of the good and P_S is the price of a substitute good. What is the partial derivative of this demand function with respect to (a) the price of the good; (b) the price of the substitute good? Interpret the meaning of each partial derivative.

Appendix summary

1. Diagrams in economics can be used as pictures: to sketch a relationship so that its essentials can be perceived at a glance.

2. Tables, graphs and charts are also used to portray real-life data. These can be time-series data or cross-section data or both.

3. In order to get a true picture from economic data it is important to be aware of various ways that statistics can be abused: these include a selective use of data, a choice of axes on a graph to make trends seem more or less exaggerated or to make a curve more or less steep, confusing absolute and relative values, ignoring questions of distribution, confusing nominal and real values, and selecting the time period to make the statistics look the most favourable or unfavourable.

4. Presenting time-series data as index numbers gives a clear impression of trends and is a good way of comparing how two or more series (perhaps originally measured in different units) have changed over the same time period. A base year is chosen and the index for that year is set at 100. The percentage change in the value of a variable is given by the percentage change in the index (I). The formula is

$$\left(\frac{I_t - I_{t-1}}{I_{t-1}} \right) \times 100$$

Several items can be included in one index by using a weighted value for each of the items. The weights must add up to 1, and each weight will reflect the relative importance of that particular item in the index.

5. Functional relationships can be expressed as an equation, a table or a graph. In the linear (straight-line) equation $y = a + bx$, the a term gives the vertical intercept (the point where the graph crosses the vertical axis) and the b term gives the slope. When there is a power term (e.g. $y = a + bx + cx^2$), the graph will be a curve.

6. *Differentiation can be used to obtain the rate of change of one variable with respect to another. The rules of differentiation require that in an equation of the form

$$y = a + bx + cx^2 + dx^3$$

the a term disappears, the bx term simply becomes b, the cx^2 term becomes $2cx$, the dx^3 becomes $3dx^2$ and so on, with each extra term being multiplied by its power term and its power term being reduced by 1.

7. *To find the value of the x term at which the y term is at a maximum or minimum, the equation should be differentiated and set equal to zero. To check which it is – maximum or minimum – the second derivative should be calculated. If it is negative, then setting the first derivative equal to zero has yielded a maximum. If the second derivative is positive, then setting the first derivative to zero has yielded a minimum value.

Appendix 2: Websites

All the following websites can be accessed from this book's own website (http://www.pearsoned.co.uk/sloman). When you enter the site, click on **Hot Links**. You will find all the following sites listed. Click on the one you want and the 'hot link' will take you straight to it.

The sections and numbers below refer to the ones used in the websites listed at the end of each chapter. Thus if the list contained the number A21, this would refer to the Moneyextra site.

(A) General news sources

As the title of this section implies, the websites here can be used for finding material on current news issues or tapping into news archives. Most archives are offered free of charge. However, some do require you to register. As well as key UK and American news sources, you will also notice some slightly different places from where you can get your news, such as the St Petersburg Times and Kyodo News (from Japan). Check out sites number 38 Refdesk, 43 Guardian World News Guide and 44 Online newspapers for links to newspapers across the world. Try searching for an article on a particular topic by using site number 41 Google News Search.

1. BBC news
2. The Economist
3. The Financial Times
4. The Guardian
5. The Independent
6. ITN
7. The Observer
8. The Telegraph
9. The Times, Sunday Times
10. The New York Times
11. Fortune
12. Time Magazine
13. The Washington Post
14. Moscow Times (English)
15. St Petersburg Times (English)
16. Straits Times
17. New Straits Times
18. The Scotsman
19. The Herald
20. Euromoney
21. Moneyextra
22. Market News International
23. BusinessWeek online
24. Ananova
25. CNN Money
26. Wall Street Journal
27. Asia News Network
28. allAfrica.com
29. Greek News Sources (English)
30. Kyodo News: Japan (English)
31. RFE/RL News
32. The Australian
33. Sydney Morning Herald
34. Japan Times
35. Reuters
36. Bloomberg
37. David Smith's Economics UK.com
38. Refdesk (links to a whole range of news sources)
39. Newspapers on World Wide Web
40. Economics in the News from Gametheory.net
41. Google News Search
42. Moreover
43. Guardian World News Guide
44. Online newspapers

(B) Sources of economic and business data

Using websites to find up-to-date data is of immense value to the economist. The data sources below offer you a range of specialist and non-specialist data information. Universities have free access to the MIMAS and ESDS sites, which are huge databases of statistics. Site 34, the Treasury Pocket Data Bank, is a very useful source of key UK and world statistics, and is updated monthly. It comes as an Excel file.

1. Economics Network gateway to economic data
2. Biz/ed Gateway to economic and company data
3. National Statistics
4. Data Archive (Essex)
5. Bank of England Statistical Database
6. Economic Resources (About)
7. Nationwide House Prices Site
8. House Web (data on housing market)
9. Incomes Data Services
10. HBOs house price data
11. Land Registry (house prices, etc)
12. Manchester Information and Associated Services (MIMAS)
13. Global Financial Data
14. PACIFIC: currencies of the world
15. Economagic
16. Groningen Growth and Development Centre
17. AEAweb: Resources for economists on the Internet (RFE)
18. Joseph Rowntree Foundation
19. Intute: Economics resources
20. Energy Information Administration
21. OECD Statistics
22. CIA world statistics site
23. UN Millennium Country Profiles
24. World Bank statistics
25. Economic Data: FRED
26. Ministry of International Trade and Industry (Japan)
27. Yahoo Finance
28. Nanyang Technological University, Singapore: Statistical Data Locators
29. Davidson Data Center and Network
30. Oanda Currency Converter

31. World Economic Outlook Database (IMF)
32. Economist Country Briefings
33. OFFSTATS links to data sets
34. Treasury Pocket Data Bank (source of UK and world economic data)
35. Economic and Social Data Service (ESDS)
36. The official yearbook of the UK
37. NationMaster
38. Statistical Annex of the European Economy
39. Business and Consumer Surveys (all EU countries)
40. Gapminder
41. WebEc Economics Data
42. WTO International Trade Statistics database
43. UNCTAD trade, investment and development statistics

(C) Sites for students and teachers of economics

The following websites offer useful ideas and resources to those who are studying or teaching economics. It is worth browsing through some just to see what is on offer. Try out the first four sites, for starters. The Internet Economist is a very helpful tutorial for economics students on using the Internet.

1. Economics Network of the UK Higher Education Academy
2. Biz/ed
3. Ecedweb
4. Study Economics
5. Economics and Business Education Association
6. Tutor2U
7. Economics America
8. The Internet Economist (tutorial on using the Web)
9. Oxford School of Learning
10. Teaching resources for economists
11. Resources for University Teachers of Economics (University of Melbourne)
12. Federal Reserve Bank of San Francisco: Economics Education
13. Federal Reserve Bank of Minneapolis Economic Education
14. WebEc resources
15. BibEc papers
16. Online Opinion (Economics)
17. The Idea Channel
18. History of Economic Thought
19. Resources For Economists on the Internet (RFE)
20. Classroom Expernomics
21. VCE Economics (Economics teaching resources – Australian)
22. Why Study Economics?
23. Economic Classroom Experiments

(D) Economic models and simulations

Economic modelling is an important aspect of economic analysis. There are a number of sites that offer access to a model for you to use, e.g. Virtual economy (where you can play being Chancellor of the Exchequer). Using such models can be a useful way of finding out how economic theory works within an environment that claims to reflect reality.

1. Virtual economy
2. Virtual factory
3. Virtual Learning arcade
4. About.com Economics
5. Classic Economic Models
6. Economics Network Handbook, Chapter on Simulations, Games and Role-play
7. Estima (statistical analysis)
8. SPSS (statistical analysis)
9. National Institute of Economic and Social Research

10. Software available on the Economics Network site
11. RFE Software
12. Virtual Chancellor
13. Veconlab: Charles Holt's classroom experiments
14. EconPort
15. Denise Hazlett's Classroom Experiments in Macroeconomics
16. Games Economists Play
17. Finance and Economics Experimental Laboratory at Exeter (FEELE)
18. Classroom Expernomics
19. The Economics Network's Guide to Classroom Experiments and Games

(E) UK government and UK organisations' sites

If you want to see what a government department is up to, then look no further than the list below. Government departments' websites are an excellent source of information and data. They are particularly good at offering information on current legislation and policy initiatives.

1. Gateway site (Directgov)
2. Department of Communities and Local Government
3. Central Office of Information
4. Competition Commission
5. Department for Children Schools and Families
6. Department for International Development
7. Department for Transport
8. Department of Health
9. Department for Work and Previous
10. Department for Business, Enterprise and Regulatory Reform
11. Environment Agency
12. UK euro information site
13. Low Pay Commission
14. Department for Environment, Food and Rural Affairs
15. Office of Communications (Ofcom)
16. Office of Gas and Electricity Markets (Ofgem)
17. Official Documents OnLine
18. Office of Fair trading (OFT)
19. Office of Rail Regulation (ORR)
20. The Takeover Panel
21. Sustainable Development Commission
22. OFWAT
23. National Statistics (ONS)
24. National Statistics Time Series Data
25. HM Revenue and customs
26. UK Intellectual Property Office
27. Parliament Website
28. Scottish Government
29. Scottish Environment Protection Agency
30. Treasury
31. Equality and Human Rights Commission
32. Trades Union Congress (TUC)
33. Confederation of British Industry
34. Adam Smith Institute
35. Chatham House
36. Institute for Fiscal Studies
37. Advertising Standards Authority
38. Business Link
39. Campaign for Better Transport

(F) Sources of monetary and financial data

As the title suggests, here are listed useful websites for finding information on financial matters. You will see that the list comprises mainly central banks, both within Europe and further afield.

1. Bank of England
2. Bank of England Monetary and Financial Statistics
3. Banque de France
4. Bundesbank (German central bank)
5. Central Bank of Ireland
6. European Central Bank
7. Eurostat
8. US Federal Reserve Bank
9. Netherlands Central Bank
10. Bank of Japan
11. Reserve Bank of Australia
12. Bank Negara Malaysia (English)
13. Monetary Authority of Singapore
14. Bank of Canada
15. National Bank of Denmark (English)
16. Reserve Bank of India
17. Links to central banks from the Bank for International Settlements
18. The London Stock Exchange

(G) European Union and related sources

For information on European issues, the following is a wide range of useful sites. The sites maintained by the European Union are an excellent source of information and are provided free of charge.

1. Economic and Financial Affairs: (EC DG)
2. European Central Bank
3. EU official Web site
4. Eurostat
5. Employment and Social Affairs: (EC DG)
6. Booklets on the EU
7. Enterprise and Industry (EC DG)
8. Competition: (EC DG)
9. Agriculture and Rural Development (EC DG)
10. Energy and Transport: (EC DG)
11. Environment: (EC DG)
12. Regional Policy: (EC DG)
13. Taxation and Customs Union: (EC DG)
14. Education and training: (EC DG)
15. European Patent Office
16. European Commission
17. European Parliament
18. European Council

(H) International organisations

This section casts its net beyond Europe and lists the Web addresses of the main international organisations in the global economy. You will notice that some sites are run by pressure groups, such as Jubilee Research, while others represent organisations set up to manage international affairs, such as the International Monetary Fund and the United Nations.

1. Food and Agriculture Organisation
2. International Air Transport Association (IATA)
3. International Labour Organisation (ILO)
4. International Monetary Fund (IMF)
5. Organisation for Economic Co-operation and Development (OECD)
6. OPEC
7. World Bank
8. World Health Organisation

9. United Nations
10. United Nations Industrial Development Organisation
11. Friends of the Earth
12. Jubilee Research
13. Oxfam
14. Christian Aid (reports on development issues)
15. European Bank for Reconstruction and Development (EBRD)
16. World Trade Organisation (WTO)
17. United Nations Development Programme
18. UNICEF
19. EURODAD – European Network on Debt and Development
20. NAFTA
21. South American Free Trade Areas
22. ASEAN
23. APEC

(I) Economics search and link sites

If you are having difficulty finding what you want from the list of sites above, the following sites offer links to other sites and are a very useful resource when you are looking for something a little bit more specialist. Once again, it is worth having a look at what these sites have to offer in order to judge their usefulness.

1. Gateway for UK official sites
2. Alta Plana
3. Data Archive Search
4. Inomics (search engine for economics information)
5. RePEc bibliographic database
6. Estima: Links to economics resources sites
7. Intute: Social Sciences (Economics)
8. WebEc
9. One World (link to economic development sites)
10. Economic development sites (list) from One World.net
11. Biz/ed Internet catalogue
12. Web links for economists from the Economics Network
13. Yahoo's links to economic data
14. OFFSTATS links to data sets
15. Excite Economics Links
16. Internet Resources for Economists
17. Google Web Directory: Economics
18. Resources for Economists on the Internet
19. UK University Economics Departments
20. Economics education links
21. Development Gateway Foundation

(J) Internet search engines

The following search engines have been found to be useful.

1. Google
2. Altavista
3. Overture
4. Excite
5. Go.com
6. Search.com
7. MSN
8. UK Plus
9. Yahoo
10. Teoma
11. Kartoo
12. Blinkx (for videos and audio podcasts)

Threshold Concepts and Key Ideas

THRESHOLD CONCEPTS

Page

1. Choice and opportunity cost   8
2. People gain from voluntary economic interaction   23
3. Markets may fail to meet social objectives   24
4. Markets equate demand and supply   44
5. People respond to incentives. It is important, therefore, that these have the desired effect   50
6. Governments can sometimes improve market outcomes   52
7. Elasticity: of a variable to a change in a determinant   68
8. Rational decision making involves choices at the margin   100
9. People's actions depend on their expectations   105
10. General equilibrium: when all markets are in balance   307
11. Allocative efficiency: private and social   310
12. The distinction between real and nominal values   395
13. Short-term growth in a country's output tends to fluctuate   402
14. Long-term growth in a country's output depends on a growth in the quantity and/or productivity of its resources   404
15. Cumulative causation: economic effects can snowball   487

KEY IDEAS

Page

1. **Scarcity** is the excess of human wants over what can actually be produced. Because of scarcity, various choices have to be made between alternatives.   5
2. The **opportunity cost** of any activity is the sacrifice made to do it. It is the best thing that could have been done as an alternative.   8
3. **Economic efficiency** is thus achieved when each good is produced at the minimum cost and where individual people and firms get the maximum benefit from their resources.   10
4. **Equity** is where income is distributed in a way that is considered to be fair or just. Note that an equitable distribution is not the same as an equal distribution and that different people have different views on what is equitable.   10
5. **Changes in demand or supply cause markets to adjust**. Whenever such changes occur, the resulting 'disequilibrium' will bring an automatic change in prices, thereby restoring equilibrium (i.e. a balance of demand and supply).   21
6. **The importance of the positive/normative distinction**. Economics can only contribute to policy issues in a positive way. Economists, as scientists, should not make normative judgements. They can make them only as individual people, with no more moral right than any other individual.   27
7. The **income and substitution effects** are useful concepts as they help to explain why people react to a price rise by buying less. The size of these effects depends on a range of factors. These factors determine the shape of the demand curve.   33
8. **Equilibrium** is the point where conflicting interests are balanced. Only at this point is the amount that demanders are willing to purchase the same as the amount that suppliers are willing to supply. It is a point that will be automatically reached in a free market through the operation of the price mechanism.   43

Page

9. **Elasticity**. The responsiveness of one variable (e.g. demand) to a change in another (e.g. price). This concept is fundamental to understanding how markets work. The more elastic variables are, the more responsive is the market to changing circumstances. — 67

10. **People's actions are influenced by their expectations**. People respond not just to what is happening now (such as a change in price), but to what they anticipate will happen in the future. — 71

11. **People's actions are influenced by their attitudes towards risk**. Many decisions are taken under conditions of risk or uncertainty. Generally, the lower the probability of (or the more uncertain) the desired outcome of an action, the less likely people will be to undertake the action. — 75

12. **The fallacy of composition**. What applies in one case will not necessarily apply when repeated in all cases. — 84

13. **The principle of diminishing marginal utility**. The more of a product a person consumes, the less will be the additional utility gained from one more unit. — 97

14. **The equi-marginal principle**. The optimum amount of two alternatives consumed (or produced) will be where the marginal benefit ratios of the two alternatives are equal to their marginal cost ratios:

$$\frac{MU_A}{MU_B} = \frac{P_A}{P_B}$$

— 102

15. **Good decision making requires good information**. Where information is poor, decisions and their outcomes may be poor. — 106

16. **Output depends on the amount of resources and how they are used**. Different amounts and combinations of inputs will lead to different amounts of output. If output is to be produced efficiently, then inputs should be combined in the optimum proportions. — 124

17. **The law of diminishing marginal returns** states that when increasing amounts of a variable factor are used with a given amount of a fixed factor, there will come a point when each extra unit of the variable factor will produce less extra output than the previous unit. — 125

18. The **'bygones' principle** states that sunk (fixed) costs should be ignored when deciding whether to produce or sell more or less of a product. Only variable costs should be taken into account. — 131

19. **Fixed costs and the time period**. Fixed costs occur only in the short run, since in the long run all inputs can be varied. — 146

20. **Market power**. When firms have market power over prices, they can use this to raise prices and profits above the perfectly competitive level. Other things being equal, the firm will gain at the expense of the consumer. Similarly, if consumers or workers have market power, they can use this to their own benefit. — 164

21. **People often think and behave strategically**. How you think others will respond to your actions is likely to influence your own behaviour. Firms, for example, when considering a price or product change will often take into account the likely reactions of their rivals. — 190

22. **The nature of institutions and organisations is likely to influence behaviour**. There are various forces influencing people's decisions in complex organisations. Assumptions that an organisation will follow one simple objective (e.g. short-run profit maximisation) is thus too simplistic in many cases. — 216

23. **The principal–agent problem**. Where people (principals), as a result of a lack of knowledge, cannot ensure that their best interests are served by their agents. Agents may take advantage of this situation to the disadvantage of the principals. — 217

24. **Stocks and flows**. A stock is a quantity of something at a given point in time. A flow is an increase or decrease in something over a specified period of time. This is an important distinction and a common cause of confusion. — 260

25. **The principle of discounting**. People generally prefer to have benefits today rather than in the future. Thus future benefits have to be reduced (discounted) to give them a present value. — 262

26. **Allocative efficiency (simple formulation) in any activity is achieved where marginal benefit equals marginal cost**. Private efficiency is achieved where marginal private benefit equals marginal private cost (MB = MC). Social efficiency is achieved where marginal social benefit equals marginal social cost (MSB = MSC). — 306

27. **Social efficiency (equi-marginal formulation)** is achieved where the marginal social benefit ratios are equal to the marginal social cost ratios for any two alternatives. In the case of two alternatives X and Y, this will be where:

$$\frac{MSB_X}{MSB_Y} = \frac{MSC_X}{MSC_Y}$$

— 310

Page

28. **Markets generally fail to achieve social efficiency**. There are various types of market failure. Market failures provide one of the major justifications for government intervention in the economy. — 313

29. **Externalities are spillover costs or benefits**. Where these exist, even an otherwise perfect market will fail to achieve social efficiency. — 313

30. **The free-rider problem**. People are often unwilling to pay for things if they can make use of things other people have bought. This problem can lead to people not purchasing things that would be to the benefit of them and other members of society to have. — 316

31. **The problem of time lags**. Many economic actions can take a long time to take effect. This can cause problems of instability and an inability of the economy to achieve social efficiency. — 320

32. **Economies suffer from inherent instability**. As a result, economic growth and other macroeconomic indicators tend to fluctuate. — 388

33. **Societies face trade-offs between economic objectives**. For example, the goal of faster growth may conflict with that of greater equality; the goal of lower unemployment may conflict with that of lower inflation (at least in the short run). This is an example of opportunity cost: the cost of achieving one objective may be achieving less of another. The existence of trade-offs means that policy-makers must make choices. — 389

34. **The principle of cumulative causation**. An initial event can cause an ultimate effect that is much larger. — 463

35. **Goodhart's law**: Controlling a symptom (i.e. an indicator) of a problem will not cure the problem. Instead, the indicator will merely cease to be a good indicator of the problem. — 585

36. **The law of comparative advantage**. Provided opportunity costs of various goods differ in two countries, both of them can gain from mutual trade if they specialise in producing (and exporting) those goods that have relatively low opportunity costs compared with the other country. — 673

37. **The competitive advantage of nations**. The ability of countries to compete in the market for exports and with potential importers to their country. The competitiveness of any one industry depends on the availability and quality of resources, demand conditions at home in that industry, the strategies and rivalry of firms within the industry and the quality of supporting industries and infrastructure. It also depends on government policies and there is also an element of chance. — 682

38. **The distinction between nominal and real figures**. Nominal figures are those using current prices, interest rates, etc. Real figures are figures corrected for inflation. — A:6

Glossary

Absolute advantage A country has an absolute advantage over another in the production of a good if it can produce it with less resources than the other country can.

Accelerationist theory The theory that unemployment can only be reduced below the natural rate at the cost of accelerating inflation.

Accelerator coefficient The level of induced investment as a proportion of a rise in national income: $\alpha = I_i/\Delta Y$.

Accelerator theory The *level* of investment depends on the *rate of change* of national income, and as result tends to be subject to substantial fluctuations.

Active balances Money held for transactions and precautionary purposes.

Actual growth The percentage annual increase in national output actually produced.

Ad valorem tariffs Tariffs levied as a percentage of the price of the import.

Ad valorem tax A tax on a good levied as a percentage of its value. It can be a single-stage tax or a multi-stage tax (such as VAT).

Adaptive expectations hypothesis The theory that people base their expectations of inflation on past inflation rates.

Adjustable peg A system whereby exchange rates are fixed for a period of time, but may be devalued (or revalued) if a deficit (or surplus) becomes substantial.

Adverse selection The tendency of those who are at greatest risk to take out insurance.

Aggregate demand Total spending on goods and services made in the economy. It consists of four elements, consumer spending (C), investment (I), government spending (G) and the expenditure on exports (X), less any expenditure on imports of goods and services (M): $AD = C + I + G + X - M$.

Aggregate demand for labour curve A curve showing the total demand for labour in the economy at different levels of real wage rates.

Aggregate expenditure (E) Aggregate demand in the Keynsian model: i.e. $C_d + J$.

Aggregate supply of labour curve A curve showing the total number of people willing and able to work at different average real wage rates.

Aggregate supply The total amount of output in the economy.

Allocative efficiency A situation where the current combination of goods produced and sold gives the maximum satisfaction for each consumer at their current levels of income. Note that a redistribution of income would lead to a different combination of goods that was allocatively efficient.

Alternative theories of the firm Theories of the firm based on the assumption that firms have aims other than profit maximisation.

Ambient-based standards Pollution control that requires firms to meet minimum standards for the environment (e.g. air or water quality).

Appreciation A rise in the free-market exchange rate of the domestic currency with foreign currencies.

Arbitrage Buying an asset in a market where it has a lower price and selling it again in another market where it has a higher price and thereby making a profit.

Arc elasticity The measurement of elasticity between two points on a curve.

Assets Possessions, or claims held on others.

Assisted areas Areas of high unemployment qualifying for government regional selective assistance (RSA) and grants from the European regional development fund (ERDF).

Asymmetric information Where one party in an economic relationship (e.g. an agent) has more information than another (e.g. the principal).

Asymmetric shocks Shocks (such as an oil price increase or a recession in another part of the world) that have different-sized effects on different industries, regions or countries.

Authorised institutions The institutions comprising the monetary (or banking) sector.

Automatic fiscal stabilisers Tax revenues that rise and government expenditure that falls as national income rises. The more they change with income, the bigger the stabilising effect on national income.

Average (total) cost Total cost (fixed plus variable) per unit of output: $AC = TC/Q = AFC + AVC$.

Average cost pricing or **mark-up pricing** Where firms set the price by adding a profit mark-up to average cost.

Average fixed cost Total fixed cost per unit of output: $AFC = TFC/Q$.

Average physical product Total output (TPP) per unit of the variable factor in question: $APP = TPP/Q_v$.

Average rate of income tax   Income taxes as a proportion of a person's total (gross) income: T/Y.

Average revenue   Total revenue per unit of output. When all output is sold at the same price average revenue will be the same as price: $AR = TR/Q = P$.

Average variable cost   Total variable cost per unit of output: $AVC = TVC/Q$.

Balance of payments account   A record of the country's transactions with the rest of the world. It shows the country's payments to or deposits in other countries (debits) and its receipts or deposits from other countries (credits). It also shows the balance between these debits and credits under various headings.

Balance of payments on current account   The balance on trade in goods and services plus net investment income and current transfers.

Balance on trade in goods   Exports of goods minus imports of goods.

Balance on trade in goods and services (or balance of trade)   Exports of goods and services minus imports of goods and services.

Balance on trade in services   Exports of services minus imports of services.

Balancing item (in the balance of payments)   A statistical adjustment to ensure that the two sides of the balance of payments account balance. It is necessary because of errors in compiling the statistics.

Bank (or deposits) multiplier   The number of times greater the expansion of bank deposits is than the additional liquidity in banks that causes it: $1/L$ (the inverse of the liquidity ratio).

Bank bills   Bills that have been accepted by another institution and hence insured against default.

Barometric firm price leadership   Where the price leader is the one whose prices are believed to reflect market conditions in the most satisfactory way.

Barriers to entry   Anything that prevents or impedes the entry of firms into an industry and thereby limits the amount of competition faced by existing firms.

Barter economy   An economy where people exchange goods and services directly with one another without any payment of money. Workers would be paid with bundles of goods.

Base year (for index numbers)   The year whose index number is set at 100.

Basic needs approach   The attempt to measure development in terms of a country's ability to meet the basic requirements for life.

Basic rate of tax   The main marginal rate of tax, applying to most people's incomes.

Behavioural theories of the firm   Theories that attempt to predict the actions of firms by studying the behaviour of various groups of people within the firm and their interactions under conditions of potentially conflicting interests.

Benefit principle of taxation   The principle that people ought to pay taxes in proportion to the amount they use government services.

Benefits in kind   Goods or services which the state provides directly to the recipient at no charge or at a subsidised price. Alternatively, the state can subsidise the private sector to provide them.

Bilateral monopoly   Where a monopsony buyer faces a monopoly seller.

Bill of exchange   A certificate promising to repay a stated amount on a certain date, typically three months from the issue of the bill. Bills pay no interest as such, but are sold at a discount and redeemed at face value, thereby earning a rate of discount for the purchaser.

Bretton Woods system   An adjustable peg system whereby currencies were pegged to the US dollar. The USA maintained convertibility of the dollar into gold at the rate of $35 to an ounce.

Broad money in UK (M4)   Cash in circulation plus retail and wholesale bank and building society deposits.

Budget deficit   The excess of central government's spending over its tax receipts.

Budget line   A graph showing all the possible combinations of two goods that can be purchased at given prices and for a given budget.

Budget surplus   The excess of central government's tax receipts over its spending.

Buffer stocks   Stocks of a product used to stabilise its price. In years of abundance, the stocks are built up. In years of low supply, stocks are released on to the market.

Business cycle or **Trade cycle**   The periodic fluctuations of national output round its long-term trend.

Capital   All inputs into production that have themselves been produced: e.g. factories, machines and tools.

Capital account of the balance of payments   The record of the transfers of capital to and from abroad.

Capital adequacy ratio (CAR)   The ratio of a bank's capital (reserves and shares) to its risk-weighted assets. Under the Basel II Accord, a bank's CAR should be a minimum of 8 per cent.

Capital expenditure   Investment expenditure; expenditure on assets.

Carry trade   Borrowing at low interest rates and then using it to buy assets that earn higher rates. In foreign exchange markets, the carry trade involves borrowing money in a currency of a country where interest rates are low and exchanging it for another currency where the country pays higher interest rates.

Cartel   A formal collusive agreement.

Central bank   Banker to the banks and the government.

Centrally planned or command economy   An economy where all economic decisions are taken by the central authorities.

Certificates of deposit (CDs)   Certificates issued by banks for fixed-term interest-bearing deposits. They can be resold by the owner to another party.

Ceteris paribus Latin for 'other things being equal'. This assumption has to be made when making deductions from theories.

Change in demand This is the term used for a shift in the demand curve. It occurs when a determinant of demand *other* than price changes.

Change in supply The term used for a shift in the supply curve. It occurs when a determinant *other* than price changes.

Change in the quantity demanded The term used for a movement along the demand curve to a new point. It occurs when there is a change in price.

Change in the quantity supplied The term used for a movement along the supply curve to a new point. It occurs when there is a change in price.

Claimant unemployment Those in receipt of unemployment-related benefits.

Classical model A macroeconomic model that assumes prices and wages are fully flexible

Clearing system A system whereby inter-bank debts are settled.

Closed shop Where a firm agrees to employ only union members.

Coase theorem By sufferers from externalities doing deals with perpetrators (by levying charges or offering bribes), the externality will be 'internalised' and the socially efficient level of output will be achieved.

Cobb–Douglas production function Like other production functions, this shows how output (TPP) varies with inputs of various factors (F_1, F_2, F_3, etc.). In the simple two-factor case it takes the following form:

$$TPP = f(F_1, F_2) = AF_1^\alpha F_2^\beta$$

If $\alpha + \beta = 1$, there are constant returns to scale; if $\alpha + \beta > 1$, there are increasing returns to scale; $\alpha + \beta < 1$, there are decreasing returns to scale.

Collusive oligopoly Where oligopolists agree (formally or informally) to limit competition between themselves. They may set output quotas, fix prices, limit product promotion or development, or agree not to 'poach' each other's markets.

Collusive tendering Where two or more firms secretly agree on the prices they will tender for a contract. These prices will be above those which would be put in under a genuinely competitive tendering process.

Command-and-control (CAC) systems The use of laws or regulations backed up by inspections and penalties (such as fines) for non-compliance.

Command economy An economy where all economic decisions are made by a central planning process.

Commercial bills Bills of exchange issued by firms.

Common market A customs union where the member countries act as a single market with free movement of labour and capital, common taxes and common trade laws.

Comparative advantage A country has a comparative advantage over another in the production of a good if it can produce it at a lower opportunity cost: i.e. if it has to forgo less of other goods in order to produce it.

Competition for corporate control The competition for the control of companies through takeovers.

Complementary goods A pair of goods consumed together. As the price of one goes up, the demand for both goods will fall.

Compounding The process of adding interest each year to an initial capital sum.

Compromise strategy One whose worst outcome is better that the maximax strategy and whose best outcome is better than the maximin strategy.

Conglomerate merger When two firms in different industries merge.

Consortium Where two or more firms work together on a specific project and create a separate company to run the project.

Consumer durable A consumer good that lasts a period of time, during which the consumer can continue gaining utility from it.

Consumer sovereignty A situation where firms respond to changes in consumer demand without being in a position in the long run to charge a price above average cost.

Consumer surplus The excess of what a person would have been prepared to pay for a good (i.e. the utility) over what that person actually pays.

Consumers' share of a tax on a good The proportion of the revenue from a tax on a good that arises from an increase in the price of the good.

Consumption The act of using goods and services to satisfy wants. This will normally involve purchasing the goods and services.

Consumption function The relationship between consumption and national income. It can be expressed algebraically or graphically.

Consumption of domestically produced goods and services (C_d) The direct flow of money payments from households to firms.

Convergence in GDP per head The tendency for less rich developed countries to catch up the richer ones. Convergence does not apply to many of the poorer developing countries, however, where the gap between them and richer countries has tended to widen.

Convergence of economies When countries achieve similar levels of growth, inflation, budget deficits as a percentage of GDP, balance of payments, etc.

Core workers Workers, normally with specific skills, who are employed on a permanent or long-term basis.

Cost–benefit analysis The identification, measurement and weighing up of the costs and benefits of a project in order to decide whether or not it should go ahead.

Cost-plus pricing (full-cost pricing) When firms price their product by adding a certain profit 'mark-up' to average cost.

Cost-push inflation Inflation caused by persistent rises in costs of production (independently of demand).

Countervailing power When the power of a monopolistic/oligopolistic seller is offset by powerful buyers who can prevent the price from being pushed up.

Cournot equilibrium Where the outputs chosen by each firm are consistent with each other: where the two firms' reaction curves cross.

Cournot model of duopoly A model where each firm makes its price and output decisions on the assumption that its rival will produce a particular quantity.

Crawling peg A system whereby the government allows a gradual adjustment of the exchange rate.

Credible threat (or promise) One that is believable to rivals because it is in the threatener's interests to carry it out.

Credit crunch A sudden reduction in the availability of loans or credit from banks and other financial institutions.

Cross-price elasticity of demand The percentage (or proportionate) change in quantity demanded of one good divided by the percentage (or proportionate) change in the price of another.

Cross-price elasticity of demand (arc formula) $\Delta Q_{Da}/$ average $Q_{Da} \div \Delta P_b/$ average P_b.

Cross-section data Information showing how a variable (e.g. the consumption of eggs) differs between different groups or different individuals at a given time.

Cross-subsidise To use profits in one market to subsidise prices in another.

Crowding out Where increased public expenditure diverts money or resources away from the private sector.

Cumulative causation (principle of) When an initial change causes an eventual change that is larger.

Currency union A group of countries (or regions) using a common currency.

Current account balance of payments Exports of goods and services minus imports of goods and services plus net incomes and current transfers from abroad. If inflows of money (from the sale of exports, etc.) exceed outflows of money (from the purchase of imports, etc.) there is a 'current account surplus' (a positive figure). If outflows exceed inflows there is a 'current account deficit' (a negative figure).

Current expenditure (by the government) Recurrent spending on goods and factor payments.

Customs union A free trade area with common external tariffs and quotas.

Deadweight loss of an indirect tax The loss of consumers' plus producers' surplus from the imposition of an indirect tax.

Deadweight welfare loss The loss of consumers' plus producers' surplus in imperfect markets (when compared with perfect competition).

Debt servicing Paying the interest and capital repayments on debt.

Deciles Divisions of the population into ten equal-sized groups (an example of a quantile).

Decision tree (or game tree) A diagram showing the sequence of possible decisions by competitor firms and the outcome of each combination of decisions.

Debentures (company bonds) Fixed-interest loans to firms. These assets can be traded on the stock market and their market price is determined by demand and supply.

Deduction Using a theory to draw conclusions about specific circumstances.

Deflationary (or recessionary) gap The shortfall of national expenditure below national income (and injections below withdrawals) at the full-employment level of national income.

Deflationary policy Fiscal or monetary policy designed to reduce the rate of growth of aggregate demand.

Demand curve A graph showing the relationship between the price of a good and the quantity of the good demanded over a given time period. Price is measured on the vertical axis; quantity demanded is measured on the horizontal axis. A demand curve can be for an individual consumer or group of consumers, or more usually for the whole market.

Demand function An equation which shows the mathematical relationship between the quantity demanded of a good and the values of the various determinants of demand.

Demand-management policies Demand-side policies (fiscal and/or monetary) designed to smooth out the fluctuations in the business cycle.

Demand schedule (market) A table showing the different total quantities of a good that consumers are willing and able to buy at various prices over a given period of time.

Demand schedule for an individual A table showing the different quantities of a good that a person is willing and able to buy at various prices over a given period of time.

Demand-deficient or **cyclical unemployment** Disequilibrium unemployment caused by a fall in aggregate demand with no corresponding fall in the real wage rate.

Demand-pull inflation Inflation caused by persistent rises in aggregate demand.

Demand-side policies Policies designed to affect aggregate demand: fiscal policy and monetary policy.

Demand-side policy Government policy designed to alter the level of aggregate demand, and thereby the level of output, employment and prices.

Dependency Where the development of a developing country is hampered by its relationships with the industrialised world.

Depreciation (of a currency) A fall in the free-market exchange rate of the domestic currency with foreign currencies.

Depreciation (of capital) The decline in value of capital equipment due to age, or wear and tear.

Deregulation Where the government removes official barriers to competition (e.g. licences and minimum quality standards).

Derived demand   The demand for a factor of production depends on the demand for the good which uses it.

Destabilising speculation   Where the actions of speculators tend to make price movements larger.

Devaluation   Where the government re-pegs the exchange rate at a lower level.

Differentiation   A mathematical technique to find the rate of change of one variable with respect to another.

Diminishing marginal rate of substitution   The more a person consumes of good X and the less of good Y, the less additional Y will that person be prepared to give up in order to obtain an extra unit of X: i.e. $\Delta Y/\Delta X$ diminishes.

Diminishing marginal returns   When one or more factors are held fixed, there will come a point beyond which the extra output from additional units of the variable factor will diminish.

Diminishing marginal utility   As more units of a good are consumed, additional units will provide less additional satisfaction than previous units.

Diminishing marginal utility of income   Where each additional pound earned yields less additional utility.

Direct monetary transmission mechanism   A change in money supply having a direct effect on aggregate demand.

Direct taxes   Taxes on income and wealth. Paid directly to the tax authorities on that income or wealth.

Dirty floating (managed flexibility)   A system of flexible exchange rates but where the government intervenes to prevent excessive fluctuations or even to achieve an unofficial target exchange rate.

Discounting   The process of reducing the value of future flows to give them a present valuation.

Discretionary fiscal policy   Deliberate changes in tax rates or the level of government expenditure in order to influence the level of aggregate demand.

Diseconomies of scale   Where costs per unit of output increase as the scale of production increases.

Disequilibrium unemployment   Unemployment resulting from real wage rates in the economy being above the equilibrium level.

Disguised unemployment   Where the same work could be done by fewer people.

Disintermediation   The diversion of business away from financial institutions which are subject to controls.

Disposable income   Household income after the deduction of taxes and the addition of benefits.

Distribution of income by class of recipient   Measurement of the distribution of income between the classes of person who receive it (e.g. homeowners and non-homeowners or those in the North and those in the South).

Diversification   This is where a firm expands into new types of business.

Dominant firm price leadership   When firms (the followers) choose the same price as that set by a dominant firm in the industry (the leader).

Dominant strategy game   Where different assumptions about rivals' behaviour lead to the adoption of the same strategy.

Dualism   The division of an economy into a modern (usually urban) sector and a poor traditional (usually rural) sector.

Dumping   When exports are sold at prices below marginal cost – often as a result of government subsidy.

Duopoly   An oligopoly where there are just two firms in the market.

Econometrics   The science of applying statistical techniques to economic data in order to identify and test economic relationships.

Economic and monetary union (EMU)   The adoption by a group of countries of a single currency with a single central bank and a single monetary policy. In the EU the term applies to the countries that have adopted the euro.

Economic discrimination   When workers of identical *ability* are paid different wages or are otherwise discriminated against because of race, age, sex, etc.

Economic efficiency   A situation where each good is produced at the minimum cost and where individual people and firms get the maximum benefit from their resources.

Economic model   A formal presentation of an economic theory.

Economic rent   The excess that a factor is paid over the amount necessary to keep it in its current employment.

Economies of scale   When increasing the scale of production leads to a lower long-run cost per unit of output.

Economies of scope   When increasing the range of products produced by a firm reduces the cost of producing each one.

ECU (European Currency Unit)   The predecessor to the euro: a weighted average of EU currencies. It was used as a reserve currency and for the operation of the exchange rate mechanism (ERM).

Effective rate of protection   The percentage increase in an industry's domestic value added resulting from protection given to that industry.

Efficient (capital) market hypothesis   The hypothesis that new information about a company's current or future performance will be quickly and accurately reflected in its share price.

Efficiency wage hypothesis   The hypothesis that the productivity of workers is affected by the wage rate that they receive.

Efficiency wage rate   The profit-maximising wage rate for the firm after taking into account the effects of wage rates on worker motivation, turnover and recruitment.

Elastic demand (with respect to price)   Where quantity demanded changes by a larger percentage than price. Ignoring the negative sign, it will have a value greater than 1.

Elasticity   A measure of the responsiveness of a variable (e.g. quantity demanded or quantity supplied) to a change in one of its determinants (e.g. price or income).

EMS (The European Monetary System, mark 1) A system whereby EC countries co-operated to achieve greater exchange rate stability. It involved use of the exchange rate mechanism (the ERM).

Endogenous growth theory A theory that the rate of economic growth depends on the rate of technological progress and diffusion, both of which depend on institutions, incentives and the role of government.

Endogenous money supply Money supply that is determined (at least in part) by the demand for money.

Endogenous variable A variable whose value is determined by the model of which it is part.

Engel curve A line showing how much of a good people will demand at different levels of income.

Entrepreneurship The initiating and organising of the production of new goods, or the introduction of new techniques, and the risk taking associated with it.

Envelope curve A long-run average cost curve drawn as the tangency points of a series of short-run average cost curves.

Environmental charges Charges for using natural resources (e.g. water or national parks), or for using the environment as a dump for waste (e.g. factory emissions or sewage).

Equation of exchange $MV = PY$. The total level of spending on GDP (MV) equals the total value of goods and services produced (PY) that go to make up GDP.

Equilibrium A position of balance. A position from which there is no inherent tendency to move away.

Equilibrium price The price where the quantity demanded equals the quantity supplied: the price where there is no shortage or surplus.

Equilibrium ('natural') unemployment The difference between those who would like employment at the current wage rate and those willing and able to take a job.

Equi-marginal principle Consumers will maximise total utility from their incomes by consuming that combination of goods where $MU_a/P_a = MU_b/P_b = MU_c/P_c \ldots = MU_n/P_n$.

Equities Company shares. Holders of equities are owners of the company and share in its profits by receiving dividends.

Equity A distribution of income that is considered to be fair or just. Note that an equitable distribution is not the same as an equal distribution and that different people have different views on what is equitable.

ERM (the exchange rate mechanism) A system of semi-fixed exchange rates used by most of the EU countries prior to adoption of the euro. Members' currencies were allowed to fluctuate against each other only within agreed bands. Collectively they floated against all other currencies.

Excess burden (of a tax on a good) The amount by which the loss in consumer plus producer surplus exceeds the government surplus.

Excess capacity (under monopolistic competition) In the long run, firms under monopolistic competition will produce at an output below their minimum-cost point.

Exchange equalisation account The gold and foreign exchange reserves account in the Bank of England.

Exchange rate The rate at which one national currency exchanges for another. The rate is expressed as the amount of one currency that is necessary to purchase *one unit* of another currency (e.g. $1.60 = £1).

Exchange rate band Where a currency is allowed to float between an upper and lower exchange rate, but is not allowed to move outside this band.

Exchange rate index A weighted average exchange rate expressed as an index where the value of the index is 100 in a given base year. The weights of the different currencies in the index add up to 1.

Exchange rate mechanism See ERM

Exchange rate overshooting Where a fall (or rise) in the long-run equilibrium exchange rate causes the actual exchange rate to fall (or rise) by a greater amount before eventually moving back to the new long-run equilibrium level.

Exchange rate: real A country's exchange rate adjusted for changes in the domestic currency prices of its exports relative to the foreign currency prices of its imports. If a country's prices rise (fall) relative to those of its trading partners, its real exchange rate will rise (fall) relative to the nominal exchange rate.

Exchange rate regime The system under which the government allows the exchange rate to be determined.

Exchange rate transmission mechanism How a change in money supply affects aggregate demand via a change in exchange rates.

Exogenous money supply Money supply that does not depend on the demand for money but is set by the authorities.

Exogenous variable A variable whose value is determined independently of the model of which it is part.

Expansion path The line on an isoquant map that traces the minimum-cost combinations of two factors as output increases. It is drawn on the assumption that both factors can be varied. It is thus a long-run path.

Expectations-augmented Phillips curve A (short-run) Phillips curve whose position depends on the expected rate of inflation.

Expenditure changing (increasing) from depreciation: the income effect Where depreciation, via the substitution effect, will alter the demand for imports and exports, and this will, via the multiplier, affect the level of national income and hence the demand for imports.

Expenditure changing (reducing) from deflation: the income effect Where deflationary policies lead to a reduction in national income and hence a reduction in the demand for imports.

Expenditure switching from deflation: the substitution effect Where deflationary policies lead to a reduction in inflation and thus cause a switch in expenditure away from imports and also towards exports.

Expenditure switching from depreciation: the substitution effect Where a lower exchange rate reduces the price of exports and increases the price of imports. This will increase the sale of exports and reduce the sale of imports.

Explicit costs The payments to outside suppliers of inputs.

External balance (in the economy) Narrow definition: where the current account of the balance of payments is in balance (and thus also the capital plus financial accounts). Loose definition: where there is a total currency flow balance at a given exchange rate.

External benefits Benefits from production (or consumption) experienced by people *other* than the producer (or consumer).

External costs Costs of production (or consumption) borne by people *other* than the producer (or consumer).

External diseconomies of scale Where a firm's costs per unit of output increase as the size of the whole *industry* increases.

External economies of scale Where a firm's costs per unit of output decrease as the size of the whole *industry* grows.

External policy objectives Objectives relating to the economy's international economic relationships.

Externalities Costs or benefits of production or consumption experienced by society but not by the producers or consumers themselves. Sometimes referred to as 'spillover' or 'third-party' costs or benefits.

Factor price equalisation The tendency for international trade to reduce factor price inequalities both between and within countries.

Factors of production (or resources) The inputs into the production of goods and services: labour, land and raw materials, and capital.

Fallacy of composition What applies to the individual does not necessarily apply to the whole.

Final expenditure Expenditure on goods and services. This is included in GDP and is part of aggregate demand.

Financial account of the balance of payments The record of the flows of money into and out of the country for the purposes of investment or as deposits in banks and other financial institutions.

Financial crowding out When an increase in government borrowing diverts money away from the private sector.

Financial deregulation The removal of or reduction in legal rules and regulations governing the activities of financial institutions.

Financial flexibility Where employers can vary their wage costs by changing the composition of their workforce or the terms on which workers are employed.

Financial intermediaries The general name for financial institutions (banks, building societies, etc.) which act as a means of channelling funds from depositors to borrowers.

Fine tuning The use of demand management policy (fiscal or monetary) to smooth out cyclical fluctuations in the economy.

First-best solution The solution of correcting a specific market distortion by ensuring that the whole economy operates under conditions of social efficiency (Pareto optimality).

First-degree price discrimination Where a firm charges each consumer for each unit the maximum price which that consumer is willing to pay for that unit.

First-mover advantage When a firm gains from being the first one to take action.

Fiscal drag The tendency of automatic fiscal stabilisers to reduce the recovery of an economy from recession.

Fiscal policy Policy to affect aggregate demand by altering the balance between government expenditure and taxation.

Fiscal stance How deflationary or reflationary the Budget is.

Fixed costs Total costs that do not vary with the amount of output produced.

Fixed exchange rate (totally) Where the government takes whatever measures are necessary to maintain the exchange rate at some stated level.

Fixed factor An input that cannot be increased in supply within a given time period.

Flat organisation Where the senior management communicate directly with those lower in the organisational structure, bypassing middle management.

Flexible firm A firm that has the flexibility to respond to changing market conditions by changing the composition of its workforce.

Floating exchange rate When the government does not intervene in the foreign exchange markets, but simply allows the exchange rate to be freely determined by demand and supply.

Flow An amount of something occurring over a *period of time*: e.g. production per week, income per year, demand per week. (Contrasts with *stock*.)

Flow-of-funds equation The various items making up an increase (or decrease) in money supply.

Forward exchange market Where contracts are made today for the price at which currency will be exchanged at some specified future date.

Franchising Where a firm is given the licence to operate a given part of an industry for a specified length of time.

Free trade area A group of countries with no trade barriers between themselves.

Freely floating exchange rate Where the exchange rate is determined entirely by the forces of demand and supply in the foreign exchange market with no government intervention whatsoever.

Free-market economy An economy where all economic decisions are taken by individual households and firms and with no government intervention.

Free-rider problem When it is not possible to exclude other people from consuming a good that someone has bought.

Frictional (search) unemployment Unemployment that occurs as a result of imperfect information in the labour market. It often takes time for workers to find jobs (even though there are vacancies) and in the meantime they are unemployed.

Full-employment level of national income The level of national income at which there is no deficiency of demand.

Functional distribution of income Measurement of the distribution of income according to the source of income (e.g. from employment, from profit, from rent, etc.).

Functional flexibility Where employers can switch workers from job to job as requirements change.

Functional relationships The mathematical relationship showing how one variable is affected by one or more others.

Funding (in monetary policy) Where the authorities alter the balance of bills and bonds for any given level of government borrowing.

Future price A price agreed today at which an item (e.g. commodities) will be exchanged at some set date in the future.

Futures or forward market A market in which contracts are made to buy or sell at some future date at a price agreed today.

Gaia philosophy The respect for the rights of the environment to remain unharmed by human activity. Humans should live in harmony with the planet and other species. We have a duty to be stewards of the natural environment, so that it can continue to be a self-maintaining and self-regulating system.

Game theory (or the theory of games) A mathematical method of decision making in which alternative strategies are analysed to determine the optimal course of action for the interested party, depending on assumptions about rivals' behaviour. Widely used in economics, game theory is also used as a tool in biology, psychology and politics.

GDP (gross domestic product at market prices) The value of output (or income or expenditure) in terms of the prices actually paid. GDP = GVA + taxes on products – subsidies on products.

General equilibrium A situation where all the millions of markets throughout the economy are in a simultaneous state of equilibrium.

General equilibrium diagrams (in trade theory) Indifference curve/production possibility curve diagrams that show a country's production and consumption of both imports and exports.

General government debt The combined accumulated debt of central and local government.

General government deficit (or surplus) The combined deficit (or surplus) of central and local government.

Geographical immobility The lack of ability or willingness of people to move to jobs in other parts of the country.

Giffen good An inferior good whose demand increases as its price increases as a result of a positive income effect larger than the normal negative substitution effect.

Gini coefficient The area between the Lorenz curve and the 45° line divided by the total area under the 45° line.

GNY (gross national income) GDP plus net income from abroad.

Gold standard The system whereby countries' exchange rates were fixed in terms of a certain amount of gold and whereby balance of payments deficits were paid in gold.

Golden-rule saving rate The rate of saving that maximises the level of long-run consumption.

Goodhart's law Controlling a symptom of a problem or only one part of the problem will not *cure* the problem: it will simply mean that the part that is being controlled now becomes a poor indicator of the problem.

Government bonds or 'gilt-edged securities' A government security paying a fixed sum of money each year. It is redeemed by the government on its maturity date at its face value.

Government surplus (from a tax on a good) The total tax revenue earned by the government from sales of a good.

Grandfathering Where each firm's emission permit is based on its *current* levels of emission (e.g. permitted levels for all firms could be 80 per cent of their current levels).

Green tax A tax on output designed to charge for the adverse effects of production on the environment. The socially efficient level of a green tax is equal to the marginal environmental cost of production.

Gross domestic product (GDP) The value of output produced within the country over a 12-month period.

Gross national income (GNY) GDP plus net income from abroad.

Gross value added at basic prices (GVA) The sum of all the values added by all industries in the economy over a year. The figures exclude taxes on products (such as VAT) and include subsidies on products.

Growth maximisation An alternative theory that assumes that managers seek to maximise the growth in sales revenue (or the capital value of the firm) over time.

Heckscher–Ohlin version of comparative advantage A country has a comparative advantage in those goods that are intensive in the country's relatively abundant factor.

H-form organisation (holding company) Where the parent company holds interests in a number of subsidiary companies.

Historic costs The original amount the firm paid for factors it now owns.

Hit-and-run competition When a firm enters an industry to take advantage of temporarily high profits and then leaves again as soon as the high profits have been exhausted.

Horizontal equity The equal treatment of people in the same situation.

Horizontal merger When two firms in the same industry at the same stage in the production process merge.

Households' disposable income The income available for households to spend: i.e. personal incomes after deducting taxes on incomes and adding benefits.

Human capital The qualifications, skills and expertise that contribute to a worker's productivity.

Human Development Index (HDI) A composite index made up of three elements: an index for life expectancy, an index for school enrolment and adult literacy, and an index for GDP per capita (in PPP$).

Hysteresis The persistence of an effect even when the initial cause has ceased to operate. In economics, it refers to the persistence of unemployment even when the demand deficiency that caused it no longer exists.

Identification problem The problem of identifying the relationship between two variables (e.g. price and quantity demanded) from the evidence when it is not known whether or how the variables have been affected by *other* determinants. For example, it is difficult to identify the shape of a demand curve simply by observing price and quantity when it is not known whether changes in other determinants have *shifted* the demand curve.

Idle balances Money held for speculative purposes: money held in anticipation of a fall in asset prices.

Imperfect competition The collective name for monopolistic competition and oligopoly.

Implicit costs Costs which do not involve a direct payment of money to a third party, but which nevertheless involve a sacrifice of some alternative.

Import-substituting industrialisation (ISI) A strategy of restricting imports of manufactured goods and using the foreign exchange saved to build up domestic substitute industries.

Incidence of tax The distribution of the burden of tax between sellers and buyers.

Income effect (of a price change) The effect of a change in price on quantity demanded arising from the consumer becoming better or worse off as a result of the price change.

Income effect of a rise in wage rates Workers get a higher income for a given number of hours worked and may thus feel they need to work *fewer* hours as wage rates rise.

Income effect of a tax rise Tax increases reduce people's incomes and thus encourage people to work more.

Income elasticity of demand The percentage (or proportionate) change in quantity demanded divided by the percentage (or proportionate) change in income.

Income elasticity of demand (arc formula) ΔQ_D/average $Q_D \div \Delta Y$/average Y.

Income–consumption curve A line showing how a person's optimum level of consumption of two goods changes as income changes (assuming the price of the goods remains constant).

Increasing opportunity costs of production When additional production of one good involves ever increasing sacrifices of another.

Independence (of firms in a market) Where the decisions of one firm in a market will not have any significant effect on the demand curves of its rivals.

Independent risks Where two risky events are unconnected. The occurrence of one will not affect the likelihood of the occurrence of the other.

Index number The value of a variable expressed as 100 plus or minus its percentage deviation from a base year.

Indifference curve A line showing all those combinations of two goods between which a consumer is indifferent: i.e. those combinations that give the same level of utility.

Indifference map A graph showing a whole set of indifference curves. The further away a particular curve is from the origin, the higher the level of satisfaction it represents.

Indifference set A table showing the same information as an indifference curve.

Indirect monetary transmission mechanism A change in money supply affecting aggregate demand indirectly via some other variable.

Indirect taxes Taxes on expenditure (e.g. VAT). They are paid to the tax authorities, not by the consumer, but indirectly by the suppliers of the goods or services.

Indivisibilities The impossibility of dividing a factor into smaller units.

Induced investment Investment firms make to enable them to meet extra consumer demand.

Induction Constructing general theories on the basis of specific observations.

Industrial policies Policies to encourage industrial investment and greater industrial efficiency.

Inelastic demand (with respect to price) Where quantity demanded changes by a smaller percentage than price. Ignoring the negative sign, it will have a value less than 1.

Infant industry An industry that has a potential comparative advantage, but which is as yet too underdeveloped to be able to realise this potential.

Inferior goods Goods whose demand *decreases* as consumer incomes increase. Such goods have a negative income elasticity of demand.

Inflationary gap The excess of national expenditure over income (and injections over withdrawals) at the full-employment level of national income.

Informal sector The parts of the economy that involve production and/or exchange, but where there are no money payments.

Infrastructure (industry's) The network of supply agents, communications, skills, training facilities, distribution channels, specialised financial services, etc. that supports a particular industry.

Injections (J) Expenditure on the production of domestic firms coming from outside the inner flow of the circular flow of income. Injections equal investment (I) plus government expenditure (G) plus expenditure on exports (X).

(Injections) multiplier The number of times by which a rise in income exceeds the rise in injections that caused it: $k = \Delta Y/\Delta J$.

(Injections) multiplier formula The formula for the multiplier: $k = 1/mpw$ or $1/(1 - mpc_d)$.

Input–output analysis This involves dividing the economy into sectors where each sector is a user of inputs from and a supplier of outputs to other sectors. The technique examines how these inputs and outputs can be matched to the total resources available in the economy.

Insiders Those in employment who can use their privileged position (either as members of unions or because of specific skills) to secure pay rises despite an excess supply of labour (unemployment).

Interdependence (under oligopoly) One of the two key features of oligopoly. Each firm will be affected by its rivals' decisions. Likewise its decisions will affect its rivals. Firms recognise this interdependence. This recognition will affect their decisions.

Interest rate transmission mechanism How a change in money supply affects aggregate demand via a change in interest rates.

Intermediate exchange rate regimes Where the government intervenes to influence movements in the exchange rate.

Internal balance (of an economy) Where the equilibrium level of national income is at the desired level.

Internal policy objectives (national) Objectives relating solely to the domestic economy.

Internal rate of return The rate of return of an investment: the discount rate that makes the net present value of an investment equal to zero.

International harmonisation of economic policies Where countries attempt to co-ordinate their macro-economic policies so as to achieve common goals.

International liquidity The supply of currencies in the world acceptable for financing international trade and investment.

International trade multiplier The effect on national income in Country B of a change in exports (or imports) of Country A.

Intervention price (in the CAP) The price at which the EU is prepared to buy a foodstuff if the market price were to be below it.

Interventionist supply-side policies Policies to increase aggregate supply by government intervention to counteract the deficiencies of the market.

Investment The production of items that are not for immediate consumption. This can include investment in plant and equipment; such investment builds the stock of firms' capital and yields a flow of future output. Investment also includes adding to stocks of goods or resources which are not sold or used in the current period, but will be in the future.

ISLM model A model showing simultaneous equilibrium in the goods market ($I = S$) and the money market ($L = M$).

Isocost A line showing all the combinations of two factors that cost the same to employ.

Isoquant A line showing all the alternative combinations of two factors that can produce a given level of output.

J-curve effect Where a devaluation causes the balance of trade first to deteriorate and then to improve. The graph of the balance of trade over time thus looks like a letter J.

Joint float Where a group of currencies pegged to each other jointly float against other currencies.

Joint supply Where the production of more of one good leads to the production of more of another.

Joint venture Where two or more firms set up and jointly own a new independent firm.

Just-in-time methods Where a firm purchases supplies and produces both components and finished products as they are required. This minimises stock holding and its associated costs.

Kinked demand theory The theory that oligopolists face a demand curve that is kinked at the current price, demand being significantly more elastic above the current price than below. The effect of this is to create a situation of price stability.

Labour All forms of human input, both physical and mental, into current production.

Labour force The number employed plus the number unemployed.

Land (and raw materials) Inputs into production that are provided by nature: e.g. unimproved land and mineral deposits in the ground.

Law of comparative advantage Trade can benefit all countries if they specialise in the goods in which they have a comparative advantage.

Law of demand The quantity of a good demanded per period of time will fall as price rises and will rise as price falls, other things being equal (*ceteris paribus*).

Law of diminishing (marginal) returns When one or more factors are held fixed, there will come a point beyond which the extra output from additional units of the variable factor will diminish.

Law of large numbers The larger the number of events of a particular type, the more predictable will be their average outcome.

Lender of last resort The role of the Bank of England as the guarantor of sufficient liquidity in the monetary system.

Liabilities All legal claims for payment that outsiders have on an institution.

Libertarian school A school of thought that advocates maximum liberty for economic agents to pursue their own interests and to own property.

Limit pricing Where a monopolist (or oligopolist) charges a price below the short-run profit maximising level in order to deter new entrants.

Liquidity The ease with which an asset can be converted into cash without loss.

Liquidity preference The demand for holding assets in the form of money.

Liquidity ratio The proportion of a bank's total assets held in liquid form.

Liquidity trap The absorption of any additional money supply into idle balances at very low rates of interest, leaving aggregate demand unchanged.

Lock-outs Union members are temporarily laid off until they are prepared to agree to the firm's conditions.

Long run The period of time long enough for *all* factors to be varied.

Long run under perfect competition The period of time that is long enough for new firms to enter the industry.

Long-run average cost curve A curve that shows how average cost varies with output on the assumption that *all* factors are variable. (It is assumed that the least-cost method of production will be chosen for each output.)

Long-run marginal cost The extra cost of producing one more unit of output assuming that all factors are variable. (It is assumed that the least-cost method of production will be chosen for this extra output.)

Long-run neutrality of money Changes in money supply over the long run will only affect prices and not real output or employment

Long-run profit maximisation An alternative theory of the firm which assumes that managers aim to *shift* cost and revenue curves so as to maximise profits over some longer time period.

Long-run shut-down point This is where the *AR* curve is tangential to the *LRAC* curve. The firm can just make normal profits. Any fall in revenue below this level will cause a profit-maximising firm to shut down once all costs have become variable.

Lorenz curve A curve showing the proportion of national income earned by any given percentage of the population (measured from the poorest upwards).

Macroeconomics The branch of economics that studies economic aggregates (grand totals): e.g. the overall level of prices, output and employment in the economy.

Managed flexibility (dirty floating) A system of flexible exchange rates but where the government intervenes to prevent excessive fluctuations or even to achieve an unofficial target exchange rate.

Marginal benefit The additional benefit of doing a little bit more (or 1 unit more if a unit can be measured) of an activity.

Marginal capital/output ratio The amount of extra capital (in money terms) required to produce a £1 increase in national output. Since $I_i = \Delta K$, the marginal capital/output ratio $\Delta K/\Delta Y$ equals the accelerator coefficient (α).

Marginal consumer surplus The excess of utility from the consumption of one more unit of a good (*MU*) over the price paid: $MCS = MU - P$.

Marginal cost (of an activity) The additional cost of doing a little bit more (or 1 unit more if a unit can be measured) of an activity.

Marginal cost (of production) The cost of producing one more unit of output: $MC = \Delta TC/\Delta Q$.

Marginal disutility of work The extra sacrifice/hardship to a worker of working an extra unit of time in any given time period (e.g. an extra hour per day).

Marginal efficiency of capital or **internal rate of return** The rate of return of an investment: the discount rate that makes the net present value of an investment equal to zero.

Marginal physical product The extra output gained by the employment of one more unit of the variable factor: $MPP = \Delta TPP/\Delta Q_v$.

Marginal productivity theory The theory that the demand for a factor depends on its marginal revenue product.

Marginal propensity to consume The proportion of a rise in national income that goes on consumption: $mpc = \Delta C/\Delta Y$.

Marginal propensity to import The proportion of an increase in national income that is spent on imports: $mpm = \Delta M/\Delta Y$.

Marginal propensity to save The proportion of an increase in national income saved: $mps = \Delta S/\Delta Y$.

Marginal propensity to withdraw The proportion of an increase in national income that is withdrawn from the circular flow: $mpw = \Delta W/\Delta Y$, where $mpw = mps + mpt + mpm$.

Marginal rate of factor substitution The rate at which one factor can be substituted by another while holding the level of output constant: $MRS = \Delta F_1/\Delta F_2 = MPP_{F2}/MPP_{F1}$.

Marginal rate of income tax The income tax rate. The rate paid on each *additional* pound earned: $\Delta T/\Delta Y$.

Marginal rate of substitution (between two goods in consumption) The amount of one good (Y) that a consumer is prepared to give up in order to obtain one extra unit of another good (X): i.e. $\Delta Y/\Delta X$.

Marginal revenue The extra revenue gained by selling one more unit per time period: $MR = \Delta TR/\Delta Q$.

Marginal revenue product (of a factor) The extra revenue a firm earns from employing one more unit of a variable factor: $MRP_{factor} = MPP_{factor} \times MR_{good}$.

Marginal tax propensity The proportion of an increase in national income paid in tax: $mpt = \Delta T/\Delta Y$.

Marginal utility The extra satisfaction gained from consuming one extra unit of a good within a given time period.

Market The interaction between buyers and sellers.

Market clearing A market clears when supply matches demand, leaving no shortage or surplus.

Market for loanable funds The market for loans from and deposits into the banking system.

Market loans Short-term loans (e.g. money at call and short notice).

Market-orientated supply-side policies Policies to increase aggregate supply by freeing-up the market.

Mark-up A profit margin added to average cost to arrive at price.

Marshall–Lerner condition Depreciation will improve the balance of payments only if the sum of the price elasticities of demand for imports and exports is greater than 1.

Maturity gap The difference in the average maturity of loans and deposits.

Maturity transformation The transformation of deposits into loans of a longer maturity.

Maximax The strategy of choosing the policy which has the best possible outcome.

Maximin The strategy of choosing the policy whose worst possible outcome is the least bad.

Maximum price A price ceiling set by the government or some other agency. The price is not allowed to rise above this level (although it is allowed to fall below it).

Mean (or arithmetic mean) The sum of the values of each of the members of the sample divided by the total number in the sample.

Means-tested benefits Benefits whose amount depends on the recipient's income or assets.

Median The value of the middle member of the sample.

Medium of exchange Something that is acceptable in exchange for goods and services.

Medium-term financial strategy (MTFS) The policy of the Conservative government in Britain during the 1980s of setting targets for the PSBR and the growth of money supply for the following four years.

Menu costs of inflation The costs associated with having to adjust price lists or labels.

Merit goods Goods which the government feels that people will underconsume and which therefore ought to be subsidised or provided free.

M-form (multi-divisional form) of corporate organisation Where the firm is split into a number of separate divisions (e.g. different products or countries), with each division then split into a number of departments.

Microeconomics The branch of economics that studies individual units: e.g. households, firms and industries. It studies the interrelationships between these units in determining the pattern of production and distribution of goods and services.

Minimum price A price floor set by the government or some other agency. The price is not allowed to fall below this level (although it is allowed to rise above it).

Minimum reserve ratio A minimum ratio of cash (or other specified liquid assets) to deposits (either total or selected) that the central bank requires banks to hold.

Mixed command economy A planned economy that nevertheless makes some use of markets.

Mixed economy An economy where economic decisions are made partly by the government and partly through the market.

Mixed market economy A market economy where there is some government intervention.

Mobility of labour The willingness and ability of labour to move to another job.

Monetarists Those who attribute inflation solely to rises in money supply.

Monetary base Notes and coin outside the central bank.

Monetary base control Monetary policy that focuses on controlling the monetary base (as opposed to broad liquidity).

Monetary policy Policy to affect aggregate demand by altering the supply or cost of money (rate of interest).

Money illusion When people believe that a money wage or price increase represents a *real* increase: in other words, they ignore or underestimate inflation.

Money market The market for short-term loans and deposits.

Money multiplier The number of times greater the expansion of money supply is than the expansion of the monetary base that caused it: $\Delta Ms/\Delta Mb$.

Monopolistic competition A market structure where, like perfect competition, there are many firms and freedom of entry into the industry, but where each firm produces a differentiated product and thus has some control over its price.

Monopoly A market structure where there is only one firm in the industry.

Monopsony A market with a single buyer or employer.

Moral hazard The temptation to take more risk when you know that other people (e.g. insurers) will cover the risks.

Multiplier (injections multiplier) The number of times a rise in income exceeds the rise in injections that caused it. $k = \Delta Y/\Delta J$.

Multiplier effect An initial increase in aggregate demand of £xm leads to an eventual rise in national income that is greater than £xm.

Multiplier formula (injections multiplier) The formula for the multiplier is $k = 1/mpw$ or $1/(1 - mpc_d)$.

Mutual recognition The EU principle that one country's rules and regulations must apply throughout the EU. If they conflict with those of another country, individuals and firms should be able to chose which to obey.

Nash equilibrium The position resulting from everyone making their optimal decision based on their assumptions about their rivals' decisions. Without collusion, there is no incentive for any firm to move from this position.

National debt The accumulated budget deficits (less surpluses) over the years: the total amount of government borrowing.

National expenditure on domestic product (*E*) Aggregate demand in the Keynesian model: i.e. $C_d + J$.

Nationalised industries State-owned industries that produce goods or services that are sold in the market.

Natural level of output The level of output in monetarist analysis where the vertical long-run aggregate supply curve cuts the horizontal axis.

Natural level of unemployment The level of equilibrium unemployment in monetarist analysis measured as the difference between the (vertical) long-run gross labour supply curve (N) and the (vertical) long-run effective labour supply curve (AS_L).

Natural monopoly A situation where long-run average costs would be lower if an industry were under monopoly than if it were shared between two or more competitors.

Natural rate of unemployment The rate of unemployment at which there is no excess or deficiency of demand for labour.

Natural wastage When a firm wishing to reduce its workforce does so by not replacing those who leave or retire.

Near money Highly liquid assets (other than cash).

Negative income tax A combined system of tax and benefits. As people earn more they gradually lose their benefits until beyond a certain level they begin paying taxes.

Neo-Austrian/libertarian school A school of thought that advocates maximum liberty for economic agents to pursue their own interests and to own property.

Net investment Total investment minus depreciation.

Net national income (NNY) GNY minus depreciation.

Net present value of an investment The discounted benefits of an investment minus the cost of the investment.

Network (business) An informal arrangement between businesses to work together towards some common goal.

Network economies The benefits to consumers of having a network of other people using the same product or service.

Neutrality of money (long run) Changes in money supply over the long run will only affect prices and not real output or employment

New classical school The school of economists which believes that markets clear virtually instantaneously and that expectations are formed 'rationally'.

New Keynesians Economists who seek to explain the downward stickiness of real wages and the resulting persistence of unemployment. They argue that governments may have to expand aggregate demand when demand-deficient unemployment is persistent.

Nominal national income National income measured at current prices.

Nominal values Money values measured at *current* prices.

Non-accelerating-inflation rate of unemployment (NAIRU) The rate of unemployment consistent with a constant rate of inflation. (In monetarist analysis this is the same as the natural rate of unemployment: the rate of unemployment at which the vertical long-run Phillips curve cuts the horizontal axis.)

Non-bank private sector Households and non-bank firms: in other words, everyone in the country other than banks and the government (central and local).

Non-collusive oligopoly Where oligopolists have no agreement between themselves either formal, informal or tacit.

Non-excludability Where it is not possible to provide a good or service to one person without it thereby being available for others to enjoy.

Non-price competition Competition in terms of product promotion (advertising, packaging, etc.) or product development.

Non-rivalry Where the consumption of a good or service by one person will not prevent others from enjoying it.

Normal goods Goods whose demand increases as consumer incomes increase. They have a positive income elasticity of demand. Luxury goods will have a higher income elasticity of demand than more basic goods.

Normal profit The opportunity cost of being in business: the profit that could have been earned in the next best alternative business. It is counted as a cost of production.

Normal rate of return The rate of return (after taking risks into account) that could be earned elsewhere.

Normative statement A value judgement.

Numerical flexibility Where employers can change the size of their workforce as their labour requirements change.

Occupational immobility The lack of ability or willingness of people to move to other jobs irrespective of location.

Oligopoly An market structure where there are few enough firms to enable barriers to be erected against the entry of new firms.

Oligopsony A market with just a few buyers or employers.

Open economy One that trades with and has financial dealings with other countries.

Open-market operations The sale (or purchase) by the authorities of government securities in the open market in order to reduce (or increase) money supply or influence interest rates.

Opportunity cost Cost measured in terms of the best alternative forgone.

Optimal currency area The optimal size of a currency area is the one that maximises the benefits from having a single currency relative to the costs. If the area were increased or decreased in size, the costs would rise relative to the benefits.

Optimum tariff A tariff that reduces the level of imports to the point where the country's marginal social cost equals marginal social benefit.

Organisational slack Where managers allow spare capacity to exist, thereby enabling them to respond more easily to changed circumstances.

Output gap The difference between actual and potential output. When actual output exceeds potential output, the gap is positive. When actual output is less than potential output, the gap is negative.

Outsiders Those out of work or employed on a casual, part-time or short-term basis, who have little or no power to influence wages or employment.

Overheads Costs arising from the general running of an organisation, and only indirectly related to the level of output.

Pareto improvement Where changes in production or consumption can make at least one person better off without making anyone worse off.

Pareto optimality Where all possible Pareto improvements have been made: where, therefore, it is impossible to make anyone better off without making someone else worse off.

Partial derivative The partial derivative of a function of two or more independent variables is the derivative with respect to just one of those variables, while holding the others constant.

Partial differentiation A mathematical technique used with functions containing two or more independent variables. The technique is used to find the rate of change of the dependent variable with respect to a single independent variable assuming that the other independent variables are held constant.

Participation rate The percentage of the working-age population that is part of the workforce.

Partnership A firm owned by two or more people. They each have unlimited liability for the firm's debts.

Peak-load pricing Price discrimination (second or third degree) where a higher price is charged in peak periods and a lower price in off-peak periods.

Perfect competition A market structure where there are many firms, none of which is large; where there is freedom of entry into the industry; where all firms produce an identical product; and where all firms are price takers.

Perfectly contestable market A market where there is free and costless entry and exit.

Phillips curve A curve showing the relationship between (price) inflation and unemployment. The original Phillips curve plotted *wage* inflation against unemployment for the years 1861–1957.

Picketing When people on strike gather at the entrance to the firm and attempt to persuade workers or delivery vehicles from entering.

Plant economies of scale Economies of scale that arise because of the large size of the factory.

Point elasticity The measurement of elasticity at a point on a curve. The formula for price elasticity of demand using the point elasticity method is: $dQ/dP \times P/Q$, where dQ/dP is the inverse of the slope of the tangent to the demand curve at the point in question.

Poll tax A lump-sum tax per head of the population. Since it a fixed *amount*, it has a marginal rate of zero with respect to both income and wealth.

Polluter pays principle The principle that polluters ought to be charged (e.g. through green taxes) for the external environmental costs that they generate.

Pooling risks (for an insurance company) The more policies and insurance company issues and the more independent the risks of claims from these policies are, the more predictable will be the number of claims.

Portfolio balance The balance of assets, according to their liquidity, that people choose to hold in their portfolios.

Positive statement A value-free statement which can be tested by an appeal to the facts.

Post-Keynesians Economists who stress the importance of institutional and behavioural factors, and the role of business confidence in explaining the state of the economy. They argue that firms are more likely to respond to changes in demand by changing output rather than prices.

Potential growth The percentage annual increase in the capacity of the economy to produce.

Potential output The sustainable level output that could be produced in the economy: i.e. one that involves a 'normal' level of capacity utilisation and does not result in rising inflation.

Poverty trap (for developing countries) When countries are too poor to save and invest enough to achieve real per capita growth.

Poverty trap (for individuals) Where poor people are discouraged from working or getting a better job because any extra income they earn will be largely taken away in taxes and lost benefits.

Predatory pricing Where a firm sets its prices below average cost in order to drive competitors out of business.

Preferential trading arrangements A trade agreement whereby trade between the signatories is freer than trade with the rest of the world.

Present value approach to appraising investment This involves estimating the value *now* of a flow of future benefits (or costs).

Price benchmark A price which is typically used. Firms, when raising prices will usually raise it from one benchmark to another.

Price discrimination Where a firm sells the same product at different prices.

Price elasticity of demand (arc formula) ΔQ/average $Q \div \Delta P$/average P. The average in each case is the average between the two points being measured.

Price elasticity of demand (P_{ϵ_D}) The percentage (or proportionate) change in quantity demanded divided by the percentage (or proportionate) change in price: $\%\Delta Q_D \div \%\Delta P$.

Price elasticity of supply (P_{ϵ_S}) The percentage (or proportionate) change in quantity supplied divided by the percentage (or proportionate) change in price: $\%\Delta Q_S \div \%\Delta P$.

Price elasticity of supply (arc formula) ΔQ_S/average $Q_S \div \Delta P$/average P.

Price mechanism The system in a market economy whereby changes in price in response to changes in demand and supply have the effect of making demand equal to supply.

Price taker A person or firm with no power to be able to influence the market price.

Price-cap regulation Where the regulator puts a ceiling on the amount by which a firm can raise its price.

Price–consumption curve A line showing how a person's optimum level of consumption of two goods changes as the price of one of the two goods changes (assuming that income and the price of the other good remain constant).

Prices and incomes policy When the government seeks to restrain price and wage increases. This may be in the form of a voluntary agreement with firms and/or unions, or there may be statutory limits imposed.

Primary labour market The market for permanent full-time core workers.

Primary market in capital Where shares are sold by the issuer of the shares (i.e. the firm) and where, therefore, finance is channelled directly from the purchasers (i.e. the shareholders) to the firm.

Principal–agent problem Where people (principals), as a result of lack of knowledge, cannot ensure that their best interests are served by their agents.

Principle of cumulative causation An initial event can cause an ultimate effect that is much larger.

Prisoners' dilemma Where two or more firms (or people), by attempting independently to choose the best strategy for whatever the other(s) are likely to do, end up in a worse position than if they had co-operated in the first place.

Private efficiency Where a person's marginal benefit from a given activity equals the marginal cost.

Private limited company A company owned by its shareholders. Shareholders' liability is limited to the value of their shares. Shares can only be bought and sold privately.

Producers' share of a tax on a good The proportion of the revenue from a tax on a good that arises from a reduction in the price to the producer (after the payment of the tax).

Product differentiation When one firm's product is sufficiently different from its rivals' to allow it to raise the price of the product without customers all switching to the rivals' products. A situation where a firm faces a downward-sloping demand curve.

Production The transformation of inputs into outputs by firms in order to earn profit (or meet some other objective).

Production function The mathematical relationship between the output of a good and the inputs used to produce it. It shows how output will be affected by changes in the quantity of one or more of the inputs.

Production possibility curve A curve showing all the possible combinations of two goods that a country can produce within a specified time period with all its resources fully and efficiently employed.

Productive efficiency A situation where firms are producing the maximum output for a given amount of inputs, or producing a given output at the least cost. The least-cost combination of factors for a given output.

Productivity deal When, in return for a wage increase, a union agrees to changes in working practices that will increase output per worker.

Profit (rate of) Total profit ($T\Pi$) as a proportion of the total capital employed (K): $r = T\Pi / K$.

Profit satisficing Where decision makers in a firm aim for a target level of profit rather than the absolute maximum level.

Profit-maximising rule Profit is maximised where marginal revenue equals marginal cost.

Progressive tax A tax whose average rate with respect to income rises as income rises.

Proportional tax A tax whose average rate with respect to income stays the same as income rises.

Prudential control The insistence by the Bank of England that recognised banks maintain adequate liquidity.

Public good A good or service that has the features of non-rivalry and non-excludability and as a result would not be provided by the free market.

Public limited company A company owned by its shareholders. Shareholders' liability is limited to the value of their shares. Shares may be bought and sold publicly – on the Stock Exchange.

Public-sector net cash requirement (PSNCR) which used to be known as the **Public-sector borrowing requirement (PSBR)** The (annual) budget deficit of the public sector (central government, local government and public corporations) and thus a measure of the how much the government needs to borrow.

Public-sector surplus or **Public-sector debt repayment (PSDR)** The (annual) surplus of the public sector, and thus the amount of debt that can be repaid when public-sector income exceeds public sector expenditures.

Purchasing-power parity theory The theory that the exchange rate will adjust so as to offset differences in countries' inflation rates, with the result that the same quantity of internationally traded goods can be bought at home as abroad with a given amount of the domestic currency.

Purchasing-power standard (PPS) GDP GDP measured as a country's PPP exchange rate.

Pure fiscal policy Fiscal policy which does not involve any change in money supply.

Quantiles Divisions of the population into equal-sized groups.

Quantitative easing Where the central bank increases the monetary base by a deliberate amount through the open-market purchase of government bonds or other securities from banks. When banks lend the money, broad money expands by a multiple of this through the process of credit creation.

Quantity demanded The amount of a good a consumer is willing and able to buy at a given price over a given period of time.

Quantity theory of money The price level (P) is directly related to the quantity of money in the economy (M).

Quasi-rent Temporary economic rent arising from short-run supply inelasticity.

Quintiles Divisions of the population into five equal-sized groups (an example of a quantile).

Quota (set by a cartel) The output that a given member of a cartel is allowed to produce (production quota) or sell (sales quota).

Random walk Where fluctuations in the value of a share away from its 'correct' value are random: i.e. have no systematic pattern. When charted over time, these share price movements would appear like a 'random walk': like the path of someone staggering along drunk!

Rate of discount The rate that is used to reduce future values to present values.

Rate of economic growth The percentage increase in output over a 12-month period.

Rate of inflation The percentage increase in the level of prices over a 12-month period.

Rate of profit Total profit ($T\Pi$) as a proportion of the capital employed (K): $r = T\Pi/K$.

Rational choices Choices that involve weighing up the benefit of any activity against its opportunity cost.

Rational consumer A person who weighs up the costs and benefits to him or her of each additional unit of a good purchased.

Rational consumer behaviour The attempt to maximise total consumer surplus.

Rational economic behaviour Doing more of activities whose marginal benefit exceeds their marginal cost and doing less of those activities whose marginal cost exceeds their marginal benefit.

Rational expectations Expectations based on the *current* situation. These expectations are based on the information people have to hand. Whilst this information may be imperfect and therefore people will make errors, these errors will be random.

Rational producer behaviour When a firm weighs up the costs and benefits of alternative courses of action and then seeks to maximise its net benefit.

Rationalisation The reorganising of production (often after a merger) so as to cut out waste and duplication and generally to reduce costs.

Rationing Where the government restricts the amount of a good that people are allowed to buy.

Reaction function (or curve) This shows how a firm's optimal output varies according to the output chosen by its rival (or rivals).

Real balance effect As the price level rises, so the value of people's money balances will fall. They will therefore *spend* less in order to increase their money balances and go some way to protecting their real value.

Real business cycle theory The new classical theory which explains cyclical fluctuations in terms of shifts in aggregate supply, rather than aggregate demand.

Real exchange rate A country's exchange rate adjusted for changes in the domestic currency prices of its exports relative to the foreign currency prices of its imports. If a country's prices rise (fall) relative to those of its trading partners, its real exchange rate will rise (fall) relative to the nominal exchange rate.

Real income Income measured in terms of how much it can buy. If your *money* income rises by 10 per cent, but prices rise by 8 per cent, you can only buy 2 per cent more goods than before. Your *real* income has risen by 2 per cent.

Real national income National income after allowing for inflation: i.e. national income measured in constant prices: i.e. in terms of the prices ruling in some base year.

Real values Money values corrected for inflation.

Real-wage unemployment Disequilibrium unemployment caused by real wages being driven up above the market-clearing level.

Recession A period where national output falls for six months or more.

Recessionary (or deflationary) gap The shortfall of national expenditure below national income (and injections below withdrawals) at the full-employment level of national income.

Recognised banks Banks licensed by the Bank of England. All financial institutions using the word 'bank' in their title have to be recognised by the Bank of England. This requires them to have paid-up capital of at least £5 million and to meet other requirements about their asset structure and range of services.

Rediscounting bills of exchange Buying bills before they reach maturity.

Reflationary policy Fiscal or monetary policy designed to increase the rate of growth of aggregate demand.

Regional Development Agencies (RDAs) Nine agencies, based in English regions, which initiate and administer regional policy within their area.

Regional multiplier effects When a change in injections into or withdrawals from a particular region causes a multiplied change in income in that region. The regional multiplier (k_r) is given by $1/mpw_r$, where the import component of *mpw*, consists of imports into that region either from abroad or from other regions of the economy.

Regional unemployment Structural unemployment occurring in specific regions of the country.

Regression analysis A statistical technique which allows a functional relationship between two or more variables to be estimated.

Regressive tax A tax whose average rate with respect to income falls as income rises.

Regulatory capture Where the regulator is persuaded to operate in the industry's interests rather than those of the consumer.

Relative price The price of one good compared with another (e.g. good X is twice the price of good Y).

Replacement costs What the firm would have to pay to replace factors it currently owns.

Resale (or retail) price maintenance Where the manufacturer of a product (legally) insists that the product should be sold at a specified retail price.

Restrictive practice Where two or more firms agree to adopt common practices to restrict competition.

Retail banks 'High street banks'. Banks operating extensive branch networks and dealing directly with the general public, with published interest rates and charges.

Retail deposits and loans Deposits and loans made through bank/building society branches at published interest rates.

Retail price index (RPI) An index of the prices of goods bought by a typical household.

Revaluation Where the government re-pegs the exchange rate at a higher level.

Reverse repos When gilts or other assets are *purchased* under a sale and repurchase agreement. They become an asset to the purchaser.

Risk When a (desirable) outcome of an action may or may not occur, but the probability of its occurring is known. The lower the probability, the greater the risk involved in taking the action.

Risk averse Where a person is not prepared to take a gamble even if the odds of gaining are favourable.

Risk loving Where a person is willing to take a gamble even if the odds of gaining are unfavourable.

Risk neutral Where a person is willing to take a gamble if the odds are favourable and is unwilling if the odds are unfavourable.

Risk transformation The process whereby banks can spread the risks of lending by having a large number of borrowers.

Sale and repurchase agreement (repos) An agreement between two financial institutions whereby one in effect borrows from another by selling it assets, agreeing to buy them back (repurchase them) at a fixed price and on a fixed date.

Sales revenue maximisation An alternative theory of the firm based on the assumption that managers aim to maximise the firm's short-run total revenue.

Say's law Supply creates its own demand. In other words, the production of goods will generate sufficient demand to ensure that they are sold.

Scarcity The excess of human wants over what can actually be produced to fulfil these wants.

Search theory This examines people's behaviour under conditions of ignorance where it takes time to search for information.

Seasonal unemployment Unemployment associated with industries or regions where the demand for labour is lower at certain times of the year.

Second best (problem of) The difficulty of working out the best way of correcting a specific market distortion if distortions in other parts of the market continue to exist.

Second derivative The rate of change of the first derivative: found by differentiating the first derivative.

Second derivative test If on differentiating an equation a second time the answer is negative (positive), the point is a maximum (minimum).

Secondary action Industrial action taken against a company not directly involved in a dispute (e.g. a supplier of raw materials to a firm whose employees are on strike).

Secondary labour market The market for peripheral workers, usually employed on a temporary or part-time basis, or a less secure 'permanent' basis.

Secondary market in capital Where shareholders sell shares to others. This is thus a market in 'second-hand' shares.

Secondary marketing Where assets are sold before maturity to another institution or individual. The possibility of secondary marketing encourages people or institutions to buy assets/grant loans in the primary market, knowing that they can sell them if necessary in the secondary market. The sale of existing shares and bonds on the stock market is an example of secondary marketing.

Second-best solution The solution to a specific market distortion that recognises distortions elsewhere and seeks to minimise the overall distortionary effects to the economy of tackling this specific distortion.

Second-degree price discrimination Where a firm charges a consumer so much for the first so many units purchased, a different price for the next so many units purchased, and so on.

Securitisation Where future cash flows (e.g. from interest rate or mortgage payments) are turned into marketable securities, such as bonds. The sellers (e.g. banks) get cash now rather than having to wait and can use it to fund loans to customers. The buyers make a profit by buying below the discounted value of the future income. Such bonds can be very risky, however, as the future cash flows may be less than anticipated.

Self-fulfilling speculation The actions of speculators tend to cause the very effect that they had anticipated.

Semi-strong efficiency (of share markets) Where share prices adjust quickly, fully and accurately to publicly available information.

Sensitivity analysis Where a range of possible values of uncertain costs and benefits are given to see whether the project's desirability is sensitive to these different values.

Set aside A system in the EU of paying farmers not to use a certain proportion of their land.

Shares (equities) A part ownership of a company. Companies' distributed profits are paid to shareholders in the form of dividends according to the number of shares held.

Short run (in production) The period of time over which at least one factor is fixed.

Short run under perfect competition The period during which there is insufficient time for new firms to enter the industry.

Short-run shut-down point This is where the AR curve is tangential to the AVC curve. The firm can only just cover its variable costs. Any fall in revenue below this level will cause a profit-maximising firm to shut down immediately.

Short selling The practice of borrowing an asset (for a fee) and selling it, hoping that the price will fall so that it can then be purchased and returned to the lender. The difference between the sale and purchase price (minus the fee) is thus profit to the short seller.

Short-termism Where firms and investors take decisions based on the likely short-term performance of a company, rather than on its long-term prospects. Firms may thus sacrifice long-term profits and growth for the sake of a quick return.

Sight deposits Deposits that can be withdrawn on demand without penalty.

Size distribution of income Measurement of the distribution of income according to the levels of income received by individuals (irrespective of source).

Social benefit Private benefit plus externalities in consumption.

Social cost Private cost plus externalities in production.

Social efficiency A situation of Pareto optimality: where all possible Pareto improvements have been made: where, therefore, it is impossible to make anyone better off without making someone else worse off.

Social efficiency (improvement in) A Pareto improvement: where changes in production or consumption can make at least one person better off without making anyone worse off.

Social rate of discount A rate of discount that reflects *society's* preferences for present benefits over future ones.

Social-impact standards Pollution control that focuses on the effects on people (e.g. on health or happiness).

Sole proprietorship A firm owned by one person. That person has unlimited liability.

Special drawing rights (SDRs) Additional liquidity created by the IMF. SDRs give countries the right to borrow a certain amount of additional funds from the IMF, with no requirement for extra deposits (quotas).

Special purpose vehicle (SPV) Legal entities created by financial institutions for conducting specific financial functions, such as bundling assets together into fixed interest bonds and selling them.

Specialisation and division of labour Where production is broken down into a number of simpler, more specialised tasks, thus allowing workers to acquire a high degree of efficiency.

Specific tax A tax on a good levied at a fixed amount per unit of the good, irrespective of the price of that unit.

Speculation Where people make buying or selling decisions based on their anticipations of future prices.

Speculators People who buy (or sell) commodities or financial assets with the intention of profiting by selling them (or buying them back) at a later date at a higher (lower) price.

Spot price The current market price.

Spreading risks (for an insurance company) The more policies an insurance company issues and the more independent the risks of claims from these policies are, the more predictable will be the number of claims.

Stabilising speculation Where the actions of speculators tend to reduce the magnitude of price fluctuations.

Stagflation A term used in the 1970s to refer to the combination of stagnation (low growth and high unemployment) and high inflation.

Stakeholders (in a company) People who are affected by a company's activities and/or performance (customers, employees, owners, creditors, people living in the neighbourhood, etc.). They may or may not be in a position to take decisions, or influence decision taking, in the firm.

Standardised unemployment rate The measure of the unemployment rate used by the ILO and OECD. The unemployed are defined as persons of working age who are without work, available to start work within two weeks and either have actively looked for work in the last four weeks or are waiting to take up an appointment.

Steady-state growth path The growth path for a given saving rate (where growth results from technological progress).

Steady-state level of national income The long-run equilibrium level of national income. The level at which all investment is used to maintain the existing capital stock at its current level.

Sterilisation When the government uses open-market operations or other monetary measures to neutralise the effects of balance of payments deficits or surpluses on the money supply.

Stock An amount of something (inputs, goods, money, etc.) existing at a point of time. (Contrasts with *flow*.)

Stock (or inventory) appreciation The increase in monetary value of stocks due to increased prices. Since this does not represent increased output it is not included in GDP.

Stop–go policies Alternate deflationary and reflationary policies to tackle the currently most pressing of the four problems which fluctuate with the business cycle.

Strategic alliance Where two firms work together, formally or informally, to achieve a mutually desirable goal.

Strategic trade theory The theory that protecting/supporting certain industries can enable them to compete more effectively with large monopolistic rivals abroad. The effect of the protection is to increase long-run competition and may enable the protected firms to exploit a comparative advantage that they could not have done otherwise.

Strong efficiency (of share markets) Where share prices adjust quickly, fully and accurately to all available information, both public and that only available to insiders.

Structural public-sector deficit (or surplus) The public-sector deficit (or surplus) that would occur if the economy were operating at the potential level of national income: i.e. one where there is a zero output gap.

Structural unemployment Unemployment that arises from changes in the pattern of demand or supply in the economy. People made redundant in one part of the economy cannot immediately take up jobs in other parts (even though there are vacancies).

Structuralists Economists who focus on specific barriers to development and how to overcome them.

Sub-prime debt Debt where there is a high risk of default by the borrower (e.g. mortgage holders who are on low incomes facing higher interest rates and falling house prices).

Subsistence production Where people produce things for their own consumption.

Substitute goods   A pair of goods which are considered by consumers to be alternatives to each other. As the price of one goes up, the demand for the other rises.

Substitutes in supply   These are two goods where an increased production of one means diverting resources away from producing the other.

Substitution effect of a price change   The effect of a change in price on quantity demanded arising from the consumer switching to or from alternative (substitute) products.

Substitution effect of a rise in wage rates   Workers will tend to substitute income for leisure as leisure now has a higher opportunity cost. This effect leads to *more* hours being worked as wage rates rise.

Substitution effect of a tax rise   Tax increases reduce the opportunity cost of leisure and thus encourage people to work less.

Sunk costs   Costs that cannot be recouped (e.g. by transferring assets to other uses). Examples include specialised machinery or the costs of an advertising campaign.

Supernormal profit (also known as **pure profit, economic profit, abnormal profit**, or simply **profit**).   The excess of total profit above normal profit.

Supply curve   A graph showing the relationship between the price of a good and the quantity of the good supplied over a given period of time.

Supply schedule   A table showing the different quantities of a good that producers are willing and able to supply at various prices over a given time period. A supply schedule can be for an individual producer or group of producers, or for all producers (the market supply schedule).

Supply-side economics   An approach which focuses directly on aggregate supply and how to shift the aggregate supply curve outwards.

Supply-side policy   Government policy that attempts to alter the level of aggregate supply directly (rather than through changes in aggregate demand).

Sustainability (environmental)   The ability of the environment to survive its use for economic activity.

Sustainable output   The level of national output corresponding to no excess or deficiency of aggregate demand.

Tacit collusion   Where oligopolists take care not to engage in price cutting, excessive advertising or other forms of competition. There may be unwritten 'rules' of collusive behaviour such as price leadership.

Takeover bid   Where one firm attempts to purchase another by offering to buy the shares of that company from its shareholders.

Takeover constraint   The effect that the fear of being taken over has on a firm's willingness to undertake projects that reduce distributed profits.

Target real wage theory   The theory that unions bargain for target real wage increases each year irrespective of the level of real growth in the economy.

Tariff escalation   The system whereby tariff rates increase the closer a product is to the finished stage of production.

Tariffs (or import levies)   Taxes on imported products: i.e. customs duties.

Tax allowance   An amount of income that can be earned tax-free. Tax allowances vary according to a person's circumstances.

Tax avoidance   The rearrangement of one's affairs so as to reduce one's tax liability.

Tax evasion   The illegal non-payment of taxes (e.g. by not declaring income earned).

Taylor rule   A rule adopted by a central bank for setting the rate of interest. It will raise the interest rate if (a) inflation is above target or (b) real national income is above the sustainable level (or unemployment is below the natural rate). The rule states how much interest rates will be changed in each case.

Technological unemployment   Structural unemployment that occurs as a result of the introduction of labour-saving technology.

Technology-based standards   Pollution control that requires firms' emissions to reflect the levels that could be achieved from using the best available pollution control technology.

Terms of trade   The price index of exports divided by the price index of imports and then expressed as a percentage. This means that the terms of trade will be 100 in the base year.

Third-degree price discrimination   When a firm divides consumers into different groups and charges a different price to consumers in different groups, but the same price to all the consumers within a group.

Tie-in sales   Where a firm is only prepared to sell a first product on the condition that its customers by a second product from it.

Time deposits   Deposits that require notice of with-drawal or where a penalty is charged for withdrawals on demand.

Time-series data   Information depicting how a variable (e.g. the price of eggs) changes over time.

Total consumer expenditure on a product (TE) (per period of time)   The price of the product multiplied by the quantity purchased: $TE = P \times Q$.

Total consumer surplus   The excess of a person's total utility from the consumption of a good (TU) over the amount that person spends on it (TE): $TCS = TU - TE$.

Total cost   The sum of total fixed costs and total variable costs: $TC = TFC + TVC$.

Total currency flow on the balance of payments   The current plus capital plus financial account balance but excluding the reserves.

Total physical product   The total output of a product per period of time that is obtained from a given amount of inputs.

Total (private) surplus   Total consumer surplus ($TU - TE$) plus total producer surplus ($TR - TVC$).

Total producer surplus (TPS)   Total revenue minus total variable cost ($TR - TVC$): in other words, total profit plus total fixed cost ($T\Pi + TFC$).

Total revenue A firm's total earnings from a specified level of sales within a specified period: $TR = P \times Q$.

Total revenue (*TR*) (per period of time) The total amount received by firms from the sale of a product, before the deduction of taxes or any other costs. The price multiplied by the quantity sold. $TR = P \times Q$.

Total social surplus Total benefits to society from consuming a good minus total costs to society from producing it. In the absence of externalities, total social surplus is the same as total (private) surplus.

Total utility The total satisfaction a consumer gets from the consumption of all the units of a good consumed within a given time period.

Tradable carbon permits Each firm is given a permit to produce a given level of pollution. If less than the permitted amount is produced, the firm is given a credit. This can then be sold to another firm, allowing it to exceed its original limit.

Trade creation Where a customs union leads to greater specialisation according to comparative advantage and thus a shift in production from higher-cost to lower-cost sources.

Trade cycle or **Business cycle** The periodic fluctuations of national output round its long-term trend.

Trade diversion Where a customs union diverts consumption from goods produced at a lower cost outside the union to goods produced at a higher cost (but tariff free) within the union.

Traditional theory of the firm The analysis of pricing and output decisions of the firm under various market conditions, assuming that the firm wishes to maximise profit.

Tragedy of the commons When resources are commonly available at no charge people are likely to over exploit them.

Transfer payments Moneys transferred from one person or group to another (e.g. from the government to individuals) without production taking place.

Transfers (by the government) Transfers of money from taxpayers to recipients of benefits and subsidies. They are not an injection into the circular flow but are the equivalent of a negative tax (i.e. a negative withdrawal).

Treasury bills Bills of exchange issued by the Bank of England on behalf of the government. They are a means whereby the government raises short-term finance.

U-form (unitary form) of corporate organisation Where the managers of the various departments of a firm are directly responsible to head office, normally to a chief executive.

Uncertainty When an outcome may or may not occur and its probability of occurring is not known.

Underemployment Where people who want full-time work are only able to find part-time work.

Underground markets Where people ignore the government's price and/or quantity controls and sell illegally at whatever price equates illegal demand and supply.

Unemployment The number of people who are actively looking for work but are currently without a job. (Note that there is much debate as to who should officially be counted as unemployed.)

Unemployment rate The number unemployed expressed as a percentage of the labour force.

Unit elastic demand Where quantity demanded changes by the same percentage as price. Ignoring the negative sign, it will have a value equal to 1.

Universal benefits Benefits paid to everyone in a certain category irrespective of their income or assets.

Util An imaginary unit of satisfaction from the consumption of a good.

Value added tax (VAT) A tax on goods and services, charged at each stage of production as a percentage of the value added at that stage.

Variable costs Total costs that vary with the amount of output produced.

Variable factor An input that can be increased in supply within a given time period.

Velocity of circulation The number of times annually that money on average is spent on goods and services that make up GDP.

Vent for surplus When international trade enables a country to exploit resources that would otherwise be unused.

Vertical equity The redistribution from the better off to the worse off. In the case of taxes, this means the rich paying proportionately more taxes than the poor.

Vertical merger When two firms in the same industry at different stages in the production process merge.

Vertical restraints Conditions imposed by one firm on another which is either its supplier or its customer.

Wage–price spiral Wages and prices chasing each other as the aggregate demand curve continually shifts to the right and the aggregate supply curve continually shifts upwards.

Wage taker An employer or employee who has no power to influence the market wage rate.

Wages councils Independent bodies which used to set rates of pay in certain low pay industries.

Weak efficiency (of share markets) Where share dealing prevents cyclical movements in shares.

Weighted average The average of several items where each item is ascribed a weight according to its importance. The weights must add up to 1.

Wholesale banks Banks specialising in large-scale deposits and loans and dealing mainly with companies.

Wholesale deposits and loans Large-scale deposits and loans made by and to firms at negotiated interest rates.

Withdrawals (*W*) (or leakages) Incomes of households or firms that are not passed on round the inner flow. Withdrawals equal net saving (*S*) plus net taxes (*T*) plus expenditure on imports (*M*): $W = S + T + M$.

Working to rule Workers do the bare minimum they have to, as set out in their job descriptions.

Yield on a share The dividend received per share expressed as a percentage of the current market price of the share.

Index

Pages with definitions are in **bold**.

absolute advantage **673**
absolute values A:5
abundance 13
abuse of power 368
ACAS 250
accelerationist theory 620–3
accelerator coefficient **496**
accelerator theory 482, **496**–7, 498, 569, 620, **621**
  interaction with multiplier 497, 499
acreage controls 89
Action Plan (EU) 700
active balances **528**
actual demand and supply 5
actual economic growth 398, 398–402
  causes of fluctuations in 401, 495–9
actual growth **398**, 408
actual output 398–400, 447–8
ad valorem tariffs **683**
ad valorem tax **77**, **291**
ADI/ASI model 556–60, 606, 618
adaptive expectations hypothesis **620**, 622–3, 626, 627, 635
adjustable peg system **714**, 729–30
administrative barriers to trade 684
adverse selection **108**
advertising 62, 188, 203
aggregate demand 5, 6, 390, 447–9
  and economic growth 393, 401, 408
  and exports 393
  and imports 393
  and inflation 393, 556–9, 616–19
  and interest rates 426, 586
  Keynesian economics 468, 590–2, 612
  and labour markets **420**–1
  and monetary policy 586, 590–2
  and national income 475
  and prices 425–9, 471
  and unemployment 393, 471, 634
aggregate expenditure **475**
aggregate labour market 420–5, 614–6

aggregate supply 5, **6**, 408, 427–8, 611–19
  and expectations 614, 627–30
  flexibility 455
  and inflation 556–9, 616–19
  and investment 613–14
  Keynesian economics 612
  and labour markets **420**–1, 614–15
  long-run 613–16
  short-run 612–13
aggressive tactics 175
agricultural policy 82–91, 768
  buffer stocks **85**
  collectivisation 18
  demand 83–4
  developing countries 776–7
  European Union 88–90
  minimum prices 86–7
  price fluctuations 82–3
  production quotas 89
  self-sufficient countries 87
  set-aside **89**–90
  subsidies 85–6, 89
  supply 83, 85, 87
  support prices 88–9, 90
  surpluses 88
  tariffs 86–7, 89
aid policies 788–90
AIM (Alternative Investment Market) 265
aims of firms 124
  alternative 213, 216
  growth maximising 221–5
  long-run profit maximisation 218–9
  managerial utility maximisation 9
  multiple aims 228–30
  profit maximisation 155–60
  sales revenue maximisation 219–21airline industry 180–1
allocation of resources 7–11, 16–24, 172, 176–9, 305–12, 338–9
allocation of road space 357–9
allocative efficiency **10**, 306, 310

alternative maximising theories 225
alternative products 40–1
alternative theory of the firm **124**
altruism 103
Amazon.com 170
ambient-based standards **349**
ambient-based standards (environment) 349
animal spirits 471
APEC (Asia-Pacific Economic Co-operation) 696
appreciation of the exchange rate **444**
arbitrage **442**
arc elasticity **61**–3, **67**
area charges (traffic) 363
Argentina 784–5
ASEAN nations 696
Asian currency crisis 748
asset prices 529–30
assets of banks **507**–9
asymmetric information **217**
asymmetric shocks **753**
Athens 362
atmospheric pollution 347, 362
ATMs 528
attitudes 284, 477
  to risk 217–18
Austrian School 338–9
automatic adjustments (in free markets) 337
automatic fiscal stabilisers **565**, 575
average cost pricing **196**, **231**–3
average costs **133**, 134–5, **146**–7
average (midpoint) formula **63**
average physical product **127**, 129
average revenue **151**, 152, 153

bail out plans 517–18
balance of payments **389**, 439–7, 447–9, 465
  in the 1950s and 1960s 592
  in the 1980s 711
  capital account 439, **440**–1

balance of payments (*continued*)
  circular flow of income 393
  current account 439–**440**, 744–5
  deficits 442, 457–8, 708, 710–14,
      719
    carry trade **721**–2
    correcting disequilibrium 712
    sterilisation 710, **712**
    in the US 730, 744–5
  in developing countries 768–9
  errors and omissions 441–2
  and exchange rates 445, 706–28
    adjustable pegs 729–30
    fixed 710, 712, 716–20
    floating 712–14, 720–8
  external **706**–7
  financial account 439, **441**–2
  income flows 440
  and inflation 431, 717
  internal **706**–7
  and investment 441
  money transfers 440
  primary exporting countries 768–9
  public sector budget balance 708
  substitution effects 712–13
  surpluses 719, 722
  trade in goods account 439
  trade restrictions 686
  trade in services account 439–40
  US trade imbalance 730, 744–5
balance sheet of the Bank of England
      513
balance of trade **6**
balance on trade in goods and services
      439, **440**
balance of types of tax 291–2
balanced budgets 460
Bali roadmap 353
bandwagon effects 499
bank bills 508
bank deposits multiplier **522**, 577
Bank of England 511–15
  balance sheet 513
  bank reserve deposits 508, 514
  cash ratio deposits 508
  exchange equalisation account **515**
  government accounts 514
  independence 511–12, 574
  issue of banknotes 512, 514
  lender of last resort **515**
  liquidity provision 514, 515, 516–18
  Monetary Policy Committee (MPC)
      515, 574, 583, 602
  open-market operations 515–18,
      578, 710, 712
  overseas central bank deposits 514

price survey 232–3
  prudential control **514**
  Special Liquidity Scheme 577
  targets 574, 607
  Ways and Means advance 514
  see also central banks
Bank Rate 508, 584, 592
banknote issues 512, 514
banks 74, 503, 505–15
  assets **507**–9
  bail out plans 517–18
  capital adequacy **509**–10
  deposit taking 503, 504, 506–7, 521
  deposits multiplier **522**, 577
  inter-bank markets 506, 515, 518,
      524
  investment banks 505–6
  investments 508–9
  lending 507–9, 576
    inelastic demand for loans 584
    maturity gap **510**
    maturity transformation **505**
    risk transformation **505**
    wholesale loans **505**, 506
  liabilities **506**–7
  liquidity **509**–10, 515–18, 522–3,
      574–6
  near money assets **523**
  profitability 509, 510, 520
  regulation 514
  reserves 508, 514, 574–5, 577, 578,
      580
  retail banking **505**
  secondary marketing **510**, 511
  securitisation **510**–11, 512
  Special Purpose Vehicles (SPV) 511
  sub-prime mortgages **511**, 512–13
  wholesale banking **505**
  see also central banks; credit crisis
bar charts A:4
barometric firm price leadership **192**,
      193
barriers to market entry **173**–5, 189,
      222
  see also freedom of market entry
barter economy **15**
base year **A:6**
basic needs 762–3
basic rate of tax **289**
Bass 191
Battle of Seattle 690
Baumol, William 219
Becker, Gary 116
behaviour
  altruism 103
  in family 103, 116–17

  legislation affecting 327
  rational 7–10, 98–101, **304**, 305–12
  selfish 103
  strategic 190
  see also rational behaviour
behavioural economics 26
benefit principle **288**
benefits
  cost-benefit analysis **329**–36
  of economic growth 406
  external **313**, 314, 315
  marginal 9–10, 310
  rational choices 9
  social **314**
  transfer payments **391**
benefits in kind **298**
  see also state benefits
Bertrand model 198–9
BETTA system 380–1
Big Bang 659–60
Big Mac PPP 722–3
bilateral monopoly **246**, 248
bills of exchange **508**, 515
biofuels industry 770, 787
Bolsheviks 18
bonds and gilts **265**, 508–9, 514, 525,
      575
Brady Plan 786–7
brand loyalty 174
Brazil 770, 786
Bretton Woods system **729**–30
brewing industry 191
British Gas 382
broad money (M4) **520**
budget line **112**–13
budgets
  balanced 460
  deficits and surpluses 525, **562**,
      563–5, 575, 708
  in the US 744–5
buffer stocks **85**
building societies 506
bureaucracy 337, 689
bus fares 63
Bush, George W. 353
business cycle 6, **400**–1, 447
  bandwagon effects 499
  and fiscal policy 562
  international 746
  and investment 497
  Keynesian economics 495–500
  real business cycle theory **469**,
      630–1
  time lags 499
  turning points 631
  and unemployment 416, 418

business finance 264–7, 661, 664
business surveys 399
by-products 137
bygones principle 131

CACM 696
cancellation of debt 788, 790
capital **4**
  accumulation 642
  demand 259, 261–3
  and economic growth 403
  free movement 660
  imperfections in capital markets
    661, 664
  marginal capital/output ratio **496**
  marginal efficiency of capital **262**,
    403
  physical 263
  price determination 261
  and profit 258–9, 264
  supply 259
  see also investment
capital account of the balance of
    payments 439, **440**–1
capital adequacy of banks **509**–10
capital equipment 482
capital expenditure by government
    563
capital gains tax 290
capital intensity (developing
    countries) 777–9
car ownership 357
carbon tariffs 685
carbon trading system 355
CARICOM 696
Carillion 658–9
carry trade **721**–2
cartels **190**, 192, 194–5, 196, 370–1
cash in circulation 512, 514, 528
cash deposits *see* deposit taking
cash ratio deposits 508, 514
central banks 508, 511–15, 574
  European Central Bank (ECB) 511,
    580–1, 602–3
  Federal Reserve 566, 579, 602–3
  funding the national debt **578**
  interest rate control 583–6
  lending to other banks 577
  open-market operations **577**, 578,
    579
  rules-based policies 606–7
  see also Bank of England
centrally planned economies **16**,
    18–20, 338–9
centre-right policies 470
certificates of deposit **507**, 510

ceteris paribus **26**, 98
Chamberlain, Edward 186
Channel Tunnel 225
characteristics theory 120
Charities Act 372
charges, environmental **348**
Chicago School 116, 627
Child Tax Credit 301
China
  economic growth 774–5
  inflation 435
  investment 774–5
  overheating 744–5
choice 7–8, **9**, 10–11
Churchill, Winston 459
cinema tickets 209
circular flow of income 14–16, 390–3,
    463, 475
  and the balance of payments 393
  equilibrium 393
  export expenditure 392, 483
  government expenditure 392,
    460–1, 483
  and households 390–1
  import expenditure 391–2, 480–1
  injections **392**, 482–3, 486–9, 491,
    544–5
  inner flow 391
  investment 392, 482–3
  state benefits 391
  and taxation 391, 479–80
  transfer payments **391**, 412
  withdrawals **391**, 478–82, 486–9, 491
    marginal propensity to withdraw
      482
    total withdrawals function 481–2
  see also savings
claimant unemployment **417**
classical theories 456–61
  economic growth 405
  Great Depression 459–60
  inflation 458–9, 626–32
  labour markets 614–15
  output 457–8
  prices 458–9
  Say's law **458**
  unemployment 457–8, 459–60,
    626–32
  see also new classical theories
Clean Development Mechanism 352,
    355
clockwise Philips loops 622–3
closed-shop agreements **250**
Coase theorem **324**, 347
Cobb-Douglas production function
    140, 141

Cobb-Douglas utility function 122
Coca-Cola 174
collective bargaining 248–51
collectivisation 18
collusive oligopolies **190**–6, 369
collusive tendering **371**
command economies **16**, 18–20,
    338–9
command-and-control (CAC)
    environmental policy **348**–9
commercial bills **508**
Common Agricultural Policy (CAP)
    88–90, 697
common markets **693**, 697–8
common resources 316–17, 318
communism 18–19, 50, 339
company bonds *see* bonds and gilts
comparative advantage 672–6, 767–9,
    771
  definition **673**
  developing countries and 767–9,
    773
  gains based on 673–6, 679–80
  graphical analysis 675, 680
  and terms of trade **677**–8
competition 23, 337–8, 368–75
  abuse of power 368
  collusive tendering **371**
  contestable markets 179–83
  for corporate control 178–179
  EU policies 369–70, 697, 699
  imperfect **164**, 185
  international trade 681
  measuring degrees of 166
  monopolies **164**, 173–9, 368
  monopolistic **164**, 189–9
  non-price **188**, 200
  oligopolies **164**, 189–201, 368, 369
  perfect **32**, **164**, 165–73
  predatory pricing **210**–11
  price-fixing agreements 371–2
  in privatised industries 382
  supply-side policies 658–60
  targets of competition policies
    368–9
  UK policies 370–3
Competition Commission 370, 373,
    374
competition policy 368–74
competitive advantage
  of firms 682
  of nations 681–2
competitive rivalry 682
complementary goods 34–5, 69
compounding **262**
compromise strategy **204**

concentration of industries 166
Congestion Charge 363–4
conglomerate mergers **222**, 368
conservation 345, 346
conservatism 230
consortium **224**
constant opportunity costs 674–5
constant returns to scale 136, 140–1, 149
consumer durables **105**, 477
consumer prices index (CPI) 428, **A:7**
consumer sovereignty **172**
consumer surplus **98**–9, 319, 331
consumers
  characteristics theory 120
  price elasticity of demand 59–61
  rational behaviour 9, **96**, **99**–100, **305**, 306
  share of tax on goods **78**
  spending on domestically produced goods **390**, 478
consumption **4**, 476–8
  determinants 477
  domestically produced goods **390**, 478
  and economic growth 406
  efficiency 10, 306
  equi-marginal principle **101**–2
  and expectations 477
  external benefits 315
  external costs 314
  income-consumption curve **114**, 115
  marginal propensity to consume **477**, 479, 490–1
  optimum level of consumption 98–9, 101–2, 113–14
  price-consumption curve **115**
  and prices 32
  and production 396
  and savings 480–1
consumption function **476**–8, 479
container principle 137
contestable markets 179–83
contractionary fiscal policy **438**, 712
controlling the money supply 576–83
convergence of economies **747**
convergence in GDP per head **640**–1
core workers **250**
corporate control 178–**179**
corporate tax 290, 656
corruption 689
cost-based pricing 231–3
cost-benefit analysis **329**–36
cost-push inflation **432**–3, 592, 593, 617–19

costs 9, 40, 130–6
  average **133**, 134–5, **146**–7
  capital equipment 482
  of economic growth 406–7
  explicit **131**
  external **313**, 314
  fixed 131, **132**, 133–4, 182
  historic **131**
  implicit **131**
  of inflation 429–32
  input **132**
  logistics 160
  marginal **9**, 13, **133**, 134–5, **147**–8, 310, **A:10**
  and monopolies 174
  motoring 357–8
  output maximisation 144
  overheads 137–**138**
  and price elasticity of supply 67
  of production
    and international trade 672, 680–1
    long run 146–50
    short run 130–6, 148
  and productivity 132
  replacement **131**
  sunk 131, **182**
  of tax collection 288
  time 104
  total **132**–3, 135
  of traffic congestion 360–1
  transport 138
  of unemployment 420
  variable **132**, 133, 134
  see also opportunity costs
countervailing power **200**
Cournot equilibrium **198**
Cournot model **197**
CPI (consumer prices index) 428, **A:7**
crawling peg system **714**
credible threats **204**
credit cards 528
credit creation 520–3
credit crisis 74, 503, 512–13, 516–18, 577
  bank bail out plans 517–18
  G7 agreement 749
  interest rates 602–3
credit rationing 576, 591
crime 397
cross-price elasticity of demand **69**–70
cross-section data **A:4**
cross-subsidising prices 368, **369**
crowding out **460**, 461, 545–6, 568
cumulative causation principle 463, **487**

currency union **751**
current account of the balance of payments 439–**440**, 744–5
current expenditure by government **563**
customs duties see tariffs
customs unions **693**–5, 697–8
cutting taxes 296–7, 568, 654–6
cyclical unemployment **422**–3

data see statistics
deadweight loss of a tax **294**, 325
deadweight welfare loss **319**
death of inflation 434–5
debentures **265**
debit cards 528
debt in developing countries 783–90
  Argentina 784–5
  cancellation 788, 790
  and environmental damage 786–7
  heavily indebted poor countries (HIPC) 788, 790
  Poverty Funds 790
  rescheduling 784–7
  structural reforms 787–8
  swapping debt 789
decision making 9, 10, 345–6
decision tree **204**–5
declining industries 684, 686
decreasing costs, and gains from trade 680–1
decreasing returns to scale 136, 140–1, 149
deduction **25**–6
deep green approach 345–6
deficits in the balance of payments 442, 457–8, 708, 710–14, 719
  carry trade **721**–2
  correcting disequilibrium 712
  sterilisation 710, **712**
  in the US 730
  see also budgets, deficits and surpluses
deflationary gap **492**–3
deflationary policies **438**, 446, 459, 465, 562
  Keynesian economics 635
demand 5, 32–9
  agricultural 83–4
  for capital services 259, 261–3
  change in demand 21, **35**, 44–5
  change in quantity demanded **35**
  cross-price elasticity **69**–70
  demand schedule for an individual **33**

demand (*continued*)
  derived demand **243**
  determinants of 34–5
  economic models 36–8
  elastic 58, 59
  estimated demand equations 36–8
  income elasticity of 67–9
  and incomes 35, **67**–9, 115
  indifference analysis 109–22
  inelastic 58, **59**–60, 584
  kinked demand theory **199**–200
  for labour 242–4
  law of demand **32**, 32
  marginal utility theory **96**–104
  market demand schedule **33**
  price elasticity of 57–65
  and prices 32–3, 57–65
  quantity demanded **33**
  under risk and uncertainty 105–9
  for road space 357–8
  see also aggregate demand; elasticity
    of demand
demand curve **33**–4, 43–4, 58, 444–5
  and advertising 62
  identification problem 50–**51**
  of individuals 115–16
  labour market **420**–1
  marginal utility theory 100–1, 104
  shifts 444–5
  straight-line 65, 154
demand deficient unemployment
    422–3, 633
demand function **38**
demand management 591
demand for money 527–31, 550–1
  and expectations 529, 530–1
  and interest rates 529, 537–8,
    545–6, 551
  motives for holding money 527–8
demand-pull inflation **432**, 434, 464,
    616–17, 618
demand-shift inflation 434–5
demand-side policies 7, 102, **465**,
    591–2, 594–5
  and inflation **438**
  link with supply-side policies
    653–4
  rule-based approach 598
dependency **772**
deposit taking 503, 504, 506–7, 521
  bank deposits multiplier **522**, 577
  wholesale deposits and loans **505**,
    506
depreciation **413**
  of the exchange rate **444**, 465, 540,
    713–14

deregulation **506**, 659–60
  of money markets 507–15
  supply-side policies 659–60
derived demand **243**
deskilling 467, 468
destabilising speculation **73**–4
devaluation **714**, 729–30
developing countries 762–790
  agriculture 776–7
  balance of payments 768–9
  basic needs 762–3
  debt problems 783–90
  exports 772–6
  GNY (gross national income) per
    capita 763–6
  human development index (HDI)
    765, **766**
  infrastructure development 782
  international trade 766–76
  land reform 777
  population growth 779
  rural-urban migration 779, 781
  technological progress 777–9
  unemployment 779–81
devolved budgeting 660
diagrams 493–4, A:1–3
diamonds-water paradox 102
diesel sulphur content 334–5
differentiation A:**9**–13
diminishing marginal rate of
    substitution **111**
diminishing marginal utility **106**–7,
    279
diminishing returns **125**, 126, 128, 142
direct income support **85**, 90
direct provision of goods and services
    328, 664
direct taxes **289**–90
discount markets 515
discounting **262**, 333
discretionary policies **567**, 565–7, 595,
    600, 604–5
discrimination 256–7
diseconomies of scale **138**, 139, 695
disequilibrium unemployment **421**–3,
    454
disguised unemployment **779**
disintermediation **582**
disposable income **413**, **477**, 480–1
distribution of income 35, 177, 276–7,
    477, 772
  by class of recipient 276
  functional 276, 280–2
  and GDP 397
  geographical 282–3
  Gini coefficient **278**

  government policies 288
  Lorenz curve **277**–8
  ratio of share of national income
    279
  redistribution 276, 288, 292–4,
    298–9
  size distribution **276**, 277–80
  and taxation 277
distribution of wealth 276, 283–4
diversification **109**, 222
dividend yields 48
division of labour **137**
Doha Development Agenda 690–1
dollar exchange rate 724–5, 744
dominant firm price leadership **192**–3
dominant strategy games **202**
drugs 81–2
dualism **778**
dumping **684**, 688
duopoly **197**
durable goods **105**, 477
duration of unemployment 417–19

e-commerce 170–1
eBay 171
echo effects 499
ecocide 786–7
econometrics **38**
economic discrimination **256**
economic efficiency **10**
economic growth 6, 398–409, 447–9,
    639–45
  in the 1950s and 1960s 591–2
  actual growth 398, 408
  and aggregate demand 393, 401, 408
  benefits 406
  business surveys 399
  and capital 403, 642
  causes 641
  China 774–5
  classical theory 405
  command economies 19
  comparison between countries
    640–1
  and consumption 406
  costs 406–7
  endogenous growth theory **648**
  fluctuations 401–2
  government policies 408
  in industrialised countries 639–41
  and investment 403, 408, 497
  labour market 403–4
  and land 404
  long-term 403–9
  model 642–3
  and the money supply 466

economic growth (*continued*)
new growth theory 405
output gaps 398, **399**
potential growth **398**, 399, 408
potential output **398**, 403
and productivity 641, 646–7
rate of economic growth **388**
savings rate 643–4, 645, 648
short-term 398–403
stagflation **466**, 592–4, 598, 622–3
steady-state growth path **645**
supply-side policies 651
without technological progress
642–5
with technological progress 645–9
trend growth 399, 400
workforce increase 644
see also business cycle; growth
economic interaction 23
economic models **25**–6
demand equations 36–8
equilibrium prices 45
supply equations 42
economic and monetary union (EMU)
693, **748**–55
economic profit **159**
economic rent **241**
economic shocks
asymmetric **753**
fixed exchange rates 716–17
floating exchange rates 721–2, 723,
731–4
random shocks 41, 499, 569
reverse shocks 631
supply shocks 558–9, 617
economic systems
classifications 16–8
command economy 18–20
free-market economy 20–4
mixed economy 24, 323–8
economies of scale **136**–8, 139, 150–1,
171–2, 221, 680, 681
and customs unions 695
EU single market 699
mergers 222
monopolies 173–4, 178
economies of scope **138**, 174
ECOWAS 696
education 349–50, 643, 662–3, 777
efficiency 10, 23, 305–13
allocative 306, 310
of capital equipment 482
in consumption 10, 306
externalities **306**, 313–15, 322,
323–4, 331
in factor markets 312

in goods markets 311–12
large machines 137
Pareto improvement **305**, 306, 308
Pareto optimality **305**, 306, 308, 317
private **305**, 306, 307–8, 311
productive **139**
social **305**–8, 310–13
efficient market hypothesis 266–7
efficient wage hypothesis **251**–5
EFTPOS 528
elasticity of demand **58**, 59, 60–1
income elasticity **67**–9, 115, 717,
768
labour markets 244
price elasticity **57**–65
elasticity of supply
financial capital 737
labour markets 240–1
price elasticity **65**–7, 78
elections 448, 600, 625
electricity industry 380–1
eliminating inflation 622
embargoes 683
emission reductions 334–5
emissions charges 348
emissions trading 352, 354
EMU (economic and monetary union)
693, **748**–55
endogenous growth theory **648**
endogenous money supply **526**, 546–7
endogenous variables **475**
energy efficiency 343
Enron 224
Enterprise Act 370
envelope curve **148**
environment 342–66
command-and-control (CAC)
systems **348**–9
and developing country debt 786–7
ecocide 786–7
education 349–50
energy efficiency 343
and free trade 683
Gaia philosophy **345**
game theory 354–6
global warming 344
government actions 354–6
grandfathering **354**
green taxes **348**, 350–1
legislation 348–9
market failures 346
market-based policies 347–8
optimum decision making 345–6
population growth 342–3
public opinion 343, 352–3
sustainability **345**–6, 787

tradable permits **350**–4
traffic congestion 256–61
urban transport policies 361–5
voluntary agreements 349
waste disposal 343
environmental charges **348**
equality 244–5, 252–3
equation of exchange **458**
equations A:8–9
equi-marginal principle **101**–2
equilibrium
circular flow of income 393
economic models 45
in exchange rates 532–3, 706,
723–5, 731, 744
general equilibrium 307, 308–10,
312
in goods and money markets 531–2,
551–2
interest rate 574, 583
in international trade **680**
macroeconomic 427
national income 486, 642–3, 706
perfect competition 167–8, 169
price and output 225
prices **20**, 42–5
monopolies 175–6
and monopolies 175
partial equilibrium 44
unemployment 420–**421**, 423–5,
454, 632–3
wages 20, 423, 615
equities *see* shares
equity **10**
ERM (exchange rate mechanism) 586,
596, 749–51
ethnic groups 420
Euribor 506
euro 572, 724–5, 751–2
European Central Bank (ECB) 511,
580–1, 602–3
see also central banks
European Union (EU)
agricultural policy 88–90, 697
business finance 265
carbon trading system 355
competition policy 369–70, 697,
699
EMU (economic and monetary
union) 693, **748**–55
ERM (exchange rate mechanism)
596, 749–51
free movement of people 241
history 697
and inflation 752
investment 752

European Union (EU) (*continued*)
merger policies 370
monetary aggregates 521
monetary policy 580–1
monopolies 369–70
mutual recognition principle **698**, 699
new member states 701, 703
oligopolies 700
regional policy 697
restrictive practices 369
Single European Act 660, 698–703
social policy 698
social protection benefits 300
Stability and Growth Pact 572–3, 575, 751–2
tax harmonisation 697, 701
excess burden of tax **325**
excess capacity **188**
exchange controls 683, 756–8
exchange equalisation account **515**
exchange rate bands **714**–15, 758
exchange rate index **442**
exchange rate mechanism (ERM) 586, **596**, **749**–51
exchange rate overshooting **726**
exchange rate regimes **707**, 709–10
intermediate **710**, **714**–15
exchange rates 389, 442–7
adjustable peg system **714**, 729–30
appreciation **444**
Asian currency crisis 748
and the balance of payments 445, 706–28
adjustable peg 729–30
fixed rates 710, 712, 716–20
floating rates 712–14, 720–8
bands **714**–15, 758
Bretton Woods system **729**–30
controlling transactions 683, 756–8
crawling peg system **714**
currency union **751**
demand and supply curve shifts 444–5
depreciation **444**, 465, 540, 713–14
determination 443–5
devaluation **714**, 729–30
dollar 724–5, 744
equilibrium 444, 532–3, 706
fixed 446, 457, 541, 592, **709**–12, 716–20, 737–9
floating **443**, 541, 593, **709**–**714**, 720–8, 730–6, 739–40
fluctuations 445–6, 727, 735–6, 742, 755–9

and GDP (gross domestic product) 394–5
government intervention 515, 710–12
import substitution 771
and interest rates 446, 540, 586
J-curve effect **729**–30
joint float system **714**
Keynesian economics 468, 719–20
and the money supply 524–5, 541, 710
new classical theories 719
nominal 707, 717
overshooting **726**
real rates **709**, 717
revaluation **714**
speculation 530, 718–20, 725–7, 731, 755
sterling 731–5
targeting 595–6, 601, 706, **714**–15, 758
Tobin tax 756–8
total currency flow balance 706
transmission mechanism **536**, 539–41
yuan 775
Exchequer account 514
excise duties 291
exogenous money supply **526**, 546–7
exogenous variables **475**
expansion path **149**
expansionary fiscal policy **438**
expectations 49, 105, 471, 633–4
adaptive hypothesis **620**, 622–3, 626, 627, 635
and aggregate supply 614, 627–30
of asset price changes 530–1
and consumption 477
and the demand for money 530–1
and inflation 435, 594, 619–20
and investment 482, 484–5
and markets 455–6
of output 616
of price changes 35, 41, 71–5
rational 469–70, 626, **627**, 628–9, 635
expectations-augmented Phillips curve **619**–26
expenditure changing **712**, **713**–14
expenditure method of GDP calculation 394, 412–13
expenditure reducing **712**
expenditure switching **712**–13
explicit costs **131**
exploitation of cheap labour 676

exports
and aggregate demand 393
circular flow of income 392, 483
developing countries 772–6
income elasticity of demand 717
primary exports 767–9
substitution effect 426
world multiplier effects 689
extended warranties 374
extensive-form games 204
external balance of payments **706**–7
external benefits **313**, 314, 315
external costs **313**, 314
external diseconomies of scale **139**
external economies of scale **139**, 170
external policy objectives **706**
external shocks
fixed exchange rates 717
floating exchange rates 723, 731–4
externalities
correction by taxation 323–4
efficiency **306**, 313–15, 322, 323–4, 331
privatised industries 377–8
extreme Keynesians 470

factor price equalisation **767**
factors of production **4**, 13, 15, 21
factor price equalisation **767**
fixed factors **124**, 125, 128, 135
and international trade 677
market efficiency 312
non-human 258–9
variable factors **124**
fairness 10, 378
fallacy of composition 84, 492
family behaviour 116–17
farmers 83–4
Federal Reserve 566, 579, 602–3
see also central banks
final expenditure **563**
financial account of the balance of payments 439, **441**–2
financial capital 258, 263, 777
elasticity of supply 737
imperfections in capital markets 661, 664
and investment 264–7, 661, 664
financial crowding out **460**, 461, **545**
financial deregulation **506**, 659–60
financial economies 138
financial flexibility **254**
financial interdependence 744–5
financial intermediaries **504**

fine tuning 562, 565–6
  demise of in 1960s 592–4
  Keynesian view 590–2, 600–1
firms 14–15
  alternative theory of the firm **124**
  circular flow of income 390–1
  competitive rivalry 682
  interdependence 613
  market valuation 223
  organisational structure 214–15
  theory of the firm **124**
first-best solution **323**, 377
first-degree price discrimination **206**,
    208
first-mover advantage **205**
fiscal drag **565**
fiscal policy **438**, 562–73
  automatic stabilisers **565–7**, 575
  and the business cycle 562
  deflationary **438**, 446, 459, 465,
    562
  discretionary 565–7, **567**
  effectiveness 588–9
  fixed exchange rates 718, 737–8
  floating exchange rates 728, 739
  and the Great Depression 460
  and inflation **438**
  ISLM analysis 588–90
  Keynesian economics 464, 589
  political manipulation 600
  pure fiscal policy **568**
  reflationary **438**, 465, 562, 593
  stimulus packages 566
  supply-side 562, 565
  timing problems 569–71
  in the UK 571–3, 590–9
  see also taxation
fiscal rules 571–3
fiscal stance **563–4**
fixed costs 131, **132**, 133–4, 182
fixed exchange rates 446, 457, 541,
    592, **709**–12, 716–20, 737–9
  advantages 718–19
  disadvantages 719–20
  external shocks 717
  fiscal policy 718, 737–8
  internal shocks 716–17
  international liquidity **719**–20
  ISLM analysis 737–9
  long-term balance of payments
    problems 717–18
  monetary policy 718, 719, 738–9
  speculation 718–19, 720
  totally fixed exchange rates **709**–10
fixed factors **124**, 125, 128, 135
flat organisations 215

flexibility
  aggregate supply 455
  financial **254**
  labour market 254–5
  prices 233, 454–5, 457, 626
  wages 454–5, 615, 626
flexible firm **254**
flexible working 255
floating exchange rate *see* free-floating
    exchange rates
flow diagrams 15, 390–3
  see also circular flow of income
flow of goods 260
flow-of-funds equation **525–6**
food prices 777
foreign currency reserves 441, 442,
    446
foreign exchange markets *see*
    exchange rates
foreign-based monopolies 684
forward markets **76**, **727**
foundation trusts 660
franchising **224**, **382**
free capital movement 660
free movement of people 241
free trade 660, 671, 676, 683
  and the environment 683
  and market power 686
free-floating exchange rates **443**, 541,
    593, **709–714**, 720–8, 730–6,
    739–40
  advantages 727
  carry trade **721–2**
  disadvantages 727
  equilibrium 723–5, 731
  external shocks 723, 731–4
  fiscal policy 728, 739
  internal shocks 721–2
  ISLM analysis 739–40
  monetary policy 728, 739–40
  purchasing power parity (PPP) **395**,
    396, **721**, 722–3, 733
  speculation 725–6, 727, 731
  UK experience 731–5
  uncertainty 727
  volatility 735–6
free-market **16**, 20–4, 323, 457–8
  advantages 337–8
  Keynesian economics 468
  and sustainability **345**
free-rider problem **316**
free-trade areas **693**, 696
freedom of market entry 165, 170–1,
    186
  see also barriers to market entry
frictional unemployment **423**–4, 657

Friedman, Milton 466, 619
FSA (Financial Services Authority) 514
full-employment level of national
    income **492**, 493
functional distribution of income **276**,
    280–2
functional flexibility **254**
functional relationships A:8–9
funding the national debt **578**
future payments 504
futures markets **76**

G7 meetings 749
G8 meetings 748–9
G20 meetings 749
Gaia philosophy **345**
game theory **201–6**, 215, 354–6
  compromise strategy **204**
  decision tree **204**–5
  dominant strategy games **202**
  first-mover advantage **205**
  maximax strategy **202**, 354
  maximin strategy **202**
  multiple-move games **204**
  prisoners' dilemma **202**, 203, 354
  single-move games 201–4
  threats and promises 204
  timing 204–5
GATT 690–1
GDP (gross domestic product) 393–7
  calculation 394, 409–14
  convergence in GDP per head 640,
    641
  and crime 397
  and the distribution of income 397
  exchange rates 394–5
  GDP at market prices **411**
  inflation 394
  nominal GDP **394**, 395
  per-capita GDP 394, 396, 644
  real GDP **394**, 395
  standards of living 395–7, 410–11
  and taxation 411, 412
  underground economy 396, 397
  unrecorded goods and services
    395–6
  see also national income
gender differences
  inequality and poverty 253, 282
  unemployment 419–20
general equilibrium
  in international trade **680**
  in markets 307, 308–10, **312**
general government debt **562**
general government deficits and
    surpluses **562**

geographical distribution of income 282–3

Germany and inflation 430

Giffen goods **119**

gilts and bonds **265**, 508–9, 514, 525, 575

Gini coefficient **278**

global growth strategy 225

global warming 344

globalisation 454–5, 556, 669, 690, 743–7

GNY (gross national income) per capita 763–6

gold reserves 441, 442, 446

gold standard **457**, 459

Golden Rule 571–3, 575

golden-rule savings rate **644**

Goodhart's Law **585**, 604

goods in joint supply **41**

goods markets 544–56, 629
  changes money supply 544–7
  efficiency 311–12
  equilibrium 551–2

Gorbachev, Mikhail 19

government borrowing
  Bank of England role 514
  and interest rates 460
  national debt **562**, 578
  public sector net cash requirement **563**, 571, 575

government expenditure
  balanced budgets 460
  capital expenditure **563**
  circular flow of income 392, 460–1, 483
  cost-benefit analysis **329**–36
  current expenditure **563**
  deficits and surpluses 525, **562**, 563–5, 575, 708
    in the US 744–5
  effects of changes in 567–8
  final expenditure **563**
  Golden Rule 571–3, 575
  public works programmes 460–1
  reducing 654
  structural deficits and surpluses **564**–5
  transfers **563**
  see also state benefits

government intervention 16–17, 24, 313–22, 456, 661–6
  advantages 313–22, 661
  collective bargaining 250–1
  direct provision of goods and services 328, 664
  disadvantages 337, 667

exchange rates 515, 710–12

forms of 323–9
  grants 664
  industrial reorganisation 665
  by information provision 328
  by legislation 327–9
  national economic planning 664
  protection of people's interests 320, 327
  protectionism 688–9
  rationalisations 664
  rejection of market allocation 80–1
  research & development 665
  selective intervention 664–7
  small firms assistance 665
  by taxation 323–6
  see also legislation

government policies 26–7, 52–3, 389, 499
  in the 1950s and 1960s 464–5, 591–2
  in the 1970s 592–4, 731–2
  in the 1980s 467, 594–6, 654, 711, 734–5
  1990 onward 596–9, 735
  agriculture 82–91
  competition 370–3
  contractionary 712
  demand management 591–2
  deregulation **506**, 659–60
  devolved budgeting 660
  discretionary 595, 600, 604–5
  distribution of income 288
  economic growth 408
  and elections 448, 600, 625
  failure 336–9
  Great Depression 459–60, 689
  industrial **661**, 666
  inequality and poverty 285, 286
  internal market in the NHS 660
  international co-ordination 745–7
  mergers 368–9, 370, 373
  monopolies 372–3
  nationalisation 328, **375**, 664
  prices and incomes 51–4, 327–8, **592**
  Private Finance Initiative (PFI) 658–9, 660
  privatisation 375–82, 659
  regional 666–7
  restrictive practices 370–2
  rules-based approach 598, 600–7
  urban 666–7
  see also fiscal policy; monetary policy

government surplus **325**

grandfathering **354**

grants 664

graphs A:5, A:8

Great Depression 459–60, 689

green taxes **348**, 350–1

greenhouse effect 342, 344

Greenspan, Alan 566

gross domestic product see GDP

gross national income **413**
  see also GNY

gross value added at basic prices **409**, 411, 412

growth
  consortium **224**
  diversification 222
  franchising **224**
  global strategy 225
  internal expansion 221–2
  joint ventures **223**
  maximisation **221**
  mergers 222–3, 226–7
  networks **225**
  price and output equilibrium 225
  strategic alliances **223**, 225
  subcontracting **224**–5
  vertical integration 221–2
  of world trade 672
  see also economic growth

H-form organisations **215**

Hall, R.L. 199

harmful goods 685

harmonisation of policies **746**–7, 748–9

harmonisation of taxes 697, 701

Hayek, Friedrich von 338–9

health care 80–1, 322, 660

heavily indebted poor countries (HIPC) 788, 790

Heckscher-Ohlin theory **767**, 778

Hicks-Kaldor criterion 333, 336

HICP (harmonised index of consumer prices) 428

hire-purchase controls 576

historic costs **131**

Hitch, C.J. 199

homogenous labour 237–8

horizontal equity **288**

horizontal mergers **222**, 368

'hot money' 731–2, 736, 744–5

Hotelling, Harold 269

hours of work 284
  supply of hours curve 238, 239

households 14–15
  circular flow of income 390–1
  composition 282, 285

households (*continued*)
disposable income **413**, **477**, 480–1
sources of income 280–1
housing market 46–7
human capital **257**, 643
human development index (HDI) 765, **766**
human life, value of 332
human resources 4
human wants 4, 5
hyperinflation 430–1, 432
hysteresis **468**, 616, 633

IBOR (inter-bank offer rate) 506, 516
identical products 165
identification problem 50–**51**
idle balances **529**
illegal goods 81–2
illiquid assets 506, 508–9, 524
imperfect competition **164**, 185
imperfect information 105–6, 627
imperfections in capital markets 661, 664
implicit costs **131**
import-substituting industrialisation **766**, 769–72
imports 593, 768
and aggregate demand 393
circular flow of income 391–2, 480–1
controls 446
determinants of the level of 480–1
harmful goods 685
income elasticity of demand 717, 768
levies *see* tariffs
licensing 683
and the standard of living 688
substitution effect 426, 766, 769–72
world multiplier effects 689
incentives 50, 217, 289, 294–6, 337, 565, 655–6
under socialism 339
incidence of tax **78**
income
and the balance of payments 440
and car ownership 358
and demand 35
diminishing marginal utility **106**–7, 279
disposable income **413**, **477**, 480–1
distribution *see* distribution of income
earnings statistics 279–80
of farmers 83–4

flow diagrams *see* circular flow of income
and house prices 47
income-consumption curve **114**–5
indifference analysis 112–13, 114–15
price elasticity of demand 58–9
real income **114**
redistribution 276, 288, 292–4, 298–9, 429
rich and poor people 245, 257, 270
and share prices 49
sources of household income 280–1
spending patterns 279–80
see also distribution of income; wages
income effect **32**, 116, **117**–18, **139**, **295**, 425–6
income elasticity of demand **67**–9, 115
exports 717
imports 717, 768
income method of GDP calculation 394, 411–12
income tax 289–90, 293–4
negative income tax **298**
income-consumption curve **114**, 115
increasing opportunity costs **13**
increasing returns to scale 136, 140–1
independence **186**
of the Bank of England 511–12, 574
independent risks **109**
index numbers A:6–7
indicative planning 664
indifference analysis 109–22
budget line **112**–13
income changes 112–13, 114–15
labour market 240
optimum consumption point 113–14
price changes 113, 115, 116–19
taxation 298–9
indifference curves **110**–11, 298–9
indifference map **111**
indifference set **110**
indirect taxes **77**–9, 289, 290–1, 294
individuals' demand curve 115–16
indivisibilities **137**
Indonesia 786–7
induced investment **496**
induction **25**
industrial action 250
industrial relations 138
industry
concentration 166
declining 684, 686

effective rate of protection **771**
government policies **661**, 666
infant industries **684**
infrastructure **139**, 777, 782
inward and outward-looking industrialisation 772–3
reorganisation 665
size 139
inefficiency 178
inelastic demand 58, **59**–60
for loans 584
inequality and poverty 245, 252–3, 276–87, 321
in the 1800s 284
analysis of poverty 276–7
causes 284–6
earnings statistics 279–80
G8 summits 748–9
gender differences 282
government policies 285, 286
household composition 282, 285
inflation rate of the poor 279
poverty trap **298**, 301
types of inequality 276–7
and wealth 284
see also state benefits
infant industries **684**
inferior goods **35**, **69**, **118**
infinitely elastic demand 60–1
inflation 6, 388–9, 393, 428–38, 447–9, 556–9
in the 1950s and 1960s 591
accelerationist theory 620, **621**
aggregate demand and supply 393, 556–9, 616–19
balance of payments 431, 717
in China 435
classical theories 458–9, 626–32
cost-push **432**–3, 593, 617–19
costs 429–32
death of inflation 434–5
demand-pull **432**, 434, 464, 616–17, 618
demand-shift 434–5
demand-side policies **438**
eliminating 434–5, 622
in eurozone countries 752
expectations 435, 594, 619–20
fiscal policies **438**
GDP (gross domestic product) 394
German 430
hyperinflation 430–1, 432
and investment 429–30
Keynesian economics 463–4, 467, 492–5, 632–5
labour market 629–30

inflation (*continued*)
   and the money supply 438, 466, 471, 575–6
   and the poor 279
   rate of inflation **389**, 428, 556
   redistribution of income 429
   in Serbia 430
   stagflation **466**, 592–4, 598, 622–3
   structural 434–5
   supply shocks 558–9
   supply-side policies **438**, 652
   targeting 470, 544, 556, 596–7, 600–7, 618–19, 625
   and uncertainty 429–30
   and unemployment 436–7, 471, 494, 620–1, 632–5
   in Zimbabwe 430–1
inflationary gap **493**–4
informal sector **17**–18
information
   asymmetric **217**
   imperfect 105–6, 627
   lack of 214–15
infrastructure **139**, 777, 782
injections **392**, 482–3, 486–9, 491, 544–5
   and the money supply 544–5
inner circular flow of income 391
innovation 179, 404, 651
input costs 132
input-output analysis **18**–19
insider dealing 266–7
insiders **250**, **468**
insurance 107–9
integrated transport policy 364
inter-bank markets 506, 515, 518, 524
Interbrew 191
interdependence 21, 308–10
   of firms **190**, 613
   international trade 743–5
interest rates 264, 457, 531–2, 583–6
   and aggregate demand 426, 586
   Bank Rate 508, 584, 592
   central bank control 583–6
   and the demand for money 528, 537–8, 545–6, 551
   equilibrium 574, 583
   and exchange rates 446, 540, 586
   and government borrowing 460
   IBOR (inter-bank offer rate) 506, 516
   and import substitution 771
   and investment 482, 538–9, 546, 549
   and the money supply 526–7, 582–3
   portfolio balance **541**, 542–3

and the credit crisis 602–3
   transmission mechanism **536**–9
intermediate exchange rate regimes **710**, 714–15
internal balance of payments **706**–7
internal expansion 221–2
internal market in the NHS 660
Internal Market Scoreboard 700, 702
internal policy objectives **706**
internal rate of return **262**
internal shocks 716–17
   free-floating exchange rates 721–2
international business cycle 746
international co-ordination 745–7
international liquidity **719**–20, 730
International Monetary Fund (IMF) 729, 787–8
international trade 23
   absolute advantage **673**
   comparative advantage 672–6, 767–9, 771
     definition **673**
     and terms of trade **677**–8
   competition 681
   competitive advantage of nations 681–2
   costs of production 672, 680–1
   developing countries 766–76
   economies of scale 680, 681
   factor markets 677
   free trade 660, 671, 676
     and the environment 683
     and market power 686
   general equilibrium diagrams **680**
   globalisation 454–5, 556, 669, 690, 743–7
   growth of world trade 672
   interdependence 743–5
   multiplier **743**
   opportunity costs 674–5, 677
   preferential trading 692–7
   restrictions 683–92
   specialisation 672, 677
   terms of trade **677**–9, 769
   trade creation **693**–4, 699
   trade cycle **400**–1
   trade diversion **694**–5, 700
   US trade imbalance 744–5
   welfare gains 679–80
intervention price (CAP) 86–7, 88
interventionist policies 424, **653**, 661–7
intimidation 175
inventories *see* stocks of goods
investment **14**, **261**
   and aggregate supply 613–14

and the balance of payments 441
and the business cycle 497
in China 774–5
circular flow of income 392, 482–3
and economic growth 403, 408, 497
in eurozone countries 752
and expectations 482, 484–5
financing 264–7, 661, 664
imperfections in capital markets 661, 664
and increased consumer demand 482
induced investment **496**
and inflation 429–30
instability 496–7
and interest rates 482, 538–9, 546, 549
internal rate of return **262**
net present value **262**
present value **261**–2
rate of return 261
risks 263
tax incentives 656
investment banks 505–6
inward-looking industrialisation 772–3
ISEW (Index of Sustainable Economic Welfare) 410–11
ISLM analysis **548**–56
   fiscal policy 588–90
   fixed exchange rates 737–9
   free-floating exchange rates 739–40
   monetary policy 588–90
   money markets **548**–56
isocost approach **143**
isoquant analysis **140**, 142, 148–9
issue of banknotes 512, 514

J-curve effect **729**–30
Japan, flexible working 255
Jevons, William Stanley 102
joint float system **714**
Joint Implementation (Kyoto Protocol) 352, 355
joint ventures **223**
just-in-time **229**–30, 255

Kaldor, N. 333
Keynesian 45 degree line 475–6, 491, 494–5
Keynesian economics 454, 462–5, 615–16
   aggregate demand 468, 590–2, 612
   aggregate supply 612
   business cycle 495–500
   deflationary policies 635

...nomics (*continued*)
...e rates 468, 719–20
...e Keynesians 470
...l policy 464, 589
...ee market 468
government and industry
cooperation 468
inflation 463–4, 467, 492–5, 632–5
labour market 462, 615–16
market for loanable funds 462–3
moderate Keynesians 470
Monetarist-Keynesian debate
466–9, 470, 589–90, 592, 595
monetary policy 464, 589
new Keynesians **470**
post-Keynesians **471**
reflationary policies 634
structural policies 467, 468
supply-side policies 652
unemployment 422, 463–4, 467,
492–5, 632–5
kinked demand theory **199**–200
Kyoto Protocol 347, 352–3

labour market **4**
aggregate demand **420**–1
aggregate supply **420**–1, 614–15
classical theories 614–15
demand for labour 242–4
discrimination 256–7
division of labour **137**
and economic growth 403–4
elasticity of labour demand 244
elasticity of labour supply 240–1
flexibility 254–5
homogenous labour 237–8
indifference analysis 240
and inflation 629–30
marginal cost of labour 242
marginal revenue of labour **242**
mobility of labour **240**–1, 424
movement of labour 237
natural wastage **248**
output per employed person
639–40, 646
participation rate **644**
perfect knowledge 237
perfect labour market 237–8
primary labour market **254**–5
secondary labour market **255**
shirking 252–3
skilled workers 282
supply of hours curve 238, 239
supply of labour curve 238–41, 423
and tax cuts 654–6
turnover rates 253

workforce increase 644
see also trade unions; wages
labour movement 249–51
labour theory of value 238
Laffer, Art 295
Lagrangian multipliers 114, 144
laissez-faire policies 456
lamb consumption 36–8
Lancaster, Kelvin 120
land **4**, 258–9, 268–70
and economic growth 404
property rights 324
reform 777
large numbers, law of 109
law of comparative advantage **673**
law of demand **32**
law of diminishing returns **125**, 126,
128, 142
law of large numbers **109**
leakages **391**
least-cost combination of factors
139–40, 143–4
legal protection 174
legislation
anti-competitive 369–73
Charities Act 372
environmental 348–9
price-cap regulation **379**
privatised industries 377–82
trade union 250–1
traffic congestion 362
lender of last resort **515**
lending by banks 507–9, 576
central banks 577
inelastic demand for loans 584
maturity gap **510**
maturity transformation **505**
risk transformation **505**
wholesale loans **505**, 506
liabilities of banks **506**–7
libertarian theories 338–9, **652**
LIBOR 506, 516
limit pricing **175**
linear functions A:8–9
liquidity
banks **509**–10, 515–18, 522–3,
574–6
international **719**–20, 730
liquidity preference **528**, 540
liquidity ratio **510**
liquidity trap **538**
LM curve 550–1
loanable funds 263–4, 457, 457–8
loans *see* lending by banks
location of production 138
lock-outs **250**

logistics 160
London Club 786
London Congestion Charge 363–4
London Inter-bank Offered Rate
(LIBOR) 508, 516–7
long run
aggregate supply 613–16
average cost curve **146**–7
equilibrium 186–7
marginal cost **147**
neutrality of money 575–6
under perfect competition **166**
production **124**, 136–50
profit maximisation **218**–19
shut-down point **159**, 160
long-term finance 264–5
long-term loans 508
long-term monetary control 574–5
Lorenz curve **277**–8
loss minimising output 159
Lucas, Robert 627

M-form organisations 214–**215**
Maastricht Treaty 572, 698, 751
macroeconomics **6**
MacSharry reforms 90
Malthus, Thomas Robert 126–7
managed floating **714**, 730–5
managerial utility maximisation 219
manufactured resources 4
marginal benefits **9**–10, 310
marginal capital/output ratio **496**
marginal consumer surplus **99**
marginal costs **9**–10, 13, **133**, 134–5,
147–8, 310, **A:10**
of labour 242
marginal disutility of work (MDU) **238**
marginal efficiency of capital **262**, 403
marginal external benefit 313–5,
323–4, 330
marginal external cost 313–5, 323–4,
346
marginal physical product **127**, 129,
141
marginal private benefit 314–5
marginal private cost 314–5
marginal product approach 139–40,
144
marginal productivity theory **242**, 251
marginal propensity
to consume **477**, 479, 490–1
to import **480**
to save **479**
marginal rate of factor substitution
111, 142
marginal rate of transformation 311–2

marginal revenue **151**–2, 153–4
of labour **242**
marginal social benefit 308–9, 311–2,
314–5, 323–4, 346, 348, 359
marginal social cost 308–9, 311–2,
314–5, 323–4, 345–6, 348,
359–60, 377–8
marginal tax propensity **479**
marginal utility theory **96**–104
demand curves 100–1, 104
marginal rate of substitution **111**
mark-up cost pricing **231**–4
market clearing **43**
market demand schedule **33**
market distortion and taxation 289
market failure 313, 320–2
environmental 346
and property rights 326
see also government intervention;
social efficiency
market for loanable funds **457**, 462–3
market loans **508**
market power 32, 164, 317–19, 368
and free trade 686
and wages 246–8
market share 193
market valuation 223
market-based policies
environmental 347–8
supply-side **652**, 654–61
unemployment 424
markets 15, 44
contestable 179–83
costless exit 182
entry barriers **173**–5, 189, 222
and expectations 455–6
freedom of entry 165, 170–1, 186
general equilibrium 307, 308–10,
312
interdependence 21, 308–10
perfect markets 32
social efficiency 306, 308
social objectives 24
underground 53, **54**
see also free-market
Marx, Karl 102, 238
maturity gap **510**
maturity transformation **505**
maximax strategy **202**, 354
maximin strategy **202**
maximisation of growth **221**
maximum price **52**, 53, 54
maximum/minimum point of a curve
A:11–12
May Committee 460
mean A:5–6

means-tested benefits 298, 299
median A:6
medium of exchange **503**
medium-term finance 264
Menger, Carl 102, 338
menu costs of inflation **429**
mergers 174
government policies 368–9, 370,
373
and growth 222–3, 226–7
monopolies 223
takeover constraint 221
takeovers 174, **199**
merit goods **320**
microeconomics 5–6, 7–11
choice 7–8, 9, 10–11
definition **6**
flow diagrams 15
marginal costs and benefits 9–10
objectives 10
opportunity costs 8, **9**, 11, 13–14,
130–1
minimum efficient plant size 150–1
minimum efficient scale 150–1, 699
minimum prices **51**, 52–4, 86–7
minimum reserve ratio **574**–5, 578,
580
minimum wage 52, 287
minimum/maximum point of a curve
A:11–12
Mises, Ludwig von 338–9
mixed economies **16**, **24**
mobility of labour **240**–1, 424
models *see* economic models
moderate Keynesians 470
moderate monetarists 470
Monetarist-Keynesian debate 466–9,
470, 589–90, 592, 595
monetary aggregates 521
monetary base **520**
monetary base control **581**–2
monetary policy **438**, 542, 574–87
aggregate demand 586, 590–2
effectiveness 588–9
in Europe 580–1
fixed exchange rates 718, 719,
738–9
floating exchange rates 728, 739–40
ISLM analysis 588–90
Keynesian economics 464, 589
medium and long-term 574–6
and national income 536–44
policy targets 574
political manipulation 600
short-term 576
in the UK 590–9

Monetary Policy Committee (MPC)
515, 574, 583, 602
money 4, 503–4
demand for money 527–31
long-run neutrality **576**
multiplier 522–4, **523**, 582
printing extra money 460
quantity theory **458**, 460, 462–3,
466, 536
money illusion **436**, **614**, 616
money markets 515–18, 548
Bank of England operations 515–18
equilibrium 531–2, 551–2
ISLM model **548**–56
money supply 463, 466, 471, 520–27
broad money (M4) **520**
changes in 536, 541–4
controlling 576–83
credit creation 520–3
economic growth 466
endogenous **526**, 546–7
and exchange rates 524–5, 541, 710
exogenous **526**, 546–7
flow-of-funds equation **525**–6
goods market changes 544–7
increase in injections 544–5
inflation 438, 466, 471, 575–6
interest rates 526–7, 582–3
long-run neutrality of money **576**
and national income 503
portfolio balance **541**–2
public-sector deficits *see* budgets
quantity theory of money **458**, 460,
462–3, 466, 536
rise in the money supply 524–5
sterilisation 710, **712**
targets 585, 601
velocity of circulation 536, 542–4
money transfers and the balance of
payments 440
monopolies 164, 173–9, 368
advantages 178–9
barriers to entry **173**–5
correction by taxation 324–5
costs 174
cross-subsidising prices 368, **369**
deadweight welfare loss **319**
definition 173
disadvantages 176–8
economies of scale 173–4, 178
equilibrium prices 175–6
EU policies 369–70, 700
foreign-based 684
import substitution 771
mergers 223
natural monopolies **173**–4, 181, 376

monopolies (*continued*)
  network economies **174**
  price discrimination 179
  public interest 176–9, 188–9
  regulatory bodies 327
  UK policies 372–3
  vertical restraints **373**
monopolistic competition **164**, 189–9
monopsony **246**, 247, 686
Mont Pelerin Society 338–9
moral hazard **108**, **512**
morale 253–5
mortgages 47
motoring costs 357–8
movement of labour 237
multinational companies 215, 223–5,
    684, 770–2, 777–9
multi-stage production 137
multiple aims (of firms) 228–30
multiple-move games 204
multiplier effects **463**, 497
  bank deposits **522**, 577
  international trade 689, **743**
  money multiplier 522–4, **523**, 582
  national income **486**–91, 569
    formula **488**, 490
  regional multiplier **666**, 700
mutual recognition principle **698**, 699

NAFTA (North American Free Trade
    Association) 696
Nash equilibrium 198–**199**, 202
national debt **562**, 578
national economic planning 664
national income 393–7, 486–92
  aggregate demand 475
  effect of monetary changes 536–44
  equilibrium 486, 642–3, 706
  flow concept 503
  full-employment level **492**, 493
  gross national income **413**
  Keynesian 45 degree line 475–6,
    491, 494–5
  and the money supply 503
  multiplier effect **486**–91, 569
  multiplier formula **488**, 490
  net national income **413**
  steady-state level **643**
  see also GDP (gross domestic
    product)
National Loans Fund 514
nationalisation 328, **375**, 664
natural level of output **615**
natural level of unemployment **421**,
    423–5, **615**, **621**
natural monopolies **173**–4, 181, 376

natural resources 4
natural wastage **248**
near money assets **523**
negative income tax 298
neo Austrian school 652
neoclassical theory 238, 242, 309,
    336–7, 652,
net national income **413**
net present value **262**
network economies **174**
networks **225**
new classical theories **469**, 626–32
  exchange rates 719
  growth 405
  supply-side policies 652–3
  wages 238
new Keynesians **470**
new products 179
NHS (National Health Service) 80–1,
    322, 660
NI (National Insurance) 290
nominal exchange rate 707, 717
nominal GDP **394**, 395
nominal values A:6
non-accelerating inflation rate of
    unemployment (NAIRU) **621**
non-bank private sector **523**, 524
non-collusive oligopolies **190**,
    196–200
non-excludability **315**–16
non-human factors of production
    258–9
non-linear functions A:9
non-monetary externalities 331
non-price competition **188**, 200
non-renewable resources 269, 343
non-rivalry **315**
non-tariff barriers 683, 698
normal goods **35**, **69**, **117**
normal profit **157**–9
normal rate of return **264**
normative statements 27
Northern Rock 503, 517
number unemployed **416**
numerical flexibility **254**

occupations 281–2
odds in gambling 106–7
OECD Environmental Outlook 343
OFT (Office of Fair Trading) 370,
    372–3, 374
oil prices 59, 593, 731, 731–2, 734,
    783–4
oligopolies **164**, 189–201, 368, 369
  barriers to entry 189
  Bertrand model 198–9

cartels **190**, 192, 194–5, 196,
    370–1
  collusive **190**–6, 369
  countervailing power **200**
  Cournot equilibrium 198
  Cournot model **197**
  duopoly **197**
  and the EU single market 700
  health care 322
  interdependence of firms **190**
  kinked demand theory **199**–200
  Nash equilibrium 198–**199**, 202
  non-collusive **190**, 196–200
  price leadership 192–3
  public interest 200
  quotas **192**
  reaction functions **197**
  regulatory bodies 327
  restrictive practices **369**
  tacit collusion **192**, 193
oligopsony **246**
OPEC 194–5
open economies 439, **440**
open-market operations **577**, 578, 579,
    710, 712
opportunity costs 8, **9**, 11, 13–14,
    130–1
  and international trade 674–5, 677
optimal currency area **753**, 754
optimum level of consumption 98–9,
    101–2, 113–14
optimum production point 143–4
optimum savings rate 643–4
optimum tariff **686**, 687
organisational economies 137
organisational slack **229**–30
organisational structure 214–15
output
  classical theories 457–8
  and expectations 616
  input-output analysis 18–19
  loss minimising 159
  marginal capital/output ratio **496**
  maximisation and costs 144
  natural level of output **615**
  per employed person 639–40, 646
  under perfect competition 168
  potential output **398**, 403
  and prices 42–51, 225
output gaps **398**, **399**
outsiders **250**, **468**
outward-looking industrialisation
    772–3
overheads 137–**138**
overheating 744–5
oversinuting (exchange rates) 726

Paish, Frank 570
paradox of thrift 492
parallel money markets 515, 518
Pareto criterion 333
Pareto improvement **305**, 306, 308
Pareto optimality **305**, 306, 308, 317
Paris Club agreements 784–5
parking restrictions 362
partial derivative **A:13**
partial differentiation **A:12**–13
partial equilibrium 44
participation rate **644**
Paulson Plan 517
peak-load pricing **206**, 207
per-capita GDP 394, 396, 644
perfect competition **32**, **164**, 165–73
    compared to monopolistic
        competition 188–9
    economies of scale 171–2
    long run equilibrium 169
    long run supply curve 169–70
    long run under perfect competition
        166
    and output 168
    and pricing 167
    and profit 168
    public interest 172
    short run equilibrium 167–8
    short run supply curve 168–9
    short run under perfect competition
        165
    wages 237–45
perfect knowledge 165, 170, 237
perfect markets 32
    labour markets 237–8
perfectly contestable markets **179**–80
performance measurement 230
perks 219
petrol sulphur content 334–5
PFI (Private Finance Initiative) 658–9,
    660
Phillips curve **436**–7, 465, 466–7,
    494
    clockwise Philips loops 622–3
    expectations-augmented **619**–26
    rightward shifts 623
physical capital 263
picketing **250**
pie charts **A:4**
planned economies **16**, 18–20, 338–9
planning 18–20, 664
plant economies of scale **137**
point elasticity **63**–5
police service 316
policy harmonisation 746–7, 748–9
    taxes 697, 701

policy objectives
    external **706**
    internal **706**
    see also government policies;
        targeting
political business cycle 448, 625
poll taxes 290
polluter pays principle 324–5, 348,
    350–1
pollution 347, 362
pooling risks **107**, 109
population growth 126–7, 342–3, 779
portfolio balance **541**, 542–3
positive statements 27
post-Keynesians **471**
post-war libertarianism 338–9
potential demand and supply 5
potential growth **398**, 399, 408
potential output **398**, 403
poverty *see* inequality and poverty
Poverty Funds 790
poverty trap **299**, 301, 565, 657
power, market *see* market power
precautionary motive for holding
    money 528–9
predatory pricing **210**–11, 373
predictions 25–6
preferential trading **692**–7
Premier League 177
present value **261**–2
price benchmarks **196**
price discrimination 179, 206–11, 373
price elasticity of demand **57**–65
    arc elasticity **61**–3
    average (midpoint) formula **63**
    consumer expenditure 59–61
    cross-price elasticity **69**–70
    elastic demand **58**, 59, 60–1
    incomes 58–9
    inelastic demand **58**, 59–60
    marginal revenue 154
    motoring 357
    point elasticity **63**–5
    proportionate (percentage)
        measurement 58
    substitute goods 58
    taxation 78
    time periods 59, 71
    unit elasticity of demand **58**
price elasticity of supply **65**–7
    arc method **67**
    costs 67
    taxation 78
price index A:6–8
    see also consumer prices index (CPI)
price leadership 192–3

price makers 154
price mechanism 20, 20–1, 363
    supply and demand 32–51
price takers **32**, **152**, 154, 165
price-cap regulation **379**
price-consumption curve **115**
price-fixing agreements 371–2
prices 20–1, 425–8
    aggregate demand 425–9, 471
    agricultural 82–3
    average cost pricing **196**, **231**–3
    Bank of England survey 232–3
    benchmarks **196**
    of capital 261
    classical theories 458–9
    and consumption 32
    control 51–4, 327–8, **592**
    cost-based pricing 231–3
    and demand 32–3
    equilibrium prices **20**, 42–5
       and monopolies 175
       partial equilibrium 44
    expectations of price changes 35, 41,
       71–5
    flexibility 233, 454–5, 457, 626
    food prices 777
    indifference analysis 113, 115,
       116–19
    limit pricing **175**
    mark-up cost pricing **231**–4
    maximum price **52**, 53, 54
    minimum price **51**, 52–4, 86–7
    output determination 42–51
    peak-load pricing **206**, 207
    under perfect competition 167
    relative prices **24**
    resale price maintenance **371**
    and supply 39
prices and incomes policies 51–4,
    327–8, **592**
primary care trusts 660
primary exports 767–9
primary labour market **254**–5
primary stock market **265**
principal-agent problem **216**–17
principle of diminishing marginal
    utility **96**
printing extra money 460
prisoners' dilemma **202**, 203, 354
private efficiency **305**, 306, 307–8, 311
Private Finance Initiative (PFI) 658–9,
    660
privatisation 375–82, 659
problem of the second best **323**
procurement policies and free trade
    684

producer surplus 306–8, 319, 325, 688, 694
producers
  rational behaviour **124**
  share of tax on goods **78**
  total producer surplus **307**
product development 188
product differentiation 174, **186**
product method of GDP calculation 394, 409–11
production **4**, 475
  average physical product **127**, 129
  Cobb-Douglas production function **140**, 141
  and consumption 396
  costs
    international trade 672, 680–1
    long run 146–50
    short run 130–6, 148
  external benefits 314
  external costs 314
  industry size 139
  isocost approach **143**
  isoquant approach **140**, 142, 148–9
  just-in-time **229**–30, 255
  law of diminishing returns **125**, 126, 128, 142
  location 138
  long run theory **124**, 136–50
  loss minimising output 159
  marginal physical product **127**, 129, 141
  marginal product approach 139–40, 144
  optimum production point 143–4
  productive efficiency **10**
  scale of production 136–8, 139, 150–1
  short run theory **124**–36, 145
  shut-down point **159**, 160
  and social efficiency 306–7
  subsistence production **17**–18
  total physical product **125**–7
  very long run production 145
  very short run production 145
  see also factors of production
production function **125**–30
production possibility curve **11**–14
  and macroeconomics 14
  and microeconomics 12–14
production quotas 89
productive efficiency **10**, **139**
productivity 132, 404
  and economic growth 641, 646–7

marginal productivity theory **242**, 251
  total factor productivity 646
productivity deals **247**
profit maximisation 41, 124, 155–61, 163
  difficulties 214–16
  employment levels 242–3
  land and capital 258–9
  long run **218**–19
  price discrimination 208–10, 211
  time periods 215–16
profit maximising rule **156**
profit satisficing **216**, 228, 230
profitability 123
  of banks 509, 510, 520
  and capital 264
  definition of profit 157–9
  goods in joint supply **41**
  logistics 160
  under perfect competition 168
  rate of profit **166**–7
progressive taxes **292**
property owner-occupiers 410–11
property rights 324, 326, 347
proportional taxes **292**
proportionate values A:5
protection of people's interests 320, 327
protectionism *see* trade restrictions
prudential control **514**
public goods 315–16, 328
public interest
  alternative maximising theories 225
  contestable markets 182–3
  monopolies 176–9
  monopolistic competition 188–9
  oligopolies 200
  perfect competition 172
  price discrimination 210–11
  and satisficing 230
public limited companies **216**
public sector budget balance 708
public sector deficits 525, **562**, 563–5, 575, 708
  in the US 744–5
public sector net cash requirement (PSNCR) **563**, 571, 575
public transport 357–8, 361–2, 365
public works programmes 460–1
purchasing power parity (PPP) 395, 396, **721**, 722–3, 733
purchasing power standard (PPS) GDP 395
pure fiscal policy **568**
pure profit 159

qualifications 284
quantiles 277
quantitative easing 577, **586**, 587
quantity demanded **33**
quantity theory of money **458**, 460, 462–3, 466, 536
quintiles 277
quotas 89, **192**, 446, 683

racial discrimination 256–7
radical left policies 471
raising taxes 296–8, 569
random shocks 41, 499, 569
random walk theory **267**
Rank Xerox 174
rate of discount 262
rate of economic growth **388**
rate of exchange *see* exchange rates
rate of inflation 389, 428, 556
rate of interest *see* interest rates
rate of profit **166**–7
rate of return 261, 528–9
rational behaviour **305**
  choices **9**
  consumers 96, 99–100, 306
  decision making 9, 10
  producers **124**
rational expectations 469–70, 626, **627**, 628–9, 635
rationalisation **137**, 664
rationing **54**
raw materials **4**, 404
  see also resources
reaction functions **197**
Reaganomics 655, 734
real balance effect **426**
real business cycle theory **469**, 630–1
real exchange rate **709**, 717
real GDP **394**, 395
real income **114**
real values A:6
real-wage unemployment **421**–2
recession 6, 499, 539, 639, 719
  see also business cycle
recessionary gap **492**–3
rediscounting bills of exchange **515**
redistribution of income 276, 288, 292–4, 298–9, 429
reflationary policies **438**, 465, 562, 593
  Keynesian economics 634
regional multiplier effects **666**, 700
regional policies 666–7, 697
regional unemployment 419, **424**, 424
regression analysis **38**
regressive taxes **292**
regulation of banks 514

regulatory bodies 327, 379
  see also legislation
regulatory capture **382**
rejection of market allocation 80–1
relative prices **24**
rent 258, 268–70, 410–11
repeated games 204
replacement costs **131**
repo markets **507**, 515, 516–17, 584
  reverse repos **508**
resale price maintenance **371**
rescheduling debt 784–7
research & development 665
reserves
  banks 508, 574–5, 577, 578, 580
  government 441, 442, 446
resource crowding out **460**, 461
resources 4, 13, 342–3
  common resources 316–17, 318
  competitive advantage of nations
    681
  full use 6, 14
  non-renewable 269, 343
  productivity 404
  raw materials **4**, 404
restrictive practices **369**
  EU policy 369
  UK policy 370–2
  see also trade restrictions
retail banking **505**
returns to scale 136, 141–2
revaluation of the exchange rate **714**
revenue 150–5
  and logistics 160
  sales revenue maximisation
    219–21
reverse repos **508**
reverse shocks 631
Ricardo, David 102
rich and poor people 245, 257, 270
risk **75–6**
  attitudes 217–18
  in cost-benefit analysis 332–3
  and demand 105–9
  and investment 263
  transformation **505**
  see also uncertainty
risk averse people 106
risk loving people 106
risk neutral people 106
road building 361
road pricing 363–5
Rowntree Foundation 285
RPI minus X formula 378–9
rules-based policies 598, 600–7
rural-urban migration 779, 781

salaries *see* wages
sale and repurchase agreements 507
sales revenue 150–5
  and logistics 160
  maximisation **219–21**
Sargent, Thomas 627
satisficing **216**, 228, 230
saving 391, 392, 457, 478–9
  and consumption 480–1
  and economic growth 643–4, 645,
    648
  golden-rule saving rate **644**
  optimum saving rate 643–4
  paradox of thrift 492
Say's law **458**
scale of production 136–8, 139,
    150–1
scarcity 4, **5**, 8, 13
school fees 372
Scottish & Newcastle 191
search unemployment **423–4**
seasonal unemployment **425**
Seattle 690
second derivative **A:12**
second derivative test **A:12**
second-best solution **323**, 324, 377
second-degree price discrimination
    206
secondary labour market **255**
secondary marketing **510**, 511
secondary stock market **265**
secondary union action **251**
securitisation **510–11**, 512
selective intervention 664–7
selective use of data **A:5**
self-fulfilling speculation **72**
selfish behaviour 103
semi-strong stock market efficiency
    266
sensitivity analysis **332**
Serbia 430
set-aside 89–90
Setanta 177
shares **265**
  short selling **74**
  speculation 527–9
  yield on a share **267**
  see also stock market
shirking 252–3
shocks *see* economic shocks
short run
  aggregate supply 612–13
  equilibrium 186
  production **124–36**, 145
  shut-down point **159**, 160
  under perfect competition **165**

short selling **74**
short-term economic growth 398–403
short-term finance 264
short-term loans 508
short-term monetary policy 576
short-termism **266**
shut-down point **159**, 160
sight deposits **507**
Singapore 364
Single European Act 660, 698–703
single-move games 201–4
size distribution of income **276**,
    277–80
skills 282
  deskilling 467, 468
Sky 177
small firms assistance 665
Smith, Adam 22, 102
Snowdon, Philip 460
social benefit **314**
Social Charter 698
social cost **313**
social efficiency **305–8**, 310–13
  and production 306–7
  and sustainability **345**, 346
social implications of choice 10–11
social indifference curves 311–3
social justice 328
social objectives 24
social policy, European Union (EU)
    698
social protection benefits 300
social rate of discount **333**
social security contributions 290
social-impact standards **349**
socialism 18–19, 50, 339
socially efficient road space 360
socially efficient road usage 359–60
Soviet Union 18–19, 50
Special Liquidity Scheme 577
Special Purpose Vehicles (SPV) 511
specialisation **137**, 672, 677, 774
specific taxes 77, **291**
speculation 47, **71–5**, 528–30
  and exchange rates 530, 718–20,
    725–7, 731, 755
  in futures markets 76
  in shares 528–30
  short selling **74**
  stabilising speculation **72–3**
spending patterns 279–80
spot prices 76
stabilising speculation **72–3**
stability of economic growth 401–2
Stability and Growth Pact 572–3, 575,
    751–2

stagflation **466**, **592**–4, 598, 622–3
stakeholders **228**, 229
Stalinist system 18
standardised unemployment rate **417**
standards of living 395–7, 410–11, 688
state benefits 286, 298–301
  benefits in kind **298**
  and the circular flow of income 391
  equity between recipients 288
  income redistribution 298–9
  means-tested **298**, 299
  poverty trap **299**, 301, 565, 657
  tax credits 301
  unemployment 565, 657
  universal **298**
statistics A:1–A:13
  absolute values A:5
  bar charts A:4
  base year A:6
  consumer prices index (CPI) 428, A:7
  cross-section data A:4
  diagrams A:1–3
  differentiation A:9–14
  equations A:8–9
  functional relationships A:8–9
  graphs A:2–4, A:8
  index numbers A:6–7
  linear functions A:8–9
  maximum/minimum point of a curve A:11–13
  mean A:6
  median A:6
  nominal values A:6
  non-linear functions A:9
  partial derivative A:13
  partial differentiation A:14, A:15
  pie charts A:4
  proportionate values A:5
  real values A:6
  second derivative A:12
  second derivative test A:12
  selective use of data A:5
  tables A:2–4
  time periods A:6
  time-series data A:2–4
  weighted average A:7–8
steady-state growth path **645**
steady-state level of national income **643**
sterilisation 710, **712**
sterling exchange rate 731–5
Stern Report 344
stimulus packages 566
stock appreciation **410**, 412

stock market 48–9, 265–7, 661
  Big Bang 659–60
  efficient market hypothesis **266**–7
  random walk theory **267**
  see also shares
stocks of goods 260, 269, 409–10
  fluctuations in 497, 499
stop-go policies **465**, **592**, 730
straight-line demand curve 65, 154
strategic alliances **223**, 225
strategic behaviour 190
strategic trade theory **684**, 685
strong stock market efficiency 266
structural deficits and surpluses **564**–5
structural inflation 434–5
structural policies 467, 468
structural reforms 787–8
structural unemployment **424**, 632–3
sub-prime mortgages **511**, 512–13
subcontracting **224**–5
subsidies 288, 323–6, 689
  agricultural 85–6, 89
subsistence production 17–18
substitute goods 34, 58, 69
substitutes for cars 357–8
substitutes in supply **40**–1
substitution effect 32, 116, **117**, 118, **239**, 426
  and the balance of payments 712–13
  exports 426
  imports 426, 766, 769–72
  and taxation **295**, 565
sugar production 90
sunk costs 131, **182**
supernormal profit **159**, 169
supplier numbers 41
supply 5, 39–42
  agricultural 83, 85, 87
  of capital services 259–63
  change in quantity supplied 41
  change in supply 21, **41**, 45
  determinants of 40–1
  economic models 42
  of finance 263
  goods in joint supply **41**
  and price 39
  price elasticity of supply 65–7
  of road space 358–9
  substitutes in supply **40**–1
  see also aggregate supply
supply curve 39–40, 41, 43–4
  identification problem 50–**51**
  labour market **420**–1

perfect competition 168–70
  shifts 444–5
  supply of labour 238–41, 423
  supply of hours 238, 239
supply schedule **39**
supply shocks 558–9, 617
supply-side policies **7**, 102, 446, **455**, 467, 631
  competition policies 658–60
  and economic growth 651
  fiscal policy 562, 565–7
  and inflation **438**, 652
  interventionist **653**, 661–7
  Keynesian approach 652
  link with demand-side policies 653–4
  market-oriented **652**, 654–61
  new classical approach 652–3
  Reaganomics 655, 734
  Third Way 653, 658–9, 667
  and unemployment 651–2, 665
  and wages 656–7
support prices 88–9, 90
surpluses
  agricultural 88
  on the balance of payments 719, 722
  consumer surplus 98–9
surveys 417
survival strategy 217–18
sustainability **345**–6, 787
swapping debt 789
Sweezy, Paul 199

tables A:8
tacit collusion **192**, 193
takeover constraint **221**
  see also mergers
targeting
  exchange rates 595–6, 601, 706, **714**–15, 758
  by firms 228
  inflation 470, 544, 556, 596–7, 600–7, 618–19, 625
  money supply 574, 585, 601
tariff escalation **770**
tariffs 291, 446, 683, 687–8
  agricultural 86–7, 89
  carbon tariffs 685
  optimum tariff **686**, 687
tastes 34, 477, 481, 685, 768
tax allowances **289**, 297–8
tax avoidance **289**, 293
tax credits 301
tax cuts 239, 296–7, 568, 654–6
tax evasion **289**, 293

taxation 323–6
  balance of types of tax 291–2
  capital gains tax 290
  circular flow of income 391, 479–80
  corporate tax 290, 656
  correction of externalities 323–4
  correction for monopolies 324–5
  cost of collection 288
  customs duties 291
  cutting taxes 239, 296–7, 569,
    654–6
  deadweight loss of a tax **294**, 325
  direct taxes **289**–90
  disincentive effects 289, 294–6
  distribution of income 277
  and employment 654–6
  excess burden **325**
  excise duties 291
  and GDP calculation 411, 412
  government surplus **325**
  green taxes **348**, 350–1
  harmonisation 697, 701
  horizontal equity **288**
  incentives 289, 294–6, 565, 655–6
  income effect **295**
  income redistribution 288, 292–4
  income tax 289–90, 293–4
    negative income tax **298**
  indifference curve analysis 298–9
  indirect taxes 77–9, **289**, 290–1,
    294
  labour supply 654–6
  marginal tax propensity **479**
  market distortion 289
  monopolies 324–5
  of motorists 363
  poll taxes 290
  price elasticity of demand 78
  price elasticity of supply 78
  progressive taxes **292**
  proportional taxes **292**
  raising taxes 296–8, 568
  regressive taxes **292**
  requirements of a good tax system
    288–9
  social security contributions 290
  subsidies 288, 323–6
  substitution effect **295**, 565
  traffic congestion 363
  VAT (Value Added Tax) **291**, 701
  vertical equity **288**
  wealth taxes 290
  windfall tax 324
  see also fiscal policy
Taylor rule **604**, 606–7
teamwork 255

technical inefficiency 178
technological unemployment **424**
technology 147, 594, 642–9, 651, 768,
    777–9
technology-based standards 349
terms of trade **677**–9, 769
Thatcher, Margaret 594–5, 654
theory of the firm **124**
Third Way supply-side policies 653,
    658–9, 667
third-degree price discrimination **206**,
    208, 210
threats and promises 204
thrift 492
Thurow, Lester 685
tie-in sales **373**
time costs 104
time deposits **507**
time lags
  in the business cycle 499
  in demand elasticity 59, 71
  in factor markets 320
  in fiscal policy 569–71
time-series data A:2–4
tit-for-tat 204
tobacco taxes 79
Tobin tax 756–8
tolls 363–5
total consumer expenditure on a
    product **59**
total consumer surplus **99**, 319
total costs **132**–3, 135
total currency flow balance 706
total factor productivity 646
total physical product **125**–7
total private surplus **308**
total producer surplus **307**
total quality management (TQM) 255
total revenue **150**, 152, 154
total revenue per period of time **59**
total social surplus **308**
total utility **96**, 97–8
totally inelastic demand 60
tradable permits **350**–4
trade blocs 692–3, 696
trade creation **693**–4, 699
trade cycle **400**–1
trade diversion **694**–5, 700
trade in goods account 439
trade restrictions 683–92
  arguments in favour 684–7
  methods of restricting trade 683–4
  problems with 687–9
  retaliation threats 684, 689
  strategic trade theory **684**, 685
  and unemployment 688

World Trade Organisation (WTO)
    689–92
  see also international trade
trade in services account 439–40
trade unions 249, 656–7
  closed-shop agreements **250**
  collective bargaining 248–51
  industrial action 250
  legislation 250–1
  productivity deals **247**
  restrictions on 657
  secondary action **251**
  union monopoly or oligopoly
    247–8
traffic congestion 256–61
  allocation of road space 357–9
  atmospheric pollution 362
  complementary services 358
  costs 360–1
  demand for road space 357–8
  environmental damage 360
  integrated transport policy 364
  new road building 361
  parking restrictions 362
  public transport provision 357–8,
    361–2, 365
  regulation and legislation 362
  restricting car access 362
  socially efficient road space 360
  socially efficient road usage
    359–60
  substitutes for cars 357–8
  supply of road space 358–9
  taxation 363
  time costs 359–60
  tolls 363–5
tragedy of the commons **317**, 318
train fares 207
training 253, 662–3, 666
transactions demand for money
    527–31, 541
transfer payments **391**, 412
transfers **563**
transmission of funds 505
transmission mechanisms
  exchange rates **536**, 539–41
  interest rates **536**–9
transport costs 138
transport policies 256–61, 361–5
transposition deficit (EU) 700–1
Treasury bills **508**, 515, 577
trend growth 399, 400
turning points in the business cycle
    631
turnover rates in the labour market
    253

U-form organisations 214, **215**
uncertainty **75**–6, 221–2
   floating exchange rates 727
   and inflation 429–30
   and mergers 223
   see also risk
underemployment **779**
underground economy 396, 397
underground markets 53, **54**
unemployment 7, 388, 416–25, 447–9
   in the 1950s and 1960s 591
   age groups 420
   aggregate demand 393, 471, 634
   business cycle 416, 418
   claimant **417**
   classical theories 457–8, 459–60,
      626–32
   command economies 19
   costs 420
   cyclical **422**–3
   definition 416–17
   demand deficient **422**–3, 633
   in developing countries 779–81
   disequilibrium **421**–3, 454
   disguised **779**
   duration 417–19
   equilibrium 420–**421**, 423–5, 454,
      632–3
   ethnic groups 420
   frictional **423**–4, 657
   gender differences 419–20
   geographical differences 419, 424
   hysteresis **468**, 616, 633
   and inflation 436–7, 471, 494,
      620–1, 632–5
   inflow and outflow rate 418
   interventionist policies 424
   Keynesian economics 422, 463–4,
      467, 492–5, 632–5
   market-oriented policies 424
   natural level **421**, 423–5, **615**, **621**
   non-accelerating inflation rate
      (NAIRU) **621**
   number unemployed **416**
   and protectionism 688
   real-wage **421**–2
   regional **424**
   search **423**–4
   seasonal **425**
   standardised rate **417**
   stock concept 417
   structural **424**, 632–3
   supply-side policies 651–2, 665
   surveys 417

   and taxation 654–6
   technological **424**
unemployment benefits 565, 657
unemployment rate **417**
unit elasticity of demand **58**, 61
United States trade imbalance 730,
   744–5
universal benefits **298**
unrecorded goods and services 395–6
urban policies 666–7
   traffic congestion 256–61
   transport 361–5
Uruguay Round 691
user charges 348
util **96**
utility
   managerial utility maximisation 219
   marginal utility theory **96**–104

vacancies 423, 454
value chain 682
value for money 9
variable costs **132**, 133, 134
variable factors of production **124**
variable road pricing 363–5
VAT (Value Added Tax) **291**, 701
velocity of circulation **458**, 536, 542–4
vent for surplus **767**
vertical equity **288**
vertical integration 221–2
vertical mergers **222**, 368
vertical restraints **373**
very long run production 145
very short run production 145
volatility of floating exchange rates
   735–6
voluntary environmental agreements
   349
voluntary interaction 23

wage setters 246
wage takers **237**
wages
   distribution by occupation 281–2
   efficient wage hypothesis **251**–5
   equality 244–5, 252–3
   equilibrium wages 20, 423, 615
   exploitation of cheap labour 676
   firms with market power 246
   flexibility 454–5, 615, 626
   in imperfect markets 247–58
   and import substitution 771
   labour with market power 247–8
   managerial utility maximisation 219

   minimum wage 52, 287
   and morale 253–5
   neoclassical theory 238
   under perfect competition 237–45
   real-wage unemployment **421**–2
   rises in wage rates 238–9, 614–15
   substitution effect **239**
   supply-side policies 656–7
   tax cuts 239
   see also income; inequality and
      poverty; labour market
Walras, Léon 102
wants 4, 5
waste disposal 343
Ways and Means advance 514
weak stock market efficiency **266**
wealth 49, 276, 283–4, 477, 503
   idle balances **528**
   and inequality 284
   medium of storage 503–4
Wealth of Nations 22
wealth taxes 290
weighted average A:7–8
welfare gains from international trade
   679–80
Whitbread 191
wholesale banking **505**
wholesale deposits and loans **505**, 506
Williamson, John 758
Williamson, O.E. 219
windfall tax 324
withdrawals **391**, 478–82, 486–9, 491
   marginal propensity to withdraw
      482
   total withdrawals function 481–2
women
   equality 253, 282
   unemployment 419–20
workforce increase 644
Working Families Tax Credit 301
working population 403–5, 423
Working Tax Credit 301
working to rule **250**
world multiplier effects 689
World Trade Organisation (WTO)
   689–92

X inefficiency 178

Yeltsin, Boris 19
yield on a share **267**
yuan exchange rate 775

Zimbabwe 430–1